PORTRAITS: 9/11/01

PORTRAITS: 9/11/01

THE COLLECTED "PORTRAITS OF GRIEF" FROM *THE NEW YORK TIMES*

Foreword by Howell Raines

Introduction by Janny Scott

TIMES BOOKS

Henry Holt and Company, New York

Times Books
Henry Holt and Company, LLC
Publishers since 1866
115 West 18th Street
New York, New York 10011

Henry Holt® is a registered trademark of Henry Holt and Company, LLC.

Library of Congress Cataloging-in-Publication Data is available.
ISBN: 0-8050-7222-5

Henry Holt books are available for special promotions and premiums.
For details contact: Director, Special Markets.

First Edition 2002

Designed by Fritz Metsch

Printed in the United States of America
10 9 8 7 6 5 4 3 2 1

Foreword

HOWELL RAINES

Nothing published in the *New York Times* during my twenty-four years on the newspaper has elicited a reader response like the one we've gotten on "Portraits of Grief." Those who've been here longer say the same thing. I'm convinced that the core of the portraits' appeal lies in our metropolitan desk's decision to cast these stories as snapshots of lives interrupted as they were being actively lived, rather than in the traditional obituary form. Bill Moyers suggested during a journalism conference at Columbia University that the impact of these stories would change the form of newspaper obituary writing. I can't predict whether that's right. In fact, I rather doubt it, since the traditional *New York Times* obituary is a powerful storytelling format in itself and is entirely appropriate to the task of recording the key facts of prominent (or notorious) lives.

But "Portraits of Grief" reminds us of the democracy of death, an event that lies in the future of every person on the planet. The scary force of that universal fact sometimes inspires in the most sober soul an impulse to flee into a carpe diem mood of headlong hedonism. I think, however, that the 1,910 stories reported in our paper and collected here in *Portraits 9/11/01* stir an entirely different feeling. When I read them, I am filled with an awareness of the subtle nobility of everyday existence, of the ordered beauty of quotidian life for millions of Americans, of the unforced dedication with which our fellow citizens go about their duties as parents, life partners, employers or employees, as planters of community gardens, coaches of the young, joyful explorers of this great land and the world beyond its shores. These lives, bundled together so randomly into a union of loving memory by those terrible cataclysms of September 11, remind us of what Walt Whitman knew: "The United States themselves are essentially the greatest poem."

There was poetry, too, in watching my colleagues on the metropolitan staff report and record these stories. The glory of a great newsroom is its each-one-teach-one ethos. They taught and learned together, as Christine Kay conceptualized the project, Wendell Jamieson managed the complex task of tracing hundreds of stories, and their leader, Jon Landman, the metropolitan editor, resisted any suggestion that we abandon our rhythm of a page or two pages every day until the end of 2001. Among the reporters, another kind of democracy — the democracy of craftsmanship — came into play. Often, on so huge a story as the World Trade Center disaster, the writing of shorter pieces falls to younger reporters. On the "Portraits" project, it became an emblem of pride to join in the largely anonymous labor of creating these pieces; some of our most senior correspondents insisted on participating.

I have seen reporters crying at their telephones, even as they summoned the professional discipline to keep reporting, keep writing until the task was done. They were inspired and sometimes driven by an awareness of what these pieces had come to mean to the grieving families and friends and to that larger community of Americans who mourned for all the World Trade Center victims, strangers to them or not, just as in an earlier day their parents mourned for the dead of Pearl Harbor. We received thousands of letters and e-mails from our readers. On the very morning I sat down to write these words, the following e-mail showed up on my screen from a lawyer in San Francisco. I thought it caught the national spirit that collected around the "Portraits of Grief" and in a quiet, sincere way validated the work of our staff:

Dear New York Times:
I am a San Francisco Bay Area resident. I have received the NY Times (Monday through Friday) for the last 16 years. I love your paper. My respect for your staff has grown even further in the last four months.

Your coverage of the September 11 tragedy has been compelling, thorough, and profoundly compassionate. Your section, A Nation Challenged, and the mini-biographies of the victims of September 11, in particular, have been invaluable tools to understand the depth and scope of what has happened. Our nine-year-old son reviewed the biographies every day. It held special importance for him because of his two uncles, aunt, and cousin who live in Manhattan. All of them, thankfully, are safe.

Another dear friend's brother was not so fortunate. In the midst of this tragedy, the Times was like a trusted, old friend.

Thank you. You have delivered something far more complex than the news.

In an important sense, the Times has been part of the healing process in our family. For that, you have my deepest gratitude and respect.

James M. Schurz

That letter reaffirmed to me that we had accomplished the core mission of the *New York Times*, which is to serve the information needs of a thoughtful, engaged readership that spans all regions of the country and indeed all ages and interests. In short, we set out to make worthy journalism, not to create a memorial. If in the course of doing our jobs we created a monument in words to those who were lost, we are proud to have honored them and their families with our labors.

Introduction

JANNY SCOTT

Few aspects of the *New York Times*'s coverage of September 11 and of all that has followed have attracted as much comment as a page or two at the back of the "Nation Challenged" section every day for fifteen weeks—a series of miniature profiles of people who died in the hijackings and in the destruction of the World Trade Center, appearing under the heading "Portraits of Grief."

Readers inundated the paper with letters about those tiny snapshots and the complex feelings they evoked. Television and radio stations around the world broadcast reports on the project. A psychologist at the University of Michigan assigned the portraits as required reading, as a source of life lessons for his students and therapy groups. Offers of help for the families poured in.

For many people, reading the profiles became a daily ritual—observed at breakfast tables, on the subway, before computer screens late at night. The stories became a source of connection and consolation, a poignant reminder of the individual humanity swallowed up by the dehumanizing vastness of the toll, a focus for the expression of unfocused sorrow.

"Never before in my forty-plus years as a reader have I been moved to close my eyes, place my palm on the page of a newspaper, shed a tear, and say a prayer," Jack Bogdanski, a professor at Lewis and Clark Law School in Portland, Oregon, wrote in an e-mail message to the *Times*. Pamela A. Mann, a lawyer in Manhattan, wrote, "Reading these portraits is my act of Kaddish." Jeff Bray, a communications specialist for an energy company in Sioux Falls, South Dakota, wrote, "Nothing—and I mean NOTHING—I have ever read in my life has moved me as much as these riveting windows into the lives of ordinary people." Without having read them, one woman told the *Times*, she had found she could not drop off to sleep at night.

The profiles came into being almost haphazardly in the immediate aftermath of the disaster, a product of the inconceivable thoroughness of the destruction. In the first few days, it became clear that it would be months before there would be an official list of all the dead, the kind of list newspapers usually use to begin writing about the victims of a disaster.

With few identifiable bodies, there could be no confirmable list. Yet thousands of people were gone; homemade missing-persons flyers had begun to paper the city. Because it seemed impossible to write about the dead without confirmation, we decided simply to start writing about the missing. And we decided to do it one by one.

On September 14, a half-dozen reporters divided up a stack of one hundred missing-persons flyers, collected from the friends and family members haunting lower Manhattan. We began dialing the phone numbers on the flyers. What we wanted were stories, anecdotes, tiny but telling details that seemed to reveal something true and essential about how each person lived.

The profiles were never intended to be obituaries, at least in the traditional sense of the word—the taking stock of accomplishments, their length determined by an editor's opinion of the impact of a life. They were closer to snapshots—concise, impressionistic, their power at least as much emotional as intellectual. And they were utterly democratic.

There was Neil D. Levin, the executive director of the Port Authority of New York and New Jersey, the World Trade Center's landlord, along with Roko Camaj, an Albanian-born window washer just back from vacationing in Montenegro. There was Heather Ho, famous pastry chef; and David Alger, Harvard-educated chief financial officer; and Tawanna Griffin, cafeteria cashier.

So many were men, traders and brokers, in their thirties and early forties, people who had ridden the bull market out of the lower middle class and into comfortable homes in suburban New Jersey. And there were the battalion chiefs, the newlyweds, the aging basketball stars, the fiancées, the doting fathers, the unfortunate few doing an early shift that morning as a favor to a friend. Like a panoramic photograph, the project gathered everyone it could and attempted to bring each one fleetingly into focus. To many readers, it captured something of the energetic, optimistic, aspiring spirit of that place and time. Some 143 reporters eventually took part in the project; some worked on it for a few days, others for many weeks. It was heartbreaking work.

But there was something uplifting in it, too. One reporter who had lost a cousin in the attacks found that interviewing other families enabled her finally to face her own loss. When her stint was done, she asked to stay on. She ended up writing profiles for months, finding strength in the courage of strangers on the other end of the line. By the end of the year, the paper had profiled some eighteen hundred of the approximately three thousand people believed to have died in the attacks. In addition, reporters had contacted, or tried to contact, relatives and friends of most of the rest. Some could not be reached, some asked to wait, others declined to take part. The project continued into 2002.

For many readers, there was something mysteriously inspiring about the portraits: all those affectionately recounted stories, acts of kindness, expressions of love. Perhaps it is, as one reader put it, the divinity brought to the commonplace, a reminder of what she called "life's wildly textured poetry" and the preciousness of each life's path.

"I would hope that you will publish these as a book once the cycle is done," Charles Zachary Bornstein, a symphony orchestra conductor who lives in Fairfield, Connecticut, and performs around the world, wrote in an e-mail. "It would be one I would always travel with for the rest of my life, as there is something consoling to know these people, each out of the mass."

PORTRAITS: 9/11/01

GORDY AAMOTH
Looking Good

Gordy Aamoth was at the top of his game. His golf was improving, and he had a membership in the Creek Club in Locust Valley, N.Y. He had girlfriends. And on Monday, Sept. 10, in his hometown of Minneapolis, he completed his biggest merger deal as an investment banker at Sandler O'Neill & Partners. The deal was to be officially announced the next day at the firm's World Trade Center office.

Mr. Aamoth, 32, was always a good athlete. He was the captain of his high school football team and played hockey. He went to Babson College in Wellesley, Mass., and earned a business degree. "He always knew he wanted to go to Wall Street," said his father, Gordon.

Gordy Aamoth also loved parties and how he looked. "Every situation was more fun when Gordy was there," said his mother, Mary. "He was always beautifully put together."

Despite entreaties to consider returning to Minneapolis, Gordy Aamoth was determined to stay in New York, even if it was far from his family. "He loved New York," his father said. "He often said, 'You had to know it to love it, and most people don't.' "

But there will be a touch of Gordy Aamoth at home. His high school, the Blake School, has decided to name its new football field the Gordy Aamoth Memorial Stadium.

EDELMIRO ABAD
One Office, Two Families

As the father of three girls who had gone to dancing school since they were toddlers, Edelmiro Abad, widely known as Ed, was a proud fixture at dozens of recitals. So it was with delight that he supported his middle child's aspiration to open her own dance studio someday.

"He was right there with me," said his daughter Jennifer, 23. "This was something he wanted as much as I did."

Mr. Abad, 54, who lived in Brooklyn with his wife, Lorraine, and three daughters—including Rebecca, 26, and Serena, 19—was also a fixture at Fiduciary Trust Company International, where he was senior vice president and had worked for 26 years. The company was a second home, his relatives said, and its staff another family.

His family members have met with co-workers who shared offices with Mr. Abad on the 90th floor of 2 World Trade Center. "Some of the people who survived are devastated," Ms. Abad said. "They don't know how to go on."

ANDREW and VINCENT ABATE
Brothers at Work and Play

By day, Vincent and Andrew Abate traded bonds at Cantor Fitzgerald. In the evenings, after long days, the brothers unwound by shooting hoops or batting handballs together. On summer weekends, Andrew and his

A makeshift memorial for the lost, at Houston Street and the Avenue of the Americas in Manhattan. (*Sarah Krulwich*)

wife, Carolyn, often drove to Vincent's rented house on the Jersey Shore for Vincent's barbecue or Andrew's grilled teriyaki.

Vincent, 44, a longtime Cantor Fitzgerald employee, brought Andrew, 37, into the company three years ago. Vincent lived alone in a brownstone in Brooklyn. Hard-driving and impulsive, he was known to hop a plane to Las Vegas for the weekend, on the spur of the moment.

Andrew and Carolyn had a house in Melville, N.Y., that they were enlarging and renovating. They liked to relax in scenic places and had just returned from a tour of Route 1 on the California coast. "They did a lot of things," said Joe Vito, a cousin. "They had good lives."

ALONA ABRAHAM
A Great Time in the States

The first 10 days of September were giddy ones for Alona Abraham, who was in Boston on her first trip to the United States. She went whale-watching, shopping and walking in Cambridge, said Dror Veisman, a college friend with whom she stayed. "She said, 'Oh, Mommy, I'm having a great time,' " said Miriam Abraham, her mother, who lives in Ashdod, Israel. "She was laughing and talking about going on picnics and sightseeing with her friends."

Ms. Abraham, 30—the eldest of three children and daughter of Israeli immigrants from Bombay—worked long hours at Applied Materials, where she was an industrial engineer. So she took her vacations seriously, spending weeks in Paris and Amsterdam and going on African safaris. Independent and religious, she often traveled alone and kept kosher wherever she happened to be.

Seeing America was one of her dreams. She liked the cool weather, the low prices, the cosmopolitan cities. And for a few weeks, she could escape the bombings and shootings at home in Israel. She planned to return again and again. She was on United Airlines Flight 175, which struck the south tower on Sept. 11.

WILLIAM ABRAHAMSON
The Linchpin of His Friends

In his 58 years, William Abrahamson generated enduring circles of friends. There was the Public School 8 school-yard group, from his childhood in Brooklyn Heights. There were his colleagues from the Federal Reserve Bank, who met in the late 1960s and remained closest friends ever since.

As the men scattered to different states, it was Mr. Abrahamson, a business analyst at Marsh & McLennan, a financial services conglomerate, who kept the group together.

"He was the quieter guy, very secure about who he was," said Ann Abrahamson, his wife of 25 years. In a group of strong personalities, she said, "he was the mediator, always above the squabbles."

When their son, Erik, was born 11 years ago, Mr. Abrahamson, like many older fathers, looked upon the boy as a gift and a mission.

"Erik was his pride and joy," Mrs. Abrahamson said. "All he wanted was to see him grow up."

PAUL ACQUAVIVA
A Hotshot with a Soft Spot

You could put together a credible story about the good-looking star jock from Wayne, N.J., who was nabbed by the prettiest girl in high school and who continued to do well—rising hotshot in the financial world, monthly Friday night cards-and-beer with the guys, the house in Glen Rock, N.J., strewn with empty water bottles and bottlecaps. You would certainly be accurate in describing Paul Acquaviva, 29, a vice president at eSpeed, a division of Cantor Fitzgerald, but you would not be right.

For you would also have to talk about the guy who was so bright that he knew the one question on his math SAT that he missed, who graduated Phi Beta Kappa from Rutgers, and from Columbia Law School. A man so tender that when he learned that his first child was a girl, he jumped up and down with untrammeled joy, who would tell Courtney—that high school girlfriend, later his bride—that she became only more beautiful to him over the years, never more so than when she was pregnant and ungainly.

Then you could meld those stories—the macho jock with the sensitive scholar—and you would see the outlines of a gifted friend and family man, father to Sarah, 2, and to Sarah's brother, who is expected to begin his own story in December.

DONALD ADAMS
Gaining Entry to Happiness

In the summer of '92 he was a bouncer, 6 feet 5 inches tall, at some long-gone beach bar on the Jersey shore. She was cute and underage, hoping to sweet-talk her way through the door. "He was nice and let me in," Heda Adams said of the day she met her husband, Donald Adams.

Turned out that both were students at Fairleigh Dickinson University. He was a fraternity boy, No. 77 on the offensive line. "Yes, I was pinned," Mrs. Adams said, laughing.

In the spring of 2001 they had their first child, Rebecca,

who, it is already clear, shares her father's outgoing, extroverted personality.

On summer evenings, Mrs. Adams and Rebecca would sit on the porch of their home in Chatham, N.J., waiting for Mr. Adams, a 28-year-old vice president at Cantor Fitzgerald, to walk up the road from the train station. "There's my girls," he would call out.

After dinner they would sometimes take a stroll through the neighborhood, sharing their day in the intimate shorthand of couples who are both lovers and best friends.

"I was H. He was D. Just the first letters. That's all we needed."

PATRICK ADAMS
Greetings for the Fish

When Patrick Adams would return home from work at Fuji Bank, he would greet not only his family, but the fish in the aquarium at the Adamses' apartment in Flatbush, Brooklyn, said his daughter Balynda Adams. "He would come home and say to them, 'How are you doing?'" she said. "He would call them 'the boys.'"

Mr. Adams, 61, was a security officer in Fuji's offices in 2 World Trade Center, working on the 81st floor. After one of the hijacked airliners struck the building and ignited a raging fire, "he called and said he was trapped in the World Trade Center," Ms. Adams said. "We got it on the answering machine."

"He was basically a family man," Ms. Adams said. "He would make sure everything is O.K., everybody is happy." As for his relationship with marine life, it was not limited to the home aquarium. "He liked fishing, and would go to Connecticut to fish," his daughter said.

SHANNON ADAMS
Finding Something Bigger

"He had his business card that gave his address as Tower 1, 101st Floor, World Trade Center," Gwyn Adams said of her son, Shannon. "He was so proud of that, coming from a town where his high school class had 34 kids. It doesn't even have a red light. It has a couple of stop signs."

It was his longstanding dream to leave Star Lake, N.Y., population 860, for something a little bigger.

"He was going 100 miles an hour all the time, it seems like," said his father, Lew Adams. "The city seemed to satisfy that a lot better than the northern Adirondacks."

Shannon Adams, 25, a fixed-income accountant at Cantor Fitzgerald, set up the perfect bachelor pad in Astoria with two friends in the finance world.

"They had their huge big TV screen with all their sports,

their full music wall," his mother said. "They had a huge fish tank with man-eating fish or whatever they're called." And they had a favorite bar where his friends gathered for an Irish wake. And when they went up north for his memorial service, they filled up all the motels in a 15-mile radius.

STEPHEN ADAMS
"An 18th-Century Man"

It was not always easy for Stephen Adams. He had majored in philosophy at college, but could not figure out what he wanted to do professionally. His tastes were from another time; his greatest interest a form of ritual English dance with hankies, sticks and swords.

"He was an 18-century man," said his wife, Jessica Murrow, a musician, who met her husband, who was 51, at this kind of ritual dance, known as morris dance. She had journeyed to Marlboro College in Vermont to accompany a group of dancers on a drum, but had left her drumstick at home. "Someone said to ask Steve. He'd have one." He did.

"Steve loved Irish poetry and James Joyce and old English ballads," she said. "He had very old-fashioned values. He believed in being honorable, honest and loyal. He forgot to put himself first. His career faltered. Making money and work frustrated him."

It was only recently, Ms. Murrow said, that her husband found himself professionally. A graduate of the French Culinary Institute, he had been named beverage manager at Windows on the World and was on the road to becoming a sommelier. "It was the first time he had a job where he was appreciated and happy."

IGNATIUS UDO ADANGA
Energy and a Helping Hand

Ignatius Udo Adanga was born 62 years ago in Nigeria. As a young man, he left home for Lagos, the capital. He moved on to Liberia and then Germany before migrating to New York some two decades ago.

Mr. Adanga's quest for a better life led him through a series of city and state jobs in housing, probation, children's services and, finally, the planning department of the Metropolitan Transportation Council, at the World Trade Center.

For all that, Mr. Adanga struck those who knew him as energetic rather than restless. He always seemed to have spare time to help family members—his wife, Afiong, and three daughters—friends and co-workers.

"Your country or your nativity was immaterial," said McLord Obiora, a friend, at a memorial service in November. Judith Wilson, a co-worker for the past year, said Mr. Adanga not only took the time to help her settle in but also became a mentor for her son Kareem, 10, when he learned she was a single parent. "I was always going to him for advice," she said.

TERENCE E. ADDERLEY Jr.
Business in the Blood

Some grandfathers teach grandsons to fish. Terence E. Adderley Jr.'s taught him to read the *Wall Street Journal*. Mr. Adderley, known as Ted, was born with business in his blood and relished it. His grandfather, William Russell Kelly, founded Kelly Services, a temp agency based in Michigan.

By the time Mr. Adderley was 12, he was picking his own stocks. He went to his grandfather's university—Vanderbilt—and joined his grandfather's fraternity, Sigma Chi. In the summers, he worked at Kelly and practiced dry wit. He teased co-workers about trivial mistakes by signing letters to them in a script similar to the company's chief executive—his father, Terence E. Adderley.

At 22, he found Wall Street an easy fit. He shared a preference for French cuffs and collars with his new boss, the veteran Wall Street money manager David Alger.

Mr. Adderley planned ahead and family always figured prominently. His sister Elizabeth's 17th birthday fell in October. From her brother, she received a watch with a blue band (her favorite color) and gloves. Mr. Adderley had bought them for her by August, along with a pink scarf. It was not pashmina.

"He didn't care for pashmina," said Mr. Adderley's mother, Mary Beth. "If he was going to buy something for his sister, it was going to be cashmere."

SOPHIA B. ADDO
Lottery, Then Hard Work

Luck, in the form of an immigration lottery, brought Sophia B. Addo to the United States from Ghana in 1996: a teacher of schoolchildren in Africa, she decided to take a chance and come to New York to further her own education.

But getting into school here was not as uncomplicated as winning a lottery. She had her working papers, and landed a succession of housekeeping jobs while she improved her English. Already having passed an oral exam, she was due to take a written test on Sept. 12 to see if she was entitled to a G.E.D. certificate and college eligibility.

"She wanted to learn how to pronounce the language so she could express herself better in interviews," said her husband, Joseph Ameyaw. Ms. Addo's aim was a career in teaching or nursing. In the interim, the 36-year-old tidied

Windows on the World, commuting from their Bronx apartment. "She liked to read her Bible; she was a person who would comfort you, and when you were unhappy with life, she would use the word of God to make you happy," said Mr. Ameyaw. "To me, she was justice."

LEE ADLER
The Girls in His Family

At work, Lee Adler could write complex computer programs off the top of his head, never needing to write anything down. He took great pleasure in shaving nanoseconds off the time his elegant programs took to run, said his wife, Alice. Mr. Adler, 48, was a systems programmer at eSpeed, a division of Cantor Fitzgerald. He also coached his daughter's basketball, soccer and softball teams and was a trustee of Temple Beth Ahm in Springfield, N.J., Mrs. Adler said.

At home in Springfield, Mr. Adler liked being surrounded by all girls. The family consisted of one daughter, Lauren, a sheltie, Meghan, and two cats, Lindsey and Brenda. Mr. Adler and the animals had birthdays a few days apart, in March, and they celebrated together. He would take the dog to the pet store, and whatever she sniffed first was her present.

Mrs. Adler recalls his most recent birthday fondly. He had given her a pair of earrings for Valentine's Day, and for his (yes, his) birthday, he gave her the pin to match, a bear climbing on a piece of lapis. "He definitely loved all his girls," she said.

DANIEL AFFLITTO
Host of Patio Parties

Daniel Afflitto loved to show off his large new house in Manalapan, N.J. There was the tree-trimming party, the barbecues, and over Labor Day weekend, a luau, complete with piña coladas and a hula dancer. "His was the place where everyone went, to take a swim, watch a game, and hang out on the patio," said his father, Joseph T. Afflitto.

But Mr. Afflitto, 32, was also a hard worker, often putting in 12-hour days at Cantor Fitzgerald, which made him a partner in 1999. On Sept. 10, Mr. Afflitto and his wife, Stacey, flew home from Santa Barbara, Calif., after a friend's wedding. His wife had wanted to extend their trip, but "Danny hated taking days off," she said. On the plane, Mr. Afflitto guessed that she was pregnant with their second child, but the home pregnancy test she took that night turned out negative. On Sept. 12, however, Mrs. Afflitto found out that her husband was right.

After a funeral Mass for Officer Dominick Pezzulo in the Bronx September 19, Gianna Pezzulo, his daughter, holds his hat. (*Angel Franco*)

"God is giving me something," she said, "because he took something away."

MUKUL K. AGARWALA
"Here's Lookin' at You, Kid"

After he folded an Internet company in San Diego in the spring of 2000, Mukul K. Agarwala moved back east to be near his parents in Kendall Park, N.J., because they were in failing health. His sense of family extended to his friends' children, too.

"He would call every month to ask for a new photo of our daughter, Riya," said Neeraj Mital, a friend since college. Mr. Agarwala's widow, Rhea Shome, said that his sense of concern went even further. Not long after they met in Hong Kong in 1993, she said, he saw a newspaper article about a mistreated domestic worker who, like Mr. Agarwala's parents, had come from India. He went to the Indian diplomatic mission and paid her fare back home.

Ms. Shome said her husband's enthusiasms ranged from snowboarding to reading history to old movies. She could not remember how many times they had watched *Casablanca*. On Sept. 11, Mr. Agarwala, 37, was in his second day as a research analyst on software for Fiduciary Trust.

JOSEPH AGNELLO
Family, Sports, Dogs, Fires

Joseph Agnello was a firefighter with Ladder Company 118 in Brooklyn Heights with a 36th birthday coming up in October. But he was not a man who was defined by his job—he was a guy who loved his kids, his dogs, his life.

"People on my block didn't know my husband was a fireman," said his wife, Vinnie Carla Agnello. "He never needed to talk about himself or the job. He wasn't the type of person who needed attention."

Mr. Agnello loved to spend time with Chelsea and

Durante, the boxers he and his wife doted on before their sons Salvatore, who was 3 in November, and Vincent, 19 months, came along.

"Those dogs have been all over the country with us," Mrs. Agnello said. But he was also into boogie boarding with his wife in the summer, skiing and snowboarding with a small group of friends in the winter.

"We spent some time together on the slopes," said Anthony Carbone, a firefighter who met Mr. Agnello at Ladder Company 118 eight years ago. "He turned into a pretty good skier, but then he felt it was time to move on to snowboarding. He was a quiet, very confident and very determined guy."

DAVID AGNES
"Just a Good Man"

Carmen Agnes sat in her home in Flushing, Queens, wondering what to say about her son, David. "I don't want to make him a saint," she said. "He was just a good man."

His photograph sat on her desk, and she described it. He wore a blue shirt and a mustache and stared straight ahead with a half-smile. The photograph, though, did not speak of his good nature, the devotion he showed to his daughter, Adrienne, 24, the intimate friendship he had with his sister Leslie, 43, the days on end that he spent at the side of the hospital bed of his father, Frank, 81.

Mr. Agnes, 46, was an assistant vice president at Cantor Fitzgerald. That's what his card says, a small, token leftover from a decent life. Perhaps the possession that speaks more to the soul of her son, said Mrs. Agnes, 71, was a lock of his daughter's hair found in his safe-deposit box. "That's the sort of thing a woman keeps," she said. "But that tells you what David's daughter meant to him."

JOAO AGUIAR
A Love on Horseback

Last year, while sailing off the coast of New Jersey, Joao Aguiar was knocked unconscious by the flying boom of his catamaran and fell into a coma. The prognosis wasn't good, but he emerged from unconsciousness two days later. In two weeks he was out of the hospital. His uncle, Raymond S. Smith, said he was not surprised that his nephew defied the odds.

"J.J. is a strong, athletic guy," he said. "Just like then, I'm sure he'll pull through."

Mr. Aguiar, 30, of Monmouth Beach, N.J., worked for KBW Investments on the 86th floor of the south tower. Mr. Smith said he had learned from co-workers that his nephew made it to the 76th floor.

"He's resourceful, a really smart kid," said Mr. Smith, who raised his nephew after his parents returned to Portugal while Joao was still in high school.

Mr. Aguiar was crazy about horses, and he recently met a woman while riding. He was planning to move in with his girlfriend, who owns a horse farm in Colts Neck, N.J., Mr. Smith said. "For the first time in his life, he was in love," he said.

JEREMIAH J. AHERN
"He Didn't Like Dancing"

Jeremiah J. Ahern, a Bronx-born son of Irish immigrants, went to work in 1946 after getting out of the Army and never stopped. He put himself through Baruch College while working for the Post Office.

After 10 years at the Post Office, he began a second career at the Internal Revenue Service. And when he retired from there at age 55, he went right back to work at the New York State Department of Taxation and Finance.

Mr. Ahern was 74 and working as an auditor in the state's sales tax office on the 86th floor of 2 World Trade Center on Sept. 11. "Dad was a very quiet person, not too outgoing, and he was always concerned he'd have nothing to do in retirement," said Geraldine Ahern Scott, his daughter.

Mr. Ahern had an equally unhurried approach to romance. He was 42 when he married his wife, Beatrice. They met at a Roman Catholic singles dance he attended with courtship in mind. "He didn't like dancing," said Mrs. Scott.

JOANNE AHLADIOTIS
Going All Out, All the Time

Joanne Ahladiotis never did anything halfway. She dressed impeccably and had her nails done once a week. She entertained regularly, making all the food herself. She took great pride in her small apartment in Forest Hills, Queens. "At Christmas," said her sister, Effie Salloum, "she would decorate her apartment like it was Macy's windows."

Fluent in Greek, Ms. Ahladiotis, 27, traveled to Greece every two years to visit her grandmother, who lives in Crete, and returned home laden with gifts of icons, jewelry, books and cookies. In fact, Ms. Ahladiotis could scarcely go anywhere without buying presents for her family and friends. "If she was out shopping and she found something she liked but they didn't have it in her size, she would buy it for me," her sister said.

The week before she died, Ms. Ahladiotis, who worked for the eSpeed division of Cantor Fitzgerald, had to travel to Las Vegas on business. She invited her parents to accompany her. "It was the most beautiful week of my life," said her mother, Eleni. "She was a very loving person."

SHABBIR AHMED
Fishing Getaways

Shabbir Ahmed had worked as a waiter in his share of elegant city restaurants since immigrating from Bangladesh in 1981, but Windows on the World was such a favorite that he stayed 11 years. His son Thanbir, 16, thinks it was because the management and customers treated him the same way he treated them: nicely and politely. Also, he was earning a salary that made his dream in life—providing a college education for his three children—a real option; his oldest daughter, 19, attends Brooklyn College.

Fishing excursions to Gerritsen Creek and Sheepshead Bay were his favorite getaways: they reminded him of his boyhood. While he preferred to let his wife, Jeba, and his children clean whatever trout, catfish or bluefish he caught, he did lend a hand with the grilling.

When Mr. Ahmed, 44, was not off fishing in his leisure hours, he was tending to the backyard vegetable garden in Marine Park, Brooklyn, a responsibility he traded with his brother on an annual basis. This summer it was his turn: chilies, squash, eggplant and tomatoes made up this year's crop, but not all of them flourished. It seems he was more vigilant pursuing fish than he was yanking weeds and spreading fertilizer.

TERRANCE AIKEN
A Jaguar Fixer-Upper

Terrance Aiken's youngest baby was a burgundy Jaguar, a four-door sedan he had bought secondhand and painstakingly restored. Every weekend, he piled his children, Terrease, Kanan and Andre, into the backseat and set off for a leisurely drive. He often bragged to his wife, Kimberly Trimingham-Aiken, that he looked good driving that car. He told her that she looked good, too, on the few occasions that he let her drive.

A former pro basketball player in the Philippines, Mr. Aiken, 30, taught himself about computers by taking apart a clunky I.B.M. desktop that he salvaged from the Salvation Army. He later filled his home in Staten Island with computers, and had, in September, just started working as a computer consultant for Marsh & McLennan.

Mr. Aiken had wanted to save enough money for a larger house, and another Jaguar fixer-upper for himself. "We were making plans," Mrs. Trimingham-Aiken said. "You never think that tomorrow you won't be here to follow through on those plans."

GODWIN AJALA
An American Family Dream

Godwin Ajala was proud of being a lawyer in Nigeria. But because of hard times there, he immigrated to the United States in 1995, hoping to earn far more to support his family. At first he bounced between jobs, but ultimately he landed a steady position as a security guard at the World Trade Center. Still, he was frustrated, and he began pursuing his dream of becoming a lawyer in America, setting his sights on passing the New York State Bar Exam.

His roommate, Christopher Onuoha, said Mr. Ajala worked from 6 A.M. to 2 P.M., went home for a nap and then studied for the bar for six to eight hours, often late into the night. Co-workers said he was last seen helping people escape from the trade center.

"When he was living here, he was suffering in terms of always working and studying," said a close friend, Christopher Iwuanyanwa.

Every September, Mr. Ajala visited Nigeria, and he was planning to travel there again this past September to visit his wife, Victoria, and their three children, Onyinyechi, 7, Uchechukwu, 5, and Ugochi, 1. His friends said he was planning to apply for visas to bring them to the United States.

"His dream was that he would take the law exam, pass it, and with that bring his family here and invite them to the swearing in," Mr. Iwuanyanwa said. "He would have been much happier if his wife and kids were around."

GERTRUDE ALAGERO
The Luckiest in the World

She always had time for a friendly chat with the corner newsdealer and the counterman at the deli, and she was sometimes forgetful about paying parking tickets and bills. But Gertrude Alagero, nicknamed Trudi, was also a determined competitor. After she taught her fiancé, Peter B. Walther, to snowboard, she never let him beat her when they raced down Okemo Mountain in Vermont.

Ms. Alagero, a senior vice president at Marsh Private Client Services, a division of Marsh & McLennan, and Mr. Walther, who was her supervisor before they began dating in 1998, had planned to marry in Boston on Jan. 5.

A few days before the terrorist attack, Mr. Walther said, she pressed her fingers to his mouth while they were walking toward the subway from their Upper West Side apartment.

"Shhh," she said, "I need to tell you something: I am the luckiest woman in the world."

On Sept. 7, the day that Ms. Alagero turned 37, she gave Mr. Walther a Nikon camera so he could become adept at using it before their honeymoon in Africa. He snapped two rolls of pictures, mostly of her.

ANDREW ALAMENO
The Little Golf Clubs

Andrew Alameno loved the guys on his desk at Cantor Fitzgerald. "They were not like a frat house," said his wife, Sally Cohen Alameno. "But they were." They would get together in Westhampton in the summer with their families. At Christmas, they brought their young children into the office to eat candy and throw around a football. No one got any work done during those visits, Mrs. Alameno said.

Years ago, Mr. Alameno saw Sally Cohen walking down Washington Street in Hoboken nearly every night for months. She was heading home from her step aerobics class wearing a University of Miami sweatshirt, and he was lifting weights in his apartment. One night, he saw her in a bar. He sent a friend to ask her if she owned a University of Miami sweatshirt. The next day, he asked her out.

They had two children: Joe, 5, and Nina, 2. Mr. Alameno, 37, was home in Westfield, N.J., every night by 6 P.M., in time for dinner with the kids. He joked about retiring to North Carolina and becoming a golf pro. He had begun teaching Joe how to play. "My husband had a hobby of making golf clubs in the basement," Mrs. Alameno said. "He made Joe a set of his own clubs. They're fit for a 5-year-old. It'd make you cry to look at them."

PEGGY ALARIO
Time for Her Sons

Because Peggy Alario's Bronco was always the first one in the commuter lot and the last out, her friends on Staten Island staved off alarm as the hours passed on Sept. 11 and her little green truck was still parked there. But Mrs. Alario, a manager at Zurich North America, had been at a meeting on the 105th floor of 2 World Trade Center.

With only a high school diploma and some college courses, Mrs. Alario, 41, put in 12-hour days and Sundays, proudly building a career that had her working on national and international corporate policies.

Her most successful partnership, however, was her 18-year marriage to James Alario, who worked at home so he could watch their two sons. "I did everything around the house for her so she wouldn't have to worry and could spend time with the boys," Mr. Alario said of his vivacious, outgo-ing wife, whom he met on the dance floor and who still loved dancing at Rod Stewart concerts.

Mrs. Alario always got home for the final Little League innings, to supervise homework and put the boys to bed, making the sign of the cross over their foreheads. Only then would she put on running shoes and tool around the neighborhood for a good 45 minutes. "She worked so hard so we could retire early together," Mr. Alario said.

GARY ALBERO
A Hand for the Unfortunate

Never judge a broker by his collar. Take Gary Albero. He was a good insurance broker: urbane and vigorous, and he could sell. That's what led him to 2 World Trade Center for a breakfast meeting. But it was not the money or the numbers that appealed to him, said his wife, Aracelis. "He liked talking," she said. "He liked people and the job fit him."

Consider the private life of Gary Albero, who was 39 and lived in Emerson, N.J. He often volunteered at a local homeless shelter and sometimes slept there because he was interested in the lives of the homeless. He would come home, put on a white collar and go off to conquer Wall Street.

Gary Albero met a boy some years ago who came from a troubled family. Mr. Albero took him under his wing, took him to ball games and coached him in football. When it was time for the young man to go off to college, Mr. Albero was there to help pack his belongings and drive him to his dormitory. They hugged; the man gave the boy some money and reminded him that he could be anything he wanted to be.

The Alberos had their own child, a boy, a year and a half ago. "That was the happiest day of his life," Mrs. Albero said.

PETER CRAIG ALDERMAN
They'll Always Have France

Elizabeth and Stephen Alderman will always treasure the priceless September week they spent with their sons Peter and Jeffrey, and their daughter, Jane, in a rented house in Roussillon, France. But Peter Craig Alderman had to fly back on Saturday, Sept. 8, in time to prepare for a conference in Windows on the World, which he attended for Bloomberg L.P., where he worked in financial services.

When his parents learned that Peter Alderman, 25, was missing after the terrorist attack, they tried to return; no flights were available. So Michael R. Bloomberg sent his personal jet to fly them back. The Aldermans know that their son was trapped on the 106th floor; Jane got an e-mail message from him at 9:35 A.M. He said that there was a lot of smoke, and that people were afraid. "We knew there was no hope for him," said Mrs. Alderman.

And so, that month, in their home in Armonk, N.Y., they threw a party: Champagne, kegs of beer and tons of food, "a celebration of his life, by his friends," said Mr. Alderman. Over 100 came from as far away as Portland, Ore.; Mr. Bloomberg was there as well. "We ate, drank and laughed," Mr. Alderman said, "and we told stories."

JACQUELYN ALDRIDGE
The Sister Connection

Jacquelyn Aldridge's family called her "the connector" because she was the one who always knew what everyone was up to. Ms. Aldridge grew up in Tampa but moved to Staten Island in 1979, joining a sister who was living there at the time. She worked as an accountant for Marsh & McLennan, and was in constant touch with her two sisters and brother, even though none of them lived in New York.

"She was always one of those who pulled folks together," said her oldest sister, Delores P. Aldridge, who lives in Atlanta. Their parents, who always emphasized to their children that they should get good educations, died in the '90s. The siblings remained close; Delores Aldridge said she talked to Jackie, as her family called their youngest sibling, once or twice a week. Jackie Aldridge was married three years earlier, to Lafayette Fredericks, and continued living in Staten Island. She would have turned 47 in October, said her longtime friend, Stephanie Wright. She was someone who raced to take advantage of everything New York City had to offer—jazz concerts, plays, new restaurants. "I used to tease her that she was a girl from Tampa who got New Yorkanized," Ms. Wright said.

GRACE ALEGRE-CUA
Romance and the Towers

Grace Alegre and Ildefons Cua found romance at the south tower. Fresh out of graduate school from the University of Massachusetts, Ms. Alegre applied for a job as an accountant at Metropolitan Bank and Trust on the 17th floor, where Mr. Cua was the accounting manager, in 1986.

"She didn't get the job, but she found a husband," Mr. Cua said. They married shortly after the interview and she became Mrs. Alegre-Cua. They have two children, Nicole, 13, and Patrick, 9. Mrs. Alegre-Cua did not have any trouble finding employment elsewhere. Two weeks after the interview, she was hired at Chuo Mitsui Trust & Banking Company, where she worked for 14 years, most recently at 2 World Trade Center.

The only reason she did not get the job at Metropolitan was that the position had just been filled recently and Mr. Cua had conducted the interview as a favor to the general manager, he said. "She was very smart," he said, "but I couldn't hire her. I don't know if we were in love right away, but I was interested because of her beauty and sweetness."

DAVID ALGER
Tales from a Lunch Table

For a generation of up-and-comers in the money world of lower Manhattan, the scene was deeply familiar: David Alger's lunch table. Nothing fancy about it—Mr. Alger seemed to thrive on cheeseburgers and apple pie, and any nondescript Wall Street coffee shop would do. His stories are what live on, and the lessons embedded within them about the stock market, and about life.

"I can see him chewing apple pie and telling these stories," said Rob Lyon, who worked for Mr. Alger at Fred Alger Management in the 1980s and remained close. One of Mr. Alger's lunch lessons was that big companies cannot possibly grow as fast as little ones, and that problems in a company—or a life—can never fully be solved in one three-month reporting period. You have to look to the horizon, he would tell the young Turks.

Mr. Alger, who was 57, took over operations at Alger Management from his brother, Frederick, in 1995. But by then his impromptu lunch seminars were Wall Street lore, former pupils like Mr. Lyon said. And strangely, all the stories seemed to have the same opening line: "That reminds me of something," he would say.

EDWARD L. ALLEGRETTO
Always a Song

Edward L. Allegretto loved to sing. He sang at his own wedding, he sang at his niece's first birthday party, he sang in his backyard to entertain all his friends. Louisa Allegretto said that while her husband was dedicated to his job as a convertible bonds broker at Cantor Fitzgerald, what he loved the most was spending time with family and friends. He was big in stature—at 51 years old, he was six feet tall. "He was a family man," said Mrs. Allegretto, his wife of 17 years, with whom he had two children. "He loved life."

The family had frequent parties at their home in Colonia, N.J., where Mr. Allegretto made everyone laugh as he barbecued or they swam in the pool. And he always sang. "He sang a cappella in high school, and he always grabbed a

A vintage fire truck carries the coffin of Firefighter William Henry down Thirty-first Street in Manhattan after funeral services for him on September 20. (*Krista Niles*)

mike and sang," said one of his wife's five sisters, Marlena Simone.

At family dinners, he always sat at the head of the table.

"He'd rather make a joke than get mad at anyone," Mrs. Simone said. "He said he couldn't waste his time on that."

JOE RYAN ALLEN
A Knack for Connecting

Joe Ryan Allen was one of those guys who still had his friends from first grade. His brother-in-law described him as "the family ambassador" because of his knack for connecting with people.

Mr. Allen, 39, had done well in his career as a bond broker at Cantor Fitzgerald. But the centerpiece of his life was his many friends and his family—a younger sister, three older brothers, six nieces and nephews.

His sister, Jennifer D'Auria, said Mr. Allen was single and thinking about settling down after seven years in Los Angeles trying to be an actor, and many more years of being

an inveterate world traveler. "He did everything he wanted to do," Ms. D'Auria said. "He was always out with friends, he was always getting together with the family."

He was her rock, she said, when their mother died of cancer in 2000.

"He would be depressed because other people around him had problems; they weren't his problems," said Robert Diodato, his best friend. They grew up in Bronxville together and met in fourth grade. "He was one of those friends you speak to four or five times a day. He left a tremendous void in a lot of people's lives."

CHRISTOPHER ALLINGHAM
The Giants' Biggest Booster

Christopher Allingham loved his family, and he loved the Giants. A season ticketholder, he never missed a home game. He even roped his sons, Christopher, 6, and Kyle, 4, and various relatives and friends into joining him. "He was like a kid," said his brother-in-law, Craig Kepple. "He was just having a good time."

The night before a game, Christopher, 36, would usually pack up the portable grill, marinate the steaks, and dig out his Giants T-shirt, sweatshirt and ball cap at his home in River Edge, N.J.

The next day, he would round up the fans for a tailgate party at the stadium before the kickoff. A few weeks ago, he took his sons to a preseason game. "They loved it," said his wife, Donna. "He was a good husband and a wonderful father."

The regular season was supposed to start on Sept. 16.

ANNA S. ALLISON
From Wine, a Beginning

Love blossomed over crushed grapes.

Blake Allison was a wine appreciation instructor at the Cambridge Center for Adult Education in Massachusetts. His future wife, Anna, was a student. "She took a couple of courses before we went out," said Mr. Allison, a professional wine-taster. "I was slow to get the hint."

Anna S. Allison was on the plane that struck 1 World Trade Center. She was on her way to visit a client in Los Angeles.

Mrs. Allison was an independent, spirited adventurer, who loved to travel, Mr. Allison said. Last year, she started her own company, A2 Software Solutions in Boston, where she and her husband lived.

When they "could swing it," they would travel together, Mr. Allison said. In 2000, they went to France, visiting Paris and Alsace. They also toured the Beaujolais district of southern Burgundy and Champagne, where the original Champagne is made.

"Every day was a new opportunity for her," Mr. Allison said. "Because there were new opportunities, there was always hope of doing something good. That's the way she lived her life."

JANET ALONSO
A Miracle Motherhood

The next-to-last phone call Janet Alonso made on the morning of Sept. 11 was typical: its genesis was maternal anxiety, and its focal point was her second child, Robbie, born with Down's syndrome in 2000. She was not only checking in with her mother-in-law, Margaret Alonso, who handled the baby-sitting during the three days each week that Janet spent as an e-mail analyst for Marsh & McLennan. She was also making sure Robbie's foot braces, misplaced on Sept. 10, had been located and returned to him; he finds it impossible to take his baby steps without them.

"Check his stroller," Janet Alonso suggested. Bingo.

Grandma discovered the braces. Janet and Robert Alonso were also the parents of Victoria, 2, a miracle baby of sorts. After 10 years of trying to conceive, using methods increasingly clinical, Ms. Alonso had all but surrendered her dream of becoming a mother when Victoria was conceived—surprise—the natural way. Ms. Alonso was so ecstatic she wrote her husband a letter, thanking him for this greatest gift. He was so moved he put the letter in a safe to preserve it.

Though her children were her passion, Ms. Alonso was a diligent homemaker—literally. She loved painting and refinishing furniture, and spent the weekend before the disaster sanding the porch they had added to their house in Stony Point, N.Y. Her final phone call was to her husband; she told him that the office was filling with smoke and that she could not breathe. And she told him she loved him.

ANTHONY ALVARADO
A Stroke Strengthened Him

Anthony Alvarado lived for his son. He suffered a stroke when his son was a newborn, and was paralyzed on his right side and lost his memory. It was as if he were a child again, said his mother, Sonia Irizarry. He could speak Spanish, his first language, but had forgotten English.

Ms. Irizarry nursed her son back to health. "Little by little, he came back," she said. After that, Mr. Alvarado could not take his baby for granted.

As the boy, Anthony Joshua Alvarado, now 10, grew older, his father took him everywhere. They walked to Yankee Stadium, not far from their apartment in the Bronx, for baseball games. They played dominoes, they went to the movies, to two amusement parks and to the beach. "My son is a good son, a good dad, a good grandson, a good brother, a good friend," Ms. Irizarry said.

Mr. Alvarado, 31, worked for Forte Food Services, in the cafeteria at Cantor Fitzgerald at 1 World Trade Center. He had planned to interview for another job as a security guard. "He needed more money," his mother said. After all, he had a son to support.

ANTONIO ALVAREZ
Learning on the Job

Antonio Alvarez and his wife, Filiberta Barragan, met more than five years ago at a garment factory in Queens. His job was to unpack and distribute the pieces of garments that came bundled together. Her job, after seamstresses had stitched them together, was to repackage them to send off to another factory.

The two were newly arrived immigrants from Mexico. They both believed in hard work and family closeness. "He was very serious, but always in a happy mood," Mrs. Barragan said.

They began living together, and four years ago had a son, Giovanni. They married in 2000. Mr. Alvarez, 23, liked to play soccer with friends or join in pickup basketball games in his neighborhood in Jackson Heights, Queens.

At one point, Mr. Alvarez was laid off from the garment factory, and he went to work for a restaurant. About a year ago, a friend helped him get the job as a grill cook at Windows on the World. He went to work at 6:30 A.M. on Sept. 11, earlier than usual, because there was a special event. "He was very happy working there," his wife said. "He said he was learning so much."

VICTORIA ALVAREZ-BRITO
Exploring the World

Just before school started in the fall of 2001, Victoria Alvarez-Brito and her husband, Mario, took their children on a weeklong vacation to Cancún, Mexico. It was a yearly ritual: pick a part of the world and explore it.

In the past, the family had traveled to the Dominican Republic and to Disney World, in Florida. Next year, the Britos were planning to visit the Netherlands. "She wanted to get to know Europe, and we have relatives in Holland, so that was a good place to start," Mr. Brito said.

During the Cancún vacation, the Britos took pictures and made a video. Watching the video or putting the pictures in the album with the children, Jamie, 8 and Raúl, 5, was sometimes as fun as the vacation itself.

On Monday, Sept. 10, Mr. Brito took the pictures to be developed. On Tuesday, Sept. 11, Mrs. Alvarez-Brito, 38, left home early for the long commute from Elmhurst, Queens, to her job in the finance department of Marsh & McLennan in the World Trade Center.

Mrs. Alvarez-Brito promised her daughter she would get cod on the way home from work that night to cook her favorite meal, cod and potatoes in a thick creole sauce. "She didn't get to see the pictures," Mr. Brito said. "Now we can't bear to watch that video."

TELMO ALVEAR
An Early Shift, as a Favor

At 25, Telmo Alvear, who emmigrated from Ecuador as a teenager, was assembling the pieces of a good life. His son, Steven, had just turned 1. His wife, Blanca, was studying computerized accounting at a Midtown technical college.

And in August 2001, he quit a busboy job to become a waiter at Windows on the World, for much higher tips. He

liked serving fancy meals and was beginning to learn about wine.

Off duty, Mr. Alvear was usually at home with his family in Queens, watching soccer on television or cooking dinners of seafood or pasta for relatives and friends. On weekend afternoons, he joined his team at Flushing Meadows-Corona Park for some hard-hitting volleyball. When he and his friends went dancing with their wives and girlfriends, he would make a point of dancing with as many of the women as he could.

Mr. Alvear was assigned to the night shift at Windows on the World. But on Monday, another waiter told him he could not make the breakfast shift, and Mr. Alvear agreed to cover for him. The friend promised to return the favor soon.

CESAR ALVIAR
A Lifetime Romantic

Cesar Alviar used to tell his wife, Grace, that everyone is born with a fate, and "your fate was to marry me." He saw her dancing, long hair swaying, at a party in their native Philippines and asked where she lived. He was quiet and modest, she said, but very handsome.

It took him three years to win her heart. But he stayed romantic. After 28 years, he still brought her flowers and opened doors for her. He loved to take her ballroom dancing. Three years ago, they renewed their vows. Mrs. Alviar wore an embroidered Filipino wedding dress. Their friends teased them, "You still answered 'yes,' in spite of everything?" Mr. Alviar pointed out that they had been married three times, in a civil ceremony, the religious service, and then this one.

His wife always drove Mr. Alviar, 60, to the bus station in Bloomfield, N.J., so he could get to his job as an accountant at Marsh & McLennan on the 94th floor of 1 World Trade Center. "He always kissed me before he got out," she said. But on Sept. 11, he hesitated after the kiss. "It was like he wanted to say something, but because I was rushing, I just said good-bye."

TARIQ AMANULLAH
Always in Demand

As a boy in Karachi, Pakistan, Tariq Amanullah was obsessed with building things. Whenever his father went away on business, he would ask him to bring back a "how to" book of some sort. He played with Lego building blocks for hours. He built himself a chair, to place in his father's study.

As a man living in Metuchen, N.J., Mr. Amanullah, 40, couldn't say no. And so his talents—as handyman, tax preparer, investment adviser—were spread far and wide among family and friends.

If his sister, Nilofer Usman, needed a garage door opener installed, Mr. Amanullah insisted on doing it. If a niece needed help selecting college classes, Uncle Tariq's advice was solicited. If anyone needed help selecting an insurance policy or figuring out an investment strategy, his phone rang. In springtime, so many friends and relatives sought his help on filing taxes that his family sometimes jokingly suggested that Mr. Amanullah, a vice president at Fiduciary Trust and the father of a boy and a girl, hang a shingle out front.

"Even though he was younger than me, I always had that feeling—he'll give me the right advice," Ms. Usman said. "Even his friends, if anybody needed anything, he would take the time out and help them. He would never say, 'I don't have time, I'm sorry.' "

ANGELO AMARANTO
Opportunity Perceived

When the World Trade Center became a part of Manhattan's jagged skyline in 1973, Angelo Amaranto saw opportunity. He left his job as a janitor at the Nasdaq and went to work at the twin towers in the same capacity. "He told me the pay was better and if they took him, he would have to work nights for a little while," said his wife, Maria. "He said it was worth it because it was a better building. He switched to days after two years or so. He loved those buildings."

Mr. Amaranto, 60, of Borough Park, Brooklyn, worked on the 87th, 89th and 91st floors of 2 World Trade Center, said his daughter, Rosanna. A native of Salerno, a city in southern Italy, Mr. Amaranto loved to provide for his family. He had three grown children. "He showed his love through work and buying gifts," said his daughter, who lives upstairs in the family's house. "He loved to buy apple juice for the kids and sometimes he would call one of my nieces to put it away. 'Sara, I have a job for you.' I keep waiting for him to walk in the door and say that."

JAMES AMATO
"A Fireman's Fireman"

Capt. James Amato, a member of Squad 1 in Brooklyn, loved putting out fires. No sitting around the firehouse for him; he wanted to be in the middle of the action, wherever it was. After years as a firefighter in one of the busier ladder companies, he applied for the elite rescue division, so he would always be one of the first people responding to a crisis.

"He liked to be one of the guys who made a difference," said his brother, Lee Amato, a firefighter from Cooper City, Fla. "He liked to get off the piece and run in with the men. He was a fireman's fireman."

The brothers spent vacations together, sometimes in Florida and sometimes on the ski slopes. Lee Amato, the elder of the two, called his brother "my dearest friend."

Captain Amato, a father of four who lived in Ronkonkoma, N.Y., and was a college wrestler, had close calls throughout his life. As a toddler, he barely survived a bout of spinal meningitis. And earlier this year, he told his men to file out of a burning building while they waited for a hose line to be set up. A few seconds after they got out, there was an explosion. "He was laughing about it," said his brother. "He said, 'Timing is everything.' "

JOSEPH AMATUCCIO
From Tollbooths to Towers

Joseph Amatuccio was hired by the Port Authority of New York and New Jersey as a toll collector right out of high school. For some people, that might be a dead-end job. For him it was only a beginning. Over the years, Mr. Amatuccio, 41, moved from toll collecting to carpentry and from there to management.

He used the agency's education plan to get an undergraduate degree in business management, taking classes at night, and was 18 months from a master's degree at Baruch College.

As a manager of operations and maintenance at the World Trade Center, he was on the phone every weekend from his home in Ozone Park, Queens, making sure that things were being done right, that subordinates were treating his beloved towers just so. "I'd argue with him, 'What do you think, you're going to own those buildings?' " said his wife, Debra.

Mr. Amatuccio was seen on the street outside the twin towers at one point on the morning of Sept. 11. Someone yelled, "Let's run!" Ms. Amatuccio was later told. He ran back in.

CHRISTOPHER C. AMOROSO
A Letter to Sophia Rose

The other night, after Sophia Rose Amoroso had her bath, she looked at her tiny hands, wrinkled from the bath water, and told her mother, Jaime, "I have Daddy's fingers."

Her father, Christopher C. Amoroso, used to tell his wife that two of his favorite things in the world were taking their 19-month-old baby for a walk, and bathing her, and he used to wiggle his wrinkly fingers at Sophia Rose.

The baby is too young to understand that her father, 29, a Port Authority police officer, died when he went back into the World Trade Center's north tower after leading a group of people to safety. She will not remember the thousands of people, including hundreds of police officers, who spilled out of Our Lady Star of the Sea Church in Staten Island for his memorial service.

But she will always have the letter he wrote her when she was 10 weeks old: "Sometimes it makes me cry, as I am overwhelmed by the joy I've been given by you and your mother. I want you to know that I consider myself the luckiest man to ever walk the face of this earth. If anything were to happen to me, I could honestly say I've known true love and happiness in my life. I've known that because of your mother and now you."

CALIXTO ANAYA Jr.
Doing Things Right

Calixto Anaya Jr.'s wife, Marie, remembers the New York City firefighter everyone knew as Charlie as "very attentive to the little things that keep love alive," whether it was taking days off for activities with their three children or showing up with flowers when she did not expect them.

"Charlie always wanted to do things the right way," Mrs. Anaya said. When they were married in 1990 in a simple civil service, Mr. Anaya insisted that they begin saving for the big church wedding her parents could not afford. Six months later, they marched down the aisle of St. Rita's Roman Catholic Church in Brooklyn.

Mr. Anaya, a former marine who re-enlisted when the Persian Gulf War broke out in 1991, believed true patriotism meant flying the American flag, not only in front of their home in Suffern, N.Y., but also wherever the family came to rest on camping trips or jaunts to the beach.

Mr. Anaya, 35, loved the Yankees in baseball and the Giants in football with similar exuberance. He preserved the hole he punched in his basement ceiling while celebrating the Yankees' World Series victory over the Mets in 2000.

JOSEPH P. ANCHUNDIA
Friends, Together Again

Joseph P. Anchundia, Judd Cavalier and Ian Crystal were best friends from grade school. They went off to different colleges, but after graduation it seemed only natural to get back together in a four-bedroom duplex in Midtown Manhattan. "When I mention Joe, I have to mention Judd," Mr. Crystal said. "We always pictured ourselves growing old together, hanging out. We never got sick of each other."

As children, their bond was going to Flower Hill Elementary School in Huntington, on Long Island. Later, it was bars. Still later, it was the monthly rounds of theaters and steakhouses. Mr. Anchundia loved Filli Ponte's lobster; Mr. Cavalier, who worked with Mr. Anchundia, a trader at Sandler O'Neill & Partners, an investment-banking firm, liked Smith & Wollensky so much he wanted to decorate their apartment the same aristocratic shade of green.

But among them, Mr. Anchundia, 26, stood out for being sweet and happy. So happy, he would wake up at 6 in the morning, crank up Steely Dan, and enter the shower whistling.

Mr. Anchundia was a middle child and a momma's boy. His last note to Mr. Crystal, who had gone away to business school, said, "I love you bro bro broski bro bro. Joe."

JUDSON J. CAVALIER's portrait is on page 78.

KERMIT C. ANDERSON
Walking Together

Kermit C. Anderson made the most of his lunch hour. Almost every day, for half an hour or so, he would descend from his 93rd-floor office at the World Trade Center and walk, usually along the Hudson in Battery Park City, gazing out toward New Jersey. He loved places where the boundaries come together: city and river, humanity's creation and nature's.

Mr. Anderson, 57, a systems analyst at Marsh Inc., was a math major at Pennsylvania State University who married another Penn State math major, the former Jill Grashof. Together, the Andersons, who lived in Green Brook, N.J., walked for 36 years of married life.

Last year, for their 35th anniversary, they walked the mountains of British Columbia. Deposited every morning by helicopter with a guide, they would hike all day and arrive in the evening at a lodge in time for dinner and a soft bed.

"He probably would have camped, but for me he would stay in lodges with running water and lights," Mrs. Anderson said.

YVETTE ANDERSON
Master of the Feast

Here are dishes Yvette Anderson might have served someday in her dream restaurant: corn pudding, barbecued chicken, fried chicken, turkey wings, collard greens mixed with kale and turnip greens, banana pudding, lemon meringue pie, peach cobbler. And her daughter Rasha McMillon's favorite, yellow and green squash with onions.

For years, members of White Rock Baptist Church in Harlem, where Mrs. Anderson prayed, praise-danced and tended to the elderly, were nourished by her feasts. Mrs. Anderson, 53, hoped to give the public a taste soon after she received her bachelor's degree in hotel and restaurant management next May. In the meantime, she was saving her earnings from two jobs: as a waitress at a soul food restaurant on weekends, and during the week, as a keyboard specialist at the New York State Department of Taxation and Finance, in the World Trade Center.

Orphaned at 15, Mrs. Anderson pressed upon her children the importance of self-reliance and hard work. But she was also a joyous, generous woman, animated by faith. On the night of Sept. 10, she braided her daughter's hair, saying, "I don't know why, but I have a nervous feeling." Then, Ms. McMillon said, "She called a friend from church and talked about loving God."

MICHAEL ANDREWS
Surprise up His Sleeve

Michael Andrews, 34, was the "grouchiest nice guy you would ever want to meet," his fiancée, Liz Smith, said. He talked tough and acted sweet—a "walking oxymoron."

He had graduated from Xavier High School and Fairfield University and worked at Cantor Fitzgerald. He also owned a Manhattan bar, Coppersmith's, with five friends. He was such an obsessive Yankees fan that if they hit a home run while Ms. Smith was in the kitchen, she would have to stay there, for luck.

They grew up together in Rockaway, Queens, and began dating in the spring of 1999. Soon after, Ms. Smith's brother was murdered.

"I feel he was totally supposed to be in my life," she said. "He was so strong for me, so wonderful. And I think I was meant to be in his life to make him happy."

He called her Morty, as in "Morty, I love you guy"—his farewell the morning of Sept. 11. Mr. Andrew's family—he is one of seven brothers and sisters—calls Ms. Smith his fiancée, but she says she wasn't, yet. One of his co-workers told her after the attack that he was planning to propose that month.

JEAN ANDRUCKI
Row, Row, Row Your Boat

Why waste time on TV when you could read or bike or help somebody out? Jean Andrucki did not even own a set. Instead, she played on two Irish women's teams: soccer on one and Gaelic football on the other. She kayaked with her 3-year-old nephew. "She's paddling," said Laura Andrucki-Izzo, her younger sister. "And he's belting out 'Row, row, row your boat.' That says it all about Jean."

Her job was doing risk assessment for the Port Authority of New York and New Jersey. After hours, Ms. Andrucki, 43, was usually either helping to care for developmentally disabled children or elderly neighbors in Hoboken, N.J., or she was jogging or hiking. Her passions were nature and animals—the wildlife of South Africa and Peru, which she visited, and of Hoboken, which she fed. "The squirrels would

climb seven floors to her terrace," Ms. Andrucki-Izzo said.

"She loved animals and gardens and writing and poetry," she continued. "She had a British heart. But it was more Oscar Wilde than Jane Austen. More a smart, tough American woman with a soft spot."

SIEW-NYA ANG
Missing Mommy

It has been at least eight years since Siew-Nya Ang saw an R-rated movie. Ms. Ang relished family time and since her daughters Jeanee, 8, and Winnee, 4, were too young for movies with grown-up themes, she only watched family-oriented films.

Ms. Ang, 37, also discouraged her husband, Kui-Liong Lee, from doing yardwork when he could be spending time with the family. "She would say: 'Wake up early in the morning. You can mow the lawn when we're asleep,' " Mr. Lee said.

On weekdays, Ms. Ang left for her job as a technical analyst at Marsh USA while her family was sleeping. But every morning around 8, she called home to make sure her girls were properly equipped to handle a day of school and dance, piano, ice skating or gymnastics lessons.

Since Sept. 11, the girls say good night to a picture of Ms. Ang, which hangs on the bedroom wall. Some nights, they complain to it, too. "Sometimes I have to let them know that Mommy is in heaven and other than that I just don't know what to say," Mr. Lee said. "Sometimes if they say 'I want mommy,' I can't do anything."

JOSEPH J. ANGELINI and JOSEPH J. ANGELINI Jr.
The Veteran and His Son

He would not have wanted it any other way.

Joseph J. Angelini Sr. and his son, Joseph Jr., were firefighters, and neither survived the twin towers' collapse. "If he had lived and his son had died, I don't think he would have survived," said Alfred Benjamin, a firefighter at Rescue Company 1 in Manhattan who was partnered with Mr. Angelini for the last six months.

The elder Mr. Angelini, 63, was the most veteran firefighter in the city, with 40 years on the job. He was tough and "rode the back step" like everyone else. His 38-year-old son, who worked on Ladder Company 4 on 48th Street, was on the job for seven years.

"If you mentioned retirement to Joey, it was like punching him," Mr. Benjamin said. Joseph Jr. was proud of his father's reputation and tried to copy him any way he could, said Joseph Jr.'s wife, Donna.

And they never gave up their tools. "Think about climbing

20 stories with bunker gear, ropes, hooks, halogens and other different types of tools and somebody wants to borrow a tool—no way," Mr. Benjamin said. "You ask them what they need done and you do it for them. You carried that tool all the way up there, so you're going to use it. If they thought they were going to need a tool, they should have carried it up. Joey Sr. always said carry your own weight. He always carried his."

Joseph Jr. applied to the department 11 years ago. He got called seven years ago. "It was the proudest day for my father-in-law. It was a great opportunity," said Donna Angelini. "His father was a firefighter and he wanted to be one, too."

Mr. Angelini, who had four children, taught Joseph Jr. carpentry. Often they worked on projects together, including a rocking horse. Joseph Jr., who had three children, had started building a dollhouse for one of his daughters. Unfinished, it is sitting on his workbench.

DAVID L. ANGELL
His Heart Was in Cape Cod

David L. Angell piled up Emmy Awards for his work on shows like *Cheers, Wings* and *Frasier*, but he was known for keeping his heart firmly on Cape Cod and for his closeness to his wife. "Lynn supported him for five years while he wrote and looked for a break," said Sally Reeder, a friend. "They used to say they had one suitcase packed and were ready to return to New England when he finally caught on."

Mr. Angell, 54, wrote compelling scenes, said Tom Reeder, a co-writer on *Cheers*. "He picked his spots to say anything very carefully, but more often than not he had the perfect words when he spoke," Mr. Reeder said. And Mr. Angell valued golf performance—he had a two handicap—over appearances. "He got his golf shirts at Penney's," said Mrs. Reeder. "He didn't care about designer labels."

The Angells, who celebrated their 30th anniversary this summer, had been excitedly watching the last stages of construction of their new home in Chatham, Mass., before boarding American Airlines Flight 11 in Boston to return to California.

LYNN EDWARDS ANGELL
And Hers Was There, Too

John Hitchcock was surprised when Lynn Edwards Angell walked into his office at Hillsides School, a Pasadena, Calif., home for abused and emotionally disturbed children, and described herself as a "retired librarian" willing to do the volunteer library work he had advertised. "She seemed awfully young to be retired," he said.

That was more than a decade ago. Mr. Hitchcock, the school's director, soon learned that Mrs. Angell, a soft-spoken native of Birmingham, Ala., was married to David Angell, a rising star in Hollywood's community of television writers and producers.

He also quickly discovered that Mrs. Angell had the dynamism and financial resources—she gave the money anonymously—to play a major role in transforming a small collection of books in the corner of the auditorium into a much larger library with its own building.

Weeks after Mrs. Angell's death at 52 in the hijacking of American Airlines Flight 11, Mr. Hitchcock continued to discover new dimensions to her contributions.

"She quietly did things like paying for golf lessons for a child who expressed an interest to her," Mr. Hitchcock said. "She knew all 66 kids by name. She sent each one a postcard from Cape Cod this summer."

DOREEN ANGRISANI
Inspired by Classic Rock

Led Zeppelin, Pink Floyd, Janis Joplin. When Doreen Angrisani was at her home in Ridgewood, Queens, the air vibrated with classic rock. In her opinion, there was nothing like a piercing Jimi Hendrix guitar riff to mellow the atmosphere in the house. Rock, said Gina Giovanniello, her sister, was not just party music; it was a "source of strength and inspiration."

By day, Ms. Angrisani, 44, was a finance manager for Marsh & McLennan. She began as a clerical worker and, over 23 years, rose to management. Her job was her job, but what really mattered to her were music, the Mets and Mike Piazza—and most of all, her family.

She lived with her sister and brother-in-law in the neighborhood they were raised in. She taught their two teenage children the beauties of great rock and contributed to her nephew's guitar lessons. "He actually knows who Led Zeppelin is," Mrs. Giovanniello said. "He must be the only 13-year-old who does."

LORRAINE ANTIGUA
In the Garden, under the Sea

The plan, Brian Wilkes said with a gentle laugh, was that he and Lorraine Antigua would marry at a drive-through chapel, maybe in Las Vegas, maybe this fall, while on a Harley-Davidson. "She said she would buy the Harley," he said.

Mr. Wilkes met Ms. Antigua, 32, at a going-away party two years ago, on the cusp of a move to North Carolina. They nurtured a long-distance relationship, until he decided to return north to marry Ms. Antigua.

Ms. Antigua loved working in the securities lending arm at Cantor Fitzgerald so much that she refused other job offers. At 8:50 A.M. on Sept. 11, she left a message for Mr. Wilkes on his mobile phone, saying a plane had rammed her building but she was O.K. He never managed to reach her.

They lived together in a house Ms. Antigua had bought in Middletown, N.J., where they had planned to make a new family with her two children from a previous marriage. They filled the garden with azaleas and sunflowers. To hear Mr. Wilkes tell it, Ms. Antigua was all good things—an avid reader, a scuba diver and a dear friend. "She's awesome," he said, slipping from habit into the present tense. "She ruined me for other women."

PETER A. APOLLO
And Then They Were Silent

It had been a year of dizzying change for Peter A. Apollo. In August 2001 he became a full-fledged securities trader at Cantor Fitzgerald. Two weeks before he was lost, his older sister, Denise, was married. In September he was to turn 27, and on Nov. 16, he and Debbie Johnson were to be married in West Orange, N.J.

"He was having the time of his life," said his mother, Cecile Apollo. "He loved his friends, loved his job, and he loved Debbie."

Mrs. Apollo said she had found some solace in reports that her son died huddling with co-workers on the 104th floor of 2 World Trade Center. Employees in the company's Connecticut office had an open line through a "squawk box," and said thick smoke rising through the stairwells had prevented Mr. Apollo and his co-workers from fleeing. Long before the building collapsed, they told Mrs. Apollo, the voices faded and then ceased altogether. Mrs. Apollo said she believed her son died before the building fell.

"At least that's what I'm hoping," she said. "I'm trying to find comfort in the fact that he was with the people he loved."

FAUSTINO APOSTOL
A Firefighter Who Baby-Sat

When both of his daughters-in-law became pregnant in the spring of 1999, Faustino Apostol took a rooting interest. "I was due a month after," said Jennifer Apostol, the wife of Mr. Apostol's younger son, Christopher, "but Faust said he had his money on me."

Mr. Apostol, 55, was the chief aide in Battalion 2 of the Fire Department, with 28 years on the force; he joked that he would quit only when the job stopped being fun. For the last 33 years, he had been married to his high school girlfriend. When they heard about the attacks on the World Trade Center, his family knew that he would be in the middle of the action.

"That's how he was," Ms. Apostol said. "When my son was born, the hospital wouldn't even let my mother in. Faust made up a story to sneak in. I couldn't believe he was there. But he'd do anything for you. You didn't have to ask. My neighbors used to ask us, 'Where'd you find a baby-sitter who also mowed the lawn?' "

FRANK THOMAS AQUILINO
A Crackling Imagination

If Frank Thomas Aquilino could have invented a 27-hour day, he would have gotten right on it.

Mr. Aquilino—F.T. to most, just F. to the closest dozens—was, like many Cantor Fitzgerald traders, young (26) and whoppingly successful (vice president and partner), a fellow in perpetual motion. What set him apart was that crackling imagination.

The boy who played cards with his sisters on the top of the refrigerator, who "borrowed" wood from construction sites to build multistory tree houses, grew into the man who was building a gambling Web site where visitors could bet on anything from sports to the weather.

That loopy inventiveness would not quit. What next from a short guy from Staten Island who danced tall and confident, who owned a red velvet shirt and black Reeboks, one of which he spray-painted white?

The ideas did more than serve financial gain and good times. As a teenager, Mr. Aquilino's best friend, Anthony Palumbo, had to use a wheelchair. "F., how can I keep my newspaper route?" he asked.

First, Mr. Aquilino tied the delivery bag to the wheelchair. Then he tied a jump rope to his bicycle, and, with Mr. Palumbo holding on to the rope's other end, Mr. Aquilino pedaled hard, towing his buddy, day after day.

PATRICK M. ARANYOS
"Mr. Smiley" Grows Up

As a child, Patrick M. Aranyos, a bond broker with Euro Brokers at 2 World Trade Center, was known as Mr. Smiley. As an adult, his life revolved around an enormous cast of companions.

He would ask them, "How are you doing?" and expect an answer. "There was a tilt of the head and a look in the eye," said John Minardo, who met him at Boston College, "that said he really wanted to know."

They flocked to his Halloween parties, where he dressed as a flamenco dancer one year. They knew he loved football; he insisted on participating, even as a skinny 16-year-old dwarfed by bulkier players. "He was like a knife, he was so thin," said his mother, Winnie, remembering the lineup at his school in North Palm Beach, Fla. "But he persevered."

In New York, they came by the dozens to go out with him at night or rolled into town from Europe, knowing they would always have a place to stay—at Patrick's. "You know how so many people in New York are so work-driven?" said his girlfriend, Alex Kearney. "He wasn't like that."

"He would give his right arm for anybody," said Ted Franchetti, one of his roommates.

DAVID ARCE
Stray Cats, Dogs, Kids

When Margaret Arce opened up her son's apartment in Stuyvesant Town, she found remnants of his generosity, letters to Santa Claus from poor children. David Arce, a firefighter, would answer them by delivering wished-for toys, year after year.

"He has always been like that, always bringing home stray cats, stray dogs, stray kids," she said. "Growing up, it was the same thing; he was always bringing someone home to me who needed a meal, or who needed a coat."

On Sept. 11, he jumped on the fire truck, Engine Company 33, on Great Jones Street, even though his shift had ended.

She described her son, 36, as a bit of a fatalist. "He always had this belief that destiny was waiting there," she said.

Firefighter Arce, whose nickname was Buddha, was an enthusiastic fan of Joseph Campbell and would have long discussions at the firehouse about the writer's research into myth and religion. "I think what resonated was the overall belief that in the bottom line, everybody's religion is the same," she said.

"Everybody is the same. It just comes down to one being. No matter who you are and what you are, we're all underneath the same sky."

MIKE ARCZYNSKI
A Tree for an Outdoorsman

Mike Arczynski's family will plant a tree next spring in his memory, and that seems exactly right. Mr. Arczynski, 45, was born to be outdoors. He was an aggressive but graceful skier, the sort people would stop to watch, said his wife, Lori. He grew up in wild places, first in Canada, and spent much of his childhood in Australia, where his father was an engineer helping build a dam on the Snowy River.

When in London, where he and Mrs. Arczynski lived for nine years before returning to New York last year, the Alps became their playground. Back in the United States, he loved where the family settled, in Monmouth County, N.J., partly because from there he could take a bracing, high-speed ferry ride every day to work across New York Harbor to his job as a senior vice president at Aon, in 2 World Trade Center.

But the family is in a quandary now about what kind of tree would best represent him: Canadian maple seemed perfect at first. "But I like the idea of an evergreen, too," his wife said.

LOUIS ARENA
Scent of a Firefighter

Louis Arena loved being a firefighter, and one of the ways he showed it was this: He would return to his Staten Island home from Ladder Company 5 and tell his wife, Wanda, "Smell my head."

Mrs. Arena, 31, was crazy about the way her husband smelled, especially after a fire. She would rub his hair and breathe the smell of smoke and sweat from his pores. The two had been friends since grade school, and married for the last six years, yet this was one of the rare times she had her husband to herself. "I used to be so jealous" of the other firefighters, she said. "I'd tease him, 'You love them more than me.' "

The couple had two children, Nina, 4, and Joseph, 3. They dreamed of retiring to Key West, sleeping on the beach and listening to Jimmy Buffett. Over the summer, she bought him tickets to a Jimmy Buffett concert in November.

Now Mrs. Arena is left with the unused tickets, and with the shirt he wore their last day together, on a trip to a Long Island beach. She has not washed the shirt, she said. She lost her husband, who was 32, but she cannot part with the last traces of his scent.

ADAM P. ARIAS
A Lover and a Fighter

After 15 lymphoma-related surgeries, Margit Arias never thought she would live to see as much of the world as her husband, Adam P. Arias, wanted to show her. So for their third wedding anniversary on Sept. 5, Mr. Arias, 37, surprised her with a globe encrusted with semiprecious stones.

They had married 18 months after the stark diagnosis. He prodded and cajoled her through treatment. During chemotherapy week, he did everything around their Staten Island apartment. But he would deliberately put his cigar ashtray in the wrong place, to jolt Mrs. Arias, a neatness fanatic, out of her chemo stupor. When she felt stronger, Mr. Arias would take her to a movie, on trips out of town; he even nudged her onto a golf course.

He was determined she would make it. A workaholic, he rose to a vice presidency at Euro Brokers with only a high school equivalency diploma. He was scary-smart—at 7, he knew the names of all the presidents, their wives and their parties—but not intimidatingly so, with a wicked wit and another life as a bar balladeer, covering songs from Tony Bennett and Meat Loaf.

On Sept. 11, he was determined that others would make

Rich Lambert, who lost three friends in the trade center attack, watches the funeral for firefighters at St. Patrick's Cathedral. (*Librado Romero*)

it, too. He lingered, prodding colleagues to leave. In October, Mrs. Arias had her 16th operation. "I didn't want to," she said. "But Adam fought too hard to keep me alive."

MICHAEL J. ARMSTRONG
Counselor Without Portfolio

Michael J. Armstrong had an uncanny way of looking people deep in the eyes and telling them things that stuck with them, that sometimes changed their lives.

There was the mixed-up, rambling Grateful Dead fan whom he met in 1993, on a train, who was stuck on drugs and on the run from his parents.

The young man wrote Mr. Armstrong a letter shortly after their meeting that Mr. Armstrong's family found stashed in a drawer when they cleaned out his Upper East Side apartment in mid-September. "After talking to you," the young man wrote, "I've worked everything out with my my parents and will be returning to work for them and continuing a drug-free life. I have positive goals but I almost threw them away. I just want to thank you for helping me."

There was the man from the Upper East Side who served time in prison. When he got out, he was shunned by most people; Mr. Armstrong, 34, went out of his way to talk to him, to make him feel welcomed.

"Since Sept. 11, we've realized what a great impact he's had on people's lives," said Catherine M. Nolan, whom Mr. Armstrong, a vice president of sales at Cantor Fitzgerald, was to marry on Oct. 6.

JACK CHARLES ARON
A Salt Baron's True Riches

After 24 years with the telephone company, Jack Charles Aron found himself with a few months off between jobs and was never happier. Staying at home meant he could spend all day taking care of his son, Timothy, which was especially important for Mr. Aron because his own childhood had been very unhappy.

It was also important because he and his wife, had been forced to wait years before having their son. More recently, Mr. Aron, 52, worked in information technology at Marsh

& McLennan, leaving before dawn and traveling by car, train and ferry so he could be home in Bergenfield, N.J., in time to coach his son's Little League and basketball games.

Although he was often so dour at home that his wife, Evelyn, referred to him as Mr. Grumpy, he was very easygoing on the ballfield or the court, she said.

Four years ago, the couple bought some land in the Philippines, where Mrs. Aron is from, and developed a salt farm. They called it Jet Farm (using the first letters of Jack, Evelyn and Timothy), and Mr. Aron told people he might like to live there after he retired.

The investment earned Mr. Aron a new nickname at work: Jack Aron the Salt Baron.

JOSHUA ARON
Reveled in Life's Details

At age 7, Joshua Aron would sit at the kitchen table bent over a copy of the *Wall Street Journal,* analyzing the stock tables with his chocolate milk. "I explained what makes it go up and down," said his mother, Ruth Aron. "He loved to do puzzles, and to him it was just another puzzle."

Fast-forward two decades. Mr. Aron was an equities trader at Cantor Fitzgerald, facing a bank of computer screens. When there was a break in the action, he sent love notes to his wife, Rachel, by instant messenger. "We were best friends," Mrs. Aron said. "Everything just came naturally."

Mr. Aron's intense, childlike enthusiasm made him a blur of activity in the kitchen, on a bike, or researching new fascinations on the Internet. He delighted in life's details, repainting his Upper West Side apartment, installing a 200-bottle wine closet and a 90-inch projection-screen television.

Even in the high-stakes world of finance, Mr. Aron, 29, remained playful, quoting liberally from Austin Powers movies ("Would they be ill-tempered sea bass?"). If Mrs. Aron was upset, he would cheer her up by promising to help get back at her tormentors. "You want to get 'em?" he would ask with mock intensity. "Come on, let's get 'em right now."

RICHARD A. ARONOW
A Sensei to His Friends

Richard A. Aronow was always so eager to share the fact that his lunch buddies at the Port Authority, where he worked for more than 18 years, called him sensei, Japanese for teacher. "Whatever they knew, or thought they knew, he knew more," his wife, Laura Weinberg, recalled.

Among the things Mr. Aronow, 48, of Mahwah, N.J.,

knew a lot about was markets, whether it was the stock market or the intricacies of frequent-flier plans, and he was forever switching long-distance companies to find the best deal.

As a deputy chief of the agency's law department, Mr. Aronow worked on some huge legal deals, most recently, the lease for the new $1.4 billion International Arrivals Terminal at Kennedy Airport, and he knew the details of all the Port Authority's leases, documents so voluminous that they are called telephone books.

Mr. Aronow was considered a fair adversary; about 20 lawyers who had been on the opposing side of his deals attended his memorial service, his wife said.

MYRA JOY ARONSON
French Food and Friends

Once, when Myra Joy Aronson was visiting her brother and his family in Washington, she found out about the Bastille Day celebrations at the French embassy and managed—at the very last minute—to get herself invited.

It was characteristic both of her love of all things French, and her spontaneous energy. She had fallen in love with France during a year abroad in college, and in recent years she held annual French-themed dinners with 15 or 20 friends, where they would prepare an elaborate Gallic feast with excellent wines. She also organized trips to Cape Cod with her friends in the summer.

Ms. Aronson, 50, loved music, and did volunteer work for the Handel & Haydn Society in Boston. A manager for Compuware in Cambridge, Mass., she was a passenger on American Airlines Flight 11 on Sept. 11.

Her family and friends have established a scholarship at Miami University, her alma mater, to help students who want to study in France.

YAPHET J. ARYEE
Taxes and Taxis

Yaphet J. Aryee was the person everyone went to for advice. "He was born in Ghana so he was the expert on that," said Ely Yulman, who worked with Mr. Aryee as an auditor with the State Division of Taxation and Finance, on the 86th floor of 2 World Trade Center. "He made his furniture when he got married, so people asked him how to fix the stairs in their house, or how to fix the engine in their car. But first of all, he was the smartest corporate tax auditor in the department. Millions and millions he brought in."

Like many other new immigrants, Mr. Aryee, 49, drove a cab when he first arrived in New York as a young man; hacking paid for bachelor's and master's degrees in business administration from Adelphi University. He and his wife, Maria, moved to Rockland County to raise their four children. But Mr. Aryee never forgot his taxi, and in August he bought his own cab so he could begin driving again.

"Only on weekends," Mr. Yulman said. "It was his hobby."

CARL ASARO
One Day, a Speaking Part

When Jerry Garcia of the Grateful Dead died in 1995, Carl Asaro was devastated. A self-proclaimed Deadhead, Mr. Asaro held a memorial service and barbecue in honor of Mr. Garcia in his backyard, complete with 50 guests, candles and the band's T-shirts hung along the side of the deck.

When his wife and six children realized that Mr. Asaro, a 39-year-old firefighter at the Ninth Battalion in Manhattan, was not coming home to Middletown, N.Y., they decorated his memorial service with some of the band's paraphernalia: T-shirts, Christmas ornaments, pictures. Songs like "Touch of Gray" and "Friend of the Devil" were played. It was a fitting tribute, they said, to his love for music. Mr. Asaro played the piano, the guitar and the piccolo.

A firefighter since 1987, Mr. Asaro also enjoyed playing one on television. He was an extra in several movies including *15 Minutes, The Siege* and *Frequency*. He played a paramedic on *The Sopranos, Law and Order* and *Third Watch*.

He dreamed of having a speaking part. "He always said one day he might go to Hollywood and be famous," said Heloiza Asaro, his wife. "And I said, 'Yes, you go to Hollywood and leave me here with all the kids.' He said no, I would be his agent."

MICHAEL ASCIAK
Many Facets of Competence

While on vacation early in September, Michael Asciak picked up his toolbox and followed his wife, Elaine, to the elementary school where she teaches. After asking if anyone needed anything, he put together tables, mounted pencil sharpeners and adjusted blackboards. "He just wanted to do it," his wife said. "He was always helping someone."

Though Mr. Asciak, 47, crunched numbers for Carr Futures, he was just as adept at fixing things with his hands. "Any kind of construction, heavy work, he liked that," Mrs. Asciak said. "It's interesting that he ended up in an office."

At their home in Ridgefield, N.J., Mr. Asciak converted the attic into a family room and spent hours maintaining the yard. He often teased the neighbors about their own efforts before eagerly showing them short cuts. But his best student was his 11-year-old daughter. Not long ago, she fixed the VCR by herself.

MICHAEL ASHER
A Daily Good-bye Kiss

On the evening of Sept. 10, Michael Asher called his son, Jeremy, into the den to show him a sleek computer image of an old Jaguar, whose engine he wanted Jeremy to help him replace and rebuild. Jeremy, 18, was eager to work on the project. But that day may never come. Mr. Asher, 53, who worked on the 101st floor of 1 World Trade Center at eSpeed, a spinoff of Cantor Fitzgerald, is missing.

"I was really into it even though I don't know that much about cars," Jeremy said of rebuilding the engine. "It was a chance to spend time with my father."

Mr. Asher was not only good with cars. He was a family man who enjoyed spending time with his son and daughter, Rachel, 16, at home in Monroe, N.Y., as well as rebuilding computers, creating software programs and listening to jazz.

He was also a man of habits, said his wife, Dana. One of them was "to kiss me good-bye before leaving for work at 6:30 A.M. while I was still asleep," she said.

JANICE ASHLEY
A Renaissance Woman

Janice Ashley was a modern-day Renaissance woman: literary, artistic and skilled in finance, as comfortable on Rollerblades as ordering a meal in a fancy restaurant. She was also outspoken and bubbly, someone who kept her friends from elementary school but relished new experiences, like a trip to Turkey in August.

"She marched to her own tune," said Richard Gallo, a friend she had dated for over five years. "She wouldn't have chicken or beef when she went out to eat—she'd order the antelope steak or ostrich burger." In a letter of condolence to the Ashley family, another friend recalled how Ms. Ashley was their only high school classmate to compliment her unconventional Sweet 16 party, at a Manhattan comedy club. "She just got things," Risa Lewak said. "There was nothing phony about her."

Ms. Ashley, 25, lived with her mother, father and 18-year-old brother in Rockville Centre, N.Y., and worked as a research associate at Fred Alger Management. She returned home tired from 12-hour days but found time to talk about her dreams, like eventually opening a florist gift shop, said Carol Ashley, her mother. She misses her daughter the most in the evenings. "She just sparkled," Mrs. Ashley said.

THOMAS ASHTON
Sharing Old Memories

It was home movies night on Monday, Sept. 10, at the Ashton household in Woodside, Queens. No one is quite sure why the family decided to break out the old videotapes after so many years. But there they sat, glued to the screen: Thomas; his sisters, Colleen and Mary; and their parents, John and Kathy Ashton.

There were a lot of laughs, especially at the scenes of Thomas, barely out of a diaper, whipping the Frisbee at his father with the precision of someone 10 times his age. Monday was also Thomas Ashton's first day at electrician's school, part of his apprenticeship with Local 3 in Manhattan. The second day on the job, Mr. Ashton, 21, was sent to the 95th floor of the north tower.

"We hope that wherever he is, he is able to have those memories from the home movies in his mind," Colleen Ashton said. "It was special that we were able to share that time together."

MANUEL ASITIMBAY
A Dream Realized

Manuel Asitimbay's life revolved around his children—two 13-year-old twin boys he had not seen since they were 6 months old, an 8-year-old boy he supported financially even though he was not his biological father, and a 4-year-old son who lived with him and his wife, Carmen Mejias, in Sunset Park, Brooklyn.

Mr. Asitimbay, 36, was an immigrant from Ecuador who was proud to work as a cook at Windows on the World. He took such joy in the food he prepared and carefully arranged on the plates of his customers that he would take pictures of his favorite dishes to show to friends and relatives.

But Mr. Asitimbay's obsession was his children. Every month for the last 12 years, he sent part of his salary to Ecuador to help support the three older boys, who were cared for by an aunt. He often sent them packages and once sent an upright piano and a guitar because he wanted them to appreciate music as much as he did. His dream was to bring them to the United States, said Dennis Diaz, a union organizer with Local 100 of the Hotel Employees and Restaurant Employees International Union, who has befriended the Asitimbay family.

Mr. Asitimbay's goal was accomplished because of what happened on Sept. 11. With help from Local 100 and Senator Charles Schumer's office, the children arrived in New York a month later.

GREGG ATLAS
Hero to the End

"Everybody ran to the stairs," recalled Gregory Warnock, a 20-year-old broker trainee who worked on the 39th floor of the north tower of the World Trade Center. "We started making our way down, landing by landing."

At the 18th floor, "there was an older fireman one floor below me. He gave me a smile. He was huffing and puffing, laughing to himself, making a joke about his age."

The 44-year-old lieutenant accepted Mr. Warnock's offer to help carry gear up about 25 flights of stairs, and he jokingly asked if the broker trainee was a firefighter. Told that Mr. Warnock was a broker, "he said, 'you stay doing that, it's better money.' "

"People were coming down, saying people were trapped on the 72nd floor. He said to me, 'Go down, you did a great job.' "

Before Mr. Warnock left, he asked the firefighter's name. "He was like, 'Gregg Atlas,' and he bent down and flexed like Atlas the bodybuilder."

GERALD ATWOOD
To Florida with Family

"Why don't we drive down to Florida," Gerald Atwood suggested on the spur of the moment last spring.

"You're crazy," said his wife, Barbara Swat-Atwood—not with a 2-year-old boy and a baby daughter in tow. But he talked her into it, and they were off.

For if Mr. Atwood, 38, a firefighter with Ladder Company 21 in Manhattan, loved anything as much as fixing up their house in Marine Park, Brooklyn, his wife said, it was getting out and "seeing new things, meeting new people." In Florida, those new people included a retired New York firefighter working there as a bartender; Mr. Atwood reveled in talking to him and "finding a common bond."

Her husband had an infectious laugh, she said, and regularly dressed up as the firehouse Santa Claus. And while a lot of firefighters had second jobs, "he was able to work it out without that," because his time at home was so precious.

"He always said that if money wasn't an object he'd have 20 kids," she said. "His daughter was just becoming Daddy's little girl." A third child, the couple learned in July, is on the way.

JAMES AUDIFFRED
Feeling Maine's Glow

James Audiffred was nutty over lighthouses. And not just any lighthouse. Again and again, he was drawn to the lighthouses of Maine. He studied their history and their architecture. In July, he packed his wife, his son and his sister-in-law's family into a rented minivan and took them to see the Cape Elizabeth Light, a majestic 67-foot lighthouse south of Portland. With childlike delight, he made everybody pose for pictures.

"My sister's oldest thought it was a little boring, but he didn't care," Robin Audiffred said of her husband. "He was having a ball."

The other day, Mrs. Audiffred received a check for $12,313 from Dennett's Wharf, a lobster restaurant in Castine, Me. The owners, Carolyn and Gary Brouillard, have been collecting dollars from customers for 11 years. Each time someone asked how they ended up with so much money taped to the ceiling, Mr. Brouillard would reply, "All you need to do is give me a dollar and I'll be more than happy to show you."

Carolyn Brouillard decided the money should go to a victim who was not in the limelight. On the Internet, she read a posting about Mr. Audiffred, 38, a World Trade Center elevator operator from Brooklyn who took tourists up to Windows on the World.

They had no idea that Mr. Audiffred was in love with Maine lighthouses—not to mention Maine lobsters. "A total surprise," Mr. Brouillard said. "A total surprise."

LOUIS F. AVERSANO Jr.
A Morning Chat with Fish

Louis F. Aversano Jr. liked to take care of everybody and everything. Especially his fish. At his home in Manalapan, N.J., Mr. Aversano, 58, kept a suburban-sized aquarium with five fish that he doted on.

"Those were his babies," said Lisa Aversano, Mr. Aversano's youngest daughter. "He would sneak in to see them early in the morning, and he would talk to them as if they were people. He would say, 'Hi fishies, good morning. Your sister is here to visit. Be nice to her. You guys look so nice today.' "

He couldn't help it, she said. After all, he exuded the same sunny disposition when helping to raise his four children or organizing neighborhood block parties.

There is a lot of father in daughter, Ms. Aversano said proudly. People call her "Little Lou" because they were best friends; they were former colleagues at Aon, where he was director of operations support; and they looked remarkably alike (except for the receding hairline and the mustache). And these days, she and her boyfriend find themselves the new parents of five fish. They spend time talking to them, just as her father did.

SANDY AYALA
The Sadness of 36

Sandy Ayala stayed close to his mother and three siblings. So close, in fact, that after he married, he insisted that he and his wife live with the family in the apartment where he was raised on East 113th Street, in East Harlem.

After he and his wife, Leyda Ayala, separated, he often took his daughter Samantha to the gym where he worked part-time as a personal trainer, and during the summer he would take her and her new half siblings to Coney Island and Orchard Beach.

On Sept. 11, he was working overtime as a banquet arranger at Windows on the World—after his usual all-night shift—to save money for a gift for Samantha's 12th birthday.

But that dedication was mixed with anxiety. "He was always afraid he would die young and never live to see his daughter grow up," Mrs. Ayala said. "He used to say he wouldn't live past 36." There was no real reason for it, since he had been weight training all his life and was in superb physical condition, she added.

He died a month after his 36th birthday.

B

E. RUDY BACCHUS
From Dancing to Deacon

E. Rudy Bacchus thought becoming a member of the Securities and Exchange Commission was one of his greatest accomplishments.

"He passed the exam on his first attempt," said his sister, Dr. Avril Anthony-Wilson. "He was pleased."

Mr. Bacchus, 48, was a successful independent trader at the American Stock Exchange and lived with his wife and two children in Metuchen, N.J. About 10 years ago, he made some changes in his life, giving up going to clubs and dancing, and becoming a deacon at his church. He used some of his earnings to help parishioners pay mortgages and college tuition, and he helped them define their financial goals.

He was attending a breakfast meeting at Windows on the World on Sept. 11.

Mr. Bacchus recently provided emotional support to Dr. Anthony-Wilson as she made plans to open a private medical practice in their childhood home in Cambria Heights, Queens. The week before the attack, she reminded him of the date of the opening celebration.

"Sept. 22, I'll be there," he said.

JOHN J. BADAGLIACCA
Mr. Fix-It for Life

Not that many people get to be somebody's soul mate. John J. Badagliacca truly did, says his wife. It began when they were 10 and she fell over his bicycle in their Staten Island school yard. They became friends that day and were married in 1992.

O.K., they did break up a few times. Sort of. Mr. Badagliacca wanted to date others when he took a share in a summer house and when he got his first car.

"All the convenient times," Nancy Badagliacca said with a laugh. "But we had all the same friends, were always together. We were perfect for each other. The first kiss was his, the first everything."

They enjoyed the same things, especially spending time with their children, Nikki, 6, and John, 4, at their summer home. Mr. Badagliacca, 35, a bond salesman with Cantor Fitzgerald, rebuilt that old house in Brick, N.J., from the beams out with his brother-in-law.

He kept their house in Staten Island in good shape, too.

"He was soooo organized," Mrs. Badagliacca recalled. "If a bulb went out he would have to change it in the next minute. If my cabinets got messy, he would reorganize them. It would drive me nuts! And his tools—you can't touch his tools."

He was so handy that she would tell him he could change professions. "I'd say, 'You could do just that.' " She paused. "I wish he did."

JANE ELLEN BAESZLER
Staten Island Tapestry

Jane Ellen Baeszler grew up in the shadow of the Verrazano-Narrows Bridge in the Randall Manor neighborhood in Staten Island. She went to Catholic schools and earned an associate's degree in business from the College of Staten Island. She never left Randall Manor, even after she got a job as a municipal bond broker at Cantor Fitzgerald.

Her mother, Rita, lived close by and said Ms. Baeszler was attentive to her nephew, Patrick, 10, and nieces, Annie-Laurie, 13, and Molly, 12, who were the perfect age to share secrets with an aunt that they would not tell their mother.

Ms. Baeszler, 43, relaxed by doing needlepoint. She had perfected it. She gave a needlepoint tapestry of a horse's head to a childhood friend, who is an equestrian. She made a cocoa pot for an aunt who collects them. She liked Americana. She made a tapestry of a *Harper's Bazaar* cover, with a woman in a long coat with a fur collar reminiscent of the Roaring '20s. On Sept. 10, she attended a class to work on a tapestry of a teapot for her sister-in-law's 40th birthday on Oct. 10.

ANDREW J. BAILEY
Good Father, Good Listener

Miosotys Fernandez decided to go out with Andrew J. Bailey to stop his best friend from pestering her about it. He is a really nice guy, the friend would say, but Ms. Fernandez only saw a low-key, calm guy—"very tranquilo," she remembered—not really her type.

"I was used to the thugs and the cuties," she said. Mr. Bailey, a 29-year-old who was born in England of Jamaican parents and had come to the States as a teenager, was no thug but he did look a little like Michael Jordan. He and Ms. Fernandez had jobs at the World Trade Center—he was an Advantage Security supervisor for Marsh & McLennan and she was an administrative assistant with the Port Authority—and after their first lunch date they became inseparable.

They worked out in the morning, had lunch somewhere in the towers every day and went home to Queens, where Mr. Bailey helped raise Ms. Fernandez's three young daughters. He also had an 8-year-old daughter, Veronica. Ms. Fernandez said he was a devoted father, a good basketball player and an even better listener.

On Sept. 11, Ms. Fernandez was coming out of the subway and dialing Mr. Bailey on the 93rd floor of 1 World Trade Center to tell him she was getting breakfast for the two of them when the first plane hit. She lingered in the area, calling and calling his number, until the first tower collapsed.

Ms. Fernandez, 29, keeps calling and leaving messages on his voice mail.

"I like hearing his voice," she said. "I tell him that I love him."

BRETT T. BAILEY
A Broker in a Wet Suit

Having spent his teenage years near the ocean in Bricktown, N.J., Brett T. Bailey seemed to pass whole seasons wearing a wet suit—whether it was winter, spring, summer or fall.

"It was hard to get him out of the water," said his father, Kevin Bailey. "He loved surfing. He loved swimming. He loved anything athletic. He was very playful."

Mr. Bailey, 28, worked as a lifeguard when he was a teenager but there was little question that after college he would become a broker, like his father and three uncles before him.

"The financial world is kind of in his blood," Kevin Bailey said. He worked on the floor of the New York Stock Exchange before taking a job as an options broker three years ago with Euro Brokers in 2 World Trade Center.

Mr. Bailey was a determined athlete. He started the sum-

mer with a 26 handicap in golf. By September, his handicap was down to 19.

"That tells you what he was like when he set his mind to something," said his father. "But one of the most interesting things about Brett was his ability to make friends very quickly, almost upon meeting them. He had such a diverse group of friends. From the New England fisherman to the Wall Street broker, they were all equal to him."

GARNET BAILEY
Ace of "Bailey-Baisse"

When Garnet Bailey would come to scout a game in Worcester, Mass., he would announce himself by saying, "table for two, please" as a tribute to the legendary meals served when the IceCats were at home.

That is how Bill Ballou, a hockey writer for the *Worcester Telegram and Gazette,* remembers Mr. Bailey, adding that he was "a pretty aggressive player on the ice, but a sweetheart off the ice."

Mr. Bailey, 53, known as Ace, played 11 seasons in the National Hockey League, and was a scout for 20 years, the last seven as director of pro scouting for the Los Angeles Kings. The team's general manager, Dave Taylor, said Mr. Bailey had a gift for measuring the intangibles that a player could "bring to the table."

Food mattered at home in Lynnfield, Mass., too, according to his sister-in-law, Barbara Pothier. For his wife, Kathy, his son, Todd, and friends, he would cook a dish called "Bailey-baisse, with "every kind of meat you could think of—tenderloin tips, chicken, pork chops, sausages." Sautéed, then baked with onions and tomatoes, Ms. Pothier said, "it was fall-off-the-bone delicious."

Mr. Bailey took a Los Angeles flight, United 175, from Boston on Sept. 11. It struck the World Trade Center.

MICHAEL BAKSH
Swinging to Abba

Michael Baksh would turn up the stereo after dinner at his home in Englewood, N.J., and swing his wife, Christina, and their two young children, Ava and James, to the sounds of Abba. They would dance until they dropped.

"It wasn't every night," said Mrs. Baksh. "But it was a lot of nights. It was a lot of fun. He really appreciated his life."

Mr. Baksh, 36, a Pakistani immigrant who grew up in Washington Heights, loved all kinds of music. He even wrote songs and performed with a rock band, Sage, in the early '90s. The band recorded a dozen or so songs, including "What Color Is a Soul?", which was played at his memorial service. Mr. Baksh had just started his first day as an insurance executive at Marsh & McLennan on Sept. 11.

An exuberant man, with dark handsome looks, he could be hard to forget. He caught his future wife's eye in a geology class at Hunter College in 1985. She introduced herself, and asked him out for a soda.

During their courtship, they went dancing every weekend.

SHARON BALKCOM
A Bookworm's Toughness

Sharon Balkcom, raised on the scrappy streets of East Harlem, was in the third grade when her teachers realized that she had a gift for mathematics, said her mother, Rosalie, who was not surprised.

Ms. Balkcom, 43, the second of three children, attended some of the city's most rigorous and selective secondary schools: Robert F. Wagner Middle School on East 76th Street, Manhattan, and the Bronx High School of Science. She received an M.B.A. from Pace University and a bachelor's degree in political science from Colgate University.

Ms. Balkcom's academic aptitude and varied education prepared her to tackle most jobs. She was a computer systems manager at Marsh & McLennan, where she had worked for about three years, her mother said.

"She was motivated," said her brother Gordon, a publicist. "Whereas I might need someone to kick-start me, she was self-motivated."

As a child, that motivation helped Ms. Balkcom, a resident of White Plains, overcome teasing from neighborhood children about being a bookworm. "She held her head up and continued to do what was right," Mrs. Balkcom said.

"My husband and I brought our children up the best we could. We tried to instill in them the importance of having an education. We taught them that things were not handed to them. If they wanted something, they had to work hard to get it."

MICHAEL ANDREW BANE
Unconventional Success

J. Donald Bane believes there are debts we owe our forebears. His first wife, a professional pianist, died in childbirth, but Michael Andrew Bane, the son born of that tragedy, carried on traits of the mother he never knew. Like her, he loved to play music, and was focused and driven in everything he did.

Sometimes what he did went against the grain, like dropping out of high school and working as a dishwasher and chef before enrolling in college. The younger Mr. Bane later married, worked in insurance and last year was promoted to assistant vice president for Marsh & McLennan's casualty

claims unit. Along the way, his father and stepmother, Arline Peabody, celebrated each step.

"It was just wonderful to see him blossom like that," his father said. "He had become my adult friend as well as my child that I'm very proud of."

In August, at home in Yardley, Pa., he and his wife, Tara, played host to a family reunion. On Sept. 9, the couple sat on the porch with their dogs and had a strangely prescient conversation. "He said, 'Would you stay in the house if I died?' and I said, 'I don't think I could,'" Mrs. Bane said. "But it feels good to be in the house. Because it's not eerie. It's comforting."

GERARD BAPTISTE
Treats for Dogs, and Himself

There is a decent chance that Gerard Baptiste had dog biscuits in his pockets when he died. A New York firefighter, he routinely carried treats to give to the pets that walked past Ladder 9 in SoHo. That helped start conversations with the children—or the women—that the dogs towed with them.

The abundance of beautiful women was one reason Firefighter Baptiste loved New York, and especially his job site. "Being American, he thought New York was the most beautiful city in the world," said Delphine Leymarie, his girlfriend.

On his fifth birthday, March 11, 1971, he flew to the United States from his native Santo Domingo. As soon as the plane reached cruising altitude, "he said, 'Now we're in America,'" recalled his mother, Gladys Rodriguez.

Mr. Baptiste studied one thing after another to get ahead in life. He tried graphic arts and computers, he joined the New York National Guard, and he was working to became an officer in the Fire Department. After postings in the Bronx and Brooklyn, he finally seemed happy with the place where he worked.

And then there were the dog biscuits. "I always found crumbs in his pockets," Ms. Leymarie said.

GERARD BARBARA
A Dad and Yankees Lover

Since Sept. 11, scores of well-wishers have packed the small Staten Island home of Gerard Barbara, assistant chief of the New York Fire Department. Mr. Barbara's wife and two children recognize many of the faces, but not all of them. In an odd twist, they end up consoling some of the visitors, who appear lost. Many just want to hang on to any memory of the chief, who was widely respected and loved for his humanitarian spirit, said his wife, Joanne.

"People I've never seen before are saying, 'You don't understand, I loved your dad,'" said a son, Paul, 23. "I say, 'I do understand, he was my dad!'"

Chief Barbara, 53, a 31-year veteran of the Fire Department, was one of the city's highest-ranking supervisors. He was walking toward the lobby of the second trade center tower when the building collapsed.

Paul said that when he and his sister, Caren, were growing up, they had no idea that their father was an important member of the Fire Department, because he was just a dad who was wild about the Yankees.

Caren said: "If the terrorists think they have won, they haven't. This whole thing just drove my dad deeper into our hearts. He died doing one of the things he liked best, trying to save people."

PAUL BARBARO
Trailing Two Little Boys

Even as a boy growing up on Staten Island, Paul Barbaro was always taking care of other people. He would shovel the snow off a neighbor's driveway free of charge and would often stay up late into the night to comfort an ailing grandmother, said his father, Nicholas.

Mr. Barbaro, 35, was a soft-spoken man and a perfectionist, whether he was painting his parents' kitchen or labeling moving cartons. An hour-and-a-half drive with Mr. Barbaro could take three hours.

"He would have to pull over at every scenic lookout," said Daniel Macri, a friend since high school. "He had to be a pain in the neck a little bit."

Mr. Barbaro, a software engineer, designed trading platforms for some of the biggest companies on Wall Street. In December, he joined eSpeed, and in August, he and his wife, Kim, moved from Staten Island to Holmdel, N.J. When he worked around the house, his sons, Paul William, 5, and Joseph Nicholas, 2½, would trail after him wearing toy tool belts.

"Anything he did, they were right behind him," said Mr. Barbaro's brother, Nicholas Jr.

JAMES W. BARBELLA
"He Would Never Give Up"

James W. Barbella was a former United States marine, and that made certain of his habits—the day-to-day decisions he'd be likely to make, the course he might be expected to take in a crisis—quite predictable, said his widow, Monica.

It was not enough, for example, for Mr. Barbella, a 53-year-old property manager for the Port Authority, to simply climb 110 flights of stairs during his fitness routine, which he often fitted into his lunch hour. That would be wimpy. Instead, he would go down all the way to the subbasement of the World Trade Center and begin his climb there. And it

was also not enough to simply climb to the top. He would descend by the stairs as well.

Mr. Barbella, who was responsible for floors 9 to 40 in the south tower, lived in Oceanside, N.Y., on Long Island, and had worked for the Port Authority for 28 years. He was last seen ushering three police officers up the stairs during the evacuation of the trade center just before its collapse.

"I knew, as soon as I heard, that that's exactly where he would be," Mrs. Barbella said. "He would never give up."

CHRISTINE J. BARBUTO
A Practical Joker

Christine J. Barbuto was one of those people whom everyone else wanted to be around. Her friends from the University of Rhode Island recalled how they hung out in 106 Barlow Hall, where she lived with Jennifer Tice in her freshman year. Erik J. Granskog, a college friend, spoke of the good times they had "playing charades, wearing stupid hats, watching *Cheers,* dancing and singing to the Violent Femmes over and over, inventing silly drinking games."

Dianne Walsh, one of Ms. Barbuto's two older sisters, recalled an old family tale: when someone praised Ms. Walsh's singing at a concert, Ms. Barbuto asked, "How long have you had this problem with your hearing?"

"She was probably 9 at the time," Ms. Walsh said.

Ms. Barbuto was also a practical joker. Her former roommate, now Jennifer Tice-McClain, said the two of them would hide behind the curtains when they saw male students heading for class and make catcalls until they turned red and ran.

"The sad thing is that Christine and I were not done

The altered Manhattan skyline forms the backdrop for a memorial service at Liberty State Park in Jersey City, on the night of September 23. (*Chang W. Lee*)

being roommates," Ms. Tice-McClain said. "We always joked about how we were going to live together at the same old lady home and put Ex-Lax into the brownies and Saran-Wrap the toilets."

Ms. Barbuto, 32, of Brookline, Mass., was a buyer for the TJX Companies and was on American Airlines Flight 11 on Sept. 11.

COLLEEN BARKOW
Building a Dream House

Colleen Barkow's job at Cantor Fitzgerald was to help oversee the building of things—including, most recently, the firm's cafeteria.

"She was very proud of that," said her father, Thomas Meehan. But over the past several months, she was using her talents to help oversee the building of something that mattered much more to her: a new home, for her and her husband, Daniel Barkow, in a virtual forest of a plot in the Poconos.

The couple were so proud of their project that they even started a Web site so friends and family could watch it rise. They were going to brave the two-hour-plus trips to work because they loved the place so much. They were supposed to move in on Oct. 1.

"I have an empty house now that she designed and built and she'll never get to live in it," Mr. Barkow said. Dates have become very important for him. He and his wife, 26, were married on Sept. 17, 2000. Rescue workers recovered Ms. Barkow's body on Sept. 17.

The only recent consolation for him has been that his wife's rings—her engagement ring, wedding ring and the diamond ring he had just given her for their coming anniversary—were found and returned to him.

Mr. Meehan said that his son-in-law had the rings repaired and now wears them on a chain around his neck.

DAVID BARKWAY
Engaged on a Ski Slope

He was a rising star in the Toronto financial world, but David Barkway, a managing director of BMO Nesbitt Burns, the Bank of Montreal's investment firm, was not all business. He was known on Bay Street in Toronto for his determination to improve his golf game, his cigars and his practical jokes. Colleagues would return from lunch to find a flashing message on their computer screen that was impossible to delete.

He became engaged in 1996 on a ski slope, presenting a diamond ring to Cindy McLennan after they had both taken a spill in the snow.

Mrs. Barkway, who is pregnant with the couple's second child, accompanied her husband on his final business trip to New York and was on her way to SoHo when the World Trade Center was attacked. Mr. Barkway, 34, had an appointment at Cantor Fitzgerald. If the baby is a girl, Mrs. Barkway said, she will have to name her Zoe.

"That's the name my husband wanted," she said. "I wasn't that keen on it, but he's going to get his way."

In Greek, she recently learned, Zoe means "life."

MATTHEW E. BARNES
Compassion Came Easy

On a March afternoon two years ago, Matthew E. Barnes climbed to the top of a 100-foot aerial ladder to rescue 6-week-old twins from a furious blaze on the Upper West Side. The ladder swayed in the crisp breeze as Firefighter Barnes took Isabella and Jacob Kalodner from the hands of their distraught mother, Linda.

Firefighter Barnes, who was honored at City Hall for the rescue, said at the ceremony that he had tried to convince Mrs. Kalodner to wait for firefighters to reach them from inside the building.

"She advised me she wasn't going to do that," he said. "I figured if she's willing to pass her baby out a 10th-story window, I should take it."

Mrs. Kalodner told him: "You treated our children like they were your own. There's nothing I can say but thanks."

The compassion was easy.

Firefighter Barnes, 37, of Monroe, N.Y., loved children, said Sean O'Brien, a friend and fellow firefighter from Ladder Company 25. Firefighter Barnes and his wife, Susan, had three boys of their own, Matthew Jr. 12, Jesse, 10, and Thomas, 8. He loved to take them fishing.

"Sue always had a project for Matt to do around the house, but somehow Matt would manage to slip out and go fishing with the boys instead," Mr. O'Brien said. "But the projects around the house always got done. They were proud of their home.'"

SHEILA BARNES
Crazy about Coupons

Just the other day, Colgate toothpaste was on sale at a local pharmacy and Zulema Barnes-Chung thought of her mother, Sheila Barnes. That was because Ms. Barnes was a bargain hunter extraordinaire, who transformed the routine of buying household goods into a competitive sport.

"My mom would go so far as to take other people's flyers just to get the coupons," Ms. Barnes-Chung said. "I guess that was stealing, but she did it so she could have three of each coupon. That's how bad it was."

And it was never really about the money. No, Ms. Barnes, who was 55 and worked for Aon, did not cut coupons because she was miserly.

"It was a game for her to see who could save the most, a game mostly between her and my aunt," Ms. Barnes-Chung said. "They kept the receipts to show the whole family 'Look what I got!'"

"My aunt says it's not so fun anymore," she continued. "But when I saw the toothpaste on sale, I thought about my mom. I almost dialed her number, before it hit me."

EVAN BARON
The Determined Type

Jeannine Spinella, a receptionist at Elders Futures, was shy. Evan Baron, a floor trader at the same company, was not. One Friday night 16 years ago, he asked if she wanted to go to a Mets game after work. She agreed.

Then she got cold feet. When it was time to leave, Mr. Baron found a temporary receptionist sitting at her desk. The young woman told him that Ms. Spinella had gone home sick. That should have been that. But he called her at home.

"He didn't believe me," she said. "So he said: 'I'm going to pick you up tomorrow, and we're going to Central Park. We'll throw a Frisbee and then have a barbecue on my friend's roof deck.' I said O.K. He was from New Jersey. I didn't think he would find my house in Midwood, Brooklyn. But he did, and we've been together ever since."

She became Mrs. Baron eight years ago. They had two children, Ethan, 6, and Julia, 2. Four years ago, Mr. Baron, 39, started working at Carr Futures, where he was a senior vice president and an energy specialist. He loved working as an oil trader, leaving college to take up the job full time.

"He was determined," Mrs. Baron said. "He worked his way up until he was in an office instead of the floor of the stock exchange."

ARTHUR T. BARRY
10,000 Miles by Motorcycle

Arthur T. Barry had an irrepressible joie de vivre.

Last year, he drove his motorcycle on a 10,000-mile trip diagonally through Canada to Fairbanks, Alaska, and returned traveling across the country.

That was just one example. Firefighter Barry, 35, a lifelong resident of Westerleigh, in Staten Island, spent his youth zipping across the country on road trips, said his mother, Audriene Barry.

Firefighter Barry's zest for life was apparent in his work, she said. He was in the business of saving lives as a New York City firefighter for the last seven years. Before becoming a firefighter, he had worked as an elevator mechanic and a machine-tool technician. He was a member of Ladder Company 15 near the South Street Seaport, and his colleagues frequently relied on him to repair elevators during high-rise fires.

"He truly loved the Fire Department," Mrs. Barry said.

Firefighting was in his blood. His father, Bertrand, retired as a fireboat pilot after 20 years on the job, Mrs. Barry said. For a time, Bertrand Barry patrolled the waters of New York Harbor in the shadow of the World Trade Center.

DIANE BARRY
At Ease with Her Life

Diane Barry loved growing up in Pompton Lakes, N.J., and dreamed about returning there someday, her cousin Maureen O'Keefe said. The families of Mrs. Barry and Miss O'Keefe lived in one big house, and the children would entertain themselves in the winter by baking potatoes over open fires, and in the summer by splashing in the town swimming hole "till our lips turned blue," Miss O'Keefe said.

When her cousin married Edmund Barry, she moved to Staten Island, raised three children and attended every Irish sing-along that came along. Mrs. Barry also taught first-graders every Sunday at the Holy Rosary School of Religion. During the week, she worked as an administrative assistant at Aon, the insurer. On July 11, to celebrate her turning 60, family members treated her to lunch at Windows on the World.

"It was a beautiful day, and you could see for miles," said Miss O'Keefe, who said the conversation turned to the 1993 bombing of the trade center. "I said, 'Oh my goodness, Diane. This building is so big. Aren't you afraid?'"

She said her cousin calmly replied, "I'm not afraid. When God is ready to take you, he'll take you."

SCOTT BART
Start of a Marriage

Scott Bart and Elizabeth Cappell conducted their courtship in a 96th-floor office at 1 World Trade Center. He was an up-and-coming vice president at Marsh & McLennan, she a student teacher at the nearby High School for Leadership and Public Service. When school let out, Ms. Cappell would grade papers alongside her future husband so that work would not separate them.

Often, Mr. Bart read the books his fiancée was teaching so they could talk about them. And he tried to confine business trips to one day.

The couple set a wedding date for Aug. 4, 2001, planned a Mexican honeymoon and bought a house in Malverne, close to his family and hers. Mr. Bart, 28, loved carpentry projects, learned at his father's knee, and had already built a chest of drawers and sketched plans for a deck. Mrs. Bart, 24, got a job teaching English at a Long Island High School.

The Barts' wedding day was vintage Scott, Mrs. Bart said. He did not want friends to spend a fortune for hotel rooms. So he turned over their new house—Hotel Bart, they called it—to a score of celebrators, who slept on couches, in sleeping bags and on the floor of rooms as yet unfurnished. He also rented a yellow school bus to transport everyone from the church to the reception.

"He made sure everything was taken care of," Mrs. Bart said.

CARLTON W. BARTELS
Wraparound Buddha

Her father was aghast: there on the doorstep of her family's West Brighton home in Staten Island stood Carlton W. Bartels, suitor.

"Carl had thick, wavy brown hair, down to his shoulders," Jane Bartels, the object of his affection, recalled decades later. "And a suede fringe jacket."

The couple managed to date and grow close, but then careers separated them. While in his 20s, Mr. Bartels took an 18-month trip around the world with his savings. He asked her to join him in Jakarta, where they inched toward Europe. They married in 1988. Mr. Bartels was an electrical engineer by training and had become, at 26, one of the top utility regulators in Vermont. At 44, he was a partner at Cantor Fitzgerald, specializing in using the commodity markets to encourage the reduction of greenhouse gases.

Mr. Bartels had his antic side, Mrs. Bartels recalled. While on his epic trip, living in a Thai village, Mr. Bartels took to wearing a favorite sarong, a black-and-white skirt with Buddha figures. But one day, the villagers giggled. He was wearing a sarong for a woman. Unfazed, he continued to wear it, even back home, years later, when the couple had settled back in Staten Island. Their daughters—Melina, 8, and Eva, 4—loved it.

GUY BARZVI
Planning a Birthday

Guy Barzvi was excited about turning 30 in February 2002. He told his younger sister, Lori, that he was spending too much time on work and too little time on himself. But that was about to change.

"He was trying to figure out how he could have more quality of life," Lori said.

The son of Israeli immigrants, Guy often wandered far from his home in Forest Hills, Queens. He had traveled to Seville, Spain, and yearned to return sometime soon. In the meantime, he learned to salsa and strum flamenco on a guitar. Not long ago, he began making plans for his birthday. He had heard of a party scheduled for that day at the Intrepid Sea-Air-Space Museum, and wanted to join the festivities. His sister planned to invite his friends along to sing "Happy Birthday."

"He's just the best guy that I've ever known," she said. "We're still hoping that we'll find him."

INNA BASINA
A Second Life of Freedom

In Russia, Judaism was Inna Basina's nationality. In New York City, it was her religion.

"Here it was not a problem," said Inna's husband, Vladimir Basin. Inna found her second life when her family settled in Bensonhurst, Brooklyn, as refugees in 1994. "It was freedom for her, freedom for our son," he said.

Inna took a job as a translator for AT&T. It wasn't an ideal job, but it made ends meet. The couple made it a point never to be on welfare; they were in the United States for the opportunity, not handouts. She worked nights while studying for a master's degree in accounting at Pace University. She was a sharp student, and a professor found her an accounting position at J. P. Morgan before she graduated. She moved to Cantor Fitzgerald in 1999.

Vladimir Basin would drop her off at the World Trade Center on his way to work. On the morning of Sept. 11, she was eager to buy a present for her son, Boris, whose 12th birthday was three days later.

"Our son is the first thing in our lives," Mr. Basin said. "Everything for America was for family and son, not because she liked accounting."

ALYSIA BASMAJIAN
In Two Years, a Full Life

Alysia Basmajian and her husband, Anthony, used to marvel to each other that theirs were lives lived in fast forward. They became parents at 21, just before the start of their senior year at the College of William and Mary, when their daughter, Kaela Grayce, was born. They graduated in May 2000, were married in June that year, and found jobs in Manhattan—he on the floor of the stock exchange, she as a staff accountant at Cantor Fitzgerald.

In the summer of 2001 their pace seemed to have slowed. They moved to an apartment in Bayonne, N.J., in

August. Mrs. Basmajian began painting again and her favorite subject was her daughter. For Kaela's second birthday, on Sept. 2, the little girl received her first bike; the family spent the day in the park.

At about the time they moved, Mr. Basmajian said, the couple found a list of life's major stresses and realized they had done nearly everything on the list within the previous 18 months.

"We'd gotten married, graduated, raised a child, found a job, moved to a new city," he said. "It was stressful, but it was O.K. because we faced it together."

The last item on the list was "the death of someone you love."

STEPHEN J. BATES
An Automatic Brotherhood

Although Stephen J. Bates liked the solitude of athletic competitions like running, swimming and bicycling, he was a team player. Period. That was why he worked for 18 years as a New York City firefighter. The lieutenant liked the way firefighters relied on one another while sticking to their vows to save lives and put out fires.

Most of all, Lieutenant Bates liked the automatic brotherhood of the job. It gave him the family he always wanted. His mother died when he was 15, and he was estranged from his father, said his girlfriend, Joan Puwalski. He frequently took family-style dinners with the firefighters at his stationhouse, Engine Company 235 in Bedford-Stuyvesant, Brooklyn. He liked cooking family dinners for the gang; sauerbraten was his best dish.

The other members of his family were two big dogs who lived in the home that he shared with Ms. Puwalski in Glendale, Queens: Samantha, 8, a 105-pound yellow Labrador retriever, and Norton, 8, an 85-pound mutt.

"He called them his babies," Ms. Puwalski said. "Sometimes the four of us would sleep together in our queen-size bed." That was a squeeze, considering that Lieutenant Bates, 42, was a big man, standing exactly 6 feet and weighing 235 pounds.

PAUL J. BATTAGLIA
A Knack for Numbers

Paul J. Battaglia's mother, Elaine Leinung, likes to say that her son was "born at age 40."

Even as a preschooler, Mr. Battaglia, who was actually 22, had a knack for numbers. How else to explain a 4-year-old tallying the correct amount of change due even before the cashier at the grocery could? It happened a lot, Ms. Leinung said, and by age 10, he was balancing checkbooks.

"I would have such difficulty with it and complain," Ms. Leinung said. "It all started with his Commodore 64 computer when he was 9. He found his niche: numbers."

By his senior year at Regis High School in Manhattan, Mr. Battaglia had earned an internship with Marsh & McLennan. After he graduated from the State University of New York at Binghamton, his internship turned into a position as a risk consultant. He was so proud of his job on the 100th floor of Tower 1 that he posted pictures of his office and his view of the Brooklyn Bridge (his home borough) on his Web site, Battaglia.org.

One snapshot was mostly gray. "Cloudy day!" he wrote underneath.

W. DAVID BAUER
Sports and Learning

W. David Bauer took part in a triathlon the weekend before the World Trade Center was attacked. At 45, he did better in the bicycling, running and swimming competition than he had expected to, said his wife, Ginny. He went to his sons' football scrimmage. He grilled steaks and drank cabernet wine with friends they entertained at their Rumson, N.J., home.

"It was a perfect weekend," Mrs. Bauer said. It was also the sum of what he loved best: sports, family, friends and competition.

Mr. Bauer was head of global sales for eSpeed. The job came a year ago after a series of promotions at Merrill Lynch, Lehman Brothers and Credit Suisse.

Mrs. Bauer said sports was a big part of their family life. But her husband was constantly telling his children that lifelong learning was important, too. To one son who loved playing basketball, he would say: "Just be the smartest basketball player."

IVHAN LUIS CARPIO BAUTISTA
Things Were Going So Well

Sept. 11 was Ivhan Luis Carpio Bautista's day off at Windows on the World. It was also his birthday. But with an extended family back in Peru depending on his paycheck, Mr. Carpio, 24, did not hesitate when a co-worker called that Monday night asking if he would cover a shift.

"He worked all the overtime he could," said a cousin, Rita Tatiana Palacio. "Too many people needed the money, including a niece whose school he paid for."

In the two years since arriving in New York speaking only Spanish, Mr. Carpio had made enviable strides. His English was nearly fluent, he had found the perfect job and in August he had moved into his own place, having previously shared an apartment with his cousin in Queens.

The day before the attack on the twin towers, he learned that he had been accepted to John Jay College of Criminal Justice. It was a day of triumph, as he had been uncertain whether the school would accept credits from his two-and-a-half years of law school in Peru.

"He was so excited, so happy," Ms. Palacio said. "I remember him saying how he was so lucky, that everything was going to be so good from now on."

MARLYN BAUTISTA
A Born Organizer

Rameses Bautista said the cleaning crew at Marsh & McLennan loved his wife, Marlyn. She was the kind of worker who kept her cubicle and everything around it so neat "that they didn't have anything to do," he said.

Mrs. Bautista, 46, was a born organizer. She worked in the accounts payable department and liked to get there early "just to get things started" and stay late "to make sure everything was finished all right," her husband said. "That was her style, always making sure everything was in its place."

When she was a girl, Mrs. Bautista helped sponsor a town festival in Dagupan, in her native Philippines. Mr. Bautista was visiting from another part of the country, saw her, and they became childhood sweethearts, he said. Ten years ago, she became his wife. They moved to Iselin, N.J., and in 2000, she received her naturalization papers. When she was not working, Mrs. Bautista enjoyed nature walks.

"She was always amazed by what God could do," Mr. Bautista said. "She's with him now."

MARK BAVIS
Scouting Hockey Talent

Mark Bavis, a hockey scout, was on his way to work on Sept. 11, flying west for the Los Angeles Kings training camp, where he would be checking on the progress of players the team had drafted on his advice.

He took United Airlines Flight 175 from Boston.

Mr. Bavis, 32, had starred for the Boston University Terriers from 1990 to 1993. He was "a great defensive forward and a real smart playmaker," said his coach, Jack Parker. The coach used Mark and his twin brother, Mike, as a team to kill penalties.

"The Bavi, we called them," Mr. Parker said. "They were always together."

Mike Bavis, an assistant to Mr. Parker, agreed. "We were very close," he said. "But we were competitive."

The scouting job, after a few years in minor league hockey and turns as assistant coach at Brown and Harvard, delighted his brother because of the travel it involved.

"He really enjoyed some of the finer places in our country and loved to have a good time," his brother said.

JASPER BAXTER
A Needy-People Person

Jasper Baxter was a needy-people person. He once made it his Saturday-morning routine to deliver meals from a food bank to hungry homes in Philadelphia, where he lived with his wife, Lillian. When he heard of a mortgage lender who was charging an old woman monthly payments that exceeded her Social Security income, he took his outrage all the way to the Pennsylvania legislature, where there was enough interest in the matter to make the company back down, said a brother, Dennis Baxter.

Jasper Baxter, 45, ran twice for state representative and lost both times. But he had a job that still allowed him to lend a helping hand. He was a consultant at Lee Hecht Harrison, a career services company at which he helped people who had lost jobs find work or start their own businesses. On Sept. 11, he was conducting a two-day seminar on the 93rd floor of 2 World Trade Center.

"He was really good at getting people excited and motivated to get out there and find employment," said Elva Bankins, senior vice president and general manager of the company's Philadelphia office, where she said condolence cards and calls had poured in from grateful clients.

The youngest of seven children, Mr. Baxter grew up as the baby who everybody felt should be told what to do, his brother said. That meant he learned fairly early in life how to stand his ground, his brother said.

"We all offered him advice," he said. "He learned how to defend his position."

PAUL F. BEATINI
Barbie's Best Customer

Paul F. Beatini told his 3-year-old daughter, Daria, that Tuesday, Sept. 11, wasn't her first real day of preschool. It was only orientation. There was no way Daddy would miss Daria's first day of school, so he would bring her on the first real day, Thursday.

That rationalization made sense for both of them and it made Mr. Beatini, who worked with FM Global, an insurance company, feel better about keeping his morning meeting at Aon. When Daria woke up on Thursday, she still remembered that Daddy was supposed to take her to school.

For Daria and her older sister, Julia, Daddy was the consummate playmate. He was a ravenous customer at Barbie's bakeshop, ordering multitudes of baguettes and fruit pies. The 6-foot-6-inch man would pretend to be a rock star in the living room while his little brown-haired girls danced.

After a fulfilling day of play with his daughters, he used to say, "If I died tomorrow, I would die a happy man."

JANE BEATTY
Surviving with a Smile

Jane Beatty was a survivor. When her first marriage broke up, she was thrust into the job market for the first time and found work as a cocktail waitress in Toronto, where she was raised. Then she learned computer skills and switched careers, eventually becoming a technical supervisor at Marsh & McLennan in New York.

Ms. Beatty, 53, faced another challenge more recently when she was found to have breast cancer. By that time, she had left Canada and moved to Belford, N.J., to marry the retired police officer she had met on a blind date while visiting a friend. The friend, Lorraine Greskow, said Ms. Beatty remained upbeat, even after her mastectomy.

"She always had a smile on her face, even through all that," she said.

In August, Jane Beatty and her husband, Bob, went to Atlantic City to privately mark her fifth anniversary of being cancer-free. She told her mother it was too early to make a big fuss.

"She said she wasn't going to celebrate until she was clear for six years," said her mother, Beth Chrystal.

LARRY BECK
A Cousin's Faithful Cards

Larry Beck liked his job in the mailroom at Cantor Fitzgerald, because his appointed rounds let him talk to his co-workers, philosophize about the Mets' performance the night before and, with special joy, show off pictures of his nieces, Isabel and Michaela.

Mr. Beck, 38, who grew up in Bellmore, N.Y., and lived in Manhattan, always sent the most beautiful and touching birthday, anniversary and Mother's and Father's Day cards, his aunt and uncle recalled. He was particularly thoughtful when his cousin Ilene Fallas gave birth to her son, Evan.

"Larry had bought him a blanket, and my son loved that blanket so much," Ms. Fallas, who lives in Panama, wrote in a tribute to Mr. Beck on the Internet. "That made me happy, because one of the things that was so cherished by my son was given to him by Larry, who stood for all of those things that that blanket was to my little boy: warm, lovable, comforting and dependable.

"Knowing that I won't hear Larry's voice on the phone on the day my family and I arrive home to New York to visit is just too much to bear."

CARL J. BEDIGIAN
Living with an Angel

Sometimes, Carl J. Bedigian did not seem real to the woman who had been his wife for less than a year. A firefighter with Engine 214 in Brooklyn, he once donated his bone marrow to a 4-year-old boy in Europe he had never met, Michele Bedigian said.

He had a "magical" smile, and "a beautiful way of making people comfortable around him," she said. "Sometimes I think he's an angel. Sometimes I think he wasn't really a person."

In 1998, Firefighter Bedigian fell ill with a rare condition that paralyzed him, but he defied the odds and walked again within weeks out of the sheer power of his will, Mrs. Bedigian said. The experience made the couple live every day as if it were their last. They traveled, they planned a family. And Firefighter Bedigian, 35, stayed committed to the Fire Department and had "a constant ambition to do more to help people," she said. Mr. Bedigian was buried Nov. 5.

"That was Carl's calling," his 31-year-old widow said of his life as a fireman. "As painful as it is, I'm incredibly proud of him."

MICHAEL BEEKMAN
Authoritative and Calm

Amidst the frenzy of the New York Stock Exchange, Michael Beekman, 39, was a rare figure of calm. His job was righting errors from the previous day's trading. He might spend a workday with a trader or two, explaining how they had actually lost hundreds of thousands of dollars on trades they had thought were profitable.

"A kill-the-messenger job," said John Furman, a co-worker at LaBranche & Company. But Mr. Beekman would walk across the trading floor without hurrying and speak in a low voice. "He would research something until he knew it completely," said Mr. Furman. "He was very organized, with his little notes all lined up. When he presented the information, people knew he was right and so they never were angry with him."

He lived a calm and orderly life in Staten Island, too, said Theodora, his wife. He spent most of his off-duty time with her and their two children—Michael, 10, and Theresa, 8. If he went golfing, he would take his son. Occasionally he would disappear for a while—and turn up at his sister-in-law's house, playing with her toddlers.

YELENA BELILOVSKY
Proud in a New Country

Hers had been the dream of so many immigrants—to find a better life for herself and her family: a comfortable home, a good school for her son, a good job. And find it, she did. Indeed, in many ways, Yelena Belilovsky, who immigrated to this country from Kiev in 1993, had found all that she ever wanted.

"She loved living in this country," said Ross Tisnovsky, her younger brother.

Mrs. Belilovsky, 38, lived with her husband, Boris, and son, Eugene, 13, in Mamaroneck, N.Y. Despite an early struggle with English, she managed to go back to school, received a Master of Library Sciences degree and landed a job at Fred Alger Management, where she had recently been named assistant vice president for information. She took pride in her job and the fact that everyone at work knew her by her Americanized first name, Helen.

She was so enamored of her new life in the United States that she eventually persuaded Mr. Tisnovsky and their parents, Leonid and Emma Tisnovsky, to leave the familiar surroundings of their homeland and to take a big gamble on this country as well.

"It is devastating," Mr. Tisnovsky said. "The only reason our parents came here was to be with Helen and me."

NINA BELL
Air Force Child

Nina Bell was every inch a fighter pilot's daughter—slender, athletic and looking even taller than her 5 feet 8 inches. Born in the Netherlands, the first stop in a nomadic Air Force childhood, she grew up confident, smart, "the It girl," as a friend once put it.

A bachelor's degree in business administration from the University of Colorado at Boulder led her to become a manager of information systems and, most recently, into project management.

But to her friends and family, there was also the side that was not all business. With her brother, Lowell Bell, 40, she kept up a private banter, sometimes based on the dim Canadian duo the Mackenzie brothers, from the 1970s television show *Second City TV*. "Hey, hoser," she would call him.

In September, Ms. Bell, 39, had settled in Manhattan, in a new apartment on the Upper East Side and in a new job as a project manager with Marsh & McLennan.

In an e-mail message to her friend Lorraine Davis on Monday, Sept. 10, at 2 P.M., Ms. Bell wrote, "I am so very happy."

STEPHEN E. BELSON
Free Spirit Found a Calling

Stephen E. Belson, 51, had different nicknames from different stages of his life. At Rockaway Beach, where he worked after college as a lifeguard, he was known as Bells. But at the fire station on West 31st Street in Manhattan where he spent most of his career as a firefighter, he was given the title "Mr. Ladder 24."

"He was our ambassador, so to speak," said John Montani, another firefighter in Ladder Company 24.

Firefighter Belson attended all the functions, was always available for holiday duty and could back a fire engine into a station in five seconds flat. His last job was as a driver for one of the battalion chiefs, Orio J. Palmer. Both rushed to the World Trade Center on Sept. 11; neither returned.

Before he joined the department, Firefighter Belson was something of a beach bum, a surfer, a devotee of the Grateful Dead and Hot Tuna, or as one friend said, a free spirit. Then, one day, he and his lifeguard buddies decided to get real jobs.

"We took the Fire Department tests on a lark, and found a calling," said John Maguire, who is now chief of Battalion 54.

Firefighter Belson who grew up in Flushing, Queens, moved to Rockaway Beach, bought a house and fit right into the tightknit community of firefighters and police officers. Unlike many of his neighbors, he wasn't Irish or Roman Catholic. But that made no difference. "While he was Jewish, he was considered one of them," said his mother, Madeline Brandstadter.

"They even named a beach after him: Bells's Beach."

PAUL BENEDETTI
Always Able to Laugh

No matter what calamity befell Paul Benedetti in this life, his response was inevitable: a joke. Thus, when he escaped the 1993 bombing of the World Trade Center, fighting smoke as he made a harrowing trek down the stairs, "he never made much of it, except as an occasion for a funny story," said his wife, Alessandra.

The joke involved a very large lady ahead of him, walking down the stairs incredibly slowly, blocking the way.

Then there were all those voices from *The Simpsons,* which he loved to imitate. Not to mention the office software he rigged so Homer Simpson's distress word—

"doh"—popped up electronically whenever users made a mistake.

Actually Mr. Benedetti, 32, was a serious man, but made his wit into a management tool at Aon Corporation, where he was an assistant director of the client-relationship services department.

"I know that if he'd been trapped somewhere, he'd have been joking around, whatever the situation," his wife said. "Trying to break the tension."

DENISE LENORE BENEDETTO
Sustained by Faith

The most important things in Denise Lenore Benedetto's life were her family and her Roman Catholic faith. It was that faith that sustained her 10 years ago, after doctors diagnosed a spinal condition so serious that she had a 25 percent chance of being paralyzed from the chest down, said her husband, John Benedetto.

As it happened, she recovered fully after spending six months in a body cast, and was able to have a second daughter and eventually to work full time as a secretary at Aon in the World Trade Center. Ms. Benedetto, 40, went to Mass every weekend at St. Rita's Church, a block away from her house on Staten Island.

The church is not far from where she grew up, in a housing project down the street from her husband's childhood home. They met one evening when they were both 17, when she stood beneath his window and began talking to him. She went to get some ice cream, and when she came back it fell off the stick. They both laughed.

"It was love from that moment on," he said.

BRYAN C. BENNETT
He Filled the Time Available

Bryan C. Bennett could turn an opportunity into an adventure, and in his 25 years, he had too many of both to recount in detail. The highlights included working on a farm in Spain, teaching English to schoolchildren in Chile, visiting a remote village in Cuba, white-water rafting in Costa Rica, and backpacking in the Andes.

"He stretched the time. I don't know how he did it all," said his mother, Ondina Bennett. "Every moment was an opportunity to do something, learn something, help somebody."

Mr. Bennett, who worked in sales for eSpeed, had moved from Boston to New York in mid-2000 to spend more time with his family. As the youngest of three children and the only boy, he tried never to miss family gatherings and vaca-

tions. He was an avid tennis player who was introducing his four nephews and one niece to the sport, along with baseball and video games. In his free time, he took advantage of opportunities closer to home.

Most recently, he signed up for piano lessons at the New School and organized an engagement party for two of his closest friends.

ERIC BENNETT
Marks Chart a Life

When Eric Bennett disappeared, his missing poster offered two distinguishing traits—a tattoo of a bulldog head on his right shoulder and deep stretch marks under his arms. Both pieces of information attested to Mr. Bennett's love of football, which he played with a championship team at Kearsley High School in Flint, Mich., and also at Michigan's Ferris State University.

The bulldog was the mascot at Ferris State; on Mr. Bennett's tattoo, the dog tag read "58," his number. The stretch marks appeared when he lost his football bulk and trimmed down to 180 pounds from 255.

"Eric was always very determined, very motivated," said his mother, Betty Bennett, who lives in Flint with her husband, Terry. "He was small for a center, and he had to prove himself."

Mr. Bennett worked as a vice president at Alliance Consulting Group on the 102nd floor of the north tower. He made many new friends in New York, even while staying in touch with high school friends and teammates. At his memorial in Michigan, a couple of them also sported bulldog tattoos.

OLIVER BENNETT
Attentive and Quick-Witted

Oliver Bennett, the younger and taller of the two Bennett sons, was a passionate listener. Joy Bennett, his mother, remembers him at gatherings: his head slightly lowered and his eyes intent on the person talking to him. In his quiet way, he drew attention.

"You were always aware of Oli," a friend told Mrs. Bennett. "He was a very, very vital presence."

And, sometimes, a rather intimidating one. His withering one-liners, Mrs. Bennett said, "could take your breath away."

"You didn't cross Oli lightly. He let you know just what he thought. At 13, he'd say, 'I don't agree with you, Mom, but let's don't argue about it.'" His decisions, she said, were absolute.

He loved to draw, she said. The Bennett home in London, where he lived, is "littered" with his portraits. But he studied economics and psychology and became a financial writer for the Risk Waters Group.

On Sept. 11, he was at its conference at Windows on the World. He planned to quit journalism in a year, at 30, and open a restaurant and bar where conversation would flow easily. He saw himself as his own boss, the quiet center of the bar's hubbub, with an ever-changing parade of people to watch and listen to.

MARGARET L. BENSON
Card Games and Cruises

Books, card games and cruises were Margaret L. Benson's preferred pastimes, and her older sister, Kathy Savidge, was her constant companion. They had scheduled a Mediterranean dream cruise for 2005 and hoped to retire in North Carolina. Sibling rivals, they grew up to be best friends, and sometimes—not always—let their husbands in on their high jinks.

"We planned to become little old ladies together," Mrs. Savidge said. "She was stubborn, set in her ways. I remember in grammar school when the nuns wouldn't give her a perfect 100 average even though she got all 99s and 100s. They told her only God was perfect. She was mad!"

Marge Benson, 52, worked for the Port Authority of New York and New Jersey for 33 years, starting as a clerk and working up to a human resources post. She lived in Rockaway, N.J., with her husband, Jim, and two children, both in college. She was last seen outside a Borders bookstore next to the twin towers.

"A friend told me to think of it this way," her sister said. "She's in a back corner full of books, she's got a card game going, and she's winning. I just wish I could call and tell her that. She'd laugh."

JIM BERGER
A Fan of the Boss

In Jim Berger's car, there was only one kind of music: the raspy rock 'n' roll of the Boss. He grew up in Bruce Springsteen country along the Jersey Shore and never listened to anything else. He knew the words to "Thunder Road" by heart, and often sang it for his passengers.

"Every time you rode in Jim's car, Bruce was on, whether you liked it or not," said his wife, Suzanne.

At 6-foot-3, Jim, 44, an Aon executive, was a gentle giant who devoted his weekends to his three young sons, Nicholas, Alex and Christian. He was grooming them to be fans of the Giants, the Yankees and the Rangers.

And he made sure they listened to Bruce, too. After a prayer service at church, his family and friends gathered at his home in Yardley, Pa. They poured wine, made a toast, and sang aloud to "Thunder Road."

"He would have loved it," Suzanne said. "He taught us all a lesson in unconditional love."

STEVEN H. BERGER
Reader of Encyclopedias

Steven H. Berger may have seemed daunting to some people. He was a supervisor of corporate tax auditors at the New York State Department of Taxation and Finance. On top of that, he knew a little about everything. His wife, Susan, says he always got the answers right on *Jeopardy!* and *Who Wants to Be a Millionaire*.

To Ms. Berger, her husband was a good man who enjoyed the everyday things of life. Mr. Berger, 45, was a big reader of encyclopedias when he was not rooting for the Dallas Cowboys or working on his cooking. At the office he was known as Emeril, a reference to the well-known Food Channel chef. He was ribbed for taking his leftovers to work.

He pampered his daughter, Melissa, 12, and they did many things together, including raking leaves and shoveling the snow. He was also the repairman around their New Jersey home.

Mr. Berger also loved his job. He spent almost four hours a day getting to and from his job at the World Trade Center, said his wife, who is an auditor for New York City.

"He was pleased by little things," his wife said. "He did not need any of the big things that some people do. He loved working in the Trade Center. He had the view of the city."

JOHN P. BERGIN
Finding a New Bond

On holidays, John P. Bergin wasn't just the turkey carver. He prepared the entire turkey.

"He was good old Martha Stewart with the cheesecloth," his wife, Madeline, said. "We're going to starve without him."

Mr. Bergin, 39, honed his cooking while working as a firefighter, first with the No. 6 truck in Manhattan and more recently with Rescue Company 5. At home on Staten Island he took up other domestic chores. He changed diapers for three children and coached their teams. With his co-workers' help, he put a swimming pool in the backyard; beside it stood a beer tap, his prized possession. Most recently, he and a partner had bought a local bar, the Grand City Tavern. On Sept. 11, renovations were two weeks away from completion.

"They did everything together," Mrs. Bergin said of her husband and the other firefighters. Now, she and 10 other wives of men from his firehouse who were lost in the attack are carrying on the tradition, albeit more somberly. "We just started counseling together," she said. "We've become very close. How the guys shared a bond—now we share a bond."

ALVIN BERGSOHN
Living for the Fun of It

Every night, it seems, came the clarion call of Michele Bergsohn. It went like this: "Alvin! Make it lower! I'm trying to talk on the phone!"

For in her living room, her 48-year-old husband—adult credentials: equity trader at Cantor Fitzgerald—would be cranking up his electric guitar, careering through songs by the Allman Brothers, Elvis Costello or Hot Tuna, while watching sports on TV. Such a multitasker! When the game was over, he would traipse off to the den and catalog his Very Serious comic book collection.

Mr. Bergsohn's view of life—no expectations, no disappointments—liberated him to seize each day and squeeze the most fun from it. He worked hard, leaving their home in Baldwin Harbor, on Long Island, before 6:30 A.M., but he returned for family dinner every night. He was a nonpartisan flirt, a rock concert fan, a softball coach for his two boys, Sam, 14, and Harris, 12. That last weekend, he perched on first base, dancing and singing wildly in between shouting out coaching orders.

For someone with no expectations, joy, when it comes, tastes of delighted surprise. At Sam's bar mitzvah, Mr. Bergsohn made a speech that did go on—and on. Forgive him: his face shone with astonishment and pride, love and fulfillment.

DANIEL BERGSTEIN
Consummate Movie Fan

It hardly made sense to enter the office Oscar pool if Daniel Bergstein was in it. He was unbeatable. Year after year, he took the money.

Mr. Bergstein, 38, the corporate secretary at the Port Authority, was not just an avid movie fan. He knew just about everything there was to know about movies. Everything.

"He was always interested in how the movies were directed, the angles, what kind of close-ups," said his wife, Alicia Bergstein.

Not only did he watch countless movies, buy countless movies, devour countless movie reviews, but he read everything that told him anything about movies.

And he had this uncanny knack for predicting Oscar winners. Not that he got every category correct. Last year, he missed the best picture award, which went to *Gladiator*. He picked *Crouching Tiger, Hidden Dragon*.

"He thought that was the perfect movie," his wife said.

Among his all-time favorite films were the Godfather movies. (He felt that *Godfather II* was the best of the lot.) His birthday was coming up. He had sent his wife an e-mail message with an unsubtle hint:

"The Godfather DVD set is coming out. That would be a good birthday gift."

GRAHAM BERKELEY
A Lover of Freedom

Graham Berkeley, a Briton, had lived in the United States for 10 years, and for 10 years he had been trying to get the green card that would grant him resident status. It came at last in June, and Mr. Berkeley had started making plans to move to New York City from Boston when, on Sept. 11, he boarded United Airlines Flight 175 for a business trip to Los Angeles.

"It's like fate playing tricks on you," said his friend Christian Winslow. "His fight for that green card had been so intense."

Mr. Berkeley, 37, was director of e-commerce solutions for the Compuware Corporation, but his friends remember him as a classical violinist, an opera buff and a world traveler.

"He loved the freedom that America has," Mr. Winslow said. "He loved the openness of our society and the friends he had here. America, to Graham, was almost like the cliché—a land of endless opportunities."

MICHAEL BERKELEY
Everything Was in Place

At 38, Michael Berkeley was soaring: following in the footsteps of his cousin, John Utendahl, one of the country's most successful African-American financiers, Mr. Berkeley recently founded his own brokerage firm, with 79th-floor offices in the north tower of the World Trade Center. He had a house in the Hamptons, two young sons, and had been married for more than 10 years to Lourdes Perez-Berkeley, a top portfolio analyst who is also a former Miss Puerto Rico.

But Mr. Berkeley, the son of a homicide detective and a head nurse, "was a regular guy, the greatest," said a cousin, Ronald Culberson, who described Mr. Berkeley as upbeat, warmly generous, welcoming. Another cousin, Ellen Turner, said that Mr. Berkeley and his wife "never lost sight of themselves."

Husband and wife referred to each with a deference and respect that only seemed to increase during their marriage, Ms. Turner said. "There was a giddiness about them—they always joked and smiled around each other. They protected each other. He didn't create her and she didn't create him. They complemented each other."

A Tribute from the
Tibetans in N.Y. in
memory of all who
perished in this
senseless act of
voilence.

WORLD TRADE CE
1972-73

DAVID W. BERNARD
A Gracious Winner

David W. Bernard loved his family and he loved golf, and he liked to combine his two passions. Every July, he played in a father-son tournament—twice in one day—so he could do 18 holes with each of his sons, Mark and David Jr. Before his daughter, Jill, was married last summer, he arranged a foursome with his two boys and his soon-to-be son-in-law. And he taught his wife of 33 years, Nancy, how to play.

"He was very patient with me," she said. "He wanted me to play golf so that when we traveled together we could do it together." (In return, he went shopping with her.) Despite his low golf handicap (just nine) and his fierce competitiveness, Mr. Bernard was a gracious winner, said Mrs. Bernard: "Nobody could ever be mad at him. He just had a very easy way about him."

Mr. Bernard, 57, was an industry specialist for the Internal Revenue Service and was based in Boston.

On Sept. 11, he was on his way to a meeting at the I.R.S. offices at 7 World Trade Center when the first plane hit the towers. He was struck by falling debris and died of his injuries on Dec. 11.

WILLIAM H. BERNSTEIN
The Late Bloomer

William H. was the oldest of four sons—arriving three minutes before his fraternal twin, Robert. The two younger brothers, Steven and David, also twins, were born four years later.

Among four boys growing up in Brooklyn, life was competitive, which posed a challenge to William Bernstein—Billy, as he was known—because he was such a late bloomer physically.

"At his bar mitzvah, he was a foot shorter than his twin," said his brother Steven Bernstein. But he did fill out later, becoming about a 6-foot-2, 220-pound adult, devoted to bodybuilding and karate.

William Bernstein, 44, a mortgage bond broker at Cantor Fitzgerald, was closest to Robert. "Same grade schools," the latter said in a memorial service, "same camps, same high school, same college, Syracuse University, living in the same co-op building, working in the same neighborhood, downtown Manhattan."

Yet they were not carbon copies. Robert Bernstein is

Models of the twin towers were placed at Union Square as memorials to the victims of the attack on the World Trade Center. This model was left by Tibetans in New York. (*Ruth Fremson*)

known as meticulous in his habits, while William was more laid back, though he took great care in his appearance. Robert said his brother was more reserved, too, but once people got to know him, "they could see the genuineness, the kindness."

DAVID M. BERRAY
What to Do? Everything

David M. Berray had a "to do" list that was extraordinary, his wife, Alison Berray, said.

"He'd write down everything from taking out the trash to fly-fishing on the Housatonic River in Connecticut to climbing Mt. Fuji. He'd get up very early in the morning and start the list."

Mr. Berray managed to accomplish just about all of the things he planned. The Berrays spent five years in Hong Kong and they rarely passed an idle moment.

They boated down the Mekong River, fished in Canton and hiked in Laos, Thailand and Cambodia. Once they went to New Zealand, where the summer days stretch dangerously long.

"Giving David 16 hours a day of sunlight was exhausting," Mrs. Berray said. "It would be ten o'clock at night, the sun would still be up and David would ask, 'What do you want to do next?' "

Despite his abundant energy, Mr. Berray, 39, managed to take time off to stay home when each of his two children were born.

He had earned a master's degree from M.I.T. in technology management in 2000 and after a dozen years in banking, became chief operations officer for MoneyLine, an Internet-based financial services company.

On Sept. 11, he was attending a technology seminar at Windows on the World.

DAVID S. BERRY
A High Form of Wisdom

David S. Berry's three sons, Nile, 9, Reed, 7, and Alex, 5, have clear memories of basking in their father's full attention. When it was raining recently, Alex pointed to the water running down the gutters in Park Slope, Brooklyn, where the family lives, and said to his mother, Paula Berry, "Remember when we came home from the play and Daddy made those boats and floated them down the river?"

On another rainy day, Mr. Berry, 43, the director of research at Keefe, Bruyette & Woods, was playing with the boys at the family's summer house.

"It was raining stunningly hard, and all the kids, of course, were running around the house naked," Mrs. Berry

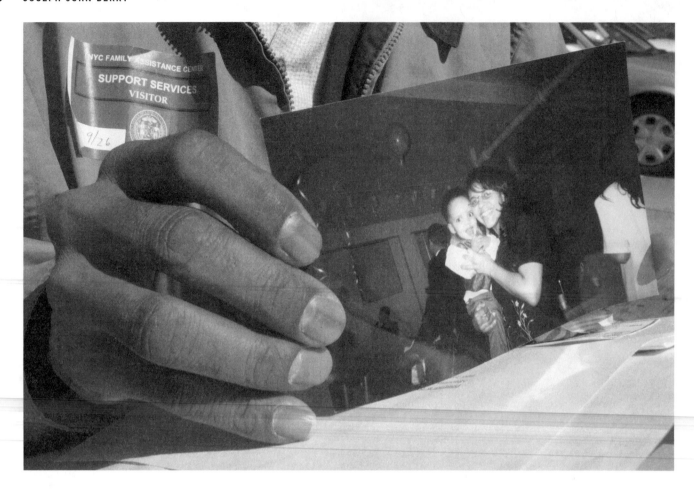

Marino Calderón holds a picture of his wife, Lizie Martínez-Calderón, and son, Nestali. Ms. Martínez-Calderón, thirty-two, was among the missing. (*Angel Franco*)

said. "David was running with them. Water was just coming down in buckets, and they remembered how it was coming down the gutter, like a faucet. David was putting his head into the drain spout."

"In playing with the children, there was no distraction," she said. "He was nowhere but right there in the moment, right there. He knew where to put his energy, and that's a form of wisdom."

"It was so elegant for him, like a fine math proof, simple and just right there, and very clear."

JOSEPH JOHN BERRY
Vacations with the Children

Joseph John Berry, a man who left big tips and who once urged a nervous friend to go through with her wedding because "marriage is a wonderful thing," simply hated the idea of a vacation without his three children. Never mind that they are all grown now, with the youngest 21 and the oldest 27.

Whether it was a trip to Italy or one of their annual pilgrimages to Aruba for New Year's Eve, "our children came with us," Evelyn Berry said. "All three of them. All the time. Wherever we go, whatever vacation. To this day, if we're going away they're there with us. "How many children do you know who spend every New Year's with their parents?"

To Mrs. Berry, this is the essential fact of her husband's life—not the honors he collected as one of the most influential Irish-Americans on Wall Street, or the professional status he enjoyed as chairman and co-chief executive of Keefe, Bruyette & Woods, an investment banking firm, but the fact that he also coached just about every team his children ever played on, from soccer to basketball.

"If anything, we were more in love today than when we first got married," Mrs. Berry said. Mr. Berry, 55, who worked on the 89th floor of 2 World Trade Center, died on his wife's 54th birthday. They would have celebrated their 32nd wedding anniversary in November.

"The fact that he's gone is the greatest pain," she said. "The day it happened is immaterial."

TIMOTHY D. BETTERLY
Behind Humor, Compassion

Timothy D. Betterly was a master of zany tricks, gag gifts and crazy costumes that family members readily acknowledge sometimes skirted the bounds of sound judgment.

Like the time Mr. Betterly, a bond trader at Cantor Fitzgerald, hopped on the back of a garbage truck passing by Madison Square Garden as he, his brother Donald and his wife, Joanne, were about to head home to New Jersey after watching a track meet. Mr. Betterly returned a half hour later in a cab.

Once when his daughters, Samantha, 12, and Christine, 9, had a sleepover party, he took the pajama-clad group on a tour of such late-night hot spots as the Little Silver, N.J., cemetery, the all-night deli and the local jail, where he persuaded the sergeant to lock up the giggling girls. The resulting photograph was a keeper.

But Mr. Betterly, 42, the youngest of four brothers, had a sober side, too. In high school, he invited a mentally handicapped girl who always ate lunch alone to sit with his table of football players.

She did, every day for two years, and the girl's mother later told Mr. Betterly's mother, Joan, that he had "made her daughter's life."

CAROLYN BEUG
Mama Bunny to the Rescue

To careful readers of *Rolling Stone* magazine in December 2001, Carolyn Beug was a force in the music business. She could be found in the Tributes section, just below Joey Ramone and just above Aaliyah. Mrs. Beug, 48, was the producer behind the video for Van Halen's "Right Now," which won an MTV Video Music Award for best video of 1992.

But to the girls' high school track team at home in Santa Monica, Calif., Mrs. Beug was something else: Mama Bunny. She raised money for track uniforms, led cheers at track meets, held track awards dinners in the backyard for a hundred or more people.

"She always called the kids on the team my little bunnies," recalled her husband, John Beug.

In 1998, she left the music industry to write a children's book. This year, she was finishing the editing of the book, about the story of Noah's Ark, told through the eyes of Noah's wife. But mostly she wanted to devote more time to Lauren and Lindsey, now 18, and Nicholas, 13.

In September, Mrs. Beug and her mother, Mary Alice Wahlstrom, helped settle the twins at the Rhode Island School of Design. The two women were flying back to California on American Airlines Flight 11 when their plane struck 1 World Trade Center.

MARY ALICE WAHLSTROM's portrait appears on page 521.

EDWARD F. BEYEA
Overcoming Obstacles

What people remember about Edward Beyea was that he was always telling jokes.

"Sometimes he laughed so hard you thought he would fall out of the chair," said Irma Fuller, his nurse's aide for 14 years. Mr. Beyea, 42, needed full-time care for the last 21 years, ever since a diving accident left him a quadriplegic. But Mr. Beyea refused to be overcome by his disability, his mother said.

"He said right from the start, 'I'll beat it, Mom,'" said his mother, Janet Beyea. "And he did, up to a point."

He learned how to type using a stick that he operated with his mouth, and worked as a computer programmer for Empire Blue Cross and Blue Shield in the World Trade Center. Even at home in his apartment on Roosevelt Island, Mr. Beyea was always busy.

"It kept his mind off himself," Ms. Fuller said. He would play computer golf, listen to music and read. He had a special tray that made it possible for him to read in bed.

The tray was rigged up by Abe Zelmanowitz, his colleague and friend for 12 years. Mr. Zelmanowitz refused to leave Mr. Beyea's side after the terror attack, as they waited on the 27th floor for the rescue workers who could not get there in time.

ABE ZELMANOWITZ's portrait appears on page 552.

PAUL BEYER
A Memorial House-Raising

Paul Beyer wanted a house. A house with a chimney. In Tottenville, Staten Island, the place where he and his wife were born and raised. So for two years, he laid the foundations for his dream: he got the necessary permits to tear down his mother-in-law's 100-year-old house, he got the blueprints from an architect, and he meticulously planned and designed every room of the two-family house that would one day be a home for him and his wife and their two boys and even his mother-in-law.

Last summer, he began to build. He had completed about 60 percent of the house when he died at the trade center. He was 37, a firefighter, a Scout leader, the father of two teenagers, Michael Paul, 15, and Shawn Patrick, 13, and, for 15 years, the husband of Arlene Beyer.

For about a week, Mrs. Beyer contemplated not finishing the house. "It was heartbreaking," Mrs. Beyer, 40, said. "I couldn't even go there."

Then she decided to go ahead. "We knew we had to finish the dream," she said. Scores of firefighters, all friends and colleagues of her husband's from Engine Company 6, are helping her. In the chimney, one of the firemen will carve a Maltese Cross, the symbol for firefighters.

ANIL T. BHARVANEY
A Knack for Fitting In

Anil T. Bharvaney's personal geography knew no bounds. Born in Poona, India, he grew up in Kobe, Japan, went to college in San Jose, Calif., worked in New York and lived in East Windsor, N.J.

"He was at home with any culture," said Pandora Po Bharvaney, his wife, a Chinese immigrant who met Mr. Bharvaney at New York University. Wherever he was, she said, he fit in. "He was soft-spoken and could calm people down," she said. "That goes well with any culture."

He was unbounded in his interests, too. At 41, he was a senior vice president in equities trading at Instinet Corporation. On Sept. 11, he was attending a conference at Windows on the World. He liked to walk in the woods around his home and take photos. He was passionate about classical jazz, like John Coltrane. And he read philosophy, taking the Tao, the Chinese way of simplicity and selflessness, to heart.

"He thought the more you give, the more you become richer," Mrs. Bharvaney said. "He very much believed in it."

BELLA BHUKHAN
All That Sparkled

Bella Bhukhan, 24, danced the part of the youngest with a certain spark. Of the three sisters, she was the most playful, the most stubborn, the bluntest—in a sense, the most western. Raised in a Gujarati family who settled in Union, N.J., after migrating from Zambia, she was the defiant one who returned from a Cancún vacation with a tattoo on her lower back.

Yet she also embraced her Indian heritage. At her eldest sister Vicky's wedding a few days before Sept. 11, she performed a traditional Indian dance wearing a long brown and gold skirt, sleeveless top and jewelry that glittered and clattered.

With her engaging smile, Ms. Bhukhan was a people-person. At the Cantor Fitzgerald memorial service, her family was struck by how many employees, especially the foreign-born, remembered how well Bella took care of them in the human resources department. That was the role this youngest sister assumed at home, too: "The three of us were best friends and she was very upset I was moving so far away," said Vicky Tailor.

"She always told my in-laws to take care of me and called every other day to see if I was being treated right."

SHIMMY D. BIEGELEISEN
Always an Altruist

It was not Shimmy D. Biegeleisen's daughter who was getting married, but that was not the kind of detail that could have stopped him from playing an essential role in the festivities.

Mr. Biegeleisen, 42, helped his niece Estee Berger prepare for the event last June by helping figure out the seating arrangements and making sure everything else was taken care of. And at the wedding he was a backup host, chatting with guests and dancing with children, recalled Shelley Berger, Mr. Biegeleisen's sister.

"We remember how extraordinary he was, in a very ordinary way," she said. Mr. Biegeleisen, thoughtful and sensitive, tried to respond to the needs of friends and family—from letting a new mother who worked with him at Fiduciary Trust telecommute, to making sure that Estee Berger's husband, Zevi Brodt, had the sports section to read in the morning when the newlyweds were living in his Brooklyn building.

BILL BIGGART
"I'm with the Firemen"

They found Bill Biggart's body among the firefighters. He was a photographer, 54, born to an American Army couple in the divided city of Berlin, and it seemed to his wife, Wendy Doremus, that a thread ran through his work. Mr. Biggart covered division and conflict: Howard Beach, Wounded Knee, Northern Ireland, Gaza, the gulf war.

"When I saw the second plane hit, all I was hoping was that my father didn't go down; I thought, 'God, I just hope he's out sailing,'" his son William said, but by then Bill Biggart was already downtown.

Mr. Biggart lived just north of Greenwich Village and he loved sailing, he loved trees. He bought people with backyards trees for their birthdays. And he spent so much time watering the trees he'd planted on Weehawken Street, near the Hudson River, that the transvestites who frequented the area were convinced he worked for Greenpeace. During the attack, his wife called him on his cell phone to tell him it was terrorism, not an accident.

"I'm O.K.," he said. "I'm with the firemen."

BRIAN BILCHER
Always to the Rescue

Captain America. That's what Tina Bilcher called her husband, Brian, a firefighter at Squad Company 1 in Brooklyn.

Firefighter Bilcher, 37, was a lot like the patriotic comic book superhero: calm, reasonable, good-looking and quick to the rescue of anyone who needed help. Car stuck on the side of the road? There was Firefighter Bilcher. Feeling sick? Like a flash, Firefighter Bilcher was at your bedside. The man liked his adrenaline rushes, said his wife.

"He once jumped off a lighthouse into the ocean," said Mrs. Bilcher. He even got her to jump with him. She says now that she did it for love—"I wanted to impress him."

A strapping 6 feet, 240 pounds, Firefighter Bilcher was working part-time as a bouncer at Coaches Cafe in Staten Island six years ago when Tina, two weeks shy of 21, showed up. He refused to let her in. He told her to come back in two weeks. She did. They talked. They were married June 4, 2000, in Staten Island. The wedding pictures show the twin towers in the background.

Grant James Bilcher was born Aug. 29, 2001. The couple named him Grant because he was a grant from God. "Brian always wanted a boy," his wife said.

CARL BINI
"I Told Him to Be Careful"

They met when they were 10, two kids from the same Brooklyn neighborhood. They married at 20 and in 23 years rarely left each other's side.

"He was my best friend," said Christine Bini of her husband, Carl, who was 43.

So it was completely in keeping with routine that Mr. Bini telephoned his wife the morning of Sept. 11 at about 8:40 A.M. while she was en route from the couple's home in Staten Island to her job in Brooklyn just to check in and say hello. Minutes later he called again.

"He told me about the plane," Mrs. Bini said. "He said he was going. I told him to be careful."

Carl Bini had been a firefighter for 18 years. Retirement was only two years away, and he and his wife had been looking forward to it very much. So were their daughters, Stephanie, 16, and Desiree, 19. That Tuesday, Sept. 11, was to have been a day off for Firefighter Bini. He and a friend

were meeting to discuss a business project for after retirement. Upon hearing the news of the attack, he and the friend, also a firefighter, went to the trade center.

"If I could have tied him down, he would have bitten through the ropes to go," Mrs. Bini said.

GARY BIRD
He Needed the Horizon

He was a corporate cowboy. Gary Bird worked in risk management, but his great joy was riding horses. He was practically born in the saddle. His mother was riding horses when she was eight months pregnant with him, until her doctor stopped her.

He lived in Tempe, Ariz., where he kept three quarter horses. He rode as often as he could, including multiday trail rides. His wife, Donna Killoughey Bird, and two children, Amanda, 15, and Andrew, 13, rode, too, but Mr. Bird was the avid one.

If he wasn't surrounded by open spaces, he would get edgy. In 1984, he was in New York for four days to attend a conference.

By the fourth day, he told his wife, "I'm really claustrophobic here, because I can't see the horizon." As she put it, "It was a case of 'don't fence me in.'"

Mr. Bird, 51, took last summer off and spent a good part of it training a new filly named Dani. On Sept. 7, he rode the filly with a saddle for the first time. On Sept. 10, he began a new job as senior vice president at Marsh & McLennan. He was to work out of Phoenix, but spent the first two days in New York for meetings.

On Sept. 11, he had a three-hour meeting starting at 8:15 A.M. at the Marsh offices in the World Trade Center. He told his wife he'd be home in Tempe by 8 P.M. for dinner.

JOSH BIRNBAUM
Turntables and Yield Tables

On Sept. 11, 1999, according to a trippy-looking flyer that Sam and Marcel Birnbaum have saved, there was a rave in Johnson City, Tenn., and DJ Samsson was on the bill. "This New York City DJ's trance set will set you off like a highly reactive chemical," the flyer promised.

Two years later, DJ Samsson, also known as Josh Birnbaum, 24 and straight out of Columbia University, had set aside his turntables for yield tables, at least for the day, and was at his job at Cantor Fitzgerald as an assistant bond trader.

But for Mr. Birnbaum, working on Wall Street was mostly a means to an end: saving up enough money to open his own recording studio. He already had a small studio set up in his apartment near Columbia.

A crowd gathered on September 27 at Liberty Street and Broadway in lower Manhattan to take in the view, solemnly, of the trade center wreckage. (*Edward Keating*)

"His dream was music, always," said Marcel Birnbaum, his mother.

Mr. Birnbaum's father, Sam Birnbaum, is no fan of techno or trance or any of the other myriad forms of dance music always pounding from Josh's speakers. But he did not mind that Josh chose a D.J. name that reflected the love and respect he had for his father.

"Are you kidding?" Marcel Birnbaum said. "He was honored."

GEORGE BISHOP
A Cliché, but Accurate

Do not tell Betsy Bishop that the description "family man" is a cliché—she knows it. Still, there is no better way to characterize her husband, George Bishop, who, she said, treasured taking his two sons to soccer games, going on beach vacations, having guests for intimate dinners and listening to music.

"He wouldn't just have music on in the background, he'd

really be listening," Mrs. Bishop said. "And he wasn't a party person, but he was a very genial host, great at bringing people together."

Mr. Bishop, who was 52 and worked for the Aon Corporation, was the kind of person who would bring you your papers on the way back from the office fax machine, or walk a seeing-eye dog three miles a day as a favor, just to give it exercise.

JEFFREY BITTNER
A Brother's Paternal Streak

If you talk to Pamela Bittner about her big brother, Jeffrey, you would probably assume that he was born at least a few years before her, the way she describes him as protective, nurturing, wise. She uses those terms as a little sister would: "He was quite a protective big brother, always concerned about making sure I was happy and safe."

The truth of the matter is, however, that Jeffrey Bittner,

27, was born all of a whopping one minute before Pamela, his twin sister. But you would never know it.

"That was the big running joke," she said. "He would always say, 'I'm a minute older!' You couldn't argue about it."

Mr. Bittner, who was a research analyst for Keefe, Bruyette & Woods, was a brotherly gentleman not only with his sister, but with everyone, she said. In the last few weeks before the attack, he had joined a mentoring program that made him a big brother to New York City schoolchildren.

BALEWA ALBERT BLACKMAN
Music by Night

Balewa Albert Blackman worked as an accountant, but that was the least of it.

"He liked a lot of different things," said his sister, Susan McMillian. Which explains, sort of, how a man with an undergraduate degree in biochemical engineering wound up working as a junior accountant at Cantor Fitzgerald by day and as a D.J. at small clubs—jazz, rhythm and blues, hip-hop—at night, which "was just something he did on the side, because he loves music so much," Ms. McMillian said.

Never one to take his sidelines lightly, Mr. Blackman had also been training since August in a Navy Seals–type fitness program, which involved getting up at dawn and getting used to swimming with fins and running in boots.

By the end of the program, Ms. McMillian said, her brother, who stood about 5-foot-5, would have been able to complete a 500-yard swim in under 10 minutes, 100 push-ups in 2 minutes, 200 situps in 2 minutes and a 1.5-mile run in under 9 minutes.

"He liked the idea of not just doing the physical work, but also learning how to think like a Navy Seal person," she said. "He likes things that are conditioning for the body, but also conditioning for the mind."

CHRISTOPHER J. BLACKWELL
Seemingly Fearless

Christopher J. Blackwell liked to live life on the edge.

"He was interested in anything that was dangerous," his mother, Frances Allen, said. "He was born with no sense of fear. When he was little he would swim underwater before he would swim on top of it. My other three children were a lot easier."

A fireman for 20 years, Firefighter Blackwell, 42, was assigned to Rescue Company 3 in the South Bronx. He was a specialist in collapsed buildings, and gave lectures on the topic to firemen across the country. Like many of his col-

leagues, he had a genetic connection to his profession: his uncle had been a captain in the New York City Fire Department. His father and a grandfather were both policemen.

When he was not on the job, Firefighter Blackwell devoted his time to his wife, Jane, and their three children, Alexandra, who is 15, Ryan, 13, and Samantha, 11. "He didn't care where we were going or what we were doing," Mrs. Blackwell said. "When he wasn't working, he wanted to spend time with the family."

He had a high-risk job, but Firefighter Blackwell "wasn't reckless," his wife said. He loved doing what he did. His mother added, "He lived and died with purpose."

SUSAN L. BLAIR
Big Laugh, Big Heart

Susan L. Blair had a work-stopping, what's-that-noise kind of laugh. Wherever she has worked, co-workers have asked her to pipe down.

"It was high-pitched and loud," said her sister Leslie Blair.

If she was telling a joke, forget it. The laugh and a joke were just too much because she was funny. For example, the day before the World Trade Center attack, she interviewed a prospective employee for Aon, where she was a team leader.

"She commented to a co-worker that the person had a fear of heights," Leslie Blair said. "She said to the co-worker, 'I'm thinking to myself that we're on the 92nd floor of the World Trade Center; you might want to rethink this job.' "

Though some of her jokes were laced with sarcasm, they were not aimed as darts, Ms. Blair's sister said. In fact, Ms. Blair, 35, from East Brunswick, N.J., had a big heart. She liked getting laughs out of cranky tollbooth workers.

"I would ask her why she cared whether that guy smiled and she would say, 'I just do.' She thought life was too short to go around with our shields up."

CRAIG BLASS
Young Man about Town

By all accounts, Craig Blass was living the high life, and he loved it. Bachelor parties in Las Vegas, summer weekends in the Hamptons, the social scene in the city. But there was one other thing he really liked to do that always seemed to surprise people.

"He loved to go shopping with me," said Mr. Blass's mother, Barbara Blass. "My friends would say, 'He still shops with you?' And I'd say, 'Oh, yes.' "

He splurged on himself, his mother and others because "he was living the good life, making good money and spending it because he made it," Mrs. Blass said. Mr. Blass, 27, worked as an institutional stock trader for Cantor Fitzgerald. He grew up in Greenlawn, on Long Island, and cheered for the New Jersey Devils hockey team.

If he was not out at an athletic event or socializing, he could probably be found on his mother's couch, flipping through the sports channels with his younger brother and their father. He also loved to gamble.

"That was one of his joys," Mrs. Blass said. "But I guess if you work on Wall Street you have that in you, you gamble all the time."

RICK BLOOD
His City Ever Since

Rick Blood grew up in Williamsburg, Va., but his heart always belonged to New York City. As a teenager, he hung subway maps on his bedroom wall and played a New York version of Monopoly.

For his 13th birthday, he asked his parents for a trip to the city. He liked it so much that he spent his next three birthdays here.

"He always loved subways and trains," said his father, Richard Blood. "He just thought that this would be the place to be."

At 36, Rick Blood had made a place for himself in one of the city's landmarks as an insurance broker at the Aon Corporation. He and his wife, Kris, were raising two children, Michael and Madeline, in Ridgefield, N.J. But every workday, he would eagerly head into the city again. Not even the crowds, the noise and the World Trade Center bombing in 1993 could scare him away.

MICHAEL A. BOCCARDI
A Loyal Scout

Taking more than a dozen 15-year-old Boy Scouts to the wilds of New Mexico for a 10-day trip on horseback might not sound like the ideal trip for some people, but it was for Michael A. Boccardi.

"It was a once in a lifetime thing," said his friend Ed Maselli, an assistant scoutmaster of Troop 40 in Mount Vernon, N.Y., which Mr. Boccardi led as scoutmaster. "Snakes, bears, the whole nine yards. He loved it."

Mr. Boccardi, 30, worked as a senior vice president of institutional relations at Fred Alger Management. Scouting captured Mr. Boccardi's imagination from the age of 10; he had been an Eagle Scout himself. A typical month might include 20 nights devoted to various activities and events, according to the Westchester-Putnam Council of the Boy Scouts of America.

Scouting was on his mind on the morning of Sept. 11.

From his office, he sent an e-mail message to a mother of one of the boys just before 9 A.M. It was the troop's revised newsletter.

JOHN BOCCHI
Prankster with a Heart

With a top broker's panache, John Bocchi presented himself as if to say, Either you love me or you don't.

He would pull up next to you in his Porsche—a 911—gesture, grin, and take off in the wind. Once, Mr. Bocchi drove by as a friend was loading his golf clubs into his car. Friend goes into the house. Comes out: clubs gone! The two search frantically. Friend calls the New Vernon, N.J., police. They take one long look at their buddy, John. Who grins and finally produces the clubs from his trunk.

Michele Bocchi loved him through 16 years of pranks, parties, Ferrari and Porsche shows, moves around New Jersey, Wall Street promotions (at 38, a managing director at Cantor Fitzgerald) and this year's 35-pound weight loss. Loved the father in him, who came home Friday nights with pizza for Matthew, 9; Nicholas, 7; Michael, 3; and Paul, the baby. His suggestion for the new license plate: "Boys 'R' Us." Only one thing she wanted to change: he chewed ice. Drove her nuts.

"And now that's what I miss," she said. "The nights are lonely. I would give anything to hear that chomp, chomp, chomp again."

MICHAEL L. BOCCHINO
A Firefighter's Scrapbook

Michael L. Bocchino kept a scrapbook of all the fires he fought and the people he helped rescue in his 22 years as a fireman. The first entry dealt with a Harlem apartment fire in June 1980—when he was 24—in which two firemen plunged to their deaths. The book's last chapter will be about the World Trade Center, his last fire. As family members compile material for it, his uncle, Leo Piro, a retired fireman, reminds people that his nephew's career started and ended with a disaster.

For the last 12 years, Firefighter Bocchino, 45, worked as a chief's aide in Battalion 48 in Brooklyn, helping deploy units at fires. He was devoted to his elderly parents, Michael and Lucy, with whom he lived, and his work, family members said.

During a memorial Mass on Oct. 13, his brother Tom talked of the scrapbook, and the people Firefighter Bocchino had saved since 1979. And he lamented the sudden end of his career.

"We may never get to meet anyone he might have rescued on Sept. 11."

SUSAN BOCHINO
Father Recalls Straight A's

It was a "little shaky" working on the 92nd floor of the south tower, Susan Bochino, who was no fan of being that high off the ground, told her father, Elmer Bochino. But she also said she thought a career move to Aon Corporation was well worth the sacrifice. Mr. Bochino remembers her saying that in the summer of 2001, when she started her new job with Aon as a client specialist.

"In her working career, I'd have to say this was the happiest she ever was," Mr. Bochino said. "She said it and I could see it."

Ms. Bochino, who was 36, loved going to the movies, to Giants football games, or just watching television shows, especially *Star Trek*. Growing up, she never spent a lot of time on her books, but her father said she did not have to. "She'd be sitting there at 4 in the morning watching television," Mr. Bochino said.

"But I couldn't get mad because she'd always come home with A's."

BRUCE BOEHM
"Incredible Zest for Life"

Bruce Boehm's love affair with the beach started when he was a teenager. Every summer, he pulled on his swimming trunks and worked as a lifeguard at Nassau Beach, in Lido Beach on Long Island. There was not much money in it, but he just loved being out there.

Mr. Boehm, 49, never outgrew that infatuation. Even when he started his career as a financial broker, he continued to lifeguard on weekends for a while. In later years, he trained for marathons and triathlons at the beach, often dragging along his daughters, Brittany, 16, and Stacey, 13.

"He always said, 'The beach is my church,'" said his wife, Irene. A born talker, Mr. Boehm made friends easily at the beach and elsewhere. At his wife's high school reunion, he danced with more people than she did.

"He had an incredible zest for life," she said. A memorial service was set for Sept. 29—at Nassau Beach.

MARY BOFFA
A Fresh View of the Future

Mary Boffa's hobby was her sprawling, close-knit family. She had 3 sisters and nearly 30 first cousins. They provided plenty to do on weekends. When she was growing up on the Upper East Side of Manhattan, there was always a cousin to play with.

Her father was a blue-collar worker at Western Electric and her mother was a school cafeteria worker. At age 45, Ms. Boffa was an associate vice president for Marsh & McLennan, in 1 World Trade Center. She had recently separated from her husband and moved into a two-bedroom apartment on Staten Island. It had a view of the Verrazano-Narrows Bridge. She had new furniture.

"She was very excited," said her nephew, Michael Trudeau. "It was renewal for her."

DARREN BOHAN
Banjos and Big Dreams

Like so many New Yorkers, there was more to Darren Bohan than met the eye. By day he was a temp and for the past few months he had worked on the 102nd floor of 2 World Trade Center, where he crunched numbers for the Aon Corporation. But Mr. Bohan would rather have been plucking a banjo or strumming his guitar, jamming with friends until late at night.

Alison Kelley, his girlfriend, said he hoped to parlay his musical talents into a full-time job, perhaps as a music teacher at a public school.

"Music was so important to him," she said.

Ms. Kelley, also a banjo player, spent many hours playing with Mr. Bohan. Their repertory ran from Irish ballads to songs by the rock band Kiss to 19th-century American roots music.

"We'd play just about anything," Ms. Kelley said. The two had been inseparable since meeting at a music jam in Brooklyn in early 2001.

Laid back, gentle and unpretentious, Mr. Bohan, 34, tried not to gripe too much about his day job, although he was not thrilled to be working 102 stories off the ground.

"He didn't like being so unnaturally high up, in a place where something terrible happened before," she said. "But he'd just try to tell people it was a nice view."

VINCENT BOLAND
Funny and Smart

Family and friends are learning a lot about Vincent Boland, who is missing from Marsh & McLennan at 1 World Trade Center.

"His friends are telling me that he was funny," said his mother, Joyce, a teacher and a nurse. "I didn't know that. At home, he was quiet. If you wanted to know something you had to ask him, you had to draw it out. He wasn't funny with his brother and sister."

On the other hand, his friend Kyle Mooney did not know that Mr. Boland was a member of Mensa, an organization for the highly intelligent. "I had no idea about that,"

Mr. Mooney said. "I'm not surprised because he was brilliant and could talk about anything in depth, even esoteric subjects. But Mensa was not something he talked about."

Among friends, Mr. Boland was known for his offbeat sense of humor; he was quick with a joke or cynical quip. Three years ago, after a friend was mugged on the subway, Mr. Boland decided that buses were safer.

For six months, Mr. Mooney said, whenever anyone asked Mr. Boland how he was doing, he would say, "There are no worries on the bus."

COLIN BONNETT
Manners and a Motorcycle

Colin Bonnett was a gentleman—a Harley-Davidson–riding, bodybuilder sort of gentleman. Born in Barbados, he had been raised with Caribbean good manners that said that a door was always to be opened for a lady and that her chair should be pulled out when she sat.

He also had deep empathy for animals, and had recently rescued a stray kitten that had been wandering around his family's home in Crown Heights, Brooklyn.

But he also had an adventurous streak that put him on horseback with his 10-year-old son, Kody, on most weekends, or on his motorcycle. He pushed himself hard with a physical fitness regimen that included weight lifting, jogging, countless situps and no junk food. Ever.

Mr. Bonnett's natural graces helped get him his job at Marsh & McLennan, where he was a telecommunications programmer. In the early 1990s he had been working as an assistant to a Manhattan veterinarian and was about to lose his job because the doctor was closing his practice. One of the customers was a Marsh executive who invited Mr. Bonnett, 39, to fill out an application. He was transferred to the World Trade Center by the company only a few months before Sept. 11.

YVONNE BONOMO
Global Traveler

Yvonne Bonomo could not have taken more seriously the word "world" in World Trade Center. Not only was she a corporate travel booker for American Express, arranging last-minute global gallivants for executives at Marsh & McLennan on the 94th floor of 1 World Trade Center, but she also loved jetting around the world on the special corporate discounts offered to those in her job.

Only days before the disaster, she returned from Las Vegas, where she had attended a close friend's bridal shower. Although Ms. Bonomo was living at home in Jackson Heights, Queens, with her mother, Sonia, and father, John, "she was really very independent," said her cousin, Richie Fabrizi.

But Ms. Bonomo, 30, had contemplated sacrificing her cherished independence over the last year; she became engaged to her boyfriend, Anthony Vaccaro.

"All we could tell him is that Yvonne's cell phone records show that she made a call to her mom at 8:51, after the plane hit," her cousin said. "That call never went through."

SEAN BOOKER
Minister to His Flock

Sean Booker was a troubleshooting technician for Xerox, but his hours away from the job were concentrated on fixing something much dearer to him than office machinery: troubled souls. Mr. Booker, 35, was an ordained minister with his own flock at the Tabernacle Outreach No. 2 in Newark. He decided to pursue the vocation during his 20s.

"Everything he did was church-related," said his older sister, Stacey Booker. "He was a true minister of God."

Three nights a week were designated for Bible study classes, he preached two services each Sunday, and he also provided an ersatz shuttle service for any churchgoers in need of transportation.

Whatever spare time was left he spent with his three children: Mr. Booker was a twin, and he and his wife, Sharon, had a set of 3-year-old twins and another son, 5. Though he'd pounded the inner-city basketball courts in Newark with the rest of the neighborhood boys and also played football, Mr. Booker abandoned sports for spirituality.

KELLY ANN BOOMS
Staying in Touch, Always

Everywhere Kelly Ann Booms lived, she made good friends, which is what you would expect of a lively, outgoing girl, the oldest in a family of four children. But throughout her childhood, she also made a point of staying in touch as she moved from Colorado to Michigan, Australia to Ohio, where her family still lives outside Cincinnati.

"She was very strong willed," said her father, Richard Booms Sr. "It was her strong personality that really made her keep up with her friends."

Ms. Booms got her first real job in Boston, working for PriceWaterhouse in 1999, soon after graduating from Miami University in Ohio with a double major in accounting and finance. Last summer she was notified that she had passed certified public accountant exams. On Sept. 11, she boarded American Airlines Flight 11 for California, where she had been sent on temporary assignment. She was 24 years old.

In Boston, as elsewhere, she had become involved in

charity work, helping out underprivileged families at Christmastime. She also loved sports, and had recently taken up the guitar.

"She was very ambitious, very outgoing," her father said. "When she was in a room, you knew she was there. She influenced a lot of people in a lot of ways."

SHERRY ANN BORDEAUX
Good Cook and Loyal Friend

There was a certain stability to Sherry Ann Bordeaux: she joined Fiduciary Trust after college and stayed there for 15 years. She got to be best friends with Nicole Lynch way back in junior high school, and stayed best friends ever since.

And she loved her cozy living arrangement in a three-family home in New Jersey, where Ms. Bordeaux, 38, lived upstairs, her mother and brother lived downstairs and her sister's family lived in the basement.

"She was close with my kids," said Ms. Bordeaux's sister, Cynthia. "She'd take them out to eat. They'd listen to music together, mostly R & B, and they danced a lot."

At Thanksgiving, while Ms. Bordeaux's mother would serve the meal, Ms. Bordeaux, an aspiring cook, would have the family—which often included Ms. Lynch—up for appetizers or dessert.

"She loved cooking and she liked to think she was the female Emeril," Ms. Lynch said. "Whenever we would travel together, she would find the good restaurants. Her wine was always merlot. She was a typical Virgo, very straight and clear and a little rigid. She always knew what she liked."

KRYSTINE BORDENABE
A Whiz in the Kitchen

Krystine Bordenabe was on the brink of an exciting life change she'd been waiting for since she had become a mother for the first time 13 years ago: she was eight months pregnant with her second child, and was counting the weeks until she could resign from her job as a sales assistant at Keefe, Bruyette & Woods and become a stay-at-home mom and full-time homemaker.

That was, for her, the noblest profession, and one she felt compelled to excel at. She was a whiz in the kitchen, loved to cook and bake, and while she was not much of a clothes hound, she occasionally indulged her passion for stylish shoes.

"She loved her shoes," said her sister-in-law, Danielle Bordenabe. "But mostly she just cared about other people, about helping out; she was my best friend."

A Jersey City girl, Ms. Bordenabe also enjoyed taking trips to the shore each summer with her extended family. She

was 33, and lived in Old Bridge, N.J., with her husband, Alfredo, and son Andrew.

MARTIN BORYCZEWSKI
Leaving Work at Work

Martin Boryczewski, 29, gave himself four years to make it into major league baseball. He played for Class A and AA teams of the Pittsburgh Pirates and the Detroit Tigers before giving it up and switching to financial trading. At Cantor Fitzgerald, he dealt energetically with the pace and stress—and at the day's end, he left it completely behind.

"If you'd so much as mentioned work," said Brian Hartigan, a friend, "you'd get this look, like, 'We're not talking about the job.' "

But he would talk about nearly anything else. "Fly-fishing to Nietzsche," said Mr. Hartigan. "Baseball to religion. He'd start with something simple and wind up saying something very deep."

Weekends were sacrosanct. First, he went to Parsippany, N.J., to see his mother and then to rural Pennsylvania to his father's place. There, he took the boat out and went fly-fishing—his passion. He felt fully at home in the woods and on the lake. His dream was to retire early and become a fishing guide in Montana. Fishing, the woods, wildlife: When he was back in the city, he could happily discuss them every evening.

RICHARD E. BOSCO
Sweet Dream of a Husband

Here was Richard E. Bosco's typical morning: He would wake about 6:30 and hop in the shower. He would be joined by Abby, his 2-year-old daughter, who had recently decided that showering with dad was a fun way to start her day. After shower time, she would stand on a stool beside him as he lathered up. With her toy razor blade, they shaved side by side, chatting away.

Mr. Bosco taught his son, Richie, 3½, how to tackle. Then he brought him inside for a glass of strawberry milk. Mr. Bosco grew up in Suffern, N.Y., where he met his wife, Traci. They started dating when she was 17.

"He just seemed genuine, like I could trust him right away," she recalled. "I just felt comfortable."

They married in 1995, and Mrs. Bosco describes him as a sweet, sweet dream of a husband: he lavished her with attention and compliments. He did not wait to be asked to do the dishes, take out the garbage or throw in a load of laundry.

"We never fought," she said. "It was total teamwork."

Mr. Bosco, 34, did not work at the World Trade Center. A financial specialist for Citibank, he was trying to cultivate new clients. On Sept. 11 his first appointment of the day was at Cantor Fitzgerald.

J. HOWARD BOULTON Jr.
A Manly Gentleman

J. Howard Boulton Jr. was a gentleman with the common touch, an outsider who made others feel at home, a man who bound together two worlds—Venezuela and Iceland—with the greatest of ease.

Mr. Boulton, 29, grew up in Caracas, the son of a prominent Venezuelan family, and spent summers working on his father's cattle farm. He attended boarding school and college in the United States and settled in New York, taking a job at Eurobrokers. A colleague introduced him to Vigdis Ragnarsson, a New Yorker whose family came from Iceland. They married in 1998.

"He had this wonderful balance of being this manly strong man, who could deal with horses and cars equally, and on the other side this kind, gentlemanly touch," said his father-in-law, Kristjan Ragnarsson.

Mr. Boulton's other great loves were his 11-month-old son, Frederick Thomas, and Formula One racing. For Frederick, he would rush home for bath time and wake at 5 A.M. to play with him before work. He would get up just as early for Formula One broadcasts from Europe.

There is surely much grief among the farmhands in Venezuela. "They watched him grow up, and were really fond of him," Mrs. Boulton said. "They are beautifully simple people but I'm sure they understand what happened, and the injustice of it."

FRANCISCO BOURDIER
Daughter Was His Life

After finishing his morning shift as a security guard at the Deutsche Bank, next to 2 World Trade Center, Francisco Bourdier always watched his 22-month-old daughter, Francesca, every afternoon and evening. He took her just about everywhere—to the stores near their home in Jackson Heights, to the park, the movies, even the auto repair shop. He put her in for a daily nap about 5 P.M., then drove with her to Manhattan about 10 each weeknight to pick up his wife, Erma, the evening office manager in a hotel.

"That was his life—his daughter," Mrs. Bourdier said. "They had a special bond."

When Francesca was an infant, her father, 40, regularly gave her the 2 A.M. bottle. More recently, he bought her Winnie the Pooh software and tried to interest her in computers, his hobby.

"Most of the time she played with the mouse," her mother said.

He also had started fixing her hair in a ponytail. "It wasn't really, like, good," Mrs. Bourdier said. "But he did it."

THOMAS H. BOWDEN Jr.
A New Jersey Native Son

Thomas H. Bowden Jr. grew up in Glen Ridge, N.J., about a dozen miles due west of Manhattan, and, like any self-respecting son of New Jersey, he was deeply, openly and emotionally loyal to Bruce Springsteen. He once argued to his skeptical father that the Boss trumped the Chairman of the Board as New Jersey's greatest voice. How, then, to explain Mr. Bowden's love of the Boston Red Sox? Even his mother, Sheilah Bowden, was a little baffled by that one. The best she could come up with is that her son had a soft spot for underdogs.

Mr. Springsteen would understand.

Mr. Bowden was 36, an equities trader at Cantor Fitzgerald. He started there in 1993, the same week as the first terror attack on the World Trade Center. He and his wife, Deborah, had two children, Sara, 22 months, and Alyson, born two weeks early on Aug. 31.

His family now views this last fact as a small gift from God.

One of his finest qualities, his mother said, was a fierce protectiveness of family and friends. He remained close to boys he first met in grade school. Early in the morning he would stand over Sara's crib, fortifying himself with her smile. Now, thanks to his friends, she has a necklace with a silver heart engraved with his initials.

VERONIQUE BOWERS
A Closet of Names

Veronique Bowers lived in Bedford-Stuyvesant, Brooklyn, and worked in accounts receivable at Windows on the World and loved beautiful clothes so much she named her son Dior, after Christian Dior. She said she needed expensive clothes because the clients were very high-class people, said her uncle, Clifford Tillman.

But the truth was, Ms. Bowers had always been a lavish spender and generous. Mr. Tillman remembers that Ms. Bowers, 26, got a Tommy Hilfiger sweatshirt for Dior last Christmas. Dior is 9 and has muscular dystrophy and uses a walker and has the mental capacity of a younger child. He and his mother lived with her grandmother.

Mr. Tillman said Ms. Bowers called her grandmother on her cell phone when the building was hit and was so hysterical she was saying that an ambulance hit the building. Then she called her mother.

"She started yelling to her mother that something is wrong, the building is shaking and smoke is everywhere,"

Mr. Tillman said. "She was saying, 'Mommy, mommy, I'm trapped' and she made a statement that she loves her. Then everything went dead."

Straightening out Ms. Bowers room this week, her family found a pair of green Gucci boots, with gold trim, still in tissue paper.

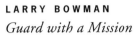

LARRY BOWMAN
Guard with a Mission

By day, Larry Bowman worked as a security guard. By night and on weekends, he did missionary work. For him, they were part of the same ministry.

His mother, Ruth Bowman White, said he loved his security job at the World Trade Center because he often helped people who were lost or stuck in elevators.

"His motto was to help people and see that they're O.K. and do what he can for them," she said. "He gave people directions and made sure that the direction was correct."

Even more important to him was his work for the Lord. On Sundays, he held services at nursing homes and at Rikers Island. Many days, he took food to the hungry. He played basketball with teenagers, and between games shared the word of God with them. Raised in a religious family, Mr. Bowman, 46, was called to God three years ago, his mother said, becoming a minister at the House of God Church Brooklyn No. 1.

"I spoke to Larry the Saturday before the tragedy," said his aunt, Lannie Williams, a senior minister at the church. "He was telling me all the good works that God is showing him and the work that he wants to do in the community. He was very good in the community. People listened to him. He pointed out that there's a better way. He said drugs is not the answer. Being out in the street is not the answer. The fast life is not the answer. God is the answer."

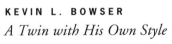

KEVIN L. BOWSER
A Twin with His Own Style

He may have been an identical twin, but Kevin L. Bowser, 45, was no carbon copy of his genetically significant other.

"We hadn't dressed alike since grade school," said Kelvin Bowser. Though people confused the two, the brothers rarely played upon their surface sameness—except as boys. When one faced a trip to the principal's office, he tended to claim that he had been mistaken for his twin.

Kevin Bowser was a vegetarian, a discipline that became more pronounced after their mother's death from cancer in 1991. Philadelphia Eagles fans since they were 5, they attended the same college, Kutztown State in Pennsylvania,

at the instigation of their high school football coach; Kevin played defensive end.

After getting his business degree, Kevin stayed in Philadelphia, married and had two children, but commuted to a Wall Street job in Marsh & McLennan's technology division, teaching brokers how to use their computer software. This year he obtained company financing for the community football team that his twin coaches in southwest Philadelphia.

"We hadn't even written the thank-you letter yet," Kelvin said.

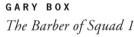

GARY BOX
The Barber of Squad 1

Gary Box was a funny man, a big kid, a roughhouser who liked laughter and pranks. When he came to the Squad 1 firehouse in Park Slope, Brooklyn, last year, he convinced everyone there that his previous profession had been that of a barber for a funeral home.

The men believed him, and in his tenure, Mr. Box, 37, managed to brutalize the coiffures of every man in the house.

"If you wanted a crew cut, he gave you a Mohawk," said his friend, Steve Iola. Eventually Mr. Box got good with the scissors and the men bought him a barber chair.

But his humor had a limit. When the men made cracks about their wives, all Mr. Box would say was: "What can I say, man? I love her." Her name is Kathleen; their children are Dalton and Bridget.

"As the other firemen make their way up to the Pearly Gates," said Lt. Dennis Farrell, "Gary Box will be there dumping buckets of water on their heads."

GENNADY BOYARSKY
Getting Things Right

The wonderful thing about Gennady Boyarsky was that he was a perfectionist who took as much pride in getting simple things right—like a backyard cookout with his wife, Jolonta, and son, Michael, 7—as in creating a travel package as an American Express travel agent. Mr. Boyarsky worked for the company at the World Trade Center for five years.

Mr. Boyarsky, 34, was known for his extensive, eclectic music collection, his ability to make detailed maps of just about anyplace, and his mischievous streak. His only sibling, Beata Boyarsky, 25, said some of her fondest early memories were of the times her brother rearranged the furniture in their home when their mother left on errands. Once, when she was 6 or 7, he dressed her up as Wonder Woman. Ms. Boyarsky said her brother never lost that fun-loving side.

"He was a simple, honest, hardworking guy."

PAMELA J. BOYCE
A No-Nonsense Life

Sometimes people would see Pamela J. Boyce's direct, no-nonsense style and take it for abrasiveness, said her partner, Catherine Anello. But Ms. Boyce, 43, refused to change.

"It was similar to slapping someone in the face," Ms. Anello said of the woman she shared a life with in Dyker Heights, Brooklyn. "If there was someone who lost a loved one and had been grieving too long, so that they were not living their life, she would say, 'Stop. It's not what they would want. They are in a better place.' She said, 'I'm not afraid to die because I know where I am going is beautiful.' "

Ms. Boyce had been the assistant vice president of accounting in the New York office of Carr Futures, on the 92nd floor of 1 World Trade Center. She was a competitive disco dancer. One of her happiest moments was serving as a Lamaze coach for her sister Desiree when her niece Kristina was born.

"She was so neurotic there she had to find something specific on the baby to make sure they got the right one," Ms. Anello said, laughing. "I think she finally found a little mark on her ear."

MICHAEL BOYLE
No Excuses for Him

He was off duty the morning of Sept. 11, but Michael Boyle, a firefighter with Engine Company 33 in Manhattan, jumped on the truck anyway when the alarms sounded.

"He cared a lot about the Fire Department," said his younger sister, Jeanne Boyle. "He was very simple in his ideas, but complex in his actions. And he could endure pain like no one I've ever known." Ms. Boyle remembered, "I would ask him, 'How do you run a marathon?' And he would say, 'Just get up every day and run.' "

That's what Firefighter Boyle did. He was a "no excuses" kind of guy, Ms. Boyle said.

A formidable athlete, Firefighter Boyle, who was 37 and also worked for the firefighters' union, clearly had a soft side for his sister. She said he was protective, but from afar. Two years ago, they both ran in the Long Island Marathon, where Firefighter Boyle, who lived in Westbury, N.Y., found her in the crowd and advised her to slow her pace for her own good. Then he disappeared. He finished at 3 hours 15 minutes.

Justinian Kfoury, pausing in September at a sandwich shop on Eighth Street in New York City, said the attack on the World Trade Center was all he thought about.

(*Edward Keating*)

"But I could see him reading this saying: 'That wasn't my good time! Tell them my good time!' " Ms. Boyle said; his good time, she said, was 3 hours 1 minute. "His goal was to break three hours in the city marathon this year. And he probably would have done it."

ALFRED J. BRACA
Romance on the Ferry

Alfred J. Braca and his wife, Jean, met on the Staten Island Ferry. He was smitten; she was not. He pleaded for a date, and she said no. But he persisted, and she finally gave in after they shared a marathon 12-hour phone conversation.

On that date, "he gave me one kiss," his wife recalled. "And I said, 'Maybe this is not so bad.' "

That first kiss bloomed into 33 years of marriage, and a good life with four children, David, Deanna, Christina and Christopher, in Leonardo, N.J. Mr. Braca, 54, was a born-again Christian who never stopped counting his blessings.

He worked as a bond broker at Cantor Fitzgerald, where co-workers nicknamed him The Rev because of his faith. In August, Mr. Braca walked Deanna down the aisle for her wedding. His funeral service was to take place in the same church.

SANDRA CONATY BRACE
25 Cats, 55 Words

Sandra Conaty Brace might have appreciated a short biographical sketch about her. After all, she herself had mastered the 55-word short story—a challenge to the most diligent amateur writer. Mrs. Brace had published much of her work on Web sites dedicated to the genre.

Mrs. Brace lived in Stapleton, Staten Island, and took the 7:40 A.M. ferry across the harbor each day to her job at Risk Insurance Solutions, where she was an administrative assistant. She shared her house with a husband, David, and 25 cats. Well, maybe not exactly 25.

"It's probably more," Mr. Brace said. "But I lose count."

Dinner for the cats always caused a minor food riot, but even a riot can have its own poetry. Mrs. Brace placed cat food on seven plates on the kitchen and dining room floors. The groups of cats arrayed around each plate formed a furry constellation of stars, with the plates at the centers and the cats as the coronas.

On Sept. 10, Mrs. Brace, 60, took the day off from work to do chores, fix the carpeting on the stairs that had been torn by a cat, and watch *Judge Judy* on television. Mr. Brace came home at 5 P.M.

He asked her: "Why don't you take another vacation day tomorrow?" She replied, "No, I think I'll go to work."

"And that's what happened," Mr. Brace said. "That's what happened."

KEVIN BRACKEN
Making the Most of It

His friends called it "the Bracken bounce." It was an expression they coined the day on the golf course when he hit a ball into the trees and it miraculously ricocheted back onto the fairway.

But it was not just on the golf course that Kevin Bracken, a firefighter with Engine Company 40 on Amsterdam Avenue and 66th Street, was known as a lucky guy. It was every time he looked for a parking spot on a busy street; or the day, two years ago, his car flipped over in a traffic accident and he escaped without a scratch. His wife, Jennifer Liang, would say Firefighter Bracken, 37, made his own luck.

"He was the most optimistic person I ever encountered," she said. "He was never unhappy. Never without a smile on his face. Whatever situation he was in, he made the best of it."

Ms. Liang, who met her husband 11 years ago on the Long Island Rail Road, said that his credo was to live life to the fullest, "to seize the moment and make everything of that moment." He enjoyed being a firefighter, Ms. Liang said. But it was not fighting fires that appealed to him. It was the comradeship at the firehouse.

"He was a real people person," she said. An avid sports fan, who coached the softball team from his local bar, Firefighter Bracken never would say "good-bye" to his friends. His parting words were always a kind of shorthand for how he believed you should live your life: "Drive fast. Take chances," he would say.

She added: "If somebody would have told him this would happen, he would have been, 'Me? Are you kidding?' "

DAVID B. BRADY
A Soccer Dad

At 41, David B. Brady had the trappings of success: an office on the 39th floor of the World Financial Center, where he was a first vice president at Merrill Lynch, and a home in Summit, N.J.

He also had his priorities: faith, family and friends. A devout Catholic, he attended Mass almost every day and occasionally wrote prayers, said his wife of 12 years, Jennifer. But he never made a big deal of it.

"He would just say, 'I'm doing a cameo,' " said Joy Fingleton, an assistant. And he made sure that his four children—Matthew, 9; Erin, 6; Mark 4; and Grace, 2—saw him every day. "If he had an evening meeting, he'd stay home for breakfast," Ms. Brady said. "Or sometimes he'd even come home for lunch."

He was an eager school volunteer. "I think it was shocking to his clients, who would call to find out that he was gone for an hour but he would be back from reading in his daughter's class out in Summit, N.J.," Ms. Brady said. On Sept. 11, he went to 1 World Trade Center to meet with a client on the 106th floor.

Now, every night his family prays for him with the words he taught them: "Thank you, Jesus, for the love you bring. Thank you, Jesus, for everything."

ALEX BRAGINSKY
With Artful Touches

You could set your watch by Alex Braginsky. And woe to the boss or relative who let dust accumulate on their computer screens: they got scolded. Having moved to Queens from the Soviet Union in 1979 with virtually nothing, he felt anyone fortunate enough to have state-of-the-art computers had better take care of them.

Mr. Braginsky, 38, was a man who picked up his shirts at the dry cleaner and, before going to work at Reuters, re-ironed them if he noticed wrinkles. A perfectionist but not a prima donna, he would pull over to help if he passed a driver with car trouble. When he traveled in Europe with his girlfriend, complete strangers would stop him on the street and ask for directions: even in foreign countries, he projected the savoir faire of a fellow who knew where he was headed. He rode a motorcycle and filled his kitchen in Stamford, Conn., with top-notch cookware.

"A three-hundred-dollar set of knives," marveled his mother, Nelly. "I'd tell him, for that much, a knife should work by itself. When Alex cooked, it was like art on your plate."

He was doing a colleague a favor and filling in at a meeting at Windows on the World on Sept. 11.

NICHOLAS BRANDEMARTI
Dazzled by the Height

It was the height that Nicholas Brandemarti used to love about his job. From his offices at Keefe, Bruyette & Woods, a financial services firm on the 89th floor of 2 World Trade Center, he could look out on all of Manhattan, and on a clear day, to Connecticut.

"What amazed him was being above the clouds, being able to see helicopters flying below his floor," said Mr. Brandemarti's father, also Nicholas.

A star football player in high school, Brando, as his

friends called him, once ran for 340 yards in a game for West Deptford High School in New Jersey, and went on to play fullback at Fordham University. Lately, Mr. Brandemarti, 21, was learning to play golf. The final Saturday of his life, his father, a more experienced golfer, took him out for a competitive round, loser buys dinner.

"We ate at Nino's," the elder Mr. Brandemarti said. "I had to pay as usual."

PATRICE BRAUT
Joyously Tenacious

At a company Christmas party four years go, Patrice Braut danced with a girl named Lupe. She fled into the night before he could learn her last name.

The next day, Lupe Mendez found a note on her desk in Midtown, saying, "You left without saying good-bye." She felt like Cinderella.

Mr. Braut, 31, loved to travel, to play soccer and to take pictures, especially of the twin towers. He took Ms. Mendez to Brussels, his hometown, to meet his parents. He excelled in his M.B.A. courses at Pace University. The first week of September, Lupe and Patrice, who lived in Riverdale, in the Bronx, went house-hunting in the suburbs. Mr. Braut was an only child, born after three failed pregnancies.

"He was the little god of the family, adored by everybody," said his mother, Paola. "We lost everything through him."

His colleagues in technology at Marsh & McLennan have endowed a scholarship in his name at the Lycee Theodore Bracops, his childhood school. It is not for the best student, but for the most tenacious.

LYDIA ESTELLE BRAVO
A Pot of Tuscan Stew

The night before the planes hit, Lydia Bravo cooked a pot of ribollita, the Tuscan stew of beans and greens. She and her fiancé, Anthony Bengivenga—"she called me Antonio"—opened a bottle of Sangiovese. They had just returned from a week in Mexico. Ms. Bravo, a nurse at Marsh & McLennan, returned to work on Tuesday, Sept. 11.

They would have been together 11 years in October, Mr. Bengivenga said. Both had been married before, both had grown children. They had found in each other a passion for all things passionate—the films of Pedro Almodóvar, flamenco music and food. All kinds of food.

Ms. Bravo, 50, was a devoted cook. She had taken classes at Peter Kump's. She had hundreds of cookbooks—some picked up at flea markets, others on trips abroad. Whenever they went to Italy she peeked into kitchens and chatted up

the cooks. At home in Dunellen, N.J., she cooked elaborate meals.

"That was really her forte," Mr. Bengivenga said. "I would help. I enjoyed being in the kitchen with her." She taught him a few things, but not nearly enough, he said.

FRANCIS HENRY BRENNAN
Larger than Life

At 6 feet 7 inches tall, Francis Henry Brennan could fill any room. But it was not just his stature that set him apart. He was good-natured, funny and generous.

The oldest of six children, he was larger than life to his younger brothers, said one of them, Brian. He had a soft hook shot that catapulted him to a starring role on the St. Agnes High School basketball team in Rockville Centre, N.Y., in the late 1960s. Teammates nicknamed him Zelmo, for Zelmo Beatty, a popular basketball player of that era, Brian Brennan remembered.

Mr. Brennan, 50, who lived in Oak Beach, N.Y., with his wife, was a senior vice president and limited partner at Cantor Fitzgerald, where he was a government securities broker for about 10 years. Before that, he owned several nightclubs on Long Island, among them Solomon Grundy's in Bay Shore.

Of all his successes, he was most proud of his affiliation with the New York Police and Fire Widows' and Children's Benefit Fund, an organization headed by Rusty Staub, the former Mets player and a longtime friend. The night before the attacks, Mr. Brennan and Mr. Staub met to review plans for a November benefit for the wives and children of dead firefighters and police officers.

MICHAEL EMMETT BRENNAN
Mikey B. the Prankster

His birth certificate said Michael Emmett Brennan, but everyone knew him as Mikey B. And if there was fun to be had, he would find it.

Growing up in a large Irish family in Queens, Mikey Brennan, 27, would delight in throwing a bucket of cold water on his brother Brian when he was in the shower. When his brother retaliated by smearing Vaseline in his hair, he could see the humor just as easily.

"He looked like the Fonz for about three weeks," Mr. Brennan recalled. And he could keep a secret. "I found out about all these little pranks after the fact," said his mother, Eileen Walsh. "And I said, 'That's my Mike?'"

As a child he was fascinated with police officers and firefighters; his favorite television show was *CHiPs*. So it was no surprise to his family when he left college in 1995 to become a firefighter.

"He had a passion for it," Ms. Walsh said, adding that he was continually working to improve his skills. He answered the call on Sept. 11 with Ladder Company 4.

"I've never been in a fire," Mr. Brennan said, "but if I were, I would want Mikey to bring me out."

Yet his hard work never took the twinkle out of the eye of Mikey Brennan, an avid snowboarder and surfer who lived in Woodside, Queens. About a year ago at a family gathering, Ms. Walsh said, one of her daughters was talking about body piercing.

"Oh, please, don't get your tongue pierced," Ms. Walsh pleaded. With that, everyone started laughing as Mikey Brennan stuck out his tongue to show off his brand-new stud.

"While living," Mr. Brennan said, "he lived."

PETER BRENNAN
A Lifelong Ambition

A librarian in the elementary school that Peter Brennan once attended found his name on a card in a library book and gave it to his wife, Erica. The book? *I Want to Be a Fireman.*

Mr. Brennan joined the Lakeland Volunteer Fire Department at 16, served for years as a volunteer, most recently in Hauppauge, and six years ago finally became a New York City firefighter.

It was his dream, even while he was a New York City police officer for several years. (Walking a beat in Queens, he rescued an elderly couple from an apartment fire.) More recently, he stopped at a fire in Ronkonkoma and—in street clothes—saved three trapped volunteer firefighters.

Bernadette Lancaster, who used to work near the World Trade Center, viewing the devastation with her daughter from the West Street footbridge. (*Marilynn K. Yee*)

On Sept. 11, Firefighter Brennan, 30, came off vacation to fill in for a colleague in Rescue 4, an elite unit that specializes in saving lives.

"He died doing what he loved at probably the greatest fire he'd ever been to," said his wife, Erica Brennan, who is expecting their second child. "I can see him on the truck being excited on the way."

THOMAS M. BRENNAN
Rock Tunes and Giggles

When Jennifer Brennan was pregnant with her first child, her husband, Thomas M. Brennan, would play Grateful Dead tapes loudly, hoping the music would reach the ears of his unborn daughter. When the baby kicked, as she invariably did, Mr. Brennan was delighted. She, too, he would say, was a fan.

On the last day he spent with his family, the Sunday before Sept. 11, Mr. Brennan, 32, played Grateful Dead compact discs in the car as the family shopped for furniture for their new house in Scarsdale in Westchester.

Strapped to her car seat, Mr. Brennan's daughter, Catherine, laughed and moved to the music. And that is how Mrs. Brennan would like to remember her husband: as the only person who could make their daughter giggle uncontrollably.

With his wife pregnant with the couple's second child, a boy who was born in October, Mr. Brennan took on many of the child care duties. He often got up early with his daughter, fed her breakfast and carried her when she needed a hug.

Mr. Brennan, an investment banker with Sandler O'Neill, treasured the time with his family, in part because he traveled constantly for work. Tuesday, Sept. 11, was the only day of that week he was scheduled to be in the office.

DANIEL BRETHEL
A Day at Disney World

Daniel Brethel, captain of Ladder Company 24 on West 31st Street in Manhattan, had had some close calls: His neck and ears had been burned when he was holding his helmet over an injured firefighter who was lying on the street; once he had required a skin graft.

Arriving at the World Trade Center after both jets had hit, he shouted a warning to his men: "Guys, be very careful, because firemen are going to die today."

He had been off duty at 9 A.M. His wife, Carol, hearing about the attack at their home in Farmingdale, hoped he was already on the train. That night, a fire chief and a chaplain came to the house and told her they had found his body. Captain Brethel, 43, had grabbed one of his men as a building started to collapse. They dived under a fire truck. Both were crushed.

The next week, Ms. Brethel went to her husband's firehouse to empty Captain Brethel's locker. Theirs is a large, close family. In April 2001, all the brothers and sisters and their children, 19 Brethels, went to Disney World, waiting until it was close to closing time so they could ride Thunder Mountain together.

At least a dozen Brethels, including Captain Brethel's children, who are 12 and 14, accompanied his wife to the firehouse. While Ms. Brethel closed the locker room door behind her, the firefighters told stories about their captain and the children had a chance to see the people stopping by and the flowers they had left. And that was good, said Captain Brethel's sister, Loretta.

GARY BRIGHT
Not a Lot of Spare Time

Gary Bright was still working flat out, usually seven days a week, sometimes at two jobs. Late last summer, he put together a combination that suited him fine: working evenings as a waiter at Spazzio's restaurant on Columbus Avenue and, during the days, as a temporary insurance analyst at Aon Insurance in the World Trade Center.

He came to New York from Indiana about six years earlier with a master's degree in therapy, and in his spare time—of which there was not much—he counseled a child pro bono.

But mostly he worked. "He was one of the hardest-working people I have ever met," said Sarah Adams, who worked with him at Spazzio's. "If anybody deserved success, it was him. He was intelligent, he was warm and he gave us all advice."

His mother, Anna Bright, said, "He wanted to get ahead, he was big on that." He had recently bought himself a house in Union City, N.J.—a "kind of a fixer-upper," said Mrs. Bright, who came east from her home in Muncie, Ind., to help with the fixing. "He turned the backyard into a little park, with a fish pond and a fountain," she said. But Mr. Bright was not planning to stay there long. "It was just a beginner house," his mother said.

JONATHAN ERIC BRILEY
Sunrises and Sunsets

Every morning, Jonathan Eric Briley watched the sunrise from New York City's highest peak—the north tower's 110th floor, where he was the audiovisual technician for Windows on the World.

"He'd tell me," said Gwendolyn Briley-Strand, his sister, "there was nothing like it."

Sunrises were one of Mr. Briley's many loves. Others were music, the Lord and the First Baptist Church of Elmsford, N.Y. As a boy, he played gospel music on the piano.

Later, he taught himself guitar and learned jazz and rock as well. Last year, he was ordained a deacon at First Baptist—a job, said Mrs. Briley-Strand, for a humble and helpful man. He drove his father, the Rev. Alexander Briley, the pastor, to church; helped him into his robes; and visited the hospital and homes of the sick and grieving.

"He was," said his wife, Hillary, "one of a kind."

The Tuesday after Labor Day, Mr. Briley, 43, nipped down to Florida for a week with his sisters.

"All we did," said Mrs. Briley-Strand, "was watch the sunrise. We took our coffee with a little Kahlúa to the beach. We relaxed and cooked. We watched the sun rise. We watched it set. It was manna from heaven."

MARK BRISMAN
Give a Little, Get a Little

Could they have had less in common?

She was an actress with traveling in her toes, an adventurous career in her dreams. He was stiff, proper Dudley Do-Right. By age 5, he had mapped out his life: lawyer with wife in the suburbs, raising their kids.

When Juliette Steuer met Mark Brisman, he was 19 going on 40.

The relationship worked, because sometimes opposites prod each other in the best ways. He gave her stability; she loosened him up. He managed to jump in a few fountains at college, and she married him, moved to Westchester and stayed home with their two young children.

Meanwhile, back at the office—Harris Beach, a law firm with a branch on the 85th floor of 2 World Trade Center—Mr. Brisman, 34, worked exhaustively, for his family's sake. If he was seen as old-fashioned in his treatment of women (as delicate flowers who need protection), he was also regarded as a can-do, meticulous guy, supersmart and assured. He was awarded his long-sought partnership posthumously.

He knew himself. "I'm not a babe magnet," he said. "I'm a baby magnet." Formal with adults, he whooped freely with small people, especially his own. A snapshot from Labor Day weekend: Mr. Brisman playing happily with children, his tall frame folded into a kiddie airplane at Adventureland.

PAUL BRISTOW
A Cheeky Blithe Spirit

Blithe spirits come in all sizes: this one was about 5-foot-6, skinny, with a smile that asserts itself in Cathy Bruneau's snapshots. There he is, Paul Bristow, cocking his head, compelling you to cast off the grumps, wearing a fright wig, kicking up a leg.

The British-born Mr. Bristow, 27—"a little cheeky person," said Ms. Bruneau, his fiancée and companion for seven years, first in London and then in Brooklyn—made sure that he never worked more than he needed to, which is not to say that he slacked off at the Risk Waters Group, where he helped organize conferences. It's just that he preserved time for the important things: shopping, friends, shooting pool, getting lost on a country road and savoring its beauty.

Funny, endearing, he could charm even the crustiest. Here is Mr. Bristow, surrounded by Ms. Bruneau's non-English-speaking relatives, rolling in their seats at a wedding in France as he repeatedly tries out his one sentence in French: "Another bottle of white wine, please?"

Like a child, he would dance impatiently around Ms. Bruneau when he wanted attention. But he reciprocated in spades when she was blue, with giant hugs to help her "get the cry out," as he would put it.

MARK FRANCIS BRODERICK
A Remarkable Smile

Mark Francis Broderick had a remarkable smile. It made everyone feel at ease with him, said Chris Dowd, his friend since they were fraternity brothers at St. John's University on Staten Island, N.Y. He had a good memory, too. He never forgot to call Mr. Dowd on his birthday. And Mr. Broderick vividly recalled the first time he saw the woman he would marry, in 1991.

"He remembered exactly what I was wearing that day," said Carolina Broderick. (It was a black skirt and pink blouse.)

Organized and thorough—traits one wants in an accountant—Mr. Broderick was also known for taking his

Liz King, at the funeral of a family friend, David Weiss, a firefighter who died in the trade center attack, is consoled by his colleague. (*James Estrin*)

time—so much so that he earned an ironic nickname, "Sparky," many years ago. The easygoing Mr. Broderick liked it and it stuck.

He joined Cantor Fitzgerald in April and when his 40th birthday came around on Sept. 2, he told his wife he wanted a family vacation, not a party. They took their sons, Matthew, 7, Andrew, 3, and James, 16 months, to Hershey, Pa.

Eulogizing his friend at a service recently, Mr. Dowd asked, "How many of us can remember him standing, smiling, with one or more of his kids hanging from his neck?"

HERMAN BROGHAMMER
Church and a Little Beer

It is true that Herman Broghammer, 58, a senior vice president at Aon, was an observant Roman Catholic. He attended weekly Mass at Sacred Heart Church in North Merrick, N.Y., was a eucharistic minister and, for 30 years, a presence at church charity events.

"But he was also a hell-raiser," said a friend, Art Dignam. The two neighbors upgraded the Knights of Columbus bar from "a stodgy old man's nickel beer setup" to "let's have fun here!" They would rise at 4 A.M. for a golf game just hours after they'd fallen into bed. At Mr. Broghammer's 40th birthday party, he allowed himself to be dressed in alpine shorts and lederhosen, as 15 couples roasted him to the strains of "The Sound of Music."

Mr. Broghammer lived deeply—husband, father, avid athlete, and, for 20 years, manager of a sprawling football pool. But his distinguishing characteristic was a sunny gentleness.

"When you were mad, he would let you have your feelings but he would never agree with the reason," said his wife, Ursula. "And eventually you would say, 'I guess I really shouldn't be angry.' "

After the towers collapsed, one mourning friend vowed a bloody vengeance. Another friend interjected: "But think what Herman would do: he wouldn't do that."

KEITH BROOMFIELD
"I'm King of the World"

To help support his 10 children in America and back in Jamaica, Keith Broomfield spent years picking apples and working as a Manhattan parking lot attendant. Three years ago, Mr. Broomfield, described by friends as having a powerful sense of integrity and a melt-your-frown smile, became a mechanic for Advent Industrial, which builds broadcast transmitters.

He had a natural fix-it ability, which he tried to impart

to his fiancée, Jennifer Morrison, with whom he lived in Brooklyn.

"He gave me the courage to do things I didn't want to do," she said—like understanding car guts. "He would say, 'I want to show you this because there's going to be times when I can't be with you and I want you to talk to mechanics in a certain way so they won't give you garbage,' " Ms. Morrison said.

Mr. Broomfield, 49, was enormously proud of his job, because he was relied upon to be a jack-of-all-trades. When he had to check an antenna site, he would clamber out on the roof of the 110th floor of 1 World Trade Center, fling open his arms and shout, "I'm king of the world!"

JANICE BROWN
No Ordinary Aunt

Janice Brown's weekends were a hullabaloo of children, her own and her sisters'. Monday through Friday, she was an accountant at Marsh & McLennan. But when Saturday rolled around, she was off to the zoo, the skating rink or the movies with her 11-year-old son, Justin Johnson; three nephews, ages 6, 3 and 1; and a 4-year-old niece.

But Ms. Brown, 34, was not a run-of-the-mill aunt. One nephew, 3-year-old Kyle, had lived with Ms. Brown, a single mother, since he was an infant. Kyle's mother, Dawn, 23, was unable to care for her children, so two live in Flatbush with their grandmother, Juanita Lewis, and the third, Kyle, lives nearby with Ms. Brown.

Janice Brown's sister Tameshia, 24, said that Ms. Brown had stepped into the breach, initially agreeing to take Kyle for a year, after Dawn had already given custody of her oldest to her mother. But, according to Tameshia, Dawn was still a street person so Ms. Brown took the boy permanently. Ms. Brown spelled her mother, who was also taking care of a third grandchild, every weekend.

Last summer, along with Tameshia, she took the whole brood to Disney World, paying for the trip and giving her mother a few days of peace and quiet.

LLOYD BROWN
Doted on His Children

Lloyd Brown liked playing basketball with friends and co-workers at Cantor Fitzgerald. He loved playing on the computer. And he also doted on his two children, even though they now lived across the country.

Mr. Brown, 28, worked as a compliance officer for institutional equities, a job he took after serving in the Navy for four years. He was born in Jamaica, and spent some of his childhood in the Bronx, said a cousin, Diane Brown.

He was living in Mount Vernon, but was searching for an apartment in the Bronx so he could be closer to his extended family. His home was filled with pictures of his children, Jacinda, 7, and Lloyd Jr., 4, who had recently moved to Texas with their mother, and he talked to them daily by telephone, said his stepmother, Iris Brown.

"He was like his dad, who is constantly cracking jokes," his cousin said. "If you met my cousin, you'd think he was quiet, but he was quite amicable."

PATRICK J. BROWN
The Bravest and Grumpiest

Yes, Capt. Patrick J. Brown was a firefighting hero. But oh, there was so much more.

"Everything he tackled, he gave 300 percent," said Sharon Watts—onetime fiancée, ever a good friend—whether firefighting, music or yoga. He squeezed a baby grand into his apartment, and once puzzled a piano teacher who had arrived looking for "Little Patty Brown." He loved Broadway shows, saying that in another life he might have been a choreographer.

Ms. Watts recalled fondly that when she and Captain Brown, 48, a Vietnam veteran, started dating, he asked her to go with him to the Vietnam Veterans Memorial in Lower Manhattan. "We saw flowers that had been knocked over, and we set them up again."

When he worked in Harlem, he bicycled from his Stuyvesant Town apartment to 149th Street, but at Ladder Company 3 on 13th Street, she said, "he could run to his firehouse and take his yoga mat with him."

He was "a deeply spiritual man," said a friend, James Remar, "but he was far too humble to advertise that."

It was hard to pull him out of the city, said his sister, Carolyn Negron, who lives on Long Island. "He had to be around that action. My father used to say, 'If our house is on fire, he ain't coming.' "

Captain Brown sometimes called himself a "grumpy old man," Ms. Watts said, so for his 47th birthday, she hand-painted a cereal bowl for him that said "To Pat: FDNY's Bravest and Grumpiest."

He never married. "He had felt so much loss," she said. "He didn't want anyone close to him to feel the pain of losing someone."

ANDREW BRUNN
The Man in Flannel

He was a tremendous pile of a man, 6-foot-2 and heavyset. His flannel shirt was tucked in, clarifying his dimension, as he flailed wildly about the dance floor of the bar in Queens. Andrew Brunn was celebrating his 23rd birthday that night five years earlier.

Sigalit Cohen watched him all evening; she had a thing for flannel. His uninhibited dancing sometimes frightened the girls away, but "Sigal actually stuck in there and danced with him," said Patrick Sullivan, a friend.

She got his number and soon made a husband of Mr. Brunn, an intensely private man. He did not bother to tell his buddies in the Air National Guard of his computer studies or even of his marriage. He made little mention of his move to the Fire Department from the Police Department.

But after Sigalit danced with him, Mr. Brunn opened his life to her, revealing his passion for the ocean and for lighthouses, for movies that seemed to reflect their own story. They worked through the clashes between his Catholicism and her Judaism. Mr. Brunn, a devoted surfer, even persuaded Sigalit, who nearly drowned as a child, to join him on a flimsy board.

"He said, 'I'll be there with you; I'll hold you if you fall,' so I trusted him," Mrs. Brunn said. "And he did."

VINCENT BRUNTON
A Picture of Inspiration

Cathy Brunton had always known that her husband, Vincent, the captain of Ladder Company 105, loved being a firefighter. He joined the department 22 years ago, the same year they got married, the same year their daughter Kelly was born.

But it was not until she received a four-page letter from a young firefighter she did not recall having met that Mrs. Brunton came to appreciate the kind of firefighter her husband had been, the lessons he was always prepared to teach and the depth of respect others had for him.

"I could go into his office at 11:30 P.M. and ask him a fire question and he would lean back in his chair and tell me countless stories," the letter from the firefighter, Will Hickey, said. "He would say the best way to learn is from your mistakes. 'If you're not making mistakes, you are not trying.'"

Even a false alarm provided an opportunity to learn. Mr. Hickey described how terrified he once had been at a fire with Captain Brunton. Flames were shooting out the windows and the roof.

"I was thinking to myself, 'This guy is absolutely crazy! What is he thinking, he's John Wayne or something?'" But Captain Brunton, 43, took his arm and showed him what to do.

"I have put a small picture of him on the underside of my helmet," Mr. Hickey said. "Sometimes I just touch it to remind me to stay calm, to keep it simple and to 'think on my feet.'"

RONALD BUCCA
Rescuer and Counselor

Ronald Bucca was nicknamed the Flying Fireman in 1986 after he fell spectacularly from a tenement fire escape, spun around a cable strung through the backyard and lived to tell the tale. And that was just one of his moments.

His specialty was rescuing mankind from smoke and flames, but he did not mind scorching certain people with his wit.

His colleagues collected "Ron-isms." An example: "This one is as sharp as a basketball." He designed hats for other firemen with details that they found hilarious (but unfortunately, that were not printable). A firefighter for 23 years, the last nine as a fire marshal, he was also a nurse and a reservist in the United States Army's Special Forces.

Fire Marshal Bucca trained as an antiterrorist intelligence expert, and when the planes hit the towers on Sept. 11, he called his wife, Eve, and said he was heading to the scene.

"He knew it was a terrorist attack," Mrs. Bucca said. "He had been expecting something like that for a very long time."

Before that day, his final investigation had involved a young woman who set her former boyfriend's letters on fire and left them to burn in a toilet. He counseled her as a father might.

"No guy is worth getting this upset over; don't be too concerned about this guy," he told her, said Keith O'Mara, his partner. "There are a lot of fish in the sea. And if this should ever happen again, think about buying yourself a paper shredder."

GREG BUCK
"He Just Amazed Me"

Where to begin with Greg Buck? Perhaps with wood. He was an accomplished woodworker. For a number of years, he had a custom cabinetry and furniture business with his father, and they restored a couple of homes, including the Victorian that his parents have in Staten Island.

He was also a classical pianist, and he played the organ at the weddings of friends. He went part of the way through cooking school and was quite proficient at the stove. He completed nursing school (where he met his wife, Catherine Morrison-Buck) and was thus a registered nurse, though he never practiced. Finally, he was a firefighter with Engine Company 201 in Brooklyn.

"He was the most talented guy I've ever seen in my life," his wife said. "He just amazed me."

He was quiet about his multiple talents. It took a while before his colleagues at the firehouse learned of his cooking skills and showed him to the kitchen. They began calling him the Silent Chef.

Firefighter Buck, 37, kept a woodworking shop in an old hotel he restored on Staten Island. He and his wife had planned to start a business selling antiques he restored and the new furniture he made. They were also in the process of buying a home on Staten Island. Mrs. Morrison-Buck closed on it in November 2001. Firefighter Buck was going to restore it.

"Now it's my job," she said.

DENNIS BUCKLEY
From Lacrosse to Pool

Dennis Buckley of Chatham, N.J., was a big man, 6 feet, 210 pounds, with an athletic build. He had been a star lacrosse player at Lynbrook High School and graduated from the University of Maryland, which he attended on a full lacrosse scholarship.

"He still walks like he's carrying a lacrosse stick," said his wife, Cathleen, speaking of him in the present tense, although she had just come from making funeral arrangements.

He was 38, a bond broker at Cantor Fitzgerald, the father of three girls ranging in age from 22 months to 6 years. A memory his wife holds dear is the massive Mr. Buckley taking his three girls, with their three pink Barbie doll towels, to the swim club. His eldest daughter, Mary Kate, had her sixth birthday 12 days after the attack, and Mrs. Buckley decided to go on with the party.

"She's 6," Mrs. Buckley said. "Not having it would be like almost taking it away from her."

She spoke of what had become a community of loss, the World Trade Center people who did not come home, and begins to weep.

"As short as it was, I was really lucky to know him. Part of me looks at these younger widows. I at least have my family."

PATRICK J. BUHSE
Living Large, Playing Hard

The yelling, screaming, posturing and power plays of the trading floor were Patrick J. Buhse's idea of nirvana. A government bond trader for Cantor Fitzgerald, Mr. Buhse, 36, scrapped his way up from entry level in "the cage" at 18 and never worked anyplace else. "College or Cantor," was his take on higher education.

He lived large and played hard: Mr. Buhse was a Budweiser man. What he liked even better than amassing money was giving it away to relatives. A car here, a fur coat there,

private school for the nieces and nephews. Sure, he drove a Honda, but it was brand-new.

"He wasn't showy, but all his toys had to be new and clean," said his wife, Susan. "And his television had to be the biggest."

Relentlessly social, Mr. Buhse looked for any excuse to entertain on the town or at home in Lincroft, N.J. He loved telling jokes, and was not above stealing other people's anecdotes and improving them. He doted on his two children and reserved Friday nights for family in Bay Ridge, Brooklyn, where he was the loudest of six siblings.

"The glass was always half full, not half empty," his wife said. "His motto was, 'Live for the moment.' "

JOHN E. BULAGA Jr.
Helping the Future Arrive

John E. Bulaga Jr. and his wife, Michelle, were three days away from closing on their first house, in Haskell, N.J., when the World Trade Center was attacked. Mrs. Bulaga bought the house a few weeks later.

She will move into it soon with their two daughters, Rhiannon, who is 6, and the baby, Alannah, who is not quite 6 months old.

"It's hard to think of what the future is going to hold," she said. "We had these plans, and now I have to make new plans or a different version of those plans."

But, she said, Mr. Bulaga, 35, would have wanted her and the girls to go on with their lives, in their new home only

After the funeral for Firefighter Jose Guadalupe in Queens, his wife, Elise, walks with her brother Andre Stanley, who held the photo. (*James Estrin*)

minutes from where he and his wife grew up. Looking to the future is what he was all about.

Mr. Bulaga was a network engineer with eSpeed. Since he was a boy watching the original *Star Trek* series, he has loved technology and all its implications for changing the world, his wife said.

"He always wanted to have a hand in that, in helping the future to arrive," she said. "He was so happy that he could do that."

MATTHEW BURKE
A Man with Connections

Matthew Burke was the kind of bartender who sensed the mood in the room, grabbed hold of it, then dialed up the energy level until everyone was part of the party. His memory for customers' names was encyclopedic, but no matter how crowded the bar and no matter how frenzied he was, he would always aim a smile toward the customers he did not know.

A blond 6-footer, he regaled patrons with sports lore and tales of his career as a quarterback at Xavier High School in Manhattan, "when he threw the most touchdowns in the league that year, and also threw the most interceptions," said a friend, Brendan McCormick.

Mr. Burke worked at the Lantern, at Rathbone's, at Sutton Place and other bars, and his tips went toward paying for his degree at Fordham University.

"It was so natural, then, for him to become a broker, because he had so many connections and he made people feel good about themselves," Mr. McCormick said. And that is why, on the morning of Sept. 11, at the age of 28, Mr. Burke was working hard at Cantor Fitzgerald, on the 104th floor of 1 World Trade Center.

TOM BURKE
Bonds: Financial and Family

Tom Burke was the quintessential Wall Street man.

He broke into the bond business this way: It was 1985 and he was fresh out of Holy Cross. Nobody wanted him. Undeterred, he put on his suit every day and attended training courses at Liberty Brokerage—uninvited. Impressed, the company hired him after three months.

Eventually, Mr. Burke, 38, became a partner at Cantor Fitzgerald, heading the government bond desk. He lived with his wife and children in Bedford Hills, N.Y.

He had a big personality. He knew how to hold his drink and when to hold his cards. He was the kind of person you wanted to be seated next to at a dinner party.

That was the Wall Street man. There was also the private man.

"He was successful, but that's not what made him happiest," said his sister, Nancy Salter. "It was his family."

That was the part the young guns did not see, the part not learned in college. Tom Burke's mother always had a happy birthday. Tom Burke's family never wondered where Daddy was. Tom Burke's friends never lay sick, alone.

WILLIAM F. BURKE Jr.
He Put His Men First

Calling Capt. William F. Burke Jr. a firefighter is a little like referring to Elvis as an entertainer. Captain Burke took the job description and set it over the high flame of his personality, rendering something else entirely.

"He always made everything better," said his brother Michael, "and in Manhattan, it's nice to be around somebody like that."

Like his father, who worked in the South Bronx in the 1960s when fires raged around the clock, Captain Burke, known as Billy, believed in putting his men first. On Sept. 11, he ordered them out of the north tower, his brother said, while he continued searching for people to rescue. In Stuyvesant Town, the Manhattan residential complex where he had an apartment, Captain Burke, 46, enjoyed a parade of admirers. Some were romantic interests, penciled into his address book, drawn by his singular charm.

"The first words out of his mouth every single time he met a woman were, 'Have you lost weight?'" his brother said. Then there were the neighbors he helped out. He liked to bicycle to his firehouse, Engine Company 21 on East 40th Street, but if he saw someone struggling with groceries, he'd screech to a halt.

He spent 25 summers working as a lifeguard at Robert Moses State Park, and a friend, Stuart Kaplan, remembered how the oldest living Jones Beach lifeguard turned up one day. The man was sickly and in a wheelchair, but his dearest wish was to swim in the ocean one last time. Captain Burke put an arm around him and helped him into the waves. Afterward, they shared a cold beer and then another. Everybody went home happy.

KATHLEEN A. BURNS
Travels Led to Home

Kathleen A. Burns was born in Staten Island, where she lived with her parents for most of her life, in a nice home in a quiet, middle-class neighborhood. If the upstairs light was on, Ms. Burns, 48, was probably reading a book. She never took work home.

"Work was work and home was home," said her mother, Eunice.

Still, Ms. Burns climbed high in the corporate world, to the upper floors of the World Trade Center, where she was a vice president with the Fiduciary Trust International.

She was good to her parents, they said. The three watched television together in the evenings and the women went shopping.

"She liked high-end things like Ann Taylor," her mother said.

Of course her life was more than work and home and shopping, her mother said. She had an interest in the wider world, and toured places like Egypt, Spain and Iceland.

JOHN P. BURNSIDE
Struck by Love's Lightning

It is 1991.

The young woman is in-line skating in Central Park on a lovely July day. The police officer is standing on duty outside the park's Summerstage, where Marshall Crenshaw is playing. She stops to chat. He asks what she is doing that night. She mentions a bar. That is how love began between Sandra Endres and John P. Burnside 10 years ago.

"He walked in the door, and I said that was it," Mrs. Burnside said. "We were like two old souls. It was absolutely meant to be."

He was a police officer for only three years, while he waited for assignment to his other true love, the Fire Department. There, Firefighter Burnside was known as mistake-free.

"When you checked in the morning and you knew John was working, it was going to be a good day," said George Kozlowski, a fellow firefighter at Ladder Company 20 on Lafayette Street.

The Burnsides lived a honeymoon life in Manhattan, vacationing often in the Caribbean and on the slopes. Recently, they started having thoughts of a more settled life.

"But just when you think you're going to get serious, buy a home and have kids, it gets taken away," Mrs. Burnside said. "I'm never going to get that back, and it stinks."

Her husband left Ladder Company 20 even before the alarm sounded, and died in the collapse of 1 World Trade Center.

Firefighter Burnside was raised in the tight-knit Irish-American world of Inwood. He had an irrational love for the Minnesota Vikings, wrote poetry and played the guitar, often in the firehouse. He was so good that another firefighter once thought his rendition of a Led Zeppelin

tune was coming out of a radio and went inside to turn it up.

He was 36.

MILTON BUSTILLO
A Wife, a Baby, a House

Life had just begun to get sweet for Milton Bustillo. In February, 2001, he and the love of his life, Laura Spordone, had a baby girl. In July, the couple married and began searching and saving for a home. Mr. Bustillo, an avid baker, set aside every penny from his job as a computer network operator at Cantor Fitzgerald. He was even planning to market his own line of cookies and cakes over the Internet. All the planning paid off, it seemed, when the couple finally found their dream house in Toms River, N.J.

But one week before the house was to be theirs, the World Trade Center was destroyed. Mr. Bustillo, 37, disappeared.

"Everything was just beginning for him," said Mr. Bustillo's younger brother, Gilberto. "He was so determined to do things right. He took his time starting a family and buying a home. He wanted to be happy."

In late September, a few days after his daughter, Alessandra, was baptized, Mr. Bustillo's body was found by rescuers at ground zero, and identified by his wedding ring. The family, his brother said, is convinced that the discovery was a gift from God.

"At least we can say good-bye to him the right way."

THOMAS BUTLER
Fire and Water

Thomas Butler liked to say that in a former life, he must have been a pirate. You could not keep him off the water.

His life basically was fire and water. He was a firefighter with Squad 1 in Brooklyn, and he had a part-time job as the bay constable in Smithtown, N.Y.

The bay constable job allowed him to be out on the water a lot, and he was entranced by water and its calming effect. Not that he needed calming down. He was the epitome of the laid-back man.

"He was my rock," said his wife, Martha. "We'd get bills and they would give me ulcers, and he'd say, 'Don't worry about it, the bills will be there tomorrow.' "

In some respects, he could be too laid back. "The grass could grow six feet, and it didn't bother him," Mrs. Butler said. "I'd try to get him to do it, and he'd say, 'The grass'll be there tomorrow.' "

Firefighter Butler, 37, lived in Kings Park, N.Y., with his wife and three children, Kelly, 4, Shawn, 6, and Patrick, 8 months.

TIMOTHY G. BYRNE
Fat Cigar and Time for Fun

Timothy G. Byrne was a classic, jet-setting investment banker, driving a black BMW that smelled like stogies the day after he bought it.

"I used to joke with him that he just didn't want to spend any time alone in his apartment," said his brother, Sean Byrne, one of his nine siblings. On Friday, Sept. 7, after finishing up work selling bonds at Sandler O'Neill, Timothy Byrne, 36, left the office with a colleague in his BMW "loaded with golf clubs and eight cigars," Sean said.

He played nine holes of golf on Long Island, came back into the city for a date, spent Saturday in Montauk with another brother and his wife, and then met Sean for a Jets game on Sunday. "That's the way it was with him," Sean said. "He always showed up, no matter how busy he was. Maybe not on time, but he was always there."

JESUS N. CABEZAS
Stone Face, Warm Heart

Jesus N. Cabezas was full of whimsy and scrappiness. At his daughter's wedding, he cast his chiseled Ecuadorean features into a stone-faced glare as he posed for a picture.

"He called it his picture face," said his daughter, Blanca I. Bowers, laughing. "You'll see a lot of pictures of him looking really serious. But if you know him you laugh, because he's just being silly."

Mr. Cabezas, 66, of Bushwick, Brooklyn, a cook at Windows on the World, was full of fight even though he was only 5 feet 5 inches tall and 150 pounds. Thirteen years ago, he won a battle with colon cancer.

Another time, he arrived home holding a knife that he had taken from a mugger during a struggle, Mrs. Bowers recalled. Mischievously, he expressed regret for not being able to return it.

" 'He ran away before I could give it back,' " she recalled him saying.

"He could have killed you," his wife yelled.

"He's not going to waste his time on me," he told her. "Don't worry. I'm going to be here for a long time."

LILLIAN CACERES
Touch of an Angel

It's very easy for Lillian Caceres's family to envision her as an angel in heaven. She was very warm and friendly, the kind of sister who would sit at the bedside of someone who was ill or lend a patient ear to someone's problems, said her younger sister Aurea de la Cruz. For 22 years Ms. Caceres, 48, made a point of incorporating her belief in Christ into her daily life, and shared her faith with family and friends, sometimes giving Bibles as gifts.

And then there's the video.

On Sept. 10, Ms. Caceres appeared in a play at Gateway Cathedral, a nondenominational church in Staten Island where she taught Sunday school and sang in the choir. In the play, *Heaven's Gates and Hell's Flames,* Ms. Caceres was one of the angels, dressed in white, who greet people in heaven after they have died in calamities like a car crash, a plane crash or a building collapse. "It was profound," said Ms. de la Cruz, "because the theme of that whole play is you have to be ready for Christ."

On Sept. 11, Ms. Caceres, a technology administrator, was at her desk at Marsh & McLennan at 8 A.M. It was her 11-year-old daughter's first week back at school; Ms. Caceres had asked for the early shift so she could meet her daughter at 4 o'clock.

STEVEN CAFIERO
Marriage, Babies, Red Wine

When Steven Cafiero took his girlfriend, Donnamarie Striano, to Las Vegas in August, he wanted her to marry him then and there. She told him she would rather wait until family and friends could be with them.

"We were more married than most, because we lived together and we were so happy," she said. "But I only wish I could have fulfilled his every wish."

Mr. Cafiero and Ms. Striano, both 31, met on the Internet three and a half years ago, and it took them a year to meet in person. He swept her off her feet.

"We had the best lives," she said. "We did everything. We traveled, we went out to fabulous dinners in the city. He taught me how to play golf."

The couple lived in Whitestone, Queens, and in August he started working as a client specialist for Aon, the insurance broker, dealing with customer service problems.

"He just wanted to be married and have lots of babies and travel and drink red wine," Ms. Striano said.

Portraits of the missing, described in words and pictures, posted on a telephone booth on Lexington Avenue at Twenty-eighth Street in Manhattan. They became a record of the city's loss. (*James Estrin*)

JOHN B. CAHILL
Good Humor in Three Languages

They called him Mad Dog.

When John B. Cahill was an undergraduate at Boston College, he was a real good-time guy, and his friends nicknamed him Mad Dog. But he calmed down and matured into a gregarious family man with a quirky sense of humor.

Mr. Cahill, 56, lived with his wife, Sharon, and two sons, Brett, 17, and Sean, 15, in Wellesley, Mass., and worked as a vice president of the systems group at Xerox. But he planned to retire at the end of the year to start his own consulting business. The name of it was MDI. His family knew what the initials stood for: Mad Dog Industries.

On Sept. 11, he was on Flight 175 to Los Angeles, where he was going to visit a friend and do some work on the new business. He had a passion for travel; the family had lived in England and Brazil. He was fond of Latin America, and planned to make it a focus of MDI.

"He loved the people," Mrs. Cahill said. "They work to live instead of living to work."

Mr. Cahill spoke Spanish and Portuguese, and his interest in languages was picked up by his children. Brett is taking three languages—French, Spanish and German.

"He got that from John," Mrs. Cahill said, "who realized the world was smaller than it seems."

MICHAEL J. CAHILL
The Renaissance Man

Michael J. Cahill had been a cross-country runner in high school 20 years ago and at 37, he was still running. In May 2001 he came in third—behind two teenagers—in a field of 100 in the annual five-mile race in East Williston, N.Y., where he lived. (His wife, Colleen, walked it with the kids, Conor, 5, and Fiona, 2, in a double stroller.) It was typical. Mr. Cahill was good at almost everything he did. That is why Marsh & McLennan, where he had worked for seven years and was a senior vice president and claims attorney on the 99th floor of Tower 1, promoted him posthumously to managing director.

That is why St. John's University Law School, from which he graduated in 1991, was giving him its Dean's Award on Dec. 1. That is why neighbors in East Williston, where he joined Halloween parades, Christmas tree lightings and other doings, were putting up a bench and plaque in his name on the village green, and why 1,000 friends attended a memorial Mass at St. Aidan's Roman Catholic Church in Williston Park on Oct. 1.

And that is why his children, with whom he shared music, sports and trips to the beach, and his wife, who met him at a Hamptons share house in 1990 and adored his wit and honesty, will miss him.

THOMAS CAHILL
A Crowded 37 Years

Thomas Cahill knew his father, Jim, really wanted to win a recent golf tournament at the Metedeconk National Golf Club in Jackson, N.J. But that did not keep him from having some fun.

He stuck a chunky cigar in his mouth, winked at the caddy and nonchalantly told his father: "Don't worry, big guy. It's all under control."

Then the younger Mr. Cahill sank the ball into a hole about 14 feet away. The Cahills, father and son, took home a trophy that day.

A natural athlete, the younger Mr. Cahill had skied in Utah and Colorado, trolled for fish in the Bahamas and putted on all the golf courses in Ireland by the time he was 37. He worked as a securities trader at Cantor Fitzgerald, and lived near his family in Franklin Lakes, N.J.

"He enjoyed life," said his mother, Kathleen. "And he fit an awful lot in during his 37 years."

GEORGE C. CAIN
Skiing Like the Wind

Life blew hot and cold for George C. Cain, in that he made his living fighting fires but spent much of his time on cold snowy mountains, skiing.

"I have pictures of him, and you'd think he could reach up and touch heaven," said his mother, Rosemary Cain. "He could ski like the wind."

Adrienne Bartolini confirmed Firefighter Cain's skiing ability. They became friends in Telluride, Colo., where the future firefighter worked for five years as a carpenter in the warm months and skied in the cold. He loved the mogul runs, and had no problem with one of the resort's toughest runs, Kant-Mak-M.

"He used to just rip down that," Ms. Bartolini said. Then he got the call to join the New York Fire Department, and they spent six weeks driving to New York in her Volkswagen van in 1994.

Firefighter Cain, 35, joined Ladder Company 7 in Manhattan and lived in Patterson, N.Y., though he grew up in Massapequa. He was in terrific shape, and ran the New York Marathon in 1999. He was training for this year's event. His mates at Ladder 7, who called him the Dude, recalled he could always beat them running up the stairs.

SALVATORE B. CALABRO
Honoring a Struggle

Here is one thing that says a lot about Salvatore B. Calabro: He wore a tattoo of a cross and roses on his right forearm, with the inscription, "In memory of Mom 11-30-89."

His mother, Connie, struggled to raise him and his two brothers on her own; he never forgot.

Mr. Calabro made his mother proud, a good boy from Bath Beach, Brooklyn, who wore a firefighters' uniform for 14 years, said his father-in-law, Francis Carillo, a retired New York City police officer. Mr. Calabro, 38, built a solid middle-class life for his wife, Francene, and two sons, Daniel, 5, and Alexander James, 2.

Another thing that spoke to his essence: He was a good son-in-law. It had nothing to do with toeing the line because he married one of two daughters of a police officer. He was just that way, Mr. Carillo said.

"When I met him, I had guarded feelings," said Mr. Carillo. "He was marrying my baby daughter. But as I got to know him, all of that went away. He became the son I never had.

"He was a gentle person, but he had the heart and courage of a lion," Mr. Carillo said.

EDWARD CALDERON
The Entertainer

Edward Calderon was always proud to wear the uniform that marked him as a security guard for the Port Authority of New York and New Jersey, but his feet felt best in dancing shoes.

"When I think of him I remember that he loved salsa," said his niece, Desiree Henley. "He was extremely outgoing, loved to dance."

He was the life of any gathering, said his sister-in-law, Sandra Calderon. And for years, he organized a regular Wednesday night salsa party in different locations at the World Trade Center for anybody who wanted to come, said his brother, Anthony.

"He liked to act and he wanted to direct—he was an entertainer," Anthony said. "That was his knowledge. That was his calling."

Eddie Calderon, 43, lived in Jersey City and worked at the trade center for 22 years. He was last seen running toward the north tower after helping guide dozens of workers to safety. He was hoping to reach a few more just before the building collapsed, Mr. Calderon's boss told his brother.

KENNY CALDWELL
The Kicknic Kid

You know how most people have to bend down to scratch their knee? Kenny Caldwell did not, because he had hands the size of baseball mitts and arms that went on forever.

"He was a little slim Jimmy," said his mother, Elsie Caldwell, from his hometown, Philadelphia, "with big hands and a big, big heart. I called him my little chocolate drop."

Mr. Caldwell, 30, liked being a technology salesman for Alliance Consulting Group on the 102nd floor of 1 World Trade Center. But what he loved was figuring out ways to get people together.

"I used to call him the C.E.O., chief entertainment officer," said his older brother, Leon Caldwell. He even invented an annual event: the International Kicknic Contest, held every August in Prospect Park in Brooklyn, for an ever-expanding circle of friends and family to play kickball and catch up.

"My neighbors used to tease me about him while he was growing up," Mrs. Caldwell said. "They'd say other kids collect stray cats and dogs, but your Kenny collects stray people."

DOMINICK ENRICO CALIA
A Special Weekend

The last weekend of his life was a special one for Dominick Enrico Calia—and typical, too.

After returning home to Manalapan, N.J., on Friday night from his job as a municipal bond broker at Cantor Fitzgerald, Mr. Calia, 40, quickly changed into gym clothes, then coached baseball practice for his son's team.

The next morning, he and his wife, Janet, ushered their two daughters to separate soccer practices. Then, for the first time in 10 years, he and his wife spent 24 hours away from the kids. They went to Cape May and Atlantic City. The next morning, they made it back for—of course—another soccer practice.

Perhaps you get the picture: Mr. Calia was very active in his children's lives, from never-ending athletics to frequent trips to New York City. And now, their son, Dominick Richard Calia, wants to change his middle name so he can be Dominick Jr.

"My son is 7 years old," Mrs. Calia said. "I tell him, 'The seven years you had with Dad is a lifetime, and some people don't even get that. It's the quality, not the quantity, that counts.' "

LIAM CALLAHAN
Many Citations for Heroism

Liam Callahan always made it out of dangerous situations. So it was fully expected that Mr. Callahan, a Port Authority police officer, would emerge from the trade center wreckage—even if days later.

So his wife, Joan, waited. They were supposed to celebrate 20 years of marriage on Sept. 12. But his homecoming was going to be sweeter, a wedding anniversary combined with a hero's welcome at their home in Rockaway, N.J., where they were raising four children: Brian, 17; Bridget, 15; Ellen, 13; and James, 11. Officer Callahan, however, died in the line of duty.

Police work was the lifeblood of Officer Callahan, 44, a 22-year police veteran who got at least a half a dozen citations for exemplary actions, including a group citation for "heroic efforts" during the first trade center bombing in 1993, the police said.

One of his first rescues as a rookie came on Sept. 9, 1982. A distraught 20-year-old man was threatening to jump from the roof of the Port Authority bus terminal.

"Suddenly, he slid closer to the edge, and I grabbed him," Officer Callahan told the *New York Post* that day. "If I didn't get him then, he would have been gone."

GENE CALVI
Mr. Fix-It on Wheels

As a teenager, Gene Calvi bought a used Honda motorcycle that promptly conked out on him. Undaunted, he studied the service manual and dismantled it piece by piece in his parents' garage. After fixing a faulty piston, he put it back together again. It rode better than ever. The year after, he moved on to a Volkswagen Rabbit. Same result.

"There was nothing he couldn't do, once he set his mind to it," said his brother, Alex. "That's exactly how he ran his life."

Mr. Calvi, 34, never ceased to surprise his family with his prowess. He was a bond trader at Cantor Fitzgerald who fixed his own car and talked about building one from a kit just for fun.

He took up running with his wife, Christine, and was soon entering five-kilometer races near their home in East Rutherford, N.J. Less than a year later, he finished his first marathon.

"He was the most serious, responsible guy," his brother said. "But he had this curiosity, and when he wanted to know something, he had to know everything about it."

ROKO CAMAJ
Working Atop the World

Roko Camaj had a job few would envy: window washer at the World Trade Center.

Several times a year, suspended 1,300 feet above earth, he and his partner would suds up the 107th-floor windows, the highest windows on the building and too wide for the building's automated window-washing system. The rest of the year, he operated the machines that crawled down the sides of the buildings.

"He wasn't scared of anything," said his brother, Kole Camaj. "He had no fear."

For years, Roko's wife thought he washed only window interiors, until she saw a newspaper account of his job. When she learned the truth, Kole Camaj said, she was furious. Roko would remind her how safe his job was, that the basket and his harness were both well tethered to the building. His son, Vincent, said his father loved his job and considered it an escape.

"He'd always say, 'It was me and the sky up here. I bother no one, and no one bothers me.'" Mr. Camaj, 60, an Albanian immigrant, had just returned home from a vacation to Montenegro, a birthday present from his daughter. All five Camaj brothers, most of them scattered around the globe, had taken the voyage together.

"It was a great pleasure," Kole Camaj said. "Everyone was so happy."

MICHAEL CAMMARATA
"Don't Mourn Me"

A day after Michael Cammarata died in the attack on the World Trade Center, his brother, Joseph, went through his things looking for a birth certificate. On the top drawer of Michael's night table, Joseph found a letter—the kind of letter that a brother never wants to read. It was a what-to-do list in case something happened to him.

No. 1 on the list: "Take care of Jenna," referring to his girlfriend of seven years.

No. 2: "Don't mourn me. This is the career I chose." Michael Cammarata, 22, was a firefighter with Ladder Company 11 in Manhattan. He died on the ninth week of a 14-week training program. He lived with his parents in Huguenot, Staten Island.

No. 3: "Make my spirit live on."

No. 4: "Remember I love you all and will be waiting for you upstairs."

From the time he was 7, Michael Cammarata wanted to be a firefighter. He was fascinated by fire engines and trucks. In his fireman's test, which he took with his brother, Michael got a perfect score; Joseph did not.

"They wanted to be together," his mother, Linda Cammarata, said of her two sons. "Thank God they didn't."

Joseph, 24, is a police officer. On Jan. 14, 2002, he, too, was to join the Fire Department.

DAVID O. CAMPBELL
Tailgating and Family Time

While rushing Delta Kappa Epsilon at Rutgers University in the late 1960s, David O. Campbell dived under a table to escape a food fight at lunch. He bumped into John Albohm down there, stuck out his hand, and introduced himself. They bonded.

"A friendship ensued of great proportions," Mr. Albohm said.

Mr. Campbell, 51, a senior vice president at Keefe, Bruyette & Woods, was a loyal friend who called Mr. Albohm at least once a week for more than three decades. He never lost his fun-loving side, and organized an annual tailgate party for his fraternity brothers. He still liked to drink beer and hang out with the guys.

As a grown-up, he once climbed onto a luggage carousel at Newark International Airport to spin around for laughs.

But Mr. Campbell always saved his Sunday nights for his wife, Cindy, and their two sons, Chip and Tim. The family would cook on the grill at home in Basking Ridge, N.J., and catch up on the week.

"Dave was an interesting combination," said his friend and brother-in-law, Fred Anthony. "He was the ultimate party animal and family man."

GEOFF CAMPBELL
A Chance Meeting

Not long after arriving in America in 1999, Geoff Campbell was sitting at a Midtown bar one night. A woman started making fun of his British accent, but instead of taking offense, he simply laughed along with her. Afterward, they e-mailed back and forth, and he asked her on a date.

"It was one of those crazy nights," recalls Caroline Burbank about that date. "You have so much to talk about that you lose track of time."

Mr. Campbell, 31, later proposed to Ms. Burbank and

A memorial service for members of the construction trades filled St. Patrick's Cathedral to overflowing on October 3. Outside, mourners listened as the names of the dead and missing were read over a loudspeaker. (*James Estrin*)

took her to visit his family in North Hampton, England. They had just returned from a trip there in August. Mr. Campbell, who worked for Reuters Consulting Group, "was just a gentle, kind soul," said Ms. Burbank, who shared an apartment with him and two cats in Chelsea.

"If someone new came to the office, he was always the one to invite them out for a drink."

JILL CAMPBELL
Teaching Baby to Crawl

Jill Campbell found out she was pregnant on her mother's birthday. At dinner that night, she gave her mother a "Happy Birthday Grandma" card signed with a question mark. When she opened the card, Ms. Campbell's mother thought it was a mistake. When its meaning dawned on her, she started crying.

Jake Campbell celebrated his first birthday in November without his mother. He falls asleep to the Baby Mozart video she bought. The clippings from his first haircut are still saved in an envelope underneath his parents' bed.

Ms. Campbell and her husband, Steven, juggled their schedules to raise Jake. Mr. Campbell worked nights as a police officer in Williamsburg, Brooklyn, so his wife cut back her hours working as an administrative assistant at Baseline, in the trade center, so she could spend more time with Jake.

Marriage to a police officer has its emotional hazards. Before Officer Campbell went to work each night, she would put her right cheek next to his and tell him to be careful.

"I promised that I would," he said.

Crawling was Ms. Campbell's latest mothering project. She helped Jake by supporting his stomach as he scurried along. She called these his "bunny foofoo" crawls. Real crawls were just around the corner.

Indeed, Jake crawled by himself for the first time on Sept. 11.

ROBERT A. CAMPBELL
Painter in the Clouds

He felt he worked on top of the world. Some days, the clouds would just pass right through him.

Robert A. Campbell was a painter, and he was assigned to the top of the World Trade Center. He found it so tranquil up there, far removed from life's struggles.

He was employed by Fine Painting and Decorating. He had been doing the observation deck and the window-cleaning equipment. On Sept. 11, his parents believe, he was on the roof.

Mr. Campbell, 25, lived with his parents, Robert and Maureen Campbell, in Brooklyn, and he was an insistent idealist. When he was a Cub Scout, he was picked to speak at a meeting of labor leaders, and he spoke of how important it was to get along with others and to be helpful.

Some day, he said, maybe he would end up being the president of a labor union. "He believed in the American dream—that everybody had a chance in life and that if you worked together you could really accomplish something," his mother said.

He enjoyed long rides in the country, where he could gaze at the trees. He kept hundreds of pictures of trees. To his parents, they looked alike; he would point out the differences.

He had begun college in the evenings to study business administration. He thought he might move into the management of a painting company. His first day of classes was Sept. 10.

SANDRA CAMPBELL
Helpful Was Her Only Gear

Early on the morning of Sept. 11, Corey Wilson took the phone when he heard that Sandra Campbell was calling from work. The 5-year-old wanted his godmother to know how much he liked the book bag she bought him for school.

The response so pleased her, she told the boy's mother, "I'm going to buy him two more."

Helping those around her was "just Sandra," said Gladys Anderson, one of Ms. Campbell's aunts. Though Ms. Campbell, 45, made a good living working for Cantor Fitzgerald as a computer programmer, she was one of those people who didn't go on vacations and made do with last year's coat. Whatever she had went to friends and her daughter, Ebony, who had just begun sophomore year at the University of Hartford.

Ms. Campbell's mother, Lendora Kearse, received $150 every month from her daughter for blood pressure medica-tion. In Fort Greene, Brooklyn, where Ms. Campbell lived, her car was at everyone's service.

"If I told her someone was in the hospital, she went," said Jacksie Smith, a friend. "The people didn't even know her, and by the time she walked out the door, they knew her."

One Saturday a month was "Aunts' Day," when she treated her aunts to a day of errands and shopping. Once Ms. Anderson casually mentioned that she needed something for the house. Ms. Campbell appeared soon afterward. She had found a Home Depot in the Bronx that was open till mid-night. Ms. Campbell had scheduled another "Aunts' Day" for the Saturday after Sept. 11.

SEAN CANAVAN
Candles from Neighbors

In some quarters of New York City, residents have an unwritten code about how to treat their neighbors: Ignore them.

But not Sean Canavan. He was one of the friendliest, most helpful people in his neighborhood, said his sister, Kathleen McKeon. The yellow ribbons, thick bouquets of flowers and white candles outside of his apartment house in Bay Ridge, Brooklyn, are testament. Neighbors placed them there when they heard he was missing.

"Everybody who knew Sean loved him," Mrs. McKeon said. Mr. Canavan, 39, a carpenter, was working for the second day at Installation Resources on the 98th floor in the south tower. He was always helping relatives, friends and neighbors with repairs and renovations. Last summer, Mr. Canavan helped his sister and her husband to build a deck on her two-story colonial house in Rockland County. He also put mahogany floors in her family room.

"Now, the family room has extra meaning," Mrs. McKeon said.

STEPHEN J. CANGIALOSI
The Great Shirt

Stephen J. Cangialosi will be remembered for "The Shirt."

Yes, he was a devoted father and husband, loyal friend, successful bond trader at Cantor Fitzgerald and a die-hard Yankees fan. But it was "The Shirt."

For years, he made fun of his Georgetown University classmate, Andy Stearns, for wearing a stained, plaid, late-1970s shirt with wide lapels throughout college. To get him back, Mr. Stearns wrapped it, threw a bow on the box and gave it to him as a gift. Not to be outdone, Mr. Cangialosi wrapped it in a big box with a bow and gave it back. That went on for about 17 years. It would turn up on holidays, birthdays and anniversaries.

"It's so ugly," Mr. Stearns said of the shirt, laughing.

Mr. Cangialosi, 40, of Middletown, N.J., will also be remembered for a horror movie, *Ghost Story,* that another Georgetown classmate produced. Mr. Cangialosi, an athletic 6-foot-1, was the star. Simply put, it was 28 minutes of horrible. But, oh, how they loved to watch it and laugh together, Mr. Stearns said.

While memorializing his friend, Mr. Stearns suddenly remembered that Mr. Cangialosi had given him "The Shirt" for his 40th birthday. He decided that it would be fitting to give it as a gift to Mr. Cangialosi's wife, Karen.

BRIAN CANNIZZARO
The Storyteller

Brian Cannizzaro would burst into a room, eyes twinkling, and you would not believe what had just happened to him.

"There was always some Herculean effort that had gone awry," said Charles Cannizzaro, a brother. "There was always something to get the ball rolling."

Once, it was the story of how Firefighter Cannizzaro, of Ladder Company 101 in Red Hook, Brooklyn, had earned the nickname Rat Boy by leaping into a Dumpster to put out a fire, then leaping right back out when a furry creature scampered into his protective clothing. And then there was the tale of heroism from his second job, as a security officer at the *Ricki Lake* show, when he had broken up a fight between two guests and then found himself encircled by autograph-seeking audience members.

Obsessed with the movie *Gladiator,* Firefighter Cannizzaro, 30, wanted to name his son after its hero, Maximus. His wife, Jacqueline, considered it, but the baby, now just over a year old, was named Christopher.

MICHAEL CANTY
Plans for a Proposal

What Michael Canty, the seventh of nine children, wanted most was to create a family like the one in which he grew up in Schenectady, N.Y. He loved having lots of like-minded people around him. He accumulated friends—from childhood, Loyola College and Carr Futures, where he was a trader—and drank beer with them at bars like Molly's and Chumley's in lower Manhattan. He was the friend his friends turned to. All of them called him their best friend.

He spent weekends at the Canty family house on a lake in the Berkshires or with Erin Clifford, whom he planned to marry. They took their first trip to Europe last summer: one day in London and 12 hours in Paris, where, Ms. Clifford said, they saw "the front of every building" and ate in the city's "only bad restaurant."

Mr. Canty, 30, was thinking of memorable ways to give Ms. Clifford the ring on which he had a deposit. He was leaning toward the Berkshire house as a setting, and here was the plan: he would take her out in the boat and drive near the shoreline, where his 16 nieces and nephews would brandish a sign: "Will you marry me?"

JONATHAN N. CAPPELLO
An Open Invitation

Jonathan N. Cappello always—even as a child—invited people into his parents' Garden City home, first to mooch food prepared by his mother and, in later years, to hang out for pizza, wings and beer. Although Mr. Cappello, 23 and the youngest of three boys, could get away with anything, older brothers Jamey and Robert say, his nickname was a result of being told no.

"First it was, 'Jonathan, no. Jonathan, no you can't do that,' " said Mr. Cappello's mother, Claudia. "Then it got to be, 'Jon, no.' Then it got to be 'Jono.' "

That was the name used by his friends, many of whom played basketball with Mr. Cappello at a nearby school. Tall, lanky and quick, Mr. Cappello would never call a foul, his brother Jamey said.

"He'd pretty much play and make shots with people—including me—bashing his arms. He just figured it was a playground."

JAMES C. CAPPERS
Joys of the Outdoors

In her junior year at Quinnipiac College, Kathleen Vieira spotted a new man on campus. He was tall. He was handsome. He was wearing a pink rugby shirt.

"Who is that guy?" she asked her friends. Nobody knew. Turns out he was a transfer student named James Christopher Cappers, a.k.a. Chris, a.k.a. Clark Kent (whom he resembled).

"Fresh from getting out of the phone booth," said Steven M. Vaughn, a friend since sixth grade. Ms. Vieira and Mr. Cappers married in 1995, on April 22, a date they selected by combining their birthdays, Sept. 4 (April is the fourth month) and Aug. 22.

It was also Earth Day, a good fit, considering that some of the Capperses' favorite times together were spent hiking, camping and introducing Alex, who turned 3 on Dec. 30, 2001, to the thrills of sleeping in a tent. Mr. Cappers, 33, was a personal client executive at Marsh & McLennan.

Mrs. Cappers recently gave Alex and Andrew, 7

months old, special teddy bears sewn from their Daddy's old shirts.

"I'm trying to find that pink rugby for myself," she said. "I think about him all the time."

RICHARD CAPRONI
Unpacking Was a Pleasure

It was just a studio apartment, but Richard Caproni had finally become a homeowner after more than a decade of renting in Manhattan and Queens. He had bought in Lynbrook, on Long Island, not far from where he grew up, and moved in shortly before Sept. 11.

His sister, Lisa, was still decorating the place in denim-blue and wood hues. He told her no fussy, floral motifs.

"He was proud of buying that apartment," she said. "Because he was on his own."

Mr. Caproni, 34, worked in the accounts payable department at Marsh & McLennan. Known as Richie to his family and friends, he was always teasing them to make them laugh.

In high school, he played football and remained a lifelong fan. He favored the Giants, but followed other teams; he had tickets to an Ohio State game in a few weeks.

His new apartment would have been the perfect place to kick back and watch *Monday Night Football.*

"He just had to unpack a little more," his sister said. "And he was good to go."

JOSÉ CARDONA
The Good Things

Pictures of José Cardona show him dancing on a conga line with his wife and friends, clowning around after getting off a horse during a vacation, having dinner with his daughter from a previous marriage—Sasha, 11—and his wife's son from hers, Miguel, 14.

He loved his family, liked the good things in life and wanted his wife, Paulina Cardona, 33, to look sexy. She said her husband was so touched he cried when she surprised him with a tattoo of a rose on her left breast, his idea. And he cried again, she said, when the couple found out that she was expecting their first child and the baby would be a son.

Knowing his family would expand, Mr. Cardona wanted to make extra money to buy a house. So on Saturdays, the couple would get up at 6 A.M. and travel around New York City in their car selling fish and products from Ecuador, their home country, to friends and friends of friends.

When his customers found out that Mr. Cardona was missing at the World Trade Center, some asked: "He sold fish there?"

In fact, Mr. Cardona, 35, had been working for Wall Street companies for 14 years, most recently as a clerk at Carr Futures.

The baby is due in January.

DENNIS M. CAREY
Living, and Cooking, Fully

Dennis M. Carey loved to cook. The family has every issue of *Bon Appétit* magazine going back 15 years, said his wife, Jean, "and you couldn't improvise with the ingredients. He had to use exactly what the recipe called for."

And he worked hard as a New York City firefighter. He joined the Fire Department almost two decades ago, and seven years ago began working with Hazardous Materials Company 1 in Maspeth, Queens. Mr. Carey's body was found, along with those of 15 of his colleagues, at the World Trade Center on Oct. 2.

When he was not on the job, Firefighter Carey, 51, loved to travel with his wife and their two children, Nicole, 25, and Dennis Jr., 22.

"We lived," Jean Carey said a day after his funeral. "A lot of people who pass on, they say about them that they lived two lives. We lived three. We've done everything with our children, traveled from Maine to Florida, went camping, went to every amusement park you can think of."

She continued: "I'm with him since I'm 17, and I'm 48 now. He was a pleaser. He spoiled me. He did for me. We had a great life. I'm so grateful to have it."

EDWARD CARLINO
Shirt-Sleeve Executive

Edward Carlino was the senior vice president in charge of running the financial reporting systems at the insurance brokerage firm Marsh & McLennan. It was a job he loved. Mr. Carlino, 46, had both technical and financial expertise, according to a Marsh spokesman, and he was responsible for assembling and analyzing financial data for the company.

"He worked hard," his wife, Marie, said. "He was at work more often than he was at home. He would be there at 7:30 A.M. and not leave before 9 P.M. He was one of the few people at his level who took off his coat, rolled up his sleeves and worked with the people that reported to him."

The couple met more than 11 years ago in a club after work when "I literally ran into him," Mrs. Carlino said. They tried to take two vacations a year, Mrs. Carlino said, but that "was like pulling teeth." Mr. Carlino liked Paris and small

Firefighters attend a funeral for Fire Captain Terence
Hatton, commander of Rescue Unit 1, on October 4 at
St. Patrick's Cathedral. (*Richard Perry*)

Caribbean islands, especially St. Barts. The two were married
and spent their honeymoon on St. Thomas in June 1995.

The latest addition to their family was Mandie, a mixed-
breed dog from the North Shore Animal League. Mr. Carlino
"didn't think he was a dog person, but he was," Mrs. Carlino
said.

DAVID G. CARLONE
Catching Up with Friends

David G. Carlone was a man who knew his
own mind and followed his own road. On
their first date 25 years ago, said his wife,
Beverly, he told her that he was going to
marry her. And he later vowed that he
would run a marathon in under three hours. He accomplished both goals.

Mr. Carlone, 46, had given up the grind of commuting
daily from Randolph, N.J., into New York City. He had
worked at the World Trade Center for many years, but
about six years ago, as his three sons (ages 12, 15 and 17) hit

the age of sports teams and after-school games, he quit and
took a job as an account executive at an insurance company
15 minutes from home.

But he still had many friends in the towers. When he
would go in for an occasional business meeting, as he did the
morning of Sept. 11 at Aon's offices on the 105th floor of 2
World Trade Center, he would actually look forward to it,
Ms. Carlone said.

It was an opportunity to catch up with the places and
people that had once been his world and that were still very
dear to him.

JOYCE CARPENETO
Bullies Beware

At the age of 6, working on a first-grade art
project in her hometown, East Northport,
N.Y., Joyce Carpeneto gave an early glimpse
of the kind of person she would become.

"We were sitting next to each other
working, and she had crayons and I

didn't," said Mary Jane Tenerelli, remembering their first encounter, in 1966. "She offered to share her crayons with me and we'd been friends ever since."

Ms. Carpeneto, who would have turned 42 on Oct. 1, was well known as the "epitome of cool," but only one thing surpassed her reputation as a great dancer and a fashion trendsetter: "She was generous to the point that people were devoted to her," Ms. Tenerelli said. "A couple of years ago, she set me up with her ex-husband. That's got to be the most generous thing ever."

Ms. Carpeneto, who worked in client services for General Telecom, was also the kind of person who would jump between a friend and a class bully, as she did in junior high when Ms. Tenerelli got into trouble.

"Joyce got in the middle and said, 'Leave Mary Jane alone,'" her friend said. "I never had a problem with that bully again."

JEREMY CARRINGTON
Larger than Life (or Death)

There is no single great story about Jeremy Carrington, 34, a man universally known as Caz. Instead there are hundreds of them, left like glittering stones along his trail.

"He did not waste a moment of his life, and he enjoyed everything about it," said his wife, Patricia Rosch Carrington, trying to sum it all up.

While they were dating, he decided to pour his considerable energy into her family's backyard football game, and ended up breaking her father's nose. When Mr. Carrington proposed to her last year, he roped her boss into the conspiracy and popped the question in the Sistine Chapel.

A British-born swaps trader for Cantor Fitzgerald, Mr. Carrington was host of a BBC program, *Manhattan on the Beach,* in which he documented the daily activities of English people summering in the Hamptons.

He charmed the conductor on his subway with the greeting, "Thank you, sir, for saving my seat."

One night in early September, he hailed a cab with a group of colleagues. When the driver refused to take all five of them, Mr. Carrington asked him to open the trunk so they could put their briefcases in it. The four other people settled into the cab. A few hundred yards up the street, the driver asked what that banging noise was, coming from the back.

"Oh, it's a Cazo," they answered. The driver pulled over, popped the trunk and discovered Mr. Carrington sitting cross-legged inside it, surrounded by the briefcases, waving his long arms and calling, "Helllooooo."

"A lot of people say that so many of these men and women were larger than life," Mrs. Carrington said. "I quite frankly think this man was larger than death."

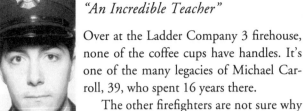

MICHAEL CARROLL
"An Incredible Teacher"

Over at the Ladder Company 3 firehouse, none of the coffee cups have handles. It's one of the many legacies of Michael Carroll, 39, who spent 16 years there.

The other firefighters are not sure why he started snapping off the handles, but just like his other habits, it could not be stopped. He also cut a hole in the wall between the ladder company's dormitory and a room reserved for the aide who drives the local battalion chief around. Late at night, if the ladder company answered an alarm and the aide stayed in bed, Firefighter Carroll would reach through the hole, open a dresser drawer and slam it, just to let the aide know they had returned.

"He was an incredible teacher for the younger firemen," said Pat Murphy, whose idea of torture was speaking to school groups touring the firehouse—until Firefighter Carroll helped him.

Michael Carroll drove the truck to the fires, coached his son, Brendan, in baseball, and doted on his wife, Nancy, and daughter, Olivia. He was "great, great and great," said his friend Gerard Brenkert. During the blizzard of 1996, he was heading uptown from New York Hospital after his father had surgery there.

"On every other corner, there was a poor soul looking for a cab," said Nancy Amigron, his sister. One by one, Firefighter Carroll picked up the snow-covered New Yorkers and drove them home.

"We were so relieved about my father that we would have driven anybody to California," said Mrs. Amigron, who is planning to send some new coffee cups—without handles—to Ladder 3.

PETE CARROLL
A Painter Who Cared

They called him Pete the Painter. Pete Carroll was really a firefighter, but he painted apartments to make ends meet. He walked into ToniAnn's life eight years ago and laid two coats of beige paint.

He had 19 years in the Fire Department. One more, and they were off to retire in California. They depended on each other, but last January, Ms. Carroll came to depend on him in very profound ways. She fell ill with a neurological disorder with no cure. It is a rapid, ravaging affliction that attacks the soft tissues.

Firefighter Carroll, 42, started to cook for his wife. He carried her to bed. Sometimes he washed her back. His last summer, on the hottest day of the year, he came home to

Staten Island from the Squad 1 firehouse in Brooklyn to see her in the backyard, frozen in a chair in the blazing sun. He saw that and wept.

"I had a beautiful fireman to rescue me," Ms. Carroll said. "Now I don't want to move at all."

In a contorted way, Mr. Carroll's wife is one of the lucky survivors. She has his ashes and his wedding band.

JAMES J. CARSON Jr.
Workstation to Playstation

James Carson spent much of the day—and often much of the evening—working with computers on the 103rd floor of the World Trade Center. When he finally did get home, he immediately headed for a different kind of computer: his Sony Playstation.

"That was how he would wind down," said his wife, Debbie Carson. She recalled that Mr. Carson, 32, would come home to Massapequa, N.Y., and relax by playing football video games in the basement. He took the games so seriously that he kept statistics on the virtual players, she said—just like the stats he kept on favorite real-life players.

"I'm not even allowed in the basement," said Mrs. Carson, who is six months pregnant with their first child. "That was his playroom."

His office was something of a playroom, too. Mr. Carson, who had worked as a computer network administrator at Cantor Fitzgerald for just over six weeks on Sept. 11, was thrilled to be so close to the heart of the world of finance.

"He always ranted and raved about his view and the work he was doing," Mrs. Carson said.

CHRISTOFFER M. CARSTANJEN
"Mr. Wonderful"

Humorist. Gardener. Motorcycle enthusiast. Philosopher.

That is how Christoffer M. Carstanjen liked to be known. His nickname for himself was "Mr. Wonderful" and the line he most identified with was from the filmmaker Federico Fellini: "There is no end. There is no beginning. There is only the infinite passion of life." These and other statements he posted on his personal Web site.

"Listen and surround yourself with positive people," advised Mr. Carstanjen, who worked in the technology office at the University of Massachusetts. The proud owner of a 1998 Honda PC800, Mr. Carstanjen, 34, was aboard United Airlines Flight 175 en route to join other bikers for a ride up the California coast.

His to-do list for the future: "Build another home. More schooling in the evenings. (Never stop learning!) Start a college or a learning/living center for elders. Build that boat, then another one! Learn to sail."

JAMES MARCEL CARTIER
The More Work, the Better

Forget about taking it easy. James Marcel Cartier loved to work. Five long days was never enough to satisfy him. He insisted on six long days.

"He loved to come home dirty," said his brother Michael. "It meant he had worked hard. He had no problem with that."

Mr. Cartier, 26, was a deep-dimpled, happy-go-lucky electrician who had been assigned to a job at the World Trade Center just two weeks before the attack. He lived in Astoria, Queens, with Michael, and was well known in his neighborhood because he had worked at so many different places. If he couldn't get enough overtime doing electrical jobs to fill up six days, then he got behind the counter at the A & F Deli.

Before becoming an electrician, starting when he was just 13, he had a succession of jobs at a mall in Jackson Heights. It would take too long to list all the stores, but he worked at a stationery store, a pizza place and a drugstore. He just worked.

So many people in Queens had encountered him on their shopping trips that they wrote in shoe polish on their windows, "We will miss you, James."

VIVIAN CASALDUC
The Hard Way to Learning

Vivian Casalduc lived to make her family's eyes light up. Each December, she would bake gingerbread for a giant candy land, where the ground was coated with thick piles of shredded coconut (snow) and the houses were studded with lollipops and licorice.

"She would make it the first two days in December and let everybody look at it all month long, and on Christmas morning, she'd let everyone ransack it," said her daughter Angilic Casalduc.

Five small grandchildren spent alternate weekends in her care, and would come home with cotton candy in a kaleidoscope of colors and shapes. Turns out, Grandma had bought a cotton candy machine.

A Brooklyn native who grew up in housing projects, Ms. Casalduc, 45, married at 16, had three children and divorced. Her job as a microfiche clerk at Empire Blue Cross and Blue Shield moved in 1999 from Brooklyn to the 28th floor of 1 World Trade Center. Her commute was longer, but the salsa concerts downstairs became a part of her lunchtime routine.

Ms. Casalduc left one prescient lesson, her daughter said: "Do everything the hard way." Why major in one subject when four would do, or take a taxi when public transportation was there? "Do it the easy way," Angilic Casalduc remembered, "and you'll never learn anything, and God forbid, anything happens, she worried we wouldn't know how to survive."

NEILIE ANNE CASEY
Runners and a Torch

There is no logic to any of it; that much is obvious. But the truth is that they did meet as freshmen, in logic class. That was at Holy Cross, and Michael Casey still remembers the sight of Neilie Anne Heffernan's long auburn hair.

They were married on Cape Cod in 1996 "because it was meant to be," he said—their "incredible bond" only intensified when their daughter, Riley Eileen, was born in early 2001.

The Caseys were both runners. On Sunday, Sept. 9, they took their daughter on her first three-mile road race (Riley was the cute one in the jogging stroller).

On the night before the attack, the Caseys played a travel video of Bermuda, planning the trip for their fifth wedding anniversary, Sept. 21.

On Sept. 11, Mr. Casey kissed his wife good-bye and watched from the bedroom window upstairs as she left their house in Wellesley, Mass., at 5:45 A.M. "I flipped the light on so she could see me, and she turned and waved back as she left."

Thus this last memory before Mrs. Casey, 32, boarded Flight 11 on a business trip to California. Later, Mr. Casey was asked to be one of the runners carrying the torch for the Winter Olympic Games in February, "in honor," he said, "of Neilie."

THOMAS A. CASORIA
On the Verge of Marriage

Thomas A. Casoria waited almost five years, after taking his exam, to be called to his job at the Fire Department. After almost three years on the job he was with Engine Company 22 on East 85th Street.

Firefighter Casoria was last heard from, according to his father, Carlo, when he radioed his captain to say that he and two other firefighters were helping a paraplegic down the stairs from the fifth floor of 1 World Trade Center and, a little later, when he radioed that a fireman was down.

Firefighter Casoria, 29, grew up in Whitestone, Queens. At Holy Cross High School in Flushing, Queens, he played second base and was captain of his baseball team and was an all-city football player. Once in the Fire Department, he switched to softball and played second base on the department team. He "made plays they can't believe he made," his father said.

Firefighter Casoria's brother Carlo, who is also a firefighter, was in the same class at the academy.

"He was my go-to guy," the brother said. "He would be there for me."

With his firefighting career under way, Thomas Casoria had time to think of his future and make his mother, Judy, happy. He was engaged on Oct. 22, 2000, and was set to be married on Oct. 13, 2001.

WILLIAM CASPAR
Steeped in Hard Work

"A Kansas farm boy"—that is how people describe William Caspar, even though he was a data processing specialist for Marsh & McLennan who could create highly detailed electronic forms.

But every summer, Mr. Caspar would return to the Kansas farm that has been in his family for five generations so he could help with the wheat harvest. At Marsh & McLennan, Mr. Caspar, 57, would often work long hours, a habit he picked up on the farm.

"You start work when the sun comes up, and you go to sleep when the sun goes down," Tony Alaimo, a colleague, quoted Mr. Caspar as saying. "That's how we were raised."

Mr. Caspar, who had been divorced for many years, spent holidays with his sister's family in Scituate, Mass.

"He was a good role model to have around my children," said the sister, Margaret Richardson.

For years, Mr. Caspar worked out of a Princeton, N.J., office with a small group of people who often socialized together on weekends and grew very close. They were transferred to the World Trade Center in February 2001.

ALEJANDRO CASTANO
A Loving Sibling Rivalry

When you are born 11 months apart, sibling rivalry can take on a whole new meaning. Alejandro Castano made an art out of torturing and teasing his sister Claudia Sanchez.

"Look at my bike, it's better than yours," he would tell her each summer while they were growing up in Englewood, N.J. And when tensions between the two got really heated, Mr. Castano would pull out his favorite taunt: "You're not really my sister. You're adopted."

For Ms. Sanchez, there was no refuge, even her Barbie dolls became victims. Those moments are cherished now.

"It was just the two of us. Alej loved to play games, to

make jokes," Ms. Sanchez said of her brother, who as a deliveryman for Empire Distribution in Carlstadt, N.J., dropped off office supplies to the World Trade Center every day. "That was just his way of saying, 'I love you.'"

Only his mother could quiet the joking. "He was always telling us, 'You can't cook,'" Ms. Sanchez said. "But as soon as he got a plate of my mother's pork chops, rice and beans and plantains, it was a different story. He was a little kid in paradise."

LEONARD CASTRIANNO
Glass Half Full

Leonard Castrianno was not really a huge country music fan. But given the right circumstances, he would load many dollars' worth of Dolly Parton songs into the jukebox at his favorite bar, an East Village watering hole where rock was favored.

"The place would just clear out, and he knew that would happen," said Garrett Davis, Mr. Castrianno's friend who was often an accomplice in the song switching. "Then we could get to the bar, no problem. He hated a crowded bar."

Despite that, Mr. Castrianno, who was 30, lived in Williamsburg, Brooklyn, and worked for Cantor Fitzgerald, was gregarious. An enthusiastic socializer, he was funny. He was also relentlessly positive.

"He would cut me off mid-sentence and say, 'Look, what's your problem?'" Mr. Davis said. "'You always see the worst in everything.'"

But not this time. Even though they had an argument shortly before Sept. 11, Mr. Davis feels Mr. Castrianno has forgiven him, and that their friendship lives on.

JOSE RAYMOND CASTRO
Comfort Food with Spice

Jose Raymond Castro began cooking at age 9 in a little house on Rosedale Avenue in the Bronx. His mother liked yellow, so she had painted the kitchen bright yellow. She let him cook eggs first. Then came rice, beans, pork, seasoning, the works. Mr. Castro, 37, was fascinated with food.

He started working at 13, delivering food, preparing food, cooking in restaurants around the city. When the World Trade Center was attacked on Tuesday, he was working as a prep cook in a food court on the 101st floor of one of the towers, readying food for the chef.

He specialized in sophisticated food, said his sister, Maritza. "Because that's what people in Manhattan liked to eat." But at home in the South Bronx, he cooked for his family: pernil, rice with gandules, lasagna, ziti, rice pudding, honey-glazed turkey on Thanksgiving.

"They had a son three years ago," Ms. Castro said of her brother and his wife, Gladys. "Oh, that's the love of his life,

and I do mean the love of his life. He looks just like him, too. He's light-skinned, dirty-blond hair, hazel eyes, and skinny just like my brother."

CHRISTOPHER SEAN CATON
Rock and the Jersey Shore

When he was a teenager in Glen Rock, N.J., Christopher Sean Caton—known as Sean—had his own band, which for some reason was called the Family Goffer.

"They once did a benefit concert for a girl who had leukemia," recalled his sister, Alison Henderson. "They were really idolized by all the other kids."

After high school, Mr. Caton moved away from Glen Rock, first to Arizona, where he attended Arizona State University, and later to Manhattan, where he got a job as a bond trader for Cantor Fitzgerald, the same company where his father had worked.

"He loved it there, he loved the people, but honestly, he wanted to be a rock star," Ms. Henderson said.

"There were many many nights down at the shore when he would be at a bar, and he would grab the microphone, and start singing," she said. "He loved being on stage; he loved being in the limelight. He always made an impression: people always remembered Sean Caton."

He would have turned 35 today.

As a boy, his favorite band was Kiss. But he soon moved on to Bruce Springsteen: Ms. Henderson found 35 ticket stubs to Springsteen concerts in his bedroom. Every summer he returned to Manasquan, on the Jersey shore, where he and his friends rented a house.

"Manasquan was his favorite place on earth," Ms. Henderson recalled.

JUDSON J. CAVALIER
The Laid-Back Approach

A couple of days after pledging his fraternity, Sigma Beta, and moving into his room at the University of New Hampshire, Judson J. Cavalier bought a bed. More precisely, said his college roommate and fraternity brother, Nathan Sloan, it was a mattress, and Mr. Cavalier never bothered to get the box spring or the frame.

"He was, like, what you would call laid back," Mr. Sloan mused.

So laid back that the university invited him to take a semester off to think about his commitment to academics. With a friend, Mr. Cavalier went to Vail, Colo., where he figured he could ski a lot, and took a job as a ski-boot salesman.

"He made phenomenal money. Everybody knew he was

a good worker," Mr. Sloan said. "He just didn't sweat the stuff he didn't have to sweat."

Mr. Cavalier, 26, did graduate, and was hired by Thomas F. O'Neill, his next-door neighbor growing up in Huntington, N.Y., and a founder of Sandler O'Neill & Partners. He was about to be promoted from bond research to salesman.

"Being a bond salesman, you made a lot of money and you played golf with the guys," said another childhood friend, Ian Crystal. "That was perfect for Judd. He was there."

MICHAEL CAWLEY
Proud to Be a Firefighter

When Michael Cawley was 3, some firefighters drove past and yelled: "Hey, Michael Cawley! How are you?"

"Mom didn't know these guys," said Brendan, 27, his younger brother. "But they all knew Michael." By the time he could walk, Michael Cawley wanted to be a firefighter.

"Wouldn't it be cool to play major-league baseball?" Brendan once asked.

"Rather be a fireman," Michael answered.

Mr. Cawley, 30, scored 100 percent on the Fire Department exam and was assigned to Ladder Company 136 in Elmhurst, Queens. He was "a walking billboard for the Fire Department," said his younger brother. He had drawers of F.D.N.Y. T-shirts and rarely wore anything else. He was furious when he was off duty during a big fire.

"I could see how happy he was," said Brendan Cawley, who is studying for the Fire Department tests. "They're buddies, hanging out talking about fires, baseball—not sitting in an office preparing for a meeting. When someone goes to a fire, they all go with him."

JASON CAYNE
In Love with Togetherness

It was this weekly ritual that Jason Cayne relished:

Every Friday and Saturday evening, Mr. Cayne and his wife, Gina, would hook up with Mrs. Cayne's sisters and brothers-in-law, along with a few other friends, and go out to bars and clubs and just have a rollicking good time. There would be as many as a dozen of them, packed into a couple of cars, traveling in the environs of Marlboro, N.J., where the Caynes lived.

"We'd be out literally every weekend," Mrs. Cayne said. "We'd meet at my mother's house. We'd fight about who would be designated drivers. And then we'd party."

Mr. Cayne, 32, a bond broker at Cantor Fitzgerald, liked togetherness.

"We could be sitting around and doing nothing, but that

was O.K.," Mrs. Cayne said. "He just wanted us to be together."

Mrs. Cayne is the oldest of four sisters. They all adored Mr. Cayne when they met him, and the fondness grew exponentially.

"My sisters always said he's the sort of man they wanted to marry," said Mrs. Cayne, who was the first of the four to marry. Two sisters have followed, with men they compare quite favorably to Mr. Cayne.

The fourth is still looking for her replica.

MARCIA CECIL-CARTER
Navy Tough, Soft at Heart

Do not be fooled by the pale pink roses Marcia Cecil-Carter holds in her Feb. 16, 2000, wedding picture.

"She was tough as nails," her husband, Ondre Carter, said proudly.

She had to be, starting out as a 17-year-old mother in Chicago, and joining the Navy to make it on her own. After 3½ years as a chef for naval officers, she moved on and up—to Carr Futures, a securities company on the 92nd floor of 1 World Trade Center.

Mr. Carter was going to the laundry when their paths crossed on his mother's street in Brooklyn in 1996.

"Our eyes met, and I made a big excuse to go to the grocery store to follow her," he recalled. Their son Devonte was 4 in 2001.

Ms. Cecil-Carter, 34, was upset when she learned that her daughter, Amber, was having a baby at 17. But she melted when she saw her baby grandson for the first time—two days before the terrorist attacks.

"Tough as nails," her husband said, "but the softest heart in the world."

THOMAS CELIC
He Made People Laugh

Cross-country running was something that Thomas Celic learned from his older brother Marty when Tom was a freshman at Monsignor Farrell High School in Staten Island and Marty was the track coach.

"Marty was the one who got him running," recalled Tom's wife, Roseanne. And he kept on running, long after Marty Celic, a New York City firefighter, was killed in the line of duty in 1977. Tom Celic ran in races in Staten Island, and in the New York City Marathon, in which he typically finished in the top 300.

"He just loved it," Mrs. Celic said. "Running was his passion."

Mr. Celic, 43, who worked at Marsh & McLennan, was close to both his families—his own and the one he joined by marrying Roseanne, a Staten Island girl whom he met when she was 17 and he was 19.

"He was a great son-in-law," said John Tasso, his father-in-law, who lived five minutes away. "Whenever they would go out, they would ask us to go, and include us."

After Sept. 11, Roseanne Celic discovered that she was not the only one who thought her husband was funny. His old clients called to tell her stories, and at the memorial service, the church was filled with firefighters from Ladder 17, his brother's company.

"He made a lot of people laugh, and when he laughed, it was really such a joyous sound that you just laughed too," she said.

ANA CENTENO
"Like a Sister"

If you could not find Ana Centeno in her office at Marsh & McLennan, then she was one of two places: at the gym, or on the track at Hudson County Park in Bayonne, N.J. An avid runner, Ms. Centeno spent so much time running that her family held a candlelight memorial service on the track at Hudson County Park, and her picture is still there.

"She had dancing eyes," her brother, Jesus Centeno, said. "She was very athletic and when she went for something, she achieved it."

Ms. Centeno, 38, was an accountant and a good friend to many. "It's hard to be without her," said Diana Rodriguez, who said Ms. Centeno "was just like a sister to her" even when she had just begun to date Jesus Centeno years ago. "Ana was just Ana, lovable, sweet. She made me feel comfortable when I first met her 17 years ago and we'd been like sisters ever since."

JEFFREY CHAIRNOFF
A Change in Priorities

From football to Food Network: that was the journey that Jeffrey Chairnoff had made over the last few years.

Before he became a father, Mr. Chairnoff, 35, liked to spend his Sundays during the fall and winter watching football games. It was the perfect way to unwind, said his wife, Helaine, after an intense workweek at Sandler O'Neill & Partners, where he eventually became managing director of the mortgage financing group. Not that he was a stereotypical type-A Wall Street guy: if anything, co-workers told Mrs. Chairnoff that her husband was a calm ballast noted for his thoroughness and attention to detail.

Still, after Sarah, 6, and Benjamin, 2, were born, Mr. Chairnoff changed his lifestyle to accommodate everyone but himself.

He was dubbed Mr. Clean by his family because of his tendency to keep the kitchen spotless. And he loved to watch the Food Network. He printed out recipes, and he was particularly fond of making peanut butter pie with his daughter. His favorite show was *Emeril Live,* because it was Sarah's, too.

SWARNA CHALASANI
Peripatetic Adventurer

When Swarna Chalasani traveled—and she traveled a lot—it was never simply a vacation. It was an adventure.

She rode white-water rapids in Colorado. She backpacked through Thailand. She taught herself Japanese and Spanish to prepare for her trips abroad. She read voluminously about her destinations weeks before she left.

Ms. Chalasani was a vice president at Fiduciary Trust and was last seen on the 94th floor of 2 World Trade Center on the day of the attack. She would have celebrated her 34th birthday on December 30, 2001.

Her first name means "gold" in Hindi, though her family called her Minny. "She was the smallest of the three girls, and the cutest," her sister Sandhya said.

If she had a taste for the exotic, she also had a knack for making her home into a comfortable palace. There were beautiful paintings and shelves full of books. There were plants and scented candles. "She treated these things like sacred objects," her mother, Lakshmi, said.

The lost echoes of her full-throated laughter. The memory of her smile across the dinner table. Her postcards mailed from distant countries. This is all that remains of Ms. Chalasani.

Her family guards them like the sacred objects they have now become.

ELI CHALOUH
Multilingual and Multinice

Fluent in Arabic, Hebrew and English, Eli Chalouh, 23, moved easily among the diverse communities to which his languages gave him access. He spoke Arabic at home, of course: he moved here with his family from Damascus, Syria, when he was 14.

At his new job at the New York State Department of Taxation and Finance, in the World Trade Center, he spoke Arabic with his Egyptian colleagues, who got a kick out of him. Mr. Chalouh was not Muslim; he was a Syrian Jew, who learned Hebrew at the yeshiva he attended in Brooklyn.

America was the country he wanted to wrap his future around. He was always in a rush, determined to cram every moment with English studies and other courses: he was so disciplined that he allotted himself only 15 minutes of television at night.

His efforts were beginning to pay off. He had just graduated with near-perfect grades from Long Island University, a member of the honor society and voted by the faculty the most outstanding accounting student of 2001.

Industrious, yes, but enormously sunny and engaging, as well. "Whatever you asked him he would do, and whatever you wouldn't ask, he would volunteer to do," said a supervisor at work, Eddie Jaeger. "He was an unbelievably nice kid."

MARK CHARETTE
The Handyman

Mark Charette, who worked as an insurance broker at Marsh & McLennan in Morristown, N.J., was handier than the handyman. Task by task, he was renovating his 120-year-old Victorian house in Millburn, N.J. He redid the heating system, much of the plumbing and put a cathedral ceiling in his bedroom.

Mr. Charette, 38, was at a morning meeting at Marsh's offices in the World Trade Center on Sept. 11. He met his wife, Cheryl Desmarais, at the University of Pennsylvania. They began as engineering majors and finished with business degrees. He was in the Navy R.O.T.C. to save his parents the expense of his college education, his wife said. Then it was five years as an officer on a nuclear submarine, while Ms. Desmarais worked as a consultant in New York.

Even with his work, travel and home renovating, he made his family the center of his life. At home in New Jersey or at their vacation house in Vermont, Mr. Charette spent hours hiking, skiing and swimming with his three children.

He made time on Saturday mornings to take Lauren, 8, Andrew, 6, and Jonathan, 2, to McDonald's for breakfast, giving his wife a break.

"This is your time," he would tell his wife. "You are not invited."

DEL-ROSE CHEATHAM
A Dream Already Realized

The family of Del-Rose Cheatham was anticipating another great party in celebration of her 49th birthday on Sept. 14. Her last big bash, in the family home in the Poconos with 55 friends and family members, was to celebrate her 2000 graduation from Queens College after years of night school, during which she worked two jobs.

She had already been working as an accounting manager at Cantor Fitzgerald, on the 101st floor of 1 World Trade Center, but the diploma was "her dream," said her

brother, Chris Forbes. He was the youngest of five children in Montego Bay, Jamaica, and Del-Rose was the oldest, "and she was a mother to me; she raised all of us," Mr. Forbes said.

His sister was a Jehovah's Witness, and loved to do field work, strolling up and down the street and talking to people about God. Now God is very much on the family's mind. "All we can do is accept," said Dunstan Forbes, her father.

PEDRO CHECO
Not Just a Car, but a Datsun

Pedro Checo was a car buff, but in particular he was a Datsun 510 buff. As a teenager he owned a 510, and as he got older he yearned for another. Three years ago, he finally bought a 1972 Datsun 510 and began rebuilding it. He had a feel for the innards of cars. He could fix anything.

He joined the Datsun 510 Club, for it was a car with a keen following, and his plan was to compete in drag races. He entered two races last year, but the car needed more power. So he installed a more potent engine and was scheduled to get the horsepower measured on Sept. 30 before returning to the drag strip. Now the car sits idle in the garage.

Mr. Checo, 35, who lived with Marmily Cabrera and their two children, Jasen, 6, and Julian, 1, in Queens, was a vice president of investment operations for Fiduciary Trust. He also had a son, Franklin, 17, from an earlier relationship. He hated the name Pedro, and Ms. Cabrera called him Frank, his nickname. At work, though, they called him Pete. He was Pete by day and Frank by night.

Something about cars seems embedded in the Checo genes. Jasen has about 250 Matchbox cars, and every time his mother takes him to the toy store, he wants another. "It's fine with me," she said. "They're only $1."

DOUGLAS MacMILLAN CHERRY
Bengals All the Way

The shoes always told Douglas MacMillan Cherry's secret. Only a devout Cincinnati Bengals fan would be seen in a pair of orange Converse sneakers painted with black tiger stripes. Sure, people stared. But Mr. Cherry did not care.

The Bengals were the team he learned to love as a boy growing up in Cincinnati. When he could steal a few days away from his job at Aon Insurance, Mr. Cherry would even fly back to Cincinnati to watch his Bengals play. He loved only one thing more, his family, his wife, Sarah, and their children, Emma, Isabel and Jack.

"He loved his family and he loved the Bengals. That was his life," said Burns Patterson, his brother-in-law.

At a makeshift memorial created near his home in Maplewood, N.J., friends posted a letter to honor Mr. Cherry.

"We all know the one thing Doug would have wanted from us. We will always take care of Emma, Isabel and Jack," the letter read. It then made a disparaging, though affectionate, reference to the Bengals.

STEPHEN P. CHERRY
A Dream House and a CD

When Stephen Cherry called his wife from work the morning of Sept. 11, he did not sound at all worried. It was 8:40, the planes were still miles away, and Mr. Cherry, an equity stockbroker at Cantor Fitzgerald, was calling to thank his wife, Maryellen, again for making his favorite dinner the night before, orange roasted chicken, and to tell her how much he loved her.

That's how life had been ever since Maryellen Pitt married Stephen Cherry. The Cherrys, who lived in Stamford, Conn., had just finished building their dream house in Westchester County. Mr. Cherry, 41, had left most of the designing to his wife.

"The only thing he wanted was to have a big great room, with the kitchen and the family room and the fireplace all in one place," she said. "He always wanted to be with me while I was cooking and with the kids when they were watching TV."

Mr. Cherry was a serious singer in his spare time—"soft-rock country blues," his wife called the style—who led his own band and played in local clubs.

Last summer he took his warm, rich voice down to Nashville and made a CD. It was never publicly released, but, "Every morning when we get in the car, my 6-year-old asks to hear Daddy's CD," Ms. Cherry said, "and Mommy's up in the front seat with tears in her eyes. But he doesn't see that."

VERNON CHERRY
The Wedding Singer

It is the singing, more than anything else, that keeps Vernon Cherry so vivid in their minds. A Brooklyn firefighter who moonlighted as a wedding singer, Firefighter Cherry, 49, sang it all and he sang it everywhere: Barry White in the firehouse, Frank Sinatra at weddings, the national anthem at Fire Department promotion ceremonies.

"He would just sing," said Raymond Thomas, a firefighter who worked with him for 11 years at Ladder Com-

pany 118 in Brooklyn Heights. "He would be walking up the stairs, in the locker room, taking a shower. He had such a beautiful voice. I used to ask him: 'Sing me a song, Vernon. Vernon, sing 'Always and Forever.' He wouldn't do the whole song, just short bits and pieces."

Firefighter Cherry, a 28-year veteran of the Fire Department, was known at Ladder 118 as Vernon Mo, because he called everybody else "Mo." And there was his lasagna, "Lasagna Mo."

"He put mushrooms in it," Firefighter Thomas said. "He used every pot in the firehouse. We tried to discourage him from cooking. I mean we loved it, but he had to use every pot in the house."

NESTOR CHEVALIER
Inseparable Brothers

Nestor Chevalier always let his kid brother, Maurice, tag along. Though the brothers were five years apart, they were inseparable growing up in Washington Heights. They worked out together at the gym, and danced to salsa at the nightclubs. They even moved out of their mother's house into an apartment of their own in the neighborhood.

"We were the best of friends," Maurice said. "We did everything together."

Nestor Chevalier, 30, verified trades at Cantor Fitzgerald and had planned to marry his girlfriend of nine years, Lillian Fermin, in October 2001. He loved to tell stories about his life, often exaggerating the details for even bigger laughs. He found a rapt audience in his family and friends. In August, Maurice took Nestor to a salsa club to celebrate his big brother's birthday. Maurice danced all night.

"I miss him dearly," Maurice said.

SWEDE JOSEPH CHEVALIER
Not Going Halfway

What is the point . . .

. . . of doing something if not all the way?

So at 10, Swede Joseph Chevalier plants pumpkin seeds, then sells his harvest to nursery schools around Middletown, N.J.

At 16, he starts a landscaping business that he keeps going by commuting home weekends from Cornell, and throughout his time at Cantor Fitzgerald, where he was, at 26, an assistant equities trader.

Don't just join a fraternity: be president for two years and then get inducted into Cornell's honor society for campus leaders.

Don't just admire cars: trade up four in six years and drive them too fast.

Don't sit back and watch sports: fling yourself at them,

Firefighter Bill Englund tends to the memorial at Engine 24 and Ladder 5 at Houston Street and the Avenue of the Americas in lower Manhattan. (*Krista Niles*)

especially speed-and-thrill ones like ice hockey and mountain biking.

Do define crash-dieting as a day fueled by 10 puny power bars, and a dinner that begins with lasagna, hamburgers, sausage and chicken and keeps on going.

Do choose a favorite song from a new CD, play it loudly, over and over, until everyone sings it in their sleep, regardless of whether they actually like it.

Do be overprotective of your mother, Elaine; sisters, Tylia and Brittany; girlfriend, Melissa Markewich.

Gamble big. Lend happily. Love fully. Never sit still.

ALEX CHIANG
A Morning Serenader

As teenagers, John and Grace Chiang had never slept in on weekends. Every Saturday morning at 7 A.M., their father, Alex Chiang, would sing hymns at the top of his voice in the kitchen to wake them and his wife, Sunny. If no one stirred after 10 minutes, he would walk into each bedroom to perform.

"We would say, 'Get out, Dad,' and he would only try to sing louder and louder until we got up," John said. "I complained about it all the time. Now I miss it."

Alex Chiang, 51, and his family traveled from their home in New City, N.Y., to Franklin Park, N.J., every Saturday to meet with other members of the nondenominational church that he helped found more than a decade ago. The Chiangs would stay the night with others and return home on Sunday evening.

"He's a very faithful person," his wife said.

Mr. Chiang, a computer specialist at Marsh & McLennan, treated other church members with such kindness, said Paul Du, a close friend, that more than 1,200 people came to his memorial service in October.

After John Chiang, 22, moved into a sparsely furnished Manhattan apartment as a young banker, he seldom visited his parents. "So on Labor Day weekend, my dad enticed me home by promising that he would bring me to Ikea," John said. "We bought a lot of heavy stuff. He dropped me off in my apartment, and then he was gone."

That was the last he saw of his father. Now John has moved back in with his mother.

DOROTHY CHIARCHIARO
A Kiss for Christmas

It was Christmas Eve, 1962, and Nick Chiarchiaro was concluding a visit to his Aunt Betty in Park Slope, Brooklyn. He gave his cousin, Rose, a peck on the cheek—when skinny Dorothy Arguelles, her friend, piped up:

"Aren't you going to give me a Christmas kiss, too?"

The reply that first sprang to mind was no. He barely knew her and had never given her a thought. But politely, he leaned over. Aiming for her cheek, he hit her lips—and was hit by lightning.

"My knees buckled," he said. "I left the house, I didn't know where I was going. I just knew I had to be with her."

Three months later—heart pounding—he asked her out. They went to a tiny cocktail lounge, on Love Lane in Brooklyn Heights, and ordered brandies. A year later, after Mr. Chiarchiaro asked her mother's permission, they were engaged.

During the 37 years that followed, he rarely experienced an hour of boredom. "Movies, dinners, friends," he said. Three children. For her, a job at Fred Alger Management—to pay for clothes filling four bedroom closets. And a constant game of sparring. They argued, he said, about everything.

"That's what kept us going. We were oil and water, black and white. In public, she called me Mr. Moroney—short for moron. The neighbor girls called us the Bickersons."

"Kind," he said, thinking of words to characterize her. "Considerate. And cantankerous."

LUIS CHIMBO
The Love of Her Life

Ana Chimbo is having trouble starting a new life without the love of her life for 20 years. Her husband, Luis, worked as a receiving attendant at Windows on the World.

"I have to let him go," Mrs. Chimbo said, sobbing. "It doesn't matter that I don't want to. But I have to."

Their 12-year-old son, Luis Eduardo, is having trouble, too. He refuses to acknowledge his father's death. He will not speak about it. He just goes to school, comes home, and plays a brutal computer wrestling game for hours.

"When I tell him to stop, he tells me I don't love him."

Mr. Chimbo, 39, of East Elmhurst, Queens, was the center of the world for his wife and son. He played, bicycled and played basketball with his son. While she was pregnant with their son, he left Ecuador to set up a new life for the family in New York. After the boy was born, he brought his family to New York. "We were so happy," Mrs. Chimbo said.

"He makes me dream," Mrs. Chimbo said. "I told him please don't go. He said, 'Don't cry anymore and let me go.' I tell him that I can't. I tell him if he goes to that place he will never come back."

ROBERT CHIN
A Cheery Morning Greeting

When Suk Tan Chin posted an inquiry about her younger brother, Robert, on the Web site of Fiduciary Trust, one reply in particular touched her heart. A woman said the two had not known each other, but from the photograph she recognized the young man who had passed by her daily, with an open smile and a ringing "Good morning!"

Robert Chin, a Xerox employee who worked at Fiduciary, was a sweet man—enthusiastic, helpful, a touch naïve. He didn't need a lot to be satisfied. At 33 and single, he lived in Brooklyn with his parents, Chinese immigrants whom he supported. He was devoted to them, and to baseball.

"Robert loved playing outfield," his sister recalled, "because to him that was freedom." And he had another great passion: karaoke. He was a weekend regular at the Point After, a Brooklyn sports bar that features the sing-alongs. Mr. Chin was an admirer of Billy Joel and the Police; he loved belting out Neil Diamond's "America."

For the last few Saturday nights, his buddy of 20 years, Billy Tsevdos, said in October, friends have been holding candlelight vigils for Mr. Chin outside the bar. "Then we go inside and sing," he said.

EDDIE WING WAI CHING
Actions Spoke Loud

He was the Cool Man.

Outwardly, he always seemed so phlegmatic. He did not talk much. He did not reveal his emotions. If anything, when you spoke to him, he would send you a stern look. But inside, Eddie Wing Wai Ching was the exact opposite—all warmth. So his family nicknamed him Cool Man.

Since Mr. Ching, 29, was the youngest of four, his relatives also liked to call him Ah-B, Chinese for baby. In truth, though, he was mature beyond his years. He had clear-cut goals of owning a home, establishing a successful career and raising a family. He had already bought a home in New Jersey when he was 27, and his intention was to propose marriage to his girlfriend by the end of the year.

As a client support administrator for UmeVoice, one of his clients was Cantor Fitzgerald, and he was at its office on Sept. 11.

To keep in shape, he liked to play basketball every week. His motto, on and off the court, was the old standard "Action speaks louder than words."

As his half sister, Patricia Liu, put it: "You would ask him a favor and he wouldn't answer you. But then he'd go ahead and do just what you asked him."

JOHN CHIPURA
For Camaraderie's Sake

After a 1981 stint in Beirut with the United States Marines, John Chipura wanted to serve the city of his birth by becoming a New York City policeman, and rose through the ranks for more than a decade to the rank of detective.

But Mr. Chipura yearned for the camaraderie of the firehouse; his brother, Gerard, was a fireman, as their father, Anthony, had been. In August, 1998, Mr. Chipura achieved his dream.

Thus it was that on Tuesday, after the terrorist attack, suiting up with Ladder Company 105 on Dean Street in Brooklyn, that John Chipura phoned his fiancée, Gina DeFalco, to ask if she had any news of his sister Nancy, who worked in the World Trade Center.

"There wasn't any news," said Ms. DeFalco, "but later, when I heard that Nancy was safe, I called John to tell him. But his ladder company had already left." John Chipura and the five other firefighters in the truck have not been heard from since.

Gerard Chipura, who survived, waits along with Ms. DeFalco, who refuses to give up hope; she and Firefighter Chipura planned to marry on Oct. 27.

"The only good thing," she said, "is that he is with the guys he worked with, and loved."

PETER CHIRCHIRILLO
A Mr. Fix-It

If Peter Chirchirillo did not care for you, he would be nice and polite. But if he really loved you, his wife said, poor you.

Mr. Chirchirillo, 47, a project manager with Marsh USA, had a knack for showing his affection in exuberant ways, his wife, Clara Chirchirillo, said. For a favorite cousin, he bought a welcome mat he put out any time she came to visit. "Go Away," it read. For large weekend gatherings of family or friends at his home, he would set at least five alarm clocks for 7 P.M. and when they all rang, he would announce: "It's time to go home, everybody. Get out."

His wife of 21 years explained, "He liked to torture people." But she said her husband was really a teddy bear. He was a regular Mr. Fix-It, always ready to help, she said. He was sentimental, and "my feelings always came first."

Lieutenant Fred Scholl of the Rescue 3 unit of the New York Fire Department takes a break at a temporary dining room at ground zero. (*Edward Keating*)

Eight years ago, he agreed to move his family from his native Canarsie, Brooklyn, to Langhorne, Pa., for a safer environment for his two sons, Michael, 18, and Nick, 14. That meant a four-hour round-trip commute to his office at the World Trade Center. Mrs. Chirchirillo said her sons were following in their father's footsteps.

"If I walk out, they lock the door and they make sure I don't have the keys with me," she said.

CATHERINE ELLEN CHIRLS
A Mother's Presence

What better tribute could a mother ask than a eulogy by her eldest child? That was the send-off for Catherine Ellen Chirls, at a memorial service in Brooklyn Heights, where her family lived for 15 years until a recent move to Princeton, N.J. The eulogy was delivered by 16-year-old Nick Chirls, the country's No. 1 squash player in his age group and his mother's partner each night when it was time to wash the dishes.

Mrs. Chirls, 47, was a banker at eSpeed. Yet at the end of her workday, and her long trip home, dinner was a special time. Best of all, her son said, was the nightly cleanup, his chore while his two younger siblings were let off the hook. His mother did most of the work, while the two talked about politics, sports, schoolwork. Once, he wondered aloud what difference it made if he got an A or a B. His mother's answer was "Never limit yourself," words that Nick said would inform the rest of his life.

So will a sparrow that joined him at the lectern on this most demanding of days. As Nick said the word "mother" the first time, the bird lighted upon his head. With hundreds of mourners gasping, the boy took the bird in his hand, then set it free.

"I'm not a religious person," he said later. "I don't believe in things like that. But there is no other explanation than that my mother was with me."

CASEY CHO
Looking Out for Mother

In the close-knit Korean-American family, the three sisters once talked about how none of them would ever want to die before their mother because of the devastation that it would cause her. But Casey Cho, the middle sister, disappeared from the 99th floor of 1 World Trade Center; now her youngest sister is trying to do what she thinks Ms. Cho would have wanted.

"I know Casey would want me to be strong," said Melissa Cho. "Casey would try to make my mother get over it."

Casey Cho, 30, shopped, traveled, wrote short stories and poems and was planning a wedding to a graphics designer next year. But she also had a strong sense of family and supported her mother, who lost her husband to a stroke seven years ago, and her oldest sister, who quit her job after becoming pregnant.

The three women, and Ms. Cho's 1-year-old nephew, lived together in New Jersey. In the summer of 2001, Casey Cho got a job doing research in the environmental claims area for Marsh & McLennan.

"She was really happy," said Melissa Cho, 24. "She never had any regrets in life."

ABUL K. CHOWDHURY
A Devoted Moviegoer

Abul K. Chowdhury and Young Kim first spotted each other in their freshman English-as-a-second-language class at the College of Staten Island. She was the willowy daughter of Korean immigrants; he was the dark-eyed younger son of a diplomat from Bangladesh. She worked as a manicurist to earn her tuition; he wanted to become a computer expert.

They began sharing the long slog by road, water and rail between school and their respective apartments. Their first kiss took place aboard the Staten Island Ferry, the Manhattan skyline in the distance.

Last April they were married, she in a long white gown, he in a tuxedo; their mothers wore traditional dress. Mr. Chowdhury, 30, had landed a job with Cantor Fitzgerald, a job he loved. He and his brother, Qaisar, cared for their parents and looked out for their four sisters. "We two brothers, we help the whole family," Qaisar Chowdhury said. "We two brothers are like two arms."

Mrs. Chowdhury taught at the College of Staten Island, and after work she would meet her husband outside the World Trade Center, the towers glowing like a pair of lanterns. Like an old married couple, they had their routines. "We loved to see movies," Mrs. Chowdhury said. "We used to enjoy the previews, and decide which ones we were going to see next."

MOHAMMAD S. CHOWDHURY
New York: The Place to Be

To Mohammad Sallahuddin Chowdhury, 38, of Queens, New York was the place to succeed—especially if you were confident, smart and very good-looking.

He was supporting his pregnant wife and 6-year-old daughter by serving banquets at Windows on the World, but that was only temporary. He had a master's degree in physics from Bangladesh, where he grew up, and had studied real estate and computer science in this country. After a few doleful years in Baltimore, he was determined to stay in New York. He knew something good would come up.

Meanwhile, he had a new baby to look forward to. It was due in September.

"If it's a boy," he told Baraheen Ashrafi, his wife, "we'll have a perfect family." On Sept. 13, Farqad Chowdhury was born—8 pounds 10 ounces, with deep black eyes like his father's. "Very expressive," said Mrs. Ashrafi. "Eyes, like he's trying to tell me something."

KIRSTEN CHRISTOPHE
Romance in an Odd Place

Romance can be ignited in the oddest places, even under the intense pressure of a bar review course, which is how Kirsten Christophe met her husband, Charles. Already a recognized expert in the field of risk management, she advised law firms on how to avoid malpractice claims. Ms. Christophe had recently moved to New York from San Francisco when they met. She spent five years working for Aon.

She left to join a competing company in Midtown Manhattan, but on Sept. 1, she returned to work at Aon, at the World Trade Center, where she had an office on the 104th floor.

During their six-year marriage, the Christophes were seldom apart, even taking business trips together. When their daughter, Gretchen Dagmar, was born last year, they brought her along, too.

Like most busy professionals, the couple, who lived in Maplewood, N.J., divided their child-care responsibilities, and it was Ms. Christophe who would put the baby to bed.

Gretchen, who turned 1 on Sept. 13, does not talk yet, but Mr. Christophe knows she misses her mother, especially in the evening.

"She cries, 'Mommy, Mommy,'" he said. "What can I say?"

PAMELA CHU
"Never Saw Her Stressed"

As a 31-year-old vice president and United States equities trader at Cantor Fitzgerald, Pamela Chu was under constant pressure.

"I never saw her stressed out," said her close friend Christiana Yu, "but she told me about customers barking, 'This is what I want. Don't sell too low. Don't buy too high.' And there was a lot of trading going at one time. And she was the only female trader and only Asian in her department, and that was difficult, but she seemed so relaxed."

Ms. Chu was born in Korea, and with her parents she moved to the United States when she was 2. After graduating from the University of Buffalo, she started working for Cantor Fitzgerald as a temporary clerk. In recent years, she counted among her clients Ms. Yu and her husband, Edwin Chan, and often joined them for dinner and weekend trips.

Last May, Ms. Chu moved from her parents' home in Queens to a recently renovated rental apartment five minutes from her office. By doing that, she said, she could get to work by 6:30 A.M.

CHRISTOPER CIAFARDINI
A Blind Love for His Job

From his older brother Dominic's vantage point, Christopher Ciafardini was "the ultimate stimulus junkie."

At the age of 9, his fascination with bicycling inspired him to complete a 100-mile race. Then he quit biking and fixated on comics and becoming a cartoonist. During his weight-lifter phase, he presented his mother with a subscription to *Muscle & Fitness* magazine one Mother's Day as a way of sharing his hobby du jour; she was thrilled when he outgrew it.

Studying was never a forte until college, when his attention turned to finance. To the family's surprise, Mr. Ciafardini found a passion that stuck and carried him through graduate school at Cornell University into a real-life version of his favorite film, *Wall Street*. He and his friends began living out a game called "Who Retires First?"

Last spring, Mr. Ciafardini, 30, joined Fred Alger Management as a financial analyst, and in August was promoted to vice president. He had a closet full of Brooks Brothers suits he could not wait to jump into each weekday morning

and had just gotten his first passport, a hint that international finance was his next niche.

"He was one of those typical Wall Street guys who worked 18-hour days and loved it," said Dominic Ciafardini. "It wasn't just a job to him; it was his identity."

ALEX CICCONE
Friendly Rivalry

Alex Ciccone was a very big fan of the New York Mets. His wife, Stephanie, whom he met on a blind date in the late 1980s, came from a family that loved the Yankees. "That was a problem," she said. "We had a lot of fun with that."

Mr. Ciccone, 38, was a vice president at Marsh Inc., the insurance brokerage subsidiary of Marsh & McLennan Companies. With a staff of eight, he was a rising star. "I had a conversation with one of my bosses about a month before Sept. 11," said Bruce Pepchinsky, who was Mr. Ciccone's boss for four years. "The strong indication was that Alex would be promoted to senior vice president. He was a great problem solver, an executive who treated his staff as students as opposed to a big bad boss."

When he was not putting in 12- or 13-hour days at work, Mr. Ciccone loved to hang out in his yard in New Rochelle, N.Y., with his son, Stephen, 6, and his daughter, Julia, 5.

He was also a big Bruce Springsteen fan. But Annette Casarella, his sister, associates her brother with another recording artist. "He wore out a 45 record of 'Lean on Me,' by Bill Withers," she said. "When we were little I can remember his playing it over and over and over. Last summer, before this happened, we talked about how much he loved that song."

ELAINE CILLO
Photographs to Remember

Elaine Cillo loved to take pictures. Her two-bedroom apartment in Bensonhurst, Brooklyn, might as well be a photo gallery, with pictures even crowding the walls in the bathroom. There are photographs of the Brooklyn and Verrazano-Narrows Bridges, of apples in a basket, of autumn leaves in upstate New York. She had a beautiful shot of the Eiffel Tower.

Elaine's twin sister, Lynne Cillo-Capaldo, was looking at the photos after Sept. 11 with her husband, Paul Capaldo. Elaine Cillo, 40, a vice president at Marsh Technology and Information Service, worked on the 97th floor of the north tower.

Over the summer, the sisters and Mr. Capaldo vacationed in Greece. Ms. Cillo-Capaldo said her husband got a great picture of Elaine: it showed the camera buff taking a photo.

EDNA CINTRON
Her Courage and Strength

For Edna Cintron and her husband, William, every evening fit into a comforting routine.

"She had everything prompt, clean, neat, organized," Mr. Cintron, a 44-year-old doorman, said of his 46-year-old wife, an administrative assistant for Marsh & McLennan. "She would come out of work, come home, cook, make sure that when I would come out of work there was food on the table and everything. And every night we would have ice cream and we would watch TV."

That simple routine in their home in East Elmhurst, Queens, was remarkable, Mr. Cintron said, because they each had been homeless, and in their 12 years of marriage they had struggled with his alcoholism.

"We started from the bottom," he said, "and we worked our way all the way up to the top," even opening a florist business, Sweet William's, in East Harlem.

Mr. Cintron said that his wife had given him the courage to go to detox and that last January he celebrated 12 years of sobriety. "She made sure that she kept me in check," he said. "She made sure that I did the things I was supposed to do. She was a very, very strong woman because she would put her foot down.

"She was more like a mother to me. She would make sure that I would eat right and she would make sure that no one would manipulate me. So she was also my backbone. She made me strong. She made me who I am today."

NESTOR A. CINTRON III
Hooked on Books

"I just want books, Ma," Nestor A. Cintron III would say.

Growing up in the Alfred E. Smith Houses in a tough part of the Lower East Side, Mr. Cintron was the resident intellectual.

"My son didn't take any drugs; he had no bad habits; his thing was reading," his mother, Alicia Leguillow, recalled. "For Christmas, I would get him $200 gift certificates to Borders and he would buy books."

Mr. Cintron, 26, a broker at Cantor Fitzgerald, read anything, but preferred books that were otherworldly: Carl Sagan, Michael Crichton and Robert Jordan were his favorite writers. He was a huge *Star Wars* buff.

Relief workers observe a moment of silence during an October 7 prayer service at the site of the World Trade Center, nearly four weeks after the terrorist attack there. (*Tony Gutierrez*)

He got his two younger brothers hooked, too, to the point where they would all sit at the dinner table reading. "They were never raised by a father, so they had each other," Mr. Cintron's mother said.

Ms. Leguillow knew her son was gifted from childhood, when a teacher at Public School 1 insisted on skipping him from the fourth to the sixth grade, because he was so far ahead in math. But he was still one of the guys.

"He had so much intelligence, he didn't need to show it," said his brother Fred Gonzalez Jr.

JUAN CISNEROS
Grand Plans for the Future

Juan Cisneros never intended to spend the rest of his life in New York. He would work as a bond trader until he could pay off his college loans and put away money for his parents. Then, said his girlfriend, Stephanie Albert, they planned to move out West. They would go to graduate school and become professors. He would teach history, she would teach English.

Mr. Cisneros, 24, who lived in Manhattan, was gentle and patient. He loved running and reading.

"You're going to do what?" Ms. Albert asked him, incredulous, when he told her he was taking a job at Cantor Fitzgerald. His parents had emigrated from Guatemala when he was 6. He went to Dartmouth College, volunteered as a Big Brother and fell in love with Ms. Albert.

One Saturday afternoon in August 2001, they found themselves in New Jersey, having offered to help a friend set up for her husband's 40th birthday party. Alone in a room with a view of Manhattan, they began dancing. They were joking, teasing, making grand plans for how they would celebrate each other's 40th when the time came.

"Thrilled with the present, excited about the future," Ms. Albert remembered sadly. "And it absolutely takes my breath away that we won't even be able to spend our 25th birthdays together."

BENJAMIN KEEFE CLARK
He Made a Mean Meat Loaf

Cooking in the Marines is not what one might think of as the best preparation for an executive chef.

But for Benjamin Keefe Clark, being a leatherneck chef was his springboard to some classes at the Cordon Bleu cooking school and finally to Sodexho, a food services company that cooked for employees at Fiduciary

Trust in 2 World Trade Center. Mr. Clark was famous for his soups and meat loaf.

Mr. Clark, 39, and known as Keefe, was last seen on the 88th floor helping a woman with three other men, according to his wife, La-Shawn. None of them survived. His son, Chaz, 17, saw the attack on the two towers from Stuyvesant High School, where he is a student.

Chaz, his three brothers and one sister would often get their parents to have a bake-off, always enjoying the results but only rarely declaring their mother the victor.

Mrs. Clark still dials Mr. Clark's office number, waiting to talk to him. They met on the subway platform at Penn Station; Mr. Clark offered to escort his future wife home late one night.

He called and sent flowers for months after, until he finally won her undivided attention. "We were so close that everybody said we looked like brother and sister," she said.

EUGENE CLARK
From the Terrace

In life, Eugene Clark observed the three D's: dance, drama and divas.

He started early: Roberta Flack was his music teacher in Washington during the 1960s. He could sing like Jennifer Holliday in the musical *Dreamgirls,* he could emote like Norma Desmond in *Sunset Boulevard* and he danced "like Tina Turner," said Larry Courtney, Mr. Clark's partner for the last 13 years. "And he had legs almost as good."

For the last four years, the couple lived in a two-story rooftop apartment on 42nd Street, with a sweeping view of the neon canyons and the bustle of Times Square. It was not that Mr. Clark did not enjoy his work at Aon Corporation, where he was an administrative assistant, but he loved his life away from the office.

He adored *Miss Saigon* and *Les Miserables,* cooked southern-style fried cabbage, and collected Waterford crystal decanters and vases. And then, there was what they called "the Terrace." Mr. Clark, 47, converted the apartment's 10-foot-by-24-foot concrete-slab patio into a thriving terrace garden, laying in latticework and a fountain. He potted red hibiscus plants, geraniums in hanging baskets, miniature cedar trees, and yellow and burgundy hollyhocks.

From the terrace, guests at their annual New Year's Eve parties could watch the ball drop in Times Square. Mr. Courtney, who has three children from when he was married, said they came to love Mr. Clark as a family member.

Mr. Courtney's daughter, Heather, 28, joined them on a gay rights march in Washington in 1993, carrying a sign that read, "I'm proud of my gay dad and my new step-queen."

GREGORY A. CLARK
A Sailor and a Gentleman

For months, the shy young Japanese woman working at the snack stand at the United States naval base in Yokohama knew Gregory A. Clark as "pizza man," the name she had given him because he always ordered the same thing.

It was the summer of 1987, and by the time that fall came, they had begun dating. Eventually, the handsome petty officer second class left the Navy and the couple married, moved to New Jersey and had four children, who are now between the ages of 5 and 11.

Mr. Clark, 40, was a computer technician for Cantor Fitzgerald.

Yuka Clark, the shy young woman who is now his widow, has written him a letter: "Gregory, you were like an angel. You always made people feel so warm with your kindness and thoughtfulness, wherever you went. You rarely demanded for yourself; you were like a selfless saint. You had so much class and you were a true gentleman and you made us feel so proud. You loved children so much and gave and gave endlessly. Your smile and happy memories will never be forgotten. You will live in our hearts forever and ever."

THOMAS R. CLARK
The Family Hug Lives On

"Big hugs!" is how Thomas R. Clark used to announce his arrivals home to his wife, Lisa—a prelude to wrapping his arms around her. When their only son, Matthew, now 2, grew old enough to speak, he asked for a piece of the action. "Me too," he'd squeal, smiling. Soon, Mr. Clark changed his opening line to "Family hugs!"

In the weeks after Matthew and the new arrival, Whitney, a girl, were born, Mr. Clark insisted on sleeping with them nuzzled up against his chest.

Saturday mornings were set aside for Mr. Clark and Matthew to breakfast together. Father and son would pick up cocoa and pastries at Dunkin' Donuts, then sit and watch the trains pass through the Summit, N.J., station.

Mr. Clark walked home from that station every day, returning from his job at Sandler O'Neill & Partners, where he was an equity sales trader. In the summer, when Matthew would play in front of the house, he could see his smiling father from halfway down the block, so he would run to him and jump into his arms. This is how the family hug became a tradition with variations.

"We still do it, the three of us," Mrs. Clark said, "and my son still smiles. He loves it."

Mr. Clark was 37.

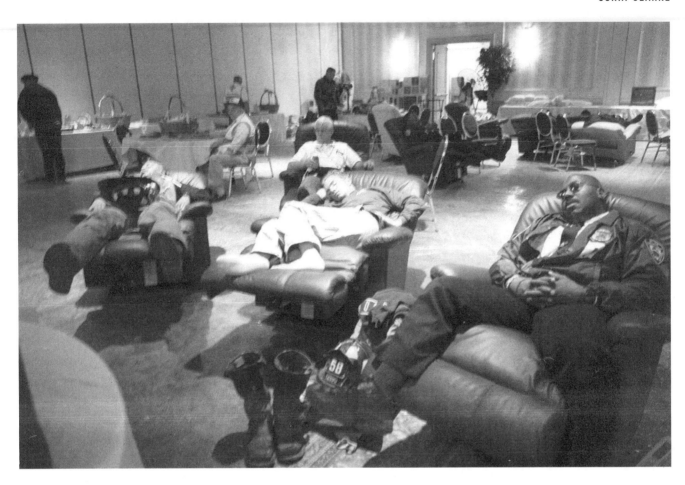

Workers cleaning up the attack site use the Marriott Financial Center Hotel, which was damaged in the collapse of the World Trade Center towers and closed to business, for rest, meals, massages and counseling. They call this area the Oasis Room. (*Edward Keating*)

MICHAEL CLARKE
Born for a Fire Truck

Jack Clarke may have been a New York City police officer, but from the very beginning his youngest son, Michael, had this affinity for firefighting.

"When he was young, he just loved to sit in the engines at the firehouse," said Michael Clarke's father, who remembers giving his son that bright red fire truck he pedaled around in.

And so, even though he became a top student at Wagner College and a star on the hockey team, it was not a surprise to his father when Michael Clarke joined the Fire Department in 1998. Firefighter Clarke, 27, was delighted in 2001 to be transferred from Staten Island to Engine 8 and Ladder 2 on East 51st Street in Manhattan, "because there was much more action in Manhattan," his father said.

Sept. 11 was a scheduled day off; Firefighter Clarke went to work because he had switched days with another firefighter.

Now, at Wagner College, they have retired Michael Clarke's hockey number—34. His father misses those regular phone calls from him, the ones that came to mean so much more after Jack Clarke's wife, Eileen, died three years ago.

"He'd call every day," the father recalls. "And he'd say, 'Hi, Pop. How you doing?' "

SURIA CLARKE
Sunny, Vivacious, Irreverent

Suria Clarke's first name means "the shining one" or "the sun" in Sanskrit, and it was as if her whole life was about living the promise of her name.

She was tall and vivacious, and somehow "she never went unnoticed," said her friend Selinde Dulckeit.

She was also "quite irreverent, whether she was talking to

the C.E.O. of a company or the mailman," Ms. Dulckeit said. The two women knew each other in Brussels, where they lived before they both moved to New York. When Ms. Clarke died, she had just started a job as a vice president for media relations at eSpeed, at the World Trade Center.

Ms. Clarke, 30, had an appetite for life, for food, for wine. On a trip to Italy with Ms. Dulckeit, the two friends fell in love with the local Tuscan wine. Ms. Clarke just had to have some to take home to Brooklyn Heights. So they bought two huge bottles of wine, almost 90 liters.

But when they got home they had to find a way to decant it. They needed 90 empty bottles. So they started drinking. "We had to drink a lot of wine," remembered Ms. Dulckeit.

KEVIN FRANCIS CLEARY
A Love of the Stage

For some film buffs, it is enough to just watch and be amazed by actors. Kevin Francis Cleary, however, decided that he would rather be one of them, and maybe one day be as good as his idol, Paul Newman. So three years ago, Mr. Cleary, a stockbroker for Euro Brokers, which had offices in 2 World Trade Center, became Kevin Cleary, the part-time theater actor.

"It was so amazing that here he was 38 and starting a second career," Cate Cleary said of her brother. Fresh from a recent production of *Waiting Station,* Mr. Cleary was gearing up to play Lenny in *Of Mice and Men.*

"He worked all day then rehearsed all night for his productions," his sister said. "Twenty-four hours just never seemed to be enough for him."

Ever the thrill seeker, Mr. Cleary took time every year for exotic trips to places like Vietnam, Cuba, Thailand and, most recently, Tuscany.

JIM CLEERE
"Good Man." Good Voice.

That October night in 1977, Jean Rieger, a divorced mother with a 10-year-old daughter, got down on her knees and prayed to God to send her "a good man" to marry.

When she got up, the phone rang. On the other end was Jim Cleere, whom she had met a year earlier. He was a divorced father of two sons, ages 12 and 10.

They married in March 1978.

Mr. Cleere, vice president of Seabury & Smith, was in New York Sept. 11 for a meeting at the insurance brokerage firm on the 96th floor of 1 World Trade Center. Mr. Cleere, 55, was across the street at the Marriott Hotel when the first plane struck the north tower. He called his wife at her office

in Newton, Iowa. They were on the phone after the second plane struck the south tower.

"He said he was O.K. and would be coming home," said Jean Cleere. "That was our last conversation." Mrs. Cleere says her husband was a man of faith. "He had a deep, rich baritone and sang all the time," she said.

She loved that voice of his. That's why she hasn't changed her answering machine tape. It has Mr. Cleere's voice on it.

STEVEN COAKLEY
The Florida Life

Steven Coakley, a firefighter with Engine Company 217 in Bedford-Stuyvesant, Brooklyn, had just finished a full shift and was preparing to leave the station house when the alarm rang on Sept. 11.

Working long hours was not unusual for him. Mr. Coakley, 36, would often work back-to-back shifts for two weeks so that he could spend the rest of the month either boating or at his house in Madeira Beach, Fla., near St. Petersburg. He liked life in Florida so much that he planned to retire and live there full time.

"He had just a few years to go," said Linda New, who had been dating Mr. Coakley for about a year. "He used to say, '41 and done.'"

He cherished his time off, but being a firefighter was also a passion.

"He liked working at the firehouse in Bed-Stuy," Ms. New said. "It was an A house, with a lot of action."

Ms. New said Firefighter Coakley never talked much about the dangerous parts of his job, but would tell stories about the lighter aspects. "He delivered five babies," she said. "Two to the same mother, but at different times."

A man who did not waste words, Firefighter Coakley worked hard and played hard. "Steve was really pretty young," said John Kauzlarich, a friend in Florida. "It wasn't easy to keep up with him."

JEFFREY COALE
Dreams of a Restaurant

His dream started when he was in college. He wanted to own a restaurant.

Training in cooking and restaurant management helps, but so does money. So Jeffrey Coale went at it methodically. He worked for a number of years as a government bond trader. At night, he attended classes at the French Culinary Institute.

He quit trading and took a job as an apprentice chef at the Louis XV restaurant in Monte Carlo. Next, he returned to New York to work at the Alain Ducasse restaurant. Wanting to refine his understanding of the wine side of the business, he then took a job as an assistant wine master at Windows on the World.

Meanwhile, Mr. Coale, 31, sifted around for a location for his restaurant. He looked at several properties in Greece and New York. He had not settled on the style of cuisine.

"He left really good money to make $10 an hour at Windows," said Leslie Brown, his sister. "But Jeff never settled for something. He followed his passion."

In recent weeks, reflecting on that devotion, two friends switched to jobs that better suited their own true interests. Two other friends broke off unsatisfying relationships.

In memory of Mr. Coale, they are going to follow their passions.

DANIEL M. COFFEY and JASON M. COFFEY
Like Father, Like Son

On Sept. 11, Daniel M. Coffey, top, and his son Jason M. Coffey planned to meet for lunch at the World Trade Center, where they both worked for subsidiaries of Marsh & McLennan. Daniel Coffey, 54, needed to have his wedding ring enlarged after 30 years of marriage. Jason Coffey, 25, was going along to pick out a surprise engagement ring for his fiancée, Colleen McDonald.

Daniel Coffey, a senior vice president at Guy Carpenter & Company, worked on the 94th floor of 1 World Trade Center. Jason, a senior accountant at Marsh Inc., was on the 98th floor. Daniel Coffey was the son and grandson of an only child and part of a family that has lived for generations in Newburgh, N.Y.

He and his wife, Francis, broke the mold with three sons, Daniel, Jason and Kevin. Daniel Coffey met his wife when she was trying to fix him up with her friend. One of his gifts was gab.

"Dad could talk to virtually anyone and get anything he wanted out of them," said his son Daniel. With his wife, the elder Coffey was fixing up the house in Newburgh.

"My mother is very particular about what she wants done, and my father was particular in how he did it," young Daniel said.

Jason Coffey was a big guy who loved to play rugby. (His mother did not want him to play football. Too dangerous.) He was also always ready to go out, including to a local bar, Pineapple Larry's.

But now he was settling down. He was in the process of buying his grandparents' house in Newburgh and he and

Ms. McDonald were going to fix it up, just as his father and mother did to their house.

Jason Coffey and Ms. McDonald had planned to be married on Dec. 7, 2002.

FLORENCE G. COHEN
A Guide Through the Maze

The offices of the New York State Department of Taxation and Finance on the 86th floor of 2 World Trade Center could be a baffling wonderland, with all the various kinds of tax returns processed and audited there. But luckily there was Florence G. Cohen, a longtime clerical worker in the sales tax department, to show the way.

"She was very helpful with people," said a colleague, Geraldine Howard-Outlaw. "She knew not only the sales tax, but all the other departments she had worked in."

Her daughter Joyce said: "She was extremely generous. She would give people the shirt off her back." Ms. Cohen, 62, loved to go to the theater.

"She had wanted to see *The Producers,* but she didn't get a chance," her daughter said. And Ms. Cohen, who was a widow, loved to travel, because "she liked to have fun and visit places and see different things," Mrs. Howard-Outlaw said. One of her favorite destinations was Las Vegas, not for the gambling, her colleague said, "but for the scenery and the atmosphere."

She had even thought about moving there permanently, once her work with taxes was done.

KEVIN S. COHEN
Friends Everywhere

When Kevin S. Cohen was 4, his family moved to a new house in Edison, N.J. Rather than being daunted by the move, little Kevin, the youngest of two boys, set out to make new friends. Soon, he was standing at his front door pointing to all the houses where he had made a friend.

"He would point with his little hands and say, 'That's my friend across the street, and that's my friend from next door, and that's my other friend from that house,'" said his mother, Marcia Cohen. "And then, he never changed. He was like a mother that way. You know how children leave home and then it's the mother who brings them together year after year? Well, it was like that with my son. He had friends from all over. He was very compassionate, a lot of fun. He loved people, and people loved him back."

On Aug. 17, 2001, Mr. Cohen, 28, who worked at Cantor Fitzgerald, took his parents to dinner at a fancy Italian restaurant to celebrate their 36th wedding anniversary. Mrs.

Cohen was reluctant at first because she figured he would be tired on a Friday, after working all week. But he insisted.

"Kevin was so proud that he could take us to a nice place like that and take out his credit card and pay by himself," Mrs. Cohen said. "He thought we had never been there before, but we had. We just didn't tell him."

MARK COLAIO and STEPHEN COLAIO
Together, Start to Finish

There are countless ways to encapsulate Mark and Stephen Colaio, but the T-shirts do it in three words. The brothers owned matching shirts that they wore every chance they got. On the front was inscribed, "Life Is Good."

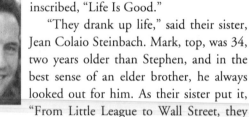

"They drank up life," said their sister, Jean Colaio Steinbach. Mark, top, was 34, two years older than Stephen, and in the best sense of an elder brother, he always looked out for him. As their sister put it, "From Little League to Wall Street, they were best friends."

Mark Colaio was a senior managing director and ran the agency desk at Cantor Fitzgerald, and he recruited his brother to work with him as a broker.

Granted, they had their distinctive sides. Stephen Colaio, for instance, adored the song "Rapper's Delight" by the Sugar Hill Gang, and knew it by heart.

Then there was that hair thing with Mark Colaio. One day last summer, he and his father, Victor, were getting their hair cut. They decided to opt for pretty short. In an impromptu moment, they decided to go the limit and shaved their heads entirely. They announced that shaved heads would henceforth become a summer ritual.

Family was paramount to the brothers Colaio. Mark Colaio lived with his wife, June, and two children, Delaney, 3, and Joseph, 22 months, in TriBeCa. Stephen Colaio, who was engaged, lived a few blocks away. So did their sister.

One recent night, Victor Colaio told his daughter, "I lost my beautiful sons, but I lost my two best friends. That's how I feel about it. They were my best friends."

CHRISTOPHER COLASANTI
The Best Way to Know God

One phrase in a book on grieving that someone gave her after her husband, Christopher Colasanti, was killed in the World Trade Center attack has stayed with Kelly Colasanti: "The best way to know God is to love many things."

She and her two daughters went to Liberty State Park, where a memorial wall has been set up for victims, and she wrote, "Chris loved many things. We love you. We miss you. You're with us."

It is a small tribute to the love of her life, to the end of what friends and neighbors often cited as the perfect family. Here are some of the moments and familiar details that stick in her mind: Christopher grew up in South Orange, N.J., and met Kelly in high school. They went to the prom together. He graduated from Dartmouth and became a trader at Cantor Fitzgerald. The young family lived in Hoboken.

The night before the attack, Mr. Colasanti gave their girls, Cara and Lauren, their baths. Then he showed Cara his baseball card collection.

"We'll be a strong family, the three of us," Kelly Colasanti said. "We have to live this way because he was so great. We can't let it not be great here because it was so great."

MICHEL P. COLBERT
More than a Good Résumé

Michel P. Colbert had the ideal résumé, the kind that might appear in a how-to book about résumés. A master's degree from the Wharton School at the University of Pennsylvania. A succession of lucrative jobs in Paris, London and Milan. Fluency in French and Spanish. A balanced range of interests, from photography to scuba diving.

"I have developed proprietary mathematical models for yield curve analysis, embedded basis options," he wrote, in the résumé that helped him secure a job as a high-level bond trader with Cantor Fitzgerald.

But did Mr. Colbert really talk like that? No. And does his résumé completely reflect who he was? Of course not.

Michel Colbert was, more than anything else, the only child of Raymond and Marie Colbert. The parents were so close to their son that all three lived in the same apartment building in West New York, N.J., and ate dinner together just about every other night, said Raymond Colbert. "And weekends, of course. And holidays."

He was 38 years old. His parents are both 79. And now time crawls. "Only child, you know?" said Raymond Colbert. "We are 16-C; he was 18-G."

KEITH COLEMAN and SCOTT COLEMAN
Three Brothers

They were as close as three brothers could be, born in 1966, 1967 and 1970. Now there is just one.

"Until Sept. 11, I have never known a day without my brothers," Todd D. Coleman, the oldest, said of Keith and Scott. "I miss them terribly."

As boys, they wrestled in their Westport, Conn., home,

had bunk beds and stole pizza off one another's plates. They went to college, to careers in finance and to satisfying romances. They dreamed of raising their children in one big family with three smart, affable uncles at the top, said their mother, Jean N. Coleman.

When Keith's equities division at Cantor Fitzgerald became wildly successful, he drafted Scott to work for him. It was there, in the 104th-floor offices at 1 World Trade Center, that Todd, 35, Keith, 34, and Scott, 31, were together for a last time in July 2001.

At a memorial service on Oct. 20, Todd told Keith's wife, Elodie, and Scott's fiancée, Jessica Nardone, that he understood why men of grace and dignity loved them so.

"I will try to live my life in a manner that will be worthy of their respect and admiration," he said. "Their memory reminds me that the world can be a wonderful place."

TAREL COLEMAN
Unbridled and Unabashed

Firefighter Tarel Coleman's friends, co-workers and football teammates called him Prozac. Not because he took the mood-balancing drug, but because sometimes he needed to calm down a little.

While many people have a childhood story involving matches, Firefighter Coleman's firebug past cost him some hair. At 5, he stuck his head into the incinerator in his family's apartment building in Queens.

"We didn't notice anything," said his brother, John Coleman Jr., also a firefighter, "until we got upstairs and saw that he had no eyebrows, no eyelashes and no hairline."

His chattiness and high-strung curiosity were viewed as charm by his friends. Whenever he prepared a lasagna dinner for his mother, Laurel Jackson, in her Jamaica, Queens, home, she would just watch her son patiently, with her head propped on her hand.

"You couldn't stop him," she said. "You had to sit there and listen."

Firefighter Coleman, 32, had an intensity that was viewed with dread by his team's opponents and by the referees of the league games he played in for the Fire Department. Everyone knew, after all, that he did not suffer bad calls gladly.

ROBERT J. COLL
Always the Peacemaker

It was perhaps inevitable that when pressures rose at work, colleagues would turn to Robert J. Coll to calm things down. Mr. Coll was born eighth out of nine children, a peacemaker amid the chaos of a big family.

"Maybe being in that position in the family made him compassionate and good with people," said Mr. Coll's older brother, Edward. "He made people feel very at ease with him."

Mr. Coll, 35, and his wife, Jennifer, led an active social life and didn't slow down even when their two children were born. They simply took the children with them, to restaurants, skiing in Stratton, Vt., and on summer trips to the beach.

Known as Woody to friends and clients because of a stubborn cowlick, Mr. Coll was a senior vice president for capital markets at Euro Brokers.

"Even though he had been successful for a while, there was really a sense that my brother was just really starting to spread his wings," Edward Coll said. "There was a transformation from being a baby brother to being one we relied on. He was starting to be a pillar in the family."

JOHN COLLINS
Future Fireman at Age 4

When John Collins was 4 years old, his father took him to a Bronx firehouse. That is when he decided what he wanted to do. It took a while, with entrance exams delayed because of a legal dispute, so he joined the Police Department first before becoming a fireman in 1990.

The oldest of five children, Mr. Collins, 42, organized family events, like two weeks each year on Long Beach Island in New Jersey, or a benefit concert on the aircraft carrier *Intrepid* in Manhattan, followed by a night on the town with his sisters and their husbands. He lived in the Bronx, lifted weights and bought groceries for neighbors who were down on their luck.

He never talked much about his work, his sister Eileen Byrne recalled, because he did not want to worry his parents.

"We teased him, said he was the only fireman who never went to a fire," she said.

That is not how they remember him at Ladder Company 25 on 77th Street. On Sept. 11, he was supposed to go to another firehouse to fill in. It was called out before he could get there. When Ladder 25 was called, he jumped on the engine.

"We had seven firemen on the rig instead of six," said another fireman, Matt O'Hanlon.

MICHAEL COLLINS
Winning Against Diabetes

Michael Collins skied and snowboarded down mountains all over the world. He went rock climbing in Japan. He rode a mountain bike, hard, on the back roads of Hawaii. Oh, and he had lived with

A woman in a Manhattan office building opposite St. Patrick's Cathedral watches a memorial service on October 9 for Assistant Chief Donald Burns, a citywide tour commander in the New York City Fire Department, who died in the attack on the World Trade Center. (*Marilynn K. Yee*)

diabetes since childhood, injecting himself with insulin three times a day.

"We would be on lift lines, and he would be checking his blood, and if he needed a shot, he would give it to himself right there," said Nina Collins, his sister-in-law.

Mr. Collins, 38, a manager with eSpeed who lived in Montclair, N.J., was even a little cavalier about his disease when he was younger, going out with the guys for beers, eating junk food. But all that changed 11 years ago, when he met his wife, Lissa, in Lake Placid, N.Y.

"He wanted to be healthy for her," said Rich Collins, his older brother. "These two were soul mates." Diabetes or not, Lissa and Michael Collins meant to grow old together.

"He would say, 'Maybe I'll be around when they cure this thing,' " she said. "We had to just keep faith." Now, she is grateful for the time they had. "I was the luckiest girl, that I could spend 11 years with him. Everyone says that I was the best thing for him, but he was the best thing for me. He was more my life support than I was his."

THOMAS COLLINS
Organizing the Weekends

It was an obvious joke, but one Thomas Collins could not resist. "Tom Collins, like the drink," he would say, introducing himself to strangers and clients at Sandler O'Neill & Partners, where he was a managing director. And when he wasn't trying to get a laugh out of someone, Mr. Collins, 36, an avid skier and outdoorsman, was busy organizing weekend adventures and outings for his friends and family.

"He was just always on," said Jennifer Hamel, his younger sister. "On Thursdays, he would start calling people, asking about the weekend: 'O.K., what are we doing this weekend, where are we going?' He loved being pulled in a million different directions."

Though Mr. Collins has been identified among the dead, Mrs. Hamel said she and her family continue to imagine him coming home, just as he did after the 1993 bombing of the World Trade Center, and telling stories about his fight to survive. "Even though I know," Mrs. Hamel said, "I keep thinking he's on a long business trip and he's going to be home soon."

JEFFREY DWAYNE COLLMAN
Happiest in Flight

Jeffrey Dwayne Collman, a flight attendant for American Airlines, had his normal flight pattern down pat: he worked the Boston-to–San Francisco route, an itinerary that linked two of his favorite cities and made for a reasonable commute home to Navato, Calif.

His presence on Flight 11 on Sept. 11 was a fluke: he had a birthday coming up on Sept. 28 and signed on for the extra trip so that he could take time off to turn 42 with a little party at home. An inspired dessert chef, he was likely planning to get creative and bake his own birthday cake.

And he didn't mind flying the extra shift: traveling was his idea of bliss. Becoming a flight attendant three and a half years ago had been the culmination of a stubborn campaign. After United turned him down, he applied to American; he was ecstatic when he was accepted on his second try.

His on-the-ground passion was tennis. The week before his death, he attended the United States Open in Queens.

"He had friends all over the world; he was a people person," said his stepmother, Kay Collman from Yorkville, Ill., his hometown.

"He'd know the life histories of his passengers after just one flight."

PATRICIA COLODNER
Family Costume Night

Patricia Colodner's world was shaped by her parents' divorce when she was just 2. So when she got married in 1990, she was determined to be the best parent she could be and offer "complete, unconditional devotion" to her family, recalled her husband, Warren.

The Colodners had two children, a 9-year-old girl and a 2-year-old boy. Mrs. Colodner, 39, who was a secretary at Marsh & McLennan, was an organized, outgoing person who created a nurturing atmosphere for the children filled with music, laughter, bicycle rides and excursions—to parks, museums, zoos, parades. She was particularly fond of Halloween, because she got to dress up with the children, and was partial to vampire getups; her daughter preferred the princess look.

On Halloween 2001, the family said, the children were still going to go trick-or-treating, but with their dad, who plans to wear a costume, too, so that he can carry on his wife's legacy. Before Sept. 11, the boy planned to dress up as a pumpkin. Now he wants to be a fireman, he says, because he wants to save his mommy.

LINDA M. COLON
Ms. Detail

Linda M. Colon was the glue at Marsh & McLennan, the person who made sure that all the logistics, the computers, the systems, the modeling, the décor—everything—were all taken care of before anyone began to complain. She was also the person who handled the relocation of the corporate headquarters from the Avenue of the Americas to the World Trade Center about a year ago.

Mrs. Colon, 46, was a senior vice president for facilities management, and she loved her job, said her sister Ivette Hernandez. Loved it so much, in fact, that she became a mentor to young people interested in the financial world.

But what Mrs. Colon, who grew up in the Bronx but lived in Perrineville, N.J., enjoyed more than anything was spending time with her husband, Robert, and two daughters, Christine, who turned 18 in December, and Tracy, who is 11.

She was especially happy that Christine had worked that last summer with her at Marsh.

RONALD COMER
Challenging Perspectives

Perhaps Ron Comer should have been an astronaut instead of an insurance executive. Pursuits that shifted conventional perspective drew him, but if he lacked a view from space, he did get to take Earth's measure from above the clouds and below the waves.

His wife, Cindy, whose first flight was with him at the controls of a Cessna when they were college students, suspected that her solitude-seeking husband flew because "only birds can be up there, not people."

Not many people in the deep, either. On a scuba vacation in Mexico in February 2001, Mr. Comer, 56, who worked at Marsh & McLennan, descended to a watery limestone otherworld the Mayans called a cenote, essentially viewing the planet from within. He told his wife it was "the dive of a lifetime."

Not all his experiments were so satisfying. He had a habit of rearranging shrubs and trees in the garden when he decided that a plant needed to be over here, say, instead of over there. Mrs. Comer had teased, "I can't go to church without coming back and a bush is gone, a tree is gone."

A favorite perspective was from the village dock at home in Northport, on Long Island, even after his daughters, Kate, 26, and Lauren, 23, no longer played in the park there. He would gaze at the birds and the boats, the water and the horizon. Mrs. Comer plans to put a bench there in his memory.

ALBERT CONDE
She "Thought He Was Safe"

At a quarter to 8 on Sept. 11, Albert Conde was on the phone with his wife as he was every morning, reporting the details of his commute from Marlboro, N.J., and promising to check in later, once he settled in to his day. When Diane Conde turned on the television at work and learned what had happened to the World Trade Center, she gasped in disbelief, not knowing that her husband, who worked at 70 Pine Street, was in 2 World Trade Center that day visiting an insurance broker.

"I thought he was safe," Mrs. Conde said. "I assumed that I was lucky."

At the Old John Street United Methodist Church in lower Manhattan on October 10, parishioners who work in the Wall Street area attend a memorial service for friends and colleagues who were killed on September 11.
(Ozier Muhammad)

At 9 P.M. that day, a friend gave her the news that Mr. Conde, 62, an avid golfer and a Roman Catholic, was among the missing. In the days since he disappeared she has tried to cling to the faith she shared for 32 years with her husband and to his own words.

"He used to tell me: 'If I die today, I'm ready. I'm at peace.' "

But peace for Mrs. Conde has not come easily, interrupted by thoughts of the milestones that were yet to come for the Conde family—son Brian's completion of graduate school, daughter Stephanie's wedding in 2002. "I just had no idea he was in that building," Mrs. Conde said.

"We were just starting to look forward to retirement. And now he's gone."

DENEASE CONLEY
Tough, with a Studious Side

The seeds of Denease Conley's toughness could be seen early on. She once had a fight with an older sister who locked herself in the bathroom, and to get her out, Denny, as she was known, threw a cherry bomb at the bathroom door.

In high school in Kansas City, she studied karate, loved Bruce Lee and even painted a poster of him on her wall. She served in the Navy for four years, and afterward became a security guard at the World Trade Center. When a supervisor taunted her by saying she was too weak to work as a firefighter, she took up his challenge and passed the qualifying exams to become a New York City firefighter. She also had a studious side, receiving a bachelor's degree in English and philosophy from Hunter College.

"Her apartment was filled with books," said her sister, Barbara Haynes. "She had a thirst for knowledge. She read everything. I called her the professional college student. And this was a child that at one time did not want to go to school."

Ms. Haynes was surprised at how many people packed the memorial service. "Several people said my sister helped save their lives," she said. "One friend said the last time he saw Denny she was holding a door open with a fireman. Knowing my sister, she had this take-charge attitude that she had to help other people get out."

SUSAN CONLON
Simple Pleasures

Susan Conlon was America's girl next door: sweet, unassuming, considerate. She was raised in Staten Island, graduated from Tottenville High School, went to work on Wall Street, married, had a daughter, loved music and sports and was always there at family gatherings with her stuffed mushrooms and laughter.

At 41, she still adored simple things—the ferry crossings, the lacquered harbor, the white butterfly sails in summer, the flaming winter sunsets, the panoramas from her 81st-floor aerie at the Bank of America at 1 World Trade Center, and quiet evenings at home with her husband, John, and Kimberly, 6.

Recalling all this, and more—her walkathons for diabetes, her steadiness under pressure, their afternoons together at Willowbrook Park, her mother, Vera Clancy, paid her a golden maternal tribute:

"She wasn't a person who needed a lot of material things to make her happy. She was like a good friend to me."

And she remembered their last conversation: "She called me that morning and said, 'You won't believe it but a plane hit my building.' I thought it was just a small plane. She said the elevators weren't running, and she was hoping to be able to walk down. Then she said they were calling her, and she had to leave, and that was the last I heard."

MARGARET CONNER
Sailing Toward Renewal

When Margaret Conner wanted to escape the chaos of everyday life, she fled her home in Bay Ridge, Brooklyn, and headed for her daughter's boat on Candlewood Lake in Brookfield, Conn. It did not matter that Mrs. Conner was prone to seasickness and could not swim. Sailing on the lake brought her peace and tranquillity.

Back home, Mrs. Conner, 57, was the gatekeeper at Cantor Fitzgerald, a receptionist who was the first person people saw when they got off the elevator on the 103rd floor of 1 World Trade Center. For many young women at the office, she was a relationship therapist.

"She was just very open and very eager to be there for anyone," said her daughter, Corrine Bounty.

Mrs. Conner and her husband, Frank Conner, were married for 13 years and spent nearly every moment of their free time together, often frequenting Broadway plays and dining out. Every day they recorded and watched Mrs. Conner's favorite soap opera, *The Young and the Restless*.

Mrs. Conner was also committed to her daily Bible study. On Sept. 11 her study passage was about the healing and renewal of God.

"I read this passage the next day and was furious with God," Mr. Conner said. "After rereading the passage, I realized that God had fulfilled his message to her. She is now in a place where His ever-renewing life is coursing throughout her body."

JOHN CONNOLLY
His Bright Irish Smile

There was something about John Connolly, known to his friends as Jack, that made people want to be his friend.

"He was a regular guy who loved people, loved life, lived for the minute," said his wife, Dawn. She has a snapshot memory of the first time the two met in a Forest Avenue pub on Staten Island. "I went up there with my cousin, and he just caught my eye with his blue eyes and bright Irish smile," she said. "I would always say we met through my cousin, and he would say we met in a bar."

Mr. Connolly, 46, was originally from Staten Island, but about six years ago, he moved the family to Allenwood, N.J. There, he would get up at 3.30 A.M. to drive to Manhattan and park his car beneath the World Trade Center, where he worked for Euro Brokers. His job in those dawn hours was to talk to London and Tokyo, where he made yet more friends. He would get home by midafternoon, in time to coach his children's sports teams and tend to his beloved lawn. Sometimes, the children—Dineen, 11, John, 8, and Patrick, 6—would tuck him into bed, rather than the other way around.

Every Thanksgiving, he would go back to Staten Island to rejoin high school friends for a touch football game and every Christmas, the Connollys would hold a party for about 90 friends, where Mr. Connolly was known to do Meat Loaf impersonations.

JAMES L. CONNOR
Golf Paved His Way

You always knew the precise moment when James L. Connor had decided that he liked you. He gave you a nickname. His wife, Jamie, was "Little." A brother-in-law was "Hitter." His youngest son, Jack, 4, rated two nicknames, "Mooshie" and "Buddha." His mother, Ruth Ann, was simply "R.A."

"If he had a nickname for you," his sister, Cathy Dodge, said, "he loved you and that was his way of expressing it."

Looking back, Mrs. Dodge said, it is now clear that golf, one of his great passions, was a "guiding force" in his life— the providential ingredient that nudged him in the direction of both his future wife and a successful career in investment banking.

By caddying at the North Hempstead Country Club he came to the attention of a Bear Stearns executive who gave him his start in the business. And by attending the College of William and Mary, where he played on the golf team, he met his wife.

Mr. Connor, 38, of Summit, N.J., was a partner at Sandler O'Neill & Partners on the 104th floor of 2 World Trade Center. But he loved to take his clients for a round of golf. Sometimes he even gave them nicknames.

JONATHAN CONNORS
A "Tip Top" Life

His license plate was "Tip Top," which was also one of his nicknames and his reflexive response to "How ya doing?"

His other nickname (having at least one is practically a prerequisite on Wall Street) was J.C., short for Jonathan Connors, a 55-year-old senior vice president of Cantor Fitzgerald who loved to make money, wear Armani, dance the Lindy, dine at Nobu and, whenever possible, be surrounded by strong, independent, beautiful women.

His wife, Susan Connors, said he greeted her not with a peck but with a full-blown kiss. He liked to hold her hand tightly. When she was diagnosed with Parkinson's disease, the two dug in together to fight off the effects.

"Whatever he did," she said, "it turned to gold, never silver."

Soon after the World Trade Center bombing in 1993, Mr. Connors constructed a diorama of his brush with terrorism. In a red-framed box, he displayed mementos of that day: the soot-covered shirt and tie he wore, the cashmere scarf he used as a mask, his train ticket, the next day's front page. He mounted the box on a wall in his house. It was, his wife said, an act of catharsis, remembrance and defiance all at once.

Mrs. Connors recently took it down. "I couldn't stand to look at it," she said.

KEVIN CONNORS
Loved to Compete, and Win

Whether it was climbing a mountain, playing charades or challenging his four brothers and his sister to a game of Monopoly, Kevin Connors would not be defeated. At work, there was the thrill of picking the next big investment for clients of Euro Brokers, where he was a vice president. At home, the simplest of family gatherings became thrill-seeking adventures. Children would be pitted against adults, and Mr. Connors, 55, would side with the team he thought had the best chance of winning.

"My brother was a voracious fan of winning at all things," said Sheila Connors LeDuc. "He once bought a boat to sail around the world. When it sank off the coast of South America, he beat the ocean by not drowning."

And when planes struck the World Trade Center, Mrs. LeDuc was certain that her brother would survive once more. Slowly, she has had to accept another probability.

"This was bigger than the boat going down," she said. "I just hope he is at peace and that those of us who mourn him can come to the same peace."

KEVIN E. CONROY
Supper Every Night

By day, he was an accountant at Marsh & McLennan, the insurance brokerage company that occupied seven upper floors at 1 World Trade Center. Evenings, Kevin E. Conroy, 47, the father of four children ages 6 to 12, insisted that his family get together at home in Kensington, Brooklyn, for supper (not dinner) that he often prepared. There was his infamous eggplant parmigiana. Salad. Pasta. Meat and potatoes. Barbecue.

"Nothing too extravagant," said a cousin, Lynn Taylor. "They were the only family I knew that cooked dinner every night. It was just important for him that the family sit together at the house."

The schedules of youth leagues and school tested the custom; some nights it was just pizza ordered in. But Mr. Conroy always looked forward to the suppers and, on weekends, playing the gracious host for gatherings of friends and family.

"We shared some great times, drank some beer, had lots and lots of laughs," said a letter from two other cousins, Tom and Oonagh, that was read at a memorial service last week. "And Kevin, the barbecues were great."

BRENDA E. CONWAY
Half of a Lifelong Team

Brenda E. Conway was hard to miss. First, because of her unique style—an avid shopper, she preferred bright colors and patterns, and made funny socks her signature—and second, because you usually saw two of her. Mrs. Conway was rarely without her twin, Linda McGee. Though they were fraternal, the sisters still looked and sounded enough alike to draw attention.

"They were always together," said their mother, Edith Watford, pastor of the Second Chance Christian Center in the Bronx.

Mrs. Conway was a native of the Bronx, and lived there with her husband, Russell, and children, Danielle Alexander, 19, and Mandell Conway, 13. A systems analyst at Marsh & McLennan, on the 97th floor of the World Trade Center, she would have been 40, and she often said that she did not need to have a lot of friends, because she had a twin.

Her sister said, "People ask me, am I dealing with it, and sometimes I say, no, I'm not dealing with it. Everything reminds me of her, because we did everything together."

The weekend before Sept. 11, the twins took a "ladies' day out" shopping trip with their daughters. Mrs. Conway bought almost a whole new wardrobe, now untouched.

"She left behind so many new things," her mother said.

HELEN COOK
Driven to Better Herself

Helen Cook was 12 when she and her brother, 10, moved to the Bronx from Honduras with their mother.

"We used to hold hands when we walked in the street," the brother, Edson Garcia, remembered. "We came over for a reason: to go to school and try to become somebody."

She loved school and wanted to become a nurse. But after three years of college in Buffalo, she took a summer job at 1 World Trade Center and met Jermaine Cook, who worked for the stock exchange. Soon his name was in a heart-shaped tattoo on her neck. Their son, Justin, will be 2 on Oct. 23, 2001. In August, the couple celebrated their second wedding anniversary in Miami Beach. Mr. Cook is distraught.

Mr. Garcia said, "He told me the World Trade brought them together, and it also destroyed them."

After the plane hit, Ms. Cook, 24, tried unsuccessfully to call her husband from the 82nd floor. Instead she reached her brother, crying. By telephone, he did his best to hold her hand.

JOSEPH J. COPPO
Every Kid's Coach

"You don't know Joe Coppo, and you do," Mike Lupica wrote in the *Daily News* two Sundays after the attacks. "Every town, if it is lucky, has somebody like him, the guy who doesn't just want to coach his own kids but all the kids."

Joseph J. Coppo, 47, a burly municipal bond trader at Cantor Fitzgerald, coached all four of his children, and hundreds of other children in New Canaan, Conn.

"He was very demanding, but he was someone you always wanted to work hard for," said his daughter, Kathleen, 22, who played center field for him on a softball team. This summer, Mr. Coppo coached his youngest son's All-Star baseball team. The players, 13 years old, attended his funeral in their uniforms.

Kathleen Coppo, who described her father as "my best friend, the first person I turned to for anything," teaches a class on social justice at a small Catholic girls' school. Recently one of her students asked her whether Sept. 11 had caused her to abandon her pacifist beliefs.

No, she replied—an answer, she said, that might have

pleased her father, who considered applying for conscientious-objector status when he was drafted just as the Vietnam War was ending. "He was not into war," she said.

GERARD COPPOLA
The Rock 'n' Roll Grandpa

Already at age 12, he was a broadcasting nut. He bought a two-watt transmitter, built a mini-radio station in his basement in East Orange, N.J., and began broadcasting, rock 'n' roll and personal musings throughout the town. His friends loved it.

Gerard Coppola's love of broadcasting and music was the central thread of his life. Mr. Coppola, who was also known as Rod and JRod, was antenna engineer for WNET, Channel 13, on the 110th floor of the World Trade Center's north tower. His Web site—NJPeople.com/jrod—lives on and features his doleful songs. Not only did he mix the songs, but he sang and played all the instruments—guitar, bass, keyboards and drums.

"Gerard was a dreamer," said his sister, Cynthia. "These are the people who are visionaries, who are risk-takers. They dare to listen to their own voices." As a teenager, he began playing in rock bands and writing songs. At family gatherings, everyone wanted to hear him tell stories. "People sought him out," his sister said. "He had a gift. He was like the Pied Piper of the family."

At home, he sought to bring his love of music to his wife, Alice, and their four daughters, Angeline, 20, Angela, 19, Delinda, 15, and Alison, 8. He was 46.

"When his first grandson, Andre, was born five months ago," his sister said in November, "he came to my house and said, 'Cindy, I can't wait for you to see him. He's a gorgeous baby.' He said, 'I'm going to be such a cool grandfather.' "

JOSEPH A. CORBETT
Not Just Picture Perfect

With their striking blue eyes and warm smiles, Felicia and Joseph A. Corbett made a stunning couple. They would walk into a room—she in a carefully coordinated outfit and he looking as if he had stepped out of a J. Crew catalogue—and they would invariably be the best-dressed couple. Their love for each another was contagious.

"They'd have barbecues, and people would crawl out of the woodwork to come," said Susan Turner, Mrs. Corbett's sister. "You'd want to be around them."

The Corbetts would often turn down invitations with friends to cuddle in front of the fireplace in their new Cape Cod home in Islip, N.Y.

"We were in our own little bubble," said Mrs. Corbett,

25. Practically the only time they separated was to go to work; Mr. Corbett, 28, was at Cantor Fitzgerald.

"I feel like they were living a fairy tale and someone closed the book," Ms. Turner said in November. "If you asked me two months ago who had the best life, it would be Felicia and Joe."

ROBERT CORDICE
"He Craved the Action"

When Firefighter Robert Cordice disappeared on Sept. 11, so did the dreams of dozens of bachelorettes. Firefighter Cordice, 28, was a handsome, hulking man, a lover of good drink, beautiful women and fast motorcycles. He was to be a pinup boy, making the cut for the 2002 Fire Department Hunks calendar.

"The picture is of him downtown on the Wall Street bull with his shirt off, wearing his bunker pants and suspenders and boots," said his longtime friend John Deliso.

Like so many other firefighters, he wanted to be in the thick of the smoke. He was stationed at Engine Company 152 in Staten Island, and decided that he wanted to work somewhere more busy and daring. He transferred to the elite Squad 1 unit in Brooklyn. He had been there only two weeks.

He was also a New York City police officer for three years before joining the Fire Department, stationed at the 13th Precinct in Manhattan.

"No matter what he was doing, he craved the action," Mr. Deliso said.

DANNY A. CORREA
Poetic Journey

Danny A. Correa wrote this: I dance in the clouds and soak in the haze. What about you?

That lyric query was in an e-mail message that Mr. Correa sent to a friend a few weeks after he started working on the 98th floor of 1 World Trade Center. The routine of ascending the building's summit quickly spawned images that fed his poetry.

"Danny loved to write," said his father, Helman Correa, who brought his family to the United States from Colombia in 1979. Danny Correa, 25, represented the fulfillment of his father's dream of a better life.

Berkeley College had placed him in a job at the accounting department of Marsh & McLennan in July; he was to receive his bachelor's degree in accounting, with honors, that fall.

He was the father of a 4-year-old daughter, Katrina, and founder of a basement rock band called Lucid-A. He played

lead guitar, but he also could handle drums, keyboard and horns.

"He was amazing, quiet and kind of mysterious," said Erin McAteer, a friend. "He never talked too much about private things, but you could tell that a lot of him came out in his music."

JAMES J. CORRIGAN
Fire and Roses

When James J. Corrigan was not fighting fires, he was smelling the roses. His house in Little Neck, N.Y., was suffused with their scent. He put them in vases; gave them to his wife, Marie; handed them to neighbors. Red, pink, yellow, white—they all flourished in the garden by his driveway.

He even gave them to the hardened men with whom he worked.

He was a New York firefighter for 25 years, retiring as a captain in 1994. He took a job the next year as a fire and safety director in 7 World Trade Center.

In August, Mr. Corrigan, 60, was promoted to oversee fire and safety operations for the entire complex. His youngest son, Sean, had just gotten married three days earlier, and his oldest son, Brendan, often ate lunch with his father.

After the planes hit, the Captain called Brendan: "Don't go anywhere. We don't know what else is going to happen." Then the line went dead.

KEVIN M. COSGROVE
"A Good Snuggler"

"Mommy, it broke my heart when Daddy died because he was a good snuggler," said 4-year-old Elizabeth Cosgrove.

She was speaking of her father, Kevin M. Cosgrove, who was vice president of claims at Aon. Wendy Cosgrove simply held her daughter close and said, "I know."

Mr. Cosgrove, 46, of West Islip, N.Y., did a great balancing act between work and home, Mrs. Cosgrove said. He could often be seen shoveling the walks of elderly widows in winter and helping elderly couples carry bulky packages throughout the year, she said.

But he especially liked to indulge his children: Brian, 12, Claire, 10, and Elizabeth.

" 'Mommy, Daddy let us eat dinner backward,' the kids used to say to me when I would come home after they had spent a day with him," Mrs. Cosgrove recalled with a chuckle. " 'We ate brownies and ice cream before dinner.' I would tell him that it made me look like the bad guy because I made them eat dinner. It was funny."

DOLORES M. COSTA
Always Giving Her All

Giving defined Dolores M. Costa. "My wife had a heart of gold—she was very soft," said her husband, Charles, who said people were drawn to her blue eyes and her smile.

"She would be up at 5 o'clock every morning to go to work, and from the minute she got up she was giving," he said. "She was giving to me, to her home, to strangers in the street. She gave herself. And when she was at her job, she was giving 110 percent."

Mrs. Costa, who would have turned 54 on Sept. 13, rose to the position of vice president at Fred Alger Management, on the 93rd floor of 1 World Trade Center.

Her evenings were spent crocheting colorful afghans for friends and talking with her husband about life. Mornings she fed finches, warblers and sparrows that lived in the birdhouses in her backyard in Port Monmouth, N.J. She was planning an 80th birthday party for her mother.

"She was really a good daughter," said Marie Barbosa of Brooklyn. "She worried about me, and now she is gone. That is the sad part of it all."

CHARLES COSTELLO
No Rights to Bragging

To Charles Costello, bragging was a criminal offense. No matter what he achieved or whom he helped, Mr. Costello never let on about it to his family. At home, he was just Chuck, doting father to four children, adoring husband to Mary and a lover of good, long bike rides.

At a recent memorial, 1,000 people turned out to tell his family of the Charles Costello they knew, the elevator technician who often on his way to work shuttled neighbors to bus stops and did other errands. On Sept. 11, despite his partner's pleas, Mr. Costello jumped out of his work truck and ran into 1 World Trade Center.

"I'll be fine," he said. "Just keep your cell phone on."

Slowly, Mrs. Costello has come to believe that her husband is safe in heaven. His spirit, she says, is still watching over his family, sending signals that life must go on. The night before his memorial service, as she prayed for a sign that it was O.K. to have a funeral without a body, Mrs. Costello was jolted from her sleep by "a pure white light and deep tingling sensation that went from my head to my toes."

The moment was meant as a message, she said. "I really believe that was his way of trying to give me peace and strength," she said. "All the hysterical crying, it stopped after that. I feel like, in a way, I've become as strong as he was."

MICHAEL COSTELLO
A Nickname That Stuck

Now how do you acquire a nickname like Stitch? Go to a party and behave yourself.

It was Michael Costello's first day at the University of Scranton. Within a few hours after his parents left, he found himself at a party in someone's basement. He was enjoying himself, not bothering a soul. Across the room, some guys were monkeying around. A hard hat came soaring through the air and smacked Mr. Costello in the face. Taken to the hospital, he had to get stitches across the bridge of his nose. Since no one knew anyone's name yet, classmates took a look at his face and called him Stitch.

Stitch stuck.

In time, Stitch Costello, 27, became an institutional equity salesman at Cantor Fitzgerald, settled in with roommates in Hoboken, and met a woman, Amy Walsh, at the beach in Avalon, N.J. They both adored the beach, and that helped forge an ongoing relationship. Every summer, they continued to rent a share in a group house in Avalon.

Activity was an absolute necessity to Mr. Costello. He could and would talk to anyone, do almost anything. When he was young, his mother, Nancy Costello, used to label him the Social Director, because one friend would be arriving to play with him just as another departed.

He liked to cook, play golf and fish. The fishing always amazed his mother, because she couldn't imagine her hyperactive son staying still long enough to catch a fish.

CONROD COTTOY
A Respectful Son

When Paula Hayes came to New York from Louisiana in the summer of 1975, she intended only to have a vacation. But she met Conrod Cottoy at the First Baptist Church in Brooklyn; on Valentine's Day 1976, they married.

"He had all the qualities I was looking for," she said. "He believed in God and education, and he respected his mother. I never met a man who respected his mother more than he did. I figured, if he respects his mother, he respects other women."

Mr. Cottoy, 50, an analyst at Carr Futures, was born in Trinidad; he had lived in the United States for more than 30 years and had settled in Brooklyn. He held degrees in accounting and history, and, like a sponge, he soaked up knowledge of the world's cultures and religions. He had traveled the Nile River and visited the Sphinx and the pyramids.

The couple's four sons knew that if they brought home

low grades, TV would be banned. And they knew that their father would not sleep until they were all home and accounted for. His affinity for Africa was evident in the names he gave his younger sons: Kojo, which means "born on Monday," and Ngozi, which means "blessing."

JOHN G. COUGHLIN
Civil Servant, Times Two

John G. Coughlin was a giving man, and that kept him very busy. Sergeant Coughlin, 43, was with the emergency services unit of the New York Police Department. In his spare time, he was a volunteer firefighter in Pomona, N.Y., where he lived with his family.

"He was always on the go," said his wife, Patricia Coughlin.

He was good at spoiling his three daughters, Erin, 16, Tara, 13, and Kayla, 6. He took them parasailing, white-water rafting and to amusement parks. He took them to baseball games, but there was a slight complication. He was a Mets fan and all three girls are Yankees fans—Mrs. Coughlin is neutral—and so they went to both stadiums. When the Yankees played the Mets in the World Series, well, that got a little tense.

A former marine, Sergeant Coughlin was active in the Rockland County detachment of the Marine Corps League, helping older veterans and doing honor guard duty at funerals.

"He loved that," his wife said. "Once a marine, always a marine."

One of his favorite times was the middle of December, when he would take a week's vacation to work on the Marine Toys for Tots Program.

"He was a firm believer that every kid should have a toy for Christmas," Mrs. Coughlin said.

TIMOTHY J. COUGHLIN
A Face Promising Friendship

Who's that guy? That's what the copy shop clerk wanted to know when a customer came to pick up the funeral photos of Timothy J. Coughlin. That's what his wife, Maura, wanted to know when she first spotted his "big Irish face" in a downtown bar. People were drawn to him before he even opened his mouth, often to tell a bawdy joke or display his distinctive vocabulary ("Great lair!" he would say to a host).

But there was plenty of substance to back up his friendly appearance. When Mr. Coughlin was not trading treasury securities at Cantor Fitzgerald, golfing, or taking his children—Ryann, 4, Sean, 2, and Riley, 9 months old—to the carousel in Central Park, he was planning social gatherings.

"I called him a friendship hawk because he was just so good at circling back and seeing how friends were doing," said Frank Coughlin, one of his three brothers.

Timothy Coughlin was the kind of man who gave the towel guy at the gym his start on Wall Street. The doorman from the Coughlins's Upper East Side building was at the funeral.

"I said something smug about how Timmy was so generous," Frank Coughlin recalled. "He said, 'No, it wasn't that. It was that Timmy was my friend.' "

ANDRÉ COX
Always on the Go

André Cox followed his brothers from St. Vincent in the Caribbean to Canarsie in search of a new future. He thought he might get into architecture by studying computer science.

So he took cafeteria jobs and enrolled in 1994 at Brooklyn College. For seven years, he worked full time and went to school full time, too. This was his schedule: up at 4:30 A.M., leave for work at 5:45 A.M.

Most recently, his job was food preparation in a cafeteria on the 101st floor of 1 World Trade Center. When he finished at 3 P.M., he would take the subway to school, go to classes and study, and be home at 11 P.M. On weekends, he studied and slept.

"That was his schedule for most of the last seven years," his brother, Nigel, said Friday. "So he really had no social life."

But that summer, he graduated. He had told his mother he was not happy in his job, Nigel Cox said, and began applying for jobs in computers. "I know he had sent out some résumés," Nigel Cox said Friday. "He was looking."

FREDERICK COX
A "Glutton for Life"

Climb into that hammock between two trees on an island in Lake Winnepesaukee, N.H. Feel the soft summer stillness. Look up.

A tile hanging from one tree reads, "Do what you love, love what you do." That was Frederick Cox's hammock, his motto, the tile he hung.

Like his motto, Mr. Cox, 27, was a full-throttle enthusiast brushed by naïveté.

Even though he sought the serenity of his family's summer home, he lived a Manhattan life of joyous clatter. Buoyantly confident, with his green eyes glowing with mischief, he made friends easily.

Who could resist that pied-piper promise of adventure, the courtliness of a Georgia-bred gentleman, the charm of a super salesman?

Not Annelise Peterson, his girlfriend, who described Mr. Cox, an investment banker at Sandler O'Neill, as a "glutton for life"—a painter, writer, golfer, shopper, food

One month after the World Trade Center was destroyed, students, officials and faculty members at City College in upper Manhattan sing the national anthem in the Lewisohn Plaza of Honor during a memorial service for those who died on September 11. (*Ozier Muhammad*)

lover. He reminded her of her older brother Davin, a trader for Cantor Fitzgerald. Both were tall, loyal, attentive.

After Mr. Cox's parents divorced when he was 8, he gave his mother a rose every Valentine's Day. His father, the son said, was his best friend.

Both Mr. Cox and Davin Peterson, who dined with Ms. Peterson on Sept. 8, worked on the 104th floor at the World Trade Center—Mr. Peterson in the north tower, Mr. Cox in the south tower.

DAVIN PETERSON's portrait appears on page 390.

JAMES R. COYLE
The Force Was with Him

James R. Coyle wanted to be Luke Skywalker. But because of certain difficulties in pursuing that career path, he decided to do what he thought was the next best thing, which was fighting fires.

Sure, there was no flying across galaxies or rescuing princesses, but joining the New York Fire Department had its own rewards. Both of his grandfathers were New York firefighters. Firefighter Coyle joined the department's cadet program while studying at Brooklyn College. He was 22 when he graduated as valedictorian of that program on a wet June day about four years before the attack.

For the next three years, he worked as an emergency medical technician. He delivered a baby in the back of an ambulance. He ducked bullets in crime-ridden neighborhoods.

In December 2000, he completed training in the fire academy and joined Ladder Company 3 in the East Village. One grandfather gave the firefighter his old fire hat.

The last glimpse his mother, Regina Coyle, had of Firefighter Coyle was on her television set on Sept. 11, when a local television station was doing a morning show on cooking in the firehouse. He had just finished a night shift, she said, and he was there to eat a meal before heading off to Chicago on vacation.

MICHELE COYLE-EULAU
A Maximum Mom

"Michele, it's 11 o'clock!" Dennis Eulau would shout. "Could you just come to bed?"

After all, her day had started at 5 A.M., with the NordicTrack workout, then the frenzy to roust, dress and feed their three little guys—ages 2, 5 and 7—and get herself to work, two days a week in the city and one at home, as a systems analyst at Marsh & McLennan. On city days, she arrived early so she could jam in a lot and leave on the dot.

Mrs. Coyle-Eulau, 38, would go home to Garden City, N.Y., dine on cereal, then supervise the boys' homework and bedtime rituals. Then she would plan weekends. A skier and snorkeler, she was the one who pushed everyone out the door for activities.

She was a to-the-max mom. A coach from an opposing soccer team asked her to tone down the cheering. Before school started, she would seek out teachers, demanding, "What can you do for my boys?"

Here is what the boys did for her: on the last Mother's Day, they cooked pancakes with red and blue food coloring. She even ate them.

What took her so long to get to bed? Packing lunches, making grocery lists, arranging play dates.

"I never understood," her husband said. "Now I do."

Malcolm I. Hoenlein, the executive vice chairman of the Conference of Presidents of Major American Jewish Organizations, led a group to ground zero in lower Manhattan for a prayer service on October 12.

(*Angel Franco*)

CHRISTOPHER CRAMER
Dreaming of Key West

Christopher Cramer had 317 days left and he would be gone for good.

Gone to Florida. Taking the buyout and retiring at 35. And just like his man Jimmy Buffett, he was going to live on an island and fish and grow fat drinking beer.

"He wanted to get down there before he went totally gray," said his friend Tracy Pereless, who knew him for four years, ever since they ran into each other in the bread aisle at the A & P. "That's what New York did to him for 11 years, turned him gray," she said. "He started at 7:10 and he hated it."

Mr. Cramer lived in commuter hell, driving more than 200 miles a day from his home in Long Beach, N.J., to the World Trade Center and back. He worked as vice president of tax operations for Fiduciary Trust Company International.

His home was on a lagoon, and on the weekends he fished from his deck and drank beer with his people and dreamed of Key West.

He was loved by his parents and three brothers and sister and friends. And if they could, they would apologize to him for forgetting to play Jimmy Buffett at his memorial.

DENISE ELIZABETH CRANT
New York, New York

Although she was born in Fort Myers, Fla., and lived in Hackensack, N.J., Denise Elizabeth Crant was a New Yorker at heart.

"I used to give her heck about not being a real New Yorker," said her brother John, of Manhattan.

But even a teasing younger brother could see that her job in the facilities department of Marsh U.S.A., on the 93rd floor of the north tower of the World Trade Center, had changed her demeanor.

"It was like having her old self back," Mr. Crant said. "She had the glow back."

Ms. Crant, 46, returned in September 2000, after taking a five-year break from the city. She first moved to New York in 1987 to get married. She left the city when the marriage broke up.

"Until she left, she didn't realize how much she truly loved it," Mr. Crant said. "Every time I ever spoke with her it was all about moving back to New York."

When she returned, she and her brother, an executive recruiter, spoke daily. Most mornings she would take the bus into the city, often arriving by 6:30 A.M. Then she would leave a voice-mail message for her brother, teasing him about his "banker's hours."

"So I would call her pretty much every morning when I got in," Mr. Crant said. "I really miss those calls."

ROBERT CRAWFORD
Modest, Helpful, "Great"

Jennifer Eppolito has dozens of reasons to call her father, Robert Crawford, great: He would stand outside Brooklyn churches in all kinds of weather, selling raffle tickets to benefit St. Rose's Home, a cancer hospital. When he was honored for his work, he would not want to be in any photographs.

He told her, when she was little, "It's more important to listen to what people are saying than it is always to talk."

He was a firefighter for 32½ years.

"You could ask him about anything, like how does a refrigerator work, and he would be able to sit there and put it into pieces you would understand," she said.

When Mrs. Eppolito's daughter, Alexandra, was born, Mr. Crawford took flowers in a vase with the Virgin Mary on it. He taught Alexandra her address by the time she was 2. He called her Poo Poo, and at 62, played Barbies with her.

"To describe my father as great, that's not even a good enough word," Mrs. Eppolito said. "I was lucky for him to be my father. There is no other man that, in my eyes, could stand up to him."

TARA CREAMER
The Perfect Life

At the University of Massachusetts at Amherst, Tara Creamer was an apparel-marketing major because, as her husband, John, said, "She knew right away what she wanted to do."

Apparel marketing it was, and Mrs. Creamer got a job as a buyer for TJX, the company that runs the T. J. Maxx clothing stores. She switched to planning manager when she had her first child and wanted to cut back on the traveling that buyers have to do. She was on one of her infrequent trips from her home in Worcester, Mass., to Los Angeles for planning sessions when she boarded American Airlines Flight 11 on Sept. 11.

Tara and John Creamer met at college, where he was captain of the football team, and she never missed a game.

"Her life, in her eyes, was perfect," said her sister, Liz Waldo. "She had a tremendous life in her short 30 years. Her smile was radiant. It was her most beautiful feature."

Tara and Liz grew up as two of the four Shea sisters in Westfield, Mass. "The four girls looked on ourselves as four sturdy legs on a table," Mrs. Waldo said, "and now we're down to three wobbly legs."

JOANNE CREGAN
Everyone's Best Friend

Joanne and Grace Cregan were sisters. The kind who moved here from Ireland and bought identical apartments, just two floors apart in the same Brooklyn Heights building; the kind who sent each other e-mail messages throughout the day and watched television together every night; the kind who were best friends.

But there was something about Joanne Cregan, 32, who worked at eSpeed, that made most people think she was their best friend. When her friends needed advice, she gave it freely. When she went home to Ireland, she took gifts for her family and friends. Her laugh and her sense of humor made bleak situations brighter.

Ms. Cregan, who loved music, also connected with children and was to become the godmother of three babies.

"She was an excellent big sister," Grace Cregan said. "Sometimes it just hits me that I'll never see her again. I won't get to grow old with her."

LUCY CRIFASI
To Be So Loved

Everybody loved Lucy.

And why not? Lucy Crifasi was the kind of woman who always seemed to have a big smile and time to solve somebody else's problems. That's basically what she did as an American Express travel coordinator assigned to the Marsh & McLennan offices in the World Trade Center.

Ms. Crifasi, 51, took care of family and friends as well. In recent months, she took off one day a week to spend more time with her 85-year-old mother, with whom she lived in Glendale, Queens. She loved to travel, and over the last few years she took her brother, Frank, to London and Antigua. The day after school ended last year she took her sister, Maria, a Roman Catholic school principal, to the Caribbean.

"She didn't like going away in the summer because it was too hot, but it was the only time I could go," Ms. Crifasi said. "She knew how stressed out I was."

The Crifasi family came to New York from Sicily in 1958. Last year, the whole family went back to visit Montevago, their hometown. Then the two sisters took a side trip to Rome, where they said the rosary with the pope and toured the city.

"She made everybody feel very, very special," said Ms. Crifasi.

Lucy Crifasi was known for her devotion to the singer

Julio Iglesias and for her classy sense of fashion. "Lucy only had two vices," said her brother, Frank. "Shoes and pocketbooks."

JOHN CRISCI
His Two Families

"The main thing about John," said Raffaella Crisci, his wife, "he was a family man." Actually, Mr. Crisci, a lieutenant who worked 23 years for the New York Fire Department, had two families: Mrs. Crisci and their three sons in Holbrook, on Long Island, and Hazardous Materials Company 1 in Maspeth, Queens. He was equally at home in both places. At each he fixed dinners of barbecued shrimp and ribs, built cupboards and shelves, and organized the paperwork.

He loved firefighting and was a rescue specialist and teacher. His shift was over on Sept. 11 when the alarm rang, Mrs. Crisci said, but "he automatically jumped in, wearing civilian clothes."

Off duty, "he liked being home with me and the kids," she said. He found plenty to do, watching his sons play hockey, nailing siding and sketching plans for a little pond.

"We didn't take fancy vacations," she said. "We just liked sitting in the backyard, swinging on the swing, drinking coffee. We had 30 years together. I want 30 more."

DANIEL H. CRISMAN
In Love with the Big City

He came from the small town of South Montrose, Pa., but he was enchanted by the inexhaustible mysteries and wonders of New York. Daniel Crisman soaked in everything about the city.

Mr. Crisman, 25, felt he was on a roll. He had labored as a carpenter in New Jersey, but yearned for something more certain and less seasonal. He found a job as a temp at Marsh & McLennan. On Sept. 1, 2001, after a year of tentative status, he was made a permanent employee as a training coordinator. When he learned the good news, he was ecstatic, flashing one of his trademark smiles.

"He really felt like he had made it," said his girlfriend, Danielle Zazula. "He felt he had achieved a level of success in his life."

Art was another side of him. He met Ms. Zazula at a poetry workshop where both of them read some of their work. They shared so many interests, including admiration for Charles Bukowski. For two years, they lived together in Chelsea.

More recently, Mr. Crisman had set aside poetry and embraced photography, taking pictures of flowers and

leaves. He also created collages, mixing his photographs with images he cut out of magazines and wrappers and bottle caps he found on the streets of the city that so inspired him.

DENNIS CROSS
Running for a Memory

The race seemed more important than ever. For 18 years, on the Tuesday before Thanksgiving, Dennis Cross competed in the Turkey Trot, a 5-kilometer race held in Flushing Meadows, Queens, where firefighters ran for charity. In 2001 he would be absent.

His wife, JoAnn, used to operate a fitness studio and induced him to run with her. But once the children arrived, she stopped running. That was 15 years ago.

Yet she felt an unshakable need to have a member of the Cross family in the Turkey Trot to honor her husband, a chief of Battalion 57 in Bedford-Stuyvesant, Brooklyn. So she concluded she would be that Cross. And she would recruit additional firefighters to run, too, in honor of all the firefighters lost in the attack.

Chief Cross, 60, known as Captain Fearless, lived with his wife in Islip Terrace, N.Y. His favorite saying was, "Take care of the men and the men will take care of you." Mrs. Cross was going to take care of his memory. She vowed she would finish this race and then begin an annual memorial run for her husband on April 27, the anniversary of the day they met.

For nine weeks, she trained, building up endurance. Race day came. She ran, as did her four children. She finished in 29 minutes.

"I thought I was going to do it in 45 minutes," she said. "I was proud of myself."

HELEN CROSSIN-KITTLE
Just Starting a Family

Helen Crossin-Kittle was the one to ask her future husband out on their first date. A good thing too, says Kevin Kittle, a high school custodian, because if she had waited for him to ask, he says, he would "still be single." The Kittles lived in Larchmont and their love story was a knew-each-other-from-childhood kind of thing.

Only, as Mr. Kittle noted, he was "just dumb"—didn't pick up on Helen's feelings until that first date, when she told him she was looking for a nice guy and had always thought he was a nice guy. They married April 7, honeymooned in St. Lucia, and did not want to wait to start a family.

Ms. Crossin-Kittle, 34, a computer specialist who worked on the 103rd floor of 1 World Trade Center, was five months pregnant at the time of the attack. She went for amniocentesis Sept. 6 and expected the results of the test in a few days.

Mr. Kittle and the couple's families have not decided whether they want to be told whether she had been expecting a boy or a girl.

KEVIN R. CROTTY
Children at the Bakery

The ladies behind the counter at a bakery in Summit, N.J., used to look forward to Saturday mornings when Kevin R. Crotty would show up with his three children. With wild candy-store looks in their eyes, Megan, 7, Kyle, 5, and Sean, 2, would load up on cookies and chocolate and glazed doughnuts and doughnut holes.

But it has been months since Mr. Crotty took his children to the bakery. Mr. Crotty, 43, worked as a bond trader at Sandler O'Neill & Partners on the 104th floor of 2 World Trade Center. Besides the bakery, he could be seen taking the children to soccer practice and dance lessons.

"I've been very open with them about it," said his widow, Lori Crotty. "The more I talk about it, the more comfortable they are. Sean is having a hard time, but it's going to take time."

THOMAS G. CROTTY
"The Energizer Bunny"

For Thomas G. Crotty the perfect day would look something like this: a run on the beach, followed by a game of tennis, perhaps a little biking or kayaking topped off with an afternoon playing with his two girls, who are 6 and 2 years old.

"Tom is somebody who on weekends never sat still," said his brother John Crotty. "He crammed his weekend with as many activities as he possibly could. We used to joke that he had it planned out in 30-second intervals."

A managing director with Sandler O'Neill & Partners, Mr. Crotty competed regularly in marathons and was scheduled to participate in a triathlon the weekend after Sept. 11. "When I think of Tom, the first thing that comes to mind is the Energizer bunny," said Tom Mulkeen, a friend of more than 20 years and running partner. "He never stopped."

Although he focused on pushing himself when it came to working out, he was also known to quietly help others, whether it was donating blood and platelets for a client with leukemia or picking up a sandwich for a homeless man. "He

always had the kindest intentions at the forefront," Mr. Mulkeen said.

WELLES REMY CROWTHER
Kindness Remembered

It is a quirk of human nature that the person who does an act of kindness may forget it, but the recipient does not. And so it was that upon the loss of their 24-year-old son, Welles Remy Crowther, his parents, Alison and Jefferson Crowther of Upper Nyack, received a note. It referred to only a few moments in their son's life, high school moments at that, but it had stayed with another young man for years.

"Welles was a big player in ice hockey," Ms. Crowther said, "and he was skating with a younger kid and nobody was passing him the puck. Welles comes up to him and says, 'Are you ready to score your first varsity goal?' He gets the puck, and passes it right to this kid and he scores his first goal."

Mr. Crowther was an equities trader with Sandler O'Neill & Partners, on the 104th floor of the south tower. He shared an apartment in Greenwich Village with his friend Chuck Platz, favored Hawaiian shirts for his evenings out. Mr. Crowther's mother speaks of her son's gallantry in escorting her to the opera.

Mr. Platz cites a very different example: the night that Mr. Crowther, when a female friend had had too much to drink, put her over his shoulder and carried her up five flights. A memorial service was held for Mr. Crowther, but neither his parents nor his roommate could bring themselves to clean out his room.

"The bed is still unmade, the dent from his head is still there on the pillow, his clothes are still on the floor," Mr. Platz says. "Sometimes I hear somebody's key turn and I think, 'Oh, Welles is home.'"

ROBERT LANE CRUIKSHANK
A Very Decent Man

The marriage proposal of Robert Lane Cruikshank was not the stuff of which a maiden dreams.

"My mother always told me how I would feel when I fell in love and I don't feel that way," he said, "but I thought about it and I decided she was wrong."

Marianne Johnson, sitting in a restaurant in her low-back black dress with the red cabbage roses, married him anyway. Why? "Because he was the most decent, the most solid—he was just a good man," she said of her husband of 38 years, from their home on Manhattan's Upper East Side.

"I make him sound dull—we had a house in Stratton that we called Mountain De Open Dour, I was the 'open,' he was the 'dour'—but he was fun. You could trust him. Grown men have been here crying. He was a rock to everyone we knew."

Mr. Cruikshank, 64, father of two, was a vice president of Carr Futures and worked on the 92nd floor of the north tower.

He and his wife had a home in Beaver Creek, Colo., and he was, his wife says, "very sportif"—he loved tennis, skiing and golf. He sometimes joked about quitting and going on the senior tennis tour, but the truth was, he loved what he did.

A special time? "He once decided to surprise me and planned a trip to Rome, the entire trip," his wife said. "It was two weeks, which for Cruikshank was a very long time, because the world was waiting for him to work."

FRANCISCO CRUZ
The Quiet Guitar Player

Francisco Cruz was not much for words—the kind of guy who would go to a party, look over the dance floor and head straight for a dark, quiet corner. When Mr. Cruz, a security guard for Summit Security in the World Trade Center, did have something to say, he let his guitar speak for him, spewing out fiery renditions of tunes by Jimi Hendrix, Carlos Santana and Jose Feliciano.

"Music was his life," said his brother Tomas Cruz. "It allowed him to escape outside of himself. He would just come alive."

Music hooked Mr. Cruz, 47, at an early age. While kids all around him were busy dreaming baseball, Mr. Cruz became mesmerized by a neighborhood kid who was learning to play the guitar, and earning lots of attention because of it. Young Mr. Cruz wanted to be cool, too.

"But we didn't have a guitar, and our mother didn't have the money to buy one," his brother recalled. "So we would steal my uncle's guitar and hang out in the hallway with it, like we knew what we were doing."

Soon, Mr. Cruz had taught himself and his younger brother how to play. "I'll never be half as good as he was," Tomas Cruz said, "but when I'm playing, it keeps me with him and takes me back to our good times."

JOHN R. CRUZ
Plans for a Wedding

John R. Cruz wasn't one of those guys who proposes marriage to his girlfriend, forks over the ring, then waits to be informed when and where to attend the wedding.

He had proposed to his bride, Susan Fereira, only two weeks before the disaster,

when they had both flown out to California for a wedding. So the whole weekend before the terrorist attack, the lovebirds took delight in discussing the complex details. It had to be at Sacred Heart Church in Yonkers, where Ms. Fereira lived. It would certainly be a large wedding: her family is Portuguese and his is Puerto Rican, with many of his relatives living around Lakewood, N.J.

Their friends from Morgan Stanley would be there, because that was where they had met, and where she still works. And certainly there must be a contingent from Cantor Fitzgerald, where Mr. Cruz was in the accounting group on the 101st floor of 1 World Trade Center. On Monday, Sept. 10, they set the date: Sept. 21, 2002.

Now she remembers all the good things. For example, "how he carried a Bible," she said, "and read a passage every morning on the way to work."

KENNETH JOHN CUBAS
In a Hero's Nature

Ken Cubas was not a fireman or a police officer, not one of the uniformed men who stormed up the stairs of the World Trade Center while fleeing office workers streamed down. Mr. Cubas, 48, was a vice president at Fiduciary Trust. Yet his wife's solace comes from hearing of her husband's bravery.

In the hours after the towers crumbled, Kerry Flood Cubas got several telephone calls from her husband's colleagues, reporting that he had helped them reach safety from 2 World Trade. One caller, Mrs. Cubas said, saw him outside the building and begged him not to return. He ignored those pleas.

"I take tremendous consolation in knowing he died so nobly," she said from the couple's home in Woodstock, N.Y. "He had a choice. He knew the risk he was taking and he wasn't deterred. His nature brought him to his death and I find beauty in that."

Ken and Kerry Cubas were together for 25 years. Mr. Cubas was a Big Brother to Oscar Zapata, an inner-city youngster, whom he befriended when the boy was 11. They remained close after Mr. Zapata joined the Army. Mr. and Mrs. Cubas were also mentoring Mr. Zapata's sister, Marlene.

"He died as he lived," Mrs. Cubas said, "helping others."

THELMA CUCCINELLO
"Nuts at Christmas"

Christmas was Thelma Cuccinello's favorite holiday, a time when she could deck her house in Wilmot, N.H., with all the ornaments and decorations she had made over the years. And not just her house. Her eldest daughter, Cheryl O'Brien, who lives in

Bedford, Mass., recently opened a box of Christmas wreaths, only to realize that every one had been made by her mother.

"She made the skirt for our Christmas tree, the decoration for our mantelpiece," Mrs. O'Brien said. "She and Dad would go nuts at Christmas."

When her three daughters were growing up in Lexington, Mass., Mrs. Cuccinello made their clothes, costumes for Halloween and other occasions, and costumes for the girls' friends as well. Later, Mrs. Cuccinello, 71, made quilts for each one of her 10 grandchildren. To her daughters now scattered around the country, she sent weekly packets of motherly advice: articles about teenage acne and the dangers of Internet access to Mrs. O'Brien, a mother of two boys, and about homemade anti-cockroach poison and bug sprays to her daughter in Florida.

Mrs. Cuccinello, who moved with her husband, Albert, to western New Hampshire, was in many ways a storybook grandmother—cozy and game. She traveled when she could—to Europe, Hawaii and California, where she was headed on Sept. 11 aboard American Airlines 11, to visit her sister and brother-in-law.

RICHARD CUDINA
Friends Around the World

Richard Cudina was the kind of guy who might have tried skiing down Mount Everest. That is, before he had hip surgery a few years ago. Of course, he still had his helicopter pilot's license and could easily distract himself by sailing or beating the pants off his friends in a game of golf.

"He had no fear and we all lived vicariously through Richie," said his younger brother, Chris. "Work was work, but when the whistle blew, he picked up another life."

When he was not calling all over the world as a bond broker for Cantor Fitzgerald, Mr. Cudina was phoning his friends in every corner of the globe. Stan Kowalski, who grew up with Richard in Cliffside Park, N.J., recalls the day his friend tracked him down at a hotel near San Francisco, just to say hello.

"He could find anyone, anywhere," said Mr. Kowalski, who shared a birthday with his friend. (The two celebrated their 46th together three weeks ago, just as they had since grammar school.) "He had a presence that made people love him. That's why he had friends all over the world."

His brother, too, remembers the time Mr. Cudina unexpectedly tracked him down. He was at the Waldorf-Astoria, and it was 7 A.M., the first morning of his honeymoon.

"He just wanted to check on his little brother," he said. "He woke me up. Of course, I'll never forgive him for that."

THOMAS CULLEN
True to His Calling

In the weeks before his death, as a member of Squad 41 in the Bronx, Thomas Cullen, 31, studied for the Fire Department's lieutenant's exam. But even without a test ahead of him, his wife, Susan, said, his idea of pleasure reading was an abstruse volume about confined rescue or some other technical aspect of firefighting. If he worked in a kind of building he was unfamiliar with, he would read up on its structural peculiarities.

The couple met in 1992 at Fordham University, where Tom Cullen took the firefighters test and the law boards as a senior. He came from a family of lawyers, but "fire was his true love," Mrs. Cullen said. He made perfect scores on the exam, she said, but then had to wait four years for an opening, "buying time" as a CPR instructor and a dean of discipline at a public school.

Firefighter Cullen's 2-year-old son, Tom, shares the passion and already can distinguish one kind of truck from another. Father and son also shared a love of electric trains. Many nights, after the toddler went to sleep, his father would add a new twist or turn to the tracks on the living room floor. Mrs. Cullen continues the tradition, but with less panache.

"Lucky for me he's not picky," she said.

JOAN CULLINAN
Memories of T.M.G.F.

It was one of those sister things, not easily understood by the outside world. Joan Cullinan was T.M.G.F.

Her sister Blaise was T.O.G.F. And the third sister, Brenda, was T.Y.G.F.

The initials could mystify others. But the sisters knew what they meant: the middle girlfriend, the old girlfriend and the young girlfriend. The girlfriends ate oysters together at the Blue Water Grill in Manhattan. The girlfriends even vacationed together—in Paris.

Throughout her life, Ms. Cullinan, an assistant to the president at Cantor Fitzgerald who lived in Scarsdale, N.Y., seemed to have a knack for making a large group of friends feel as close as sisters.

"She was kind of like a girl's girl, a woman's woman," said her husband, Tom. Ms. Cullinan, 47, who had a long career in business, was in the middle of changing directions on Sept. 11. She and her husband were married in the summer of 2000, and they had just begun filling out paperwork to try to adopt a child from China. She had also sent out applications to graduate schools to pursue a degree in clinical social work.

"Maybe, one of these days, we'll get an acceptance letter," Mr. Cullinan said.

BRIAN THOMAS CUMMINS
A Math Whiz Early On

Brian Thomas Cummins was the fourth of six boys who remained close all their lives. His four surviving brothers are married but Brian was not. He was a surfer, skier and he loved to go out.

"Some people might say he burnt the candle at both ends—and we're glad he did," said his brother Brendan.

Mr. Cummins, 38, who lived in Manasquan, N.J., was a market maker and partner at Cantor Fitzgerald. He was born in New Jersey and was known as a math whiz, winning state prizes beginning in the fifth grade.

He attended the University of Colorado and then started a seafood restaurant, the Lobster Trap, in Belmar, N.J. After he got his M.B.A. from Rutgers, he gave up the restaurant and went to Donaldson, Lufkin & Jenrette, working on the floor of the New York Stock Exchange. Then he joined Cantor Fitzgerald, where he started as an assistant trader.

"His colleagues and bosses would all probably say the same thing about Brian—he was driven to succeed," his brother Brendan said. "I believe he enjoyed the process of accomplishing and shunned the idea of his own success and replaced it with the desire to do better. He was one of the sharpest guys I've ever met."

MICHAEL J. CUNNINGHAM
Life with Micky C.

Michael J. Cunningham and his wife, Teresa, were known among their friends for their theme parties. Costumes were always a must. In June, the party had a Hawaiian theme, and Mrs. Cunningham also wore a grass skirt, even though she was seven months pregnant with their first child.

"He was just the funnest person," Mrs. Cunningham said about her husband, who was from London and came to work here with Euro Brokers 11 years ago. "You would never forget him if you met him once at a bar."

Mr. Cunningham, 39, a negotiable securities broker, lived fully. Even though he never lost what she called his "heavy East End accent," he said he preferred American football to soccer, and he rooted for the Philadelphia Eagles. He and his wife lived in Princeton Junction, N.J., with their son, William.

The couple met while working together; at first she resisted the idea of going out with a co-worker. But he won her over. "He had this fun go-for-it attitude," she said. "He made me laugh. Plus he was very handsome."

"He used to say to me, 'I'm 6-foot-2, eyes of blue, Micky C. will come after you.'"

ROBERT CURATOLO
Image Captured in a Photo

Three brothers—two firefighters and a police officer—went to ground zero on Wednesday, Sept. 12, to search for the fourth: Robert Curatolo, 31, a firefighter and the baby of the family, married only three weeks. They had a pretty good idea where he was, because rescuers had already found the helmet of the lieutenant he had been with.

Rescuers had also, it turned out, found Mr. Curatolo's body, under a fire truck.

The brothers were told it would be better if someone else made the ID. Quiet Robert, funny Robert, Robert who ironed his clothes and worked two jobs.

"He was the cautious one, I was the wild one; I still can't believe this happened," said Billy Curatolo, a firefighter with Engine 243 in Brooklyn.

Robert Curatolo, who lived in Staten Island, was off duty when the towers were hit, one of the guys whose shift ended at 9 A.M. He hitched a ride to the scene with a 19th Precinct car. After the first building collapsed he was seen dragging a man with two broken legs to safety, then—in an eerie photo snapped by another firefighter—heading back to the second building. That is the last image his brothers have of him.

"We always have birthday parties for the nieces and the nephews and he was always late and always—since he was a teenager—he would arrive saying, 'Hello, my fans!'" said brother Anthony, the cop.

"He was always late to everything," said his brother Billy. "Except the World Trade Center. He gets there on time."

LARRY CURIA
Life with the Clam

The Cantor Fitzgerald Web site has listed memorial services for about 200 people recently, but one name leaps out: "Larry (the Clam) Curia."

Mr. Curia, a broker, according to his longtime friend Peter Garofolo, used that name on the Bloomberg business site, too. The genesis of the nickname? There was a time, Mr. Garofolo explains, when Mr. Curia, 41, was very uptight. But that time seemed to be over.

"We live in a decent-sized house," Linda Curia said of the Garden City, N.Y., home she and the Clam shared with their two children, a son, 4, and a daughter, 8.

"But there's no furniture. He always said he didn't want to live in a museum—he wanted for neighborhood kids to be able to Rollerblade and bicycle through it. My living room is completely empty except for two folding chairs and a computer. He wasn't materialistic; it was more important to him that the kids have a great time."

PAUL CURIOLI
The Birdhouse Expert

The son and grandson of skilled craftsmen, Paul Curioli discovered his carpentry gene only after he married. But he quickly made up for lost time.

On weekends, when he wasn't in the bleachers cheering on his teenage sons' baseball or football teams, Mr. Curioli, 53, a vice president with FM Global, a commercial insurance company, could typically be found in the garage of his home in Norwalk, Conn., knee-deep in a woodworking project. He built dressers, tables, a blanket chest, a corner cabinet for the television, a game table with an inlaid checkerboard top. His specialty, however, was birdhouses. In the beginning, he made simple A-frame models. But over time, they became more elaborate.

"Some were shingled and stuccoed by hand," said Mr. Curioli's wife, Kathi. "They're beautiful like Colonial homes."

A family man who grew his own tomatoes, Mr. Curioli had big plans for his birdhouses. In early September, he told his wife that he thought Martha Stewart might like to see them and asked her to write Ms. Stewart a letter.

After he was lost while attending a meeting at the World Trade Center, Mrs. Curioli decided to act on his request. She sent Ms. Stewart an e-mail message relating her husband's story and describing his birdhouses.

"He had just started one," Mrs. Curioli said. "It's sitting here unfinished."

MICHAEL CURTIN
Always Ready and Thinking

Water recoveries. Auto extractions. Cajoling deranged gunmen into straitjackets. Talking jilted lovers down from a ledge on the George Washington Bridge. As squad sergeant for Truck Company 2 of the Police Department's Emergency Service Unit, Michael Curtin never knew what kind of risky rescue operation he and his men might be asked to perform on any given day.

But he believed in being prepared. On Sundays or slow days, when New York residents managed to keep themselves out of mortal peril, Sergeant Curtin, 45, a former marine who served in the gulf war, did not let his squad members just sit around. Instead, he would drill them on old skills and teach them new ones—like how to wire a police van by tapping into a telephone pole.

"If you wanted an epitome of an E cop, that would be Michael Curtin," said Robert Yaeger, an officer with Truck 2, using the police lingo for an Emergency Service Unit officer. "He was always thinking on his feet and wanted you to think on your feet, too."

Not that Sergeant Curtin was all work and no play. At the end of those Sunday morning training sessions, he would fry up an outsize Marine Corps breakfast for all: sloppy eggs, sausage and bacon seasoned with his favorite red, blue and green spices.

On Sept. 11, Sergeant Curtin, the father of three athletic teenage girls, was due back in the kitchen of his home in Medford, N.Y., again—this time, to make a birthday dinner for his wife, Helga.

GAVIN CUSHNY
All Things American

Gavin Cushny, the son of an Episcopal priest from England, considered America paradise. Randy Yates, from California, was interested in everything British. Naturally, when the two young men met, as students at the University of St. Andrews in Scotland 25 years ago, they became close friends.

Mr. Cushny complained bitterly about Britain—the dreary weather, the lack of central heating, the ancient plumbing.

"He wanted to know a lot about California—what the homes were like, how they were built, why the plumbing didn't vibrate at night," Mr. Yates said.

The two friends talked of moving to California together, but Mr. Cushny instead settled in New York City, where he eventually went to work on the 104th floor of the World Trade Center, as a programmer for eSpeed.

"He loved what he considered the emotional honesty of Americans," Mr. Yates said.

His friend had an American's devotion to self-improvement. He studied math at Columbia, with the idea of perhaps getting an engineering degree. He took acting classes as a way of overcoming his stage fright. He had regular sessions with a therapist. One of the things he was working out, Mr. Yates said, was his relationship with his strict and intellectually demanding father, who died last year.

"Gavin was committed to emotional and intellectual growth," said his fiancée, Susann Brady, who was to have married Mr. Cushny, 47, on Oct. 26, and instead buried him. "He encouraged that in other people, too. If we had differences, he was always open to talking about them."

JOHN D'ALLARA
Calming Influence

John D'Allara, a member of the New York City Police Department's emergency service office in Harlem, was a rescue specialist who pried, cajoled or otherwise extracted a broad array of life-forms from danger when he entered 1 World Trade Center on Sept. 11.

During his 14 years on the job, Officer D'Allara, who was 47, dealt with a menagerie of exotic animals. Spider monkeys. Bats. Squirrels. One time he saved an iguana. But he helped plenty of people, too.

"One time we had a kid trapped in an elevator, with his head trapped between a beam and the elevator," said Sgt. Lee Hom, who worked with Officer D'Allara for five years in the late 1980s and early '90s. "He kept the kid calm, and we got him out."

A physical education teacher before he joined the N.Y.P.D., Mr. D'Allara, who lived with his wife and two sons in Rockland County, intended to go back to teaching.

"He loved the Police Department, but he was counting his paychecks to retirement," said his brother, Dan D'Allara.

One more quirky thing: John and Dan D'Allara are twins. And John D'Allara's boys, Johnny, who is 7, and Nicholas, 3, were born on the same day in May.

JACK D'AMBROSI
Hooking the Big One

"Fishing, fishing, fishing."

That was what Karen D'Ambrosi said her husband, Jack, liked to do most when he wasn't at work, or helping out at church, or coaching one of his two daughters in soccer or basketball. Luckily, he had a friend with a lake on his property a few miles away from the couple's Woodcliff Lake, N.J., home, so almost every weekend, from April to October, he would cast a line. His best

catch came this past summer, a beautiful 32-pound striped bass. ("Or was it 32 inches?" his wife wondered. "I don't know. It was big.") She even has a picture of him with it.

"He would come back from fishing trips loaded with bags and bags of fish and fish fillets," she remembered, laughing. "And he would just give it away, up and down our street. So everywhere we'd go, all over town, there would be people thanking him for the fish, you know, saying, 'We just had a barbecue, Jack, it was great.' "

EDDIE D'ATRI
Just a Working Man

Lynda Mari was painting her porch in the fall of 2000 when she was approached by a construction worker with an extension cord.

"Hello, I'm Eddie," he said. "You mind if I borrow your power?" Eddie D'Atri was a handsome, muscular fellow. "I told him, 'You can borrow anything you want,' " Ms. Mari said the other day. She asked him if he was a fireman.

"I just felt it," she said. "Something just told me." He told her no, he was just a working man, but she didn't believe it. Her brother is a fireman, and something deep inside her made her fearful of falling in love with a guy like that.

But she did. They were engaged June 30. Mr. D'Atri was 38. He studied nursing and was a lieutenant at Squad 1 in Park Slope, Brooklyn. He was crowned Mr. Staten Island in 1987.

Sadly, steel is stronger than muscle, and Mr. D'Atri leaves behind a broken heart.

MICHAEL D'ESPOSITO
Happy Together

Michael D'Esposito and his family led quiet lives. "No fairy tales," said Grace D'Esposito, his wife. Life passed to the rhythm of daily and weekly routines. In the mornings, he would kiss his wife while

The fireboat *John J. Harvey,* on the Hudson River near Cornwall, shoots out a twisting, arching water display in memory of Kenneth Kumpel, a firefighter with Ladder Company 25 in Manhattan who was killed at the World Trade Center on September 11. (*Suzanne DeChillo*)

she was still asleep before he left for work as a consultant at Marsh & McLennan. In the evenings, his 2-year-old daughter, Ashley, would help him take off his shoes after work. Mr. D'Esposito, 32, would tickle her and throw her on the bed while Mrs. D'Esposito cooked.

After dinner they would watch television, content in being together. Conversation centered on Ashley and on all the improvements around the house that they never got to. Bedtime was 8:30 P.M. for Ashley. First came a glass of milk, then a story. Tuesdays were Ashley's swim class. Saturdays were music class. The weekend was the time for neighborhood walks with the stroller.

Mrs. D'Esposito does not remember her good-bye kiss that Tuesday morning. She was at Ashley's swim class when she first heard. Now the two are taking it day by day.

"We're trying to get back to a normal routine, which I don't think will ever be normal again," she said.

C. ARRON DACK
Poetry and Software

A deck off a garage. A handmade fish table. A long, a loe, a winding, drooping dahlia. From the moment his parents named him Arron with an RR instead of AA, C. Arron Dack always surprised.

Born in England and raised in Canada, Mr. Dack, 39, studied molecular biology, but went into computers. He wrote loopy poems and complex business software. In July he became senior vice president of a Midtown start-up called Encompys, but there was a trade show at Windows on the World he couldn't miss.

His wife, Abigail, said that after they settled in Montclair, N.J., Mr. Dack wanted to prove he was not all brain and no brawn. He built what may be Montclair's only garage deck—impractical, yes, but certainly popular with Carter, 2, and Olivia, 6. To celebrate a promotion, he promised Mrs. Dack a great fish dinner, then spent days building a unique table of cedar and granite for the fish.

And in a spare bedroom on the third floor, there is a headboard painted with words from one of Mr. Dack's poems.

"It goes, 'A long, a loe, a winding, drooping dahlia,' " recited Mrs. Dack.

CARLOS DaCOSTA
Honoring a Heritage

All the houses on his block in the Elmora section of Elizabeth, N.J., were well kept and aging in a graceful, uniform way. But Carlos DaCosta's property stood out, its individuality coming from a three-foot-high concrete-and-wrought-iron fence constructed in the style of walls in Portugal.

That fence—the only one on that side of the street—was built by Mr. DaCosta and his father-in-law. Even after more than 30 years in the United States, Mr. DaCosta, who was born in Portugal, showed off his native culture whenever possible.

"There was a special place in his heart for Portugal," said his younger sister, Celeste. "He loved Portuguese culture and Portuguese food." Mr. DaCosta, 41, regularly took friends to the Portuguese restaurants in Newark's Ironbound section. On special occasions, he would take Portuguese pastries to his office at the World Trade Center, where he was general manager of building services for the Port Authority.

Mr. DaCosta spoke only Portuguese at home to make sure that his two children learned the language, and he tried to make them aware of how big and diverse a world this is.

"Carlos was fascinated by different cultures," said Antoinette Viana, a friend since high school. "He would take his kids anywhere that would seem different."

THOMAS DAMASKINOS
Passionate Fan of Broncos

Thomas Damaskinos, his wife is quick to point out, was a passionate Denver Broncos fan long before John Elway came along. No, Mr. Damaskinos's Broncos fixation started 23 years ago, when he was 10. His brother gave him a Broncos cap, and that was that. So what if the Broncos lost every game he ever attended?

In 2000, for her husband's 32nd birthday, Jennifer Damaskinos found the perfect gift for him—the official N.F.L. John Elway Retirement Helmet, autographed and embossed with Mr. Elway's career statistics. And when Mile High Stadium was put out of commission, he simply had to have a souvenir.

"He bought two of the seats because he never got to go," Mrs. Damaskinos said in October. "They are supposed to come next month."

Mr. Damaskinos, vice president for operations at Cantor Fitzgerald, had other obsessions. He taped every single episode of *The Simpsons,* for example, and on some nights, he and his wife indulged in *Simpsons* marathons, calling out favorite bits of *Simpsons* dialogue.

And then there were his children, Jessica, 13, by his first wife, and Matthew, 1. Jessica and her father had a nightly ritual. He would tuck her in and then they would race to see who could say "I love you" the fastest and the most.

MANUEL DaMOTA
Two Languages Masterly Mixed

For Manuel DaMota, woodworking was translating. But it was a translation process that worked with images, not words. Architects would concoct fanciful designs, and Mr. DaMota would translate their elaborate visions from paper into wood. His work could be as elaborate as making jewelry—with glass marbles, aluminum and fabric that all had to be embedded into the woodwork.

As a project manager for Bronx Builders, Mr. DaMota, 43, had worked with architects like David Rockwell and Jeffrey Beers to do the interiors for fine restaurants including the Russian Tea Room, Nobu Next Door and Tuscan Steak. But he also worked for the children of the North Presbyterian Head Start program, where he built a miniature mahogany building complete with windows.

"He loved working with wood," said his wife, Barbara. "You could see it from the way he talked about it."

He always said yes when asked to do another project.

"He was busy, so we only went to the beach once this past summer," said Christopher, Mr. DaMota's 10-year-old son. Mr. DaMota had two other sons, with a fourth child on the way.

His latest project was a wine room for another top Manhattan restaurant, Windows on the World.

PATRICK W. DANAHY
Counting Down the Days

She was born on Oct. 11, a month too late to get a blurry glimpse of her father. Grace, she was called. When Patrick W. Danahy and his wife, Mary, had discussed girls' names, she suggested Grace. He was hesitant. But Grace is the patron saint of motorcyclists, she told him. (No, really. Look it up.)

"It'll have to be," he said. "She'll look out for me when I go out riding." Mr. Danahy loved motorcycles, and cars. (He bought himself an old Porsche for his last birthday, his 35th.) And mountain bikes. (He did a couple of 100-mile bikeathons.)

"He seized any sunny day," his wife said. "He wouldn't waste it inside."

But "his girls were his life," she said—before Grace, a 2-year-old and a 3-year-old. He did a weekly countdown with the oldest, saying on Sunday nights, "Five days to go," and on Mondays, "Four," till he would be home with them. He would often get up at 4:30 to go to a gym. And later, from the 90th floor of 2 World Trade Center—he was vice president for investor services at Fiduciary Trust—he would call and say, "How are my girls doing?"

He called and talked to them at 8:30 A.M. on Sept. 11, hanging up just before the first plane hit—and with no bikers' saint to protect him.

VINCENT G. DANZ
"A Special Breed"

Vincent G. Danz was a member of the New York Police Department's Emergency Service Unit's third squad in the Bronx. The elite unit's officers are experts in areas like psychology, rappelling, scuba diving, first aid and marksmanship. Officer Danz liked the excitement and challenge of the E.S.U.

Officer Danz, of Farmingdale, N.Y., was also a husband, and a father of three daughters, including an 8-month-old. With the two older girls, he liked to watch *SpongeBob SquarePants,* a Nickelodeon cartoon.

"He was a special breed," Felix Danz said of his brother, who at 38 was the youngest of nine children. "I'd always ask him if he had any good jobs lately. He'd say, 'Yeah, I had this subway "pin job," ' where some poor soul was taken out by the subway, or even worse, still alive.

"The E.S.U. guys are the ones who go on the tracks, find some way to lift up the train and get those people out," Mr. Danz continued. "He wasn't boastful. He wasn't one of those guys with the swelled chest at the bar. He loved his work and the guys that he worked with. They would die for one another. I think that goes globally for the N.Y.P.D. My brother and his partner went into the trade center without any questions. They knew what to do and how to do it. Unfortunately, this thing was bigger than either of them."

DWIGHT DARCY
Bad Memories of '93

Like many others who were there, Dwight Darcy, 55, lived with the memory of the 1993 trade center bombing. It bothered him for years, said his wife, Veronica.

"Every time there was a bang, he would jump," she said.

But Mr. Darcy was at work again on the 66th floor of the north tower, where he was a labor relations lawyer for the Port Authority of New York and New Jersey, when the trade center was struck. Mr. Darcy had been with the Port Authority for 25 years, raising two sons with his wife in their Bronxville, N.Y., home, and serving on the parish board of St. Joseph's of Bronxville Roman Catholic Church.

Opera was one of his great loves, Mrs. Darcy said, and the couple frequently attended performances at the Met and the City Opera with groups organized by Mr. Darcy's Fordham University alumni group and by the New York Athletic Club, where he was also a member.

ELIZABETH DARLING
On the Right Path

Elizabeth Darling was moved by a sermon at a Baptist church in Newark last Sunday about the struggles that make you stronger.

Ms. Darling had enough struggles to turn her into Superwoman. She was the single mother of a 2-year-old boy. She feared being laid off from her job as a business analyst at Marsh & McLennan. She worried about her mortgage payments.

The daughter of a minister, Ms. Darling, 28, was a spiritual person. She spoke to her best friend, Toyia Burks, about the sermon, and was surprised to learn that Ms. Burks had heard a similar sermon. It seemed to tell Ms. Darling that she was on the right path.

"She was going through a lot of transition and just trying to find a balance," Ms. Burks said. "She reached back to her Christian roots."

ANETTE DATARAM
"Get Me a Big Fish"

Anette Dataram worked in accounting for Windows on the World at 1 World Trade Center and planned to pursue a bachelor's degree to further her career as an accountant. But the 25-year-old's real passion seemed to be food—not that served at the famous restaurant where she worked, but her own.

"Get me a big fish, I'm going to bake it," she would tell her mother after watching one of the cooking television shows she loved. Then she would cook the new recipe for her parents, her sister and her two brothers, with whom she lived in Queens.

"Yes, it was very good," Chandra Dataram said of her oldest daughter's culinary abilities.

Mrs. Dataram said her daughter, who was engaged to be married next year, was quiet and simple, not "a dressed-up type," but was also driven and ambitious. In New York City for the last nine years, the family had come to this country from Guyana to take advantage of its opportunities, she said, and her daughter was certainly making it.

LAWRENCE DAVIDSON
His New Best Friend

Lawrence Davidson decided to go live in Israel shortly after he graduated from Erasmus Hall High School in Brooklyn, and ended up staying there for 12 years. He lived in a kibbutz, fell in love, married, had two children and joined the army, where he became a tank commander.

He traded in his uniform for a suit after returning to New York in 1980 and joining the financial services industry. Mr. Davidson, 51, had been working as a broker for Aon for only three weeks when the World Trade Center was attacked.

Around the time of his return to the United States, Mr. Davidson's marriage ended, and his children moved to Toronto with their mother. But his son Marc said something wonderful happened five years ago: Marc graduated from college and moved to New York, where he made a new best friend—his father. They moved in together, cooked dinners and even met for lunch. They got to know each other again, this time as adults.

"I feel really blessed," Marc said from Whistler, British Columbia, where he now lives. "I really got to know my father again and be a part of his life."

MICHAEL DAVIDSON
A Fight for His Beloved

"He is going to get married in July," Jeff Davidson was saying in September 2001 about his brother Michael, a 27-year-old equity options sales trader for Cantor Fitzgerald.

"Her name is Dominique DeNardo. They met in college, at Rutgers. He just saw her from a distance, fell in love with her and wanted her. So he beat up her boyfriend and took her. Caveman-like, pretty much. And they've lived happily ever after. They got engaged on Sept. 21, 2000. On her 25th birthday, he took her to Cancún to propose. He lied to her by saying he won a trip on one of the Web sites just for the weekend. About midway through, he finally popped the question. He waited until sunset on the first night.

"He's a big mush ball. He cries at commercials. But you better not put that in because he thinks he's a tough guy. He's kind of a big kid—5-foot-10, 215 pounds. But he's as sensitive as they come.

"We have a grandma down in Florida. So every chance we get, we try to get Grandma to fly up. Grandma's like, 'I don't have the money right now.' My brother's like, 'Don't worry.' He pays for it, or we all pitch in, whatever. We get her up here somehow. He cares.'"

SCOTT M. DAVIDSON
Christmas Boy

Like many adults who are still children at heart, Scott M. Davidson loved Christmas. In fact, his friends in Staten Island called him Christmas Boy.

One year he drove up to Perry Seridge's apartment with Christmas tree lights strung around his car, all lighted up. When he cautioned that wiring lights to the car battery could be unsafe, he held up a finger and began rummaging through the pile of sweaty basketball clothes in his back seat.

After a few minutes, Firefighter Davidson, 33, a member of Ladder Company 118 in Brooklyn Heights, found what he was looking for: a fire extinguisher.

Triumphantly, he proclaimed, "I got it covered."

Firefighter Davidson was also a bartender; the father of Peter, 8, and Casey, 4; a substitute teacher at Intermediate School 49 near his home in Staten Island, and an unabashed patriot long before the World Trade Center fire that he died fighting on Sept. 11.

"He loved all things American," Mr. Seridge said. "I used to think it was kind of rare, really, especially for a young guy who had never been in a war. Looking at it now, it was nice. He'd be really happy now that everyone would have flags out."

CLINTON DAVIS
Father, Model and Hero

Clinton Davis, a Port Authority policeman, was a disciplinarian. "Keep in line, stay out of trouble and stay in school" was the mantra he had for his children and his nephews and nieces.

"When one of the kids got into trouble, he would have a little talk with them," said his younger sister, Sandra Davis. The children looked up to Mr. Davis, 38, as their model, and the family savored the story of his restraining a "huge crazy man" at the World Trade Center. In the process, Mr. Davis tore his hamstring.

The knowledge that Mr. Davis died while helping others gives the Flushing, Queens, family comfort. One of his colleagues told his family that he ran in and out of the north tower to evacuate people, and when he went in one last time, the tower collapsed. His body was later found on a stairs next to his closest friend, another Port Authority police officer, Uhuru Houston.

"They knew their father died a hero," Ms. Davis said of

Clinton Davis's three chidren, ages 18, 12 and 10. "And that made it a lot easier for them to accept the facts." But still, they are on the move with their mother to Texas, where their maternal grandparents live. The memory New York evokes is just too painful.

EDWARD DAY
Warm Humor, Frozen Shoes

Edward Day did not just extinguish fires. He extinguished grouchiness.

At Engine Company 28 and Ladder 11 on the Lower East Side, where Mr. Day, 45, was a firefighter, he kept a sharp eye out for grumpy colleagues. They got the Day treatment: smiley face stickers slapped on their helmets.

Whenever he stayed at his mother's house in Newport, R.I., he would make the bed when he was ready to leave and then drop a dollar on it with a note, "For the maid." His mother liked to give what she called the last Christmas party of the year, held well into January. Mr. Day had a ritual at the parties: he collected all the bottle caps from exhausted beer bottles and deposited them throughout the house in her plants.

His wife, Bridgitte, was a fervent Clint Eastwood fan, so he would sign his cards to her, "Clint Eastwood."

"He was always ready to make you laugh," said Tim Day, his brother, "whether he knew you for 20 years or 20 minutes."

The first time Eddy Day met Tim's wife, Essie, he asked if she wanted a glass of wine. Sure, she said. He brought it out and handed it to her. "Excuse me," he said, and bent over and slipped off her shoes. As she watched, mystified, he marched into the kitchen and put them in the freezer.

JENNIFER DE JESUS
An Aunt and Confidante

Galo Perez says he practically grew up with his aunt, Jennifer De Jesus, at their grandmother's Brooklyn home.

"I'm 20, she was 23," he said. "She was more like a sister, and she affected me a lot; I could go to her about things nobody else could understand."

A year and a half ago, Ms. De Jesus got a job as a data entry worker at Morgan Stanley, on the 59th floor of the World Trade Center. The home of her extended family in Brooklyn has become a place of memories.

"She was always so sweet and thoughtful; always looking out for other people," said her sister, Wilma Perez. "She baby-sat for my kids all the time, and my kids loved her."

Ms. De Jesus leaves a 2-year-old daughter, Jacinda.

NEREIDA DE JESUS
Life with Lauren

For Nereida De Jesus, life equaled Lauren. Lauren was her daughter, a bubbly 7-year-old whom Ms. De Jesus, 30, was raising alone in Woodlawn in the Bronx. Mother and daughter would do everything together—get their hair done, go to movies, take bubble baths.

Ms. De Jesus's new job as a claims adjuster at Aon Insurance, which she started only a few months before Sept. 11, enabled her to send Lauren to a private Catholic school.

When Ms. De Jesus was not working or taking care of Lauren, she could usually be found at church, either at her sister's missionary church in Dover, N.J., or at a church near her home.

Ms. De Jesus, said her sister, Elaine De Jesus, wanted to be like her own mother, who had raised three children alone on the Lower East Side—when that neighborhood was one of the worst in the city—and somehow had them all turn out fine.

"Her job was helping her accomplish the plans that she had," Elaine De Jesus said. "She was proud."

EMERITA DE LA PEÑA and JUDITH DIAZ-SIERRA
Best Friends Forever

Emerita de la Peña and Judith Diaz-Sierra met in business school as teenagers and soon became best friends. Each was the maid of honor at the other's wedding, they vacationed together with their husbands, and they both worked as administrative assistants at Fiduciary Trust Company International, where Mrs. de la Peña had helped recruit Ms. Diaz-Sierra in 1997.

Mrs. de la Peña, 32, of Queens, known by her nickname, Emy, was the extrovert of the two. The mother of a 1-year-old daughter, Daniella, she wanted to become a schoolteacher and had been attending St. Francis College in Brooklyn part time to get a bachelor's degree.

"She's beautiful and she was a beautiful person," said her husband, Gabriel.

Ms. Diaz-Sierra was reserved but "had a great laugh, a great heart, was very high in her morals and very selective about her friends," said her husband, Ron Sierra.

Ms. Diaz-Sierra, 32, worked one row away from her best friend on the 90th floor of 2 World Trade Center. A co-worker told Mr. Sierra the two were together when he last saw them on the day of the attacks, as they held the door open for him.

Mr. Sierra rushed to the city from Suffolk County, where he and his wife lived, after learning of the attack, but could not get onto the Brooklyn Bridge. As he watched the soot-covered people walking from Manhattan, he said, "I was just hoping that Emy and Judith would come out, that they were among the thousands crossing the bridge."

FRANK DE MARTINI
Defending the Brownstone

Frank De Martini had a passion for old cars, motorcycles, sailing and everything Italian. He also loved restoring Brooklyn brownstones, and was fascinated with the World Trade Center. Mr. De Martini, an architect, started working at the twin towers when he was hired to assess the damage from the 1993 bombing. He stayed on, becoming the construction manager, the man to see when you wanted to move a wall or rearrange the plumbing. Mr. De Martini's wife, Nicole, also worked in the towers, and their children, Sabrina, 10, and Dominic, 8, could often be seen splashing around in the pool at the complex's Marriott Hotel.

Compact and athletic, Mr. De Martini, 49, once used a baseball bat to chase away an intruder who had picked the wrong brownstone.

"He was really very fearless," said Michael Prager, a long-time friend. When the north tower was struck, Nicole De Martini was just leaving her husband's office on the 88th floor. Finding a stairway that was still intact, he ushered her to safety. But he refused to follow just then because others needed help. "He saw himself very much as a protector," Mr. Prager said.

ROBERT J. DeANGELIS Jr.
Firefighting and the Church

Just because he spent his working life as a project manager for the Washington Group International—helping to build one of the biggest dams in the world, in the Philippines—Robert J. DeAngelis Jr. did not curtail his responsibilities as a district fire commissioner on Long Island. He had begun as a volunteer fireman 29 years ago, had taken decades of fire calls in the middle of the night, and this avocation was an anchor of his life.

Nor did his demanding job keep Mr. DeAngelis from 6:30 A.M. Mass every day at St. Thomas the Apostle Roman Catholic Church in West Hempstead, N.Y. In fact, Msgr. James Lisante had given him the keys so that he could open the church on mornings when the priest arrived later than the 47-year-old Mr. DeAngelis.

On Sept. 11, Mr. DeAngelis called upon his rescue expertise in evacuating co-workers in his office on the 91st floor of 2 World Trade Center and in guiding many others downstairs. Then he went back up to his office to man the phones, said his wife, Denise.

"I was still talking with him when the phone went dead."

THOMAS P. DeANGELIS
In the Thick of Things

Five years ago, when Thomas P. DeAngelis was promoted to battalion chief in the New York City Fire Department, his wife, Patty, told him: "You've been running into burning buildings for 22 years. But you're a battalion chief now, so you won't have to do that anymore."

In her heart, she knew better. Tommy DeAngelis would never send a firefighter into a building he had not personally entered and checked out. Around the East 51st Street firehouse in Manhattan, he was known as Chuckles because of his sunny good humor and his lust for life: sports, cooking, sailing, carpentry, writing. But when the alarm sounded, he would suddenly become all business.

Sometimes he would kick around the idea of retiring in a year or two—he was 51—maybe to take up writing children's books. But, again, Mrs. DeAngelis knew better.

"He loved being a firefighter way too much to ever quit early," she said.

On Monday, Sept. 10, she had lunch with him at their home in Westbury, on Long Island, before he headed into Manhattan to pull a 24-hour shift. "See you Tuesday night," she said as he left, giving him a kiss. "Be careful."

JAYCERYLL deCHAVEZ
Dreams in the Clouds

Jayceryll deChavez never came across like a know-it-all. He was smart but soft-spoken. Still, he had his ambitions. For the longest time, he had dreamed of working in one of the twin towers of the World Trade Center. He even told his mother that he wanted to build his own tower.

Mr. deChavez got part of his wish. He worked as an assistant to the portfolio manager at Fiduciary Trust, a job that his parents said he loved, in 2 World Trade Center. He was 24 and had just passed the first level of a test to become a financial analyst. He was eager to take a review class for the next level in October 2001. He lived in Carteret, N.J., with his parents, Bibiano and Asuncion deChavez.

Despite his humble manner, his parents said, Mr. deChavez never had to struggle to ace tests. He had been at the top of his class from elementary school through Rutgers, where he studied finance and economics. "He was a very ambitious guy," his father said.

SIMON DEDVUKAJ
Son of Albanian Tradition

Simon Dedvukaj, his seven brothers and sisters agree, was the good son. When his siblings had questions about Albanian history, he was the encyclopedia they turned to. As a 13-year-old he sat for hours with his grandfather learning about all things Albanian, while his brothers played pool downstairs. Although he was born and raised in New York, he remained close to Albania and its traditions.

"He was Old World in many ways," said his brother-in-law, Joey Vukaj. "Take the way he honored guests. If a visitor was at Simon's house, even for six hours, Simon would stand the whole time."

"But," Mr. Vukaj continued, "he was New World in the way he honored children." Mr. Dedvukaj, 26, who supervised maintenance workers at the World Trade Center, skimped on himself to take his nieces and nephews to McDonald's and to buy them lavish Christmas presents.

"He dressed very mediocre so he could spend his money on other people," Mr. Vukaj said. "He'd spend just $30 on sneakers for himself and then he'd spend $200 on sneakers for his nieces and nephews."

Two years ago, Mr. Vukaj and his wife, Donna, Mr. Dedvukaj's oldest sister, went to a cousin's wedding in Albania. "There was this gorgeous girl there," Mr. Vukaj said. "When we went home we told Simon, 'We met the girl for you.'" Mr. Dedvukaj soon went to Albania to meet her, and it was love at first sight. And soon his wife-to-be, Elizabeth, moved to the United States. They would have celebrated their first anniversary in October 2001.

"She was brought to a new world," said Nik Dedvukaj, Simon's brother. "And then she was hit by something like this. It's crazy."

JASON DeFAZIO
Love under His Nose

His last summer, Jason DeFazio married the girl who had a crush on him in high school. He was a linebacker on the Curtis High School football team on Staten Island; Michele Moss was a cheerleader, about three years his junior. She was in love with him; he had no idea.

But when they met by happenstance at the Jersey shore three years ago, he paid attention. He wondered aloud how he had missed her in the first place. No matter. The relationship Ms. Moss had dreamed of as a teenager blossomed under a star-filled sky.

Now he is gone again. Mr. DeFazio, 29, worked as a bond trader at Cantor Fitzgerald on the 104th floor of the north tower. Mrs. DeFazio is heartbroken that they did not have a chance to raise children. She will miss the chutzpah that helped him work his way from the mailroom to the trading floor.

"He was a joy to be around," Mrs. DeFazio said. "He made crazy faces that made everyone laugh. He was the type of person I could bring to meet new friends and he got along with everybody."

VITO DeLEO
"Never Surrender"

Vito DeLeo was in court in March 1994 when four defendants were convicted in the 1993 bombing of the World Trade Center.

A trade center mechanic who had grudgingly worn a hearing aid since the explosion, Mr. DeLeo had been fixated by the trial. He plastered his office with clippings about the case. When the verdict came, he rushed to meet his wife, Sally Ann, to have a vodka on the rocks in celebration, he said in an interview with the *New York Times* at the time.

"I had chills coming down my body when I heard it," he said. "For my colleagues who are deceased: 'We can't bring you back, but I hope now that your souls will rest in peace. Never surrender.'"

Mr. DeLeo, 42, who was 150 feet from the explosion in 1993, was partly deafened by the blast. Nonetheless, he helped dozens of people escape from the building, said his cousin Helen Potenzano. Witnesses told the family that Mr. DeLeo, a father of two, was back at it again on Sept. 11.

"He was a hero twice," Ms. Potenzano said.

COLLEEN DELOUGHERY
"She Was Not Shy"

Colleen Deloughery's tiny backyard in Bayonne, N.J., was the center of the galaxy. A pool took up most of it, leaving barely enough space for a table and chairs. But no matter how many friends and relatives showed up on weekends—dozens, scores, nobody kept count—they squeezed in somehow: kids splashing, adults yakking, beer flowing, luscious barbeque aromas swirling.

"There was always room for people," Patricia Marrese said of her sister's universe. "I called it the magic yard."

Open, spontaneous, generous, Mrs. Deloughery, 41, laughed a lot, and said "I love you" too much. Perhaps that's why everyone needed her so terribly—not just her husband, Jay, and her "shadows," Amanda, 8, and Michael, 5, or her sister and five brothers, but the menagerie of nieces, nephews and cousins, and the circus of friends and co-workers at Aon (99th floor, 2 World Trade Center).

Strangers too. Jeanette Krupinski, a friend, recalled how Ms. Deloughery had stopped one day to talk to a homeless teenage mother living with her baby on the margins of a commuter station. "After that, she started bringing things to the woman—a stroller, a carrier, clothes, food, milk," Ms. Krupinski said. "She was not shy. She did wonderful things."

MANNY DelVALLE Jr.
Carpe Diem, to Music

Manny DelValle Jr. was an organized man—he had to be to find time for his extensive family and all of his interests.

"Manny was a don't-leave-for-tomorrow-what-you-can-do-today guy," said his mother, Gricel Zayas-Moyer, of Brookline, Mass.

At home in the Bronx, Firefighter DelValle took advanced classes in salsa dancing. He loved Latin music but listened to everything. "Rap," said his brother Pete Moyer. "And R&B," added his sister Grace Nolly. "Old school," said his father, Manuel DelValle, to be specific.

Firefighter DelValle, who graduated from the University of Maryland, was also an accomplished moguls skier and roller skater, a traveler, a lover of war movies and, his family says, a lady's man. He also got Engine Company No. 5, where he was assigned, to participate in the Puerto Rican Day Parade. He was the one in the family who always sent a card and gift to siblings, half siblings and cousins.

He helped his stepfather get organized, too. "All of a sudden, my husband was remembering all this stuff, and he told me 'Manny organized my Palm Pilot,' " Mrs. Zayas-Moyer said.

ANTHONY DEMAS
Always Time for His Sons

Anthony Demas's love for his twin boys began before their birth on Aug. 5, 1993. He had been born on an Aug. 4, and he asked his wife, Violetta, to wait a day so the boys would have a birthday they could call their own.

Mr. Demas, 61, was a managing director of Aon Corporation for four years, and before that had been a managing director at Marsh & McLennan, where he worked for 31 years, including assignments in London and Milan. Colleagues described a dynamic, natural leader, a former first lieutenant in the Army, an expert in risk management and a respected mentor, who also had the most impressive collection of family photos in the office.

His secretary told Mrs. Demas that he raced through the 105th-floor office in the south tower on Sept. 11, encouraging everybody to get out. "He would never leave anyone behind," Mrs. Demas said.

Mr. Demas, whom family members called Andoni, was proud of his Greek heritage, his world-class cooking (as well as his grilled cheese sandwiches) and his 1960 Mercedes convertible, which he would drive in the Fourth of July parade, wearing a Greek fisherman's cap, in Madison, Conn., where the family has a weekend house.

But most of all, he was proud of his boys, whose names were withheld at Mrs. Demas's request. Last summer, the boys saw Greece for the first time with their parents.

"Everything was about his boys," Mrs. Demas said.

MARTIN DeMEO
A Sting That Did Not Repel

The bumblebee caught her eye.

It was Halloween, 1982, and Martin DeMeo, dressed as a bee, was buzzing around a friend's Halloween party until he saw Joan, the future Mrs. DeMeo, who, you could say, was stung at first sight.

She had dressed as "Joan," she said, because she had come straight from work. Nonetheless, her outfit was a success. And she thought Mr. DeMeo, who friends called Marty, was "pretty funny."

She learned that the jovial bumblebee was in love with nature, and he introduced her to the joys of camping and hiking and long vacations next to the sea.

After his wife, his two children, Kristen, 16, and Nicholas, 14, and the great outdoors, what Mr. DeMeo, who was 47 and a New York City firefighter, liked most was baseball.

"He would have been very happy right now," Mrs. DeMeo said Saturday, referring to the Yankees' successful fight to get into the World Series. "I'm really hoping they do it for us this year. It would have meant a lot to Marty, and we need it really bad."

FRANCIS XAVIER DEMING
Solid Man, Quiet Hero

Francis Xavier Deming was not a peacock. He was not ostentatious, flashy or loud. He was a solid man who bowed to God.

"He was the quiet hero," said his sister Rose Deming-Phalon. "He worked hard and he worked a lot. He loved his family and he is missed."

By his sister's account, Mr. Deming, 47, was one of the workaday Americans who is never celebrated. He went to his job as an accountant at the Oracle Corporation and came directly home to Franklin Lakes, N.J. He taught his five children to swim. He was active in his church, Most Blessed Sacrament. He built furniture. He was a man who did not lean on others, but whom others leaned on.

His last day on earth is a good example. There is a record of it in a message he left for his wife on their answering machine. He and a group were fleeing the 99th floor of 1 World Trade Center. "Get down low so you can breathe better," he told the group. And then: "What happened to the people who were behind us?"

CAROL DEMITZ
Made Happy by Motherhood

When Carol Demitz got home from Fiduciary Trust, where she was the chief corporate lawyer, she did not reach for a martini. She went directly to play with Annie, her 4-year-old.

"I could tell what room the girls were in by the squealing and laughter," said Fred Brewer, her husband. "Carol would be playing hide-and-seek. Carol was thin and could squeeze herself into the most amazing little cubbyholes. You could hear Annie squealing when she found her."

Ms. Demitz, 49, was thrilled with motherhood. She pored over catalogs of children's clothes and bought a dollhouse with a fireplace that crackled and birds that chirped from the windows.

"She was so enamored of that dollhouse," Mr. Brewer said, referring to his wife, not his daughter. She had long loved vacationing in Switzerland among the green valleys and vast peaks of Mount Eiger. Last summer, her pleasure there was heightened by Annie, who was old enough to do a bit of mountain hiking. She felt the same way about the weathered house on a stretch of beachfront on Long Island's North Fork that they bought last spring.

"She loved taking Annie there," Mr. Brewer said. "It gave her life balance."

JEAN CAVIASCO DePALMA
One Last Girls' Night Out

Just think of that Saturday before the tragedy as, well, girls' night out at the World Trade Center. Jean Caviasco DePalma made sure her teenagers, Drew and Jamie, were O.K., then left home in Newfoundland, N.J., to stay the night with Michele Caviasco, her baby sister, on the Upper East Side of Manhattan. "We just hung out together," Ms. Caviasco said. They even went for a run along the East River, saying all the sister things.

Then a subway delivered them to the trade center, where Ms. DePalma, 42, happened to work as a forensic accountant on the 100th floor of the north tower at Marsh & McLennan.

But this was Saturday night, so they remained downstairs on the plaza between the twin towers and watched a free performance of the Twyla Tharp dance company. Afterward,

they strolled around, past those buildings that no longer exist, on their way to ice cream at Ben & Jerry's.

Back in the apartment, they laughed a lot while watching Ms. Caviasco's tape of Madonna in concert. The sisters had always been close, even though Jean was the oldest of five and Michele the youngest, growing up in Wood-Ridge, N.J. Their friendship rekindled after Ms. DePalma's divorce two years ago.

"I remember the closeness we had that day," Ms. Caviasco said. "I feel lucky to have had that last bit of her."

ROBERT DERANEY
"Pretty Much Perfect"

When Michele Haobsh learned last year that she had breast cancer, she called Robert Deraney, her brother, and said: "What do I do?" He provided answers, finding an oncologist and surgeon and accompanying her to chemotherapy and radiation appointments. Long before she did, he joined Gilda's Club, for people with cancer and their families, and made an appointment for her and her family.

"He got me through it," she said.

Mr. Deraney, 43, a financial consultant who graduated from Princeton and the Wharton School, was at a breakfast meeting at Windows on the World on Sept. 11.

He was the "high energy" family organizer, Mrs. Haobsh said. He planned the annual reunions of 70 relatives, ordering Lebanese food and creating a game—Who Wants to be a Famillionaire?—based on Deraney trivia.

His Upper West Side apartment was furnished with family antiques. He set an elegant table with china and silver for 35 and ended evenings by playing the piano.

"He was," Mrs. Haobsh said, "pretty much perfect."

MICHAEL DeRIENZO
Half of a Duo

Michael DeRienzo, a broker at Cantor Fitzgerald, had the safe job in his family. It was his twin sister, Lisa, a narcotics detective in the New York City Police Department, who put herself in harm's way every time she went to work. Mr. DeRienzo was so nervous that he would call daily and beep her if he got no answer at her desk.

"I'm O.K., I'm O.K.," Ms. DeRienzo, who just turned 36, would assure him.

Mr. DeRienzo and his sister were close as close can be, twins and then some. Their father had disappeared years back, remarried and not maintained contact with the family. Their mother died of cancer four years ago. "It was just him and me," Ms. DeRienzo said. "We were like magnets."

As children, attending parochial school near the family's Staten Island home, she was the standout athlete. Michael would grow testy with people who considered him merely "Lisa's brother." All that changed in college, she said, when her brother reached his full growth—tall and thin, a marathoner-in-the-making, a favorite among the girls at Wagner College. "Then it was 'Lisa who?' " she said.

On Sept. 10, the twins were planning a weekend trip to Chicago for a Mets-Cubs game, to be together on the anniversary of their mother's death. Instead, with a fellow member of the narcotics task force who also lost a sibling, Ms. DeRienzo spent the doubly sad day in the bucket brigade at the World Trade Center.

DAVID P. DeRUBBIO
"Dave Was an Experience"

If you knew David P. DeRubbio—Crazy Dave or Crazy Uncle Dave to his family— you knew about the jokes and you knew about the milk.

The fifth of seven children, Mr. DeRubbio, a Brooklyn firefighter, was famous in the family for his countless ways of getting around the household rule against profanity and for the zany nicknames he gave out.

"Dave was an experience," said Angela Tiberi, his younger sister, who contended with being nicknamed Witchie Poo.

He doted on his daughter Jessica, 12. He nicknamed her Pestica.

To avoid using one profanity at home, Firefighter DeRubbio would say, "What the H-E-double hockey sticks is going on?" Callers who encountered him at the other end of the line would typically find themselves being serenaded.

Firefighter DeRubbio, 38, was such a milk hound that their mother joked about buying a family cow just to meet the demand, his sister said.

To the delight of his friends and family, none of this stopped after Mr. DeRubbio, who joined the Fire Department in 1998 and was assigned to Engine Company 226, became an adult.

"I know he's up there," Ms. Tiberi said. "And he's got everyone rolling."

CHRISTIAN L. DeSIMONE
Taking On Responsibility

When Christian L. DeSimone's father died of a heart attack in the spring of 2000, he was there for his mother, Christel. He left his position as linebacker for the Rams football team at the University of Rhode Island so he could have more time to commute to and from

his home in Ringwood, N.J. After graduation, Mr. DeSimone, 23, moved back home and found a job as a forensic accountant at Marsh & McLennan on the 100th floor at 1 World Trade Center.

"He didn't have to take on the responsibility of the house, but he wanted to do it," Mrs. DeSimone said. "He was always like that. Just the other day, a 20-year-old neighbor came to the door to tell me that my son was his hero because he carried himself so wonderfully and he was so smart."

Mr. DeSimone was to have turned 24 on Oct. 18.

CINDY DEUEL
Tracing the Line

For more than two years, Cindy Deuel had been trying to map the Deuel family line back to 16th-century England. Using the New York Public Library, the National Archives, the Internet and her brother Richard's similar passion for genealogy, she had made a few important discoveries, including great-great-grandfather Henry Deuel's unmarked grave at Cedar Lawn Cemetery in Paterson, N.J.

"It is in this location that we have chosen to erect a headstone for Cindy, whether or not we find the body," said Richard Deuel, 31. "On the headstone we are going to depict Cindy's family tree, much of it information that Cindy learned through her research."

Ms. Deuel, 28, who lived in Brooklyn with her husband, Tomas Pons, worked as an executive assistant at Carr Futures on the 92nd floor of 1 World Trade Center. But Mr. Deuel, who has another brother, Joseph, 37, said his sister dreamed of starting a genealogy business to help people with their own family research. It was fitting of someone who, he said, helped friends with everything, including their taxes.

"I don't know anyone who knows Cindy that hasn't consulted her," Mr. Deuel said.

JERRY DeVITO
"You Could Count on Him"

Among the potential dangers of hanging out with Jerry DeVito were that you would laugh a lot and find yourself blown away by his mastery of sports trivia. And one other thing: you might have gotten fat.

Mr. DeVito, 66, loved to take care of people around him, especially when it came to making sure that they were fed. He was the personal driver for David Alger, the chief executive of Fred Alger Management. When not behind the wheel, Mr. DeVito spent his days at the firm, spending time with traders and looking out for the welfare of interns, particularly making sure they knew there was left-over food from a conference or luncheon.

"He even used the interoffice mail system to send doughnuts to our New Jersey site," said Christopher W. Cheever, a former summer intern.

A native of the Bronx and a great baseball player in his younger days, Mr. DeVito was a die-hard Yankees fan, who used to joke with the Alger brothers that they should buy the Bronx Bombers and make him the team's general manager. A father of two, he planned to retire this year, though he would have missed being in the mix.

"He just liked being around people," said his daughter, Robyn Goldstein. "No matter what age you were, young or old, you could count on him."

ROBERT P. DEVITT Jr.
A Life Lived to Its Fullest

At Kutztown University in Pennsylvania people may not have heard of Robert P. Devitt Jr., but everybody knew Psycho. Rugby player and life of the party, Mr. Devitt had been known to go so far as to eat goldfish and drink beer out of his shoes to keep revelers entertained.

"There was nothing he would not do to keep a party going," said his brother, Timothy Devitt.

Although rugby took a back seat to golf after he left college, Mr. Devitt, 36, was always adventurous—skydiving, motorcycling and kayaking.

He liked to quote his father, who would say, "If you want to learn how to play poker, play it for money."

And that's how he lived his life, whether it was cooking for friends, hitting the links or working as project manager for Cantor Fitzgerald with an office on the 103rd floor of the World Trade Center. He commuted three hours a day, said his fiancée, Nicole LeMaster.

"There was nowhere else he would rather be."

DENNIS L. DEVLIN
Her Cheerleader

For 29 years, Dennis and Kathleen Devlin were man and wife, parents to four children. In a house on a small hill in upstate New York, they watched sunsets and laid plans to grow old together.

But Dennis Devlin, a battalion chief for the New York City Fire Department, is gone now, leaving Mrs. Devlin to try and hold on to their bond. So, Chief Devlin's hobbies have become her hobbies. Every morning, she's out on a three-mile run, a habit she never cared for when her husband was alive, but one she hopes now will prepare her for a coming race that she is planning in his honor.

"I can hear him sometimes telling me not to get tired, pushing me," she said.

It is also because of her husband that no day passes without Mrs. Devlin thumbing through one of the 23 photo albums Chief Devlin labored over, for decades, meticulously labeling and dating each photograph. (The last photo he ever entered, taken three months before Sept. 11, was one of him in a helicopter flying over lower Manhattan, staring at the World Trade Center.)

"We complained about him taking so many pictures, everywhere we went," she said. "But having those albums now is such a joy. We all look at them and think how blessed we are that he took the time and that we were a happy family."

GERARD P. DEWAN
Finding a Home

Gerard P. Dewan was not a New Yorker, and he would have told you that. He was a Bostonian, the son of a firefighter, who in turn was the son of a firefighter. But there were no jobs in the Boston Fire Department, and so he took the southbound bus and began his career in New York five years ago.

Gerry Dewan, 35, just wanted to be a firefighter, said his friend and landlord, Sean Cummins, also a firefighter. He was one of the first rescuers to enter the twin towers. Along with 11 others from Ladder Company 3, Battalion 6 in lower Manhattan, he never made it out.

He was the first member of his family to die in the line of duty, Firefighter Cummins said. He was not married, but had always planned to have children and move home to Boston. In the meantime, he found a family in the Cummins household in Rockaway Park, Queens, where he rented a basement apartment. Two nights before the calamity, he was helping write the names of the Cummins children on their crayons for the first day of school.

"He finally found a home with us," Firefighter Cummins said.

SIMON A. DHANANI
Humble Man of the World

"He was a man without frontiers, without borders."

That is how Simon A. Dhanani was described by the man who regarded himself as Mr. Dhanani's best friend.

"My wife called us the odd couple," Albano Martell said of his friend.

Mr. Martell, 46, was the voluble one of the pair; Mr. Dhanani, 62, the quiet, humble one. They shared a love of poetry, Andalusian music, talk of world religion. They both loved to eat. "It was the perfect marriage," Mr. Martell said.

Mr. Dhanani was a vice president at Aon, on the 99th floor of 2 World Trade Center. He lived alone in Hartsdale, N.Y. But he had a fixed chair at the Martells' dining table.

The weekend before the attack, Mr. Dhanani visited their home in nearby Ardsley. They drank a glass of wine. They listened to a new album of Andalusian music until late into the evening. They made plans to go to a Korean restaurant the following week.

"He was a humble, kind, universal man," Mr. Martell said. "He really enjoyed the mosaic of the world."

JOSEPH L. DI PILATO
Blooms to Fill the Yard

This year the chrysanthemums have not been planted in front of Joseph L. Di Pilato's home. Each morning, Phyllis Buono looks out her window in Staten Island at Mr. Di Pilato's house across the street. She notices that the impatiens, their blooms past, are still there, and she remembers that Joe Di Palato, her friend, is gone.

Mr. Di Pilato, 57, was an electrician who for the past 22 years had done work for Morgan Stanley in the World Trade Center. By avocation, though, he was a gardener. Each season he would put in new plants as if he were striving for year-round blooms.

"He set that yard up like it was a resort," Mrs. Buono said. "In the spring the flower pots would explode with blossoms."

Mr. Di Pilato's wife, Maria, met him when they were growing up in Little Italy but did not discover he was a gardener until they moved to Staten Island with their sons, Leo, now 32, and Joseph, now 31.

"He didn't like the flowers I bought, so he started planting," she said. "He loved going out in the yard. His backyard had to be impeccable."

MATTHEW DIAZ
Work and Family

Matthew Diaz was a man with a conflict on his hands.

A carpenter specializing in laying floor tile and carpets, he had a friendly wager that he could put in more hours than his foreman during 2001. But his desire to get an early start on each workday was impeded by his late-night routine: he liked to stay up until midnight or later, playing video games with his two sons.

"He couldn't stop talking about his kids," said William

Gonzalez, Mr. Diaz's friend and foreman at New York City District Council of Carpenters Local 2287. On Sept. 11, Mr. Diaz, 33, was laying tile in the elevators of the Cantor Fitzgerald offices.

Long before, he and his sons, Michael 7, and Christopher, 4, had a lot to deal with. His wife, Karen Diaz, received a diagnosis of late-stage breast cancer a year earlier. Mr. Diaz had been caring for her, and preparing their sons for carrying on without one of their parents, but not without him.

The older son still goes to the front door some days, hoping his father will come home—to build more *Star Wars* figurines, skateboard or ride bikes with him, go to his soccer practice, listen to the stereo.

"He was just a family man," said Florence Kneff, his mother-in-law. "He worked, and he came home."

NANCY DIAZ
Preparing for Caribbean Trip

Nancy Diaz loved to shop, but in her last days she was shopping with a purpose: Her daughter's birthday was coming up, and she was planning a trip to the Dominican Republic, where the girl lived with a great-grandmother.

Planning to fly to the Caribbean on Sept. 14, she started her workday three and a half hours early, at 7 A.M., the previous Tuesday so she could use the free afternoon to prepare for her trip, said her brother, Leonel Diaz. A kitchen assistant, she was tending to the breakfast buffet on the 107th floor of the north tower when the first plane hit, he said.

Ms. Diaz, 28, who lived with her sister in the Bronx and had moved to the United States from the Dominican Republic less than three years ago, liked her American life, particularly her job, her brother said. She had a boyfriend at work (he was off on Sept. 11), and she had just heard from her boss that she had promotion potential.

"They said, 'You can be a manager. You're such a hard worker,' " Mr. Diaz said.

Now Ms. Diaz's daughter is preparing to come to New York to visit her family.

MICHAEL A. DIAZ-PIEDRA III
Playing Soldier

He called his basement the war room and filled it with an array of military uniforms from around the world. He kept about 30 on mannequins; there were another 100 on racks, but they didn't just sit there. Michael A. Diaz-Piedra III loved to wear them, whether at an elaborate Halloween masquerade party or birthday parties for his son Michael, now 6.

"The uniforms called attention to him, and he liked that," said his wife, Kelly. The plumes and swords also gave Mr. Diaz-Piedra an opening to talk about the historic periods that so fascinated him.

In fact, he was crazy about all kinds of vintage things, Mrs. Diaz-Piedra said, including old cars. This gave him a kind of Old World romanticism that fit his background as son of a wealthy Cuban plantation owner exiled after the Castro revolution. "Once for my birthday, Mike rented a vintage Jaguar and picked me up at work," Mrs. Diaz-Piedra said. "He hired some violinists to play while we had dinner. Then he asked me to marry him."

Although he came to the United States from Cuba when he was 8, Mr. Diaz-Piedra maintained strong ties with the food and culture of his homeland. "Mike was not a ravenous anti-Castro Cuban," said his brother, George, but he said he had prepared a claim to recover the family's property in Cuba when the Castro regime ends.

Mr. Diaz-Piedra, 49, was a vice president with the Bank of New York in charge of disaster recovery planning. But he was happiest when the planning he did was for a mock battle of the soldiers in his collection. "Some people may have thought of Mike as eccentric," Mrs. Diaz-Piedra said. "But he was just a big kid at heart."

JUDITH DIAZ-SIERRA's portrait appears with Emerita de la Peña on page 119.

JOSEPH DERMOT DICKEY Jr.
Family Matters Most

Joseph Dermot Dickey Jr. grew up with two older brothers in the Bronx, and the three siblings became more competitive the older they got. They sparred in tennis, basketball, volleyball and golf.

Mr. Dickey, 50, who had settled down in Manhasset, was not only the best basketball player, his oldest brother admits, but was probably also the best liked of the three.

"He was extremely sociable," said Bill Dickey, 58. "Frankly, he was more easygoing and personable than me or my brother."

A managing director with Cantor Fitzgerald, Joe Dickey was also successful on Wall Street. But in his tight-knit Irish-American family, attributes as a husband and father—in Joe Dickey's case to his wife, Irene, son Joseph, 17, and daughter Liz, 15—were "the mark by which we judge each other," Bill Dickey said.

His family's verdict was that Joe Dickey was exceptional on both counts, especially with the children. The last big family gathering, which also drew Walter, 55, the middle brother, was at the wedding of Bill Dickey's daughter last August in Adare Manor, Ireland.

"We had a great time, all of us," Bill Dickey said. "We spent a lot of time playing golf."

L. PATRICK DICKINSON
Keeping It Simple

L. Patrick Dickinson loved jaunts to Hersheypark in Pennsylvania, visits to Williamsburg, Va., and trips to Las Vegas. But most of all he relished family time at home in Marlboro, N.J., sitting by the pool, relaxing on the couch while his daughter Erin, 7, fell asleep on his belly, or playing a mean game of Trivial Pursuit.

Mr. Dickinson, 35, a stockbroker on the American Stock Exchange who worked for Harvey Young Yurman, spent long days in the hectic world of futures and options trading, standing on the floor of the exchange.

On Sept. 11, he was having his weekly Tuesday morning meeting at Windows on the World. With him were five colleagues from his company, including his brother-in-law, who is also missing. With his days so frenzied, Mr. Dickinson kept it simple when he was away from work, said his wife, Linda.

"It was enough for him to look at the stars at night or relax by the pool," said Mrs. Dickinson, who met her husband 18 years ago when the two worked at a five-and-dime store in Jersey City. She is expecting their second child in December.

MICHAEL D. DIEHL
Barbecue in the Snow

Michael D. Diehl was a grill master. He grilled chicken, hamburgers, spareribs and turkeys year-round. Neither rain nor sleet nor snow could stop him.

"He would park himself in a lawn chair in front of the barbecue with a glass of wine, preparing mouth-watering foods for his family and friends," said his wife, Loisanne. "Even in the winter he would don a parka, shovel a path to the grill and sit there like he was on top of the world."

Mr. Diehl, 48, used grilling to escape the hurly-burly of Wall Street. Some days he would sit on the sprawling deck of his house in Brick, N.J., taking in the air, not saying a word to anyone, or enjoying light conversation with Mrs. Diehl. He worked at Fiduciary Trust for 19 years. He was a vice president for custody in his last position.

The couple had two children, Jason, 20, and Jeannette, 15. He pushed them to do their best and they tried. Jeannette plays 10 instruments, including the piano, flute and piccolo, while Jason plays 5, including guitar, Mrs. Diehl said.

"He would beam from ear to ear as he listened to Jeannette perform at her piano recitals," Mrs. Diehl said, "or watch Jason make a great save in the goalie net."

JOHN DiFATO
Joined at the Heart

John DiFato and Susan Giaccio fell in love at Macy's. She was working there when he walked in with a friend. She had known him vaguely from college. "He said something cute," she remembered. "I instantly fell in love with the cleft in his chin."

"We were each other's soul mates," she said. When Anthony, 10, Nicole, 9, and John, 3, were born, he called their births a miracle. Like many couples joined at the heart, husband and wife were in constant telephone contact all day. Mr. DiFato, 39, went to his job as a business security controller at Cantor Fitzgerald in the World Trade Center early, and he always phoned so he could say good-bye to Anthony and Nicole before school.

And "during the day he would be beeping me—like, where are you?" Mrs. DiFato said. Sometimes she would be running for an appointment and when she heard her beeper she would mutter, "O.K., now what?"

On Sept. 11, when she learned of the attack on the World Trade Center, she tried to beep Mr. DiFato. There was no answer.

CARL A. DiFRANCO
She Yearned to Help Him

Even as a grown man, Carl A. DiFranco's mother came first. They had dates, simple in nature, but the kind most mothers never forget. There were the spontaneous trips to Atlantic City, the surpise trip to Florida, and the quick getaways to Delaware, where Mr. DiFranco, 27, and his mom, Carole, would spend hours online buying lottery tickets and dreaming of becoming millionaires.

Of course, there were also the run-of-the-mill moments, the days when Mr. DiFranco would return from his job as an accountant with Marsh & McLennan, and go to work all over again, helping his mother around the house, trimming bushes, refinishing floors or moving furniture.

"Everytime I came up with a project, he was there for me," Mrs. DiFranco said of her youngest child.

And this year, Mrs. DiFranco had tried to repay some of her son's kindess, to help him, as best she could, through what seeemed the most difficult moment of his life. On April 1, his wife, Loren, who had been born with a chronic heart illness, died while waiting for a transplant.

"He was trying so hard to be upbeat," she said. "But their one-year anniversary was Oct. 14. I keep thinking I hear him coming in the door, that I'll have a chance to help him get through it."

DONALD J. DiFRANCO
A Quirky Perfectionist

When Donald J. DiFranco set out to replace the roof on his house, he counted out every nail and every tile he would need before starting. When he needed new windows for the house, he spent months compiling a list of virtually all the window manufacturers in the world. After he ordered the windows, he stained the wood around each pane, applying coat after coat, before installing them. But the windows did not look quite right, so he removed them, stained them again and put them back in.

Mr. DiFranco, 43, the engineer in charge of maintaining WABC-TV's transmitter on the 110th floor of 1 World Trade Center, approached the tasks of life with a quirky perfectionism. This endeared him to anyone who watched him work and to relatives, who counted on his being able to tackle anything, from broken radios to tax returns.

"He just had something you can't learn," said his sister, Lisa Pipitone. Mr. DiFranco would often work late. But before he left the building—no matter what time it was—he would slip on a pair of work gloves and do a long set of push-ups, said his co-worker Vinny Ioele.

"It was a good sign to see him put on the gloves," Mr. Ioele said. "That meant it was time to go."

DEBORANN DiMARTINO
A Ribbon for Christmas

Sometimes Joe DiMartino finds himself studying the Christmas 2000 picture from Keefe, Bruyette & Woods at 2 World Trade Center, where his wife of 16 years, Deborann, worked as an assistant trader on the 89th floor.

"It shows the whole trading department, and every one of them is now gone, except for the one girl who went in late that day," he said.

Mrs. DiMartino, 36, took the express bus to the World Trade Center each morning from their house on Staten Island; Mr. DiMartino drove over the Verrazano-Narrows Bridge each night to the Pepsi-Cola plant in Brooklyn where he worked until dawn. The only time when their schedules coincided was the evening.

And so, together, they would help their 11-year-old, Danielle, with her homework, then get her and her sister, Samantha, 5, to bed.

"I kissed Debbie good night that Monday night, and left

for work," he said of Sept. 10. "Now I can't drive over the bridge because I can't look where those beautiful buildings were."

This year, the giant lighted mechanical Christmas display Mr. DiMartino used to install outside his house has been replaced "by one lonely yellow ribbon on the tree outside," he said. "A lot of kids are going to be disappointed."

DAVID DiMEGLIO
Gregariously Gifted

David DiMeglio was a child of his digital generation. He loved computers, and was this close to turning that love into a career.

"He was just coming into himself," said his father, John.

After working as an apprentice electrician, Mr. DiMeglio, 22, recently finished computer school and was starting a business in computer services—helping people upgrade hard drives and the like (the stuff the young somehow seem best at). He was so good at it that his father was convinced that "the business would have taken off." If it had, it would have owed a lot to this young man's outgoing personality.

"He loved to help people," his father said. Mr. DiMeglio's friends were numerous, but he did not reserve his charms for his peers.

His 2-year-old nephew got so excited when he saw Uncle David that he could not stand still. And Mr. DiMeglio was no one-note computer nerd. He wrote and sang rap songs and loved to draw. He loved motorcycles, even dismantling one in the garage. And he was an avid wrestling fan.

On Sept. 11, Mr. DiMeglio, who lived with his father near Boston, headed west on American Airlines Flight 11 to help his mother move.

STEPHEN P. DIMINO
Generous from the Start

When Stephen P. Dimino turned 9, his parents organized a special birthday trip into Manhattan from their home in Bensonhurst, Brooklyn. They took Stephen and his sister to see *My Fair Lady,* and then they all stuck nickels and dimes into the slots at an Automat to get their lunch.

But then the boy spotted an old man sitting by himself who looked hungry. He brought his sandwich over to him. Then the rest of the Dimino family followed suit, said Gigi Ebert, Mr. Dimino's sister.

"We ended up giving him all of our food," she said. Mr. Dimino, 48, who was a partner at Cantor Fitzgerald, continued to be generous. "He was someone you'd want as your neighbor," said his cousin Robert Messina.

He loved to give people presents, like venison steaks from

the deer he shot and souvenirs from his travels abroad. At home in Basking Ridge, N.J., he showered his daughter, Sabrina, 15, with time, too, "hunting together, playing video games together, riding roller coasters together," Mrs. Ebert said. "He started taking her to Disneyland as soon as she was old enough to remember it. He really took delight in her and in her accomplishments. I thought he was going to burst the day she was born."

WILLIAM DIMMLING
Seeker of Perfection

When William Dimmling was 18, his father, a butcher who had emigrated from Germany, died suddenly, thrusting the teenager into adulthood. As the new head of the household, he sold the business, taught his mother to drive and became a role model for his brother, Rudy.

While a seriousness fell over Mr. Dimmling and deepened his work ethic, his father's death did not make him unduly sober. Quite the opposite. It taught him to seize each day joyfully, because the future could only be planned, not presumed.

He brought that approach to obstacles at work and home. He would let loose that smile, clap his arm around you and say, "We'll get through this!"

Mr. Dimmling could persuade executives around the world to cooperate on joint financial reporting systems, like the one he finished that last weekend for Marsh Inc. He and his wife, Leslie, had one son, Gregory, but even though infertility treatments and then adoption problems intervened, Mr. Dimmling, a doting dad if ever there was one, never doubted that their family would grow. Indeed they got through it, triumphantly bringing Nicholas to their Garden City, N.Y., home from Russia six years ago.

Mr. Dimmling, 47, was determined, but sometimes had a hard time letting go. Perfection was critical, no matter how small the task. Did you know there was a right way to tie the knot on newspaper-recycling bundles?

MARISA DiNARDO
An Angel Collector

On Monday, Sept. 10, Marisa DiNardo went out to dinner to celebrate her mother's birthday. But Ms. DiNardo, who was a trader at Cantor Fitzgerald, did not have to travel far to join the party. She played host to a group of six at Windows on the World, a few floors up from her office in the World Trade Center.

"We ordered great wine and food, danced and laughed until 1:30 A.M.," said her brother Harley. "She said she had to be back at 8:15 that morning for a meeting."

Born on New Year's Eve in 1962, Ms. DiNardo grew up in West Harrison, N.Y., and went to Harrison High School. She is remembered as a woman who was devoted to her job, who doted on her family and was very religious. "She went out of her way for family and friends," said Nella Barrese, who knew Ms. DiNardo since they were 8.

"She was ambitious in a field that was dominated by men," her brother said. "Trading came very easily to her."

Neither Ms. Barrese nor Mr. DiNardo would call it a hobby, but Ms. DiNardo collected angels. "She believed in fate and destiny and that sort of thing," Ms. Barrese said. "She had a very strong faith in God."

CHRISTOPHER DINCUFF
He Knew How to Share

What his friends and family will tell you about Christopher Dincuff, 31, an assistant trader for Carr Futures, is that he was always smiling.

"He always made people feel welcome," said his mother, Joan. "I never had to teach him how to share." He became the center of a large circle of friends, some of whom had known him since childhood in South River, N.J. All of them learned that if the Villanova Wildcats were playing basketball, he had to hear or see the game.

"He has driven his car to remote places just to get the Villanova game on the radio," said Garth Smalley, his best friend. Mr. Dincuff's father, Jim, a Seton Hall graduate, accompanied him to Seton Hall–Villanova games.

Mr. Dincuff's proposal to his fiancée, Angie Gutermuth, in February 2000 encompassed several passions at once. As Ms. Gutermuth opened the door to her apartment, exhausted after business-school exams, she discovered a trail of rose petals, illuminated by candles, that led to Mr. Dincuff, dozens of helium balloons arrayed around him. There was Champagne, and music, and a ring he had designed himself. He arranged for her to have a manicure the next day, at the same time there was a Villanova game on TV.

JEFFREY MARK DINGLE
The Missing Ring

In the days since her husband, Jeffrey Mark Dingle, went to a breakfast conference at Windows on the World and never came home, Dr. Nichole Brathwaite Dingle has relied on friends, family and humor to keep her spirit from crumbling. With two children, ages 9 and 3, she has had to be strong.

She tells friends he is not missing, but simply staying away from their Bronx apartment because he does not want to clean the bathroom. The coast is clear, she says. I've cleaned it. He can come home now.

The two had been inseparable since they met on the University of Pennsylvania campus a decade ago (he was at Villanova, she at U. Penn), although there were the few months that Mr. Dingle, 32, lived in Washington, working and taking care of the children, while his wife stayed in New York to finish medical school.

In July, Mr. Dingle found a job with Encompys, a high-tech company with offices in Midtown. That summer they moved into a new apartment.

"They were finally going to be adults," said a longtime friend, Sherry Ellerbe.

A few weeks before Sept. 11 the couple renewed their vows and Mr. Dingle told his wife he was taking her ring in for repairs. In fact, he was having the jeweler put in a higher-grade diamond. Dr. Brathwaite Dingle has been telling friends that her husband must come home for one reason:

"Only he knows where he took my ring."

ANTHONY DIONISIO Jr.
He Took Her Everywhere

The focus of Anthony Dionisio Jr.'s life was his 11-year-old daughter, Stephanie.

"On the last day of school last June, he met her at school and surprised her with a trip to Disney World in Florida," said Lucille Dionisio, his mother. "That was the kind of thing he would do. He was her best buddy," Mrs. Dionisio said. "They were inseparable. They went everywhere together, Yankee Stadium, basketball games, ice-skating shows, racetracks."

Mr. Dionisio, a divorced father, had custody of Stephanie on weekdays, and her mother had custody on weekends.

"Stephanie held out until the very end," Mrs. Dionisio said of her granddaughter's reaction to Mr. Dionisio's presence in the World Trade Center. "She said, 'I am not worried. Dad will make it out.' When we planned for a memorial service, we had to sit her down and talk her through it."

Mr. Dionisio, 38, quit college and worked his way up to become the vice president for operations at Cantor Fitzgerald. "We are Catholics, so we believe he is in a good place now. He will be our guardian angel," said his mother.

After the tragedy, she put her son's picture on the wall, and every morning when there is school, the granddaughter says, "Good morning, Dad," and the grandmother says, "Good morning, Anthony. We are going to school now."

GEORGE DiPASQUALE
Practiced What He Preached

Melissa DiPasquale has told enough stories about her firefighter husband, cried enough tears before strangers. Now, she wants peace and privacy. Another article about George DiPasquale? His wife begged a reporter to use what had already been said about him in his local newspaper, the *Staten Island Advance*: His nickname at Ladder Company 2 in Manhattan was Holy Man, more respectful than many in the rough-and-tumble world of a firehouse. The 33-year-old firefighter, one of 10 from the company who raced to duty at 9:09 A.M. on Sept. 11 and never returned, was known for his faith.

Firefighter DiPasquale, an imposing 6-foot-5, was an elder at the Kingdom Hall of Jehovah's Witnesses in the Mariners Harbor neighborhood, and shared his thoughts on religion and hope with his colleagues. He was a man who "practiced what he preached," said his father-in-law, Michael Mattei. "What he said, he meant."

Firefighter DiPasquale and his wife celebrated their ninth wedding anniversary in Cape May, N.J., just days before the attack.

"A perfect weekend," Mrs. DiPasquale said.

The couple's daughter, Georgia Rose, was 20 months old in September.

DOUGLAS DiSTEFANO
On the Threshold

Things were beginning to click for Douglas DiStefano.

He had been working as a trader trainee at Prebon Energy in Jersey City, a job he got with the help of his brother David, who worked there. It was not high pay as yet, so he also tended bar at Hobson's Bar and Grill in Hoboken, where he lived.

There he met Robert Wayne Hobson, who had quit his stockbroker's job to start Hobson's but had returned to Wall Street in 1999 and was working at Cantor Fitzgerald. He helped Mr. DiStefano become a commodities broker there. Mr. DiStefano, 24, began in August, and had not even cashed his second paycheck by Sept. 11. Mr. Hobson, too, perished in the attack.

Mr. DiStefano felt the World Trade Center was the best address in the world, and it was proving an effective lure for women. "He said it worked much better on the girls," said David DiStefano. "Saying 'I work in Jersey City' didn't go over as well as 'I work at the top of the World Trade Center.'"

One thing Douglas DiStefano had always been really proud of was his West Islip high school football team's winning the Long Island championship. (He was an offensive lineman.) He became equally thrilled about the Cantor job. He was talking about getting a new apartment, buying a car. "The toughest part is he was just turning the corner," his brother said. "He was just making it."

DONALD DiTULLIO
"Riding Free and Forever"

When the people who admired Donald DiTullio think about him, some go to the distant past, some to the recent past and some to the future, but it is always with fondness. His older sister, Janice Fleming, recalled how, as a toddler, he would go around the house fixing everything with his new wooden hammer. He hammered so hard, his indentations were left as a reminder until the home was remodeled.

His mother, Marjorie DiTullio, talks about how Mr. DiTullio, 49, a passenger on Flight 11, took good care of her, maybe even spoiled her a little. He lived in Peabody, Mass., not far from her. If she talked about something that she needed done, "It would be 'Yes, mother.' It was not what he said, but the way he said it," she said. "He would pop in, two or three times a week."

A co-worker at Smith & Nephew, a medical device manufacturer in Andover, Mass., thinks of Mr. DiTullio, a Harley-Davidson fan, in the future. "I see you riding free and forever, wind blowing in your face, leaning into long smooth turns, spitting out the occasional bug," Sue Farnsworth wrote on a family Web page. "Your bike is chromed to the max and running perfectly, with a crank on the throttle. A deep throaty blast fills the air. Ride, Don, ride."

RAMZI DOANY
Ways to Amass Friends

Ramzi Doany amassed friends. He amassed them with acts of kindness, like tutoring a woman with lupus, two children and no husband, to get her through college, or letting his college roommate and the roommate's wife live in his condo for two years so they could save money for a down payment on a house.

He amassed friends with his sense of humor, which filled a room and flourished at an early age. As a boy of 9 or 10, young Ramzi dug a hole in the backyard for a terrible report card and put a stone on top.

"He said it was dead and buried," said his sister, Dina Doany Azzam.

Mr. Doany was born to Palestinian parents in Amman, Jordan, and lived for many years in Milwaukee. At 35, he devoured the novels of Dickens, cooked Thanksgiving turkeys with great pride (even if they were just a bit dry) and had just bought a Harley-Davidson motorcycle.

He chose to work as a forensic accountant in March 2001 for Marsh & McLennan, the insurance brokerage company, because it would bring him to New York, a city he loved. The job also brought him to the World Trade Center.

It was a funny sort of journey, his sister said.

JOHN J. DOHERTY
Always Time for Golf

John J. Doherty was one of those guys who loved golf so much that he would sleep in his van to be sure and get a good tee time at Westchester County's public courses.

"John would get there at 3 or 4 in the morning," said Tom Beaudrot, a friend of Mr. Doherty's for two decades. "We would sit there in the parking lot sleeping, drinking coffee."

Mr. Doherty, 58, was a vice president for Aon in the trade center. Mary Doherty, Mr. Doherty's wife, said that on Sundays, Mr. Doherty and Barbara, his eldest daughter, who was born with developmental disabilities, would travel from their home in Hartsdale, N.Y., to a driving range. In the summers, Mr. Doherty took Barbara, now 16, and Maureen, his other daughter, now 13, for walks in Vermont.

"He would take the girls into the woods and find them walking sticks and skip rocks across mountain streams with them," Mrs. Doherty said.

But still, if there was time for a little golf, "he would sneak off to Vermont and take lessons," Mr. Beaudrot said.

BRENDAN DOLAN
A Lifelong Quarterback

The prudent know well: never do business with friends. Brendan Dolan, however, did business only with friends.

He merrily ran roughshod over that bright divide, saying, "I don't have clients, I only have friends."

He must have been doing something right: at 37, he was a senior vice president at Carr Futures, a successful energy broker who traveled worldwide for clients whom he easily befriended, with his trademark smile and wink.

In high school Mr. Dolan had been a quarterback, and he played that position for the rest of his life. He called the shots, gathering his siblings and parents together in vacation houses, throwing job opportunities at loyal buddies. He encouraged Carr brokers to move their young families to his town, Glen Rock, N.J. Who wants to live so close to the boss? They did.

On summer weekends, the gang from work would hang out at Brendan and Stacey's, for a swim and a barbecue.

Joking, flipping burgers, jumping in the pool with Samantha, 2, and Sarah, 4, Mr. Dolan reveled in his life at home.

He would tell his older brother Charles, who is still single: "Forget business. You don't get it yet. Work will never bring you the kind of satisfaction you'll have from a family."

NEIL M. DOLLARD
Connected by Telephone

His family's memories of Neil M. Dollard frequently involve a telephone. There were the calls Mr. Dollard made to his mother, Helen, from his kitchen ("How do you debeard a mussel?") and to his sister Megan ("I'm working with purple basil. Have you ever made purple pesto?") and the endless conversations on the special line that connected him to his brother Peter's office; they spoke "maybe 45 times a day" by Peter Dollard's count.

After high school, Neil Dollard, who was 28, headed straight from Staten Island to Cantor Fitzgerald, signing on as a "bluecoat" who emptied wastebaskets, and working his way up to bond broker. He embraced the lifestyle, building a wardrobe of natty suits and taking on the vocabulary of Wall Street: "waving in" bottles of wine at dinner, for example, to indulge clients. He bought a condominium in Hoboken, N.J., and had a happy relationship with his girlfriend, Kristin Ledzion. They planned to join other family members vacationing in Chiavari, on the coast of Italy, in the middle of September.

He called them there on Sept. 10. They were returning from town around midnight, and heard the phone ringing. Someone sprinted up the stairs to answer it. "He spoke to all of us, and he told me how much he was looking forward to the trip," his brother said. "He said that when he got there, we were going to wave everything in."

BENILDA DOMINGO
Bus Ride to Romance

Benilda Domingo was heading home to Laoag City in the Philippines from Manila after two years of menial work in Singapore. Relatives introduced her to the bus driver, Cefar Gabriel. While she had been working abroad, one of her brothers had married one of Mr. Gabriel's sisters. By the end of the nine-hour bus trip, they were in love.

The couple had three children—Daryl, 11, Yvonne, 5, and Lucki Angel, 2. But for 14 years they kept postponing their wedding, said Dorothy Gabriel, Ms. Domingo's sister-in-law, because Ms. Domingo's parents, living in Hawaii with their eldest son, were petitioning United States authorities to allow Ms. Domingo to immigrate, and a spouse would have slowed the process.

Last year Ms. Domingo's visa finally came through, and she brought the three children to America. She planned to return to Laoag City to marry Mr. Gabriel and to bring him over, too.

She left the two younger children with her parents in Hawaii, and took the oldest with her to New York.

Ms. Domingo, 37, found work with an office-cleaning company. "She was so proud that she was hired at the W.T.C.," her sister-in-law recalled by telephone from Canada.

Now Mr. Gabriel, still a bus driver in the Philippines, is even more desperate to come to New York.

"He was so devastated," Ms. Gabriel said. "He wants to come to see the place where it happened, and just to be with his kids."

KEVIN DONNELLY
Fun Is the Beach

Fire may have provided Lt. Kevin Donnelly of Ladder Company 3 with his livelihood, but what he loved was water.

Born under the hot July sun, he got a job as a lifeguard at the town pool in Wantagh, while still a teenager on Long Island, said his mother, Cecilia. As an adult, he found any excuse to head for the water, even when some other task beckoned.

"He kept a bathing suit, a towel and goggles in his car at all times, just in case," said his companion, Mary Coughlin, "and in the summer, he'd add two beach chairs, a towel and a bathing suit for me."

The two of them might be driving along, on their way to Home Depot or some other store to run errands. And Lieutenant Donnelly, 43, would turn to her, and say: "You know what? We can do this another time. Let's go to the beach."

He was not persnickety about his beaches, though he preferred those on the ocean. He was hoping to become a lifeguard again, on some Long Island strand. North Shore, South Shore.

"He wouldn't have cared what beach he ended up on," Ms. Coughlin said, "as long as it was on the sand and near the water."

STEPHEN S. DORF
"I'm Lost Without Him"

Michelle Dorf said she used to fight "a lot" with her brother Stephen S. Dorf. But as the two youngest among six siblings from Bensonhurst in Brooklyn, they were also very close.

He helped her get a job at Euro Brokers/ Maxcor Financial Group, where he worked as a communica-

tions technician on the 84th floor of 2 World Trade Center. When she could not afford to buy a home by herself, she said, he went in as her partner, and the two got a five-bedroom house in New Milford, N.J. Mr. Dorf, 39 and single, was also the father figure to his younger sister's 15-year-old son after her divorce.

Uncle and nephew were addicted to movies—"Everything. The hottest movie out they'd see," Ms. Dorf, 37, said—and loved nothing more than watching television together, day and night.

"He used to baby-sit a lot," she said. "He used to do everything around the house. I don't know what I'm doing now. I'm lost without him."

KEVIN DOWDELL
On Time When It Mattered

It's a slow day in superhero land. So Kevin Dowdell docks the fireboat, and, dressed in firefighter regalia, clumps over to the Mercantile Exchange. He waves proudly from the visitors' window to his teenage sons on the floor, wearing ties for their summer jobs. Patrick! James!

Then the job calls. So Lieutenant Dowdell of Rescue Company 4, Queens—trained to use roof ropes and scuba gear, to handle hazardous materials, wiggle into confined spaces—sprints into action, with a relaxed head and a racing heart. He loves rescue work so much he chooses not to try for captain, so he will not be transferred.

"Rather be a happy lieutenant," he tells RoseEllen, his wife of 21 years. He has a bravery medal and 20 citation bars.

To support the family, the happy lieutenant, 46, works days off, sanding floors. When his boys start playing bagpipes and snare, he practices with them, whomping a bass. More time with the boys, plus he gets to march in the parade, wearing his kilt. Only one thing about RoseEllen's best friend drives her nuts: first to a fire, last to a social event.

"You don't know what would have happened if we left on time," retorts the happy lieutenant, a born talker. "We could have gotten into an accident."

MARY YOLANDA DOWLING
The Voice of an Angel

Give Mary Yolanda Dowling an instrument—an accordion, a piano or a set of bagpipes—and she is likely to produce a foot-stomping tune. She may have spent her days as an administrator for Aon Corporation, on the 92nd floor of 2 World Trade Center, but Ms. Dowling's mind was often on her music.

The oldest of four children and deeply immersed in the Celtic culture she inherited from her father, Ms. Dowling,

46, spent much of her free time singing with a choir near her home in Floral Park, N.Y. Rosaleen Shea, her sister, said she received a standing ovation several years ago after singing the national anthem at a Mets game.

"She had a voice like an angel and she shared it with everyone, in good times or bad," Ms. Shea said. "Our entire family is immersed in music, but Yolanda is the most gifted."

RAYMOND M. DOWNEY
Firefighter to the Core

Raymond M. Downey was the battalion chief in charge of special operations in the New York City Fire Department.

Here's his son, Chuck, a fire lieutenant: "Dad joined the Fire Department on April 7, 1962. Coming on in the '60s, they went to a lot of fires. The war years, they termed it. In 1995 he was assigned to Special Operations Command, SOC is the acronym, as chief of rescue operations. . . .

"He was on the Gilmore Commission to fight domestic terrorism. No one's going to see it all, but I don't think anyone thought of the World Trade Center. . . .

"When the south tower went down, there was a lot of Maydays. He survived. A lot of the top brass did. These are all guys with 30-plus years. They went back in. There were two young firemen; he told them, not in the nicest language, to get out of here."

Here's Chief Downey's daughter, Marie Tortorici: "Mommy, Rosalie, is Italian. Daddy's Irish. He would have been 64 on Sept. 19. He's very spiritual. He was in Oklahoma City after the bombing. Governor Keating gave him a set of rosary beads. He wore them every day. Well, they broke, and he kept them in his pocket. He had them with him, because they're not home. . . .

"When I was a little girl, he was working three jobs to support the family, and he was always too busy to come to the school to do fire prevention week. Last year, when my daughter was in first grade, he went to the school for fire prevention week. I don't know. It's so sad, everything. But a good thing came out of this. My sister, my father called her the baby, we just found out she's pregnant. So she felt like it was a blessing from my father."

FRANK DOYLE
"I Have to Stay"

When Frank Doyle came home from his job on Wall Street, he would play with his two young children and get them to bed. Only then did Mr. Doyle pull on his running shoes, go outside and run hills in his Englewood, N.J., neighborhood to train for triathlons.

"He was a tremendous athlete," said Kimmy Chedel, his wife of four years. The couple ran their first triathlon together on Aug. 5.

Ms. Chedel said she met Mr. Doyle on an evening cruise of New York Harbor for alumni of his school, Bowdoin College in Maine, and her school, Middlebury College in Vermont. His name tag fell off and stuck to her shoe.

"I said, 'Who is Frank Doyle?' " she said. "He came over when he heard his name. It was love at first sight."

Mr. Doyle, 39, who was head of equity trading at Keefe, Bruyette & Woods, called his wife after terrorists struck the World Trade Center's north tower. "I have to stay," he said. After the south tower, which contained Mr. Doyle's office, was struck, he called her again, saying that he and many others were trapped.

"He very calmly said, 'We need your help,' " Ms. Chedel said. "Up to the last minute of his life, he was a team player."

JOEY DOYLE
Crazy about the Packers

The Sunday ritual at Bill and Camille Doyle's home would make most N.F.L. fans jealous. Four televisions, four different games and 16 rowdy young men rooting at the top of their lungs, all day long. This, the Doyles did without fail, at the request of their youngest, Joey, a Staten Island "sports nut" who made it to Wall Street but still loved mom and dad's house best. Especially mom's cooking.

"He made Sundays this big holiday for us," said Mrs. Doyle. "You couldn't be around him and not like football, any sport."

The mantel in the Doyle house is lined with trophies, newspaper clippings and certificates from the days when Joey Doyle, 25, a rabid Green Bay Packers fan, was a star pitcher at Wagner College.

Now the family is preparing to add another prize to the collection, an autographed football mailed to the family from the Green Bay Packers, a gift that Mr. Doyle would have surely coveted, and one that has helped to remind the Doyle family that they do not grieve alone.

"Every day you think, I'm not going to get through this," said Mr. Doyle's father. "But the people, strangers a lot of them, they just keep reaching out. They help more than they know."

RANDY DRAKE
Indulging with Family

Put a golf club or a fishing rod in his hand, or have a kid wake him up asking to play, and that was all it took to make Randy Drake happy.

He preferred to indulge his interests

with members of his family. He had plenty of choices. He was one of 13 children, and on his side alone, he had 30 nieces and nephews, most of whom lived near his home in Lee's Summit, Mo., which he shared with his wife, Tammy, and son, Joe, 17.

"He often said he would rather be with his family than anybody else," said Mrs. Drake.

Mr. Drake, 37, was a network integration manager for Siemens, and was assigned to a job at 195 Broadway, across the street from the World Trade Center. After the first plane struck, his building was evacuated. He called his wife to say he was all right, but he was apparently hit by debris from the impact of the second plane. He died Sept. 22.

LUKE A. DUDEK
Keeping the Tide In

Luke A. Dudek was forever proud to work at Windows on the World, where he was the food and beverage controller. He had a knack for numbers. Naturally, given the environment, he delighted in fine wine, and it was his custom when his wineglass was empty to remark to the waiter, "My tide is out."

But his special joy was Coqui Designs, the flower business he owned with his life partner, George A. Cuellar. (Coqui is Mr. Cuellar's nickname.) Mr. Cuellar operated the place and was the creative mind behind the designs they did for stores like Bloomingdale's and Gucci, and for countless weddings. The numbers, though, were the province of Mr. Dudek, 50.

"He did the books," Mr. Cuellar said. "He did my taxes. He even delivered flowers on the weekends and did weddings. I called him the core of the apple."

The two had always wanted to own their own building. In May, they bought a building in Cedar Grove, N.J., to move the store to. They spent the summer renovating. To do the final touches, Mr. Dudek recently devoted a week's vacation to the store.

His first day back at Windows on the World was Sept. 11.

CHRISTOPHER M. DUFFY
Nice Suits, Hawaiian Shirts

Christopher M. Duffy was determined. At 160 pounds, he was the fullback on his high school football team. He was captain of his lacrosse team and spent a good part of his time on the field knocking other players down.

But when his two brothers, one older and one younger, both grew to over 6 feet tall and Mr. Duffy stopped at 5-foot-10, he decided he just was not big enough. So he made up for it with muscle.

"Chris was the most ferocious of the three of them," said John Duffy, Chris's father.

Chris Duffy was known for his weekend "Duff Jam" parties in high school. When his parents went away, Mr. Duffy and his friends would play. "They covered their tracks," said his father. "But over the years we learned about the extent of the parties."

Mr. Duffy, 23, started working at Keefe, Bruyette & Woods, where his father is president, as an assistant equity trader after graduating from Villanova in 2000. His sister Kara said her brother was a smart dresser, loving to shop at stores like Hugo Boss. Still, outside the office he was often seen in flip-flops and a Hawaiian shirt. His 12 closest friends, who were honorary pallbearers at his memorial service, wore suits—and flip-flops.

MICHAEL J. DUFFY
Often the Best Man

Michael Duffy loved Dickens, a yellow Labrador who had been a Christmas puppy. But best friend? There the dog would have some competition. Mr. Duffy's big brother, for one. His little sister, too. Any of a dozen inseparable schoolmates from St. Anthony's High in Huntington, on Long Island.

He could have slept in a tuxedo, as often as he was asked to be in a wedding party. Last year he was in five. Truth is, says his sister, Mary Kay Duffy, if not for his friends' brothers, he might have been best man in each.

He was best man at the wedding of his brother, John, who says, "I can honestly say that many of the best days of my life had been spent with Michael."

He tended to invite seven or eight friends to make up one golf foursome. But he was always "expanding the group rather than eliminating," says John Duffy. His refrain was, "Who's got it better than us?"

Ms. Duffy recalls a soulful, athletic, protective brother who "used to break my girlfriends' hearts." She says, "A running joke was that Michael could always date my girlfriends but I couldn't date his guy friends."

Michael Duffy, who joined Keefe, Bruyette & Woods as a bond salesman in August 2001, was a week shy of 30.

Four years earlier, Dickens's best Christmases were past. Old, ill and in pain, the family pet needed only that last trip to the vet. Michael Duffy made the trip on his own. He kept the dog's collar over his bedpost.

ANTOINETTE DUGER
Making Time to Help

Rose Duger Duane remembers calling her brother shortly after having a baby and asking if he and his wife could baby-sit. He declined, saying they had plans. But her sister-in-law, Antoinette Duger, quickly called back. Of course they could watch the baby, Ms. Duane recalled her saying, "I don't know what he was saying."

Ms. Duane feels certain that Mrs. Duger canceled the couple's plans so they could help out. Mrs. Duger, 44, an operations associate for First Union on the 47th floor of 1 World Trade Center, was all about family. She rose at 5:30 each morning to spend time with her 8-year-old daughter, Megan, and evenings were dedicated to homework and housekeeping.

Coming from a close-knit Italian family, she was a wonderful cook. Each year she would gather with her mother and sisters to press their own tomatoes and bottle a year's worth of sauce for each.

"I think there's a line in literature that sums up Antoinette's life," Ms. Duane said. "It was a simple life, well lived."

JACKIE SAYEGH DUGGAN
She "Gapped" Generations

Nicknamed "The Gap," Jackie Sayegh Duggan was the oldest grandchild—and the only girl—in both of her parents' families.

"Grandparents to parents to cousins. She organized all the family events," said George Sayegh, her father. "The Christmas parties, the Thanksgiving dinners. She made sure everything was in order and everyone was at the right place."

Her work was only a natural extension of her family role: Mrs. Duggan, 34, booked banquets and parties for Windows on the World. "She loved that job. She thought she was on the top of the world," said Diana Sayegh, her mother.

Mrs. Duggan married Mitchell Duggan, a former colleague, last March, but the two planned to hold the reception in March 2002 when the family could gather in

Manhattan from all corners of the world. The party specialist was finally organizing something for herself. As they grieved this holiday season, her parents decided to call off the family Christmas dinner for the first time in 35 years.

SAREVE DUKAT
Living Life Joyously

When Sareve Dukat, at age 20, resolved to marry her high school sweetheart, Joel Shapiro, there was no talking her out of it—not even by her mother, who thought she was too young.

Mr. Shapiro recalled his wife's response to her mother this way: "She said, 'You have a choice: Either I will hide his socks when you come to visit, or we will get married.' "

Ms. Dukat, 53, was an opinionated woman. She knew what she liked and she went for it. She worshiped Mickey Mantle. (Her husband's preference for Sandy Koufax did not change her mind.) Early mornings, at least twice a week, she walked her "aerobics walk" along Riverside Park. On weekends, she walked along the beach at the family's summer home on Long Beach Island, in New Jersey, solving "the problems of the world," her husband said. She loved to travel. She went to every sports event she could.

And not a week went by that she did not go to the theater, usually with a colleague, Jon Schlissel. They worked for the New York State Department of Taxation and Finance, on the 87th floor of 2 World Trade Center.

As Mr. Shapiro put it, "She was committed to living her life joyously."

She was also committed to him: they stayed married for 33 years. "She was and is my emotional core," Mr. Shapiro said. "Now there's this void that someone described as a toothache of the heart. It isn't always a sharp pain. But it never goes away."

E

BRUCE EAGLESON

Attention to Detail

When Bruce Eagleson would say he would make dinner, his sons—they're 15, 19 and 22 now—would groan and say, "Now we'll never eat—it'll take hours!" It was probably worth the wait, though, because Mr. Eagleson was a perfectionist—whether at home or at work, he had to get every detail just right.

Do not think he lacked a sense of humor, though. On the contrary, he was famous for his practical jokes—with telephone impersonation being a pet trick—said his wife, Gail. If, say, he overheard his sister-in-law mention a person causing her trouble in some union negotiation, he would call and pretend to be that person, just to mix things up a bit.

Mr. Eagleson, 53, hoped to retire within seven years. He loved golfing and fishing in New Hampshire, and hoped to spend more time there.

A vice president at the Westfield Group, of Los Angeles, Mr. Eagleson, who lived in Connecticut, was at a meeting on the 17th floor of 2 World Trade Center discussing Westfield's plans to run the trade center's retail operations. His oldest son called him after the first plane hit and urged him to leave. Mr. Eagleson said he was evacuating people, but promised to get out.

ROBERT EATON

Primed for Halloween

Robert Eaton could wear a funny hat—or a Halloween costume—with style. A vice president for sales and for eSpeed at Cantor Fitzgerald, he always went along with a joke, especially on Oct. 31.

A big event for the English-born Mr. Eaton and his American wife, Jacqui, was their annual Halloween party at their home in Manhasset, on Long Island. The party was such a staple that even when his wife spent most of one Hal-

loween in the hospital following a car accident, she came home at 10 P.M. only to be greeted by Mr. Eaton and their friends waiting to begin the festivities. His costume that night? Marv Albert, the sportscaster, behind the mike and knee deep in legal trouble.

Mr. Eaton, 37, had other interests: he loved his two German short-haired pointers, Frankie and Wetherby, and was pretty good at soccer.

He and his wife did not hold a Halloween party in 2000 because they were renovating their house.

This past Halloween was difficult for Jacqui, who had met Robert on a blind date in 1991 and married him a couple of years later.

Just before Sept. 11, Mr. Eaton was already talking to his wife about possible costumes, pumpkins and party decorations.

MARGARET ECHTERMANN

"Best Summer of Her Life"

This was the plan: run in the New York Marathon and get out of town. Getting out of town would actually come first for Margaret Echtermann. She was 33, a former upstate New York girl living in Hoboken, and was pleased that her firm, Regus, was relocating her to Boston in two weeks.

Tall and athletic, with long blond hair, Ms. Echtermann had been exceptionally happy in September. "You could tell it was the best summer of her life," said her older sister, Heidi Echtermann. "She had fallen in love with this guy. She had taken a summer house out in the Hamptons and they had an amazing summer. Her birthday is in August. They celebrated Margaret's birthday every single night."

Margaret Echtermann worked on the 93rd floor of 2 World Trade Center. Heidi works at Lehman Brothers, across the street. Margaret spoke to her sister after the first plane struck and told her she was fine, then called her parents in Barneveld, a small town north of Utica, and told them the same. Then she called a friend, who recognized Margaret's phone number on her caller ID, but heard nothing. That was the moment of impact, her sister thinks.

CONSTANTINE ECONOMOS
Two Weeks, Then 23 Years

On a memorial Web page for Constantine Economos one message posted by a former colleague summed up all the others: "When he walked in the room, everything got funnier and better."

A partner at Sandler O'Neill & Partners, Mr. Economos, 41, known as Gus, was on the parish council at his church, left work early to coach the football team at Xavier High School in Manhattan and planned excursions for his children, Constantine and Katherine.

He met his wife, Audrey, in high school in Fort Hamilton, Brooklyn—across the street from where the family now lives. At first, she would date him for only two weeks, saying she was too young to date longer; at the end of two weeks, he asked, "Can I have two more?"

As it turned out, the couple shared 23 years—not enough, but as she said in her husband's eulogy: "Gus didn't live a short life, he lived a condensed life. He lived life to the fullest, and I believe he has left us with large shoes to fill."

CHRISTINE EGAN and MICHAEL EGAN
Siblings and Close Friends

Peter Pan was Michael. Wendy was Christine.

He always sang "I Won't Grow Up" from the Broadway musical, and he meant it. Despite his image of mature respectability—after all, Michael Egan was a 51-year-old insurance company executive—he sprayed shaving cream on the bedsheets and taped down the telephone of colleagues, then giggled as they struggled to pick up the receiver.

His older sister Christine Egan, 55, was the mature one, a nurse who always looked out for him and everyone else, from the Inuit of the Canadian Arctic to the Indians of Canada's central plains. They came from Hull, England, and settled in Canada. But they never surrendered their Yorkshire accents nor their Britishness. Michael collected maps of Hull and made a study of British beers. "He always reminded me of being English," said Mr. Egan's younger sister, Denise.

Christine Egan never married but she traveled extensively and was devoted to her patients. She was also determined to continue her education. In 1999, at 53, she earned a Ph.D. in community health service from the University of Manitoba.

Michael and Christine were inseparable, said Mr. Egan's wife, Anna. "At times I was jealous, that's how close they were," she said.

In September, Christine flew to New Jersey from Winnipeg to care for her brother's handicapped son Matthew, 16, while the Egans celebrated their 20th wedding anniversary in Bermuda. She arrived a few days early, and on Sept. 11 accompanied him to his office at Aon Insurance on the 105th floor of the World Trade Center for a cup of coffee and a peek out the windows.

Mrs. Egan said her husband always called her, no matter where he was. He called that morning, too. "You made it," she said. "No, we're stuck," said Mr. Egan.

Then, still on the phone, she watched his building collapse on television. "He had to call," she said. "But all we could say is, 'I love you, darling.'"

LISA EGAN and SAMANTHA EGAN
Sisters, Always Together

Lisa, right, and Samantha Egan, sisters and co-workers, did most things together: playing sports, visiting their parents on Long Island, collaborating on a Mother's Day gift. This year, they gave their mother, Elizabeth, a photo album of their moments together.

When Lisa, 31, heard there were jobs available at Cantor Fitzgerald, where she had worked for four years as a human resources manager, she suggested that Samantha, 24, apply. Early in 2001, Samantha started working steps away from Lisa.

And so their father, David, says he knows that in the minutes after the plane hit their tower, Lisa and Samantha were together. "They would have been seeking one another immediately," he said from his home in Rocky Point, N.Y. "It would have been the first thing in their minds. 'Where is Samantha?' Lisa would have said. 'Where is Lisa?' Samantha would have thought. I know they are together."

Lisa, the oldest of three, had a master's degree in psychology and was looking for another job. Samantha, who had gone back to college, planned to finish school and find work that would tap her business experience and her interest in charitable work.

"My girls," Mr. Egan said, "were outgoing, bright, articulate, giving, loving, caring. Not just my flesh and blood."

At a memorial service for Sean Patrick Tallon, a Marine Corps reservist and New York City firefighter, his boots, dog tags and helmet adorn an M-16 rifle. (*Kevin P. Coughlin*)

LISA CAREN EHRLICH
Tinkerer and Gadgeteer

After she had opened, revamped and overhauled a home computer about a dozen times, Lisa Caren Ehrlich decided to name the thing. "She called it Frankenstein's Monster, because the case wouldn't close anymore and the pieces didn't fit in," said Jonathan Ehrlich, her husband. Dauntless tinkerer, fanatical gadgeteer—she got power tools on birthdays and a blowtorch to make crème brûlée—Mrs. Ehrlich had a soft spot for useless frog paraphernalia. "As long as the frog wasn't too cartoonlike," her husband said.

Mrs. Ehrlich, 36, and her family lived in Midwood, Brooklyn, near the high school she had attended, Edward R. Murrow. On summer evenings, they would stop at a coffee bar in Sheepshead Bay, because she was as serious about her java as she was about the Mets. Somehow she managed to raise two sons, Ryan and Myles, who were devoted to the team in the Bronx. She rounded them up to make sure they saw the end of a perfect game pitched by former Met David Cone for the Yankees.

Only one of her boys loved to read, so Mrs. Ehrlich took a speed-reading course, to encourage the one who wasn't interested. And in her job as relationship manager for Aon Corporation at the World Trade Center, she was constantly taking or teaching courses. One of her students brought his best friend to meet her about five years ago. "We completed each other's sentences on the first date," Mr. Ehrlich said.

JOHN ERNST EICHLER
Magician and Joker

John Ernst Eichler believed in bringing the world some comic relief—not in a clownish way, but with his own brand of dry wit. "He had one of the greatest senses of humor on the face of the earth," said his friend Edmund Redsecker. "He could brighten your day."

Mr. Eichler, 69, of Cedar Grove, N.J., retired several years ago as director of administration for Cadwalader, Wickersham & Taft. He was at a breakfast at Windows on the World on Sept. 11.

He was a man of multiple avocations. He joined the New York Academy of Sciences, attending lectures with rapt attention. ("But you don't understand what they're saying," his friend Gene Bloch would say. "Yes, but I look like I understand it, don't I?" Mr. Eichler would reply.) He was also a member of the Society of American Magicians, performing sleight-of-hand for friends, said Rod Eichler, his son.

And he was known for his practical jokes. Once, he walked into a men's clothing store owned by a friend in Montclair, N.J. He took out a handful of black plastic ants and scattered them over the sweater table. "He started making a commotion," his son recalled, "saying, 'I can't believe it, there's an insect problem here, they're all over the sweaters.'"

ERIC A. EISENBERG
The Troubleshooter

When computers crashed or Palm Pilots failed, friends called Eric A. Eisenberg. He would laugh at them—a big, infectious laugh, his friends said—and fix the problem. Colleagues at Aon tinkered with his computer to see if he noticed. He always did.

"Everybody in the world that he knew relied on him to fix what was wrong with their computers," said Heidi Cetron, who attended school with him in Plainview, N.Y. Ms. Cetron went with Mr. Eisenberg, 32, in June to buy a car, a blue BMW. He was so excited that on the day of the purchase he wore a shirt of the same color, she said.

On Sept. 11, Mr. Eisenberg, who worked in the south tower, spoke to his mother and grandmother after the first plane hit the other tower. He assured them that he was evacuating, but his mother, Paula Shapiro, did not believe him. "I knew he was there trying to get other people out," she said.

DAPHNE FERLINDA ELDER
A Loyal, Doting Daughter

Sept. 11 was Daphne Ferlinda Elder's first day back at work after a glorious week of vacation with her sister. A business analyst at Marsh & McLennan, at 2 World Trade Center, Ms. Elder was expected in at 10 A.M. on some days, 8:30 A.M. on others. That Tuesday was an early day.

Jimmy Elder, Daphne's father, was a few blocks north of the twin towers when the first plane crashed. "I thought it was an accident but then the other plane hit," he said. His cell phone rang, but all he heard was static. "It had to be her."

All day Mr. Elder stayed as close to the scene as possible, hoping for news of his daughter, 36. He went home around 10 P.M. The family of four children that Mr. Elder and his wife, Josephine, raised in Upper Manhattan was always close. One happy memory: a 1993 trip to Disney World where they all swam, fished and picked oranges. Even though the children were scattered across the metropolitan area, all six got together for lunch every Saturday. "Daphne was a loving person," Mr. Elder said. "She called me every day to find out how I'm doing, what did I eat, did I get some rest. That's what I really miss."

VALERIE SILVER ELLIS
Fixing Shoes, and Wagon

One of the best Valerie Silver Ellis stories takes place in the early '80s when she was starting out at Cantor Fitzgerald. A senior trader asked her to take his shoes to be repaired, so Ms. Ellis had taps put on the toes and the heels extended to four inches. When the senior trader ordered the upstart young trader to redo the job, Ms. Ellis had the shoes bronzed.

"They ended up being friends," said Brian Hull, a friend and former client of Ms. Ellis. "She refused to be insulted, she refused to be intimidated. She just worked as hard as she could and she won."

Ms. Ellis, a 46-year-old equities trader, worked at Cantor Fitzgerald for 20 years, 18 of those at the World Trade Center.

"Someone said at her memorial that Val collected people," her husband, Sam Ellis, said. "She also loved to collect art. We had a place in the Hamptons and she liked the artists in the area. She loved the beach; she loved her dog Spudley. She also loved the theater and we'd often entertain clients by taking them to theater and dinner."

Mr. Hull said, "You never had to see her to know that she was in a room. You just knew her laugh. She always found a reason to laugh."

ALBERT ALFY ELMARRY
A Life on the Upswing

It was a whirlwind romance. He had been living in Toronto; she in Cairo. He had gone home to Egypt for the wedding of his brother. There they met and two weeks later were engaged.

"It was crazy," recalled Irinie Guirguis, who married Albert Alfy Elmarry, a computer specialist, one year later. "We just knew we were right for each other."

By the time they married in November 1999, Mr. Elmarry had started work in New York at Cantor Fitzgerald. Ms. Guirguis followed him. They lived in an apartment in Edison, N.J., and embarked on an exciting new life together. Although they were sometimes homesick for their families in Egypt, it was clear that the job of Mr. Elmarry, who was 30, was going well—so well that the couple decided to buy a house.

They closed on a town house in North Brunswick, N.J., on Aug. 1. Several weeks later, Ms. Guirguis discov-ered she was pregnant with the couple's first child. The baby, a girl, is due in April 2002. Now, Ms. Guirguis is not sure what to do.

"My family is in Egypt," she said. "But I feel Albert is here. I don't want to leave him."

EDGAR H. EMERY Jr.
A Runner for All Seasons

Cold and snow were never enough to keep Edgar H. Emery Jr. from going running. "He'd come back with icicles in his hair," said his wife, Elizabeth.

Mr. Emery, who worked at Fiduciary Trust, organized co-workers to run in charity races, recalled Kevin Granville, a longtime friend and colleague. "He pulled me into these 5-K runs," Mr. Granville said—and often Mr. Emery would take off, leaving Mr. Granville behind. "Only the last couple of races we ran, I guess Ed didn't have any-thing to prove," he said. "He'd stay back with me, make sure I was doing O.K., not having a heart attack."

Mr. Emery would run after work, so that he and his wife somehow frequently ended up eating late, candlelit dinners. It was a routine he stuck to even while studying for several months for the test to be a certified financial planner, which he passed shortly before Sept. 11. "He never even got a chance to see the certificate," Mrs. Emery said.

DORIS ENG
The Dream Job

Long after her friends had left the nest and set up homes of their own, Doris Eng was still sharing an apartment in Flushing, Queens, with her mother, Sui-Kam Eng. Ms. Eng, club manager for Windows on the World on the 107th floor of 1 World Trade Center, was single-minded in her devotion to her mother, a garment worker whose hus-band died last year. "Everything she did was for my mom," her younger brother, Jerry, 27, said in a telephone interview as his mother sobbed in the background. "She cared about other people more than herself."

Ms. Eng was also devoted to her work. A graduate of New York University, she had worked in some of the city's finest establishments—Le Cirque, the Mayfair Hotel and the Warwick Hotel—but her job at Windows was, he said, a dream come true. She worked from 6 A.M. until 5 P.M., and sometimes came in on the weekends.

A network administrator for the City Council, Jerry Eng was on his way to work when he saw the first plane hit. He tried to make his way into the building to rescue his sister but was rebuffed by the police. "That's the hardest part," he said. "I witnessed everything happen."

CHRISTOPHER S. EPPS
Accounting and Poetry

Geneva Epps has not given up hope that the son she had late in life is alive. "I'm just being hopeful and prayerful," she said of Christopher S. Epps, her seventh child and second son. "I just can't seem to give up. I know that I'm not considered very wise and not facing reality. But the reality is that no one has showed me any proof that he is not alive."

Sister Epps, as she is called at the Greater Zion Baptist Church in the Bronx, knows that the 29-year-old Mr. Epps, an accountant for Marsh & McLennan, was in the World Trade Center on Sept. 11. "He said, 'Bye, Mom, see ya later,'" she recalled. "And I said, 'Have a blessed day.' And that was it."

Now she focuses on a September day in 2000 when her church honored her, and Mr. Epps recited from memory a poem he had stayed up all night writing.

There were times when I was faced with danger
And fear filled my head.
Yea, though I walk through the valley of the shadow of
    death, I fear no evil;
I remember what Sister Epps said.
She asked the Lord every morning to watch over my life.
I live today because God heard her plea.
Now I go through this life as a grown man fast in your
    words.
Please order my steps, for you are the Father.
Others who love her call her Sister Epps,
But I am just proud to call her my mother.

ULF R. ERICSON
Adventurous Vacationer

At 79, Ulf Ericson was still working full time as a civil engineer at Washington Group International. On vacations, he trekked in the Himalayas and explored Antarctica. "My father saw himself as someone much younger," said his daughter Catherine. "He had a real passion for engineering. Every year I would say: 'Dad, do they know how old you are?' But he didn't see age as limiting."

Ten years ago, Mr. Ericson returned to mountaineering, which he had loved as a student at Stanford University. He and Helen, his wife of 48 years, had traveled widely. He lived for years in Guatemala and Indonesia and regularly took his family to see relatives in Sweden, where he was raised.

But he wanted to see Nepal's soaring peaks. That trip was the first of his exotic vacations, which continued with a safari in Tanzania, a South Pacific tour and the Antarctica trip.

"He didn't brag about his adventures," his daughter said. "Most people just thought he was a quiet, flexible nice guy. I don't think they knew the depths of my father."

FANNY ESPINOZA
Dedication, and Doughnuts

Fanny Espinoza was earning extra pocket money working behind the counter at a doughnut shop on Fordham Road in the Bronx when she met her husband, Luis, in 1988. At first he was there for a coffee and a doughnut. But pretty soon he was there for Fanny. "He likes doughnuts. But I don't think he likes them that much," said Harry Borrero, a younger brother of Mr. Espinoza. They were married at City Hall the next year.

Fanny Espinoza, 29, was the kind of person that you wanted to tell your problems to. Especially if you were a child. When her children, Christian, 11, and Stephanie, 9, were in the first and third grades at Public School 33 in the Bronx, she volunteered as a guidance counselor for both grades, even though she was holding down one job and studying for a paralegal degree at Bronx Community College.

"When children were sad or misbehaved, she was always there with good advice," said Karen Wilson, a teacher and guidance counselor at P.S. 33. "She'd say 'Keep trying, you can do it.' And she did that in her own life, too. She was a real go-getter. When she told me she got a job at this fancy firm, Cantor Fitzgerald, in the World Trade Center, I was so happy for her."

MICHAEL ESPOSITO
Regular Guy, and a Leader

"My Mel," her voice quivered. "Oh my Mel. He was a regular guy. But he was so much more than that."

Those were the words of a woman asked to describe the man she made a life and two children with. His name was Michael Esposito. He was 41 and a lieutenant at the elite fire and rescue company Squad 1, stationed in Park Slope, Brooklyn. Her name is Denise. The children are Andrew, 15, and Michael, 12.

"When you say regular guy that's an inside joke," she said. "What it means is that he just helped people and asked for nothing in return."

Lieutenant Esposito checked the soundness of neighbors' roofs. He shoveled the old people's snow. And when the old neighbors heard of his passing, they came to ask in a sad, friendly way, "Denise, who will shovel our snow now?"

The boys at the firehouse nicknamed him Mel, a term for an average guy taken from a Rodney Dangerfield movie.

"Mel," said a friend, Firefighter Phil Solimeo. "Best fireman in the whole house. A leader of men. He led you into flames and you knew you were coming out. Mel was a regular guy."

WILLIAM ESPOSITO
What Really Mattered

Vacations were big in William Esposito's life. When he was a boy, his family had a summer home in Budd Lake, N.J. And the summer he was 10 he met a girl named Stevie, whose grandparents also had a home there.

For a while, Billy avoided Stevie, sensing that she liked him. Finally, she told him, "I don't like you," and their friendship blossomed. By age 15 they were dating, by 23 they were married.

Mr. Esposito, 52, of Bellmore, N.Y., became a partner at Cantor Fitzgerald, where he was known as Scoop.

"He was pretty ruthless in the business world," his wife of 29 years said.

But when he was on vacation with his family, he could leave that behind. For many years Mr. Esposito, his wife, son and daughter would go to Florida over Passover and Easter.

"It would be just the four of us—no phones, no friends, no nothing—so we'd play cards," Stevie Esposito said. "And by the end of the vacation, the kids would owe him or he'd owe them like a million dollars. Of course, they never played for real money. As long as we were all together that was really all that mattered."

RUBEN ESQUILIN Jr.
Living for Sports

You wanted to talk sports? Ruben Esquilin Jr. was your man. He lived sports, he breathed sports, he ate sports for dinner.

He was a maintenance worker for Fiduciary Trust. Once the workday ended, however, he was off to play softball or basketball or football. He belonged to so many different teams around the city that his relatives could not keep them straight. Mr. Esquilin, 35, lived with his mother and one of his sisters and her son in lower Manhattan. His room was stuffed with sports equipment and trophies certifying his abilities.

"I know the Angels was the last softball team he was on," said his sister, Priscilla, "but don't ask me to name any others. He was on so many, forget about it.

"He watched sports constantly," she went on. "If he was playing a game, he'd call the house and ask me or my mother to videotape a game that was on TV. Of course, we'd do it. We spoiled him."

He was a big Michael Jordan fan. His sister said he would

have been ecstatic to hear that his beloved basketball star was returning to the game.

SADIE ETTE
A Taste for Adventure

Sadie Ette loved to show friends and family where she worked, laughing at their startled faces as the elevators whooshed off to the 106th floor at 1 World Trade Center, where she was an account representative for Windows on the World. This summer she assured her cousin Ben Edokpayi that after the 1993 bombing, security had been fortified. "It didn't cross her mind that it would happen again," he said.

Ms. Ette, 36, had a taste for adventure and risks. A decade ago, she migrated here from Eket, Nigeria, where she had studied law, but continued to skip around the world on her many travels. She fastidiously maintained contact with far-flung relatives and friends, and was at the center of a large social group of Nigerians in New York. Every week she would phone Mr. Edokpayi, who lives in California, launching into Nigerian pidgin English with her cheerful signature greeting, "How now!"

When Mr. Edokpayi was packing up Ms. Ette's Manhattan apartment, he saw a Bible on her pillow, which she had apparently read before work that final morning. It was open to the 91st Psalm: "With His wings He will cover you and beneath His wings you will find refuge; His truth is a shield, a full shield. / You will not fear the terror of night, nor the arrow that flies by day."

"That gave me some sense of relief," Mr. Edokpayi said.

BARBARA ETZOLD
The Right Number

Barbara Etzold always answered the phone whenever David Konigsberg called for a friend who never seemed to be available. On one level, this was natural; she was, after all, a receptionist at Fred Alger Management. On another, it was kismet.

Two months into this strange telephonic relationship, Mr. Konigsberg mentioned in passing that he would be stopping by the office, and Ms. Etzold popped the question: "Why don't you take me out to lunch?"

The widowed receptionist and the divorced health-benefits administrator became inseparable. In 1997, a year after their first date, the couple moved into a house that Mr. Konigsberg bought in Jersey City. They would boat together along the Hudson River, snorkel together in the Bahamas, ride stationary bicycles together at a local health club. "She and I were just livers of life," Mr. Konigsberg said, referring to Ms. Etzold, who was 43. "There wasn't enough."

Then, of course, there was their Harley-Davidson. The two of them would zoom down to the beaches of New Jersey, to an arts-and-crafts community in Pennsylvania, or to the village of Cold Spring, in Putnam County. "You go up that Route 9W and over the Bear Mountain Bridge," Mr. Konigsberg said. "Especially at this time of year, when it's the most beautiful."

ERIC B. EVANS
A Gardener with Standards

He was gorgeous. That much everybody agreed on.

But beneath his model's good looks, there were two different Eric B. Evanses. His parents, Charles and Corinne Evans, said he was reserved and quiet, a good student who had been a defensive lineman in high school, and who at 31 was determined to succeed in business.

The other Mr. Evans was a looser, self-assured guy with an infectious laugh who once roomed with three easygoing friends and set standards for them.

"He'd be the only one to have all his shirts pressed," said Keith Carlson, one of the roommates. "We'd run out of shirts and take one of his. So on any given day, there could be four Eric Evans dress shirts out in the workplace," Mr. Carlson said. "He yelled, but he never really minded."

More recently Mr. Evans roomed with Karina Almansa, the woman with whom he said he wanted to grow old.

"He was an open-doors-for-you kind of guy," she said. "He was my heart."

Mr. Evans planted tomatoes and basil behind their building in Weehawken, N.J., and recently adopted Skipper, a 70-pound mutt. Ms. Almansa said he talked of someday having a big house and lots of dogs. "Eric loved animals," she said, "but he hated squirrels. They took his tomatoes."

ROBERT EVANS
Rob, Bob or Bobby

If nicknames are a measure of affection, Robert Evans inspired plenty. "To me he was Rob, to Mom he was Bob and to the rest of the world he was Bobby," said his sister, Jeanne Evans, who lived near her brother in Franklin Square, on Long Island.

Firefighter Evans, 36, was also known as Jerry Lewis around the Engine Company 33 firehouse in Manhattan, a reference to his practical jokes and big heart. He often called his sister when he got home from work to say he was O.K.,

but once, catching her asleep, he decided to call back every 15 minutes. (To avoid retaliation, he then turned off his phone.)

"He was very, very protective, especially of me and my mom," his sister said. "I remember when he went skydiving, he didn't tell me about it. He comes over one day and says, 'Check out this tape.' I look at the TV and it's him skydiving. I said, 'Why would you go without me?' He says, 'There's only two of us, so only one can go at a time.' "

MEREDITH EWART and PETER FEIDELBERG
Quite a Birthday

Meredith Ewart, 29, and Peter Feidelberg, 34, had a romance that began in a corporate office in Montreal. They took their vows in a civil ceremony at the Municipal Building in Manhattan.

And more than a year after that, they held the reception back home in Quebec, at a country inn where friends and family danced and toasted their happiness under bright sunny skies.

"They really loved each other," said Robert Ewart, Ms. Ewart's father. "I never heard them fight, never heard them bicker."

Both worked at Aon Corporation, on the 104th floor of 2 World Trade Center. Their long-planned wedding party finally took place on Aug. 11 at an inn a few miles from Otterburn Park, Ms. Ewart's hometown, where about 90 guests gathered. The weather, so hot and sticky most of August, became clear and mild for the occasion.

"He was just a prince of a fellow, and we just loved him," Ms. Ewart's father said of Mr. Feidelberg. "At the end I went over, and I said, 'I love you, Mer,' and she said, 'I love you, Dad.' "

Mr. Feidelberg, an avid skier and bicyclist, had recently returned from a trip to Germany, where he hiked in the mountains with his father. "I was fortunate to travel with him," said his father, Michael. "It's a very big loss."

Ms. Ewart was born on June 25, 1972, her father's 33rd birthday, and they always celebrated together, with two cakes—orange for him, chocolate for her. But last year, she and her husband bought a house in Hoboken, N.J., and could not make it to Montreal for the big day.

As they went for a walk that evening, Mr. Feidelberg told her he regretted that he had never formally proposed to her. "So he got down on his knees and said, 'Meredith, will you marry me?' " Mr. Ewart said, "And he gave her this gorgeous diamond engagement ring. Needless to say, she accepted the proposal, and the birthday present."

PATRICIA FAGAN
Stopping to Chat

Patricia Fagan was a "classic gabber," said her sister Eileen. She could not pick up dinner rolls at the store without striking up a conversation about the clerk's mother's arthritis. Or board the bus from Toms River, N.J., to lower Manhattan, where she was an insurance claims officer with Aon, without chatting with the drivers. Or check an insurance claim without finding out, for instance, about the weather or the claimant's children's schools.

As a result, just about everybody in Toms River, where she grew up, knew her—the tall, exceptionally slender woman of 55 who had a word, or several, with everybody and never forgot a name. She was the official Saturday night greeter at St. Joseph's Roman Catholic Church.

After her death, letters from numerous insurance clients began to arrive: "I never met Pat," they all wrote. "I only knew her from business calls. But I feel like we've been friends for years."

KEITH FAIRBEN
Big, Fast and Reassuring

Keith Fairben was the adrenaline kid, always on the run, said his mother, Diane. He would get home from his job as a paramedic for New York Presbyterian Hospital, get on the cell phone, the home phone and his e-mail all at once, and then field calls from all his friends as they decided what movie to see that night or where to have dinner. Sometimes, to assuage the tension of his job, Mr. Fairben, 24, and his fellow paramedics would play practical jokes on their supervisor, Jack Delaney, one time smearing grease on his office doorknob so he couldn't get in.

But when Mr. Fairben was on the job he was in com-

mand, big and reassuring. And he was fast. Records of the Fire Department's Emergency Medical Service show that he and his partner, Mario Santoro, arrived at the World Trade Center within minutes after the first plane hit. They immediately got to work tending to the injured, running in and out of the building. At 9 A.M., Mr. Fairben's father, Kenneth, reached him on his cell phone, but Mr. Fairben said he was too busy to talk. The elder Mr. Fairben told his son to be careful.

That was the last time he spoke to him.

Linda Morrone, center, the wife of Ferdinand V. Morrone, superintendent of the Port Authority police, who died September 11, watches the folding of the flag after the memorial service for Superintendent Morrone at Sacred Heart Cathedral in Newark. (*Keith Meyers*)

WILLIAM FALLON

To the Shoreline of Kauai

When Kayla turned 6 in 1999, William and Laura Fallon decided it was all right to start taking long trips. The resulting trip to the Grand Canyon was Kayla's first long airplane ride and the first of a series of trips to national parks for the Fallons.

This year, they went on a sweeping 16-day trip that encompassed Grand Teton, Mount Rushmore, Rocky Mountain National Park, "and everyplace in between," Mrs. Fallon said. She and her husband had mapped the trip using an atlas to pick a principal destination, then figured out what other parks were nearby. They got back on Labor Day weekend, and Mr. Fallon returned to work at Cantor Fitzgerald.

"We went on roads we weren't even supposed to go on," Mrs. Fallon said, and recalled a prior trip she and her husband had taken to the island of Kauai in Hawaii, before they had Kayla or her older sister, Kathleen, who is 11. They followed a winding road past signs ordering them to turn around, all the way to where the beach ended at a rocky shoreline.

"We got great pleasure out of that," she said. "We went as far as we could."

WILLIAM F. FALLON Jr.

Finished What He Started

William Fallon's family was not surprised when they learned that every member of his department at the Port Authority had escaped but him. He called his wife, Brenda, from his office on the 62nd floor of the north tower at 9:25 A.M. but later made calls from the 64th floor.

They knew he had stayed to help, as he had after the 1993 bombing, when his military training kicked in and he volunteered for the rescue effort. "He did carry people out in '93," said his sister-in-law, Suzanne Fallon. "So he was probably hanging behind again."

Mr. Fallon, 53, was a general manager in charge of commerce at the Port Authority, a job that took him around the world. He was known to his neighbors in Rocky Hill, N.J., just outside Princeton, as a trim marathon runner, and he was to compete in the Philadelphia Half Marathon on Sept. 16. He came to the sport late—past 40—but he was dedi-

Port Authority police officers unfurl a torn flag that had been flying at the World Trade Center, to remember fellow officer Michael T. Wholey, thirty-four, in Westwood, New Jersey, on October 16. (*Norman Y. Lono*)

cated to it, and gradually built up his endurance to the point where he could finish a race. "He always completed what he started," said his brother, Donald.

ANTHONY FALLONE

A Joke Everywhere

Ever wonder who writes those wacky e-mail jokes that make the rounds on Wall Street? Anthony Fallone, 39 years old, was clearly one of the champs.

He had a no-nonsense style at business. He was a bond trader at Cantor Fitzgerald. But when he was not busy at work, he could be found sitting at his computer screen—roaring with laughter at either what he had just read or written. "He had an irreverent sense of humor," said his wife, Patty. "He could see the humor in anything. As one friend put it: He looked at life and got the joke."

With his deep belly laugh and quick (sometimes twisted) wit, Mr. Fallone—who everyone knew as Tony—had a personality that matched his large frame. He invented nicknames for people, punctuated jokes with ad-libbed songs and never lost the chance to poke fun at himself. But probably no one appreciated his humor more than his wife and their four children, Katie, 11; Alexandra, 10; Anthony, 7; and Patrick, 5.

"He was a larger than life guy," Mrs. Fallone said. "One of the funniest people you ever met. When I filled out the missing person's report, we laughed so hard at how he would want himself described in the report."

ROBERT J. FANGMAN

A Job That Fit

Money is little comfort when you hate your job. As a salesman for Verizon Wireless, the only part Robert J. Fangman liked about his job was the travel, said his mother, Ruth. So he kept the travel, threw out the selling, and took a 50 percent pay cut to become a flight attendant with United Airlines in November 2000.

He had found his calling, enamored with the people and the lifestyle. Thirty-three and single, Mr. Fangman traveled extensively, walking on and off planes as if they were buses. One week it would be to Texas to visit his brother, another it would be to Delaware to visit his mother. He carried flashcards so he could study the information about the various planes.

Mr. Fangman loved foreign cities, dancing and fine wine, Mrs. Fangman said. It bothered him that unfinished wine in first class had to be poured down the sink, so he would ask other attendants to do it for him.

On Sept. 11, he was assigned to Flight 175. His ambition was to be assigned to international flights and he chose to be based out of Boston because he could move up more quickly there.

He even liked the polyester uniforms, Mrs. Fangman said. When he looked at himself in the mirror, he would quip, "I always like a man in uniform."

THOMAS FARINO
The Gift of Strength

Capt. Thomas Farino was the rock on which his wife, Mary, built her life. He was the baby in a family of six boys, sons of a New York City policeman. He was captain of Engine Company 26 in Manhattan, doing a job he loved. He was posthumously promoted to battalion chief.

"I never knew anyone who woke up in the morning happy to go to work," said Mrs. Farino. And his schedule allowed for a lot of family time. For their children, Jane, 10, and James, 6, it was like having another mother—"five out of seven days they'd have Daddy at home."

"I'm not making it a fairy tale, everyone has good times and bad times," she said. But the good times were rolling recently—a new house, the fourth trip to Disney World. "He was the most content person I've ever met," Mrs. Farino said.

Throughout their 20 years together, she said, he would tell her: "Love me all you want, want me all you want, but don't need me so much. You have to get your strength from someone higher than me."

After the attack, she thought: "Wow, this is what he was talking about. It was a gift he gave me by telling me I'm stronger than I think—I know how happy he would feel to know that I believe I am stronger."

NANCY FARLEY
A Heart for Strays

Having three cats of her own did not stop Nancy Farley from feeding neighborhood strays and taking them to the veterinarian when needed. "If there was a snowstorm and she saw a cat, she would bring it in," recalled Linda Selnow, Ms. Farley's older sister. "She had the most caring heart."

Ms. Farley, 45, negotiated insurance claims at Reinsurance Solutions Inc., on the 94th floor of 1 World Trade Center. The youngest of three children, she lived with her husband, Robert, in a condominium in Jersey City; her brother lived upstairs. Her father died when she was in high school, and her mother died a decade ago. "Just the three of us were left, and we were very close," Ms. Selnow said.

Nancy and Robert married in Las Vegas a few years ago. Her sister and brother were there, front and center. "It was one of the greatest times the three of us had together," Ms. Selnow said. Except when she was cheering on her beloved Yankees, Ms. Farley was a quiet person. "We believe that she is in a better place," Ms. Selnow said. "It's just the pain of not knowing what happened or where she was."

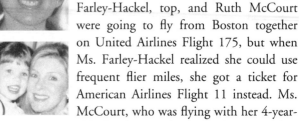

PAIGE FARLEY-HACKEL, RUTH McCOURT and JULIANA McCOURT
Taking Miss J to Disneyland

They were best friends, close as sisters, and they were headed to California. Paige Farley-Hackel, top, and Ruth McCourt were going to fly from Boston together on United Airlines Flight 175, but when Ms. Farley-Hackel realized she could use frequent flier miles, she got a ticket for American Airlines Flight 11 instead. Ms. McCourt, who was flying with her 4-year-old daughter, Juliana, and Ms. Farley-Hackel said good-bye in the early morning hours at Logan International Airport in Boston on Sept. 11, and boarded their planes.

The women had planned on meeting in Los Angeles and taking Juliana to Disneyland. Ms. Farley-Hackel's plane was hijacked and struck the north tower of the World Trade Center. Ms. McCourt's and Juliana's flight, hijacked as well, crashed into the south tower shortly thereafter.

The mother and daughter would have been a striking pair sitting together, said Ms. McCourt's mother, Paula Clifford Scott, what with Ms. McCourt's long red hair and Juliana's blond locks. She was only 4, but already Juliana, nicknamed Miss J, displayed a little sense of wit.

"And she was a nurturer like her mother," Ms. Scott said.

Ruth McCourt, who was 45 and a homemaker from New London, Conn., met Ms. Farley-Hackel at the day spa she used to own in Boston. She gave up the business when she got married six years ago, but the friendship lasted. The two women often traveled together. They shared passions for reading and cooking and learning new things.

Ms. Farley-Hackel, who was 46 and a writer and motivational speaker from Newton, Mass., was looking forward to having the first few episodes of her new radio program, *Spiritually Speaking*, hit the airwaves. She had a dream: in two years or so, she wanted to either be featured on *The Oprah Winfrey Show* or be Oprah's biggest rival, said her husband, Allan Hackel.

Recently, the *Oprah* show included a memorial segment about Ms. Farley-Hackel's friendship with Ms. McCourt and Juliana.

BETTY FARMER
Too Restless for the Duke

Betty Farmer once rejected Duke Ellington. A jazz singer who made her debut with a Dixieland band in her native New Orleans as a teenager, she toured with Mr. Ellington in the 1960s and 1970s and in 1972 performed with him in Carnegie Hall. But when Mr. Ellington offered her a long-term contract, her daughter said, she turned it down.

"My mother was a free spirit," said Kathryn Nesbit, 38. "She said, 'Duke, I love you, but I'd be bored out of my mind.'"

Ms. Farmer, 62 and divorced, performed in clubs and jazz festivals, lived in different cities and once owned a nightclub in Denver. She also had a son, Shawn Farmer, 42, who died this year. In 1997, she moved to New York City at the urging of Ms. Nesbit, who told her "you have to go. It's for you."

Ms. Nesbit was right. Ms. Farmer made new friends, started playing the guitar and, although on a singing hiatus, was preparing a comeback. David Jung, an actor and comedian, said Ms. Farmer had agreed to lend her big, sultry voice and gift for comedy to a number of sketches he was going to tape for a comedy show bound for the theater.

Ms. Farmer's most recent job was with Cantor Fitzgerald, where she worked as an executive assistant for three weeks.

DOUGLAS J. FARNUM
Jack of Many Trades

Douglas J. Farnum opened a comic-book store with a partner, tried his hand at stand-up comedy and worked at a series of bagel shops in Brooklyn, concocting sandwiches that sold like crazy.

Shortly after meeting Amy Leong, Mr. Farnum, 33, of Brooklyn, decided he wanted to be able to support a family. He asked his friend Gabriel Polmar to teach him about computers, and ended up finding work as a software specialist for Marsh & McLennan. He developed a talent for finding ways to make incompatible systems work, finding "that the incompetence of others provided him with a challenge," Mr. Polmar said.

Last year, Mr. Farnum and Ms. Leong married. Some things did not change. He continued to find pleasure in comic books, parking-lot Frisbee games and the aisles of Toys "R" Us, where the couple acted "like two big kids," Mrs. Farnum said.

Still, some things changed. Mr. Farnum quit smoking and started driving like an old man—a far cry from the stomach-churning old days, Mr. Polmar said. "I have too much to lose," Mr. Farnum had explained.

JOHN FARRELL
A Caring Klutz

By day's end, Grandma would have everyone fit to be tied as she roared with the agitation of an Alzheimer's sufferer. Then a grandson, John Farrell, would walk into the kitchen, flop next to her wheelchair and say genially, "Peg! How was your day?"

She did not know who he was, only that she could trust him. "Peg! Keep it down, there!" he would say. "Let me finish my dinner and we'll take care of it." She would relax, calmed by her broad, hulking friend.

A good-time guy, Mr. Farrell, 32, was a vice president and partner at Cantor Fitzgerald, student of all things Irish and endearingly hapless, according to his sister, Margaret. "He was so caring," she said, "and so klutzy."

He also had a way with the ladies, especially Cate, the 2½-year-old niece he pronounced the only perfect woman he had ever met. That last September weekend, as the Farrell clan gathered in Rockaway Beach, Mr. Farrell captivated the perfect woman with a gimmick leash that walked an imaginary dog. Saturday night, Cate could not sleep.

Wearing feetie pajamas, she slipped out to the backyard for a stroll with Uncle John, who carefully held the leash as he recounted tales of the inimitable, invisible Spot.

JOHN W. FARRELL
His Town, His Home

He got up every weekday morning before the sun rose, drove his beat-up truck to a Basking Ridge, N.J., train station glittering with Lexuses and Volvos, and began an hour-and-half commute to lower Manhattan. There, in an office tower that sometimes swayed in the wind, he put in long hours as a managing director for the Sandler O'Neill investment-banking firm.

It took another 90 minutes to get back to that old truck. But then John Farrell would be truly home. There, in Basking Ridge, was his wife, Maryanne, who caught his eye way back in the '70s at Bernards High School just down the road. There, too, were his four children; the oldest was 12, the youngest just 3.

"He grew up in a small town, met his wife in a small town," said Bob Bush, the best man at his wedding and a friend from high school. "He wanted his children to have the same experience that he had in a small town."

Bob Kumpf, another high school friend and now a Basking Ridge police captain, agreed: "He made the trek into the city every day, those long hours and that long commute, because it was the best thing for his family."

At 41, John Farrell knew the value of simple things. At

one of many backyard gatherings, surrounded by family members and old buddies, he leaned over and said: "You know what, Kumpfy? It doesn't get any better than this."

TERRENCE P. FARRELL
Giving His Very Self

Terrence P. Farrell lived close to the flame, said his brother Dennis. Terrence Farrell's specialty as a transit police officer had been disasters. In the Fire Department, he joined Rescue Company 4, an elite unit specially trained to do things like extricate people from collapsed buildings.

Mr. Farrell, who was 45, was not simply a New York City firefighter. He was also a volunteer fireman near his home in Huntington, N.Y., a part-time construction contractor and a father of two. And, a few years back, he helped save the life of a child in Nevada by donating his bone marrow.

Here is that story. When Mr. Farrell joined the department, his blood had been tested as part of a program to screen for potential bone marrow donors, Dennis Farrell said. Told years later that his blood matched that of a small girl dying of t-cell lymphoma, he underwent the painful process of marrow extraction.

A year later, he learned that the child was considered cured. She and her family flew to New York and had lunch with him at the World Trade Center, his brother said.

On Nov. 1, 2001, they were back. Fellow firefighters had raised $3,000 to fly them to New York for Firefighter Farrell's funeral because they did not have the money.

CHRISTOPHER FAUGHNAN
Love Behind the Wheel

It was an October Saturday morning, and Cathy Faughnan was standing in the chilling wind beside a soccer field rooting for Juliet, her second child. Just a few weeks earlier, that had been the job of her husband, Christopher Faughnan.

They met as undergraduates at the University of Colorado, where he worked as a security guard and she as a lifeguard. One day, she held up a piece of paper to him that said, "Cute Butt."

He became a perfect dad. When Mr. Faughnan got home every weekday at 6:30 P.M. from his job as a trader at Cantor Fitzgerald, "he would get the kids all crazy," Mrs. Faughnan said. "They would jump around him, laughing and kissing him."

He bought a minivan, and ferried the three children to art classes, gymnastic practice, ballet lessons and soccer games. The children are Siena, 7, Juliet, 5, and Liam, 3. One night, Liam asked his mother why Daddy could not come back, but a few days later, he told her that his father was a hero.

"I don't know where he got that," Mrs. Faughnan said. "And he told me: 'Mommy, I will take care of you. Daddy doesn't want you to be sad.' "

Halloween would have been Mr. Faughnan's 38th birthday. After the trick-or-treating, Mrs. Faughnan asked the children to write their dad a message on a piece of paper, tie it to a balloon and let it fly.

WENDY FAULKNER
A Legacy of Giving

Growing up as the daughter of missionaries in Japan and the West Indies, Wendy Faulkner always knew what it meant to be poor. Even after she became a successful businesswoman and settled in Mason, Ohio, she would regularly pack up boxes of clothing and send them to orphans and poor children whose names had been passed on to her by her parents.

"She spent thousands of dollars, but no one even knew she did it," said her husband of 21 years, Lynn Faulkner. "I know she put at least one kid all the way through school."

In fact, some of her friends did not even know she was a vice president at Aon, with people working for her in several countries, because she rarely talked about it. Several thought she was a stay-at-home mom because she spent so much time with her two daughters, her husband said.

Yet she often traveled to New York and other cities, and on Sept. 11 she was attending a one-day meeting at Aon's offices in the World Trade Center.

To continue her legacy of helping children in the Third World, her family has established a nonprofit group, the Wendy Faulkner Memorial Children's Foundation.

SHANNON FAVA
She Dances in His Heart

Frank and Shannon Fava would have celebrated their seventh wedding anniversary in October, 2001, so Mr. Fava was in a reflective mood. He remembered the first time he saw his wife. She was walking into a bagel shop in Bensonhurst, Brooklyn. She was 18, and he was shy.

"I had seen her once or twice before, and I just had to talk to her," Mr. Fava said. "I'm a shy guy, but we started talking and just clicked." What he thought might have been a fling turned into "my first true love," he said. "I watched her grow into a woman."

The woman Shannon Fava became loved to hug their 3-year-old son, Joseph Anthony, rent movies and laugh. Mrs.

Fava, 30, worked as an assistant broker for Cantor Fitzgerald and lived in Bensonhurst. Mr. Fava said he could almost still see his wife dancing around the house to whatever was on MTV. He thinks that might be because she called after the plane hit her tower and said, "Tell the baby I'll always be with him, and you."

BERNARD FAVUZZA
Model Trains a Passion

Each time his wife, Vincenza, got pregnant, Dominick Favuzza would buy a Lionel train set: engine, boxcars, caboose and tracks. This was postwar New York in the 1950s.

He did this a month before Bernard's birth. And he did it before his daughters, Janice and Anna, were born. Around Christmas, the shiny trains would clack around the tree.

Bernard Favuzza, who was 52 on Sept. 11, had taken to the hobby. He built a miniature model of Ridgewood, Queens, in his house in Suffern, N.Y.—with a train that whistled through his childhood neighborhood complete with Dietz Coal. And he took over his dad's tradition of buying the trains for those soon to be born. He bought them for his nephew Kevin, 12, and his grandson Dominick, 1.

"They were relaxing," Anna Favuzza said of her brother's train hobby. "It's stressful, right? The market. Wall Street. This was a way for him to unwind."

Mr. Favuzza was at Cantor Fitzgerald, above where one of the planes went in. Now his daughters, Donna Posta, 32, and Laura Favuzza, 24, will take care of his trains.

RONALD C. FAZIO
Still a Family Man

Ronald C. Fazio's son, Ron Jr., was getting married on Oct. 14, 2001. So Mr. Fazio spent the last few months as his son's trusted wedding consultant—touring reception halls, interviewing florists, considering limousine services. When his three children were young, Mr. Fazio never missed a baseball game, a school play or a prom.

"He was the ideal family man," Ron Jr. said.

In recent years, Mr. Fazio would ride the train from Closter, N.J., to his office at Aon Reinsurance, on the 99th floor of 2 World Trade Center, and two of his grown children would ride in with him. "He lost his father at the age of 9," said Mr. Fazio's wife, Janet. "When he had his children, he used to say to me, 'I don't know how to be a father.' Well, he did a better job than a lot of men. When my parents were sick and dying, he would be the one to go for me if I couldn't handle going because I was devastated.

He was a family man for all of us." Mrs. Fazio corrected herself: "He is."

WILLIAM FEEHAN
The Can-Do Bond

When he was not fighting fires, William Feehan walked the fields of Gettysburg, toured Churchill's War Room and read naval history. Military culture, with its embrace of tradition and tactics, appealed to Mr. Feehan much the way firefighting did, said his son, William Feehan Jr.

He remembered his father tracing the path of Pickett's Charge, mapped in his mind by accounts he had read in a novel, *The Killer Angels*. The senior William Feehan, a New York City firefighter who ascended through the ranks to serve as first deputy fire commissioner, recommended the book often.

One who read it at his suggestion, Firefighter Vincent Panaro, was there when the towers fell and Commissioner Feehan was killed. At his wake, two days later, Firefighter Panaro stood sentry in his dress blues at his mentor's coffin. "He refused to leave until he was relieved," the younger Mr. Feehan said.

It was that sort of bond, that sort of Semper Fi candoism, that Commissioner Feehan thought was intrinsic to the firefighter ranks, his family said. It explained, he thought, how people, whether they be soldiers or firefighters, found it within themselves to charge into harm's way to save complete strangers.

When he died, Commissioner Feehan, 71, was the oldest and highest-ranking firefighter ever to die in the line of duty.

FRANCIS J. FEELY
Friend of "The Far Side"

You always knew when Francis Jude Feely was around by his distinctive laugh, a deep and loud guffaw. An accountant at Marsh & McLennan, Mr. Feely was a huge fan of "The Far Side," and would bring cartoons applicable to members of the family at gatherings.

"Every year he knew one present he was getting from me, the 'Far Side' calendar," said his mother, Patricia Feely. Mr. Feely also had a talent for remembering jokes and recounting them perfectly. "Such a repertoire!" she said.

Mr. Feely, 42, grew up in Flatbush, Brooklyn, where he began dating his future wife, Lori, at 16. They both went to St. Francis College, married and eventually moved to Middletown, N.Y. He made friends with a small band of commuters on Metro-North, and they had dinner once a month or so, said his father, Francis Joseph Feely. Frank and Lori Feely separated in January, but remained amicable.

"He wasn't a saint by any means," his mother said, but he was a funny, loyal friend, and was devoted to his girls, Jennifer, 19; Lauren, 16; Stephanie, 11; and Caitlin, 7.

GARTH E. FEENEY
An Engineer's Shortcut

Earning an engineering degree from the University of Pennsylvania typically takes five years. But it was not the fact that Garth E. Feeney did it in four years while also majoring in business. It was everything else he did at the same time that amazed his family.

Mr. Feeney, 28, who was at a conference at Windows on the World on Sept. 11, tutored an illiterate adult, established a program for poor children, worked for campus security, was a dorm counselor, was a representative on the university's board of trustees and worked for Habitat for Humanity.

"He was one of these people who did everything and anything," said his mother, Judy Feeney.

Even after he moved to New York, where he was director of corporate development for Data Synapse in Manhattan, he kept up the pace of activities. He was a rock climber, a scuba diver, a kayaker and an avid in-line skater. He loved gliding through Central Park whenever he got the chance.

One thing his parents did not know, until they heard tales from friends at his memorial service, was that Mr. Feeney was exceptionally frugal. Even as he earned a decent income, he refused to take a taxi anywhere—not even to the airport—and loved using coupons, including ones for the fast-food spot Subway, where he would buy one sandwich (lunch) and get one free (dinner). "We weren't aware that he was quite that economical," his mother said.

SEAN B. FEGAN
Nurturing Strong Roots

Sean B. Fegan eventually gave up on the lettuce he planted in his family's garden in Blauvelt in Rockland County, where he visited for Sunday dinner every week.

"His scallions were his biggest success," Mr. Fegan's sister Anne Marie said; the lettuce was one of his rare defeats.

At 34, Mr. Fegan was a senior equity trader and an assistant vice president at Fred Alger Management Inc. He was meticulous about the way he looked.

"He ran and worked out," Ms. Fegan said. "He had really beautiful blue eyes."

Mr. Fegan also had to get the details right, whether in long, funny stories he loved to tell or when quizzing his parents, Colette and Peter, and Anne Marie and his other siblings, Catherine and Peter Jr., about how their lives were going.

But Mr. Fegan also liked to party in Manhattan, where he lived, to go to Jets games and to travel to Europe, often with his girlfriend, Jenny Hebeler. A favorite destination was County Cavan in Ireland, where his family came from and still maintains a home. He wanted the family to have dual citizenship and had applied for it for himself.

"He was very proud of his heritage," Ms. Fegan said. "He always made the most of life."

LEE S. FEHLING
Born to Laugh

It did not take Lee S. Fehling's mother long to know that she had a character on her hands.

"You know when the doctor slaps you on the back and the baby cries?" said his mother, Joan Bischoff. "Lee came out laughing."

Mr. Fehling, 28, relished a good telephone prank, calling his mother, an insurance investigator, and claiming to be an investigation subject, or impersonating a Nassau County official to inform a friend that her garage violated zoning restrictions.

"He wasn't ever a fan of dull moments," said his younger brother, Thomas.

This was particularly problematic for those who played bagpipes with Mr. Fehling in the American Legion band in Wantagh, on Long Island, where he lived. (Just try playing the pipes while cracking up.) Mr. Fehling, a firefighter with Engine Company 235 in Brooklyn, could always make his wife, Danielle, smile, but he could never fool her.

"I could tell a mile away if he was up to something," she said.

He adored his daughter Kaitlin, 4. But his stepsister-in-law Jennifer Bischoff thinks she knows the real reason he was pleased that the second little Fehling would also be a girl. (Megan was born Oct. 18.)

"He was afraid a little boy would be just like him," she said, chuckling. "And he wouldn't be able to handle it."

PETER FEIDELBERG's portrait appears with Meredith Ewart on page 144.

ALAN D. FEINBERG
Mr. Mom's Fire Truck

When Wendy Feinberg recalls meeting Alan D. Feinberg 21 years ago, she remembers not only the man, but also his car—a sharp Datsun 240-Z. From that encounter in the parking lot of a Sheepshead Bay diner came marriage, children and a life for Mr. Feinberg as both a firefighter and a Mr. Mom.

Mourners gather on October 17 at St. Francis Xavier Roman Catholic Church in Park Slope, Brooklyn, for the funeral of Dave Fontana, one of twelve firefighters from Squad 1 among the missing after the terrorist attack on the World Trade Center. (*Edward Keating*)

Unbeknownst to his wife, Alan Feinberg, who worked at the time as a salesman of buttons and boys' clothes in the garment district, secretly wanted to be a firefighter. Four years into the marriage, that is what he became. To compensate for a cut in salary, he took advantage of the flexible hours of firefighting to remain home with Tara, now 18, and Michael, 15, while his wife took the 6:05 A.M. into the city to work as a broker at Cantor Fitzgerald, a job she left in 1996.

His children remember Firefighter Feinberg, 48, making breakfast, putting them on the school bus and being the "class dad" who chaperoned school field trips and coached baseball and soccer. As his children got older, Firefighter Feinberg, who was the battalion chief aide at Engine Company 54 in Manhattan, took on a second job that built on his love of fancy cars: he became a transporter of new cars to the automotive press, which would then write about them. Just recently, he was thrilled to have dropped off a PT Cruiser and a red 2002 Corvette. "He would have loved that new Thunderbird if he had seen it," his wife said.

"He was doing what he wanted to do," she added. "He

was very happy. Everyone should have had such a happy life. He was the little boy who never grew up."

EDWARD T. FERGUS Jr.
The Sporting Life

Every Saturday, the first thing Edward T. Fergus Jr. did was drive to Dix Hills, N.Y., to tinker with his parents' boat and do some chores. Returning home to Wilton, Conn., he would go fishing on Long Island Sound with his 10-year-old son, Tom, and 11-year-old daughter, Shannon. Then, before dinner, he would work on the nearby house he was renovating. The question was: how?

"On-tap energy," said Allison Fergus, his sister. Working at Cantor Fitzgerald, he was home early enough for picnics in the boat with his wife, Linda, and the children. The winter sports were skiing and snowboarding, usually in Vermont.

Mr. Fergus, 40, organized the annual seaside vacation

with his parents and three sisters, and coaxed the two sisters who lived in Manhattan to get out of the city for events like the Norwalk Oysterfest. He was hard to miss, even in the church balcony. The priest always picked him out—a head above everybody, with red hair that nearly glowed.

HENRY FERNANDEZ
A House for His Mother

When he wasn't at his job making pastries at Windows on the World, Henry Fernandez was probably out playing soccer with his buddies at Flushing Park, or inviting friends to the apartment he shared with four cousins. Or he would be calling home, a small town in Ecuador, to check on his mother and other family members.

"He was very active," said one of the cousins he lived with, Hernan Calle, 29. "He would say, let's go play soccer. Let's do this, let's do that. Oh! He had so many friends, either people he worked with or *paisano*s from Ecuador that he met here."

Mr. Fernandez, who was 23, came to New York about nine years ago, and quickly found work and a home among his relatives in Elmhurst, Queens, a neighborhood that has attracted many from his country.

"A lot of people from Ecuador of that age, because of the lack of employment there, come here to seek their fortunes," the cousin said. "He and his brother Alfredo wanted to buy a house for their mother."

"He was such a good young man," Mr. Calle said. "He was like a brother to me."

ROBERT J. FERRIS
Papa Bob at the Orphanage

While many men his age pondered retiring to Florida or hitting the links in Arizona, Robert J. Ferris considered buying a house near an orphanage in Haiti.

His wife of 38 years, Susanne, demurred. "I don't know if that would have worked out," she said.

To Mr. Ferris, 63, a family vacation meant packing his wife and their three children into the family car and setting off for Columbus, Ohio, to visit relatives. If he wanted to support a local firehouse or church, he did not just open his checkbook: he went door to door in Garden City, N.Y., asking for donations. Similarly, at Aon Corporation, where he was a senior vice president, he was just as likely to befriend a secretary as he was an executive.

Mr. Ferris went to Haiti after Hurricane Georges in 1998 to visit his son, Bob, a doctor in his first year out of medical school. Mr. Ferris volunteered at a nearby Roman Catholic orphanage, where the children called him Papa Bob.

Mr. Ferris's son went on to work in the intensive-care unit at St. Vincent's Hospital in Manhattan. He was on duty Sept. 11, and from the hospital saw smoke billowing from the first tower.

"Bobby, you won't believe what I'm seeing," Mr. Ferris told his son on the telephone.

Minutes later, the second plane hit. Mr. Ferris's son was one of the doctors waiting for ambulances that never arrived.

LOUIS FERSINI
Doing Things with Flair

At St. John's University, Louis Fersini and his future wife, Cathy, dated others and saw each other at parties. "Always in a group," Mrs. Fersini said. "Laughing and playing."

When the fraternity formal rolled around, Mr. Fersini suggested that they go together and meet up with their friends. "But first," he said, "how about dinner?"

Mrs. Fersini expected to go to Charley O's for a hamburger. Instead they went to One if by Land, Two if by Sea—romantic, gourmet and expensive. And he sent a dozen roses beforehand. "I thought of him as a buddy," she said. "I guess he had something else in mind."

After, she felt like a girl in an old-fashioned romance. "I sat on the edge of my mother's bed," she recalled, "and said, 'Oh my God.' I was thrilled. I was only 19 and I'd never been treated like that. But that was Louie—everything in his life he did, he did big."

Like holidays. On Christmas Eve, Mr. Fersini—a 38-year-old Cantor Fitzgerald trader—made seafood stew and stayed up late assembling toys for his four children. "He played with them more than the kids ever did," Mrs. Fersini said.

MICHAEL FERUGIO
The Measure of a Man

"The true measure of a man is how he treats someone who can do him absolutely no good." Samuel Johnson, the 18th-century man of letters, wrote it, and Michael Ferugio lived it.

He came from Smalltown, U.S.A. Pottsville is an aging coal-mining town in the northeastern hills of Pennsylvania, and like many young people there, Mr. Ferugio, 37, left to make his fortune.

Still, he took something with him. His father was a steam-pipe fitter, his mother a homemaker. They imparted some regular folk wisdom to him that he did not abandon: "You're no better than anyone else."

"We used to fight because he said hello to strangers," said his wife, Susan, 34, who grew up in Queens and lived with her husband in Brooklyn. "I'm a New Yorker, and I told him you can't do that here."

But he did, top to bottom. As an insurance broker at Aon, he ate breakfast with chief executives at the World Trade Center, and when he was done, he made small talk with the secretaries. After his death, Susan Ferugio went through his phone book. Inside were the numbers of half a dozen janitors. His friends.

BRADLEY JAMES FETCHET
Turning the Focus to Others

To his family and friends, Bradley James Fetchet always seemed an odd fit for the dog-eat-dog world of Wall Street that became his life as an equity trader for Keefe, Bruyette & Woods. Quiet and reserved, Mr. Fetchet, 24, loathed being the center of attention, even on occasions when he deserved it. On his birthday, he preferred that the day go unnoticed, forbidding his mother to plan even the smallest celebration.

But no one could stop Mr. Fetchet from surprising other people. On a whim, Mr. Fetchet would buy and set up elaborate electronic gifts for his family or disguise simple gifts, like CDs, in multiple boxes just to elicit smiles. In letters and visits, thousands of people have recounted such stories to Mr. Fetchet's mother, Mary Fetchet, and to Brooke Stengel, the woman with whom he had begun shopping for wedding rings.

"Brad was always focused on other people, whether he knew you or not," Mary Fetchet said. "In his journal, he kept this quote: 'You can tell the character of a man by what he does for the man who can offer him nothing.' That's how he lived."

JENNIFER FIALKO
A Spiritual Journey

At 24, an age when most people are busy with first jobs and apartments, Jennifer Fialko was diagnosed with Hodgkin's disease. She was 29 before she fully recovered; by then, she felt her cancer had been a gift.

"It led her on a spiritual journey," said Bob Fialko, her father. Weakened by 18 months of chemotherapy, Ms. Fialko devoted herself to becoming healthy, with organic food and alternative treatments.

Six years later, she was not simply cancer-free, said Evelyn Fialko, her mother. She felt marvelous—strong and energetic. Her new mission was to help other sick people regain their health. She had met "her soul mate," Mr. Fialko said. And in September she started a new job at the Aon Corporation. After years in Teaneck, N.J., she was excited to be working in lower Manhattan.

Beating cancer made her glow with new confidence, Mr.

Fialko said. She felt she could do anything. "She was convinced she was now going to live to 120," said Andrew Fialko, her brother. "And we believed her."

SAMUEL FIELDS
Sports-Loving Deacon

Samuel Fields was a man of simple tastes. He loved Motown and the Beatles. He loved singing in the choir in the House of God Holy Church in Harlem, and he was thrilled to play bongos there. He also served as a church deacon, helping usher the elderly to seats.

Mr. Fields, 36, loved sports. He loved watching the Yankees on television, and the Mets, too. He often played basketball with his kids in the court just outside their apartment in the Martin Luther King Jr. Towers on 114th Street.

He also loved strolling around downtown with his wife of 10 years, Angela. Sometimes he showed her around the World Trade Center, where he worked as a $22,000-a-year security guard. "He was last seen on the first floor in the north tower helping people get out of the building," she said.

He left four children: Samuel Jr., 11; Stefan, 7; Demetrius, 5; and Sharaia, 3. Last summer Mr. Fields learned that his wife was expecting a fifth child this March. "He was at first worried that we didn't have enough money," Mrs. Fields said. "I told him God would make a way for us, and he accepted it."

ALEXANDER FILIPOV
A Desire to Know

Alexander Filipov, an electrical engineer, did not just check his sons' homework. He explained it in complex mathematical terms. He took them sailing and taught them to calculate their location by the positions of the stars.

"He had incredible math acumen," said David, a son who is a journalist. "But he was no genius whiz nerd. He would go up to anybody and start telling stories about himself."

He asked religious proselytizers about their lives and showed them the backyard goldfish pond he had carved in granite. He learned the phrase "Do you like Chinese food?" in 17 languages to open conversations with foreigners.

Mr. Filipov, 70, and Loretta, his wife of 44 years, lived in Concord, Mass. He was a passenger on American Airlines Flight 11, which was hijacked en route from Boston to Los Angeles and flown into 1 World Trade Center.

When he was 60 and on business in California, he went bungee-jumping. "I didn't like when I was done," he said later, "and nobody was looking at me."

"Every new gadget he found he had to tell you about, whether or not you understood it," said David Filipov. "He wanted very badly to learn things and know things."

MICHAEL FINNEGAN
An Impromptu Rodeo

The innumerable friends of Michael Finnegan found that one simple word best captured him: "mine." Everyone felt he belonged to them, because he made everyone feel special.

"Every one of his friends thought Mike was his," said Katherine Finnegan, his sister. "If he was talking to you, you were the only person in the world. A neighbor remarked that Mike never just beeped the horn and waved. He stopped the car and got out."

Finny, as his friends called him, was a 37-year-old currency trader at Cantor Fitzgerald, who could never let a friendship lapse. He kept up with people he had met when he was 5.

He constantly rooted for his friends. He was a scratch golfer. At a memorial service for him, a fellow golfer printed out a dozen or so recent e-mail exchanges between the two. The friend was preparing for a club championship, and Mr. Finnegan told him: "It's all in your mind. Don't play against yourself." And: "E-mail me your tee time. I'm going to be in the gallery. You're going to break 70."

If there was a chance for some impulsive fun, he took it. Once, after a golf tournament, he and some golf buddies jumped a fence encircling a horse farm, leapt on some horses and rode them merrily around the pasture.

TIMOTHY J. FINNERTY
Basketball and Hijinks

On Sept. 8, Timothy J. Finnerty's cousin was getting married. Some family was up from Atlanta. He was tired. It had been a long week. But he knew a cousin's daughter had never seen Manhattan. So at 8:30 P.M., he and his wife, Theresa Finnerty, did a tour of the entire city with her.

"He wanted her to be able to go back to her friends and say she saw it," Ms. Finnerty said. "We walked around the World Trade Center, and he even tried to get us into the office, at Cantor Fitzgerald on the 105th floor. But the office was locked."

A bond trader—and impromptu tour guide—Mr. Finnerty had one great obsession: "He lived and breathed basketball," Ms. Finnerty said. He was a guard at the University of Scranton in the late 1980s, and played in the N.C.A.A. championships, Division III. Mr. Finnerty, who was 33, loved to coach, too. At Wagner College in Staten Island, he was an assistant coach.

"When we moved to Glen Rock, N.J., he wanted to coach seventh and eighth graders," Ms. Finnerty said.

Last year, he got the chance. "St. Catherine's, my church, had a team. And those kids loved him," she said. "He was just silly and goofy. If a kid was quiet, within minutes he would have the kid laughing," Ms. Finnerty said. At the wedding of his cousin, on Sept. 8, he did goofy dances—the lawn mower dance and the sprinkler dance.

"I don't know where they came from," Ms. Finnerty said. "But I was laughing so hard I had tears coming down my face."

STEPHEN J. FIORELLI
Painting the Picture

For Robert Vitali, Stephen J. Fiorelli was the truest kind of childhood friend, the kind you stick with, commute with, talk to on the phone four times a week, and name as your baby's godfather. The two grew up four houses away from each other in Dongan Hills, in Staten Island.

"He was the best kind of best man," Mr. Vitali said.

Mr. Fiorelli, 43, was an engineer for the Port Authority, and loved buildings and bridges, said his brother Bill. He was well known in Aberdeen, N.J., for helping neighbors and friends with their home-improvement projects.

"He was really an artist in a lot of ways," said Mr. Vitali, who still has the cocktail napkin his friend used to sketch out the new second floor of the Vitali home. "He was able to paint the picture both in words and in drawings. I could watch him for hours, explaining something, sketching something out. It was amazing."

After Mr. Fiorelli's funeral, Mr. Vitali offered these words to people who asked him how he was holding up: "If you have any close friends, write a eulogy for them today, even if they're still alive. You'll look at them differently."

PAUL FIORI
The Gift of Gab

Paul Fiori was a talker. "He would talk your ear off, and he would talk to anybody," said his wife, Lynda Fiori. He talked so much to the guys working at the Mobil station where he got gas that he befriended them. After it was reported he was missing, his friends there, six of whom attended his memorial service, wrote his wife a letter, "telling me he would help them make coffee, give people directions and always talk about his two daughters."

Oratory skills were vital to the couple's courtship. After seeing Lynda speaking about football defenses in a speech class when she was a college sophomore, Mr. Fiori knew she was the one. Then he talked her into marrying him.

"He treated me like a princess," she said. "Never a day went by that he didn't tell me he loved me. He brought me flowers on no occasion and wrote me poems. He took me to Windows on the World just to express his love for me."

One year ago, Mr. Fiori, then 30, left his high school teaching position in Hawthorne, N.Y., for the equities desk of Cantor Fitzgerald so his young family could be more financially secure. On Sept. 11, their second child, Adriana, was only 3 months old. Their oldest, Debbi, 2, now kisses Daddy's picture every day.

JOHN FIORITO
Attention for "Little Johnny"

John Fiorito loved the sun and fishing and wide-open spaces. He also loved working as a broker at Cantor Fitzgerald. But he loved nothing more than being a husband and a father. At home, his wife, Karen, says, he was meticulous. Each night, he carefully pressed his clothes. Each morning, he used special clippers to groom his mustache.

At 40, he gave the same kind of attention to his 6-year-old son, "little Johnny," who three years ago was found to have leukemia.

He loved trains and boats because that is what little Johnny loved. And when his son needed special care, the family moved closer to a good hospital, where little Johnny would eventually receive a successful bone marrow transplant.

Mr. Fiorito—or "Johnny Fever" as some of his friends jokingly botched his name—also loved surprises. He proposed to his future wife in 1987, at a dinner atop the World Trade Center. A waiter brought her ring on a silver platter.

"John was fidgeting that night," she said. "After he gave the waiter the ring, I think he was worried he'd never come back with it."

And after 11 years of marriage, one of the biggest surprises was that he never forgot how to be tender.

"Till the end, he always held my hand," his wife said. "And he always complimented me on how beautiful he thought I looked. I don't know if every husband does that; but he did."

ANDREW FISHER
A Love of Laughter

Andrew Fisher was driving his family to Kennedy International Airport in August when he noticed that his newly wed sister, Maria, was still carrying her bouquet. He pulled over to the curb, opened the door, and made everyone get out. Then, as angry drivers honked, he gleefully snapped pictures of the bride tossing her bouquet.

"It was very funny," said Christina Fisher, the sister who caught the bouquet. "My brother was kind of a big kid. He always had a need for laughter and was very playful. That was the side of him that I miss most."

Mr. Fisher, 42, a sales manager for Imagine Software, was attending a seminar at Cantor Fitzgerald on the day the World Trade Center was attacked. A veteran traveler, he had lived in Amsterdam; Sydney, Australia; and Edmonton, Alberta, before settling into the East Side of Manhattan. He swam laps every morning and competed in races, but never talked about how he did. When his family unpacked his gym bag, they found a third-place medal buried under goggles and swimming trunks.

BENNETT L. FISHER
In Charge in a Purple Car

Many who escaped the Fiduciary Trust Company's offices in the south tower of the World Trade Center said afterward that they last saw Bennett L. Fisher on the 44th floor, pushing people into elevators and sending them to safety while he stayed behind.

Susan Fisher, his wife, said she was not surprised to hear it. "He was very caring and take-charge and he was probably obnoxious as hell up there," Ms. Fisher said.

Mr. Fisher, 58, was a senior vice president at Fiduciary Trust, managing his clients' assets and troubleshooting the firm's computer systems.

His son, Jamie, thought his character was reflected in the once-familiar sight of this successful businessman, a sailor and a skier, motoring about in his aged Volvo, painted an unorthodox purple, while following his favorite conservative commentators on the radio.

Ms. Fisher said the family and friends are struck by the possibility that the attack that took his life could influence the world.

"Not to make it tougher," she said, "but a little more understanding."

JOHN R. FISHER
Guiding Force from Below

It looked like the flight deck of the starship *Enterprise*. The operations control center in the World Trade Center basement was hooked up to every surveillance camera and intercom in the twin towers. Only 15 people were authorized to enter. John R. Fisher, a Port Authority security consultant, was one of them.

As debris from the first plane to hit the towers rained down, Mr. Fisher, 46, rushed to the bunker. He refused to leave so long as he could guide people out of the buildings. "John probably saved quite a few lives," said his friend and co-worker Ed Bonny.

Anyone who worked with Mr. Fisher knew he was obsessed with details and hated running into anything unexpected. But his personal life was different.

"If there was an ostrich, alligator or anything unusual on the menu, you just knew that's what John would order," said

Gail, his former wife. On a vacation to Costa Rica a few years ago, he swung through a rain forest canopy on a steel cable and climbed up the side of an active volcano.

His sister Catherine Chiola said the compass of his heart always pointed to his seven children in Beachwood, N.J. Two years ago he took all seven, then aged 4 to 14, to Disney World. He treated them royally, escorting them to every ride, hauling onto his shoulders any who were tired. He kept up that performance the whole week, losing none of them, nor the slightest bit of his patience.

THOMAS J. FISHER
A Planner and a Doer

Carving the turkey. Slipping out for a round of golf. Taking his wife and three children to a Britney Spears concert. Not to mention working, as a vice president for operations at Fiduciary Trust Company International. How did Thomas J. Fisher, 36, get it all done?

"The Bible says God created our world in seven days," Mr. Fisher's brother-in-law, Chris O'Donnell, said in his eulogy. "I think Tom could have done it in six and still gotten 18 in along the way."

The Fisher family had the most meticulously mowed lawn in their Union, N.J., neighborhood, and Mr. Fisher insisted on painting the house himself. Twice. "He was on double ladders, hanging off a slate roof. I was panicking," said Susan Fisher, his wife. "But he wouldn't hire people to do things like that."

Mr. Fisher was a planner. "Get it on the calendar!" he would cry when friends proposed a tentative get-together. And on the calendar it got. "He exhausted me," said Mrs. Fisher, 38.

Now she is the one raking the lawn and shopping for groceries. "He left me with a three-month supply of paper towels," she said. "And big shoes to fill."

LUCY FISHMAN
Antsy on First Day of School

Tuesday, Sept. 11, was the first day of school for Lucy Fishman's 3-year-old son, Jason. Her family sometimes theorizes that she stayed at her office in the trade center because she wanted to hear from her husband, Gene Springer, how it had gone: if Jason had cried, if he went willingly, that kind of thing. Whatever, when Mr. Springer called Ms. Fishman, 36, an executive secretary at Aon Research, in her 105th-floor office, he got only her voice-mail.

Family was what mattered to Ms. Fishman. That last summer she and her husband built a big pool in their backyard in Gerritsen Beach, Brooklyn, and that's where they and the kids—Jason and his sister Samantha, 11—hung out. Ms. Fishman's favorite movie? She liked action pictures, her younger sister Mary Dwyer said, but the movie did not really matter; she just liked curling up next to her husband. He agreed to talk to a reporter about her, but he began to weep and was unable to speak, so it fell to Ms. Dwyer.

"A week before this happened we went to the Bronx Zoo with the kids," Ms. Dwyer said. "I went with my two children. It started raining, everybody went running, we were just taking our shoes off, walking in puddles, and singing in the rain. That night, me and my sister went out dancing."

RYAN FITZGERALD
Man on the Town

It is not that Ryan Fitzgerald kept secrets from his family, but as the oldest of three children who had just found his own place in Manhattan, he was savoring some newfound independence. The clues were on his credit card bills.

When his mother opened his final bill, she caught a glimpse of his young, exuberant life. There were the excesses at Banana Republic, the golf games in Las Vegas, the gifts for his girlfriend, Darci Spinner, and textbooks for his M.B.A. work at Dowling College. Just as revealing were the repeated visits to the same cozy downtown restaurants.

"He obviously liked going back to places so when he walked in, they'd know who he was," said his mother, Diane Parks. Tall and blessed with gleaming blue eyes, Mr. Fitzgerald was a foreign currency trader at Fiduciary Trust.

He adored the Yankees and the Dave Matthews Band and enjoyed living slightly beyond his means. So in August, when he told his mother he was going to a friend's bachelor party in Las Vegas, she advised against it. Now she is glad he went.

"It made me feel good that he enjoyed the summer because it was the last summer of his life," she said.

THOMAS FITZPATRICK
He Made His Calls

Thomas Fitzpatrick briefly dated a woman named Marianne during his days at Boston College. Perhaps her name was Maryanne, or Mary Ann. It escapes the memory of his real Marianne, the one who lived around the corner when they were children in the Bronx, who was his steady girl in high school and to whom he wrote each day during their separation. She was the one he married in 1994, who kept their home in Tuckahoe, N.Y., and bore the two children he adored, Brendan and Caralyn.

"When we finally got married, everyone teased us about how long it took," said Mrs. Fitzpatrick.

The lengthy courtship was consistent with the 35-year-old Mr. Fitzpatrick's patient, methodical approach to his work as a bond salesman and financial adviser at Sandler O'Neill & Partners. Mr. Fitzpatrick made daily calls to clients from his office on the 104th floor of the south tower. After the first hijacked jetliner hit the north tower, he was making the calls again, assuring them he was in no danger.

"I never met a more thorough financial adviser," said Thomas Wirth, a longtime client.

RICHARD FITZSIMONS
Keeping Life Fresh

Richard Fitzsimons, of Lynbrook, N.Y., kept his Irish roots well watered. For him, a visit to Ireland was going home, said Colleen, his daughter. He last saw Dublin in the summer, when he ate, drank and danced for 13 hours to celebrate a niece's wedding.

At home, he kept busy. In his job as a fire safety inspector at the World Trade Center, he conducted drills and planned evacuations. He was, Ms. Fitzsimons said, almost certainly "saving people right from the start."

Mr. Fitzsimons golfed and coached a workingmen's ice hockey team. He belonged to the Ancient Order of Hibernians and had studied Gaelic with Patricia, his wife.

At 57, he was keeping his life interesting by starting fresh. He was toying with the idea of another career as a guidance counselor or as a travel agent. Two years ago, he began taking piano lessons. He and his wife would spend evenings at home, singing old tunes while he played along.

SAL FIUMEFREDDO
A Partner Found

Sal Fiumefreddo and Joan Chang had both been divorced for years and had just about given up on finding another partner. But the minute she saw him, her heart melted. "He had the most beautiful blue eyes and incredible head of black hair," she said.

Two weeks later, a friend got them together at a backyard barbecue. In six weeks they were flying to Las Vegas, where they were married in the Little White Chapel.

They would have celebrated their first wedding anniversary on Sept. 29. Instead, it became the day of Mr. Fiumefreddo's memorial service.

Mr. Fiumefreddo, 45, was a telephone technician who had been assigned to help out at Cantor Fitzgerald for one day. The day was Sept. 11.

The couple lived in Manalapan, N.J., with Mrs. Fiumefreddo's daughter, Rebecca, 7. His son, Anthony, 11, lived with his former wife. Mr. Fiumefreddo was a whiz in the kitchen, and made a great spaghetti sauce and pizza from scratch.

CHRISTINA DONOVAN FLANNERY
Everyone's Best Friend

Christina Donovan Flannery was not your stereotypical New Yorker; she was friendly, said Brian Flannery, her husband of three months. The couple commuted together every day from their home in Middle Village, Queens—he to a brokerage firm in Midtown, while she headed downtown to Sandler O'Neill & Partners, where she was a sales associate.

While her husband got familiar with the newspaper, Ms. Flannery made new friends. "She made everyone feel like she was their best friend," Mr. Flannery said.

Ms. Flannery, 26, grew up in Middle Village, and her dreams focused more on marriage than career. One hobby, said her best friend, Nicole Lagnese, was crashing weddings. "We used to drive around from church to church on Saturdays to see how other people had done it and get ideas for our own," Ms. Lagnese said.

Six years ago, Ms. Flannery met her future husband on the trading floor of HSBC Bank USA. He asked her to marry him one evening in July 2000 as the sun was setting at Jones Beach, the same spot they had gone on their first date.

On Sept. 11, they were waiting to sign the contract on a house on Cranberry Lane in Plainview, on Long Island. "There was lots of room," Mr. Flannery said. "A big yard for our dog, Tye. She even loved the name of the street."

EILEEN FLECHA
Business Before Voting

Eileen Flecha opted to be on time for work on Sept. 11, which is why she won the debate she had with her stepfather, who worked nearby on Wall Street, over whether they should vote in the mayoral primary that morning—his preference—or wait until after business hours. Ms. Flecha was a stickler for punctuality, and her job as a junior trader at Fiduciary Trust came first. So she got to the office early; they never made it to the polls.

Ms. Flecha, 33, lived in the Kew Gardens section of Queens with her mother and her stepfather, Robert Morris, and the family dog, Hannibal, a 102-pound bruiser.

"Now every time he sees a green car pass the house, he thinks it's her," Mr. Morris said. "He misses her terribly." A Yankees fan and a horror-movie aficionado who collected scary videos, she was engaged to a co-worker, Ivan Perez.

As a wedding present to themselves, they bought a home in Kew Gardens. As a surprise wedding present, Ms. Flecha's parents bought them enough furniture to feather the new nest. Now the house sits empty, the furniture remains in storage, and Mr. Perez is listed among the missing, too.

IVAN PEREZ's portrait appears on page 388.

ANDRE FLETCHER
Type A-Plus

Andre and Zackary Fletcher were the only African-American twins in the Fire Department. Both rushed to the World Trade Center; Andre Fletcher never returned.

"We both have Type A-plus personalities," said Zackary Fletcher, who works at Engine Company 4 in Manhattan. "Anything that reeks of excitement, adventure and danger. That was us." Andre Fletcher, 37, was a member of Rescue Company 5 in Staten Island.

The son of Jamaican immigrants, Andre Fletcher attended the Bronx High School of Science, but later transferred to Brooklyn Technical High School to be near his brother and to play on the sports teams, which Bronx Science did not have. In 1994, both brothers joined the Fire Department. When he learned that the department had no baseball team, Andre Fletcher organized one. On the department football team, both played the same positions: wide receiver and defensive back.

Today, Zackary Fletcher is watching out for Andre's son, Blair, 12. He also talks of dreams, now dashed, that the two brothers had of modeling in tandem for TV commercials. The two had located an agent and were planning a trip to California to sell themselves. Zackary Fletcher said his parents, Lunsford and Monica, were having a hard time, but it was especially difficult for him:

"I miss him more than anyone else."

CARL FLICKINGER
Golf, Gadgets and Gifts

Carl Flickinger considered his work hours at Cantor Fitzgerald to be one of the job's biggest benefits. Though he started at 7 A.M., he was home by 6:30 P.M. with his family in Congers in Rockland County.

Mr. Flickinger, 38, slid comfortably into domestic routines. Every Saturday, he shopped for groceries before taking his 11-year-old twin sons to the mall for new sneakers or jeans. In the evening, he checked his sons' homework and read to his 5-year-old daughter. On and off the job, he drove himself. He would not just play an easy 18 holes of golf—he took lessons and practiced on the driving range.

Mr. Flickinger was a gadget guy, said his wife, Kathy, and

he liked to buy the latest nifty devices as gifts for friends. Every morning before his commute, he bought coffee at the Dairy Mart and left it for his wife. And at 11 A.M., he always called home.

"Just to touch base," she said. "Just to tell me how his morning was going."

JOHN J. FLORIO
Iron and Metallica

If it was 6 A.M. and Metallica was blasting from the basement of Engine Company 214 in Bedford-Stuyvesant, it meant that John J. Florio was down there pumping iron.

Firefighter Florio, 33, was an athlete, built like a box of bricks, the kind of man who made starting halfback the first year he tried out for the Fire Department football team. He was the metalhead of his Brooklyn firehouse, an electric presence in a place that was already called the Nuthouse.

"He would have been in charge of the mosh pit if we had one," said Roddy Richards, a colleague and a friend.

Mr. Richards said one of Firefighter Florio's oldest buddies once stopped by the firehouse and joked that Firefighter Florio had been an A-student in the fourth grade—until the teacher moved the smart girl away from him. But John J. Florio cared about other things, like his wife, Shari, and his children, Michael and Kylie.

Then there was his beloved Metallica. The night that the men of Engine 214 found Mr. Florio's body, someone called to say turn on the radio. They did and they caught the opening riff of a Metallica song. Mr. Richards knew it was a message.

"We were all like, 'O.K., John.'"

JOSEPH WALKDEN FLOUNDERS
Creating a Sanctuary

Every weekday, Joseph Walkden Flounders arose at 3:30 A.M. at his home in the Pocono Mountains of Pennsylvania. He drove to Harrison, N.J., then took a train so he could be at his desk by 8:30 A.M. on the 84th floor of 2 World Trade Center, where he was a money-market broker at Euro Brokers.

"The house was his sanctuary," said his wife of 21 years, Patricia. They had slaved away, renovating it ever since they moved there three years before from Brooklyn Heights, after her health problems spurred him "to find a better quality of life for both of us," she said. "We'd been working on the house three years, and three days before he died, we finished it."

The memorial service for Mr. Flounders, 46, will be held

on Dec. 11, 2001, at Trinity Church in Manhattan, where he had worshiped, his wife said. "The reception will follow at Fraunces Tavern, because they, too, were once bombed, and we thought it would be appropriate to have it there, since they suffered, as well."

CAROL FLYZIK
A Patient Stepmother

"She sold, like, computer software to hospitals and medical companies or something," said Kristin Walsh, unsure exactly what her stepmother did.

That is how their relationship had once been, cordial but constrained. Ms. Walsh's mother, Nancy, brought Carol Flyzik home 13 years ago and introduced her as her girlfriend to Kristin and her two brothers. Ms. Flyzik, 40, was a passenger aboard American Airlines Flight 11. She was on her way to the West Coast on a business trip.

"It's hard when your parents bring a new person home," Ms. Walsh said. "The fact that she was a woman made it a little harder, but I guess I felt the same way when my dad married another woman."

The family of five lived in Plaistow, N.H., and Ms. Flyzik proved to be a patient woman. She listened to the children. She made the holidays warmer. Through the years their relationship changed from "Stay out of my life" to "I love you."

Last year was the first time that Ms. Walsh bought Ms. Flyzik a Christmas present of her own: two tickets to a Celtics game. "We had so much fun," she recalled. "It was quality time that we never had together before."

She considered the empty chair, where her stepmom used to sit and watch television. "I guess you don't know what you have until it's gone."

DAVID L. W. FODOR
Rescuer of Animals

The accountant was also a mountain man. David Lawrence William Fodor had moved from his native Staten Island to the hills of Putnam County, but the plan was to keep on heading north. He and his wife, Claudia Petrone, had started scouting possibilities in the Adirondacks last summer. For the time being they had their rocky two and a half acres in Garrison with the vegetable garden in front—tomatoes, corn, lettuces, scallions and the beginnings of an herb garden.

It all went to good use in the kitchen. Mr. Fodor's father was a restaurateur and his mother a caterer, and he was so avid a chef that he did the cooking at his own wedding, held at a friend's farm in the Catskills, using all locally grown produce and New York State wines.

His home being a long way from the city—he was a corporate tax accountant at Fiduciary Trust as well as a volunteer fire warden for his floor at 2 World Trade Center—made possible space for an ever-changing assortment of animals: three dogs and two cats at the moment. Most came from shelters, but some came from a rottweiler kennel in New Jersey where Mr. Fodor, 38, helped out to learn about breeding and showing. (One of his rottweilers won a national championship.)

"He was one of the most fully alive people I've ever met," his wife said. "He laughed fully, saw the humor and responded fully to life."

MICHAEL N. FODOR
His Best Was for the Family

Lt. Michael N. Fodor, his friends were convinced, had seen every *Jeopardy!* episode before it was on television. "He always knew the answers," said Deborah Fodor, his wife of 28 years. "He had a passion for learning" and a vast collection of antique history books, as well as original copies of the newspapers reporting the attack on Pearl Harbor and the assassination of John F. Kennedy.

Fifteen years ago, the family moved to Warwick, N.Y., because Lieutenant Fodor wanted his children—Michael, 23, Andrew, 22, and Ashley, 16—to grow up in a small town. Lieutenant Fodor, 53, of Tower Ladder Company 21 in Manhattan, was still all firefighter, and although the trip to Manhattan could take three hours, he was on the job on time when the call came from the World Trade Center.

Holidays were Lieutenant Fodor's favorite times of year, his wife said, and, like many firefighters, he loved to cook. After he was promoted to lieutenant 17 years ago, though, he saved the cooking and especially his pièce de résistance, prime rib and Yorkshire pudding, just for the family.

THOMAS FOLEY
Fame and Firefighting

Sometimes the spotlight lands on a New York City firefighter and just stays there. That's what happened to Thomas Foley, 32, a member of Rescue Company 3 in the Bronx.

Two summers earlier he helped rescue construction workers dangling from a broken scaffold 12 stories above the street. "Don't worry," he told one of them. "You'll be going home to your family tonight." He got plenty of TV time for that, which blossomed into bit parts in *Third Watch* and *The Sopranos.* Then he posed shirtless for *People* magazine's list of 100 most eligible bachelors last year.

"It was one of the most popular photos in that issue,"

said Carol Wallace, *People*'s managing editor. Firefighter Foley, who lived in Nyack, N.Y., started out shy, said Joanne Foley Gross, his sister. But as an adult, he pursued interests like bull riding and hunting and turned his German short-haired pointer, Maggie, into a field-trial champion. He was "always the life of the party," said Danny Foley, his brother and a firefighter with Engine Company 68.

When it came to firefighting, "he said it was the best job in the world and he would never give it up, ever," remembered a cousin, Christina Cimmino. "No matter how famous he got."

DAVE FONTANA
Man Among Men, and Boys

The memorial for Dave Fontana was scheduled for Oct. 17, which would have been his 38th birthday. He died at the World Trade Center on Sept. 11, on his eighth wedding anniversary.

Mr. Fontana was a firefighter with the elite Squad 1 unit, stationed in Park Slope, Brooklyn, where he lived with his wife, Marian, and 5-year-old son, Aidan. Neighbors were shocked by the news that 12 men from the small firehouse on Union Street had died, but they took his loss especially hard.

Dave Fontana was a man's man. He volunteered his time for the Boy Scouts. He read to children. He worked tirelessly to find the names of firefighters who had fallen in World War II so that dedication plaques could be hung in the firehouses where they had served.

A trained sculptor, Firefighter Fontana was known for the elaborate Halloween costumes he and his son wore in the annual neighborhood parade. "You know Dave Fontana?" Aidan asked the other day. "I love Dave Fontana."

DONALD FOREMAN
He Kept 15 Captains Happy

The picnic was intended for Port Authority police officers assigned to the PATH system. Technically, Officer Donald Foreman was assigned to the Holland Tunnel, but he was welcome anyway. Donald Foreman was always welcome.

He had spent 29 years with the Port Authority, working for many of those years as a captain's clerk, which meant he did a lot of the nuts-and-bolts administrative tasks for a superior. According to a plaque on a wall at the Holland Tunnel offices, he served 15 consecutive captains, according to his last, Robert Sbarra.

"If he could work for 15 captains without anyone trying to remove him, he must have done his job extremely well."

But Mr. Foreman, 53, had a full life outside, with a large extended family and volunteer duties that included running the youth sports program for his Roman Catholic parish, Immaculate Conception, on Staten Island. He was also a strict vegetarian, but that hardly kept him from that picnic, a hamburger-and-frankfurter feast on the Jersey shore.

"I do remember giving him french fries," recalled his companion, Cheryl Cooper-Foreman. "He loved french fries."

And Ms. Cooper-Foreman and Captain Sbarra both remember this: Donald Foreman playing basketball with kids young enough to be his grandchildren.

CHRISTOPHER HUGH FORSYTHE
It Took Three Alarm Clocks

Christopher Hugh Forsythe lived by the clock. Or rather, he lived by the three alarm clocks it took to wake him up each morning. Mr. Forsythe, a foreign-exchange money broker at Cantor Fitzgerald, was not much of an early riser, and his morning ritual of hitting the snooze bar on one clock after another tickled his wife so much that she often got up with him.

Even at 5 A.M., she said, they would joke around until it was time for her to say good-bye to him at the door. When he returned by 6 P.M., she would be waiting for him. Mr. Forsythe, 44, was a London native who settled in Basking Ridge, N.J., three years ago to work at Cantor Fitzgerald, after other jobs took him to Mexico and Madrid, where he met his wife, Tessie Molina. Though their initial conversations were awkward, they eventually grew to speak mostly Spanish at the home they shared with two children, Mrs. Molina's son Jose, 16, and Mr. Forsythe's daughter Kirsten, 15.

CLAUDIA MARTINEZ FOSTER
Proud to Be Big Sister

As the oldest in a family of girls, Claudia Martinez Foster promised her parents she would always look after her three younger sisters. One day, she told them, she was even going to give the Martinez family its big wish: a baby boy. Married almost a year, the 26-year-old assistant broker for Cantor Fitzgerald had already begun, with her husband, to pick out baby names. They were planning to buy a house and start a family later this year. She liked the name Carlos, in honor of her father. Her husband could not decide.

"My daughter was a true family person," said Blanca Martinez. "She was proud to be the big sister, always helping me with my youngest, taking her to the movies, bowling, shopping. She liked to call what she did 'sister power.'"

Watching such a young, promising life fade away has made the grieving even more trying. "She has so much to live for, and to go like this," Mrs. Martinez said. "I pray for God to give me strength to accept her death. But as a mother I don't know how to let go. I want to keep hoping for a miracle."

NOEL J. FOSTER
Blue Eyes and Red Cars

Everything was going so great for Noel J. Foster. He and his wife, Nancy, were extremely in love. They had just celebrated their 10th wedding anniversary with a two-week trip out West. Both the children were in school, with the youngest, Nicole, 5, having just started kindergarten on Sept. 6. The family had bought a house in Bridgewater, N.J., and Mr. Foster, 40, had fixed up every room but one. His wife just bought a new car.

It was as life should have been for a young couple in America. Mr. Foster was a vice president with Aon Corporation on the 99th floor of 2 World Trade Center.

"They were at a perfect time in their life," said Peggy Oblack, Mrs. Foster's sister. "Things were really good."

Mrs. Oblack admired her sister's husband. He had blue eyes. He loved music. He was full of fun. He loved red cars. He always had a project going.

"He was a wonderful family man," said Mrs. Foster. "He loved spending time with his wife and kids on the weekends. The beach, the boardwalks, the arcades."

ANA FOSTERIS
Commuting to Dress Up

Even though she was up at 4 A.M. every day to make the two-hour commute on the Long Island Rail Road from Coram to 2 World Trade Center, Ana Fosteris kept resisting the very idea of finding a job closer to home. She loved her life as an insurance broker at Aon on the 103rd floor, she loved shopping downtown, and "she liked dressing up and being around people who dressed up," said Michael Fosteris, her husband of 31 years. "She couldn't put up with the dress code on Long Island; it's so casual."

Theirs was a transcontinental love story: they met and married in Romania, and immigrated to New York shortly after. The weekend before Sept. 11, the two were listening to Verdi's "Macbeth" and Mrs. Fosteris, who was 58, happened to mention that the "Ah, la paterno mano" aria "would be the song she would like to have played for her at her funeral," her husband said. "It came out of nowhere."

Oct. 30, Mr. Fosteris was accompanied by friends as he drove back from the memorial service at ground zero. He said, "We played the aria in the car."

LUCILLE FRANCIS
"Never Liked to Sit Around"

As a seasoned housekeeper, Lucille Francis took immense pride in polishing the brass and vacuuming the much-trod carpets of Windows on the World on the 107th floor of 1 World Trade Center. She always insisted that her rooms be as perfect as the view. And although she was scheduled to come to work at 9 A.M. on Sept. 11, "she went in early as usual," said Joseph, the oldest of her four sons.

In fact, he thought, she should not have gone in at all: she had insisted on working the week before despite a bout of the flu, and the previous Thursday her boss had demanded she go home, telling her, "Don't come back until you're ready," Joseph Francis said.

But at age 62, Ms. Francis "liked to be out there working, she never liked to sit around at home," her son said. And so, on the morning of the terrorist attacks, Ms. Francis took the A train from Fulton Street as she always did, and arrived well before the first plane struck the building. Her son recalled how hard she had worked all her life, after coming to the United States in 1986 from Barbados. Her family, including Mr. Francis, his brothers Peter, Troy and Raymond, six grandchildren and two great-grandchildren, still cannot quite believe she is gone.

GARY J. FRANK
A Dolphin, a Starfish, a Shark

Though Gary J. Frank programmed computers for a living, he was not the nerdy type. He had a dolphin and a starfish tattooed on his left shoulder because he loved to hang out at the Jersey shore. And he knew his way around smoke-filled pool halls, taking down more than a few seasoned sharks over the past decade. In amateur tournaments from Baltimore to Las Vegas, Mr. Frank, 35, racked up trophies with his pool-stick-wielding teammates.

His sister, Laurie Vigeant, said that he concentrated so hard that he rarely talked when he was playing. "It's like watching the professionals," said Ms. Vigeant, who sometimes played alongside him. But even champion pool players take time out.

A divorced father, he devoted every other weekend to his 12-year-old daughter, Jessica. The weekend after Sept. 11 would have been theirs.

Nino's Restaurant, on Canal Street in lower Manhattan, serving as a relief center open all the time for those working on the recovery effort at the trade center. A volunteer staff there served about five thousand workers a day—a total of more than one hundred thousand free meals in the month after September 13. (*Nancy Siesel*)

MORTY FRANK
A Sense of Mischief

About the snake: Morty Frank smuggled it into the basement of the house in Lynbrook, on Long Island, and kept it there for three months without telling anyone, said his mother, Phyllis. "Until the day he said: 'Guess what, Mom? We have a snake in the basement.' "

She and her husband, Mel, would keep asking what kind it was, but all Morty would ever say was, "The kind you can make boots out of." He was sunny but always "a little mischievous," she added, and he did not much favor the name Morton.

"When I took him to the pediatrician for the first time, the doctor said, 'What a big name for a little boy,' " she recalled. "It was my father's name. But to everyone, he was Morty."

Morty Frank and his wife of one year, Jessica, had returned from a wedding in California on the day before the attack. When Phyllis Frank watched the images of the plane hitting 1 World Trade Center—where Mr. Frank worked at the institutional sales desk of Cantor Fitzgerald on the 104th floor—"I knew instantly by the way it hit, and where it hit, well . . ." She paused. "I knew that I was nowhere."

RICHARD K. FRASER
"Daddy Can Fly"

The focus of Richard K. Fraser's life was his 22-month-old son, Aidan, who suffers from neurofibromatosis, a disease that causes tumors to grow at the ends of nerves.

"Aidan was the joy of his life," said Mr. Fraser's wife, Suzanne. "He came home at 7 every day and played with Aidan. He would talk to him about the Giants, tickle him, everything."

Aidan called Saturday Daddy's Day, because on Saturdays Mr. Fraser, 32, took Aidan out to see the big city, where he worked as a manager at Aon. The father and son went to the Central Park Zoo, the museums, the playgrounds and the public library. "He was the kind of guy who wanted kids even when he was quite young," Mrs. Fraser said. The couple planned to have three more children, but they postponed conceiving the second one to the end of the year because of Aidan's illness.

"I told Aidan that Daddy was an angel," Mrs. Fraser said, "and he thinks it's really cool that Daddy can fly."

CLYDE FRAZIER Jr.
Making Their Dreams Real

For hundreds of young New Yorkers, Clyde Frazier Jr. was a friend with a basketball.

Mr. Frazier, 41, worked as a state tax investigator in the World Trade Center but was better known as the founder of the SlamJam Women's Basketball League. The league brought together top players from city public and Roman Catholic schools and sent countless girls off to college with basketball scholarships.

Mr. Frazier, who enjoyed films, plays and working out, also found time about 10 years ago to start the Friends of Frederick E. Samuel Foundation (named for a former city councilman). The nonprofit group in Harlem provides basketball and counseling to young people. Clyde Frazier Sr. said his son, who was married but childless, could talk to anybody about anything.

"He was passionate and committed to young people," said Shawn Dove, a friend and colleague. "For 10 years every Saturday and Sunday he traveled from Queens to open up the gym at 9 A.M. at the Countee Cullen Community Center in Harlem."

ANDREW A. FREDERICKS
The Tool of His Trade

Andrew A. Fredericks felt strongly about the best way to blast a stream of water at a fire. They called him Andy Nozzles.

In training videos, speeches around the country, trade magazine articles—even on the couch in his home—Firefighter Fredericks preached the gospel of the solid stream of water aimed hard at the source of the blaze.

"He was so proud that his 9-year-old son could tell apart the different nozzles," said Diane Feldman, the managing editor of *Fire Engineering*, a trade magazine.

It is not an academic debate. Firefighter Fredericks, 40, believed that fog nozzles, which disperse water widely, were

dangerous because the steam that they produced would burn firefighters who moved close to put out flames. Solid-bore—those were the kind that Andy Nozzles liked.

His wife, Michelle Fredericks, said that her husband relished the chance to pass on the knowledge he had gained fighting fires for 20 years, 16 of them with the New York City Fire Department, most recently with Squad 18. "It was his passion, next to me of course," Mrs. Fredericks said. "He had a passion for teaching."

TAMITHA FREEMAN
Good Times at the Dew Drop

Her mother's generation, 11 siblings in all, some in East New York, Brooklyn, and some in North Carolina, gather each Friday night in somebody's living room to rehash the ups and downs of the week. So 35-year-old Tamitha Freeman and her cousins replicated the ritual, tweaking it for their age group by meeting weekly at the Dew Drop Inn in Greenwich Village, convenient to their downtown jobs and their Brooklyn homes.

The Dew Drop Inn serves drinks in mason jars and has a down-home feel, which reminded the group, 10 cousins ranging in age from 23 to 40, of their ancestral home. They would drink and laugh, said one of Tamitha's aunts, Earnestine Keaton, catch up on jobs and marriages and "discuss things they wouldn't discuss with us."

Ms. Freeman, who had a new job at Aon in 2 World Trade Center, was the organizer, the one who would call the others to ask, "Are you coming?" She played the same role when the New York branch of the family headed south, making sure that everyone was on time and had a plane ticket.

Now, the North Carolina relatives are shuttling north, several carloads each weekend, to comfort Ms. Freeman's parents, sister, fiancé and 18-month-old son. The young ones would be helped, Mrs. Keaton said, by resuming their weekly ritual. "The thing I most want them to do is go back to the Dew Drop," she said. "To be together and talk is something they need."

PETER L. FREUND
The Amateur Astronomer

Peter L. Freund was a firefighter and a stargazer.

He built an observatory, a 10-by-10-foot wooden cube, in his backyard in Westtown, N.Y., and would look at the stars through a telescope mounted on a piece of sewer pipe. In the summer his wife, Robin, would often join him.

"But there were some winter nights when I'd sit inside with my woolens on," Mrs. Freund said, laughing. "I'd say, 'Take a picture of it, show me later.' "

When her husband wanted to see a major eclipse, she was worried, though: one of the trees in the yard was directly in front of the eclipse. "I thought I was going to lose a pine tree," she said. But Mr. Freund spared it.

Mr. Freund, 45, a lieutenant with Engine Company 55 in Little Italy, "always followed his own interests," said Arne Francis, a high school classmate. He recalled that Lieutenant Freund took up windsurfing in the early 1980s before it was popular. He would vanish for hours at a time, Mr. Francis said.

"I'd go, 'Pete, where the hell were you?' He'd say, 'I was out by Buoy 20.' And I'd say, 'Pete, there are ocean liners and tankers that go by there. Be careful,' " Mr. Francis said. "What he was into, he just put his whole soul into."

ARLENE FRIED
Always Ready with Advice

Arlene Fried, the vice president and assistant general counsel at Cantor Fitzgerald, was a hard-driving lawyer who handled multimillion-dollar initial public offerings during the dot-com era. At Cantor, she played an essential role in the creation and public financing of eSpeed. Young Wall Street hopefuls constantly sought her out for advice, and she was always willing to give it.

But there was another Arlene Fried. She enjoyed juicy gossip and shopping until she dropped—a cliché, perhaps, but her friend Nina Gaspar said it really was like that.

Mrs. Fried, 49, of Roslyn Heights, N.Y., was also a dedicated wife and mother to her three daughters. "It was not unusual for Arlene to come rushing into a parent school conference or a school play, a few minutes late, out of breath and apologetic—but she was always there," said Ms. Gaspar's husband, Andrew.

On Sept. 11, Mrs. Fried was trying to help a young lawyer who wanted to know where he should apply for a job, said her husband, Kenny. She returned the lawyer's telephone message at 8:44 A.M. He was not there, so she left a message. Four minutes later, the first plane struck.

ALAN W. FRIEDLANDER
Bikes, Photos and Family

Alan W. Friedlander was a family man with a handful of passions: bicycling, planning vacations and photography. He bought his wife, Helen, a bicycle, and the second weekend in September they headed from their home in Yorktown Heights, up the Westchester County Trail to Baldwin Place. When their daughter, Laura, was living abroad, they visited her, and he enjoyed studying books and maps whenever the family traveled.

The couple met at the Gristede's on Second Avenue at 68th Street, where he stocked shelves and she worked the checkout. They were married for 28 years, with a son, Steven, 26, and Laura, 22. Mr. Friedlander, 52, a senior vice president at Aon Corporation, had recently enjoyed taking pictures of the figure-skating competitions his wife liked to attend.

"He really did everything well, and he was a patient guy," she said, "so he took a gazillion shots." His four best pictures are displayed in a spare bedroom.

Mrs. Friedlander wanted to add one last thing: "My favorite time of day was 10 till 7 at night, because that's when he came home.'"

ANDREW FRIEDMAN
A Life of Friends

When Andrew Friedman's wife was planning his memorial service in Woodbury, on Long Island, she called the local police to ask for help directing the traffic because she had a feeling a lot of people would attend.

The police thought Lisa Friedman was overreacting. But as it turned out, more than 2,000 people showed up to remember Mr. Friedman, 44, vice president for institutional equities trading at Carr Futures. His life had been filled with friends he had known from the age of 6, college friends, work friends and neighborhood friends.

"He was the glue that held everybody together," said Ms. Friedman, who met her husband at a bar in TriBeCa when she was in college. (The two easily spotted each other, as he was 6-foot-4 and she 6-foot-1, although they always disagreed over which one of them had approached the other.)

What struck many people about Mr. Friedman, who coached several boys' sports teams on Long Island, was how much he loved children, especially his 11-year-old twin boys, Michael and Daniel. He was also known for his laid-back ways and his "Andrewisms," sayings that only he could devise.

One was his definition of a balanced meal: "An Italian hero cut in half."

PAUL FRIEDMAN
A Problem Solver

Paul Friedman, a shy, kind man with a surging mind, was always a problem solver. Of the five Friedman siblings, he was the listener, the untangler of life's knots. He would pose a zillion questions, leading his siblings toward their own solutions. Professionally, he played a similar role. With degrees in psychology, engineering and business, he became a management consultant for Emergence Consulting in Lincoln, Mass.

You could not not like him, the man who at snoozy business meetings kept his end of the table in convulsive snickers. The friend who schlepped rugelach cross-country for a pal, the human jungle gym for nieces and nephews, the husband who showered his wife, Audrey Ades, with gifts. He collected snow globes (only the tackiest!), saved his report cards (including those from Hebrew school) and gazed at the natural world, entranced, camera in hand.

At 45, he tackled his most delightful problem. In May, he and his wife adopted a Korean infant, Richard Harry Hyun-Soo Friedman (nom de nursery: Rocky).

Mr. Friedman delivered rib-tickling disquisitions on the challenge of the dirty diaper. He spent Sept. 10 with Rocky. "Did you take him to a playground?" a sister asked. "No," replied the cerebral new papa. "I took him to Starbucks."

The next morning, Mr. Friedman boarded American Airlines Flight 11.

GREGG FROEHNER
Modest Man of Action

Since he was a boy, Gregg Froehner yearned for a job where he could serve others. When he was a teenager, he became an Eagle Scout and a volunteer firefighter. After college, he became a police officer with the Port Authority of New York and New Jersey.

Mr. Froehner, 46, was assigned to the PATH system in Jersey City, and was a unit leader for the Emergency Services Unit. Yet he never bragged about the rescues he was involved in.

Many people who knew him in Chester, N.J., where he lived with his wife, Mary, and four children, did not even know what he did for a living. His wife usually only found out about his daring episodes when she overheard his nightly conversations with his boss, whom they sometimes referred to as his "other wife."

Mrs. Froehner used to work as a nurse in a nursing home, and one of her patients was Mr. Froehner's grandfather. One day, he told her, "You look like somebody my grandson should meet."

This information was passed on to Mr. Froehner's father, who urged Mr. Froehner to go visit his grandfather soon at the nursing home. Mary and Mr. Froehner clicked immediately.

When he was home, Mr. Froehner was a total family man, his wife said. "He loved his children more than anything in the world," she said in her eulogy. "This could be seen in the way he always called Katie his little smiley face, by coaching Matt's team in Little League, by laughing to himself all the way across the room at one of Heather's jokes and by teasing Meghan that she couldn't date until she was 25."

LISA FROST
In Memory of Lisa

On September 11, 2001, Rancho Santa Margarita resident Lisa Frost was a passenger on the ill-fated United Airlines Flight 175.

When Boston University went to California to recruit Lisa Frost she fell in love with the school. By the time Miss Frost was in her junior year at B.U. she was traveling the West Coast talking about the university and doing the recruiting herself. She graduated in May 2001 with two degrees, summa cum laude, one in communications and one in hospitality administration, which everyone who knew her embracing character thought was absolutely fitting.

She was awarded the Boston University Scarlet Key for extraordinary achievement in student activities and organizations.

"Everybody that comes in contact with her is just so inspired and so motivated," said her father, Tom Frost. On the B.U. Web site there are more than 80 messages sent in by people who knew Miss Frost and many who didn't but were touched by the story of how she died while taking a flight to begin her career at home in California.

Mrs. Frost's family and friends will miss her sweet smile. Peggy Burnett of Cerritos, Calif., never met Miss Frost but she knitted her family a red, white and blue afghan. "My heart just went out to them," Ms. Burnett said.

Mr. Frost recently planted a 13-foot scrub oak near his home in Rancho Santa Margarita in honor of his 22-year-old daughter. He placed a granite plaque there with an inscription he wrote detailing her life, her death and all the lives she touched.

This tree is planted in her memory and is dedicated to parents who have children that are with God in heaven.

PETER C. FRY
A Big-Handed Fisherman

Big hands were an asset to Peter C. Fry, even when he was using them to tie flies onto hooks to use as bait when fly-fishing. It was an activity on a rainy day, when fishing might be out of the question, for him and his 6-year-old daughter, Taylor. She had a natural advantage with her smaller fingers, but Mr. Fry's hands taught hers, said his wife, Meredith. Mr. Fry's friends say they will take Taylor fishing now.

Mr. Fry, who worked at Euro Brokers, was a great cook, his wife says. "Actually, he was a chef," she said, correcting herself with a laugh. He could use whatever was in the refrigerator to whip together a feast for Mrs. Fry, Taylor and 3-old Caley. The two met at the River Cat Grill in Norwalk, Conn. Mrs. Fry was trying to set a friend up with Mr. Fry but he was more interested in her, and six months later, they were engaged.

"He saw me instead," Mrs. Fry said simply.

CLEMENT FUMANDO
Mr. Wonderful

Clement Fumando met his future wife in the school yard when they were 13. They were married almost 39 years; his memorial service was on their anniversary, Sept. 30.

"We lived a very simple life, shopping and staying near home; that was it," Katherine Fumando said. "It was not going to sell a book, you know what I'm saying? But it was our life and we were so happy with it. It was perfect for us, because we both enjoyed each other so much. We had a very, very unique marriage. Like anybody could say you had a good marriage. We had a great one. Everything was great about it. He was just a wonderful person, thoughtful, and he never ever had a hard word for me. He was just a good man."

Mr. Fumando, 59, was an operations officer at Cantor Fitzgerald. He liked to bowl with his son, Stephen, 30, go to car shows and the Englishtown Raceway with his other son, Gregory, 36, and shop with his granddaughter, Brittany, 8. "She could call him up at the drop of a button," Mrs. Fumando said.

"She loved junk stores, that's what he did with her, 99 cents stores."

"Whatever needed to be done," she said, "he did it."

STEVEN FURMAN
Mr. Generosity

Math and mitzvahs—those words ran through his family's memories of Steven Furman, a broker at Cantor Fitzgerald who died two days shy of his 41st birthday.

Mr. Furman's math score on his SAT was 790 out of 800, according to his brothers, Michael and Andrew. "He always wondered where the other 10 points went," Andrew said. "He knew he'd gotten them all right." After 13 years as a trader on the New York Mercantile Exchange, Mr. Furman joined Cantor last April.

An observant Orthodox Jew, Mr. Furman and his wife, Chavi, lived in Wesley Hills, N.Y., with their four young children: Nisan, Sarah Rachel, Naomi and Menashe. "He didn't have a fancy house or a fancy car," said his sister Jayne Furman. "The more money he made, the more money he gave away."

He paid one young man's school expenses, bought another a new suit, drove neighbors on errands. He did not fit easily into the macho, big-money world of Wall Street, said his father, Marvin Furman.

"His family, his religion, the people in his community—that was his life."

PAUL FURMATO
Monologue of Heartbreak

"He adored me, and I adored him," said Cindy Furmato. "We love him, we want him back."

Cindy and Paul Furmato met 17 years ago when both were undergraduates at Florida Institute of Technology. They were taking a trigonometry class, and despite earning high marks, "I pretended that I didn't know what was going on and asked for his help," she said. "We had our first date in a Chinese restaurant, and we were in love from then on. It was just him and me.

"He was my other half, and now I have to go on without him," Mrs. Furmato said, tears in her eyes. "It's the hardest for the children. Their father had always been there for them. Paul just turned 11 last week, but Daddy wasn't there. Stephanie is 9. She always went fishing with Daddy. She says now every time she fishes, it is for and with him. Theresa is 6. She is very very bright, just like her Daddy. Every morning, I don't want to get out of bed, but I have to, because the children need me.

"He got me this house, and it was our castle. But we only had seven weeks. Now I won't be able to make love with him anymore."

Mr. Furmato, 37, was a vice president at Cantor Fitzgerald.

KARLETON FYFE
"Really Living It"

Karleton Fyfe's mother had to be bedridden for the six months before he was born; he seemed to be in a hurry to get into the world.

There was so much to be excited about. Take the birth of his own son. He and his wife made it a group project. They sent family and close friends a video titled "It's a . . ." showing them going for the sonogram, and at the end opening an envelope in which the doctor had written "boy." When Jackson turned 1, they asked the same group to write something and seal it for him to open when he turned 18.

Then, because Mr. Fyfe heard that the terrible 2s were caused by frustration at not being able to communicate, he taught his son sign language. "He was really living it," said Tristin Laughter, a longtime friend of the couple.

Mr. Fyfe, 31, really lived everything, applying the same boyishness and determination whether he was mastering Steve Martin routines or the curveball as a kid, or tackling projects as a senior analyst at John Hancock—the job for which he was traveling on American Airlines Flight 11.

G

FREDRIC NEAL GABLER

A Yearning for Community

Fredric Neal Gabler's idea of heaven was to live surrounded by his friends, on the same block or perhaps in some suburban compound. Friends sometimes thought he was joking when he talked about this dream of "communal living," but he meant every word, his family says.

It would have had to be a sizable place. More than 1,500 people, including his sister Jolie and his parents, Howard and Leslie Gabler, attended his memorial service on Sept. 23 at Temple Beth Torah in Upper Nyack, N.Y.

"He was happiest when he was surrounded by the ones he loved," his wife, Mindy, told the crowd. This dream compound would also have been neat and comfortable. (Mr. Gabler and a college roommate once traded blows over the roommate's refusal to meet his housekeeping standards.)

Mourners entering St. Patrick's Cathedral on October 19 for a memorial service for World Trade Center workers lost in the attack on September 11. The service was organized by Local 32B-32J of the Service Employees International Union. (*Nicole Bengiveno*)

And it would have been filled with the sounds of sports—part of the glue that held his friendships together.

Fred Gabler, 30, an equity trader at Cantor Fitzgerald, met Mindy when they were both 16. His sports-hardened good looks and his father's Camaro were the first attractions, she told his friends, but his loving nature, honesty and sense of humor kept her at his side. They lived in Manhattan and were expecting their first child, a daughter, in November.

At his memorial service, his father—who escaped on Sept. 11 from his own office in the World Trade Center—told mourners that the only thing missing from his son's life "was length." Taking in the overflow crowd, he said, "You are his eulogy."

RICHARD GABRIELLE
Taking Baby for a Drive

He called it his Baby P, a 1999 black Volks-wagen Passat. It was kept in a garage in West Haven, Conn., and brought out only when the weather was fine—or when it was time for Richard Gabrielle's racing lessons.

Mr. Gabrielle's wife, Monica, who was not allowed to drive the Passat, said she had little doubt that her husband's fairly recent passion for driving a souped-up little car around a racetrack at Lime Rock Park in Lakeville, Conn., was the result of a midlife crisis.

Mr. Gabrielle, a 50-year-old insurance broker at the Aon Corporation, was an extraordinarily gentle man in most ways. Even moths, when they got in the house, would be carefully ushered out, uninjured. But he would also never tell his wife how fast he went during his driving lessons, and he recently bought a radar detector, so that he could, as he put it, "practice" on the highways.

"He'd tell me, 'Better that than women, don't you think?'" she said.

ERVIN GAILLIARD
All-Army Basketball Team

Ervin Gailliard never realized one of his biggest dreams because he was orphaned as a teenager. Having grown up in the South Bronx, he hoped to go to college like his older brother and sister, but it was not to be.

"He was very intelligent, and he always wanted to go to college, but the financial situation was never right," said his brother, Ronald. "By the time he was college age, our parents were dead, and he would have had to pay for it on his own."

But Mr. Gailliard, 42, would not allow himself to be kept down. He joined the Army, served in Germany and made the all-Army basketball team, his brother said. After his brother taught Mr. Gailliard chess, he soon was not only trouncing him, but was beating computers.

When he took a job as a security guard at the World Trade Center, he grew unhappy with the low wages and the way he was bossed around, so he helped bring in a union, and soon conditions were much better. He loved to listen to soft jazz with his wife, Cynthia, and he spent hours and hours teaching basketball and handball to his stepchildren.

"What impressed me most was how he always abided by the family rules—you never fight, you never argue with each other," said his brother. "He was a very strong person. No matter how tough things got, he was always able to bounce back."

DEANNA L. GALANTE
A Knack for Hair

Deanna L. Galante had such a knack for styling hair that she attended beauty school after high school in Sheepshead Bay, and when she ran out of heads to practice on among family members, she used her own.

It was her second career, and she kept up with the trends. Braids, beads, perms and shavings, she did them all.

On Wall Street, Ms. Galante, 32, worked for eSpeed as a personal assistant. At home on Staten Island, where she lived with her husband, Anthony, she did puzzles to unwind and was busy redecorating in anticipation of their first child; she was six weeks away from going on maternity leave. "She was already like a second mom to my 12-year-old," said her sister, Tina. "They were always doing their hair and nails."

ANTHONY GALLAGHER
Student of Teenage Culture

He called it his 4 o'clock conference call. It happened every Friday afternoon. That was when Anthony Gallagher placed the call to the Adamses—Katie, Liz and Jay. Sometimes Peter Adams might participate, but he was only 7. Mr. Gallagher would start off, "What's up?" and they'd go from there.

Mr. Gallagher, 41, an energy broker at Cantor Fitzgerald, handled a lot of important phone calls during his workdays, but none meant more to him than his weekly conference call to his nieces and nephews, the 15-year-old twins, Katie and Liz, and 13-year-old Jay.

Mr. Gallagher had only recently married, at the age of 40, and during his bachelor days he had cultivated a tight and unending relationship with the children of Suzanne Adams, one of his sisters.

"He just loved them," said his other sister, Carolyn Gallagher. "When he was planning to get married, he even asked them if it was O.K. They gave him the thumbs up."

To stay in the loop, he knew he needed to be wired into teenage interests, so Mr. Gallagher faithfully watched MTV.

"He would talk to them about Eminem and all that," Carolyn said.

And he did what they did. At a family barbecue at the Adams household over the Labor Day weekend, there was a contest to see who could make the biggest splash off the diving board of the pool. Mr. Gallagher was up there doing massive cannonballs.

JOHN PATRICK GALLAGHER
Making Sense of Life

The Friday before the World Trade Center attack, John Patrick Gallagher, an electricity trader at Cantor Fitzgerald, played hooky from work so he could treat his wife, Francine, and 2-month-old son, James Jordan, to a day at the Bronx Zoo.

"He was so proud of his big boy," recalled Mrs. Gallagher. Later that evening, at dinner with his brother and friends, he told them about the jaunt. "Isn't that what dads are supposed to do with their families on a beautiful September day?" he asked.

Mr. Gallagher, 31, stood 6 feet 3 inches tall and weighed around 270 pounds, but he had an extraordinary grace about him, his wife said. He never took anything for granted, perhaps because he lost his mother when he was 1 and his father six years later. He was born in the Bronx but he and his wife loved to travel. In 1999, Mr. Gallagher asked his future wife to marry him on a trip to Ireland.

"He made my life make sense," Mrs. Gallagher said. "It's hard to make sense of things now that he's gone."

CONO GALLO
Ocho Rios Memories

A grand time is the only way to describe Cono Gallo's Jamaican vacation with his wife the week before the World Trade Center attack. There the two were, holding hands while climbing Dunn's River Falls in Ocho Rios. A reggae dancing contest? Mr. Gallo went at it solo, and was the runner-up.

The Gallos, both 30-year-olds from Maspeth, Queens, clinched a *Newlywed Game*–like couples contest at their vacation resort by giving the same correct answer to every question. (The two had been married for five years.)

What's your wife's bra size? Mr. Gallo, the contestant, was asked. "Usually a 38C," he answered, "but sometimes a 36D depending on the style of the bra."

"It was exactly right," said his wife, Vicki Nita-Gallo, a kindergarten teacher. "He had the audience hysterical. They thought it was so cute. He really paid attention to details. That's what is so fabulous about him."

Mr. Gallo, a commodities broker with Carr Futures at 1

World Trade Center, was caring and selfless, his wife said, and he believed in a true partnership. There he was, "always by my side" when she was sick, she said. And there he was again, helping out with her Avon side business.

On the eve of Sept. 11, Mrs. Nita-Gallo left a bag full of Avon hand lotion, lip gloss and other products by the door for him to take to her customers at his office. The next morning, Mr. Gallo, who started work at 7:30 A.M. and left the house while she was still in bed, picked it up on his way out, happy to distribute the orders and collect payment.

"Everything was teamwork so we could go out and enjoy ourselves," Mrs. Nita-Gallo said. "We completed each other."

VINCENT GALLUCCI
He Banished Formality

Vincent Gallucci was not one to be bound by the formality of the upper echelon of a big financial firm, his wife, Barbara, said. "A friend said that even though he was a senior vice president in a very corporate environment"—the information technology department of Marsh & McLennan—"he would pass by the desks of colleagues, people above and below him, and he would pinch them on the side or give them a big hug."

Mr. Gallucci's easygoing style apparently served him well. After his death, his wife was informed that he was to have been promoted to managing director in November. "That was something he was really looking forward to," she said. "You don't go much higher than that."

Mr. Gallucci, 36, never lost sight of what motivated him—his wife and son and daughter and their house in Monroe Township, N.J. "He was working so hard because he wanted to achieve, but really he wanted to be with the kids," Mrs. Gallucci said. "His weekends were not spent golfing with friends."

Mrs. Gallucci did not feel much like celebrating Christmas 2001, but the kids insisted on it: Daddy's Last Christmas, the 7-year-old, Joseph, called it. Now that the holidays are over, the Galluccis have plans for their Christmas tree.

"We're going to plant it in the backyard for Dad," Mrs. Gallucci said.

THOMAS GALVIN
After Hours, Soaring Drives

When it came to soaring drives, pinpoint irons, mental toughness, Thomas Galvin had the whole package. He played a mean game of golf. Fortunately for his opponents, he worked a lot, and that limited the number of tournaments he entered. A member of Winged Foot in Mamaroneck, N.Y., Mr. Galvin

At what had been a boutique on Prince Street in lower
Manhattan's SoHo district, visitors view images of the
World Trade Center. The store was converted into a
gallery selling photos of the trade center at twenty-five
dollars each, to raise money for victims of the
September 11 attack. (*Nancy Siesel*)

managed to maintain a scratch handicap even while putting
in long hours at the office. Most players would drool over
that handicap.

But as a senior vice president and corporate bond broker
at Cantor Fitzgerald, Mr. Galvin never found enough time
to play extensive competitive golf. His hope was that his
schedule would lighten up enough that next summer he
could compete in more area tournaments.

Mr. Galvin, 32, who was single and lived in Manhattan,
took up the game when he was 10, and immediately demonstrated an unusual gift. He was captain of his high school
team in Greenwich, Conn., and was named to all-state and
all-county squads. He was also captain of the varsity team at
Georgetown University.

"He always had a wonderful swing," said his mother,
Diverra Galvin. "He didn't take a lot of lessons. He just
seemed to know how to play."

On Sept. 23, Mr. Galvin was supposed to leave for Ireland, to be the co-captain of a team from Winged Foot in the

first Emerald Cup match between players from American
and Irish clubs. It would have been his first trip to Ireland, a
favorite destination, in years.

GIOVANNA GAMBALE
Finding Peace with Peace

Giovanna Gambale and her sister Antonia
both worked in 1 World Trade Center.
Antonia, who is 25 and worked on the fifth
floor, was able to get out right away. She
called her father, Anthony, in Carroll Gardens, Brooklyn, and told him she was O.K.
He told her to come home. Then he said, "What about your
sister?"

Giovanna Gambale, 27, was a vice president at Cantor
Fitzgerald, on the 105th floor. She loved the Mets, and was so
organized that even as a child she told the teachers what to do.

"Yesterday I would not have talked to you," Mr. Gambale told a reporter that week, "but we have had a lot of discussion. We are extremely sad, but we are resigned that my daughter is in heaven. We haven't heard from her in four days. I spoke to a psychiatrist at Cantor Fitzgerald yesterday and he more or less told us nobody survived.

"I loved my daughter, but I'm at peace with God. We've had three prayer services in front of my house: 300 people Wednesday, then 200, tonight about 150. There was a young man in the group whose father is a fireman, missing, caught in the rubble. And we talk about there is no greater love than to lay down your life for your friend and that is what the firemen did. I told people that never in my life did I ever imagine we would be saying prayers as a group on the street, in front of my home, and this is what God wants us to do. If we are going to destroy hatred and bigotry, what we have to do is begin being peaceful."

GIANN GAMBOA
Found Meaning at Church

Just about everything Giann Gamboa needed in his life he found at Iglesia Nueva Vida, his church in Corona, Queens. There he found his girlfriend, hundreds of pals, a weekend soccer team and a spiritual life. As often as he could, he tried to bridge his professional life, as a manager of the Top of the World Cafe, with his religious life, sometimes offering a word of prayer to a troubled colleague or an invitation to join the church's daily 6 A.M. prayer service.

Friends at church still talk about how Mr. Gamboa, 26, arranged for 70 children from the church to visit and pray atop the World Trade Center a few months ago. "He loved being a Christian and sharing his faith with people," said Fernando Montoya, his best friend.

The last time anyone saw Mr. Gamboa, he was on the 78th floor about to squeeze into a crowded elevator as the building was being evacuated. But he offered his spot instead to a young woman on his staff who was crying and anxious to flee. "I'll just take the next one," he told a friend, as the elevator doors shut.

PETER J. GANCI
A Leader with Modesty

The thing about Peter J. Ganci was, he didn't flaunt it. He was just a regular guy living with his family on Long Island, so at peace with himself that if you asked him what he did for a living, he would just say: "I'm a fireman in the city."

"He would never say that he was the highest-ranking uniformed officer in the department," said Fire Marshal Steven Mosiello, his longtime friend and executive assistant.

Most of the time, Pete Ganci, who was 54, was that regular guy down the street who happened to be a decorated hero and boss: the guy who loved to laugh, golf, go clamming in Great South Bay. On Deputy Fire Commissioner Lynn Tierney's desk is a photograph of him in formal uniform—five stars on his collar and all—and a pink headband that says "Happy Birthday." The photograph's meaning is simple, she said: "He was man enough to wear a pink headband that said 'Happy Birthday.' "

Then there were those times when Pete Ganci was Chief Ganci, as on that last morning. In the eerie calm between the collapse of the two World Trade Center towers, Deputy Fire Commissioner Michael Regan recalled, "Pete Ganci directed every civilian and every firefighter to go north. He went south."

CHARLES GARBARINI
The Family's Core

When you are smack in the middle of a family of nine children, you could, understandably, have a rough time getting attention.

Or, you could not.

Charles Garbarini's siblings would clear the coffee table so he could leap up and entertain them. He even had his sister Janet fooled into thinking that if she washed the family's dinner dishes while he just sat and talked to her, she had it good. "Nobody gets out of more work than I do!" Charley Garbarini, 44, would shout, even as a Fire Department lieutenant.

By her own admission, Andrea DeGeorge, whom Mr. Garbarini married after a decadelong engagement, was the source of his best material. Parodying her New Age–like interests, he wrote a monologue about a woman much like her who tells her husband that their new house in Westchester requires "a $10,000 deck so I can meditate and keep in touch with my lack of needs."

A softie at heart for all his wisecracking, Lieutenant Garbarini would march Dylan, now 5, and Philip, 3, into their Pleasantville, N.Y., home bearing flowers from the A&P for their mother.

He was a proud if sardonic professional. His business card read: "Firefighter Charley Garbarini. You light 'em, we fight 'em."

DAVID GARCIA
An Unexpected Present

David Garcia was a man who could make things work, albeit in the most unusual ways. Once, he patched up a pair of rundown work boots by gluing pieces of tire to the soles. And when the floor on his future wife's Chevy Malibu rusted out, he retrieved his tin sandbox and welded it to the bottom.

But Mr. Garcia could not fix his eyesight, which began

deteriorating when he was 10 years old and had, by the age of 40, left him with 20 percent of his vision. So he found ways to compensate for the independence he lost along with his view of the world, said Deborah A. Garcia, his wife.

A computer programmer, Mr. Garcia began working on a contract basis, most recently for Marsh & McLennan. He had enough vision left that he could still go boating, his family said. Mr. Garcia's older son, Davin, 8, had his own boat: a remote control toy that broke last summer. After Sept. 11, Mrs. Garcia discovered it in the basement.

"It was all put back together," she said. "He fixed it the night before this happened."

MARLYN DEL CARMEN GARCIA
Every Inch Full of Authority

When Marlyn del Carmen Garcia was 14 years old, a guy in the neighborhood offered her a marijuana cigarette. She was probably no taller than 5-foot-2. He towered over her. But Marlyn Garcia was not one to be cowed.

"She smacked the guy," her elder sister Ingrid recalled. "She was like, 'This is how you say no to drugs.'"

Ms. Garcia, 21, was regarded as the most brainy, responsible and big-mouthed of the three Garcia girls. She graduated three years ago as the valedictorian of her class at the Bay Ridge Christian Academy and was offered a scholarship to Syracuse University—but she turned it down to be close to the family. She enrolled instead at John Jay College. Every morning, she arrived at work at the 101st-floor offices of Marsh & McLennan a half hour early, so she could leave in time for school.

"I'm 33," Ingrid said, "and if she said, 'Sit,' I would sit."

Ms. Garcia aspired to travel, to be an advocate for those who could not speak for themselves, to work for the United Nations someday.

"She was a little girl who was very powerful, very determined," Ingrid said. "We used to call her an old woman trapped in a little girl's body."

CHRISTOPHER S. GARDNER
The Captain of the Ship

Christopher S. Gardner had a lifelong passion for the sea and was a born skipper.

"He was always the captain of the ship," his brother Jonathan said, "whether that was at work, around the house, or on the boat. He had an incredible amount of energy."

Mr. Gardner, 36, rose at dawn each day and drove to the World Trade Center, where he was an executive at Aon, with a large staff reporting to him on the company's global risk services. He was a combination of boss and friend—a cap-

tain beloved by his crew, even when he had to lay someone off, which he found agonizing.

When he got home, he and his wife, Susan, put their children, Christopher Trowbridge, almost 4, and Alexander, 2½, to bed, which he found delightful. "He never brought work home," Mrs. Gardner said.

"He never played golf a single weekend in his life. We really tried to maximize our time with the children."

In the summer of 2001, the family spent a lot of time in Maine, where Mr. Gardner took the boys sailing and began their seafaring education. They were too young to absorb much information, but they loved steering the ship with their dad.

"First Christopher drove the boat," said Jonathan Gardner. "Then Alexander got so excited, he just had to drive it. And meanwhile the boat is going all over the place, all over this crowded harbor."

But the captain was happy and in control. "He was never worried," Mr. Gardner said.

DOUGLAS B. GARDNER
Cards Full of Mad Love

When Joseph Gardner took his young son, Douglas B. Gardner, to watch his first Knicks game, Douglas said he wanted to play basketball in Madison Square Garden. His father told him he would have to own the team to do that.

So Douglas Gardner, who grew up to be a good athlete, playing basketball on outdoor courts across the city, became a businessman. He worked for Lehman Brothers, his father's real estate business and, finally, joined a college classmate at Cantor Fitzgerald, where he became executive managing director.

Despite his long hours at work, Mr. Gardner, 39, had the time to be the core of many groups of friends. He watched out for his younger sister, Danielle, who he even invited to Haverford College weekends while she was in high school. And he would not miss an important event for his children, Michael, 5, and Julia, 2½. He taught Michael how to ride a two-wheel bike last summer; on Sept. 10, he was at the orientation for his children at nursery school.

For his wife, Jennifer, he marked every important date with cards—often five or six for each occasion. The cards came with long personal notes and always included, "I love you madly!!!"

HARVEY JOSEPH GARDNER III
Built from Scratch

For his career, Harvey Gardner chose the computer lab over the kitchen, but both places fostered his creativity. He was a tinkerer, someone who built computers from stray parts and, evidently, built dinners the same way. Mr. Gardner, 35, did all the cooking for himself and his younger brother Mark, with whom he lived in Spring Lake, N.J. But the recipes were gleaned from the air.

"They were all his own concoctions," said another brother, Anthony, who is the founder of the WTC United Family Group (www.wtcunitedfamilygroup.org), an information network for families of the victims of Sept. 11. "It was crazy stuff. But it was good."

A practitioner of martial arts and a devotee of the History Channel, Mr. Gardner was a computer consultant for General Telecom on the 83rd floor of 1 World Trade Center.

"Mark managed to get through to him at the trade center that morning," Anthony Gardner said. "And Mark heard him comforting others, telling them it was O.K. He was being his normal, level-headed self."

FRANK GARFI
In Brother's Footsteps

After a dull time studying pharmacy, Frank Garfi, the son of an immigrant Brooklyn barber, found a job that suited him precisely. His first year as a trader at Cantor Fitzgerald was as fast-paced, demanding and as power-filled as an extreme sport.

"He was ecstatic about it," said Vito Garfi, his brother, who also worked in finance. "Coming in every day and participating in a worldwide game. Trading millions of dollars. Constantly trying to fight all the other traders and gauge the market."

After a lifetime of looking up to his older brother, Frank Garfi, 28, was meeting him as an equal, said Sabina, his sister-in-law. Vito Garfi, 33, "was big, was everything, to Frank," she said. "He loved talking about stocks and companies and the economy and financing," she said of the younger brother. "He loved that he could actually sit down with his brother at the table and talk about this stuff. He was in it, too, now."

JAMES M. GARTENBERG
Love at First Sight

"When I first met him, he was running the University of Michigan Alumni Club meeting. He was president of the New York City chapter. I was impressed with his leadership skills, how well he was organized, his intelligence, his presence, his ability to negotiate in difficult situations when there was conflict. I said to myself, 'I want to marry him.'"

That was in 1989. James M. Gartenberg, a man who would be hugely thrilled to know that Coach Lloyd Carr and the entire Michigan football squad signed a condolence card to his family, took a long time to come to the same conclusion about Jill Freeberg that she had about him.

But figure it out he surely did. Married six years ago, happily ensconced on the Upper East Side, father of Nicole, 2, with another child on the way, Mr. Gartenberg, 35, was moving out of his office at 1 World Trade Center on Sept. 11. His employer, Julien J. Studley Inc., the commercial real estate firm, was shifting him to Midtown. Mr. Gartenberg spent some of his last minutes on ABC-TV, calmly describing the situation on the 86th floor.

He was making plans to take his family to next month's Michigan-Wisconsin game. He had taught Nicole—"his heart and soul"—to yell "Go Blue!" when Michigan was on television. He secretly fantasized about wearing navy pants embossed with little maize M's when he was suitably old.

MATTHEW GARVEY
A Life Dedicated to Service

For those who are anxious or tired or losing focus on the war effort, the friends of Matthew Garvey would like you to consider his life.

"It was a life dedicated to the service of the people of America," said his friend, Rick Helton, who served with him in the Marine Corps.

Matthew Garvey enlisted in 1981 at the age of 18. In his 10-year career, he would make sergeant and become a squad leader in 2nd Anglico, an elite scout team that went into hostile territory ahead of ground troops. He served in Beirut and in operations Desert Storm and Desert Shield.

Mr. Garvey, 37, joined the Fire Department in 1995 and earned his way into the elite Squad 1 unit based in Park Slope, Brooklyn. He was recently accepted to law school, was an active Marine reservist, studied kung fu, played guitar, took photographs, climbed to the summit of Mount Rainier and was a rescue instructor for the Fire Department. Books on his nightstand included: *Don Quixote, War and Peace, The Iliad, Moby Dick.* "No one word can describe him," said his friend and station house mate Gerald Smyth.

There are three: New York firefighter.

BRUCE GARY
The Coach with a Heart

You could learn something about Bruce Gary from the way he coached a Little League team. Season after season he created good teams by focusing not on the all-stars but on the children other coaches would stick in right field and forget about.

"Every year there would be the really good kids, and some kids who weren't so good," said Thomas Gary, his 15-year-old son. "But he worked more with those kids, and by the end of the season the team would be more equal."

Mr. Gary, 51, was a firefighter with Engine 40, a part-time plumber and since his divorce a decade ago a full-time parent to his three children: Richard, 20, Jessica, 24, and Thomas. Somehow he found time to be vice president of the Little League in Bellmore, N.Y., coaching his sons and their friends. Always encouraging, never losing his temper.

"He would help boost kids' self-esteem," his daughter said. "He wanted to give everyone a chance."

PALMINA DELLI GATTI
Keeper of Helpful Secrets

Palmina Delli Gatti knew things. The secret of homemade pie crusts, for instance, and of a good thick pasta sauce. She knew. She knew the powerful people in the World Trade Center by their first names. When she traveled, she often went alone. They knew her in Paris, London, Rome.

"If there was a famous person in the room, there she was up there rubbing elbows with him," said her sister, Maria Fortuna.

Ms. Delli Gatti, 33, knew numbers. She was an accountant with Marsh & McLennan and lived with her father in Long Island City, Queens. In the evenings, she attended classes in pursuit of a master's degree in business administration, her sister said.

She never married, but hoped for a life mate. It just seemed that the career took possession of Ms. Delli Gatti's youthful years, her sister said. She liked fine things: jewelry from Fifth Avenue; good seats at Yankees games. "She was not afraid to walk through the door of life," Mrs. Fortuna said. "She knew what she wanted, and almost always she got it."

BOYD GATTON
Worldly Interests

Boyd Gatton moved to the United States in 1992 and was still discovering new interests. An operations officer at Fiduciary Trust who was born in Paget, Bermuda, he spent his free time practicing tai chi in the park near his home in Jersey City, doing carpentry work, reading and indulging his nieces when they visited from Bermuda with his two sisters.

"He just spoiled them to death," said his sister Pauline O'Connor, who has learned what kind of an impression her brother left on people while she has been settling his affairs.

He was the type of person who could walk into a store and leave with a new friend, like Wilfred Garcia, a photographer who works at a camera shop in Jersey City. "Not only was he interested in photography," Mr. Garcia said, "but just about anything in the world."

DONALD R. GAVAGAN
"I Am Here for You"

Out by his family's vacation house in Montauk, Donald R. Gavagan loved to go out in his Jeep for a spin by the sea. So did his 3-year-old twins, Donald and Lara, who imitated their father by scooting around in their own little motorized vehicles.

There is a new addition to the Gavagan family, Connor, who was born 52 days after the death of his father, a bond broker at Cantor Fitzgerald, and was christened Jan. 27, 2002. Mr. Gavagan's wife, Jacqueline, is not sure when she will be ready to return to their Long Island getaway. But she cherishes the photo she took of her husband and their children the weekend before Sept. 11: on a foggy beach, in the soft morning light, the twins sitting and watching their father cast his line into the surf.

Then there are the boxes of poems Mrs. Gavagan found as she was going through her husband's personal effects. Mr. Gavagan, 35, had a college degree in pharmacy and a career in finance, but he wrote poetry as well—while helping care for their small children, working long hours and renovating their new house. One poem read:

When life's trials overwhelm you and all you have is tears,
Please remember I am here for you now and for many
  years.
If you ever should need me when you want to run and hide,
Know I will be waiting and standing right by your side.

"It is almost," his wife said, "as though it was his last message to me."

PETER GAY
Efficient Executive

Their sheer numbers—six boys and one girl—made the Gay family hard to ignore as they grew up in the industrial city of Taunton, Mass. Their father, a longtime state representative, would march them into his law office on the occasional Saturday for dusting and polishing duties, which he watched over with a stern but twinkling eye.

While most of the children stayed in the area when they grew up, the second oldest, Peter, moved north of Boston to become a plant manager for Raytheon. But he stayed close to his family, spending summers with them on Cape Cod. And he never forgot the attention to spit and polish, in his work or play. "It doesn't shine itself," he'd reply when people admired the condition of his vintage car.

Mr. Gay, who would have turned 55 in December, was

Leslie Tapia, nine, among volunteers at DeWitt Clinton Park helping begin a citywide drive to plant one million daffodil bulbs in memory of the World Trade Center victims. Parks officials said 250,000 bulbs were planted on the first day. (*Richard Perry*)

commuting to California, where he'd been asked to increase production at a Raytheon plant producing a new military radar system. The plant had been producing 5 systems a day and the goal was 9; when Mr. Gay boarded Flight 11 for his weekly commute on Sept. 11, production was 14.

TERRENCE GAZZINI
"He Lit Up a Room"

At the end of the week's bond trading at Cantor Fitzgerald, Terrence Gazzini geared up for a weekend that was equally demanding but a lot more fun. He and a group of friends shared a beach house in Hampton Bays, where he worked as a bouncer at Boardy Barn, a popular Hamptons nightclub.

"This summer was going to be the last," said Tracy Gazzini, his mother. "He started there in college, but bouncing and working at Cantor Fitzgerald was a little bit too much. And he still had to go out."

In the city, where he lived with his parents in Bay Ridge, Brooklyn, Mr. Gazzini, 24, went to the gym after work or to restaurants and nightclubs with friends. His style was friendly and laid back.

"All his cousins wanted to be as cool as he was," Mrs. Gazzini said. "He lit up a room," she added. "I keep waiting to hear him say: 'Ma, could you have this shirt ready for me? I'm going out.' "

JULIE GEIS
The Great Motivator

Julie Geis had a way of encouraging people to do their best, whether they were in a boardroom or on a softball field.

"A pitcher from the softball team that she coaches called to tell me that whenever she was not doing what Julie wanted, she would yell at her to try harder," said Ms. Geis's mother, Betty Geis.

Ms. Geis, 44, senior vice president of Aon Corporation, where she worked for six years, was in New York City in the south tower for a monthly meeting on the day of the attacks, Mrs. Geis said. She lived in Lee's Summit, Mo., the small town where she grew up. The job allowed her to indulge a favorite pastime, traveling. Besides New York, business trips took her to London, Paris and Brazil.

"Aon was getting established all over the world," Mrs. Geis said. "She loved the challenge. She loved the people."

PETER GELINAS
Father for All Ages

The future Michelle Gelinas was 23, enjoying the single life in Manhattan. It was 1993. A friend from a cubicle near hers at work invited her to a comedy club. It turned out to be a triple date, with one Peter Gelinas. He was a broker at Cantor Fitzgerald in the trade center.

"We just hit it off," she said.

Fast-forward to 2001: Mr. Gelinas was still working at Cantor, enamored of his role as father to Jack Gerard, now 4, and Griffin Clark, 1. A few weeks before the terror attack, he took Jack camping in Pound Ridge, N.Y.

"Most people thought he was crazy for taking Jack camping. Who takes a 3-year-old camping?" Even she had her doubts, telling them, "Forget it, I'll see you at 10 o'clock tonight." But the two braved the elements, followed deer and slept peacefully in a tent.

All Michelle can do now is make sure her boys understand that she is here to protect them, and how important they were to their father. "He really wanted to be part of their lives," she said. "He was so psyched for what was coming—the bike rides, the Boy Scouts."

STEVEN P. GELLER
Kitchen Improvisations

How to describe Steven P. Geller's love of cooking? Envision a man prowling the touchstones of Upper West Side cuisine—Zabar's, Citarella and the like—looking, say, for the perfect green pepper. Imagine a Food Network enthusiast for whom an episode of *Iron Chef* was reason to drop everything.

"I have pots and pans here that are worth more than my jewelry," said his wife, Debra Geller, with complete seriousness and not a trace of resentment. Mrs. Geller suspects that she may have been the catalyst for Mr. Geller's quest for great food.

"I come from a long line of non-cooking women," she confessed. Her husband, she suggested, most likely gravitated toward the kitchen as "a sort of survival technique."

Mr. Geller, a 52-year-old institutional trader at Cantor Fitzgerald, embraced the role. Presentation—the more ostentatious the better—became a pet cause. He wore chef shirts and he cooked not by the book—heavens, no—but like a jazz artist. He made their daughter, Hali, 12, his chief assistant and partner in cuisine. "He was sort of cloning himself," Mrs. Geller said.

PETER V. GENCO
King of His Castle

People make assumptions about high-octane bond traders. You would think, for example, that Peter V. Genco, who traded government bonds at Cantor Fitzgerald on the 104th floor of 1 World Trade Center, "would have some kind of aggressive reputation," said his sister Jennifer. "But Peter wasn't into the big loud. He wasn't into the cursing, like so many traders on the desk. And I think that's what his clients really liked."

And what Mr. Genco really liked, aside from bonds and his wife, Diane, was being the father of two daughters, Annalisa, 2, and Victoria, who was born June 2.

"He was soft-spoken, so very gentle with them; he just loved his girls," Jennifer Genco said. In fact, on the Sunday before the attack, Victoria had her christening at St. Agnes Cathedral in Rockville Centre, N.Y. "There were 45 relatives in the party at his house afterwards, and I remember looking at him, and his house, and his girls, and thinking how happy he was, thinking that Peter loves to be the king of his castle."

STEVEN GREGORY GENOVESE
Those Matching Pajamas

The previous time the World Trade Center was attacked, in 1993, Steven Gregory Genovese showed up hours later at a Hoboken bar, much to his family's relief. So they held out hope last fall that he would surface once again.

His older brother, John Thomas, who lives in Manhattan, awaited his arrival with pizza. Steven's wife, Shelly, had dinner and strawberry bread waiting for him at the couple's home in Basking Ridge, N.J., every night that week.

Now when the question of his whereabouts comes up, his 18-month-old daughter, Jacqueline, chimes in. "He's up," she says.

Mr. Genovese was 37. Family and friends still cannot fathom it.

His mother, Veronica, recalls a hardworking boy who

once used his 25-cent allowance to buy her a miniature cup and saucer at a neighbor's yard sale. A so-so student, as she put it, who rose to become a partner at Cantor Fitzgerald.

His wife, a former Miss Dallas, recalls a husband quick to tell everyone that "they" were pregnant with Jacqueline so she would not feel self-conscious, and happy to wear pajamas that matched his wife's and daughter's as they opened presents on Christmas morning, a family tradition on her side. "He thought we were the biggest dorks dressing alike, but he totally went along with it," said his wife, who has pictures to prove it.

This Christmas, no one was in the mood.

ALAYNE GENTUL
She Saved 40 Co-workers

Alayne Gentul, the director of human resources for Fiduciary Trust Company, was on the 90th floor of 2 World Trade Center when the first plane hit, but she went up to the 97th, because she thought it was her responsibility to get everybody out. It was particularly difficult to get the people in technical support out, because they were backing things up. As the floor filled with smoke, she called her husband, Jack, the dean of students at the New Jersey Institute of Technology.

"She was with a colleague, Ed Emory," Mr. Gentul said. "They made a determination to wet their clothing and put it over their heads and get to the stairwell. She said she loved the kids and we said we loved each other and we said good-bye."

Mr. Gentul started to cry.

"At least we got to say good-bye," he said. "So many didn't. And I know she did something decent. The chair of Fiduciary told me at least 40 people are alive because of Alayne."

Alayne Gentul was 44, had been married for 23 years and lived in Mountain Lakes, N.J. She taught Bible school for nine years and loved Billy Joel and Louie Prima. Her sons, Alex and Robbie, are 12 and 8.

Asked about treasured moments, her husband offers two, years apart.

"We loved the ocean. Our first kiss was on the beach on Wildwood, N.J. It was a beautiful moonlit night, full moon, and thousands of horseshoe crabs were coming up on the beach to lay their eggs."

The latter: "Our son is part of a group of junior Sunfish sailors and a few weeks ago, they had a junior moonlight race. A bunch of kids gathered with boats, some decorated with little glow lights, in this beautiful, still, moonlit night. We had this feeling, in this excruciating slow race, of something of incredible beauty. One of those times in life you'll remember."

LINDA GEORGE
Love Through Volleyball

In July 2000 Linda George had no idea of what was coming when Jeff Pereira, whom she had been dating for several years, suggested they drive out to Gooseberry Island, near Westport, Mass.

It was overcast. They were strolling along, idly picking up shells. While Ms. George was distracted, Mr. Pereira hid something inside a mussel that he asked her to pick up. Inside, she found an engagement ring. Mr. Pereira dropped to his knee and asked her to marry him. Tears ran down her cheeks.

He reached into his backpack. She thought he had brought lunch. Actually, he had a bottle of Champagne chilling in ice in a Ziploc bag. He had stuffed Champagne glasses inside a pair of winter gloves so they wouldn't break. They drank a toast to their future together. There was no one else around. The sea was calm. "It was right out of a Julia Roberts movie," Mr. Pereira said. "It was the best moment of my life."

Ms. George, 27, a buyer for TJX, lived in Westborough, Mass., and was on her way to a buying trip in Los Angeles aboard Flight 11. Athletic and with countless friends, she had met Mr. Pereira on the volleyball court; they played on the same team in the company league. She was captain. Their first date had been on New Year's Eve in 1997. They went to see *Titanic*. Their wedding was arranged for Oct. 20.

SUZANNE GERATY
The Kiss Monster

Her four nephews christened Suzanne Geraty the Kiss Monster for obvious reasons: when she wasn't chasing them around the park, she was smooching them. Or tickling them. "She was the best aunt," said her sister, Erin Durkin. But Suzanne, 30, had numerous outlets for her playful nature. She always scooped up any extra concert tickets at the Cantor Fitzgerald office, where she worked in system support, and regretted missing Madonna at the Garden. She couldn't hold a tune, but she danced with abandon. She loved dining out and drinking red wine, and she was a devoted shopper for accessories: she filled her closet with shoes, hats, pocketbooks. Her collection of potions and lotions was encyclopedic.

She lived with her mother in Bay Ridge, Brooklyn, and had done volunteer work there at the Guild for Exceptional Children, a center for retarded adults, since she was 14. One of her nephews told his father, a retired firefighter, exactly how to find Suzanne at the disaster site: he was sure she had climbed a tree and was waiting to be rescued.

A makeshift shrine created by residents of West Orange, New Jersey, overlooks lower Manhattan and the gap where the towers once stood. (*Emile Wamsteker*)

RALPH GERHARDT
A Dream Fulfilled

He delighted in bungee jumping and feeding sharks. At 6 feet 2 inches tall, Ralph Gerhardt enjoyed playing the part of daredevil and strongman. He had an impish sense of humor and a reputation for practical jokes. Still, he was an affectionate son, who called his parents in Toronto every day.

He had grown up in Toronto, the son of German immigrants, but New York had always been his dream. And so February 2001—when Mr. Gerhardt, a 34-year-old bond trader, was transferred by Cantor Fitzgerald to the 105th floor of the World Trade Center—was one of the happiest times of his life. He was eager to show his parents that life— "my New York" as he was so proud to call it.

His parents came often to visit so he could show them the apartment he was fixing up on Lexington Avenue and 26th Street, the bicycle he liked to ride over to Central Park, the woman from Staten Island he had met at work, the many museums and monuments he prided himself on knowing, as well as the best tour guides.

"It was the pinnacle," said his father, Hans Gerhardt, who last heard from his son at 8:48 A.M., moments after the plane hit. "He said: 'Something just happened. I am O.K. We are evacuating. I will call you later.' "

ROBERT J. GERLICH
Family and Baseball

Last summer, Robert J. Gerlich rounded up his sons, Matt and Daniel, for an afternoon at Shea Stadium. The Mets lost again, but he didn't complain. He never complained. "He didn't care," Matt said. "He always had a good time."

A lifelong baseball fan, Mr. Gerlich, 56, worked long hours as an accountant for Guy Carpenter & Company. But his weekends were devoted to his family in Monroe, Conn., and to baseball. Though his wife of 23 years, Rochelle, never shared his passion for the sport, he found willing seatmates in his sons.

They would talk and joke in between cheers for the Mets or the Bridgeport Bluefish (he was a season ticket holder).

And no matter who won or lost, they would have a good time together.

"He's one of those guys you have to know," Matt said. "It's hard to describe him. If you knew him, you knew he was a cool guy."

DENNIS GERMAIN
Daffy Downhill Skiing

Dennis Germain, 33, a firefighter with Ladder Company 2, spent his working hours in the canyons of Midtown Manhattan and his free time on the slopes. He was a ski instructor at Sterling Forest, near Tuxedo, N.Y., where he trained high school racing teams. He skied the Rockies on department trips. And he was indispensable at the annual downhill race at Hunter Mountain, which pits firehouses against one another.

Teams of five people grab hold of a 50-foot fire hose and spread out across the trail. The goal is to ski together without letting go, falling, or otherwise messing up. No, they are not allowed to use ski poles. Yes, there are other skiers sharing the snow. Depending on the firefighters' finesse, the spectacle can be either mildly funny or completely hilarious.

"The hoses in many cases would cross and guys would go head over heels down the mountain," Lt. Neil Skow said. But not Firefighter Germain: "Dennis was always one of the better skiers we had."

His other specialty at Ladder 2 was starting enormous debates in the firehouse kitchen with politically incorrect statements he was sure would set people off. As the argument heated up, he would slip away. "He loved what he did," said his brother Brian, a firefighter in Harlem.

MARINA GERTSBERG
Pride of Her Parents

Marina Gertsberg's father did not want to serve with the Soviet forces in Afghanistan, so when she was 4, the family emigrated from Odessa, Ukraine, and settled in the Howard Beach section of Queens.

Bright and athletic, Ms. Gertsberg was everything her parents, Roman and Anna, could have hoped for in their only child. She went to the Mark Twain School for the Gifted and Talented, Stuyvesant High School and the State University of New York at Binghamton. She kept up with her Russian so she could write to her grandmother. She had her own apartment in Brooklyn, but talked with her mother several times a day. She and her boyfriend, Henry Kravchenko, seemed headed toward marriage.

For the fall of 2001, Ms. Gertsberg, 25, enrolled in a master's program at Baruch College and had to switch jobs because her employer would not adjust her schedule to accommodate her classes. On Sept. 4, she joined Cantor Fitzgerald as a junior manager.

Four days later, Ms. Gertsberg was maid of honor at her friend Clara Mazepa's wedding in Brooklyn, walking down the aisle in a purple gown that set off her blue eyes. "She was like a queen," her mother said.

SUSAN M. GETZENDANNER
Business and Buddhism

One does not often encounter a practical businessperson who is a spiritual seeker, but this was Susan M. Getzendanner. She was a vice president at Fiduciary Trust, but she also trekked all over the world, including the Himalayas, and was a serious student of Buddhism.

"I think it was the all-inclusiveness of it and the spirituality of Buddhism," said Fiona Fein, a longtime friend. "She had meetings with various Buddhist sages whom she found to be enormously spiritually powerful people. They were interested in something she wanted."

Ms. Getzendanner, 58, had a great grin, and silver-gray hair that she never dyed. She lived on the Upper East Side and worked behind the scenes for the Blue Hill Troupe, an amateur group of Gilbert and Sullivan players. On weekends, she went to her cottage at the foot of Mount Riga in Connecticut, which, like her apartment, was filled with handicrafts and art from her travels. Her brother Tom Getzendanner lamented the fact that a woman who spent her life traveling foreign lands and trusting others was killed in an act of international terrorism.

JAMES G. GEYER
The Team Is the Goal

James G. Geyer worked as a bond broker at Cantor Fitzgerald and for a catering company on weekends. But his true calling was as a friend, a father and a coach in Rockville Centre, on Long Island, where he and his wife, Cathy, grew up and settled.

A natural athlete—he played baseball and basketball as a child and lacrosse and football in college—Mr. Geyer, 41, took up soccer so he could coach the teams of his three children: Michelle, 13, Matthew, 11, and Laura, 7. He had a knack for calming overexcited parents and made a point to include all children in the game, not just the most talented players.

"There were always soccer books in his car," said his mother, Jo Ann Geyer. "He studied up on the game and learned to love it."

Shortly before Sept. 11, Mr. Geyer's best friend, Charles Rollins, happened upon an old home video. "Jimmy's holding my son Charlie like a football and playing soccer with my two girls," Mr. Rollins said. "That's Jimmy in a nutshell. He just was really into not only the athletic part of playing games, but the joy of being part of a team."

JOSEPH GIACCONE
He Knew No Stress

Not too long ago, Sondra Giaccone broke it to her husband: "Joe, you're starting to look weathered."

She meant it as a compliment. Joseph Giaccone, 43, a vice president at eSpeed, had acquired the look of a man completely at ease in his own skin.

As much as he traveled for business, work stress did not own his face. He had figured out how to find the time to coach baseball for his son, Max, and to attend countless *Nutcracker* performances with his daughter, Alex. When the Giaccones moved to Monroe Township, N.J., he made visiting his parents, Elizabeth and Vincent, in Queens, a priority.

He had developed the unusual ability to stop on a dime and relax instantly. On autumn Sundays, he would bake fresh bread while sipping a serious wine, his special Bolognese sauce bubbling on the stove. Andrea Bocelli would be soaring through the speakers; the Jets would be on TV. Bread done, Jets won, guests arriving, bliss! For nothing made Mr. Giaccone happier than feeding people.

So comfortable was he that he could laugh at his own vanity. When Mr. Giaccone saw a video of himself at a family reunion in California, learning to surf in a wet suit, he cracked up. "I look like a pregnant seal!" he shouted.

VINCENT F. GIAMMONA
Born to Be Wild

At about 1:30 P.M. on Sept. 7, Lt. Vincent F. Giammona was at Coney Island, flashing his fireman's badge and, once again, pushing the limits.

He had just spent the morning exploring the aquarium with his wife, Theresa, and their two youngest daughters—Nicolette, 4, and Daniella, 2. They had started back home to Valley Stream, when, suddenly, he turned the car around. He couldn't go to Coney Island without riding the Cyclone roller coaster.

But the Cyclone would not open until 6 P.M., Lieutenant Giammona was told. He smiled and jabbered about his upcoming birthday (he would turn 40 in four days, on Sept. 11th). Soon, the Cyclone was creaking up into the sunshine, carrying one passenger. His daughters cheered.

He lived for moments like this. Using fake buck teeth, an accent or his infamous Elvis costume, he would transform household errands or roll call at the firehouse into improv comedy. At sporting events involving his two older daughters—Francesca, 8 and Toni-Ann, 6—his cheering was an aerobic workout. At Ladder 5 on Houston Street, he taught rookies about high-rise fires and downtown bars. They called him "Lieutenant Fun."

The morning of Lieutenant Giammona's 40th birthday, his wife would hear his voice for the last time: he said goodbye during a brief phone call while hurrying to the World Trade Center. On Sept. 7, though, when the Cyclone started its descent, she heard him shout with joy.

JIM GIBERSON
Gentle Giant

Neighbors of Ladder Company 35 on Amsterdam Avenue and 66th Street in Manhattan grew to count on seeing the Paul Bunyanesque figure in the firehouse doorway with his baseball cap, bushy mustache and, always, a friendly smile.

They did not know him by name, but just as the one who would hoist their would-be firefighter toddlers into the rig, or lean down and with his oversized hands help adjust the handlebars of a bicycle.

To his colleagues, Jim Giberson, 43, was the one who organized and cooked for all their annual parties over the last 20 years. But as much as Firefighter Giberson seemed comfortable in that traditionally all-male environment, it was a different story at home. He told his wife, Susan, when they became engaged that he wanted three daughters, and she obliged. The only reason he ever missed firefighter events was to go to his daughters' swim meets, no matter how far, where he cheered them on as they became champions, or as he liked to say, future Olympic contenders.

"I used to kid him, 'You'll never be able to get into the bathroom with all those women,' " said Mike Kutula, a fellow firefighter. "But he was happy with his three girls."

CRAIG GIBSON
Treats for Daisy

Craig Gibson had a number of keen interests, starting with soccer (he played for a Manhattan team called Barnestonworth, but rooted for Liverpool) and continuing with the movies. (He had to be the first to see a new release, and there had to be plenty of popcorn on hand.) And he loved his wife, Dannielle, with whom he emigrated from Australia in December 2000.

But beginning in August, he had a new focus: Daisy, the boxer puppy he gave his wife for her birthday. "He was so obsessed with this dog," marveled Mrs. Gibson. At the office, where Mr. Gibson, 37, was a reinsurance broker for Marsh & McLennan, "instead of doing work he'd be on the Internet, looking up pet stores and buying treats for her." Sometimes he would come home in the middle of the day to take Daisy for a walk.

It was hardly a one-sided affair. "She used to sleep on his slippers every night, with her little nose tucked into one of them and her paws over the top," Mrs. Gibson said. "She was mad about him."

RONNIE E. GIES
Loved Giving, Not Receiving

One of the most difficult times in Ronnie E. Gies's life came two years earlier, when his family's home in Merrick, on Long Island, burned down.

It was not so much the destruction that upset Firefighter Gies, 43, of Squad 288 in Maspeth, Queens, but the fact that he was suddenly the recipient of favors and goodwill from neighbors, instead of being the benefactor.

"It was very difficult for him to be receiving and not giving," said his wife, Carol. "Someone would call at 3 in the morning because their toilet was clogged, and Ronnie was there."

Luckily, Firefighter Gies was also a carpenter. With a little help, in six months he built the family a new home, with a basement big enough to serve as hang-out headquarters for his sons, Thomas, 18; Ronnie, 16; and Robert, 14, and their friends.

A couple of years ago, Firefighter Gies took the lieutenant's test, after studying for hours at the dining room table. Recently, Mrs. Gies was told that her husband had been pegged for a promotion on Sept. 10. "It meant a lot to him to be promoted," Mrs. Gies said. "He never knew."

PAUL S. GILBEY
Doing It Himself

Paul S. Gilbey was "a very, very keen D.I.Y. man," as in do-it-yourself, said his wife, Deena.

"He'd be coming home, and he would call me on the cell phone and say, 'Dee, set up the paint,'" she recalled. "He'd always involve the kids in it. I don't know how he had the patience to do it all, but he always did." That patience played out on the ski slopes, too, where he would ski all day with a 3-year-old between his knees. His son Max is now 7, and Mason is 4.

"He loved those twin towers, he loved them," his wife said. Mr. Gilbey, 39, would leave his home in Chatham, N.J., at 4:30 A.M., so he could visit the gym before starting his job as an assistant vice president at Euro Brokers. "He would say to me, 'Every morning I drive over the Pulaski

Skyway, I see those towers and I quiver, they're just so magnificent,'" Mrs. Gilbey said. "In an ironic sort of way, he died doing a job he loved in the towers he loved."

PAUL GILL
An Early Trial by Fire

Several years before he became a firefighter, Paul Gill was walking down the street in Astoria, Queens, when a woman started screaming in a burning building. Smoke poured from the window as the woman clutched a baby and cried for help. With no firefighter in sight and everyone else standing around, Mr. Gill climbed the fire escape, took the baby in his arms and led the woman to safety. He was a carpenter at the time, but the incident firmed his desire to join the Fire Department, which he did in 1999. While his family worried about his safety, he assured them that fighting fires was no more dangerous than carpentry jobs that put him on steel beams 50 stories up in the sky.

"He didn't have a fear," said his father, John.

Firefighter Gill, 34, managed to blend his two careers, continuing to take carpentry jobs to help pay the medical bills of his two sons, Aaron, 14, who had received a kidney transplant seven years earlier, and Joshua, 11, who has juvenile osteoporosis.

"He was both a dad and a big brother to his kids," said Michelle Evans, his sister. "He was patient with Aaron and helped Joshua with sports."

He was also artistic. Though he never took a drawing class, he became adept at complicated line drawings and geometric designs, even toying with the idea of becoming a tattoo artist.

His best-known artwork is a big Maltese cross he designed for the front of his fire station, Engine 54 in Manhattan. Right now, it is covered in flowers.

EVAN H. GILLETTE
"We Walked Hand in Hand"

Sherri Partridge, a native New Yorker, had been searching for the right man for years, and at 39, she found Evan Hunter Gillette. They met on the Internet.

"We just really hit it off," recalled Ms. Partridge, a publicist working downtown. Mr. Gillette, 40, was a vice president at Sandler O'Neill & Partners.

After a few dates last year, the two moved in together and spent weekends in Canada, Vermont, Washington and Monticello, Va. "We did a lot of bed and breakfast," she said. "We walked hand in hand, lay on the grass and took it all in."

A wedding was in the offing. The couple roamed the

streets of Manhattan, looking for the right rings and talking about babies. "We were very, very happy," she said.

Before the attack, Ms. Partridge says, she had a dim prescience of what was to come. "Sometimes, I woke up in the middle of the night and had this gripping fear that he might die," she said. "I would tell him, please don't die, please don't die. And he would tell me, 'I'll never leave you.' "

LAURA GILLY
The Joy in Her Voice

For nine years, Laura Gilly traveled the world, all expenses paid, a perk from her life as a flight attendant. She saw Paris, she saw Rome, indulged in the exotic sights and sounds of Egypt, Jakarta and Kuwait.

But the thrill of being up in the air, away from family and friends, eventually subsided. Ms. Gilly wanted out of her job with Tower Airlines. "She wanted a 9-to-5, so she could make plans without breaking them," said Phyllis Gilly, her mother. "So many times she wasn't home for Christmas or New Year's. She was really looking forward to stability."

And in mid-2000, she found it in a job working in technical support for Cantor Fitzgerald. Life was finally sweet and somewhat predictable, and Ms. Gilly, 32, was enjoying every minute of it, her mother said, recalling a phone conversation she had with her daughter weeks before Sept. 11.

The joy Mrs. Gilly heard in her daughter's voice has made it all the more difficult accepting her death. "We spent so much time worrying about her flying here and there, and to have her go like this: killed by a plane as she sat in an office building. All she wanted was a real job at a desk in a building."

DONNA MARIE GIORDANO
Family Friends

Donna Marie Giordano liked to go to Bon Jovi concerts with her son, Michael. "Bon Jovi was her second love," he said. But the Giordanos' common interests went beyond music. "We would drive to the mountains and go hiking. Or go out to dinner," Mr. Giordano said. "We did everything together. We were more like brother and sister."

Ms. Giordano, 44 and divorced, liked having her family nearby. An insurance syndicator for the Aon Corporation in 2 World Trade Center, she had gotten jobs for her son and her sister, Elaine Barrett, at the company. Though they were in the building on Sept. 11, Mrs. Barrett and Mr. Giordano escaped.

Generous and warm, Ms. Giordano could also be single-minded. "She made everything she became interested in a priority," her son said.

One priority was raising money for charity. On Sept. 7, Ms. Giordano helped organize an event to benefit Urban Pathways, a program for the homeless, at a bar near her office. As usually happened when Ms. Giordano got involved, she had persuaded executives at Aon to show up. That night, they raised $2,500.

JEFFREY GIORDANO
He Shared His Bounty

His wife's beloved stepfather, clinging to life in the burn center at New York Hospital, made Jeffrey Giordano promise to become a firefighter. And so he spent 14 years at Ladder Company 3 in the East Village, where he was decorated for bravery last spring after rescuing a woman from a burning apartment.

Firefighter Giordano, 45, also became a devoted friend of the burn center, where adults and children go to heal and where his wife, Marie, worked. He took ice cream to the children there, and endlessly raised money for the New York Firefighters Burn Center Foundation, which buys equipment and contributed $700,000 in 2001.

On weekends, Firefighter Giordano loaded his van with T-shirts to sell at firefighting conferences, often taking his children—Victoria, 12; Nick, 9; and Alexandra, 6—with him. That was for the foundation, too.

He and his wife met when he was 15 and she was 13. "I miss his arms around me," Mrs. Giordano said. "I thought we would grow old together."

On Jan. 22, 2002, the hospital will open a children's playroom in the burn center. It will be named for Firefighter Giordano, who sped to the World Trade Center in the battalion chief's car on Sept. 11, even though it was his day off.

STEVEN A. GIORGETTI
Family First

Steven A. Giorgetti worked for Marsh & McLennan for 20 years. Dashing, hardworking and unfailingly in a good mood, he worked his way up to senior vice president. And beyond.

Recently, Mr. Giorgetti, 43, had been nominated for a promotion to managing director. He worked at the company's Midtown offices, but was at the World Trade Center for a meeting on Sept. 11. He was promoted posthumously.

Mr. Giorgetti lived in Manhasset, on Long Island, with his wife of 18 years, Arminé, and two children. On a rare occasion when he had to miss one of his son's Little League games for a business dinner, Mr. Giorgetti telephoned his wife not once but three times, asking for updates.

His daughter was his princess. "Who's going to push me on the swings?" she has wondered lately.

Mr. Giorgetti decorated his home office with pictures of Joe DiMaggio and Mickey Mantle. At work, his office was unmistakably that of a Daddy, adorned with arts and crafts projects galore.

Walk inside, said Patricia Hagemann, a longtime colleague, and you knew where Steven Giorgetti's heart was.

MARTIN GIOVINAZZO
Home to the Daily Ambush

The muffled engine of the 11-year-old Chevy Blazer was always the cue for the Giovinazzo children to scramble to hide under the table or behind the front door. "Raaa!" Theresa, 5, and Ashley, 3, would scream, attacking their father, Martin, as he walked in. Sixteen-month-old Andrew even made a baby attack.

But what Andrew liked most was standing on Mr. Giovinazzo's lap and dancing to "Who Let the Dogs Out."

Mr. Giovinazzo, 34, of Staten Island had worked in the maintenance department at Marsh & McLennan for two years, said his wife, Dorothy. He was happy to have landed the position after job-hopping for years.

Things were looking up. Marsh officials had approached him about attending air-conditioning school. The couple were saving to buy a house. As Mr. Giovinazzo had always been the main breadwinner, Mrs. Giovinazzo now wonders how to go on. She worked part-time in a drug store, but mostly took care of the children. "I've always daydreamed of having a house where the children can have their own rooms," Mrs. Giovinazzo said. "Now I'll never have it. I'm clueless about what to do."

SALVATORE GITTO
Spirit in the Sky

The Gitto family did everything as a unit. They raked leaves together. They painted together. They fixed lights together. And everyone piled into the car for trips to the supermarket.

The only thing Salvatore Gitto did by himself was pilot planes. He had been flying airplanes longer than he had been driving cars. But being a risk manager for Marsh & McLennan, he was cautious not to take his wife along as a passenger.

Yet even his weekly trips were planned around his family. On Sunday mornings, Mr. Gitto, 44, would fly out of the local airport, in Old Bridge, N.J., and be back home by noon to spend the rest of the day with his wife, Angela, and two sons, Stephen, 4, and Gregory, 10.

His next big step was to buy his own plane. Being a pilot let him see the world spread out below him, not through the tight oval window of a Boeing 747 but in a glorious panorama.

Now, Stephen knows that his father is in heaven and that heaven is in the sky. When he is bigger, he says, he's going to go up and bring Dad back down.

MON GJONBALAJ
"Keep the Family Together'"

His workmates often called him Jambalaya because his Albanian last name was so hard to pronounce. Mon Gjonbalaj (pronounced JAHN-buh-lie) liked the Cajun nickname even though he was always proud of his Albanian roots.

He was a janitor at the World Trade Center and he loved the camaraderie, often showing up an hour before work started to chat with friends.

"He was supposed to retire last year," said his son Sal. "He was going to turn 66 on Oct. 31, but he wanted to continue working. He was so attached to that building. He didn't want to let go. It was his second home."

Mr. Gjonbalaj stuck close to his family in New York and in Europe. He lived with his three sons in a three-family house in the Bronx, while his daughter worked as a translator for NATO forces in Kosovo. Last year, he went to Kosovo to help his brother rebuild a house destroyed in the war there.

After the twin towers were attacked, Sal said, his father called home and said, "I'm trapped. I don't think I'm going to see you guys again. Keep the family together. Be strong."

DIANNE GLADSTONE
On-the-Money Instincts

At 24, Dianne Gladstone, the meticulous young tax official, followed her romantic instincts. She would marry this fellow who had offered—on a blind date no less—a pricey dinner at Maxwell's Plum, in Manhattan's archetypal 1970s singles spot. A year later, she was a Mrs.

And as in her public life—37 years at the New York State Department of Taxation and Finance—her instincts were right on the money. She and Herb Gladstone, a crane operator, skied, hit the Broadway shows, traveled. Each year they celebrated the holidays at the Queensboro Hill Jewish Center, where they were married, and then it was off to the Caribbean.

Even at home, she was "organized, maybe too organized," Mr. Gladstone recalled. In their Forest Hills home she had tax files going back to when they had met, he said,

An October 23 memorial service at State Supreme Court
in Brooklyn for court employees' relatives lost in the
terrorist attack. (*Justin Lane*)

recalling her fondness for her tax work as section chief in 2
World Trade Center, 86th floor.

Yet in her favorite photo, on the beach at Provincetown
at sunset last Labor Day, Dianne Gladstone, at 55, looked
as happy as Mr. Gladstone could ever remember, perhaps
because her thoughts were far away from tax codes, the
paper shredder and the job she treasured. She had decided
to retire—to their new house, near the water, on the north
fork of Long Island. The moving date was the next April.

KEITH GLASCOE
Big Man, Big Heart

Keith Glascoe was a big man—roughly 6-
foot-4, 270 pounds—but maybe the
biggest thing about him was his heart.

"He was the sort who would stop and
pick up a hurt animal in the street, take it
to a doctor and pay for it," said his father,
Benjamin Glascoe.

Given his size, football was inevitable. He started playing
organized ball when he was 8 and twice made it to the New
York Jets training camp. The second time, he was injured,
but he played for a year in Italy, and learned to speak excellent Italian.

Back in New York, he caught the acting bug. Soon, there
he was doing commercials and appearing on *One Life to Live,
Law and Order* and *100 Centre Street*. He also had a part in
the TV movie *Assault on Devil's Island*, but the best of all was
playing Benny in the movie *The Professional*.

He married Veronica Squef, and he yearned for a more
regular job. His kindly nature meshed perfectly with the Fire
Department, and he joined Ladder Company 21. Naturally,
he played on the department's football team.

Firefighter Glascoe, 38, lived in Brooklyn with his wife
and their two children, Nolan, 3, and Owen, 15 months.
Ms. Squef is expecting a third child in April 2002. Off duty,
he continued to go to casting calls. But his sons had discovered modeling, and so Firefighter Glascoe had a new role
escorting them to their own auditions.

THOMAS GLASSER
Not Typical Wall Street

If Thomas Glasser had filled out an occupation form, it would have looked something like this: philosophy major–track star–stand-up comic–restaurant owner–bartender–partner at Sandler O'Neill. Mr. Glasser was not a typical Wall Street guy, said his wife, Meg. That was all right with her, since she had an aversion to them until she met Mr. Glasser, a moment she said was like time-lapse photography.

"I looked at him and I saw everything," she said. "He walked in the door, and I knew that he was my husband."

By 40, Mr. Glasser had added husband and father to his résumé. He could have also added wallet-rescuer: Mr. Glasser earned a do-gooder reputation in high school when he returned a teacher's lost wallet. Years later, he witnessed a robbery and chased after the culprit. Again, the wallet was returned to its owner.

Mr. Glasser's children, Dylan and Luke, are still a bit too young to appreciate their father's focus on education, but other children are not. Mr. Glasser and his father, Gerald, had for years planned to start a charitable family foundation. After Sept. 11, Mr. Glasser's father decided to continue with their plan. The Thomas Glasser Foundation will begin awarding scholarship money this year. "I can't think of a better memorial to him," said Gerald Glasser.

STEVEN GLICK
Wanted Time with Family

Steven Glick was one of 11 graduates of Harvard Business School who all somehow ended up in Greenwich, Conn., and found their way to each other's dining tables once a month. But Mr. Glick sometimes missed the group's dinners because of work that took him overseas for weeks at a time.

"Every once in a while, it feels like he's just in Tokyo," said Tom Stark, a friend and dinner buddy by way of marriage to one of the Harvard graduates, describing his emotions since the attack.

Earlier this year, Mr. Glick, 42, took a new job to avoid the extended travel and be able to spend more time with his wife, Mari, a Broadway theater producer; his son, Colin, 6; and his daughter, Courtney, 4. He was at a financial technology seminar at the World Trade Center in his new position as managing director with Credit Suisse First Boston when the planes hit.

At Greenwich Associates, the financial consulting firm where Mr. Glick worked for 10 years before joining Credit Suisse First Boston, former colleagues remembered him as driven, straightforward, not afraid to speak his mind. But among the couples who formed his dinner group, Mr. Glick was mostly viewed as kind, cheerful and loyal. "He didn't need to be the center of attention," Mr. Stark said. The dinners, he added, will go on.

HARRY GLENN
He Pursued His Dream

Harry Glenn was the pride of his family, the fourth of five boys, the son who said he was going to college to learn all about computers, and then went and did it. Mr. Glenn's father, Roosevelt, loved to brag about his boy Harry, 38, how he kept his promise and how he managed to get a good job looking after Marsh & McLennan's elaborate network of computers.

"A lot of people didn't believe he could come out of Harlem and do as well as he did," Mr. Glenn said. "But Harry had a goal that he set for himself, and he followed it. I don't think he had any idea how many people were proud of him."

Mr. Glenn continues to hope that his son's body will be found amid the ruins of the World Trade Center. He hopes for that day, just as he does for the day when he can forget what he saw on television on Sept. 11.

"I stopped watching the news. But I don't think I'm ever going to get seeing that plane hit his building out of my mind. It just won't go away."

JOHN GNAZZO
Making Work Easier

Work did not seem like work if your boss was John Gnazzo. It seemed like fun. What else could you think if you sat down at your desk and heard a whoopee cushion emit its inimitable sound? Yes, John Gnazzo was up to his tricks.

Mr. Gnazzo, 32, was vice president for operations at Cantor Fitzgerald, and his sunny disposition and impish inclinations enabled people to get their work done efficiently but also amply enjoy themselves. One of his co-workers suggested that Mr. Gnazzo made every day at the office seem like a Sunday afternoon.

Mr. Gnazzo, who lived in Manhattan with his wife, Helene, and their children, John Vincent, 3, and Jule, 8 months, had deeply etched memories of the World Trade Center. During the 1993 bombing, he helped a woman who was in a wheelchair down 60 flights of stairs. Several years ago, his father, an electrician, had a heart attack while working in the trade center and died. And for reasons he couldn't explain, Mr. Gnazzo seemed to have premonitions of his own destiny.

He would tell his wife: "You're going to live into your 80s. I'm going to die young."

But nothing inhibited his innate generosity. It showed up early. When he was 11, he made deliveries for a cheese shop in Greenwich Village. Anytime he made a delivery to an old woman, he never accepted any money. When he got back to the shop, he paid for those orders out of his own pocket.

WILLIAM R. GODSHALK
For Love of Wild Bill

James Bond Godshalk had five children and William R. Godshalk was the wildest. When Bill Godshalk was 10 and playing shortstop in Little League, he caught a ball only to drop it when the base runner hit his glove. Bill attacked the other player. James Godshalk walked onto the field and pulled his son back.

"He needed me," Mr. Godshalk said. "And I needed him, I did so much."

James Godshalk taught his son sports, and in the process taught him how to calm himself. But Bill Godshalk kept his wild and adventurous heart, even as a 35-year-old vice president at Keefe, Bruyette & Woods in the World Trade Center, said his fiancée, Aleese Hartmann. At a memorial service for his son, James Godshalk was reminded of a verse by James Whitcomb Riley:

Old man never had much to say—
'Ceptin to Jim,—
And Jim was the wildest boy he had,
And the old man jes' wrapped up in him!

When he recited the poem, he substituted "Bill" for the name Jim, and told the story of a wild boy and the father who loved him.

BRIAN GOLDBERG
Birthday for the Handyman

Jodie and Brian Goldberg started dating in high school. After seven years—going to the movies, roaming the New Jersey suburbs, eating out in Manhattan—they got married in May 2000 at a temple in New Jersey.

"We danced," Mrs. Goldberg said. "We were just so happy."

They moved into a new town house in Union, N.J., after the wedding, and he hung the fans, wired the stereos and "made everything work." He was the handyman in the extended family. He fixed a broken wall unit at his sister's house and made a microwave stand for Jodie's sister.

On weekends, he was often hired to photograph weddings, bar mitzvahs and birthdays, a sideline he had gotten into when he was 13. It suited him well. "He wasn't really able to sit still," said Mrs. Goldberg.

"He had to go from place to place."

Having a first baby, Mrs. Goldberg said, was in their "five-year plan." Mr. Goldberg, who worked at Fiduciary Trust, would have turned 27 on October 17, 2001.

MICHELLE GOLDSTEIN
Blessed to Be Dazzled

Michelle Goldstein was a small-town girl. She was still dazzled by the ordinary big-city indulgences—getting Chinese food at any hour, eating sushi, popping into a Banana Republic store just below her East Side apartment.

And she was still—blessedly, as her husband, Ed, saw it—untarnished by the big-city ways. She smiled a lot, a big, beaming smile. She thanked him for the little things he did, typing up something for her, picking up something at the store. She liked to tell him they were blessed.

"She always was positive," Mr. Goldstein said. "She symbolized life more than anyone I've ever met." He would tell his friends: "I had to go to Florida to import her. She was so different from a lot of people you meet around here."

They met on a blind date. She lived in Coral Springs, Fla. He was visiting his family. His mother set them up. And within six months, the woman whom her sister, Annete Herman, described as "the queen of three-, four-, five-year relationships," was packing her bags to move to New York, where she found a job in brokerage services at Aon at 2 World Trade Center.

Michelle and Ed, both 31, were married last February. But Michelle and Annete still spoke every day, without fail.

MONICA GOLDSTEIN
Concerns about Elevators

Monica Goldstein never worried about working so high in the twin towers before the elevators began behaving badly. In recent weeks, she told her older sister, Adrienne Triggs, weird things had happened: elevators skipped floors and were unpredictably out of service, and then everyone heard that rumor about the elevator that was stopped by emergency brakes after going into free fall. After a touch of anxiety, Ms. Goldstein laughed it off.

She was good at calming others' fears, too. On the morning of the attack, Ms. Goldstein, 25, commuted from her sister's home in Bay Terrace on Staten Island, taking the No. 3 bus to her job at Cantor Fitzgerald on the 101st floor of 1 World Trade Center.

"We watched a scary movie together Monday night," Mrs. Triggs said, "and Monica asked me, 'Are you scared?' I said, 'A little.' And she said, 'I'll stay with you tonight.'"

Her sister still does not know whether Ms. Goldstein ever made it into those cranky elevators on that fateful morning.

STEVEN GOLDSTEIN
Who Wants a Horsey Ride?

The portrait that emerged of Steven Goldstein at his memorial service was that of the kind of guy who would give "horsey rides" to any neighborhood kid who showed up on his lawn, the kind of man who would even listen to long-winded telemarketers' speeches so as not to be rude.

He had season tickets to the Knicks, but would rarely go to the games. "He'd say, 'I just want to be with you guys,' " said his wife, Jill. The couple had a baby boy and a daughter, 3. "People would think we were crazy because we never had a baby-sitter. He would say, 'Why do we need to go out?' "

Mr. Goldstein, 35, had been working at Cantor Fitzgerald for only two weeks. Prior to that, he spent his working days in his basement office at home in Princeton, where he had developed an Internet company that Cantor recently purchased.

ANDREW H. GOLKIN
An Evening Remembered

Knowing that Andrew H. Golkin had so many friends, his family planned a memorial service in the spacious second-floor ballroom of the Harmonie Club in Manhattan, which seats 400. Then more than 750 friends, schoolmates and co-workers showed up, overflowing the room and spilling so far down the staircase that loudspeakers were set up so they could hear the service.

"He had a special heart, and was a good listener, which made him very good at his job," said his mother, Janet, of her son's work as a vice president at Cantor Fitzgerald on the 105th floor of the World Trade Center. Only the Sunday night before the disaster, she and her husband, Gerald, and their daughter, Susan, had dinner with Andrew at their favorite neighborhood Italian restaurant, Parma, on the Upper East Side.

"It's some comfort to have had this lovely, joyous evening," his mother recalled. "He was planning his 31st birthday, Nov. 3. He was planning a large party, and he was planning on having a good time."

ENRIQUE GOMEZ and JOSE GOMEZ
Two of a Kind

In life and in tragedy, Enrique and Jose Gomez were brothers determined to share every moment together. They worked together, slicing vegetables and cleaning seafood, in the kitchen of Windows on the World. At times they lived together. Even when they did not, Enrique 42, and Jose 44, both fathers of teenagers, always made time to dream together, envisioning themselves one day sitting in the stands at Yankee Stadium, just like the people on television, sharing beers and rooting for the boys in pinstripes.

For the Gomez family, there is peace in knowing that the brothers disappeared as they lived. "So many people down there, they had no one," said Maglais Gomez, a niece. "At least Enrique and Jose, they had each other to comfort."

And there is also this: On Sept. 11, Miguel and Ramone Gomez, who also worked in the kitchen with their older brothers, Enrique and Jose, had been scheduled to work, but were not there when the planes hit.

MANUEL GOMEZ Jr.
Loving Adventure

Manuel Gomez Jr. could hardly pass up an adventure. A vice president at Fuji Bank, Mr. Gomez, 42, spent his off hours scuba diving, mountain climbing, motorcycling, golfing and piloting his own Cherokee Piper.

His wife, Lori, said that on one of their first dates, Mr. Gomez took her on an aerial tour of Puerto Rico, where she was living. Mr. Gomez hired a pilot to take them out in a small plane, and it was then that he decided to take flying lessons. They would have celebrated their 10th wedding anniversary in November.

"He had such beautiful, warm eyes," Mrs. Gomez said through sobs from her home in Brooklyn.

On Sept. 11, Mr. Gomez called his wife from the 80th floor of 2 World Trade Center, where he worked, and told her about the attack, and how he was helping to evacuate people. When she saw the attack on television, she called him to tell him to get out immediately. He told her he would.

A year ago, he flew his mother, Gladys Alma, to Virginia in his plane. "I saw him so confident, so intelligent," Ms. Alma said. "I was so proud of him. I gave him a kiss."

WILDER ALFREDO GOMEZ
Feet in Two Countries

Wilder Alfredo Gomez's family was split between New York City and Colombia, and after the first plane hit the World Trade Center, one of his brothers in South America reached him by telephone. On any other day, Mr. Gomez would have told his brother not to worry, that his shift as a waiter, sometimes bartender, at Windows on the World did not start until afternoon. But on Sept. 11 he had been filling in for a co-worker since early morning.

"He told his brother he was trapped on the 103rd floor and that there was a lot of smoke," said Rosario Piedrahita, an aunt in New York.

Mr. Gomez, 38, had come to the city 10 years ago and lived in Brooklyn with his mother and his 7-year-old daughter, Stephanie. "He was a hard worker, a good father," his aunt said. "He loved to dance and play soccer."

But while he planned to become a United States citizen in January, he kept one foot firmly planted in his native country. His ties to Colombia included his father, three brothers and one son and two daughters whom he financially supported, Ms. Piedrahita said. And on a trip this year to Cali, his hometown, she said, he had also reunited with a childhood girlfriend whom he had decided to marry next year.

JENINE GONZALEZ
Entrepreneurial Dreams

At 28, Jenine Gonzalez already knew that life could be short. In February, her mother died of pneumonia after a long bout with cancer. Then, in late August, the singer and actress Aaliyah, 22, died in a plane crash. Ms. Gonzalez, who loved music and dancing, looked up to Aaliyah as a role model, even styling her hair—long, black and wavy—the way the singer did.

When her mother died, Ms. Gonzalez decided to start taking steps to build her own business. She wanted to be an events coordinator, the kind of person who organizes concerts for Latin and hip-hop bands, said Orlando Diaz, who is married to a cousin of Ms. Gonzalez and knew her for 10 years.

"She always had a smile on her face," Mr. Diaz, 28, said. "From the moment she set her eyes on you, she made you feel special."

During the day, Ms. Gonzalez worked as an executive assistance for Aon Insurance, but the rest of the time, she was busy planning her business.

"She would bring home stacks of books from Barnes & Noble," Mr. Diaz said. "She also started to attend business seminars and she made it a point to introduce herself to every band manager and party planner she met. She was on her way."

MAURICIO GONZALEZ
A Fan Named Moejiggy

Mauricio Gonzalez had such skill on the basketball court that he earned the name Moejiggy from other players, from Greenwich Village to Harlem to his native Washington Heights, said his wife, Evan van Dommelen-Gonzalez. "Basketball was his passion," Ms. van Dommelen-Gonzalez said. "He played on every city court and everybody knew him."

A New Yorker through and through, Mr. Gonzalez was a Knicks fan. "He was almost in tears when Patrick Ewing was traded. He was looking forward to this season to see what was going to happen with Michael Jordan's comeback. I watched opening night without him and cried," his wife said.

He was priming his 15-month-old daughter, Nina, to play for the Women's National Basketball Association, Ms. van Dommelen-Gonzalez said. "She has all the right moves."

Mr. Gonzalez was a carpenter. He was installing furniture at Aon, in 2 World Trade Center, on Sept. 11.

ROSA JULIA GONZALEZ
"Take Care of My Daughter"

After the attack, when Rosa Julia Gonzalez telephoned her sister Migdalia from the offices of the Port Authority of New York and New Jersey on the 66th floor of 2 World Trade Center, these were her last words: "I love you," she said. And then: "Promise to me that you are going to take care of my daughter."

That is because to Rosa Gonzalez, 32, a single mother who worked as a secretary, her 12-year-old Jennifer was everything. Certainly, Migdalia tried to reassure Rosa. But she was never sure her words had registered. The call was cut off. Only a little while later—10, maybe 15 minutes—the building collapsed.

"Of course, Migdalia will take care of Jennifer," said Rosa's older sister Maria. "We will all take care of Jennifer." The "we" refers to the six Gonzalez sisters who are not missing. Every day they and the rest of the family have been gathering in Jersey City, where Rosa lived. "The situation is," Maria said, "we have to be strong for Jennifer."

LYNN CATHERINE GOODCHILD
and SHAWN M. NASSANEY
Inseparable Travelers

It was supposed to have been a quick getaway for Lynn Catherine Goodchild and Shawn M. Nassaney, a four-day trip to Maui, Hawaii, before they hunkered down to study for their M.B.A. degrees at Providence College.

So they woke early on Sept. 11 to board United Airlines Flight 175, which was to take them to Los Angeles, where they would take a connecting flight to Maui, said Ellen Goodchild, Ms. Good child's mother. They had almost decided against the trip, considering a vacation in Sydney, Australia. But they decided to visit a place where neither had traveled before. (The couple had lived in Sydney briefly after Mr. Nassaney was transferred there last year by his job.)

Now, both families wonder what would have happened if

the couple had gone to Sydney instead of Maui. But they find serenity in the fact that the two were together. The couple had been almost inseparable since they met at Bryant College in Smithfield, R.I., more than four years ago, traveling frequently.

For Mr. Nassaney's 25th birthday in July, Ms. Goodchild took him to Disney World in Florida for four days. They spent four days in London for Valentine's Day. And in January, they went to Palm Beach Gardens, Fla., where Ms. Goodchild attended a birthday party for one of her college roommates.

Ms. Goodchild, 25, worked at Putnam Investments as a 401(k) plan administrator. Mr. Nassaney worked in the sales department at American Power Conversion.

Ms. Goodchild and Mr. Nassaney had a lot in common. Both were athletic and came from close-knit families. Ms. Goodchild practiced karate, while Mr. Nassaney was a runner. Ms. Goodchild lived with her brother, Neil Goodchild, 27, in Attleboro, Mass. Mr. Nassaney lived in his grandmother's three-story apartment building in Pawtucket, R.I., along with his two brothers.

"Just because Shawn is not there, it will still be his apartment," said his grandmother, Barbara Shaw. "It will be a little sanctuary for me."

CALVIN GOODING
Finding Love with a Haircut

Whenever Calvin Gooding went to the barbershop, he would stare wistfully at the photo of the Broadway and television actress LaChanze (*Ragtime, Once on This Island*) hanging on the wall. He pleaded for an introduction, but the barber always refused. Then one night, Mr. Gooding spied LaChanze, who did not use her last name, Sapp, professionally, in a Manhattan nightclub. He managed to introduce himself, and was instantly smitten. Two years later, they were married. At the wedding in August 1998, the barber took credit for the match. But it was Mr. Gooding, 38, a financial trader, who did all the work.

"I was hoping maybe this would be the one," said his mother-in-law, Rose Sapp-Hines, about the first time her daughter brought her beau home. "They were a perfect match. They just seemed right for each other." The Goodings had one daughter, Celia Rose, and Mrs. Sapp-Gooding is expecting another child in October 2001.

PETER MORGAN GOODRICH
A Selfless Boss

Peter Morgan Goodrich was a burly, 6-foot-1, all-American shot-putter who also threw the hammer and discus during the late 1980s at Bates College. He was an avid Boston Red Sox fan.

Mr. Goodrich, who overcame dyslexia to achieve a double major in math and physics, was also drawn to cerebral pursuits like chess and studies of the behavior of ants and dragonflies. The child who delighted in feeding wolf spiders grew into a man who welcomed them into his Cambridge, Mass., home, according to Rachel Carr Goodrich, the college sweetheart he married in 1992.

"He was nice to everybody and everything," said Mrs. Goodrich, confessing she could have done without the eight-legged housemates.

Mr. Goodrich, 33, a passenger on United Airlines Flight 175, was also a protective boss. A manager of software product development at struggling Upspring Software, he was told to cut $200,000 from his budget last winter. He eliminated his own job rather than break up his programming team. His selflessness was rewarded: when MKS, another software firm, acquired Upspring, the company rehired him.

HARRY GOODY III
Mountain Bikes and Sci-Fi

Rain or shine, Saturdays were always the same for Harry Goody III. He would wake up early, break out a can of wax for his silver and chrome mountain bike, then take his favorite ride, through the streets of Coney Island all the way to Prospect Park.

For Mr. Goody, 50, few things were sweeter, except perhaps sitting in front of the television watching the Sci-Fi Channel for hours at a time, his way of shedding the stress that came with working in the state's tax and finance office on the 86th floor of 2 World Trade Center. The addiction was one so intense that Mr. Goody's three children nicknamed him Sci-Fi Man and told jokes about his penchant for buying science-fiction–themed gadgets—the pen he loved because he could use it standing upside down just like the astronauts, or the Superman ring he wore nearly every day.

"If love could bring him back," said Mr. Goody's daughter, Alexis, 24, "then just from the way we felt and from what his friends, neighbors, workmates, have told us, then my daddy would be right here watching *Star Trek* and shining his bike."

LISA FENN GORDENSTEIN
A Kiss Before She Left

Lisa Fenn Gordenstein had a way of doing things to make the people in her life feel special, whether it was branding them with silly nicknames or slipping motivational notes under an office door.

She called her husband, David Gordenstein, Chez. (No relation to the French word for house, he said.) She also called him "Jessica."

"Go figure," Mr. Gordenstein said of his nicknames. She

called her sister, Debby Fenn, "Garmy," he said. "I often wondered why this phenomenon took place," Mr. Gordenstein said. "It came to me the other day that this was the way Lisa made everyone feel a little extra special. She had a great sense of people."

Mrs. Gordenstein, 41, had worked in the clothing industry for years, most recently as an assistant vice president of the TJX Companies. She was traveling on business on American Airlines Flight 11 on the day of the attacks. But before she left her home in Needham, Mass., at 5 A.M., she insisted on waking her two daughters, Samantha, 7, and Carly, 3½, and kissing them good-bye. "Thank God she did," her husband said.

The night before, Mr. Gordenstein found a note that his wife had slipped under his office door. It was a poem about maintaining a positive attitude no matter what happens in life.

THOMAS E. GORMAN
Final Celebrations

Some people like to imagine how they would spend their days if they learned that they had only one week to live. Thomas E. Gorman seems to have spent his last seven days as if he had some inkling of what was to come.

The week began on Sept. 4, which happened to be the day that Officer Gorman's eldest daughter, Laura, turned 15. Before he left for his job as a police officer with the Port Authority's emergency services unit in Jersey City, he left Laura a "Happy Birthday" note on the kitchen table of their home in Middlesex, N.J. He cooked dinner that night and passed around slices of cake to his wife, Barbara, and their three children.

The family of Firefighter James Raymond Coyle after a memorial Mass on October 24 in Brooklyn.

(*Kevin P. Coughlin*)

Two days later, Officer Gorman, 41, invited his friends to a golf outing to raise money for the Middlesex Little League. Fathers of Little League players showed up, as did some of his co-workers. That same week also found him celebrating his wife's birthday, the two of them riding in his motorboat up Barnegat Bay. They stopped at a lighthouse and collected seashells and driftwood. Their getaway ended with dinner at a seashore restaurant as darkness settled.

Days later, Mrs. Gorman watched from her car on her way to work as an airplane crashed into 1 World Trade Center. Miles away, her husband climbed into a rescue truck. It was the end of a very full week.

MICHAEL E. GOULD
Family and a Fast Ride

Michael E. Gould loved little children, guitars, beautiful women, fast cars and Mountain Dew. He had them all, almost.

"You opened his refrigerator, and there would always be Mountain Dew and leftover pizza," said Jeff Anderson, his stepfather of 21 years. Mr. Gould, 5-foot-11 and 260 pounds of muscle—he was an avid bodybuilder—traded equities for the San Francisco branch of Cantor Fitzgerald until June 2001, when he was transferred to New York. On the West Coast, he roamed highways with his girlfriend, Vanessa Mills, in his silver BMW M5, which was fast "like a rocket ship," Mr. Anderson said.

In his solitary moments, Mr. Gould played guitar; Les Paul was his hero. He had no children of his own, but he was waiting to produce some. In the meantime, he snuggled with the kids of Ms. Mills's friends.

"But despite his strong, macho appearance, he called me every day," said Kathie Anderson, Mr. Gould's mother. "We just had a special connection. He confided in me everything, sometimes even more than I want to know."

JON GRABOWSKI
Love, Philosophy and Plato

It was a love story that began at a bagel shop in Maryland, over a conversation about Plato. Jon Grabowski, a student at the University of Maryland, managed to make sense of philosophy for the woman he later married, Erika Lutzner, a classmate and co-worker at the bagel store, when her professors could not.

He was enigmatic, devilish, selfless, "too smart for his own good"—as she wrote in his eulogy—and he could always make sense of the world, of himself, of her, she said. His friends and colleagues said that, too, in interviews and memorial e-mails filled with recollections of his wry wit, helpfulness and deep love for his wife, a chef.

Mr. Grabowski, 33, was vice president for technology

information at Marsh & McLennan, a job in the World Trade Center that he had begun only a week before the Sept. 11 terrorist attack.

Mr. Grabowski and Ms. Lutzner were together for 12 years. He won her over during their second week of dating, when he brought her Tylenol and orange juice after she came down with the flu.

"I felt like we were one soul," she said. "Plato wrote about searching for your other half. Jon was my other half."

EDWIN J. GRAF III
His Last Mountain

When he was hugging the side of a mountain was when he felt most capable and in control. Transport Edwin J. Graf III to the Grand Tetons or Yosemite, and he was instantly at peace.

"It was the most therapeutic thing he could imagine," said Bill Eydt, a longtime friend and his frequent climbing partner.

In his work life, noise and commotion would build up, and his answer was to climb. In February 2001, on the coldest weekend of the winter, he felt the need and traveled to the Green Mountains in Vermont and camped out for two nights. He came back renewed.

Mr. Graf, 48, had been a skilled mountain climber since college, and perhaps it was apt that he also worked high up, as a vice president at Cantor Fitzgerald on the 104th floor of the World Trade Center.

Naturally, friends worried about him hanging from pitons, but not sitting at the office. "We always feared something would happen on a mountain," said Polly Perkins, a friend since high school. "He did fall off a mountain. It just happened to be a mountain in New York City. That's not what we expected."

Mr. Graf was divorced and lived in Rowayton, Conn. He had three children, Kristin, 15, Tyler, 14, and Wesley, 12. Not long ago, he took the two boys to a Go Vertical gym so they, too, could scale a mountain. Now when Tyler sees the face of a mountain, he calls out to his dad, because he knows that's where his dad's spirit is.

DAVID M. GRAIFMAN
Dozens of Watches

David M. Graifman had a sense of humor and a passion for watches. He owned dozens. Not your basic expensive watches; a Rolex would be too ordinary.

"He liked ones that didn't have hands, or with unusual mechanisms," said his brother, Gary Graifman.

An equity analyst at the investment firm of Keefe,

Bruyette & Woods on the 89th floor of 2 World Trade Center, David Graifman, 40, often contributed his thoughts to a watch lovers' Web site called Timezone.com. Early in September he wrote about the trip he and his wife of one year, Christine Huhn, had just taken to Alaska, including a photograph of the bear they encountered at close range.

CHRISTOPHER STEWART GRAY
His Big Moment Came to Be

Just for a moment, Christopher Stewart Gray lived his greatest dream. He became a professional football player—a strong-armed quarterback no less—for the Miami Dolphins, the team he rooted and raved for while growing up in New Jersey. His big moment came in 1992, when the team offered him, a former University of West Virginia quarterback, a free agent contract.

The moment lasted only a month, but Mr. Gray, 32, took the lessons he learned all the way to Wall Street, where he became a foreign exchange broker for Cantor Fitzgerald. Work hard, he believed, and anything is possible.

"Chris was a goal setter," said his father, Jim Gray, recalling how his son declared that he would one day play for the Dolphins while watching them in the Orange Bowl when he was six. "He wanted a shot and he got it. When it was over, he wanted to have a good job and he got it. And he even found a beautiful young woman to be his wife."

Mr. Gray and his fiancée were to be married in May 2002. His father says he grows weak just thinking of the family his son might have had. But he manages to fight back the tears, remembering all the goals his son did reach. "He truly lived his life. We were lucky we had him for 32 years."

LINDA MAIR GRAYLING
One Hot Summer

The Hotfoot Marathon, as everyone called it, began with a Bugs Bunny cartoon, during one of those endless summers at Linda Mair Grayling's grandmother's house on 139th Street in the Bronx. The idea was to emulate Bugs himself when he put a match between the toes of the snoozing Elmer Fudd: lighting it always produced a startling amount of jumping up and down.

"I don't know how it started, but it got so bad we were all afraid to go to sleep," said Aaron Mair, Ms. Grayling's first cousin. He remembers that he was maybe 9 and Linda was maybe 12, and that her brother and his brothers were all culprits. "Nobody really won, but nobody burned the house down, either," he said with a laugh.

The very large Mair family—which counts many police

and correction officers as members—tried to keep alive such golden memories as they searched hospitals and ground zero itself for the 44-year-old Ms. Grayling after the terrorist attacks. A single parent, she was so proud of the new job she had just gotten as a receptionist at Marsh & McLennan on the 100th floor of 1 World Trade Center. She so adored the view.

Now her 7-year-old daughter, Isa, is living with Ms. Grayling's sister Yvonne, who takes Isa to Our Lady of Refuge Roman Catholic Church. "That's near the Grand Concourse," Mr. Mair said, "and it's the very same church that her mother went to."

JOHN GRAZIOSO and TIMOTHY GRAZIOSO
Two Brothers, Always Close

Timothy Grazioso, right, the older brother, was considered the sensitive one; John Grazioso hid his sensitivity under a caustic wit. Born 18 months apart, they remained close, playing football together for the Clifton (New Jersey) Junior Mustangs and the Clifton High School varsity and, later, working for Cantor Fitzgerald.

And they were protective of their little sister.

"Johnny taught me how to fight to protect myself," said Carolee Azzarello, two years John's junior. She recalled when a neighborhood tough bloodied her nose with a snowball. "They both went running," she said. "I don't know if they found the kid, but they wanted to beat him up."

Timothy Grazioso, 42, a math whiz, went to work for Cantor Fitzgerald, rising to chief operating officer for over-the-counter trading; John Grazioso, 41, a supervisor for U.S. Air, was encouraged by Timothy to join the company and eventually became a salesman for eSpeed.

Timothy Grazioso moved his wife, Deborah, and twin daughters, Lauren and Briana, now 12, to Florida; he thought the climate would help Lauren, who has diabetes. During the week, he lived alone in a Brooklyn apartment where he kept a complete set of his children's schoolbooks to do homework with them over the phone. Each weekend, he flew to Florida.

"When he came down here he was a hundred percent with us," Deborah said. "He'd put the kids to bed, he made breakfast for them—French toast and omelets were his thing. We went out as family on Saturdays and Sundays. We loved the beach."

John Grazioso's specialty was silver dollar pancakes in their Middletown, N.J., home for daughters Kathryn, 7, Kristen, 4, and Michael, 11 months, the first boy born in the Grazioso family in 41 years. "He always seemed to squeeze in his golf game no matter where he went, but he always made time for his family," said his wife, Tina.

At a christening recently, he told a relative, "I've got it all. I've got a beautiful wife, two beautiful daughters and I've got a son. What else is there?"

WADE B. GREEN
From Rascal to Gentle Giant

As a boy, Wade B. Green was a mischievous rascal until his sister, Alicia, was born. "One night he stayed up with me when I was feeding the baby and he said, 'Mommy, did you have to do that with me, too?' " said his mother, Wilhelmina. "When Wade realized how much care an infant required, he decided he would be my helper."

A kindness marked his remaining years. His was known as the gentle giant.

Mr. Green, 42, did not work in the trade center regularly. But he was there on Sept. 11, as a Thomason Financial employee, setting up computers for a conference at Windows on the World, said his wife, Roxanne. He was handsome, clean-cut and not afraid of hard work, she said. In a storm last winter, he shoveled snow from the driveway of a pregnant neighbor in Westbury, N.Y.

"He was very well liked," his wife said. "He had a smile that was to die for."

ELAINE MYRA GREENBERG
The "Cool Aunt"

Elaine Myra Greenberg loved sending people postcards.

"She would call you up to tell you she had sent you one," said her sister, Karen Rappleye. "Then she would call you up when you got it. She wanted to see if you were enjoying it."

The cards were often funny, her sister said. "She sent my husband a birthday card that said, 'Don't worry about getting older, I'll come over and dust you.' "

Ms. Greenberg, 56, was known as the "cool aunt" in her family. And why not? How many aunts teach their nieces and nephews to drink and gamble? Her sister did not mind. "She was doing it so she could keep an eye on them," she said.

While she enjoyed some vices, Ms. Greenberg also loved New York City's cultural offerings. She had season tickets to the Metropolitan Opera, often went to the theater and spent many hours at her favorite museum, the American Museum of Natural History.

A financial services consultant for Compaq, she was attending a technology conference on the 106th floor of 1 World Trade Center on Sept. 11 when it was attacked.

Mrs. Rappleye remembers one card in particular that her sister sent. One day, Ms. Greenberg played hooky from work and went to Atlantic City with her roommate, Susan Price. She sent her sister a card. It read: "Having a wonderful day. Ferris Bueller."

GAYLE GREENE
Two Trips a Year

In 2001, for the first time, the Christmas lights outside Gayle Greene's town house in Montville, N.J., were red, white and blue. Inside, however, nothing had changed: the holly arrangements were scattered about, as were Ms. Greene's cherished antique ornaments and the holiday-themed carousel horses that she collected.

"Every nook and cranny of everywhere she ever lived was covered with Christmas stuff," said Eileen Carey, Ms. Greene's best friend and roommate. "So this year, in her honor, every decoration she ever had is going up."

Ms. Greene, 51, worked as a vice president at Marsh & McLennan, commuting two hours each way to the World Trade Center and hauling out her laptop many nights to finish projects as she watched *Eco-Challenge* and other adventure shows on television.

But to satisfy her lifelong wanderlust, Ms. Greene always made time for two trips a year. She adored Alaska, Las Vegas, the Outer Banks of North Carolina and especially Hawaii.

The finest day of her life, she often said, was spent on a catamaran off the emerald-hued Na Pali coast of Kauai. In her will, she asked that her ashes be scattered there.

JAMES GREENLEAF
Devoted to History

James Greenleaf might have been expected to be a little impressed with himself. He was strikingly handsome, a former high school football star who had recently run a marathon in under three and a half hours, and who made a very nice living as a foreign exchange trader at Carr Futures.

But Mr. Greenleaf, 32, was not only a golden boy. He was a nice, considerate guy, the social glue that held his high school friends from Connecticut together, the type who thought nothing of spending a week's vacation helping an old friend build his new house.

"He was everybody's idol," said David McBride, the friend in question. "He was brilliant but he wouldn't rub it in your face, and he could get along with people from all levels."

Over the summer, when Mr. Greenleaf, a history buff, decided to learn more about the conflict in the Middle East, he sought out a book written by an Israeli and a Palestinian.

"He always wanted to see both sides," said his girlfriend, Lisa LaGalia.

ELIZABETH GREGG
History Before Finance

Elizabeth Gregg was not in her brownstone in Cobble Hill, Brooklyn, when a neighbor walked by on the morning of Sept. 11.

"We had talked the day before about voting," said Joseph Igneri, who had lived near her for more than 20 years. She was always punctual, so he figured she had already left to vote, or was at work on the 93rd floor of 1 World Trade Center, where she was an analyst for Fred Alger Management. "Then I went around the corner," Mr. Igneri said, "and disaster happened."

Mrs. Gregg, 52, who was known to her friends as Lisa, had no family in the area, so Mr. Igneri took it upon himself to search for his neighbor. "Somebody had to show for her," he said. He searched the hospitals and rescue sites, pasted up flyers and tracked down her dentist for records.

Mrs. Gregg had worked at Alger for 18 years, but finance was not her first career choice. Before she moved to New York in the late 1970s and earned an M.B.A. from New York University, she eagerly studied history, receiving a doctorate in medieval studies from Yale. Her specialty was defense spending in 15th-century France.

DONALD H. GREGORY
A Family Man's Gifts

Amanda Gregory had her father's sense of commitment. Her sister, Sara, had his creativity. And their brother, James, had his love of sports.

Donald H. Gregory, 62, gave many gifts to his children, one of which was loving their mother. He kissed her at the start and end of each day. "He was just a man of quiet faith," said his wife, Maureen. "He had a generosity of spirit that extended to all in our family. Most importantly, he taught to believe in yourself."

He believed in Amanda, 20, who wants to work for NASA; Sara, 19, who loves art; and James, 14, who plays soccer, basketball and baseball with a passion.

Since the trade center fell with him in the 104th-floor office of Cantor Fitzgerald, in the north tower, people have sent notes to Mr. Gregory's family in Ramsey, N.J.

"Because I was not with him during the day, I didn't know the extent to which he raved about the children," his wife said. "That is the essence of a family man to me."

FLORENCE M. GREGORY
The Stylings of Disco Flo

Seated in what she thought was too formal a restaurant last winter at Christmas, Florence M. Gregory announced to companions that she was going outside to ask the Salvation Army band on the corner if they knew a certain song. Moments later, the band arrived at the restaurant, took the table next to hers, and played songs for everyone.

"That was my sister," Maureen Petronis said. "She could break the ice anywhere."

Miss Gregory, who was known as Disco Flo because of her taste in music, loved people. "She was always smiling and laughing and joking," Mrs. Petronis said. "People were drawn to her."

When she was not working at Aon, where she was a specialist in marine insurance, Miss Gregory, 38, could be found golfing, fishing, cooking, traveling and spending time with her two nieces and three nephews. A longtime resident of Breezy Point in Queens, she was one of three children of Florence and John Gregory.

She was an excellent cook and took particular pleasure in preparing meals for family and friends. Her favorite holiday was St. Patrick's Day, when she would pull out all the stops with corned beef and cabbage.

"She was a fabulous aunt," Mrs. Petronis said.

JOHN GRIFFIN
Springing into Action

As an engineer and director for operations for Silverstein Properties, the company that leased the World Trade Center in July, John Griffin first thought something big—maybe a transformer—had blown up. He threw a fire extinguisher through the glass wall of his 88th-floor offices in 2 World Trade Center, looked up at the havoc on the floors above, and knew that it had been a plane. Survivors said he quickly handed out wet towels.

"He was at the back of about 30 people they were evacuating," his wife, June Griffin, related from the accounts of survivors. "He had been in fires before—he should have gotten out."

Before that day, Mr. Griffin, 38, focused on other pas-

Firefighters from New York and other states attend a memorial service on October 25 for Captain William F. Burke Jr. at St. Patrick's Cathedral. He was with Engine Company 21 and was one of twenty-one fire captains who died in the trade center collapse. (Ting-Li Wang)

sions—the Rangers, the Yankees and the Giants; doing school projects back in Waldwick, N.J., with his children, Jenna, 11, and Julie, 9.

Mrs. Griffin speculated that her husband, instead of running for the exits, headed for the fire control center, where his training as a fire safety officer would have directed him. "He was an engineer," Mrs. Griffin said. "He must have thought, 'Buildings don't just fall down.' "

TAWANNA GRIFFIN
Family Meant Everything

Tawanna and Bobby Griffin met in the kitchen of a Wendy's restaurant in East New York, Brooklyn, where they had after-school jobs in high school. Romance blossomed over the deep fryers, and their life together began soon after.

Theirs was a tight bond, said Mr. Griffin's sister Juanita Inniss, who saw it in the little things the Griffins did together, like the daily ritual of Mrs. Griffin's predawn trip to work. She had to be at Cantor Fitzgerald, where she worked as a cashier in the company cafeteria, by 6 A.M., so at 5 A.M., without fail, Mr. Griffin, a plainclothes security guard who worked evenings, got up and drove his wife the eight blocks to her subway stop.

When she got home, Mrs. Griffin, who was 30, doted on their 5-year-old son, Bobby Jr., and when the weekend came, home was the only place she really wanted to be.

JOAN D. GRIFFITH
"Joan on the Job"

Joan D. Griffith had two identities. As an office manager at Fiduciary Trust, she was known as Joan. But with her family and friends in Willingboro, N.J.—where her pasta improvisations attracted a fan club—she went by her middle name, Donna. Her husband, Peter, is not positive why, but he has a theory: "She was Joan on the job, I guess, because it sounded more official."

She was the mother of their 16-year-old daughter and a mother to his 24-year-old daughter, raising both girls as her own. "That we were madly in love for 20 years is a tribute to her," he said.

Her weekly routine rarely varied: Saturdays she went to the library and loaded up her book bag with romance novels to read, two per day, on her 90-minute commute to and from work. Reading was one escape from the stresses of Wall Street. She also had a rule that the home front was to be computer-free. They met in 1980 at Merrill Lynch, married in 1981 and moved out of Brooklyn in 1992 so that their children could experience an environment dominated by cornfields rather than concrete.

WARREN GRIFKA
Took Care of Mother

Nine years ago, the health of Warren Grifka's elderly mother began to deteriorate. Mr. Grifka, a Marsh & McLennan computer specialist who lived with her in Brooklyn, took on her care. "He'd be up all night with her," said Bonnie Montellaro, his older sister. "Then he'd go to work in the morning."

He quit taking vacations or going out with friends. Mrs. Montellaro said she and Henry, their younger brother, wanted to help or hire round-the-clock help. But Mr. Grifka, 54, would not hear of it, she said. "His feeling was that this was his job and that was it," she said.

Last year, Frances Grifka, who had been bedridden and largely unable to communicate for three years, died at 86.

"He was just starting to live again after my mother died," Mrs. Montellaro said. "He was back seeing his friends and going to movies." He went to Florida to see friends and relatives—his first vacation in a decade. An accomplished baker, he spent a Saturday showing a Brooklyn chef how to make his famous cheesecake.

"He was out, which was so nice," Mrs. Montellaro said. "Out to dinner at night, out on the weekends. He had just got his life back."

JOSEPH GRILLO
Six Feet of Loyalty

He called himself Jumping Joe. He was 6 feet even, but bite your tongue if you think that is short for a basketball player. How tall do you think Allen Iverson is?

Joseph Grillo, as his wife, Mary Jo, put it, "was a maniac basketball player." He played three times a week, with friends from Brooklyn on Friday and with a group on Staten Island, where he lived, on Wednesday and Saturday. He played hard. He played exceptionally well. He would not stop, even as the game gnawed at his 46-year-old body. "It took his knees, his ankles, his wrists," his wife said. "But he loved it so much."

Mrs. Grillo supported his commitment, though she established certain fouls of her own. He wanted to play on their wedding day. Forget that. The Saturday game took place in the morning, and the men liked to return home and collapse on the couch.

"A lot of them slept all day," Mrs. Grillo said. She made it clear that he had to do things with her and the two boys. So he would have a hearty lunch and keep his eyes open.

Another thing about Mr. Grillo, a risk finance analyst for the Port Authority, was that he was intensely loyal to a wide network of friends. He was great at listening to their problems. "He was aware of whose wife had breast cancer, whose kid was giving his parents a hard time," Mrs. Grillo said. "I heard from so many people, 'Oh, I had just talked to Joe the week before,' 'I just talked to Joe the day before.' I started to wonder, 'Did he ever do any work?' "

FRANCIS E. GROGAN
Taking the Charitable View

He served as a sonar expert on a Navy destroyer during World War II. But the Rev. Francis E. Grogan spent the rest of his days sowing peace as a chaplain, a teacher and a parish priest.

He was not the kind of priest who lived to unravel theological contradictions or who sought power on a higher plane. He disliked confrontation and tried to take the charitable view, said the Rev. J. Robert Rioux, who met him when both were studying for the priesthood in North Easton, Mass., and remained his friend for the next 50 years.

"His approach to life was, 'Don't sweat the small stuff,' " he said. "You could witness this tendency in his clothes." More than once, he showed up for chapel in his bedroom slippers.

Father Grogan, 76, was most recently the head of the Holy Cross Residence in North Dartmouth, Mass. On Sept. 11, he was aboard United Airlines Flight 175, planning to visit his sister in California, when the hijacked plane smashed into the World Trade Center.

Father Rioux envisioned his friend ministering to others until the last moment. In the cockpit of the jet, "evil was personified," Father Rioux said, "but personified goodness entered the scene, a person who loved people, a person of great faith."

KEN G. GROUZALIS
He Was in Love

This is a love story. It begins and ends with the Port Authority, which is not known for amorous liaisons. It involves a mail deliverer, a secretary and the skyscrapers of New York.

The deliverer was named Ken G. Grouzalis. He was 18 when he began working for the authority. This was in 1963, when the authority had its headquarters at 111 Eighth Avenue. Mr. Grouzalis raced from floor to floor, dumping packages here, picking up letters there, but he lingered in the purchasing department. There sat Frances Zacharski, a secretary. Like Mr. Grouzalis, she commuted in each day from New Jersey. Like Mr. Grouzalis, she was young and single and full of dreams.

"In the beginning, he would say thank you, good morning, how are you," she said. "And then he'd start hanging around my desk a little bit longer than necessary."

Within two years they were married. Mr. Grouzalis was drafted into the Marines, served in the Vietnam War and came back to the Port Authority and a host of departments: stockroom, real estate, accounting.

He was proof that one could also fall in love with an institution. "The sun rose and set on the Port Authority," Mrs. Grouzalis said.

He moved to the World Trade Center when it was built and became a property manager there. In his wife's words, "He often referred to it as his building." It was a lot like love.

JOSEPH GRZELAK
Firefighting with Research

Around the firehouse, they called him Joe Knows.

The chief of Battalion 48 in Brooklyn, Joseph Grzelak had been fighting fires for 28 years and memorizing trivia for even longer. During slow shifts he could be found at his computer, researching everything from home repair to bowling strategies. He was a history buff who read two newspapers a day, breezed through crossword puzzles and answered all manner of arcane questions for friends and colleagues (hence the nickname).

"We encouraged him to try out for *Jeopardy!*, Chief Grzelak's wife, Joanne, said. "He'd watch it, and most of the time he was right on the money."

Chief Grzelak, 52, had a mathematical mind that benefited the men he supervised. "He was very rational about fighting fires," Mrs. Grzelak said. "When the younger guys would ask him how to approach a certain situation, he always came up with the best advice."

When he raced to the World Trade Center on Sept. 11, Chief Grzelak took a binder full of research he had compiled over the years about fighting high-rise fires. It was found, Mrs. Grzelak said, in his crushed car.

MATTHEW J. GRZYMALSKI
"They Just Fit Together"

In winter, when his father died, he brought a steady girlfriend around. It was notable for Matthew J. Grzymalski, 34 and the quintessential bachelor. Before, there had been golf with his three brothers, the triathlon in Montauk, a house in the Hamptons, the Allman Brothers and Giants games. Now there was Kaleen Pezzuti. His five nephews and two nieces delighted in sharing him with her.

"When you ask my daughter, Kelly, 'Where's Uncle Matt?' her answer is, 'In Grandpa's heaven with Kaleen,' " said Mr. Grzymalski's sister, Patti Ann Valerio. "They were a match, like a left shoe and a right shoe. They just fit together."

They were together on the 105th floor of 1 World Trade Center on Sept. 11, working on the same trading desk at Cantor Fitzgerald.

At Easter, Mr. Grzymalski had taken his father's seat at the dinner table in New Hyde Park, N.Y. He threw the kitchen towel over his left shoulder the way his father did. He cooked the kielbasa and stood at the sink afterward, just like his dad. Ms. Pezzuti was there, too, and Mr. Grzymalski's family secretly hoped for a wedding.

KALEEN PEZZUTI's portrait appears on page 391.

GEOFFREY E. GUJA
The Mayor of Gilgo Beach

Big and loud, Geoffrey E. Guja always made sure that life was fun for everyone around him. He built tiki huts for parties at the beach and took his golden retriever, Simba, with him to the bars. He even kept a yellow-feather chicken costume in the closet that he donned for special occasions, like his daughter's sweet 16 party in August. It always got laughs.

Lieutenant Guja, 47, was a New York City firefighter for 15 years, and lived with his wife, Debbie, and two daughters, Jamie and Kelly, in Lindenhurst, N.Y. He surfed every summer at Gilgo Beach, and was so popular there that he was called the mayor. At his funeral, his wife arranged for a flower replica of his chicken costume to be laid on his grave.

"There's nobody else like him," she said. "The world is going to be very quiet and boring without him."

BABITA GUMAN
The Best Catch of All

Babita Guman was the type who "doesn't back down," said her husband, Deodat Guman. When a fellow shopper at a market once told her to go back to her country, Mrs. Guman, 33, threw the question back at her. "Why don't you go back to your country?" she asked.

A native of Guyana who moved to the United States as a teenager, Mrs. Guman was a smart, aggressive and flag-waving American who also took charge at home in the Bronx, said her husband and father of her two daughters, ages 6 and 7. "Most guys would say they're the men of the house, but my wife did everything," said Mr. Guman, a bus driver for New York City Transit. "She cooked, she cleaned, she paid the bills. I just went to work and came back."

Mrs. Guman was a computer specialist at Fiduciary Trust Company International on the 97th floor of 2 World Trade Center, but she was about to take a test to become a schoolteacher, Mr. Guman said. Two weeks before the attacks, Mr. Guman took his wife and the girls fishing for the first time. Mrs. Guman, of course, caught a fish. It took Mr. Guman a little longer to catch his, but as he noted to his daughters, "I ended up catching the big one."

DOUGLAS B. GURIAN
Barefoot for Days

Douglas B. Gurian, 38, found pleasure in simple things like two-inch-thick steaks, the ocean, his two young children. He would call his friends out of the blue, put the receiver up to the stereo speaker, say, "Listen to this riff, man," and just as abruptly hang up. He went to West Point, but he was anything but straitlaced.

In the summers, when he took his family to Fire Island, Mr. Gurian would take his shoes off before they reached the shore and not put them on again for days. Each morning started with a jump into the ocean.

"He was the most quirky, fun-loving guy," said Susan Gurian, his wife of almost 10 years.

Mr. Gurian worked at Radianz, a financial services technology company. On the morning of Sept. 11, he was at Windows on the World, at a technology conference.

Mr. Gurian loved his children—Tyler, 7, and Eva, 4—most of all, his wife said. Eva is too young to understand what happened to her dad, but Tyler told his mom, "I just don't feel I'll be happy again."

PHILIP GUZA
Free-Form Vacations

The rules of life according to Phil Guza: Cats are the worst, never waste time planning and never ever leave home without your suspenders.

At 54, Mr. Guza, a client specialist for Aon, the insurance brokerage, did not seem to mind that his habits made some people laugh. He loved to live life his way, arranging vacations with his sons, Tom and Pete, where the only arrangement he would actually bother to make was buying plane tickets. The rest of the details—the hotel, the rental car—were left to chance.

"It was hilarious the way we'd get on a plane and just show up," said Mr. Guza's oldest son, Tom. "He'd get a car and we would just drive until we found a cheap motel or some interesting museum. Dad wasn't much for planning."

Except when it came to his diet, a buffet of burritos, potato chips, Ragú pasta sauce, pickled herring, canned mackerel and loads of Tabasco sauce on everything, especially crabs. The crabs he insisted on catching himself several times a month, with his sons in tow of course, during trips along the Shrewsbury River in New Jersey.

No one is sure how Mr. Guza, a native of Philadelphia, came upon crabbing as a hobby. It was just one of his many quirks, like his hello and good-bye hugs or the voice-mail message he left for his son Tom as he watched smoke gush from 1 World Trade Center.

"It's a great show up here. I can see the whole thing," the message said.

BARBARA GUZZARDO
"She Pulled Herself Up"

At the age of 4, Barbara Guzzardo was forced to work in the sugarcane fields of Cuba. At 5, her father, a plantation owner, was stripped of his property and deported from the country with his family. After landing in Brooklyn with no money and only two bags of clothes, her father, educated and once wealthy, eked out a living doing maintenance work.

Perhaps that is why Mrs. Guzzardo, 50, took such pleasure in homey routines like housework and child rearing. "She pulled herself up," said Anthony, her husband of 20 years. "She established herself. She made a home and a family."

She usually spent her vacations from Aon, where she was an insurance underwriter, at home in Glendale, Queens. She cooked lavishly and well—from empanadas to macaroni with long-simmered Italian sauces. She liked to putter in the garden, trying, without much success, to grow flowers.

"She kept them surviving," Mr. Guzzardo said. "But eventually they drooped. You have to love a fanatic."

She also preferred her own homey spiritual life over the more formal one at church. "She prayed every night before bed," Mr. Guzzardo said. "I can see her now, sitting on the edge of the bed, saying her prayers."

PETER GYULAVARY
A Tool Belt as a Symbol

"I always knew Australia would bring me something special and magical," said Jane Gyulavary. So it did in 1986, when, after traveling there nine times in less than 10 years, she met Peter Gyulavary, a strapping Australian graduate student 11 years her junior, who in an instant convinced her that soul mates do exist.

They married, had a child, Geniveve, now 13, and returned to New York. They settled into a three-story Victorian in Orange County, which Mr. Gyulavary, a 44-year-old environmental engineer for Washington Group International, insisted on painting yellow and green, the colors of Australia.

"All week he would work in an office, writing these massive reports," Mrs. Gyulavary said. "And then he would come home and put up a roof, paint the porch or sand a floor. He loved the physical part of life, getting his hands dirty. I'd have to ring a gong to get him to come in for a cocktail and dinner."

For weeks, she has hoped her husband would come home once more. Now she has resigned herself to saying good-bye to "his physical presence" by honoring him with a memorial service, where there will be no coffin, just a photo, draped with his tool belt, hard hat and a picture book of their beloved Australia.

H

GARY HAAG
Following His Lead

Gary Haag was the Pied Piper of the neighborhood. Children would flock to his house when they saw him drive home from work. He would lead the children off to games of baseball, soccer or hockey. Bicycles and scooters would be left scattered in the Haag driveway, their owners off playing with Mr. Haag and his kids.

It was never about winning, or competing to be strongest and fastest. Everyone was invited. Even Mr. Haag's 2-year-old daughter, Molly, would join in and kick the ball when she could.

He would get home to Ossining, N.Y., from his job at Marsh & McLennan at 6:30 P.M., change clothes, and rush through dinner so he could play with the children until the sun went down—or until his wife, Mary, put her foot down. His sons, Michael and Kevin, started homework right after school so they would be ready when dad came home.

Mr. Haag, 36, loved sports and adored children. Coaching united the two. He coached a peewee football team before he got married and he coached a T-ball team after he had children. He was an avid sports fan and would bring his children to Yankees and Rangers games. Sports was a glue for Mr. Haag and his children.

"It was something special they shared together," his wife said.

ANDREA HABERMAN
Planning for Two

Andrea Haberman and Allen Kolodzik were engaged in April 2001 in the gazebo at St. Norbert's College in Wisconsin, where they met freshman year. At first, she thought he was weird, Mr. Kolodzik said, but by sophomore year they were dating.

Sixteen months was not too much time to plan a wedding scheduled for September 2002. By the end of the summer, Ms. Haberman—snap-tight organized—had booked the rooms, bought the dress, planned the honeymoon, made hundreds of lists. They had bought a house in Chicago, where they moved after college, and Ms. Haberman was in the thick of decorating.

"We had it all down," said Mr. Kolodzik. "As far in advance as 25-year-olds can—marriage and family and so on and so forth."

Ms. Haberman grew up in rural Wisconsin, where her parents own a restaurant. She grew to love Chicago after taking a job there with Carr Futures, but she had never visited, or wanted to visit, New York. But when her company asked her to go there for a day of meetings, she steeled herself. She arrived late Monday night, Sept. 10. She had a 9 A.M. meeting in the north tower on Tuesday. She was there 20 minutes early.

BARBARA HABIB
A Steady Worker and Friend

Barbara Habib, 49, was a senior vice president in the aviation division of Marsh Inc. who worked in Midtown. Known for her steadiness and dedication, she had worked for the company for 30 years, and was visiting the World Trade Center for a meeting on Sept. 11.

She was planning to slow down in her work, said her husband, Raymond: "She was going to enjoy the quietness of Bay Ridge, walking along the shore. She loved to walk."

The couple had planned a weekend trip to Boston to spend time in the North End, enjoying Italian food, the kind she liked to cook. She also missed the chance to enjoy the house in Brooklyn they had recently bought and renovated—they moved in during August, but the new furniture did not arrive until the week after her death. She took care of her aging parents before they died, and was a source of strength for her two brothers.

"She put others ahead of herself," he said. "That was Barbara. That was my wife."

PHILIP HAENTZLER
Steadfast Loyalty

Philip Haentzler left for work early on Tuesday the 11th so he could take Wednesday off to help his 90-year-old mother, Madeleine, of Woodside, Queens, work out a winter lease for a Florida condo.

"He was the kind of guy who would work two extra days so he could take off one," said his companion, Patricia Thompson. "He was the most loyal person I knew."

Mr. Haentzler, 49, showed his loyalty in staying on as one of the last administrators working out the final details on dissolving the brokerage firm of Kidder Peabody after its acquisition by PaineWebber Group and then, last year, PaineWebber's sale to UBS, the Swiss banking giant. And he showed it with his plants, which cluttered his office on the 101st floor of 1 World Trade Center and his home in Staten Island. Ms. Thompson stood among them in their home on Sept. 11, watching the towers burn across the harbor.

NEZAM A. HAFIZ
Mild-Mannered Cricket Star

During the week, Nezam A. Hafiz was a mild-mannered analyst for Marsh & McLennan, the insurance giant. On the weekend, he was something else: a cricket star.

But a mild-mannered cricket star. "He was a proper gent, as we like to say, on the field and off the field," said Lesly R. Lowe, president of the Commonwealth Cricket League, of which Mr. Hafiz was captain. Mr. Hafiz, 32, was a member of the United States national team, which in 2000 actually defeated an English team on its home turf. He had also been captain of the American Cricket Society.

In Guyana, where he was born, Mr. Hafiz played on the under-19 national team, said his sister, Debbie Ally. He moved to New York about a decade ago, she said, and lived with his parents in South Ozone Park, Queens.

Mr. Hafiz was admired for his cricket skills, but "more than that, he was a very likable guy," said Atul Rai, president of the United States of America Cricket Association. "People liked him for his manners. In cricket, those things are also important."

KAREN ELIZABETH HAGERTY
"She Was Really Tough"

Karen Elizabeth Hagerty threw a birthday party recently for her horse, Ricardo. A caterer brought a carrot cake in the shape of a horseshoe. There were 40 non-equine guests, and goody bags for every horse in the barn.

"My sister loved her animals more than life," Deborah Anne Hagerty said yesterday. "She called them her kids."

Karen, 34, was a senior vice president for Aon Risk Services in the World Trade Center. She was loud and funny and inclined to take charge. When two of Deborah's friends called Karen to begin planning a bridal shower they were giving for Deborah, they found that Karen had already done it all.

Years ago, Deborah told Karen about a homeless shelter in the Bronx; Deborah was looking for people to buy presents for children who had written to Santa.

"Give me the whole shelter," Karen said. Her office would overflow with donated toys. "She just hounded everyone in her office," Deborah said. "She had to hire a moving truck last year because she had so much stuff. She told everybody, 'I want you to buy something and it has to be good.' She was really tough: 'Don't give me a scarf. Kids don't like scarves.' "

STEVEN M. HAGIS Jr.
Love to Fill a Doorway

When Steven M. Hagis Jr. was 2, the family pediatrician told his parents that if they doubled his height at the time—3 feet 4 inches—they could figure out how tall he would eventually be. So they braced for a giant son. As it turned out, Mr. Hagis, who was 31 and a vice president at Cantor Fitzgerald, grew to 6 feet 10 inches.

Naturally, he was drawn to basketball—and coaches were

Visitors write notes to the fallen, the rescuers and all those affected by or involved in the World Trade Center disaster. A memorial banner was placed near ground zero, at St. Paul's Chapel on Broadway between Fulton and Vesey Streets in lower Manhattan. (*Angel Franco*)

drawn to him. More than 60 colleges tried to recruit him, said his father, Steven Hagis, but he wound up at Fairfield University in Connecticut, where he and another very tall teammate were known as the "twin towers." He seriously injured his knee during his sophomore year and stopped playing, focusing on a degree in finance. He wound up as a trader.

After graduating from college, Mr. Hagis met his wife, Gloria (she is 5 feet 3 inches tall), while he was working as a bouncer at a sports bar. As she was leaving, Mr. Hagis said, "Where are you going?"—the first line in what became a three-hour conversation. She interrupted the conversation about 90 minutes through, called her mother and said, "I'm going to marry this man," recalled Mrs. Hagis.

When she got home that night she told her mother that she had forgotten what he looked like, except that he was as tall as their front doorway. "Go stand in the doorway," her mother said. So she did, and they both decided that she could live with a foot-and-a-half difference.

MARY LOU HAGUE
Not Just Any Kind of Love

Mary Lou Hague was a West Virginia girl who had come to New York three years ago and loved it. Or maybe it should be said that she loved it. Because, as her friend and onetime sorority sister Heather Fain remembers, when Ms. Hague, 26, loved something, she loved it big. She loved Michael Jackson, and spent $1,500 to see him the last weekend of her life. She loved 1980s music. She loved Twizzlers.

"She had given them up for Lent, I guess two Easters ago, and we went to church, but she had a pound bag of Twizzlers in her bag to take out as soon as we got out," Ms. Fain said. "I took one, and took a bite and threw it away. She was, 'What did you just do?' "

With her shoulder-length hair and Miss America smile, she got her share of attention. There was a little romance, on New Year's Eve 2000, with a scuba diving instructor at Club Med Martinique, but Ms. Hague, who lived near Gracie Mansion with a roommate, was thinking that she would like to meet a Southern guy, move back home to Parkersburg, W. Va., and have a dog.

She worked as a financial analyst at Keefe Bruyette & Woods, on the 89th floor of the second tower to be hit. Her entire floor, according to Ms. Hague's mother, Liza Adams, was wiped out. Better to remember Ms. Hague doing what her friends called her happy dance, waving her arms in the air and, the minute she heard the music, hollering, "Woo-hooo!"

DAVID HALDERMAN
A Shy Son, a Hero

"I love you, take care of yourself." That was how David Halderman always ended his telephone conversations with his mother.

And this year his mother, Geraldine Halderman, had come to rely more than ever on hearing those words, uttered from her serious, shy and loving son, who she said would have been "embarrassed by all the fuss that's been made over him" since he was killed on Sept. 11. He was a firefighter with Squad 18 in Manhattan, a nine-year veteran.

Firefighter Halderman's father, who was also a firefighter, died last August, six days after his son's 40th birthday. The younger firefighter spent his summer vacation accompanying his mother to the hospital, and he called her every night to check on her.

A belated birthday celebration—nothing fancy, because Firefighter Halderman did not "like to be in the forefront," his mother said—was still being planned when he perished.

At a memorial service in Brooklyn on October 27 for Lt. Paul Martini of Engine 201, his wife, Lisa Martini, is given his helmet. (*Nancy Siesel*)

MAILE RACHEL HALE
A Renaissance Woman

Well-rounded is too pale a term for Maile Rachel Hale. Her heart was in dancing—ballet and, later, modern. She was a chemistry major in college. And at 26, she was the chief operating officer and vice president of Boston Investor Services, overseeing the management of billions of dollars.

On Sept. 11, she was attending a conference at Windows on the World. As a young woman, she made peace with her shyness, said Carol Ann Hale, her mother.

"She was calm and quiet and really, really sweet," said

Kimberly Gilbert, a college roommate. "She would put together a party and do all the work," said Mrs. Hale. "And when it was going, she'd be standing by the side, watching and enjoying people."

Along with dance, her passion was the ocean, acquired while growing up in Honolulu. And chocolate—M&M's, Dove bars, desserts.

"She was the craziest chocolate person ever," said Ms. Gilbert. "But she thought, as an adult and professional, she wasn't supposed to be so excited about chocolate.

"So she was always sneaking it."

RICHARD B. HALL
Nights with Shawn

Richard B. Hall liked to tell his wife, Donna, that life was good. " 'I'm a happy guy'; that's what he used to always say to me," she said. At 49, he was a senior vice president at the Aon Corporation, enjoying work, staying in shape by shooting hoops and playing golf with such dedication that he dreamed of one day joining the senior pro tour.

But his greatest joy came from his family. His son, Shawn, 15, from a previous marriage, was "the light of his life," Mrs. Hall said. Mr. Hall would pick up his son once a week and take him home to Purchase, N.Y., for dinner and television. He called the evenings with his son his "Shawn nights," said Al Willbee, who considered Mr. Hall his best friend. "You couldn't get him to break those appointments for the life of you," Mr. Willbee said. Mr. Hall regularly took his son to see his grandparents, Ruth and Herman Hall.

Mr. Hall was devoted to his stepdaughter, Katie Holster, Mrs. Hall's daughter from her first marriage. He talked about her so much that people were surprised to learn that she was not his own daughter. As Ms. Holster progressed through high school, Mr. Hall would tell his wife not to worry about college expenses, because wherever she wanted to go, they would find the money for it. When it came to what he would do for his stepdaughter, "the sky was the limit," Mrs. Hall said.

In June, Ms. Holster was her high school's valedictorian. Mr. Hall, his wife recalled, said jokingly, "I wish I could take credit for her brains, but I can't."

VASWALD HALL
"Can't You Ever Say No?"

Vaswald Hall would leave home at 6 A.M. and put in a 12-hour day delivering packages, a job that often took him to the World Trade Center. Despite the long hours, he was the one who usually made dinner for the family, preparing oxtail, curried chicken or other dishes from his native Jamaica.

On weekends, when one of his neighbors in St. Albans, Queens, needed help hauling boxes, Mr. Hall, 50, would turn off the stove and run out the door. "My mom would say, 'Can't you ever say no'?" said his stepdaughter, Jacqulyn McNally. "We had a problem with it because it's not in our nature. He never had a problem with it."

A police officer in Jamaica, Mr. Hall came to this country 17 years ago. He had been making plans to switch jobs and had recently passed the Civil Service exam with high marks. Mr. Hall, who left behind four children in Jamaica, was particularly attached to Ryan, 6, the grandson of his wife, Beverly.

"Ryan says that Grandpa was his special friend, his best buddy in the whole world," Ms. McNally said.

ROBERT HALLIGAN
Shopping across the Pond

To a proud Englishman, America is a country of vexing insufficiencies. Its supermarkets know not of H.P. (House of Parliament) sauce and tins of steak and kidney pie. Marmite, sadly, remains a mystery.

Several times a year, London-born Robert Halligan, 59, a vice president at Aon, would cross the pond to stock up on such indelicacies. He would cheer on his beloved Tottenham Hotspurs, visit his sprawling family, including five adult children, and drop by a specialty shop to add to the locomotive steam engine models he had been collecting since his trainspotting boyhood. Every weekend he brought the old country to his wife, Jerrie, and their son, Trevor, in Basking Ridge, N.J., by cooking a lard-loving British breakfast (sloppy bacon, fried bread, eggs splashed with grease) and Sunday lunch (roast, two vegetables, potatoes, Yorkshire pudding).

Yet for someone who clung to his British identity, Mr. Halligan flourished in America, where he moved with Jerri, his American wife. He gardened here, played golf and danced beautifully. He was a kind, solicitous grandfather of 10 with a knack for joke-telling. And here he celebrated the holiday he loved even more than Christmas: as a citizen of two countries, Robert Halligan adored Thanksgiving.

VINCENT HALLORAN
Five Children, No Problem

A lot of firefighters have second jobs. Vincent Halloran had a nonpaying but extraordinarily rewarding second job in his children. He and his wife, Marie, had five of them (she is expecting a sixth on May 17, their wedding anniversary).

Around the firehouse, some of his colleagues would say, "I can hardly handle my two kids. How do you do it with five?"

He would just laugh. He did just fine with five. He had a

cool demeanor that left him unruffled if one of the kids was crying while another was running his toy truck over his foot and one of the others had to eat, and eat immediately.

Lieutenant Halloran, 43, who was with Ladder Company 8 in TriBeCa and lived with Mrs. Halloran and the children in North Salem, N.Y., took it all in stride. He ran the house, as his wife put it, like a camp. There was a wide age range—Jake, 15, Conor, 13, Aidan, 12, Kieran, 9, and Declan, 2—but he arranged activities for all of them.

They'd go fishing, boating, camping, swimming. Crowded as these activities could get, when Lieutenant Halloran took the children camping, he told each of them to invite a friend along. If that wasn't enough, during the summer, the Hallorans welcomed children from Ireland to stay with them, further swelling their ranks. "What can I say," Mrs. Halloran said. "He just loved kids."

and Christine, 8. She knew the importance of warming up the barracks, considering a firefighter's grim occupation.

"The brothers would take the fire truck and get the tree," Mrs. Hamilton said. "It was a big deal. My Christmas couldn't start until they had that party organized, and my husband was the main organizer.

"The party usually happened in the first or second week of December. So we always had our time together as a family. He made sure of that."

About 6 feet tall, with broad shoulders and a muscular build, the 43-year-old Mr. Hamilton was charming and outgoing, said his wife, whom he met at Christ the King High School in Queens their junior year. "At parties, he would work the room with his cigarette, asking everyone if they were having a good time and if he could get them anything," she said. "Everybody knew him. He was bigger than life."

JAMES DOUGLAS HALVORSON
Meticulous in Work and Play

As a managing director at Marsh & McLennan, the insurance brokerage company where he worked for 30 years, James Douglas Halvorson was meticulous in structuring complex deals for construction projects in Pakistan, Indonesia and other third world countries. He was similarly methodical in his pleasures.

When he decided to run in the New York City Marathon about 10 years ago, for example, he cut back on the good meals and wines that he loved. "He was very meticulous about keeping to his training schedule," said his son, Douglas James Halvorson. "He was totally focused on the job at hand. It was the only marathon he ever did, and he was very proud of doing it."

Douglas James Halvorson said his father, an avid Giants fan, had season tickets near the 50-yard line, and had a system for attending games, sometimes with his wife, Maureen, and often with his son. He would arrive by 11:30 A.M., park right by the Stadium Club entrance and eat lunch there at a table just to the left of the bar—usually a turkey sandwich, "lite mayo on whole wheat toast," his son said.

As for the game, much as he liked the action, Mr. Halvorson, 56, would usually leave at the end of the third quarter. "He wanted to beat the rush," his son said. "He had it all rigged."

ROBERT HAMILTON
Firehouse Tree Came First

The Christmas tree at the Squad 41 firehouse in the South Bronx always went up before the tree at Firefighter Robert Hamilton's cozy home in upstate New York. His wife, Elizabeth, never balked, even after the births of their two children, Robert Jr., 12,

CHRISTOPHER JAMES HANLEY
He Liked What He Saw

He had an eye for special objects—a street grate in Paris, a license plate in the Virgin Islands, a gondola in Venice. Christopher James Hanley's photographs always looked like postcards. He loved taking pictures around the world, but he lived in Manhattan and some of his favorites were of his city—a chandelier in Grand Central Terminal, a street sign in Greenwich Village, a fried chicken restaurant in Harlem.

Mr. Hanley, 33, was a child of the news media. Both his mother and father had long sales careers in radio, newspapers and television. They watched him grow into a young man who had an affinity for finance, good music and a penchant for responsibility. He called his parents every morning, and at the request of a friend, he had recently agreed to be the godfather of the child of a couple he had never met.

Although he worked as a sales representative at Radianz, a financial services technology company at Rockefeller Center, he attended a management conference at Windows on the World on Sept. 11.

"Had he been late, he'd be here today," said his mother, Marie Hanley. "But because he was an early bird . . ."

VALERIE JOAN HANNA
At Home on the Farm

Just 10 minutes before the first plane struck the World Trade Center, Valerie Joan Hanna called Glenn Hughes, her husband of 29 years, to remind him "to take care of the animals," he recalls. That would be Ramses the goat, Quito the llama and the flock of assorted ducks, chickens and turkeys they had been assembling on their 23-acre farm in Dryden, N.Y., near Ithaca.

The couple moved there from Brooklyn two years ago because "she couldn't take the city anymore," he said. She remembered growing up at her family's farm upstate, and, at 57, dreamed of retiring to the region. And so, Ms. Hanna had kept her job at Marsh & McLennan, where she was a senior vice president for information technology, while she looked for comparable work in Ithaca. Each weekend she returned to the farm, the animals, the vegetables and the herb garden. The phone call to look after the animals was the last her husband heard from her. The farm "isn't for the both of us anymore," Mr. Hughes said.

"I don't know what to do. Life doesn't make any sense."

THOMAS HANNAFIN
In a Brother's Footsteps

Thomas Hannafin was a high school and college basketball star on Staten Island. When he followed his eldest brother, Kevin, into the Fire Department, he joined Ladder Company 5 in Greenwich Village. The captain there, John Drennan, a football coach on Staten Island, was building the firehouse into an athletic powerhouse, Kevin said.

Then Captain Drennan and two others in the company died from injuries in a 1994 fire. "Being so young on the job, it affected him deeply," Kevin, a member of another company in Brooklyn, said of his brother. On Friday, Kevin was part of a search team, including members of Ladder 5 that found the bodies of Thomas, 36, and four other members of his group in the mound of trade center rubble.

Kevin carried his brother's helmet out of the wreckage. "It was the proudest moment of my life," he said.

"It means a lot for firefighters, in firefighter tradition, that members of their company carry them out. That day, I was part of that company."

KEVIN J. HANNAFORD
Youth and Maturity

He bent over to kiss his sleeping 2-year-old son. He patted the belly of his pregnant wife, and told her again that he loved her. Then Kevin Hannaford melted into the predawn darkness. That was the routine— reassuring, expectant—in one house in Basking Ridge, N.J.

Some three hours later, Eileen Hannaford was standing in the shadow of the World Trade Center's north tower, where her husband worked as a commodities broker for Cantor Fitzgerald, 105 stories above. The first plane had hit, she and other commuters had been evacuated from the PATH station below, and now she was frantically trying to

reach him on her cell phone. Finally, she decided it was best to go to her office across town.

"If Kevin had been looking for me, which he would have done, he would have gone directly to my office," she reasoned.

Kevin James Hannaford was 32 years old, young enough to enjoy playing soccer, mature enough to be an attentive husband and father. In the delivery room after the birth of Patrick two years earlier, he had thanked her for her friendship, and for their son.

On Jan. 9, four months after her husband died, she gave birth to their second son. He is healthy, wonderful, and his name, of course, is Kevin James Hannaford.

DANA HANNON
Deer Hunter with a Heart

Dana Hannon lived to hunt. While his family knew he would always be there for them, they knew better than to ask favors on the first day of hunting seasons for deer, ducks and geese. So it is no surprise that he knew how to track down a quarry. Maybe that explains why he waited until he got to the top of the Sydney Harbor Bridge in Australia to propose to Allison Dansen. He smuggled the ring on a string around his neck. They were to be married next fall.

Dana Hannon, 29, wanted to be a firefighter for almost as long as he wanted to hunt. After high school, he worked as a carpenter to support himself while he served as a volunteer firefighter in his hometown, Wyckoff, N.J., where he rose to the rank of captain. He got his first paying job as a firefighter in Bridgeport, Conn., where he was awarded the medal of valor for a rescue. Seven years after taking the exam, he joined the Fire Department of New York. He was with Engine Company 26.

"He was the best brother anybody could ask for," said his sister, Kyle. "Just the right mix of friend and tormentor."

VASSILIOS G. HARAMIS
Soothing Ferry Rides

There was gardening, Greek music and food, soccer, keeping his two Audis in pristine condition and, of course, the children. These were all passions of Vassilios G. Haramis, a mechanical engineer for Washington Group International who lived on Staten Island.

But it was the water that truly moved Mr. Haramis, 56, who grew up by the sea in southern Greece and, later, relished commuting in the morning on the Staten Island ferry, said his wife, Gloria. "I think it reminded him of Greece," she said. "The water was calm and it was soothing."

But Mr. Haramis was deeply devoted to living in the

United States. An immigrant who had come to New York in the 1970s as an engineering student at New York University, he received a master's degree from Columbia University and eventually wound up working at the World Trade Center. There, he survived the 1993 parking garage bombing. He and several colleagues waited until a helicopter came and rescued a pregnant woman before they descended more than 90 flights of stairs.

Even after that, Mr. Haramis still adored working at the World Trade Center and riding the ferry to work, Mrs. Haramis said. "He loved the building, he loved being down there," she said. "That was his place."

JAMES A. HARAN
Home and Family

Some of James A. Haran's happiest moments were spent in the backyard of his home in Malverne, on Long Island. It was there that he held countless barbecues with his family and friends, sometimes with as many as 100 people playing volleyball and table tennis and eating hot dogs and hamburgers. It was there that he splashed in the pool with his four children. And it was there, two years ago, that he spent a weekend planting 30 evergreen trees around the yard to make it into the haven he dreamed of.

Mr. Haran, 41, was a broker at Cantor Fitzgerald, but his life was centered on his home and family. He was tall and broad and gentle, the kind of man who loves dressing up as Santa to entertain the kids, as he did at a party last Christ-

mas. He took his mother to church every Sunday, and he and his wife, Carol, would have celebrated their 20th wedding anniversary in March.

"Jim's biggest accomplishment, in his eyes, was marrying his best friend, Carol, and raising their four children," said Mary Haran, his sister.

JEFFREY P. HARDY
Musician Turned Chef

Jeffrey P. Hardy was a musician from a musical family, but after he had been at it for a few years he decided to look for a better-paying career, and went to cooking school. After working at a number of New York City restaurants, he and his wife, Suzanne Gabriel, started a family, and he looked for a way to spend more time with them. Being a corporate chef was the answer, because someone who worked the breakfast and lunch shift could be home early.

For the last two years, Mr. Hardy, 46, was an executive chef at Cantor Fitzgerald, whose offices were high in the World Trade Center. On Sept. 11, as every day, he left his Brooklyn apartment before 5 A.M. to get to work cooking breakfast for bond traders.

"He had such tremendous energy," said Ms. Gabriel, a public relations executive. "He got up so early, and he was on his feet all day, but when he got home he was the one getting the kids to kick a soccer ball." Then, she added, he would cook dinner for the family.

At a party last year, he talked of the pleasures of watching his sons, Max, now 11, and Duncan, 7, grow while still having time to play the bass, which he did primarily in Greenwich Village, sometimes accompanying his brother, Jack Hardy, a singer-songwriter.

"If he knew I was talking to you," Ms. Gabriel told a reporter, "he would want me to mention that he was a huge Mets fan and that he had not given up on them this year."

TIMOTHY J. HARGRAVE
Soccer Dad

Timothy J. Hargrave—known to all as T. J.—started working at age 6 and didn't stop until Sept. 11. As a child, his work was acting: he was in many television commercials, made regular appearances on *Guiding Light* and starred in a made-for-television movie called *The Prince of Central Park.*

As an adult, Mr. Hargrave, 38, worked at Cantor Fitzgerald. But most of his prodigious energies went to those close to him: his wife, Patty; the friends they had made as far back as the Wayne, N.J., high school they both attended; his

Mourners at the World Trade Center Family Memorial Service on October 28, held at the site of the disaster in lower Manhattan. (*Fred R. Conrad*)

seven older siblings; his three young daughters; and all the girls on the soccer teams he coached.

"He was passionate about everything, and he was an everlasting friend," his wife said. "Once you were in his life, you stayed there. And he was the most devoted father you can imagine. He'd never played soccer a day in his life, but he wanted the girls to be involved in team sports, so he learned. I tell them, 'Some parents have their kids in soccer so they can have some time by themselves, but your father had you in soccer because he wanted to be with you.' "

DANIEL EDWARD HARLIN
Offered the Best to Others

Daniel Edward Harlin looked forward to the start of deer-hunting season all year long. But when he and his friends finally arrived in the Catskill woods in November, he always offered up the best spots to someone else.

"He was a very unselfish guy," said Charles Foulds, who grew up with him and had hunted with him every year since they were both teenagers. "He never took the best for himself."

A quiet man with a contagious laugh, Firefighter Harlin, 41, had worked with Ladder Company 2, Battalion 8, on East 51st Street for more than a decade. But he loved the outdoors so much that he and his wife moved to rural Putnam County 10 years ago, settling in Kent, before having their three children.

"He looked forward to taking the boys hunting when they got old enough," said his wife, Deborah.

This year his friends held their annual deer-hunting gathering in a Catskill cabin without him for the first time. "There wasn't a dry eye in the house," Mr. Foulds said.

AISHA HARRIS
Keeper of Confidences

Aisha Harris had a plan for her life, and she told her mother, Arvette Harris, that she was on schedule. At 22, she enjoyed her job at General Telecom as a customer services representative, dealing with accounts and troubleshooting. She switched her major at New York Technical College to telecommunications because she saw a future in the field.

She had a lot of friends, and took trips with her girlfriends. They went to Florida last summer. Many had been with her at Adlai Stevenson High School in the Bronx, where she wrote for the newspaper and the poetry magazine, played saxophone in the band, and was an honor student and treasurer of the student government.

But more than that, said Tanisha Robinson, who knew her since preschool, "she was the kind of person you could

talk to about anything—school, boyfriends, money problems, family—and she would keep it to herself. But she'd give you her honest opinion."

She had a boyfriend, Curtis Noel, who also worked for General Telecom at 1 World Trade Center. They were thinking about marriage, her mother said, but he also died on Sept. 11.

CURTIS NOEL's portrait appears on page 362.

STEWART D. HARRIS
Serious Fun

Stewart D. Harris had a serious job on Wall Street—and a season pass to the Six Flags Great Adventure amusement park. Which, said his wife, Sheila, he used all the time. When the Batman ride first opened at the park, in Jackson, N.J., Mr. Harris left the house in Monmouth County early one morning, went on the ride "and came home, happy as could be," Mrs. Harris said. "He was truly a kid at heart."

Mr. Harris, 52, was the chief credit officer at Cantor Fitzgerald. But he was devoted to his family—whenever anyone had a special occasion coming up, Mrs. Harris said, he bought cards weeks in advance. He also made time for fun. He taught his wife to ski, and took her camping and rafting on the Delaware River. He used to laugh when they saw cars with bumper stickers boasting about having climbed Mount Washington in New Hampshire.

"We did it—and not with the car," Mrs. Harris said.

JOHN C. HARTZ
Giving to the Causes

As they do in so many households, the letters seeking charitable donations piled up. But John C. Hartz would not throw them away unopened. One by one he would go through them; carefully, thoughtfully, he would choose which charities he would send money.

"He was inclined to go through all the solicitations and would consider giving to them all," said his wife, Ellie Hartz. "Many times, he would send them something." The causes ranged from endangered species to local community services.

She and Mr. Hartz, 64, a senior vice president at Fiduciary Trust, started their romance with a blind date in January 2000. They married that November. The couple, who lived in Basking Ridge, N.J., hiked on nearby trails and biked along the Delaware River. "I was so much looking forward to the rest of our lives together," Mrs. Hartz said. "It was too short a time. We were basically just newlyweds. I couldn't think of growing old with anybody but him." For their honeymoon, the Hartzes took their grown children to Bermuda.

EMERIC HARVEY
A Memorable Voice

As a young man, Emeric (Ric) Harvey sold truck rides to children with his friend Ray in Sheepshead Bay, Brooklyn, where he grew up. "Come swing and sway with Rick and Ray!" he'd bellow. Eventually, that voice was heard on the trading floor of the American Stock Exchange, where he became a force as founder and president of Harvey Young Yurman Inc.

His relentless energy made him a natural leader, though at times it was hard to keep up, said his daughter Jennifer Castelano. Part of it came from having lived through some close calls: as a young man in Texas, he nearly boarded an Air Force plane that crashed, killing everyone on board. And he narrowly missed being in the World Trade Center when it was bombed in 1993. On Sept. 11, Mr. Harvey, 56, of Montclair, N.J., was at a weekly breakfast meeting at Windows on the World.

His drive and generosity remain an inspiration, a loud one. "That's how I get out of bed every morning, because I can hear him yelling, 'What are you doing lying there crying?' " said his wife, Jennifer Harvey.

THOMAS HASKELL
Creating Tiny Wonderlands

In some ways, Thomas Haskell seemed like everyone's idea of a firefighter. The battalion chief for Ladder Company 132 in Brooklyn, he loved football—"God help you if you got in the way of the TV on Sundays," said Dawn Haskell-Carbone, his sister—and he played on the Fire Department team, like his brothers, Kenneth and Timothy. Timothy Haskell also died in the World Trade Center attack.

But he had another side. Every year just before Thanksgiving, Mr. Haskell, 37, would start disappearing into the basement of his home in Massapequa, N.Y., for hours, forbidding anyone else to come down. "He'd stay up till 3 A.M.," said his wife, Barbara Haskell. Then, about two weeks before Christmas, his wife, daughters, friends and other relatives would be invited downstairs to see an elaborate winter landscape with hundreds of tiny ceramic figures, surrounded by ski chalets, with three separate train sets running through it all.

In 2000 he built three miniature towns—Meaghanville, Erinburg and Taratown, named for his

daughters—along with Barbara's Garden, for his wife. Behind them all was a dark blue night sky, lit up with electric stars.

TIMOTHY HASKELL
Prepared for Emergencies

Timothy Haskell trained his Dalmatian, Blaze, to "stop, drop and roll." He took the dog to the school where his sister, Dawn Haskell-Carbone, teaches. "Timmy would say to the dog, 'Your clothes are on fire! What do you do?' " she recalled yesterday. "She would stop, throw herself on the ground and roll. He would ask the kids, 'What if you smell smoke?' The dog would crawl on her belly over to a door. Timmy would say, 'Feel the door first to see if it's hot.' And the dog would put her paws on the door."

Timothy grew up in Seaford, N.Y.—on a skateboard, then a dirt bike, and always on the water. As an adult, he loved scuba diving and extreme games; he was getting his pilot's license.

Timothy, 34, and two of his brothers, Thomas and Kenneth, followed their father into firefighting.

"All my brothers, they all got perfect scores on their physical, and their tests were almost perfect," his sister said. "It was that important to them, that they worked hard at it."

Timothy's brother, Thomas, also died in the World Trade Center attack.

LEONARD W. HATTON Jr.
Into the Flames

Leonard W. Hatton Jr. was on his way to work in a downtown Manhattan office building on Sept. 11 when he noticed smoke billowing from the north tower of the trade center. A volunteer firefighter and an agent for the Federal Bureau of Investigation, he changed course "and went straight there," said his wife, JoAnne Hatton. He radioed the F.B.I. and relayed what he was seeing, one of his supervisors recalled, "then tried to pitch in and help as best he could."

For Mr. Hatton, 45, that meant going into the burning buildings and getting people out. "He didn't have to do that, but that was my husband," Mrs. Hatton said. "He joined right in with the Fire Department to help people and gave his life for it."

Mr. Hatton's mother, Marilyn Hatton, said he learned a lot from his father, who was a Ridgefield Park, N.J., police officer, and that he strove to instill the same values in the children he left behind: Courtney, 11, Jessica, 16, Lenny, 20, and Tara, 21.

TERENCE S. HATTON
Knowing the Drill

Terence S. Hatton did not like surprises. A captain in the Fire Department, he took his squad to tour buildings when there were no smoke or flames, or people to rescue.

"He was very knowledgeable about the history of Manhattan and its buildings," said Alfred Benjamin, a firefighter who was a member of the captain's squad at Rescue Company 1 in Times Square. Captain Hatton was a 20-year veteran of the department.

The firehouse is an elite force of about 25 firefighters, whose mission is to perform rescues. It is one of the busiest houses in the city, with 10 runs a day—very few of them are false alarms. Captain Hatton, 41, once took his rescue team on a drill to a small theater on 43rd Street, off Eighth Avenue, so that they would know what to expect.

"The theater looks small from the outside, but it's a tremendous building," Mr. Benjamin said. "It has subcellars, and the performers have dressing rooms in one of the basements. We wouldn't have known that if we hadn't done the drill."

MICHAEL H. HAUB
Calling Out for Father

Kiersten Edda Haub, 17 months old, said "Dada" for the first time on Sept. 11. She seemed to sense the tension in the living room as her mother, Erika Haub, and some friends gathered in front of the television.

They did not expect "Dada"—Michael H. Haub, 34, a New York City firefighter—to come back home. As she called out to her father, the little girl pointed at his picture. "I was like, 'Oh, my God, she has never said that before,' " Mrs. Haub recalled. Kiersten, who was 15 months old at the time, has been calling out to him ever since. It is not surprising: he was a dedicated father, who had a 4-year-old son, Michael Andreas.

As much as Mr. Haub gave to his family, he also gave to the job. He was a member of Ladder Company 4 in Midtown, one of the busiest in the city. Being an only child, he enjoyed the camaraderie of the firehouse.

"He liked helping people," his wife said. "He was happy to be at such a busy house because he really wanted to be working all the time."

TIMOTHY A. HAVILAND
Promotion to the 96th Floor

Titanic was just hitting theaters when Timothy A. Haviland earned a promotion from computer programmer to project manager at Marsh & McLennan, a jump that took him from an office on the Avenue of the Americas in Midtown to the 96th floor of 1 World Trade Center.

Just like Jack, the movie's hero, Mr. Haviland thought that he had it all. "After his first day, he was jumping around the house saying, 'This is New York! I'm king of the world!' " said his wife, Amy L. Haviland. "This man, you couldn't get the smile off his face when his position moved to the World Trade Center."

Mr. Haviland, 41, met the future Mrs. Haviland online almost five years ago. They hit it off immediately but had one big problem: he was in St. Paul, Minn., and she was on Long Island. He decided to visit. She said their love affair began in the baggage claim area at La Guardia Airport and led to a wedding two years ago. It was a four-ring ceremony: one each for the bride and groom and a ring for each of Mrs. Haviland's children, Nicholas, 14, and Jesse, 12.

Mrs. Haviland's brother, Robert W. Spear Jr., a firefighter, also died in the attack.

ROBERT W. SPEAR Jr's portrait appears on page 472.

DONALD G. HAVLISH Jr.
A Love That Almost Wasn't

As love stories go, the tale of Fiona and Donald G. Havlish Jr., well, it almost never happened. While a mutual friend pleaded for months with Mrs. Havlish to meet her future husband, a senior vice president at Aon, she resisted, convinced, though she had never seen him, that the relationship would never work.

"Guys do not like women with two kids," Mrs. Havlish told the friend.

But the friend persisted, cleverly arranging a meeting of the two at a corporate picnic. Mr. Havlish was the tall, dark-haired stranger with the quick laugh and the bouquet of spring flowers. "I just fell in love with his sense of humor," Mrs. Havlish said. Two months later, the two were engaged. They married a year and half later, on a beach in Bermuda, at sunset. Mrs. Havlish's children became his children, soon joined by a daughter of their own.

It is a story, one of many that Mrs. Havlish is saving for Michaela, 4, whose smile would send her 53-year-old father racing home to Yardley, Pa. "I tell her that Daddy is still watching over us, that he'll always love her."

ANTHONY HAWKINS
On Tuesday, the Clock Broke

Anthony Hawkins always made sure that his day started with a laugh. At 5 A.M., he would rouse his mother, brother and sisters to watch reruns of his favorite comedy, *Good Times*. He never missed it.

At 30, Anthony had settled into a life of comfortable

routines. He always listened to hip-hop music while taking the subway to his job as a maintenance worker. He always picked up newspapers on his way home to Brooklyn, sharing them with his family. He always walked his mother to the market to buy the fixings for the Sunday dinner.

"He was the clock for our family," said his cousin, Byron Haynes. "He set the tone for the day." The only time that Anthony broke his routine, his cousin said, was when he did not come home that Tuesday. Like clockwork, he always stepped through the front door at 6 P.M.

NOBUHIRO HAYATSU
Each City an Adventure

In a world of the reserved and the circumspect—Japanese banking—Nobuhiro Hayatsu stood out: he was outgoing, sunny, loquacious. He embraced foreign assignments as a vice president of Chuo Mitsui Trust and Banking Company with alacrity, for each tour of duty was a chance to make even more friends, party in a new town. At 36, Mr. Hayatsu had already lived and worked in Taiwan, Tokyo, London, Hong Kong and, as of this spring, New York City.

With each city, a clutch of memories. In Taiwan, Mr. Hayatsu learned Mandarin and became enamored of classic Chinese literature. In London, his wife, Yoshiko, gave birth to their son, Ryo, whom Mr. Hayatsu held so long, so adoringly in the birthing room that the doctor yelled at him. He loved Hong Kong's noise, convenience, dynamism.

Life in New York was intriguing, but he was looking forward to sightseeing with his family soon. Every morning he'd leave their Scarsdale apartment at 6:30 for the World Trade Center, returning at 10 P.M. Weekends, he'd flop on the couch and hug his son, murmuring gently to him.

For a city enthusiast, Mr. Hayatsu had an unusual dream: to retire to a country home where his family could gather. He had bought the land on which to build it, near Mount Fuji.

JAMES E. HAYDEN
The Love Stayed Young

Looking back on their nearly 25 years of marriage, Elizabeth Gail Hayden credits James E. Hayden with bringing her much joy, to say nothing of chicken and fish.

When they met in 1972 as freshmen in college, the only dinner entree she would eat was beef. Mr. Hayden, though, was adventurous about food.

Determined and focused at work, Mr. Hayden, 47, was chief financial officer of Netegrity, an Internet security company in Waltham, Mass. He was aboard United Airlines Flight

175 when it hit the south tower. He rarely talked of work at home, but instead was a great listener, helping solve the workaday issues for his children, John, 17, and Elizabeth, 19.

The family ate dinner together every night. He liked to cook on weekends, frequently making salmon on Saturday nights. He sought out new restaurants to try, and when he traveled he chose exotic foods. He even got his wife to try them, too.

"I moved beyond beef," Mrs. Hayden said, with a laugh. There was one thing she hadn't moved beyond: the feeling that they were young, and in love. "He made me feel like I was 18," she said. "I loved that."

PHILIP T. HAYES
A Protector to the End

On Sept. 11, Philip T. Hayes rescued children from a day care center in 5 World Trade Center. Then, as debris fell from the sky, he ran into the south tower to redirect people out of harm's way.

It had always been that way. Mr. Hayes, 67, the second oldest of 16 children, was the cornerstone of his family and its great protector. He was the patriarch.

"I had a feeling that he had no fear of anything," said his son, Philip T. Hayes Jr. "To him, anything was possible."

A New York City firefighter from 1959 to 1979, Mr. Hayes lived in East Northport, N.Y., and had worked as fire safety director at the trade center since 1995. He loved that building. He loved those firefighters. On Oct. 1, his daughter, Laura, gave birth to a son who weighed 9 pounds 11 ounces and was immediately given his grandfather's name.

"The weight, 9-11, correlates to the Sept. 11 date," Mr. Hayes's son said. "We all said, that's Dad, telling us in his own way, 'I'm still here, watching over you.' "

ROBERT HAYES
The Man with the Surfboard

Robert Hayes sported a year-round tan because almost everywhere he went, he also sported his surfboard. It did not matter whether he was headed for business or pleasure. In fact, his wife, Debbie Hayes, said it was not uncommon to see him walking through Logan International Airport in Boston in a business suit with a briefcase in one hand and his black-and-white surfboard in the other.

"It was kind of funny to see him," she remembered.

It was at Logan Airport that she saw him for the first time, actually, although she did not think he was so much funny-looking as cute, she said. It was 1989 and he had missed his flight. She was the Trans World Airlines customer service agent who had the pleasure of re-booking him. She said that after he returned from his trip, he began to call her at the ticket counter—and it had nothing to do with air travel.

Twelve years and two children later (Robbie is 4 years old and Ryan was 5 months in September), Mr. Hayes, who was 37 and lived in Amesbury, Mass., devoted his time to his family, his work in sales at Netstal Machinery, a maker of compact disks, and, of course, surfing.

He walked through Logan Airport for the last time on the morning of Sept. 11, headed to Los Angeles on American Airlines Flight 11 for a business meeting.

W. WARD HAYNES
Sold on the Car

W. Ward Haynes really wanted the car. Not that it made a whole lot of sense. The car was a Porsche Boxster. Two people could squeeze in it, and that was about it. But there was the matter of the golf clubs. Both he and his wife, Ann, played golf. It did not look like two bags could even fit in the trunk. Ward-O, as he was known, insisted they could, if they were square-bottomed bags rather than round-bottomed ones.

And then there was the matter of the children: three of them. Where would they go? Well, the family had a larger vehicle for full-family trips. And starting in August, Mr. Haynes, 35, was no longer commuting by car from his home in Rye, N.Y., to his office in Stamford, Conn., but taking the train to his new job as a broker at Cantor Fitzgerald. So why shouldn't he have a fun weekend car? At least, that was his argument.

Hesitantly, Mrs. Haynes surrendered. He got his car the weekend before Sept. 11. "The family could not fit in it—ever," Mrs. Haynes said. "But he really wanted it."

He went zipping around, giving everyone a ride. He picked up his 85-year-old grandmother. Mrs. Haynes figured that ride would not last long. They were out for two hours.

SCOTT HAZELCORN
Dream of an Ice Cream Truck

At a memorial service for Scott Hazelcorn, his father learned that there were at least a dozen people who considered his son their best friend. This was not the result of duplicity, Charles Hazelcorn said, but rather a function of Scott's open heart and sunny nature. Each eulogist put it differently: your problem was his problem; he made each person feel he was the only one in the room; he taught people to hug each other; he was the one who made work fun.

"Nobody enjoyed life more, from the minute he got up to the minute he went to sleep," his father said. And to that end there were "Haz's Rules," which included setting the clock radio to a Spanish language station, which he could not understand, so he never had to start the day listening to bad news.

The younger Mr. Hazelcorn, 29, was a trader of long-term treasury bonds at Cantor Fitzgerald; his girlfriend, Amy Callahan, was a special-education teacher. The pair had plans for a summer camp for needy kids. Scott often told his parents that he wanted to buy an ice cream truck, so he could hear the squeals of children all day.

When Cantor Fitzgerald spun off a company called eSpeed, which allowed clients to do their own trading, Mr. Hazelcorn's work group shrank from 30 to 4. In a few months, it was to disappear altogether, his father said. To his son that was good news: between yearly raises, bonuses and stock options in eSpeed, he was planning to buy that ice cream truck.

MICHAEL K. HEALEY
Cleaning on the Job

Michael K. Healey used to clean the bathroom at home. He was married for 20 years to Theresa Healey, with whom he had three children and who said that he cleaned everything from the bathroom to the bedroom to the kitchen without putting up a fuss. He even did the laundry. Mr. Healey, a lieutenant in the Fire Department, did not mind cleaning on the job, either. (An aside: Firefighters clean the station house bathroom on a rotating basis.)

When Firefighter Healey became a lieutenant four years ago, he stopped changing bedsheets and washing dishes. Officers become so burdened with paperwork that officials discourage them from doing household chores. "It took him a while to get used to the new rules," Mrs. Healey said. "The guys do a lot of bonding while doing their work."

Lieutenant Healey, 43, was an 18-year veteran of the Fire Department and a member of Rescue Squad 41 in the South Bronx.

ROBERTA BERNSTEIN HEBER
Second Career

Roberta Bernstein Heber could appear to be all business, but those close to her knew that she was a soft touch, the kind of person who briskly went down her "to do" list but had smiles and hugs to spare at the end of the day.

Ms. Heber was an assistant vice president and a systems analyst at Marsh & McLennan. Her two daughters and son were proud that the mother who stayed at home with them when they were growing up went back to school at night for a master's degree in computer science, and a second career.

"That was very brave of her," said Melissa Bernstein. "We used to say to her, 'We should get some of your salary because we trained you by letting you boss us around.' "

"She was really impressive, actually," Ms. Bernstein said.

CHARLES FRANCIS XAVIER HEERAN
Staying for Family

Charles Francis Xavier Heeran gave up a promotion to stay in New York City. Only 23 and a little more than a year out of college, Mr. Heeran had risen quickly as a bond trader at Cantor Fitzgerald. But when he was offered a promotion that meant moving to the company's London office, he declined.

"He wanted to stay near his friends and family," said his father, Bernard Heeran. A natural extrovert, Mr. Heeran loved to get together with people. His great-aunt Bernadette Hay Griffin said, "He was a great organizer of parties. He would gather 30 people and go to *Tony and Tina's Wedding*," the long-running Off Broadway show.

He was also generous with his friends. His father said: "He was always buying cocktails to get the party going. He wasn't tight with a buck."

Mr. Heeran grew up in Rockaway Beach, Queens, and went to Xavier High School in Manhattan. He was one of 10 Xavier graduates and 16 twins who disappeared in the World Trade Center on Sept. 11.

H. JOSEPH HELLER
A Broker and a Fixer

Whenever H. Joseph Heller felt strongly that he should do something, he went out and did it. That's how he ended up owning a yellow turn-of-the-last-century farmhouse on a hilly acre in Ridgefield, Conn., a house that his wife, Mary Jean, calls "a major fixer-upper."

Mr. Heller, a commodities broker at Carr Futures, saw the potential in the house and set about restoring it himself. He installed new woodwork, nailed in the window trim, hung the doors, replaced the stair rails. Even when the outside needed a coat of paint, he climbed a ladder with a brush in his hand and did the job. He was self-taught, with only some Time-Life books and television to help him. And, of course, his wife.

"We watched a lot of Bob Vila on TV," Mrs. Heller said.

The house became home for the Hellers and their four children, ages 8, 6, 4 and 16 months. The only part Mr. Heller, 37, did not build was the new wing put on a few

years ago, which included enormous windows—his idea— that frame the view of trees and old stone walls. "So much of him is right here," Mrs. Heller said. "He fell in love with this house and convinced me. I never really fell in love with it until it started taking shape. He was the one who had the vision."

MARK F. HEMSCHOOT
What Penny Knows

Penny knows he's gone; the chocolate Labrador shows she senses this. Her master, Mark F. Hemschoot, 45, is not there to walk her in the morning. Penny can't greet him at the door each night. And he'll never again feed her slices of bologna or ham while he makes his next day's lunch.

"The first two weeks she didn't eat," said Mr. Hemschoot's wife, Debora. "She moped in the house. The veterinarian was concerned. The dog actually lost 10 pounds." They had always had dogs, since they got married in 1979. They had Chad, a collie, and Kelsey, a black Labrador, who died eight years ago. That's when they took a drive to a farm and picked out Penny. The couple's sons, Jeffrey, 19, and David, 16, thought of the pets as family.

These days, Penny has begun to eat again. She has accepted the way things are now and she is getting back to normal. Humans have their own way. "I sit down and look over at the recliner chair and he's vanished," Debora said of her husband, a senior vice president at Aon Corporation on the 105th floor of 2 World Trade Center. "It's hard. I know he is gone but he has literally vanished. But Penny is at my side and my sons are here."

RONNIE LEE HENDERSON
An Abundance of Family

He may have been earning a fireman's salary, but Ronnie Lee Henderson planned all along to turn that into more. He pared money from his paycheck and put it into bonds and mutual funds. In the quiet hours at the Engine Company 279 firehouse in Red Hook, he could be found reading books with titles like *How to Make Money Buying and Selling Houses*.

"I'd say to him, 'What are you doing? You're a fireman, you know what we get paid,' " said a friend, Gary Kakeh.

The father of four children, Mr. Henderson also helped raise his five younger siblings. His advice to all of them was consistent: stay in school, save your money. He figured out travel routes that enabled him to avoid paying bridge and tunnel tolls, and would stand in line for hours to get the store specials, said his sister, Sharon.

As a teenager, he got a job in a Frito-Lay factory and got

to bring home the extra potato chips. Naturally, he shared them with the rest of his family. "And he'd charge us a nickel," she added.

"He was always telling us he was going to be a millionaire," Ms. Henderson said. "He was a millionaire, by his heart."

EDWARD R. HENNESSY Jr.
Mad about Guitars

Edward R. Hennessy Jr. tried baseball and hockey and all the other sports his dad loved, but as a little boy he told his father that sports simply did not interest him. Then in second grade he found his true love: music. He took up the clarinet first, then the saxophone and later keyboards bass drum and guitar.

At Belmont High School in Massachusetts and at Harvard, where he graduated cum laude in 1988, he played in the marching bands. He wrote part of the 1989 Hasty Pudding Club musical-comedy show at Harvard. At the Kellogg School of Management at Northwestern University, where he studied information science, he arranged musical numbers and even conducted the orchestra.

"Ted was mad about screaming guitars," recalled Melanie Salisbury, his wife of 10 years. "The Ramones was his favorite and Spinal Tap a close second. He recorded a lot of his own music."

At family gatherings he would often slip away to the piano with his niece and nephew.

"He would teach them basic notes and the fundamentals of playing the piano," said his brother-in-law, Jim Kelleher.

Mr. Hennessy, 35, father of two, was on his way to Los Angeles on American Airlines Flight 11 on Sept. 11 to consult on a distribution system for AOL Time Warner's Elektra records.

MICHELLE HENRIQUE
Keeping Her Focus

As a child, Michelle Henrique's life had revolved around her family and church—and at 27, she saw no reason to change her focus. A secretary at Fiduciary Trust, she split her week between her parents' home and her grandparents' home in Staten Island, lending a hand at each. At her grandparents', she was a house-sitter. At her parents', she helped care for her orphaned cousins, 5 and 8, who were being adopted by the family.

At the Church of the Holy Child, she was president of the Columbettes, the women's Knights of Columbus group. She mainly organized and helped run benefits—grilling hamburgers, singing Broadway hits and doing a bit of acting.

She played, for instance, an over-the-top mother of a male bride in drag.

With discount tickets from her fiancé, Craig Castro, a Continental Airlines employee, she vacationed in Hawaii, the Bahamas and the Dominican Republic. She did not know it, but Mr. Castro had bought a ring, a surprise for her birthday in December.

JOSEPH PATRICK HENRY
Celebrating Youth

Joseph Patrick Henry never played professional baseball, but there were plenty of people who thought he did. And some of them have his autograph. By all accounts, Mr. Henry, a firefighter, who at 25, had worked only 11 months for the department, bore a striking resemblance to the pitcher David Cone. So much so that often people would whisper "Is that David Cone?" and ask for his autograph. A fervent baseball player and Yankee fan, Firefighter Henry could not help but oblige a few of those requests, said his mother, Alice Henry.

When his mother was cooking dinner, Mr. Henry would go out onto the terrace and shout, "Mom's cooking my favorite stew!" so loudly that Mrs. Henry would jokingly threaten to call the police. (This continued even after he moved into his own apartment in the same building, in Bensonhurst, Brooklyn, his mother said.)

One of six children in a family of many firefighters—his grandfather, father, uncle and two brothers—Mr. Henry could be the frivolous one. "He was usually the first to arrive at a party and the last one to leave," said his longtime girlfriend, Julia Corrales. "He always said, 'We're young, we should enjoy these days.'"

WILLIAM L. HENRY Jr.
The Big Red Truck

William L. Henry Jr., who was known as Bill or Buddy, had a galaxy of friends and admirers that stretched from the Ladder 24 firehouse on West 31st Street to the paddle tennis courts at windswept Jacob Riis Park in the Rockaways. He spent his vacations in places like Brazil, and his free time fixing up houses for people like his mother, Ethel. People would compliment his work; Mr. Henry tended to agree with them. "Yeah," he'd say, "it's a beautiful thing."

His competitive streak ran deep. "He would say to me, you know, I go to more fires than you do," said John Dopwell, a former colleague at Ladder 24, where Firefighter Henry was assigned before moving on to Rescue 1, also in Manhattan.

He also let all kinds of post-conflagration messiness build

up on his coat and helmet, as a sign of how hard he worked. "Outside of his family, that job was what he lived for," said another friend, Paul Stewart.

For a while, he moonlighted as a security guard at Laura Belle, a nightclub in Times Square. "I was his boss, but in all honesty, he was my boss," said Joanne O'Connor, the club's director of catering and special events. "He was always telling me what to do."

Once Ms. O'Connor made a demand of her own. "I asked him, when are you going to take me for a ride in the fire truck?" It became a joke between them. Then one day, the huge red Rescue 1 pulled up in front of Laura Belle, packed with firemen on their way back from a call. In clomped Mr. Henry, who said, "Let's go for a ride."

JOHN HENWOOD
He Loved Spain

A lot of the young bond traders at Cantor Fitzgerald were looking forward to earning enough to move on to a more relaxed life. John Henwood, 35, was one of them. He had met his wife, Concha Munoz, in Spain when he was in Madrid for I.B.M., and the couple, married for nine years, had already begun making plans to move back, perhaps to a Mediterranean shore front, with their two children, Alejandro, 5, and Claudia, 2.

"Every year they'd go to Spain for four weeks, and those were probably the best days of John's life," said David Keefe, a friend. In the meantime, the Henwoods lived on Manhattan's Upper East Side. "I think the most important thing I could say about John is that he was the guy you looked forward to being with," Mr. Keefe said. "When we were in Boston and right out of college and working three or four different jobs, no matter how tedious something might be, if John was there, it was fun."

ROBERT A. HEPBURN
Comforting Routines

Every morning, Theresa Hepburn and her two girls would drive Robert A. Hepburn to the train station in Union, N.J., where they lived, for his commute into the city. It was just one of the many routines that defined their family life.

Another unfolded after he settled into his office. He would call every day around 8 A.M. to make sure that Allyson, 6, and Jennifer, 4, were ready for school. And he would always ask what they wanted him to bring them that night. "They always wanted gum or candy," his wife said.

When he returned home, he would take care of the girls so their mother could go to her evening job. Mr. Hepburn, 39, was an office service manager for Marsh

USA, a job he had held for only two months. He worked on the 93rd floor of 1 World Trade Center, and his desk was against a window with a view of the Statue of Liberty and Ellis Island, and of course he shared it with his family. During the summer, Mrs. Hepburn and the girls took the train into the city every Thursday for lunchtime concerts downtown.

"He would go down to our train and meet us and put us in our seats, and then he'd go back upstairs to work," she recalled. "Then he'd come down during his lunch hour and watch the rest of the show with us."

MARY HERENCIA
A Wit with a Purpose

Mary Herencia is remembered for her cough, a theatrical, throat-clearing "a-hem!" she used every morning to get her four boys out of bed and on their way to school. The sound, uttered from the living room of their apartment, was all it ever took. The boys knew that malingering in bed beyond that signal, unless you were really, truly sick, would not be wise.

"She was very tough, but she was also gentle, and that captured it for me," said her son Joseph.

Ms. Herencia, 47, known as Molly, raised four boys, including a set of twins, by herself in Manhattan, without a lot of money, and it was not until much later that her children realized that the blunt, firecracker Irish wit that defined her was also sometimes a front for the struggles she had faced.

An insurance broker at Aon for the last 10 years, she had lost none of her edge to middle age. At dinner one night last summer, she eyed Joseph's girlfriend, Sara Walter, over the table. "So," she cracked, "when you getting married?"

LINDSAY C. HERKNESS III
Man About Wimbledon

There are few bons vivants who work for a living, and should you doubt that Lindsay C. Herkness III, senior vice president at Morgan Stanley, was among them, you have only to consider his Christmas cards, showing Mr. Herkness in top hat at Ascot, or at Wimbledon, being hustled away by two bobbies. The captions reflected his humor, too.

"I only recommended to Her Majesty that she fund an IRA account," read the Wimbledon card.

Fun-loving Lindsay. There was never a cloud in his sky, his old friend Bunny Whiteley said. He lived in the Upper East Side of Manhattan in a "totally male" apartment. He was witty and charming. Women adored him. Even the way he got into the business made an amusing tale: He was fresh out of business school, gave an investment seminar on a cruise ship in exchange for free passage, and at the end of the cruise a dozen well-heeled widows beseeched him to manage their funds. Two true loves, in addition to business and the ladies, were the Union Club and his basset, Beauregard Hound.

Ms. Whiteley said it was Mr. Lindsay's decision not to leave the building. "We understand that when the plane struck—he was around the 70th floor—his statement was, 'This is the strongest building in America,' and he went back to his desk."

HARVEY HERMER
The Incredible Harve

"It's the Harve!"—Harvey Hermer would always shout out that greeting when he phoned. Mr. Hermer, 59, was an ebullient person, single, and loved to make friends, said Joel Beja, who married Mr. Hermer's niece, Susan. If someone liked the Yankees, he did. If they liked the Mets, he would switch.

"He just wanted to have a good time with you," said Mr. Beja.

Mr. Hermer was an electrician. He was raised in Brooklyn. He had been a body builder, and was proud that he worked out at the same gym as Lou Ferrigno, who played the Incredible Hulk on television. Mr. Hermer was also a fight fan, and had season tickets for the Columbia University football team. He never went to college, but regarded Columbia as his home team.

As an electrician, he was dependable. On Sept. 11, he was working at Cantor Fitzgerald at 1 World Trade Center and his boss left him in charge of a crew on the 105th floor. Sometimes Mr. Hermer would just disappear for a while, said Mr. Beja. Then the phone would ring, and there he would be:—"It's the Harve!"

NORBERTO HERNANDEZ
Cooking with Love

Norberto Hernandez, a pastry sous-chef at Windows on the World, whipped up his first dessert in his mother's kitchen at age 12. Only he used too much flour, and the chocolate-chip cookies turned out to be too hard to eat. His family still laughs about that one. Mr. Hernandez, 42, cooked even on his days off; though he rarely devoured sweets himself, he relished nothing more than plying his wife and three daughters in Elmhurst, Queens, with cookies, cupcakes, muffins, cheesecakes, homemade ice cream. On birthdays and graduations, he baked a two-layered chocolate mousse cake.

"We gained a lot of weight," said his daughter, Catherine. "That was a problem."

Mr. Hernandez, a quiet man, never explained to his daughter exactly why he liked to cook so much. But it went without saying that it was always done with love. "He knew everybody liked the desserts," she said. "So he would make them."

RAUL HERNANDEZ
Always Helping the Family

Raul Hernandez was happiest at home having dinner and watching the New York Mets with his brother, or just talking on the telephone with his three sisters. No matter how tough his days were as supervisor of maintenance for Cantor Fitzgerald, Mr. Hernandez, 51, was never too tired to check in, sometimes talking for hours at a time. It was his duty, he used to tell his sister Gladys Estepan, trying to explain his need to be provider and protector.

He yearned for the day when his two other sisters, who live in the Dominican Republic, would make their way to New York to be with the rest of the family. Even when money was tight, he would send $400 a month back home for them.

"We are only five children, a small family," Mrs. Estepan said. "He was to us like our mother and father, always wanting to help for the family. We hope in our hearts that he will come home and we can help him."

BRIAN HICKEY
Unspoken Devotion

There is no telling how many New Yorkers are walking around because Capt. Brian Hickey became a New York City firefighter 20 years ago. He commanded Rescue Company 4, which rushes to every major fire in Queens, not to fight flames, but to save trapped civilians and firefighters.

It has always been among the department's most dangerous jobs. Two of his men were killed in Astoria last Father's Day, and another died with him at 2 World Trade Center on Sept. 11.

Yet the 47-year-old captain, who had suffered burns and other injuries many times on the job, never dwelled on the dangers. Instead, he spoke with pride of the brotherhood (women included) of firefighters.

"It means they are ready to lay down their lives for one another," his wife, Donna, said. "They all knew it. It was something unspoken among them."

He was also a volunteer firefighter in Bethpage, N.Y., where he grew up, married his high school sweetheart and had four children: Danny, 23; Dennis, 18; Jaclyn, 16; and Kevin, 10.

In 1992, Captain Hickey and his only brother, Raymond,

created *Brothers in Battle*, a 45-minute video documentary about firefighting. It is still used in training.

In 1993, Raymond died of cancer. "Brian was at his side for 11 months," Mrs. Hickey recalled. "I've never seen such love and compassion."

YSIDRO HIDALGO-TEJADA
Seasoning with Love

Ysidro Hidalgo-Tejada had a gentle touch that he applied to making dinner for his huge extended family, planting flowers, or taking care of his 90-year-old diabetic mother when he visited his native Dominican Republic.

Mr. Hidalgo-Tejada, who was 50, worked in food preparation at Windows on the World. Even though he worked around food all day, he would often go home and prepare something special for his wife and three daughters, said his eldest child, Anyela Hidalgo, 18.

"I miss him every day," Ms. Hidalgo said softly. "I'm not going to have my dad with me anymore. My little sisters, they don't want to talk about him much." "One of the last things we did together was to go to the Statue of Liberty. We had to wait in line for a long time but my dad said it was worth it."

In his down time, Mr. Hidalgo-Tejada enjoyed playing dominos and watching the Discovery Channel. His family kept him busy, too; he had 10 siblings and more than two dozen nieces and nephews.

ROBERT D. W. HIGLEY II
The Three Boys

When he was just 4 years old, Rob Higley moved to Ridgefield, Conn., and soon made friends with three other little boys: Carl and Erik Abrahamson and Dan Kish. When he was 8, Rob's family moved away. But he kept his friends.

In fact, he built his life around them, said his wife, Vycki Higley. He decided to go to the University of Connecticut because one of his pals was going there too, and they could room together. Through his old friends, he met his wife and her parents, who also live in Ridgefield.

"The boys," as Mrs. Higley calls them, went mountain biking together in recent years and took their families camping every summer, sleeping in tents and cooking over an open fire.

Though his jobs in the insurance business took them all over the country during their seven-year marriage, the Higleys always dreamed of moving back to Connecticut, "close enough so he could be around these guys all the time," Mrs. Higley said. In the spring of 2001, their dream came

true when Mr. Higley got a job at Aon in the World Trade Center. He started work there on June 11.

Mr. Higley was just 29 when he died. His three dear friends are godfathers to his daughters Amanda, 4½, and Robyn Elizabeth, who was born on Nov. 3.

CLARA HINDS
Courtesy and Humility

Clara and Hubert Hinds met in Trinidad. At 14, she could sew a wedding dress. "As the years go by, we were getting closer and closer," he said. They moved to Far Rockaway in Queens after marrying.

"Everything was for the family," said Mr. Hinds. "She would bake and cook up a storm. She would go to work and would hustle home to be with the family for dinner. When the boys were young she took them to baseball. She was like a big kid rooting for them when they ran bases."

Ms. Hinds, 52, worked as a seamstress at the Rainbow Room and Windows on the World. "She believed in being polite and humble," said Mr. Hinds. She sewed for family and friends and repaired a 1929 gown for a Broadway play as a favor. "She thought: 'God made colorful things, flowers, animals, trees,'" he said. "'Why should we be prejudiced?' She thought: 'Life is too short to be sad. She hated people to be down.'"

"I was pretty fortunate," he said. "Most people say marriage is heaven and hell. For me, it was 31 years of heaven."

NEIL O. HINDS
Striving for His Family

Neil O. Hinds was the type who could laugh the loudest and dance the longest at any party, but he had a serious side, too, and had settled down to providing for his wife, Karen, and 2-year-old son, Jameer.

Mr. Hinds, a personal banker for the Bank of New York, was attending a seminar on Sept. 11 when he was killed by falling debris from the trade center.

As part of his effort to keep doing better for himself and his family, Mr. Hinds, 28, was a semester away from graduating from Baruch College with a bachelor's degree in computer information systems, his father, Collin Hinds, said.

The elder Mr. Hinds said his son had come to New York at 19 from Kingston, Jamaica. The two played dominoes together and watched basketball, baseball and football on television.

"He was fun-loving and outgoing," said Karen Greene, Mr. Hinds's older sister. "I was like a mom to him and my younger sister. He was always concerned about our well-being, if we got sick or something like that."

Mr. Hinds went home to Jamaica as often as he could to

visit their mother. Two weeks before he died, she had requested a photograph of all the siblings. They put it off, thinking they had time, but a friend happened to snap all four one night after a party. "That was the last picture of Neil," Ms. Greene said. As usual, he was smiling.

MARK DAVID HINDY
Bridging the Generation Gap

Mark David Hindy, 28, was 6 feet 4 inches, 250 pounds. His niece Olivia, 22 months old in November, was 2 feet 11 inches and weighed 30 pounds. That's a big difference—a 3-foot-5-inch, 220-pound difference, to be exact—but somehow a bond had grown between them when she was even smaller.

"His hand was the size of her, but you could see the gentleness of his big hand supporting her back when he held her," said Ginny Hindy, Mr. Hindy's mother.

Olivia smiled at him when she was 6 months old—before she had smiled at anyone else. When the family watched television, Olivia always crawled to Mr. Hindy's lap instead of her father's.

"She felt very secure with Mark," Ms. Hindy said.

Greg Hindy, Mr. Hindy's brother and Olivia's father, said that Olivia clearly missed her favorite uncle after the attacks destroyed the offices of Cantor Fitzgerald, where he worked.

"After 9/11, she would ask for Mark. 'Markie, hug, Markie, kiss,' she would say," he said. "Then I would say, 'Hug Daddy. Mark will hug you through Daddy.' Now she points to his picture, and says 'Markie, angel.' "

Because of the pair's special relationship, the Hindys have created the Mark Hindy Charitable Foundation to help, among other things, fight diseases that afflict children.

HEATHER HO
Always Room for Dessert

There can be no doubt that Heather Ho, the award-winning pastry chef at the Windows on the World on the 107th floor of the World Trade Center, had a sweet tooth.

"We would go to a restaurant and she would order only the desserts," said Daniel Roorda, her boyfriend for the last two years. "But she was petite. She ate more than I did, and never gained a pound. I don't know how she did it. I think it's that her energy level was so high."

High enough to have propelled Ms. Ho, 32, from Honolulu to premier New York restaurants that included Jean Georges, Gramercy Tavern and Clementine, and Boulevard in San Francisco. She came to Windows in June 2001, but her dream was to open her own pastry shop, said Michael Lomonaco, the restaurant's executive chef.

"In mid-August she gave me notice, but offered to stay until we could find a replacement."

TARA Y. HOBBS
A Queen of E-Mail

Tara Y. Hobbs was crowned the "e-mail queen" by her friends. "She kept in touch with everybody—everybody from middle school, high school, college, work, social life—through e-mail," said her sister Sherian Hobbs. "She was always planning get-togethers."

And some of her best friends were her brothers and sisters. As the youngest of five children growing up on Long Island, Tara Hobbs was very close to Sherian, the oldest. "When Tara was 8 and I was 16, I took her with me on my dates," Sherian said. "The three of us ate ice creams and walked around in the neighborhood. She smiled a lot, never got into the way, and we didn't mind having her."

When Tara became an adult, she and her sister still belonged to a threesome, but the third person was new: Tara's boyfriend, Paul Lalanne, with whom she lived in Brooklyn. The three planned to open an office for Primerica, an insurance company under Citigroup. The week before the disaster, Tara, 31, who worked in the insurance branch of Aon, received her license to sell health and life insurance. She and Mr. Lalanne were planning to marry next year.

JAMES HOBIN
A Friend of Little League

James Hobin coached children for 21 years, long before his two sons started to play baseball and basketball. "I used to get so upset with him. He hadn't mowed our lawn yet, but he was out there mowing that Little League field," said his wife and high school sweetheart, Sheila Hobin of Marlborough, Conn.

"People will remember him with that lawn mower hanging out of his truck." He helped get electricity, a dugout and a concession stand for the local field. He could even be counted on to set up the grid for a local charity's cow chip auction—people bought squares and would win money if a cow deposited a chip on their particular square.

Mr. Hobin, 47, a vice president with Marsh & McLennan, was at the World Trade Center for a meeting. "The morning of the 11th he had called me at work just to make sure I was there O.K., to tell me he'd be home later that evening," she said. Often, after she dropped him off at the train station, he would call her at her office from the train.

"He was always thoughtful," she said. "He always cared a lot about what we all did, and how we were."

ROBERT WAYNE HOBSON
Unlimited Energy

Robert Wayne Hobson—universally known as Wayne—talked a lot, dreamed big and was so lighthearted about everything that his wife, Cindy, made him propose three times just to make sure he was serious.

"He called me a hundred times during the day, always with some new idea or big plan for the future," Mrs. Hobson said.

Five years ago, Mr. Hobson, 36, left a job as a broker at the World Trade Center to fulfill one of his dreams—he opened Hobson's Bar and Grill in Hoboken, N.J. It soon became the place for his friends to get together after the stock market closed for the day, said Mrs. Hobson, who told her husband a more appropriate name for the bar was "Wayne's World."

In 1999, Mr. Hobson returned to the trade center as a broker for Cantor Fitzgerald, but he kept the bar. "He loved to be around people," Mrs. Hobson said. "He had unlimited amounts of energy."

She said that when she went out golfing with her husband, he, not the game, was the draw. "It was the only time I had five hours straight of his undivided attention."

DAJUAN HODGES
A Dancer and a Ham

DaJuan Hodges never gave his mother any trouble. "He had every opportunity to stray, and he chose not to," said his mother, Pamela Dixon, who raised two sons in Harlem.

As a child, Mr. Hodges loved to dance and ham it up for family pictures—"He was always ready to show the latest dance," Ms. Dixon said—and as a teenager he was a good student and did volunteer work. When his daughter Jatair, now 8, was born, he embraced fatherhood with determination. "It was like, O.K., I have a child now," his mother said. "He just knew he had to stay up on things because he had this responsibility."

Mr. Hodges, who lived with his daughter and fiancée in the Bronx, did everything with his family, particularly going to movies, one of his passions. He worked in management services at Marsh & McLennan, on the 96th floor of 1 World Trade Center.

Ms. Dixon, who works for the same company in Midtown as an executive secretary, watched from her 42nd floor window as the first tower—2 World Trade Center—collapsed on Sept. 11. "I just went crazy," she said. As she screamed, "My son, my son," and co-workers tried to calm her down, the other tower, where he was, also disappeared in a storm of smoke and dust.

Not having her son to bury has made the experience even more devastating. "You have nothing except good memories," Ms. Dixon said.

PATRICK ALOYSIUS HOEY
Always First to Volunteer

Patrick Aloysius Hoey was never far behind his four children: Brian, Robert, Michael and Sharon. When they played Little League baseball, he was right there as the coach. When they went to high school, he was the president of the parent-teacher's association.

"He was very active in our lives," Brian said. "All my siblings aspire to be just like him." Patrick Hoey, 53, married his high school sweetheart, Eileen, and raised his family in Middletown, N.J. If anyone needed help, Mr. Hoey, a civil engineer for the Port Authority, was always the first one to volunteer. And he was as generous with his love as with his time. When he stepped through the door at night, he always made sure to greet the family dog, a Maltese named Casey.

"Everybody loved my dad," Brian said.

STEPHEN HOFFMAN
Drawn to the Surf

Stephen Hoffman met his wife, Gabrielle, during his freshman year in college when he checked out the girls living below his floor in a coeducational dorm. They dated for more than eight years, and a daughter, Madeline, was born five years after their wedding.

"We loved it, loved it, loved that life," Gabrielle Hoffman said. "We had a great marriage, and we were very much in love."

An avid surfer, Mr. Hoffman, 36, would sometimes get up at 5 A.M. to surf near their house in Long Beach, on Long Island. For that, he was willing to commute an hour each way to and from Cantor Fitzgerald, where he was a trader.

And he doted on Madeline, 5, whom he taught to surf last summer. "She's a little peanut, but she got onto the surfboard six times in one day," Mrs. Hoffman said. Madeline misses Daddy. She now puts cologne on his old T-shirts and sleeps in them every night.

"It's very hard for her," her mother said. "He tucked her in, kissed her goodnight the previous night. The next day, he got up, went to work and she never sees him again. We are heartbroken."

Mr. Hoffman had an identical twin, Gregory. "Now it's a thrill to see Gregory," Mrs. Hoffman said. "It makes me feel I were seeing Stephen again."

FREDERICK J. HOFFMANN and MICHELE L. HOFFMANN
All Too Much in the Family

There was a piece of favorite banter between 5-year-old Derek Leohner and his grandpa, Frederick J. Hoffmann. The grandfather would ask, "Who loves you?" Derek would reply, "Pop Pop." "How much?" Mr. Hoffman would ask, and the answer would come back, "Too much."

"I only hope that Derek knows how true this was," said Nicole Leohner, Derek's mother and Mr. Hoffmann's daughter.

The day after Derek was born in Ohio, six weeks premature, Mr. Hoffmann hopped into his car and drove nine hours straight through, getting a speeding ticket along the way. When he saw the baby, lying in an incubator and connected to tubes, he said he looked like a movie star.

When Derek was less than a year old, his parents moved back to Freehold, N.J., where his grandparents live. Mr. Hoffmann's wife, Gail, said that over breakfast last week, Derek said he wished he had a magic pebble, so he could "make a wish, and Pop Pop and Aunt Shelly will be with us, and we will be a happy family again."

Aunt Shelly was Michele L. Hoffmann, Mr. Hoffmann's younger daughter. She went with Derek to his school Halloween parades and class trips. She took him to movies. She teased him. And she was beautiful. She made people's heads turn. "People were drawn to her dazzling smile and bright blue and green eyes," her sister said.

Four years ago, Mr. Hoffmann, a partner at Cantor Fitzgerald, brought Michele, then 23, into his firm. He also brought in two other members of the family—Ms. Leohner's husband, Bart, and Thomas Cosenza, Mrs. Hoffmann's nephew. On Sept. 11, Mr. Leohner was out sick and Mr. Cosenza was late for work. Michele and Frederick Hoffmann were there.

"I always thought it nice to have the family members work together," Mrs. Hoffmann said, "but who knew this would happen? Our loss is heavy, but it could have been heavier."

JUDITH HOFMILLER
The Simple and Treasured

After sixteen years and more than a few hurdles and health scares weathered together, Judith Hofmiller and Robert Winkis had discovered themselves in the right kind of mood—an upbeat mood—to make their union official and segue into marriage in October 2001. They intended to tie the knot the same way they lived:

"No muss, no fuss," he said—a trip to Town Hall in Brookfield, Conn., an after-the-fact gathering of friends, maybe a pseudo honeymoon at Christmas.

Ms. Hofmiller, 53 and a computer whiz, had put in for vacation at Marsh & McLennan, where she was a senior software consultant. At home, she ironed to the crooning of Backstreet Boys and 98 Degrees, and her passion was cross-stitching—she conjured up baby bibs, towels, and bottle-holders for pregnant friends. On weekends, the couple puttered, collaborated at mealtime, and rented a Saturday night movie.

The couple spent their last Saturday together in the yard, pulling weeds; suddenly it has become a cherished memory of what they were all about. "It was quiet time together; just talking," Mr. Winkis said. "Appreciating the simple things."

THOMAS WARREN HOHLWECK Jr.
A Fast Engine, an Easy Pace

Boys will have their toys, and Thomas Warren Hohlweck Jr. had his. Starting with a used Fiat in high school, Mr. Hohlweck loved to tool around in racy vehicles, although he could not be described as a racy driver.

"He liked to rev the engine but he was no speedster," said his wife, Pamela. "In fact, he was the best driver I ever met." Cars alone could not keep Mr. Hohlweck's attention when he wasn't working at Aon Risk Services as a vice president. There

After September 11, many children turned to art as a medium for expressing grief over the terror attacks and support for the victims. This was part of a memorial wall at the Union Square subway station in New York City. *(Ruby Washington)*

were the daily jogs through Battery Park, the weekend tennis and golf games and the endless tinkering that—next to the New York Philharmonic—made a visit to Home Depot one of his favorite excursions. Mrs. Hohlweck indulged all her husband's hobbies, even allowing him to set up a workbench in the kitchen. "When we weren't outdoors hiking or gardening, he was inside doing some project," she said.

But all of Mr. Hohlweck's hobbies took a back seat to his children, Randy, Robin and Todd. All three inherited his love for running.

A few years ago, while the Hohlwecks were on vacation in Virginia Beach, a fire destroyed their home in Harrison, N.J., including a score of woodworking accomplishments and the beloved Jensen-Healy that sat in the garage. But if Mr. Hohlweck was devastated, he never let on. "He was just happy no one was hurt," Mrs. Hohlweck said.

JOSEPH HOLLAND
He Made Everybody Laugh

Joseph Holland could always poke fun at his life. He would be the first one to joke about his golf scores, his in-laws and his newborn boy. And his zingers, delivered just right, were a constant source of laughter for his family and friends.

"He could get everybody to laugh," said his mother-in-law, Ellen Mahoney. "He was insightful and quick-witted."

Mr. Holland, 32, started working in finance after college, and later became a broker for Carr Futures. He lived with his wife, Kathy, and their son, Joseph IV, in Glen Rock, N.J. Though Mr. Holland saw humor in most things, he was serious about being a father. He was in the delivery room when his son was born on Sept. 1, and even cut the umbilical cord himself. He could not wait to pass out cigars to his co-workers. "He was really looking forward to being a dad," said his mother-in-law.

ELIZABETH HOLMES
Hard to Keep Up With

One morning in June, Elizabeth Holmes called her fiancé and informed him that she was ready to take him up on his offer to go ring hunting on 47th Street, so off they went. In no time at all, she found the diamond of her dreams: a $6,500 beauty.

"I looked at the price tag and started to sweat, and when she asked me what was wrong, I told her it must be the bright lights in the store," said Ron Harden, who had hoped to present her with the ring at Christmas.

They planned to marry next year and move in together in Harlem, where she lived with her son, Miles Travis; they were also in the process of buying a car she picked out during

a trip home to visit relatives in South Carolina this summer, a Toyota Highlander.

A devoted runner, Ms. Holmes, 42, circled Central Park every day, and often put in a second run if she felt dissatisfied with her morning jog. "I'm a runner, too, but I couldn't keep up with her," said Mr. Harden. She sewed her own clothing, sang in the choir at the Canaan Baptist Church of Christ, and was always halfway through a book. She worked in the communications department at Euro Brokers.

TOM P. HOLOHAN
Dream Job, Dream House

Colleen Fitzpatrick was introduced to Tom P. Holohan 12 years ago through a mutual friend at a bar. "A big blond guy named Eric came to greet me as I walked in the door," she said, "but I wanted Tom"—he was the guy leaning back in a seat, quiet and smiling.

When they were newlyweds, Mr. Holohan, an auditor at Manhattan Trust, became eligible for a firefighter's spot. "I didn't want him to go," said his wife, now Colleen Holohan. "But he was so happy. Being a firefighter was his boyhood dream."

When Mrs. Holohan was pregnant with their third child, Liam, the young couple bought a piece of land in Chester, N.Y., and started building their dream house. It was a two-story colonial with four bedrooms.

"In June 2000, we moved into a new house with a new baby."

He was the soccer dad who helped coach the football team of Thomas, 7, and brought Caitlyn, 5, to the soccer fields. He took them to see *How the Grinch Stole Christmas*, the *Pokémon* movies and *Shrek* as soon as they were released, and read them bedtime stories, tucked them in and kissed them good night every night he was home.

"He enjoyed every minute of being with us," said Mrs. Holohan. "I just wish it were longer." Firefighter Holohan, 36, was a member of Engine Company 6 in Manhattan.

MICHAEL J. HORN
An Extra Yearbook Picture

A picture of Michael J. Horn is featured in the Lehigh College yearbook in 1993. It was a nice tribute, considering Mr. Horn was in high school at the time. Mr. Horn, from Lynbrook, N.Y., visited his older brother, Charles, so often at Lehigh just to hang out that friends, acquaintances and the yearbook staff assumed he went to school there too.

It was a typical performance for the younger Mr. Horn, 27. His looks opened doors, but his charisma, zest for life and supreme confidence gave him a grand entrance wherever he went and made him a welcome fixture. A software support technician for Cantor Fitzgerald, he loved to camp and ski, and spend time outdoors.

He had a big network of friends, who were accustomed to his practical jokes. He left amusing phone messages for friends, singing songs he had written and putting on accents. He liked to entertain himself, and people around him.

"He's not one of those guys who wanted to conquer the world—he wanted to enjoy life," said his brother, Charles H. Horn. "He was a good guy with a great heart."

MATTHEW HORNING
Setting, and Meeting, Goals

At an office Christmas party in 1999, Matthew Horning told a colleague he had two goals: improving at guitar and finding someone to love. In January he started taking guitar lessons. In August he met Maura Landry, who also lived in Hoboken, N.J.

"Hi," he called down the table at a Mexican restaurant where mutual friends had gathered. "We're neighbors." In the following months, Mr. Horning's grin grew into what his family called the "Maura smile." He started getting sappy, observed his sister, Dana.

A database administrator for Marsh & McLennan, Mr. Horning, 26, aspired to write a fantasy novel or a comic book. His dreams were simple and sincere. "We didn't have to live in the biggest house on the street, but the people inside had to be happy," said Ms. Landry, 24.

Though not yet engaged, the couple were planning a life together. She wanted four children; he talked her down to three. He wanted her to walk down the aisle to the *Star Wars* theme. She said, "We'll see."

ROBERT L. HOROHOE Jr.
In Love with His Work

Robert L. Horohoe Jr. was literally reared to be a corporate bond broker. His father, a former senior executive at Cantor Fitzgerald, kept a Telerate machine in their house and introduced him early to terms like "bid" and "offer."

So when Mr. Horohoe graduated from college and went to work for Cantor Fitzgerald in 1992, it was a natural and seamless progression. "He loved it there," said his brother Michael, who once worked at Cantor as a bond broker. (One sister, Donna Erskine, is also a former Cantor employee.) "People would gripe all the time, but Bobby never complained about going to work so early and leaving late. He was team Cantor."

After 10 years in Battery Park City, where he could see his office from his apartment, Mr. Horohoe, 31, had decided to buy a home in his native Holmdel, N.J., where he spent nearly every weekend at his mother's house, relaxing with his fiancée, recounting tales of earlier days with his high school buddies, and playing tennis with fellow weekday city dwellers.

Now, his mother, Patricia, said, "On Friday when I come home, the house is a little empty. Maybe I'm just waiting for him to come through the door and say 'Ah, it was a hoax' or something."

AARON HORWITZ
Bad Day Was Still Good

Once, Aaron Horwitz had a supremely lousy day. A friend asked, "From 1 to 10, with 1 as the worst, how would you rate it?"

"Eight," he replied.

You could get a contact high from Mr. Horwitz, 24, a bond broker at Cantor Fitzgerald with the enviable responsibility of entertaining clients to make them feel as if they were the most important people in the world.

As if anyone had to pay him.

For Mr. Horwitz was not just a showman, who did the Michael Jackson moonwalk on bar tops, who, at a museum, drew his own masterpiece on a mist-coated window next to a Rembrandt.

He seized souls, not letting go until he made them merry: Met a guy in a toy store and, moments later, the two were having a hula hoop contest. Insisted a concierge stop weeping over a bad breakup and called her at 2:30 A.M. to make sure. Sweet-talked hostesses at four-star restaurants into producing tables for eight, and their phone numbers for dates. Persuaded a Chinese street masseur to let Mr. Horwitz give him a massage.

"You could talk to a brick wall," a friend told him. Yes, Aaron said, but he preferred chatting with a mirror. He often did so, then fell over, laughing.

CHARLES JOSEPH HOUSTON
A Mush Around Children

Charles Joseph Houston was 6-foot-1, weighed 225 pounds and had a thick mustache. "He had a rough exterior, but inside, he was such a mush, especially around children." said Linda Houston, his wife. He frolicked in his backyard pool with his 2-year-old nieces, read to his 9-year-old nephew, and in general "snuggled with them." He went for walks with them and took them to movies and malls. "He was like a second father," she said.

"But he was a pull-no-punches type of guy," she added. "What you see is what you get. He wouldn't sugarcoat on anything. If you asked him for an opinion, he'd tell you what he really thought, sometimes even things you didn't want to hear."

He and his brother-in-law, Otto Diodato, the father of his nieces and nephew, used to be efficient handymen in their two houses, merely a few yards apart. They'd be constantly concocting projects—redoing the kitchen countertops, building fences, changing the bathroom tiles—and actually finishing them.

But shortly before the September attack, they had become more like "Fred Flintstone and Barney Rubble," his wife said. "They would joke around, enjoy each other's company, and the projects would last forever." Mr. Houston, 42, worked at Euro Brokers. He and his wife were planning to adopt a child next summer.

GEORGE HOWARD
Going to Work on a Day Off

Sept. 11 was the second time that George Howard, a Port Authority police officer, was enjoying a day off when he heard that there was trouble at the World Trade Center. It was also the second time that he raced to work, voluntarily, into the midst of the chaos. The last time was 1993, when the trade center was bombed. "He always did that," said his mother, Arlene Howard. "He heard about it and called up and said, 'I'm on my way.'"

Officer Howard, who was 44 and lived in Hicksville, N.Y., worked in the Port Authority's emergency services unit, an elite group he helped found. To him, Mrs. Howard recalled, the unit combined the best of police and rescue work.

In his spare time he volunteered for the local fire department and he trained other police and fire departments in safety and rescue work. And he loved coaching children, including his own two sons, Christopher, 19, and Robert, 13.

When President Bush visited ground zero just after the attacks, Mrs. Howard was asked if she would like to present him with her son's silver shield. When the president mentioned the shield in a subsequent speech, and said he could carry Officer Howard's memory forever, Mrs. Howard said, "That made me very proud."

MICHAEL C. HOWELL
Boundless Energy

Michael C. Howell rarely took vacations or sick days. He simply found it hard to slow down at Fred Alger Management Inc., where he was the director of management information systems. His high energy also was evident in his tennis game: he played

to win. He used to be on the courts nearly every weekend with his 29-year-old son, Kevin, also a computer network engineer. His son was wary of his father's very good forehand.

Mr. Howell, 60, had to make a rotten choice recently. He had been handed a ticket to the United States Open. Should he go? He reluctantly decided that he had too many meetings planned and clients to see.

His wife, Emily, remembers how he did the funniest thing. He left his office on the 93rd floor of 1 World Trade Center and drove to his home in Bayside, Queens, staying just long enough to deliver the ticket to her. "He startled me," she says. Then he went straight back to work.

STEVEN L. HOWELL
A Short Ride Lasts 10 Years

They met 10 years ago on the Staten Island Ferry on a half-hour ride to Lower Manhattan. She was a secretary. He was a technician, the fellow who often got beeped when computers at Marsh USA went on the blink.

And although they married two summers before Sept. 11, Steven L. Howell and Debra Upton still behaved like newlyweds. The weekend before Sept. 11, he surprised his wife with three days at Mount Airy Lodge, a Poconos resort famous for its heart-shaped tubs. The resort, which shut down in October, was on its last legs, but she took no notice. "We loved being with each other," Ms. Upton said.

On Sept. 11, the express bus from Staten Island dropped them off at 8:15. He reported to the 97th floor of 1 World Trade Center. She went to the 40th floor of 2 World Trade. They had been apart all of 15 minutes when she called to see how his day was going.

When the first plane hit, she said, she made it out, but he never had a chance. Lost, too, was his best friend, Martin Giovinazzo, who was hired by Marsh about a year before.

Mr. Howell, 36, who left Ms. Upton with a roomful of Nascar collectibles, was helping support his father, so they were not sure they would have children. "He was my kid," his wife said.

MARTIN GIOVINAZZO's portrait appears on page 185.

MILLIE HROMADA
At Home in the Vertical City

Everyone in the family knows that to Wendy Breban, Millie Hromada has always been "my Millie." True, there were five sisters and two brothers, but Millie and Wendy were the only two born in Puerto Rico, and their bond was incredibly close. Millie, 35, loved Manhattan—Wendy called her "city girl"—and was addicted to the bustling life in the vertical city of the World Trade Center, where she was a secretary at Aon Corporation.

Luckily, she was able to take the train from Flushing every day with her husband, Joseph, an electrician who often also worked in the trade center. In fact, that's where he had a job that Tuesday. Millie and Joseph were "like glue," Wendy said, and so, when the plane crashed into 1 World Trade Center, Millie was terrified for Joseph. Wendy and her sister Doris called Millie on her cell phone. There on the 98th floor, Millie had a horrifying view of "the people jumping out," Wendy said.

It wasn't until the second plane hit Millie's building that she reached her husband on the phone. He was downstairs, but it was O.K., he said. He was coming to get her. "Millie told him, 'I'll see you later tonight,' " Wendy said, "but then she never came home.'"

Joseph survived and is now looking for Millie. "I feel her, we are so close," Wendy said.

MARIAN HRYCAK
Their Time Together

"This was supposed to be our time now," Joanne Hrycak said of her husband, Marian Hrycak, who went to work as usual on Sept. 11, but never came home. The couple had been getting ready to take their annual trip to Vermont, were sprucing up their home in Flushing, N.Y., and had just bought a puppy.

Now, she said, she has learned things she never knew about her husband of 32 years. It was no secret that the 56-year-old collected books, stamps, coins and Conan comic books. But she had also found tuna fish cans and toothpaste tubes he had squirreled away for some far-off reason.

When they met in 1967, she could not bring herself to call him by his given name. What was his mother thinking? "I just couldn't," she said. "He was Marty."

He took her ice skating on their first date and nearly broke his neck, but it did not matter. They married in 1969, raised two children, and he eventually went to work for New York State's Department of Taxation and Finance. His specialty was investigating shopkeepers who charged consumers tax on items that are tax-free.

Shortly before 9 A.M. the day of the attacks, he called to say he was safely out of the building. She later learned he was not. He was last seen on the 78th floor of the south tower, helping some elderly co-workers evacuate, before the second plane hit.

PAUL R. HUGHES
The Ultimate Technophile

Paul R. Hughes was a computer guy. "And our house looked like it," said his wife, Donna Hughes. "He put together most of the electronics in our house. He built all our computers from scratch and was in the middle of building another one. He would go to computer shows or visit online auctions to get parts. U.P.S. visited my house quite frequently."

Only a few things took Mr. Hughes, 38, away from computers. One was a hot tub, installed about a year and a half ago. If he could have found a way to safely tinker with electronics while immersed in the bubbling warm water next to his wife and 10-year-old daughter, he might have tried it.

Another passion was the Yankees. Because Mr. Hughes rose at 5 A.M. to catch an early train from his home in Stamford, Conn., to his job at Marsh Inc., on the 97th Floor of 1 World Trade Center, he frequently could not stay up to watch the end of a game. So he taped them, and woe to the person who even hinted that she knew the outcome.

Some technophiles have trouble communicating their passion to the uninitiated. But Mr. Hughes had the ability to give simple directions on tackling a technology problem, usually sight unseen, said John Humen, a colleague in the data systems department at Marsh. "He would say do this, do that, and your problem would be solved."

THOMAS F. HUGHES Jr.
A Life in Pictures

Thomas F. Hughes Jr.'s wife and children assembled dozens of photographs for collages they displayed at Mr. Hughes's funeral services.

There were several pictures of dolphins kissing them during a family vacation in the Bahamas. Another one captured Mr. Hughes laughing, because he had fallen in the snow on a skiing trip. There was another one of a tailgate party when he and his wife, Rosanne, went to see Bruce Springsteen at Giants Stadium.

The largest picture was of him in a tuxedo, at his sister's wedding. "He had the smirk on his face that everyone recognized," Mrs. Hughes said. "I wanted people to laugh when they saw these pictures. That's how he would have liked it. He lived life to the fullest."

Mr. Hughes, 46, owned a company called Colonial Art Decorators, a painting and decorating company based in New York City. On Sept. 11, he was at Windows on the

World, for what was supposed to be a 15-minute meeting with a client.

The Hugheses, married for 17 years, lived in Spring Lake Heights, N.J., with their children Ashley, 15, and Patrick, 12. "I don't have the words to say good-bye," Mrs. Hughes said. "He will always be a part of my life."

TIMOTHY ROBERT HUGHES
Large-Scale Loving Care

When it came to hobbies, Timothy Robert Hughes had one as big as a house.

He and his wife, Karen, liked to buy tattered older homes and, with elbow grease and loving care, restore them to life.

Take the century-old late Victorian house they bought in 1999 in Madison, N.J. "It had been vacant for many years," Mrs. Hughes said. "Basically, it needed everything." So the couple put in new Sheetrock, plaster, plumbing, bathrooms and a kitchen. They had experience, having done such work on every home they had owned in 17 years of marriage. This time, their efforts so impressed a local historic preservation society that it gave the Hughes an award last May. "There was a huge banner on the front of our house for a month," Mrs. Hughes said.

Still, Mr. Hughes, a currency options trader in emerging markets at Cantor Fitzgerald, had enormous zest for his work and his children, Tim, 15; Ken, 13, and Chrissy, 8. "He always found time to coach all his kids in baseball, soccer, sports," said Donald M. Burns, the best man at the Hugheses' wedding.

Mr. Hughes was thrilled when Ken won a county baseball tournament last summer, cleanly laying down 10 consecutive bunts. Mr. Hughes spent his 43rd birthday, Sept. 3, golfing with Tim. "In retrospect," his wife said, "I'm glad they had that time."

WILLIAM HUNT
Little Brother's Protector

What Dan Hunt remembers best about his older brother William is that during Dan's senior year in high school, William, then a college senior, went to every basketball game he played. When Dan's team lost its final game, and Dan fell two free throws short of a milestone of 2,000 points, his brother was right there to protect him.

"Some newspeople wanted to come down and ask me how I felt, not to have made that," Dan Hunt remembered. His brother, he said, kept them away, approaching one of them and saying, "Buddy, I really don't think it's a good idea right now, and if you wouldn't mind, I'd appreciate it if you wouldn't do this." Dan Hunt said of William, who worked at Euro Brokers in 2 World Trade Center and was 32, "He's very protective of everyone that he loves."

That included his wife of three years, Jennifer, and their 15-month-old daughter, Emma, whom William called Lovebird. "Now I call her Lovebird, too," Dan said.

KATHLEEN HUNT-CASEY
A Friend, a Sister

Kathleen Hunt-Casey was a careful friend, who listened and acted on what she heard. "She would call me at least three or four times a day, and then she'd have to get off the phone because of work, but when she called back she would continue talking where she left off," said Virginia Lemmerman, who knew Ms. Hunt-Casey since she was 10. "If I was feeling down, going through hard times or rocky days, she always tried to make me feel better about myself."

And if someone mentioned they had had a baby and needed, say, a picture frame, she would find one, and never take anything in return, Ms. Lemmerman said.

Ms. Hunt-Casey, 43, worked on the trading desk at Sandler O'Neill & Partners, and lived in Middletown, N.J., with her husband, Kevin, and son Matthew, 14. She was a devoted mother, Ms. Lemmerman said: "He was her life."

Ms. Lemmerman said, "I didn't just lose my best friend, I lost a sister."

JOE HUNTER
Destined for Firefighting

Long before he understood the dangers, Joe Hunter was love-struck by the sights and sounds of firefighting, the shiny red trucks with their bright lights and whirring sirens. The trucks from the South Hempstead Fire Department, whose firehouse was at the end of his block, could not pass his house without him racing behind on his Big Wheel. At age 8, Mr. Hunter would coax friends into mock rescue drills, using the family's water hose and a ladder.

"He was just a kid," said Teresa Labo, his sister. "But whenever it came to anything about firefighting, he was always oh so serious. It was like he was destined."

So by the time he was old enough to go off to college, to Hofstra, Mr. Hunter, 32, was no longer just dreaming of fighting fires. He had become a volunteer with the very department that fueled his passion. It was a feat that meant as much to him as the day in 1996 when he graduated from the New York City Fire Department's academy. His family, though proud, never stopped worrying.

"God bless you," his mother would say on days when he rushed off to be with his squad, 288 in Maspeth, Queens.

Hoping to comfort her, Firefighter Hunter would always pause long enough to say: "Mom, don't worry about me. If anything ever happens, just know I loved the job."

ROBERT HUSSA
Sharing Hobbies, and Values

Robert Hussa's hobbies eventually became his family's hobbies. He took up golf and got his oldest son, Robert Jr., hooked. His wife, Kathryn, was taking lessons, too. And though his youngest son, Thomas, did not play golf, Mr. Hussa managed to interest him in skiing and riding mountain bikes. Those were his hobbies, too.

"Every season, there were different activities," said Kathryn Hussa. "We were rarely home.'"

Mr. Hussa, 51, a senior vice president at Carr Futures, shared more than just his hobbies with his family. He believed in honesty and integrity, and stressed the importance of those values to his children.

"He led by example," said Robert Jr. The weekend before the World Trade Center attack, Mr. Hussa joined Thomas and his friends for a barbecue at the family's home in Roslyn, N.Y. The next day, he rounded up Robert Jr. for an outing to a Jets game at the Meadowlands.

"He was very content with his work and his family," said his wife. "He had a life that was full."

THOMAS E. HYNES
No Moment Worth Missing

To Thomas E. Hynes, an account manager for the Vestek division of Thomson Financial, every moment was a golden opportunity and every person he met was sure to be a friend. Was somebody going somewhere, to a bar, a Yankees game, a wedding out of town? Mr. Hynes, 28, wanted to be there, too, and invariably, he was. He set his alarm clock early, "to get into the day, because the day was going to be happy, it was going to be glorious, and it was going to be fun," said his mother, Fran.

He grew up in Pelham, N.Y., playing ice hockey with his older brother, John, as well as soccer and, eventually, baseball. "When he was a senior in high school, he found out the baseball team was going to Florida for spring training, and he wanted to go to Florida," said his father, Bill. "So he tried out for the team, and he made it."

He met his wife, Carolyne, on St. Patrick's Day in 1996. He proposed to her in 1997, beside the tree in Rockefeller Center. It was Dec. 19, his birthday, and "he told me he wanted to propose to me on his birthday because he wanted to give himself the best gift he could think of," Mrs. Hynes said.

He had bright blue eyes and a broad smile. When the sky is the right color these days, his parents call it "a Thomas sky."

"I feel Tom was an angel among us," his wife said. "He was so cheerful and loving and understanding and generous and kind, and nobody could light up a room like he could." They had just bought a house in Norwalk, Conn.

Their baby is due in April 2002.

WALTER HYNES
Handyman and Lawyer

Capt. Walter Hynes was the person his extended family relied on for everything. If you needed your plumbing fixed or a room painted, he would do it. He would change your tire. He was the family lawyer. He even met his wife while lending a hand: he was helping another firefighter, Richard Fanning, move into a new house and was introduced to Mr. Fanning's sister.

Captain of Ladder Company 13 at 85th Street and Lexington Avenue, Mr. Hynes lived in Belle Harbor, Queens, with his wife, Veronica, and their three daughters. He had worked as a firefighter in Brownsville, Brooklyn, and put himself through law school at St. John's University at night.

"He had no free time," a family member said yesterday, "because he was always doing for everyone else."

I

JOSEPH IANELLI
A Life Taking Off

Joseph Ianelli's personal and professional lives were taking off. The 28-year-old Hoboken resident and his fiancée, Monica Palatucci-Lebowitz, had decided they would marry next September. In the summer of 2001, Mr. Ianelli, an accountant formerly with an architectural recruiting company, went to work for a financial services conglomerate, Marsh & McLennan, on the 98th floor of 1 World Trade Center, the complex's north tower.

Normally, Mr. Ianelli arrived at work at 9 A.M., said his sister, Jennifer Thompson, but because he was preparing for a meeting on Sept. 11, he got there earlier. The last communication from him of which his family is aware is an e-mail message he sent to a friend at 8:35, 13 minutes before one of the hijacked planes smashed into the north tower.

Mr. Ianelli, the son of Joseph and Barbara Ianelli of Staten Island, was 6 feet 2 inches and about 200 pounds and an avid sports enthusiast, playing as well as watching baseball and basketball. His family, which also included two grandparents, Anthony and Theresa Capozzi, "was very important to him," Ms. Thompson said. Her 7-month-old son gave Mr. Ianelli plenty of opportunity to get a taste of life as a future father. "When he was here, he always played with him," she said.

ZUHTU IBIS
In the Thick of Things

Zuhtu Ibis was born and raised in a small city in the middle of Turkey. So it is perhaps understandable that when he made his way to the United States, at 18, with his father, he was not overjoyed about working in New Jersey.

"He came so far and he was from such a small place, that he did not want to be in New Jersey," said his wife, Leyla Uyar. "He wanted to be working in New York, in the middle of everything." But the only way for a brand-new immigrant to get there, he knew, was to work. And so that is what he did—delivering pizza, pumping gas at his father's station, putting himself through technical school in North Brunswick.

Then, three years ago, he finally made it across the river, working on a temporary computer project at Cantor Fitzgerald. They liked him; they hired him. Suddenly, he was not only in the middle of everything—from his window on the 103rd floor, he could see everything, too.

"His window looked out to New Jersey, and he told me he could see our house and he was keeping a watch over me," said Ms. Uyar, tending to their 2-year-old son, Mert, in their house in Clifton, NJ. Ms. Uyar and Mr. Ibis were high-school sweethearts, married when she was just 18, and he was 20. In a new country, with a new language, it was not always easy for them. "We have terrible times, you know, but the thing was that we were together," she said. "I was with him in all the times, good and bad. And we worked so hard."

JONATHAN L. IELPI
Honoring No. 16

Take a walk out to the Saddle Rock Bridge over Udalls Pond in Great Neck, on Long Island, and you will see the Manhattan skyline, forever altered by a terrorist attack. Look down from the vista toward the railing of the span and you will see a North High School Blazers hockey jersey, No. 16.

The jersey belonged to Jonathan L. Ielpi, 29, a New York City firefighter from Great Neck who was among the first to reach the twin towers. Mr. Ielpi's sister, Melissa, put it there just 24 hours after the disaster. It was still tacked to the railing in November, among flowers and candles. "Jonathan loved playing hockey, but he gave it up when he joined the Fire Department," Ms. Ielpi said. "He was just very nervous that he'd hurt himself and wouldn't be able to do his job."

That was Jonathan Ielpi—more concerned about others than he was about himself. He not only worked for Squad

288 in Queens; he also served as the chief of the Volunteer Vigilant Fire Department in his hometown.

If you cannot find Saddle Rock Bridge or Udalls Pond, just head over to Great Neck's skating rink. There, from the rafters, hangs an enormous banner emblazoned with Mr. Ielpi's name and jersey number, which the Blazers recently retired.

MICHAEL IKEN
One Night to Count the Stars

It would be hard for anyone who came to Michael Iken's 37th birthday party, on the Saturday right before the disaster, ever to forget it. Michael, a bond trader at Maxcor/Euro Brokers on the 84th floor of 2 World Trade Center, insisted that that night's celebration be at home on the terrace of the garden apartment in Riverdale, the Bronx, he shared with his wife, Monica.

"It just had to be surf and turf," she said, "so I got his favorite teriyaki beef, and the lobster tails, and ordered his favorite key lime pie from Florida, because you just can't get decent key lime around here," she said.

Of course, close friends Jennifer and Andrea were there. The food and conversation were so great that even the neighbors stopped by.

Then all four of them sat on the lawn "and hung out till the wee hours," his wife said, "and counted the stars."

She cried for a bit: "I am so grateful to have that memory. Because he was so happy."

FRED ILL Jr.
Everything over the Top

Fred Ill Jr. was a skinny kid from the Bronx, and he made up for it by being better than you. A captain in the New York Fire Department, he gained fame two years ago for saving the life of a man who was pushed onto the subway tracks. The duty of a firefighter ends right about there, but simple lifesaving was not enough for Captain Ill. He later stayed nearby as the man learned to walk on artificial legs, and he helped to find scholarships for the man's children.

He put in extra effort as a father of three, a baseball and basketball coach, a reservist in the Army Corps of Engineers and, of course, a firehouse leader.

"Everything he did, he did it over the top," said Chris Flatley, a firefighter at Ladder Company 2 in Manhattan. The men there, on East 51st Street, say that Captain Ill, 49, was the first captain to dedicate himself to the house, which officers are wont to treat as a stressful, temporary steppingstone.

The firefighters could not resist occasionally pulling pranks on such a man. Once they watched as Captain Ill

called in a report of a suspicious package, though they knew he was looking at a newly installed sculpture.

ANTHONY INFANTE
An Inspector in Shape

Anthony Infante, an inspector for the Port Authority Police, had gotten in shape for the New York City Marathon after laying off the race for a few years. His regained slimness came in handy as he ran up the stairwell of 1 World Trade Center, aiding victims. He was seen giving his coat to one man to protect him from burning materials.

Mr. Infante, 47, became a cadet with the Newark Police Department at 18. After staff cuts, he joined the Port Authority Police. As he progressed through its ranks, he attended college and then graduate school at night.

His last post was as the highest-ranking policeman at La Guardia and Kennedy Airports, when Mayor Rudolph W. Giuliani was campaigning for the city Police Department to take over the job. Mr. Infante marshaled evidence to show his force was doing well.

"There is no issue with the police departments," he said. "It's with the mayor."

The mayor went to his funeral, where Mr. Infante was remembered as a nice guy. Paul Brady, a friend, recalled how Mr. Infante nursed him through a divorce. He had tried to say thanks.

"What, are you nuts?" Inspector Infante answered. "We're friends."

CHRISTOPHER INGRASSIA
A Concern for Others

Sure, Christopher Ingrassia was a Wall Street whiz and a terrific athlete. But what stood out about him to many was the deep kindness he poured out on friends and strangers alike.

Even in high school, where he played three sports and was very popular, his sweet concern for others was evident.

One day, when a group of girls stood up and left the table after a girl they didn't like dared to join them, Mr. Ingrassia went over and sat with the abandoned girl. "The mother of that girl told us about it," said his father, Anthony Ingrassia. "There are so many stories like that."

Recently, as a trader at Cantor Fitzgerald, Mr. Ingrassia, 28, who lived in Watchung, N.J., was at a business dinner with several of his bosses and several clients, when he could not help but overhear the argument between the man and woman at the table behind them—and noticed when the man got up, threw the napkin in the woman's face, and left the restaurant.

"Chris turned around and said, 'Don't worry about it; you're with us now,' " his father recalled. "He told her he wasn't a very good dancer, but he asked if she'd like to dance. And he danced with her that night."

PAUL INNELLA
Man of Enthusiasms

"He was like me," said Lucy Aita about Paul Innella, her fiancé. "He talked too much."

They talked daily for weeks before their first date (they had "met" through a singles Web site). After Mr. Innella moved in with Ms. Aita, her son, and her parents in East Brunswick, N.J., he would call "a zillion times a day."

"Hi, honey! Are you O.K., really? Talk to you later!" "Hi honey, I'm 15 minutes from home!"

He was a bright man and knew it—"That's O.K., honey, I'll do it!"—but he was also boyishly enthusiastic. He loved food, giving surprise gifts, bowling and bouncing hard and high on a trampoline with Ms. Aita's son, Kyle, 10. In the first flush of courtship, rather than leave her to drive home to Brooklyn for clean clothes, Mr. Innella would happily swing over to the nearby Macy's to buy some.

He was a hard-working adult—33 and a systems analyst with eSpeed at Cantor Fitzgerald—but also a childlike Disney fanatic. He had been to Disney World nine times, collected hundreds of Disney movies and cartoons, and let's not even talk about the memorabilia. "He was so excited about *Snow White* coming out on DVD," said Ms. Aita. "Because it would have all the extras."

STEPHANIE IRBY
The Expert on Captain Kirk

Stephanie Irby would have fit right in on the Starship Enterprise.

"Her collection of *Star Trek* videotapes just blew my mind," said Addison Irby, an older brother. As soon as a tape was released, she bought it. "When I tried to debate with her about what Captain Kirk did, she would take out a tape, find the exact spot and show me that I was wrong," he said.

Ms. Irby, 38, an accountant for Marsh & McLennan, who always wore "a big, bright smile," microwaved the food for her dog, Charlie, a golden retriever, said Kenneth Irby, another older brother. And she doted on her 2-year-old niece, Cecelia Melton.

Ms. Irby, who was single, shared a house in Queens with Cecelia and her mother, Stephanie's older sister, Pam Irby.

"Stephanie was like a second mother to Cecelia," Ken-

neth said. "Before she died, she was about to use her own savings to open up a college fund account for the baby."

On Sept. 11, Stephanie Irby had planned to take the day off, but "she was too conscientious to miss work," Kenneth Irby said. "In the last minute, she decided to go in."

DOUG JASON IRGANG
Love on the No. 4 Train

Doug Jason Irgang had the kind of jaw-dropping luck that could win a lottery, or save a life. A financial trader, he was there when the trade center was bombed in 1993. And he was on board the Long Island Rail Road train when Colin Ferguson went on a rampage.

"Talk about somebody who was able to get out of touchy situations," said his friend Lisa Saffian. "We're hoping that his luck holds." Mr. Irgang, 32, was even lucky in love.

Riding the No. 4 train to work daily, he noticed that the same young woman was reading his newspaper over his shoulder. This being New York, they barely exchanged hellos.

Then one day, the woman, Kristin Ladner, scribbled her phone number on the newspaper and told him to call. He did. They were engaged a year and a half later, and set a wedding date for Dec. 22, 2001.

TODD ISAAC
A Kick out of Everything

From college on, it was Todd Isaac and Troy Dixon. Two young black men navigating the mostly white world of Wall Street traders. They played golf, they went to the Hamptons, but Mr. Dixon drew the line at skiing. "Todd said: 'Why don't we learn to snowboard? That way we can say we've been skiing all along, and we're just trying something new,' " Mr. Dixon said.

So they did, and when they were on top of Whistler Mountain, Mr. Isaac, who grew up in the Bronx and worked for Cantor Fitzgerald, would say, "Look at us!" And when they were in South Beach, or in the V.I.P. lounge of a swank Manhattan nightclub, or at the Super Bowl, he would say it again. "Look. At. Us."

It was persistence and charm that got him there. Those qualities got him his girlfriend, Sandra Perez, too. A quiet foil to his boisterous humor, she did not like him when they met, at a Valentine's dinner for singles. She is Puerto Rican, and Mr. Isaac made one too many jokes about flan.

But it was not long before she was picnicking in Central Park with him, poring over the real estate ads to plan where they would live. "Todd would make you love him," said his

A wall of American flags and photographs of people missing since the World Trade Center towers fell attracts passers-by near ground zero. People on their way to and from work invariably stop for a moment to reflect or to look at the disaster site through the fence. (*James Estrin*)

brother O'Dell Isaac. "If you didn't love him right away, he would work on you until you did."

ERIK ISBRANDTSEN
Giving His All, All the Time

Erik Isbrandtsen's approach to life was "Do it 150 percent or don't do it at all," said one close friend, Scott Foster. "Whether it was working, working out, playing basketball, playing golf, playing soccer or going out at night, he gave it his all."

Mr. Isbrandtsen, a 30-year-old equity sales trader at Cantor Fitzgerald, always hoped to move back to the Boston area, where he had grown up, where he had starred for the Babson College soccer team. But he stayed in New York, Mr. Foster said, because in his industry, the greatest success could be achieved here.

Another Babson soccer player, David McEachern, remembered how Mr. Isbrandtsen, a midfielder, had come back from a bad junior-year injury in better condition than anyone else on the team the next fall. That drive was evident throughout his friend's life. "If anybody could do 80 years in 30 good ones, he could," Mr. McEachern said. "Good restaurants, good clubs; he enjoyed the finer things in life."

WALEED J. ISKANDAR
An Adventurer at Heart

He was supposed to be studying for his M.B.A. at Harvard. Where was he? Water-skiing with his brother. Was that a problem? No. Waleed J. Iskandar was so sharp that he could study less, achieve high grades and squeeze in plenty of water-skiing. Classmates remembered him wandering in late for a study group and rapidly rattling off solutions to a thorny case before dashing off to the water.

Known for his zest for life and his devotion to Pink Floyd, Mr. Iskandar enchanted people—a lot of people. His contact list on his Palm Pilot consisted of thousands of names. As one of his relatives put it, "Wherever he was, that became the best place in the world to be."

He was an inveterate adventurer. Among innumerable excursions, he had biked the 400 miles from San Francisco to Santa Monica, gone on safari in Africa, explored the rain forests of South America and stayed with monks in India.

Mr. Iskandar, 34, chief of digital strategy for Europe for the Monitor Group, lived in London, and was on Flight 11 from Boston to Los Angeles to visit his parents. He and his fiancée, Nicolette Cavaleros, had been visiting his brother in Boston. She was going to fly to California the day after he did. They were going to be married in July.

JOHN F. ISKYAN
The Surprise Party

John F. Iskyan got up regularly at 5 A.M., rode the train in from Wilton, Conn., and was at his desk in the World Trade Center by 7 A.M. He would return home at 7 or 8 P.M. "Everything John did, he researched it, he studied it, he looked hard at it," Bob Keeling, a brother-in-law, said yesterday. "He didn't want to do it half-baked."

John Iskyan was competitive and loyal, Mr. Keeling said. He played high school lacrosse in Manhasset and became an avid skiier and hiker at St. Michael's College in Colchester, Vt. He joined Cantor Fitzgerald out of college and worked his way up to partner. After the 1993 trade center bombing, Mr. Keeling said, Mr. Iskyan disliked the building. But he would not leave the firm.

On Saturday, Sept. 8, he held a surprise 40th birthday party for his wife, Margaret, at the Old Town Hall in Wilton, with about 50 friends and family members, a two-piece band and a lot to eat. He had started planning the party a year ago, Mr. Keeling said. Even the Iskyans' children, Peter, 12, and Carolynn, 9, kept the secret.

"It was a great night," Mr. Keeling said. "John had done such a beautiful job. And it thrilled his wife."

KAZUSHIGE ITO
Loving New York

Kazushige Ito was born in Hiroshima, but he loved New York. "I think he loved New York more than a lot of native New Yorkers," said his wife, Yuko Ito.

Living on the corner of 66th Street and Columbus Avenue, he jogged regularly in Central Park, visited Lincoln Center every weekend and explored the city's French, Italian, Vietnamese and Indian restaurants. Last year, he ran in the New York City Marathon. "He was in heaven," Mrs. Ito said.

In Japan, Mr. Ito used to spend $600 for an opera ticket; a fraction of that got him some of the best seats at the Metropolitan Opera. Last year, he watched more than 20 operas. His favorite was *Aida.*

He was training to run in the Philadelphia Marathon. "Last year, it took him four hours and 18 minutes to run the New York City Marathon," Mrs. Ito said. "He wanted to finish in four hours this year. I think he could have done it. It would be Nov. 18, one day before his birthday." He would have been 36.

For Fuji Bank, where Mr. Ito was a planning specialist, the couple had relocated from Yokohama to Tokyo to Manila. They came to New York in 1998. "If this hadn't happened, we would have settled here," Mrs. Ito said. "He loved New York the best."

VIRGINIA M. JABLONSKI
The Early Bird

Virginia M. Jablonski, an assistant vice president at Marsh & McLennan, liked to get up at 5 A.M. and catch an early bus from her home in Matawan, N.J., to her office on the 94th floor of 1 World Trade Center. In recent months, that often meant slipping out while Barry, her husband of 21 years, was enjoying the extra sleep made possible by his recent retirement from Lucent Technologies.

Fortunately, Mr. Jablonski is an astronomy buff. Having noted that the International Space Station was scheduled to pass directly overhead shortly before sunrise on Sept. 11, he got up with her that morning. He recalls their standing in their garden, marveling at the stars in the clear sky and sharing the feeling that it would be a good day.

"She was a bubbly person who was always smiling," Mr. Jablonski said. "Most people wouldn't know if she was angry."

No one could miss her passion for cats, though. Mrs. Jablonski, a 49-year-old Brooklyn native, filled their home with cat-themed decorations and doted on her two feline companions, Fred and Bill.

BROOKE JACKMAN
Family Historian

Brooke Jackman had a photographic memory that earned her, at 23, an unofficial role as family historian. If her mother wanted to remember a decade-old conversation, she'd dial up Brooke, her youngest daughter, at her Murray Hill apartment. Usually Ms. Jackman recalled not only what was said, but what everyone was wearing at the time. In late August, she organized a family birthday outing: she, her parents and two siblings went to dinner in Greenwich Village, then to an Off-Broadway play.

She forever had her nose in a book, read everything from Sylvia Plath to *Sex and the City*–style fluff, and stopped by the Borders bookstore almost daily on her way home from her new job as an assistant bond trader at Cantor Fitzgerald. She was, said her brother, Ross, literally the kind of person who would not hurt a fly. "There were times I'd try to kill a bug, and she wouldn't let me."

She grew up in Oyster Bay, N.Y., graduated from Columbia University in 2000 on the Dean's List, and gravitated to Wall Street, where her father and brother worked, after a year in publishing. But she was not completely fulfilled at Cantor Fitzgerald. "She decided there were more important things in life than making money," said her brother. A master's in social work was her goal, and she was in the process of applying to Berkeley and Columbia to achieve it.

AARON JACOBS
Well-Traveled at 27

Aaron Jacobs wanted to retire at an early age and travel. He had already backpacked through Europe, taught English in Cozumel, Mexico, spent a semester in Madrid, climbed a volcano in Greece and vacationed with his family in Central America and the Caribbean.

But Mr. Jacobs, 27, was making plans for the ultimate trip––his honeymoon with his bride-to-be, Jeannine McAteer. "He was leaning toward Africa," Ms. McAteer said. "He loved animals," and wanted to go on a safari.

Still, for Mr. Jacobs, who lived on Manhattan's Upper East Side, there was no place like home. A vice president and partner on the international trading desk at Cantor Fitzgerald, he was a fan of the city as an institution. He sought out ethnic restaurants, skated and jogged through Central Park and loved visiting museums. He also taught job skills to welfare recipients.

"He knew that he had achieved something with his life, but he was never someone to rub it in anyone's face or to feel like the fact that he was in this lucrative business made him any different," said his older brother, Josh Jacobs. "He just remained a really loving and loyal person."

ARIEL LOUIS JACOBS
Working the Room

Watch the salesman work the room. His banter is interrupted because his cell phone rings incessantly, but every comer's gaze is met. The people in this room feel important; they feel at ease. They like this guy. This skill has made him a success.

The room this time is called Dave & Buster's. Today is Saturday and business is not at hand, but the salesman's skills are at work. He sips his Grey Goose martini as the partygoers fete him with gifts for his 30th birthday. He slowly unwraps each offering. "He loved his friends and family and loved entertaining them and making people more comfortable," said his wife, Jenna.

She gave birth to the salesman's son, Gabriel, on Sept. 17. That was nine days after the party, one day after the salesman's birthday and six days after his death. It was six days before their first wedding anniversary.

Ariel Louis Jacobs, known to friends as R-E and to family members as Airy, used his charm to climb from Radio Shack clerk to chief of United States operations for a multinational company, Caplin Systems, in the space of a decade.

JASON JACOBS
He Found His Happiness

Jennifer Jacobs has done her share of crying and praying for her husband, Jason, who disappeared in his office at Fiduciary Trust on the 97th floor of 2 World Trade Center.

But now she is mostly trying to celebrate the good times, sifting through memories made with Mr. Jacobs, 32, a man who loved her at first sight, but whom she could initially regard only as nice. The memories are everywhere. In the kitchen of the new home they bought in January, on a quaint little block in Randolph, N.J., she stares at the cookbooks and gourmet magazines that her husband loved more than Monday night football but not nearly as much as his little girl, 13-month-old Zoe. In every room of their home, she remembers watching him strip and paint the walls over and over, promising that they would be perfect.

In the memories, she said, there are only smiles and laughter. "There are no regrets. We had an incredible relationship. We have this beautiful child. We got the house we wanted and we always said 'I love you,' even that day when he should have been trying to get out, he called to say 'I love you and I love Zoe.' "

"I wish I could spend the rest of my life with him, but I know Jason had already reached all of these great places in his life. Most people, they live their whole lives without ever being that happy."

MICHAEL G. JACOBS
An Office with a View

Michael G. Jacobs had been taking his four children to the World Trade Center since 1983, for visits to his office and for special occasions, like seeing the renovated Statue of Liberty or viewing the parade for the Olympics in 1984.

"We have pictures of all of that," said his oldest son, Michael Brady, 27. "It always fascinated me how high up we were."

Their father was an accountant, working as vice president for tax operations at Fiduciary Trust, with an office on the 90th floor of 2 World Trade Center. But Mr. Jacobs, 54, was interested in much more than the arcane laws of withholdings and deductions. At home in Danbury, Conn., where he was born and raised, he was rebuilding a Volkswagen bug and learning to play the bagpipes. And he had a wry sense of humor, Mr. Brady recalled. "I'd ask him, 'How's the World Trade Center today?' because I used to love going up there, and he'd say: 'It's still here. Still here.' "

"He loved history so much," his son said. "Now he's a part of world history. I think he would like that, that his name is going to be remembered forever because he was a part of this."

STEVEN JACOBSON
A Transmitter Marvel

He worked up top. He liked it up there, with his transmitter.

Steven Jacobson was an engineer for WPIX-TV and worked in a room on the 110th floor of 1 World Trade Center, usually by himself, tending to the station's transmitter. Mr. Jacobson, 53, had a deep fidelity to that transmitter. He cared for it like a sick baby the occasional time it would "dump" and take the station off the air. Once he used his shoelaces to get it going.

During the 1993 trade center bombing, he stayed until midnight, to make sure the transmitter operated properly once power was restored. When the bomb exploded, Victor Arnone, a WPIX maintenance engineer and a close friend, went to the concourse to get lunch for him. He called Mr. Jacobson and yelled: "Steve! Explosion! Smoke! People are running out!"

Mr. Jacobson said, "Does this mean I don't get my egg roll?"

Mr. Jacobson had a dry humor. It was a routine for him to invite Jewish friends to lunch at his Manhattan home on Yom Kippur, when, of course, they were fasting. He loved to prowl through ham radio flea markets. Unfailingly, he would ask a vendor, "Do you have a used logbook and a big eraser?" He had a habit of not using turn signals when he drove. When questioned, he would respond, "It's nobody's business which way I'm turning."

RICKNAUTH JAGGERNAUTH
Happy to Be a Grandfather

Every day when he came home to Brooklyn from his construction job, Ricknauth Jaggernauth would grab a beer and sit in his front yard, and play with his grandchildren and other neighborhood children until it was time for dinner. "My father was a happy, loving, giving man," said his daughter Anita, 31. "He loved to talk to young people about their lives and about how important it was to get a good education."

He would have only one or two beers, but his wife, Joyce, teased him and called him "drunkie grandpa," a nickname the children used for him. He came here from Guyana 19 years ago, and worked for a company that was renovating offices in the World Trade Center. The day it was attacked, they were working on the 104th floor of the first tower.

Mr. Jaggernauth, 58, planned to retire in two years and wanted to visit his homeland. He had five children and three grandchildren, and all lived together in the family's two-story house on Pennsylvania Avenue. His daughter said that if his body was recovered, the family would have a traditional Hindu funeral for him. "It's what he did for his own mother," she said.

JAKE JAGODA
The Fishing Life

Right from the beginning, Jake Jagoda believed that he had a special knack for fishing, and so he was willing to put up with certain inconveniences. For instance, he was scared of worms.

He got into fishing when he was about 4, but those worms! When he was 9, his sister Mary, who was 3, had to attach the worms to the line. Of course, before she did, she tormented him with them.

He moved on to other lures. He became proficient at fly fishing. "If he saw feathers on a hat of mine and he liked the color, he would take one off and make it into a fly," Ms. Jagoda said. He went deep-sea fishing. He went ice fishing. He trapped lobsters.

Mr. Jagoda, 24, grew up in Huntington, on Long Island, and every chance he got he grabbed his pole and went fishing. One Mother's Day, his gift to his mother, Anna, was to take her to Connetquot River State Park to fish. Afterward, he complained that she didn't care enough about catching a fish—she just liked the scenery.

When he was 13, he started working on a fishing boat. After college, he became a tackle salesman, working weekends on a party boat that took groups fishing off Long Island. "This last year, Jake was sort of growing up," his sister said. "He wanted more of a regular job that you would commute to and where he could have more of a future." So, at the beginning of the summer, he became a trader at Cantor Fitzgerald.

For the first time, he learned how to use a computer. He continued to live in Huntington, and every chance he got he went fishing.

YUDH V. JAIN
Finishing What He Started

Yudh V. Jain was his wife's dream. He encouraged her to buy clothes. He did the grocery shopping and showered her with flowers and greeting cards on not-so-special days. And every night, he remembered to make her a cup of tea.

Despite her husband's devotion, Sneh Jain often joked that Mr. Jain's first wife was his studies. Long after he finished his formal schooling, Mr. Jain, 54, who had doctorates in computer science and chemical engineering, continued to study and upgrade his skills. His discipline rubbed off on his two daughters and Mrs. Jain, who sometimes struggled with her accounting job.

"He used to make me calm down," Mrs. Jain said. "He said nothing is difficult if you put your mind to it."

Mr. Jain was also an ethicist. He had only been at his job as a senior project manager at eSpeed Inc. for a little over a month when he decided the position was not a good fit for him. But rather than leave immediately, he decided to stay on and finish a project he had begun.

A few weeks after Sept. 11, Mrs. Jain received medicine for her migraine headaches in the mail. She was surprised because her husband usually bought it for her. "I said, 'Oh my God, maybe he's hiding somewhere, and maybe he's teasing me,' " she said. But it was just Mr. Jain being Mr. Jain; he had ordered her medicine on Sept. 10.

MARIA JAKUBIAK
Getting It Just Right

Kazimierz Jakubiak is uneasy about that urn of trade center ashes on a table in his Queens living room. "It's mixed with the people who did this," he said.

His wife, Maria, loved this house, had tried so hard "to get it just right." That brick fireplace? He had promised to build it by Christmas, and now he has. Next to it hangs a picture of the couple on a cruise in 1997, just before a flood engulfed her parents' house in Poland. "She was crushed," he said. "It was the house she was born in."

In 1989, the Jakubiaks had the chance to emigrate to either the United States or Canada. "I want to see the Statue of Liberty," she had said, and it was decided.

When their youngest was 3—their boys are 11 and 16 now, their daughter, 17—Maria Jakubiak itched to go to work. After studying English and receiving an associate's degree, she got an accounting job at Marsh & McLennan, later studying nights for a bachelor's degree. Everything was clicking.

In August, shaken by a ride in a plunging, out-of-control elevator, Ms. Jakubiak, 40, took a few days off.

"You could quit," her husband had said. But she loved her job, and especially the co-workers who were fresh out of college. "She was like a mother to them," he said. "It was her first job in the U.S., and she was proud of it."

AMY N. JARRET
Taking Care of Others

Amy N. Jarret, a flight attendant on United Airlines 175, loved to travel. But the 28-year-old Ms. Jarret also kept flying because it gave her the resources and free time to divide herself between Philadelphia, where her longtime boyfriend, Kyle Rusconi, lives and the home she shared with her father and two brothers in her native Rhode Island.

The men in Ms. Jarret's life marveled at her organizational skills. "When she was around, everything ran smoothly," said Marc Jarret, her brother.

"I told her she had to start thinking more about her own needs, but she liked taking care of others," said Mr. Rusconi, who met Ms. Jarret at the 1995 homecoming of their alma mater, Villanova University. She enjoyed slot machines and betting on racehorses, but fretted that she was spoiling herself if she was lured by a clothing sale.

"We assumed we would get married when it came time to have children," said Mr. Rusconi, who had recently completed a two-year job in Australia. "We just needed to be in the same place a little longer."

MAXIMA JEAN-PIERRE
No Doubt Who Was Boss

Sometimes those big guys on Wall Street needed to be handled like babies. That is where Maxima Jean-Pierre came in.

In spite of her maximum name, Ms. Jean-Pierre was not tall and gorgeous. She was short and gorgeous, about 5-foot-4, a size 2. But when she walked into the 105th floor executive offices of Cantor Fitzgerald, watch out. "She was very small, but so are hurricanes until they start," said her husband, Michael Zinkofsky.

If Ms. Jean-Pierre, a food-service administrator, noticed that one of the executives had not eaten all day, she would bring him a plate with a note on it saying, "Please eat this. You might get sick. When I come back, it better be gone." They always ate it. "They knew who was boss," her husband said.

Ms. Jean-Pierre, 40, and Mr. Zinkofsky were both on their second marriages, and had been together for two years, sharing a house and six children in Bellport, New York. Naturally, the big shots became very attached to her. Once, Howard W. Lutnick, the president of Cantor Fitzgerald, was in London during a videoconference. On the screen, he noticed Ms. Jean-Pierre walk into the room in New York. He paused for a beat, said "Hi, Maxima," and calmly went back to business.

PAUL JEFFERS
A Guitar Man

This is how passionate Paul Jeffers was about the guitar: when his nephew J.P. was about 10 years old and showed some interest in learning to play, Mr. Jeffers gave him lessons—strumming his own guitar into the phone from his office at Cantor Fitzgerald, since J.P. lived in North Carolina.

And this is how passionate he was about his 3-year-old son: He let his living room be dominated by a big table filled with Thomas the Tank Engine trains and track.

And then there was his house in Westhampton, the one that was nearly swallowed up in the fires that raged across the Hamptons a few summers back. "He planted all the trees himself," said his girlfriend, Nancy Evans. "Weeping willows, silver birches, even a Christmas tree that we bought with the roots." On weekends, hordes of Cantor colleagues traveled out to play basketball and tennis and swim.

Here's how Mr. Jeffers, who was 39 and lived in Manhattan, combined everything he loved on a single day last August: He organized a 50th-anniversary party for his parents, inviting his three siblings, nine nieces and nephews and assorted friends to convene in Westhampton. Everyone got T-shirts in different brilliant colors. Toward evening, he disappeared into the basement, to play Beatles songs with his nephews on their guitars.

JOHN C. JENKINS
Eclectic Collector

When you walked into the apartment of John C. Jenkins, you had to beware of the toasters. The floor was littered with them.

No, he wasn't a toast fanatic. He collected things: old coffee pots, glassware, copies of the *New York Times Magazine* (he had all the issues going back about 20 years). He collected anything (pots,

Children at Public School 138 Annex in Crown Heights, Brooklyn, donating small change to the American Red Cross to help victims of the World Trade Center attack. The children started collecting the money in mid-September and raised about two hundred dollars. (*Marilynn K. Yee*)

knives) that had handles made of Bakelite, an early plastic. He would tell friends that if you rubbed a Bakelite handle, it smelled like Vaseline, because it was petroleum-based.

"The degree of clutter in his apartment was remarkable," said Jeff Levy, a friend. "You could barely move."

Mr. Jenkins, 45, lived in Cambridge, Mass., and was operations manager for Charles River Associates. He was on his way to the Charles River office in Los Angeles on Sept. 11, aboard Flight 11.

One aspect that friends most relished about Mr. Jenkins was his knack for finding humor in anything. He once worked for an architectural firm that was opening a new office, and the architects were fastidious about making it perfect. Once they moved in, they discovered that a dance studio was above them, and no one could get any work done because of the constant thumping. He thought that was hilarious.

PREM NATH JERATH
He Stayed to Help

Meena Jerath remembers exactly what her husband was wearing that day: a summer suit, with a blue striped shirt and a blue tie with a white design. She had picked it out as part of their morning ritual. He would rise first and start the tea and put her bagel in the toaster oven. Then, he would be running a little late, and she would follow him out to the car with his tea.

Prem Nath Jerath came to the United States from India in 1970. He and his wife married after a bit of encouragement from their parents. Both got M.B.A.'s. They had a son, Neel, in 1982. In their backyard in Edison, N.J., Mr. Jerath would barbecue for friends.

In the last few years, the number of visitors from India increased, and they would take them on tours to Niagara Falls, Florida, and Washington.

"On their vacations, we would have our vacations too," Mrs. Jerath said. As a structural engineer for the Port Authority, Mr. Jerath, 57, had great faith in the twin towers. That might be why, Mrs. Jerath said, her husband apparently stayed behind to help an injured colleague. During the bombing in 1993, she said, he had walked a woman down 30 flights of stairs.

"Sometimes we get angry" that he sacrificed his life, Mrs. Jerath said. "But I don't think I would have liked him to run away from that sick person."

FARAH JEUDY
A Focus on Religion and Fun

Her religion was the most important thing in Farah Jeudy's life. "Everything revolved around that," said her sister-in-law, Suzette Jeudy. Three times a week, Ms. Jeudy, who lived with her parents in Spring Valley, N.Y., attended a Jehovah's Witnesses meeting with her mother.

But while she was religious, she was far from somber. She loved traveling in the Bahamas and being with friends. "Anyone who ever heard Farah relate a story may not remember the story," according to a tribute read at her memorial service, "but they can remember laughing until their sides hurt."

Born in Haiti, Ms. Jeudy, 32, came to this country as a child and later graduated from Baruch College. For eight years, she left home at 6 A.M. to commute to her job as an administrative assistant at the Aon Corporation. But if one of her nephews was taking part in a Jehovah's Witnesses meeting, Ms. Jeudy would always be there, not caring that her trip home would be even longer.

ELIEZER JIMENEZ Jr.
Filling In for a Co-worker

Eliezer Jimenez Jr. was supposed to be on vacation that week, but his bosses at Windows on the World called him at home on Sunday, and asked if he would fill in that week for someone else. "My son was such a good worker, of course he said he would do it," said his father, Eliezer Jimenez.

The younger Mr. Jimenez had worked as a chef's assistant at the restaurant for less than two years. He had begun working there part-time, his father said, while he worked at another restaurant in Midtown, because he needed the money to support his four children. When the other restaurant closed down, Mr. Jimenez went to work at Windows full time.

When he was not working, Mr. Jimenez, 37, was usually at his Disciples of Christ church. When he was 6, his mother died while giving birth. His father moved with his three sons to Puerto Rico, and they returned to New York a few years later. The younger Mr. Jimenez lived in Washington Heights with his wife and children. "He was my son, my friend, my everything," Mr. Jimenez said. "He was my firstborn. They have stolen him from me."

LUIS JIMENEZ Jr.
Minding the Details

By the end of the year, Luis Jimenez Jr. was planning to be a married man on his way to graduate school. Everything seemed to be adding up for Mr. Jimenez, a 25-year-old Marsh & McLennan accountant who lived in Corona, Queens. As a boy, he was so bent on a future in finance that he would go to the grocery store with his parents and figure up the bill on his little wrist calculator before the shopping was done.

The details were everything. He couldn't propose on just any day, so he set his girlfriend's birthday in November as the moment to pop the question. Two weeks before the attack on the World Trade Center, he asked her parents' permission and started laying plans to buy the perfect ring.

"When he was a boy, 10, he told me, 'Daddy, I want to be an independent man, to take care of myself,'" said Mr. Jimenez's father, Luis Sr. "He reached his dream. He made his family so happy. In every room, there is a picture of him. He was a son to be proud of."

LASHAWANA JOHNSON
For the Children

Lashawana Johnson's name was the stuff of family legend. When her mother sat down to print the name on her birth certificate, she inadvertently inserted an "a" between the "w" and the "n." Spelled "Lashawana" but pronounced "Lashawna," the name was a constant source of confusion to people.

Not that Ms. Johnson, 27, minded. She extended the same consideration to co-workers and strangers that she showed to her three children, whose photographs lined her cubicle on the 83rd floor of 1 World Trade Center, where she worked as a customer service manager for General Telecom. A single mother to 7-year-old Jade Ashley, 5-year-old Jerrard Maurice and 2-year-old Jordan Timothy, Ms. Johnson spent most of her free time either with her children or devising ways to surprise them.

"Many times, she would come in with packages from the World Trade Center mall—shirts, blouses, pants, outfits— all for those kids," said Willie Borrero, who worked with Ms. Johnson.

Tru Trimingham at the funeral held on November 3
for his brother-in-law Terrance Andre Aiken, who
worked for Marsh & McLennan. During the service,
at the Love Fellowship Tabernacle in Brooklyn, Mr.
Trimingham held Mr. Aiken's three-year-old son, Andre.
(*Aaron Lee Fineman*)

To support her family, Ms. Johnson, who lived in East
New York, Brooklyn, awoke at 4 A.M., got her kids dressed
and off to the sitter's by 5:30 A.M., and often arrived at her
office in time to see the sun rise. On weekends, she was up
early and out the door with her children again. "She made
sure that every weekend they were very active," said Ms.
Johnson's mother, Lois Johnson. "They never stayed
home."

SCOTT JOHNSON
Song of a Wayfarer

Because Americans rarely travel to Cuba,
Scott Johnson had to go. He and his friend
Steve Selwood spent five days in Havana in
1998, listening to music in one bar after
another. Because he graduated with a
minor in Jewish Studies from Trinity College in Hartford,

he had to explore Egypt. There, Scott and his friends made
their way into a pyramid off-limits to tourists. And before a
second jet crashed into 2 World Trade Center, where Mr.
Johnson worked as an analyst for Keefe, Bruyette & Woods,
he was making plans to visit South America next summer to
explore a culture that fascinated him.

Mr. Johnson, 26, played golf with his father in Montclair, N.J., where he grew up, and cheered the Yankees
from his couch. He was cherished for his quiet, firm sense
of what was important: family, friends, knowledge and
adventure.

For Eric Kusseluk, Mr. Johnson was the best friend who
took calls at 3 A.M. when Mr. Kusseluk's mother was dying of
cancer. For Mr. Johnson's father, Tom, he was the child
devoid of any meanness. For friends who loved music as he
did, he was a generous investor in a new live-music club in
Williamsburg, Brooklyn.

The fire of his passions changed you, people said. His

brother, Tom, is still reading the book he recommended a few months before Sept. 11: a biography of Che Guevara. And Mr. Selwood is still hoping to take that trip to South America someday.

WILLIAM R. JOHNSTON
Soccer and Football Whiz

For a while there, a large firefighter was walking around with one eyebrow. That was thanks to William R. Johnston of Engine Company 6 in Manhattan.

It happened while the Fire Department football team was on the road, and Firefighter Johnston shaved off his teammate's eyebrow while the fellow was sleeping: part of some undetermined high jinks, said Firefighter Johnston's sister, Diane Cuff.

He was the quiet one in a North Babylon, N.Y., family of four siblings, but could be mischievous outside of it. While on a date at a Ground Round restaurant one night, Mrs. Cuff said, she heard a familiar-sounding croon.

It was Firefighter Johnston, singing "Roxanne" into a microphone. "He was a character, and everyone loved him for that," she said.

The Fire Department and sports grabbed Firefighter Johnston more than anything else. He joined the football team as a kicker because of his soccer prowess. His friend since age 5, Eugene Masula, said that Firefighter Johnston played professional indoor soccer and had "a rocket of a right foot." On their amateur team, Firefighter Johnston was the center midfielder, or playmaker.

Until joining the Fire Department nearly two years ago, Firefighter Johnston worked for the Transit Authority as an ironworker, tending to elevated subway tracks. A high-school friend, John Kolich, joined the New York Police Department around the same time as Mr. Johnston.

"We both were really ecstatic for each other," he said. Not long afterward, Officer Kolich found himself attending Officer Johnston's funeral in full dress. "I never thought in a million years I'd wear my uniform for my best friend," he said.

ANDREW B. JORDAN
Loving the Eye of the Storm

It was Hurricane Gloria in 1985 that led Andrew B. Jordan into the firefighting life. With the power out, a neighbor in West Islip, on Long Island, lighted a kerosene lamp that wound up igniting the house. Mr. Jordan thought to back the neighbor's car out of the garage, so there wouldn't be an even bigger catastrophe, then led a disabled woman to safety.

He became a New York City firefighter in 1994 and was assigned to Ladder Company 132 in Brooklyn, nicknamed the Eye of the Storm. Every day was a joy, despite his two-and-a-half-hour commute. "He loved the firehouse and all the guys that worked there," said his mother, Ellen. He loved even the unromantic parts of the job, like fire inspections, said his father, Thomas, because he saw them as one more way to save lives.

A 36-year-old father of four, he was keenly aware of the risks he faced. When the ladder truck pulled up at a burning building, he was often the first one raised high into the air to battle the flames. "Andrew was going into the bucket at one fire, and this guy said to him, 'Thank God it's you and not me,' " his mother recalled. "Andrew said, 'Thank God it's me and not you.' "

ROBERT T. JORDAN
Abstract and Focused

Robert T. Jordan had a laugh that friends said was a little louder and lasted a little longer than anyone else's. Behind that laugh was a 34-year-old man who by turns was kind and caring, imaginative and spontaneous, yet determined and focused.

"Rob was on his own tangent," said David Wick, a friend since high school. "There was nothing too abstract for his imagination. But when it came time to train for something, he pushed himself harder than anyone I have ever seen."

An expert surfer who learned the sport as a teenager in Hawaii, Mr. Jordan, who was 6-foot-4, rowed heavyweight crew at the University of California. He subsequently turned his competitive interests to golf, and was a very competent nine-handicap golfer when he was not working as a partner at Cantor Fitzgerald.

It was at the end of his college days at Berkeley that Rob Jordan met his life companion. "We were milling about backstage, waiting to go out to get our diplomas," his wife, Elizabeth, recalled. "I had seen him on campus, but we never hooked up. He thought my name was Jennifer. I thought his name was Ted. We talked the entire time. Neither of us remember anything about graduation."

KARL JOSEPH
Taking the Ribbing

Karl Joseph was a "probie," a probationary firefighter, at Engine Company 207 in downtown Brooklyn after joining the department in October 2000. The senior guys played pranks on him—a throwback to high school days—but he took it well. "When you're a probie, you really can't respond back to the veterans," said

Michael Beehler, a firefighter who went through the fire academy with Mr. Joseph and worked with him at 207.

"Karl had a way of shrugging off the ribbing. He had a great smile and a great laugh," Mr. Beehler said. "As far as the job, he was top-notch."

Mr. Joseph would have turned 26 on Nov. 5. He was a native of Haiti. His parents fled the chaotic country with their nine children to stake their claim in America, said Lucy Bouciquot, a family friend. "He liked Haiti," she said, "but America was his home.'"

STEPHEN JOSEPH
Helped the Good Times Roll

The Pied Piper's allure was so strong that whenever he went to New Orleans for Mardi Gras, grown men clambered into a closet, trying to resist his dare for a sixth shot of tequila. But that booming laugh, the one you heard in the trading room of Fiduciary Trust before you saw him, beckoned: Stephen Joseph, who had a faint Trinidadian accent and the party-with-me magnetism of a world-class barkeep, could not be denied.

Even when he and his wife, Gillian, moved to Franklin Park, N.J., from Brooklyn, private time was rare with Mr. Joseph, 39, who had started as a messenger with a high school education and worked up to operations officer. The party followed him everywhere: 14 friends would arrive at their house for a barbecue; at restaurants, he would introduce Mrs. Joseph to all the diners he had met while she was in the ladies' room.

There was one Pied Piper whom Mr. Joseph himself found irresistible: his long-awaited child, Tristan Anthony. He had already taken Tristan, 2, to Disney World and to a Nets game, sat his son on his lap and driven around the block. "If you do all this now, what will you do when he's older?" Mrs. Joseph would ask. Mr. Joseph would just smile.

JANE JOSIAH
Have Friends, Will Travel

Last year, Jane Josiah began a series of visits to far-flung family and friends that did not end for nearly a year. She did not begin looking for work after being laid off last winter. Instead she flew from Texas, where she had moved seven years earlier, to Seattle to see her brother and sister-in-law.

Soon after, she went to Washington for a few weeks with Jennifer and Kelly, her daughters. Then she stayed with friends in Philadelphia and Long Island.

Ms. Josiah, 47, had a gift for making friends, loving them and kicking up her heels with them, said Debra Potash, who knew her 20 years.

The visiting culminated with Ms. Josiah's 30th high school reunion in Levittown, on Long Island, where old friends persuaded her to come home. After one found her a job at Fiduciary Trust, she drove north to Mrs. Potash's home on Long Island. Her first day was Aug. 27.

All the traveling had made Ms. Josiah's daughters a bit impatient. "It was supposed to be a month," Jennifer said. "Then two months. Then four."

Now, she said, the months her mother spent with the people she loved seem like an unmatchable gift.

ANTHONY JOVIC
A Special Plaque

Anthony Jovic videotaped his sons, Matthew, 10, and Peter, 9, at every swimming meet they entered. He went to their practices. And he took them along when he and his wife, Cynthia, went on a cruise in the Caribbean. And whenever he came home from work, the boys would rush up to him and say, "What did you do? Did you fight any fires?"

He was a 39-year-old lieutenant, studying for October's captain's exam. Though on the rolls at Ladder Company 34 in Washington Heights, he was assigned on Sept. 11 to Engine Company 279 in Red Hook in Brooklyn, and was among the first men to arrive at the World Trade Center.

At Ladder Company 34, Capt. Arthur DePew recalled, Lieutenant Jovic is also noted for a kind of remembrance that predates videotape—the brass plaques in firehouses that honor men who died in the line of duty. He did research on some who had never been remembered, like Eugene J. Caffrey, who died in 1921. Next Sept. 11, a plaque will go up with Lieutenant Jovic's name.

As for the boys, Mrs. Jovic still takes them regularly to swimming and meets, but she says, "Their hearts aren't in it."

ANGEL JUARBE
A Pinup and a Sleuth

The sun seemed to shine on Angel Juarbe, a firefighter with Ladder 12 in Chelsea. He was an animal lover, with eight formerly stray dogs, who visited Tanzania to see lions and zebras, then left just two days before the bombing of the United States embassy in 1998. Single and handsome, he was one of 12 New York firefighters chosen to pose for the calendar "Firehouse Hunks 2002."

A week before the Sept. 11 disaster, Mr. Juarbe, 35, was the winner in an eight-part game show on the Fox network in which 10 contestants, chosen from 3,000 applicants, competed to solve a fake murder. The show was called *Murder in Small Town X*, and Mr. Juarbe tracked down the killer. He won a Jeep and $250,000.

He kept the secret from his family until Sept. 4, when the final show was broadcast. After the terror attacks, the show's entire cast visited his family. His mother, Miriam, recalled what his friends said. "If only I could live one day of your life, even an hour." She added, "Most of them are married, you know."

KAREN HAWLEY JUDAY
Following Love

At 48, after two bad marriages and a lifetime in Elkhart, Ind. (pop. 45,000), Karen Hawley Juday fell in love and moved to New York City, which she had seen only in movies. She found a world unlike anything she had imagined. The streets of Bensonhurst in Brooklyn were crowded with people and lined with small shops. She gazed down at the city from her job at Cantor Fitzgerald on the 101st floor of 1 World Trade Center.

"She couldn't believe we don't have malls," said Richard Pecorella, the Wall Street manager Karen followed to New York.

She loved the neighborhood restaurants and Italian bakeries and devoured pastries. On weekends, she and Mr. Pecorella went to the ocean or gambling in Atlantic City. They planned to grow old together. But they had only four years.

"She left everything to move in with this tough little Brooklyn guy," he said. "Her children said she'd never been happier."

MYCHAL JUDGE
Where He Was Needed

The Rev. Mychal Judge never shut his door at the Midtown Franciscan friary, literally or emotionally. Anybody with the slightest need for the contents inside—be it a warm jacket or his attentive ear—was welcome.

Not that Father Judge was often in. As chaplain to the New York Fire Department, Father Judge, 68, could be found joking or comforting firefighters or driving hellbent to emergencies. When a boatload of Chinese refugees were shipwrecked in the Rockaways, he was one of the first there, "handing out blankets and coffee and telling them jokes," said Peter Johnson, a friend. "They didn't know English, but he was doing pantomime and they were laughing."

He had "movie-star looks and a tremendous ability to speak and sing," said Mr. Johnson. "And that was tempered by his absolute consistent devotion to being a priest." He wore his friar's robes to soup kitchens, to Gracie Mansion, to the White House, to countless baptisms and funerals.

He had no use—none—for physical things, said Steven McDonald, the police officer paralyzed by a gunshot who accompanied Father Judge on peace trips to Belfast. Give the father a cashmere sweater, he said, and it would wind up on the back of a homeless person. Go to him with a troubled soul and he would listen intently for as long as it took. He went where he was needed. On Sept. 11, he faced the inferno with the firefighters.

PAUL JURGENS
A Hero Once Again

Those who knew Paul Jurgens said his life was divided into three parts: family, work and practical jokes. He excelled at all three.

He joined the Port Authority police in 1980 and developed such expertise as a rescuer that he was made an instructor at the authority's Rescue Training Center. On the morning of Sept. 11, Mr. Jurgens, 47, was driving from Kennedy International Airport to Jersey City, but he detoured and was last seen speeding to the World Trade Center to help. In 1992, he rushed onto a burning jumbo jet that had crashed on takeoff at Kennedy and helped usher all 292 passengers to safety.

"What he did was unusual and heroic," said Sgt. Mike Florie, one of his supervisors. "It's hot and smoke-filled, and you're risking your life."

On weekends, he loved to shoot baskets and throw softballs with Paul Jr., 17, June, 15, and Lindsay, 9. He and his wife, Maria, also loved inviting friends over to barbecues.

"He always used to say, 'I got it made. I got the greatest wife, the greatest kids and the greatest job,' " she said. As for practical jokes, his brother-in-law, Tony Liotta, recalled that when he woke up after dozing off one evening after dinner, he found "Paul Jurgens is my hero" written on his arm.

At a memorial service in Levittown, N.Y., Mr. Liotta said, "Now I realize how true that is."

THOMAS E. JURGENS
A Sentimentalist

The night that Joan Jurgens met her future husband, Thomas, at a bowling alley, they sat and talked for hours. When the evening was over, she gave him her phone number on a little slip of paper.

But when he called, she was reluctant to go out. He was 19, she was 24. He told her age did not matter to him. They went out to a movie, *Murder in the First*, and to dinner and sat for hours, the conversation never flagging. From then on, they were inseparable. After seven years, they married last June.

He was in the Army reserves. Every year, he went away for two weeks for training exercises. She wrote to him every day but did not send the letters because he would be home before they arrived. When he got home, he would read every one.

Four years ago, he took Civil Service exams to become a police officer and a court officer. He passed both. They talked it over and decided he would become a court officer. "It was supposed to be safer," she said.

Officer Jurgens, 26, who worked near the World Trade Center, was one of three court officers who disappeared while helping victims of the Sept. 11 attacks. Afterward, Mrs. Jurgens went through his papers. She found all of her old letters to him. And, in a carefully folded piece of plastic, she found two ticket stubs to *Murder in the First* and the slip of paper with her phone number.

K

SHASHI KIRAN KADABA
A Penchant for Charity

Indian weddings are often extravagant affairs that can last as long as a week.

So friends and family of Shashi Kiran Kadaba were taken aback when he and his fiancée decided to have a modest wedding, donating whatever money they saved to orphanages in their hometown, Bangalore, in southern India.

"He was that kind of person, the kind of guy who would wait before everyone got out before leaving a burning building," said his fiancée, Pushpa Sreenath, 26, who drove 30 hours to New York from Texas as soon as she learned about the World Trade Center collapse.

Mr. Kadaba, 26, a software designer for an Indian company, had recently come to New York to do consulting work for Marsh USA, whose offices were on the 97th floor of 1 World Trade Center. Ms. Sreenath, also a software designer, said her fiancé was taken with tennis, Formula One racing and big, brash Bollywood movies.

"He was very energetic and skilled at making people laugh," she said. Since 1996, the couple had been largely separated by half a world, although they always remained in communication through phone calls and e-mail messages.

"It was hard, but not impossible because I knew I would see him again," she said. "This is different."

SHARI KANDELL
Her Parents Came First

About the only major disagreement Shari Kandell had with her parents was over her admiration of Reggie Jackson. Her father, Jan Kandell, could not abide him. But Ms. Kandell commemorated her admiration long after Jackson's retirement by including his number, 44, in her e-mail address.

She was 27 and lived with her parents in Wyckoff, N.J.

Since March she had worked at Cantor Fitzgerald in support of traders. She was also going to school at night to finish her bachelor's degree. But she found the time to enjoy New York. On her last weekend, she took her mother, Beatrice, to see *A Chorus Line.*

Her brother, Steven Kandell, said she was "the least judgmental and cynical person I have ever known." He added, "I can't think of a single fight we ever had about anything."

Her mother and father came first, said an aunt, Barbara Weinberg, but Shari Kandell went out of her way to do things for friends, like arranging a 30th-birthday dinner for a girlfriend's husband because the couple had nothing left over for a party after buying a house.

And she listened, said Ms. Weinberg, recalling that a few months after telling her niece that David Letterman and Jay Leno were not up to the standards of Johnny Carson, she received a gift of *The Best of Carson.*

HOWARD LEE KANE
No Words for the View

Having struggled with Crohn's disease, an intestinal illness, for most of his life, Howard Lee Kane had little patience for anyone in a bad mood. His tonic was laughter, and whether it was a new joke he would e-mail to friends or a funny story about that day at the office, he had the gift to make people smile.

Mr. Kane, 40, was the comptroller at Windows on the World, a job he loved, said his wife, Lori, because it combined his passion for cooking with a view he called "halfway to heaven." Mr. Kane, who lived in Hazlet, N.J., put in long days that began at 4:30 A.M. He commuted more than an hour each way. But his only complaint about work, his wife said, was that he lacked the words to describe the sunsets and view.

He had little time during the week to cook or chat with the couple's 11-year-old son, Jason, so Sunday mornings became a father-son-only time for waffles and fishing down at the dock.

"They were best friends," said Mrs. Kane.

JENNIFER L. KANE
A Sisterhood Forged

Her years at Villanova University gave Jennifer Kane, 26, both her career—she was an accountant at Marsh & McLennan—and her best friend, Constanca Fonseca Vescio, who grew up in Portugal.

"We were like sisters, always. I swore in our sophomore year that she would be my maid of honor someday," Ms. Vescio said. She kept that promise last year when she got married in Sintra, near Lisbon. "She had memorized a sentence in Portuguese, but she was too shy to make her speech," Ms. Vescio said. "She wanted to tell me personally." But in the festive uproar, she never did.

Ms. Kane's photograph has been used in many media accounts of Sept. 11, which gives some tiny comfort to her parents, Faye and George Kane of Plymouth, Mass., and her brothers, Matthew and Timothy Kane.

But she was more than the beautiful face the photos show, said her mother. She was full of humor and warmly affectionate, with "strong family values."

Ms. Vescio said. "She was my heart."

VINCENT KANE
Strumming in the Park

Among the city's thousands of firefighters, Vincent Kane stood out. He lived on the Upper East Side and spent hours in the galleries of the Metropolitan Museum of Art. And he went to performances of the New York Philharmonic—something that still amazes his friends in Engine Company 22. "Most firefighters don't even know what the Philharmonic is," said one of them, Michael Ruddick.

He was also an environmentalist who regularly patrolled the firehouse trash bins for recyclables. And not long ago, he became a vegetarian—though the other firefighters insisted on piling red meat onto his plate anyway. "My daughter would be serving turkey on a holiday, and he would have the artificial kind," said his mother, Joan. "We had to laugh when he'd do that."

Firefighter Kane, 37, grew up in Breezy Point, Queens, where he became a volunteer fireman at 17. "He was always giving," Mrs. Kane said. He loved to play tunes by the Grateful Dead or the Beatles on his guitar. His neighbors on East 80th Street, who nicknamed him the Mayor, listened for the music wafting softly from his apartment late at night.

He kept a guitar in his locker at the firehouse, too, and would sometimes announce to his colleagues that he was heading out to play it in the park. "I used to tell him he was straying as far away from the normal firefighter stereotype as he possibly could," Mr. Ruddick said.

JOON KOO KANG
The Thousand Cranes

In the grogginess of early mornings, Dohee Kang often feels her husband, Joon Koo Kang, next to her. She tries to talk to him, only to realize he is gone.

The couple met when Mrs. Kang visited New York as a college student in 1994. She soon returned to Korea, but he followed her back to Seoul the next year, and proposed to her the day after she graduated.

"He gave me a thousand origami cranes, and said when he missed me, he would make a crane," she said. "He also showed me a photo album of me growing up. I don't know how he got the pictures. At the end of the album, there was a card, which said, 'Will you marry me?' "

The couple have two daughters, Ariel, 4, and Diane, 2. Mr. Kang, 34, was a computer analyst at Cantor Fitzgerald. He took his daughters to swimming pools and parks and read them the Bible every night

"I told my little ones that Daddy is in heaven. Then my older girl asked me, 'Could I call him?' " Mrs. Kang said. "I said no. If you wanted to see Daddy, you had to pray."

SHELDON R. KANTER
Mad for Mantle

A little boy was born in Brooklyn on a late-July day in 1948, and though there were still plenty of innings left to play at Ebbets Field, and even a World Series to win, in his heart time had run out for the Dodgers. By the time he was old enough to count base hits, the boy, Sheldon R. Kanter, had turned to the Bronx, where Mickey Mantle was playing center field, and attached his affection to Mantle for keeps.

"He was so easy to buy presents for," said Mr. Kanter's wife, Tami. "Just get anything that had a 7 on it." Over the years he accumulated autographed cards, baseballs and—his favorite—a replica of his hero's pinstriped jersey.

Mr. Kanter, who was 53 and a vice president for system support at Cantor Fitzgerald's eSpeed division, stubbornly stood by the Yankees, even when his two sons, Evan and Adam, turned out to be Mets fans.

"The subway series was not a happy place in this house," Mrs. Kanter said.

But there were other opportunities for harmony, like

Giants and Knicks games. The family bowled together, taking home trophies. And every year for Father's Day, the Kanter sons gave their father tickets to the Yankees old-timers game. They went as a family, the boys gritting their teeth and Shelly Kanter happy as could be in his jersey with the 7 on the back.

DEBORAH KAPLAN
Gathering for the Feast

She set up the tent.

Anyone who has tried it knows the frustration of erecting a tent in the woods with children waiting. But during a vacation at Niagara Falls the summer of 2001, Deborah Kaplan snapped together her family's brand-new ripstop shelter without breaking a sweat.

"She was the best at that stuff," said her husband, Harold. "She was the engineer. That was her domain."

It was a peculiar domain for an Orthodox Jewish woman from Brooklyn, one of only three women engineers in her graduating class at Cooper Union. She went on to work for the Port Authority, but Mr. Kaplan said engineering was not her passion. Her family was.

For years, Mrs. Kaplan, 45, worked only part time. Even after she was transferred from Journal Square in Jersey City to the World Trade Center this spring she took the 3 o'clock train home to be with her four children, he said.

When the family moved to Paramus, N.J., Mrs. Kaplan discovered that the local yeshiva did not give the children the traditional items used to celebrate the Jewish holiday of Sukkot. She did not complain. Instead, she found a wholesale supplier of the lulav, a palm branch, and the etrog, a citrus fruit from Israel. She sent forms to parents, took orders and collected payments.

Mrs. Kaplan was so efficient she ended up ordering lulavs and etrogs for five area synagogues. "If you had to count on someone for anything," said Nina Glaser, a friend, "you knew you could count on Debbie."

ROBIN KAPLAN
The Peacekeeper

When Robin Kaplan's friends bickered, she would chime in, "Harmony." She was the peacekeeper. And if they kept fighting she would put her hand to her temple and say, "Oh, my head."

"She had tons of phrases," said Andrea Nardini, a friend of Ms. Kaplan's since they were in sixth grade.

Although by nature a peacemaker, Ms. Kaplan hated to be the center of attention. She did not want to talk about what was going on with her; she wanted to talk about what others were doing.

"She made everyone feel welcome," Ms. Nardini said.

Ms. Kaplan, 33, of Westboro, Mass., was a senior equipment specialist at TJX Companies in Framingham, Mass. Her job required her to fly around the country setting up new clothing stores, and on Sept. 11 she was aboard American Airlines Flight 11.

"What you saw is what you got—she didn't put on airs," said Francine Kaplan, her mother, who also works at TJX.

ALVIN KAPPELMANN Jr.
Thinking of Others

Alvin Kappelmann Jr. sold insurance and worried about saving lives. Mr. Kappelmann, 57, was an insurance executive at Royal and SunAlliance. His office was in downtown Manhattan, though he was at a business meeting held by Aon in 2 World Trade Center when the attacks occurred.

Blessed with a powerful generosity, Mr. Kappelmann was a proud member of the volunteer fire department in Green Brook, N.J., where he lived. In fact, he joined when he was 16, and had logged 41 years of service. His interest was undoubtedly stimulated by his father, who had been a volunteer in the department for 70 years. An uncle also belonged. It was what they did.

"He enjoyed helping other people and educating people on fire safety," said his daughter Melanie Kappelmann, who believes that he tried to help evacuate workers in the towers, drawing on his training.

She remembered a moment at the Jersey shore when she and her sister were young.

"We were at a parade," she said, "when my father noticed there was smoke coming from a house. He went into the house before the fire department even got there. He wanted to make sure no one was inside. That was him, putting others before himself."

CHARLES HENRY KARCZEWSKI
Loved Wine, Hated Silence

Charles Henry Karczewski did not have children, but he might as well have. His two dogs, Princess, a yellow Labrador, and Baby, a cocker spaniel, are devastated that he is gone, said his wife, Philomena.

"Every male person that walks in the house they look at, and you see the disappointment in their eyes," she said. For comfort, they are sleeping with one of Mr. Karczewski's dirty shirts.

His dogs and his wife were only two of Mr. Karczewski's passions. He loved "that stupid trade center," as she put it, where he had worked for three years as a benefits consultant for the Aon Corporation. Every time they drove by the buildings, he would say, "I work there."

He loved to talk, and hated silence. He loved wine and the beach. He loved the stock market, even when it was on the downswing ("You never marry a stock," he liked to say), and had started a stock club.

Mr. Karczewski, 34, loved to vacation, often in adventurous ways—sky-diving, canoeing, kayaking. He had been to Italy, Bermuda and Alaska, among other places. In October 2001, he and his wife were planning to go to Arizona. The books he had ordered about hiking the Grand Canyon arrived in late September.

WILLIAM ANTHONY KARNES
Discovering New York

William Anthony Karnes made his living as a software trainer for Marsh & McLennan. But his life's passion was praising the virtues of his adopted hometown, New York, regaling his sisters with stories about the wonders of living in the city where anything is possible, a place grander than anything he imagined growing up back in tiny Corryton, Tenn.

At least twice a week, Mr. Karnes, 37, would phone home to Tennessee, as much to say "I love you" as to brag about his latest favorite restaurant, usually some Indian place. "He loved that there was so much to discover in New York," said John Winter, his domestic partner.

And he made sure to share his favorite discoveries. "It was a big kick for him to show us around his city," said his sister, Gayle Barker. "He'd take us to the Empire State Building, the top of the World Trade Center, Rockefeller Center or just walking through the streets."

The one thing Mr. Karnes couldn't find in his beloved Manhattan was true Southern cooking. His love of a good plate of pinto beans, corn bread, mashed potatoes and biscuits always managed to guide him back home to one of his sisters' dinner tables. In her mind, Mrs. Barker still imagines her brother sitting around the table.

"I just keep thinking that this isn't really happening, that he's not dead. He's just on a long, long trip somewhere."

DOUGLAS G. KARPILOFF
Security and Sweetness

After the World Trade Center was bombed in 1993, the Port Authority of New York and New Jersey made Douglas G. Karpiloff the director of security and life safety for the center. He installed an array of protective systems, including huge concrete planters around the towers, a strict set of building passes and an identification and tracking system for vehicles entering the basement.

He was also called in to consult about security in Denver before Timothy McVeigh's trial for the Oklahoma City bombing and on how to protect the White House and other federal buildings. Last year, his industry trade group named him security director of the year.

"He was always trying to think out of the box," said Alan Reiss, the former director of the Port Authority's World Trade Department. "Doug set up all kinds of procedures that became the new norm for signature office buildings."

As he increased security, Mr. Karpiloff, 53, was concerned that the tenants he was trying to protect still be treated as people. That meant getting security guards to say good morning and putting out candy near the guard desks at Halloween. "Even if you were turned away, he wanted it to be a positive experience," Mr. Reiss said. "He came to me with all of these ideas, like, 'I'm going to spend $2,000 on candy.' All of these little things made a dramatic difference."

After Silverstein Properties took over operation of the towers in July, Mr. Karpiloff had remained for a few months as a member of the transition team.

CHARLES L. KASPER
Granddaddy's Trains

At Christmastime 2000, Deputy Chief Charles L. Kasper of the Fire Department's Special Operations Command went out and bought a set of trains.

They were not for his 425-person division, which races to the scene whenever there is a major catastrophe and already owns a huge collection of red-painted fire trucks, fireboats and other exciting toys for grown-ups. No, they were for his grandson, but when the chief linked the track pieces into a circle and sent the locomotive huffing and whistling around it, Dylan, then only 7 months old, was too young to appreciate the spectacle.

Never mind, thought Chief Kasper. There's always next year.

On Sept. 11, the 54-year-old veteran of dozens of rescues was having a day off when he heard about the World Trade Center attacks. He scrambled into a spare fire engine parked near his home in Staten Island and sped to the towers. He had a motto: "Drive it like it's stolen," recalled Jim Ellson, a retired captain.

Recently Chief Kasper's wife, Laureen, and their children unpacked the trains, set them up the same way he had and watched while Dylan reacted with delight.

"We say that he's playing with Granddaddy," who was "always on duty for his family," Mrs. Kasper said. "And we know that Charlie's circle will always encircle us."

ANDREW KATES
A Life Enjoyed to the Fullest

On the Saturday morning before Sept. 11, Andrew Kates woke up to find his three children bouncing on the bed, all ready to play.

"He just looked right at me and said, 'I love our family,' " said his wife, Emily Terry.

He spent every spare moment with his two daughters and son, ages 5, 3 and 1. He gave them piggyback rides around their Upper West Side apartment. They played hide-and-seek. Every weekend last winter, he packed hot chocolate and took the two older ones, Hannah and Lucy, ice skating for hours in Central Park.

An athletic 37-year-old, he had brown hair, green eyes and dimples creasing both cheeks. His son, Henry, looks a lot like him. He managed to see the best in every situation, whether it was at home or on the job at Cantor Fitzgerald in 1 World Trade Center, where he was a senior managing director.

Perhaps it sounds like a cliché, his wife said, but he did manage to enjoy life to the fullest. "He is one of the people I know who had very few regrets about his life."

JOHN KATSIMATIDES
Everything in Technicolor

Cool New Yorkers drape themselves in black. Guess someone forgot to tell John Katsimatides. Because he was very cool and lived utterly in Technicolor.

His Jet Ski and his Jeep were bright yellow. His Harley was baby blue. During his Travolta-esque period, he cruised Astoria Park strip in Sweet Sensation, his blindingly white 1982 Eldorado Cadillac; no black leather jackets could rub against its snowy seats.

At a macho Super Bowl party, the underwear he flashed was hot pink.

A bonds broker at Cantor Fitzgerald, Mr. Katsimatides, 31, had a cocky strut and melted even the most self-conscious women with, "Hey good-looking, what's up?" He could also be tender—"Agape mou" (my love), he addressed family members, shouldering them through private tragedy. He attended Greek Orthodox services every Sunday at a different church. He was something else.

Johnny Bodacious, they called the guy who would do back flips off windowsills to impress the girls, who would do Greek dances on tabletops, fall, break his wrist, and keep on dancing. Johnny Cash, they called the guy who would borrow $20 to get into a club and end the night with $40 in his pocket, an endearing moocher who also ran up $500 on his credit cards from a night of buying drinks for the bar. (You can't imagine how many people thought he was their best friend.)

ROBERT M. KAULFERS
"Bob Was a Minstrel"

Men and women of the Port Authority of New York and New Jersey, friends and family members: soon, the famed lyrics of Sgt. Robert M. Kaulfers may be available. These are the tunes you know and love from retirement parties, wedding receptions and slow days on the job. Take it from Sgt. Mark O'Neill: "Bob was a minstrel."

You'll get "The Hat," the famous ode to Officer Mike Barry, set to the tune of the theme from *The Cat in the Hat*, and "Carnevale Time," the paean to Lt. Mike Carnevale. And who could forget the tribute to Sgt. Bernard M. Poggioli, a world-renowned expert on runaway children, "I'm Much Taller Than Poggioli"?

Many of the lyrics were found in Sergeant Kaulfers's locker. His wife, Cookie, thinks she may soon be strong enough to go through his papers at home to meet requests for the other songs. "I would hear him in the shower singing and laughing to himself," she remembered.

Sergeant Kaulfers, 49, also found time to study world history, keep the rookies on the right path and raise two children. His friends said he never held a grudge; perhaps the best evidence of that was his 25-year marriage to the girl who beat him in the election for sixth-grade class president.

DON J. KAUTH
"Find Something You Like"

After the early deaths of his father and brother and his divorce 10 years ago, Don J. Kauth, a bank analyst, focused intently on his four children.

"It made him a much better father," said Matt, the oldest.

Mr. Kauth bought a house near the children and their mother in Saratoga Springs, so they could spend weekends with him, and a camper for vacations in the Adirondacks.

"He told us, 'Find something you like to do and the money will come,' " Matt said. But he was immensely proud when Matt worked at a homeless shelter with the Jesuit Peace Corps, a job rich in everything but money. And when Kathleen, his daughter, won a place on the United States national hockey team, he was "crying, he was so overjoyed," said Winifred Kauth, his mother.

On Mondays, he rose at 3 A.M. to commute to Manhattan, where he kept an apartment and worked at Keefe, Bruyette & Woods.

"He'd say: 'That's where the money is,' " Mrs. Kauth said. "He was making it for his children."

HIDEYA KAWAUCHI
A Love for Clothes

Tomoko Kawauchi's husband, Hideya, loved three things: her, of course, the beach and shopping. On Sept. 8, the two packed a picnic lunch and went to Belmar Beach in New Jersey. They spent half the day there since Brooks Brothers closes at 6 P.M. on Saturdays. And nothing made Mr. Kawauchi happier than spending part of his day shopping for the latest in men's casual wear.

"He changed frequently," says his wife. "He had a lot of clothes. Much more than me. He had 15 shoes. I have maybe 5."

Mr. Kawauchi, 36, was born in Chiba, Japan. After he graduated from the Wharton School of the University of Pennsylvania in 1993, he wanted to work in New York but could not find a job in the city. He returned to Japan and got a job at Fuji Bank, where he met his wife. They were married in 1995. In 1997, Mr. Kawauchi, a general affairs officer, was transferred to the Fuji Bank division at 2 World Trade Center. The Kawauchis moved to Fort Lee, N.J., because they had friends in the area.

"There is also a Japanese restaurant and supermarket," Mrs. Kawauchi said. And Brooks Brothers only minutes away.

EDWARD KEANE
Too Restless to Retire

More than three years ago, Edward Keane retired. He had had a long and satisfying career as a mechanical engineer, and it made sense. He was 62.

He enjoyed the outdoors, and so he busied himself hiking and puttering around the garden.

His mother-in-law died, and there was a lot to do, selling her house and otherwise wrapping up her affairs. He sold his sailboat—it was too big to handle—and was going to buy a smaller boat. After a while, though, he got restless. He was in perfect health, and wanted to do more.

"He kept watching a neighbor walk his dog three times a day," said his wife, Barbara Keane. "He knew that wasn't for him."

So in May 2001, he resumed the work life as a consultant with Hill International, assigned to the Port Authority. Mr. Keane, 66, lived with his wife in West Caldwell, N.J., but he was enthralled by lower Manhattan.

Whenever a friend or relative came in from out of town, he had to show them around the area.

He made a point of being considerate. The week before Sept. 11, a neighbor was moving. She had a lot of stuff to throw out. He got a hand truck and carted it out to the curb, as some of the young residents of the block watched and egged him on. He did not need any help.

RICHARD M. KEANE
A Life Lived to Music

Here are pictures of Richard M. Keane: tending a garden in exceptionally grubby clothes while a boom box blasted out Orbison or Puccini; coming home from a business trip and telling his wife, Judy Keane, about the man he met on the plane; riding the commuter bus from his home off the village green of Wethersfield, Conn., to the Marsh & McLennan office in Hartford. (Mr. Keane, a senior vice president, was making a rare trip to Marsh's World Trade Center office for a meeting on Sept. 11.)

Mr. Keane, who exuded friendliness, loved to collect stories about people on his constant business travels. He believed in public transportation as a public good. He loved to garden, bringing to life 80 tomato plants this year and growing Connecticut field pumpkins every fall for the children in his extended family.

"Dick was always trying to foist vegetables off on people," Mrs. Keane said.

And his life was done to music. "If I ask him to put up a picture for me, he can't do that until the music is going," she said. He was not the greatest singer, but sang in the choir of Sacred Heart Church, where he would shuttle several blind women on most Sundays.

A brother-in-law, Dr. Thomas C. Dolan, remembers Mr. Keane's constant coaching as the father of five sons, the marathons he started at age 40, the communal house paintings every year.

"The glass of water was always half-full for this guy," Dr. Dolan said.

LISA KEARNEY-GRIFFIN
She Could Calm the Angry

It's crazy, she'd tell her daughter. Here she was, 35, and her best friend was 13. Flip a few cruel calendar pages back and imagine Lisa Kearney-Griffin dancing and singing in the kitchen with that daughter, Brityne, that best friend, who wants so, so badly to be a singer.

Ms. Kearney-Griffin, who also had a 1-year-old daughter, loved to dance and sing. With her piercing hazel eyes, she was "vibrant, larger than life," said her husband, Craig Griffin. "She could sell snow to Eskimos."

That glow could come in handy. When she worked at Delta Air Lines as an agent coping with travelers' preboarding problems, one passenger grew irate at a delay. No one could calm him down. Except her. She talked to him and soon they "became the best of friends," Mr. Griffin said. Until his plane left, "he refused to talk to anyone but her."

Ms. Kearney-Griffin, who worked for American Express Corporate Travel at Marsh & McLennan's office at the trade center, shared her love of travel with her husband, and they took trips all over. He did not like ships, but she got him to take a cruise to Aruba, and he loved it.

It "left a lasting impression," he said, quickly adding, "Everything about her left a lasting impression."

DONNA BERNAERTS KEARNS
Soft Heart, Sharp Tongue

Even after she became a successful computer programmer, Donna Bernaerts Kearns never forgot what it was like to grow up poor. So each Christmas, she would get her colleagues at Accenture to participate in the Postal Service's Secret Santa drive for needy children.

"She would go out and buy coats, boots and puzzles," said her older sister, Rosemarie D'Amato. "She would spend her lunch hours doing these things."

Ms. Kearns, 44, who was known as Donna Bernaerts at work, had a soft heart, but she also could have a sharp tongue. "She didn't let anybody take advantage of her," her sister said. "She was honest about how she felt."

Often, what she felt was the weight of a stressful life, Ms. D'Amato said. Ms. Kearns frequently worked late into the night from her home in Hoboken, N.J. She would get to her office at 1 World Trade Center by 8 A.M. so she could spend more time with her son, Joseph, who is mildly autistic. Now, her husband, Edward, is learning how to take care of Joseph, now 11, on his own.

"It's all on one shoulder now," Ms. D'Amato said.

KAROL ANN KEASLER
Ever the Social Butterfly

She was reared in a two-stoplight town in Arizona, but Karol Ann Keasler was hardly a small-town girl.

"One of my friends said, 'I always knew Karol would not live the life of the girl next door, fall in love with her high school sweetheart, live in that little world,' " her mother, Denise Keasler, recalled. "And she didn't."

Ms. Keasler traveled the world. She lived in Africa for two years and visited countries from Cambodia to Sweden to Bosnia. On Sept. 9, she had just returned from a trip to Tuscany with her fiancé, Michael Weinstein. The couple planned to live in Mr. Weinstein's native city, St. Petersburg, Russia.

At 42, Ms. Keasler was a bride-to-be; a Fire Island regular; a reader to her elderly next-door neighbor in Brooklyn Heights; a volunteer at a soup kitchen on the Upper East Side. Ever the social butterfly, Ms. Keasler was perfect for her job as an event planner at Keefe, Bruyette & Woods on the 89th floor of 2 World Trade Center.

"Karol had probably the biggest zest for life that I've ever seen," said her friend Elizabeth Coss. "Sometimes I wonder almost if she didn't know inherently that her life was going to be short. She just really packed so much in."

PAUL H. KEATING
Wit That Won People Over

Paul Keating went to a carpet store for something to put on his floor for $100, but the rug that caught his eye cost $119. As the salesman launched into a pitch about why it could not leave the store for $100—stain-guard and padding and such—Mr. Keating grabbed the tag.

"See, it says right there," Mr. Keating said. Then he said, as if reading aloud: "Go ahead. One hundred dollars." The salesman laughed; Mr. Keating got his bargain.

That kind of scene was repeated often in Paul Keating's 38 years. He could annoy, persuade or reassure with his one-liners.

"Very few people had the gift of giving you a relentless amount of ribbing while making you laugh," said Jeffrey Borab, a friend. Mr. Keating tried jobs as a plumber's assistant and surveyor before joining the New York Fire Department six years ago.

Because he played down his heroic exploits and won friends with his wit, many people recall his charm before his sacrifice. He was off duty on the morning of Sept. 11.

"It is noted that he wasn't working when he went there, isn't it?" asked a colleague at Firefighter Keating's firehouse in SoHo.

L. RUSSELL KEENE III
"I Know Just Where He Is"

L. Russell Keene III, a 33-year-old equities analyst at Keefe, Bruyette & Woods, was such an avid sportsman that he once hiked through New Zealand for two solid months.

"He has plenty of stamina to survive," said his wife, Kristen, who is offering him more than just spiritual support. The other day his wife, who lives in Westfield, N.J., was escorted by Union County sheriffs to the disaster site outside 2 World Trade Center.

Instead of standing there offering respectful witness, "I wanted to go dig him out," she said, "but they wouldn't let me. I know just where he is."

Two other employees from Bruyette escaped from an elevator jammed near the lobby, and reported that Mr. Keene and 15 others were alive inside. Then the building collapsed. And so, while his wife and other Bruyette relatives tried to lobby the rescuers to dig near the elevator, she remembered the man she met six years ago in Ocala, Fla., saying simply: "I loved him from the start."

JOSEPH KELLER
His Motto: "Let's Do It!"

On that last Sunday, Joseph Keller, bona fide grown-up—father, husband, home-owner in Park Ridge, N.J., and department head at the Marriott World Trade Center Hotel—had what would be a final fling with his daredevil teenage self. He and two buddies from high school got together and dusted off their old bicycle freestyling stunts. Mr. Keller, 31, who had competed in the extreme sport, still had the chops to pull off a funky chicken. (Don't ask.)

"If you were looking for someone to egg you on," said his friend Prentice Chang, "Joe was like: 'Let's do it!' A lot of people followed his direction."

Some lucky ones did on Sept. 11. When his wife, Rose, called, urging him to flee, he told her he was helping with the evacuation. Later, when he phoned his boss, he sounded cool, but concerned about the two injured firefighters with whom he was trapped.

"Joe was always reassuring, the one who made things O.K.," Mrs. Keller said. "You'd think you couldn't do something, but he made you believe you could. He made me think things were possible."

PETER R. KELLERMAN
Dogs, Drums, Motorcycles

Robi and Peter R. Kellerman planned to have children, but first they had dogs.

Mrs. Kellerman was more like Maverick, the excitable black Labrador retriever. Mr. Kellerman, his wife said, "was totally Bosco," the mellow chocolate Lab with the adorable face.

A slight problem: some of Mr. Kellerman's six nephews were scared of Bosco and of Taylor, the German shepherd. The nephews range in age from 5 to 13, and Mr. Kellerman played with them so enthusiastically that their friends' moms wanted to book him for birthday parties.

"He was just pure fun," said Pam Fox, a sister. "Whose uncle plays PlayStation all day?" Uncle Pete, 35, was also a partner at Cantor Fitzgerald.

A drummer and motorcyclist, he gave one set of nephews, the Dicksteins, his old helmets and once gave each of the Fox nephews a set of real drumsticks—not toy ones—then initiated a jam session on the coffee table.

Mr. and Mrs. Kellerman grew up three blocks apart on the Upper East Side but did not start dating until they met at a basketball game at Madison Square Garden in 1998.

The Fox boys now sleep with the drumsticks under their pillows. One is afraid to cry, because the tears might never stop.

But they have since warmed up to the dogs, Mrs. Kellerman said. "He'd be so proud."

JAMES J. KELLY
Castle Keep

Nearly every room in the Kelly family's home in Oceanside, N.Y., has some sort of feminine touch or floral print, which is not surprising, considering the women outnumbered the men five to one.

But not the family room.

That was the space known as Kells's domain, where James J. Kelly, 39, was king.

He hung photographs of his college fraternity brothers and the Cantor Boys, his buddies at Cantor Fitzgerald,

At 1 Police Plaza on November 4, a memorial organized by the New York State Fraternal Order of Police honored those in law enforcement who died in the trade center attack. As part of the ceremony, officers from across the country presented flags. *(Frances Roberts)*

A memorial wall in honor of victims stands alongside the heavily guarded temporary morgue adjacent to Bellevue Hospital Center, near Thirtieth Street and the Franklin D. Roosevelt Drive in Manhattan. The tents behind the wall shelter trucks arriving from ground zero. (*Lonnie Schlein*)

where he worked on the mortgage desk. He furnished it with plum-colored couches and a 55-inch television with multiple remote controls.

"It's just very Daddyish," said Joanne, Mr. Kelly's wife and high school sweetheart. And when it came to the kitchen, Mr. Kelly had his own specialties. He was renowned for his popcorn and M & M mixtures.

He made Mets fans of his four young daughters—"the squad," he called them—by serving waffles and milkshakes for Sunday breakfast after Saturday victories.

Now, the girls take turns sitting in his spot at the kitchen table, and Mrs. Kelly dreads the times of day that she used to cherish, like 6:30 P.M., when Kells would return to his domain.

"I still think he's going to walk up the driveway swinging his keys," she said. "He would walk through the door and everything would change."

JOSEPH KELLY
A Compulsive Do-Gooder

Joseph Kelly's friends and family knew never to praise anything he showed them. If they did, they were sure to find the items at their homes the next day.

"He was like that—he had a big heart," said Mr. Kelly's brother, James, a New York City firefighter. "He would just give it away."

Joseph Kelly, 40, who lived in Oyster Bay, N.Y., was a broker for Cantor Fitzgerald, a husband and the father of four children, ages 8, 6, 5 and 2. His wife, Susan, is pregnant with their fifth child, who is due in May. He was also one of six siblings and a compulsive do-gooder.

"He once left a brand-new car on my parents' driveway

because he was going to London for a few days and just never picked it up," his brother said.

At the memorial service, Jim Kelly said he learned that his brother's generosity extended beyond the family. People spoke of his kindness, and told how, at auctions for various charities, he bought the leftovers.

"Whatever people didn't buy, he got, so he had a room full of stuff, a lot of sports memorabilia," his brother said. Luckily, Mr. Kelly was a sports fan. On the last night of his life, he took his two older children, Christopher and Thomas, to a Yankees game.

MAURICE PATRICK KELLY
Finding Happiness

Maurice Patrick Kelly, a carpenter who was patching a ceiling for Cantor Fitzgerald on the 103rd floor of the World Trade Center on Sept. 11, had a tattoo of the Grim Reaper on his arm, a symbol of a harrowing life that only now, after 41 years, seemed to be improving.

Mr. Kelly raised himself in a family of alcoholics, said his younger sister, Claire Dawson. A grandmother in Pelham, N.Y., put the children through parochial school and looked after them whenever their mother, divorced when the children were small, disappeared—out of money or on the prowl with a new boyfriend.

On one visit to their grandmother, when Maurice was 16 and Claire was 12, a chilling telegram arrived: "Due to unforeseen circumstances I will not be able to pick up the children."

A year later, Mr. Kelly's mother reappeared, with a man in tow, himself a drinker and gambler. She wanted to take the children to Maryland, but Maurice refused. Instead, he lived on his own, an 11th-grade dropout, trying to care for his father, who died of complications of alcoholism. Years later, when his mother was dying, Mr. Kelly refused to say good-bye.

Mr. Kelly's own marriage ended in divorce, with a 17-year-old daughter remaining with her mother, and two sons, 7 and 10, living with Mr. Kelly on City Island. But by then, he had apprenticed as a carpenter, loved his trade, worked shifts that allowed him time with his boys and had fallen in love again, with 33-year-old Melissa Sponheimer.

"He had a very sad life," said Mr. Kelly's aunt, Dorothy Gould, "and was finally finding happiness."

THOMAS R. KELLY
Tom Kelly, Meet Tom Kelly

Everything about Thomas R. Kelly's life springs from his summers in Riverhead on Long Island. He spent all his vacations in a family bungalow there, riding his bike to the beach and swimming.

Eventually he followed in his father's

footsteps and joined the Fire Department, but his world continued to revolve around water and bike trails. He swam in the shark tank of a nearby aquarium. He went deep sea diving in Belize. After his divorce last year, he moved into a house around the corner from where his family had summered, and where his parents, Sue and Emmet, now live year-round.

When he was not swimming, he was biking, and on a 400-mile charity ride from New York to Boston last June he met Kate Zona. The couple planned to pedal through Europe in the summer of 2002 to raise money for AIDS research. But instead their last bike ride was on Sept. 9, through all five New York boroughs.

Because Ms. Zona's pace was slower, Firefighter Kelly waited for her at a bar, where he sat down next to another man named Thomas Kelly—also a firefighter—and they marveled that two Tom Kellys happened to be in the same place at the same time. Two days later, both Tom Kellys died at the World Trade Center.

TIMOTHY C. KELLY
A Dapper Throwback

The youngest of five children and the last to leave home, Timothy C. Kelly cultivated a taste for the chivalry and silk handkerchiefs of his parents' generation.

"He was a man who enjoyed the finer things in life," said his wife, Julie. "He sort of lived in the '40s. He was a Dapper Dan."

Mr. Kelly, 37, griped when Cantor Fitzgerald, where he worked as a municipal bond broker, switched to more casual business attire. He insisted on dressing up several times a week in butterscotch loafers or a camel's-hair coat.

He plied his siblings with restaurant recommendations and instructed his friends on the importance of proper shoe storage. "The loveliest of the lovelies" is what he called his wife.

"His life was short," Mrs. Kelly said. "So I'm glad he had all those things to enjoy." Recently, Mr. Kelly had happily parted with one cherished luxury: his golf membership at the Plandome Country Club, on Long Island. He was saving to put his children—Kevin, 6, Mary Kate, 3, and Caroline, who was born Sept. 4—through Catholic school.

WILLIAM H. KELLY Jr.
Mr. Long Beach Island

If you lived on Long Beach Island in New Jersey, you knew William H. Kelly Jr. Although Mr. Kelly grew up in Bucks County, Pa., his family spent summers on the island, where he was able to indulge his passion for the water, learning to sail and surf.

"My friends would joke around; they used to call him

A New York City police officer plays taps at a memorial
service on November 7 for a fellow officer, Robert Fazio,
at St. Agnes Cathedral in Rockville Centre on Long
Island. (*Ed Betz*)

'Mr. L.B.I.,' " said his girlfriend of three years, Sue Magee,
an employee of Bloomberg L.P., where Mr. Kelly also
worked.

In fact, even if you did not live on Long Beach Island, you
may have known Mr. Kelly, or the type of person he was.

"He wasn't a loud, life-of-the-party kind of guy, but he
always sought out the person in any situation who wasn't
comfortable, and made them feel welcome," said his sister
Colleen Kelly.

Mr. Kelly, 30, who lived in Stuyvesant Town, was a
favorite uncle to his many nieces and nephews. Once,
instead of giving them all individual Christmas gifts, he
rented an ice rink for an afternoon, and invited his whole
family.

After Sept. 11, his mother, JoAnne Kelly, was surprised
to receive an envelope full of a 4-year-old Billy's dark curls,
from an early trip to the barber. She had given the envelope
to a beloved neighbor, whom Mr. Kelly had nicknamed Pal,
as a joke, and Pal had saved it for 26 years. Now Mrs. Kelly
has something of her son left to treasure.

ROBERT C. KENNEDY
A Proud Father

Robert C. Kennedy loved to laugh, mostly
at silly things. His laugh was so huge and
his face grew so red that people sometimes
worried he was having a heart attack.

"When we were younger," said his
daughter Meredith Andrews, "we were so
embarrassed." But Mr. Kennedy was also the father who
made her and her older sister, Catherine Miller, feel like
women rather than girls. "He was proud of our relationship
and the fact that he was able to teach us so young that you
can be friends with your parents," Ms. Miller said.

"His daughters were his hope," Maureen Kennedy, his
wife of 32 years, said. "He took them to work before it was
the thing to do." He was also a quiet, steady mentor to
women at Marsh & McLennan, where he worked.

Mr. Kennedy, who was 55 and lived in Toms River, N.J.,
was also a tease. "He loved his view from the World Trade

Center," Mrs. Kennedy said. "He would tease that he could see Pennsylvania on a clear day. When we drove to Staten Island, he'd look back across the bridge and say he had left the lights on in his office."

THOMAS J. KENNEDY
Last Wishes, First Steps

Thomas J. Kennedy had the sort of welcoming face that babies and children love. Wherever he went, they would try to make friends. "He would treat kids as if they were adults," said a brother, Bob. "Then he could play the kid himself, at the same time."

A firefighter with Ladder Company 101 in Brooklyn, Mr. Kennedy, 36, wanted five children of his own. He and his wife, Allison, had two children and planned to have another. Michael is 2, and James turned 1 on Nov. 17.

As a father, Firefighter Kennedy cherished his children's bedtime rituals, administering evening baths and reading *Goodnight Moon*. He and Michael would drop coins into a piggy bank, because the father was teaching the son the value of saving. This winter, Firefighter Kennedy had hoped to take Michael skiing and ice skating, and to see James walk. On Sept. 14, the baby took his first steps. "Now he runs and climbs," said Mrs. Kennedy. "Tom would have loved that."

JOHN KEOHANE
Spirit of a Traveler

One year, before he moved to New Jersey, he took his mother to New York. One year he took her to Washington for a tour of the White House. Some years, she would simply visit his apartment and cook.

This year, for their annual vacation, Mary Keohane and her son, John, 41, were planning to meet in Florida on Saturday, Sept. 15.

He had loved the idea of travel since he was a boy building model airplanes and visiting his grandmother's house, which sat in the flight path of San Francisco International Airport. As an adult, Mr. Keohane—an energetic, good-humored yet quiet lawyer at the Zurich company, according to his sister, Darlene—liked to say he had visited everywhere except Antarctica.

Mary Keohane's bags were already packed when her phone rang in Northern California around 7 A.M. on Sept. 11. It was her son saying he had safely left 1 Liberty Plaza, where he worked, and met up three blocks away with his partner, Mike Lyons, who worked nearby.

Hearing a loud noise, Mr. Keohane told his mother that

a third plane had hit a building. The connection was lost. The second tower was collapsing, spreading darkness through the streets—Mr. Keohane became separated from Mr. Lyons and was hit by debris. Weeks later, the Keohanes received a letter from a priest at a downtown church, saying he had found Mr. Keohane about two minutes later and performed last rites.

RALPH F. KERSHAW
A Yachtsman's Best Friend

After he married his high-school sweetheart, Hedi, 30 years ago, Ralph F. Kershaw built a two-story colonial house at Manchester-by-the-Sea, a town 30 miles north of Boston. In the years after, as the kids were born, he kept adding rooms to the original house: a playroom, a bedroom, a study. The family still lives there. Mr. Kershaw, at 6-foot-3 and 250 pounds, had big hands that were also adroit at the culinary art.

"He made a great, great salsa," said Mrs. Kershaw. She said he also chopped cabbages, peppers and lots of garlic, and "made the most delicious soups."

A surveyor of yachts, he knew the boats inside and out. He would tell you what was right or wrong with your boat and know how to fix the problems, too.

"He was very well respected in his field. He knew what makes a boat tick," said Mrs. Kershaw. Ralph had followed his father into this trade, and he wanted his own twin sons, Matthew and Jason, both 25, to continue the in the same tradition.

"Daddy knew everything about every kind of boat," said Matthew Kershaw. "Tankers, wooden, fiberglass, steel, aluminum." He and his brother work at a boatyard repairing fiberglass boats.

On Sept. 11, Mr. Kershaw, 52, was on United Airlines Flight 175 when it struck the World Trade Center's south tower. He was en route to Singapore, via Los Angeles, to inspect a yacht.

HOWARD KESTENBAUM
For Experience, a Shelter

Howard Kestenbaum worried about the homeless. He spent nights in a shelter to see what it was like, and would respond to a request for a dollar with a five, along with a suggestion to get some soup and a sandwich.

He was involved with his temple, Beth Ahm in Verona, N.J., and was impressed that so many there had been through crises like the Depression and World War II. His friends and relatives speak of him as unassuming and friendly.

Lauren, his 24-year-old daughter, said she remembered him at home in Montclair, "standing in my doorway, trying to get me to go do something with him, like go for a walk. "Him in a flannel shirt," she said. "My dad was a good guy, he was a really good guy."

He met his wife, Granvilette, when they were both graduate students at Columbia. He was studying astrophysics; she was in social work. At Aon Risk Services, Mr. Kestenbaum, 56, used his training to develop models to help clients understand how real certain risks were.

In his office on the 103rd floor of the south tower, he hung a lightly weighted paper cup from the ceiling—and noted how it and the building swayed in high winds.

DOUGLAS D. KETCHAM
He Just Started Climbing

Douglas D. Ketcham climbed the corporate ladder. Literally.

A few years ago, Mr. Ketcham was summoned into the office of a high-ranking supervisor at Cantor Fitzgerald. He saw a ladder in the middle of the room and started climbing, figuring he had been invited in to change a light bulb.

"The boss said, 'Doug, what in the hell are you doing?'" recalled his mother, Raenelle. Turns out the ladder was there for someone else. He was being given a bonus. But that was Mr. Ketcham for you: humble.

"He was never too high to do anything," said his girlfriend, Evelyn J. Abeles. "He liked the finer things in life, but he was also very down to earth."

Mr. Ketcham was remarkably close to his mother. He would call her, even at 2 A.M., if he had just spotted a celebrity, and even told her about his love life.

She had an uncanny knack for sensing, long distance, when he was feeling down. "He told me stuff," Mrs. Ketcham said from her home near Orlando, Fla. "I'd say, 'Son, remember, I'm your mother. I'm not old enough to know that.'"

In her son's briefcase, Mrs. Ketcham found an envelope on which he had scrawled an itinerary for a visit to New York that she had planned but postponed. "I was going to be taken everywhere," Mrs. Ketcham said. "I was going to be the queen of New York."

RUTH E. KETLER
Heard on the Street—Ruth

Ruth E. Ketler once said she thought it was possible to be an executive who was liked and admired, instead of respected and feared. At Fiduciary Trust, where she was director of research, and in her daily life around the city, she tried to make that come true.

"Ruth made you want to give something back to her," said

Robert Dow, her longtime companion, who called her Beautiful Ruth. She generated compliments, but studiously avoided becoming self-important. Her fans included doormen, artists and cabdrivers. She built a strong following among her investment banking peers, people who not easily impressed.

"In a business that can be dehumanizing at times, she always had a heart," said John R. McMillin, an analyst for Prudential Securities. If there was one bit of shared wisdom around Wall Street, said Heidi Albert of Lehman Brothers, it was: "Nobody didn't like Ruth."

Ms. Ketler might counsel an infuriated friend, visit a sick colleague, remember a small child's birthday. She loved to fish in the surf off Cape Cod, to sink difficult shots on the golf course, and to pick the winner in the Kentucky Derby. And she liked to have a big group over for dinner, which she would cook, and she would listen intently as her guests chatted around the table.

"It wasn't that she was a free spirit," said Jan Meissner, a friend. "She was a very large spirit."

BORIS KHALIF
A Tiny, Rapt Audience

Boris Khalif moved to the United States from Ukraine at the age of 10, loved computers and devoured everything he could find about them. When he got his first computer in high school, he took it apart and then put it back together.

At first it did not work, so he kept fiddling until it did. Friends and relatives brought their computer problems to him and he fixed them. Mr. Khalif, 30, who lived in Brooklyn, was working as a computer consultant at Marsh & McLennan in 1 World Trade Center on Sept. 11.

Although his son, Steven, was still only 2, Mr. Khalif had already begun to buy him children's games for the computer. But Steven was fascinated watching Mr. Khalif play his own computer games.

"War games, fighting, monsters, our son liked to watch them all," said Mr. Khalif's wife, Ella. "That's how I fed my son. He was too busy watching what my husband was doing to feed himself."

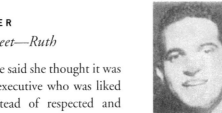

TAIMOUR KHAN
"He Cannot Be Taken Down"

As a child in Woodbury, N.Y., Taimour Khan doggedly practiced his BMX bike tricks until he could balance on his front tire, on his back tire, and even essay long bunny hops.

One day he raced his brother Shaan so fiercely down Fairbanks Boulevard that their pedals tangled, they crashed, and went flying "for 20 yards," Shaan said. Later, although

Taimour weighed but 150 pounds and stood 5 feet 11 inches tall, his determination propelled him to the captaincy of the Syosset High School football team and a celebrated 90-yard touchdown run.

It was this drive that made Mr. Khan, 29, a commodity futures trader at Carr Futures, heading his own desk on the 90th floor of 1 World Trade Center.

"He has the determination to be a really major player," his brother said, "and he cannot be taken down. I know that he's going to make it."

SEI-LAI KHOO
Providing a Lifeline

Yeng Leng Khoo was used to seeing his big sister Sei-Lai Khoo quoted in the press about hot public offerings and tech stocks. At 38, she co-managed some of the best-known mutual funds at Fred Alger Management and was often sought out for her views about market trends.

But for all her success, she always had time for family, friends and co-workers, they say. When Yeng Leng arrived in New York from Malaysia, where they grew up, to start college, she treated him to his first Broadway show. She also taught him survival skills like which subways to take—and how to use Zagat's to find the best dumplings in town.

"She always remembered what she ordered and what was good the last time we ate someplace," said her brother. He said she was also first to "fight for the bill."

Ms. Khoo provided the same lifeline to young colleagues, once professing shock that a subordinate of Vietnamese descent had never sampled Vietnamese cuisine. Off they went.

MICHAEL VERNON KIEFER
From Boyhood, a Fireman

Michael Vernon Kiefer wanted to be a New York City fireman as long as anyone can remember.

As a toddler, he and his father, Bud, would visit the firehouse in Franklin Square, N.Y., so little Michael could sit on the trucks.

As a schoolboy, he once caused a bus driver to pull over abruptly because Michael's impression of a siren was a little too convincing, and his sisters were often drilled on how to rescue their dolls from pretend fires in the backyard shed.

And as a teenager about to undergo an appendectomy, Michael was anxious, not about the operation, but whether the surgery would keep him from passing the New York Fire Department's physical someday, his parents recalled.

As a young man, Michael Kiefer worked as an emergency medical technician and met his fiancee, Jamie Huggler, a physician's assistant.

When he finally got the chance in late 2000 to be a full-fledged New York City firefighter at age 25, he was all nerves until he learned he had been assigned to Ladder Company 132, one of Brooklyn's busiest.

"He was lucky in a way," said Bud Kiefer, "because a lot of people today are 50 years old and don't know what they want to be when they grew up. He knew. "

ANDY J. KIM
The Spiritual Sort

As a child, Andy J. Kim developed his musical talents. He played piano, clarinet and guitar. During high school, he was in the marching band, the jazz band and the orchestra. At Columbia University, where he studied engineering and finance, he developed his spiritual side, working with the Campus Crusade for Christ.

After college, Mr. Kim, 26, was a research analyst for Fred Alger Management; in late July 2001, he passed the certified financial analyst exam.

Although he lived in Leonia, N.J., he spent every moment he could at the Bethany United Methodist Church in Wayne, where his musicality and spirituality came together. He worked with the youth group and led the band that played during church services. Some said he was the best worship leader they had known.

He was especially excited when he was asked early in 2001 to lead worship at Autumn Blaze, a gathering of about 6,000 young people scheduled for Oct. 13 in New Jersey. He even formed a special band for the event.

But they played without him. "We felt we should continue," said his companion, Michele Jhun, who sang in the band. "That is what Andy would have wanted."

LAWRENCE KIM
Appetites for Food and Life

Nov. 22, 2001, would have been Lawrence Kim's 32nd birthday.

His appetite for food mirrored his appetite for life. He loved doughnuts, wine, hot dogs from New York City vendors and his sister's pancakes. But his favorite was General Tso's chicken, which he would cook for his father.

He also had an appetite for knowledge. He drank in the world around him—teaching himself German so he could read Freud in the original. He also owned several versions of Martin Heidegger's *Being and Time* and could quote from Goethe's *Faust*.

But he embraced pop culture along with philosophy. One time, his co-workers opened the door to his office to find him blasting Celine Dion and singing along at the top of his lungs. He could recite the lines from the movie *Philadelphia* after watching it two dozen times.

He was a chronic workaholic. Security guards at Time Warner's Tampa offices were once alarmed because Mr. Kim's car had been parked in the same place for eight straight days while he had been continuously working on a project.

That discipline carried over to his new job at Marsh & McLennan. Parking records show that he arrived between 7:30 and 8 A.M. on Sept. 11, his second day of work.

MARY JO KIMELMAN
"Time Out New York," Live

Whenever friends or friends of friends came to town, Mary Jo Kimelman eagerly became their tour guide. She knew so much about happenings in New York City that her mother once called her "Time Out New York," after the magazine.

Ms. Kimelman, 34, was always a taker when people had an extra ticket to concerts or sporting events. She often read poetry at clubs in Greenwich Village and ran up on stage when bands invited audience members to sing. About two years ago, Ms. Kimelman impressed her friends by belting out a Melissa Etheridge tune at a bar near Wall Street.

"At the beginning she was a little nervous," said her friend Carolynn Kutz. "But once she started going, she let it rip. The band helped her along and she shined."

Ms. Kimelman was passionate about photography and travel and was particularly smitten with Paris. She mused about getting executives at Cantor Fitzgerald, where she worked as a volume control clerk, to transfer her there.

"We always got a kick out of that," said her stepmother, Pat Kimelman. "I said, 'Mary, maybe you should learn to speak French first. You should go to London.' But she happened to like Paris better."

AMY KING and MICHAEL TARROU
Wanting to Be Together

Amy King and Michael Tarrou, United Airlines flight attendants, were on Flight 175 when it crashed into the south tower. Working on the same flight was not uncommon: Ms. King and Mr. Tarrou had been dating for more than two years. They had recently started living together in Stafford Springs, Conn.

"They tried to get the same schedule so they could be together more," Deborah Lloyd, Ms. King's sister, said from her home in Naperville, Ill. "They were supposed to have a long layover in Chicago beginning Sept. 12. We were going to have dinner."

The youngest of three sisters, Ms. King, 29, grew up in a small town near Jamestown, N.Y. In high school, she ran track and cross-country. She liked to paint and was interested in clothing design. She started working for United in Chicago in 1993.

Mr. Tarrou, 38, grew up in Wantagh, on Long Island. He loved flying, but making music was a stronger love. "Originally we started playing in bands in Queens and on Long Island in high school," said Tom Divine, a friend. "He was great at guitar, bass and keyboards and was pretty much the best vocalist I have ever worked with."

During layovers in the Bay Area, Mr. Divine said, he and Mr. Tarrou would spend time in the recording studio.

So far as anyone knows, Mr. Tarrou never asked Ms. King to marry him. But no one doubts that would have happened.

"They were engaged, in their own way," said Dr. James Tarrou, Michael's father. "We were encouraging him, because she was a remarkable person."

ANDREW M. KING
A Real Golfer

A lot of the Cantor Fitzgerald crowd played golf. And a lot of them were good at it. But Andrew M. King was REALLY, REALLY good. He had a four handicap and had shot three holes-in-one.

"He had a beautiful swing," said his wife, Judy King.

Mr. King, 42, a bond trader, played the world's great courses, but last summer he led his wife and three children, 14 other family members, and his best friend, Tom Pritchard, to golf nirvana—the storied St. Andrew's in Scotland. "We teed off, and Andrew said, 'We're here!' " said his sister-in-law, Jackie Szafara.

It was typical of Mr. King that he had been the one to organize the trip. "He was the head-in-law," Ms. Szafara said. "The family get-together started when Andrew got there."

And while he left his home in Princeton at 5:30 A.M. for the World Trade Center, and often entertained clients until midnight, he never missed a family gathering.

He spotted his future wife at the Denver airport 16 years ago, and talked his way into the limousine she and her friends were taking to Vail for a skiing vacation.

"I thought, 'Oh, God, he's so cute, he's so nice,' " Mrs. King, 41, recalled. Skiing with him the next day—watching him ski, he was a superb skier—she was hooked.

They were married 14 years.

"I never saw him down in his life," Ms. Szafara said. "It was always how great Judy was, how great the kids were, how great the house was."

CHRIS MICHAEL KIRBY
"He Would Help Anybody"

At Yankee Stadium last summer, Chris Michael Kirby raced up and down the escalators looking for a young boy who had wandered off. The boy's father had been frantic, and Chris had offered to help.

Finally, Chris spotted the boy stepping into the women's bathroom. He ran in after him, calling out, "Coming in, girls!"

The son of a Bronx firefighter, Mr. Kirby grew up in a family used to helping strangers. "He was a great kid—he would help anybody," said his father, Mickey Kirby.

Chris, 21, was born on New Year's Day and was nicknamed Happy because of his happy-go-lucky nature. He was working as a carpenter while taking classes to become a firefighter like his father. A few days before he disappeared, he called his family, who now live in Middletown, N.Y. His father told him, as he always did: "Be good. I love you." And Chris responded, as he always did, "Dad, I love you, too."

GLENN KIRWIN
Fit as a Fiddle, Full of Love

Glenn Kirwin was fit. Triathlon fit.

Over the years, he competed in a number of triathlons, and though he stopped the endurance events after the children arrived, he kept himself in enviable shape.

"He was a fitness freak," said his wife, Joan. "He did 50-mile bicycle rides." When they were dating, she tried to keep up, but it was hopeless. "I once did 30 miles with him," she said, "but I couldn't sit for a week."

Mr. Kirwin, 40, lived in Scarsdale, N.Y., and was up at 5:15 in the morning to catch the 6:30 train to New York, where he was the head of product development at eSpeed. It was usually 8 at night when he arrived home. It was his practice, though, to always do something with the children, Miles, 10, and Troy, 7, before they went to bed. He would read them a story or play checkers or engage in a game of Go Fish. Sometimes they would go outside and play catch or shoot baskets.

On weekends, he would take the boys golfing with him, even if that meant they did little more than steer the cart. Miles had gotten into running, and Mr. Kirwin would take him jogging for three or four miles. In mid-October 2001, Miles came home from school beaming. There had been a mile run that day as part of the National Physical Fitness Award program. Miles told his mother that he had finished first among the fifth graders.

Mrs. Kirwin said to him, "Well, Daddy was up there watching you and rooting for you."

RICHARD J. KLARES
At Worst of Times, a Giant

When the going gets tough, some men fold, some turn to the bottle and others wallow in self-pity. Not the case with Richard J. Klares, a solid and ethical man, both morally and physically upright in the manner of the old school.

"When he died in that absolute massacre, a piece of America died," said his son, Doug Klares.

The son of a German immigrant who laid tracks for the subway system and a stenographer, Mr. Klares, 59, grew up in Harlem and the Bronx. He went to merchant marine college at Fort Schuyler in the Bronx, and in the fashion of the old days, married his high school sweetheart, Veronica Bavoso.

He was a risk engineer for Marsh & McLennan, and had a meeting Sept. 11 on the 105th floor of the south tower to tell a client how to make its factories more safe.

It is easy to admire a man who is a success, his son said. It's when a man is down that you can take his true measure.

"When I was in high school, he lost his job and was out of work for a year," Doug Klares said. "Every day I'd come home, and he'd be there with his head held high. He never ever gave up. He used to say, 'No matter what's in front of you, attack it, deal with it, be a man.'"

ALAN DAVID KLEINBERG
Skate Park for a Son

On Sept. 10, Alan David Kleinberg spent the evening at the Township Council in East Brunswick, N.J., urging it to move forward with a community skate park, a nod to his oldest son's affection for in-line skating. The park proposal was a hot-button issue known to provoke emotions, but Mr. Kleinberg won respect as a negotiator and mediator who helped gain acceptance for the idea.

"He did this for his child," said Jacque Eaker, special assistant to the East Brunswick mayor. At 39, Mr. Kleinberg thrived on his job as a securities trader at Cantor Fitzgerald, but family was the focus of his time off.

Whether it was planning a trip for his wife, Mindy, coaching 10-year-old Jacob's basketball team, taking his 7-year-old daughter, Lauren, to dance or a Saturday afternoon ice skating with the children, including 3-year-old Sam, "whatever was good in this world he took and gave to them," said Gail Rubin, his mother-in-law.

Firefighters line the procession route on November 8 for a funeral held at St. Patrick's Cathedral for Firefighter Durrell Pearsall of Rescue 4. Firefighter Pearsall had been a member of the Fire Department's Emerald Society Pipes and Drums. (*Nancy Siesel*)

On Oct. 15, the council endorsed a plan to build the skate park. Work is scheduled to start in the spring.

KAREN JOYCE KLITZMAN
A Woman of the World

At 38, Karen Joyce Klitzman had seen more of the world than any 10 people do in a lifetime. After Princeton, she taught for several years in Macao, near Hong Kong. Living in a house wedged between a pig farm and a brothel, she escaped to Hong Kong on the weekends. Then she taught English in Beijing, where she lived in a hovel with a suspicious landlady, and where a bicycle ride to the public bathhouse was a luxury.

"It was a completely exotic environment," said Joan Klitzman, her mother. "So far removed from the Upper West Side, where we lived."

After graduating from the Columbia University School of International Affairs and Public Policy, she began work-

ing at the New York Mercantile Exchange. An energy specialist, she traveled in Siberia and throughout the Middle East. Recently, she started at eSpeed.

She was quick-witted and played a crackerjack tennis game, said Donna, her twin sister, a New Jersey doctor. "Like having a built-in best friend."

RONNY KLOEPFER
Founder and Leader

Within the tight fraternity of the New York City Police Department is an even tighter fraternity—the 25 men, from officers to lieutenants, who wear the blue jerseys of the department's lacrosse team. Ronny Kloepfer, 39, a sniper with the Emergency Service Unit, was their leader. He was founder, coach and midfielder of the six-year-old team, which had a 4-2 record in the annual charity game against its arch-rival, the New York City Fire Department.

Officer Kloepfer, who played for Seewanaka High School and then Adelphi University, somehow fit the team into a schedule that included his elite police position, a side job as a contractor and the demands of a young family. His wife, Dawn, and three children—Jaime, 11; Taylor, 9; and Casey, 5—were always on the sidelines, as Officer Kloepfer was when his two daughters played their games. Casey was still too young, Mrs. Kloepfer said, but had his own stick from the day he was born.

From March to May, the team practiced two or three times a week, from 5 to 7 P.M., at an abandoned junior high school near Officer Kloepfer's home in Franklin Square, N.Y. Now that he is gone, three teammates will run the team, a task Officer Kloepfer managed alone.

"We don't know how he did it," said Detective Craig Carson. "We took him for granted almost."

REBECCA KOBORIE
Music and More Music

Rebecca Koborie's passion was music, whether she was singing in a musical, doing a cabaret act or leading a chorus. She did it all. Ms. Koborie, who was 48, was an executive secretary for Marsh & McLennan in the World Trade Center.

"She really, really put her life into music," said her father, John Koborie. "She sang. She played piano. She started at 4 or 5, singing and dancing. At age 10, she made the *Ted Mack Amateur Hour.*"

Ms. Koborie adored the spotlight but she was far from self-centered, her father said. She was kind-hearted, too, toward animals and people. She had a couple of cats she adored and one was hit by a car. Rather than follow the doctor's advice to euthanize the cat after it lost the use of a leg, Ms. Koborie decided to let it live on three legs.

"She was really a positive, positive person," said Dorothy Fox, a friend for more than 30 years. "She directed church choirs and her job was high-powered, high-strength. I never saw her terribly angry and I never saw her discouraged, really."

DEBORAH KOBUS
Open to Adventure

Being downsized is no fun at all, unless you have the Deborah Kobus perspective on things. Ever since her days at New Utrecht High School in Brooklyn, she was the sort who knew how to cheer herself up, lately by sailing to Tahiti or going skiing in Argentina.

So her response to being abruptly laid off during the economic downturn just over a year ago was to jump into her Ford Explorer and drive to Colorado, figuring the skiing would be great. Work would take care of itself. It always did. She walked into the St. Regis Hotel, arguably the best ski hotel in Aspen, and walked out with a switchboard job that left weekends free for skiing and who knows what else?

The what else was meeting the man who would become her fiancé, Alexander Setzler, who also worked at the hotel. When the skiing ended, Ms. Kobus, 36, returned to New York to help her brother, Robert, care for their mother, who has Alzheimer's disease.

She soon found a job on Wall Street, as assistant vice president at Chuo Mitsui Trust and Banking Company, on the 83rd floor of 2 World Trade Center. On Labor Day, Mr. Setzler proposed, successfully. Ms. Kobus planned to tell her mother and brother the happy news the following week.

GARY KOECHELER
A Reticent War Hero

Gary Koecheler was awarded the Bronze Star in Vietnam, but few of his friends or acquaintances knew about it until his memorial service last week. He was not the kind of man to brag. He never even told his children what he had done to receive the medal; they still do not know.

The son of a railroad worker, Mr. Koecheler, 57, put himself through college and law school and worked at Euro Brokers Inc. He and his wife, Maureen, raised their sons, John and Paul, in Harrison, N.Y., and tried to give them the easy life that he never had. He often teased them by saying that he was a simple man and not a part of the social elite, as they were.

"I love him very much, and I'm proud to be his son," John Koecheler said. "I hope I can step up to the challenge of carrying out his legacy."

FRANK KOESTNER
Every Other Weekend

For the last eight years, Frank Koestner was a stock trader for Cantor Fitzgerald, leaving home at 6 A.M. and trying to leave his office by 7 P.M. At 48, there was never enough time for jogging or skiing or hiking or biking or whitewater rafting.

Since his divorce two years ago, there was never enough time with his 5-year-old daughter, Carolyn. He would spend alternate weekends with her. In summer, they would go to a park or zoo or swim in a backyard pool he put in for her. In winter, they would shovel snow together, even if there had been only flurries, because she thought it was fun.

He was planning to marry Michelle Stabile on Oct. 28. During the week of Sept. 11 they were supposed to close on a three-bedroom house in Massapequa Shores on Long Island.

"He was articulate and educated and ethical," said Dominick Schook, his friend for 31 years. "He was the type of person where you could go away and leave a million dollars on the coffee table and when you got back there would be a million dollars plus interest."

RYAN KOHART
Time for a Nice Vintage

The two couples stumbled back to the apartment at 2:30 A.M., laughing and slightly tipsy. The men collapsed on the couch.

The women kicked off their heels. Ryan Kohart dragged out his prize case of red wine that he had brought in Italy in March. He took a taste and penned in his wine journal: "First bottle was sharp. A little aftertaste, but it tastes great. It needs more time to age."

The bottles would be opened over the next 20 years.

The four toasted to the future and to a great night. Earlier that evening, friends and family had gathered on the rooftop of Sotheby's to celebrate the engagement of Mr. Kohart and his fiancée, Melissa White. He had proposed on that Italy trip on the island of Capri. The ceremony would not take place until the next year because Mr. Kohart, a 26-year-old trader at Cantor Fitzgerald, wanted the best wedding he could afford.

By 4 A.M. they all dozed off, but Mr. Kohart and Ms. White managed to make it to Sunday brunch at Tavern on the Green with his parents.

It was the morning of Sept. 9. The bottle is still in the apartment, but what little wine is left has probably now turned to vinegar.

VANESSA KOLPAK
Letters for a Mother

"What has been so beautiful in the last three months are the letters I've gotten," Vivian Kolpak said in December, about her daughter, Vanessa, 21, a financial researcher at Keefe, Bruyette & Woods. "Those are the things that say more about her than even I could say." Some excerpts:

"I had difficulty believing that she would not appear in some unexpected place to comfort our aching hearts," her music teacher wrote.

"I can't think of a more brilliant young woman, someone who had so much poise and grace, and someone who made people melt with her smile," a former employer wrote.

"I feel that Vanessa's presence in my life allowed me to see the beauty, kindness and good that could only emanate from someone higher," wrote a friend from college.

"Vanessa said, 'If I knew that of all of my friends, someone had to have something bad happen to them, I would want it to be me,' " wrote a confidante from high school. "I was shocked by her statement, what did she mean?

She explained that she had been so blessed with a great family, all of her needs had been met, she was healthy, bright, and had known good friends, and so she was comfortable with one day having to suffer."

IRINA KOLPAKOVA
Watching the Leaves Turn

Irina Kolpakova loved New England. Cape Cod. Anywhere in Rhode Island or Vermont. She loved being there when the leaves changed and she could jog or people watch.

Ms. Kolpakova, 37, worked at the Harris Beach law firm on the 85th floor of 2 World Trade Center. Her only child, Arsen Kolpakov, 19, a legal studies student at John Jay College of Criminal Justice, recalled that his mother had started working there less than a year ago. She was an assistant to the lawyers, he said, performing mostly clerical duties.

Ms. Kolpakova was divorced. She had a sister and a brother but no other relatives in the city, so she and her son, of whom we was proud, were very close. She had enough of her own life that she could often be seen jogging around Bensonhurst, Brooklyn, or working out at the gym, and in her down time, she tuned in to movies.

"She was a great person," Mr. Kolpakov said, his voice quiet but resonating with the enormity of his loss.

DOROTA KOPICZKO
Sunny Personality

Bugoslawa Kopiczko's words about her daughter Dorota come in a torrent of tearful Polish. "We came in September 1992," she said, with a neighbor, Ewa Kowalski, interpreting. "Dorota was 17. She loved it right away. She wanted to know everything."

Dorota Kopiczko embraced the American way from the start. After teaching herself English and working her way through Montclair University in New Jersey by cleaning offices and waiting on tables, she got an accounting job at a firm in Parsippany, N.J.

When the firm was acquired by Marsh & McLennan and she started working on the 100th floor of 1 World Trade Center, Ms. Kopiczko was overjoyed. She bubbled through the office every day—she was known there as Sunshine, for both her ebullient personality and her blond hair—and made friends with everybody.

At night she prepared for the C.P.A. exam. She had already fulfilled her dream of owning a home—a town house in Nutley, N.J.—at age 25. But she wanted more.

"She was all the time dreaming to get a higher position at

work," her mother said. "One time she took me to Franklin Lakes, one of the most beautiful towns in New Jersey. We looked at the houses, and she said, 'Mommy, don't worry. One day we will have this.' "

BOJAN KOSTIC
All Set for Citizenship

It was Grand Army Plaza, in front of the Plaza Hotel, that hooked Bojan Kostic on New York. He had grown up in Belgrade in Yugoslavia, and moved to Iowa in the mid-1980s for college. During his first semester, on a school trip to New York, he stepped off the bus in Grand Army Plaza.

"That's when he decided to move here," said his fiancée, Susanna Ferm. "He loved it—the energy, the excitement, everything about the city."

He soon dropped out of school and took a job painting houses in Connecticut, and he eventually enrolled in Baruch College. That was typical of Bo, as people called him. He was straightforward, honest and reliable. He knew what he wanted.

An example: on his first date with Ms. Ferm, in 1998, he asked her to move in with him. "I held off for three weeks," she said.

He liked to arrive at his office at Cantor Fitzgerald by 6 A.M. In early September, Mr. Kostic, 34, went home to his West Side apartment each day and eagerly sorted through the mail, looking for the letter telling him that he was eligible to become a United States citizen. On the night of Sept. 10, Ms. Ferm quizzed him for his citizenship test, asking him to name the original 13 states.

"He got them all," she said. "He was ready."

DANIELLE KOUSOULIS
Always Thinking of Others

Danielle Kousoulis was a vice president at Cantor Fitzgerald with enough fire to earn an M.B.A. from New York University while working, but her admirers say her success as a bond broker was one prism in a spirit of amazing generosity.

The youngest girl in a close family of three girls and one boy from Haddon Township, N.J., she delighted in treating her parents to a vacation in their native Greece or throwing a New Year's party for a sister sidelined by a broken leg. Ms. Kousoulis, 29, was an ardent runner and skier who had enjoyed the city's museums and nightlife since coming to work at the World Trade Center in 1993.

"She cared more about other people's feelings and other people's problems than her own," said Tricia Lippincott, a friend since kindergarten.

That love was returned. A friendship with Christopher Mills, whom Ms. Kousoulis knew from her Villanova University days, had just turned serious. Hundreds showed up at Ms. Kousoulis' memorial service. "She was the most exciting, fun-loving person I'd ever met," Mr. Mills said.

DAVID KOVALCIN
Portraits in the Mist

There are little ghosts of Daddy in the mirrors of the Kovalcin house in Hudson, N.H.

David Kovalcin had a habit of drawing smiling portraits of the whole family—his wife, Elizabeth, and their daughters, Rebecca, 4, and Marina, 1—on the steamy glass in the bathrooms. Now Rebecca draws her own, with only three people.

Mr. Kovalcin, 42, was a passenger on Flight 11, on a business trip for Raytheon, where he was a senior mechanical engineer. Mrs. Kovalcin said they had carved out a *Father Knows Best* kind of life, with him coming home at six every evening, choosing to know his family well rather than to work longer hours for more money.

She remembers that her husband had trouble sleeping two nights before his departure. "He woke me up at 3 A.M., and said 'I'm pacing the house. I can't sleep,' " she said. "I rubbed his head and tried to calm him down. He was very distressed, but had no idea what it was. Then three days later I remembered, and thought, 'Holy cow, I wonder what that was about.' "

The morning he left home he had written a note for his family: "Rebecca, Marina and Mommy, I will miss everybody very much. See you Friday night." At the end he added, "I fed the dogs but not the fish."

WILLIAM E. KRUKOWSKI
Pedal to the Metal

When William E. Krukowski gave up his motorcycle—and, by the way, skydiving—he took up with a bicycle. He got his exercise: he rode the bike to work most days at Ladder Company 21 in Manhattan from his home in Bayside, Queens.

He was a firefighter for about three years. He grew up in Bayside and went to Holy Cross High School and Nassau Community College. While he was waiting to be called to the Fire Department, he worked in construction and with the New York Department of Sanitation at Fresh Kills landfill in Staten Island, where, more recently, the rubble from ground zero has been taken.

Firefighter Krukowski was separated from his wife but spent a lot of time with his son, William Lee, 10. "I am so proud of the kind of father my brother was to his son through all the difficulties of his personal relationship," said his sister, Virginia.

His other love was souping up a car and then trying it out on a drag strip, his mother, Barbara, said. His father, Walter, said his son would also be remembered as a collector of junk, most of which Firefighter Krukowski brought to his grandparents' place in Connecticut, where there was more room.

"Thanks, Bill," his father said. "I know what I'll be doing someday when I retire."

LYUDMILA KSIDO
It Was Family That Counted

When her eldest son, Robert, had his first child, Lennox, a year ago, Lyudmila Ksido was thrilled beyond words. Her first grandchild!

"It was huge, huge, colossal," said her middle son, Barry, who is 19. "She would be stressed out and she would spend a few hours baby-sitting for him and it would change her. I was in college in Buffalo and I would talk to her on the phone and I could just hear her smile."

Family was so important. Life had been tough, and then, through forbearance, it had gotten better. She arrived in this country from the Soviet Union in 1979, on the heels of a horrible tragedy. Her husband and brother were killed in a plane crash on their way to get immigration papers for the trip. But she had Robert, and she was determined to forge a better life.

In time she married Felix Ksido, and had Barry and Lawrence, 9, and they settled in Brooklyn. Mrs. Ksido, 46, worked as a consultant for Accenture.

When he was in college in Buffalo, Barry made a point of calling his mother almost every day. "If I missed a day," he said, "when I called her she would say, 'Oh, now you remembered you have a mother back home?'"

On Sept. 10, he got back to his room late. It hit him that he hadn't called his mother that day, but it was much too late. He told himself he'd better make sure he spoke to her on the 11th, when he knew she'd kid him about missing a day. He never got the chance.

KENNETH KUMPEL
Fixing Up the House

Raised by his mother and grandmother, Kenneth Kumpel, 42, spent much of his adulthood filling in the gaps left by an absentee father. He was a self-taught handyman and craftsman around the house; an endlessly patient, delighted father of Gregory, 11, and Carl, 9; a buddy who sought, through work, the camaraderie of other guys, first as a New York City police officer and then, more happily, as a firefighter.

Because firefighters can have a few days off between shifts, Firefighter Kumpel, a steady, warm presence, had time for his sons. He cooked, cleaned, coached, volunteered and endlessly fixed up their house in Cornwall, N.Y., perfecting his stained-glass windows, tiling and floors.

That was his castle, his home. But the firehouse—Ladder Company 25 on Manhattan's Upper West Side—was Firefighter Kumpel's home away from home. He would fix up the firehouse, too. Oh boy, would he.

Why is that bed slowly sinking to the floor when a firefighter flops on it? Someone propped it on empty soda cans! Who switched the handles and hinges on the refrigerator door? Smeared peanut butter on the phone receiver? "The Fire Department definitely helped complete him," said Nancy Kumpel, his wife of 18 years.

FREDERICK KUO Jr.
Part of Church's Soul Is Gone

At the Community Church of Great Neck, Frederick Kuo Jr. was always at the center of everything. His parents had also been active there and so he just grew up with it.

"He poured a lot of everything he has into the church," said Fred Kuo, the oldest of Frederick's four children. "So many people were dependent on him for everything."

Frederick's contributions ranged from helping to set up for services to giving occasional readings to arranging for members to get there, even when it meant enlisting his children or driving them himself.

Recently, the church merged with a Chinese congregation, to bring new young members into its aging congregation. As usual, Frederick, whose mother is Filipino and whose father is Chinese, was right there to help bridge the gap. His son said that the new members identified with his father even though he was Asian-American and didn't speak any Chinese.

"I've often thought to myself," Fred Kuo said, "that church wouldn't run without him."

PATRICIA KURAS
Faithful Daughter

"My brother and I try to fill the gap she left behind, but it's just not the same," Tom Kuras said of his sister, Patricia Kuras, a 43-year-old facilities manager for Marsh & McLennan. "She always put herself second, so that the family's needs came first."

So no one was surprised by what happened five years ago when Ms. Kuras's mother had a stroke. Without being asked, she up and sold her beloved little red Nissan sports car and the quaint house in Brooklyn that she had just remodeled. In the Grant City section of Staten Island, Ms. Kuras bought a smaller home to share with her mother. She took the basement while her mother and a live-in nurse occupied the rest of the house.

"She gave so much of herself," Mr. Kuras said of his younger sister. "She lived for my mother."

Ms. Kuras's body has yet to be recovered. But in January, searchers delivered a small bit of closure to her family: her mother's insurance cards. She carried them everywhere.

RAYMOND KWOK
The Perfect Son

Raymond Kwok was the best son any Chinese parents could hope for. At age 31, he worked as a network administrator for Cantor Fitzgerald and lived in Flushing with his parents as well as his wife and their 9-month-old daughter, following the Chinese tradition to serve his parents in old age.

"Everything they asked for, he gave it to them," said Yunyu Zheng, his wife. "When they berated him, he never talked back." The couple bought a three-bedroom condo just before Ms. Zheng gave birth, and he moved his parents out of their apartment in Chinatown, where the family had settled after they immigrated to America 20 years ago.

"I know the worst thing for him would be not to see his daughter growing up," Ms. Zheng said. "He was very content. Our child is cute, and his parents really care for us. The two of us really loved each other. We had never fought. We only wished to have a few more children."

Karen, their baby, has just learned to say "baba" in the past week.

ANGELA KYTE
Organized and Precise

At 49, Angela Kyte was planning to retire in a year or two. She and her husband, Roger, had saved money and were fixing up a retirement home on Cape Cod.

"We went there in the summer," Mr. Kyte said. "We loved bicycling along the National Seashore."

Mrs. Kyte, who lived in Boonton, N.J., started at Marsh & McLennan when it was a young company and worked her way up to managing director.

She was very organized, taping a two-week list of dinner menus on the refrigerator for Mr. Kyte, a retired precision toolmaker, to prepare. And she had a lock-snap memory, which enabled her to make a shopping list with a time-efficient supermarket map—up aisle two for canned tomatoes, down aisle three for paper towels.

The Kytes were putting away money for a scholarship fund at Lycoming College in Williamsport, Pa., where Mrs. Kyte graduated cum laude. Her husband intends to donate more in her memory.

AMARNAUTH LACHHMAN
Big Spike, Big Clint

Don't be on the other side of the net. That was the sound advice opposition volleyball players learned about Amarnauth Lachhman. He possessed a devastating ability to spike the ball. Small wonder. He was 6-foot-2, 220 pounds. Who would want to be on the other side of the net? "He was just awesome at spiking," said Gopaul Lachhman, one of his brothers.

A strong but gentle man, Mr. Lachhman, 41, started playing volleyball when he was a teenager in his native Guyana. He became so proficient that twice he was selected to play on the national team that competed against teams of other countries.

In the early 1980s, Mr. Lachhman settled in the United States, and eventually got into construction work. He was employed by PM Contracting, and was doing office renovations for Cantor Fitzgerald.

In Valley Stream, on Long Island, where he lived with his wife, Kamee, and their two children, Andrew, 13, and Stephanie, 7, he continued to indulge his knack for volleyball. He played with his son in the backyard, and he put together periodic adult games in the park. Everyone always wanted to be on his team, because it invariably won.

Whenever there was a big play, they would go to him," Mrs. Lachman said.

In the evenings, his interest switched to Clint Eastwood, whose movies he adored. Each time *The Good, the Bad and the Ugly* came on, volleyball yielded to the television set.

ANDREW LaCORTE
Salad for Every Party

Andrew LaCorte, 61, was never married. But there was a woman and there were children whom he loved.

"He loved Barbra Streisand," said Joanne Fletcher, his younger sister. "Barbra Streisand was his girl. And my children were very close to him. They were just like Andrew's children."

Mr. LaCorte had about 20 CDs of Ms. Streisand, which he played over and over. And for as long as his nieces and nephews can remember, Mr. LaCorte, a trader at Carr Futures, was a fixture at family parties—on Thanksgiving, Christmas, Easter, Fourth of July, Labor Day and birthdays.

"He always made one thing," said Randi Fletcher, an 18-year-old niece. "He made a salad. Olives, artichokes, peppers and anchovies. The Italian kind that grandma used to make. He never cooked anything else."

And he did not shop much, either, so he gave the kids money as gifts for special occasions—"$100 for graduations and $50 for birthdays," Randi Fletcher said. "He was really really funny. He was witty." she added. "For instance, when someone died and we were really sad, he would pop up with something and make us all laugh."

She said the Fletchers could use Andrew right about now.

JAMES LADLEY
Pleasure in the Mundane

Simple things made James Ladley happy. Things like little activities with the kids. He would take Elizabeth, 4, and James, 2, to pick up the mail. Or to get the newspaper. Or just run around the yard.

He was a soft target. He would be watching baseball, and his son would yell from his bed, "Daddy, get me out of the crib. I want to watch the Yankees." Mr. Ladley would fetch James and plop him down beside him, where James would watch a few pitches and promptly fall asleep.

"It didn't take much to make Jimmy happy," said his wife, Sheri.

Mr. Ladley, 41, a bond broker at Cantor Fitzgerald, would not miss dinner with the family. "We always waited for him," Sheri said. "He got home at 7, and we always ate together and then he would help give the children a bath and he and I would read them stories. It was a group effort."

He had succeeded enough at work that he was contemplating retiring within three years. "He wanted to take the kids to school," Sheri said. "He wanted to coach their sports. He wanted to spend more time with me. He wanted to downsize his load."

Dinner at the Ladley home has not been the same. The meal never started until he was there. Every night, Elizabeth and James ask for Daddy.

JOSEPH A. LaFALCE
Played the Odds

Joseph A. LaFalce, 54, lived a life of simple routines. He prided himself on being on time for work. He could talk endlessly about college basketball. He enjoyed a drink at pubs like the Killarney Rose, not far from the World Trade Center, where he helped the brokers at Cantor Fitzgerald settle their accounts at the end of the day. "He was one of those guys, and there are thousands of them in New York, that make the city work," said Ted Outwater, who struck up a friendship with him years ago when Mr. LaFalce admired his aging dog.

A native Manhattanite, Mr. LaFalce came to love thoroughbred racing: both the personalities involved and the art of figuring out a horse's chances in a particular race. "He could tell you when the horse was born, when he died, how fast he ran," said his brother, Dominick. "He could tell you who won the Preakness 20 years ago."

Once, Mr. LaFalce came close to snaring his dream job, with the *Daily Racing Form*. "But there was a hiring freeze," said Noel McPartland, the bartender upstairs at the Killarney Rose, where Mr. LaFalce used to order a rye-and-ginger-ale and respond to jokes and stories with: "Give me a break! I'm tired!"

Now his friends are trying to organize a horse race at Belmont or Aqueduct in his memory. "We'd probably call it the Joe LaFalce Handicap or the Middle Move Handicap," Mr. McPartland said. "That was his big thing—if the horse made a good move in the middle of the race."

JEANETTE LaFOND-MENICHINO
For Art and Mother

Jeanette LaFond-Menichino was the kind of woman who took pictures of sunsets. She would take her car, leave the city and drive for hours, enjoying nature. Later, her observations—the blossoming flower, the flowering tree, the imposing mountain and the sparkling waterfalls—would end up on the canvases that surrounded her at home in Brooklyn. Ms. LaFond-Menichino, 49, an accounts analyst for Guy Carpenter Insurance Company in the World Trade Center, was an artist at heart.

"I guess that if you don't have flowers and trees around you, you become fascinated by them," said Dina LaFond, 77, who keeps dozens of her daughter's paintings in her home. "Her winter scenes are out of this world and she painted Halloween pumpkins that looked so alive they seem to come out of the painting."

Ms. LaFond-Menichino, who lived with her parents until her late 30s and married four years ago, was especially close to her mother. The two went shopping every weekend. Mrs. LaFond, who relied on her daughter for matters of taste in everything from winter coats to furniture style, calls Ms. LaFond-Menichino her "second right arm."

MICHAEL P. LaFORTE
Competitive and Gentle

Michael P. LaForte had an algebra grade on the cusp of C and B at Glen Ridge High School in New Jersey two decades ago. The teacher, who was also his golf coach, gave him a C. He was upset, but days later they were out together on the course again. Competitive yet easygoing: he always seemed to find the right balance.

Mr. LaForte's competitive spirit came out at Syracuse University, where he graduated in 1984; in his five years as a Marine Corps artillery officer; in a dozen years as a broker at Cantor Fitzgerald; and in his tenacious golf game.

His gentle, easygoing side was more apparent in his relationships with his deaf parents, Samuel and Nancy, who raised him with sign language, and his wife, Frances, and children, Andrea, 5, and Raymond, 4, who often went fishing with him on weekends.

Mr. LaForte turned 39 on Sept. 11. He usually took off on his birthday, but this year was at his desk on the 105th floor of the north tower. He had planned to leave early for Holmdel, N.J., and spend the evening with his children and pregnant wife. His third child, a son born on Nov. 14, was named Michael Patrick LaForte Jr.

JUAN LAFUENTE
Simple Needs

Juan Lafuente, 61, was a vice president at Citibank, near the World Trade Center. Here is his wife, Colette, the mayor of Poughkeepsie: "He loved his family, his work, his home. He constantly strove to improve himself professionally, and never considered retirement after leaving I.B.M. in 1993 . . .

"Juan did not need things—he had the same jackets, shirts and slacks for years and years. He lived a simple life—good food and a night out with family or friends. After his morning paper and coffee at the deli, his weekends were spent mowing or raking or painting, bill paying, watching the Mets (his love for baseball he brought from

Cuba), storming out of the room when they really screwed up . . .

"He had great joy in his daughters' accomplishments and supported them through all of their struggles."

NEIL K. LAI
Seeking Political Stability

In 1958, Neil K. Lai left Shanghai by himself at the age of 16. His father was dead, and his mother wanted Neil to flee for security to Hong Kong. Their family had been turned upside down by the Communist Party rule that started in 1949. Mr. Lai's father, a former factory owner, had been branded a capitalist.

Neil Lai worked for two years in his uncle's tailor shop in Hong Kong before attending night school. He learned English, which landed him a series of relatively well-paying jobs through the mid-1970s. But the sight of Vietnamese boat refugees in the waters around Hong Kong made him realize that the Asian political situation was unstable. So at the age of 34, he came to the United States to study at a community college in Arizona.

He transferred to Arizona State University, where he studied accounting—a skill that eventually led to his job at the New York State Office of Taxation and Finance.

Mr. Lai wanted his two teenage children to maintain straight A's in school. "His experience had told him education is a path to success," said his wife, Yvonne.

FRANCO LALAMA
"Go Ahead. I'll Follow."

For Franco Lalama, every season had its tradition, and autumn was the season for making wine. As soon as the leaves started to swirl, Mr. Lalama, 45, and his brother Mario headed to the Italian market to buy crates of fresh grapes. Using an old press that belonged to their father, the brothers proudly followed a family recipe handed down from generation to generation.

"Those things were very important to him," said Mr. Lalama's sister Teresa Sweeney, in whose basement the wine press is now lovingly kept. "Frank was a very traditional kind of guy."

Born in Italy, Mr. Lalama, of Nutley, N.J., came to New Jersey in 1963, when he was 7. Tradition held that as the oldest boy in an Italian-American family of seven children, Mr. Lalama was responsible for the others. When he became manager of structural integrity for the Port Authority, taking care of the agency's bridges and tunnels came naturally to him.

"He was very responsible, maybe too much so," said his wife, Linda. "He put himself last and everyone else first." A co-worker told Mrs. Lalama that on the morning of the attacks, Mr. Lalama cleared everyone out of the engineering office on the 64th floor of 1 World Trade Center. Then he turned back to make sure no one was left behind. "Go ahead," he told the others. "I'll follow."

STEPHEN LaMANTIA
Big Laugh, Big Personality

On the 6:36 A.M. out of Darien, Conn., protocol dictates that commuters talk in murmurs, something that Stephen LaMantia could never get the hang of. His bellowing laugh and his tales of his latest practical jokes and feats in golf, tennis and paddle ball would reverberate through the train car he took to work as a bond broker at Cantor Fitzgerald.

"Steve could not be quiet," said Jim Hughes, his brother-in-law. Mr. LaMantia, 38, was an energetic, hard-charging financial warrior during the week, but weekends were reserved for his wife, Kim, and two young children. He was one of the few men whom the mothers on the cul-de-sac trusted to watch over the children as they gamboled from yard to yard.

Mr. LaMantia had been president of his fraternity in college, and was the self-proclaimed captain of the cul-de-sac. When newcomers moved in, he would tell them the most important, if unofficial, rule: "It's unacceptable to mow your own lawn—you'll have to hire someone to do it," he would say, "because otherwise, my wife will make me mow ours."

ROBERT T. LANE
A Son's Cake and Candles

Robert T. Lane was a man whose size might have been intimidating were it not for his magnetic smile. Name a sport, and this towering firefighter played it, but his favorite hobby was cooking.

"He'd go to restaurants and try to duplicate their food back at the firehouse," said his mother, Janet Lane. Firefighter Lane started work at Engine Company 55 in November 1998. That was fitting, because November was the month his parents married and the month he and his sister were born. In November 2001, on their anniversary, the Lanes dined at Trattoria Romana, a restaurant near their Staten Island home. They ordered shrimp fra diavolo over linguine—their son's favorite dish. They paid the check with a gift certificate he had given them.

Mr. Lane would have turned 29 on Nov. 29, and until mid-November his family planned to take a cake, lighted with candles, to the site of the World Trade Center on that day. But they learned that their son's body might have been among a group retrieved from the rubble. So now they will have their cake at home, his mother said, "and hope he isn't down under there anymore."

BRENDAN LANG
Hardworking and Ambitious

On Sunday, Nov. 23, Sandy Lang came by her in-laws' home and told her father-in-law, William Lang, that she was going down to Long Beach Island to leave some candles where her husband, Brendan, had proposed to her. "I asked, do you want company, and she said, 'Absolutely,' " Mr. Lang said. So together they drove through a pouring rain. As soon as they got to the beach, the rain stopped.

"See, he's speaking to you," Mr. Lang told his daughter-in-law.

Brendan Lang, 30, was a project manager for Structure Tone, and was doing work at the World Trade Center on Sept. 11. He called his parents to tell them about a plane hitting the first tower, and that he had a "plan." They believe that after calling them he went to help his aunt Rosanne Lang, who worked in the first tower. Neither of them made it out.

Brendan and Sandy Lang were married for three years. They had recently purchased a home, next door to Middletown. Brendan was hardworking and ambitious, Sandy Lang said, but family was everything to him. They had just gotten a puppy, a golden retriever they named Tucker.

ROSANNE LANG
Encircled by Family

Even in a family of 12 siblings, Rosanne Lang stood out.

"She danced the longest, sang the loudest—even though she couldn't carry a tune—and she loved the fiercest," said her brother, Gerard.

At 42, Ms. Lang was an equities trader at Cantor Fitzgerald, a job that afforded her a nicely landscaped home with a pool in Middletown, N.J., and a share, with two siblings, in a beach house in Sea Bright, N.J.

She was the first girl after her parents had six sons. They grew up in Brooklyn, but eventually most of them, including the parents, Rose and William, ended up in the Middletown area. Ms. Lang moved to Los Angeles with her husband and infant son, Michael, but after a divorce, she moved to New Jersey, and forged a life for herself and Michael, now 17, surrounded by family.

"Rosanne was a self-made, successful woman," said William Lang, the oldest of her 11 siblings, who also lives in Middletown. "She was successful in spite of the fact that we all had our preconceived notions about her. After all, she

had six older brothers. She was this amazing woman, always smiling."

The Lang family experienced a double tragedy on Sept. 11: William Lang's son, Brendan, 30, also died.

VANESSA LANGER
Setting the Agenda

Tim Langer was hesitant about the baby his wife, Vanessa, wanted so badly. He gave her a golden retriever and a cat. But Vanessa, who adored her two younger brothers, James and Jackson, knew she was right. Shortly after their first anniversary, she was pregnant. By then, Tim was pleased, too. "As time went on I was so in love," he said. "It felt like we should have a family."

Vanessa Langer, 29, an office manager at a trade center company, usually set the agenda. She was "fast and furious," said Mr. Langer. She did not walk—she darted. She competed fiercely at computer games and the family football pool and screamed when the Yankees or Giants scored. "Oh goodness," Mr. Langer said, and laughed. Before Vanessa, he used cruder expressions. She got him to stop that. Four months pregnant, she was having "the easiest time of her life," he said.

"She gave me a book," he said. " 'How to Pamper Your Pregnant Wife.' At night I had to go out and get Fig Newtons and Stella D'oros for her."

PETER LANGONE and
THOMAS LANGONE
On the Job, Together

A neighboring volunteer fire company called the one in Roslyn, N.Y., for help on Thanksgiving Day 2000. A rescue specialist was needed to extricate a young man from a wrecked car. The company, and the driver, were lucky. Two rescue specialists, Peter and Thomas Langone, arrived and cut him loose.

In their time off, Firefighter Peter Langone, top, and Police Officer Thomas Langone were leaders at the Roslyn Rescue Fire Company, training other volunteers in the skills they learned at work.

Peter Langone, 41, a driver with Engine Company 252 in Bushwick, Brooklyn, a specialty unit, was the "elder statesman" at the firehouse, according to Firefighter James O'Connor. He drove the truck and showed rookies the ropes, speaking bluntly at times. "He never beat around the bush," Firefighter O'Connor said.

His wife, Terri, and his daughters Nikki, 9, and Karli, 5, were often seen around the firehouse, and they took weekend

Firefighters load a flower arrangement onto a truck after
the November 9 services for Captain Patrick Brown of
the New York City Fire Department. The funeral was
held at the Frank E. Campbell Funeral Home at
Eighty-first Street and Madison Avenue in Manhattan.
(*David Paler*)

trips to the country. They were planning a family trip to Disney World this winter. He also liked to hunt, and in good years that meant venison stew in the firehouse.

Thomas Langone, 39, of Emergency Squad 10 in Brooklyn, went to Oklahoma City in 1995 to help with recovery efforts after the bombing of the Alfred P. Murrah Federal Building. "His entire day went at a million miles an hour," a fellow officer said. "He didn't wait to be called." He also taught firefighting techniques for Nassau County, and was working toward a bachelor's degree from Empire State College's distance learning program so he could teach when he retired from the department.

With his wife, JoAnn; his daughter, Caitlin, 12; and his son, Brian, 10, Thomas Langone took a trip to Rhode Island last summer, touring mansions and enjoying the cliff walk in Newport.

Their jobs brought the brothers together. In 1990, the Roslyn volunteers went to the scene of the Avianca crash in Oyster Bay. In 1993, working for New York City, the brothers went to the World Trade Center bombing. On Sept. 11, they arrived separately not long before the twin towers collapsed.

CAROL LaPLANTE
True Believer

Security cameras caught Carol LaPlante going to early Mass on the morning of Sept. 11, before she made her way to the office of Marsh & McLennan at the World Trade Center.

It was a good start for her last day on earth, said her friend and fellow parishioner, Ann McCarthy. For Ms. LaPlante's real calling, "the star of her life," Ms. McCarthy said, was St. Francis and the art gallery in the lobby of the friary. Ms. LaPlante ran the gallery as part of the St. Francis Creativity Group for many years, and it was recently renamed for her. She would have been 60 on Dec. 30, 2001.

"She was a poet and an artist, and while her paintings tended to be very cheerful and flowery, the poetry we found after her death seemed to say she was ready to go," said Ms. McCarthy. "She wrote about going back to God, and of being a star in God's heaven." One of her poems, "Alice O'Connell's Candle," was written after the death last Christmas of another parishioner, a woman who wept as she lighted candles in the sanctuary. But Ms. McCarthy thinks it could be about Ms. LaPlante. Here is the final stanza:

So God has blown your candle out.
He has relit its light, no doubt,
Some place our eyes must wait to see:
A heaven's star he made of thee.

INGEBORG LARIBY
International Friends

In the hours after the attack, her voice mail brimmed with more than 40 messages, in several languages, from almost every continent. Ingeborg Lariby—native of the Netherlands, citizen of everywhere—collected friends across the globe like postcards.

After years of wanderlust, Ms. Lariby, 42, put down roots in New York to work for Regus Business Centers, which had offices in the trade center. She gloried in being a New Yorker, taking up in-line skating (she had the scrapes to prove it) and zipping around the city.

She spoke five languages and was never known to date a man without an accent. Her favorite toast was "Carpe diem!" Her birthday was July 5, and when the fireworks began, she would joke that it was her adopted nation heralding her special day.

"Somehow, she managed to be at home in any part of the world, and then return to New York, to share her pictures and experiences with her less bold friends who lived vicariously through her," said a friend, Gerard Cunningham, a Scottish venture capitalist who lives in California and met her in Belgium.

ROBIN LARKEY
Keeping Everyone Laughing

Some days were boring. At the Cantor Fitzgerald offices, the trading would be lackluster because everyone was awaiting a Federal Reserve announcement or some such market-epochal event. So the brokers would be grumpy.

Not Robin Larkey. Unfailingly, he would resuscitate the mood with one of his *Monty Python*-esque one-liners. "He kept everyone laughing nonstop," said Patrick Edwards, a good friend. "What a sense of humor he had."

Mr. Larkey, 48, was a Cantor currency broker, who lived with his wife and three sons in Chatham, N.J. Another thing about him was that he always stood up for the underdog. Mr. Edwards remembers being in a bar some years ago when a loud-mouthed drunk was really giving it to the female bartender. She tried to quiet the drunk, but he got more boisterous. Mr. Larkey stood up and very effectively upbraided the man. The man left. Good thing. Back in his native England, Mr. Larkey was a skilled boxer. Legend has it that he once knocked out a future Olympic silver medal winner.

Mr. Larkey had to be at work early, but he always abided by a little ritual. At 6 A.M., before he left, he would make tea and toast and take it to his wife, Tracy, in bed. In truth, she might doze off without eating, and then later put the tea in the microwave, but she adored the thought. As he left, using his nickname for her, he would say, "I love you, Plum."

JUDY LAROCQUE
Her Business, Her Retriever

Judy Larocque founded and led a small company in Framingham, Mass., called Market Perspectives, and she had a golden retriever named Naboo. They were pillars in her life, said her daughters, Carie and Danielle Lemack. More than that: the dog and the company were her children, too.

That realization brought responsibilities. Carie Lemack went to the company's offices to tell employees that Ms. Larocque's plane, American Airlines Flight 11 out of Boston, had crashed. Danielle Lemack, a lawyer in Chicago, met with board members. Naboo needed to be walked, and loved, and perhaps consoled, too.

"The company was her creation," Carie Lemack said. "I would say it was her third baby, but that would be Naboo, so it was her fourth."

Ms. Larocque, 50, had been seeking a new balance of work and life recently, and did so with the intensity she brought to everything. She walked 60 miles for a breast cancer fund-raiser in May, and had rediscovered a passion of her youth: yoga.

CHRISTOPHER LARRABEE
Putting Life in Focus

Christopher Larrabee was a Californian, raised with the sun and the sea, who had just come to New York in March to start on the bottom rungs at Cantor Fitzgerald. He was 26 and decided to trade his breezy California lifestyle for a career in finance, just like his father and older sister, Nicole.

Mr. Larrabee gave up a small beach house on the Pacific for a Manhattan studio apartment. The move came about after a health crisis. At 18, he underwent brain surgery after suffering a series of seizures. Earlier this year, after quietly stopping his daily medication, seizures—and more hospitalizations—returned. He decided to put more focus in his life.

His father, Stephen, an equity trader at Cantor Fitzgerald in Los Angeles, helped get his son the job. On a trainee's salary, life was tough for the newcomer. He appreciated it when older colleagues treated him to dinner and he took advantage of museums when they were free.

"He left a lot behind to follow this dream of his," said his twin sister, Paige. "He was scared and nervous to move so far away. But he was adjusting pretty well and getting into the scene."

JOHN ADAM LARSON
Out of Big Sky Country

You couldn't take the Montana out of the boy, at least not entirely. Adam Larson went East for college and stayed, yet he did what he could to keep his home state in his life—taking his two children back to Big Sky country for horseback riding at a dude ranch, and even carting his family to Yankee Stadium and Camden Yards in Baltimore to cheer his beloved Minnesota Twins. (When you're a teenager in Cut Bank, Mont., the concept of a local team has to be pretty elastic.)

Still, his job as a senior vice president at Aon, and his suburban life in Colonia, N.J., suited Mr. Larson perfectly. His wife, Patti, talked of the cinnamon pancakes he made for the children every weekend, the boogie boarding at the shore near her family home in Brigantine, the coaching of his daughter's school basketball team, which is adding a patch in his honor to its uniforms this season.

The family moved into a new house in July, and Mr. Larson, 37, had not finished work on the backyard. Since then more than 100 family members, neighbors and local firefighters and police officers have pitched in to build perhaps the only treehouse in North Jersey decked out in the vibrant purple of the Minnesota Vikings.

N. JANIS LASDEN
The Strong One

Her passion was her dogs. She had three of them. Two German shepherds and a Rottweiler. She spoke of Shilo, Jessie and Sasha as if they were her children. She loved country-western line dancing and was a crackerjack quilter. She had worked for 27 years at General Electric and was a whiz on the computer. But to her one and only younger sister, N. Janis Lasden was always the strong one "who told me what to do."

"I'm lost without her," said the sister, Linda LeBlanc, who lived not far from Ms. Lasden in Peabody, Mass. Ms.

Lasden, 46, was a passenger on American Airlines Flight 11. She and her boyfriend, Donald A. DiTullio, were traveling to Los Angeles on vacation. Mrs. LeBlanc, who spoke to her sister daily, had known of Ms. Lasden's plans, and upon hearing the news on Sept. 11, rushed to her sister's home to see if she could find an itinerary.

What Mrs. LeBlanc found instead was a typed letter. It was addressed to her. In it, Ms. Lasden said that if she were to die, she wanted the house maintained for the benefit of her dogs. The discovery stunned Mrs. LeBlanc and was made all the more haunting by what was in the mail that day: a will that Ms. Lasden had executed the day before. It repeated her wishes.

"I guess even now she is guiding me with what I'm supposed to do," Mrs. LeBlanc said.

NICHOLAS LASSMAN
Life Was Like a Sailboat

"Make this a sweet story," Ira Lassman said the other day, "about one little kernel of a human being whose life will be sorely missed."

He was talking about his son Nicholas, who worked for the eSpeed unit of Cantor Fitzgerald, and was 28 years old. Nicholas's life had been like a sailboat, catching the right breeze here and there, and always being led to a happy situation. He had been a golf pro at clubs in Florida and New York before teaching himself computer programming. That turned into a temporary job at Morgan Stanley, and then a full-time role at eSpeed. In between, he learned Russian and German, and the guitar, all on his own. He lived in an apartment in Cliffside Park, N.J., and loved his job, where his boss, Abul Chowdhury, was also his best friend.

"He was bright beyond his years," his father said. "He had a charming smile and a quick wit. People flocked to him." At a memorial held for him in September, the 400 mourners included a row of caddies from the Alpine Country Club, where his parents were members and where he had once worked as a caddy. "He never hung out with the members," Mr. Lassman remembered. "He always hung out with the caddies."

PAUL LASZCZYNSKI
A Hero Who Loved the Flag

Paul Laszczynski (pronounced la-ZIN-ski) had a box full of honors from his career as a Port Authority police officer, most notably a Fraternal Order of Police Valor Award for helping to carry someone down more than 70 flights of stairs after the 1993 bombing of the World Trade Center.

But his position with the Port Authority's honor guard carrying the American flag meant more to him, said his girlfriend, Charlene Talarico. "That was probably one of the more important things to him, more important than most of his commendations," she said.

At 6 feet 5 and 240 pounds, Mr. Laszczynski, 49, of Paramus, N.J., was a striking flag-bearer. "He was into the snap, he liked to look right," Ms. Talarico said. "I don't think anybody looked better in the uniform."

He kept his turquoise Harley-Davidson Wide Glide just as spiffy, and even named one of his Lhasa Apsos Harley. He rode the bike with the Renegade Pigs, a motorcycle police group that raises money for children's charities.

"He was a hero with a heart," Ms. Talarico said.

JEFFREY LaTOUCHE
Energy from the Church

For Jeffrey LaTouche life was church, family and work. A banquet captain at Windows on the World for more than 15 years, Mr. LaTouche, 49, happily returned to work when the restaurant reopened after the 1993 bombing.

"He loved that job," said his wife, Virginia LaTouche. "The people he worked with were like family to him."

A born-again Christian, he had begun to focus increasingly on the church as he became involved at the Pentecostal Winner's Chapel in Queens. A trip to see the evangelist T. D. Jakes last year had left him even more inspired. "That really turned his life around," she said. "He came back with so much energy and zeal to really do something for the Lord."

He served as president of the men's fellowship, was on the chapel's building committee and worked with the children's ministry, said Peter Kpapharo, pastor at Winner's Chapel. The chapel is open three days a week, he said, and "almost every time the doors were open he was here."

CHARLES A. LAURENCIN
Broadening Minds

Charles A. Laurencin's idea of a vacation was buying a van and rounding up his wife, Barbara, and their four daughters and one son, as he did for one cross-country adventure in 1987. He made so many stops along the way that it took them a full three weeks to reach California.

"My dad was rich in culture," recalled his youngest daughter, Birther. "He always wanted to broaden our minds and our horizons."

Mr. Laurencin, 61, was an immigrant from St. Lucia who later saved lives as an Air Force medic in Vietnam. He started his own business designing and making fire sprinklers, and put all his children through college before retiring.

Two years ago, he took a job as a security guard at Mor-

gan Stanley in 2 World Trade Center to save enough money to move to St. Thomas in the Virgin Islands in November. Mr. Laurencin used to tell his youngest daughter that the best part of his post-retirement job was meeting all the new people. "He would talk you to death," she said.

STEPHEN LAURIA
He Looked Only Forward

That was no mere December snowstorm. Screaming wind, blankets of snow, visibility zilch. Blizzard.

So where else would Stephen Lauria be on that day in 2000 but in the thick of it, the first one at the road race, the volunteer timekeeper? After all, it had been two whole days since he had been released from the hospital following minor heart surgery.

Mr. Lauria, 39, who had moved a few years earlier from Binghamton to Staten Island, where he had grown up, resumed the running he had last done seriously in parochial school. Only now, he approached it wholeheartedly: he volunteered at races every Saturday, he socialized with runners, he gave pep talks to high school runners and, running daily after work as a project manager for Marsh & McLennan, he flew around courses with the intensity of a man aware that his own father had died of a heart attack at 44.

Although he ran after life with a single-mindedness, planning 20 years ago to learn about computers and finance, Mr. Lauria was funny and upbeat, like his mother, Antoinette. Girlfriends leaned on him for support; buddies tapped him for financial advice.

He loved giving advice, too, especially to fellow human greyhounds: Don't look over your shoulder during a race, he would say. You'll lose 10 seconds.

MARIA LA VACHE
Just the Girls

It was a perfect summer night. Aug. 28, 2001. The 60th birthday of Maria La Vache: wife of 38 years to Joseph, mother of Mary Jane, 36, and Bernice, 33. Mrs. La Vache did not want anything fancy or special, she insisted—just a nice quiet dinner with the family. They went to the River Cafe in Brooklyn.

"We had a beautiful time," recalled Mary Jane La Vache. "We laughed, talked and celebrated our lives together."

Mrs. La Vache worked as a receptionist for Marsh & McLennan, on the 99th floor of 1 World Trade Center. Her daughters will miss their "girls' night out," when the La Vache women would take in a movie or go to the theater or out to dinner.

They could talk to her about anything, they said. That is

why they never moved out of their parents' home in the Dyker Heights section of Brooklyn. Mrs. La Vache enjoyed meeting their friends. And her Italian cooking.

Which reminded Mary Jane La Vache of some unfinished business. Her mother recently redesigned the family kitchen. All it needs now are shutters for the windows.

DENIS LAVELLE
A Mother's Devoted Son

Denis Lavelle idolized Rush Limbaugh and had cleared rooms at many a family gathering arguing his hard-line conservatism, but the last thing his relatives expected him to do was run for public office. But there was Mr. Lavelle over the summer, 42 and an absolute newcomer to retail politics, going door to door around Yonkers, where he was born and raised, collecting signatures for a run for the City Council on the Right to Life line.

"He had no chance," said his brother-in-law, Alex Dziadek. "But the party picked him because they knew he wouldn't take it lightly."

Mr. Lavelle, an accountant at Marsh & McLennan, had a ready smile, but he took his responsibilities seriously, and his greatest one was caring for his 75-year-old mother, who, widowed when he was 16, had become severely arthritic.

Mr. Lavelle, who never married, lived with his mother all his life, escorted her to Mass every Sunday and to the Italian restaurants on Central Avenue just about every weekend.

"He was so devoted to her," said Mr. Lavelle's sister Marie Paprocki. "He was a dedicated son."

JEANNINE M. LaVERDE
A Soft Spot for Snow

When the snow comes, the real stuff, deep enough to keep most Staten Islanders indoors, the hardy few on skis or sleighs in the hills of LaTourette Park will remember a joyful Jeannine M. LaVerde on her sled. Her dream, she said, was to tackle some real snow, Alaska. She was fearless, her Aunt Janet recalls. Her response to the fiercest of snowstorms was to trudge out to take somebody fresh bread and milk.

Ms. LaVerde drew on her courage last year to take a tougher job, in new accounts at Keefe, Bruyette & Woods, on the 89th floor of 2 World Trade Center. So high, her mother-in-law fretted. "Don't worry," replied Ms. LaVerde, 36. "I can run down the stairs. Any problem, I'm out of there."

She had a son, Christopher Sodano, 10. The whole family would gather each Labor Day at Daniels, a Poconos resort, where she would cheer as Christopher socked home

runs on the softball diamond. When he took home this year's batting trophy, she pronounced the vacation "the best ever." Then, back to work.

ROBERT LAWRENCE
Athlete and Organizer

Robert Lawrence was infused with energy, and boy, could he organize. He lived in Summit, N.J., where he happened to have grown up, an area scattered with parents, cousins, aunts, uncles. He was the nucleus.

"He would organize a Christmas lunch that started at noon, and before it ended it would be midnight," said his wife, Suzanne.

A talented athlete, Mr. Lawrence played competitive tennis in college. As an adult, he continued to play tennis as well as hockey. He liked to win. He imparted this competitive spirit to his son, Bobby, 9, as he coached him in his own hockey beginnings. The two of them went to a father-son hockey camp during the summer.

He was attentive, as well, to his daughter, Toland, 11. He liked to play the guitar to wind down, but also to entertain her. At night, he would invent songs for her. When she was a little younger, the two collaborated on the not overly well-known number "I Love Noodles."

Mr. Lawrence, 41, used to work in New Jersey for a financial firm, and wanted nothing to do with heights. Nonetheless, he took a new job as a managing director at Sandler O'Neill & Partners, on the 104th floor of 2 World Trade Center. His first day was Sept. 10.

NATHANIEL LAWSON
The Knicks and the Gospel

The day before the World Trade Center was attacked, Nathaniel Lawson called his sister, Betty Moore, excited to tell her about his new cable television service. "He wanted to be able to watch the Knicks and other games, and to watch the gospel shows," said his niece and Mrs. Moore's daughter, Brenda Weaver.

Mr. Lawson, 61, was a waiter and cook for Forte Food Service, and had been transferred to the World Trade Center just three months before. It was a heady experience for a man who was born and raised in Georgia in a family of 19 children.

"He was a very spiritual man," Ms. Weaver said. "He always kept a smile. And he was helpful. Anytime you would call to talk to him about a problem, he was always willing to give good advice and willing to pray with you about anything that was bothering you."

Mr. Lawson lived alone in a tidy apartment in Flatbush, Brooklyn. His grown daughter, Pamela, lives in Germany.

He was close to his sister Betty. "For my mother, it's like losing another half of her," Ms. Weaver said.

OLABISI SHADIE LAYENI-YEE
The Cord That Bound Them

The telephone was the umbilical cord that connected Olabisi Shadie Layeni-Yee to her mother, Edith Layeni. Her mother lived in Newark. Ms. Layeni-Yee worked in 1 World Trade Center as an assistant manager for International Office Centers. But when they talked on the phone, it was as though they were sitting next to each other.

Ms. Layeni-Yee, whose first name means "love and joy" in Yoruba, would call every day when she arrived at work to check on her two "munchkins," for whom her mother babysat. Then she would call at 2 P.M. to say good afternoon. Then again at 5 P.M. to say she was leaving.

The two hurled jokes at each other. "Mother, are you dead yet?" Ms. Layeni-Yee, 38, the eldest of four daughters, would say. "No, I'm not dead yet, and I'm going to kick your little girl out the window if she doesn't be quiet," was the reply.

In 1993, Ms. Layeni-Yee's mother watched on television as people raced from the World Trade Center to escape a terrorist bombing. She prayed. Then came the phone call, "Mom, I'm fine." Her daughter had helped a pregnant woman walk down from the 79th floor.

On Sept. 11, her phone rang again. Her daughter told her to turn on the television. "If worse comes to worse, I'm just calling to say good-bye to all of you," Ms. Layeni-Yee said. Then she said the lights were going out and the floor was shaking. Ms. Layeni-Yee's mother whirled around to see the tower collapse on television.

EUGEN LAZAR
Hunger for Answers

Eugen Lazar was a child with a million questions. How does our body work, his mother once recalled his asking their pediatrician back in Bucharest when he was 3. When we stop walking, what makes us stop?

"All these questions," said Siu Chong, his girlfriend. "He was always wondering how everything works, always seeking for knowledge."

A programmer at eSpeed, Mr. Lazar, 27, had graduated from Cooper Union with a degree in engineering. Fascinated by music and how people hear it, he was building his own speakers. He was a cook and a baker. He and Ms. Chong liked to make crepes together; in Paris, they watched closely to see how they were made. They had even tackled chocolate fondue.

An only child, Mr. Lazar lived in the Glendale section of Queens in an apartment in the home of his parents, Alecsandru and Elena, who immigrated from Romania in 1985.

He met his girlfriend, a graphic designer, on a camping trip in the Catskills years ago. When he learned years later that she no longer had a boyfriend, he sent her an e-mail message and asked her out for pizza.

On Sept. 9, they returned to the restaurant, Lombardi's in SoHo, and remembered their first date. "He was so perfect for me," Ms. Chong said.

JAMES P. LEAHY
Lessons Learned Young

James P. Leahy learned responsibility at a tragically early age. A New York City police officer, he was 13 and the eldest of five children when his father, a Parks and Recreation Department employee, was murdered while on duty at a city golf course.

Officer Leahy, 38, became the head of his family then and there, said Officer Tim Duffy, a colleague at the Sixth Precinct in Greenwich Village. His youngest sister, Danielle, describes James Leahy as the only father she knew, from the time she was a toddler until he walked her down the aisle.

Losing his father shaped Officer Leahy's devotion to his own family: his childhood sweetheart and wife, Marcela, and his sons, James Jr., 18, Danny, 13, and John, 6. To ensure his children's educations, he worked two part-time jobs, as a security guard at New York University and at a J. C. Penney store near his Staten Island home.

He coached his sons in football and was always on the sidelines for their Little League games. A die-hard Pittsburgh Steelers fan, Officer Leahy fulfilled a dream by taking his boys to the Pro Football Hall of Fame in Ohio last summer for the induction of Lynn Swann, his favorite player.

JOSEPH LEAVEY
The Pleasure of Looking Up

Joseph Leavey had a crush on skyscrapers. He could stand for hours outside a highrise and marvel at it. He always wanted to become a firefighter, but he became an engineer in the construction industry because of his affection for buildings. Then he became a firefighter. His favorite spot was Battery Park City. His favorite buildings: the World Trade Center. It was his habit to take his family to lower Manhattan, so he could soak in the dimensions of the trade center. He took endless pictures of the buildings, sometimes lying flat on his back.

As a lieutenant with Ladder 15 in the South Street Seaport, Mr. Leavey, 45, was one of the first firefighters to reach the trade center on Sept. 11.

He lived in Pelham, N.Y., with his wife, Carole, a son, Brian, 16, and a daughter, Caitlin, 10. A stepdaughter, Kerri, 26, lives in Manhattan.

"Joe was a real people person," Carole Leavey said. "There wasn't a person in Pelham Joe didn't know." For the family Christmas card, he often tried to get a family portrait set somewhere amid New York's skyscrapers. No one forgot the time he hustled them to the top of the Citicorp building so he could shoot them with the New York skyline in the background.

"I swear it must have been 20 degrees below zero," said his stepdaughter. "The winds were like 100 miles an hour."

It turned out the picture was overexposed. So Mr. Leavey substituted a photo of the family in front of the New York Stock Exchange.

NEIL LEAVY
A Firefighting Heritage

Neil Leavy was very familiar with the World Trade Center. For a number of years in the 1990s he traded commodities, first oil, later gold, on the futures exchanges there.

But Neil Leavy, 34, had a firefighting heritage. His uncle was a firefighter. So was his godfather, who was a captain. Two of his cousins are currently on the job. "He always wanted to be a firefighter," his cousin Michael Leavy said. And so he became one, working at Engine Company 217 in Bedford-Stuyvesant, Brooklyn.

When he was not on the job, Firefighter Leavy could often be found in the basement of his parents' house in Bayonne, N.J., pumping iron. When he was not there, he worked part time as a bartender at Memories, a Staten Island tavern. "He was a workout maniac," his brother Mark said. "He was a strong, strong guy."

Firefighter Leavy, who was single, had agreed to be best man at his brother's wedding next year. The ceremony is scheduled for Oct. 4, a year to the day after Neil Leavy was buried. There will be no best man. "I look at that day with mixed emotions," Mark Leavy said. "It's the day I start a new life, but the day he was laid to rest."

ROBERT LeBLANC
An Insatiable Globetrotter

He had the itchiest feet. Robert LeBlanc's insatiable desire to see the world meant he would not even have embarked on one trip when he would already be sketching out the next.

"We were due to leave for Argentina right after Sept. 11," said his wife, Andrea LeBlanc. "Then we had tickets on the desk to go to India. We were planning to go to Sweden in the summer. Last year, we celebrated his birthday in Burma."

Mr. LeBlanc, 70, was a professor emeritus of geography at the University of New Hampshire, and lived in Lee, N.H., with his wife. Though he had retired from teaching nearly there years ago, he remained an active and restless scholar. On Sept. 11, he was on United Airlines Flight 175 to a geography conference in Los Angeles.

"He didn't just want to read books about people," Mrs. LeBlanc said. "He wanted to go there. He wanted to smell the smell and taste the food and talk to the people."

There were not many places he had not been. Granted, he had never set foot in Antarctica. But he did live on an ice island near Greenland on two occasions when he was in college. And he worked once on a glacier, taking core samples.

Now his wife faces the considerable task of sorting out his frequent-flier mileage. "There are seven different airlines he has frequent-flier mileage with," she said. "It's impossible."

LEON LEBOR
Universal Sign for Laughs

He was deaf, but Leon Lebor certainly got to see the world. Born in London, he moved to New York and worked as a furrier. Then he moved to Jerusalem, where he was a florist at the King David Hotel. Having problems signing in Hebrew, he returned to New York and became a janitor at the World Trade Center.

"He managed to live his own life and take care of himself," said his brother, David.

Mr. Lebor, 51, was one of the most popular janitors at the trade center. He was known for telling jokes and making hilarious faces that rivaled Emmett Kelly's.

"He loved what he did, and the tenants loved him because he did what he had to do and then some," said Frances Ramirez, a former supervisor. "He worked very hard and he took pride in it. He just loved to make friends."

ALAN LEDERMAN
Man on a Mountaintop

Alan Lederman and his wife, Nancy Zuckerman, had not spent a vacation apart in the 10 years they were together. But he really wanted to climb Mount Whitney in California. They talked it over. She gave him the go-ahead.

Mr. Lederman, 43, hiked a lot and had done some modest mountain climbs, but nothing like Mount Whitney. A friend, Ed Gilroy, was going to make the attempt, too. They had met in fifth grade.

"My brother had very long friendships," said Roni Salkin, one of Mr. Lederman's sisters. He got himself as fit as he could. Every day, he went up and down the 14 flights of his Manhattan apartment building, listening to his Walkman.

In July, he and Mr. Gilroy traveled to the West Coast and began climbing. It was not easy. Some altitude sickness stopped Mr. Gilroy short of the top, but Mr. Lederman went on and made it. On his cell phone, he called his wife at her office and breathlessly announced his achievement. Mr. Lederman was a senior client specialist for Aon, a job he had started just two months before Sept. 11. His wife had returned from her own trip to visit friends on Sept. 7. Awaiting her in their apartment was a picture showing Mr. Lederman at the peak of Mount Whitney, his route and his signature in the visitors' log. He had written, "Where is the snack bar?"

"I have it high on the wall in my bedroom, above his desk," Ms. Zuckerman said. "I feel my husband is peering at me from heaven."

ELENA LEDESMA
A Family's "Source of Light"

Elena Ledesma was the heart and soul of her extended family. On camping trips, she was the first to pitch the tents. She was the one who administered insulin to her 66-year-old diabetic mother and took her to the doctor. She was raising two daughters and working full time.

Ms. Ledesma, who was 37, worked at the World Trade Center as a maintenance coordinator at Marsh & McLennan. She was responsible for maintenance on Floors 93 to 99. The divorced mother of a 12-year-old and a 17-year-old, she lived in Williamsburg, Brooklyn. Her mother, aunts and cousins all lived in the same building.

"My sister was a giving person," said Nelson Hernandez, her older brother. "She was always the one we turned to for anything. I had a lot of dreams. We were going to buy a house together for our mother."

Belkis Mercedes, a friend, said she believed that many family members still expected Ms. Ledesma to reappear. "She was their source of light," Ms. Mercedes said.

ALEXIS LEDUC
A Born Father

Some people are made to be fathers. Alexis Leduc, a maintenance supervisor for Franklin Templeton on the 97th floor of 2 World Trade Center, was like that. He and his wife, Isa, had Adolfo, 23; Cindy, 21; Elvis, 21; and Alexia, 10.

Then there were the neighborhood children in the Bronx that Mr. Leduc, 45, was father to. Eddie and Freddie Perez across the street have nice parents, but sometimes when they

were younger it was easier for them to discuss things with an outsider.

And there is another Elvis, also 21. Elvis Castillo has a good mother, but got into trouble and went to jail. After he was released, he asked to live with the Leducs. He has no siblings, his mother works all day, and the Leduc children are close to him in age. Mr. Leduc made a deal with him: Elvis could stay, if he got a job and helped himself. He found a job, and has lived there since.

Mr. Leduc's other great love went right along with being a father. He collected toys. "He was a big kid when it came to Christmas," Mrs. Leduc said. He grew up poor in Puerto Rico and had few toys. When he died, he left behind 100 Spawn figures, 500 toys from McDonald's, 500 toy antique cars and thousands of baseball cards.

DAVID S. LEE
Expectant Father

David S. Lee's wife was three months' pregnant when he died on Sept. 11.

"He was so excited about the baby that he actually bought almost the whole collection of Warner Brothers Beanie Babies," said Angela Lee, his wife. The child was going to be the couple's first. "He tried to talk to the fetus. He would say: 'Hello! Can you hear me? I love you.' He came up with two names, one for a girl and one for a boy."

Since Mr. Lee's death, a sonogram has shown that his wife will have a son. The Lees, both Chinese, did not care much about the sex of their child, but traditional Chinese families prefer to have at least one son to carry on the family name. "Under the circumstances, it is a joy that I am carrying a son," Mrs. Lee said.

Mr. Lee, 37, a senior vice president at Fiduciary Trust, was looking forward to taking time off and helping his wife when the baby was born.

"He wanted to give our children what we didn't have as children," she said. "You know, the Chinese generational thing. They will learn swimming at a much younger age, interact with other children early on and have a lot more toys."

GARY H. LEE
The Incurable Collector

Bayonets. Eagles. Baseball cards. Hess trucks. Vinyl records. Matchbooks. Coins. Stamps. Old record players. These were some of the things Gary H. Lee collected. Just about anything might meet his criteria and turn into a full-blown collection.

Mr. Lee, 62, and known variously as Uncle Dude, Big Gary or Pop Pop, lived with his wife, Eileen, in Lindenhurst, on Long Island, where the attic was very full. There is all this

World War II gear up there—helmets, uniforms, bayonets. He had something like 150 bayonets and swords, 40,000 baseball cards, dozens of statues and pictures of eagles, every birthday and anniversary card he ever received.

"He was collecting his whole life," said Gary A. Lee, his son. "And he never sold anything."

Mr. Lee, a senior vice president at Cantor Fitzgerald, did not collect cars, but he always wanted a Studebaker. About 15 years ago, he bought a 1948 model that he lovingly restored and took to car shows, winning several first- and second-place trophies.

His wife and son are trying to sort through his myriad collections. Some of the bayonets are being donated to a new World War II museum that the town of Babylon is opening in Lindenhurst. As for the baseball cards, the eagles and the Hess trucks, his son is going to continue those collections.

"I think he would want me to," he said.

KATHRYN BLAIR LEE
Holiday Extravaganzas

Kathryn Blair Lee was never one to do things halfway. Consider Thanksgiving. "There had to be at least 25 people and dinner had to last three to five hours," said her husband, E. Philip Lee, noting that there were always a theme and printed menus. "None of this gobble up the turkey and go back and watch football."

At 55, a senior vice president with Marsh Inc. who had recently moved to New York, she was a self-taught elder stateswoman in her information technology group. But in a field dominated by youth she stayed a step ahead.

"Her energy extended to every aspect of her life," said Richard Shewmaker, who had worked with her since 1993. "I remember a breathtaking cluster of California poppies on her floating home in Portland, Ore., the goldfish pond with a rocky stream and waterfall she designed at another.

"When I think of Kathryn in her office on the 96th floor of the trade center, I can see the pretty teacup and saucer she had brought with her. Those touches were wherever she was."

LINDA C. LEE
Everyone's Best Friend

Linda Lee knew how to make a friend feel special. She knew just how to make you feel like you were the most important person to her.

"She listened with her fullest attention," said Tiffany Norwood, her friend since kindergarten. "She wanted to know exactly what was going on in your life."

Ms. Lee, 34, was a senior associate at Jennison Associates, a financial services firm. On Sept. 11, she was attending a technology conference at the trade center.

Ms. Lee had a love of adventure, Ms. Norwood said. In high school, the two girls would sneak off from their homes in Camp Springs, Md., to New York for the weekend. As young women, they would sweet-talk New York cabbies into letting them drive the taxi.

"She had an amazing ability to make and nurture friendships," said Stacey Harris, another close friend. "She made you feel like you were her only friend."

LORRAINE LEE
Too Happy at Work

In the end, it was all of those heart-stopping miseries with the elevators at 2 World Trade Center that prompted Joan Greene to tell her daughter, Lorraine Lee, "to leave that building, to get a job somewhere else," Mrs. Greene said.

There were the elevators that stopped unexpectedly. The elevators that dropped a few floors. Then there was the elevator that actually zoomed up when it was supposed to go down—then plummeted a bit before stopping, safely, as if nothing had even gone awry. And since Ms. Lee, 37, regularly went out to the plaza for a smoke, it was annoying to spend all that time taking the elevator down from her office on the 101st floor.

But Ms. Lee would not listen to her mother because she loved her job as an administrative assistant at Aon Consulting, even though she traveled each day from Eltingville, Staten Island. And it was also true that Ms. Lee had quit smoking for eight months before the terrorist attack, and did not need to make all those trips to the plaza anymore.

"She loved the people there," Mrs. Greene said. "She loved her boss. And she loved the view."

RICHARD YUN CHOON LEE
Time for a Playroom

Richard Yun Choon and Karen Lee had just started a new life as first-time suburban parents. Their son, Zachary, was approaching his second birthday, and they had moved to their dream house in Great Neck, N.Y., in July. From there, Mrs. Lee would e-mail a steady stream of digital photos of Zachary's days to Mr. Lee at his offices at Cantor Fitzgerald, on the 104th floor of 1 World Trade.

"Even though he was so big and intimidating, he was just so cute and loving," said Lynne Engelke, Mrs. Lee's sister. "He worked such long hours, but when he had to leave on a trip he would make a pan of lasagna for Karen, because he was afraid she wouldn't eat while he was away."

Mr. Lee, who was 34, played football at Yale, where he

met his future wife, and he was head of equities technology for Cantor Fitzgerald. He kept London hours—up at 3 A.M., but home by 5 P.M., in time to put in some work building shelves and toy boxes for Zachary's new playroom.

STUART LEE
Always on the Move

A safari last year. Paris in May. Skiing in Chile in July. Did Stuart Lee ever sit still? Apparently not. On Sept. 10, in fact, he and his wife returned from a trip to Japan and his native Korea. Good thing he had a travel agent handy—his wife, Lynn Udbjorg.

"He loved the best of everything," whether Champagne, Cuban cigars, or sushi, his wife said. (She had a sushi chef at his memorial service.)

For all Mr. Lee's travels, New York was his favorite city—especially the neighborhood where they lived, the East Village, with all its diversity. "He always liked Scandies"—Scandinavians—said Ms. Udbjorg, a native of Norway. "And he ended up marrying one."

After growing up in Vancouver, Canada, where his family moved when he was 6, Mr. Lee, 30, came to this country, later becoming a bond analyst and then a vice president at DataSynapse, a software company.

On Sept. 11, jet lag and all, he was up early for a technology conference at the trade center.

An avid skier, he had long talked of going to Whistler, north of Vancouver, with a group of skiing pals.

Now the others will do it. "This year we're going for him," his wife said.

YANG DER LEE
Family, Charity and Temple

Yang Der Lee, 63, was easy to miss on the coursing sidewalks of Wall Street and along the shiny gum-slicked subway platform, where he took the train each morning from his house in Richmond Hill, Queens, to lower Manhattan.

The small-built man often wore a baseball cap and a fraying suede jacket that he brought from Taiwan when he emigrated to New York City with his wife and three children 16 years ago. "It's good quality," Mr. Lee would tell his family, when pressured to buy new clothes, said his son, Philip. "It doesn't wear out."

The $10 an hour that he earned as a delivery clerk at Windows on the World was for family, charities and the Buddhist temple where he worshiped, Philip Lee said. Mr. Lee worked the day shift, hauling deliveries of fresh meats, fish and vegetables.

His children, who have successful careers and contribute to the household, cajoled him into agreeing to retire when he reached 65. "My father never wanted to be a burden on us," Philip Lee said. "He would have liked to come up with down payments for our houses. That's how great he was. We finally got him to agree to quit working at 65. Now, it's too late."

STEPHEN P. LEFKOWITZ
Natural Big Brother

Throughout his life, Stephen P. Lefkowitz was always doing something for somebody: participating in the Big Brother program as a young man, buying his parents a car, providing someone in need with a place to stay. "He always had time for other people even if that meant he didn't have time for something he wanted to do," said Eric Migdal, who was 10 when Mr. Lefkowitz became his Big Brother and who remained in touch even as an adult.

But after his marriage five years ago when he was 45, Mr. Lefkowitz seemed to expand his reach as he raised his son, Daniel, and became more active in family, politics and Judaism. A mediator with the New York State Department of Taxation and Finance who worked at 2 World Trade Center, he had helped organize a solidarity march for Israel in his Belle Harbor, Queens, community during the summer and had volunteered as co-treasurer for the City Council campaign of Lew M. Simon in the fall. "In many ways," said his wife, Sara, "he was just starting his life."

ADRIANA LEGRO
A Strong Determination

On Super Bowl Sunday, Adriana Legro ran a five-kilometer race in Central Park. It was her first time out with the New York Road Runners Club, but those who knew her never had any doubts that she would finish. She did, of course.

The youngest of four children of Colombian immigrants, Ms. Legro, 32, was known as the achiever in the family, the one who had accomplished the most in the shortest time. She was the only one of her siblings born here, and the only one to graduate from college.

"She was strong-willed," said her sister, Maria. "She was really determined to make something of her life."

Ms. Legro worked as an institutional sales broker at Carr Futures. She lived in Elmhurst, Queens, with her 92-year-old grandmother, Beatriz Molina, and her Pekingese, named Lucky. Ms. Legro's mother had died when she was a teenager, and she often turned to her grandmother for advice. "I know she talked about getting her own place and leaving the nest," her sister said. "But she never did."

EDWARD LEHMAN
The Running Man

Edward Lehman loved to run. He would run in the morning. He would run in the evening. He would run on the weekends, sometimes for three and one-half hours. He belonged to a running club, and anytime there was a benefit run, he would be there. He especially liked to run for causes in and around Glen Cove, N.Y., where he lived. He ran for the local hospital. He ran for the local orphanage. He ran.

The funny thing was, the running started out as the idea of his wife, Joanne, who had done sprints back in school. A couple of years ago, she announced to him that she'd like to start running again on a regular basis. Long jogs, she discovered, were nothing like short sprints.

"I stopped," she said. "But he tried it and kept it up. I guess you could say, he took it and ran with it."

Mr. Lehman, 41, an assistant director in the risk management area at the Aon Corporation, really got into the fine points of the sport. He subscribed to running magazines. He bought books on running. He elaborated on his discoveries to his wife. "The man would just not stop talking about it," she said. "I'd tease him, 'Ed, enough.' He'd talk about the pace for hills and all that. He'd talk of the technical things. I'd say, 'Ed, layman terms, please.' "

ERIC LEHRFELD
Comic Collector

Eric Lehrfeld was always crazy about comic books. As a kid. As an adolescent. And as a 32-year-old husband and father. "He had the largest collection I have ever seen," said John Tabbone, Mr. Lehrfeld's best friend. "He had thousands and thousands."

Mr. Lehrfeld, who was director of business development for Random Walk Computing, a computer consulting company in New York catering to investment banks, was at a breakfast conference at Windows on the World on Sept. 11.

A finance major at the Stern School of Business at New York University, Mr. Lehrfeld liked to dunk french fries in gravy. He loved movies and the movie business. And Brooklyn Heights—where he, his wife, Hayley, and daughter, Laura Elizabeth, lived—was a big part of his life.

"We met in the winter of 1996 at a Jewish singles party at the Roxy, on West 18th Street," Mrs. Lehrfeld remembered. "We loved to talk about the day we met."

A perfect "Eric day," Mrs. Lehrfeld said, would be something like this: "It's Saturday. Pick up the paper. Go to the farmers' market, pick up produce. Bring it back to me to cook it while he was reading his comic books. And then he would eat it all."

DAVID R. LEISTMAN
Avatar of Sportsmanship

Scores of lacrosse players, old and young, came to David R. Leistman's memorial Mass in Garden City, on Long Island, on Sept. 22. Many were in their early 40s. They had played with Mr. Leistman in high school and at Adelphi University, where he was an all-American midfielder who helped the team win national championships in 1979 and 1981.

Many others, both boys and girls, were teenagers and younger. Mr. Leistman, 43, had coached them over the last 10 years in Garden City.

"More than skills, he taught love of the game and the values of competition, team work and sportsmanship," said Dennis Barry, the director of the Garden City Rams Lacrosse program. "Winning was not the only thing."

Besides achieving stardom at Adelphi, Mr. Leistman, a bond trader and partner at Cantor Fitzgerald, met his wife, Maryclair, there. They married in 1983 and had two children, Brian, 13, and Katie, 12.

DAVID LEMAGNE
Motivator and Prankster

He pushed. Whatever you thought you were capable of, he thought higher. David Lemagne loved to help people, and especially to push them to become all that they could. "He pushed people to get the grades, to get moving, to get motivated," said his sister, Magaly Lemagne Alfano. "He pushed a lot of friends, and they went further in life because of him."

Officer Lemagne, 27, lived in North Bergen, N.J., and was a police officer for the Port Authority, as well as a part-time paramedic in New Jersey. He had begun riding around in ambulances when he was only 11, learning to care for others. He was assigned to PATH in Jersey City, and when the attack occurred he was told to stay put. But he asked to be sent to the trade center, because of his training as a paramedic.

Officer Lemagne was a notorious prankster, and friends never found it dull in his company. He loved to kid around. "He would tell my husband, in front of me, 'If you ever have a problem with her, I'll help you get rid of her,' " Mrs. Alfano said. "He would say, 'Don't worry, no one will ever have to know.' "

For all his paramedic training, he was not always entirely comfortable with blood. When he was young, he and his close friend decided they would become blood brothers. Fine. Officer Lemagne was handed a knife.

"I'm not cutting myself," he exclaimed in horror. They became spit brothers.

JOSEPH A. LENIHAN
Talent for Drawing Laughs

Joseph A. Lenihan was a master mimic, and everyone he met was fair game.

"No one was safe from it," said John J. Lenihan, one of his older brothers. "But it was never to belittle someone or make them feel bad. It was always uplifting."

Making people laugh was a talent Mr. Lenihan, 41, developed as the youngest of six children and one he perfected as an executive vice president and director of fixed income at Keefe, Bruyette & Woods. A businessman's businessman, Mr. Lenihan possessed an ever-present smile and engaging personality that made everyone from taxi drivers to chief executives feel special.

"He was really into relationships," said his wife, Ingrid. "He couldn't even garden outside without talking to half of the neighbors on the street."

Mr. Lenihan, who lived with his wife and three children in Cos Cob, Conn., had a reputation for being lucky. When an earthquake shook the San Francisco Bay area in 1989, he was hovering above it all in an airplane. He took the day off from work to move into a new house when the World Trade Center was bombed in 1993.

But during the week of Sept. 11, he made sure that he was in town so he could attend an open house at his daughters' school.

JOHN LENNON
A Perfect Mesh

When your name was John Lennon, you had to go with a nickname. John Lennon's father, also John, went by Jack. John Lennon himself went by Jay. His own son, John III, is sticking with John, though his mother, Patricia, said, "I tell him, watch what you do."

With the other children, Melissa, Katie and Christopher, there's no issue. Mr. Lennon, 44, was a Port Authority police officer who worked out of Jersey City and served as a court liaison who transported prisoners. He lived with his family in Howell Township, N.J. Patricia and John met when they were 15, living in nearby neighborhoods of Brooklyn. He went to an all-boys school and she went to an all-girls school. A mutual friend introduced them. She was quiet. He was gregarious. A perfect mesh. Soon after, they became a permanent item.

"It was love at first sight," Mrs. Lennon said. "I never had a desire to look at anyone else and neither did he. We saw each other every day." They were married at 23.

"He made a comment to a friend a few years after we met that at 16 he knew I was the girl he was going to marry," Mrs. Lennon said. "When I heard that, I thought he was crazy. But he knew. He knew."

JOHN ROBINSON LENOIR
Dad the Dancing Bear

At his daughter's birthday party, John Robinson Lenoir donned a pink tutu and skated onto the ice rink. For one time only, he turned into "Dad the dancing bear." It was just the kind of thing he would do for his children, Courtney and Andrew.

Mr. Lenoir, 38, a vice president at Sandler O'Neill & Partners, was never embarrassed about showing his love. A former defensive tackle at Duke, he married his college sweetheart, Susan, and moved to Locust Valley, N.Y.

During the summers, he presided over clambakes and cookouts at the beach, and even found his way onto a boogie board. In quieter moments, he challenged his family and friends to games of Scrabble. They called him the "lord of the board" because he sat with a dictionary handy to check their words. Even so, he never had to play alone.

"He was a lovable teddy bear," said his father-in-law, Allan Haack.

MATTHEW G. LEONARD
A Lawyer Helping Others

Matthew G. Leonard was the kind of lawyer who would join a homeless man in singing Christmas carols in downtown Brooklyn, successfully drawing contributions from charmed passers-by.

"He probably was the kindest law clerk I ever had," said Peter Leisure, a federal district judge in Manhattan.

Mr. Leonard, 38, had done well as a lawyer, rising to director of litigation for Cantor Fitzgerald. But he was also known for extensive pro bono work, largely at MFY Legal Services. He started working there as an intern, helping poor Chinatown residents while he was at Columbia Law School, and served for more than a decade on its board, including five years as vice chairman.

On Sept. 11, he rose early, as he always did, well before his 7-month-old daughter, Christina, had awakened. "He said he got more work done before the phones started ringing at 9," said his wife, Yolanda Cerda Leonard, who had met him when she was a paralegal and he a lawyer at Willkie Farr & Gallagher, a Manhattan law firm. As he left their Brooklyn apartment to go to his office high in the

World Trade Center, his wife looked at the clock. It said 7:11 A.M.

MICHAEL LEPORE
A Life of Homey Pleasures

Since Sept. 11, Michael Lepore's friends have been pruning his rose bushes, clearing wayward ivy off stone walls, planting bulbs for next spring. It is the perfect act of kindness, said Mr. Lepore's partner of 18 years, David O'Leary. Their house and garden in Yonkers had been Mr. Lepore's pride and joy and are now Mr. O'Leary's primary source of comfort.

"We used to say nothing bad could ever happen here," Mr. O'Leary said. "And it's still the most important thing. It's where I see most of Michael."

The house, designed by Edgar Tafel, Frank Lloyd Wright's apprentice, is a Usonian ranch with windows everywhere, opening onto the terraced garden. It is the ideal setting for the couple's collection of mission-style furniture, for their three cocker spaniels, for the fabulous meals that Mr. Lepore cooked for friends and family, for the wedding they were in the middle of planning for the youngest of the four Lepore brothers.

Mr. Lepore, 39, a project analyst in the technology division of Marsh & McLennan, and Mr. O'Leary, controller for the publisher Penguin Putnam, chose a life of homey pleasures. Looking back, Mr. O'Leary fixes on one glorious late August day. The house bustled with family: his parents, Mr. Lepore's mother and stepfather, Anthony Lepore and his fiancée. The garden was in full bloom. Michael Lepore had prepared three different entrees for dinner. "Everything was so perfect in our lives," he said. "Just so perfect."

CHARLES LESPERANCE
A Lesson for His Daughter

Charles Lesperance loved the good life, and he loved to learn. He was a pro at cooking salmon, had season tickets to the opera, and could take a computer apart and put it back together again. He had an M.B.A. from Columbia and enough credits for a second bachelor's degree. The Saturday after Thanksgiving, Mr. Lesperance, 55, was supposed to marry Renee Alexander, whom his daughter described as "like the love of his life."

"I really tried to go about being as normal as I possibly could," Ms. Alexander said of that day. "I just didn't know what to do. I did not know what to do. I figured it's just a day; it'll come and go. But then his birthday was right after that. Holidays are very difficult."

Mr. Lesperance had spent his early childhood in Haiti, and he and Ms. Alexander enjoyed traveling to the Caribbean, especially St. Martin, Jamaica, the Dominican Republic, Martinique and St. Lucia.

"We were always very at peace and comfortable back there," she said. "He wanted to go back to the blue water of the Caribbean. He loved it," she said of her fiancé, who had spent his early childhood in Haiti.

Nilaja Shealy, the second of his three daughters, remembers the lesson she learned from her father, who was a systems analyst with the State Department of Transportation. "The biggest thing that my father did, that anyone should try to do in their life, is to always improve, to always continually seek to be better," she said. "I think he did that."

JEFF LeVEEN
A Teenage Rocker at Heart

See them there, those five adult children at the Dave Matthews Band concert? The ones huddled together, mortified? And note that blissful, aging teenager next to them, about 55 actually, in khaki pants and Docksiders, blue eyes blazing as he jumps up and down, bellowing his request: " 'Proudest Monkey'! 'Proudest Monkey!' "

By day, Jeff LeVeen of Plandome, N.Y., was a chieftain in the financial world, a partner at Cantor Fitzgerald, an Ivy Leaguer and the owner of two well-appointed homes and a golf handicap of three. By night, he was a rock groupie who attended nearly a dozen Dave Matthews concerts a year.

You allowed a father like that his nuttiness. He plunked down and listened to Phish because one son asked him to. He negotiated with his wife, Christine, about discipline, pleading for leniency. He swept up his bucketful of kids to take them fishing, clothes shopping, to N.B.A. games.

He kept his privileged background and considerable achievements to himself, but boasted like crazy about the children. A happy man with a year-round tan, he would sing, "Now I am the proudest monkey you've ever seen!"

JOHN DENNIS LEVI
A Cop Who Rode a Harley

Debralee Scott walked into the Greenwich Village bar Hogs & Heifers on Dec. 15, 1995, and there he was—a cop who rode a Harley. The rugged, tattooed man who wore a cowboy hat asked her to dinner. "It was love at first sight," said Ms. Scott, an actress.

Five years later, on a cross-country trip, John Dennis Levi, a police officer with the Port Authority of New York

Mourners look up as a police helicopter flies over St. Patrick's Roman Catholic Church in Smithtown, New York, on November 10, to honor Lieutenant Daniel O'Callaghan, a firefighter who died on September 11. His widow, Rhonda Lee, left, looks away, while his son, Connor Daniel, sleeps. (*Kevin Coughlin*)

and New Jersey, proposed to her in a hotel room in Winslow, Ariz., the town mentioned in an Eagles song. It was to be a March wedding.

But he took the call for overtime at 6 A.M. on Sept. 11, because he liked to be with her on the weekends. He called her when the first plane hit. He called again from the basement of the World Trade Center, as he searched for evidence.

He was thoughtful like that. He even made a beauty parlor for his mother, Joanne Priavity, below her Brooklyn home. He loved his children, Dennis, 23, and Jennifer, 26.

"He'd like a lot of bikes at his funeral," said Michelle Dell, the Hogs & Heifers owner. "He'd really like that."

ALISHA LEVIN
Loved Work and Her Family

Alisha Levin lived alone in her own apartment and loved New York—the lifestyle, the rhythms of the city. She loved her job as vice president for human resources at Fuji Bank. Loved working at the World Trade Center and looking out the window on a clear day.

"She hated it when it rained because she couldn't see through the windows," said her aunt Marlene Roseman, who lives in Philadelphia. "She just enjoyed getting up every day and going to work."

She worked very hard, sometimes seven days a week. But every other week, Ms. Levin, 33 and single, would go home to Philadelphia to spend time with her parents, Audrey and Marvin; her sister, Mindy Gottenberg; and her adored nephews, Jacob, 5, and Alex, 2.

"There was a special bond between Alisha and those boys," her aunt said. "She never came home without bringing them toys. She spoiled them rotten, and they loved her."

NEIL D. LEVIN
A Consensus Builder

Neil D. Levin had plenty of friends in important places: two of them, Gov. George E. Pataki of New York and Acting Gov. Donald T. DiFrancesco of New Jersey, made him executive director of the Port Authority of New York and New Jersey. He watched over New York City's three major airports, its port facilities, most of the area's bridges and tunnel crossings, as well as the agency's crown jewel: the World Trade Center.

In his career, Mr. Levin was appointed to other high-level posts, first as state banking commissioner and then as state insurance commissioner. He was chairman of the Federal Home Loan Bank Board of New York and a vice president at Goldman Sachs.

But arguably the most important appointment he ever received was one arranged by Senator Alfonse M. D'Amato,

A candlelight ceremony in lower Manhattan on November 11 honors firefighters from Battalion 1 who were killed on September 11. The flames were lighted with a candle delivered by a fire chaplain from Germany, who offered it to show the support of German firefighters. (*Nancy Siesel*)

with an assist from Claudia Cohen, then Mr. D'Amato's girlfriend: a blind date with Christine Ann Ferer, a style correspondent for NBC. The two were married in May 1996.

"Neil was part of my family," Mr. D'Amato said. He added that Mr. Levin was a consensus builder—a trait that helped him significantly on one of his latest projects, as head of the Commission on the Recovery of Holocaust Victims' Assets, which arranged for restitution of property taken from families during World War II.

ROBERT M. LEVINE
Too Busy to Retire

Robert M. Levine would occasionally think ahead to retirement. After all, he was 66 and a vice president for finances at Baseline Financial Services, a division of Thomson Financial. He and his wife, Roberta, even took up golf, a sport he had played as a younger man.

"It was something we could do together if and when he ever retired," Mrs. Levine said. But he never did retire, largely because he liked his work too much. He could have worked flexible hours, yet he still commuted every day from Edgewater, N.J., to be at his desk in a corner office on the 78th floor of the south tower of the World Trade Center by 7:30 A.M. Mr. Levine used to marvel at the beautiful view.

"I remember him telling me that he could see the helicopters flying below," Mrs. Levine said. "But I hated him working there."

When they could, Mr. and Mrs. Levine traveled. The two made a trip to Europe last summer, and the summer before that. They went to Florida once a year to visit his 88-year-old mother and to California to see his sister and her family.

"He used to tease me about having a good day, about California food," said his sister, Carole Levine. "He was a meat and potatoes guy," Roberta Levine said. "He used to joke that all he could eat out there was lettuce."

JUAN JOSE BORDA LEYVA
He Kept to Himself

Juan Jose Borda Leyva was stingy with words. "If someone said good morning to him, he would say good morning," said his mother, Ana Borda. "If someone said good afternoon, that's what he would say, too. He wouldn't say more. He wanted nothing to do with anyone; he didn't want to get into their business."

Mr. Borda, 59, was born and raised in Colombia, and came to this country with his widowed mother about 35 years ago, she said. He did odd jobs—painting, maintenance work, working in restaurants. They lived together in a small apartment in the Bronx.

He helped her with the rent and with grocery money, but both mother and son were independent and kept to themselves, said Mrs. Borda, who is 81. When he came home from work, she said, "He would say hello, bathe, eat his dinner, watch a little TV and then go to bed—that's all."

Did he have many friends or a girlfriend? "I told you, he kept to himself," she said. She does not have a photograph of him. On Sept. 11, he told her he was going to the trade center for a job interview. He did not tell her what job, with whom, or what floor. Still, his mother said, "He was my everything."

ADAM LEWIS
He Wanted More Children

Adam Lewis couldn't imagine a family that was too big. With his wife, Patti, he had four children, but he would have been happy with more.

It was his reaction to having grown up in such a small family. For much of his youth, it was just him and his father, sharing one room in the Bronx. There were two single beds against the walls at one end of the apartment and a tiny black-and-white television set resting on a folding chair at the other end. The miniature kitchen contained a round table where the two ate dinner and Mr. Lewis did his homework.

"He was a poor kid in the Bronx, and he got a full scholarship to Dalton and Hamilton College, and achieved the American dream," said Stephen Sander, a close friend.

Mr. Lewis, 36, was a senior trader at Keefe, Bruyette & Woods, but the three biggest things in his life were family, friends and food. He didn't care much for fancy wines or designer clothes or expensive stereo systems, but he did care for the relationships with his family and friends. He loved music but owned maybe five CDs that were played repeatedly: Simon and Garfunkel, Billy Joel, Fleetwood Mac, Creedence Clearwater Revival and the sound track to *Forrest Gump*.

Mr. Lewis dearly loved his father, who died in his arms after battling cancer. "I can only pray that they are with each other now," Mr. Sander said at the memorial service for Mr. Lewis, "sitting on a comfy leather couch watching football on a wide-screen TV."

RALPH LICCIARDI
"Handsome Son of a Gun"

Ralph Licciardi could stuff his ear lobe into his ear and then wiggle the ear until the ear lobe fell out. Few people can do that. Mr. Licciardi was pretty funny, but not in looks. He was "a handsome son of a gun," his father, Sebastiano, said, and a very much a family-oriented person.

Every weekend, Ralph's mother, Jo-Ann, would cook all day. Ralph; his wife, Jennifer; their children, Ralph Jr., 2 and Michael, 1; the other grown children, Anthony and Carmelanne; their spouses and offspring would go to their parents' house in Queens for a family feast. After they left, Sebastiano Licciardi said, "My wife would sit and talk about how lucky we were."

Ralph Licciardi, 30, was an electrician for the P.E. Stone Company. "I am lucky enough to do what I like to do, and get paid for it," he used to say. And on the morning of Sept. 11, he was doing just that, working on a job at the Aon Corporation, which was in the south tower of the World Trade Center.

EDWARD LICHTSCHEIN
The Favorite Uncle

Edward Lichtschein had master's degrees in physics and engineering, designed software for eSpeed, and prided himself on solving challenging computer glitches that stumped others. He was also a favorite uncle to nine nieces and nephews, ages 8 to 33.

"He was 35, but in certain ways he was a kid at heart," said Vera Glatt, his sister.

With his older nieces and nephews, Mr. Lichtschein, of Park Slope, Brooklyn, swapped videos and CDs, and critiqued movies, *The Simpsons* and rock music. With the younger ones, he took nature walks in a wildlife preserve behind his brother Mark's home in Teaneck, N.J. Everybody always received cartoon sketches from him parodying family members and family life.

Two cousins, Yoni Glatt, 19, and Avi Lichtschein, 15, have been particularly despondent over his death, Ms. Glatt said. "They were angry at us for accepting it."

CARLOS LILLO
Tale of Two Pictures

At a friend's housewarming back in 1993, Cecilia Lillo paged through a wedding album and spotted a familiar face in the group pictures. Years earlier, back in high school, Carlos Lillo had been a gymnast and a baseball player, the handsome older boy who dated a girl in her homeroom.

Now he was a paramedic in Queens and she was working for the Port Authority at the World Trade Center. They resisted being set up, until a party on New Year's Eve of 1997. They talked in a cafe until 7 the next morning. They bought a house together in Babylon in 1999. She finished her degree at Baruch. He worked extra shifts on private ambulances to save for a new fence and a pool. In April, they married. She is 35; he was 37. Even after being together four years, he had kept her e-mail valentines.

"He was very romantic. We had our candlelight dinners at

home, we used to act silly," Ms. Lillo said. "He wanted us to go to Disney World. I said, 'Let's wait until we have kids.' " They had an appointment with a fertility doctor for this week.

On the morning of Sept. 11, Ms. Lillo escaped from her office in 1 World Trade Center, just as the building collapsed. "Then I saw an article in Newsweek, and his picture was there," she said. "He was helping someone."

CRAIG LILORE
Nothing Stood in His Way

Buy a preposterously depleted house and revitalize it in your spare time? Why bother? But that was Craig Lilore. Mr. Lilore, 30, who worked in institutional sales at Cantor Fitzgerald, believed that nothing was beyond him.

"If you wanted to get him to do something, you just told him that he couldn't do it," said his father, Ralph Lilore. So a few years ago he found this house in Lyndhurst, N.J. "It could only be charitably described as a handyman's special," his father said. "I looked at it and said, 'Oh, Craig, this is a two-year job, and not for one person.' "

It was a two-year job, and basically for one person— Craig Lilore. Sure, he relied here and there on a specialist, but he essentially did almost all of it himself. He had no training in the trades of home building. Yet he had an intuitive knack that enabled him to figure out almost anything. His wife, Caroline, was duly amazed.

Challenges were his thing. Though he always knew he was going to work on Wall Street and graduated from college with a finance degree, he got a law degree as well. Then he took the New York and New Jersey bar exams back to back, and passed both.

"He was an expert skier," his father said. "He started to scare me when he began talking about doing this helicopter drop into a remote area you can't get to except from the air. But that was Craig."

DARYA LIN
Stayed Behind to Help

Darya Lin was not easy to rattle. Growing up in Iran in the early 1980s near a border under heavy bombardment by Iraq, she nevertheless had a "very, very healthy childhood," said her mother, Nahid Mashayekhi Lin. "She never had any fear or any bad memories."

So it makes sense to her friends and family that on Sept. 11 Ms. Lin, a 32-year-old senior manager with Keane Consulting Group who was advising clients that day at Aon, stayed on the 78th floor to help a pregnant client while others in her group ran downstairs to safety.

But Ms. Lin was also aware of her mortality. Over the summer, when she returned a pair of running shoes she had borrowed from her mother, one of them had a note with her name and personal information inside. "She said, 'Yeah, mommy, because when people die, the first place they look is in their shoes.' "

Ms. Lin, whose father is Burmese, moved with her parents to Ann Arbor, Mich., when she was 11; as an adult she traveled in Europe and the United States, eventually settling in Chicago. She never returned to Iran, but kept up with the language and was considering a return visit with her mother. "She had very good handwriting in Persian and she used to write me in Persian," her mother said. "In her letters, she would thank us for everything we'd done."

THOMAS V. LINEHAN
Stealing Quiet Moments

If anyone had asked Thomas V. Linehan what his idea of a perfect vacation was, he would have said that it was a week spent at home in Montville.

"He was a quiet person," Carol Linehan said of her husband of almost 10 years. "We were basically homebodies. He was very private." A senior vice president at Marsh & McLennan, Mr. Linehan enjoyed working on his yard and playing with the couple's two children, Melissa, 7, and Tommy, 4. They would frolic in the treehouse in the backyard, he would make picnics for them and he would take them on walks. "My daughter always knew how to get a laugh out of him," Mrs. Linehan said.

Mr. Linehan, 39, was not without friends. His memorial service last Saturday in Montville was attended by hundreds of friends, from his high school days in Vernon, his days at the Assumption College in Massachusetts, and by friends from jobs. There were even people there from the men's softball team he belonged to in Vernon, the Mud Chickens. The Linehans met on a blind date, arranged by Mrs. Linehan's brother-in-law, Dennis Taormina, who worked with Mr. Linehan and was also on the 98th floor of 1 World Trade when it was attacked.

When they met, "it was like love at first sight," Mrs. Linehan said. "We met in June, were engaged by October, and married in February. We had almost 10 wonderful years together."

ROBERT T. LINNANE
Friends Around the World

Robert Linnane was a horrible dresser. With the ridiculous bright red shorts that he jogged in while training to join the Fire Department and the mismatched get-ups that he called evening wear, he was a walking affront to the eyes.

"We would have to make him go inside and change," said Al Belfiore, a friend.

This shortcoming was tolerated by Firefighter Linnane's friends all over the world because of his cheerful, easygoing and tolerant personality. An enthusiastic traveler, he had worked for Delta Air Lines for nearly a decade before becoming a firefighter. He took every opportunity to fly off and meet new people, and he often had a pass to bring one of his New York friends along.

"It was a life that people liked hearing stories about," said his brother Vincent. It was a life that ended at 33 as a New York firefighter—he had passed the daunting physical tests and joined the department after his 30th birthday.

His body was identified by the Grateful Dead tattoo on his ankle. His favorite song, a Dead standard titled "Sugaree," says:

I'll meet you at the Jubilee
If that Jubilee don't come
Maybe I'll meet you on the run.

DIANE LIPARI
"Nothing Left Unsaid"

Diane Lipari had a sustaining relationship with joy: she ate it for breakfast and served it to others for lunch. Her knack for drawing out the best in even the most difficult people allowed her to say something good about everyone. Her friends teased that when she woke in the morning, birds chirped around her.

When Ed Tighe, her husband, asked what kind of golf clubs she wanted for her 42nd birthday this summer, she replied merrily, "They just have to be pretty."

The small gesture was unknown: when her niece had a school dance, Ms. Lipari, a commodities trader for Carr Futures, bought a half-dozen pairs of shoes for the teenager to select from. Mr. Tighe said the couple, married only since 1999, felt grateful to have found each other. "We traveled a lot for business and the last thing we always said to each other was, 'Nothing left unsaid.' "

FRANCISCO LIRIANO
Always Trying to Get Ahead

Francisco Liriano liked to set goals for himself. Every month, he would think about a way to move up his work. He was always taking exams for licenses that might enable him to do things like sell insurance or real estate.

"He was always looking for the next opportunity," said Yvette Toribio, a friend of Mr. Liriano's sister, Maribel Paulino. He worked his way up to the position of assistant to a vice president of Citibank in an office in the World Trade Center, Ms. Toribio said. A Dominican immigrant, he had earned a bachelor's degree in business administration and, two years ago, married Shirley Somwaru, originally from Guyana.

On Tuesday morning, Mr. Liriano, 33, was not in his fifth-floor office in the trade center. He had gone looking for the next opportunity. According to Ms. Toribio, he had gone to a meeting hoping to explore the possibility of landing an even better job. The meeting was on the 105th floor.

LORRAINE LISI
Joy in Caregiving

"We had a last day together, just that Saturday," Enrica Naccarato said about her younger sister, Lorraine Lisi. They had last-minute tickets to a concert at the PNC Bank Arts Center, formerly the Garden State Arts Center, and packed up Ms. Naccarato's daughter and two friends. "We spent the whole day there. It was like God saying, 'Here, have your last day.' "

Ms. Lisi, 44, had an apartment in Manhattan, but used it only when she had to work late. The rest of the time she lived with and cared for her parents in Bensonhurst, where she grew up.

"Lorraine was always checking in with the people she loved," Ms. Naccarato said. "She would call everybody; she was everybody's mother. She loved children, and was always ready with candy. She was everybody's aunt. She found so much joy watching people opening the gifts she gave." And in her office at Fiduciary Trust International, she displayed the pictures of her co-workers' children. "I can't believe it," Ms. Naccarato said. "It's like she vanished. It's like somebody kidnapped her almost."

VINCENT LITTO
A Very Large Group of "Us"

When Vincent Litto's sister was stricken with multiple sclerosis in 1979, she was no longer able to care for her daughter. So Mr. Litto and his wife, Linda, took the daughter in and raised her as their own. She was one of four girls Mr. Litto doted on.

"Although I was not born his daughter, he treated me as nothing less," said Michele Reitano, 33, as a thousand friends and relatives at a recent memorial service mourned Mr. Litto, 52, a vice president at Cantor Fitzgerald. "I was privileged to be part of his family, his home and to have him as my father."

Ms. Reitano's sisters—and that is what they consider themselves—told their stories, too. Kimberly Litto, 20, spoke of the crowd around their Staten Island dinner table. "I'd ask who was coming for Sunday dinner," she said, "and he'd answer 'You know, just us.' "

"Just us," to Mr. Litto, meant "Grandma, Grandpa, Poppy, Katie, Peter, Vincent, Michele, Joey, Lauren, Julia, Robbie, Stacey, the Tolkins, the Sorrentinos, the Roccobonos, the Laskys, the Palmisanos and Steve."

Catherine Litto Petras recalled the many ways her father taught his girls to "do the right thing," some as simple as "making sure to say hello and good-bye to everyone who came in out house, whether it be the sprinkler guy or our grandfather."

And Kristen Litto, 22, asked mourners to close their eyes and conjure a special moment with her father. "The way you felt at that moment," she said, "is the way our father made us feel every single moment of every single day of our lives."

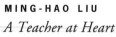

MING-HAO LIU
A Teacher at Heart

If he had not been an engineer for the Washington Group International in the World Trade Center, Ming-Hao Liu would probably have been content teaching children or planning parties. After all, that is precisely what he did during most weekends as the principal of the Livingston Chinese School, near his home in Livingston, N.J.

Last year, Mr. Liu, 41, persuaded four busloads of parents and students to go to Tennessee for a field trip, after emphasizing that the journey, not the destination, mattered most. Seizing the microphone, he encouraged students to get up in the front of the bus and talk in Mandarin about these questions: "Why do you love your parents? What do you want to do for your parents?" recalled his wife, Jiun-Min.

Another time, during a trip back to his native Taiwan, he was planning to return with some gifts for his two young sons. But when he stumbled upon new textbooks for his Chinese school, he stuffed all 150 books into his suitcase. His sons' gifts did not fit. He left them with his mother-in-law. His wife understood. His sons are still learning.

"They didn't know why Daddy spent so much time for other people and for the school," Mrs. Liu said. "I tell them: 'It's not for himself; it's for other people. He always wants to make things good.' "

HAROLD LIZCANO
Wanted: A New Web Site

He wanted something else, something new, something more. Yes, he was a dreamer.

Harold Lizcano liked working with numbers just fine. He was an accountant at Carr Futures. But at 31, newly married, he was thinking about a business of his own, something he could operate out of home once he began raising a family.

He was already talking with his wife, Emily, about having children. He wanted a big family, maybe four kids, and a big

house somewhere. He had never had that. His father left home when he was 5, and he never saw him again. He had no siblings. It was just him and his mother.

"The latest thing he had on his mind was to open up a Web site," said Mrs. Lizcano. "His new idea was a site with classified ads for jobs and cars."

On Monday night, Sept. 10, he stationed himself before his computer and spent the evening surfing the Internet researching his dream. He was getting excited. "I was less excited," Mrs. Lizcano said, "because I was watching Spanish soap operas and they're hard to compete with. He kept calling me in to look at something. I'd say, 'Wait till the commercials.' "

MARTIN LIZZUL
An Easygoing Best Friend

Martin Lizzul wanted to be everyone's best friend. You could not force a nasty word out of him. "He was so easygoing," said his sister, Susan Lauria. "He never said a bad word about anyone. Even if he didn't like someone, he wouldn't say a bad word."

Mr. Lizzul, 31, was an account executive for Kestrel Technology, a software company, and for months he had been spending the mornings—usually from 7:30 to 11—at Cantor Fitzgerald, a client that was using Kestrel products.

He had married Jean Lucido in June. His parents lived in Dix Hills, on Long Island. It wasn't often that either of his parents made it into Manhattan, where he lived. But on the Wednesday before the attack, his mother came into the city, and they had dinner with other friends and relatives. He walked his mother to her car. He walked off. For some reason, they both turned around toward each other at the same time. They looked into each others' eyes and said, "I love you."

It was his practice to call his parents every Wednesday to see how they were. For some reason, he called on the following Monday, Sept. 10.

GEORGE LLANES
A Poet of Bensonhurst

George Llanes was a sensitive, studious child, the kind that classmates often teased. His mother, Eugenia, wanted him to have an outlet, a safe place to express himself, so as he approached the painful years of adolescence, she bought him a journal and encouraged him to "unburden yourself."

From that modest beginning, a writer was born. A few years back, after Mr. Llanes began working as a clerk at Carr Futures, he gave his mother a bound volume of his poetry. After his death, when Mr. Llanes's parents cleaned out his apartment in Bensonhurst, Brooklyn, near their own, they found his poems everywhere.

Mr. Llanes, who would have turned 34 on Sept. 13, lived with his parents until recently. He was their only child and did not leave the nest until he took up smoking and decided to get a dog, both of which gave his mother allergy attacks. When he went apartment hunting and found one he liked, he told the landlady, "I have to talk to my mother first." The landlady repeated the exchange to Mrs. Llanes, saying, "That's when I knew he was a good boy."

Mr. Llanes's devotion to the dog, a pug named Mae Mae, persuaded him to rejigger his work schedule. He switched to a schedule of 7 A.M. to 3 P.M. from an ordinary one of 9 A.M. to 5 P.M., despite a lifelong aversion to getting up early.

Had he been on his old schedule, she noted, "We wouldn't be having this conversation now."

CATHERINE L. LoGUIDICE
And Lilies at Her Back

Exit the caregiver, Catherine L. LoGuidice, 30, of Bay Ridge, Brooklyn. The one who quit high school to look after her grandfather who had cancer; the one who took in the stray cats and helped out at a veterinary hospital on weekends; the one who, according to her fiancé, Erick Elberth, a tugboat captain, would do "all sorts of nutty things" for her friends. They had dated, more off than on, but always stayed friends, since they were teenagers at Canarsie High School, and were supposed to marry in October 2001.

Ms. LoGuidice—who earned a high school equivalency degree—was an assistant bond trader, working at Cantor Fitzgerald on the 105th floor of 1 World Trade Center. She had survived the 1993 bombing while working at the same office and feared another attack, according to her neighbor Kathryn S. Wylde, but she worried that she could not get as good a job with only a high school degree.

Ms. LoGuidice's family is planning a remembrance service, her fiancé said, but they do not want a coffin until her body is found or the last stone is overturned. Meanwhile, Mr. Elberth has filled out a nine-page form to help identify her. It describes the tattoos of the girl who loved Led Zeppelin and The Black Crowes, the purple lilies across her lower back, the rose and sword on her right ankle.

JÉRÔME R. LOHEZ
Vive l'Amérique!

Jérôme R. Lohez was French, Dening Wu was a Francophile, and their first date was a film at the Paris Theater on West 58th Street.

But they decided to build a life together in America.

Mr. Lohez, 30, had the sort of open, trustworthy face that prompted strangers to ask directions. He loved to cook,

once carrying two trays of homemade cherry clafoutis, a creamy French dessert, from Jersey City to the PATH train to the subway to Central Park, where he met friends for an outdoor concert.

The couple married in 1998, and in August, when Mr. Lohez got his green card, they flew to Europe to visit his relatives and sign the marriage certificate of a couple they had introduced. But it rained too often, they agreed. And Paris, though beautiful, suddenly seemed distant.

"New Yorkers may seem cold, but people are just in a hurry," Mrs. Lohez said. "They have softer hearts. That's what we concluded."

When they returned home on Sept. 9, Mr. Lohez declared, "Only in New York do we have so much sunshine."

A software architect at NexxtHealth, an Empire Blue Cross and Blue Shield subsidiary in the World Trade Center, he had recently helped develop an online claims system that was to go into effect on Sept. 11.

SALVATORE P. LOPES
Worked in Two Worlds

Salvatore P. Lopes retired from the New York Police Department after he fell off a roof while trying to help someone down, and hurt his back.

So he started working as a travel agent, getting a thrill out of finagling hotel and airline upgrades for friendly customers. "Everybody was going on vacation, everybody was in a good mood," said his wife, Lorraine.

Mr. Lopes, 40, had long thought he might like to work on Wall Street, so when he found a job as a travel consultant for Sandler O'Neill & Partners, it was the perfect fit. "That was the best of both worlds for him," Mrs. Lopes said. "To be doing a job that he liked, but to be surrounded by people who were doing a job he thought he might have liked."

Back home in Franklin Square, on Long Island, Mr. Lopes was the softball and basketball coach for his daughters, Alexandra, 11, and Nicole, 8. "He had a huge heart," said Leane Romeo, a family friend. "He'd talk to you like he knew you forever."

DANIEL LOPEZ
Pushing Jokes to the Limit

Daniel Lopez had about 15 best friends. He collected them from elementary, middle and high school and old jobs. He was close to all of them. "Even before he passed away, I was like, I've never seen a man with such good friends," said his wife, Elizabeth. "He was my best friend."

Mr. Lopez, 39, of Greenpoint, Brooklyn, loved a good joke. So what if it occasionally went too far? For instance, he once pretended to fall from a ladder. A blood-curdling scream brought Mrs. Lopez to his side. She found him on the floor in the fetal position, holding his ear. She kneeled before him to comfort him, only to see what looked like a piece of his ear in his hand. She screamed and cried. He laughed. It was the melted butt of a pink candle. Finally, she laughed.

"I thought he was really hurt," Mrs. Lopez said. "I was so upset with him. But you couldn't stay angry at him."

He also pulled some good ones on his friends. When he was the best man at one of his best friend's wedding three years ago, he presented the bride with a ring box containing a Viagra pill. Mr. Lopez was a financial analyst at Carr Futures.

MACLOVIO LOPEZ
Falsely Gruff Exterior

People sometimes wondered why Maclovio Lopez, known as Joe, always wore sunglasses when his picture was taken. The answer: they weren't sunglasses at all. Hiding his eyes were photogray lenses, the same way his demeanor covered his heart.

"He was kind of rough and gruff and I don't think you could really print anything that he would have said," said Rhonda Lopez, his wife of 22 years. "He always had a standing joke about how he got 11 Christmas cards," she said, "because there were 12 bad blah-blah-blahs in the world" who exchanged cards only with one another.

A 41-year-old construction worker who specialized in pipelines, he had been working in Boston and was on United Airlines Flight 175 on his way home to Norwalk, Calif., to visit his wife, his 21-year-old daughter, Dannette, and his 18-year-old son, Joseph. "He loved children," Ms. Lopez said, remembering how he ran behind his daughter when she was learning to ride a bicycle.

But he didn't trust people easily. "If you weren't a little kid you had to wait until he liked you," she said.

"People always saw hard, but really he was soft on the inside," she said. "I think that anybody who really knew him knows what they're going to miss. Anybody else, it wouldn't have mattered to him anyway."

MANUEL LOPEZ
Craving Greens and Gadgets

When Manuel Lopez was not putting in long days as a corporate tax manager for Marsh & McLennan in 1 World Trade Center, he liked to tend the big garden he and his wife had in Jersey City. The backyard plot bore beans, tomatoes, mustard greens—the last an important ingredient in sinigang, a tangy soup of Mr. Lopez's native Philippines.

But while Mr. Lopez, 54, liked vegetables, he was crazy about gadgets and electronics. DVD players, laser discs, cameras—"Everything that came out, he had to be the first to get it," said his daughter, Minnie Morison. "We have five or six televisions and there's only three bedrooms in this house."

Mr. Lopez often trawled the Internet in search of hot deals. "There was this DeWalt drill that kept being auctioned on uBid," his daughter said. "He wanted it so bad, but he was stubborn and he was always outbid. I was like, 'Why don't you just go to Sears and buy it, and I'll pay the difference?'

"A couple days after the World Trade Center, a drill showed up in the mail. It was really weird for us. No one's opened it."

JOSEPH LOVERO
Fan of the Firefighters

Joseph Lovero was the ultimate fire buff. He fell in love with firefighting as a child hanging out at the firehouse a few doors down from his family's house on Bergen Avenue in Jersey City. His brother and friends became firefighters; but a heart problem disqualified Mr. Lovero. So he joined the Jersey City Gong Club, a fire buffs' group, and turned up at every fire, often with the club's canteen, helping out the firefighters.

Several years ago, the Jersey City Fire Department began hiring civilian dispatchers. Mr. Lovero, who had worked in construction and hoped for a cameo role in *The Sopranos*, got one of the jobs. Late Tuesday, his family learned that he was in St. Vincent's Manhattan Hospital, where he later died.

Firefighter Lovero went to the World Trade Center soon after the first plane hit. He was struck by debris when the south tower collapsed.

SARA ELIZABETH LOW
Poise, and a Silly Streak, Too

For Sara Elizabeth Low, a career as a flight attendant was a birthright. Family vacations meant piling in the back of her father's small plane and heading from Batesville, Ark., to the Gulf Coast or Rocky Mountains.

"Sara didn't think there was too much difference between being in the plane and being in a car," said her mother, Bobbie Low.

Poised, collected, yet prone to sudden streaks of silliness—she had a personality to calm even the most enraged traveler. And her job sated her wanderlust, her need for cosmopolitan glamour.

"She would call us from the different destinations and give us a hard time," said her older sister, Alyson, a teacher in Fayetteville, Ark. "In the summer she'd phone from San Francisco or

Vancouver because she loved that she had to wear a sweater, rubbing it in about how hot and humid it is in Arkansas."

Yet one aspect of the itinerant life wore on Sara Low: in her first two years as a flight attendant she had about two dozen roommates. So at age 28 she had finally found a place of her own in the Beacon Hill area of Boston, the city from which she boarded Flight 11. "It had a fireplace and wooden floors," Alyson said.

"Our mother went to Boston in the summer to help her clean it up, and it was going to be a real home.'"

MICHAEL W. LOWE
Working for a Better Life

Although Michael W. Lowe loved junk food, he cut back three years ago after learning he had diabetes. "It changed his life completely," recalled his wife, Vivian Lowe. "He said he wasn't going to be a casualty."

Mr. Lowe, 48, also hung out with friends less and focused more on his family and future, his wife said. The couple gave up renting what she called "slum apartments" in East New York, Brooklyn, and bought a house in Canarsie, where there were better schools for their children: Charisma, 6; Jasmine, 11; Gary, 12; and Donovan, 14. And Mr. Lowe clocked as many hours as possible at his delivery job at Liberty Electrical Supply, showing up even when sick. The first stop on his daily route was a loading dock underneath the World Trade Center, said Liberty's chief financial officer, Stephen Mayer.

Mr. Lowe kept at least one indulgence: his beloved white 1993 BMW, which only he drove. On Sept. 10, he drove his wife to work, arriving a half-hour before her overnight cleaning shift at Amtrak began. In the car, they discussed renovating the house so Mrs. Lowe could open a day care center there, partly to see more of her children.

"I'm still thinking about it," she said. "Because after everything that's happened, I believe that my children need me."

GARRY LOZIER
Baths and Bedtime Stories

Garry Lozier, 47, a managing director at Sandler O'Neill & Partners, on the 104th floor of 2 World Trade Center, had risen to the top of the investment world.

But he still put his family first. He cheered on Evan, 10, when he played hockey and tennis. Without fail each night, he bathed his two girls, Karoline, 7, and Olivia, 4, following up with bedtime stories. He and his wife, Kathleen, had just bought a sailboat they planned to take out on Long Island Sound.

Mr. Lozier was a man who loved the women in his life,

starting with his wife. He adored his mother, Patricia Lozier, who died of cancer when he was 25. After that, he grew especially close to his two sisters, becoming a paternal figure to them. "He had a big, beaming, sunny smile," said Diana DeBartlo, his sister-in-law. "Everything he did was for his family."

When the trade center was bombed in 1993, Mr. Lozier escaped and acquired a new zest for living. A recent health scare made him appreciate life even more. "He had overcome so much, and for this to happen . . ." said Ms. DeBartlo. "He had finally achieved all of his dreams."

CHARLES LUCANIA
Man with a Beach Bug

On weekends, the gang gravitated to Charles Lucania's small but serene bungalow just a block off the surf at Atlantic Beach. His friends turned up with burgers for the barbecue. His nephews turned up with toys and bathing suits. Someone usually brought a backgammon board, not that Mr. Lucania, 34, ever sat still long enough to play.

But accompanied by Jake and Sugar, two playful pit bulls raised to be lovers, not fighters, he was always primed to play host. He liked having people around; maybe that's why 2,000 turned up on Oct. 13 at St. Luke's Church in Whitestone to say good-bye at a memorial service. His mother received the last of her daily phone calls from him on Sept. 11: Mr. Lucania, a union electrician two weeks into a job for PE Stone Electrical on the 98th floor of the south tower, told her something was amiss at the north tower, and promised to high-tail it to street level.

He bought his beach pad in 1997, gutted it, rebuilt, and planned further renovations for next year. Unless he was at work or at a Rangers game, he was probably home, where an open-door policy prevailed. And it was not just his two young nephews who continually shouted "Let's go to Uncle Charlie's house!" Not long after Mr. Lucania moved to the shore, several buddies caught the beach bug and followed suit.

"If there's one thing that gives me peace, it's knowing he didn't want for anything," said his sister, Joann. "He was living the life. He had his friends nearby. A big smile, a kiss, and a warm embrace: that was him. Always happy."

EDWARD H. LUCKETT
The Adrenaline Hound

Here's the wind blowing at 50 miles an hour and the sailboat tossing like a lettuce leaf in a salad bowl, up and down, 30 feet at a time. And here's Edward H. Luckett, raising and lowering the sails, expertly tweaking them, never panicking.

"He was very cool under pressure, always laughing," said Jeff Beneville, Mr. Luckett's longtime sailing companion. "He was a tremendous sailor."

The two sailed together in numerous New York Yacht Club "maxi-yacht" races, which originate in Newport, R.I. Mr. Luckett's wife, Lisa, called the maxi-yachts, which are 75 to 85 feet long, the "ultimate racing machines." They carried her husband and other sailors to Bermuda many times.

"It's a passion," Mrs. Luckett said. "It's the ultimate rush. The wind and salt and speed in your hair, and the mixing with the elements." At Mr. Luckett's memorial service, she served Dark and Stormies—rum and ginger beer.

Mr. Luckett, 40, of Fair Haven, N.J., went into equities trading in his late 20s and was a product manager at Cantor Fitzgerald. "It's the same young-male-bonding business," Mrs. Luckett said. "It's the same rush. It's about doing a million things at the same time and all the guys staying together."

MARK LUDVIGSEN
A Titan in New York Rugby

Within days, the news went out in e-mail messages across the world of rugby. Mark Ludvigsen, a driving force behind the New York Athletic Club Rugby Team, had been lost in the World Trade Center.

Mark, known to many friends as Lud, was a 32-year-old bond salesman at Keefe, Bruyette & Woods. He was one of three members of the same firm who played on the New York City rugby team. All three died in the attack.

Mr. Ludvigsen not only carried his weight at his second-row position, but he formed a recruiting network in which he befriended players from around the world, helping them get visas and find employment so they could pursue rugby in New York.

"Everybody was drawn to him," said Mr. Ludvigsen's wife, Maureen Kelly. "He was amazing on and off the field."

That is apparent from the messages that have flowed from rugby players in Sydney, London, and elsewhere. In one, a player from Dublin tried to capture Mr. Ludvigsen's influence by quoting George Bernard Shaw.

"I am of the opinion that my life belongs to the community," the message says, "and as long as I live, it is my privilege to do whatever I can."

Firefighters attend another funeral on November 13, at St. Catherine's Church in Pelham, New York, for a September 11 victim. This is for Lieutenant Joseph Leavey of Ladder Company 15. (Suzanne DeChillo)

SEAN T. LUGANO
A Disciplined Winner

"I called him my perfect child," Eileen Lugano said of her second of five, Sean. He was the one who slept through the night, the one she never had to yell at to do his homework. Even as a small boy, he had unusual discipline. After his first swim meet, when he practically drowned, he vowed he would beat the kid who had won by the next meet. And he did.

Sean T. Lugano, who was 28, was a fierce competitor and a born winner. He was captain of the Xavier High School football team and captain of the Loyola College rugby team. He had more than 50 swimming medals. But, given a chance to try for the Olympics in swimming, he declined, his mother said; he enjoyed too many other sports.

Mr. Lugano loved a challenge. He was a snowboarder, he had parachuted, he ran the New York City Marathon. But he was also the only child who never missed the weekly Sunday dinner in the Luganos' apartment in Stuyvesant Town in Manhattan.

He was a trader with Keefe, Bruyette & Woods and a partner in several bars, but he still toyed with the idea of becoming a teacher, like his mother.

"He was very, very charming, too," his sister Kristen said. "The ladies in Stuyvesant Town just adore him. Ladies in this building were just distraught about this whole thing."

DANIEL LUGO
Too Proud Not to Work

Daniel Lugo's asthma was acting up, and his physician had detected the advent of prostate cancer and was debating the most effective course of treatment. Everybody gave him the same advice: leave his job as a Summit security guard at the World Trade Center and concentrate on getting healthy. But Mr. Lugo, 45, didn't listen.

Instead, he switched from the night to the day shift on Sept. 10, and asked his supervisors to give him lobby duty rather than the usual spot shifts throughout the towers. That was his only concession to his iffy health. He told his sister Eneida Lugo that he had no intention of dozing on the living room sofa collecting disability: "I'm a man," he said. "I need to work."

She cannot remember a time when he wasn't industrious on all fronts: back in Puerto Rico, their mother had taught him to cook, clean and fend for himself. A bachelor until a few years ago, when he met his wife, Olga, at a Pentecostal church in upper Manhattan where he served as a pastor, Mr. Lugo kept up with his mother's lessons.

"He even did his own laundry," Ms. Lugo said. "He was taught that you don't depend on anybody else." But anybody could depend on him, his sister said.

WILLIAM LUM Jr.
Partying Heartily

Organizing surprise parties was William Lum Jr.'s specialty. For the 60th birthday of his mother, Grace Lum, for instance, he surprised her with a big dinner party at Windows on the World, the restaurant at the top of the north tower of the trade center.

"It was exhilarating," remembers his father, William Sr. "The view was just incredible." Mr. Lum wanted to introduce the city to his septuagenarian parents, who are both of Chinese descent.

"Whenever he got a chance, he would call us and take us to the nice restaurants, Broadway shows and Central Park," Mrs. Lum said. His parents live at his childhood home in Rockland County, and William Jr., 45, had an apartment on the Upper West Side.

Normally at this time of the year, he would start making plans to take his parents to Rockefeller Center to window-shop and see the big tree.

"There are times when I walk around and I see things that remind me of Billy," William Sr. said. "My eyes would be filled with tears."

And the World Trade Center, where Mr. Lum worked for Marsh & McLennan, was his favorite building in the city—every time friends would visit from out of town, he would take them to the observation deck.

MICHAEL P. LUNDEN
The Perennial Best Man

Michael P. Lunden's friends always said he was worth waiting for, an assertion he tested frequently. "They called him the Human Rain Delay," said Michelle Lunden, who married him even though he was 20 minutes late to their first date.

People would wait for Mr. Lunden, 37, because, basically, no event could start without him. He was the constant center of an ever-widening social circle, a member of 26 wedding parties, a hyperfriendly guy in a loud Brooks Brothers shirt who introduced himself to each and every waiter, bartender and vineyard keeper he came into contact with.

When Mr. Lunden was not cocooning (loudly) with his wife and their 10-month-old son at their Manhattan home or their weekend place on the North Fork of Long Island, or playing Friend's Best Man for the umpteenth time, or touting a new merlot, he was an energy trader at Cantor Fitzgerald.

The night before Mr. Lunden's memorial service, a few of his pals—about 85 of them, actually—got together at his favorite steakhouse, Smith & Wollensky. "Somebody said that only Michael would have a rehearsal dinner for his funeral," Ms. Lunden said. Mayor Rudolph W. Giuliani happened to be

eating there. He went over to see what all the noise was about and ended up donning a baseball cap that said "Lundo!!" and giving a speech about the indomitable spirit of the city.

CHRISTOPHER LUNDER
Welcome to Club Lunder

Christopher Lunder found cause for celebration in life itself, so much so that with the strong encouragement of his wife, Karen, he converted their home in Manasquan, N.J., into Backyard-Barbecue Central. He babied the propane-gas grill. He built the pond and stocked it with large goldfish. He even designed the built-in pool.

Friends would come to join in the celebration, so many friends: from high school on Long Island, from college in Florida, from Cantor Fitzgerald, where he worked as a bond broker—all mingling together at the home dubbed Club Lunder.

"Now they're all friends," Karen Lunder said. "He just loved to entertain."

Last summer he renewed his commitment to fun by buying a 37-foot boat. It was christened KC, an appropriate name given that Karen and Christopher had been together for so long, with a decade-long courtship and the wedding in 1997. The boat's potential for entertainment—treating clients to rides, commuting on summer weekends with Karen—was only just beginning to be explored.

"He worked hard, he played hard, he liked the best of the best—and he was so cute." Karen Lunder said. Between sobs she added: "And he left me with a beautiful place."

ANTHONY LUPARELLO
Lunch and a Phone Call

For the 14 years that he was a maintenance worker at Aon, Anthony Luparello called his wife, Geraldine, every day at 1:45 P.M., the end of his lunch break. "Just to let me know what's going on," Mrs. Luparello said. " 'What are we getting for dinner? What did you do? Who did you hear from?' " And when the evening buses got him home to Corona, Queens, later than usual, he would be very upset.

"He felt it was his time home to be with me, and he shouldn't be sitting on a stupid bus," she said. "I would tell him, 'What's the matter that you are home late? You came home safe.' "

Mr. Luparello, 62, was equally serious about his work. Every morning, he got up at 3:30 to start work at 6 A.M. "He'd rather be half an hour early than be stuck in traffic," his wife said. "He would never take a day off. Headache, flu, cold, you name it. He went to work.

"I would ask him, 'Tony, is the tower going to fall without you?' It was just a joke. But you know, it came down with him."

LINDA LUZZICONE
Japan, Hawaii and Romance

In an era when people change jobs with the seasons, Linda Luzzicone was remarkably devoted to Cantor Fitzgerald, where she worked as a broker. At 33, she had worked for Cantor most of her adult life, having joined the firm as a clerk soon after graduating from high school. Many of her best friends worked there, as did Ralph Gerhardt, a colleague who sat in a nearby cubicle on the 104th floor and who later became her boyfriend.

"It was a young group there and they had a lot of fun," said her older sister, Debra Luzzicone. "She was happy with what she was doing."

She loved work, but Linda Luzzicone, who grew up in Staten Island and lived on the Upper East Side, was especially passionate about yoga, cycling and travel. In recent years she had made it to Japan, Hawaii, Canada and many spots in between. The inspiration for a trip was usually a friend or family member who happened to live somewhere other than New York.

"She loved the idea of visiting people and seeing a new place at the same time," her sister said.

In the summer of 2001, Ms. Luzzicone's relationship with Mr. Gerhardt started to become more serious. He told his mother he was "ready to take it to the next step" and in August both sets of parents met for the first time in New York. When the plane struck 1 World Trade Center, both of them were working on the same floor. "At least they were together," her sister said.

RALPH GERHARDT's portrait appears on page 180.

ALEXANDER LYGIN
His Love Was His Camera

Alexander Lygin's day job was computer programming at Cantor Fitzgerald on the 104th floor of 1 World Trade Center. But his passion was his 35-millimeter camera, and nature photography and portraits. He had a studio at home, and contributed photographs to Web sites. Mark Rogov, a close friend, said, "One of his long-term dreams was to get hired by a magazine to go to Africa for a couple of months to shoot pictures of animals."

Mr. Lygin, 28, became a citizen in 2001. He came to the United States from Tbilisi, Georgia, in 1994 with many relatives. They included his parents, whom he supported. He lived with them in Brooklyn, and then moved just a few blocks away this year when his fiancée, Anna Klekl, arrived

from Moscow. Mr. Rogov said, "Among our little company of friends, Alex was probably the kindest and nicest person." Ms. Klekl called him "an incredibly kind person" and recalled joining him when he was out taking pictures, going to lots of movies together, and camping in a tent on the Delaware River on the weekends.

FARRELL P. LYNCH and SEAN P. LYNCH
Strivers, Like Their Parents

Whatever their achievements, the Lynch boys were products of their upbringing. The children of Irish immigrants, Farrell P. Lynch, top, and his brother Sean P. Lynch were strivers like their parents.

"They never forgot where they were from," said their sis-ter, Ellen Lynch. Growing up in a family of seven in a two-bedroom house—"all the boys slept in the attic," she said—they were a tight-knit group, and as adults with families, they often gathered in that same house, where their parents still live, for traditional Irish breakfasts.

The brothers both worked at Cantor Fitzgerald; Sean Lynch was an interest rate options broker and Farrell Lynch, who had worked there long enough to be around for the 1993 bombing, was a partner.

Farrell Lynch lived on Long Island with his wife, Eileen, and daughters Katie, 13, Meghan, 11, and Annie, 7. The couple met as sophomores in high school, and they were looking forward to their 15th anniversary in November. Farrell Lynch also looked forward to a day when he could retire and coach high school basketball, said his wife. "He wanted to get into coaching one day—that was his dream. Simple, but that's what he wanted," she said.

Sean Lynch, 36, lived in Morristown, N.J., with his wife, Lori, and daughters Mary, 3, and Grace, 17 months. "He was a very thoughtful person," said his wife. "He was already saying to Mary, 'Be kind to your sister; always treat people well.' "

MICHAEL LYNCH
Perpetual Motion

At 34, life was great for Michael Lynch, known to friends as Morty. He was always on the move—running on the shore at the Jersey beach, doing chores, carrying his 1-year-old daughter, Caroline, working out at a downtown Manhattan gym, dealing with corporate bonds and trusts at Cantor Fitzgerald in the World Trade Center or putting his 6 feet, 6 inches on a basketball court anywhere.

He played basketball at Manhattanville College in Purchase, N.Y., and earned a degree there in business and finance. During high school and college summers, he would fly to Ireland and play in a league in Dublin, not far from his father's family.

If clients wanted to mix basketball with business, they found the right broker. At 6:30 A.M. on Sept. 11, he and a client played basketball at Chelsea Piers. At 8:33 A.M., he was on the phone with his mother making plans for a birthday party a week later for his wife, Michelle, and a nephew and a niece. Later that morning, his mother kept calling his office number. No answer.

MICHAEL LYNCH
Lightening the Mood

In a family of 10 children like the Lynches—this one Democrat, that one Republican, some of them independents— disagreements happen. And at family dinners, Michael, the seventh oldest, was peacemaker. He would don a silly hat, utter a one-liner, and "they would just realize we shouldn't take ourselves too seriously," said his father, Jack.

Michael Lynch, 31, was a firefighter with Ladder Company 32 in the Bronx, and diffused the tension there too. Every time a Federal Express truck drove by station, he would yell, "WILSON!" and run after it like Tom Hanks in *Cast Away*. Out on call, he would scream at his friend Bill Owens from the back of the truck, "O-WEN!"—as the horrible mother does to Danny Devito in *Throw Momma from the Train*.

In November, Firefighter Lynch was scheduled to marry Stephanie Luccioni. But the Lynch family has a news video of Michael and firefighters from Engine Company 40, where he was on rotation on Sept. 11, responding to the World Trade Center attack. In it, Michael Lynch's face is somber. It was about 9:44 A.M. The men were rushing down a stairwell in 4 World Trade Center, and heading underground toward the south tower.

RICHARD LYNCH
A Shared Strength

"These past few weeks, so many people have said to me, 'Oh, my God, I can't believe how strong you are,'" said Christina Lynch, whose husband, Richard, 30, was a bond trader at Eurobrokers.

She brushes off the praise. The strength, she says, is Richard's. And she is borrowing it now as she did throughout their four-year marriage, and perhaps for many, many years before, when the golden couple grew up together in the leafy precincts of Douglaston Manor in Queens.

Mr. Lynch, one of six children, dreamed of a houseful of his own and exuded confidence, his wife said, and his positive attitude was contagious. "I got stronger when I married him," she said.

When their first child, Olivia, was born in 2000, Mrs. Lynch said her joy was often swamped by fear that she "didn't have a clue how to take care of this little tiny baby." Her husband would calmly reassure her: "He was like, 'Look at you with this baby. You're a natural. You're doing it already.' I needed him to tell me that."

These days, when Mrs. Lynch feels herself slipping, she listens for her husband's voice, reminding her that "Olivia needs you so you can't lose it." When she goes running, as she and Rich used to do together before the baby was born, she pushes Olivia in a jogging stroller and talks to her husband inside her head. "O.K., Rich," she tells him. "You have to give me a sign, give me some guidance. You have to get me through today."

ROBERT H. LYNCH
"Bob the Builder"

Elisabeth Lynch did not think much of Robert H. Lynch's baseball card collection until he presented her with an engagement ring. "Wow," said the future Ms. Lynch, "what did you do, rob a bank?" He had not. He had sold his treasured stash of Ricky Henderson cards.

Years later, Mr. Lynch, 44, one of the World Trade Center's many property managers, still bought a complete set of baseball cards every year to pass on to his kids. He passed on more valuable things too, teaching his son Patrick to whistle by age 4. The summer of 2001, on a family trip to the Jersey shore, he outfitted his three young children (he had two others from a previous marriage) with kites and guided them aloft.

"Even the 18-month-old was standing on the beach holding a kite," Ms. Lynch said.

Around the Lynch home in Cranford, N.J., Mr. Lynch played master carpenter. "He rebuilt most of this house," Elisabeth Lynch said, "and he was always teaching the kids how to do things. They liked to sing that song"—the theme from a Nickelodeon TV show—" 'Bob the Builder, can he fix it? Bob the Builder, yes he can.' "

SEAN LYNCH
Red Sox and Best Friends

Sean Lynch was the uncle with the cool cars.

The fourth of five siblings, Mr. Lynch, 34, took joy in watching his nephews' soccer and hockey games and playing tic-tac-toe with his nieces. Then he would be off, often taking trips to other cities with friends to attend sporting events. One year it was the Super Bowl, another year the Final Four.

Mr. Lynch went to college in Boston. A devoted Red Sox fan, he counted among his accomplishments converting his best friend at Cantor Fitzgerald, a lifelong Yankee fan, to a Red Sox fan.

Mr. Lynch had known since high school that he wanted to be a stockbroker, and shortly before Sept. 11 he was promoted to senior vice president for equity trading.

"He used to say he was paid to hang out with his friends," said his older brother, Mike. "He loved it."

MICHAEL J. LYONS
The Best Job to Have

Even as a child, Michael J. Lyons hung out at a firehouse in his South Yonkers neighborhood. He always thought firefighting was the best job to have. At 32, he had grown up to be a firefighter himself with Squad 41 in the Bronx, and before that, with Engine Company 44 on the Upper East Side.

But Firefighter Lyons was good not only at putting out fires. A graduate of Manhattan College, he worked as an engineer on the side to make extra money. His other jobs included fixing roofs, driving a hot-dog truck and taking counter orders at the Yonkers deli where he met his future wife, Elaine (she was a waitress there).

"He was always working," she said. "There would be spans of two days when I wouldn't see him."

Firefighter Lyons had started slowing down, though, after his daughter Caitlyn was born in 2000 on his birthday. He never had the chance to meet his second daughter, Mary, who was born in November 2001 and named after his late mother. Mrs. Lyons gave the baby the middle name Michael.

M

ROBERT MACE

Hoping to Be a Novelist

This was the dream for Robert Mace: retire by 50, buy a little place on Nantucket and write novels to rival those of John Grisham, the Mississippi novel-writing lawyer. Mr. Mace, 43, also a lawyer, had collected his share of stories over the years, first as a lawyer with the National Labor Relations Board and most recently as a labor lawyer for Cantor Fitzgerald.

The tales he would use to regale his family and friends at dinner parties and golf outings. He especially loved to tell friends about the various circuit courts in which he had a chance to argue cases, making sure to point out that he planned to visit them all before retiring.

"He was in his glory being an attorney," recalled Mr. Mace's brother, Ken. "Even his girlfriends over the years knew he was married to the law. Nothing could beat it for him." Except a Philadelphia Eagles game. But only if his childhood team was winning.

MARIANNE MacFARLANE

Haircuts at Disney World

The MacFarlanes of Revere, Mass., did everything together. They lived side by side in two houses built by their Irish immigrant ancestors after the Civil War. Marianne MacFarlane, 34, the middle child and only girl, was a customer service representative for United Airlines at Logan Airport. She lived with her mother, Anne, also a customer service representative in the same terminal at Logan.

Marianne MacFarlane's brother, George, his wife, her children and George's brother, Joseph, lived next door. Except for the children, they all worked at Logan Airport at one time or another. The MacFarlanes took advantage of the free flights that are offered to airline employees to travel together.

Marianne MacFarlane—tall, blond, vivacious—and her mother flew to Disney World just to get their hair cut by a hairdresser at the Contemporary Resort Hotel.

On Sept. 11, Ms. MacFarlane was traveling alone on United Flight 175, headed for the West Coast for a vacation.

JAN MACIEJEWSKI

A Guy Just Like Him

Jan Maciejewski had a knack for being in the right place in the right time.

In 1990, when Mr. Maciejewski was still living in Poland, a friend got a visa to study in the United States. The friend could not go, but Mr. Maciejewski could, so he postponed his plans to be a soccer coach and immigrated to the land of his dreams.

In 1995, a young woman named Mary DeFranco was at a restaurant in Midtown where her bartender friend wanted to introduce her to a man named Chuck.

"I said, 'I don't want to meet a guy named Chuck,'" she recalled. "'I want to meet a guy with an odd name and an accent. Like him.'" She pointed at a good-looking waiter with brown-green eyes and a distinctly European air. It was Mr. Maciejewski's twin brother. He was already married, so Ms. DeFranco was introduced to Jan Maciejewski instead. They married the next year.

Mr. Maciejewski, 37, an avid soccer and tennis player, was always running. He would run from his main job as a waiter at Windows on the World to catch the subway to his other job as a computer consultant. He would run back to the subway to get home to his wife in Astoria, Queens. When she looks through the pockets of his pants, she often finds the Band-Aids he wore on his well-traveled feet.

A colleague at Windows on the World had asked Mr. Maciejewski to fill in for him on the breakfast shift on Sept. 11. Sure, Mr. Maciejewski had said, and gone off to work.

SUSAN MacKAY
A Dress Transformed

Susan MacKay, a vice president at the TJX Companies, a discount apparel and home fashion retailer, had been looking forward to her business trip to Los Angeles for weeks when she and some colleagues boarded American Airlines Flight 11 in Boston on Sept. 11.

"She loved the travel part of the job, and had been looking forward to this California trip all summer," said her husband, Douglas. "They have a good time when they travel."

Ms. MacKay, 44, spent her entire professional life in retailing, first for Jordan Marsh, then for Marshalls, a retailer that was later bought by TJX. But she was much more than a working woman.

"She loved her job, but she was so excited about having children," said Nan Alphen, a longtime friend and neighbor in Westford, Mass., about 25 miles northwest of Boston. "They were the highlight of her life."

Ms. Alphen recalled that Ms. MacKay, an accomplished seamstress, transformed her wedding dress into a christening gown for Matthew, 13, and Lauren, her 8-year-old daughter. "She loved to sew," Mr. MacKay said. "Everything in the house, she made. The comforters, the pillows. Her youngest sister got married last fall. She made her wedding dress."

CATHERINE FAIRFAX MacRAE
Capturing Cat in Words

The question, at last, was put to Andrew Caspersen: Did your girlfriend have any flaws? Long pause.

Catherine Fairfax MacRae, granddaughter of a founding partner of the law firm LeBoeuf, Lamb, Greene & MacRae, won the math prize at the Brearley School, was editor of its newspaper, and was a ferocious field hockey player. At Princeton she made varsity squash and graduated magna cum laude in economics, with concentrations in math and finance. She never pulled an all-nighter and usually finished her work a week ahead, said Channing Barnett, a friend.

Ms. MacRae was never late and expected the same when you met her for dinner. She was inexhaustibly thoughtful, always checking in, sending small gifts, and fretting that she was not being a good enough friend, seemingly to hundreds. She was beautiful and funny and charmingly self-deprecating and talked on the phone to her mother at least three times a day.

People always wanted her at their parties.

She was 23, and a stock analyst at Fred Alger Management on the 93rd floor of 1 World Trade Center.

Mr. Caspersen?

"She was not great with driving directions and we'd get lost quite often," conceded Mr. Caspersen, a Harvard law student. "But that was a bonus. It allowed us to spend more time together."

RICHARD B. MADDEN
His Flag Is Still Flying

Richard B. Madden's daughter, Patricia, was only 19 months old when she kissed her father for the last time. But already they had their little jokes.

Every morning, before setting off for his job as an insurance broker at Aon, he would warn her, "I'm going to work. Don't grow up on me now." Then, when he got home, he would chide her for having disobeyed him.

Mr. Madden, 35 and a first-time father, would also forbid her to mess with his still-full head of hair, which, of course, she took as an invitation.

And as only a dad can do, he taught her how to clink her juice bottle to his beer glass and say, "Cheers."

Father and daughter shared one other little ritual long before it became fashionable. Mr. Madden would take down the flag outside his home in Westfield, N.J., each night before bed and take it indoors. Each morning, little Tricia would shout, "Flag! Flag!" to remind him it was time to hang it again.

"My husband was a strong Republican," said Mr. Madden's wife, Maura. "He was very proud that at her age, his daughter wanted the flag outside."

On Sept. 11, he had called Mrs. Madden from the 100th floor of the south tower, afraid he would not make it out. The authorities later identified his body in the rubble from the inscription on his wedding ring, which read, "Rich, all my love, Maura."

SIMON MADDISON
Kept His British Habits

Simon Maddison liked his Marmite. He was British, and it was not easy to find the spread—which is made from yeast—in America, so he carried his own jar.

It was one of the routines his wife, Maureen, found so endearing. He kept a jar at her parents' house. He kept a jar at her parents' shore house. He carried a jar on vacations. One thing must be clear: she liked his habit, but she hated Marmite. It's an acquired taste and smell, and she never acquired it. "It's gross." she said.

Mr. Maddison, 40, a software consultant for the eSpeed

division of Cantor Fitzgerald, lived in Florham Park, N.J., making sure not to wake his wife when he left at 6 A.M., and making sure he got home in time to play with his three children before their bedtime. Their favorite game was "sandwich," with pillows as the bread and the children as the ingredients.

Mrs. Maddison sees traces of her husband in the children. Caileigh, 7, has his sense of humor. Kyle, 4, has his enormous heart. Sydney, 1, has his unwavering determination.

They also have picked up some British expressions. They say "serviette" instead of "napkin," "boot" for the trunk of the car. When Kyle said he was going to play with his trucks, Mr. Maddison would correct him: "No, you're going to play with your lorries."

All three children have also acquired his fondness for Marmite. Holding her nose, Mrs. Maddison spreads it over their toast and bagels. She'll never remove it from the house.

"Actually," she said, "it sort of smells better now."

JENNIEANN MAFFEO
The Giving Gene

It is easy to dwell on Jennieann Maffeo's misfortune—she did not even work at the World Trade Center—but first, some words about the life she had.

She had the giving gene. She volunteered for all kinds of charities, helping children learn to read, raising money for juvenile diabetes research and regularly providing meals for a handicapped co-worker.

Joseph Rall, sixteen, leaving the memorial service for his father, Edward, forty-four, who was a New York City firefighter. About fifteen hundred firefighters and police officers lined up in Holbrook, New York, to pay tribute on November 14 as the funeral procession passed. (*Joyce Dopkeen*)

When her goddaughter was born, she was so eager to pitch in that she offered to baby-sit even though she had no experience with newborns. The result: a contented baby, diapered backward.

She was 40, single and a senior programmer at UBS PaineWebber in New Jersey. That morning, she was waiting for a bus in the shadow of the towers, one leg of her commute from her home in Bensonhurst, Brooklyn, to her job, when the first plane hit, dousing her with flaming jet fuel. She spent 41 days in a burn unit before succumbing.

"We had a short miracle," said her sister, Andrea Maffeo. "We were able to be with her. We talked to her, although she couldn't talk to us. They said they had never seen more visitors in the hospital."

JOSEPH MAFFEO
"Joey Pockets"

There was always a project under way when Joseph Maffeo, T. J. Beinert and Robert Melloy got together. Which was pretty much always. As teenagers, the friends spent a summer cruising Staten Island in a Cadillac they made into a convertible by sawing off the roof.

Mr. Maffeo was the handyman. "He always had the right nut or the right bolt," Mr. Beinert said. As a firefighter, Mr. Maffeo, 30, was called Joey Pockets because he sewed so many onto his bunker gear to make room for gadgets. He carried a black duffel bag with rope, gloves, water and a can of tuna. Just in case. That is why his wife, Linda, kept hoping, even after many other missing firefighter's wives had given up on any hope that their husbands would survive.

"Joey's got his tuna and water," Mrs. Maffeo, 26, had said. "Joey's probably rationing it out," the wife of another firefighter at Ladder Co. 101 in Red Hook, Brooklyn, had added. The Maffeos, who have a 1-year-old son, Christopher Joseph, met while she was working as a bank teller. He asked her out. She agreed.

"I wouldn't usually do that," Mrs. Maffeo said. "You know when you can look at someone and tell they're a sweetheart?"

JAY MAGAZINE
Food as the Music of Love

For all of Jay Magazine's achievements as a chef and then as catering sales manager of Windows on the World, his happiest moments were spent with his 13-year-old daughter, Melissa, and 10-year-old son, Andrew. His wife, Susan, is convinced that her husband's desire to hold his children close sprang from the early loss of his parents.

Mr. Magazine, 48, was involved in every aspect of his

children's lives, she said. Last spring, he watched Melissa—playing with her school's team in the Junior Knicks program—sink a layup in front of 19,000 people during halftime at a Knicks-Celtics game at Madison Square Garden. Mr. Magazine loved to cook with Andrew. Their specialty was hot salsa, a recipe that Andrew is now teaching his mother. The couple would have celebrated their 19th wedding anniversary on Oct. 17.

"This year," Mrs. Magazine said, "Andrew, Melissa and I shared gifts, dined with my brother and Jay's sister, toasted a wonderful family life, and spent the evening looking at photos and celebrating our 19 years of happy marriage."

CHARLES MAGEE
A Risk-Taking Rationale

Charles Magee was flying a single-engine plane to the Grand Canyon when the radio died and the gas gauge went from full to empty. He diagnosed the problem fast—loss of electric power—looked over his flight charts, and set down safely at a nearby airfield.

"He was like that," said Janet Wexler-Magee, his wife of 13 years. "He said, 'Let's move forward with a rational plan.'"

Such were the nerves and skill that catapulted Mr. Magee from budding technician 30 years ago to chief engineer for the World Trade Center complex. Mr. Magee knew how things worked. He oversaw the hundreds of miles of ventilation ducts, pipes and electric wires of the complex—the arteries of what amounted to a small city.

Mr. Magee, 51, started the job six weeks before Sept. 11. Though he was expected to wear a tie, he still loved to roll up his sleeves and fix things, and teach the buildings' younger engineers. Ms. Wexler-Magee, who shared in many of her husband's nervy pursuits, now plans to take up another. "I've started taking flying lessons," she said.

JOSEPH V. MAGGITTI
Tickets to Paradise Island

Joseph V. Maggitti met his future wife, Pam, in high school, and he took her to the senior prom. Dec. 4, 2001 would be their 25th wedding anniversary, and Mr. Maggitti had already bought the tickets for their return to Paradise Island, where they had honeymooned.

"But Joe went to Paradise ahead of me," said Mrs. Maggitti. "My husband was a Christian; I am a Christian and so are my children. That is the great hope that we have and one day I will be there with him."

Mr. Maggitti, 47, who lived in Abingdon, Md., worked for Marsh & McLennan, and was in the trade center for a morning meeting on Sept. 11. When Mrs. Maggitti turned on the television that day, she said, all she could think of was something he told her after another meeting there: "I can see the planes flying beneath me."

Mr. Maggitti was born in Baltimore and was always a jock. He was a midfielder on the University of Baltimore soccer team that won the Division II N.C.A.A. championship in 1975. Lately, he had shifted his athletic passion to golf.

He cooked stuffed peppers for his daughter, Lauren, 14, on Sundays. He would go to the Fells Point area of Baltimore with his son, Christopher, 22, where they would drink local beer and eat oysters.

"He was a best pal to me," Christopher Maggitti said.

RON MAGNUSON
Golf and Other Loves

Twelve years ago, on a July morning at a golf club in River Vale, N.J., Ron Magnuson shot a hole in one. Afterward, he attached the ball and day's scorecard (82) to the congratulatory certificate and hung it in his rec room in nearby Park Ridge—in the center, where nobody could miss it.

"It was his proudest moment in his golf life," said Audrey Magnuson, his wife of 31 years.

Mr. Magnuson, 57, pursued golf with single-minded passion. He played every Saturday, rising before 7 to drive to a course about an hour away in New York State. He made his own clubs, ordering the parts and gluing them together. He played a serious game, adhering strictly to the rules. His best score was 77.

His goal was 75.

But he was a player, not a fanatic, his wife said. Golf was certainly not his only love. After some 40 years working on Wall Street, most recently as a Cantor Fitzgerald consultant, he was still thrilled by the neighborhood's pace and power. He raised his children—Sheryl, 20, and Jeff, 23—to love conversation as much as he did. His idea of a great night out was a rousing talk over a restaurant dinner, with any or all of the members of his family.

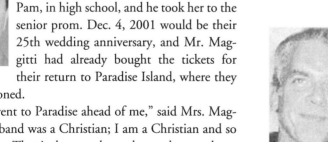

DANIEL L. MAHER
Coming Around to Sports

Daniel L. Maher was a reluctant sportsman. Not for him were the sweating and grunting and locker-room camaraderie. Then along came his sons.

Daniel Jr., now 24, and Joseph, now 20, were not ones to shy away from athletic endeavors. But they also wanted their father alongside them.

So Mr. Maher, a 50-year-old executive at Marsh & McLennan, gradually became an avid sports fan and a participant.

There were his sons' 3 A.M. hockey practices. There were the football games and golf matches and fishing trips. But perhaps most memorable were the hunting trips in the woods near Hamilton, N.J., where the family lived.

"They would try and get something, but they never did," Mr. Maher's wife, Kathy, said with a laugh. (He had an easier time catching her. They met more than 25 years ago in a Queens diner, where she served him grilled-cheese sandwiches.)

Mr. Maher had triple-bypass heart surgery two years ago, but he stayed as active as ever with his family. For their 25th anniversary, Mr. Maher took his wife to Aruba. The family spent a weekend in August water-skiing and fishing at a lake in upstate New York. They even began looking for their own lakeside home.

In the fall of 2001, Mr. Maher's sons went hunting and killed a deer with a bow and arrow. It was their first one ever.

THOMAS MAHON
Moving for Shay

After 14 years in Manhattan, Thomas Mahon packed his bags and headed home. Though the big city still thrilled him, he was no longer the carefree, single guy who moved here to be a financial broker. The oldest of five children, he had married and had a young daughter of his own. He wanted his daughter, Shay, to grow up in Oyster Bay, on Long Island, the way that he had, with playgrounds, beaches and family sprinkled within a few blocks.

On warm, summer evenings, Thomas, 37, who worked at Cantor Fitzgerald in 1 World Trade Center, always hurried home to take out his girl. He pulled out his mountain bike, strapped Shay into a child seat, and glided through the neighborhood. He stopped every so often for relatives and friends.

"Tom took it day by day," said his brother, Gerald Mahon. "I think his grand plan was to create a good life for his daughter."

JOSEPH D. MAIO
A Meticulous Dresser

Joseph D. Maio had a bit of a competitive streak. His wife, Sharri, remembers playing Monopoly with him one Christmas: he was hoarding real estate, so she cashed in and quit in disgust. When she sat near him at the blackjack table in Las Vegas, covering her eyes, he suggested she move away rather than bring him bad luck.

Mr. Maio was tall, hazel-eyed and a meticulous dresser. In his mid-20s, he headed a desk for Cantor Fitzgerald in Tokyo; by his early 30s, he had started a lucrative new desk for Cantor in New York. He was fair-minded, Mrs. Maio said. Friends sought his advice. And he never complained about anything—except his dry cleaning.

But there was another side to Mr. Maio, who was 32. When the Maios' not-yet-house-trained puppy came down with a cold, Mr. Maio slept on the kitchen floor in his pajamas rather than let the dog sleep alone.

When his son, Devon, was born in the summer of 2000, Mr. Maio wept with joy. He would take baths with Devon until his hands were wrinkly. "He was just a beautiful man, inside and out," Mrs. Maio said.

DEBBIE MALDONADO
Mighty Mouse

Her husband, Otilio, nicknamed her Mouse, but that was because Debbie Maldonado was short, not because she was timid. She was not shy. "Miss Miriam," she would start on her older sister, "You're too fat, you need to lose weight!" And heaven protect the salesman who stood between her and a bargain: "Whaddaya nuts? Lower it, lower it!"

Feisty, warm, shopoholic, chocoholic Mrs. Maldonado, 47, an executive secretary at Marsh & McLennan, called her sister in Miami every day before lunch—"There's a sale at Strawberry's! What size are you now?"—and spent every Sunday with her mother, was a woman of constancy. Same boyfriend, later husband, since she was 14; same boss for 21 years; same summer vacation year after year to visit Miss Miriam.

Even so, she had her jolts. For 16 years, Mrs. Maldonado fought infertility with high-tech intervention and no-tech prayer. But she became pregnant the old-fashioned way, with Krystal, now 11, and then Cris, 9. This August in Miami, she went on a shopping spree.

"You never know what's going to happen tomorrow," said Mrs. Maldonado. "What are you talking about?" asked Miss Miriam. Mrs. Maldonado replied: "I'm going to enjoy my life now."

MYRNA MALDONADO
Years Later, Romance Again

While growing up in a Rockland County children's home, Myrna Maldonado learned that Wilfredo Agosto liked her, because he threw rocks at her. Somehow his routine worked, and she liked him back, but for one reason or another, the two did not became a couple.

"I was a little crazy back then," Mr. Agosto said. "She was a lot more mature than I was."

After leaving the home—where they had ended up with their siblings because of dead or ill parents—they each found partners, had children and barely heard about each other. It was not until last year, when Ms. Maldonado, 49 and single in the Bronx, was told by one of her sisters that Mr. Agosto was divorced and living in North Carolina with his three children, that they acted on what she called "this-meant-to-be thing."

"Hi Wilfredo. This is Myrna—a blast from the past," he recalled hearing on his answering machine one day. He said, "I knew my time finally came." In April, 40 years after they had first met, they were married. Ms. Maldonado initially planned to retire from her job as a systems designer for the Port Authority of New York and New Jersey at 1 World Trade Center and move down with him by next June, after the youngest of her two sons graduated from high school. Then she moved up the date to December 2001.

"She always said to me, 'Do it right and enjoy it all, because you don't know how much time you've got,' " her new husband said.

GREGORY J. MALONE
A Bachelor Settling Down

Gregory J. Malone was the personification of Wall Street—hard-working, fast-living, a risk taker. And he had found his soul mate.

"He was a real guy's guy, but that's O.K. because he was scared to death of me," his fiancée, Fiona Fitzgerald, who is Irish and works for a biotechnology company, said with a laugh. "He loves fishing, and he's particularly fond of hockey and the New York Yankees. He wouldn't miss a game of the Yankees whether he was at the stadium or watching it on TV in some bar, much to my dismay."

The two met three and a half years ago in Hoboken, N.J., where Mr. Malone had a house. Mr. Malone was 42, and worked as a bond broker for Maxcor/Euro Brokers. His friends knew him as someone they could party with. But they also saw that Ms. Fitzgerald brought out the romantic side of the longtime bachelor.

One of Mr. Malone's last phone calls was to his friend of 18 years, Kevin Croutier, a broker at Lehman Brothers. They talked about the first plane that had hit. "He was about to settle down," Mr. Croutier said. "He'd just gone to look at lawn furniture, which surprised me. The last place I could imagine him was at Home Depot looking for lawn furniture. But I bet he's happy now, because the Yankees are going to win."

JOSEPH E. MALONEY
We Hardly Knew Ye

You probably think you know Firefighter Joseph E. Maloney. Son of a cop; grandson of a fireman; married forever to Kathy, the pretty, tough-talking nurse; father of Joe, 10, and Megan, 7.

Sure, you know Firefighter Maloney, 45, of Farmingville, N.Y. He is the tall, dark and handsome type who keeps the muscles pumped and the prankster side buffed. Every firehouse has one—or a dozen—like him. He's driving the Ladder Company 3 truck in Manhattan, spots a yuppie couple sipping lattes outdoors, and blaaatt! he smacks that horn, rattling them and their cups. And he's wearing a "borrowed" chief's uniform, baby powder graying his hair, haranguing a quivering probie (new firefighter).

You know him? Not at all. Meet Firefighter Maloney, who never mentioned fear or death, who cared more about being a hero dad than a hero firefighter, although he was both.

Recently, Mrs. Maloney was going through paperwork—he was fastidiously organized—and found a note, stuck between the kids' birth certificates, dated 1995. "Honey, if I die and if on the F.D.N.Y.," he wrote, "you will fare O.K." Tax instructions followed, and an admonition to a giddy shopper: "Don't spend a lot of money."

It concludes: "I love you, Joseph and Megan. Sorry I had to leave you so early. Your father and husband, Joseph E. Maloney."

TEDDY MALONEY
A Name to Carry On

People at his memorial Mass kept using the same words over and over about Teddy Maloney. Loyal. Modest. Magic with kids. A true friend.

At 32, Mr. Maloney was the kind of young husband who called his wife, Brinley, three or four times a day, especially since she was seven months pregnant with their second child—another girl, they had learned. He had already made his morning call home to Darien, Conn., at 8:40 that Tuesday from the TradeSpark offices of Cantor Fitzgerald on the 104th floor, just minutes before the attack.

"I'm not sure he liked his work that much," his mother, Sally Maloney, recalled. "If he had had his way, he would have opened a string of carwashes. He always wanted to be in control of his own business."

And to be closer to home and his extended family, the girls' hockey and lacrosse teams he coached. He took the job in the city only because Cantor Fitzgerald had promised a transfer to the Darien office in February 2002, just after the baby's arrival. Her name will be Teddy Bray Maloney.

GENE EDWARD MALOY
One Last Talk with Mom

When he was a senior in high school, Gene Edward Maloy had an open block in his schedule. He needed a subject to fill it. His mother, Merlyn, thought she had a good idea: typing. He looked at her, stunned, and said, "Typing is for girls." But nothing else fit, and so typing it was.

Years later, he thanked his mother. The course came in handy as he became enraptured by computers. "Computers were his passion," she said. When he visited his parents as an adult, it would be, 'Hi, Mom; hi, Dad,' and he would vanish into the room with the computer and not be heard from for hours.

Mr. Maloy, 41, who lived in Brooklyn and was an analyst for Marsh & McLennan in the company's technology department, had an unusual bond with his mother.

"Gene and I had like a psychic relationship," Mrs. Maloy said. "I would be meaning to call him about something, and before I did, he would call me up and say, 'O.K., Mom, what's up?' He would just know."

On the morning of Sept. 11, Mrs. Maloy felt this urge and decided she didn't care if she was late for work. She had to speak to her son. She got him on the phone, they chatted, and she went off to work. "I'm glad I did that," she said. "I had that last conversation."

CHRISTIAN MALTBY
Glamorous, with Grace

Christian Maltby was so handsome that his college friends used him as bait. They would take him to a bar, wait for the girls to flock around him, and then move in to flirt with them. Mr. Maltby was usually too reserved to make any moves of his own.

"He was very handsome, but he didn't believe it," said his younger brother, Jason Maltby.

With his dark brown hair, blue eyes and unassuming manner, the elder Mr. Maltby was a reluctant heartthrob who signed with Wilhelmina Models to help pay his way through Fordham. He appeared in *Rolling Stone* magazine, and on the covers of teenage romance novels. He later became a vice president for currency trading at Cantor Fitzgerald. Mr. Maltby, 37, gravitated toward a quiet life in Chatham, N.J.

He spent weekends with his wife, Jane, and their three children, Max, Morgan and Samuel, in the backyard. He was

training to be a Sunday school teacher at his church, and liked to read novels that he swapped with his brother.

FRANK MANCINI
They Loved Him in Astoria

It seemed as if everyone in Astoria knew Frank Mancini. He might as well have been living in a Greek or an Italian village instead of the big city of New York.

He met his future wife, Anastasia, in first grade at Public School 17 in Queens. They went to the prom at Long Island City High School. By the time they were married on May 21, 2000, they considered it their 10th anniversary—of dating. Frank was Spanish and Italian. Anastasia was Greek. They went to Mykonos for their honeymoon. Six feet tall, red-haired, riding a motorcycle and laughing, he stood out.

"Everybody loved Frankie in Astoria," said his doting mother, Lea. "Frankie was No. 1." Mr. Mancini, 26, had been a laborer with Local 79, his dad's union, since he was 18. When his father retired, Frank continued working construction at the World Trade Center, the only job he had ever known. About two weeks before the plane hit the north tower, he had moved from the basement to the 107th floor. Mr. Mancini couldn't wait to take his 3-month-old daughter, Sophia, to Disney World.

"How old does she have to be?" he asked his wife. "I think we should wait till she's 3 or 4, at least," she said. He was also planning her wedding.

JOSEPH MANGANO
Where the Deer Wander

Last summer Joseph Mangano went on a fishing excursion in northern Canada, staying on a remote island without running water or electricity. Kathy Mangano, his wife of 33 years, did not go along.

"What woman would be dumb enough to go on a trip like that?" said Mrs. Mangano, who did not share her husband's love of "back-to-nature survival stuff."

But Mr. Mangano, a software engineer, was also very sociable.

"Everybody who knows him calls him his best friend," said Tony Alaimo, a colleague at Marsh & McLennan, still lapsing into the present tense. When Mr. Alaimo was out of work for 12 weeks while recovering from a heart attack, Mr. Mangano called him every day.

Earlier in 2001, the Manganos moved to Jackson Township, N.J., into what his wife described as their "dream house." It has a large yard, where deer sometimes wander, and an extended driveway that doubles as a basketball court.

Mr. Mangano, 53, had planned to install his model train set in the basement. He also had a room built for a pool table, but he never got around to buying it.

"Now the room is sitting there," his wife said, "and I can't stand to go down there."

DEBBIE MANNETTA
Knowing What Is Important

Debbie and Kenny Mannetta had what they wanted. Their only aspiration was to keep it. "We had both lost parents," said Mr. Mannetta, a police sergeant on the Upper West Side. "We wanted to see our children grow up."

Their home was a brown Cape in Islip, on Long Island, where they strolled after dinner with 1-year-old Ashley and 3-year-old Jessica. Since Mrs. Mannetta was working part time at Carr Futures, they arranged their schedules so one or the other was home with the girls. Every summer, they vacationed at a lakeside family camp in New Hampshire.

"People asked: 'Why go to New Hampshire every year?' 'Why go to the same restaurant?' " he said. "Because we knew what we liked and did it."

Both were unabashedly sentimental, becoming weepy at the sight of Jessica at nursery school or their hundredth viewing of *On Golden Pond*. "We're here today, together," Sergeant Mannetta said. "We knew what was important. Until Sept. 11th turned my home into a house."

MARION MANNING
The World Beyond Queens

Those girls in Springfield Gardens were just tight like that. They grew up together and went to school in the neighborhood. They became young women and found husbands and homes near where the Q5 bus stops. They were starting to have little ones of their own, right there in Springfield Gardens.

Marion Manning, known as Vick or Vickie, was no exception. She was close to her old friends, including one named Sean who had become her husband in April 1997. And her 2-year-old daughter, Lauryn, was so close to her in looks and in her heart that she sometimes called the girl Mini-Me. But her dreams carried her outside of Queens.

"She just wanted to see the world," Mr. Manning said.

And she was taking her friends along. Mrs. Manning, an executive secretary at Marsh & McLennan, had arranged trips for her friends and their husbands to Cozumel, the Bahamas and Cancún.

"She would get the best deals; she would get everybody's ticket," said Tina Corbett, a friend.

TERENCE MANNING
A Knack for Persuasion

Every sunny day last summer, Terence Manning would take his two daughters, Mairead, 3, and Trinity, 1, to the beach down the street from their home in Point Lookout, on Long Island. "They'd go for hours," said his wife, Megan. "He would put Mairead on a throne and make a sand castle around her. And he would try to get Trinity to put her toes in the water. They loved it."

Mr. Manning, 37, used his prodigious energies to make everything an adventure: skiing in the Alps, proposing to his wife under the Eiffel Tower, going cross-country with her on a motorcycle or persuading his brothers to run the New York City Marathon with him—and crossing the finish line holding hands.

"He could do anything he put his mind to," his wife said. "He could build a house if he decided to. He'd been a trader his entire career, but then he decided he wanted to do computer consulting, learned how, and made the change."

That career change at ARC Partners led him, finally, to a conference Sept. 11 at the World Trade Center. "His life was full of laughter and adventure," his wife said. "He left us with no regrets."

JOSEPH MARCHBANKS Jr.
Someone to Brag About

Joseph Marchbanks Jr. was a Battalion Chief in a Harlem firehouse, but he preferred to be called a firefighter. A 22-year veteran, Chief Marchbanks garnered four promotions by the time he died at age 47, but "he wasn't one to brag," said his wife, Teresa.

Still, Chief Marchbanks had a lot to brag about. A Bronx native, he qualified for the police force and the Fire Department in the same week, chose the Fire Department, never looked back.

"He loved his job," said his friend (and stickball teammate) Frank McDonagh.

Chief Marchbanks was justifiably proud of his daughter Lauren's softball team, which he helped coach to a championship in Nanuet, N.Y., where the former city boy lived with his wife and children, Lauren, 14, and Ryan, 8.

At the firehouse, he organized study groups to help others pass tests for promotions. "He taught without you realizing you were learning," said his friend and colleague, Lt. Kevin Guy.

Now Lieutenant Guy would like to do the bragging for

him, more than willing to relate more stories about his friend.

"Anything for Joe, anything," he said.

LAURA MARCHESE-GIGLIO
A Loyal Fan and Friend

Laura Marchese-Giglio was "the boy my father never had," said her older sister, Cathy Marchese-Collins. As a baby she looked like a little boy. And she was a sports fanatic, who loved skiing and watching football.

But she also loved boys, from an early age. She always had a boyfriend, but she wasn't a player, her sister said—she was "true blue." She was equally loyal to her friends. Born and raised in Freeport, on Long Island, she kept the same group of friends her whole life, although she couldn't help but add many more along the way.

"She exuded friendliness," her mother, Lorraine Marchese, said.

Ms. Marchese-Giglio, 35, made friends at the gym and on the train, where she met her fiancé, Joseph Mendez. They had just bought a house in Oceanside. As of Sept. 11, she had lived in it for 10 days.

She was the baby of the family, her mother's best friend and a godmother to her nephews. She loved her job, as executive assistant to the chief executive and president at Alliance Consulting.

And she lived to eat—she would come to her parents' front door sniffing the air for dinner. She wasn't a cook, her sister Cathy said, but she almost never visited without baking a batch of brownies.

PETER E. MARDIKIAN
At Long Last, Together

Peter E. Mardikian had both good and bad timing: good, because he met his future wife, Corinne, at Ohio State University, where they lived in the same dorm; and bad, because, try as he might, after graduation, there never seemed to be a good time for her to move to New York to be with him.

Mr. Mardikian, who worked at Imagine Software, traveled a lot in his job after college. Corinne Mardikian—graduated after him and did not want to be in New York unless they could be together.

"It was very tough to live apart," said Mrs. Mardikian. "The time was never right to actually be together." But Mr. Mardikian, 29, had grown up in Princeton, N.J., dreaming of living in Manhattan and working on Wall Street. Though he never made it to Wall Street, less than two years ago, the timing was finally right, and his future wife moved in with him.

"His closure was her coming to Manhattan," said his friend and former roommate, Eric Boucher. "He wouldn't have been complete without getting married to Cori."

On Sept. 11, Mr. Mardikian was attending a conference at Windows on the World. He had been married for six weeks.

CHUCK MARGIOTTA
An Obligation to Fill Up Life

When he left Staten Island to attend Brown University, Chuck Margiotta told classmates that he would return to New York to become a fireman. He did just that, serving 15 years in Harlem and then the last 4 with Ladder 85 in Staten Island. He also became a substitute teacher. A private investigator. A coach of his children's soccer and basketball teams. And he was a member of the Screen Actors Guild, winning small roles in the movies *Frequency* and *Hannibal*.

"He was usually the guy who got shot," said Steve Gallira, a friend since childhood. "Nobody knows when the guy slept. We don't think he did."

Early on Sept. 11, Lieutenant Margiotta, 44, was returning to Staten Island after filling in for another firefighter in Brooklyn. Once he heard the news of the attacks, he turned around, caught a ride with Rescue 5 near the Verrazano-Narrows Bridge and headed for the towers.

That was Chuck Margiotta: all drive. Always doing the unexpected. Like becoming tight end for his high school football team when he could hardly catch a pass. Like saying unabashedly in the company of other men how he had done the right thing by marrying his wife, Norma.

Mr. Gallira said, "I felt all this work he did, Chuck believed it was his obligation to life, to fill it up."

KENNY MARINO
A Devout Baseball Fan

Kenny Marino was a Mets fan and a Seattle Mariners fan, but his all-time favorite ballplayer was Ken Griffey Jr. So Katrina Marino, his wife, e-mailed the Cincinnati Reds wondering if Mr. Griffey could hit a home run for her husband because he would be "looking down with a big grin."

On Sept. 25, Mr. Griffey, in his second at-bat against Philadelphia, obliged Mrs. Marino. He said it would always stand out as one of the most memorable he had hit. The bat was later given to Mrs. Marino and her two children, Kristin, 3, and Tyler, 1. Mr. Marino, 40, was a firefighter with Rescue 1 in Manhattan. His family happened to visit him at the firehouse the morning of Sept. 11, shortly before the summons to the trade center.

Firefighter Marino whispered into Kristin's ear, "If you

are a good girl, when I get home I will get you a prize—a Wizard of Oz prize."

A few weeks later, Mrs. Marino found the prizes, a Dorothy doll for Kristin and a Scarecrow for Tyler. And there was a Fireman Santa Claus ornament for Mrs. Marino. She mentioned those treasured final prizes at the memorial service for him on Long Island. As Rescue 1 led the mourners out, the organist played "Take Me Out to the Ballgame."

The members of Rescue 1 had to smile. They knew that was so Kenny.

LESTER MARINO
Days on the Boat

This is a fish story about one that did not get away. Lester Marino was fishing for bluefish off Long Island in the early 1970s when he hooked a 250-pound mako shark. He had only light tackle aboard, so he radioed a friend with a bigger boat. The friend came from 20 miles out in the ocean, and they were able to cut the line, reattach it to a heavier rod and reel and land the shark.

"They steaked it out and it was eaten, for sure," said his son, Peter Marino.

At 57, Mr. Marino loved to get up at 5 on summer mornings in North Massapequa, N.Y., stop for a bacon-and-egg sandwich on a roll and spend the day on his boat. Sometimes he fished with one or more of his four children. Other times he went out with his companion, Gay McKenna, and her 87-year-old mother, Grace. He fished the Great South Bay, Jones Inlet, Oyster Bay, wherever the codfish, bass, fluke and flounder were running.

Mr. Marino had worked for most of three decades as an electrician at the World Trade Center, most recently at Cantor Fitzgerald; on the water he used the towers as a landmark.

"Look at the World Trade Center," he would say. "It's so clear it looks like you can reach out and touch it."

JOSE J. MARRERO
The Pleasure of Pigeons

Last summer, Jose J. Marrero rediscovered one of the joys of his childhood. He bought some pigeons.

Always handy—he had fixed up a dining room at his home in Old Bridge, N.J., and an upstairs room that lies unfinished—Mr. Marrero built a pigeon coop in the backyard. He'd come home from his job at EuroBrokers, where he was a facilities manager, and spend an hour or so out back just watching the birds, his wife, Jodi, said. He was making plans to race them, just as he had when he was growing up in Brooklyn.

Mr. Marrero, 32, was the fire warden for his floor—the 84th, in the south tower. He had helped a man down the stairs, Mrs. Marrero said, when he got a call on his walkie-talkie from someone else who needed assistance. He went back in.

"In the bombing of '93, he did the same exact thing," she said. "Helped people right to the end."

Now, the pigeons are having babies like crazy, Mrs. Marrero said. There are about 20 of them, and they provide plenty of entertainment for the couple's three children. One bird in particular has taken a fancy to their 3-year-old, coming right up to her and eating out of her hand.

"We named him Jose," Mrs. Marrero said.

JAMES MARTELLO
Big Man with a Big Heart

Jimmy Martello wrote a lot of checks he did not have to. This foundation, that foundation, this friend in need, that stranger with the brain tumor and three children. He had grown up solidly middle class, a hefty Jersey guy—6 feet 3 inches, 240 pounds—who became a varsity linebacker at Rutgers and an impressively successful trader at Cantor Fitzgerald. Feeling blessed, he was always thinking of ways to give back.

His credo, said his wife, Sheila, was, "If it needs to be loved, love it; if it needs to be given, give it; if it needs to be done, do it."

In late August, the Martellos moved to Rumson, N.J., to be 10 minutes from an office that the company was readying. Mr. Martello, 41, hoped to scale back in a few years to attend more of his two sons' activities. He had already been coaching the 7-year-old's football and roller hockey teams.

The boys were robbed of that dream. They will keep the images of Mr. Martello tossing them in the air in the backyard pool, and playing King of the Basement, scooping them up and whirling toward the couch.

MICHAEL A. MARTI
A Chum to the Underdog

In Glendale, Queens, where Michael A. Marti lived, neighbors might not have known the bond trader from Cantor Fitzgerald. But they probably knew his car. Mr. Marti, 26, wouldn't have minded. He cherished his red 1985 Camero IROC, and was known to wash and wax it whenever he got a free moment, even if the free time was at 6 A.M., or midnight.

"The first word he ever said was 'daddy,' " said Rosalie A. Marti, his mother. "His second word was 'car.' "

As a flag is unfurled over the Rockefeller Center
Christmas tree on November 15, Kaitlyn Hucszko,
seventeen, watches with her brother Aidan, five. Their
father, Stephen Hucszko, a Port Authority police officer,
died in the World Trade Center collapse on September
11. (*G. Paul Burnett*)

He liked to lift weights. He loved to play and watch basketball. He was a popular, gregarious guy, who did well with the girls. But he was also quick to count loners among his circle of friends, to see interesting people and companions where others saw nerds and geeks.

"He would see someone who was unpopular and stick by their side and make sure they were taken care of," said Cris C. Italia, 23, a friend. "He would always favor the underdog."

KAREN MARTIN
They Liked Her Style

Karen Martin's friends say she was not just a Type A personality, she was a Type A+. Competitive. Organized. In charge. On the stick to a fault.

She did her Christmas shopping during the summer, had it all wrapped up and out of the way by first frost. When water skiing, she would dip and slip a little lower than most people. On snow, she always took the steeper, riskier route down. Golfing? She hit from the men's tee.

Back in the 1980s, Ms. Martin, from Danvers, Mass., worked for a while as a bartender at the Hard Rock Cafe in Boston—a Type A+ bartender. She set up her glasses and bottles just so, kept a precise inventory of everything and ragged on all the other bartenders to do likewise. They grumbled. But it was good-natured grumbling because at heart they liked Karen Martin's style. They went along.

In 1989, Ms. Martin became an American Airlines flight attendant and, jumping up onto a chair, proclaimed to her friends: "There is now something special in the air." She liked to work the long, hard hauls, especially the coast-to-coast "transcons."

On Sept. 11, she was the head attendant on American Airlines Flight 11, bound out of Boston for Los Angeles. She was 40 years old.

PETER C. MARTIN
He Still Speaks to Her

Lt. Peter C. Martin had plenty of interests. He liked to watch Nascar races, "glued to the TV," said his friend, Lt. Peter Lund. He also kept track of how many fires he had been to, perhaps inspired by a book, *20,000 Alarms*, that was lying around the Rescue 2 firehouse in Brooklyn.

And once a month, he would take out the antique rifles he collected, put on a cowboy hat and take aim at the buffalo silhouettes set up on a field in the Hamptons with other members of the local Single Action Shooting Society. There he was known as Sidewinder Pete, a true aficionado to whom the group dedicated a memorial shoot in October 2001.

But mostly, Mr. Martin, 43, cared about being a father to his three boys, ages 13, 9 and 6. His own father had died when he was 11 months old. "As much as he loved the Fire Department, his first love was ours," said his wife, Alice. "He would race home from work so he could put the boys to bed. He'd sing to them, and tell them stories. He had a whole routine."

Now Mrs. Martin is taking care of things on her own. "I get a lot of strength from Peter," she said. "I can almost hear him saying to me, 'Everything's O.K.' "

WILLIAM J. MARTIN Jr.
Big Brother to All

After illness took both their parents, Laura and Billy Martin had only each other. And for the six years that they lived together in a Hoboken, N.J., apartment, that was enough.

William J. Martin Jr., 35, was Laura's big brother, but she said he was "duty bound" to take the place of their father. Any boyfriend she brought home had to pass muster with Billy, and he wasn't afraid to tell them not to come back if he thought they were wrong for her. Part of that sense of responsibility came from his Navy years, and part from working at a big Wall Street firm, Cantor Fitzgerald. But his concern for others was genuine. After just a year of marriage, he agreed to take in his wife Debbie's 90-year-old grandmother to live with them in Denville, N.J.

"He could never do enough for family or friends," Ms. Martin said. On game days, those friends counted on Billy to show up at Giants Stadium hours early with steaks, fresh mozzarella from Hoboken and plenty of beer. The same group tailgated again this season and presented Ms. Martin with a banner for her husband's Jeep. It said: Billy Martin: A True Giant.

BRIAN MARTINEAU
King of the Wisecracks

Brian Martineau was a big guy and a funny man, with a brash sarcastic way about him that cracked people up. But though he was hardly shy about sharing his opinions, especially about the British underground bands in his collection of 5,000 CDs, Mr. Martineau, 37, could still make room for people to be heard. He was the self-appointed one in a crowd who would welcome newcomers at the door, the genial host and all-purpose cook at so many family get-togethers.

His new job as a benefits consultant at Aon opened the way to several firsts: first time in a New York City taxi and a subway, first time as part of the skyline he used to see from his old job in New Jersey, featuring those towers he thought were exciting but kind of intimidating.

He just was not a city person. Mr. Martineau was most comfortable reigning on familiar turf. He grew up in Edison, N.J., and was raising his young family there. He was king of the kitchen, where he prepared Sunday breakfasts and dinner every night for his wife, Bettyann, who got home from work after he did. Home was where a wisecracking king could show his gentle side: every night before he went to bed, Mr. Martineau made sure he kissed his two children, even though they were asleep.

EDWARD J. MARTINEZ
A List of Things to Love

This is how much Edward J. Martinez of Elmhurst, Queens, knew how to appreciate the banquet of life: he carried a blanket in his car trunk so he would always be ready for a picnic. And with one of those aluminum-looking things that folds up into nothing, said his wife, Helen, wherever they went, biking in Connecticut, up to Vermont, he was ready.

Also, there was a great list of things Mr. Martinez loved. He loved skiing, loved ice skating, loved to sky-dive, loved the opera. He lived, at 60, in the house he had grown up in on Cornish Avenue. He and his childhood friends from the block, now grown and married, formed themselves into an unofficial gang: the Screwball Club.

Mr. Martinez was an operations manager at Cantor Fitzgerald. His daughter Stephanie turned 18 four days after the attack on the World Trade Center. Mr. Martinez's 20th wedding anniversary would have been Sept. 19. Friends came over on both occasions and, on the anniversary, took Mrs. Martinez and her daughter out to dinner.

A Navy veteran, Mr. Martinez could not bear two things: people who "dissed" America, and racist remarks. He draped a flag on his house on Memorial Day and kept it out all summer. As a memorial to her husband, Mrs. Martinez plans to leave the flag out year round.

ROBERT MARTINEZ
A Niche for Helping

Robert Martinez believed that he had finally found his niche and was doing what he was destined to do. It had been only about three months since he had said goodbye to fast-food jobs and he was working as a security officer for Summit Security, patrolling the lobby of the World Trade Center.

This was a job that fulfilled him, because he had always been keen to help others. Which is why he managed to get out of the buildings after the planes struck, but told other workers that he had to hurry back to the towers and direct people out. He was inside when the buildings came down.

Mr. Martinez, 23, lived in Astoria, Queens, with his parents, Marie and Gabriel Martinez, and he had a son, Jonathan, 5, with a former girlfriend. He made a point of visiting his son on the weekends and taking him to the park, the beach or a movie.

He was a rabid sports fan, and when he was not playing basketball or baseball in the park, he would be planted in front of the television with his father and brother, absorbed in one game or another. He was one of those rare New Yorkers in that he rooted for both the Yankees and the Mets.

LIZIE MARTÍNEZ-CALDERÓN
A Mother's Love

On Tuesday, Sept. 11, Lizie Martínez-Calderón woke up early and headed for the kitchen. From their bed, her husband, Marino Calderón, saw that their 4-year-old daughter, Naomi, had also woken up and was following her mother down the hall. Their 20-month-old son was still sleeping. It was 10 minutes before 6.

"I said, 'Go back to bed, Naomi. It's too early,' but she kept going towards her mother," Mr. Calderón said. So, he got up, followed their daughter and found his wife sitting on the living room sofa, gently cradling their little girl. Again, he told Naomi to go back to bed. But his wife pleaded with him, "Let her be, just leave her with me for a little while," Mr. Calderón remembers she said. Ms. Martínez-Calderón, 32, a secretary at Aon Insurance who immigrated to New York from the Dominican Republic almost three decades ago, was a woman of faith, her husband said. She sang in the choir of their Adventist church in Washington Heights and was a member of a church group trained to assist victims in times of tragedy.

"I think they were saying their good-byes," Mr. Calderón says, still haunted by the last image of his wife mothering their little girl.

PAUL MARTINI
Maxims, but No Wristwatch

Lt. Paul Martini had his cherished mottoes, and he stuck to them. One was, "Don't sweat the small things." He was always saying that, whenever anyone got frazzled over something minor. His other favorite was, "If it's not broken, don't fix it." Take going to the dentist. He didn't abide by the notion of visiting the dentist every six months. If he didn't have a toothache, why bother: "If it's not broken, don't fix it."

Then again, he was pretty fastidious about his teeth. "I swear he would spend an hour in the bathroom," said his wife, Lisa. "I'd say, 'When are you going to be done?'"

Lieutenant Martini, 37, was with Engine Company 201, and lived with his wife and daughter, Lindsay, 6, in Staten Island. He was so laid back that he never wore a watch. He would say he could look at the position of the sun and have a good idea of the time. In any event, he was never late for work.

He liked to call people "mook," which was his euphemism for "idiot." If someone messed up, he would say, "Oh, you're such a mook." Except many people didn't know what he meant.

Once, sitting around the firehouse, the talk turned to another firefighter going through a tough divorce. Asked what he thought, Lieutenant Martini said: "Oh, Lisa and I have it all figured out. We would split everything 50-50. Lisa would get the inside of the house, and I would get the outside."

BERNARD MASCARENHAS
An Anonymous Benefactor

Bernard Mascarenhas was a zealous bridge player, an executive who had risen steadily up the corporate ladder, and a man who liked to take it easy on weekends with his wife and two kids. But it was what he was not known for that is worth remembering as well.

Deeply committed to education, Mr. Mascarenhas, 54, used to make anonymous donations to a number of different charities, in particular to scholarship funds. Among his causes, he would send anonymous scholarship donations to his native Pakistan, to assist Roman Catholics, a religious minority in that country.

Mr. Mascarenhas's influence was felt in the corporate world too. He was the chief information officer at Marsh Canada, a subsidiary of Marsh & Mclennan, in Toronto, and was in New York for a meeting on Sept. 11.

Mr. Mascarenhas's work on computer systems at the company was known as particularly innovative and wound up being used not only in Canada but in Marsh offices around the world.

"He made sure everything he worked on was a first-class product," said Thomas J. Grimes, managing director at Marsh Canada.

NICK MASSA
Betting and Breaking Even

Nick Massa had clearly defined interests. They were golf, the racetrack and cards, not necessarily in that order. He was on the golf course every chance he got. Each year, he and his golf buddies would go on a couple of four-day outings, often to Florida. They would play golf in the morning and often follow up with tennis in the afternoon.

Then he had a card group that would assemble every couple of months and play poker.

The horses were a longtime fixation. He kept a box at Monmouth Park in New Jersey, and attended once a week during the season. You could also find him at Belmont and Aqueduct, if not elsewhere, though he wouldn't bother with the trotters.

His dream had been to own racehorses, and some years ago he managed to buy several, and he did get into the winner's circle a few times.

Mr. Massa, 65, lived in Manhattan and was a senior vice president at Aon. There were times he spoke of retiring next year, and there were times he would say, "I'll never retire."

"He was a friend to all," said his daughter Donna Mercurio. "Anyone who became his friend, he took a big piece of your heart."

Between golf, the horses and poker, there was a lot of betting going on in his life. So how did he do on those golf trips?

"He said he broke even," his daughter said. What about at the racetrack? "Broke even," she said. And poker? "Another break-even," she said, "According to him."

PATRICIA A. MASSARI
The Family Was Starting

She had found out early that morning that she was pregnant—news that was at once thrilling and unsettling since it was neither planned nor expected.

There were still so many things Patricia A. Massari, 25, had wanted to do before starting a family. Still in school at night, she wondered out loud that morning, as she raced to get dressed for work, if the home pregnancy test was wrong. She told her husband of two years, Louis, that she would buy another.

"She called me at 8:40 A.M. to tell me she got the second test," Louis Massari recalled. The couple stayed on the telephone several minutes.

Mrs. Massari, who worked during the day on the 98th floor of the World Trade Center at Marsh & McLennan, had been studying for an exam that night in world civilization at Berkeley College in Manhattan. A bubbly, outgoing woman, she had been looking forward to getting the test behind her and was excited about visiting the television set of Emeril Lagasse's cooking show on the Food Channel. A lifelong resident of Queens, Mrs. Massari had sent in her name last year to a lottery and won two seats for the Sept. 14 show. She and her husband were also looking forward to a vacation in October.

"Everything was cut short," said Mr. Massari, who was on the phone with his wife when the plane hit.

MICHAEL MASSAROLI
Avid Bowler and Mets Fan

Tuesday night was his night. Bowling night. Virtually his whole life, Michael Massaroli bowled. As a young boy, he would tag along with his father to the alley and keep score. Once he started knocking down the pins himself, he never stopped.

A memorial set up in the New Jersey Transit station parking lot in South Orange, New Jersey, honoring Christopher Faughnan, who died September 11. Mr. Faughnan, thirty-seven, was a trader at Cantor Fitzgerald. Among his survivors are a wife and three children. (*Dith Pran*)

He lived in Staten Island with his wife, Dianne, and their children, Michael Jr., 6, and Angelina, 6 months.

He bowled once a week from September to May, as a regular in the Tuesday Night Mens Triples league at the Bowling on the Green alley. He maintained an average of about 190, and his constant bowling companion was his best friend, Paul Colletti. They had bowled together since they were 10.

Sept. 11 was a bowling night that didn't happen, and Mr. Colletti has not bowled since then and doesn't know if he ever will again. As a tribute to his friend, the alley has renamed the Tuesday night league the "Mike Massaroli Memorial Triples."

Mr. Massaroli, 38 and a vice president of operations at Cantor Fitzgerald, was a fanatical Mets fan. His wife estimated that out of 162 games, he would catch—in person, on television or on radio—at least 160.

It was never a good idea to raise the subject of the Yankees. As Mrs. Massaroli put it, "He used to say his two favorite teams were the Mets and whoever was playing against the Yankees."

RUDOLPH MASTROCINQUE
Soccer Was His Life

He did not want to miss a minute of the soccer goalie clinic he was running later that night, so Rudolph Mastrocinque arrived at his office in the World Trade Center early on the morning of Sept. 11. As his wife, Meryl, put it, "soccer was his life."

It started out as something for the children, Peter, 11, and Amy, 16. But one day a group of parents got together to play and someone noticed how quick Mr. Mastrocinque's feet were. He went on to become one of the most enthusiastic members of the Kings Park Soccer Club on Long Island, and coached several children's teams.

When he was not playing soccer, "he'd be telling me joke after joke after joke," Mrs. Mastrocinque said. "Rudy was very funny."

Mr. Mastrocinque was 43 and a vice president for property claims at Marsh & McLennan. Mrs. Mastrocinque talked him into buying a boat "to find some relaxation on the water" after his long hours at the office. He did, and fishing on Long Island Sound became one of his favorite things to do—second only, perhaps, to soccer.

JOSEPH MATHAI
Thinking Forward

Words like "gentle" and "unassuming" are not often used to describe those who work on Wall Street or in the financial services industry. But colleagues of Joseph Mathai were struck by his humor and modest, unpretentious demeanor. "We have an open-door policy and

I could always hear his laughter," said Eric-Jan Schmidt, a colleague at Cambridge Technology Partners in Massachusetts, where Mr. Mathai was a managing partner.

His pleasant nature was matched by an insatiable interest in business technology. Using algorithms, Mr. Mathai, 49, developed a system to detect insider trading after the New York Stock Exchange scandals in the mid-1980s.

He read so much that 20 magazines a week came to the family home in Arlington, Mass. "He knew more about the underpinnings of the stock market than almost anyone I ever met," said Doug Brockway, a former colleague at Fidelity Investments.

Married, with two children, Mr. Mathai divided his time between New York and Boston during his career. The World Trade Center had been a signpost for his personal and professional life. He had dated his wife, Teresa, at Windows on the World, where he was attending a conference on Sept. 11, and he started his first commercial venture at the World Trade Center after getting his M.B.A. from Columbia University in 1976.

"He was definitely a forward thinker, one of the few guys I know in the technology business who had the ability to sift through the tea leaves of the present and discern the direction of future events," said Larry Scott, a former colleague at Cambridge Technology Partners.

CHARLES MATHERS
In Crisis or Comedy

Here is the man you want in a crisis: while everyone squawks, he is listening. A great bear of a fellow, his eyes bright blue and calm, white-haired head nodding, he says, "Hmmmm." Then, "I'll take care of it." And he does.

Charles Mathers, 61, whose quiet sparkle attracted innumerable friends, clients and employees, spent a lifetime handling crises. As a young man he served in the Navy for six years, much of it in a nuclear submarine. In Sea Girt, N.J., where he and Margaret, his wife of 39 years, raised three children, he was a volunteer firefighter for a quarter-century. He traveled around the world, consulting on insurance for utilities, including nuclear power plants.

But for all his responsibilities, Mr. Mathers, a managing director at Marsh & McLennan, was hardly slathered with gravitas. On the contrary. Last summer, at a conference of utility clients, insurers and brokers in Chicago, Mr. Mathers's company was host to a dinner. Mr. Mathers made brief remarks and introduced an executive client.

"And here's one risk Chuck may not have considered," the client said, then planted a shaving-cream pie in Mr. Mathers's face. Several hundred otherwise staid people gasped and fell all over with laughter.

Mr. Mathers had planned the entire stunt.

MARGARET MATTIC
Dimples Right and Left

Margaret Mattic was the only one of the five Mattic girls of Detroit to have dimples. Right and left, the dimples set off the shy smile and the lilting, gentle voice that everyone remarked on. As a young girl, in elementary school productions, she played Snow White as well as Gretel in *Hansel and Gretel.*

The love of performing stuck with Ms. Mattic, a surprise since she seemed so quiet. She studied theater at Wayne State University. After college, more productions followed, mostly in community theater, often in plays like *Sty of the Blind Pig,* the 1971 work by Phillip Hayes Dean about a black family in Chicago.

Eventually, Ms. Mattic wound up in Manhattan to pursue acting. She usually took temporary jobs, typically as a receptionist, so she could go to auditions.

Recently, she talked to friends about producing and starring in a one-woman play she had written, called *The Vision,* about how the gift of prophecy changed several generations of a family. At 51, she also wanted the comfort of a permanent job, so she became a customer service representative for General Telecom in the World Trade Center.

"Every employer she ever worked for always loved her voice," recalled her sister, Jean Neal, 56. "It was so soothing and gentle and soft."

ROBERT D. MATTSON
A Hero in 1993

Robert D. Mattson did not seek out danger. But danger seemed to have a way of finding him. A lot of his friends managed to avoid Vietnam. He ended up over there in the Army, smack in the middle of harm's way, came home with a Bronze Star for valor and some memories he would never share, not even with his wife, Elizabeth.

"He would just slough it off as not worth talking about whenever I asked," she said.

Then, in 1993, when terrorists attacked the World Trade Center the first time, with a truck bomb, Mr. Mattson, a banker with Fiduciary Trust Company International, found himself in harm's way again. One of his co-workers in the stricken tower was eight and a half months pregnant, unable to make her way down 96 flights of stairs to the street after the elevators stopped. He was one of a handful of people who helped carry her up more than a dozen flights to the roof, where a helicopter plucked her to safety.

On Sept. 11, when the trade center was attacked again, Mr. Mattson called Mrs. Mattson on his cell phone a few minutes after the first plane had struck and told her not to worry, he was in no danger, the plane had hit the other tower. But just to be on the safe side, he said, he was leaving his building and, in fact, was already down to the 90th floor.

He was 54 and lived in the Green Pond section of Rockaway Township in New Jersey.

CHARLES A. MAURO Jr.
Turning Down Retirement

Charles A. Mauro Jr. had been working for the Aon Corporation on the 92nd floor of the north tower for a little over two months. The surprise to those who knew him was that he was working at all.

In May, Mr. Mauro, who was 65, had taken a buyout from his previous employer, Associated Aviation Underwriters, when it was bought by a British company. He had been asked to stay on, but did not want to commute to Short Hills, N.J., from his home in Staten Island, his wife, Dorothy, said. Retirement beckoned.

"I told him and my husband told him to enjoy his life and not go back to work," his sister, Nancy Sparozic, said. "But he wanted to go back and work with people. Staying home was boring to him. He liked to be with the young ones."

It was not as if Mr. Mauro did not have other interests. A history buff, a voracious reader of newspapers and periodicals, Mr. Mauro was also an avid sports fan. He loved following the Rangers and Knicks, but baseball and football were special; he was a New York Giants season ticket holder for 30 years. Mrs. Mauro said she put the emblems of the Giants and the Yankees on his headstone.

Kathy Mazza's family attend her memorial Mass on November 17 at Maria Regina Roman Catholic Church in Seaford, New York. Ms. Mazza was a captain with the Port Authority Police. (*Kevin P. Coughlin*)

One more thing: his life was bracketed by historic events. The day he was born, July 9, 1936, it was 106 degrees in Central Park, a record that stood for 30 years. And then there was Sept. 11, 2001.

CHARLES J. MAURO
He Supplied the Bucks

As director of purchasing for Windows on the World, Charles J. Mauro worked his food vendors indefatigably for their finest vegetables, fish and meat. But he was never averse to being his own supplier. Since the age of 14 he had hunted with his father, Vincent, in Hancock, N.Y., "and during hunting season he'd be up there every weekend, going for the big six-point bucks," said his wife, Barbara.

Charlie, 38, was a proud member of the National Rifle Association and the president of the Bambi Rod and Gun Club in Hancock. Charlie did have one of the six-pointers mounted, "but now it's stashed away somewhere, because we're in the middle of moving," Ms. Mauro said.

Charlie was also passionate about riding his Custom 883 Sportster Harley. Ms. Mauro added, "That six-point buck is going to be up on the wall, and Charlie's picture is going to be next to it."

DOROTHY MAURO
A Chill for a Twin

The friends of Dorothy and Margaret Mauro must have envied their relationship. As twins, they played the kind of tricks and had the kind of friendship that others fantasize about. When blind dates took them dancing, they switched partners mid-evening—and the men never guessed. Throughout elementary and junior high school, they sat beside each other in class. "When they separated us," said Margaret, "it was like being split in half."

"You always have a playmate, a companion," she continued. "She was somebody to talk to who understood me completely."

Eventually Margaret, 55, moved to Nashville, while Dorothy, a state tax clerk working at the World Trade Center, remained in Brooklyn. But they talked every day— after arriving at work, when they returned home, before bed. On Sept. 11, they spoke at 8:30 A.M. "about what I was planning to cook," said Margaret. "About how busy I was going to be."

After hanging up, she said, she felt a chill. "I told myself it wasn't true," she said. "But when I tried to call, the phone was dead."

NANCY MAURO
A Radar for Sales

She concocted the gourmet spreads at home in Forest Hills, Queens; he chopped the ingredients. She cultivated the flower garden in Dutchess County; he whacked the weeds. Compatibility was the essence of Don and Nancy Mauro's 18-year marriage. Mr. Mauro recalls falling in love with his future wife at first sight. Introduced by her sister one wintry Friday during happy hour at a Manhattan bar, they became an item in the course of an evening that ended with him walking her to the subway and kissing her good night—but not good-bye— beneath the twin towers.

Nancy Mauro, 51, studied fashion design and spent two years on Seventh Avenue, then switched to computer technology after realizing that she did not enjoy the clothing trade backbiting (though she never lost her radar for a good sample sale). Mr. and Mrs. Mauro both worked for Marsh & McLennan; he at Marsh Aviation in Midtown, where his office windows faced downtown toward hers on the 97th floor of 1 World Trade Center. His office provided a grotesque vantage point on Sept. 11; he watched as the unspeakable happened, the whole time surrounded by screaming colleagues.

Early on they agreed that theirs would be a childless marriage. Both city kids who had never known anything but apartment living, they fulfilled a dual dream two years ago by buying a weekend house in Red Hook. Naturally, both fell in love with the same place at the same moment.

"The second one we looked at," said Mr. Mauro. He has trouble going there now. "That house is really her."

TYRONE MAY
The Music, and Party, Man

Tyrone May's music collection was vast: hundreds and hundreds of records and CDs, running the gamut from reggae and disco to rhythm and blues. And his apartment in Rahway, N.J., was littered with the announcements for record fairs he received in the mail each month. Naturally, people leapt to conclusions.

"Everybody comes into the apartment and says, 'Who's the D.J.?'" said Mr. May's wife, Marva May. The truth is that on any given day, Mr. May, 44, an auditor with the New York State Department of Taxation and Finance, was more likely to be crunching numbers than spinning records. But he had an expert ear and, more important, the party-planning skills of a born impresario.

Nearly every December, Mr. May would rent a club somewhere in the city and throw a huge dance party for a few hundred friends and family members. By early Septem-

Pictures of the fourteen firefighters from Engine Company 4 and Ladder Company 15 who died on September 11, on display in a shrine outside the firehouse on South Street in Manhattan.
(*Suzanne DeChillo*)

ber, he had a date (Dec. 15) and location (a club in Brooklyn). On Sept. 11, before he left home for 2 World Trade Center, Mr. May told his wife to keep an eye out for a fax from the agency that was designing the tickets for the event.

"I still have the fax," said Mrs. May, who is saving many of her husband's possessions for their son, Tyrone Jr., 2. "Everything is the same way since he left."

KEITHROY MAYNARD
A Role Model by Choice

Keithroy Maynard was black. He was also a firefighter. Those two things meant everything to him, said his twin brother, Kevin.

"People do look to you," he said. "You're like a role model in a sense, especially in the black community where there aren't many black firefighters." The New York Fire Department has been criti-cized for its lack of diversity. Firefighter Maynard was one of those determined to change that. After becoming a fire-fighter in 1999 at age 28, he joined the Vulcan Society, a group of black firefighters.

Mr. Maynard visited predominantly black neighbor-hoods to encourage others to take the Fire Department test. He worked with the Vulcan Society to train applicants to pass the department's physical exam. He was part of Engine 33 in the East Village, but he wanted to be posted to a fire-house in his home neighborhood of East Flatbush, Brooklyn, so that children there could know the life of a firefighter, his brother said.

Mr. Maynard was recruited by his father, a New York firefighter of 36 years. His father drove him to the fire acad-emy at 5 A.M. on the first day of classes. Months after Mr. Maynard graduated, his father died, his final dream ful-filled.

Mr. Maynard's dress uniform and spare work jacket now sit in his mother's house. His nametags are on them. His brother said the only person who will be able to fill them is Mr. Maynard's 6-year-old son, Keithroy Jr., another firefighter in the making.

ROBERT J. MAYO
Notes to His Son

Robert J. Mayo used to leave notes on the breakfast table for his 11-year-old son, Corbin. He worked an early shift as a deputy fire safety director at the World Trade Center, so he got up about 4 A.M. He would drink coffee, check the sports scores and include them in his note to Corbin. "I love you," he might add. "Good luck on your test."

Mr. Mayo, who was 46, was warm and affectionate, said his wife, Meryl. He would take in stray animals, bring them back to health and find them homes. He loved planning family expeditions and undertaking home-improvement projects like landscaping and working with Sheetrock.

Mr. Mayo and Corbin were obsessed with the Giants. They could never afford tickets, so they watched the games on television in the family room in what Mrs. Mayo describes as their Giants shrine. They would wear Giants caps and drink from Giants glasses in the midst of Giants paraphernalia. On Sept. 11, Mr. Mayo's note to Corbin included a losing score.

"He wrote, like, 'Sorry. I love you. Have a good day, I'll see you later,' " Mrs. Mayo recalled. The notes were always on scratch paper or the back of an envelope, nothing fancy. "I would kill for a few of those notes now," Mrs. Mayo said.

KATHY MAZZA
The "Family Fisherperson"

When Kathy Mazza threw her line into the water, fish couldn't resist. At least, it always seemed that way. Ms. Mazza didn't get to fish as much as she would have liked in recent years, but she was known as the "family fisherperson" because of her chronic success.

When she was growing up and went fishing with her brothers, she was the one who came home loaded down with all the fish. "On our honeymoon, we went to Acapulco and we went deep-sea fishing," said her husband, Christopher Delosh. "No one got anything, except her. She hooked a sailfish. It took her 90 minutes to reel it in, but she did it."

Ms. Mazza, 46, lived in Farmingdale, N.Y., with Mr. Delosh. She was a police captain with the Port Authority, and the first female commander at its police training academy. Trained as a nurse, she taught emergency medical service at the academy, a fact not lost on her neighbors.

"Everyone in the neighborhood would come to the house when anything was wrong," Mr. Delosh said. "Like, a young man across the street hurt his hand and he was with his grandmother, who didn't know what to do. Another neighbor was having chest pains. It turned out she was having a heart attack." Some years ago, Ms. Mazza saved her own mother's life. Her mother complained of chest pains, and Ms. Mazza recognized that her arteries were blocked.

EDWARD MAZZELLA
Leaving a Legacy

Edward Mazzella worked on Wall Street for over 40 years, the last few as a senior vice president for equity sales at Cantor Fitzgerald. He was killed three days before his retirement date, Sept. 14. His life's other enduring constant was family. Mr. Mazzella, 62, and his wife, Kay, were married for 40 years. Since early in their marriage, they had held a grand family dinner every Christmas Eve. About two dozen people always came for a spread of crabmeat sauce on pasta, shrimp scampi and cold fish salad, and plenty of fun.

"They were always very gay, very animated, wonderfully boisterous times," said Ann LoPresti, his sister-in-law. In 1993, to everyone's surprise, Mr. Mazzella took to watercolors. Since then, he had done about 100 paintings of flowers, apples, sailboats, treehouses, even a bird cage and a top hat and cane. He framed the paintings and gave them to family members. His children, Susan and Michael have the most, 15 each.

"It's almost like he had a need to leave a legacy," Ms. LoPresti said. "He didn't know, but that's how it's turned out."

JENNIFER MAZZOTTA
Keeping Her Standards High

At 8, Jennifer Mazzotta cut out magazine photos of big, luxurious kitchens and bathrooms to tape to the refrigerator door. "For my house," she said. "When I grow up."

Amused and slightly alarmed, Catherine Mazzotta said: "You shouldn't set your standards so high!" But Jennifer replied firmly: "No, Mom. I'm going to have these."

Fifteen years later, Jennifer Mazzotta, of Queens, was one of Cantor Fitzgerald's youngest traders and engaged to Anthony Roman, a student at the police academy.

"They were on a roller coaster of making their plans," Mrs. Mazzotta said. "He was graduating in February. They were looking for a house. Their wedding was in the summer. They each were saving."

But then, Ms. Mazzotta had been making meticulous plans since age 5. She got ready for kindergarten by selecting a special outfit, sharpening several number two pencils and packing a new box of crayons.

At the school doorway, Mrs. Mazzotta steeled herself for her daughter's tears, "but she just gave me a kiss and said 'Good-bye, Mom,' and walked in without looking back. I was the one who cried."

KAARIA MBAYA
Informality Suited Him

When Kaaria Mbaya was a young boy in Kenya, he threw a stone at his housekeeper's cat, breaking its leg. He was so pained by what he had done that he walked nearly three miles, with the wounded cat in his arms, to a veterinary clinic that is part of the University of Nairobi. He got the cat admitted using the name of his mother, a biochemistry professor at the university. She was confounded when she received a medical bill for a cat.

Mr. Mbaya's mother, Vertistine Mbaya, had looked forward to seeing her shy, compassionate son next summer, when he was to visit Kenya. He was raised there, where his father was a member of Kenya's first Parliament after the country became independent of British rule. His mother is American.

At 38, he was a computer analyst at Cantor Fitzgerald in 1 World Trade, a job that suited him. It was informal. And Mr. Mbaya, who lived in Edison, N.J., did not like to dress up.

JAMES J. McALARY Jr.
"Jimmy Mac" the Leader

James J. McAlary Jr. was always a civic-minded sort of guy and a natural leader. A transplant from Upper Manhattan, he coached his kids' sports teams in Spring Lake Heights, N.J., and led trips to the Bronx Zoo.

"If he was in charge, you felt safe," said his wife, Jeanne. "If Jimmy Mac said 'Let's go to Afghanistan,' you'd go."

Mr. McAlary, 42, a heating-oil trader at Carr Futures, was immersed in the life of his small town. In the summer, he would go from work straight to the town pool, changing from suit to swim trunks in the locker room and launching his 6-foot-4-inch self into the water with a mighty cannonball. "All the kids would wait for Mr. McAlary to show up on the diving board," his wife said.

When he considered running for the school board a while back, she said he did so for selfless reasons. "Jimmy said to me, 'When I was a young kid, I lived in Washington Heights and a lot of people did a lot of things for me they didn't have to do. They opened the gym at night, they

coached baseball, they led the Boy Scouts and they made a big difference in my life. I have an opportunity now to help not just our own children but all the kids in our neighborhood.'"

PATRICIA McANENEY
Like a Firefighter

As a little girl, Patricia McAneney was rarely without her toy fireman's hat. She grew up honest and conscientious, embodying the firefighter ideal. Ms. McAneney never joined the Fire Department, but her strong principles brought loyalty from friends and admiration from co-workers. She was the fire marshal of her floor of 1 World Trade Center, where she worked for the insurance company Guy Carpenter.

"If one of us committed a crime, Pat would be the last person we could go to because she would turn you in," said Margaret Cruz, who shared a home with Ms. McAneney for nearly 20 years. Ms. McAneney's droll sense of humor shined through when Ms. Cruz teased her about this. "She said she might give me a few hours' head start," Ms. Cruz said.

Phyllis Libretti, a friend since childhood, cherishes a plaque given to her by Ms. McAneney. It says:

> The reason why we're such good friends/ is very plain to see
> I understand the things you do/you have respect for me
> No complicated folks are we/no striving to be clever
> Yes, friends may come and friends may go/but we'll be friends forever

JOHN McAVOY
Power and Grace on the Rink

John McAvoy, a firefighter assigned to Ladder Company 3 in Manhattan, did not hesitate to speak his mind—even when it made him sound opinionated. But his wife and two brothers have even more to say than he did.

Paula McAvoy remembers her handsome husband as a figure of power and grace on the rink. Firefighter McAvoy, 47, coached hockey teams on Staten Island, where he lived with her, their children Kate and Kevin, and the family dog, Zoo. Mrs. McAvoy had to drag him onto the dance floor. "And yet he skated beautifully," she said.

Michael McAvoy, the youngest McAvoy brother, said Firefighter McAvoy "never gave up on me when there were times I gave up on myself." George McAvoy, the oldest one, recalled that the "incredibly protective" John, out on a jog, once pulled two elderly people out of a burning house, went back for their cat, then continued on his run.

Kristin Brethel, whose father, Captain Daniel Brethel, died in the September 11 attack, before a news conference at his firehouse. (*Frances Roberts*)

BRENDAN McCABE
"Daddy Did This with Us"

Whenever Brendan McCabe went out to business dinners, he ordered an extra dessert, took it home to his wife, Terri, and shared it with her. Some other images from Mr. McCabe's life: holding Jane, 10 months old, while walking around the house and calling her "my gorgeous, beautiful, wonderful girl," and playing baseball and football with his sons, ages 8, 6 and 4.

When Mr. McCabe got home every evening from his job as a vice president at Franklin Templeton, the boys would stop what they were doing and run to Daddy. Jane would crawl to him, and he would scoop her up.

On Sept. 10, Mr. McCabe, 40, took the day off and played in the pool with Connor, his youngest boy. Then he called for the older boys at school and bought them cleats for soccer. "Now my kids cry themselves to sleep," Mrs. McCabe said, "because they want their daddy. They say to me, Mom, remember Daddy did this with us, Daddy did that with us."

MICHAEL J. McCABE
Unpretentious and Happy

It had been a golden summer.

After 18 years at Prudential Securities, Michael J. McCabe quit in June 2001. He took a trading job at a Cantor Fitzgerald office near his Rumson, N.J., home so he could convert commuter time into family time. And he decided to take the summer off so he could spend it with his wife, Lynn, and their three children. There were lazy days at the Jersey shore, barbecues, swimming. There was a glorious late-summer stay at a rented house in Provence with his best friend of 40 years and their wives.

He started work for Cantor at the World Trade Center exactly one week before the attack. The stint was supposed to last only a month or so, while the company completed work on its Shrewsbury, N.J., office.

Mr. McCabe, 42, was an unpretentious man with a ready laugh, happy in his own skin, his family and friends said. He was a big guy, strong enough to rescue several people over the years from the surf.

"We sort of thought that if anybody could come out of this, Mike could," said his sister Mary Ellen McCabe.

JUSTIN J. McCARTHY
Competitive and Caring

Justin J. McCarthy and his friend Bill Marmo never won the shark-fishing tournament that they entered every summer, but it didn't matter. Mr. McCarthy just liked being on Mr. Marmo's boat off Freeport on Long Island, where he grew up, drinking a few Heinekens and hanging out.

That is not to say that Mr. McCarthy was not competitive. A trader at Cantor Fitzgerald, he was ambitious and determined to advance in his career. He was known for his quick comebacks and sharp sense of humor. But Mr. McCarthy had a creative, dreamy side, too. In his spare time he carved sculptures out of wood and came up with ideas for inventions.

Mr. McCarthy, who died in the World Trade Center attack one week before his 30th birthday, had reunited with his high school girlfriend, Megan Cromer, last year. Ms. Cromer had a 9-month-old son from a previous relationship and was overcome by the kindness Mr. McCarthy showed him.

"You could never find a man that comes into your life to be so good to your own child," Ms. Cromer said.

KEVIN M. McCARTHY
An Unabashed Confidence

First think of him and Cape Cod. For Kevin M. McCarthy, the man with the catching smile who never encountered a conversational pause he couldn't fill, the salty air, sand dunes and lapping waves of Cape Cod constituted paradise. He found serenity there as a boy, and it was where he took his own family for vacations.

Then think of his facility with his hands and his knack for MacGyver-like solutions. "You gave him a string and he could create a universe," said his wife, Debra.

Then consider his unabashed confidence in himself. Risks didn't register. The proof was 98 stitches. Like the hockey stitches. The stitches from his service days when the antenna of an Army tank sliced off his eyebrow. And the box spring stitches. Unable to maneuver a box spring up three flights of stairs, he cut it in half, meanwhile sawing the inside of his hand. That was 23 stitches.

Mr. McCarthy, 42, who lived in Fairfield, Conn., with his wife and three children, Chelsea, 12, and Andrew and

Stephanie, 5, was also the master of reinvention. He ran a personal service business, then became a stay-at-home father when the twins were born, and then emerged as a bond trader for Cantor Fitzgerald.

On the night of Sept. 10, just before they went to sleep, he told his wife, "This is just too good to be true."

MICHAEL McCARTHY
Trader with the Gift of Gab

Michael McCarthy, as he was known to his colleagues, was the tough, competitive trader, at 33 an assistant vice president at Carr Futures who worked from 2 A.M. to 10 A.M., following the London exchanges.

But his family always called him Desmond. Desmond was the happy-go-lucky rugby player who liked a pint and a good tale to chase it. He was a big talker, speaking heatedly about history and politics, or dazzling them with his high-flying deals in Nice and Monaco. "He would try to explain what he did in the business world, but we never did catch on," his father, Bill McCarthy, said.

To his parents, first- and second-generation Irish immigrants, Desmond was the epitome of New World success. You could see Ellis Island and the Statue of Liberty from his 27th-floor apartment in Battery Park City. When he worked in London, he thought nothing of flying home for the night for a family wedding, or to celebrate St. Patrick's Day in Manhattan.

And though Desmond had been commitment-phobic, he seemed serious about the latest girlfriend he took home to Huntington, N.Y. "We were looking forward to watching Desmond move through life," his father said. "Now, every morning hurts. But we love talking about him. It's a way of honoring him."

STANLEY McCASKILL
Proud to Be a Mama's Boy

Stanley McCaskill was called a mama's boy in the housing projects on West 112th Street, where he lived from the time he came into this world. Everyone knew that his 77-year-old mother, Ella Mae McCaskill, had a tight hold on him.

But he did not mind being picked on about it. Neither did she. Mr. McCaskill would call his mother every day from his job at 1 World Trade Center, where he was a guard for Advantage Security. She told him to. She gave him a prayer cloth and a tiny red Bible for his wallet. His mother knew the size of his belt, his pants, his shirt, even the name of his barber.

At age 47, he had not moved out, even though his mother did not care for some of his girlfriends. "He loved her," said his cousin, Carolyn Louallen. "He just didn't want to leave her."

KATIE MARIE McCLOSKEY
Simply Awesome

Even in grade school in South Bend, Ind., Katie Marie McCloskey and Cherese Djakiewicz were best friends, and somewhere along the way—maybe it was at Indiana University together—they both began sharing a dream: to move to New York City.

And so, when Ms. Djakiewicz moved to Manhattan a couple of years ago, it was inevitable that her friend would follow. It took a while, but Ms. McCloskey finally arrived to share the apartment in 2001. That summer Katie found a job on the 97th floor of 1 World Trade Center, staffing the computer help desk of Directfit Inc., rushing to the aid of employees.

Now her sisters, Leslie and Julie, her brother, Noah, and her father, Richard, are in Manhattan searching for her. The other night, they discovered Katie's journal in Cherese's apartment.

"She wrote 'I made it!' and that she loved it in New York," said her mother, Anne. Actually, Ms. McCloskey's exact words were that she had found "an awesome job in an awesome place in an awesome city."

TARA McCLOUD/GRAY
At Home in Brooklyn

Tara McCloud/Gray was a Navy communications veteran of the Persian Gulf war. She had friends who were on the Cole, the destroyer that was bombed in Yemen in October 2000.

On Sept. 11, she was working as a switch technician for General Telecom on the 83rd floor of 1 World Trade Center.

Ms. McCloud/Gray, 30, grew up in Bay Ridge in Brooklyn, her mother's only child. She married Lawrence Gray just before getting out of the Navy. After her discharge, she took the test for the Central Intelligence Agency but then decided to stay in Brooklyn.

She was a sharp dresser, recalled Maria Gonzalez, a colleague at General Telecom. And her mother, Doris McCloud, said that if she wasn't careful how she dressed, Ms. McCloud/Gray would comment—not positively—on what her mother was wearing.

"She was a precise person, with everything in its place," her mother said. "She was a no-nonsense girl. I know she is gone but there are times I have picked up the phone and dialed her number."

RUTH McCOURT and **JULIANA McCOURT**'s portrait appears with Paige Farley-Hackel on page 148.

CHARLES AUSTIN McCRANN
A Past in the Movies

Charles Austin McCrann was a levelheaded, respected executive, devoted to his wife, Michelle, and children, Derek and Maxine. But beneath his responsible exterior beat an auteur's heart. He loved film, whether the comedies of W. C. Fields or horror movies.

And so it was that Charlie McGrann, graduate of Princeton University and Yale Law School, senior vice president at Marsh & McLennnan, was also the writer, producer, director and star of *Toxic Zombies*, a comic horror film that was shown twice on the USA cable network. The movie was made while Mr. McCrann was on hiatus in the late 1970s; its plot turned on a group of hippies who turn into those toxic zombies after a drunken crop-duster oversprays their marijuana field.

Toxic Zombies epitomized a sense of humor that even now makes Mrs. McCrann laugh out loud. Charlie McCrann would surprise someone taken in by his straight appearance with a funny duck walk as he left the room. He would tease her relentlessly, so that after an angry derelict spit on her once, he said, "You mean your Uncle Spitty did that to you?"

He brought her cappuccino in bed every morning. He did his children's chores behind her back.

"He was a character, that's for sure," Mrs. McCrann said.

TONYELL McDAY
Energetic Family Booster

They may be aunts, cousins, nephews and nieces, but the three dozen members of the McDay family prefer to see one another as a nuclear family. Once a month, they would come together in one big, boisterous gathering, and invariably, Tonyell McDay was at its creative and energetic nucleus.

An artist and gospel singer, Ms. McDay, 25, was devoted to her sprawling family, and she was just starting on her next project: a Caribbean cruise next year for the entire group. "She just loved being part of this huge family," said her aunt, Ladora Knight. "She loved bringing everyone together."

Ms. McDay was also deeply spiritual. Her grandfather and uncle are bishops, and her father, Rufus, is a deacon in a local church. Her choir, Voices of Praise, was about to make its first recording.

A computer technician for Marsh Technologies on the 97th floor of 1 World Trade Center, she lived with her parents in Colonia, N.J. Since the Sept. 11 attack, the house has somehow accommodated dozens of relatives, who have been holding a round-the-clock vigil.

"We're just sleeping all over the house," Mrs. Knight said. "Tonyell would have wanted it that way."

MATTHEW McDERMOTT
Together for 16 Years

Matthew McDermott's message impressed his mother-in-law: "I'm going upstairs," he would call from the 104th floor of the World Trade Center, where he was a partner at Cantor Fitzgerald. Matt's working late, his mother-in-law thought. Mr. McDermott's wife, Susan, translated. "Upstairs" meant Windows on the World, two flights up the back stairs. "Matt's going for cocktails with the guys," Mrs. McDermott said drily.

Mr. McDermott, 34, partied well and often with those guys, a desk of five traders who worked together for nearly a decade. Families dined and vacationed together: the gang had just spent a golf weekend at Mr. McDermott's home in Basking Ridge, N.J., where he lived with Kara, 3, Kelly, 2, and Susan, who is pregnant.

Although Mr. McDermott might complain that his career interfered with his handicap—he was a 7, down from 4—he was a fortunate fellow and he knew it. His dawn ritual included three or four clothing changes (he usually settled on his original ensemble), the rumble of the garage door, which functioned as the girls' alarm clock, and his good-bye kiss.

"This is a good story," Mrs. McDermott said. "We were together for 16 years. Kara has Matt's smile, Kelly has his eyes—they are wonderful reminders. A lot of people look for this and never find it. How lucky am I?"

JOSEPH McDONALD
Brainy, Brawny, Balanced

To mere mortals, people with natural gifts seem to stroll down easy street. Certainly Joseph McDonald appeared that way. He towered over his six siblings athletically and intellectually, said his brother Paul.

A perennial captain, he had the generosity of soul to pick the dorky kids for his team. During high school he was courted by scouts for Major League Baseball, but he chose college.

As he aged, Mr. McDonald was no longer the best athlete, but he was usually the smartest. He could always figure out a way to win. And winning was everything.

Most people knew him as a modest, funny, social fellow. Those closest saw an occasional moodiness that would come upon Mr. McDonald, 43, a bonds broker at Cantor Fitzgerald. He felt, said Paul McDonald, that he was not fulfilling his potential.

But about three years ago, Mr. McDonald suddenly got it. He stopped competing with himself. He cut back the socializing with clients and embraced the family: his wife, Denise; his daughters, Kathleen and Brigid; his parents, Joseph and Mary. Weekends he hiked with the family and coached girls' soccer and softball in Livingston, N.J.

"He accepted that there were other ways to define himself," Paul said: he seemed imbued with faith and fresh joy, and he strolled with the lightness of a man who had found his way to easy street.

BRIAN McDONNELL
"A Cop's Cop"

Maggie McDonnell is trying to keep Christmas normal for her two children. Their Long Island lawn is decorated in lights and they will have a tree. The tree will be decorated in red, white and blue, and Daddy's police cap will stand atop it.

Brian McDonnell was a member of the Emergency Service Unit Truck 1, stationed on East 21st Street in Manhattan. He was last seen heading into the south tower.

"Brian was a cop's cop," Mrs. McDonnell said. "When people get in trouble they call the police; when the police get in trouble they call Emergency Services."

But more important to him than the job were his children, Katie, 8, and Thomas, 3. When his daughter was born, he was there in the delivery room holding his wife's hand, gently weeping.

A former Army paratrooper, Officer McDonnell, 38, was never decorated in his 15-year career because he never wrote himself up for a commendation. "He wasn't showy," his wife said. "It wasn't his nature. He just wanted to help people."

Once, he saw a little girl waving to him and the mother pulled her in the window and scolded her: " 'Don't wave to him, police are bad,' " Mrs. McDonnell recalled. "It crushed him."

JOHN FRANCIS McDOWELL Jr.
Determined to Live in Style

There was never a time when John Francis McDowell Jr. did not care about living in style. "He got his first Polo golf shirt in elementary school, and he just thought it was the cat's meow," said his sister, Megan.

"He'd buy Ralph Lauren cologne, boxer shorts, dress shirts, everything. And he loved Hermès ties."

For some years after college, Mr. McDowell was more intent on golf, skiing and partying than on making a career. But eventually, the connections he made caddying in the Hamptons helped land his dream job at Sandler O'Neill, in the World Trade Center.

As his father tells it, Mr. McDowell was on the golf course six years ago, with a man who had previously interviewed him, when it began to rain. Mr. McDowell got him under a tree and kept talking about the job until the man finally said that if he would just stop talking, he could start Monday morning.

"When he got the brokerage job, and he had to go to Brooks Brothers and buy a dress suit, he was on top of the world," his sister said.

"He never did anything halfway, or quietly, or without thinking of those he cared for," said his fiancée, Bebe Morrissey. Shortly before Sept. 11, she said he told her: " 'I have no regrets and I don't intend on living life where I will create any. It's no way to live.' "

EAMON McENEANEY
A Man with a Secret

Sometimes a wife learns things about her husband after he is gone, and this is how it has been with Eamon McEneaney's wife, Bonnie. She knew that Mr. McEneaney, a senior vice president at Cantor Fitzgerald, had escaped from his office on the 105th floor after the 1993 bombing of the World Trade Center, but she did not know he had been a hero.

"He saved the lives of 63 people," Ms. McEneaney said from their home in New Canaan, Conn. "They were hysterical, and he pulled them together and wet paper towels for them to put over their faces and made them form a human chain and took them down the stairs. All he ever told me was that he came down the stairs with some friends."

Eamon McEneaney, 46. A star lacrosse player at Cornell University who had been painted by LeRoy Neiman; a father of four; a man, his wife says, who was very much like a leprechaun. He is not on the list of the dead, but his family has released his obituary and his wife says she has had enough conversations with other Cantor Fitzgerald wives who spoke with their husbands at the time of the attack to know what happened: there was fire, the stairs were engulfed in flames and the heat was bad.

Ms. McEneaney did not get the opportunity to speak to her husband. She was on the way to her office, and he left a message with her assistant: A plane had hit the building; tell Bonnie that he loved her, that he loved the children, and that he was on his way out.

JOHN T. McERLEAN Jr.
The Games of Life

He admitted that it was a silly T-shirt, but for John McErlean Jr. it tapped into a deeper truth. The words emblazoned on it were "Life Is Good," and he bought it last summer when he and his wife, Beth, returned to Nantucket, where they had spent their first vacation together 15 years earlier. On that earlier trip, though, they did not have four children in tow.

"John said, 'It seems so simple, but it's true: I've been blessed with a wonderful family and everything I wanted from life,' " she recalled.

The entire family agreed that last summer's was the best vacation they had ever had—they biked, flew kites, kayaked and built a bonfire on the beach one evening with some of Mr. McErlean's colleagues from Cantor Fitzgerald, where he was a partner. Still, returning home to Larchmont, N.Y., was hardly a letdown. It was where he had grown up, where he and Beth had dated in high school.

Girard Smith, who was Mr. McErlean's neighbor, paddle tennis partner and close friend since the fourth grade (they even chose the same college, St. Michael's in Vermont), said the finest testament to Mr. McErlean was "how many people called John their best friend."

He talked of Mr. McErlean's a joyous belly laugh and good-natured competitive streak.

"Johnny could make games out of anything," he said. "Traveling to college we would play Name That Tune on the radio for three hours. He always did things like that with his wife and kids, making a game out of life to make it more fun."

DANIEL F. McGINLEY
Singing for Parties

Every March 17, Daniel F. McGinley took the day off from work, got his children out of school and took them and his wife to New York City for the St. Patrick's Day Parade. A devoted Roman Catholic and proud Irishman, Mr. McGinley was known for singing at every party he attended or gave, with "Danny Boy" his most requested number.

"He was always working his beads," said his wife, Peggy. She told the authorities that they would probably find a rosary on him at the World Trade Center, where he worked as a senior vice president at Keefe, Bruyette & Woods.

Mr. McGinley met his wife at Seton Hall University, where he graduated with a degree in theology. They married 12 years ago, had five children, and lived in Ridgewood, N.J. Mr. McGinley, 40, coached his children's soccer, baseball and ice hockey teams, and he himself was a passionate hockey player, said his sister-in-law, Mary Lou Margel.

MARK RYAN McGINLY
In the Heart of It All

From his days in high school in Vienna, Va., Mark Ryan McGinly had eyes only for New York City. He told anyone who would listen that one day, he was going to live and play in Manhattan. And Mr. McGinly, a 26-year-old trader for Carr Futures, wound up living in the heart of the city, on the Upper West Side in a little apartment on 68th Street, near Columbus Avenue. It was the life he dreamed of—no need for a car, a party on every corner and a job with overnight hours that came with one irresistible perk: he could work and watch the 11 P.M. edition of *SportsCenter* without interruption.

"I'd call him every Monday morning to make sure he made it through the weekend," said Mr. McGinly's best friend from high school, Brian Cramp. "He loved that he was in a city where he could be out until four or five in the morning doing whatever. The only thing he didn't like was Times Square."

At a recent memorial service planned for 500 relatives and friends, 1,500 people from around the world came to celebrate Mr. McGinly's life and say good-bye. It's something his family and Mr. Cramp are still waiting to do.

"There is no closure yet," Mr. Cramp said. "He was on the 92nd floor, where the plane hit directly. It would help if they could somehow find his body. But I think we'd be happy just knowing that he didn't suffer, that when the plane hit it took him out in a matter of seconds."

WILLIAM E. McGINN
Firefighting, Not Engineering

William E. McGinn was a civil engineering major at Hunter College. But he spent much of his spare time hanging out at the firehouse in Spanish Harlem where his uncle Kevin was a lieutenant. Some time around sophomore year, he took an exam that was not in any of his courses: the firefighter's test. By the time he graduated, he had decided that being a civil engineer would be boring, so he became a firefighter.

Eighteen years later, in September 2001, Firefighter McGinn was Lieutenant McGinn of Squad 18, a special operations command based in Greenwich Village, a father of two, Cub Scout leader and the only male member of the school leadership team at his children's school in Riverdale in the Bronx.

Lieutenant McGinn, 43, used his engineering skills mostly to demolish parts of the house, but he used them on the job, too. "He understood how structures and materials fail," said Dr. Anne Golden, an epidemiologist, who was Mr.

McGinn's college sweetheart and who later became his wife. "He would have had a field day with this one."

Squad 18 was one of the first on the scene on Sept. 11 and lost all seven men, but Lieutenant McGinn had already passed on the firefighting itch. For the past two years, a kid from Staten Island named Sean Bradley spent much of his spare time hanging around Squad 18, where his uncle Billy was a lieutenant. Now Sean, 17, has decided that he wants to be a firefighter, too.

THOMAS H. McGINNIS
Sports and Reading

After Thomas H. McGinnis and his wife, Iliana, scrimped, saved and bought their dream house in Oakland, N.J., in 1999, he left the decorating details to her, all except for the entertainment center. That demanded extensive research, his specialty, and he ended up with a wide-screen television with reception sufficient to zero in on practically every sporting event in the world. Besides loving sports, especially Rangers hockey, Mr. McGinnis, 41, was a voracious reader: he scoured five newspapers a day, a habit that met with disbelief from his fellow brokers at Carr Futures.

"He read everything," said his wife. "If he wanted to know more about Ben Franklin, he'd pick up four books and read them all."

A city kid, he thrilled to the rhythms of suburbia: the new house; Havana, the golden retriever; and his daughter Caitlin, at 4 a seasoned traveler who accompanied her parents on business trips to Europe and made yearly visits to Disney World. On her first, when she was just starting to toddle, she walked hand-in-hand with Snow White in the Halloween Parade and Mr. McGinnis proudly recorded every step on his video camera.

They planned another Disney visit for fall 2001, with Caitlin dressed as Sleeping Beauty. "I think he would want us to still go," said Iliana McGinnis. "We'll see."

MICHAEL G. McGINTY
Finally Putting Down Roots

Growing up in an Air Force family, Michael G. McGinty moved many times, so when he and his wife, Cynthia, bought their first house in Foxboro, Mass., he put down roots, planting flowers to attract birds and butterflies, and becoming a chairman of the deacons of the Bethany Congregational Church.

But his great joy in life was being the father of David, 7, and Daniel, 8, Mrs. McGinty said. "I'm the one to say it's time to do homework, but he would come in and it would be a game."

The night before Mr. McGinty, 42, left for a meeting of the global power group of Marsh USA at the World Trade Center, he and his wife had a great conversation where everything clicked, and they felt really good about their family and children.

"I'm so glad that's the last conversation we had," Mrs. McGinty said. "I really hang on to that. It could have been about calling a plumber, but it wasn't."

ANN McGOVERN
The Light of Her Life

On a return trip from Long Island to her apartment in Manhattan just before Sept. 11, Terry McGovern had the sudden idea to surprise her mother, Ann McGovern, with a visit. In her arms, she carried her newborn, Liam Andrés.

To her delight, Mrs. McGovern, who was in the shower, ran to meet them at the door, half dressed and dripping water, and began yelling for her husband: "Larry, Larry, look who is here! Liam is here! Liam is here!"

And that's how Ms. McGovern says she will remember her mother: exuberant, happy, full of life. Mrs. McGovern, who lived in East Meadow on Long Island, was a claims analyst for the Aon Corporation and worked on the 93rd floor of 2 World Trade Center, the first tower to collapse. A native of the Bronx, Mrs. McGovern drove a black sports car and was an avid golfer who had recently made a hole in one.

But her biggest thrill, Ms. McGovern said, was her youngest grandson, Liam Andrés, born in the summer of 2001. Several times a week, she would leave her job and sneak in a visit with her daughter and the baby in the Upper West Side.

"She'd drive me crazy," Ms. McGovern said. "She would show up at all hours, saying she just had to see him. She called him the light of her life."

SCOTT M. McGOVERN
A Secret Santa Revealed

On Christmas morning 1989, a struggling waitress and single mother living in a dreary basement flat in Staten Island woke up to find a set of Matchbox cars and a snowsuit on the doorstep for her son, accompanied only by a card that said: "To Eric. Love, Santa."

The woman, Susan Trainor, did not know who had left the presents. Everyone she knew denied having anything to do with them. Then, in September 2001, she picked up a newspaper and saw a memorial notice for an old friend, Scott McGovern, written by his mother. "He had his silent charities," Ms. Trainor said she read from the notice.

"He knew a woman with a toddler, and on Christmas Eve . . ." Ms. Trainor stopped reading and began to cry.

That was Scott M. McGovern to a T, said his wife, Jill McGovern. Mr. McGovern, 35, a trader at Euro Brokers in 2 World Trade Center, was always trying to figure out how to make someone happy.

Just before bedtime, Ms. McGovern said, her husband would pick up Alana, the older of their two daughters, wrap her in a blanket and walk out to the driveway of their house in Wyckoff, N.J. "Where are you going?" Ms. McGovern would ask them. Scott would whisper back, "We're going to wish on a star."

STACEY S. McGOWAN
Known by Her Embrace

Stacey S. McGowan was known for her hugs—just part of a comfortable feeling she engendered that a friend chose to call "Staciness."

"Hers was a hug that would essentially render every other hug you'll ever receive in your life a complete insult to hugging," said the friend, Patrick Corry, in a eulogy.

Tom McGowan, her husband, elaborated from their home in Basking Ridge, N.J.: "She made those around her feel better about themselves and the life they're in, just through the enjoyment of them, you know?"

Stacey Sennas McGowan, 38, a managing director for Sandler O'Neill Partners, was president of her class each year at Nyack High School and played for its varsity lacrosse team and later, for Boston College. It was at college that Tom McGowan, now an executive in foreign exchange marketing for Reuters, first saw her and fell in love. They were married nearly 10 years ago and had two daughters, Ryan, 5, and Casey, 4.

"She had no pretensions and she loved life every day," he said. "She was just warm and giving and happy and funny, proud, strong and graceful. I never met a saint, but this girl certainly was a saint."

FRANCIS McGUINN
Show Tunes and History

Everyone knew to be there at 5 o'clock, no excuses. They came. They listened. They had great fun. When Francis McGuinn was growing up, his entire family—including aunts, uncles, his grandmother—assembled at 5 P.M. each day to listen to music. Show tunes were the emphasis. The McGuinns were major Gershwin lovers. They played Cole Porter. Naturally, they played Sinatra.

That attachment to show music never left Mr. McGuinn. He had quite a voice, and as his wife, Lynn, put it, "If we were out to dinner and there was a combo, he didn't need much prodding to go up there and sing."

Mr. McGuinn, 48, a managing director and bond trader at Cantor Fitzgerald who lived in Rye, N.Y., with his wife and three daughters, also had an abiding interest in military history, especially the Civil War and World War II. He still had his collection of hand-painted soldiers from his childhood.

Though slightly too young to be drafted into the Vietnam War, he badly wanted to volunteer. His parents talked him out of it, yet he regretted not having served. "He always talked about it," his wife said.

"He'd be going on: 'I should have. I should have. I should have. I know how to take a hill.' At work, he'd tell his co-workers, 'Let's go grab that hill.' I have to tell you, if he were alive today, he'd be going over to Afghanistan. He'd be there."

PATRICK McGUIRE
Envelope of Jokes

There it was, filed under I-J, when Danielle McGuire was looking for the insurance papers of her husband, Patrick. A big manila envelope of jokes. The Wall Street kind, from 1988. And even though her home in Madison, N.J., had been like a funeral parlor for days, "everyone just had a laugh," she said. "It was true Pat. It was almost like they were planted there on purpose."

Mr. McGuire, 40, was a money broker at Euro Brokers but had wanted to be remembered for a more important role: father to Sean, 10, Ryan, 8, Mara, 4, and Shea, 3.

"He had told the boys years ago, when they would bust his chops, 'On my tombstone I want Best Dad Ever because I spend so much time with you,' " Mrs. McGuire said. He would paint his girls' nails when they were in a giddy mood to help calm them down, his wife recalled.

"He was known by everyone for his sense of humor, his great Irish sense of humor. He could make any bad situation better by telling a joke," she said. "He was very, very devoted. He was my best friend."

THOMAS McHALE
The Happy Athlete

Thomas McHale's notions for paying his college tuition ranged from taking chances at the gambling tables in Atlantic City to working behind the counter at his parents' deli on Long Island.

Both worked, as did his romance with his wife, who said it was love at first sight on her second day at college at Oneonta State University in upstate New York. "I would never believe it was possible," Taryn McHale said of falling in love on the spot, "but it was."

They were married in 1996 and their son, Collin Thomas, was born on Oct. 18, five weeks after Mr. McHale was killed in his office at Cantor Fitzgerald, where he was a mortgage security broker.

Collin is going to follow his father as an athlete, Mrs. McHale predicted—her husband played basketball at Holy Trinity High School in Hicksville and at college and was a winner in golf tournaments.

"He has my husband's disposition," Mrs. McHale said of her son. "He is calm, laid back and happy. And he has my husband's hands."

KEITH D. McHEFFEY
An Anchor in a Crisis

Keith D. McHeffey was flying home from France in 1999 when one of the jet's engines failed and the pilot was forced to drop fuel, turn around and head back toward Ireland. In the panic, distraught flight attendants plucked Mr. McHeffey from his seat, gave him a crash course in emergency landings and assigned him the unenviable job of operating the emergency door and slide.

Mr. McHeffey, 31, inspired confidence. Friends called him for help in the middle of the night and he would come; if a house got flooded, he would be there at midnight helping.

"These kind of things sort of happened to him," his mother, Sherry McHeffey, said of the incident on the plane, which landed safely at Shannon Airport. "We were assuming this was one of the worst things that would ever happen to Keith."

The son of a broker, Mr. McHeffey had become a trader. He lived in Monmouth Beach, N.J., played in a softball league, skiied and snowboarded, played basketball and rode a mountain bike in Atlantic Highlands, near his home. In the summer of 2001, he took a job at Cantor Fitzgerald. He was planning to work in the firm's new office in Shrewsbury, N.J., which, his mother said, had been expected to open early that September but turned out not to be ready.

DENIS McHUGH
Time for Fun and Faith

It was with delight that Denis McHugh spent two weeks with his mother, Bernadette, in Italy four years ago. He took her to Florence and climbed to the top of Santa Maria del Fiore, the spectacular duomo, where he took in views of the city's skyline. They went to Rome and visited the Sistine Chapel, where they gazed upon the image of God and Adam touching fingertips in one of Michelangelo's most famous frescoes, *Creation of Adam*.

But it was not by accident that Mr. McHugh visited some of the world's most famous Catholic churches. He was devoted to his faith, said his sister, Bernadette McHugh Torres. Mr. McHugh, 36, was an Eucharistic minister at St. Peter's Church in Lower Manhattan. He gave out Holy Communion at the 9:30 A.M. Sunday Mass.

But Mr. McHugh, who worked at Euro Brokers and lived near South Street Seaport, was not Mr. Fire-and-Brimstone.

"He had a great sense of humor and he liked a good party," Mrs. Torres said. "He was always looking for a good time. But he was just really close to God."

DENNIS P. McHUGH
The Man Who Did It All

There wasn't much that Dennis P. McHugh, 34, couldn't do. He ran the New York City Marathon, played Gaelic football, married the beautiful Una Hinch- cliffe and became the proud father of Chloe, 5, and Sophie and Joseph, who both turned 1 in November. When he became a firefighter with Ladder Company 13 three years ago, "he was about as perfect as you can get," said his friend Chris Gainer, who graduated from the Fire Academy with him and, in longstanding firehouse tradition, became "the bad probie" while Firefighter McHugh was "the good probie."

On summer mornings at the family place in Montauk, Fiefighter McHugh's brothers-in-law would wake up and rush to the window, "to see if he'd done all the chores," said Rob Hinchcliffe. "By the time we'd woken up at 11 o'clock, this guy had already painted the house and mowed the lawn. It was an ongoing joke. Dennis always made us look bad as sons."

For the twins' birthday, Mrs. McHugh asked everyone in the family to write down their memories of her husband. She has created a Web site, www.nyfdwidows.net, listing infor- mation about books and other ways to cope with loss, as another tribute to him. "He was always so optimistic," she said. "He always saw the glass as half full."

MICHAEL McHUGH
Greener Grass Was Here

Michael McHugh could have stayed in London. Cantor Fitzgerald had sent him there in January to open the firm's energy desk. It meant more—possibly a lot more—money and a new future, and his wife, Maria, was ready for it.

But Mr. McHugh, 35, the sales director of Cantor's TradeSpark division, had sunk his roots too deep in Tuckahoe, a village in Westchester County. He started as an adjunct member of the village's planning board and quickly moved up to chairman. He loved the town because it was so

pleasant and because of all the "normal, unpretentious peo- ple" who live there, Mrs. McHugh said.

So in April, Mr. McHugh returned, to Maria and the three kids and the fixer-upper they had bought before they thought they could afford to live in Tuckahoe. Mr. McHugh came back so that his son Michael would not have to change soccer teams and so that he himself could run for the county board of legislators. Now his widow is running in his place.

"I thought, 'I really can't leave this hanging out,'" she said. "I have to finish it up. To complete a journey that we started."

ROBERT G. McILVAINE
Only One Dream Short

Growing up in Oreland, Pa., Robert G. McIlvaine had three dreams: to get a degree from Princeton, to experience life in New York City and to work at the heart of the financial universe.

"Bob achieved all three dreams," said Andre Parris, who was his college roommate for all four years before they graduated in 1997.

An assistant vice president for media relations at Merrill Lynch in the World Financial Center, Robert, 26, was repre- senting his company in a banking conference on the 106th floor of 1 World Trade Center when the attack occurred.

"To him, New York was the center of everything, the place to be," said Mr. Parris, adding that Robert was about to make another dream come true: he and his fiancée, Jennifer Elizabeth Cobb, were making plans to marry.

"I've known Bob eight years," Mr. Parris said, "and I feel that he had finally come into his own as a person."

DONALD J. McINTYRE
Mr. Fix-It to the End

A multitasker before the term became trendy, Donald J. McIntyre never seemed to run short on energy or good inten- tions. A Port Authority police officer for 15 years, he was also a union trustee—a vigilant, wave-making trustee, said his wife, Jeannine.

But around the house in New City, he was the sort of husband even the neighbors couldn't seem to get enough of: he shoveled driveways, ran errands, played Mr. Fix-It.

"People were always calling me up and asking if they could borrow my husband," she said. "It seems like there's nobody he hasn't done a favor for."

Mr. McIntyre, 39, banked enough overtime to take December off to stay home for the birth of their third child. He was on duty for the 1993 World Trade Center bombing, escorting workers to safety, and was on the scene of the Sept.

11 disaster. As usual, he was multitasking: when he ran into the towers with his unit, he called his wife and promised to try and get to the 84th floor to search for his brother-in-law, John A. Sherry, a missing EuroBrokers trader. And he told her to skip work that night because he would not be home in time to baby-sit.

BARRY J. McKEON
Leading by Example

Barry J. McKeon and his wife, Ginnie, were high school sweethearts. They met working at a movie theater in Levittown, N.Y.—he was an usher, she sold candy. His best friend dates back to kindergarten. "That's how he was, he was just loyal," said Tom Shannon, the kindergarten pal from 42 years ago.

Mr. McKeon, 47, was out the door at 6:30 each morning for his trip from Westchester County to Fiduciary Trust International, at the World Trade Center. When he walked back in the door, 7:30 P.M. at the earliest, if one of his four children needed help with homework, he was ready to sit down and help out.

A gifted athlete (and avid golfer), Mr. McKeon always led by example, Mr. Shannon said. "I'm totally convinced if Barry had thought of himself on Sept. 11, he'd still be alive," he said. "If he saw someone struggling, he'd be the last one out."

DARRYL L. McKINNEY
Wanting to Go Further

When Darryl L. McKinney was growing up in Soundview in the Bronx, his mother used to call him Dennis the Menace. He was the type of child who, as she puts it, "always ventured out." He wanted to go further, discover new things. He seemed to sense that no matter what he thought about doing, he might actually be able to pull it off.

Mr. McKinney's childhood was not easy. His parents split up, and he and his brother and sister spent eight years living with relatives, apart from each other. Mr. McKinney dreamed of becoming a professional basketball player. He took his team at Elmira College to the college finals and got a bachelors degree in political science and a master's degree in education.

Mr. McKinney, 26, worked as director of a youth program in the Bronx, then as a district manager for Coca-Cola, said his mother, Rubina Cox-Holloway. Several years ago, he became a brokerage clerk at Cantor Fitzgerald. He was preparing to take the test on Sept. 22 to become a broker, and was engaged to a fellow Cantor employee, Angela Rosario, who was also lost in the attack.

"He would have had his license and would have begun his career," Ms. Cox-Holloway said. "I think he did pretty good, coming out of the South Bronx, an African-American man."

GEORGE PATRICK McLAUGHLIN
Psst, It's a Secret

George Patrick McLaughlin grew up as the middle child and only boy among four sisters. He was the peacemaker, the practical joker, the one who could never keep a secret.

"Mom, I'm not supposed to tell you this," he would say if a surprise party was being planned. "But we're having a birthday cake."

His college major was girls, said his mother, Dorothy McLaughlin. When he had a graduation party in Ocean City, N.J., where the family goes for the summer, a family friend remarked that he had never seen such a mixed group, all getting along. "He's the core of many of his friends," Mrs. McLaughlin said. "He likes to keep people happy."

On Sept. 9, Mr. McLaughlin, 36, and his sisters celebrated their parents' 40th anniversary by going to Mass in Somers, N.J., where they were married. Afterward, Mrs. McLaughlin remembered, "His father told him he should get a girl like me. And I told him he always had one. He looked at me and said, 'What do you mean?' And I said, 'You've got me.' And he smiled and hugged me. And he went home.'"

ROBERT C. McLAUGHLIN Jr.
Tough Guy and Poet, Too

Robert C. McLaughlin Jr. ran with the bulls in Pamplona, visited the killing fields in Cambodia and sailed the South China Sea.

He played rugby and lacrosse in college, and later, as vice president for emerging markets at Cantor Fitzgerald, romped the playing fields of American capitalism. He was a man of adventure and action, a tough guy.

He also wrote poetry. This wasn't something he shared with many people, and he didn't do it often. But every now and then, when he felt particularly moved, he found his voice in verse. It happened in 1999, the night before his wedding, recalled his wife, Liz. And it happened again in April 2001, when he began a new poem about their first child, Nicholas, then 4 months old. Like many new fathers, Mr. McLaughlin, 29, of Pelham, N.Y., was endlessly fascinated by the infinitesimal ways in which Nicholas was growing and becoming. He wrote:

Open your eyes young Nicholas
Open and see the colors
Of the world around you
Roll over young Nicholas
Roll over and see the light

Of day that awaits you
Crawl young Nicholas
Crawl and peer over the edge
Of experience that awaits you
Walk young Nicholas
Walk and find—

The last verse was a work in progress. "That's as far as he got," Mrs. McLaughlin said.

GAVIN McMAHON
A Life of Adventure

Gavin McMahon was awfully adventuresome for an insurance executive. He loved Formula One racing, followed an Irish punk rock band called Stiff Little Fingers, and fractured his skull once when he fell out of a window where he had been playing air guitar.

A world traveler, Mr. McMahon, of Bayonne, N.J., made friends wherever he went. Since he disappeared Sept. 11 from the 105th floor of 2 World Trade Center, where he was meeting with colleagues at Aon, his girlfriend, Bridget Fitzpatrick, said she had heard from friends in Singapore, Australia, Paris, London and Mr. McMahon's hometown, Chester-le-Street, England.

Mr. McMahon, 35, moved to New York five years ago, but he was still the Sunderland Football Club's biggest fan. The team, based in northern England, is expanding its stadium and Mr. McMahon's chums are building a wall there in his honor.

A celebration of Mr. McMahon's life was held recently at the North Moore Bar in lower Manhattan, just as he had wanted it.

"He was never, ever sad," Ms. Fitzpatrick said. "He squeezed every bit out of life that there was. His catchphrase was, 'I hope I live before I get old.' And he really did."

EDMUND McNALLY
The Joy of Shopping

Edmund McNally was in the market for a new car. He was thinking about a Volvo, but he wanted to be sure. He read up on other options in the automobile magazines. He went to dealerships and drove some of the possibilities. A BMW. A Mercedes. This research went on for a year. Finally, he knew the best car for him—a Volvo.

Mr. McNally loved cars but he also loved shopping, so what difference did it make how long it took to buy something? He enjoyed the process. In particular, he got a thrill out of finding the absolute best price.

"We had role reversal," said his wife, Liz. "I shop under pressure. He enjoyed shopping." Mr. McNally, 40, a senior vice president and director of technology at Fiduciary Trust, lived in Fair Haven, N.J., with his wife and three children, Brienne, Erin and Shannon, and in a lot of ways he was an oversized child. He relished playing tennis with his wife and going to the beach to ride his body board in the water with the children. Last year, the family took its first trip to Disney World.

"He went on all the rides and had the most fun of all," Mrs. McNally said. The next thing he had his eye on was getting a sailboat. "He was warming me up to getting one," Mrs. McNally said. "I think he had a ways to go. But he knew me. It took time, but he would get his way."

DANIEL W. McNEAL
The Heart in the Three-Piece Suit

Daniel W. McNeal wore a three-piece suit in high school. He followed the stock market, loved Ronald Reagan and considered politics as a profession. His mother advised against it. So Daniel went to business school at Georgetown University and one year ago became an analyst for the firm of Sandler O'Neill on the 104th floor of 2 World Trade Center. His plan was to make a name for himself on Wall Street, then write books and become a professor at Georgetown, his sister, Kathleen, said.

In the meantime, his annual Christmas present to his family in Towson, Md., was a trip to New York City and a night on the town.

"He was so proud of New York and the people he had met and the places he had been," she said.

Daniel liked helping people. Once, on a golf course, he threw himself between a hurtling ball and a woman who was about to be hit, Kathleen said. The woman emerged unscathed; the gentlemanly Daniel ended up bleeding from the head and apologizing profusely to the golfers, whose ball he had intercepted, for having interrupted their game.

SEAN PETER McNULTY
Planning Family Business

The mother wept when she learned she given birth to a boy.

It was 1971, and the nun at the Roman Catholic hospital assured her there would be no more Vietnams by the time her son grew up. The mother, Rosanne McNulty, took comfort in those words for years to come.

"But war came and got him anyway," Mrs. McNulty said. Her son, Sean Peter McNulty, 30, was a trader on the international desk at Cantor Fitzgerald.

He was the first boy of five children in a close-knit family—so close that Mr. McNulty was unable to stay at State University at Albany for longer than a month because he missed his family.

He was also eager to start a career on Wall Street, where he began as a gofer at Prudential Securities. He eventually worked his way up to the trading desk, and later moved to Société Générale Crosby Securities. He turned down a job offer from another company to work in Hong Kong because it was too far from home.

He lived just blocks away from his childhood apartment at 68th Street and York Avenue. He recently told his family that he was looking forward to quitting Wall Street and joining his mother and father, Gerald McNulty, in Venice, Fla., where they retired in 1996. He and his brother, Richard, had talked about opening a family business in Venice.

ROBERT McPADDEN
"Fireman Bob"

Robert McPadden liked to be tested. He did not wait to see if he could withstand challenges—he sought them out.

He liked comparing his personal favorites to the critics' Top 10 lists. He was so good at *Jeopardy!* that other firefighters thought he was watching reruns of shows he had seen. He was confident enough to marry a woman almost as tall as he and as much of an athlete: when Kate and Bob McPadden played one-on-one basketball, he won the scrambles, she beat him on the foul line.

Could he best his late father, a New York City Fire Department lieutenant? For years, he waited to be accepted into the department and dreamed of making captain.

Confident, yes; attitude, no: although Firefighter Mc-Padden, 30, had a master's degree in criminal justice, as a new member of the crew he happily peeled potatoes, washed everyone's dishes and led schoolchildren around Engine Company 23 in Manhattan, saying, "Hi! I'm Fireman Bob!"

Last summer was truly his championship season. He hit the tying run that helped Engine Company 38 win the Bronx title. His young marriage glowed. Kate and he were a day away from moving to Pearl River, N.Y., near his mother and siblings. So excited was Firefighter McPadden about life that he would shout, "We won, Kate, we won!"

TERENCE McSHANE
The Friend Collector

The life of Terence McShane, so full and so brief, could be measured by his friendships. There were the buddies from Sts. Cyril and Methodius parish, St. Anthony's High School, lifeguarding, Siena College, rugby, his decade as a New York police officer, and the two years he spent as a city firefighter.

"Terence was still friendly with guys he went to nursery school with," said his older brother, Kieran. "He'd bump into someone and start talking, and I'd say, 'Who was that?' "

"Some girl I went to third grade with," he would answer.

What drew people to him? Maybe it was the way he had mastered the art of drawing the best from small moments. Take one of his approaches to fatherhood: pushing a kids-packed stroller while in-line skating. Shirtless. Along Montauk Highway.

Firefighter McShane, 37; his wife, Cathy; and their three children—the oldest of whom is 7—had been living at a relative's house while their home in West Islip, on Long Island, underwent a wholesale renovation. And when he disappeared in the firestorm of Sept. 11, the Buddies of McShane banded together to finish the job.

Cathy McShane was back at the house about two months later, preparing it for her family's first night there in months, when four men in uniform appeared at the door with the awful but welcome news: they had found her beloved Terence's remains. "I told everyone all along that I didn't want to come back to the house without him," she said. "And in a way, I didn't."

TIMOTHY McSWEENEY
Everyone's Gentle Giant

Timothy McSweeney was a big man—6-foot-3 and far from spindly—but sweet as the day is long. "They called him the Big Guy, or the Gentle Giant," said his wife, Debbie. "Everyone was drawn to him."

He spent 14 years as a firefighter with Ladder Company 3 in the East Village, and eventually was in charge of so many things: paying the bills, going to the grocery store, cooking elaborate roast beef dinners for the company.

His best friends were other veteran firefighters from Ladder Company 3, Mrs. McSweeney said, but he also looked out for the new firefighters, the ones who are often awkward and nervous about the job.

He loved being part of a busy firehouse. He won six awards for heroism, but hardly anyone knew it, said his father, Dennis, a retired battalion chief. "He didn't brag about it," he said.

And he raced back to Staten Island at the end of every shift to be with his children: Dennis, 4, Margaret, who was 2 in December, and Patrick, 1.

When his wife got home from work, there they would be: Firefighter McSweeney, 37, in his brown armchair with one child perched on his shoulder, another cradled in the crook of his arm, the third nestled on his lap.

"Like one great big person," Mrs. McSweeney said.

MARTIN McWILLIAMS
Jack-of-All-Trades

There are men who are handy around the house, and then there was Martin McWilliams. At age 4, he grabbed a screwdriver from his father's toolbox—correctly choosing a Phillips head—and dismantled the neighbors' storm door. When he grew up, there was no stopping him from tiling kitchens, installing new windows and siding, or putting up wallpaper.

"He could do just about everything," said his mother, Mary, said. "He was always ready to help."

Firefighter McWilliams, 35, a member of Engine Company 22 on the Upper East Side, had many other talents. He knew his way around cars and left behind several, including a 1967 Mustang, at his mother's house in Kings Park, N.Y. He was a fine skier and an accomplished cook, whose chicken francese was a family favorite.

But there was one skill Firefighter McWilliams lacked. "He could appreciate a joke, but he could never tell one," said his younger sister, Lynn McWilliams. "He would always mess up the punch line."

Toward the end of Firefighter McWilliams's life, he became a father for the first time. The baby, Sara, was 4 months old in September. "I'm in love with her," he used to tell his family.

ROCCO MEDAGLIA
"A Way about Him"

The class couple way back when, a couple with two grown daughters now, Rocco and Marian Medaglia were the talk of their high school reunion last summer: "People we hadn't seen in 30 years said, 'Oh my God, you're still together!'" Marian Medaglia recalled from their home in Melville, N.Y.

They shared the same bus stop in grammar school, started dating in junior high, married not long after high school graduation in Massapequa. "Any time we broke up, he'd tell me, 'You know we're going to get married someday.' He had a way about him."

He was a jokester, a storyteller who did not mind embellishing details. It was only natural that the Army chose him as a recruiter in the 1970s: "He could charm the pants off anybody, even make you want to join the Army," said his wife. Around Melville, she was known as Mrs. Rocco, his daughters as Rocco's kids. When ordering takeout or dropping clothes at the dry cleaner, the family never used their last name: Rocco was enough.

Rocco Medaglia, 49, was a construction supervisor for G.M.P. Inc. and was putting the finishing touches on a renovation for Cantor Fitzgerald. The project kept him so busy

over the summer that he missed the annual family vacation in Moodus, Conn., but he kept up with the weeding and transplanting in his beloved perennial gardens. And he always tended the barbecue.

ABIGAIL MEDINA
Bible Stories and Dinner

Picture the children of Bushwick, Brooklyn, hundreds of them, speaking several languages, filling little chairs, singing of love and God's mercy. It's 10 A.M. at the Saturday children's ministry. More songs, and prayers, and Bible stories. A woman moves among the young and restless, giving them treats to keep them quiet and attentive. She soldiers on, through all three preschool sessions, long past twilight.

By 6 P.M. a now weary Abigail Medina, 46, would make the eight-block journey from Metro International Church on Evergreen Avenue to her home on Jefferson, to cook: "Arroz con gandules; that's yellow rice and pigeon peas. Served with pork—we call it pernil. Hey, we are Puerto Rican," said Mrs. Medina's daughter, Enid Marie, 18, who, along with her sister, Amy, 14, and father, Eli, constituted the other focus of Mrs. Medina's life. Such Saturdays, even more than the Sunday services, were the happiest moments in her week, Enid Marie remembered.

Mrs. Medina's life in Bushwick was blessedly far from the pace of Wall Street, where she worked at Guy Carpenter reinsurance brokerage on the 94th floor of 1 World Trade Center. What helped her through many workdays were hymns, and one that she especially loved, Enid Marie said, starting to hum: "I am running to the mercy seat, where Jesus is calling."

ANNA MEDINA
She Loved to Laugh

Anna Medina had 10 brothers and sisters, perhaps 60 nieces and nephews, and the circle of grief is even wider if you count the cousins, aunts, uncles and friends in Brooklyn and her native Puerto Rico. But those she held closest were her 11-year-old son, Leonardo Acosta, and her mother, Monserrate Gonzalez, 87, with whom she lived in Park Slope.

"She loved dancing and salsa; she loved to laugh," Yvonne Mendez said, recalling two decades of friendship. "She had such a good sense of humor. And she was a strong woman. If she had problems, she never showed them. But she was really dedicated to her mother and her son. That's what she lived for."

Ms. Medina, separated from the boy's father, had cheered all summer at her son's baseball games, and recently organized a barbecue for 35 family members in Prospect Park for her mother's birthday. On Sept. 11, she arrived at Aon Consulting, an insurance company on the 101st floor of 2 World Trade Center where she was an administrative assistant, at 8:30 A.M., a half-hour early, as was her habit.

She would have been 40 years old on Oct. 6. Her family had planned a surprise party, but was to gather instead at a small Pentecostal church she attended. "She was so kind and generous," a brother, Freddy Medina, said. "We will pray for her soul."

DAMIAN MEEHAN
Golfers and Brothers

The summer of 2000, Damian Meehan celebrated a milestone best appreciated by other rookie golfers struggling for some semblance of par: he finally broke 100.

And his foursome included three of his six brothers, so the feat did not pass unverified. Several brotherly beers were shared that day, recalled his brother Michael. The Meehan boys had played Gaelic football since childhood, but recently five of them took up golf and made a habit of getting away for a weekly game, followed by a nice dinner and animated reminiscences.

Mr. Meehan, 32, was the baby of the brothers. As they grew up in the Inwood neighborhood of Manhattan, they bossed him unmercifully, but he took it in stride. Last year the brothers pitched in and completely renovated the house he shared in Glen Rock, N.J., with his wife, Joanne, and their 18-month-old son. Another baby was on the way.

In a family of police officers and firefighters, he was the quiet and serious brother, the only one of his nine siblings to wind up on Wall Street. He was an up-and-coming trader at Carr Futures, and he loved his job all the more, said his brother Michael, because so many of his bosses and co-workers were from the old neighborhood.

"Everything with us," he said, "is family."

WILLIAM J. MEEHAN
Wall Street and Harry Potter

William J. Meehan liked to say he had the ideal job. "All he had to do was give an opinion," said his wife, Maureen. But when Mr. Meehan opined, Wall Street listened: he was chief market analyst for Cantor Fitzgerald.

The job was ideal if you did not mind rising at 4:30 A.M., which Mr. Meehan, 49, did to write his column for the *Cantor Morning News*, an online newsletter. He was a fixture on the proliferating financial shows and got to banter with Louis Rukeyser on *Wall Street Week*.

A Meehan opinion was grounded in books. "He would read everything and anything," his wife recalled, "not just financial but also biographies and Harry Potter, too." He bought the early Potter books for his daughter, Katie—and ended up reading them himself. But for a man who spent many a vacation day between hard covers, Mr. Meehan was also big on the Internet.

"He was the first guy I knew to buy his Christmas tree online," said Steven Montano, the *Morning News*'s managing editor. Mr. Meehan initially worked for Cantor in Darien, Conn., where he lived, getting home in time to coach his three children in Little League, flag football and basketball. But in August, as his TV appearances became more frequent, he shifted to the World Trade Center.

ESKEDAR MELAKU
"She Didn't Judge People"

"What frustrated me," said Nurya Bond about Eskedar Melaku, her closest friend, "was that she didn't dislike the people I disliked." It was no good trying to get a satisfying complaining session going, Ms. Bond said. "She'd just say, 'That's the way people are.' She didn't judge people."

Ms. Melaku and Ms. Bond, who immigrated from Ethiopia to attend Queens College, met during their first year. Ms. Bond, who was alone, wanted to quit, but Ms. Melaku persuaded her to stay and invited her to meet her relatives.

Ms. Melaku did favors often and quietly. She signed Ms. Bond's name as well as her own to a baby gift—which mystified Ms. Bond when she was thanked. She asked after the ailing mother whom an acquaintance had mentioned months before. Ms. Melaku, 30, was an assistant vice president at Marsh & McLennan, and three-quarters through her C.P.A. exam.

Off duty, she tried some new things. "Would you like to suffer through the opera?" she asked Ms. Bond recently. Unsurprisingly, they found something else to do.

ANTONIO MELENDEZ
A Dream for His Children

Antonio Melendez had worked in the kitchens of some of the fanciest restaurants in town, and he could have taken his daily meals there, too.

He chose not to.

Every day, after an eight-hour shift that began at 6 A.M. in the kitchen of Windows on the World, Mr. Melendez, 30, rode the train back home to Hunts Point in the Bronx. That is what his wife, Julia Hernandez, 27, remembered of his ritual: "He wouldn't eat at the restaurant. He would wait to come home and eat with the kids."

They had four children together, the eldest, 11, the youngest, barely 1. The couple had been together since they were practically children themselves back home in Acatlan, a village in Puebla, Mexico: he was 18, she 15. He was the first to head north, first to California, then with her, to New York.

A month before the trade center attack, the family moved to a new apartment. All six of them, plus a dear friend who also worked at Windows on the World, squeezed into a one-bedroom apartment. Now, Ms. Hernandez said, it is just her and the children. Both her husband and his friend, Leobardo Lopez Pascual, are missing.

And what did he want for the children? Nothing but a life different from his own, Ms. Hernandez said. "To study, to be somebody in life," she said, "so they didn't have to be like us, to work like us."

LEOBARDO LOPEZ PASCUAL's portrait appears on page 383.

MARY MELENDEZ
A House for the Late Years

Mary Melendez doted on her husband and four children. In early 2001, she moved her 9-to-5 work schedule at Fiduciary Trust up an hour so she could spend more time with them in the evenings.

Her 18-year-old son, Ricky, was graduating from Marine training on Sept. 13 in North Carolina, and she was eager to attend. "Ricky wasn't here, but she wrote to him every day about everything, including the traffic, or what the family had for dinner," said Kathi Olivo, her niece, "Once, he asked her not to describe their dinners in so much detail because she made him hungry."

Mrs. Melendez, 44, and her husband, Raymon, recently left Jersey City and bought a four-bedroom ranch-style house in Stroudsburg, Pa. "They were looking forward to growing old together in that house," her niece said. "We all miss her, especially Raymon. They were together for so long. He applied for her death certificate on Sept. 27, their 26th wedding anniversary."

CHRISTOPHER D. MELLO
Cartoons at Conference Calls

Christopher D. Mello was handsome. (He had "a kinetic smile," said his father, Douglas Mello.) He was athletic. (He led his high school football team to the New York State finals.) He was polite. (He wrote a thank-you note to his interviewer after getting into Princeton.)

At 180 pounds, he was too slender even for Ivy League

football, so he turned to rugby at Princeton. In Boston, where he worked as an analyst for Alta Communications, he took up boxing. But Mr. Mello was also a poet, a film buff and an artist.

"If there was one thing Chris would have wanted to do, it was be a cartoonist," said his girlfriend, Kristy Walsh. An aficionado of "Garfield" and "Calvin and Hobbes," Mr. Mello created his own cartoon characters and would doodle during pauses in his countless conference calls.

A father and a girlfriend see a man through different lenses, but both agreed that Mr. Mello was exceedingly loyal to friends. Ms. Walsh recalled the day she and Mr. Mello drove four hours to see her sister perform a three-minute dance piece. Two thousand people came to the wake after he died on Flight 11. He was 25.

After Sept. 11, Ms. Walsh learned that Mr. Mello had saved a valentine she sent him in fifth grade.

DIARELIA MENA
A Line of Strong Women

Strong women they make in Diarelia Mena's family: matriarchs, and lots of them, too—six sisters in Diarelia's mother's generation. And who can count all the cousins between here and Panama City who keep in touch through a sprawling e-mail group? Diarelia Mena was the youngest, the baby, the much fussed-over little princess, and didn't she know it, with her winning smile, her spontaneous three-day jaunts to the Bahamas?

She became a mother herself—her daughter, Karelia, is 2—and she married the toddler's father, Victor Barahona, whom she had known from her childhood visits to Panama from Brooklyn. But like other mothers in her family, Ms. Mena, 30, worked hard outside the home, too: she was a computer programmer at Cantor Fitzgerald, regularly arriving there around 10 A.M., after household chores were done, and staying late. On Sept. 11, she showed up before 9 A.M. so she could leave early, to begin graduate courses at Columbia.

She needed to make more money for, among other life necessities, shoes. Ms. Mena was a tall woman who craved stiletto heels, wedges, sandals, boots; the more the better, the higher the better yet. Now see her as her mother remembers her: after midnight on Christmas Eve, visiting family in Panama City, her long hair loose as she moves from house to house, nibbling tamales, dancing the merengue until sunrise, swaying confidently on those towering shoes.

The scaffolding used by workers who decorate the Christmas tree at Rockefeller Center, draped with a three-by-fifty-foot American flag in memory of the terror victims. (*Don Hogan Charles*)

CHARLES R. MENDEZ
"I Have No Regrets"

Charles R. Mendez was a reed of a boy who grew up to be a "good-sized" man with a heart to match, said his mother, Doris Mendez. When Mr. Mendez's father died, he was a tremendous help to his mother, even though he was only 21.

Mr. Mendez was a firefighter with Ladder Company 7 in Manhattan. His last job was at the World Trade Center. He was 38.

"He was sort of quiet but well-liked all over," Mrs. Mendez said. "He wanted to be a policeman, first. Then he was working for a bank but when the Fire Department called him, that was his glory. He loved that job."

Firefighter Mendez's wife, Kelli, said her husband so enjoyed his job that there were many mornings he rose early to leave home in Floral Park, on Long Island, to get to work. When he was not working, he renovated their old house, she said. He learned how to be handy by reading books.

"He was always doing something," she said. "We had a million friends and we were always out doing something. We probably vacationed five times a year. I have no regrets—we never canceled, we never said we can't go, we just did it.

"He was just a wonderful, wonderful person. If I'd known five years ago this would happen, I still would have married him. He was it. He was my best friend."

SHEVONNE MENTIS
The Youngest Grocer

At an age when most girls are focused on boys and lip gloss, 17-year-old Shevonne Mentis had not only decided that she wanted to go into business for herself, she had also opened her own grocery. It was called Shevonne's Super Center. And from opening day, it was the talk of the little seaside town of Vryheid's Lust, Guyana.

"Everybody in the neighborhood thought it was strange, a girl running a store," said her longtime boyfriend, Gary Garroway. "All the other shop owners were 45, 50 years old. But people kept pouring in."

She also ran a fleet of taxis. Mr. Garroway said she succeeded in business through a combination of toughness and sweets. "She was very strict, very formal about getting things done," he said. "But she had a very good relationship with children. She kept a wide range of confectionery, and the children would always come in after school."

In 1999, after six years at the helm of the Super Center,

Ms. Mentis left her boyfriend in charge, joined her family in Bedford-Stuyvesant, Brooklyn, and enrolled in a business management program at Borough of Manhattan Community College. She worked days as a clerk for a division of Marsh & McLennan to pay her tuition. She was 25.

Mr. Garroway closed Shevonne's Super Center to come to New York and attend her memorial, but promised that it would reopen soon. "We want that name to live on," he said.

STEVE MERCADO
Keeping a Hand in Baseball

While growing up in the Bronx, Steve Mercado wanted to play for the Yankees. And even though he ended up becoming a firefighter, he did not exactly leave his boyhood dream behind. He played softball with other firefighters. He presided over a stickball league. And he was helping to create a baseball and stickball league for children under 9.

"He had his fingers in everything," said his mother, Mary Mercado. "Every time someone calls, I say, 'I didn't know that.'"

But Mr. Mercado, 38, who remained in the Bronx with his wife and two sons, also loved being a firefighter, his mother said. He is now one of 11 firefighters missing from Engine 40, Ladder 35 in Manhattan. His parents, who live in Florida, visited the firehouse recently and were greeted with hugs and kisses from firefighters and strangers alike.

"They cry with us," Mrs. Mercado said of the strangers dropping off flowers, food and money at the firehouse. "New York City has been great. They feel the pain." But none more than her son's Fire Department brothers, she said. "The firemen are the ones that are hurting," Mrs. Mercado said. "They say they have to have hope." That is why she still spoke of the oldest of her three sons in the present tense. "I'm very proud of him," she said. "He's a great son."

WESLEY MERCER
A Veteran of Many Crises

Wesley Mercer, the vice president of corporate security for Morgan Stanley, had a way of making people feel safe. A quiet man, he often got lost in a noisy crowd. But in times of crisis, he was always the one who took charge. He was helping to evacuate employees when the towers collapsed.

"It put a hole in my stomach," said his life partner, Bill Randolph. "But I knew that's what he would have done."

At 70, Mr. Mercer had already weathered many of life's crises. A war veteran turned security officer, he was divorced and helped to raise two daughters. In later years, he lived with Mr. Randolph in the Hamilton Heights neighborhood in Harlem. Mr. Mercer dressed to inspire confidence, and even wore a sports jacket to walk the dog or shop at Pathmark. He did not own sneakers or jeans.

"He always thought the way he carried himself was important," Mr. Randolph said.

ALAN H. MERDINGER
Tae Kwon Do for Stress

After his two hours of commuting from the World Trade Center, where he was an accountant for Cantor Fitzgerald, Alan H. Merdinger spent almost every evening at Lehigh Valley Taekwondo in Bethlehem, Pa.

"It was a way to release his energy, to release any stress. He just loved being there," said Barbara Merdinger, his wife of 23 years.

His teacher, Lee Arnold, remembered a helpful, strong and funny student. "Often I would grapple with him and frustrate him," Mr. Arnold said. "He knew what to do to get me, but he was not strong enough to do it. He would get very frustrated with that, but he was a good student."

Mr. Arnold plans to present Mrs. Merdinger with the blue belt her husband, who was 47, would have earned in September.

GEORGE MERINO
Cuba on His Mind

The smell of Little Neck Bay reminded George Merino of Cuba. He lived in Bayside, Queens, but the town of Matanzas, east of Havana, on the Straits of Florida, was his real home.

Mr. Merino fled his homeland in 1968, and he came to New York City with his family to begin a new life. He was a securities analyst for Fiduciary Trust in 2 World Trade Center and would have been 40 on Dec. 18.

As he approached his 40th birthday, his mind had started to turn once more toward Cuba, said Olga, his wife. "He was thinking of getting into politics," she said. "He always kept abreast of the Castro regime and wanted nothing more than a free Cuba and to go back."

Ms. Merino, too, is Cuban. She's a city slicker from Havana. She came to America in 1970, two years after her husband came. They met at a party in New York when she was 19 and he was 20. They were married for 15 years.

Mr. Merino used to teach their daughter, Tania, 11, all about their island country, reading her Spanish news articles

he found on the Internet. They also went biking together at the Bayside Marina, where the salt air reminded him of a homeland he would never see again.

YAMEL MERINO
Fulfilled by Acts of Kindness

Yamel Merino had a soft, sweet voice and a gentle smile, yet she could be as strong as a bull. She had to lift heavy patients onto gurneys in her job as an emergency medical technician. She knew her job was dangerous. Every night, she prayed for God to protect her 8-year-old son, whom she was raising on her own.

She felt most fulfilled when she was helping people. She was one of the first people to reach the trade center complex before the first building collapsed.

The 24-year-old mother lived with her son in Yonkers. Her big goal was to return to school to become a nurse. She had struggled mightily to get where she was. She didn't finish high school, though she eventually got her general equivalency diploma. She had worked at Metrocare, an ambulance company, for more than three years. A close friend recalls she had been nervous about whether she would get the job. She need not have worried.

"They loved her," said the friend, Maureen Niciu.

RAYMOND METZ
Boston and Barbies

Raymond Metz took merciless ribbing at work for his taste in sports teams. What could he expect? He worked in New York and yet rooted enthusiastically for Boston. Not just the Red Sox; the New England Patriots were his football team. The Bruins were his hockey team. Mr. Metz even had season tickets to the Patriots.

"So he was very popular in downtown Manhattan," said his wife, Patrice. "It made for a lot of sports bets." One of the reasons Mr. Metz and his wife picked Trumbull, Conn., to live with their two young daughters was that it made the trip to the New England football games more palatable.

Mr. Metz, 37, a currency broker for Euro Brokers, was born in Ohio, but his family moved to the North Shore of Boston when he was young. He was the state champion in the hurdles in high school and continued to play hockey and ski as an adult.

When you're a Boston sports fan, you need to protect the tradition, so he was methodically indoctrinating his daughters, Natalie and Halie. "It was working," his wife said. "He used to get them all the paraphernalia from the Boston teams."

But he would settle for indulging in their interests. As

his wife put it, "He was equally happy painting the girls' nails and playing with Barbies while watching a hockey match."

NURAL MIAH and SHAKILA MIAH
The Voice of a Deer

Long ago in Bangladesh, Nural Miah's grandfather hunted birds in the jungle. The tradition lapsed when the family came to New York, until Mr. Miah, an audiovisual technologist at the World Trade Center, took it up with a fire-hot passion. He taught hunting to Mohammed Sadat, his 15-year-old cousin, and took him on week-long hunting vacations.

"We expressed our feelings," Mohammed said. "We both talked about whatever we had on our minds. Three years ago, he talked about this girl, Shakila. The parents didn't want her to get married to him. So he would leave a deer caller on the machine and when she heard the deer's voice, she'd know."

But Mohammed worried last year when Mr. Miah said he and Shakila were to be married. She was a computer technician who also worked at the trade center. "I confronted my cousin," he said. "I said, 'You're going to be married and leave me?' "

Instead, Mrs. Miah drew Mohammed in, inviting him into their new Brooklyn home, furnished with antiques and eight-point antlers. The hunting in the woods, just Mr. Miah and Mohammed, continued.

"It was peaceful," he said. "All about nature. All about relaxing. He watched out for me. He was like a brother."

PETER T. MILANO
Kind and Attentive

Thoughtful. He was always thoughtful.

The son of a good friend was starting high school. On the morning of the first day of classes, Peter T. Milano called the young man to wish him luck. At the end of the day, he called again to see how things went.

Arriving to take the commuter ferry to New York, Mr. Milano spied a pregnant young woman waiting at the end of a very long line, carrying a package. He whisked the package from her arm and escorted her to the front of the line and onto the ferry.

He never missed his son's basketball games, never missed his daughter's dance recitals. "He was an incredibly thoughtful guy," said William McGarr, a close friend.

Mr. Milano, 43, was a corporate bond broker at Cantor Fitzgerald and lived in Middletown, N.J., with his wife, Patti, and their two children, Jessica, 13, and Peter, 16.

About 20 years ago, he played in a pretty serious touch football league in Brooklyn. The field was asphalt; when the game ended, you felt it. After a championship game, he was introduced to Patti, who had come to watch. He spoke to her only briefly. When he got home, he told his aunt, "I met the girl I'm going to marry."

During every workday, even the busiest and most stressful ones, he found the time to call his wife several times, just to hear her voice and see how she was. "It always boosted his spirits," Mr. McGarr said.

GREGORY MILANOWYCZ
A Bundle of Energy

When Joseph Milanowycz visited ground zero on a late October Sunday, he roamed around, wondering where his son, Gregory, was. "We don't have anything but an urn," said Joseph Milanowycz. "He was a bundle of energy, and now there is no energy."

His 25-year-old son, a manager at Aon, lived with his parents in Cranford, N.J. He was the household handyman, fixing plumbing and electric appliances, but his true love was golfing.

"Whenever he had time, he would go to the golf courses and team up with whoever was there to play," Joseph Milanowycz said. "He could socialize with anyone. It doesn't matter whether you are a teenager, or middle-aged, or 102."

And he often traded golf clubs with friends. "When he got a golf club in the mail, he would walk around in the house, showing it to people," said Amy Verdi, Gregory Milanowycz's girlfriend of five years. "It would be like his birthday all over again. He would hold onto the club, swinging it and pretending to play. You cannot stop him from playing golf."

After his golfing friends learned that he was missing, a few dozen got in touch with his parents and donated $10,000. "These were friends we had never known," said his father, who has decided to donate the money to a New Jersey first aid squad.

LUKASZ MILEWSKI
His First Job in America

On July 11, 2001, Lukasz Milewski landed in the United States for the first time. His parents, who emigrated from Poland to New York City a year earlier, had left him and his sister, Kamila Milewska, behind to finish college.

Mr. Milewski, 21, found a summer job serving food at the Cantor Fitzgerald canteen. "He was the only Polish guy, and soon everybody knew him," said Ms. Milewska, who had come to the United States with her brother. "He was the best brother in the world. Last year, we only had each other. When I broke up with my boyfriend of six years, only he could find a way to help me. He told me that life was too short to worry."

Proud to be working in the World Trade Center, Mr. Lukasz sent many photos of himself in front of the towers to his girlfriend in Poland. He told his sister that he would keep going to school and find a permanent job in the trade center.

The family was returning to Poland in November 2001 to plan for his funeral. "We will put in the coffin his favorite CDs and T-shirts, letters from me, his girlfriend and our parents, photos and teddy bears," Ms. Milewska said. "In a way, I don't want them to find his body. I want to remember him handsome and smiling."

SHARON CHRISTINA MILLAN
A Romance Broken, Lovingly

"I used to play baseball with her older brother, Richie," Tommy Demaris was saying of Sharon Christina Millan, 30, his ex-fiancée, who worked the last two months at the trade center in the human resources department of Harris Beach, a law firm.

"This was in school, when we were young, in Astoria. One day I saw her in a little restaurant, a cafe. I asked a friend of mine who she was. And my friend said, 'Richie Villa's sister.' I thought she was stunning, a beautiful girl. She was always worrying about making other people happy," Mr. Demaris said. "She was the type like if you told her something, she'd always believe you. She'd always give you the benefit of the doubt." He added: "I'll put it to you this way.

"The day that Sharon and I finally let each other go, we sat in a restaurant in Long Island that was filled to capacity. I remember sitting there for 45 minutes, not saying a word, and both of us crying. Because we knew we loved each other, but we had to let each other go. We were best friends. That never ended."

COREY MILLER
Hobnobbing with the Past

If you wanted to find Corey Miller on a summer weekend, you usually had to look for him in Tuxedo, N.Y., where he and his fiancée, Stacy R. Rosen, would regularly hobnob with people who looked as if they had just stepped out of the 16th century.

Aside from the annual Renaissance Faire, Mr. Miller, 34, enjoyed more modern pastimes like attending Devils games or going to parties with his large circle of friends, Ms. Rosen said. And it was sometimes hard to pry him away from his computer.

Mr. Miller, the supply manager for Cantor Fitzgerald, lived in Queens with his widowed mother and was close to his younger sister Cara, who has cerebral palsy. He and Ms. Rosen were introduced by mutual friends in 1994 and started a telephone friendship that eventually blossomed into romance. Although they got engaged in December, they did not plan to get married until 2004.

Their more immediate goal was to save enough money to buy an apartment in Queens and get it set up. "A wedding is just one day," Ms. Rosen said. "An apartment is someplace you'll be the rest of your life."

DOUGLAS C. MILLER
Putting Up the Lights

Elizabeth, Rachel and Katie Miller miss their daddy. They miss sitting on Daddy's lap—all three—and watching the movie *Ghostbusters*. They miss Daddy lying in bed to keep them warm. They miss Daddy hanging them outside of windows by ropes during the family "fire drills," making small baskets under their hips. They wonder who will put the lights on the chimney this year.

Their daddy, Douglas C. Miller, 34, was a firefighter in Rescue Company 5 of Staten Island. He and their mother, Laurie, met when he was 15, she 16. He visited relatives over the summer in Mill Rift, Pa., where Laurie grew up. When he returned home to Long Island, he sent her audio tapes of his voice, telling her he missed her.

"We were young, and we were in love," she said. They married seven years later. Now in the bedroom, she hangs a 20-by-15-inch picture of him, in uniform. "I am trying to be strong for the girls," she said.

A local council member has volunteered to climb their three-story house to put the lights on the chimney.

HENRY MILLER Jr.
Gentle Procrastinator

With one exception, Henry Miller Jr., 51, made his way through life slowly, meticulously. He took maddeningly long to finish anything—woodworking, roofs, stories. His Massapequa, N.Y., garage was a testament to the potential of broken objects, the dream of a thousand somedays when he would get around to fixing them. (Enduring mystery: just how old was that slice of pie found under the scuba gear and fishing tackle?)

Yes, he took his time. Spent 28 years at the job. Countless hours giving pep talks to a woman who lived on the street; she would later credit him with her decision to get off welfare, find work, start a bank account. He was 45 before he married. And like all his projects, this one glowed: "I dunno, fellas," Mr. Miller would say to holdout bachelors, "marital bliss, it's the way to go!"

He was a steady, gentle man, slow to anger, who covered his wife Diane and her children with a mantle of security. He understood the value of time and unwavering persistence: he beat back bladder cancer and smoke inhalation, too.

What's the exceptional rush? Only to a fire: Henry Miller drove the truck for Ladder Company 105 in Brooklyn.

MICHAEL M. MILLER
No Time Like the Present

Michael M. Miller planned to get engaged on New Year's Eve 2000. But he could not wait. So he popped the question just after Christmas instead, said Patricia Skic, his fiancée.

"We were going to a wedding, and everybody at the wedding knew, and he was afraid I would find out," Ms. Skic said.

It was not the first time Mr. Miller, 39, of Englewood, N.J., had moved quickly. A three-sport athlete in high school, he was recruited to be a wide receiver at the University of Pennsylvania, said his mother, Betty Ann Miller. After college, he fulfilled his passion for speed by skiing and riding his Harley-Davidson.

A bond trader at Cantor Fitzgerald, Mr. Miller had planned to marry Ms. Skic in October 2001. "We were just going to elope and throw a party," she said. "We didn't want to spend the money for a big wedding—we were saving to buy a house in the Hamptons."

Said his mother: "He brought pleasure to a room. He was a joy to be around."

PHIL MILLER
A Call Every Morning

Years ago, Phil Miller walked two hours from his home in upper Manhattan across the 181st Street bridge to pick up his date in the Bronx because he could not afford the train and the cost of the date, too. He worked delivering newspapers so he would have enough money to take her to Greenwich Village, a big deal at the time.

After 33 years of marriage, Mr. Miller's devotion to his wife, Arlene, never wavered. Nor did his devotion to hard work, or long commutes. He was proud of being one of the youngest members of the Casualty Actuarial Society and of his position at Aon. In the summers, when the Millers left their home in Staten Island for their vacation home in the Poconos, Mr. Miller, 53, got up at 4 A.M. to take a bus to his office at the World Trade Center.

And each morning he would call his wife after he got to work, just to check in. On Sept. 11, he called from his office in the south tower. He told her he had seen the crash and was leaving; he got as far as the 78th floor.

Had he lived, the couple would have retired in four years to Orlando, Fla., near his daughter, son-in-law and two granddaughters. Now Arlene Miller is moving south sooner than expected. "My windows face the World Trade Center; I can't stay here," she said. "He wouldn't have wanted it."

ROBERT MILLER
Sports, Food and TV Shows

He was the simple, reserved, all-American type. He would talk, but not for long. Yet if you hit him with a trivia question, you got his attention. He was matchless.

Robert Miller knew his stuff. "He just absorbed a lot," said his wife, Faith. "He was very well versed. He loved sports, especially his Mets and his Jets. He loved food. People called him a restaurant guide. He knew where all the restaurants were and how good they were."

A television buff, he was attracted to good comedy, relishing everything from *The Honeymooners* to Jerry Seinfeld to Howard Stern. He'd sit for hours watching classic movies. Whatever he watched, whatever he read, the information entered his mind and stuck.

"If you needed the answer to a trivia question, you'd call him," said Steven Miller, his brother. "I have trouble remembering my kids' names. He knew everything. TV programs, you name it."

Mr. Miller, 46, was a conferee for the New York State Department of Taxation and Finance, and lived in Old Bridge, N.J., with his wife and two daughters. "He didn't have a sport or a hobby," his wife said. "He didn't fish or paint or anything. My husband was a simple, quiet type of guy who knew a lot."

CHARLES MILLS
A Lifetime of Pearls

At the end of a family barbecue on that last Sunday, the young man asked old-fashioned Charles Mills whether he had a moment for a private conversation—about his only daughter, Kari Mills.

It was to be another pearl of a moment to add to the strand of Charles Mills's life: that night in Manhattan when he first laid eyes on his wife-to-be, Mae. The purchase of their home in Brentwood, on Long Island. The birth of each of their five children. His promotion to assistant chief on the city's transit police force.

Now he was 61 years old, overweight, flirting with thoughts of retiring as an enforcement director for the State

Department of Taxation and Finance. And a young man named Keith Favarulo was seeking permission to be his son-in-law. Charles Mills said yes, of course, then went into the backyard to be with his daughter.

He gave her a bear hug, and he joked that he would have to lose weight so that he could dance with her at her wedding.

He also asked whether she was happy.

At that very moment, with a future as clear as that beautiful September night, she said that she was.

RON MILSTEIN
Cats and Calligraphy

In a most unusual way, Ron Milstein combined a love of animals and a love of calligraphy. The 54-year-old bachelor from Queens would take pro-animal sayings from famous people, inscribe them on cards and give the cards as gifts.

One quote carried this observation from Leonardo da Vinci: "The smallest feline is a masterpiece."

Another was from Abraham Lincoln: "I care little for a man's religion whose dog and cat are not the better for it."

And this from Mark Twain: "If man could be crossed with a cat, it would improve man, but it would deteriorate the cat."

Mr. Milstein was a temporary administrative worker at Fiduciary Trust at 2 World Trade Center. His cousin, Douglas Mann, said Mr. Milstein was an intelligent person who preferred short-term jobs, but work was not the main thing about him.

"He was very concerned about animal welfare," Mr. Mann said. "He was a vegetarian. He would not buy leather clothes or other animal products. He loved to come to baby-sit our cats. He wrote poetry. He had strong opinions, but if he liked you he really liked you."

WILLIAM MINARDI
The 48-Hour-a-Day Man

William Minardi lived 48-hour days. "He never sat still," said Stephanie Minardi, his wife. "He didn't want to miss anything."

And he did not. Mr. Minardi, 46, of Bedford, N.Y., got up at 4:30 A.M. every morning and worked out; traded derivatives for Cantor Fitzgerald; kept up with friends—dozens of them—from Wall Street, college and high school; played golf with clients on weekends; coached the basketball team of his 12-year-old son, William Jr.; and followed the Louisville Cardinals, the basketball team of the University of Louisville, coached by his best friend and brother-in-law, Rick Pitino.

He followed them to Tennessee, Georgia, Florida, California, Utah. Mr. Minardi and Mr. Pitino had been best friends since high school. And Mr. Pitino used to tease his wife, Joanne Pitino, Mr. Minardi's sister, that he married her "only to be close to Billy," Mrs. Minardi said.

LOUIS J. MINERVINO
A Very Quiet Life

Louis J. Minervino didn't really have hobbies. He had a job and he had a family. At work, he calculated figures as an accountant for Marsh USA on the 98th floor of 2 World Trade Center. At home, in Middletown, N.J., he helped his young daughters, Laina and Marisa, tabulate their schoolwork. Now they are college graduates.

Mr. Minervino, 54, was dedicated and disciplined. He was married for 26 years. "He was quiet, so quiet," his wife, Barbara, recalls. "He was so quiet we once asked him if he was in the witness protection program."

Saturdays were for chores around the house—chores he did with quiet precision. On Sundays, he would pile his papers on the dining room table to do office work. Some of the other habits he left behind: rotating his socks in the drawer, to put the most recently washed in the back; sharpening pencils to a perfect point; and knowing how to say good-bye.

"He never left the house without kissing everyone good-bye," his wife says. "He made a trip to each of the girls' rooms to say good-bye. And then he came to me."

Ryan Vasel, four, at a tribute to his father, Scott C. Vasel, thirty-two, November 19, at Fort Lee High School in New Jersey. Mr. Vasel died on September 11. (*Dith Pran*)

Firefighters from Engine Company 74 load a mural for their firehouse made by students at Abraham Joshua Heschel School. (*Don Hogan Charles*)

RAJESH MIRPURI
A Beloved Only Son

Rajesh Mirpuri was working in Tokyo in the summer of 1995 when his parents were celebrating their 29th wedding anniversary at their home in Englewood Cliffs, N.J. Rajesh told them he was about to take a vacation in Hawaii.

"On the day of the anniversary, he called us and told us he had arrived in Honolulu," said his father, Arjan Mirpuri, 61. "Half an hour later, the door bell rang, and it was him."

As Arjan Mirpuri told the story, tears welled in his eyes. Rajesh Mirpuri, 30, was his only child. Arjan and his wife, Indra, Hindus who immigrated from India, have built a small temple inside their house to burn incense to remember their son. "His pictures are hung all over the place," Mr. Mirpuri said.

On Nov. 2, the Mirpuris traveled to Pier 94 in Manhattan to pick up an urn of ash, provided to the victims' families by the city. Following the Hindu tradition, the parents will sink the urn in the Ganges River in India.

"When night falls, I turn the outside lights on. Maybe he will open the door and come in," Mr. Mirpuri said. "But I know it has been seven weeks. It will be very difficult."

Rajesh Mirpuri, a sales manager at Data Synapse, was attending a conference in the World Trade Center during the attack.

JOSEPH D. MISTRULLI
Building and Bonding

As a union carpenter, Joseph D. Mistrulli was good at putting things together, and he made a career of putting together some of the best-known places in New York City: the Russian Tea Room, Madame Tussaud, Niketown, Windows on the World.

But his life's work was not a building at all. It was his family. "He worked all the time, not for himself, for us," said his son, Joseph Jr. "I can't tell you the last time he did something for himself."

The elder Mistrulli, 47, was adding a second floor to the

ranch house in Wantagh, N.Y., that he shared with his wife, Philomena, and their three children. He had left his and his wife's bedroom for last.

PAUL T. MITCHELL
Mentor to the Probies

In every firehouse in New York, somebody like Paul T. Mitchell takes the probies under his wing, nurturing them and giving them just enough grief to make sure they can endure. In Fort Greene, Brooklyn, at the Tillary Street firehouse, Big Daddy Mitchell taught everything: how to jump in when trouble calls, what to grab when you hear seven bells—the code sending Ladder 110 on a run.

Lieutenant Mitchell, 46, was someone the first-year probationers looked up to. Senior man on the truck, on the back step as a fireman, in the front seat after his promotion to lieutenant. He would go in with the inside team: the guys who cut through doors, looking for people needing help. That's the kind of guy they remember on Tillary Street: husband of Maureen; a sports fan if daughter Jennifer, 20, or Christine, 18, was competing; holder of three citations for valor.

But on Sept. 11, the truck rolled without him.

Off duty, he had stopped by for coffee around 8 A.M. When seven bells rang and the truck left, he soon realized it was trouble, the worst.

Without thinking, he grabbed somebody else's bunker pants, black coat with the yellow stripes, boots, helmet. And he was rolling, too.

RICHARD MIUCCIO
Dreams of Retirement

He survived combat in Vietnam and it appeared that he had finally beaten prostate cancer after a rough siege of chemotherapy. Richard Miuccio and his wife, Joyce, were finally at the brink of their retirement dream to camp across the country in an R.V.

"He always used to say as soon as he turned 55 he would retire," said John C. Bilotti, a friend from their teenage years in the South Beach housing projects in Staten Island. "He counted the days."

But Mr. Miuccio, who turned 55 in May, never got around to filing the necessary papers with the State Department of Taxation and Finance, where he had worked for 35 years, rising to audit supervisor.

"He just kept putting it off," Mrs. Miuccio said. He was generally meticulous and methodical, whether it was at work or while playing poker, handicapping horse races or visiting his mother at St. Elizabeth Ann's nursing home every day without fail for three years.

Mrs. Miuccio, who first met her husband when she was 13, now gravitates to his home desk, where he often worked instead of going to the office—there was a meeting on Sept. 11—feeling closest to him there. "He was my whole life," she said. "He was everything to me."

JEFFREY MLADENIK
Living His Faith

Jeffrey Mladenik leaves a wife, Suzanne, two daughters, Kelly, 21, and Grace, 4, two sons, Joshua, 18, and Daniel, 17, and a baby in China named Hannah, whose exact age is unknown to her parents. Her adoption was under way on Sept. 11, when Mr. Mladenik, 43, was a passenger on Flight 11. Mrs. Mladenik plans to bring the little girl home in the summer.

Mr. Mladenik was the interim chief executive of eLogic, an Internet publishing company in Los Angeles. At home in Hinsdale, Ill., he worked with Christ Church of Oak Brook, leading discussions about faith in the workplace, using real-world cases, to solve problems from a Christian perspective.

"You couldn't be around him without being affected by his enthusiasm for God," Bill Cirignani, a friend from church, said. "I had been a Christian for six years, and had gotten stale, a little bit awry," but Mr. Mladenik, an ordained minister, reignited him, he said.

"He was actually seeking to live this radical vision of Jesus Christ, set out for us as human beings," Mr. Cirignani said. "He calls you to an extreme level of justice."

"I hope we can help Hannah learn about her dad."

FRANK V. MOCCIA Sr.
Laughter, Win or Lose

Frank V. Moccia Sr. was content to come away even. On a recent trip to Las Vegas with his wife, Elaine, and on countless trips to the Foxwoods Resort Casino in Connecticut, it suited him just fine. In fact, it didn't even matter much to Mr. Moccia if he lost—as he often did to his son and golf partner, Frank Moccia Jr., a police officer.

"Whether he won, lost, broke even, it didn't matter," said Officer Moccia. "Whatever he did, he had a good time."

Mr. Moccia was a big believer in doing things for only as long as they were enjoyable, which is why he spent 26 years working for Washington Group International, as a facility planner in the World Trade Center.

It's also why Mr. Moccia would not consider a retirement away from his home in Hauppauge, N.Y., which was near his daughter, Donna Marie Velazquiz, and her children.

His wife described her husband as "a big teddy bear" and Mr. Moccia was just that to his grandchildren.

The weekend before Sept. 11, for a granddaughter's seventh birthday, Mr. Moccia took the family on a trip to Six Flags Great Adventure. Unexpectedly, Mrs. Moccia decided to accompany her husband on one of the scarier roller coasters.

"I said the Lord's Prayer from the minute the ride started," Mrs. Moccia remembered about that day. "I squeezed his hand so tight, but he was laughing for the whole ride."

Mr. Moccia was 57.

LOUIS MODAFFERI
Modest Winner

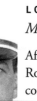

After they took the captain's test, Lts. Robert Dimperio and Louis Modafferi compared notes. Lieutenant Dimperio knew he'd aced it; Lieutenant Modafferi knew he'd done badly.

Results: Lieutenant Dimperio missed it by a point. Lieutenant Modafferi was among the top 10 scorers in the Fire Department.

Captain Modafferi, 45, who was awaiting assignment as a battalion chief, was so modest that many people had no idea about his accomplishments—although they knew all about those of Christine, 18; Michael, 16; and Joseph, 12. The captain led Staten Island's Rescue 5, an elite company that saves people from a horrendous array of precarious situations.

Captain Modafferi also worked on a federal rescue team, racing to aid victims in plane crashes and Caribbean hurricanes. To make extra money, he fixed dents in cars. As a boss, he was good-humored and fair-minded. If he was teaching you something, he acted as if you knew it already and he was just reminding you of some details.

He was a man of many loyalties: married to Joanne and the job for about 20 years; played softball with childhood friends, three of whom worked with him at Rescue 5. Rarely rattled, when he got home he relieved job stress fervently but safely: he vacuumed.

DENNIS MOJICA
A Dream Accomplished

"The first time I met him, I told people I had met a man that was 10 feet tall," said Maria Barreto about her fiance, Lt. Dennis Mojica, who was 5 feet 11 inches tall. She carefully outlines the story of his life: his mother died when he was a year old, he graduated from the competitive Aviation High School, served in the Navy for 6 years, and in the Fire Department for 29.

"It was his dream, it was his life, it was his first love," she said of firefighting. "I admired him even more because he knew what he was here for in this life. He really knew."

Lieutenant Mojica, 50, proposed five days before Christmas 2000, at her favorite restaurant, Gino's in Bay Ridge, with a ring hidden inside a walnut shell on a tortoni covered with fresh raspberries and powdered sugar. "For an old guy, I'm still trying to be romantic," she remembers him saying.

The couple enjoyed bicycling and skiing together on days off, sometimes with his 14-year-old daughter from a previous relationship. "He was always trying to extend it, one more hour, one more day," said. "Both of us appreciated so much having each other."

JUSTIN J. MOLISANI
Host with Huge Dimples

To family and friends alike, Justin J. Molisani was "as loyal as a puppy dog," said his wife, Jodi. A sizable puppy dog, mind you—a 6-foot-3, nearly 300-pound weightlifter—and undeniably loyal.

When his best friend moved into a new house, he spent four or five weekends helping with the finishing touches. When his wife's stepfather ran for office, he was there pitching in. When Bob Cecere Jr., his college roommate, was out of work, Mr. Molisani got him a job interview. When, on a "miserable, long and exhausting day," Mr. Cecere moved, Mr. Molisani was there all day helping. And if the job was demolition, he'd be there in a flash.

Mr. Molisani, 42, a senior vice president at Euro Brokers, loved to entertain. Their house in Lincroft, N.J., his wife said, was "the Christmas party house," with Mr. Molisani—known to all as Jud—the jovial host with the huge dimples, making sure every glass was full.

But the "center of his universe," she said, was his 3-year-old daughter. They could play for hours with her pretend kitchen, as she reveled in making him imaginary coffee or sandwiches.

BRIAN P. MONAGHAN Jr.
The Archetypal Good Kid

His friends nicknamed Brian P. Monaghan Jr., "slick"—but not the deceptive, smooth-talking, street-smart kind of slick. Around Inwood, where he lived, Mr. Monaghan was known as the archetypal good kid, a 21-year-old who helped elderly women across streets and went to the store for neighbors who could not.

No, they called him Slick because of the way he wore his hair: smoothed back, matinee-idol style. He grew up playing baseball and handball on the courts near 207th Street. The older guys use to tease Brian Sr., the Little League coach, that Junior was not going to be a New York Yankee. But if the former World Champs drafted on the basis of heart, Brian Jr. would have been wearing pinstripes for a living.

He chose carpentry as a profession. Sept. 11 would have been his second day on the job at Certified Installation Services on the 98th floor of 2 World Trade Center. Mr. Monaghan had already made an impression on his co-workers.

After Sept. 11, his new colleagues said what those who have known Brian Jr. all his life have said: he was a good kid.

JOHN G. MONAHAN
Bastion of the Beach

No matter what else was going on in his life, John G. Monahan always had the beach. The beach where he went jogging and swimming. The beach where he read the newspaper before taking the train to his accounting job at Cantor Fitzgerald in 1 World Trade Center. The beach where he and his wife, Diane, courted and committed to each other and returned year after year, just the two of them, just for a few days.

These were along the shores of New Jersey, the state where Mr. Monahan lived his entire life. Five years ago, at age 42, he and his wife moved from Bayonne to Ocean Township, where they lived only two miles from the ocean and where they raised their two sons, Terrence, now 6, and CJ, now 3.

But it was farther south, at Cape May, where he and his wife found their escape. They went alone once a year, "adults only," she said. The first time was in 1991; the trip was what Mrs. Monahan called a "relationship-test kind of thing."

"You're at that point when nothing the other person does gets on your nerves," she said. "In life, things get deeper as you move on, but that beginner phase is a really good spot too."

KRISTEN MONTANARO
The "Devilish" Twin

Karen Montanaro was the cautious twin. Kristen, her identical sibling, lived life with gusto. Their personalities. That's how their mother, Ellen, could always tell her twin girls apart. Kristen Montanaro, 34, was quick to spend the money she earned as an administrative assistant at Marsh & McLennan at 1 World Trade Center, shopping for clothes or traveling with her twin and her younger sister, Jamie.

"Who's going to treat me better than me?" Kristen Montanaro often told family and friends.

"If she had a dime, she would spend it on herself," said Karen Montanaro. Now, she said, her "devilish half" is gone.

Kristen was the one who sneaked out at night and then tried to con her mother into thinking she was Karen. The memory is sweet and makes Karen laugh.

They did everything together: grade school, high school, college. When Karen found a job in the Wall Street area, the twins rode the subways together. "We could go into a mall, go our separate ways and come out with the same outfits," said Ms. Montanaro.

CRAIG MONTANO
Offbeat Interests

Craig Montano met his wife by cutting in line. On the first day of college at Syracuse University, Caren Mercer was waiting to register. She had risen early to get a good spot. He had gotten up later, and was looking around for a convenient place to cut in. "Since he was cute, I let him," she said. They began seeing each other; they never stopped.

Mr. Montano, 38, a partner at Cantor Fitzgerald, lived in Glen Ridge, N.J., with Caren Montano and their three children, Christa, 7, Lukas, 4, and Liam, 10 months. He had a touch of wanderlust, for he loved to pack everyone into the car and head off somewhere for the weekend, often with no notice.

He was a man of eclectic interests. At one point, he had a specialty painting business. Then he enrolled in brewers school and worked for a brewery. He opened his own

People in Manhattan for Thanksgiving Day events stop at Engine Company 54, at Eighth Avenue and Forty-eighth Street, to pay their respects to victims of September 11. The station lost fifteen firefighters in the World Trade Center disaster. (Edward Keating)

restaurant, where he served beers he concocted. "He always had certain offbeat interests, and he always excelled," Mrs. Montano said. "But he always returned to family. That was his No. 1 interest."

SHARON MOORE
Laughing at Her Stumbles

For all of Sharon Moore's beauty and elegance—a slender 5 feet 9 inches, she was a sometime model whose photo was featured in an issue of *Esquire*—she lacked a certain physical grace. "She was a very clumsy person," said Barbara Bridges, Ms. Moore's mother. "She was always falling."

But Ms. Moore, 37, and a native New Yorker, was not embarrassed by her many stumbles. "She would come home and tell us how she fell," said her brother, Raybury Moore. "She was able to laugh at it."

Though her relationship with gravity was undeniable, Ms. Moore, a vice president at Sandler O'Neill, had another side that was less evident. "At her memorial service, I said a few words, but one thing I didn't convey is how funny she was," said her brother. She was even thinking of pursuing a career as an actor or comedian, he said.

With her gone, there is less to laugh about. Ms. Moore's son, Lance, was a Thanksgiving baby, said his grandmother. He is 15. "But I don't think there will be a Thanksgiving here this year," said Ms. Bridges. "I don't really feel like Thanksgiving."

KRISHNA V. MOORTHY
A Call That Never Came

Krishna V. Moorthy's life was just beginning to feel settled down, said his daughter, Anitha.

He viewed his job as a technology consultant at Fiduciary Trust, on the 97th floor of 2 World Trade Center, as a wonderful opportunity. A devoted if overprotective father who would come running with an Ace bandage for a scratch, he had successfully shepherded his daughter and son, Sriram, into adulthood. All this after Mr. Moorthy, 59, took a chance 11 years ago by immigrating to the United States from India with his family.

"He was one of those people never afraid to change," Anitha Moorthy said. "All of us would say, 'You're not 30, you're 59,' and he would say, 'So what?'"

On Sept. 11, Mr. Moorthy was at his desk by 7:45 A.M., and had placed his customary call to Saradha, his wife of 31 years, telling her that he had arrived safely. After the plane struck the north tower, Mr. Moorthy called his wife again, leaving a message that he was evacuating the building, and

that he would call again when got downstairs. That much is known.

But Mr. Moorthy's name later appeared on a hospital list in New Jersey, and his family does not know if that means that he may be safe somewhere. For now, they are holding on to that uncertainty.

LAURA LEE MORABITO
Manilow and Ice Cream

Laura Lee Morabito, 34, the national sales manager for Qantas Airways, met her future husband in the Jacuzzi at an apartment complex where they were neighbors. They shared an appreciation for Barry Manilow's singing, and they sat on the pool deck sharing a bottle of wine and a pizza all evening, even as rain began to fall.

"She just had a beautiful smile," Mark Morabito said.

The beautiful woman he met that night eight years ago had been a tomboy. Her older brother, Jeff DeFazio, was protective of her, and she learned to protect her younger brother, Craig DeFazio. Once, she knocked a tooth from the mouth of a child who picked on Craig.

Perhaps because Jeff had scared away her potential suitors earlier in life, she never told him about Mark until they were engaged.

"I said, 'Tell me about this guy,'" Jeff DeFazio said. He quickly decided that she had found the right match, though, and told his sister, "You guys are probably the only two people I know in the country who like Barry Manilow."

This is how Mrs. Morabito ate ice cream: she would eat only half of her portion, letting the rest melt and then drinking it slowly.

"She would just kind of savor it, as long as she could," Craig DeFazio said.

ABNER MORALES
The Biggest Dreams Remain

"The man with the golden fingers."

That is how most everyone knew Abner Morales at Fiduciary Trust, where he worked for 11 years as a Lotus software programmer.

"He's a huge loss," said his wife, Norma Morales. "He could program anything."

Mr. Morales, 37, a Brooklyn native, honed his skills at work to provide a comfortable lifestyle for his family. His earnings allowed his wife to stay at home to raise their two children, a girl, 11, and a boy, 2. The couple, who were each other's first love from high school, had been together for the last 20 years, 17 as husband and wife.

They bought their first house three years ago in Ozone

Park, Queens. They looked forward to watching their children grow up on a leafy street with neat lawns and backyard barbecues.

"We had a lot of dreams," Mrs. Morales said. "The biggest dream was having our children. I have them now. I could look at the attacks as in a negative way. But the only thing that keeps me strong are the beautiful things to remember him by. He had a great outlook on life. To know him, you would never forget him."

MARTIN MORALES
An American Dream

Martin Morales moved from a small Mexican village to New York City three years ago, seeking the storybook American life. Living in a cramped basement apartment with a half-dozen relatives in Elmhurst, Queens, he scoured Spanish-speaking newspapers for jobs, working here and there until about a year ago, when he landed a job as an assistant chef at Windows on the World, said his brother, Gonzalo Morales.

The picturesque views of Lady Liberty and Governors Island allowed Martin Morales, 22, to reflect daily on the mission ahead of him. He wanted to learn English and earn enough money to build a house in the countryside back home, his brother said.

His 9-year-old niece, Diana Narvaiz, said she would miss playing soccer with her uncle and his sense of humor. "He would always say he was going to Mexico," she said. "It was funny because he was really going to work or the store."

JOHN MORAN
Firefighter with Law Degree

John Moran was a Fire Department battalion chief and his cousin Joseph Crowley was a congressman. But when they united their voices that last Saturday afternoon, at the block party in the Rockaways—well, "The Star of the County Down" never sounded sweeter.

At 42, Chief Moran was a kayaking, tin-whistle-playing firefighter with a law degree. But he never put himself before others. When his wife, Kim, was working out of town, he fed, bathed and smothered with love their two children—Ryan, 7, and Dylan, 4—all the while ensuring that Peggy Moran, his mother who lived above him, never went wanting.

"When I saw his car outside, back home from work, that was a comfort to me," his mother said. People may never forget the taunt that Michael Moran, John's younger brother and fellow firefighter, delivered to Osama bin Laden during a nationally televised concert in October, a taunt so profane and yet so eloquent, full of Irish anger and grief.

But Kim Moran will remember the late afternoon of Sunday, Sept. 9, the day after the block party and two days before the disaster that swallowed him. Trudging up from the beach came her beaming husband, pulling his sons on that wheeled contraption he had built for his kayak.

His wife grabbed a camera and caught it: John Moran in his glory.

LINDSAY MOREHOUSE
A New York Archetype

Lindsay Morehouse, 24, was the archetypal young New Yorker: starting a career as a research assistant at Keefe, Bruyette & Woods, sharing an Upper East Side apartment with two roommates, jogging in Central Park, spending summer weekends at her childhood home in Connecticut, organizing friends to go hear her favorite band.

Ms. Morehouse was an only child who had recently volunteered to be a Big Sister. She was unusually close to her mother, Kathy Maycen, and her best friend, Sara Sparks, whom she met at boarding school. "When she had boyfriend trouble, I'd ask what her mom said before giving her my advice," Ms. Sparks said. "Her mom was her bestest, bestest friend. They talked five times a day."

Ms. Morehouse was the event planner in her circle, and she brought so many friends to hear her favorite band, Seeking Homer, that the band agreed to play at her graduation from Williams College two years ago. On Oct. 18, 2001, they will play for her again, at a tribute at the Mad River Bar and Grill, an Upper East Side hangout.

GEORGE MORELL
"He Collected Friends"

At a Giants playoff game last year, George Morell introduced himself to the legendary halfback Frank Gifford, without knowing who he was. Even when Mr. Gifford said his own name, Mr. Morell still did not know. When his friends ribbed him, Mr. Morell replied, "Well, he didn't know who I was either."

Mr. Morell, 47, a bond broker at Cantor Fitzgerald, was the kind of man who shook hands with strangers and made them his friends. It did not matter if they were celebrities or not. "George made the shoeshine guy feel like a million bucks," said his younger brother, Mark. "He didn't collect cars or postage stamps. He collected friends."

The elder Mr. Morell lived with his wife, Roberta, and their children, Nancy, George Jr., Kelsey and Harrison, in Bedford, N.Y. He liked to hunt and fish, and often took his family along. But his favorite pastime was telling stories about his encounters with life. He always had just one more to tell.

At Grand Central Terminal, passers-by stop to look at a memorial wall for World Trade Center victims. The display included fliers with photographs and descriptions of the missing that were posted in the weeks after the attack. (*Edward Keating*)

STEVEN P. MORELLO
The Silver Band

There was something about the way Steven P. Morello looked at you, grinning, that just made you want to be near him.

So much so that the woman who handled the insurance for his family's New Jersey condominium continued to take his telephone calls years after she was promoted into another division. So much so that once, his children swear, a homeless man offered him money.

"When he was talking to you it was like he was only concentrating on you," said his daughter Jessica, 24. "He was just a sparkle." He married his wife, Eileen, young, and grew up alongside his three children. He introduced them to music by playing "Puff the Magic Dragon" on the guitar and, years later, clipped articles about heavy metal bands he had heard them mention.

Mr. Morello, 52, was a facilities manager at Marsh &

McLennan. Several years ago, his grown children pitched in to buy him a silver ring. He never took it off. "It just turned out to be like a wedding band from his kids," Jessica Morello said.

YVETTE NICOLE MORENO
A Devoted "Sister"

Yvette Nicole Moreno, 24, was a gawky junior high school student when she was paired with a Big Sister, who volunteered to take her on outings to the beach, the ballet or the mall. The match was perfect. Joanne Alicea, 41, had also grown up in a single-parent home, went to Roman Catholic schools and lived in Pelham Bay Park in the Bronx.

For four years, the two saw each other at least every other weekend. They got to know each other's friends and family. And long after the formal relationship was over, they stayed in touch. Over the summer, Ms. Alicea joined Ms. Moreno and her mother for dinner at Cabana, at the South Street Seaport. Ms. Moreno was bubbling with news. She was working as a receptionist at Carr Futures, in the World Trade Center, and finishing college part time. She was dressed like the successful professional she was becoming, made-up and manicured. She was thinking about buying a car. "She was doing everything she set out to do," Ms. Alicea said.

After the trade center attack, Ms. Alicea visited her friend's mother with condolences. There was a shiny Mitsubishi outside, so new it still had temporary plates and that leathery smell. Ms. Moreno's 21-year-old brother was desperately, hopefully, polishing the chrome.

DOROTHY MORGAN
Warm Comfort in Routine

Dorothy Morgan never dressed up in stunning gowns like those in her Holiday Barbie doll collection. The fairy tale extravagance of the dolls seemed to contradict her own more conservative style. She wore solid colors and had a keen eye for bargains—Deloryce Bright, a longtime friend, called her the Coupon Queen—and preferred Chinese takeout to cooking at home.

Ms. Morgan, 47, was the fifth of nine children of working-class parents, growing up in Hempstead, N.Y. She worked in Marsh & McLennan's confidential service department, where she was a broker, assisting celebrities and high-profile clients.

She found warm comfort in routine, visiting her mother on Fridays and shopping with her daughter, Nykiah, on Saturdays. Sunday morning was always spent at church in Jamaica, Queens, in the same seat of the same pew.

Though she was a loving grandmother, buying clothes and toys for her 4-year-old grandson, Dante, and paying for his preschooling, she preserved her own independence. "She was no baby-sitter," said Nykiah Morgan.

NANCY MORGENSTERN
Cycling and Determination

Five years ago, Nancy Morgenstern tried a new kind of vacation—a bicycling tour in the West. On the most strenuous day, she pedaled from Bryce Canyon to the Grand Canyon, 110 miles. After that, bicycle racing became her passion.

But Ms. Morgenstern, 32, was also an Orthodox Jew, which, in its way, is as demanding as bicycle racing. Some people might look at the seemingly conflicting requirements of each and give up one or the other. But Ms. Morgenstern embraced them both, fully. Instead of traveling on the Sabbath, she drove for hours on Saturday nights to a race. Or she stayed in motels with her cell phone off, while the others competed on Saturdays. When the others went out for dinner, she ate the kosher food she had packed.

Last spring, Ms. Morgenstern, the eldest of five siblings and a travel agent, began working at Cantor Fitzgerald. Her sole experience in high finance was balancing her checkbook. But an executive, impressed by her determination in the face of airline snarls and efficiency in untangling them, hired her as his administrative assistant.

She was, said her Jewish friends, a me'rachim al ha'brios—a person whose compassion extended beyond her family to acquaintances and strangers, including those stuck in airports on overbooked flights.

BLANCA MOROCHO and LEONEL MOROCHO
Bringing a Family Together

About a year ago, Leonel Morocho, a sous chef at Windows on the World, got an offer he almost could not refuse: more money and a less stressful job at a top hotel.

He ended up refusing, though, because Mr. Morocho, an undocumented immigrant from Ecuador, was using his job at Windows to legalize his status in the United States. If he changed employers, he would have to persuade a new employer to petition the government on his behalf, delaying his dream of bringing his two older daughters, ages 12 and 14, from Ecuador. So he stayed, working the early shift so he could be home when his younger daughters, 8, 7 and 5, came home from school.

"At home, he was the father and the mother," said his wife of 15 years, Marta Morocho, 33. "I basically followed him around, watching what he did. He took the girls to the park, did the grocery shopping."

Mr. Morocho's sister, Blanca, died with him. He had helped bring her to the United States five years ago and had found her a job preparing salads at Windows. She was married and had one daughter, Catherine Victoria, who was 8 months old when her mother died.

The Morochos were close. On July 7, Blanca Morocho helped her sister-in-law prepare a surprise party for her brother, who turned 36. The day the towers fell was Mr. Morocho's first day at work after a two-week vacation, which he used to work as a cook for the United States Open. As always, he was saving money to bring his daughters to the United States.

Eight days after his death, his dream became a reality. The girls arrived with a humanitarian visa. They are with their mother now, in Sunset Park, Brooklyn.

"It cost him his life," Mrs. Morocho said. "But he brought them to me."

DENNIS MORONEY
The Fantastic 40

Maybe it was a bit of ego at work. Or maybe it was an early attack of male midlife crisis, sparked perhaps by one of those fleeting thoughts about mortality. Then again, maybe it was just, hey, time to boogie!

Whatever it was, starting last spring, Dennis Moroney began to talk a lot about making a big deal out of his 40th birthday, which would fall on Nov. 7, 2001. First, he told his wife, Nancy, that he wanted her to throw a big bash for him and invite all his friends from Eastchester, N.Y., where he lived, as well as friends from his office at Cantor Fitzgerald.

Then he began to change the way he lived.

"He started to work a lot harder and longer at his job," Mrs. Moroney recalled. "And he went on a diet and started exercising a lot more. When he started, he weighed maybe 215 pounds and loved to eat cheeseburgers, five or six a week. But all of a sudden he was seriously into eating veggies and regular jogging, sometimes 10 miles or more. He dropped at least 25 pounds. He was still the sweetest man who ever lived, but he also seemed to have this fresh new focus on life."

Mrs. Moroney reserved space at an Eastchester restaurant for a birthday celebration and drew up a guest list. Invitations were to go out on Oct. 1. Most of the people on the list ended up gathering in Immaculate Conception Church in Eastchester on Sept. 22 for a memorial service.

LYNNE I. MORRIS
Teaching, or Trading?

Lynne I. Morris was a cat person. Growing up in Monroe, N.Y., she and Frisky were inseparable and shared their own special pillow. At Oneonta College, she named her new cat after her dormitory, Matteson.

She worked hard on her tan each summer and during spring break sprees in Florida and Cancún, but according to her mother, Pat, that was her only glimmer of vanity.

"She always worried about everyone else's feelings more than her own," said her older sister, Chrissy, "and she said it sometimes got her in trouble."

She vacillated between wanting to teach—she did some substitute teaching in Monroe—and hankering after a business career with a more hectic pace, which was what took her to Cantor Fitzgerald straight out of college. Ms. Morris, 22, spent her first several months logging other brokers' trades into the company computers, but her goal was to make those trades herself, sooner rather than later. In mid-2000 she rekindled her relationship with her college boyfriend, Mark Chabus; the reunion took, and they were on the verge of announcing their engagement.

SETH MORRIS
All His Waking Hours

Seth Morris didn't sleep.

Well, he didn't sleep much. Four hours a night was it. His wife, Lynn, preferred eight, so while she and the three children were still in bed, he would be up doing projects.

Five years ago, the Morrises had bought a house, and he undertook renovations during the early morning hours. Mrs. Morris would wake and find that a room had been painted. New bathroom fixtures had been installed. The dining room molding had been done. He would pay bills in the middle of the night. Once, he sent an e-mail message to his great-grandmother at 2:30 in the morning.

He knew all the 24-hour businesses. On weekends, he would visit a 24-hour bagel shop and have bagels ready when everyone else awoke. He often did his shopping at Home Depot at 2 in the morning. He knew the clerk on duty on a first-name basis.

Having extra hours meant a lot to Mr. Morris, 35, a managing director at Cantor Fitzgerald. "He would actually calculate how many more hours and days and years of living he was going to have than I was," Mrs. Morris said. "The last time he did it, he said he was going to have five extra years."

His skimpy amount of sleep became a running joke. The children began to imitate his sleep patterns. They'd get up at 3 in the morning, and when Mrs. Morris complained, they'd say, "Well, Daddy's up." Mrs. Morris would tell her husband, "You need to get more normal sleep patterns." He would reply, "You can sleep when you're dead."

JORGE MORRON
A Citizen in the Making

Sonia Morron said the only thing that came between her and her husband, whom she described as "honest, humble, a gentleman," was religion.

Jorge Morron, 38, was Baptist, she is Roman Catholic, and on Sundays they would go to their respective churches and meet up after services.

After begging her for months to accompany him to his church, he got her to agree the last Sunday of his life. "He made me stand up and he said, 'This is the woman that for years I prayed God for.' He was so happy."

Mrs. Morron, who met her husband in 1999, said both were immigrants from Colombia who set out to discover New York together. The couple lived in Queens with one of Mr. Morron's brothers. "We visited museums, went to concerts, took advantage of everything," she said.

Mr. Morron, a security guard with Summit Security Services, was assigned to the concourse level between the twin towers. He also taught Spanish at Manhattan Community College. He was scheduled to become an American citizen on Sept. 17 and had wanted his wife to wear her best dress and to bring a video camera to the ceremony, she said. The event, Mrs. Morron said he told her, would be in her honor and that of their baby, due in March. Mrs. Morron lost the baby less than a month after her husband died.

FRED V. MORRONE
A Hidden Spirituality

Fred V. Morrone enriched the graduate level course in public management that he taught at Seton Hall University with his experience as superintendent of the 1,300-member Port Authority police force. But his most important lesson was the one he never lectured about: living a moral life.

"My husband wasn't a saint," said Linda Morrone. "but he was a spiritual person, and he lived his life according to that." It was well known that Mr. Morrone, 63, was a 30-year veteran of law enforcement, a tough former New Jersey State Police lieutenant colonel who ran the casino gaming and intelligence services sections.

But hardly anyone knew that several times a week he attended 6:30 A.M. Mass near his home in Lakewood, N.J., before boarding a train into the city, or that he prayed at the start of each and every morning. All that was visible of Mr. Morrone's spiritual side was an occasional glimpse, like the time he had to decide what to do with a young new employee who had gotten into serious trouble.

"Most other people would have given up on him," said Mrs. Morrone, "but my husband took the time to pray about it, and he came away with a feeling that he should act in favor of that person."

"Fred did that with a lot of different aspects of his jobs," Mrs. Morrone said, "but most people who worked with him would not have guessed that at all."

BILL MOSKAL
Fitness with Finance

Bill Moskal's business and personal lives were wrapped around sports and fitness. As a risk consultant for Marsh & McClennan, he made sure potential clients were insurable. In recent months, his projects included proposed new stadiums for the Cincinnati Reds baseball team and the Cincinnati Bengals football team.

At home in the Cleveland suburbs, he worked out daily. He would run with his dogs. At age 50, he boxed and wrestled once a week. He coached teams in every sport his 13-year-old son, Andy, played. He juggled business trips, including a Sept. 11 meeting at the World Trade Center's north tower, around family activities.

As his wife, Lorraine, said, "He was always available to us. He was truly the other half."

"He loved opera," his wife added. "When we had a memorial service for him, I joked with the priest that he would have loved to have had Andrea Bocelli sing 'Ave Maria' because he adored him. There was a memorial service the next day at ground zero in New York. I couldn't make it, but I watched on television. Andrea Bocelli was there and sang 'Ave Maria.' Quite a coincidence."

MARK MOTRONI
He Became Everything

Mark Motroni took a ribbing for the protective goggles he wore over his glasses when he showed up at the community courts to shoot hoops with his sons, but that did not stop kids from wanting the elder statesman on their team.

Same thing happened on the baseball diamond. When his son Christopher, 23, was looking for a pitcher to fill in last summer in Central Park, he tapped his 57-year-old dad, a broker-trader at Carr Futures. They won; Mr. Motroni went two-for-three at the plate.

Whatever he did—trading crude oil options at the Mercantile Exchange, singing and touring with a busy salsa band, Orquesta Novel, or playing ball with his three sons, all of whom followed him to Wall Street jobs—Mr. Motroni put his heart into it.

Mr. Motroni, who arrived from Cuba when he was 12 knowing no English, felt blessed for the chance to reinvent himself in the United States. He went to Mass every morning before hitting the trading pit. His presence Sept. 11 at Carr's 92nd floor office was a fluke: he was there for a twice-a-year meeting.

"He came here with nothing and he turned himself into everything," said Christopher, who lives at his parents' home in Fort Lee, N.J. "Every day after work he'd come up to my room and ask what I learned today."

CYNTHIA MOTUS-WILSON
Instiller of Love

Cynthia Motus-Wilson was a people person, according to her husband, William Wilson, and her daughter, Patricia Motus-Chan. "She was very caring," Mr. Wilson said. "A small woman, 5-foot nothing. But a heart bigger than Alaska."

Ms. Motus-Wilson, 52 and the head receptionist at International Office Centers Corporation in the World Trade Center, was proud of the culture of her native Philippines but had recently become an American citizen.

She was an accomplished craftswoman, creating everything

from delicate flower arrangements to wall hangings. She was about to move with her husband into her first house, where she would have a studio, in Warwick, N.Y.

After her death, Ms. Motus-Chan and her brother Braulio Jose found a loving note from their mother attached to a life insurance policy and adorned with a drawing of a smiling face. She had highlighted her request that the two take care of each other.

"She really trusted myself and my brother," Ms. Motus-Chan said. "This is still hard. But it's easier because she made us independent and strong."

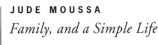

JUDE MOUSSA
Family, and a Simple Life

Jude Moussa did not keep a lot of clutter in his apartment in Battery Park City. It was clean and sparse and uncomplicated, and that's the way he liked it.

Mr. Moussa, 35, had lived in New York for eight years but grew up in Lebanon, where terrorist bombs were a part of life. He had escaped death more than once, and when he was 19 most of his family left the country and scattered around the globe—to Guadeloupe, Paris, California, London, Monte Carlo.

"His life in Lebanon probably had a lot of chaos in it," said Janel Guerrero, his girlfriend of two years. "His life here was simple. He focused on things that brought him joy. He didn't try to fill his life with material things."

Mr. Moussa was a successful bond trader at Cantor Fitzgerald and a lover of the basic pleasures of love and friendship—he was always the guy who was calling at an odd hour, just to say hello. Keeping in touch with his family, around the world, was of the utmost importance to him. Early on the morning of Sept. 11, he called his mother in Guadeloupe. And on Saturday, Sept. 8, he got a call on his answering machine from an aunt and uncle in California. It said simply: "Jude, we love you and miss you."

PETER MOUTOS
A Lot of Bear Hugs

If the sailboat hadn't gotten lost, they might never have met. If the red-haired nurse hadn't noticed his deepening sunburn and offered him sunscreen, they might not have talked so much. And if the shy man hadn't screwed up the courage to ask for her number, the sweet daily routines of Peter and Meg Moutos would never have evolved.

"He'd say, 'I love you, gorgeous woman,' and I'd say, 'I love you, handsome young man,' and he'd go off in the morning," Mrs. Moutos said of her husband, 44, a systems consultant at Marsh & McLennan who lived in Chatham, N.J. "At 5 he'd call me: 'How's my gorgeous woman?' 'How's my handsome young man?' and tell me what time to pick him up at the train, and then we'd go to the Y together in Madison."

They would work out, pick each other up in a bear hug to crack each other's spine, then he would carry her gym bag as they left. "If we had an irritable day, we wouldn't discuss it until after we were done, because we were always in such better moods after we worked out," she said.

They were married less than a year and a half.

A memorial to Brian Patrick Monaghan Jr., twenty-one, who was installing an air conditioner at the World Trade Center on September 11, stands near his home and the nearby courts where he played handball, at the edge of Inwood Hill Park near Manhattan's West 207th Street.
(*Nancy Siesel*)

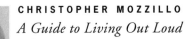

CHRISTOPHER MOZZILLO
A Guide to Living Out Loud

Some people live life out loud. Christopher Mozzillo lived life out louder.

How to Stop Your Mom and Sister From Fighting at the Dinner Table: Take a fork, pretend to ram it in your forehead and shout, "You're driving me nuts!" Or bang your head against the wall, whimpering, "Help me, help me!"

How to Get Your Girlfriend out of the Ocean for Lunch: Roll her, soaking wet, up the sand, laughing as you yell, "Chicken cutlet here!" (Escort her to the showers, please.)

Cook only masterpieces. Ski only black diamond trails. Drink till someone else passes out first. Be president of your fraternity at St. John's, a king of the bar scene at the Jersey Shore, the best at trivia because you have a photographic memory.

Take the firefighter's exam at 18 and wait impatiently all those years, working as an environmental scientist, until you are called—finally!—at 25. Be so upbeat that, at 27, you think you know what the future holds: husband, father, upstate homeowner, lieutenant, captain, chief.

Love being in the fraternity known as Engine Company 55 in Manhattan's Little Italy so much that you come home to Staten Island boasting, "Today the captain let me hold the knob of the hose!"

STEPHEN V. W. MULDERRY
Family and Basketball

Stephen V. W. Mulderry, the sixth of eight children, had a way of making his presence known. "If you met him, you would remember," said his younger brother, Andrew Mulderry. "He was just a ball of energy in the most casual of circumstances."

Mr. Mulderry, 33, a vice president for equity trading at Keefe, Bruyette & Woods, commanded attention with his quick wit and willingness to meet new people. He was also hard to miss, at 6 foot 2 and 180 pounds. His lanky frame lent itself well to his favorite sport, basketball. A point guard, he graduated in 1990 as an all-American from the University of Albany.

"He loved basketball," Andrew Mulderry said. "But he had four passions: friends, family, work and basketball. He was an incredible source of love and support for me. Even in the midst of this horrible circumstance, I feel nothing but blessed for the older brother I have."

MICHAEL D. MULLAN
Things We'll Never Know

Michael D. Mullan honored his father by following him into the military, he honored his mother by following her into nursing, and he honored himself by becoming a firefighter, his brother, Patrick, said in a eulogy.

Sometimes Firefighter Mullan combined his vocations, like when he told a young boy named Steve who had a 106-degree fever that if he let him put in an I.V., he would get a trip to the firehouse.

Steve has a picture of himself with Firefighter Mullan, 34, who worked at Ladder Company 12 in Manhattan's Chelsea section, next to the fire pole.

"Michael loved to play the piano," said his mother, Theresa. "He played the piano like Jerry Lee Lewis, and when he got up, the piano went into cardiac arrest."

A captain in the Army Reserve, he was planning to become a nurse practitioner. He lived with his parents in Bayside, Queens, and had a girlfriend.

"I know what his goals were, but what would he have attained and achieved?" Mrs. Mullan said. "Would he have married, and been a father? We'll never know."

PETER MULLIGAN
A Bachelor Extravaganza

Two weeks before Peter Mulligan and his wife, Sara, were married, his entire trading desk and other friends—about 40 people—took him to Las Vegas for his bachelor party. There were duffel bags printed with "Pete's Bachelor Party." There were key chains and cocktail stirrers. One trader had spent six months taping stickers on cigars for the occasion.

"It meant the world to him that people would travel that distance for him," his wife said. For the wedding, Mr. Mulligan, 28, an associate vice president for international equity at Cantor Fitzgerald, thought about having fewer groomsmen but could not get below 14.

"That was just him," Mrs. Mulligan said. "Our friends meant the world to us. It was a lot of fun. We had two full large stretch limousines, and two guys walked down the aisle with every girl. So it was very funny, but it worked out."

That was May 5, 2001. They had a two-week honeymoon in Hawaii. He stayed home from work for a few days in August after hurting his back. Mrs. Mulligan keeps wondering, what if that had happened a few weeks later.

MICHAEL MULLIN
Mother Awaits a Son's Call

Football, wrestling, snowboarding, baseball. There was not a sport that Michael Mullin, 27, would not eagerly throw himself into. The same went for spectator sports, and Mr. Mullin was thrilled to have finally secured season tickets to the Giants after years of trying.

"My boy just loves sports," said his mother, Lynn. "He loves to have fun, and he loves to make everyone laugh."

A trader with Cantor Fitzgerald, Mr. Mullin worked on the 104th floor of 1 World Trade Center and lived in Hoboken, N.J., with one of his brothers. There were five children in the Mullin family, and all of Mr. Mullin's siblings have been spending recent days in Manhattan, father and son volunteering to remove rubble, the other three children canvassing the city for information about their brother. Mrs. Mullin has been staying home in Holbrook, N.Y., awaiting what she believes will be a call from her son.

"He used to call me every day just to check in," she said through tears. "I'm just waiting for the phone to ring, to hear his voice."

JAMES MUNHALL
Surrounded by Friends

Between the commute from Ridgewood, N.J., to New York and the time at work, a 12-to-14-hour day was normal, but James Munhall didn't mind. He enjoyed his job at Sandler O'Neill & Partners, an investment banking firm, where he was a managing director on the 104th floor of 2 World Trade Center, and besides, he was surrounded by close friends.

But it was the sensitive husband and devoted father who looked forward to the weekends with his wife, Susan—whom he met in 1988 when she was working as a vice president for Lehman Brothers—and his 7-year-old daughter, Lauren.

"He and my daughter renamed Saturdays "Dadurdays," Susan Munhall recalled. "He spent all his free time with her anyway, but that was their special day. They'd get bagels and the newspaper together in the morning, or work around the house or ride bikes together." Or Mr. Munhall, 45, would sit with his daughter at the dining room table, poring over the sports pages. "He was such a Yankee fan," she said. "And he taught her how to read the baseball stats."

NANCY MUNIZ
Improving Self, and Others

Her son, now 8, was born with a developmental difficulty and could not walk at first. But Nancy Muniz had taken a course in massage therapy and supplemented the therapy he received through his school with some of her own. Now, his aunt Ada Muniz said, he walks just fine and "everybody says he's real intelligent."

"We both had a real interest in helping others, and in helping to better ourselves," she added.

Toward that end, Nancy Muniz, who was working as an administrative assistant at the World Trade Center, liked to watch Oprah Winfrey's show and to read self-help books. She would also get together with Ada Muniz for the occasional spirit- and body-toning yoga class.

The two sisters even tossed around the idea of starting a physical therapy business together. "But on account of cir-

cumstances," Ada Muniz said, "I never got a chance to pursue it."

THERESA MUNSON
Traveling Grandmother

Theresa Munson—Terry to friends—was a gypsy with her daughter, Christine Hayes, and her granddaughter, Kaitlyn, hitting the road to places like Walt Disney World in Florida or Pennsylvania Dutch country.

The trio temporarily disbanded with the birth of Ms. Hayes's son, Patrick, about 9 months before the attack. When the telephone rang in the Hayeses' Houston home on Sept. 11, Patrick said "Nana," his word for his grandmother, for the first time. But it was a call reporting the collapse of 2 World Trade Center, where Ms. Munson, 54, worked as a technical assistant at Aon on the 92nd floor.

"Her whole world revolved around the three of us and my husband," said Ms. Hayes, an only child. She said Kaitlyn, 6, was devastated by the loss of her grandmother, who used to telephone twice a day from her home in Broad Channel, Queens. Ms. Hayes called her mother, who was divorced and who leaves behind her own 88-year-old mother, "a great parent and a great friend."

CESAR A. MURILLO
A Dance All His Own

Cesar A. Murillo, 32, lived in TriBeCa and used the West Side Highway as his backyard. Along this road, Mr. Murillo used Rollerblades to get to work at Cantor Fitzgerald. He was proud of his Colombian heritage, flying a Colombian flag on his scooter during World Cup matches. He played volleyball on Pier 25 and kayaked near the same dock with his new bride, Alyson Becker.

And he danced. He was nicknamed Lawn Mower for the particular way he moved. "It wasn't any style. It was his own style," Ms. Becker said. "It was a mixture of hip-hop and Latin moves. He loved dancing. He danced when he was asleep. Literally, his feet would be moving when he slept. His mom said he danced in his crib."

Once, when the couple was visiting Fire Island with a group of friends, Mr. Murillo sneaked back to the dance club after Ms. Becker fell asleep in the hotel. Soon, their friends discovered a crowd laughing and staring. At the center of it was Mr. Murillo, dancing as only the Lawn Mower could. "It was so typical of him," Ms. Becker said.

Then there was the "Cesar Murillo factor" when it came to finding a parking spot in Manhattan. He drove his Toyota

Jack Lynch, the son of Firefighter Michael F. Lynch, is carried past the honor guard at his father's memorial service on November 24 at Notre Dame Roman Catholic Church in New Hyde Park, New York. Firefighter Lynch died at the World Trade Center after the terrorist attack. (*Andrea Mohin*)

Land Cruiser everywhere, and "there was always a parking spot waiting for him," Ms. Becker said. "It was just unbelievable."

MARC A. MUROLO
"He Had Come of Age"

Marc A. Murolo never used a napkin, even when he was eating at his favorite restaurant, Morton's steakhouse. His sister, Cathy Lynn Roberti, said, "I can go through three napkins in one sitting. He never used one, even when he ate a rack of ribs, so I would usually steal his."

Bright and quiet with a ready smile, Mr. Murolo, 28, worked as a bond trader at Cantor Fitzgerald on the 105th floor of 1 World Trade Center. He loved his job. He also loved the city. He liked to go out to restaurants with friends.

And to Mets games. Mr. Murolo, who grew up in Englewood Cliffs, N.J., moved to the city shortly after graduating from Fairfield University in Connecticut.

"He was really proud of his apartment," his sister said. "In July, for my dad's 70th birthday, we went to the Water Club for lunch. Afterward, he entertained the family at his apartment. He had come of age."

BRIAN MURPHY
Knowing the Answers

The first thing Brian Murphy would say when he got home from work was, "Where are my girls?" There were three of them: his wife, Judith, and their two daughters, Leila, 4, and Jessica, 5. Mr. Murphy, 41, coordinated electronic bond trading for Cantor Fitzgerald.

But as his wife made clear, "He would always talk about his three girls. That was his priority." He was always planning trips, teaching them things, springing little surprises. One of the last things he did was take everyone apple picking.

Mr. Murphy's mind was stuffed with facts. You name it, he knew it. "He knew a lot about nature—different birds, insects, plants," said Steven Bram, his brother-in-law. "He knew all about gadgets and was great at fixing things. He was like a *Jeopardy!* contestant."

When friends got lost—and it could be just about anywhere—they called Mr. Murphy. He knew which roads to take. And he knew the answers, with great precision. Once, Jessica said to him, "How come you know so much more than Mommy?"

He answered, "I know a little bit about everything, and Mommy knows a lot about a few things." But his wife said that he was being modest. He truly knew a lot about everything.

CHARLIE MURPHY
"Absurdly Generous"

After growing up in Ridgewood, N.J., with four older sisters, Charlie Murphy somehow emerged as transcendently normal. "We wanted to move to the suburbs," said Lynna Huie, his fiancée, who worked with him at Cantor Fitzgerald. "He wanted a big porch. A deck in the back with a pool and a fireplace were necessities."

He was "relentlessly funny," said one sister, Nancy. He ruled the family's holiday Trivial Pursuit games. "He'd insult you and you'd be laughing so hard you didn't care," she said.

At 38, he was finally making some money, which he spent on presents.

"He was absurdly generous," Nancy said. "He'd come at Christmas with the car loaded with gifts. He'd bring bags and bags of steaks and salmon to family parties. He'd do all the cooking and all the cleaning and if you tried to thank him, he'd insult you and make you laugh."

CHRISTOPHER MURPHY
Happiest at the Helm

For all of Christopher Murphy's impressive accomplishments on land (Yale B.A., Emory J.D., William & Mary M.B.A., budding inventor), he was probably most comfortable on the water, with a smile on his face, and a Bob Marley tune pulsating on deck.

Mr. Murphy was the captain of the Yale sailing team, and he had an easygoing and egoless style that classmates still recall fondly. He raced a sailboat across the Atlantic after graduation. He also taught teenagers how to sail as a long-time instructor at a program called Sail Caribbean.

"There was something about Murph that was so comforting," said Dr. Bradford Burke Worrall, a classmate of Mr. Murphy's at Yale and Emory. "He was the sort of person you'd want at the helm of anything."

Mr. Murphy, 35, had just started working at an investment bank in New York, Keefe, Bruyette & Woods, but he planned eventually to do most of his work from his new home in Easton, Md. That way, he would be closer to his wife, Catherine, and their two young daughters, Hope, 2, and Hannah, 5 months. And closer to a sailboat, too: already, Mr. Murphy had done a lot of sailing this summer with the children. Hannah was learning to sail before she could walk.

EDWARD C. MURPHY
Defying Easy Categorization

Edward C. Murphy's life brimmed with contrasts and deep loyalties. He was a staunch Republican who invested in real estate and racehorses. But he also helped nonprofit groups raise money for food and clothing for poor children in his native Clifton, N.J.

He loved the vitality of Manhattan but insisted on living in Clifton, where he headed a town board that improved traffic safety, especially around schools. Mr. Murphy, 42, was a managing director at Cantor Fitzgerald and was as busy as the job title implies, but every morning at 9 sharp, he called his mother Evelyn, a 77-year-old widow. On Sept. 11, her phone rang on schedule, minutes after the first jetliner hit.

"He said, 'Mom, I'm O.K., I'm getting out,' " said Mr. Murphy's brother Daniel. "She just cherishes that moment."

Mr. Murphy's girlfriend of 17 years, Maryann Flego, called him a "quick-witted maverick" who jogged for years and loved both classical and rock music and the works of Andy Warhol, Jackson Pollock and R. C. Gorman, a Navajo artist in the Southwest. He delighted in haggling to cut prices of many of his purchases, whether a pearl ring for Ms. Flego or a pretzel at a ball game.

JAMES MURPHY
Faithful to Family

James Murphy, a Cantor Fitzgerald trader, kept his eye on the basics. His family were his friends, and together they were a big crowd. He and his wife, Mary, had two children and were expecting a third. He had 10 brothers and sisters, between the ages of 44 and 30, and 13 nieces and nephews. Most of them lived within a 20-mile radius of the Jersey shore.

Mr. Murphy, 35, was the "ringleader," said Bill, his eldest brother. "His favorite thing was to get together with a big

Mementos dangle from a fence at Seventh and Greenwich Avenues in one of the many September 11 memorials that lingered in the city. (*Earl Wilson*)

group of our family, with all our children. He'd everybody to come have lunch on the beach and then go hang out on our parents' deck and cook out. He'd call people on the spur of the moment to go to watch football games, go to a bar and have lunch. At Christmas, he was the Santa Claus."

He liked to ski in Vermont and Vail, but otherwise was a homebody, Bill Murphy said. "He was innocent in a way. He was very apolitical, very low-key about most things. He was very happy to go home to his house. He was very happy to tell us that he and Mary were having another baby."

JAMES F. MURPHY IV
"A Smiling Soul"

On Friday, Sept. 7, James F. Murphy IV got up early to catch a flight to Dallas. His limo never came. So at 6 A.M., he woke his mother, Helen Marie Murphy, and asked her to take him to the airport. Except that he insisted on taking his car, a beloved new Volkswagen Passat, and doing the driving himself.

"It was hysterical," said Mr. Murphy's mother, recalling how he wove in and out of the traffic at a furious speed. "I said, 'Jimmy, if you don't slow down, you won't have a mother, a car or a flight.' "

But Mr. Murphy, a 30-year-old account manager at Thomson Financial who was habitually late for everything, was coolly confident, arriving at the airport with six minutes to spare. By Sunday night, he was back at his parents' kitchen table on Long Island—where he and his wife, Jeanine, and four gregarious older sisters liked to gather—with a pair of turquoise and silver earrings and an apology for his mother. "I know it was the ride from hell," he told her, more amused than contrite.

It was his upbeat, teasing manner that won over his wife, whom he met at college in Maryland. As she put it: "He was a very genuine person, warm and comfortable to be around. He was not a saint, but he had a smiling soul."

Married in 1999, Mr. Murphy and his wife were living temporarily with his parents while repainting a new apartment in Mineola, N.Y. But on Sept. 11, Mr. Murphy attended a trade show at the World Trade Center.

KEVIN J. MURPHY
His Wife's Cheerleader

"Look! They're cleaning my office," he had said, pointing from the deck of the *Spirit of New York* as it cruised beneath the twin towers. Not that he could really see his desk pressed against the window at Marsh & McLennan on the 100th floor, where he drank in the inverse view daily.

It was Sept. 7, a welcome night out for Kevin J. Murphy and his wife, Beth. Melanoma is a slippery cancer, and hers had returned in May 2000. On Valentine's Day, she had her last treatment. He took her to *Beauty and the Beast*. But then a virus took hold. Before the diagnosis the couple feared the worst: more cancer, worse cancer. The boat ride came when she had again recovered, again with him as her chief cheerleader.

"This will be my birthday present," said Mr. Murphy, a newly 40-year-old Long Islander.

They met on another of his birthdays: She sneezed. He said, "God bless you." There is a son now, Connor, 7, and a daughter, Caitlyn, 4. Mr. Murphy helped Connor assemble an "All About Me" collage on Sept. 10. Caitlyn asks to watch *It's a Wonderful Life*, to see "if Daddy gets his wings."

His absence is "like an amputated leg," said Mrs. Murphy, who knew what she was talking about: two dozen lymph nodes were sliced from her thigh; it is permanently numb. At her sickbed, he wept for her. He ordered her to live. She did.

PATRICK SEAN MURPHY
A Motto to Live By

Sometimes, you learn the most about someone from the silence. From what people who knew them best do not say. With Patrick Sean Murphy, they don't talk about his job much, as successful as he was.

No, those closest to him emphasize other pieces of his life. Because he did. They all say he had three loves: his family, basketball and fishing. Summer weekends at the family cottage in Beach Haven, N.J., would find Mr. Murphy, 36, fishing on the 20-footer named *Nothin' But Net*. Because, though only 5-foot-9, he could drop a basketball into a net without hitting the rim.

Mr. Murphy, a vice president at Marsh & McLennan, formed basketball leagues. He was a regular at Knicks games. He even taught his daughter, Maggie, only 2 years old, to dribble (with both hands). But he wasn't dogmatic. His son, Sean, 4, somehow wasn't charmed by basketball, so father and son would find projects. They'd fix things around the house in Millburn, N.J. They'd search Internet sites for information about trucks, Sean's passion, and Mr. Murphy would bookmark them.

"He enjoyed his success," said his wife, Vera. "But Patrick had a motto. He'd say he worked to live. He didn't live to work."

JOHN MURRAY
Very Much in Charge

It was in character, the way John Murray came down to the Sky Lobby and then went back upstairs to help get people out of the building, Joe Sacco said of his boss, whom everyone knew as Jack.

Mr. Murray, who ran corporate services for the Industrial Bank of Japan, was in charge of facilities, purchasing, security and communications, among other things. "He was running the properties for the bank," Mr. Sacco said. "He would've always been the last person out, to make sure everyone else got out. He was very serious about those issues."

Mr. Murray, 52, was also a key person in the bank's disaster recovery team, and one of the leaders of the business contingency committee. "Because he was so good at managing, he had everything set up so we could follow the plans," Mr. Sacco said. "His departments were able to do what they needed to because of his leadership."

Mr. Murray, who had one son, John, had a particular laugh, said his wife of 28 years, Patricia. That laugh would have come in handy when the bank was trying to recover from Sept. 11. "Life goes on, the way he would've wanted it," Mr. Sacco said. "He set up for this."

JOHN J. MURRAY
Enamored of Fatherhood

John J. Murray was not one to put things off. He would fill his weekends visiting friends and family and he would make that one last phone call even if he was exhausted, said Rory, his wife of two years. Mr. Murray, of Hoboken, N.J., was a partner at Cantor Fitzgerald.

"There was no complacency about him," she said of her husband. "He didn't take life for granted. His father said of him after the attack on the World Trade Center, 'He probably lived more in his 32 years than most people live in 100.'"

For example, shortly after they were married, Mrs. Murray had an opportunity to take a job in London. He sought a transfer and they lived abroad for about a year. The couple moved back to the New York City area late in 2000 to be close to family after she became pregnant with Alyson, who was 5 months old in September.

"He was enamored of his daughter and fatherhood," Mrs. Murray said. "For so many people, becoming a father changes their lives, but he loved every minute of it."

N

ROBERT NAGEL
History and Sci-Fi Buff

His wife used to tease Robert Nagel that he never watched any television channel below the number 13. He could not stand commercials, and so he could not stand commercial television.

Instead, he watched black-and-white movies on cable (though the spread of commercials to cable did not please him), and he was faithful to the History Channel, no matter what was on it. His wife, Janet, has not been able to bring herself to watch that channel since Sept. 11.

Lieutenant Nagel, a member of Engine Company 58, lived in Manhattan with his wife and their daughter, Bridget. The other thing that captivated him was science fiction; hundreds of science-fiction books were spread around the house.

He was the type of person who let people know what was on his mind. He was blunt. He was opinionated. "He didn't like things to be bottled up," Mrs. Nagel said.

He could discourse at considerable length on almost any subject. It was not unknown for his monologues to well exceed the listening patience of his friends. When he sensed a distinct waning of interest, he would quickly inject the phrase, "and furthermore," and then stop talking. It became his little joke. Sometimes, someone would say something and he would interject, "and furthermore," and then immediately clam up. Those who knew him just chuckled, and so did he.

MILDRED NAIMAN
Thumbed Her Nose at Age

At 81, Mildred Naiman kept the pedal to the metal. "She had a little bit of a lead foot," said her daughter-in-law Carol Naiman. "She had been stopped for speeding and was totally insulted the officer would give an old woman a ticket."

Despite the number of birthdays that had passed, she lived her life at full tilt. She called her apartment in an Andover, Mass., community for the elderly her bachelorette pad, and she kept her friends there busy, organizing shopping excursions, dinners out and weekend trips. She headed to California twice a year to visit her sons, usually taking American Airlines Flight 11, as she did on Sept. 11. "You'd sort of have to see her between her little excursions," Carol Naiman said.

All this despite two knee replacements, cataracts and a variety of other health problems. "If something was wrong with her," said her son Russ Naiman, "she'd go to the doctor and say, 'Fix me up; I've got a lot of traveling to do.'"

FRANK J. NAPLES
From Cook to Broker

Frank J. Naples was a shy man who defied the norm, but did it quietly. He knew his hard-core Republicanism had made him a bit of the black sheep in his family and in the old neighborhood in Bensonhurst, Brooklyn. It even aggravated his high school sweetheart and future wife, Heidi, but he stuck to it. The day that Rudolph W. Giuliani, then a prosecuting attorney with a reputation as a tough cookie, visited Madison High School and posed for a photograph with him sealed the deal: Mr. Giuliani became an inspiration. Mr. Naples scraped his way to success at Cantor Fitzgerald the odd way: he hired on as a cook 12 years ago and worked his way up to broker.

He and Heidi eloped to Hawaii in 1998 after an eight-year courtship that was initially frowned on by their families, who feared they had become too serious too young. "We kind of sneaked around together during high school," his wife said. He collected soccer jerseys from Italy and loved '70s disco music; on weekends, he moonlighted as a D.J. at various Brooklyn fetes. He retained his knack for cooking despite his promotion from the corporate kitchen, and liked to watch cooking shows.

The couple lived in Cliffside Park, N.J., and were house-hunting and planning a family. "We met when I was 16; I knew we were soul mates," she said.

JOHN P. NAPOLITANO
Living Life His Own Way

John P. Napolitano won enough awards, medals and citations from the New York Fire Department and the Lakeland Fire District in Ronkonkoma, N.Y., where he lived, to fill a box.

And a box is where he kept them.

"He didn't have to wear medals on his chest," said his father, John. "I really admired him, not for what he did for a living, but for how he lived his life."

Lieutenant Napolitano—he was promoted posthumously—was a fireman's fireman. He showed up as an experienced rookie in 1991, having started as a junior volunteer with the Lakeland district when he was 17. He eventually became chief and commissioner there.

Robert Galione worked with Lieutenant Napolitano at Rescue 2 in Brooklyn, following him into some tough fires. "He'd go into a fire that was roaring so loud we couldn't hear anything," Firefighter Galione said. "I was right behind him humping the hose, so I know he never took a step back."

Firefighting was his life's work, but not his life. "What did he do outside the firehouse?" said his father.

"That's the easiest question to answer. Being with his wife and kids. Period. End of story."

To please his two little girls, Elizabeth and Emma Rose, Lieutenant Napolitano, 33, would do almost anything. The image that sticks in the mind of his wife, Anne, is of him trying to fly a kite on a windless day to make the girls smile.

They did.

CATHERINE A. NARDELLA
Someone to Lean On

On Sept. 10, with her parents about to return home from a senior citizens' bus outing to Atlantic City, Catherine A. Nardella stopped by their home in Lincoln Park, N.J., to the make sure everything was in order. She knew it was their habit to have a cup of coffee as soon as they got in the door, but the electricity was temporarily out. So she went to a Dunkin' Donuts for a carafe of hot coffee, and had it waiting for them.

That's the way she was about her large Italian-American family. "Cathy always thought of others," said her sister Grace Samek. Another sister, Lavinia Wilson, said Miss Nardella "was the kind of person that just gave and didn't think she was going to get anything in return."

Miss Nardella, 40, was an insurance consultant at Aon Corp. Single, she owned her own house in Bloomfield, N.J., and was active in her local parish. She was a member of the choir and a regular lector, distinguished by her professional manner of dressing and speaking, and by a certain gentle kindness.

"Every Sunday after Mass she'd wait for this old man to come out and she'd help him walk down the steps of the church," said Msgr. William Hatcher, pastor of St. Thomas the Apostle.

MARIO NARDONE
Nothing Too Good for Mom

Mario Nardone called his mother that Tuesday morning to say he had found just the doctor for her. Linda Nardone has serious knee problems, and her son, a 32-year-old bonds broker, had done a little research. "He said he found a doctor who took care of the pope and the doctor doesn't take insurance, but it doesn't matter," his mother said.

Mr. Nardone was the guy with the million-dollar smile and the million-dollar heart. He worked at Euro Brokers at 2 World Trade Center, but told his mother that he planned to quit in seven years so he could give back to humanity. Single and the oldest of three children, he split his time between his Upper East Side apartment and Staten Island, where he supported the Nardone household for two years.

When his father fell gravely ill with cancer, he cut a check for his mother every month and opened a restaurant account for her. "There was nothing he didn't think of," she says.

SHAWN M. NASSANEY's portrait appears with Lynn Catherine Goodchild on page 190.

KAREN S. NAVARRO
Always in High Style

Every day, top to bottom, Karen S. Navarro looked like a million bucks. Even when the rest of her friends were schlepping to Sunday brunch with their eyes barely open, Ms. Navarro would join them fully coiffed, nails enameled, makeup perfect, and in heels, said her former roommate Patricia Antogiovanni.

"Everyone who knew Karen knew about her obsession with her hair," Ms. Antogiovanni said. "She had very thick, curly hair and always tried to straighten it. The blow dryer was always on in our apartment. Then when she bought her apartment in Queens, she had a standing appointment twice a week to get her hair blown out professionally. She wanted long, straight hair, and with a lot of work and money she accomplished it."

Ms. Navarro, 30, worked just as hard at everything she did. She had studied to be a teacher and loved children, but went to work in finance instead. She was an assistant on the foreign exchange trading desk of Carr Futures, a fast-paced job that required a high energy level and suited her personality just fine.

"It was a very demanding job, but she enjoyed the challenge," said her father, Edward. "You have to be young and motivated to work those kinds of hours."

Ms. Navarro returns every night in Ms. Antogiovanni's dreams. Recently she was there, restless as ever, complaining about the long wait to get into heaven.

"You can't believe the lines up here," Ms. Antogiovanni said Ms. Navarro told her in the dream. "I can't just wait around. I have to do something. I have to get a job."

JOSEPH NAVAS
Making the Hours Count

Given that the days Joseph Navas worked fluctuated—his schedule was four days on, two days off—and given that his overriding interest was doing things with his wife and three children, he had to improvise. That was O.K. He knew how to make hours count.

If he was off on weekend days, it was easy. He might play ball with Joey, 9, or help coach his Little League team or his ice hockey team. He would take Jessica, 12, shopping, or watch her perform with her cheerleader squad. He might ride bikes with Justin, 3. When he was off on weekdays, school preoccupied the children, but he would make the most of the hours he had with them. He would drive them to school, or pick them up for lunch, or even bring them lunch.

Mr. Navas, 44, was a Port Authority police officer, part of the emergency services unit, assigned to PATH. He worked out of Journal Square but was summoned to the World Trade Center after the attack. He was broadly trained. He had been to chemical identification school; he had learned how to deal with hazardous materials; he knew how to rappel; he was schooled in scuba diving.

"He wanted his family to be safe," said his wife, Karen. "He wanted everybody to be safe. That was why he was a police officer."

LUKE NEE
Bronx in His Blood

As a boy, Luke Nee played all the games that a Bronx sidewalk offered to kids on Minerva Place, just off the Grand Concourse: stickball, of course, and off-the-point and street hockey.

Right out of Cardinal Hayes High School, he answered a help-wanted advertisement for people with math skills and landed a job at Drexel Burnham Lambert. Before long, a half-dozen guys from the block followed. It was a small world, he would say, but he would not want to paint it.

At Drexel, he met Irene Lavelle, and they were married Sept. 11, 1982. After he had shifted to Cantor Fitzgerald, he would chew through a couple of novels a week on the train ride from Stony Point, N.Y., said his brother, John Nee. His Bronx roots showed: he shared a ticket plan for Friday night Yankee games with boyhood friends from St. Philip Neri School.

Mr. Nee, 44, made the simple pleasures glow. "He treasured Irene and loved bringing their son, Patrick, to ballgames," said his brother. On summer weekends, he, his wife and Patrick would jump in the car, pick up a few relatives and head for the beach. And on Sept. 11, he made a final call of farewell and love to his family.

"Luke was just a friendly, kind, peaceful, and unaffected guy," said Mr. Nee. "Meatball heroes, watch a movie with Patrick—that was a Saturday night."

ANN N. NELSON
"My Dear Little Friend"

She was a small-town girl with her sights set on the world. She grew up in Stanley, N.D., population 1,000, but eventually traveled to China, studied in England and hiked on her own around Peru. Ann N. Nelson loved grand plans and had little patience for details—a quality that sometimes left dinner guests hungry in the living room while she was still reading recipes off the back of boxes in the kitchen.

"Life's purpose is not to find a fun party, it is to make one," was the quote Ms. Nelson had selected for the yearbook her senior year at Carleton College.

Exuberant. Spontaneous. Ambitious. Determined. Introspective. Passionate. Irreverent. Brilliant. That is how friends and family remember Ms. Nelson, a 30-year-old bond trader at Cantor Fitzgerald. She had worked at the firm less than nine months, after having worked five years at an investment firm in Chicago.

"She was my dear little friend," said her mother, Jenette Nelson.

DAVID W. NELSON
French Horn to Finance

David W. Nelson was a maverick and an iconoclast in the best way, friends and family say. He was also intellectually and emotionally adventurous. "You don't have to have just one career in your life," he once told his mother, Betty. And he didn't.

Most recently, Mr. Nelson, 50, was a senior vice president at Carr Futures. But high finance was not always in the cards for Mr. Nelson, who lived in Park Slope, Brooklyn, with his wife, Elizabeth Crawford, and two children, Ingrid and Frederick. After graduating from Johns Hopkins in

1973, he became a social worker in Baltimore. He quit a year later after an alarming accident.

"He was shot in both legs as he stepped out of a phone booth," Mrs. Nelson said. "He was looking up an address for his next client, but someone must have thought he was reporting a drug deal."

He fully recovered, but decided to move to Boston, where he tended bar and tried to earn a living playing the French horn. "By 1980, he realized that the demand for French horn players was far smaller than the supply," Mrs. Nelson said. He then went to work for his father at Clayton Brokerage in Clayton, Mo., eventually reaching Wall Street.

GINGER RISCO NELSON
Striving for the Best

William A. Nelson remembers his wife, Ginger Risco Nelson, as someone who always strove to be the best and never did anything casually. They met on a bicycling trip in the Napa Valley of California, when she joined him and his friends because they always opted for longer routes over shorter ones.

A senior vice president and senior analyst at Fred Alger Management, Ms. Risco Nelson, 48, covered retailing stocks like Nike and Home Depot. The job allowed her to combine a love for design with her hunger for always knowing more. "When someone made a statement, she instantly had 10 questions," Dr. Nelson said. Evenings, she stretched out on their bed surrounded by reports about the companies she followed while he made dinner.

Although they had been married almost 10 years, they still did many things together, from buying photographs for their growing collection (she liked black-and-white abstracts) to running the New York City Marathon (they had planned to run it again next year) to shopping for her designer clothes (he would go into the dressing rooms with her and she often consulted him about what she wore).

When he filed a missing person report, he was able to describe her in detail: a redhead, very lean, about 110 pounds, wearing a black pinstriped Gucci suit with tapered pants and a white cotton blouse with a spread collar. He even knew the color and make of her underwear. "Their mouths were open," Dr. Nelson said.

PETER A. NELSON
A Marriage Proposal

When Gigi Vega attended the funerals of Harry Ford and Brian Fahey, members of Rescue Company 4 who died in a Father's Day explosion in Astoria, Queens, she was deeply touched. Her boyfriend, Peter A. Nelson, also a member of Rescue 4, had been scheduled to

work on Father's Day, and had the day off only because he had worked overtime the week before. It could have been him.

"So I asked him, 'Will you marry me, Peter?' " she said. Mr. Nelson had asked for her hand numerous times before, but she had demurred. They were married Aug. 22.

Gigi was already pregnant with the couple's first child when she proposed, and Mr. Nelson, 42, was a gleeful expectant father. "He talked to my belly every day. 'I love you, Lyndsi. Treat Mommy well today,' he would say. I had a very rough pregnancy."

On the night of Sept. 10, Rescue 4 called Mr. Nelson, who lived in Huntington Station, N.Y., to work overtime the next day, his day off.

Lyndsi was born three hours after her father's memorial service ended on Oct. 5. More than 20 days later, the rescuers found Mr. Nelson's body, and Lyndsi saw her father for the first time at his funeral.

GERARD T. NEVINS
Fireman and Farmer

Gerard T. Nevins lived a life of sweet contradictions. His primary job was fighting fires. But when he was not pulling people from burning buildings, he was tending to his small farm in the backyard of his house in Campbell Hall, N.Y.

"It was a way he could totally disconnect from all the madness of Manhattan," his brother Stephen Nevins said. "He would just make his way through the community every day as if he was just a farmer."

In his neighborhood, people recognized Firefighter Nevins, 46, as the man who raised pigs, goats and chickens and sold fresh eggs. He was also known as a doting father to Daniel, 7, and Andrew, 5.

Among the men at Rescue 1 in Midtown Manhattan, Firefighter Nevins was a keeper of traditional values. He was an 18-year veteran of the department who vehemently opposed ordering take-out food because he thought that cooking together helped to cement the brothers' bond.

To his wife, Marie, Firefighter Nevins was simply a devoted husband, whom she fell in love with at first sight in 1979. "It was just one of those things where he looked at me, and I melted and that was it," she said. "It was that way for the next 20 years."

JODY TEPEDINO NICHILO
No Complaints, Just Smiles

Jody Tepedino Nichilo, 39, never wanted anyone to worry about her. She would smile and insist that everything was all right, even if it was not. When she was thrown from a horse as a teenager, she just walked away with a hurt shoulder. "She was walking crooked," said her older brother, Vincent Tepedino. "That was typical. She would do her thing, and make sure everyone else was O.K."

She was a single mother raising a 13-year-old daughter, Jaclyn, in the same neighborhood in Bay Ridge, Brooklyn, where she had grown up. She worked as an executive assistant at Cantor Fitzgerald.

Though she never asked for help herself, she was known for helping others. She volunteered with the Meals on Wheels program, and recruited her daughter, brother and mother as well. Last Thanksgiving, they delivered turkey dinners before sitting down to one themselves. "She would make everybody feel special," her brother said.

MARTIN NIEDERER
Selfless and Self-Disciplined

Martin Niederer, a gifted athlete, was an all-star point guard while growing up in western New Jersey. He was a point guard in life, too, bringing a passionate yet disciplined and selfless kind of style to everything he did.

After playing basketball at the University of Vermont, Mr. Niederer, 23, began working last year as a securities trader at Cantor Fitzgerald. He loved his job, always showed up at 7 A.M. on the dot, and always worked long hours, said his mother, Marilyn.

He was still dating his college girlfriend. He called a tiny apartment in Hoboken home. And he loved to play host to friends and family. In June, his parents, who now live in Richmond, Va., visited, and Mr. Niederer had scouted out the martini bars in Lower Manhattan. His father loves martinis. Martin found the perfect place in SoHo.

No matter how busy he was, he conducted his life with precision and aplomb. The day after the attacks, Mr. Niederer's parents visited his apartment in Hoboken. They found the bed made, the pillows fluffed.

ALFONSE J. NIEDERMEYER III
Ever the Rescuer

"One day we were at a busy intersection in Brooklyn," Nancy Niedermeyer recalled. "An elderly gentleman tried to get across the street but he was disoriented. Al stopped the car, got out and helped him across."

That was the moment she decided that Alfonse J. Niedermeyer III, all 6-foot-4, 220 pounds of him, was somebody she could marry.

Mr. Niedermeyer, 40, was a Port Authority police officer, a big man with a booming New York accent who was a gen-

uine hero even before he rushed into the World Trade Center on Sept. 11. In 1992, he received a special citation for rescuing passengers from a US Airways jet that skidded off a runway at LaGuardia Airport.

Robert A. Fischer, a retired Port Authority police officer who worked with Mr. Niedermeyer for 16 years, called him "a born rescuer." He made friends quickly and kept them for a long time, said Kevin R. Quinn, who met Mr. Niedermeyer in the sixth grade.

Mrs. Niedermeyer asked that this article end with mention of how, a week after her husband's memorial service, she found out she was pregnant with their second child. (The first is Alfonse J. Niedermeyer IV.) "I just want people to know," she said, "that through all of this tragedy there is hope."

JUAN NIEVES
Inseparable from His Kids

For nearly 30 years, Juan Nieves, 56, of the Bronx, worked in the kitchen of the Russian Tea Room, making salads and appetizers. But when the restaurant was renovated he lost his job. He had four children. His wife, Irma, had postpartum depression and could not work. He was about 50 at the time, had no pension and had not finished high school.

But in 1994, he found a job making salads at Windows on the World for $7 an hour. When he died he was up to $12 an hour.

Every weekend he took his children to the beach or the park or the pool. He drove a mint-condition 1967 Mustang, which was new when he bought it.

He liked to be with his children so much that Carmen De La Cruz, his older sister, had to give him hints that they were teenagers now and wanted to be with their buddies.

If he was not with his children he was with his brother and sister. Two days before his death they went to South Street Seaport, where he pointed to the top of the north tower. "That's where I work," he told them.

TROY E. NILSEN
"People Took Daddy"

Every day at 6:30 P.M., when Scott Nilsen, 5, and his brother, Ryan, 3, heard their father's footsteps approaching their home in Staten Island, they would race to be the one to open the door. Sometimes Scott won, sometimes Ryan did, and the other would be left crying. So Troy E. Nilsen, home after a long day of work as a network engineer at Cantor Fitzgerald, would walk out, re-enter, greet the second one first, and make both boys smile.

Scott is autistic, "but he loved him no matter what,

unconditionally," said Jennifer Nilsen, Mr. Nilsen's widow. And because of Scott's autism, Mr. Nilsen, 33, lavished more attention on him than on Ryan. He put Scott to bed every night, read him books, taught him the alphabet, taught him to swim and even went down slides with him.

"Troy helped Scott to become who he is today," said Mrs. Nilsen, who now tucks Scott in every night. "But now after I put Scott to bed, he would come out and look around. He's used to his daddy putting him to sleep. He misses him."

And when Mrs. Nilsen tells Ryan that his daddy is an angel flying in the sky, the boy is incredulous. "He would say, no, Daddy is working," she said. "And then, I would tell him: 'Daddy cannot come back. People took Daddy; they stole him away from us.' "

PAUL NIMBLEY
A Father to His Team

Paul Nimbley had four daughters and a baby boy of his own, and as if that were not enough, he also adopted a squad of teenage basketball players. He recently bought a Ford Expedition just so he could cart more kids around. "He was not the kind of dad to leave his kids at home," said his wife, Cheri.

Mr. Nimbley, 42, was a vice president at Cantor Fitzgerald, who doubled as a coach for the Hot Shots, a girls' basketball team in his hometown of Middletown, N.J. The players called him the "voice of reason."

"If they had problems, Paul would be the one the kids listened to," Mrs. Nimbley said.

The morning of the World Trade Center attack, Mr. Nimbley called home to check on his wife and kids, the way he always did. He has not called since then, and the Ford Expedition sits empty in the driveway.

JOHN BALLANTINE NIVEN
An Oyster Bay Getaway

John Ballantine Niven lived for weekends with his family in the country. An insurance executive at Aon, he shared an Upper East Side apartment with his wife, Ellen, and their 18-month-old son, Jack. But when the work ended, the Nivens always escaped to a gray-shingled house in Oyster Bay, N.Y.

Mr. Niven, 44, had grown up there and still played tennis with childhood friends. He carried his son everywhere, taking him along to wash the car or go for a dip in the pool. He would even hunker down with his son's toy cars. In quieter moments, he liked to read about history and philosophy.

"He would say that although his life was short, he was really blessed in the years he had," his wife said. Just that summer, the Nivens vacationed in the British Virgin Islands. Mr. Niven never got a chance to see the photos from that trip.

KATIE McGARRY NOACK
A People Person

When people met Katie McGarry Noack at parties, they remembered her. She had a knack for turning strangers into acquaintances and acquaintances into friends. "We were at a party in Australia for just a few hours," said Brad Noack, her husband, who grew up in Sydney. "But they all still remember the Yank."

Mrs. Noack, 30, made use of her charm: talking her way out of a speeding ticket, for instance. Her verbal adeptness was famous among family and friends.

So was her consideration for them. She would go to school meetings with her sister and autistic godchild, and on the spur of the moment, drive 45 minutes at night to comfort a grieving friend. She was married only six months, and had worked at Telekars USA for only six weeks. She was at a breakfast meeting at Windows on the World on Sept. 11. She was full of plans, for children and perhaps for a career in forensics. "She was just starting her life," Mr. Noack said.

CURTIS NOEL
Class Clown and Big Tease

Curtis Noel loved to tease his mother. Once Theresa Noel dropped some chicken on the floor, and her son shouted, "Nasty, nasty!" Then he said that was where he got his clumsy genes. That sense of humor got him voted class clown at James Monroe High School in the Bronx. He also loved his job as a switch engineer at General Telecom in the World Trade Center.

The company had sent him to training courses, and was always calling him in on weekends when something went wrong.

Mr. Noel, 22, could never bulk up. He would go to the gym, or eat a lot, but he was always skinny. So he would tell his husky friend Garvin Richardson, "You're my bodyguard." He had got Mr. Richardson a job at another office of General Telecom, but they rode most of the way from the Bronx to work together.

The last time he told Mr. Richardson about bodyguard duty was the morning of Sept. 11, when they arranged to go to the bank at lunchtime. They shook hands when Mr. Richardson got off at the Brooklyn Bridge stop on the No. 4 train.

Mr. Noel and his girlfriend, Aisha Harris, were thinking of getting married. She worked at General Telecom, and she died that day, too.

DANIEL NOLAN
The Ultimate "Fun Guy"

Daniel Nolan thought of himself as invincible. Danger did not scare him. It sounded like fun. He was an expert skier, and his idea of a good time was to ski down a mountain that did not have any trails carved out of it. When he went scuba diving, he would descend as deep as possible, and would grab on to whatever fish were down there and ride them.

"He would take things to the extreme," said his wife, Renee. "He was never afraid to take risks. He would always talk about how nothing could hurt him."

He enjoyed fast trips in his motorboat on Lake Hopatcong, N.J. near where he lived, and friends labeled him the Fun Guy, because of his adventuresome streak and his abiding passion for jokes. He belonged to a joke circuit of sorts on the Internet, and e-mailed friends fresh jokes every day. His wife got them too. "There were a lot of blonde jokes," she said.

But Mr. Nolan, 44, an assistant vice president for computer technology services with Marsh & McLennan, had a more placid dream for himself and his family—a splendid house on Lake Hopatcong. They had begun building it and it is nearly finished. Now it is for sale.

ROBERT NOONAN
"Send a Star up to Daddy"

Each night before bed, Chance Noonan jams his chubby 3-year-old feet into some tight sneakers and scampers outside his home in Rowayton, Conn., to "send a star up to Daddy."

The ceremony starts as his mother, Dana, hands him a sparkler. Picking out what he imagines is his father's star, Chance then whizzes around his yard like a comet, shouting "Yea, Daddy." His father, Robert, 36, a broker for Cantor Fitzgerald on the 105th floor of 1 World Trade, never came home on Sept. 11. His wife and child have since gone through boxes of sparklers. "We haven't missed a night yet," said Mrs. Noonan.

The ache is everywhere. There were 15 pictures of Robbie, as they called him, on the refrigerator alone. When Chance was born, it was his father who tended him at night, charting how much formula was consumed on his watch. When Chance grew, Mrs. Noonan slept in on Saturdays, while Mr. Noonan made the pancakes. And when Chance outgrew his sneakers this year, they put off buying a new pair because his father had wanted to help pick them out.

Mrs. Noonan lost her childhood sweetheart as well. When she first caught his eye at Greenwich High School in 1984, he had already been named Mr. May, and was pictured leaning against a goalpost in that year's "Men of Greenwich" calendar. Girls' schools as far away as Avon, Conn., had Robbie fan clubs.

Dana McGowan, however, won the prize, and the two made a striking bride and groom, she in immaculate white, he in full Highlands regalia.

DANIELA NOTARO
"She Was Full of Life"

Daniela Notaro was a receptionist and secretary with Carr Futures and worked on the 92nd floor of the World Trade Center in a job she held for about five years. She lived with her parents in Bensonhurst, Brooklyn, and had an older sister, Rosaria, and a boyfriend of several years.

"She was full of life," said her father, Carlo Notaro. "It was a very simple, normal, peaceful and joyful life."

Ms. Notaro, 25, took a vacation in August to the Bahamas, and her favorite holiday was Christmas. "She would wrap gifts for friends, for everybody in the family," he said.

And she was a perfectionist, particularly at the office, where her good manners and character made her a valuable worker. "She used to like to go to work," her father said. "Every morning she would get up very early, and never be late. If she would be late, maybe she would've saved herself.

"But she was never late. They took my life away."

BRIAN NOVOTNY
Romantic Touches

Brian Novotny first glimpsed Theresa Thomas as he and some Cantor Fitzgerald clients were leaving the Monkey Bar on the East Side of Manhattan. He shook their hands, said good night and made a beeline back inside.

Ms. Thomas, visiting from Los Angeles for the weekend, had been in New York less than an hour when she noticed a tall, soft-eyed young man smiling at her. Soon they were deep in conversation. "The chemistry was very strong—no question," she said. "When you have that chemistry, it's unavoidable." Two years ago, after numerous cross-country visits, she moved to New York, and fell more in love with Mr. Novotny, 33, than ever.

One day she remarked of the weather, "It's getting hot," and returned home the next day to find a new air conditioner humming in her apartment. Feeling out of sorts while vacationing, she comforted herself with a long bath—and emerged to a room filled with candles and soft jazz.

But then, this was a man who surprised his parents by

painting the entire exterior of their house while they were away for the weekend.

A week before Sept. 11, Theresa Thomas and Brian Novotny were engaged. For a few days, the future seemed to unfold joyously before them.

SOICHI NUMATA
On Weekends: At Home

Soichi Numata put in long hours at Fuji Bank, where he was a senior vice president. His office was on the 82nd floor of 2 World Trade Center, and his day usually began early and ended late. "He worked so hard," said his wife, Noriko. "But he spent the weekends with us."

The 45-year-old Mr. Numata loved to play golf, and the summer of 2001, when their daughter Mayu, 14, was away at camp, he and his wife spent plenty of time on public and private courses near their home in Irvington, N.Y. A former ice hockey player for Keio University, Mr. Numata relished all kinds of sports. His favorite baseball team was the Yankees, but this year, he began rooting for Ichiro Suzuki, the Seattle Mariners pitching ace. He also made sure he and his family took in the arts, including the Metropolitan Opera and the ballet.

The Numata family still owns a house in Tokyo, and Mr. Numata was planning to begin renovating it when he went back to Japan on home leave later this year. He expected to be transferred back to Tokyo before long, his wife said, after seven years in London and five years in New York.

BRIAN NUÑEZ
Coming into His Own

He was one of those kids who turned his mother, JoAnne Lovett, into a regular apologizer at the principal's office. He's almost a genius, they would say, but would you please send him somewhere else? He's taking care of everyone's business but his own.

Smart, mischievous and scattered, Brian Nuñez took a while to find his footing. He was canny and cool-headed, more logical than emotional. "Play the cards you were dealt," he would remark. He had a comment for everything.

But in his early 20s, he began settling into himself. He lived in Staten Island, putting himself through college. After graduation, he joined eSpeed as a statistical analyst, work that left him proud and exhausted. At 29, Mr. Nuñez was still solid with his mother and two brothers, and had grown into a tall, funny, dependable man with a girlfriend, Donna Corbett, whom he would kiss on the forehead and promise never to leave.

Of course he was still a prankster, still blunt, still outspoken, but on occasion his heart would tiptoe onto his sleeve. At his brother Eric's wedding, Brian stood to give the best man's toast. And stood. And stood. Overcome with love, he was finally tongue-tied.

JEFFREY NUSSBAUM
The Mayor of the Hamptons

Jeffrey Nussbaum's friends called him the Mayor of the Hamptons. After 10 or 12 summers there, he knew more people than many meet in a lifetime. "If there were 300 people in a bar," said Arline Nussbaum, his mother, "he knew 200." Friends say he liked to get one group together with another—and then introduce the combined group to a third. Given another 10 or 15 years, he might well have managed to introduce one half of the Hamptons to the other.

A trader at Carr Futures, he was a big man—6-foot-4, 230 pounds. His talent—besides making friends—was sports with balls. "Basketball, baseball," said Melissa Brunschwig, his sister. "Tennis, golf. Give him any kind of ball, he was good. It sickened his friends."

A die-hard New Yorker, Mr. Nussbaum, 37, played ball with teams in city parks. Afterward, he went to bars, restaurants, clubs—anyplace where people mingled. "He was really, really social," said Mrs. Brunschwig. "We were shopping together in Secaucus. We went to two stores and he met people he knew in each. Everywhere he went—everywhere—he knew people. And if he didn't, he'd meet them."

O

DENNIS O'BERG
Just out of the Academy

Dennis O'Berg never meant to become a firefighter like his father, but after a few years of feeling shackled to his job as an accountant at a big firm, he entered the fire academy. He graduated in 2001, and was assigned to a firehouse in Park Slope, Brooklyn.

Though his salary was lower than in the old job, his new career was more exciting and the hours more reasonable. He was 28, recently married, and wanted to start a family on Long Island. "He was so much more cheerful when he came home," said his wife, Christine. "Now he is a hero, but he was a good man back then."

She has put off a memorial service, hoping that his remains will be found.

Firefighter O'Berg's father, Lt. Dennis O'Berg, was also at the disaster site. After the towers fell, he searched for his son, but located only his fire truck, smothered in debris. He decided to retire on that day, after 31 years on the force.

JAMES P. O'BRIEN Jr.
He Was "Totally Normal"

"For the seven years I've known him, we've basically done nothing but be at home together," Lisanne MacKenzie said of James P. O'Brien Jr. "There were two children in the house, babies when he moved in, and we live really modestly in a three-room apartment. We don't have a country house, he doesn't golf, he was totally normal: come home from work, hang out in the house, do nothing, watch TV, hang out with the kids on the weekend."

Their first child together, Aiden, was five weeks old on Sept. 11.

Mr. O'Brien, 33, started out in the mailroom of Cantor Fitzgerald when he was 22, but soon moved up to become a bond broker.

"He was very disciplined," she said. "He walks into the house at 6:10 on the dot, and was up every morning at the same time. He was very structured with his time."

And every evening, from 6:30 to 8 P.M., he would take the couple's Rhodesian ridgeback, Roadie, known as the Road Dog, for walks in Prospect Park, near their home in Park Slope, Brooklyn, where he grew up.

"The dog cried every single night, all night long, for two weeks after this happened," Ms. MacKenzie said. "The dog was very attached to him."

SCOTT J. O'BRIEN
A Final Message of Love

Scott J. O'Brien had lived in Brooklyn for 13 years, but he had never seen Manhattan by boat until Sept. 8, when a friend with a powerboat showed him and his family around. "We had this fabulous picnic, and we went all around the harbor," recalled Kelly Hayes, Mr. O'Brien's wife. "He was so happy. We never knew there was a lighthouse under the George Washington Bridge. He was like a little kid. Every single thing was new to him."

A Connecticut native, Mr. O'Brien, 40, had met his wife at the University of Connecticut and moved to New York after an employer transferred him here. He was an active soccer and baseball coach for his 9-year-old son, Liam, and his 7-year-old daughter, Chloe. Liam had recently taken up fencing, a sport his father used for exercise.

On Sept. 11, Mr. O'Brien, a regional sales manager for Slam Dunk Networks, which provides Internet networks for companies, attended a conference at Windows on the World. "I didn't even know he was in the building," Ms. Hayes said. "I knew he had this conference, but I didn't know where it was."

She learned of the attack while dropping her children at school. When she returned to their Park Slope home, the message light was blinking on the answering machine. "Scott was on the phone," she said. "He said: 'I love you. There has

Our Dearest Dennis,
We miss your gentle face and patient smile,
With sadness we recall,
You had a kindly word for each
And died beloved by all.
The voice is mute and stilled the heart
That loved us well and true,
Ah, bitter was the trial to part,
From one so good as you.
You are not forgotten loved one,

been an accident. We're waiting for help. I love you and I'll see you soon.' "

TIMOTHY M. O'BRIEN
Love at First Sight

Timothy M. O'Brien was a comfortingly confident man who smiled with his eyes, and this is why, when Lisa D'Arpino first saw him, she thought, "This is it."

Mr. O'Brien interviewed Ms. D'Arpino for her first job, at a Wall Street securities firm. "I didn't hear a word he said—I was just thinking, 'O.K., this is my husband,' " said the woman who in 1994 became Mrs. O'Brien.

The oldest of seven children, Mr. O'Brien gave his siblings career advice and taught his children—John, who turns 7 today, Maddie, 5, and Jacie, 4—to dribble a basketball and to swim.

His wife called him Captain Catholic because he regularly attended church and refused to curse. "He would spell it if he had to, and he would only spell the first two letters," Mrs. O'Brien said.

"If he was really mad, it would be, 'Man alive!' We laughed about it."

A partner at Cantor Fitzgerald, Mr. O'Brien, 40, would say "Stay here" when work intruded on a telephone conversation with a relative.

"It just gave you a feeling of, 'I'm here and I'm going to come back to you,' " Mr. O'Brien's brother Sean said. "It was just a nice feeling."

DANIEL O'CALLAGHAN
Always at the Ready

Summer and winter, morning, noon and night, Lt. Daniel O'Callaghan wore his thick black bunker pants around the Ladder Company 4 firehouse in Midtown Manhattan. "It would be 102 degrees out, and he'd be wearing his bunker gear," said Al Schwartz, a firefighter who drove the truck with the lieutenant sitting up front beside him. "He was always ready to charge in."

This was a man who set the Fire Department like a seal upon his heart as well as a seal upon his arm. But he also taped paintings by his 6-year-old daughter, Rhiannon Rose, to his office walls at the firehouse, and when he left his house would

back his pickup truck up the street just to wave good-bye one more time to his 17-month-old, Connor Daniel. And when he left their home in Smithtown, N.Y., to work a 24-hour shift, he left a trail of Post-It notes in places where his family would find them: the dresser drawers, the refrigerator, the pillows.

"He'd draw smiley faces on them," said his wife, Rhonda, who married him on his 31st birthday, "and he'd write 'I love you' or 'I miss you' on them."

A lot of firemen work second jobs to make ends meet. But not Lieutenant O'Callaghan, who would have turned 43 on Feb. 3, 2002. "He was always with us," his wife said. "I'm glad, because my daughter has all these special memories."

He usually carried a battered prayer card with a book of matches stapled to it in his jacket pocket. It was his good-luck charm. On Sept. 11, he left it behind.

RICHARD O'CONNOR
From Dirt to the Sky

There's a patch of land in upstate New York called Kendrew Corners, where Rick O'Connor's forebears scratched out a living as dirt farmers. In scarcely two generations, one of their ambitious descendants had climbed to the 100th floor of the World Trade Center as a senior vice president for risk management at Marsh & McLennan. To Rick O'Connor, that meant a lot, his brother Bill recalled.

Raised in rural Watertown, N.Y., Mr. O'Connor had an itch for adventure. In college, he drove a white '56 MG and went hang gliding on weekends. When his engineering-related jobs took him around the country, he explored new terrain hungrily. (He became a connoisseur of Texas barbecue.)

His restless, demanding mind was always cooking up schemes. As a teenager, he began swapping Boy Scout patches, an activity that became a business and a newsletter. Years later, he scoured flea markets for vintage postcards and sold them over the Internet. Enamored of the chocolate cake his wife, Lynne, made, he envisioned a cake business.

Despite his love of sassy cities, Mr. O'Connor, 49, settled in the small town of LaGrangeville, N.Y., believing it was a sweet, safe place to raise Matthew, Erin and Lauren. He commuted two hours each way between his touchstones: his children and his tower.

AMY O'DOHERTY
Promise of City Life

To Amy O'Doherty, in her first job and apartment, Manhattan's streets emanated excitement and its air, promise—of new friends and smart conversations over steaks at Morton's, and of unlimited success. Of what Geraldine Davie, her mother, called "the largeness of life."

Outside the November 26 service in Melville, New York, for Dennis Scauso, Theresa Furrelle holds a picture of him, his wife, Janlyn, and their children, Juliette, Donny, Gabrielle and Darcie. Mr. Scauso, a New York City firefighter, was among the missing from September 11.
(Joyce Dopkeen)

Ms. O'Doherty, 23, loved her job as a broker's assistant at Cantor Fitzgerald. "Financing, trading, bonds," said Liz Gallello, a childhood friend. "She wanted to take it—the career, the city woman lifestyle—as far as far it could go."

She was delighted with her five-story walk-up—so small, said Ms. Davie, that "Lilliputians should live in it." She filled it with dozens of framed photos of friends from Pelham, N.Y., where she grew up, and from camp, college and work.

"She was soaking up that great New York style," said Ms. Davie. "Picking up that New York language. She didn't know it but she was living her bliss."

MARNI PONT O'DOHERTY
Focused and Looking Ahead

Marni Pont O'Doherty was so focused that while she was still in college, she opened accounts to pay for her wedding and to buy a car with cash, even though she had neither a boyfriend nor a job at the time.

At 31, Ms. O'Doherty was the optimistic baby in a family of three children. She indeed married (outside, in an off-the-shoulder gown on an unseasonably cold fall day) and landed a fabulous job. She was a senior vice president at Keefe, Bruyette & Woods.

She had her silly side, too, and was always the one with the funny story, said her brother and sister, Steven and Stefanie Pont. Their younger sister threw herself into a series of hobbies, from needlepoint to painting to gardening, and delighted in researching amusing information and e-mailing her find-

ings. "From the time she was 2 and learned to talk, she never shut up," Mr. Pont said. "Personally or professionally, she'd tell you every single thing. She always made it interesting."

JAMES ANDREW O'GRADY
A Place for Everything . . .

James Andrew O'Grady kept his shirts arranged by color. He lined up his cuff links just so. And he liked his towels in a certain place. His love of order and ritual might have seemed out of place in the tumultuous world of the bond market, where Mr. O'Grady, 32, was a managing director of fixed-income sales for Sandler O'Neill & Partners.

Yet even there, in his 104th-floor office in the World Trade Center's south tower, "there was rarely a scrap of paper out of place," said Rich Tuohey, a friend and colleague.

As a boy, Mr. O'Grady's focused intensely on swimming, and he won a swimming scholarship to U.C.L.A., where he earned four letters, traveled three times to the N.C.A.A. finals and, in his senior year, was selected as a co-captain of the team.

"He liked things the way he liked them," said Rachel Uchitel, Mr. O'Grady's girlfriend and, since Aug. 5, his fiancée. Early in the morning on Sept. 11, Andy, as he was known, called Ms. Uchitel at work to needle her with a running joke. She had left the towels, he said, in the right place.

THOMAS G. O'HAGAN
On a Different Path

When Thomas G. O'Hagan was 7, he tried to stamp out a fire in the Riverdale section of the Bronx, but his pants caught fire. He ended up with second- and third-degree burns. "Even with all that," said his brother Raymond, "and all the pain that burns cause, Tommy wanted to be a fireman."

In a family of 11, with his grandfather, father and two brothers being police officers, Thomas O'Hagan's decision to become a firefighter, and later be promoted to lieutenant, set him apart.

"Tom was very different from the rest of us," said the eldest of the five O'Hagan brothers, Frank, a banker. "While the rest of us are kind of quiet, Tom was very loquacious and extremely generous with his time, money and advice."

Lieutenant O'Hagan, 43, lived in Riverdale, where he grew up, and was an enthusiastic firehouse chef who knew all the best recipes because they were his own. He had been assigned to Engine Company 6 a few weeks before Sept. 11.

If anyone needed a hand, his brothers said, Tom O'Hagan's voice was first to be heard. He was dedicated to his wife, Andrea, and their twins, Patrick and Pierce. After his mother died in May, Lieutenant O'Hagan visited his father

Residents of Levittown, New York, taking part in an illuminated remembrance walk on the night of November 27 to honor the victims of the September 11 attacks.

(*James Estrin*)

at least three times a week and often more. "He was there for dad a lot," Frank O'Hagan said. "That speaks volumes about his generosity."

MATTHEW O'MAHONY
No Waster of Sleep

Matthew O'Mahony, 39, refused to let sleep usurp time that could be put to better use. The hours he could allot to pleasure were limited enough, without sleep cutting into them. On his annual Paris vacation, for instance, he was ready to start the day at 4 in the morning. "Let's go for a walk in the Tuileries," he would say, nudging Lauren, his wife, awake. "Let's go see it when no one else is there, so we can appreciate it."

They lived downtown, near his work as a Cantor Fitzgerald trader, but spent weekends at their farmhouse in Columbia County. They would squeeze every last hour of their time in the country by driving back very early Monday morning.

Mrs. O'Mahony remembers awakening at 4:30 one Monday, looking out the window and seeing her husband, out on the lake in the boat, fishing for bass. "He had an extra 15 minutes," she said. "So he was going to enjoy them."

He had a flair for drama, and used it to heighten the spectacle of gift giving. They locked horns on the question of buying a horse. He loudly, adamantly opposed it. That made his choreographed anniversary scene all the more satisfying. He led an Arabian chestnut out; she stared incredulously until he finally said: "Are you dense? Look at the ribbon around its neck!"

His real success was keeping it a surprise. Only close friends knew—which, for Mr. O'Mahony, meant at least 50 people.

JOHN O'NEILL
The Head of Security

John O'Neill of the Federal Bureau of Investigation was a relative newcomer to New York, but nearly everybody saw him as New York to the bone. And not just any New Yorker, but a New Yorker of a certain pure strain—the gregarious, high-living, deeply curious Irish cop, who loved wit and companionship and, most of all, investigating crimes.

During his six years as head of national security at the New York F.B.I. office, he seemingly became acquainted with half the population of the city. One after another, said Valerie James, his companion, people would stop by his table at Elaine's or Bruno's or at one of the other restaurants he frequented nearly every night. He would order a Chivas with water and a twist and a hearty meaty meal, smoke a Dominican cigar and talk—to cops, colleagues, movie stars, kitchen workers, musicians.

He was a complicated man, with a life full of contradictions. Long estranged—but not divorced—from Christine O'Neill, his wife in New Jersey, he lived with Ms. James, a fashion sales director he met in Chicago. A driven F.B.I. investigator, he was, said Ms. James, a well-studied lover of jazz and French Impressionism. He led the agency's investigations into the terrorist attacks on the American embassies in Kenya and Tanzania in 1998 and the World Trade Center in 1993 and was its foremost expert on Osama bin Laden. In August, he retired from the F.B.I. to become head of security at the World Trade Center, which he intended to protect against the enemies he had studied so deeply.

PETER J. O'NEILL Jr.
Like Father, Like Son

Their firstborn's name was debated and decided, but the baby looked too much like his father to be a Brendan. He was a Peter J. O'Neill Jr.—case closed—his mother, Jeanne, decided when she caught her first glimpse. Peter O'Neill shared all of his father's interests and an extra virtue: enamored of firemen from the time he was 2, he joined his local volunteer crew in Amityville, N.Y., at 17.

At home, he and his father were known as the Twins. Handy and outdoorsy like dad, Peter Jr. knew his way around the family boat, the basement toolbox, the lawn mower; he also hunted duck and shot skeet, a bonding ritual for the O'Neill men.

He considered working alongside his father, a Wall Streeter-turned-painting contractor, but realized his business degree from Bentley College would get a better workout at his uncle's firm, Sandler O'Neill & Partners, at 2 World Trade Center. He was a natural there, too, and he and four friends were stockpiling their salaries in hopes of renting a Manhattan apartment.

Shoe-shopping on the Sunday before the attack, Mr. O'Neill, 21, told his mother he intended to take classes to become an emergency medical technician. When she asked why he wanted to do that rather than go to graduate school, he said, "Because, Mom, I want to help people."

KEVIN M. O'ROURKE
Kids' Best Friend

All the kids knew. If their bike was broken—a flat tire, a loose chain—then all they had to do was take it to the firehouse and see Kevin M. O'Rourke. He would dig his tool kit out of his locker, where the other firefighters had taped up a sign saying "Kevin's Bike Shop," and he'd fix it. And while the kids were there, he invariably taught them fire safety. He would unroll a rug and demonstrate how to do the stop, drop and roll technique when one's clothes caught fire.

Firefighter O'Rourke, 44, lived with his wife, Maryann, and their daughters, Corinne, 20, and Jamie, 17, in Hewlett, N.Y. Each year, his family and his wife's family would converge for a ski trip and a golf outing.

He also was a regular in the annual firefighter ski races at Hunter Mountain. There would be five-man teams, and they would be in their jackets and helmets and have to cling to a fire hose and swoop down the mountain. There were innumerable teams, but one year Firefighter O'Rourke's came in fifth, and it made him very proud.

TIMOTHY F. O'SULLIVAN
A Caring Negotiator

Tim O'Sullivan remembers going to his father's office at the Bronx Zoo one night as a child and discovering that his father knew the night janitor's entire family by their first names. When the son expressed amazement, his father said, "Here at the zoo, we have tremendous scientific minds, but what good would they be if they were buried up to their necks in wastepaper?"

His father, Timothy F. O'Sullivan, who was 68, worked as a personnel manager, then as an administrator and specialist in labor relations at the Wildlife Conservation Society. His success as a negotiator, his children believe, stemmed from his ability to make everyone he encountered feel like the only person on the planet and from an unshakable respect for working folks.

He was 6-foot-7 and had stood eye-to-eye with an elephant. He loved military history, jokes and Geraldine, his wife of 43 years, whom he met at a St. Patrick's Day firemen's dance in the Bronx. After he retired and moved to the Poconos—"just me and my girl," he would say—he worked as a consultant to the Cultural Institutions Retirement System, commuting one day every six to eight weeks to the trade center.

"What did somebody say to me?" Mr. O'Sullivan's daughter, Denise, said recently, alluding to where her father would be headed next. " 'There's nobody better to lead the other 5,000 in—to negotiate their way in.' "

JAMES A. OAKLEY
A Volunteer for Gettysburg

Jim Oakley was a Civil War buff, so he was happy to be a parent volunteer when one of his daughters went on a class trip to Gettysburg. In fact, he had such a good time camping and re-enacting the great battle that "he insisted on bringing the whole family down" to Gettysburg that summer, said his wife, Denise I. Oakley.

That trip was rivaled perhaps by the class trip he took with another daughter to Fort Ticonderoga to re-enact a battle of the Revolutionary War. "That time, they gave him a uniform," Mrs. Oakley said, adding that her husband had been looking forward to accompanying his youngest daughter on her class trip. James A. Oakley always found time for his four daughters, ages 26 to 11, despite a daily three-hour round-trip commute from Cortlandt Manor in northern Westchester County to the World Trade Center, where he worked for Marsh & McLennan as senior vice president for information technology.

One of those daughters is starting to share his interest in history. "We have Civil War books all over the house, and the nice part is that she's started to pick up some of them," Mrs. Oakley said. "So she's going to carry on that interest."

JOHN OGONOWSKI
Captain on the Farm

John Ogonowski wore two uniforms: his navy blue senior captain's uniform for American Airlines and the blue jeans and denim shirt he wore while working on his 150-acre farm in Dracut, Mass., where he lived with his wife and three daughters.

Twelve days a month, Mr. Ogonowski, 50, flew transcontinental flights. On off days, he tended the farm's peach orchard, with acres set aside for corn, pumpkins and hay. After supper he often sat in his favorite chair, reading agricultural journals late into the evening.

Mr. Ogonowski joined the Air Force at the height of the Vietnam War. He flew C-141 transport planes, taking equipment to Asia, and sometimes flying back to the States carrying the bodies of American soldiers. He became a commercial pilot in 1979, and met a pretty flight attendant named Peggy, whom he later married.

The morning of Sept. 11, he left his wife at home, still in bed. It was already dawn as he turned down the road in his dusty green Chevy truck, to start his drive to Boston and to Logan International Airport. As he passed his uncle's nearby house, he tooted his horn. Mr. Ogonowski was the captain of Flight 11, the first plane to crash into the World Trade Center.

JOSEPH J. OGREN
Rambunctious Brothers

Joseph J. Ogren and his brother Lance were always close.

Tall and athletic, Joseph, who was called Jay, and Lance earned swimming scholarships to St. John's University. They both ran the New York City Marathon—twice. They

Children from suburban Philadelphia who brought toys to
Manhattan for the children of the uniformed
personnel killed September 11 (*James Estrin*)

both loved music and played guitar. And they rented a house in Staten Island and lived upstairs-downstairs from each other.

"We knew each other inside and out," said Lance Ogren.

The youngest of five children, the two brothers enjoyed each other's company, sometimes a little too much. Their mother, Dorothy Ogren, said that when they visited their siblings and nieces and nephews, the siblings sometimes said the brothers "were too wild for their children."

In 1992, the brothers took the exam to become firefighters and both scored well. Even so, it was four years before there was an opening for Lance Ogren. Jay Ogren had to wait another two years.

Once he joined the Fire Department, Jay Ogren was assigned to Ladder Company 3, one block south of Union Square, where he was working on Sept. 11. Lance was off-duty that day.

Mrs. Ogren was surprised by their career choice. "Of my children, I never expected them to go into the Fire Department," she said. But once Lance Ogren became a firefighter, it was likely that Jay Ogren would, too. After all, they were twins, born 31 years ago.

CHRISTINE A. OLENDER
Yankee Doodle Sweetheart

No, she did not sing the song.

But Christine A. Olender was a Yankee Doodle sweetheart, born on the Fourth of July. It was her best day. But when she grew up, it was her worst—the only time when the petite, long-haired, effervescent former pompom girl, elected homecoming queen for Archbishop Weber High School, an all-boys Catholic school in her native Chicago, felt a little bit lonely.

When she moved to the Upper West Side of New York, Miss Olender, 39, discovered that the Fourth was the day when New Yorkers fled town. Even the bakery was closed. So she and a friend who had the same birthday, Melissa Trumbull, would make sure to order Miss Olender's favorite birthday treat—strawberry shortcake—a day in advance. Then the two of them put candles on the cake, got a bottle of Champagne from Windows on the World, where Miss Olender was assistant to the general manager, and celebrated.

Part of the ritual was a call from Miss Olender's mother, Stella. Don't worry about being left behind on your birthday, Miss Olender's mother would croon. "You're my little firecracker."

But Miss Olender, known for being practical in all things except shoes, did not sing the George M. Cohan song. "Christine was way too cool for that," Ms. Trumbull said.

LINDA OLIVA
Taking Charge with a Smile

She was a take-charge woman, but she did so with the upbeat fervor of a cheerleader, which she was in high school. Linda Oliva would march into her mother's home a few times a week, cook meals, shop, organize and fuss sweetly over her brother Frankie, who has special needs.

Ms. Oliva, 44, was like that at work, too. Temp agencies would send her to a job and she would have things running so smoothly that positions would open for this suddenly indispensable woman. She had been executive assistant to the president of the New York office of Carr Futures.

She succeeded not only because she was capable, but because she exuded joy: she would dance happily to Rod Stewart or Tony Bennett, her laughter bubbling forth without prompting. "I knew she had a great sense of humor because she thought everything I said was hilarious," said another brother, Chuck Oliva, whose young daughter, Alexandra, adored her.

Divorced, Ms. Oliva, who lived in Staten Island, had begun dating a family friend, Tom Donovan, last summer.

On their first date, he recalled, "There she was in a beautiful cream-colored outfit. She wore her brown hair long, and she was a knockout. And I thought, I can't believe this girl is going out with me."

EDWARD OLIVER
A Long-Distance Romance

Sheryl Budke of Cincinnati had no intention of trying to meet a guy when she and her sister went to Daytona Beach on vacation, but two grandfatherly men kept nagging them, so Ms. Budke finally took a walk on the beach with Edward Oliver, from Staten Island. They knew by the next day that they would marry, and they kept the romance going long-distance for two years. They were married for seven.

Mr. Oliver, 31, lived in Jackson, N.J., and was a commodities broker for Carr Futures. He had a 2½-year-old daughter, Emily, and a 4-month-old son, Eddie. Mr. Oliver loved golf and *The Honeymooners* and, most of all, sitting on the couch with Emily, eating reduced fat Cheez-Its. (He was careful about his health.)

His offices were at the New York Mercantile Exchange building, but on Sept. 11, he had an early meeting at the main office in the World Trade Center.

Ms. Oliver received an odd phone call that morning, in which her husband's phone number came up on caller ID but she did not hear his voice. She did not begin to worry, however, until her sister-in-law called.

"I said, 'Oh, but he had a meeting,' " Ms. Oliver said. "Then I ran upstairs and looked in his nightstand drawer and found a business card that said, '1 World Trade Center, 96th floor.' I thought I would die.

"The struggle we did to stay together for two years, and this is all we get," Ms. Oliver said. "It's just not fair."

MAUREEN OLSON
Getting Back to Manhattan

She moved to a Long Island suburb to raise her family, but Manhattan was the nexus of Maureen Olson's life.

"We met in 1979 on a blind date in New York," said her husband, John Eric Olson. At that time, "She lived on 65th Street and First Avenue. But in the 1960s and 1970s she lived up in the high East 90s. "In the past year or so she had been looking around to move back to the city. I am sure we would have."

The professional part of that goal was already in place.

Three years ago, with son Christopher and daughter Maeve in high school, Mrs. Olson took a job as a business librarian in the World Trade Center offices of Marsh Inc., a risk and insurance subsidiary of Marsh & McLennan, commuting to Manhattan with her husband from Rockville Centre, N.Y.

Mrs. Olson, who was a month and a day shy of 51 on Sept. 11, graduated from Manhattan Marymount College. She loved Broadway. She and her husband ran in the New York City Marathon.

"We met in college," Marian Masone, a friend for roughly 30 years, said. "Her sister and my sister were two years ahead of us. We even dropped out of college the same day, in the middle of our junior year. Eventually, we both went back."

STEVEN OLSON
"The Rock" of Ladder 3

Every firehouse has an array of personalities, from pranksters to perfectionists. At Ladder Company 3, on East 13th Street, Steven Olson was known as the Rock.

Cheerful, optimistic, diligent, reliable, Firefighter Olson arrived in 1989, fresh out of the Fire Academy, and never left. He proved to be an excellent probie, short for probationary firefighter. Lately, whenever the older firefighters would try to push a little extra work out of the newest recruits, they would hold him up as an example.

"We'd say, 'There hasn't been a good probie here for 12 years, not since Steve Olson,' " said Rob Burmeister, a friend and fellow member of Ladder 3. "He was full of energy. He never sat down."

Firefighter Olson, 38, turned himself into a top fireman. In the 12 years they spent together, his colleagues watched him marry and become the devoted father of two daughters, ages 2 and 7. In the quieter moments at Ladder 3, he'd work on crossword puzzles, usually with a pen.

"He was a confident guy," Firefighter Burmeister said. At fires, "you always felt comfortable working with him," he added. "If you were in trouble, he was coming to get you."

SEAMUS ONEAL
Many Names, Many Faces

For Seamus Oneal, the idea of having one career and one name was much too timid. By 52, he had worked in five widely different professions, using three different names. As James, he studied drama at the University of Oklahoma, and as Seam, he acted, danced and sang in Off Broadway shows. "It would be fair," said John Oneal, his brother, "to call him a hippie."

Seam Oneal the hippie joined the Army, became Captain Oneal and won medals for his work in hospital administration. Nevertheless, after converting to Mormonism, he and Janet Kaye, his wife, and their three children moved into a bed and breakfast by a big Maryland temple and ran it together. Eventually, though, he returned to college to study advanced computer science, moved to Manhattan and took a job with eSpeed.

Along the way, he composed liturgical choral works that were played by the Mormon temple's orchestra. And he dropped Seam and became Seamus.

"He said, 'There might be other Jameses,' " said his brother, " 'but there won't be other Seamuses.' He was something. A piece of art."

MICHAEL C. OPPERMAN
A Hardworking Man

The annals of workaholism will hold a special place for Michael C. Opperman. It is one thing to leave the house at 3 A.M., as Mr. Opperman, a senior vice president at Aon Insurance, routinely did, so that he could get a head start on his own work before people started coming to him for help.

It is another thing to try to keep working after a jet hits the building across the plaza. Around 9 A.M. on Sept. 11, when a colleague said urgently, "I'm going now, Mike, are you coming?" Michael Opperman replied, "O.K. I've just got a few loose ends to tie up here."

Deborah Opperman said that her husband, 45, who grew up the son of a truck driver in the Bronx and who never got further than his associate's degree in college, was driven by a fear that his accomplishments in life could be taken away.

"I think he always had in the back of his head that he could lose it," she said from their home in Selden on Long Island. "He'd say, 'My God, Debbie, there are so many people out there that are so educated.' "

Mr. Opperman left an 18-year-old son and a 12-year-old daughter. His son, Mike Jr., had just started school at Wagner College in Staten Island. "They're good kids, thank God for that," Ms. Opperman said. "Except I sort of see my husband's drive in my son. That sort of frightens me."

CHRIS ORGIELEWICZ
Straight Arrow

Chris Orgielewicz's 18th birthday was one to remember. When he returned to Fairfield University, he told his roommate, Martin Sullivan, all about it. He went bowling with his father, Mr. Sullivan recalled. He had cake with his family. Then he visited his grandfather and had cake all over again.

Not exactly the wild and crazy party some teenagers might prefer. But that, Mr. Sullivan said, was the kind of guy Chris Orgielewicz was. "Sweet," he said, "innocent and kind."

During the 17 years that followed, Mr. Orgielewicz married (though it required patience and time to get his sweetheart to take him seriously). He and his wife, Olga, had three children and he became a research analyst at Sandler O'Neill & Partners, specializing in the Middle East. But what struck Mr. Sullivan was how much, at 35, he resembled what he was at 18: hardworking and kind, a quintessential straight arrow.

PETER ORTALE
An Unprompted Giver

Peter Ortale did not need occasions to send people presents. He just sent them when the desire percolated in him. That was often.

One of five siblings, he regularly liked to pick out something that caught his fancy and mail it to each of the others, as well as his mother. In the spring, the relatives got a book, *A Short Guide to a Happy Life,* by Anna Quindlen. Just before the summer, he sent them a box of chocolates with a note, "Have a happy summer." His mother was constantly getting flowers.

"He did things without provocation, because he liked to," said his sister Mary Malitas.

When not working or sending presents, Mr. Ortale, 37, a bond broker at Euro Brokers, was often playing lacrosse. He was one of the best players on his high school team in Philadelphia, and again at Duke University. After he graduated, he played in Australia, and once he began his career, he continued to play for various leagues on weekends.

A few years ago, he took up cooking. He found it therapeutic. When friends and relatives visited him and his wife in SoHo, he would often turn out an elaborate meal, sometimes trying things not everyone might. Once he steamed a fish in the dishwasher. He thought it came out great.

ALEXANDER ORTIZ
A Big Heart to Help People

Alexander Ortiz was the security guard with the grin, usually there at the entrance to Blue Cross and Blue Shield on the 28th floor of the north tower. His dedication would become known best after Sept. 11.

Mr. Ortiz worked for Grubb & Ellis Inc., a property management company, and was assigned for seven years to the insurance carrier's offices. He died after assisting several people out of the north tower, and returning to direct traffic in the building's lobby. "He loved his job, because he loved helping people," said Lourdes Dominguez, Mr. Ortiz's former wife and mother of his 5-year-old son, Alexander Jr.

Mr. Ortiz, who lived in Ridgewood, Queens, was adjusting to life as a bachelor. "Dating wasn't easy for him," said Moises Lorenzi, a friend and weight-lifting buddy. "He had such a big heart, he would let himself get hurt."

Ms. Dominguez said Mr. Ortiz and his son were together on alternate weekends, which started with breakfast at a Chinese restaurant in Ridgewood and often included outings to a park or museum. "Those of us who saw them together will always remember the radiant smiles," Ms. Dominquez said.

DAVID ORTIZ
The Fish Didn't Flee

When David Ortiz was not working overtime on weekends at his job as a locksmith at the World Trade Center, sometimes he would take his 14-year-old son, Richard, fishing in upstate New York. His catches or lack thereof were legendary at the third-floor Port Authority shop at 4 World Trade Center.

"What was it, boy, that he used to catch?" said David Achee, a friend and colleague, struggling to remember the type of fish. "Oh, teeny-tiny striped bass. And he would catch just one. He had expensive fishing rods. I told him in my country that we use a cork, a can and some rope and catch more fish." Mr. Achee is a native of Trinidad.

Mr. Ortiz, 37, was easygoing, and took the teasing in stride. He worked hard and knew the ins and outs of the trade center like the back of his hand, Mr. Achee said. He used his overtime earnings to pay for renovations on his new house in Rockland County, N.Y., where he lived with Richard, his wife, Lillian, and daughter, Crystal, 6.

"The reason he is missing is because he was trying to help people," Mr. Achee said. "We didn't know it was an attack. I went to give backup batteries to the other workers on the West Side Highway, and he stayed back to prevent people from going into 4 World Trade Center."

EMILIO ORTIZ
Suddenly Silly

At Emilio Ortiz's wedding reception three years ago, his best man, Daniel Lopez, gave an emotional toast that caused people to get weepy. Suddenly, he turned to the bride, reached into his tuxedo jacket, pulled out a ring box and handed to her. Everyone in the room grew quiet, wondering what it was.

"It was a Viagra pill," the blushing bride, Wanda Ortiz, recalled, laughing. "Those two together were so silly. They were always playing jokes on each other."

Mr. Ortiz, 38, who everyone knew as Pete, was always playing jokes on his wife, too. He was supposed to draw the curtain after every shower, she said. One time, he forgot and she reminded him by asking, "What's wrong with this picture?" Instead of closing the shower curtain, he adjusted a picture on the wall and said: "It was a little crooked."

Mr. Ortiz, who worked at Carr Futures and lived in Corona, Queens, was the father of twins, Amanda and Emily. "I've never seen such a proud man," Mrs. Ortiz said. "The attacks happened three days shy of their first six months. We tried for a year to have a child. When we finally had one, God blessed us with two. It makes me angry that he only had five months with his children."

Mr. Ortiz and his best friend, Mr. Lopez, worked together. Both are missing.

PABLO ORTIZ
The Paradigm of Patience

Pablo Ortiz had been a military man, a Navy Seal, and he had a military discipline. He was fussy. He was relentlessly neat. "He liked his clothes ironed a certain way," said his wife, Edna Kang-Ortiz. "They had to be ironed legs first and the crease had to be perfect. The shirts couldn't have any wrinkles. I tried to do it and couldn't please him."

Fine. He handled the laundry. He ironed her clothes too, and did they look good.

Before they got married in March of last year, they compared their strong and weak points. Mrs. Kang-Ortiz confessed she was a terrible cook. No problem. He did all the cooking.

Mr. Ortiz, 49, superintendent of construction for the Port Authority, lived in Staten Island with his wife, and she liked to say, "People come into your life to teach you a lesson. He taught me a lot of lessons. I was materialistic. I have become less materialistic. I learned from his strength. I learned from his patience."

In May, the sister of Mrs. Kang-Ortiz had some difficulties and needed to move to the Ortiz home with her two children. Mr. Ortiz was entirely supportive. "He would say to me, 'As long as you're happy, it's cool,'" his wife said. "His feeling was, 'You make the wife happy, you're happy.'"

PAUL ORTIZ Jr.
"He Took Care of Us"

At 21, Paul Ortiz Jr. was already on his way to getting everything he wanted. He doted on his wife, Star, whom he had met in college, and was immensely proud of their baby, Rebecca Brianna.

Mrs. Ortiz said her husband carried around pictures of his daughter to show to everyone, and spent much of his time at home in their Brooklyn apartment playing with her and feeding her. "He took care of us," she said. "Whatever we needed, he would get, no matter what he had to do to get it."

And he loved his job at Bloomberg, where he was a computer technician. The first gift he gave Rebecca was a toy truck with the Bloomberg logo on it, Mrs. Ortiz said. "He loved his company so much, and he loved the fact that the truck said Bloomberg Company on it," she said. "I told him, 'No, don't give that to her because that's for a boy,' but he didn't care."

Mr. Ortiz worked at the company's offices on Park Avenue, but on Sept. 11, he was setting up a conference to be held at Windows on the World.

SONIA ORTIZ
With Her Son Again

In her native Colombia, Sonia Ortiz was forced to work as a seamstress from an early age. After she immigrated to the United States in 1971, she landed a job as a janitor at the World Trade Center and eventually was promoted to run the freight elevator serving Windows on the World.

With her earnings, she bought a tidy two-story brick house in Flushing, Queens, that she filled with fanciful knicknacks, including place mats with pictures of cherubs, and porcelain figurines of fairy tale characters. "Everything we have today is because of her," said her son, Victor.

In the photograph that her children have posted on bulletin boards of the missing, Mrs. Ortiz is dressed demurely in her work outfit—white blouse and black bow tie—and is holding a Spanish-language book about life after death. Her children said she became fascinated with that subject after her son, Wilson, died of a brain aneurysm nine years ago, at 26.

"She was absolutely convinced there is a God and an afterlife," said her daughter, Alexa Ortiz. "She always said she wanted to be up there with my brother. If there's any comfort, it's knowing that she's with him now."

ELSY C. OSORIO-OLIVA
Spoiled Her Siblings

Elsy C. Osorio-Oliva was the oldest sibling in her Flushing, Queens, household, but she acted like a mother hen. She doted on her younger brother and sister—Kate and Anthony Umanzor, 10 and 8—with whom she lived, along with her mother and stepfather. And she doted on her mother, Feliciana Oliva-Umanzor, who left college and a war-ravaged El Salvador in 1983 for a new living in the United States cleaning apartments.

A junior translation engineer with General Telecom on the 83rd floor of 1 World Trade Center, Ms. Osorio-Oliva, 27, spoiled her sister and brother with toys, outings and weekend breakfasts of pancakes and French toast. She paid for her mother to take courses in computer and tax preparation so she could get an enjoyable job. The daughter, who was known by her middle name, Carolina, even lent her mother some clothes for the office, and planned to buy her a car so she could be more independent.

But there was so much independence that Ms. Osorio-Oliva wanted for herself. Engaged for the last two years, her mother said, she wanted to get married and have a house big enough to move in her whole family.

"She said, 'Mami, I can't live without you or the children,'" her mother said.

JASON DOUGLAS OSWALD
New York, His Second City

Jason Douglas Oswald had moved to New York only in June. But he and the woman he was seeing, Nancy Prentis, also a fresh arrival from the Midwest, were already consummate New Yorkers. They ran at dusk in Central Park. They frequented the public tennis courts beneath the George Washington Bridge. And they spent hours moving the broken-in Ford

Explorer he had brought from Chicago, just to keep up with maddening parking rules. Apparently, said Jane Oswald, Mr. Oswald's mother, "you can't have a job and a car in New York because you have to keep going to move your car."

Her 28-year-old son was not thinking that far ahead in June when he quit his job in Chicago and drove east, ending up in Manhattan. All he knew was that he wanted to be with Ms. Prentis. The job would come later, he told his mother from somewhere on the Pennsylvania Turnpike. When he finally landed an accounting job in August at Cantor Fitzgerald, on the 101st floor of 1 World Trade Center, the Explorer was parked at a friend's home.

The S.U.V. got some exercise before Labor Day, when Mr. Oswald took Ms. Prentis to Merrill, Wis., to meet his parents. After Mr. Oswald's disappearance on Sept. 11, Ms. Prentis and her parents made the trip one last time from the big city to attend memorial services for Mr. Oswald and return the Explorer.

TODD OUIDA
The Strength in That Smile

Whether he was mischievously finagling another stroke at golf or beaming over his infant niece, Todd Ouida's smile touched people. "A great smile that could light up a room," said his mother, Andrea.

It was not a smile he came by easily.

He was not big enough, his older brother, Jordan Ouida joked, to be a water boy. But he persisted and became a starting defensive back on the River Dell High School football team in New Jersey. He overcame a panic disorder that began in the fourth grade and made him terrified to go to school for several years. But he received a degree from the University of Michigan.

Todd Ouida, 25, became a foreign currency option trader for Cantor Fitzgerald on the 105th floor of the north tower. He was hired on his own merits after a summer internship arranged by Jordan Ouida, a vice president in the London office. He and his father, Herbert, executive vice president of the World Trade Centers Association on the 78th floor—he survived the attack—commuted together from River Edge, N.J.

"Todd was always amazing us; whatever the obstacle, he was able to overcome it," Jordan Ouida said. "There was a lot of family support, but it was also the inner strength that he had in himself."

ADIANES OYOLA
"She Gave Me Vision"

Adianes and Felipe Oyola were at work when they fell in love seven years ago and when they last saw each other on Sept. 11. They had met as teenagers—she was a cashier at the Brooklyn fast-food restaurant where he was a cook. "She gave me vision and motivation to better myself," said Mr. Oyola, who married her last year.

The couple made plans to save money, clear debts and move to Florida, where her parents and 13-year-old brother live. Both native New Yorkers, they craved a house almost as badly as they did children. "We didn't want to raise our kids here," Mr. Oyola said. "We wanted to give them things we never had. We've always lived in apartments, never having control. We wanted something of our own."

The Oyolas commuted together from their Brooklyn home to their jobs with Fuji Bank at 2 World Trade Center. She went to the 82nd floor, where she worked in human resources and payroll, while he went to the 81st floor, where he was supervisor of mail services. When the first plane hit the tower next door, the Oyolas found each other by a bank of elevators on the 78th floor. They were hugging when the speakers announced that it was safe to return to their offices.

Mr. Oyola went back first, leaving his wife with her boss and a co-worker. Then the second plane hit, and he barely made it out. His wife is missing. "She was crying," Mr. Oyola, 24, said of the last moments with his 23-year-old wife. "I told her everything was going to be O.K."

P

ANGEL PABÓN
Defying Stereotypes

When Angel Pabón gave up Marlboro Lights six years ago, his 5-foot-8 frame grew from 185 pounds to 205 pounds. "He had these chubby cheeks that I used to love to grab," said his wife, Yvette. "When he gained that weight, it made me love him just a little bit more."

Mr. Pabón, 53, a manager of international equities at Cantor Fitzgerald, achieved his position through will and talent. A native of Puerto Rico, he loved to defy ethnic stereotypes. More than 30 years ago, an employment agency sent him to interview for a position as a teletype operator at Drexel Burnham Lambert. He got the job, but was intrigued by traders, who were screaming in a nearby office. He asked an Anglo colleague what was going on, Mrs. Pabón said.

"The guy told him not to worry about it because he would never work there," Mrs. Pabón recalled. "My husband was furious. He wanted to say something to him, but he didn't. But within a year, my husband was trading for the company on the Japanese market. That was his response to the guy."

ROLAND PACHECO
A Wedding That Wasn't

Roland Pacheco's pickup line when he met Annie Guerrero eight years ago was, "What's the matter with you?"

He asked it softly, but it was still a bold question to ask a stranger. They were both teenagers hanging out with their respective groups of friends when he spied her hanging back on a bustling corner a couple of blocks away from Washington Square Park.

"Nothing," Ms. Guerrero recalled saying. "I'm just tired. And we just started talking."

The meeting sparked a fine romance. Now, eight years later, they were engaged to be married and have a 2½-year-old son, Ryan.

Mr. Pacheco, 26, was a pretty good catch, Ms. Guerrero said. He was an employee of Alliance Consulting on the 102nd floor of 1 World Trade Center. Ms. Guerrero is disconsolate that there will never be a wedding. They had other plans: they were going to open a lounge together on the West Side.

"He was so outgoing and happy," Ms. Guerrero said. "I wish he had gone in later."

Geraldine Davie reading to some of her students in the library at Barnard School in New Rochelle, New York. Many of the books were bought with money raised by Ms. Davie and coworkers of her daughter, Amy O'Doherty, who worked at Cantor Fitzgerald in the World Trade Center. (*James Estrin*)

MICHAEL B. PACKER
Musical and Mechanical

Michael B. Packer had a Ph.D. in mechanical engineering from the Massachusetts Institute of Technology, which came in very handy at his children's science fairs and birthday parties.

"When you walked into the house, you usually walked into a scientific experiment," said Ronald Soiefer, a close friend who had met Mr. Packer when they were Harvard undergraduates. One contraption had a microphone hooked up to a laptop computer, which recorded human voices and showed them as sound waves on a colored screen.

Mr. Packer, 45, of Hartsdale, N.Y., had many other sides. He played the piano and, in his spare time, made harpsichords, a trade he had learned as a student at Phillips Exeter Academy and Harvard. He made sure that his children—Sarita, 11, and Jonathan, 7—were steeped in the classics.

In June, he and his wife, Rekha, took the children on a tour of the Aegean Islands, following in the footsteps of Homer's Ulysses. Mr. Packer, who was to be the keynote speaker at a technology conference at Windows on the World on Sept. 11, joined Merrill Lynch in 1999 as a leader of a major e-commerce initiative.

"He was very good at managing things," said Mrs. Packer, who remembers most vividly how he coped with the family, the house, his job and her convalescence when she suffered a brain injury in 1990. "Nothing really got him down. We really miss him for that now."

DEEPA K. PAKKALA
Determined to Do It All

Deepa K. Pakkala was a perfectionist. She went to work early and returned late to her home in Stewartsville, N.J., and then she often cleaned. Every last spot of dirt. She was a consultant for Oracle and was working for a client at the trade center. The morning of the attack, she was at her desk before she had to be.

Her husband, Sampath, whom she met in Bangalore, the technology center of India, realized that her drive was an essential part of her, but he often tried to persuade her to scale back, if just a little. He said he would always ask her to go in a little later. "She would say that 'if I do that, I would have to leave my job.'"

November 29 at ground zero: the charred shell of a building that was once a part of the World Trade Center complex. Remnants of steel beams form the shape of a cross. (*Michelle V. Agins*)

Ms. Pakkala, 31, did slow down for the birth of their first child, Trisha, last January on the couple's ninth anniversary. She took two months off, but then it was back to work. "She didn't want to stay at home and do nothing," Mr. Pakkala said. "She wanted to contribute to the family."

THOMAS PALAZZO
A Clockwork Life

Thomas Palazzo was perpetually in a rush, but only because there was so much he longed to do. At 5, he harassed another boy, Mark Morell, for holding up the water fountain line at the Westchester Country Club. "We were friends ever since," Mr. Morell said. "Tommy would basically tell me what we were doing every minute of the day."

Mr. Palazzo, 44, typically rose at 4 A.M. and headed to the gym, where he would furiously pedal his favorite exercise bike. He prized his 23-foot boat, a Mako, and it was not unusual for him to indulge in a 5 A.M. water-skiing or fishing trip on Long Island Sound. Yet he always got to his desk at Cantor Fitzgerald by 8:30.

"He would shower on the dock with a hose, then hop on a train," Mr. Morell said. "He ran like a clock." Mr. Palazzo, who lived in Armonk, N.Y., also coached lacrosse and golfed, skied and snowboarded. He whisked his wife, Lisa, and three daughters off to Nantucket every summer. In the winter, they spent weekends on the slopes of Stratton, Vt.

"You know how they say, 'He who dies with the most toys wins'?" Mr. Morell said. "That was Tommy. He had a big energy level and a big heart."

RICHARD PALAZZOLO
A Difference on Beatles

Just eight minutes after he was born, Richard Palazzolo met his lifelong companion: his twin brother, Ronald. The two were identical in every way: looks, mindset, careers, everything. They shared an apartment in Manhattan, owned a home together upstate, and both worked in the World Trade Center.

Richard Palazzolo, 39 and known as Rico, was a mortgage security broker at Cantor Fitzgerald, and Ronald Palazzolo was a government security broker at Garban Intercapital. "I wouldn't think about doing something without including my brother in it," said Ronald Palazzolo. "I would have to be with him."

Were there any differences? Mr. Palazzolo thinks for a long time. Finally, it occurs to him: although they both loved the Beatles, "my brother always liked George Harrison. I liked Paul McCartney."

ORIO JOSEPH PALMER
Letter to a Father

Orio Joseph Palmer, 45, a 20-year veteran of the New York Fire Department, was the battalion chief of Engine Company 3 and Ladder 12 in Chelsea. He lived in Valley Stream, N.Y., with his wife, Debbie, and their three children, Dana, 14, Keith, 12, and Alyssa, 9. Dana wrote a letter to him in her journal. Here are excerpts:

Dear Dad,
A friend gave me the idea of writing to you. She said it might help. Oh, how I wish you could write back, or I could hear your voice again, or see you—even if it's just a quick glimpse. I hate knowing that you're really not coming home this time, and all I remember about when I saw you last was that I was doing my homework when I got up and kissed you good-bye. I didn't know it would be forever, though.

When I was listening to all your favorite music the other day, I thought I would feel sad and I'd miss you. But instead, I felt closer to you, and it was quite comforting because there's not one time that I can remember when you didn't have the radio on. You were the music man.

Always know that you're my hero. I could never compare any man to you because that would be unfair to him. For, like Keith said, you're one of a kind—the very best there is out there.

My birthday is coming up, but I'm sure you already knew that. It won't be the same without you, and I'm not really looking forward to it. I feel that way about a lot of things, though. I would do anything to have you back.

Love always, Dana

FRANK PALOMBO
Earnest and in Dissent

"It was hard to dislike Frank, but he sure could get on your nerves," chuckled his brother-in-law, Michael Courtien. "He was always trying to do the right thing. But he was no diplomat."

An example, perhaps burnished by memory: union delegates are about to vote on a proposal, considered a done deal. Predictably, Firefighter Frank Palombo's hand shoots up. Unpredictably, he announces his support. Buzz, buzz. The proposal fails: If Frank says yes, let's rethink, because disagreement is normal for Frank.

There was no arrow straighter than Firefighter Palombo, 46, of Ladder Company 105 in Brooklyn. His moral outlook was shaped by studying for the priesthood; his degree in philosophy; the Roman Catholic prayer group with whom he worshiped twice a week; his wife, Jean, and their eight sons and two daughters, ages 1 to 15. Mrs. Palombo would look down the dinner table and catch him weeping. "I'm so fortunate to have all these children," he would say.

Firefighter Palombo, who joined the department in 1979, believed God would provide. Since his death, Brooklyn neighbors who never said hello stop by and towns in far-away states send gifts. The family is well, reports Mr. Courtien. They believe that God is providing and that good is flowing from the tragedy. As a point of view it was quite Frank-like.

CHRISTOPHER PANATIER
An Adventurous Spirit

Christopher Panatier embraced his spirit of adventure and determination at an early age. At 3, he clambered behind the wheel of his father's 1959 Cadillac and managed to put the car in neutral, said an older sister, Patricia. The car rolled down the family's sloping driveway and into the cul-de-sac, and crashed into the neighbor's bushes.

"I ran to the car, thinking the worst," Ms. Panatier said, "but there he was with a big smile on his face. He was ready to go. He was ready to do it again."

On the eve of a benefit triathlon in Sag Harbor, N.Y., he realized that he had forgotten his bicycle helmet. Instead of skipping the race, he wore his hockey helmet. "It was ridiculously funny," Ms. Panatier said.

Mr. Panatier, 36, of Rockville Centre, N.Y., was a foreign-currency trader for Cantor Fitzgerald on the 104th floor of 1 World Trade. He married his high school sweetheart, Carolyn, and they had two children, Annie, 6, and Christopher, 4. His ample esprit drew many lifelong friends. "People just gravitated to him," Ms. Panatier said. "He was a great husband and father, which was paramount to him."

EDWARD J. PAPA
The Center of Five Families

Edward J. Papa, 47, was lost Sept. 11. Not one, but five families were devastated.

It started after graduation from Boston College in 1976. Mr. Papa and four friends went to Cape Cod for a vacation. Then came girlfriends, wives, kids. They moved the gatherings to Martha's Vineyard. The group never missed a summer—25 consecutive vacations together. The children, including Edward and Patti Papa's four daughters, became de facto cousins.

One of the five friends, Russell Hawkins, called Mr. Papa

the focal point of the gatherings. "He made everybody feel good," he said. "He was a subtle creator of good times." He did that partly through food—one of Mr. Papa's great affections was for cooking and taking his friends on restaurant expeditions. Golf was his other great pursuit. "He stunk at the game of golf, but he absolutely loved it," Mrs. Papa said.

The circle of friends exploded outward from that original five over the years, Mrs. Papa said. Many worked with him at Cantor Fitzgerald, where no one could remember seeing Mr. Papa lose his temper. His brother, the Rev. Charles E. Papa, said Mr. Papa was a deeply committed Roman Catholic who respected others' beliefs. He also helped people, including the elderly woman he carried down 10 flights of smoke-filled stairs in the 1993 attack on the trade center.

With the girls nearly all out of the house in Oyster Bay, it had been time to buy a summer place, Mrs. Papa said. On the Vineyard.

SALVATORE T. PAPASSO
Never Too Old for Toys

Think tax investigator, and if you do not envision a man who relishes birthdays and spaghetti with the zeal of a child, perhaps you did not know Salvatore T. Papasso.

Mr. Papasso worked as a special investigator for the revenue crimes bureau of the New York State Department of Taxation and Finance, on the 86th floor of 2 World Trade Center.

He liked bringing white-collar criminals to justice, but he also drew pleasure from simpler things. Take the Lego pirate-ship set he received as a gift after complaining, in his late 20s, that people no longer gave him toys. "He actually put it together," marveled Vincent Papasso, one of his brothers (and the bearer of the gift).

Mr. Papasso, 34, and his wife, Christine, celebrated one another's birthdays for an entire month, with multiple cakes and dinners out. They married on May 12, 2000, then marked their union on the 12th of each month, sometimes nudging one another awake after midnight to be the first to wish a happy anniversary. "He celebrated life," Mrs. Papasso said. "My outlook on everything changed with him."

MARIE PAPPALARDO
Protector of Cats

Marie Pappalardo's passions were deep and varied. Once, with a friend, she finagled her way into the stall of Affirmed, the Triple Crown–winning racehorse, and hugged him. "Because he always ran with such love, and he was strong, he was something she always loved," said Ms. Pappalardo's daughter, Maria Koutny.

She was profoundly devoted to the Feast of the Three Saints, celebrated on Labor Day weekend at her home church, the Holy Rosary in Lawrence, Mass. When she neared the end of her pregnancy and was told that her daughter would be born that Sunday, she said she would not give birth until she had been to the feast. And she was right.

Ms. Pappalardo, 53, who was returning home to Paramount, Calif., on Flight 175 after visiting the Boston area—for the feast and Ms. Koutny's birthday—was also a devoted protector of cats, catching wild ones and taking them to her vet for shots and spaying.

"She made a hole in her garage so they could come in and eat and get out," Ms. Koutny said. "One was Goofy, one was Daisy, one was Minnie; they all had those kinds of names. Hopefully the person living there now is still feeding the feral cats."

NITIN PARANDTER
He Wanted to Go Home

Over the Labor Day weekend, Nitin Parandter and some of his friends ended up in Staten Island enjoying the view of lower Manhattan from across the water. "That's where I work!" Anand Srinivasan, a friend from Mr. Parandter's native India, remembers him saying.

It had only been four months since Mr. Parandter, 28, took a position as a software consultant at Marsh McLennan. He loved New York because it reminded him of Bombay, the busy city where he had honed his computer skills early in his career, Mr. Srinivasan said.

"He always wanted to return to the Bombay life," Mr. Srinivasan said. "He wasn't a crazy party guy, but he liked the night life and always wanted to return to his home country."

Otherwise, Mr. Parandter did not talk much about his plans, and he seemed content with his new life in New York. He spent weekends shopping at Indian stores in Woodbridge, N.J., renting Indian movies and watching them with friends, and praying at Hindu temples. But he did have a penchant for one thing a lot of his friends did not—American pop music. Mr. Srinivasan laughed, explaining part of the fascination in two words: "Jennifer Lopez."

JAMES PARHAM
From Prankster to Officer

The joy of being the older brother is that you can do whatever you want simply because you're older. Or at least that's the way James Parham, 33, used to justify the pranks he pulled on his younger brother.

"When I was about 7 he got me to stick

a coat hanger in the light socket," said Kevin Parham. "All I remember was the hallway looking blue to me and him sitting there tickled to death." Of course, not all the pranks between the two were so painful. The boys would race one another home from school determined to win control of the television. But big brother always managed to come out on top, mainly because of a scheme.

"He'd take the knob off the television so that even if I beat him, I couldn't turn to my channel," Kevin Parham said. "It was stuck on his show, *Little House on the Prairie*."

But Mr. Parham the prankster eventually became Mr. Parham the proud United States marine, the proud father of a 3-year-old, Resa, and the respected law enforcement officer. Shortly before he disappeared, he had been promoted to an academy instructor for the Port Authority. "He had so much to be proud of," Kevin Parham said. "But he'd give up everything to help somebody. He was always on the job."

DEBBIE PARIS
General Factotum

Debbie Paris, an executive assistant, scheduled her bosses' flights, kept their calendars and managed payments, construction, staff and insurance on their three yachts and several homes—to list some of her duties. "When I needed an autographed photo of Sting," said Suzanne Murphy, a colleague, "I called Debbie. 'No problem,' she said."

When Herman Sandler, president of Sandler O'Neill, bought his yacht, he turned everything over to Mrs. Paris, saying, "Let me know when the money runs out." She did the rest, from hiring a captain to paying the marina. No Problem was his name for the boat—fitting, no doubt, from his point of view, but only because of Mrs. Paris. Mr. Sandler, too, died on Sept. 11.

At home, she managed the gigs for Jimmy, her husband, a rock musician, and was helping him with an album. "She was his muse and inspiration," Ms. Murphy said.

Mr. Paris put it more strongly: "She was like my wife, my child, my mother, my best friend," he said. "And I was a husband and father and child and brother to her." Even now he will not reveal her age. "Just say," he said, "she looked 15 years younger than she was."

PHILIP PARKER
Several Joys, One Headache

Next to his wife, Joan, and daughter, Stephanie, Philip Parker had two great loves: music and his green MG convertible, which he bought in 1977 when he and Joan were dating.

By day, Mr. Parker, 53, was a senior vice president of Aon Corporation, which took him fre-

quently to Aon's office on the 99th floor of the World Trade Center. But on weekends, he was transformed. He became a D.J., at least in the privacy of his home, mixing CDs to entertain friends, or just his wife. He played banjo and guitar.

And then there was the car, his constant joy and headache—"a mechanical nightmare," Mrs. Parker said. "He said he was going to either give it up or have someone restore it." In the end, he couldn't bear to let it go, and had it restored. Mrs. Parker could never drive it because it has a standard transmission. Now she plans to learn.

"There might be a few thunderstorms up there," said Mrs. Parker, imagining her husband looking down from heaven as she struggles to drive the thing. She can just hear him yelling, " 'Don't burn the clutch!' "

MICHAEL PARKES
He Just Wanted to Help

At first, the personnel director at Marsh & McLennan thought Michael Parkes had—to put it gently—embellished his job application. A scoutmaster? A leader of a church youth group? A volunteer camp counselor? A member of the church managing committee? Please.

"They said, 'You don't have to say these things to get a job here,' " said Stanley Edme, a friend who roomed with him at New York University. " 'We're going to check these things out, you know.' "

Turned out that Mr. Parkes, 27, was telling the truth. He worked as an accountant, but his goal was to help young people on a grand scale—to guide young black men into top colleges and corporations and teach them true friendship. Among his friends, he was the diplomat, the mediator. "When you talked to him," Mr. Edme said, "you felt stronger and taller. He'd have been a great politician."

But his heart was with the Episcopal Church, said his twin sister, Monique. "We thought he'd be a bishop," she said, "and go home to Jamaica and build a school." Already, she said, they were making plans.

ROBERT PARKS Jr.
Of Home and Home Runs

Robert Parks Jr. was called the sports trivia specialist on Wall Street. "He had an unbelievable memory if you ever wanted to know who had the first home run or who was the first guy to get the Triple Crown," said his younger sister, Carol Parks Clancy. And though his mind simply brimmed with facts about sports, he was also no slouch on the movement of the stock market since 1929.

He was a bonds broker at Cantor Fitzgerald in 1 World

Trade Center, and liked the energy of New York City. But he was really a homebody. At 47, he was the married father of two teenagers. He was content to barbecue burgers on the pool deck of his home in Middletown, N.J. His enthusiasm for sports played out through his children.

His 16-year-old daughter, Bridgette, is a big swimmer, and he would go to her meets, checking out her times. He was also a coach for the basketball team of his 14-year-old son, Kevin. He himself had played high school varsity basketball and football at St. Peter's Preparatory School in Jersey City.

HASMUKH PARMAR
Making a Gift of the City

Hasmukh Parmar had a smile to cast away darkness, and that is what his wife, Bharti Parmar, misses the most these days. She can see that smile when she recalls the Friday before the twin towers fell, when the couple went on a nighttime cruise around Manhattan. It was like a second honeymoon, with the city as a wedding gift of a jeweled skyline, the September breezes like soft brush strokes.

The following Tuesday morning, Mr. Parmar, 48, the father of two boys, was back at his job on the 103rd floor of the World Trade Center. He was kept busy as a computer systems manager for Cantor Fitzgerald but always found time to chat with friends or lavish attention on his sons.

"He was everything to us," Mrs. Parmar said. "Everything."

At his 14-year-old son's school, Mr. Parmar was a basketball coach. Guitar was the special bond between Mr. Parmar and his 16-year-old. The father taught the son to play, amusing him with the songs of Jimi Hendrix and Carlos Santana. They played together every night when Mr. Parmar came home from work.

LEOBARDO LOPEZ PASCUAL
Lives in Pictures

It had been four years since Leobardo Lopez Pascual had seen his wife and four children. That was when Mr. Pascual left them on the family farm in a small town in Puebla, Mexico, for the trek north to New York.

It wasn't long before he was working the morning shift in the kitchen of Windows on the World. Stretching his money as far as he could, he lived with a co-worker and his family in a one-bedroom apartment in Hunts Point, the Bronx. He wired money to his wife every week, and parcels of clothes and shoes three or four times a year.

Every now and then Mr. Pascual, 41, received envelopes stuffed with photographs; it was how he watched his children grow up. He sent home a picture a couple of years ago too: He is sitting in a ferry on the way to see the Statue of Liberty. That's where he took his sisters when they were visiting from Mexico. He took them to his restaurant, too.

MICHAEL J. PASCUMA Jr.
Immersion in Everything

Golf was Michael J. Pascuma Jr.'s consuming passion. He played every Saturday with a group of friends from work, at courses all over Long Island. He watched golf endlessly on television.

Michael, 50, immersed himself in everything, whether it was golf, his family in Massapequa Park or his work as a stockbroker on the American Stock Exchange. Work and family were entwined: he and his 92-year-old father, Michael J. Pascuma Sr., possibly the oldest broker in the United States, had their own firm, M.J.P. Securities, which recently merged with Harvey, Young & Yurman.

"You would think it was a stressful job, but he was never stressed," said his 23-year-old daughter, Melissa Pascuma, whom he called his little princess. He also had two sons, ages 20 and 17. "As soon as he came home, he detached from it and his family was No. 1."

JERROLD PASKINS
Up to 58 Pushups

There were two things Jerrold Paskins never left home without: the ring his wife, Inez, gave him for his 40th birthday and a 1976 silver dollar issued for the nation's bicentenial. Mr. Paskins, 57, a reinsurance executive with the Devonshire Group in Anaheim Hills, Calif., was a stickler for routines and mementos.

He was in the office every morning by 6, never stopped for lunch, and never let a day go by without doing pushups—one for every year of his life and "an extra for good luck."

"The work ethic was very important to him," said Inez Paskins, who met her husband of 31 years when they were college students. The couple had one son, Robert, who lives in San Francisco.

On Sept. 9, Mr. Paskins came to New York for what was supposed to have been a three-day business trip—an insurance audit on the 78th floor of the trade center. His remains were identified Nov. 11. The 1976 silver dollar and the special birthday ring were also found and returned to the family.

AVNISH PATEL
On the Road with a Camera

There is Avnish Patel, beaming from astride a rented scooter in Thailand. There he is again, skimming through the powder at Snowbird in Utah, hiking 3,000 feet above Lake Wakatipu in New Zealand, decked out in Mardi Gras beads and surrounded by his four best college buddies at a Cajun restaurant in New Orleans.

Mr. Patel, a research analyst for Fred Alger Management, was only 28, but he had already been everywhere, "probably 20 to 30 countries," in his older brother Yogesh's estimation.

The proof can be found on the Web site where Mr. Patel, a talented photographer, posted elegant images from his travels (along with nuggets of wisdom culled from his favorite novels). But despite his voracious appetite for the rest of the world, there was no question in Mr. Patel's mind that New York City was home.

As an 11-year-old living in London, he had persuaded his parents to let him cross the Atlantic alone and move in with an uncle in Connecticut. From then on, he was hooked, eventually graduating from—where else?—New York University.

"His love for New York City was immense," his brother said. "We tried to get him to live out in Long Island, but he just wanted to be there."

Three black-and-white pictures taken from the 93rd floor of his office in the north tower attest to the depth of that love. Next to one, a moody tribute to the Statue of Liberty—glimpsed as a proud dark silhouette across an expanse of glinting water—Mr. Patel had written: "Freedom! Liberty! The ultimate symbol of the greatest city in the world."

DIPTI PATEL
Outspoken and Maternal

Dipti Patel was a warm mother hen of a woman who minced no words.

"She'd tell you right in your face if she liked you or not," said a sister, Vibhuti Patel. "She would yell at you for some-

A memorial service for Firefighter Michael Carlo of Engine Company 230 held November 30 at Holy Trinity Catholic Church in Queens. Firefighter Carlo was killed on September 11. (*Nicole Bengiveno*)

thing, but the next minute if you needed her, she'd do anything for you."

Ms. Patel, 38, a database administrator at eSpeed, would tell you exactly what she thought about your new dress or the price you were considering paying for a house. And then she would get on the phone with everyone she knew to find you a better one.

After telling her future sister-in-law that the wedding dress she had selected was not sufficiently bridal, Ms. Patel ordered an elegant champagne-colored gown from a dressmaker in India.

"You have to look better than all your sisters-in-law," she advised the bride.

Discouraged by seeing friends and relatives endure the pain of divorce, Ms. Patel, who emigrated from India as a child, never married. She lived in New Hyde Park, on Long Island, with her parents, her sister Vibhuti and two nephews.

"She was like a son to my father," Vibhuti Patel said. "She took care of everybody."

STEVEN PATERSON
Getting What He Aimed For

Steven Paterson was so sure he was going to succeed as a bond trader that he skipped college out of Raritan High School in New Jersey and headed straight for Wall Street. In April, that journey landed him a job on the bond trading desk with Cantor Fitzgerald, on the 105th floor of 1 World Trade Center. He was 40.

"He was such a straight-ahead guy, he always got what he aimed for," said his wife, Lisa, from their home in Ridgewood, N.J. "The first time he saw me he said, 'I want to marry you,'" she said. "I always thought, 'If anyone was going to get out of there, he was.'"

But for all Mr. Paterson's focus on career, the family agreed that the moment he walked in the door each night at 6 was the best time of the day. He would help cook dinner and give the twins, Lucy and Wyatt, their baths while his wife relaxed for a change. "He got laid off for five months last year and he really had a great time," Ms. Paterson said. "I think he secretly would have loved to be a stay-at-home dad."

JAMES PATRICK
Anticipated Fatherhood

James Patrick envisioned his future as filled with children—shouting, playing, bouncing around the house. "He really liked the noise, the chaos, the Sunday morning with everyone jumping in bed with you," said his wife, Terilyn. "I was bargaining for three kids. He didn't want to settle for any less than four."

But Mr. Patrick, a bond broker at Cantor Fitzgerald, died seven weeks before his first child, Jack, came into the world. "We would talk about that stuff all the time," Mrs. Patrick said. "He really loved the thought of teaching them to play hockey and going to all their games, and in college, going up to their games and tailgating with them."

Mr. Patrick, 30, grew up with five siblings in a noisy Irish family, and he wanted to repeat the experience from a dad's point of view. Last spring, a few weeks after Ms. Patrick learned she was pregnant, the couple moved from the Upper West Side to a condo in Norwalk, Conn. It was to be a brief stop on the way to a big house in Fairfield County.

"They have great hockey there, for the kids," Ms. Patrick said. "Darien has great hockey."

MANUEL PATROCINO
The Things He Built

He was extremely adept with his hands. And he approached furnishings with a dose of imagination. Skilled at carpentry, Manuel Patrocino built a smart-looking console for the television and stereo. He made shelves to hold cassettes. The sofa? He took it apart and redid it three times. A neighbor needed chairs. No problem. He built them.

"If he saw something that he wanted, he would build it," said his niece, Martha Martinez. His most distinctive creation? He built a clock out of a CD, carefully installing a watch face in its center.

Mr. Patrocino, 33, was in charge of uniforms for Windows on the World, and lived in Manhattan with his wife, Sandra, and their two children, Keyla and Alex. He normally reported to work early, and would be home in the afternoon, when he would head to the kitchen to cook a meal before the children arrived from school.

On the weekends, he liked to play dominoes with his friends. "If you saw a view of the family, he was always the happy person," said Ms. Martinez. "He always had a joke for us. When he told a joke, people would drop on the floor laughing."

JAMES R. PAUL
Finding Their Place

In 1993, when James R. Paul decided to move to New York after two decades in Chicago, he was walking around Gramercy Park one day with a real estate broker when a building caught his eye. Built in 1883, it appealed to Mr. Paul's taste for the old and beautiful. "I wish we could find a place there," he told the broker, pointing to the red-brownish brick facade. They did.

Then, two years ago, Mr. Paul and his wife, Pat, decided to begin looking for what one day would be their retirement home. The two got in a car and drove south, hugging the Atlantic coast. They found their place in a condominium in Savannah, Ga., where Mr. Paul could play golf and his wife could enjoy the city's architecture and cultural life.

That is how Mr. Paul, 58, lived his life: with one foot on the gas pedal and the other on the brakes, making plans, but also letting his impulses guide him. He drove too fast, skied even faster, and loved being on top of the world, on the 92nd floor of 1 World Trade Center, where he was an executive vice president of Carr Futures. He called his wife, an accountant, "the bean counter."

"He was working very hard, six days a week, to make enough money to retire early," Mrs. Paul said. "He wanted to have enough years and energy in him to play golf."

RICHARD PEARLMAN
Trained to Save People

It was only supposed to be a way of keeping a teenage boy off the streets and out of trouble. But soon after Richard Pearlman's mother signed him up, the Forest Hills Volunteer Ambulance Corps unlocked a life's passion. For four years, no matter the weather, he was always there, riding two buses from his home in Howard Beach to Forest Hills, Queens, determined to learn as much as he could.

On Sept. 11, he put that training into action, almost by accident. An 18-year-old office clerk for a Queens lawyer, Mr. Pearlman had been sent to run an errand at 1 Police Plaza. While there he learned of the World Trade Center attack and raced there alongside police officers.

"He dreamed of becoming an E.M.T.," said Dori Pearlman, who last saw her son in a photo in a newsmagazine surrounded by emergency workers at ground zero. He was scheduled to begin emergency medical technician classes in October.

"He used to always say, 'I'm going to be a famous person one day, Mom. I'm going to help save the world. You'll see.'"

DURRELL V. PEARSALL Jr.
Imposing Yet Inviting

His name was Durrell V. Pearsall Jr., but everyone called him Bronko. At 6-foot-2, 285 pounds, Firefighter Pearsall could bench press 455 pounds as easily, said someone who witnessed the feat, as if "it was nothing."

"As soon as he walked into a room, everyone noticed," said Liam Flaherty, a fellow firefighter at Rescue Squad 4 in Queens. But while his facade was fierce, Firefighter Flaherty said, his smile "could warm a room right up."

Firefighter Pearsall had played offensive tackle for C. W. Post during college. He slimmed down to 230 pounds to take the firefighter's test but put the weight back on after he joined the department in 1993. He played tackle for the Fire Department's football team. "Bronko had just unbelievable power and strength," said John Szczech, a firefighter who roomed with Firefighter Pearsall in Hempstead, N.Y. He was fiercely proud of his Irish heritage. He played snare drum in the department's Emerald Society Pipes and Drums, and the band's logo was tattooed on his calf.

On his upper right arm—big as a billboard, some said—he had tattooed his family crest, pierced with the legend Death Before Shame in Gaelic. "And he certainly lived up to that," Firefighter Szczech said.

THOMAS PEDICINI
Attached to His Guitar

Thomas Pedicini never strayed too far from a guitar. His brother-in-law Raymond Morace's earliest recollection of him is as "a skinny 13-year-old kid jumping around his room playing air guitar" to Van Halen. In his mother's last memory of him, he is strumming and teaching his 11-year-old cousin how to play, a few days before his death.

In between, Mr. Pedicini, 30, an easygoing sort and a seemingly effortless golfer, studied business and had been working as a trader at Cantor Fitzgerald since 1998, a job he got through another brother-in-law, Mark Colaio, who died with him.

After Sept. 11, in Mr. Pedicini's apartment in Woodside, Queens, one of his roommates found a tape of him strumming and singing his way through some of his favorite tunes. "He was too shy even to show it to me, but I could hear him in there singing and playing so I knew he was up to something," said the roommate, Jordan Zed. He gave the tape to Mr. Pedicini's parents. More musical memories.

But Mr. Zed remembers Mr. Pedicini mostly as a decent human being whose life was going somewhere. "You'd sit around and talk about where you see yourself in five years," he said. "He had dreams and goals. He wanted to eventually find the right girl and settle down and have a family and work his way up in the firm. It seems so sad."

TODD D. PELINO
The Natural Father

You always found Todd D. Pelino surrounded by the children. Fatherly—that was him, his wife's girlfriends said. The other men kidded him for it, though they knew in their hearts that it was true. They were five couples, with nine kids among them, whose houses were close but not too close.

Home was Fair Haven, N.J. Work was Wall Street, Cantor Fitzgerald, and it was tougher than the muddiest soccer match Mr. Pelino, 34, ever played at Colgate. Come Saturdays at 5 P.M., Todd and Megan Pelino put their children, Bennett, 2, and Annie, 9 months, into a double stroller and wheeled them to the redbrick church down Hance Road, where they sat with other young families in a back pew.

"Once he did say to me that he was praying for life and everything to be as good as it is now, meaning then," said Ms. Pelino, whose sister, Kaleen Pezzuti, was also killed in the Sept. 11 attack. "We hoped there would be more kids. He was always first to hold the newborns. My friends said, 'Of all these guys, Todd is the natural father.' "

KALEEN PEZZUTI's portrait appears on page 391.

MIKE A. PELLETIER
A Private Language

Since Sept. 11, there's been a mystery in the Pelletier household. "Tigi, tigi, tigi," 2-year-old Sydney says. "Papa said, 'tigi.' "

Her mother doesn't know what it means. It is a private word that Sydney's father, Mike A. Pelletier, made up with her. "They developed all these inside jokes," his wife, Sophie, said. Mrs. Pelletier can relate; she and her husband had a trove of their own private jokes. "He was my laughing buddy," she said.

From the night they met at a Manhattan party, the couple also had their own secret language: French. She came from France via Los Angeles. He was a former professional hockey player from a tight-knit family in Quebec. They fell in love "almost immediately," marrying in 1998 in a tiny glass chapel jutting over the Pacific Ocean.

Mr. Pelletier, 36, commuted from Greenwich, Conn., to work as a commodities broker for Cantor Fitzgerald—"but his priority was his family," his wife said. "He ran home every night to be with us." Now, she aches for the little things. "I miss going to Costco with him," she said. "Everything we did was fun."

ANTHONY PELUSO
Modest Despite Assets

Whenever Anthony Peluso pulled out the saxophone and played his favorite song, "I've Got the World on a String," his listeners could only nod in agreement. Successful and athletic, good-looking and in love with life, he seemed to have everything—except an attitude.

"He was so gorgeous, but he never strutted around," said his fiancée, Ann Marie. "I couldn't believe it."

Yet the bigger surprise was how silly he could be: making Ann Marie, who admits she's prim and proper, walk down an up escalator or help him crash a wedding. "We laughed every time we wondered what the newlyweds thought when they saw us on their wedding video, dancing with drinks in our hands," she said in her eulogy.

Mr. Peluso, 46, worked long hours as a construction supervisor for Structure Tone, but he always found time to check in on his mother, Lillian Peluso. He was overseeing work inside 2 World Trade Center on Sept. 11— a Tuesday, so he had his sax with him for his weekly music lesson. At his memorial service in Carroll Gardens, his teacher, Vincent Della Rocca, played the old standards Mr. Peluso loved, like "My Funny Valentine" and, of course, his favorite:

Life is a beautiful thing.
As long as I hold that string
I'd be a silly so-and-so
If I should ever it go.
I've got the world on a string.

ANGEL R. PENA
Rain or Shine

Rain. More rain. So much rain that ball fields became too soggy even for the fairy-light footsteps of a little girls' softball team. But the season had already begun, and the Eagle Paint Minors' coach wanted his girls to be ready.

So Angel R. Pena held batting practice in his backyard.

Mr. Pena was the Joe Torre of River Vale, N.J., girls sports. Whether it was softball, basketball or soccer, whether his girls Melissa and Sara played or not, he dedicated himself to his teams. "He had a sense of magic about him," said Walter L. Slasinski, president of River Vale's Baseball/Softball Association. Mr. Pena, 45, and his wife, Michele, lived across from Alexander Field, and he sometimes borrowed a lawn tractor to groom the diamond before a game. He ran a bilingual law practice for 16 years and then in August went to work at the insurance company Aonat the World Trade Center.

That same month, before the last game of the season, Mr. Pena hung American flags and bunting around Alexander Field.

The girls played well, but Melissa's team lost. They celebrated anyway.

RICHARD A. PENNY
Love of Work and Learning

Even during the 10 years he was homeless, Richard A. Penny loved to work. Even when he slept on a Harlem shelter cot, or dozed upright near Grand Central Terminal, he still rose to polish the brass at St. James' Church, scrub floors or sweep city streets. Three years ago, he found a steady job in the World Trade Center recycling program, now run by Project Renewal, and rented a room in Brooklyn.

"He totally went against all the stereotypes of homeless folks," said Jon Bunge, a caseworker with Project Hope, another of the social service agencies that found work for the "soft-spoken, incredibly thorough" man who listed his best quality as his love of learning.

Mr. Penny, who was 53, told his story as a fall from grace. An only child, he was the 1966 valedictorian of Metropolitan High School. He married young, had a son and worked as a communications craftsman for AT&T for seven years.

Then heroin and a 1975 robbery conviction swept it all away. After 14 months in prison, Mr. Penny retreated to his parents' Brooklyn brownstone. But they died, he was evicted and eventually he lost his metalworking job.

The hard climb from homelessness led to the upper floors of the twin towers, where he was collecting paper on Sept. 11. His memorial service drew more than 100 people. "We loved him," Mr. Bunge said.

SALVATORE F. PEPE
For Family, a Tomatofest

Salvatore F. Pepe was an assistant vice president for technology at Marsh & McLennan, but to the Pepe clan he will be remembered as the originator of Tomatofest and the Pepe family calendar.

Mr. Pepe's mother used to can tomatoes every August. So after she died in 1992, he organized a messy, joyous annual get-together where the next two generations of Pepes would gather to cut, skin, cook and can enough tomatoes to last everyone through the winter. "It was like Little Italy," said his sister Leonida Pepe.

The calendar was another way Mr. Pepe, 45, kept the family connected. He would put together a photo-filled calendar marking the birthdays and anniversaries of the 60-odd members of his, his wife's and his six siblings' families and hand it out to everyone.

Not everything he did involved huge numbers of people, though. Mr. Pepe loved watching the stars, which was hard if you live in Elmhurst, Queens. So on a cold, clear winter day, he would call his wife, Cathy Ng Pepe, and say, "Let's go." They would take the afternoon off work, drive out with the telescope to the Delaware Water Gap and stand beneath the sky, bundled up in hunting suits and warmed by the sparkle of the stars.

The Pepes had not done much stargazing since their son, Salvatore Loong Pepe, was born early in 2000. But Big Sal hoped to take Little Sal to Quebec someday to see the northern lights. "Maybe when he gets older, we'll take him out there," Cathy Ng Pepe said.

ROB PERAZA
A Run to Glory

The number is 18416. That is the number that Rob Peraza was to wear while competing in the New York City Marathon in November 2001. It was to have been his first marathon, and family members say that his diligent long-distance training—often accompanied by his dog, Otis, through Central Park—spoke to the determination and future plans of a man only 30 years old.

This year seemed to bring a certain maturity to Mr. Peraza, who had been living the 20-something life on the Upper West Side. His job as a bond trader with Cantor Fitzgerald was going well. His relationship with Megan Cressy, his girlfriend of nine months, was getting serious. And his mind, more accustomed to anticipating hits on a rugby field, was focused on completing that marathon.

"A lot of things were falling in place for Rob," said his younger brother, Neil Peraza. "He was just starting to, I think, come into his own as a person."

Mr. Peraza's parents live in Ohio, his sister lives in North Carolina and his brother lives in Florida. But they were still planning to attend the marathon, and to see Rob's uncle from Virginia, Steve Comber, cross the finish line—wearing No. 18416.

JON A. PERCONTI Jr.
Food Hatched from the Egg

Jon A. Perconti Jr.'s prize possession was a green oval-shaped backyard grill that he called the Egg. As a boy, he spent hours watching his grandmother in her kitchen. As a man, Mr. Perconti, a 32-year-old trader at Cantor Fitzgerald, had become a great cook.

"He was just a natural," said Tammy Perconti, his wife, who is expecting the couple's child. "When we ate out he would taste something and say 'I can make this.' And he would come back home and make it even better."

Mr. Perconti's cooking became high art on the Egg. At Christmastime, he cooked prime rib on it. In the summer, he used it to smoke the perfect rib.

"I am getting hungry just thinking about it," Mrs. Perconti said.

Outside Giants Stadium, people would stop and gape, lured by the sweet smoky smell of Mr. Perconti's ribs cooking on a mini Egg. "Most people do hot dogs at the game," said Alfred Savastano, a lifelong friend.

"He was doing roast pork, deep-fried turkey, London broil, ribs, steaks anything. It was crazy and it was good."

ANTHONY PEREZ
Sold, but Not on the Car

When Mary Gola walked into the Westbury Mazda dealership eight years ago, she knew which salesman she wanted: Anthony Perez. Six feet tall with dark Latin looks, he was exceedingly handsome. The trouble was, he knew less about Mazdas than she did. Mischievously, Ms. Gola peppered him with requests for features she knew did not exist. Mr. Perez (who was helping out a friend that week) assured her he could meet her demands.

Needless to say, he failed to sell her a car. He did persuade her to join him for coffee and—the following year—to marry him. Mazdas, it turned out, were about the only gap in Mr. Perez's storehouse of practical knowledge. He could wire a house, solder a pipe, and paint and spackle like a pro. When it came to computers, he was a whiz.

Each of his three children had a state-of-the-art model assembled from castoff hardware that Mr. Perez, 33, a computer specialist at Cantor Fitzgerald, brought to his home in Locust Valley, on Long Island, from the office on the 103rd floor of 1 World Trade Center.

"Sometimes I got jealous of the computers," said Mrs. Perez. "He loved fiddling with them."

IVAN PEREZ
Using Weekends for Fun

If you ask people what Ivan Perez was like, the first thing they say is how he loved being with his children, Darleen, 12, and Ivan Jr., 11. Mr. Perez did not live with them and their mother, but every Saturday he would show up at their apartment in Brooklyn, and Darleen and Ivan would literally knock him over in excitement. Then the fun began. Usually, there was lunch, a movie, roller-skating. The three made a lively group. There were arguments because Darleen loved the Yankees, and the two Ivans were Mets fans. Mr. Perez, 37, was a hugger, too.

Last December, Mr. Perez got engaged to Eileen Flecha, a co-worker at Fiduciary Trust International, and everyone remarked how nice she was with the children. On Sept. 11, Mr. Perez was on the 97th floor of 2 World Trade Center in operations, and Ms. Flecha, a trader, was on the 94th. Mr. Perez's family speculates that after the first plane hit, he delayed leaving so he could get Ms. Flecha. Now they are both missing.

On Saturdays now, Mr. Perez's brother, Edgard, goes to see the children. "I try to keep their minds busy," he said.

EILEEN FLECHA's portrait appears on page 159.

NANCY PEREZ
Many Things for Children

A classic Nancy Perez story is about how she started taking karate in the late '90s and one day met a class of deaf children at her karate school. Intrigued, Ms. Perez, left, began learning American Sign Language and ended up teaching karate to the children she had befriended.

"She would do anything for anyone," said Marie Roman, one of her best friends. "I don't remember what level she got to in karate but she learned sign language in six months." "She was an upbeat person," Ms. Roman said. "We did country line-dancing, we went to Graceland, we took boxing lessons."

Ms. Perez, 36, was a Port Authority supervisor at 1 World Trade Center. Single and childless, she doted on children. She even wrote a book about a little boy afraid to go to school for her 8-year-old cousin, Kyle McCann. It was printed by a friend who was a graphic artist.

Ms. Perez was always learning something new, said Maritza Conti, her older sister. She enjoyed traveling and also got a kick out of taking their parents around New York, especially the Broadway shows. The family of three girls came to New York from Cuba in 1970.

"Nancy was a wonderful person, sister, aunt, godmother and daughter," Ms. Conti said. "She just lived life to the fullest."

BERRY BERENSON PERKINS
The Touch of an Angel

Hers was a life of almost fairy tale proportions. She was a granddaughter of the French couturier Elsa Schiaparelli. She was an intimate of Halston; a photographer for *Life* and *Vogue*; a model with Vermeer-blue eyes and golden hair; an actress; the sister of Marisa Berenson; the wife of Anthony Perkins; the mother of their two handsome boys.

But ask friends and family members what Berry Berenson Perkins was, and the answer comes to one word: angel.

"If there was ever a person who could be called a living angel, I think Berry was," said Gale Parker, a friend. Her sister, Marisa Berenson, used the word, too. "She touched everybody who met her," she said.

Mrs. Perkins, 53, was devoted to her two sons, Oz and Elvis. But she had experienced her share of pain, having nursed her husband for two years before his death in 1992.

Seven years ago, while visiting Jamaica, she met Albert Parchment, whom friends know as Coot, at a party.

"We stayed up all night talking," he said. Then he took her back to her hotel and went home. "I couldn't wait for daylight to come to get to see her in the morning."

The two fell in love, and soon she was living between homes on Cape Cod and in Jamaica, where they ran a bar in Treasure Beach. After spending the summer on the Cape, she said goodbye to Mr. Parchment at the airport as he returned to Jamaica. Then she boarded American Airlines Flight 11 to see Elvis, a musician, perform in Hollywood.

Despite her travels, she was always there for her friends. One of them, Nuala Boylan, said, "Berry, darling, you will be with us always."

EDWARD J. PERROTTA
A Grower of the Green

Ever since he was a child, Edward J. Perrotta could make things grow. Money, specifically. And plants. As an 8-year-old, Eddie lent Laura, his sister, money with interest. Once, he gave her change to buy ice cream in exchange for a 1935 silver dollar she had been given as a baby. (His mother made him return it.) He started his Wall Street career as a money broker and ended it managing the energy desk at Cantor Fitzgerald.

"He liked to make money, and he was good at it," Laura Perrotta said. "It wasn't so much the amount of money as it was the thrill of acquiring it."

A recently remarried father of two teenagers, Mr. Perrotta, 43, spent his weekends fishing with his brothers, nurturing a shared dream that they would one day catch a 50-pound striped bass.

Mr. Perrotta inherited his mother's love for gardens, doting on the one at his home in Mount Sinai, on Long Island, and the one at her grave, which he would visit every weekend, planting mums in the fall, tulip bulbs in the spring, impatiens in the summer.

"He loved beautiful things," said his wife, Josephine.

JOHN W. PERRY
A Full Life, and Then Some

John W. Perry was not your typical police officer. He spoke French, Spanish, Swedish and Russian, and was learning Albanian. He was a graduate of New York University School of Law. He ran in three marathons and took part in a swim around Manhattan. He was an extra in Woody Allen films. He volunteered one day a week for the Kings County Society for the Prevention of Cruelty to Children. He was in the New York State Guard and was a board member in the New York Civil Liberties Union. He collected bulletproof vests from retired police officers and gave them to officers in Moscow.

On the morning of Sept. 11, Mr. Perry was filing his retirement papers at 1 Police Plaza, intent on becoming a medical malpractice lawyer.

When he learned of the attacks, he ran the few blocks to the World Trade Center. Colleagues said he disappeared in the rubble when the south tower collapsed, just moments after he tried to help a woman who had fainted.

"I always wondered why John did so much," said his mother, Patricia Perry. "As a child he was classified as having a learning disability, but he rose above it. He always felt he had something to prove."

FRANKLIN PERSHEP
Like a Kid, with Bagels

To his co-workers at the Aon Corporation on the 93rd floor of 2 World Trade Center, Franklin Pershep was the Bagel Man. First he would bring in two or three dozen to celebrate someone's wedding, promotion or new baby, said his daughter, Stacy, then later, for no reason. He bought them at a shop near his home in Bensonhurst that Stacy also visited. "They'd say, 'Oh Stacy, your dad was here, he paid for your bagel and coffee this morning,' " she recalled.

"Oh, he was so corny, so corny," she said. "As a little girl I remember saying to my father, 'When are you going to grow up, Dad?' and he would say, 'Why? Why do I have to grow up?' " Mr. Pershep, 59, loved his story of the Incredible Shrinking Cubicle. He knew his co-workers were pushing in the walls of his office a tiny bit each day, but he wouldn't let on that he noticed, even when he had to turn sideways to get inside.

His daughter didn't know what he had done first to deserve such a prank, but she thinks it was probably something good.

MICHAEL J. PESCHERINE
The Green Plaid Shirt

The shirt caught Lynn Beckman's eye as she was sitting at an Upper West Side bar five years ago.

"It was hideous," she said recently. But the man wearing the green plaid shirt was looking her way so intently that she approached him. "I really like the shirt you're wearing," she told him.

Michael J. Pescherine's answer goes unrecorded, but the two talked until 2 A.M., started dating and were married in 1999. Mr. Pescherine, 32, was a bond trader at Keefe, Bruyette & Woods and worked on the 89th floor of 2 World Trade Center.

Michael and Lynn Pescherine were inseparable. They ran the 1999 and 2000 New York marathons together. In their Upper West Side apartment last summer, they watched as the telltale lines on her pregnancy tests got bluer and bluer. "You're getting more pregnant by the minute," he screamed in delight.

Such moments more than made up for Mr. Pescherine's awkward confession that he had not really noticed his future wife at the bar that first night. He was actually watching a Knicks playoff game on the television set above her.

His family—his parents, one sister and three brothers—are awaiting the birth of Mr. Pescherine's son in March. Lynn Pescherine's friends are making the baby a quilt with the green plaid shirt at its center.

DAVIN PETERSON
A Clear-Headed Giant

It felt natural to look up to Davin Peterson: he was 6 feet 6 inches tall. But he was also comfortable as a leader and mediator of the four Peterson kids, his mother's stalwart and confidant when the family was cracked by divorce. He was calming, clear-headed, an old soul since childhood, but possessed of an exquisite sensitivity: when one sister was going through a rough time, he wept about it openly at work.

At 25, he was a trader at Cantor Fitzgerald, although notions of his future were still forming. His travel lust had taken him to Vietnam, China, Scandinavia. With a deep interest in human rights, politics and economics, he considered starting a business in an impoverished country.

Mr. Peterson was also possessed of an antic sense of humor. He cooked anti-Thanksgiving meals—one year, fajitas, another year, steak.

He had an elaborate scheme for the secession of his native California, featuring himself as the head of a military coup. And he vowed to leave his life insurance to Rambo, his mother's beloved five-pound Yorkshire terrier.

Really?

Ah, got you!

And whenever he did, Mr. Peterson, enormously pleased with himself, would dance a little jig, a gentle giant with size 16 feet.

WILLIAM R. PETERSON
Full of Shenanigans

A few years ago, James Morris finally beat his uncle William R. Peterson at basketball. Mr. Peterson was 6-foot-2 and so good that he inspired Mr. Morris to play better. Though Mr. Peterson was more of a brother than an uncle to his nephew, in this case he believed that age made a difference. "He claimed he was getting too old," said Mr. Morris. "I said I was getting too fast."

Otherwise, Mr. Peterson, 47, was not one to act his age. At family holidays, "there's a voice that's missing. Some of the shenanigans are missing too," said Mr. Morris.

A claims examiner at Marsh & McLennan, Mr. Peterson had been practicing those shenanigans since he was a child in Bay Ridge, Brooklyn. "He was a brat," said his father, Robert. Still, everybody loved him, and the father ended up giving him the family's summer home in Breezy Point, Queens. Mr. Peterson lived there with his wife, Robin.

The house sits so close to the shore that Mr. Peterson could watch for the bluefish to start running from his front window. He called his father three times a day, and his early morning phone call on Sept. 11 was special.

"He was really on cloud nine that day," said Robert Peterson. He had caught some bluefish from his front yard the night before.

MARK PETROCELLI
At Long Last, a Broker

Mark Petrocelli toyed with the idea of becoming a guidance counselor, a teacher or a firefighter like his father. But he got hooked by the hurly-burly of the commodities trading floor and chose a raucous occupation that members of his close-knit circle in Staten Island say seemed out of character for a kindhearted man who loved entertaining his friends and family.

"People would say, 'I can't believe that's what he does for a living,' " said his wife, Nicole.

After six years as a phone clerk delivering orders to the brokers in the pit, Mr. Petrocelli, who was two days short of his 29th birthday, had finally become a broker himself, starting in his new position just days before the attack.

The Petrocellis normally had breakfast together before he left for work at the World Financial Center, where his job with Carr Futures was based. But on Sept. 10, Mr. Petrocelli told his wife that he planned to leave the house at 6:30 A.M. the next morning to go to the World Trade Center. It was his first brokers' meeting, he said, and he did not want to be late.

GLEN PETTIT
The Smile Behind a Camera

Glen Pettit took on a lot and never let it slow him down. In addition to being a New York City police officer, he was a TV news cameraman, a freelance photographer, a volunteer firefighter and a devotee of Irish tradition and music.

Then there was the endless flood of gifts: from packages of Skippy peanut butter for friends in East Asia to the prize seat he arranged for his mother at a Christmas Eve Mass at

St. Patrick's Cathedral, just a row from the mayor and the police commissioner. "If he loved you he loved you completely, and he was going to take care of you," recalled Tara Felice, one of his five siblings.

Officer Pettit, 30, had joined the department's video production unit, which makes training and promotional videos. "His greatest love was being behind a camera, composing a shot," said his partner, Officer Scott Nicholson. The video unit responded to the World Trade Center attack hoping to get footage for an annual promotional tape it makes called "Heroes."

"Glen was telling us, 'I'm gonna get in close; you stay and get the establishing shots, get the rescue workers responding,' " Officer Nicholson recalled. "I looked over and Glen was running past me, camera in hand, heading toward the towers."

DOMINICK PEZZULO
The Unusual Was Typical

Two kids from the Bronx just out of high school on their first date: Let's take the train to Manhattan and walk around, they say. Approaching a fountain, he's afraid she's not paying attention. He steps in front to block her, and falls right in. "We had to ride home with his brand-new sneakers squeaking," recalls Jeanette Pezzulo, with a laugh. And after that, she said, there was no way she could avoid marrying Dominick Pezzulo.

It happened at the World Trade Center.

Through the succeeding 18 years, Mr. Pezzulo fixed airplanes for T.W.A., taught shop at Herbert Lehman High School, restored a Porsche 944 (it is on hold for 7-year-old Dominick Jr.), pumped iron regularly, went on dinner cruises and just slipped under the 35-year-old age limit for the Port Authority police force.

Officer Pezzulo, who lived in the Bronx, was assigned to the bus station. "He knew everybody in there, from the maintenance guys to the elevator operators to the store owners," said Officer Michael G. Placido, a close friend. On Sept. 11, he commandeered a bus with some other officers, and died under the first tower collapse while digging out a fellow officer. "I would say that's typical," said Frank Augello, a boyhood friend.

KALEEN PEZZUTI
Laughter and Loyalty

She graduated from Cornell University and backpacked around Europe with some sorority sisters. In fall 1995, she got a job at Cantor Fitzgerald. It was there that Kaleen Pezzuti met Matthew Grzymalski and fell in love. And there they died together.

"We are certainly hoping they were holding hands or

Amber Amundson, whose husband, Craig, was killed at
the Pentagon, flanked at a Union Square peace vigil
December 1 by Mr. Amundson's brother, Ryan
Amundson, at left, and David Potorti, whose brother,
James Potorti, died in the World Trade Center.
(*Frances Roberts*)

hugging or wrapped in each other's arms somehow," said
Mr. Grzymalski's sister Patti Ann Valerio.

At Mr. Grzymalski's memorial Mass, his mother gave
Ms. Pezzuti's mother, Kathleen E. Pezzuti of Fair Haven,
N.J., a card from Ms. Pezzuti she had found in Mr. Grzy-
malski's dresser. "My mom was right," she wrote. "Happi-
ness agrees with me. I owe that all to you. I love you, K.
XOXO."

Ms. Pezzuti, 28, was a loyal friend. She had blond hair,
dark eyebrows, blue eyes. She never needed mascara. She
played soccer. She painted. She had a contagious laugh.
"On the night before, on Sept. 10, she spoke to one of her
best friends and told her, 'He's the one,'" said Mrs. Pezzuti, whose other daughter, Megan, lost her husband in the
Sept. 11 attack. "It would have been a really wonderful
family."

MATTHEW GRZYMALSKI's portrait appears on page 199.

KEVIN PFEIFER
Shouting with His Life

To the casual acquaintance, Kevin Pfeifer
had a manner—a quiet, thoughtful
demeanor—that seemed of a piece with all
the philosophy courses he took at Marist
College. His gift for abstractions, though,
was far exceeded by his taste for the concrete. And adventure.

He learned to fly, and logged 400 hours of flying time.
He learned to sail, and loved to bring his friends out to race
the tankers around Sandy Hook or his nieces and nephews
out on Jamaica Bay. He loved to drive, and managed to
sneak onto the secure grounds at Kennedy Airport, where he
sped along a runway.

Mr. Pfeifer, 42, shouted with his life, not with his
mouth. Growing up in Middle Village, in Queens, and
spending many summer days in Breezy Point, he developed a

close circle of friends who ate at Beefsteak Charlie's and joined him for his capers on the ground, at sea, in the air. He knew that fun was where you made it: he organized a legendary bash at an abandoned missile silo near Floyd Bennett Field in Brooklyn.

In Mr. Pfeifer's work as a city paramedic and later as a fire lieutenant, he had a knack for quietly bringing out the best in people, his brother Joseph said. Joseph Pfeifer was among the first battalion chiefs at the trade center on Sept. 11. He spotted his brother coming in with Engine Company 33, and the two Pfeifers exchanged a quick word, and then glances as they parted.

LUDWIG J. PICARRO
He Loved to Commute

Ludwig J. Picarro had always worked in the suburbs, so he was absolutely thrilled four years ago when he got a job as an insurance executive across the street from the World Trade Center.

"He felt he was in the center of business," said Susan Picarro, his wife. "He just felt so much energy, and he thrived on that."

Mr. Picarro, 44, relished the daily routines that other suburban commuters simply tolerate. A resident of Basking Ridge, N.J., where he lived with his wife and sons, Andrew, 15, and Matthew, 9, he actually liked the ride on the PATH train or the ferry. He thrilled at the sight of the twin towers. He grew up in New Castle, Pa., where he married his junior high school sweetheart, Susan, and found work in the suburbs of Pittsburgh and Cleveland.

In New York, he was the senior vice president for diversified products at Zurich American Insurance Group, in 1 Liberty Plaza. On Sept. 11, he was attending a business meeting at Aon Insurance.

As much as he loved the fast pace of the city, his wife said, he had his priorities straight. Without hesitation, he would rearrange his business schedule to attend his sons' sporting events.

MATTHEW PICERNO
Wine by Night

Try, now, to envision a municipal bond broker, in his 104th-floor office, who dreams the green and bacchanalian dream of being a winemaker. That was Matthew Picerno, 44, of Holmdel, N.J. By day he worked at Cantor Fitzgerald, rising at 5:30 A.M. Six months of the year, when the day job ended, he headed over to Jersey City, to his Bacchus School of Wine franchise, and worked there until 11 P.M. It

was a former two-truck garage, well scrubbed, with Italian flags and piped-in Sinatra. The students turned out 200 barrels of wine a year, the school only broke even financially, but what does money matter in an affair of the heart?

"This was a hobby," said his wife, Petrina Marie, "but he really enjoyed it. Municipal bond broker at day, winemaker at night. He was pretty wild, very loud. This was a man if you told him this was a rule, he would try to break it just because it was a rule. Anything. Driving. He lost his license at least twice in his lifetime."

Mr. Picerno, who leaves three children, aged 9, 12 and 14, had planned to pursue winemaking full time when he left Wall Street.

JOSEPH PICK
A Special Christmas Memory

There was something about that Christmas nearly four years ago that inspired Joseph Pick to go beyond the normal holiday routine. Not only did Mr. Pick decorate his home in Hoboken, N.J., and buy the usual assortment of presents (hiding them in black garbage bags) for his wife, Marie Puccio-Pick, and his daughter, Jeannette, but he also decided to pose as Santa Claus.

It was a major undertaking that involved secretly buying a Santa suit, slipping into it unnoticed and arriving at his in-laws' house on Christmas Eve. And it went off so well that he even surprised his wife. But he made one little mistake: The label on his sweatshirt was visible through a seam in the suit. Jeannette, now 9, and her cousin, Julianna Antonucci, recognized it right away.

Mr. Pick, a vice president at Fiduciary Trust, was quick with an explanation when confronted afterward: Because Santa was far too busy, the visitor was actually an elf. In fact, Mr. Pick went on, he was an elf.

After her father became missing on Sept. 11, Jeannette reminded her mother about that Christmas Eve. "Is Daddy still an elf?" she asked. "I said, 'Sure, he is,' " Ms. Puccio-Pick recalled. Though it was months before Christmas, Jeannette went about making her Christmas list.

CHRISTOPHER PICKFORD
The Rocking Firefighter

He was the rocking firefighter.

When Christopher Pickford was a toddler, his mother remembered, he sang merrily along to a song on *Sesame Street* about a fireman.

That became his goal: to grow up to be a firefighter.

But he was captivated by music, too. "I've got baby pictures of him with a guitar," said his mother, Linda Pickford. So he fought fires during the day and played rock music at night. And he always found time for his girlfriend of 11 years, Amy Whalley.

Firefighter Pickford, 32, who lived in Queens and was in Engine Company 201, had his own band, called Ten Degree Lean. He was the lead guitarist and wrote most of the music. An earlier band was called Riboflavin and the Vitamin D's.

At his funeral, a special tribute CD was distributed to mourners that contained songs from both of his groups, as well as several songs written by Ten Degree Lean in his honor. Also on the CD are four messages from Firefighter Pickford that the lead singer of the band had saved on his answering machine.

The first one was to give the big news that he had met the requirements and was finally going to become a firefighter.

BERNARD PIETRONICO
Brotherly Devotion

Bernard Pietronico was Michael Pietronico's older brother, his only brother—his hero, he says. As kids playing basketball in the courtyard of St. Joseph's School, there on Pavonia Avenue in Jersey City, Bernard always picked his kid brother to be on his team. Always.

Bernard played basketball for Hudson Catholic High School, then so did Michael. Bernard got a job on Wall Street, then so did Michael. Bernard married, had two children, and moved to Old Bridge, N.J. So did Michael.

"He began losing his hair, and so I decided I would too," Michael Pietronico joked, before turning serious. "I just watched him rise up through the ranks and make a wonderful career for himself and be a great provider for his family. That's something that I thought was an exceptional thing."

On weekdays, Bernard Pietronico, who was 37, was a corporate bond trader at Cantor Fitzgerald. The rest of the time he was a husband, a son, a father, a coach in his Roman Catholic parish's youth-basketball league. And a brother, to two sisters and to Michael, who still proudly remembers his schoolyard nickname: "Little Bernard."

NICHOLAS P. PIETRUNTI
Everybody's Nicky

Everyone seemed to know Nicholas Pietrunti, who earned the nickname the Mayor.

In Staten Island, in Manhattan, or anywhere in New Jersey, "there would always be someone who knew him," said his sister, Janet Ciaramello. "I'd say my maiden name and people would say, 'Oh, do you know Nicky, are you related to Nicky?' Everybody knew him."

Mr. Pietrunti, 38, an equities clerk at Cantor Fitzgerald, lived alone in Belford, N.J., where he coached roller hockey, golfed and treated his nieces and nephews like his own children.

John Pietrunti said the future would not have necessarily been easy for his brother, who was deaf, but that his life was starting to improve.

"That's the sad part. You don't build to a crescendo of happiness, it comes and goes, but the only thing I believe is that on Sept. 11 he was happy. He was looking forward to going to work the next day. Work didn't define him, but he felt good about where he was."

Students and teachers from the Hanahan Middle School in Hanahan, South Carolina, bring boxes of gifts for the families of firefighters from Ladder Company 118 in Brooklyn Heights who were killed in the collapse of the World Trade Center. (*Justin Lane*)

JOSEPH PLUMITALLO
From A&P to Wall Street

Hey, tell the guys in Bensonhurst: Joe's horse came in first at Freehold the other day.

Yeah, the same Joseph Plumitallo who used to be the stock boy at the Stillwell Avenue A&P, where at 17 he caught the eye of Doreen Manno, 16, the meat wrapper. Got married and lived in a room in his parents' house on Lake Street. Talked his way into a bottom-rung job on Wall Street. Rode the F train to his future, as a Cantor Fitzgerald bond broker. Went from a polyester suit at the 1976 Lafayette High prom to wearing pinstripes, buying a few horses, and, at 45, treating clients to Super Bowls.

He was quite a talker. He would start that story of how Ms. Manno nodded off after one drink on a date at Dangerfield's, slept through dinner, dessert, "the whole show, asleep" and—here's where his smile would widen, eyes locked on Ms. Manno's, for the punch line—"in the ladies' room." And so many other stories.

Dressed impeccably, he would take his daughters, Genna, 11, and Lisa, 9, in new white outfits, to the hometown Father-Daughter Dance in Manalapan, N.J. He would drive his son, Joseph Jr., 5, over to the stable at Gaitway Farm on a Saturday to watch his favorite, El Diablo, get ready to race.

Are Diablo and the others still racing? You bet. It was Genna's wish, and Lisa's, and Joe Jr.'s. And you have to believe it would have been Joe's.

JOHN POCHER
He Arranged the Trips

John Pocher was a details guy, the one in any group who could be counted on to make all the arrangements. When he and his wife, Laura Grygotis, went to London a few years ago, they flew first class, stayed at the best hotels and ate at five-star restaurants. He planned it all. When he and a couple of friends from his alma mater, Seton Hall, took a weekend road trip to Georgetown to catch a basketball game, he scouted out hotels and restaurants, and picked the best route.

"John didn't want to leave anything to chance," said Michael P. Donelan, a friend and road-trip warrior. "He wanted to make sure things were done professionally."

As a bond trader for Cantor Fitzgerald, Mr. Pocher, 36, had to pay close attention to detail, knowing when and where the bonds in his sector were trading. "But John didn't let his job rule his life," Mr. Donelan said.

In a testimonial, Mr. Pocher's sister Joanne captured his spirit this way: "He loved to throw a party, and he loved to be around his family and friends."

Said Ms. Grygotis: "When I think about John, I think about a very thoughtful person."

WILLIAM H. POHLMANN
Living Every Day as the Last

The night William H. Pohlmann met Linda Fata in a bar at Rockefeller Center in April 1973, he told her he just knew they would end up married. They did, seven months later. The children came quickly: Craig, now 27, Christopher, 26, and Darren, 23.

But Mr. Pohlmann, who was born in the Bronx, also sensed that he would die young. "He was devastated by his father's death when he was 15, and always thought he wasn't going to get much time with his own children," Mrs. Pohlmann said.

And so, Mr. Pohlmann lived every day as if it were his last. He coached his children in Little League baseball and in soccer. He helped them with homework. He worked hard, but played harder. He was funny and, his wife said, when he drank, even funnier. He liked to have big family dinners and backyard barbecues with neighbors and friends.

At 56, he was still a volunteer firefighter and a lieutenant colonel in the Army Reserve. Mr. Pohlmann, a lawyer, worked as an assistant deputy commissioner for the New York State Department of Taxation and Finance in the trade center. But his real love was politics. He was a perennial Republican candidate in Ardsley, N.Y., where he lived for 28 years. He lost every time.

"It was very difficult for him to lose," Mrs. Pohlmann said. "But what can you do? He always kept going."

LAURENCE MICHAEL POLATSCH
No Date, but a Good Story

Laurence Michael Polatsch, an equities trader at Cantor Fitzgerald, hardly lacked for chutzpah, and may just have raised the meaning of the word to a new level. He was a free spirit who was able to talk his way into companies' holiday parties at Manhattan hotels year after year.

Forget the pride he felt at having successfully crashed the Plaza Hotel wedding of Michael Douglas and Catherine Zeta-Jones. He truly met his Everest on the day he was browsing at a magazine store in downtown Manhattan and the actress Julia Roberts stopped by. Mr. Polatsch said hi, then asked her out "for dinner or a cup of coffee," recalled his mother, Linda. The actress paused, then declined—but made a point of thanking him.

A few months later, in an *Entertainment Tonight* interview, Ms. Roberts wondered over the airwaves why she did not go out with that guy who tried to pick her up by the magazines. Mr. Polatsch called the show, which then broadcast him re-enacting his proposition at the same store.

Remembering the incident in the current issue of *Esquire* magazine, Ms. Roberts recalled that "there was a certain charm to his chutzpah."

Many of those who attended Mr. Polatsch's memorial celebration in Woodbury, on Long Island, where he grew up, told the story about the big date with the movie star that was not to be, and many others. "He was charismatic and fun-loving," his mother said, "and made everyone feel terrific."

A union memorial to victims of the September 11 terrorist attack, erected on West Street near the World Trade Center site. (*James Estrin*)

STEVE POLLICINO

Living in the Moment

Any evening, Steve Pollicino, 48, might call his home in Long Island to say: "Get ready! I've got tickets to the Knicks!"

Or *The Producers*. Or 'N Sync. In August, he announced that he was taking his wife, Jane, and his 12-year-old, Celeste, to the Bahamas—in a couple of days. "Can you imagine planning a vacation a year in advance?" he once said incredulously.

A trader at Cantor Fitzgerald, he did not head for his easy chair after work. He might take Celeste to get an ice cream after her religion class or shoot pool with his 19-year-old son, Steven, during college holidays. He could turn a humdrum gathering into a party just by showing up. Once, on a summer morning, he headed for his usual 6:10 A.M. train, turned around at the last minute and spent the day at the beach with his wife and sister-in-law.

His big worry was Celeste. He could not bear to think of her leaving childhood, home and him. Four days before he died, he picked her up at a friend's and she emerged in giggles. "Promise me," he said, catching her mood, "that you'll never stop giggling."

JOSHUA POPTEAN

Inspiring Hard Work

To pass the "Josh test" at Bronx Builders, a new employee had to be very good. Of all the project managers, Joshua Poptean was known as the most exacting, the man with the most indefatigable appetite for work. He came across as defiant and argumentative, but new employees and clients alike quickly realized that his crustiness masked his fairness, loyalty and hearty sense of humor.

Mr. Poptean, 37, moved to Portland, Ore., from Romania with his family when he was a teenager, and he embraced his new country. He joined the National Guard; at a family reunion this Fourth of July, Mr. Poptean, an adored uncle, was the first to leap up and sing the national anthem. In New York City, he became deeply religious. He drove a taxi, learned carpentry and made his way to Bronx Builders, where he rose, eventually overseeing sites, including a bar for Windows on the World, on the 106th floor of the World Trade Center.

In the chaos of Sept. 11, Bronx Builders' supervisors around the city reported they were shutting down for the day. Finally, one supervisor, an immigrant himself and a protégé of Mr. Poptean's, called in from Brooklyn. His crew, he said emphatically, was continuing to work.

GIOVANNA PORRAS
Living the Life She Wanted

Giovanna Porras realized many of her dreams in 2001. In January she received an associate accounting degree from Baruch College, and about three months later she landed an accounting job at General Telecom.

Ms. Porras, 24, lived in Queens with her mother and was proud to be working at the famous World Trade Center, said her older sister, Roxana Batista. Ms. Porras planned to study for her C.P.A. degree in a few months and was sticking to her diet by working out.

"She was just a happy, cheerful person," Ms. Batista said, the type who was there for everyone. She was like a second mother to her nephews and pulled for her boyfriend, Demetrios Xanthopoulos, at softball games. Mr. Xanthopoulos, also an accountant, said Ms. Porras pushed him to do his best.

She was the kind of young woman who was as comfortable escorting her mother, Adela Romero, around town as she was nightclub-hopping with her friends. "There was not one person in the world she wouldn't get along with," Mr. Xanthopoulos said.

ANTHONY PORTILLO
Photography and Calypso

Anthony Portillo had a habit of deferring to his wife, Minerva Mentor-Portillo, to express things that he could not put into words. He was quiet, a bit on the shy side. But that is not to say that he was not deeply moved by what he heard and saw. A native of Trinidad, Mr. Portillo considered himself a serious collector of calypso music, particularly 1930s albums that were recorded in remote corners of the island.

An architect for Raytheon in 2 World Trade Center, Mr. Portillo, 48, also was an amateur photographer. On weekends, he would take his family to places like the Brooklyn Botanic Garden and set up his tripod. His devotion to his children was obvious. Practically every time they sneezed, he was snapping photographs of his sons, Elijah, 7, and Isaiah, 5. He had an older daughter, Zarifa, 22, from a previous marriage.

Mrs. Mentor-Portillo said the family budget was tight, but even so they enjoyed the city's cultural life through its museums, parks and libraries. And every night in their Brooklyn apartment near Ocean Avenue, Mr. Portillo would curl up in bed with his sons, taking turns with them in reading aloud their favorite children's books.

"The Bible said many have entertained angels unawares," his wife said. "I strongly believe that Anthony was an angel that God brought into my life."

JAMES E. POTORTI
"Je T'Aime, Jim"

Paris, 1988. Nikki Stern is napping and the new love in her life, James E. Potorti, a sweet soul with penetrating eyes, is painting. For days they have been exploring Paris, and discovering each other in its art galleries, cafes and, inevitably, the Eiffel Tower. Now, as she sleeps, he arranges fresh oranges and grapes in a bowl, and he paints his simple still life with a purpose made clear by the inscription on his canvas, "Paris à Nikki—Je t'aime, Jim, 1988."

"That," Ms. Stern recalled with a warm laugh, "is when I knew I had him."

Cayuga Lake, N.Y., 2001. It is Labor Day weekend, and Mr. Potorti, 52, is kayaking side-by-side with Ms. Stern, his wife of 10 years. They bought kayaks this spring, took lessons together, and now, on a clear, cool day, they are exploring Cayuga Lake, and discovering each other. Near the middle of the lake they drift for a moment, basking in the intimacy of being so alone, and so together. Ms. Stern reaches for her husband's hand. He leans close to her. They kiss.

"The best day of my life," Ms. Stern said.

These words come through tears. Mr. Potorti, a vice president at Marsh & McLennan who worked on the 96th floor of 1 World Trade Center, has left behind a wife who loved the way they ignored birthdays, Christmas and Valentine's Day because they much preferred surprising each other with gifts throughout the year. What does she miss most?

"I definitely miss his physical presence," she said, again with that warm laugh. "We were close that way."

DAPHNE POULETSOS
The Party House

Big holidays usually meant big parties at Daphne Pouletsos' house in Westwood, N.J. On Mother's Day, she decorated her tidy three-bedroom house with flamingos and invited all of her relatives—including those who were not mothers. At Christmastime, she decked the house with Christmas toilet paper and holiday napkins. She invited her relatives on Christmas Day, followed by her friends and colleagues from Aon Corporation the day after.

She was, according to her brother-in-law, John Krachtus, "the family's social director." But what Ms. Pouletsos, 47 and single, was really famous for was her Halloween extravaganzas. The decorations included witches flying through trees, gravestones on the lawn and sound effects at every door. Everyone was invited. Sometimes, 200 people would pass through her doors.

She would prepare weeks ahead of time. Before Sept. 11, she had already begun to take the Halloween decorations out of the closet.

STEPHEN POULOS
Finding Opera Again

Stephen Poulos spent most of the last year loosening up. He was starting to enjoy opera again after tuning it out for five years. "The louder, the higher and more Italian, the better," his wife, Lisa, of Basking Ridge, N.J., said of his preference for operas. "I knew not to get him Mozart and things like that. They are more on the pretty side versus the powerful side."

A high achiever, Mr. Poulos, 45, stopped listening to opera out of frustration when he realized that he could not earn a living as an opera singer after 20 years of training as a baritone. But as he rose quickly in his career in information technology, recently becoming a manager at Aon Corporation, he began to ease up on himself. He even joined the Opera Forum, an Internet discussion, using the alias billybobives, chastising members for their opera preferences.

A service for Harlem residents who served in uniform and died on September 11, held December 4 at the Bonner Youth Center on West 124th Street in Manhattan by Ministers of Harlem. (*James Estrin*)

"It was hard for him to get over leaving the opera," Ms. Poulos said. "On good days during that time, I would say, 'Oh, you seem happy today.' He would say, 'Lisa, I'm never happy. I may be happier, but I'm never happy.'"

"This summer, I reminded him about that phrase, saying you must be happier now," she said. "He said, 'No, I'm actually happy.'"

SHAWN E. POWELL
His Glass Was Full

Shawn E. Powell was the firefighter with the light touch. Whether working at Engine Company 207 in downtown Brooklyn, at home in Crown Heights, or camping with his 5-year-old son, Joshua, he had a way of lifting spirits.

"If there wasn't any fun going on, he would find a way," said Matthew Dwyer, a fellow firefighter. "With Shawn, the glass was half full, never half empty."

Firefighter Powell, 32, brought unusual skills to the Fire Department. An artist and woodcarver, he had built props and volunteered at several New York City theaters, including the Apollo Theater, and studied architecture at New York Technical College.

At Engine Company 207—where the slogan is The House of Misfit Toys because of the company's specialized, somewhat bizarre-looking fire-fighting equipment—Mr. Powell made the point in comic relief with a poster that includes a square-wheeled fire engine.

Firefighter Powell and his wife, Jean, who had been teenage sweethearts in Brooklyn, married in 1989 and moved immediately to Germany, where he served four years in the Army.

In 2001, Firefighter Powell's passion had been camping with Joshua.

On several trips to lakes and state parks in New Jersey, he was teaching the boy to make a campfire and put up a tent and had planned another father-son outing soon after Sept. 11.

GREG PREZIOSE
"Tow'" and His Big Dreams

Greg Preziose's road to the world of high finance started behind the wheel of a tow truck. He was a driver, and a big dreamer. "My husband was very determined," Lori Preziose said. "Whatever he set his mind to, he proved it."

At Cantor Fitzgerald, where Mr. Preziose, 34, traded bonds, he was known simply as Tow, a nod of respect from colleagues who marveled at his journey. At home he was superdad, a father never too tired to help coach baseball or football practice or just to embrace his three children.

Mourners at a memorial Mass in Staten Island on
December 3 for Joseph Maffeo, thirty, who was among
the 343 firefighters who died September 11.
(*Mary DiBiase Blaich*)

"He had a full-time job, but he was as close to the children as any stay-at-home parent," his wife said. When the twin towers collapsed, she posted a flyer with a picture of her husband being hugged tightly by his children. In bold letters, it read, "Please find our daddy."

WANDA PRINCE
Coffee Healed All Wounds

Wanda Prince had a weakness for coffee. Whenever she was upset with her husband, Edward, about leaving his dirty clothes on the bathroom floor (again) or leaving his dirty dishes in the sink (again), Mr. Prince would woo her back with a strong cup of Joe. "She just loved coffee," said Mr. Prince.

They were opposites who attracted.

Mrs. Prince was "a neatnik." He left clothes on the floor. She was a Mets fan. He loved the Yankees. She loved her cat, Lucky. Lucky got on Mr. Prince's nerves.

They first met at a tailgate party at Giants Stadium. Both

were involved with other people. They fell in love, the second time they met, after their other relationships had fallen apart.

Mrs. Prince, 30, worked long days as a trader at Fiduciary Trust Company on the 94th floor of 2 World Trade Center. She was at her desk at 7:30 A.M. and often did not return home to Staten Island until 7:30 P.M. Mr. Prince, a firefighter, would have dinner waiting for her.

Along with a cup of coffee.

VINCENT A. PRINCIOTTA
The Essence of Cool

First there was the blue van with the surfboard strapped to the roof. Then there were the bright Hawaiian shirts, the flowing hair, the perpetual tan. Soon there was no doubt: Vincent A. Princiotta was cool.

Starting in the late 1970s, Mr. Princiotta, a firefighter with Ladder Company 7 in Manhattan, led a band of surfers from their landlocked Bronxwood Avenue neighborhood into the big waves off Gilgo Beach.

"I think he watched too much Don Ho," said Dave Breiner, a Connecticut firefighter who knew him as Vinny Van. When he visited his sister Bernadette at college in Hawaii, her friends were amazed, she said, that a non-Hawaiian, "this haoli from the Bronx," was so able on the longboard.

Even as the years rolled by, and he married the lovely Karen and became the adoring father of Christina, now 16 months old, Firefighter Princiotta, 39, who lived in Orangeburg, N.Y., maintained his profile. He invested in phony winning lottery tickets, which he would distribute to his fellow firefighters and watch while they shrieked and kissed the firehouse floor. But he also helped the younger ones get familiar with firefighting tools, said Patty Boylan, a friend and colleague at Ladder 7, and cooked heaps of Italian food for the entire company.

And he kept on surfing. "He was just supercool," Mr. Boylan said. "We called him the Vin Man."

EVERETT PROCTOR III
A Jokester's Gentle Heart

Everett Proctor III had a big heart and made for a good friend, but his dry humor came with the package. If he noticed an opportunity to do a little tormenting, he took it. Being six years younger, his sister, Mary Griffin, took plenty of teasing growing up. They would go to an amusement park and he would announce that they were going on a nice, gentle train ride. Before she knew it, she was buckled into a roller coaster screaming for help. "He'd say we're going on a Ferris wheel," she said, "and it would be one of those ones that went upside down and all around."

When he was in the Boy Scouts with his cousin, they had to row across a lake. Mr. Proctor could row; his cousin could not. So Mr. Proctor rowed to the middle of the lake and told his cousin, "O.K., your turn." He sat there and laughed as his cousin rowed in circles.

Mr. Proctor, 44, was single and lived in Manhattan. He was an avid music and movie fan, and relished traveling. He had been working in Connecticut, but in January had switched to a new job as equities controller at Cantor Fitzgerald.

His sister lives in Massachusetts, and he would speak with her every day, often multiple times, just to see how things were. "On Sept. 10," she said, "I spoke to him three times."

CARRIE PROGEN
Telling Sketches of Strangers

As the A train gently rocked her, Carrie Progen would sit with a small pad in her lap and sketch hurried portraits of the commuters sitting and standing around her in silence. These fleeting moments were among life's truest, she told her boyfriend, Erik P.

Sharkey, "the moments when New Yorkers were thinking the most."

In all, she filled four notebooks with sketches that seemed to reveal the thoughts of strangers. But they also reflected a young artist's passion for her adopted city, Mr. Sharkey said. "The one thing, if you could, is to say how much she loved New York."

Ms. Progen, 25, came from Ashburnham, Mass., where she celebrated her high school graduation by getting a Celtic-style tattoo. "The correct terminology for Carrie is free-spirited," recalled her mother, Kathleen.

Ms. Progen, who lived with Mr. Sharkey in Fort Greene, Brooklyn, was an administrative assistant at the Aon Corporation. But her passion was her art, including illustrations she had just completed for a children's book about "two parents trying to find their little girl who's hiding from them," he said.

An exhibit of her artwork—including her subway sketches—was to be held at 8 P.M. on Nov. 17, 2001, in Manhattan at Anderson's Martial Arts Academy, 35 West 31st Street.

DAVID PRUIM
A Lifelong Honeymoon

David and Kate Pruim were married 28 years ago, and Mrs. Pruim talks about him as if they were newlyweds. "We had an 18-year honeymoon and then our daughter was born and then more joy came into our lives," she said. "We just thought it would go on for another 28 years."

Mr. Pruim, 52, a senior vice president for the Aon Corporation, worked on the 103rd floor of 2 World Trade Center. "He was the kindest, nicest, most gentle 6-foot-4 person there ever was," she said. "He made everyone he came into contact with feel good about himself, from children to adults."

The two were from Michigan, and were introduced by friends, Mrs. Pruim recalled. "I just liked his personality, and he was gorgeous," she said, with a full-throated laugh. They enjoyed being together, even just sitting next to each other, reading. They lived in Montclair, N.J., with their daughter Carrington, who is 10. A memorial service is being planned.

"We're calling it a celebration of his life," Mrs. Pruim said. "And if he walks in in the middle of it, boy, will I be the happiest person there."

RICHARD PRUNTY
Answering a Daughter's Call

Richard Prunty's world revolved around two families. There was his family in Sayville, on Long Island, and there was the Second Battalion of the New York City Fire Department.

Mr. Prunty, the battalion chief, would explain to his

wife, Susan, that his life depended on his firefighters. They depended on him, too. When he received promotions, his firefighters did not want him to move on. "It truly was a brotherhood," she said.

Mr. Prunty was heading into 1 World Trade Center with his firefighters, but his wife thinks he probably had tried to call them out because he was so conscious of their safety. At 57, he was a tall, unassuming man, never the type to dominate a conversation or even brag. But when he did have something to say, his soft-spoken words were usually the strongest and most effective that could be said.

Despite his sometimes gruff exterior, his family knew he was a teddy bear. He was protective of his two children, Lisa, 25, and Christopher, 21. His daughter recalls her father's visit when she became so ill at Dartmouth College in New Hampshire that she couldn't finish classes during final exams. He stayed for one week, sleeping on the floor. "I almost didn't graduate and that put me through it," she said.

games to attend. Although his long trip prevented him from taking the lead in coaching his children's teams, he still kept score or coached at third base.

When Mr. Pugliese's three children became teenagers, he took on a new role as their personal chauffeur, often driving them to and from part-time jobs. Sometimes he took them in his 1978 Thunderbird, a rust-brown hulk of a car with a peeling interior that he inherited from his father in 1993.

"Everybody knew him because of that car," his wife, Maureen Pugliese, said. "As long as he put his key in the car and it started, that was fine with him. He didn't care what kind of a car he had."

The car, which is no longer running, is parked on the street in front of the family's home. It is a daily reminder of Mr. Pugliese. "Nothing was a problem," his mother, Josephine Pugliese, said. "He would say, 'Mother don't worry. As long as I've got my health, I'm the richest person in the world.' "

JOHN F. PUCKETT
From Sinatra to Windows

John F. Puckett's father, back in the '60s, had been a Marine drill sergeant, and Mr. Puckett was a long-haired hippie musician, so their home life, in Las Vegas, was not always tranquil. There was, on the other hand, a constantly changing group of show business players in Las Vegas, which is a good thing for an audio engineer. That came to be Mr. Puckett's line, and he was good at it. His family said there are gold records by Frank Sinatra, B. B. King and Johnny Mathis that list Mr. Puckett as the recording engineer.

"Don't mention Sinatra," Mr. Puckett used to say. "It makes me sound old."

He was 47, tall and lanky, and lived in Glen Cove, N.Y., with Regina Bogan, an office manager, and their four children. He had a Harley and a Chrysler LeBaron convertible and liked going on day trips with Ms. Bogan to Lake George; freewheeling trips on the bike where he was always the lead, though he never knew where he was going. He had a band that played locally, and he worked frequently for Windows on the World, setting up the sound system for conferences. There were no final messages from the audio man after the attack. The last time Ms. Bogan saw him, they were having morning coffee.

PATRICIA ANN PUMA
Two Days a Week

Two things about Patricia Ann Puma made her co-workers at the brokerage company Julien J. Studley smile: her penchant for decorating her fingernails according to the season and her insistence on eating her food—preferably chicken—plain.

"She was one of the pickiest eaters you ever saw," said Barbara Kennish, a longtime friend and colleague. "We would always have to order a separate meal for her."

Shy and quiet, Ms. Puma, 33, was someone that people could count on for common-sense advice, said her boss, Don Schnabel. She was also known for being generous with her time—for spending Christmas morning, for example, visiting a friend's mother at the hospital. Her own mother did not like to drive, so Ms. Puma took her on weekly shopping trips.

But above all, Ms. Puma, who was married to a New York City Transit worker, wanted to be with her children, now 10, 5, and 18 months. So in 1994, when Ms. Kennish suggested they share a secretarial job, Ms. Puma was only too happy to accept. She worked only on Mondays and Tuesdays.

ROBERT PUGLIESE
Suburban Dad

Robert Pugliese was a true suburban dad. He took the two-hour trip from his job as an assistant vice president at Marsh & McLennan to his house in East Fishkill, N.Y., in stride. As soon as he got home, there were bowling matches, basketball games and softball

EDWARD R. PYKON
Fast Eddy from Lehigh

Life was proceeding more or less on schedule for Edward R. Pykon and his wife, Jackie. They met 10 years ago on the Fourth of July, and last August they celebrated their fifth wedding anniversary. In 2000, again on the Fourth of July, they found out that they were going to be parents. By the time their daughter, Jordyn, was born in 2001, they had already bought a house in Princeton Junction, N.J.

"We came here to raise a family," Jackie Pykon said. "Our plan was to buy a beautiful home, fix it up and have a baby. Everything was going along just as planned."

Mr. Pykon, 33, worked at the World Trade Center offices of Fred Alger Management, where he was a senior vice president with a specialty in health care. "What was great about Ed was that he was brilliant, but not stuffy or boring," Mrs. Pykon said. He was very down to earth, modest, and a lot of fun to be around."

As an undergraduate at Lehigh University, Mr. Pykon was known as Fast Eddy, a nickname he picked up as the D.J. at his fraternity. "We still have the turntables in the basement," Mrs. Pykon said. "He had a real adventure for life."

Q

CHRISTOPHER QUACKENBUSH
Christmas Carol *All Year*

Most people think of *A Christmas Carol,* the Charles Dickens classic, only during the holidays. But the tale of greed and redemption was on Christopher Quackenbush's mind his entire life.

As a founding principal at Sandler O'Neill & Partners, Mr. Quackenbush, 44, thrived on sharing his wealth. He created the Jacob Marley Foundation, which provides scholarships and programs for poor children on Long Island, including annual trips to Shea Stadium for Mets games. The Mets themselves once played Tiny Tim to Mr. Quackenbush's Scrooge: he flew some team members to Washington on his company jet last June to meet President Bush.

In keeping with the story that haunted him, Mr. Quackenbush's generosity peaked at Christmas. "He would give us all a trip somewhere," his sister, Gail, said. "A ticket to whatever we really wanted to do."

Not only that, but Mr. Quackenbush took his wife, Traci, their three children and a throng of relatives to see *A Christmas Carol* at Madison Square Garden every December, reminding them not only of the importance of spreading good fortune, but of having fun doing it. They have resolved to go without him this year. "We're not going to have a good time," Gail Quackenbush said, "but we're trying."

LARS QUALBEN
The Giving Trees

The abandoned lots were originally strewn with rusty cars, decrepit refrigerators and rubble. But over the years, the land became a secret garden, a tree-lined oasis with winding brick paths in the middle of Brooklyn.

With his free weekends and evenings, Lars Qualben slowly nurtured frail foot-high seedlings in Carroll Gardens into a backyard of sturdy giving trees for his family. When his two sons could barely walk, Mr. Qualben hung swings from the branches of the mulberry tree so they could fly through the air. Once the boys could scamper, he pruned the branches so they could climb up and build their own treehouse. His sons, now 15 and 14, have graduated from middle school. The family celebrated with a party under the tree canopy. Even dead tree trunks were made into garden benches.

Mr. Qualben's trees now display a radiant fall palate of reds and yellows. The garden offered Mr. Qualben, 49, a senior vice president at Marsh & McLennan, some solace for urban living. It now offers his family some solace for their pain. "We feel him in our lives by being there and looking at it," said Martha Qualben, his wife. "It's a place where he is a living presence."

LINCOLN QUAPPÉ
All-Star Father

It would not be accurate to say that Lincoln Quappé attended every one of his son's baseball and soccer matches; his job as a firefighter with Rescue 2 in Brooklyn required him to work all hours. But he never missed a game, thanks to the Quappé Broadcasting Service, otherwise known as his wife, Jane. "If I was at a game and Lincoln was working, I would call and give him the play by play," she said.

And when Firefighter Quappé, 38, was at home, in Sayville on Long Island, he was all kid-business—"a true sit-down-on-the-floor-play-G.I.-Joes-play-Barbies-build-Legos-100-percent kind of dad," Ms. Quappé said.

On weekends, taking care of the children, a son and daughter, often meant nature trips on the boat the firefighter's stepfather kept behind his house in Brookhaven and pointing out the herons and egrets and osprey nestled in the reeds or soaring overhead.

Firefighter Quappé, who, like his father, was also a volunteer firefighter in his town, showed the same devotion to his job as to his family. "Being a firefighter defined him," Ms. Quappé said. "It was his blood. It was his life. I've said to many people that if he had to die at such a young age, this is how he would have wanted to go."

BETH QUIGLEY
Balancing Work and Play

Beth Quigley never turned down an invitation, whether it was to a movie, a party, or a waterskiing trip. A loyal and generous friend, she packed her calendar with social outings and family visits. She held dinner parties at her apartment near Lincoln Center, and treated her guests to filet mignon wrapped in bacon and imported cheeses. "Her hors d'oeuvres were famous," said her sister, Suzanne. "She never skimped on them."

At 25, Ms. Quigley had struck a balance between work and play. She was a trader at Cantor Fitzgerald, and had just started an M.B.A. program at night. But even when things got hectic, she never forgot to call. A few weeks before Sept. 11, she invited her sister to the United States Open match between Lleyton Hewitt and Andy Roddick. Only the sisters were too busy catching up to pay attention. Finally, the other fans turned around and shushed them.

Lieutenant Dennis Farrell, a firefighter based in Park Slope, Brooklyn, and a surfer, putting up a Rockaway Beach memorial to the victims of the World Trade Center attack. (*Nancy Siesel*)

MICHAEL THOMAS QUILTY
Giving Away His Time

If it moved, he was on it. If it was water, he was in it. Michael Thomas Quilty, 42, flew a plane, owned a boat and rode his bike from his home on Staten Island to Ladder House 11 in lower Manhattan, where he was a lieutenant in the Fire Department.

On Sept. 5, Lieutenant Quilty celebrated his 20th anniversary with the Fire Department. Most of his career was spent at Engine 282 and Ladder 148 in Brooklyn. A year ago, he moved to Ladder 11. "There's a picture of him in uniform there," but not in his gear like the rest of the firefighters, said his wife, Susan. "He wasn't there long enough to have a new picture."

The Quiltys met 23 years ago. "He was a lifeguard at my pool," Mrs. Quilty said. "My mother said, 'Go out to the pool. There's a cute lifeguard there.' "

The sports didn't end there. The Quiltys had a boat for waterskiing and fishing. They kayaked in the ocean.

Last summer, Mr. Quilty took their son, Daniel, 15, to learn to scuba dive, and for eight years he coached the soccer team that his daughter, Kerry, 13, played on. Now the girls on the team have his initials on their jerseys.

JAMES QUINN
At the Center of Things

Since childhood, when he sneaked train rides to the hotel where the famous baseball players stayed, James Quinn would find a way to be at the center of the action with celebrities, and he had dozens of photographs to prove it. There was Jimmy with Wayne Gretzky, Jimmy with Michael Jordan, Jimmy with Will Smith.

"You never knew how he would get in," said Noreen Quinn, his mother. "He would just walk in like he belonged."

But he was interested in less famous people too, and closely followed the basketball career of his younger brother Joseph, a West Point cadet. Though James Quinn, 23, loved the excitement of being a fledgling trader at Cantor Fitzgerald, he did not mind entertaining a young cousin or an elderly aunt.

Late one night when he was a teenager, his mother remembered, he called to say he had gotten a ride to the end of the Marine Parkway Bridge. When she arrived to pick him up on the Brooklyn side, she discovered that the bridge was closed for construction. But there came Mr. Quinn; he had persuaded the workers to radio to those on the other side to let him across, telling them his mother was waiting.

"I really thought he would come out of the darkness this time," she said. "I really did."

R

CAROL RABALAIS
Forgiving and Optimistic

Carol Rabalais and her elder sister Patricia Tate exchanged harsh words during the summer when Ms. Rabalais mistakenly booked some standby plane tickets instead of reserved ones for a family vacation to their native Jamaica. But by the next day, Ms. Rabalais was her usual sunny self, the standby upset seemingly forgotten.

How very Carol, Ms. Tate said. Whether she was struggling as a single teenage mother in Brooklyn raising three children, or relishing her new job as an administrative assistant at the Aon Corporation, Ms. Rabalais, 38, never held a grudge, never lost her optimism, never doubted God.

"The running joke was that although we fight, she would still come to my house and walk in and say hi, and play with the kids, and eat what she wanted to eat, and then say, 'Bye, I'm not here.' "

The two sisters were planning a cruise vacation next year, without children. And though Ms. Tate can still travel with her three other sisters, the dynamics will not be the same.

"I've been telling my sisters, 'I can't even get into a good fight with you all, because you guys won't talk to me for a week,' and Carol would say, 'Forget it. Let's move on.' "

CHRISTOPHER A. RACANIELLO
Chasing Tradition

In a family of Wall Street types, traders and bond brokers, Christopher A. Racaniello found it hard not to chase tradition. Like father, like son was the plan: the 30-year-old was working his way through the ranks at Cantor Fitzgerald.

"He was hoping to make his way to the trading desk," said his father, Frank Racaniello, a retired trader. "I was proud of him the way a parent always is. But it felt good watching him work his way up. He had a bright future ahead of him."

Nov. 24, 2001, was to be a particularly big day—his wedding day, the moment Mr. Racaniello, who was forever a best man or an usher in friends' weddings, planned to walk down the aisle with Lisa Greco, an old friend from the neighborhood. For his father, it is impossible not to wonder what might have been for the kid who grew up in Douglaston, Queens, but fancied himself a beach boy.

"My wife and I had finally got our Christopher to the point where we could see the things we taught him and the things he worked for coming to fruition," Frank Racaniello said. "Sometimes I second-guess myself. I think maybe it was my fault. He wouldn't have been there if he hadn't been trying to follow family tradition."

EUGENE J. RAGGIO
Big Man, Tiny Dog

When Eugene J. Raggio said he was taking his dog, Tinkerbell, out for a walk, it meant driving her around in the car through their Staten Island neighborhood.

"Big man, tiny dog, we used to say," said his daughter, Melissa Raggio, recalling her tall father doting on his three-pound Yorkshire terrier.

About the only place Mr. Raggio did not take the dog was to the World Trade Center, where he worked as a building operations supervisor for the Port Authority of New York and New Jersey since the day the towers opened.

"He absolutely loved those buildings," his daughter said. "The people he worked with were his second family. He was even good to the homeless people who hung around the tower."

Her father, who was 55, called his wife, Francine, just after the first plane hit the north tower. There was no question that he would stay to help. It was his job.

"If he hadn't been working that day, he would have been

just as affected if the towers had collapsed and he hadn't been there to help," his daughter said. "His life would never have been the same."

MICHAEL PAUL RAGUSA
W.W.M.D.?

Michael Paul Ragusa was not a mountain climber, a sculptor, a scholar. He was not anything like that, his loved ones say. Being a firefighter was enough for him. "He did things to make others happy," said his fiancée, Jennifer Trapani. "That's how he made himself happy."

Mike Ragusa, 29, joined the Fire Department about two years before Sept. 11. He was assigned to Engine Company 250, but was working at Engine Company 279 that day.

He was single-minded, said his sister, Christine Saladeen. "If we all lined up outside the World Trade Center and yelled, 'Mikey stop!,' he still would have ran in."

When word of Firefighter Ragusa's disappearance percolated through his neighborhood of Bergen Beach, Brooklyn, dozens of people camped out on his parents' lawn, on their patio furniture and on their living room floor. Strangers who did not know his name came by with fruit baskets to tell of how he helped fix their fences or change their tires.

He may not have been a sculptor, but he was a plumber, and if a friend's pipe burst at midnight, he was there. He may not have been a scholar, but he was a good man. His friends had a saying about him—W.W.M.D.: What Would Mikey Do?

PETER F. RAIMONDI
Life in Perspective

The day after Thanksgiving, Peter F. Raimondi would always put up the family's Christmas tree, and by the weekend he had turned his attention to his mother.

"Mama, put the hot chocolate on and play the Christmas music," said his mother, Candida Raimondi, recalling his words. "He was always trying to make life special for everyone."

Whether it was his open-door policy as first vice president of Carr Futures on the 92nd floor of 1 World Trade Center, games of basketball and chess with his sons or home decorating with his wife, "Everybody was a priority to him," said his wife, Lenore. The 46-year-old father of two didn't just take the family on vacation, she said. He would do exhaustive research for the trip and serve as tour guide.

Above all, he believed in taking life in stride, and he made a plaque for the refrigerator with this motto: "It

Doesn't Really Matter." When last heard from, he was stuck in a trade center elevator. "Anytime I worry about anything now, I look at the refrigerator," his wife said. "That's helped get me through."

HARRY RAINES
Stones in the Office

Those who didn't know Harry Raines by name called him "the guy with the kids." He had three of them, Jillian, 8, Kyle, 6, and Kimberly, 2. For his vegetable garden, they each made him steppingstones, plates of concrete inlaid with colored decorative glass. Mr. Raines wanted the stones at his office, where he was the vice president of global networking for eSpeed. He lined them up on the windowsill of his office at the World Trade Center.

"He enjoyed life," said his wife, Lauren. "He was always up at the crack of dawn. He would go out to the dead end of the street and play soccer with his son or splash in the pool with the children. Or he would go running and dirt-trail biking at Jones Beach with his twin brother, Mark.

"Kids were the focus of our lives," Mrs. Raines said. But lately, she said, "we found we were missing each other, too." On Sept. 9, Mr. Raines, 37, asked her to come for a Sunday walk. She had a lot of things to do, but he told her, "Slow down, slow down." She recalled: "He just came and grabbed my hand. We were always holding hands."

EHTESHAM RAJA
No Fan of Fundamentalism

Ehtesham Raja loved to party and loved his $70,000 BMW 740iL. He was a Muslim from Lahore, Pakistan, and worked for TCG Software in Bloomfield, N.J. Like many Muslims from India and Pakistan, Mr. Raja, 28, loved Hindi music. He sang it in the shower, and was also crazy about the Hindi movie star Amitabh Bachan.

His best friend in the United States was Maneesh Sagar, a Hindu from India. Mr. Raja talked about how some friends from Pakistan had become fundamentalists. "He hated how fundamentalism rears its ugly head," Mr. Sagar said. "To all of us, religion is more a spiritual and personal thing than dogma."

Recently, said Mr. Sagar, Mr. Raja was thinking of giving up partying and marrying his girlfriend, Christine Lamprecht, an American.

On the weekend before he was to attend a conference at the World Trade Center, he and Mr. Sagar went partying. They talked about their dreams, and at 5 A.M. ended up at an Indian restaurant for tea and tikkas, skewered lamb.

"It was a guy's night out," Mr. Sagar said. And that's how he would always remember his friend.

LUCAS RAMBOUSEK
Annual Host and D.J.

Every year in late September, Lucas Rambousek would invite his friends to his parents' vacation house in the woods in Pennsylvania. They slept in tents or in a trailer, ate junk food all day, and at night Mr. Rambousek would spin dance records.

The party was called Junkfest, and it grew out of the parties that Mr. Rambousek, who would have turned 28 today, had at his parents' house in Williamsburg, Brooklyn, just about every Friday. "It was the best thing," said Jesica Vilett, his longtime friend and sometime girlfriend. "Five or 10 people in the apartment and Luke in the bedroom with his turntables."

Mr. Rambousek, who was working as a computer temp at Cantor Fitzgerald on Sept. 11, was obsessed with what his mother, Jindra Rambousek, calls "that crazy music"—techno, trance, anything with a huge beat. He once worked as a quality-control checker for a record-pressing company, listening to CDs all day long.

Junkfest 2001 was scheduled for Sept. 28. Mr. Rambousek's father decided it should go on, as a tribute to him. A big bottle of dandelion wine, made by father and son, sat on a table in the trailer. "We were all sitting around the fire and I went into the trailer and got 12 cups out," Ms. Vilett said. "We all packed into this little trailer and we all did a little toast to Luke. It was good. The wine messes you up. It's got a bitter aftertaste."

MARIA ISABEL RAMIREZ
Taking Care of Mozart

As a child, Maria Isabel Ramirez was always bringing home stray cats and dogs, but could never keep them because of her mother's allergies. When Ms. Ramirez got her own apartment five years ago, on 96th Street in Canarsie, one of the first things she did was to go to a kennel and pick out a dog. She named him Mozart. He was black and brown—the vet called him brindled—and he was part German shepherd and part pit bull.

"She brought him home on her palm, he was so tiny," said her mother, Elsie Cintron. "She treated him like a little baby. She used to feed him well. He was a fat little dog." Her mother said that Ms. Ramirez often asked what would happen to Mozart if anything happened to her. "I used to say, 'I don't know, Maria. I'm allergic. But don't worry about Mozart. He will be fine.' "

And he is. Ms. Ramirez, 25, died in the elevator at 90 West Street, where she worked for Langan Engineering and Environ-

mental Services, when the building was damaged by falling debris from the World Trade Center. Mozart, now 82 pounds, is in Orlando, Fla., with Maria's mother. "I have to keep the dog," Ms. Cintron said. "Even though I am very allergic to it, I have grown used to it. It's something I have to do for her."

HARRY RAMOS
A Quest for Green Eyes

Migdalia Ramos remembers that she had just broken up with her boyfriend on her 18th birthday and was too despondent to dance. All evening, men asked her, and all evening she said no. Finally, the girlfriends trying to cheer her up told her, "If you don't dance with the next person who asks you, we're going to embarrass you."

Up through the crowd came Harry Ramos.

"He was a great dancer," she said. "He had a lot of hustle." He was also delighted when she told him she was Puerto Rican, and spoke Spanish to prove it. "He said, 'I have to marry you then, because I've been looking for a Puerto Rican girl with green eyes,' " she said. "I didn't believe him, but he was all excited. He said, 'Look! Look!' " and he pulled out photographs of the green-eyed Puerto Ricans his two brothers had already married.

She was somewhat alarmed, and considered giving him the wrong phone number. But he persisted. They dated for eight years and were married in 1986.

When Mr. Ramos was laid off from his job as a carpenter, he remade himself in financial services, working his way

A memorial mural for September 11 attack victims, created by Tats Cru, graffiti artists, on Tenth Avenue in upper Manhattan. (*James Estrin*)

up to head trader at the May Davis Group, a small investment bank on the 87th floor of 1 World Trade Center. "He got that break and he ran with it," Mrs. Ramos said.

VISHNOO RAMSAROOP
Daughters' Dream Vacation

When Vishnoo Ramsaroop moved from Trinidad to New York 17 years ago, he roamed excitedly around Manhattan his first week here, and when he visited the twin towers, he fell in love with their size and majesty.

"So he told himself he wished he could get a job in the World Trade Center," said his brother Sahadeo. "So he went down there the next week, and he got a job there. He just liked the building. He never worked nowhere else in America, not even one hour."

Mr. Ramsaroop, 45, helped run the towers' elevators, and when his brother visited, he unfailingly took him to the top to proudly show the view. He felt compelled to work six days a week to support his eight daughters and stepdaughters.

One of his happiest times came in August when he took a week of vacation. On successive days, he took his daughters Tiffany, 8, and Ashley, 5, to Great Adventure, the Bronx Zoo, the New York Aquarium and, on one day, not just one movie, but two.

"The day they went to the movies, they came home very late and I was very worried," said his wife, Shrimatti. "I got a little angry at him, but the girls were so happy. They said, 'Guess what, Mommy! Daddy sneaked us into a second movie. We had so much fun.'"

LORENZO RAMZEY
King of Chess, Not Golf

His nickname was Grandmaster. For anyone who dared to move a pawn against him, the reason was obvious. Lorenzo Ramzey played a daunting game of chess.

Every day during his lunch hour, he challenged anyone to play. If no one was willing, that did not stop him. He dragooned an opponent into a game. Could you beat him? Forget it.

When he went home to East Northport, N.Y., where he lived with his wife, Volteen, it was often back to the chessboard. He would log on to the Internet and play against cyberspace opponents, sometimes until 3 in the morning. Relatives would call, and the phone line would be busy for hours. Mrs. Ramzey's grown children were planning to get her a second phone line.

Last summer, two relatives in Florida played an epic game against Mr. Ramzey on the Internet and, for the first time, beat him. "They never let him forget that," said Jennifer Fontus, his stepdaughter. "They said they had dethroned the Grandmaster." He was supposed to visit them for Thanksgiving for a rematch.

Mr. Ramzey, 48, came to America from Panama when he was in his late teens, and worked his way up in the insurance business, eventually becoming a casualty broker at Aon. He also loved golf, but was less proficient with woods and irons than with knights and bishops; friends who had been humbled at chess were quick to remark, "Did he tell you about his golf game?"

A. TODD RANCKE
A Community Fixture

When A. Todd Rancke knocked you down, you did not want to get back up, because you were too busy laughing. Mr. Rancke, a managing director at Sandler O'Neill, had a teasing sense of humor that played on people's flaws but did not generate any ill will, said his sister, Cindy Bienemann.

"He could crack on you in a way without making you feel bad," she said.

In fact, it seemed that he did just the opposite. Mr. Rancke, 42, was such a fixture in the Summit, N.J., community where he lived that people teased him about being mayor someday, said his wife, Deborah. He was so well loved by his clients that they would sometimes join him on family vacations with his wife and children, Christina, 11; Brittany, 9; and Todd Jr., 7.

For all his jocularity, Mr. Rancke was a gentleman at heart, a caring man whose primary concern was his family's happiness. Mrs. Rancke sees that same quality in her children, especially her son. Now little Todd puts his arms around her when she's sad, Mrs. Rancke said, "just like big Todd used to do."

ADAM RAND
Doing What Came Naturally

Adam Rand always wanted to be a firefighter. When he graduated from high school, he joined the volunteer fire department in his Bellmore, N.Y., neighborhood. Even after Mr. Rand, 30, became a member of the New York City Fire Department in 1995, he continued to volunteer in Bellmore. For Mr. Rand, fighting fires was a calling.

He reveled in the camaraderie and in learning new techniques that he could teach to younger firefighters. Firefighter Rand's specialty was rescue. On Sept. 11, he joined his fellow members of Squad 288 from Maspeth, Queens, at 2 World Trade Center. He was trying to evacuate people when the building collapsed.

"If he had to die, he died doing something he loved," his mother, Mary Ann Rand, said.

Mrs. Rand said that in addition to his devotion to fire-fighting, her son lived a life of full appreciation for other activities, like skiing, fishing, hunting and preparing for his forthcoming wedding.

At the firehouse in Bellmore, Firefighter Rand will be remembered for his legendary Halloween costumes. He once arrived at the annual party wearing a red wood box. Mr. Rand had cut out a square hole on the back of the box so that his face could be seen. He was supposed to be the missing child on the back of a milk carton.

JONATHAN C. RANDALL
Committed to His Daughter

It is late Saturday morning at Kensington Stables, on the edge of Prospect Park in Brooklyn. Jonathan C. Randall sits patiently, smoking a cigar, waiting for his 11-year-old daughter, Katharine, to finish her weekly riding lesson.

It is a calming routine for both father and daughter, a treasured escape from times made hectic by divorce and a thousand other pressures. It is what Mr. Randall, 42, lived for.

"Jonathan had been bouncing around for a while until Katie was born, but then he got his life together," said Gindy Bladen, his former wife. "He was completely committed to her."

He also got more involved with a local church, the Zion German Evangelical Lutheran Church in Brooklyn Heights. He was assistant treasurer at the church council, and some-times moderated discussions after prayer services.

"He was very definitely a peacemaker," said the Rev. Dr. George R. Muenich, its pastor. "He had that gift." Mr. Randall also led a Bible study group at Marsh & McLennan, where he was a manager. But he always reserved time for Katie.

"Whenever he was with her you could tell that he was totally enjoying the moment," said Matthew Steffanie, a neighbor. "He seemed to have an inner peace."

SHREYAS RANGANATH
Bollywood and Nan

They call Bangalore the Silicon Valley of India, and when the city, in southern India, became a hot place for high-tech enterprise several years ago, Shreyas Ranganath, 26, threw himself into the world of software design. "For him, it became an addiction," Manoj

Baalebail, a longtime friend, said. "He had a great love for software."

In August 2001, that love brought Mr. Ranganath to New York on a three-month project for Marsh & McLennan, on the 97th floor of 1 World Trade Center. Mr. Baalebail, who works for the same consulting company, put him and another software designer, Shashi Kiran Kadaba, up in his Hacken-sack home, where they spent their evenings cooking elabo-rate Indian meals or watching Hindi films. "He appreciated Hollywood movies, but he had a great taste for Indian movies."

Monday night, the men shared a feast to celebrate the birthday of Krishna, the Hindu god. "It was a wonderful dinner we had," Mr. Baalebail said. "I just don't want to think of it as his last."

SHASHI KIRAN KADABA's portrait appears on page 244.

ANNE ROSE RANSOM
"A Subtle Adventuress"

When her husband's chatter about buying a sailboat turned serious two years ago, Anne Rose Ransom—who disliked being on the water about as much as did her overweight pet, Pig Cat—decided it was time once again to stare down her fears. She signed up for a sailing class for women in Annapolis, Md.

When she came back home to Edgewater, N.J., a week later she still was no sailor, but she had gained her sea legs. She did not get seasick anymore, and she even threw out a couple of nautical terms that disguised her nervousness about falling into the water when the boat tacked hard.

Forcing herself to take risks was the way Mrs. Ransom, 45, lived many aspects of her life. It was a part of how she showed her concern for others, from her co-workers in the travel department at American Express to her oldest and best friends.

"She didn't really like sailing, but God, she tried," said Michelle Glynn, a friend since high school. Over the years Ms. Glynn learned that in her own understated way, Mrs. Ransom ruled out almost nothing. "She was a subtle adven-turess," she said.

Once they went skiing, but it was only when the lift reached the top of the slope that Ms. Glynn learned that her friend was afraid of heights. As a lark they once bought dirt bikes. Only when the bikes were delivered did Mrs. Ransom admit she'd never been on one before. Learning to sail was the same. "She knew how much I enjoyed sailing, and she wanted to learn how to enjoy it, too," said her husband, Robert.

Last spring he did buy his sailboat, a 27-footer. Mrs. Ransom wanted to call it Pig Cat. Mr. Ransom called it the *Anne Rose*.

FAINA RAPOPORT
A Grateful Refugee

Faina Rapoport carried a mental portrait of New York City for years. It was a means of survival while she and her family waited to hear from the United States goverment about whether they qualified for the refugee program. Her family, Jews from Moscow, wanted to escape religious persecution.

In 1994, New York City was no longer a painting in the gallery of Mrs. Rapoport's mind. It became real—the family received refugee status. They were free to worship as they pleased.

They settled in Brighton Beach, Brooklyn, a bustling Russian Jewish community near Coney Island.

Mrs. Rapoport, a computer programmer, studied English, while her husband, Yuriy, a civil engineer, became a construction inspector. Their children, Alex, 25, and Elena, 19, attended school.

Soon Mrs. Rapoport, 45, learned enough English to pursue a job. Eventually, she became a computer programmer at Accenture at the World Trade Center. Her salary helped buy a condominium near the beach.

The job also let her see two things featured in her mental portrait of the city: Ellis Island and the Statue of Liberty. "I know my mother is still happy about coming to America," Elena Rapoport said. "She accomplished things that she never would have been able to do in Russia. No one misses Russia."

AMENIA RASOOL
Dining as a Twosome

How did Amenia Rasool do it all? her mother-in-law now wonders. She would rise at 5 to do laundry before kissing her four children goodbye, leaving a tidy house in Queens to go to work as an accountant on the 95th floor of the World Trade Center. Every evening, she and her husband, Sadiq, a city accountant, would wash and feed the children as a team, dine as a twosome while the little ones watched TV, then help with schoolwork and put them all to bed.

Yet somehow, at the end of the day, after a husband-wife cleanup that included vacuuming and wiping down all the rugs in the Muslim household, Ms. Rasool, 33, found time for a small indulgence: catching up on tapes of her favorite soap operas and doing her nails.

Thousands of bronze tiles, each representing a victim of the trade center attack, suspended in towers at the New York State Museum in Albany as a memorial. (*David Jennings*)

As a young woman, she had come to America with her parents from rural Guyana, much like her husband. Their marriage was arranged by their parents, and flourished on a mix of Islamic tradition and American opportunity.

"They were really, really happy," said Fahida Rasool, her mother-in-law, who recently left her job in a bank to help with the children, 8, 6, 3 years old and 10 months.

R. MARK RASWEILER
Father, Son and Canoe

R. Mark Rasweiler bought a canoe about a year ago—a 14-footer, fiberglass—partly because he wanted to get out on the water more, and partly "because he wanted to spend more time with me," said his 18-year-old son, Michael. Mr. Rasweiler's daughters—Caryn, 27, and Lindsey, 24—had their own lives, but Michael was still at home. So father and son would take the canoe to a tributary of the Delaware River near the family house in Flemington, N.J., and head out for the Delaware, fishing for smallmouth bass and the occasional trout.

"We took the canoe out a couple of times," Michael Rasweiler recalled, "went fishing a couple of times, but I was so busy—and he was so busy in his job"—a vice president at Marsh & McLennan on the 100th floor of 1 World Trade Center. The floor plan shows that Mr. Rasweiler, 53, sat exactly where the first plane hit.

"It's sad," his son said, "we didn't have the time to take the canoe out more."

DAVID A. J. RATHKEY
The Proof Is in the Ducks

David A. J. Rathkey wanted all the soccer he could get. So he played year-round on an over-40 team. Naturally, his twin sons, Matthew and Ian, played, and so did his daughter, Emma. Who was their coach? Him. If there was practice and that meant leaving work early, well, soccer was that important.

The last few years, it was too overwhelming to coach everyone, so he concentrated on his daughter's travel team, the Mountain Lakes Electrics. "If anyone was injured or upset, he always made a point to call them later to see how they were," said his wife, Julia. "They were very fond of him."

Mr. Rathkey, 47, a sales executive at IQ Financial Systems, lived in Mountain Lakes, N.J., a small place with only 4,000 residents, many of whom Mr. Rathkey touched. The proof was in the ducks. To raise money for the Rathkey children and the children of Alayne Gentul, another Mountain Lakes resident killed in the attacks, a competition known as the Great Duck Race was staged, with hundreds of rubber ducks in a local stream. A duck could be bought for $250 or a smaller contribution. Some 800 people showed up. The race raised more than $100,000.

WILLIAM RAUB
The Creator of Surprises

William Raub loved arranging surprises for his family—a birthday party for his wife, Maureen, a surprise 10th anniversary trip to Little Palm Island in the Florida Keys, and that was just last year.

"He loved planning big surprises and special gifts," Mrs. Raub said. "He really got a lot of happiness doing that." "He liked to play with his daughter a lot, and take her with him when he did errands, and cook dinner to give me a night off," she said on the phone from her home in Saddle River, N.J., as her 6-year-old daughter prompted her, then corrected her: "He liked to make reservations at restaurants." The couple also has a 5-month-old son.

Mr. Raub, 38, an institutional stock trader at Cantor Fitzgerald, almost didn't go to work on Sept. 11, because he had a stomach bug, but decided to try putting in half a day. He thought the World Trade Center was the safest building to work in, thanks to security measures after the 1993 bombing, when he helped a flagging co-worker down 104 stories, stopping to rest with him every few flights. "That was just so Will, to always be thinking of other people," Mrs. Raub said.

"I'll never forget, on the night before our wedding, at the rehearsal dinner, he said, 'Tomorrow I'm marrying my best friend,' " she said. "That said it all."

ALEXEY RAZUVAEV
Laughing over Broken Glass

Alexey Razuvaev left Russia and came to the United States in 1994—just about the same time, as it happened, as Natalia Loginova. They knew each other casually, through mutual friends. But it was not until the end of 1997, when he and Ms. Loginova, the mother of two girls, got together.

"I was working in a Laundromat and he was there fixing a computer program, and he was always asking me so many questions," she recalled. "I said, 'Why do you ask so much?' and he said, 'Because I want to marry you.' I said I would never marry him. But he said, 'I love you and I love your children, and maybe I won't have any other chance here to love someone.' "

They married the next year, on Valentine's Day, and Mr. Razuvaev, 40, went on to work at Euro Brokers in the World Trade Center. Their romance never faded, his wife said.

"He always made us laugh," she said. "One night, he brought me flowers, but I dropped the vase and it broke.

He started picking up the pieces, while I was still saying, 'Oh no!' When a friend called, he said, 'My wife is in a very bad mood, she threw things at me, and I am picking up the glass,' and we all began laughing, so it was a joke, and not sad."

GREGORY REDA
Ordre et Beauté

The little things mattered to Gregory Reda. For instance, that little flourish he prepared for his marriage proposal to Nicole, at her 21st birthday party. She spoke French. He spoke no French. So he got her brother to teach him to say, "I love you; will you marry me?" in French.

Once they were married, they jointly pursued their interests in photography, and eventually many of their pictures tended to focus on their two children, Nicholas, now 2, and Matthew, 6 months.

Mr. Reda, 33, who was in charge of e-mail for Marsh & McLennan, lived with the family in New Hyde Park, N.Y., and among the little things that mattered to him was extreme orderliness. He was neat, really neat. Everything had to be in the right spot.

"All my friends admired it," Mrs. Reda said. "Their husbands were leaving dirty socks around the house and he would clean up after me."

He even rotated things so they got used evenly. He made sure he wore T-shirts and underwear in proper rotation. He kept the kitchen ordered so the plates and silverware were used to the same extent, preventing some dishes from wearing out before others in the set. There were six chairs at the dining table, and Mr. Reda and Mrs. Reda always sat in the same place, so he would rotate the chairs, and that way the cushions softened equally. A little thing, but he noticed.

MICHELE REED
Weekends on the Farm

Michele Reed's idea of a good time was getting muddy in her black-and-white all-terrain vehicle. On weekends, Ms. Reed, 26, and her twin sister, Jennifer, would escape the city for their family's dairy farm in Plymouth, N.Y. After the kisses and hugs, they would dust off their A.T.V.'s and race through the woods. Sometimes, they were joined by a brother, an aunt, or another relative. Everybody in the family had their own vehicle.

"Those two girls can keep up with the best of them," said their aunt, Darlene Beckwith. Ms. Reed, who worked at Aon, even talked her grandmother into tagging along in August 2001. "We have a lot of fun doing things as a family," Darlene said. "We like to try to go through mud to see who gets stuck." That day, no one did. In the past year, Michele started taking a boyfriend to the farm. He had his own A.T.V., too.

DONALD REGAN
Keeping Tabs on Family

The post office people in Pine Bush, N.Y., knew Donald Regan well. Every Saturday, he mailed parcels to the two of his four children who did not live nearby. He took requests: an old pair of baseball cleats; the spaghetti sauce he and his wife made and canned; money. Sometimes just a letter. He had always kept close tabs on his family. "If there were four sporting events at one time, he would be there for an inning of each game," said his son Shane.

Donald Regan was a firefighter from Rescue Company 3, a 17-year veteran who knew every tool and was considered fearless by his squad mates. His sleep was so deep that he had to sleep in the firehouse kitchen so the alarm would wake him, and he was famous for drifting off in the most contorted positions.

"He was the consummate blue-collar person," Shane Regan said. "He worked until he couldn't work any more. He made sure everybody else was taken care of." For his drive to work, his son added, he would buy clunkers with at least 100,000 miles. "My dad was famous for having nasty cars. He called them classics."

But with his brood out of the house, he had bought himself a 2001 Chrysler Sebring, and he washed it as if that were his paying job. "He finally broke down and said, 'Now I'm going to do something for myself.' "

ROBERT REGAN
A Real "Mr. Mom"

When Robert Regan first met Donna Wells, he was 21 and she was 15. He was tall, dark-haired, and "had the most beautiful blue-green eyes that you ever wanted to see," she remembered. She was having trouble with geometry, and he helped her with her homework. They started dating. "It was a big scandal back then," she said.

But Mr. Regan was the quietly determined sort and a friend of Donna's older sister, so her parents eventually gave their permission for them to go out. They married, and Mr. Regan became a civil engineer. But when Caitlin, their daughter, was born, Mr. Regan quit his job to join the Fire Department so he could have more flexible hours and spend more time with the baby. Four years later, Brendan was born.

"He was Mr. Mom," Mrs. Regan said of her husband's delight in his children.

Lieutenant Regan, 48, was a member of Engine Company 205, Ladder Company 118 in Brooklyn Heights, and when word came of the World Trade Center attack, he and his fellow firefighters sped to the scene.

"There was never a day that went by that we didn't know what we had," Mrs. Regan said. "We told our kids not everybody gets to be as happy as we are."

CHRISTIAN REGENHARD
Determined to Follow Father

Graduates of the Bronx High School of Science generally do not enlist in the marines, but Christian Regenhard, 28, resisted easy categorization. He was determined, said his mother, Sally Regenhard, to follow his father into the elite branch of the armed forces, despite a 146 IQ and an array of artistic talents.

Mrs. Regenhard "practically had a nervous breakdown" when Christian announced his intentions, a week before his 19th birthday. But his military accomplishments, and the medals to prove it, are now among her proudest memories.

After his discharge, Mr. Regenhard spent a year at San Francisco State University, studying art and trying writing. But he continued with the daring pursuits he had learned in the marines: rock-climbing, scuba diving, running marathons, traveling—and disappointing a parade of women.

"He was a babe magnet," Mrs. Regenhard said. "He spoke the language of love."

In January, Mr. Regenhard, the son of a retired police detective, again chose the adventurous route and joined the Fire Department. The long shifts on duty alternated with extra days off and time to pursue his art and his climbing.

Mr. Regenhard was still a "proby" on Sept. 11, assigned to Ladder Company 131 in Red Hook, Brooklyn, which shares a firehouse with Engine Company 279. He was covering for someone in the engine company that morning, his mother said.

GREGG REIDY
Making Sure to Live

The words were written on a small scrap of paper, found in Gregg Reidy's car. "Every man dies. But not every man lives."

The quotation, spoken by Mel Gibson in the movie *Braveheart*, compelled Mr. Reidy to approach life with zest and vigor. "A few people said he was 25, but as far as how much he did with his life it was like he lived a life of a 50-year-old," said his sister, Ann Curti.

After graduating from college in 1998, Mr. Reidy immersed himself in the culture of Wall Street. He loved the stress and excitement of his job as a trader at Cantor

Fitzgerald. Spending time with friends and family was also a priority.

His ingenuity was fodder for countless family tales.

Three years earlier, when his parents bought a house in an adult community in Holmdel, N.J., Mr. Reidy moved in too. Although his living quarters were much smaller than they had been in the family's previous house, he would not be undone. Mr. Reidy built a bed in his room that stood high enough to fit a sofa underneath.

"My dad said if Gregg was not gone when it first happened, he would have made a parachute, and he would have figured a way to get out," Mrs. Curti said. "So we really believe it was the impact that took him."

JAMES B. REILLY
The Coolest Uncle

James B. Reilly became godfather to his niece, Katherine, in February 2001 and he took it seriously. "Can I please have my goddaughter," Mr. Reilly would demand whenever Katherine—8 months old—was around. The 25-year-old bond trader would then swoop her from the arms of whoever was holding her and coo as if he was the father.

Mr. Reilly, who worked at 2 World Trade Center at Keefe, Bruyette & Woods, liked to make his other nieces and nephews laugh. In May, he folded his 5-foot-11-inch, athletic frame into the car of a red electronic train that chugged around a cul-de-sac at a birthday party for his 3-year-old nephew in Atlanta, said his mother, Virginia. The children squealed with laughter.

"It was very funny to see him squeezed in the seats with the children," Mrs. Reilly said. "The children loved it. He made sure that he had plenty of time for his nieces and nephews. Unfortunately, they won't remember him, but they will certainly know about him."

TIMOTHY E. REILLY
The Talker in a Big Family

Timothy E. Reilly was the toastmaster, the speechmaker, the mayor of the family—the gregarious and easygoing fourth of six children in a clan that counts 48 first cousins on his mother's side alone.

He made it his business to know them all; and he loved nothing more, his siblings say, than giving everyone else a great time.

A vice president at Marsh & McLennan, Mr. Reilly spent little on himself. At 40, he lived in what had once been his grandmother's one-bedroom apartment in Brooklyn Heights, still furnished with her old couch, table and chairs. He skied, flawlessly, in boots held together with duct tape.

He spent his money on his family and on taking people out to dinner and picking up the tab at the bar. After he died, his sister, Maureen, created a Web page in his honor. The message board brims with letters from cousins and friends. In one, a cousin recalls how Mr. Reilly had saved him from suicide, then helped him through his hospitalization, regularly driving 90 minutes each way after work to bring clothes, books, cigarettes and the desire to live.

"His outpouring of love was the life preserver that kept me afloat in my hour of greatest need and deepest pain," the cousin wrote. He added later, "He made me believe in myself. He made me happy to be alive."

JOSEPH REINA Jr.
The Thrill and the Agony

His teams gave him unending joy and unending heartbreak. He rooted for the Yankees and the Jets. With the Yankees, of course, Joseph Reina Jr. had an abundance of warm memories, a few of them interlaced with his marriage. He was married on the day of Game 1 of the 1999 World Series, and so a friend took a small TV to the reception so Mr. Reina could check the progress. His wife, Lisa, did not mind, though if he had tried to go to the game, that would have been it.

The Jets were a different story. Mr. Reina watched their games, too, but more often than not found himself cursing at the team. Mr. Reina, 32, a manager of operations for Cantor Fitzgerald, lived with his wife in Staten Island, along with his collection of eagle statues and pictures. Their first child, Joseph Robert, was born in October.

One of the bonds between the Reinas was their dual worship of the sun. Mr. Reina adored vacations, and they had to be somewhere hot. "He was the first guy I'd met who liked to take the sun as much as I did," Mrs. Reina said.

Mrs. Reina believes that the Yankees could not quite win that final World Series game in 2001 because her husband, and his Cantor friends who worshiped the team, were not there. But she has some little Yankees outfits for her son, whom she intends to raise as a loyal fan.

THOMAS REINIG
Lust for Life

"Follow me, Dad."

With just those words—part request, part challenge—Christopher and Scott Reinig could get their father, Thomas, to do most anything. Like swoop down the slipperiest ski slopes behind them. Or climb the Grand Tetons with them. Or spend Father's Day competing in a triathlon that taxed the 48-year-old's stamina and his sense of humor.

"He beat me on the running part but of course I had the better overall time," said Scott Reinig, 20, a competitive swimmer. "He blamed it on the swimming."

Mr. Reinig, a vice president with eSpeed, was not a sore loser, even when it came to being beaten at golf by his wife, Jeanne. "He always had fun and laughed," she said. She described his big, gap-toothed smile as infectious. "He wasn't a good-time Charlie. He just enjoyed life."

And he did everything for his family. When the boys were small, Mr. Reinig moved them all to London for three years after he took a job there so they would learn to appreciate the world. They returned to New Jersey, but when the boys enrolled in a private school in Morris County a few years later, Mr. Reinig moved to Bernardsville to shorten their commute.

"My Dad was always calling home, a couple of times a day, every day, and all he'd say is, 'I'm just checking in,' " Scott Reinig said. "There wasn't any other reason than that."

FRANK REISMAN
The Perfect Daddy

When Frank Reisman was single, mountain climbing was his passion. The summer after the end of college, he hiked the Appalachian Trail alone from Maine to Pennsylvania, picking up dry food that his parents, George and Evie, mailed to him at post offices along the way.

After Mr. Reisman married, family was his focus. Every evening around 6:15 he returned home, where his wife, Gayle, and their two children, Kasey and Dillon, always waited for him to have dinner.

Living in Princeton, N.J., and working at Cantor Fitzgerald on the equities desk, Mr. Reisman, 41, was the perfect suburban daddy, his wife said. He coached Kasey's softball team and took Dillon to golf on the weekends. He taught them how to download music from the Internet and ferret out useful information. Because he left home before the children got up for school, he always sent them online messages from work.

On the morning of the attack, he phoned his wife, who happened to be out jogging. He reached his mom. "He said: 'I'll be fine. Don't panic, Mom. I love you,' " Evie Reisman said, as tears welled up in her eyes.

JOSHUA REISS
Born to Be a Bond Trader

Joshua Reiss was practically born a savvy dealer. At 10, though he was too young, he talked his way into a paper route and won a trip to Disney World as the top paperboy in Yardley, Pa. But when the managers discovered his age, they took the award away and offered him

$300 as a consolation prize, an amount that would greatly impress most fifth graders. Not Joshua. He did a bit of bargaining and they upped it to $500.

Bond trading at Cantor Fitzgerald was ideal for him. "The action, the people," said Gary Reiss, his father, at the family home in Yardley. "He was 23 and making six figures." And, after only five months at Cantor, he was spending it freely on his family. He covered one brother's varsity football expenses and sent another, who was away at college, two blank checks. "If you need more, call me," he said. "I don't want you to have to work. Just study. And don't tell Dad."

As a teenager he told his father: "You never take time off. When I get some money I'm going to make you go on a vacation." He had it all planned: the next summer he and his father and three brothers were going whitewater rafting in Colorado. And he was paying. Period.

KAREN RENDA
Handling Travel, and Crafts

Two years ago, Karen Renda decided it was too boring at home. With her two boys—Daniel, 19, and Matthew, 15—pretty much grown up, she traded her full-time homemaking career in Staten Island for a job as a travel agent.

But working for American Express, arranging trips for executives at Marsh & McLennan on the 94th floor of 1 World Trade Center, did not mean Mrs. Renda, 52, forgot her crafty side, her husband said. She still made silk flower arrangements and wreaths for Christmas.

And in February 2001, for her youngest son's Valentine's Day school dance, she was in charge of the centerpieces for the tables—stuffed bunnies in pink and white that needed to be decorated with hearts and bows and arrows.

"One day I come home and the whole table was full of these bunnies staring at me," said her husband, Charles Renda. "There were about 100 of them."

Mr. Renda said he knew she was the one the minute they met on a blind date in 1972. "We immediately hit it off," he said. "She was very ladylike, very different from the girls I met in New York."

JOHN REO
Striking Out on His Own

Twenty-eight-year-old John Reo was just about to strike out on his own. He had recently started a job as a bond trader at Cantor Fitzgerald and he was scheduled to move into an apartment in the East Village in October.

"He was so excited," said his brother-in-law Richard McGuire. "It was his first important job." But he was most excited about working alongside another brother-in-law,

At the Lexington School for the Deaf, in Jackson
Heights, Queens, local firefighters from Engine
Company 307 and Ladder Company 154 were honored
December 7. One student there, Dahiana Gonzalez,
tried the coat of a firefighter, Eugene Reaccuglia.
(*Suzanne DeChillo*)

John Swaine, a veteran of Wall Street who got him the job on the 104th floor of 1 World Trade Center, Mr. McGuire said. Mr. Reo, of Troy, N.Y., was living temporarily in Larchmont with his sister Suzanne, who was married to Mr. Swaine. He also died in the attack on the trade center.

"He looked up to Swaine because he had been there for so long," Mr. McGuire said. "He really wanted to make him proud."

JOHN SWAINE's portrait appears on page 486.

COL. RICHARD C. RESCORLA
A Hero's Life (and Death)

Legendary Vietnam warrior. Poet and quoter of Shakespeare and Proust. Criminal justice professor. Screenplay author.

Col. Richard C. Rescorla, the head of security for Morgan Stanley Dean Witter's individual investor group, was a big man who lived large and died a hero, barking out orders on a megaphone in a smoke-choked stairwell and personally seeing to it that Morgan Stanley lost only 6 of its 3,700 employees on Sept. 11. Colonel Rescorla, 62, was carrying out the evacuation plan he had drawn up and repeatedly rehearsed after the 1993 bombing.

He grew up in England, joined the British Army, and moved here in 1963 to fight with the United States Army in Vietnam. He led a platoon through the notorious valley of Ia Drang, where more than 200 American soldiers died; a battlefield photo of him graces the cover of the 1992 bestseller *We Were Soldiers Once . . . and Young*.

At a gathering of Ia Drang veterans in 1992, Colonel Rescorla, who leaves a wife and two children in Morristown, N.J., described his vision of facing death: "A man is dying down there in the valley, and what do you do? You hold him in your arms and you say to him—it's all you can say to him—you say: 'You're not alone, son. You're not alone.' And he's gone."

JOHN RESTA and SYLVIA SAN PIO RESTA
A Fancy Proposal

The marriage proposal was famous in the Resta family. John Resta already had a reputation as a hopeless romantic, relatives said, but on this one he outdid even himself. Mr. Resta and his wife, Sylvia San Pio Resta, had traveled to Florida several times, and there she found a seafood restaurant that she adored.

So on the day he was to propose, he took the day off work. He had a meal—lobster and other dishes—and menus flown into New York City from the restaurant. He rented a tuxedo, a top hat and a cane, and spent the day setting up their apartment in Bayside, Queens, with candles, a fancy tablecloth and flowers.

Needless to say, the answer was yes, and they were married in the summer of 2000. When the two—both traders for Carr Futures—were killed in the Sept. 11 terrorist attack, she was seven months pregnant with their first child.

Mr. Resta, 40, adored children, said his sister Chris Mazzeo, and he was obsessed with his wife's pregnancy, voraciously reading every childbirth book he could get his hands on and doting on her constantly. Mr. Resta's cousin Kenneth Bynoe said that as soon as Mr. Resta met Ms. San Pio Resta, 26, he was so smitten that he could not stop talking about her, especially about her habit of reading cookbooks on the train, from cover to cover, as if they were novels.

Ms. San Pio Resta was artistic, yet she had a mind for numbers, said her sister Martiza Mure. In college, she majored in both mathematics and ceramics, and she had recently inspired her husband to take up oil painting.

Ms. Mazzeo said: "My brother was an angel on earth. Now, he's an angel in heaven. Now he has wings." Ms. San Pio Resta's sisters, who were planning her baby shower when she was killed, said that when they planned her memorial service, they chose the theme song "In the Arms of an Angel."

DAVID E. RETIK
Cheering People Up

David E. Retik's office in Boston looks as it did Sept. 10, before he boarded Flight 11. His screen saver shows fly-fishing, his special joy. There is a gallery's worth of pictures of his family. And on his desk, a little box has pictures of Ben, 4, and Molly, 2, on one side. Press the button on the other side, and their voices emerge: "I love you, Daddy. I miss you."

"David was an oxymoron," said Timothy Dibble, like Mr. Retik a general partner at Alta Communications, quoting a remark at his memorial service. "He was a venture capitalist who everybody liked."

Whether leaving a recording of "Gettin' Jiggy with It" on his mother's answering machine or visiting his sister in the hospital after an appendectomy and asking, "Did you save it?" Mr. Retik, 33, knew how to cheer people up.

"He played practical jokes on every single person he knew," said his wife, Susan, who met him in their freshman year at Colgate, where he was a varsity soccer player. Their third child, Dina, was born in November. In 2001, for the first time, Alta was inviting children to its holiday party, Mr. Dibble said. Ben and Molly could see Daddy's office one last time, just the way it was.

EDUVIGIS REYES
Wrestlemania Shirts

Eduvigis Reyes's name was too big for him so everyone called him Eddie. He was a 5-foot-4-inch wisecracking Mets fan who spent his working life in the paperwork sector of the shipping industry and loved wrestling, bowling and beer.

"He was a happy-go-lucky guy, always had a smile on his face," said his friend and former boss Max Reyes, no relation. "Many times he was the joke of the party."

Mr. Reyes, 37, was close to his three daughters, who split their time between his house in Richmond Hill, Queens, and their mother's in Brooklyn. Over the summer, Max Reyes stopped by Eddie's, just before Eddie started a new job at Rohde & Liesenfeld in the World Trade Center, and there were Eddie and his 13-year-old, Tiffany, dressed in matching Wrestlemania T-shirts.

Eddie could be a bit of a troublemaker, Max Reyes said. "But for all that he was, you needed a favor, he'd do it for you."

BRUCE REYNOLDS
The Man Behind the Camera

Somehow, most of the pictures from that last weekend are of Brianna Reynolds at the Bronx Zoo, coasting above the trees on the safari ride, or back in her grandparents' apartment in Inwood for her fourth-birthday cake. Her father, Bruce Reynolds, must have stayed on the business side of the camera.

That weekend, Brianna and her baby brother, Michael, played in the rooms where their father had grown up, a city kid in a sixth-floor apartment in northern Manhattan who loved nature. A bird cage ran from the floor to the ceiling. Down the street was the garden in Isham Park that Officer Reynolds's parents, J. A. and Geri Reynolds, had cultivated, and where Bruce, their only son, planted cherry plum trees.

When Bruce Reynolds met Marian McBride, they settled

in Knowlton, N.J., not far from the Delaware Water Gap. There, they could fish, grow vegetables, swim in their own pool.

It was a long ride for Officer Reynolds, 41, to the George Washington Bridge and his work as a Port Authority police officer, but he was undaunted by big journeys. "They often went to Donegal in Ireland, where Marian is from," said his father. "Bruce loved it there. That gave me joy."

His father has planted bulbs at the garden in his son's memory, and the Port Authority has promised a flagpole. "Maybe they'll raise it in the spring," Mr. Reynolds said. "When the daffodils bloom."

JOHN F. RHODES
Late-Blooming Golfer

By the time they reach their 50s, many dedicated golfers muse about the scores they used to shoot with ease and cannot quite match anymore. Not John F. Rhodes. He was avid about golf, but since he had taken up the game in his 40s, he found he was still improving.

Jack McAleese, four, watches a helicopter fly overhead after a memorial Mass on December 7 in Baldwin, New York, for his father, Brian McAleese, a firefighter who died in the attack on the trade center. Firefighter McAleese, thirty-six, was a member of Engine Company 226. *(Kevin P. Coughlin)*

"I know he was very excited about getting under 100 recently," said his son, John F. Rhodes IV. On a business outing not long ago, he won the award for longest drive, one more milestone in his progress.

The other thing that meant a lot to Mr. Rhodes, 57, a senior vice president for Aon Risk Services, was family. He methodically scheduled his business trips so he would return home to Howell, N.J., on Friday and not have to work on the weekend. He would always tell his wife, Linda, "Make sure you take care of family, because without family you have nothing." In 2001, he became a grandfather for the first time, when his son's wife gave birth to twin boys. He couldn't talk enough about them. Co-workers heard the latest details every day.

"He really enjoyed the journey rather than the destination," his son said. "He didn't talk about where he would be in 10 years. He truly lived for the moment. He would say, 'Don't worry about down the road.' "

FRANCIS S. RICCARDELLI
Planner of Family Fun

Francis S. Riccardelli was the vertical transportation manager at the World Trade Center complex, the man in charge of all the elevators and escalators. He loved his job so much it scared his colleagues.

"One guy said, 'I used to duck Francis all the time because he would come up with all these projects and they would always involve so much work,' " said his wife, Theresa Riccardelli.

At home in Westwood, N.J., with Theresa and their five children, though, Mr. Riccardelli, 40, had no problem enlisting volunteers. When he went to Home Depot, 5-year-old Genevieve would ride in the shopping cart and help pick out tools. When he was taking down a wall in their house, 3-year-old Zachary would bang away at it with his plastic hammer.

"He was always planning fun thing to fun thing," Mrs. Riccardelli said. "He'd get up Saturday morning and make pancakes. Friday was movie night—we'd all pile into our bed with popcorn and watch a movie together. Saturday was game night."

Mr. Riccardelli had just bought a huge trailer and hoped the whole family would hike the Grand Canyon someday. "It was going to be the start of a new project," Mrs. Riccardelli said. "Exploring America."

RUDOLPH RICCIO
Knowing What Matters

When Rudolph Riccio was a teenager, his parents got sick and died 13 months apart. His older sister, Meg, took care of him and of their younger sister. One day when Mr. Riccio was 17, he approached Meg and asked her for $80 to buy a pair of boots.

"I said to him, 'Rudy, I can't give you money for boots. I don't have that kind of money,' " said Meg Durrance, now 44. "He looked at me and said, 'If I work, can I then buy the boots I want?' I said yes. It was his money."

So, Mr. Riccio worked a paper route for a few weeks and saved up the $80. But he did not buy the boots. Instead, he left the money for his sister in an envelope on the kitchen counter. A note inside the envelope read, "We need the money to buy food, not to buy boots."

Ms. Durrance cried. She still cries, retelling the story so many years later. Mr. Riccio went on to finish high school and take some computer classes in college. Eventually, he got a computer job with Cantor Fitzgerald's eSpeed division. He was 40, married to Joanne Riccio, and lived in the Bronx, where he had lived all his life.

"It's like I've lost a child," Ms. Durrance said. "We had a connection most brothers and sisters don't have. We learned to rely on one another."

DAVID RICE
Turning Things Around

David Rice was the student with the grade point average of less than 2, who was voted most likely to succeed in high school. He was constantly in trouble. He would do things like rent a warehouse in Oklahoma City, hire a rock band, charge $10 a head and make thousands of dollars before the police broke up the party.

Still, as a teenager in Oklahoma City, he read biographies of Donald Trump and told his family that that was the kind of entrepreneur he would be. At age 31, David was an investor in bonds at Sandler O'Neill & Partners, in the south tower.

"He drove his clients crazy but they loved him to death," says his younger brother, Andrew. "He was a pistol."

His life was marked by huge turnarounds. He had hit bottom in his early 20s from alcoholism and drug use. He dropped out of college. Then he began his recovery. He became a Fulbright scholar in Zimbabwe and South Africa. He earned a master's degree from the London School of Economics. Last February he transferred to New York from Chicago, where he had lived for 10 years.

"He was very real," his brother says. "He wasn't perfect but he was so wise for his age."

EILEEN M. RICE
"A Good Friend to Many"

Eileen M. Rice was a woman of many passions. Politics. Clothes. Latin. Her dog, Mozart. Her family described her as sophisticated, opinionated and caring, a woman who worked on behalf of animal rights and poor people but also indulged her fashion moods by owning 11 bathrobes.

Ms. Rice, 57, raised her son, Brian Keegan, and her daughter, Lesli Rice, largely as a single mother. She was an executive assistant for Marsh & McLennan.

"She was meticulous in her home and in her work and in her person," recalled Patrick Keegan, her younger brother. "I'll miss our conversations. She always talked about the underdog. She was unbelievably caring."

Lesli Rice said her mother was her foundation, and self-reliance was one of the many life lessons her mother taught. Her mother also passed on a love for the classics and for the Latin she learned during the Roman Catholic Masses of a bygone era. "She had a strong sense of values," said Lesli Rice. "She took pride in her work and everything she did. I don't think I'd be where I am without her. She was a good friend to many."

VERNON RICHARD
Roller Coasters and Choir

Vernon Richard, his wife, Dorothy, recalled, "loved anything that had to do with roller coasters." His daughter, Vernessa, a college student, recalled the same thing.

"When I'd come home for the summer, we'd go to Great Adventure," Vernessa Richard said, "and he'd look up at the roller coaster and go 'Wow! Let's go on that!' The excitement on his face!"

Lieutenant Richard, 53, was a 24-year veteran of the Fire Department. A member of Ladder Company 7 in Manhattan, he was to have been promoted to captain in November, an elevation that occurred posthumously. A weight lifter and jogger (he ran six New York City Marathons), he sang in the choir at the First Baptist Church in Spring Valley, N.Y., near his home in Nanuet. His voice, a deep baritone, was memorable.

"When I played high school ball, and there were maybe 500 people in the stands, I'd hear nothing but his voice," said his son, Vernon II. "He'd be saying, 'Go to work, Vernon.' "

CLAUDE RICHARDS
Bombs Were His Business

If ever a man was to the bomb squad born, it was Detective Claude Richards of the New York Police Department. Fearless, meticulous and disciplined nearly to a fault, Detective Richards, 46, the bomb squad's intelligence coordinator, spent his off-duty hours working, working out and planning his next workday. When he took some time off, it was to defuse land mines in Bosnia with a United Nations peacekeeping force.

All the way from boyhood, Dan, as Detective Richards was known, "always wanted to charge up to the front," said his brother, Jim, "just to prove himself." He was in the Rangers in the Army, and on the bomb squad his command presence allowed him to give orders to colleagues who far out-ranked him as he oversaw security logistics for events ranging from presidential visits to the United States Tennis Open.

Detective Richards, who lived in Greenwich Village, was a complicated man. True, he could yell at a co-worker who borrowed his stapler and put it back in the wrong place, but he also didn't think twice before taking his shoes off on the street and giving them to a vagabond, Jim Richards said.

Detective Richards's work ethic left him little time or space for relationships, his brother said, but added, "He was so devoted to his work I don't think he had a problem with it."

GREGORY RICHARDS
The Call of the City

Gregory Richards just could not stay away from New York. He was born here, grew up in Greenwich Village and went to Stuyvesant High School. When he went off to the University of Michigan, he longed to come home. When he went to Florida to work for a hedge fund, he wanted to come back.

Even after he left Cantor Fitzgerald, moved to Michigan in 1998 to live near his wife's parents and started his own real estate investment business, he dreamed of concrete, sky-scrapers, Central Park, the trading floor.

"He missed the pace of Wall Street; he missed the cama-raderie of being around the guys all the time," said his wife, Erin. "He was a true city kid. All the things that made people crazy about New York, he liked."

So Mr. Richards, 30, returned to the city in 2000 and rejoined Cantor Fitzgerald, this time working for eSpeed, its electronic subsidiary. He now had a son, Asher, 2, and could run in Central Park on a weekend morning and meet Asher and his wife at the playground.

Mrs. Richards, who is spending time with her parents in Michigan, said she would also return to New York. But the city, she said, will be empty without her husband. "He had New York's cocky charisma about him," she said. "He was cool."

MICHAEL RICHARDS
Giving Bronze Flight

It is most likely that Michael Richards, a well-regarded sculptor, was doing the thing he loved most Tuesday morning, Sept. 11, in his studio on the 92nd floor of the north tower. "He would work through most of the night and into the morning," said Kira Harris, a friend.

Mr. Richards, 38, who was born in Kingston, Jamaica, worked a lot in bonded bronze, and his sculptures often had the look of life-size human figures. "We had scheduled that I

would see his new work this week," said Christine Y. Kim, assistant curator at the Studio Museum in Harlem.

His creations often dealt with "technology such as avia-tion, ironically," she said, then read aloud the words of another curator, Jorge Daniel Veneciano, about Mr. Richards's sculpture: "Each of his works engages the notion of flight in at least two important senses: as a form of flight away from what is repressive, and as a form of flight toward what is redeeming."

VENESHA RICHARDS
A Dream of Paris

When Venesha Rodgers caught a short ride home from work at Bradlees in North Brunswick, N.J., her lift, Hopeton Richards, instantly realized she was just the person he had been looking for: fun, smart, an active Christian and, like Mr. Richards, an émigré from Jamaica. Not only that, she lived around the corner. In July 1998, four years after that five-minute car ride, they were married.

Mrs. Richards was a one-woman power plant. As a young mother, a student in technology systems at Pace University, holding a full-time job, she still helped run trips for her church youth group.

Before baby Kayla was born last year, she and Mr. Richards traveled to Mexico; Key West, Fla.; the Bahamas; and the Poconos. "Ven always wanted to go to Paris," Mr. Richards said.

Mrs. Richards, 26, "was more of a mama to me than I was to her," said Lelith Grant, her mother, who worked night shifts as a nurse so she and Mrs. Richards could swap child-minding chores. On school holidays, Mrs. Richards took her little brother and sister to work at Marsh & McLen-nan on the 100th floor of 1 World Trade Center.

Heading home, she always made a beeline. "She couldn't wait to see Kayla take her first step," said Mr. Richards. "She took it three days after the incident."

JIMMY RICHES
A Way with Women

Among the firemen sifting debris at ground zero is a battalion chief, James Riches, who is searching for his son and namesake, known to his family as Little Jimmy.

Jimmy Riches, who would have turned 30 on Sept. 12, was the oldest of four brothers in a family in which uniformed service is a way of life. He served seven years in the Police Department before joining the Fire Department in 1999.

Rita Riches, Big Jimmy's wife and Little Jimmy's mother, does not bemoan her fate. Her second son, Timothy, is a police officer who expects to join the Fire Department early in 2002. Her third, Danny, a college sophomore, placed high on the police exam, which boys like these routinely take as teenagers. Her fourth, Thomas, is a junior at Xavier High School.

Jimmy Riches was a basketball star in high school and college, a gregarious bartender on his nights off. He drove a Mercedes convertible, had a share in a beach house on the Jersey Shore. And he had a way with women. A parade of girlfriends have paid condolence calls, Mrs. Riches said, each wearing a firehouse T-shirt from Jimmy.

"They all think they're the only one that has one," she said. "I'm dying the whole visit, hoping another one doesn't show up at the same time."

ALAN RICHMAN
Life's Small Pleasures

Alan Richman was never much of a social animal. Mr. Richman, 44, a vice president for employee benefits at Marsh & McLennan, liked to go to the opera and the theater on occasion, said his sister Jane Gewant. But for the last two years, his life outside work had revolved around his parents, who lived near him in Riverdale in the Bronx.

Mr. Richman was by his father's side for two years, helping him battle cancer. After his father died in April, he moved in with his mother. "He just said, 'I think Mommy needs me and I think I'll help her,' " Ms. Gewant said. Mother and son had five months of quality time, going to the botanic gardens at nearby Wave Hill or simply relaxing together, before the widow Ruth Richman lost her son, too.

"Alan lived a quiet life," Ms. Gewant said. "He wasn't a risk taker. He didn't ski. He lived a very simple life. For him, going to Wave Hill and reading the newspaper was wonderful. He was very content in his own world, in Riverdale, and in family. And so to me it's unbelievable that his death would be so violent."

JOHN RIGO
Coffee and the Man

John Rigo liked to pose as the lovable curmudgeon. "That's Mr. Rigo to you," he would say, when somebody wanted something.

His two great loves were his wife, Elizabeth, and his work as senior vice president at Marsh & McLennan, where he specialized in workers' compensation claims, and put in 50- to 60-hour workweeks.

Mr. Rigo, 48, and his wife had no children, and they were particularly fond of their nieces and nephews. Mr. Rigo loved to play the subversive uncle. Last summer, the Rigos took Mrs. Rigo's nephew, Jackson Meredith, 10, to Rome and Paris.

Jackson was too young for many things he would have

liked to do, among them drinking coffee. But every morning, Mr. Rigo and Jackson would sneak out of the hotel, arms around one another, and have a cup together, man to man. On the plane back, the stewardesses were enchanted with young Jackson, Mrs. Rigo said.

Jackson wanted to know how come he could attract older women, "but I can't get the girls in my class interested in me," he said. "Come back to me in a couple of years and I'll give you a couple of tips," Mr. Rigo told him.

FREDERICK RIMMELE III
Doctor with a Ponytail

The first time Kimberly Trudel met Frederick Rimmele III, he was far ahead on a hiking trail in New Hampshire, a dot in the distance. Gradually, he kept dropping back to others in the group, until, walking with his shirt off, he found himself chatting with Ms. Trudel.

"Those hiking boots look awfully small," he said, using a pickup line straight out of an L. L. Bean catalog. She responded, "If you want to check out my feet, you could give me a foot massage at the end of this hike."

He did, and a romance blossomed. That was the summer of 1994. A year later, they became engaged on the side of a mountain in Maine. In June 1997, they married, settling in Marblehead, Mass. At 32, Dr. Rimmele was a physician who directed a residency program affiliated with Beverly Hospital in Beverly, Mass. He was popular with his patients, who, when they could not remember his name, asked for the doctor with the beard and the ponytail.

"He recognized that life was a precious gift and he never took it for granted," Ms. Trudel said of Dr. Rimmele, who was a passenger on United Airlines Flight 175. "He took advantage of every opportunity, whether it was travel or educational."

MOISES RIVAS
"Some Kind of Moves"

When Moises Rivas first laid eyes on Elizabeth, it was at a local beauty pageant in Queens, and he was the lead singer of the band. He was smitten, and made a $50 bet with another band member that he would get her to go out with him.

"When he finished singing he came down from the stage and started talking to me," Elizabeth recalled. "He asked for my phone number. Two weeks later we were going out, and we were still together six years later."

Moises Rivas had dreams, big ones. He imbibed life in big gulps. And he went after want he wanted. Of course he got the girl, and he and Elizabeth married and had two children, Moises Jr., 4, and Moesha, 2. A 29-year-old immigrant from Ecuador, he wanted to be the next Emeril, so he took a job as a chef at Windows on the World. He also wanted to be the next Ricky Martin, so he wrote songs and became lead singer for an up-and-coming band that recorded a CD. "And, boy, he knew how to dance," his wife said.

"He had some kind of moves. He could attract any girl. He was so-o-o cute. I just wish he could come back. I wish he was with me right now. It's the only thing I wish." There was another woman—his mother in Ecuador. "She couldn't see him for 10 years because he was in New York, and then when she came up here after Sept. 11, she couldn't see him either," Elizabeth said.

CARMEN A. RIVERA
Wearing Many Hats

On the night after the collapse of the twin towers, a co-worker of Carmen A. Rivera called her husband at the couple's Orange County, N.Y., home and left a message saying that the two women had been heading down the stairs from the 96th floor of 2 World Trade Center together but lost each other. "She was O.K.," the co-worker said. "She's alive somewhere."

Luis Rivera, a circulation manager for the *New York Times,* clung to that thought more than two weeks after the tragedy, and continued putting up posters and checking hospitals long after most others had resigned themselves to the loss of a loved one. Mrs. Rivera, 33, an assistant vice president for Fiduciary Trust Company International, worked full time and raised three children, but also found time for the gym and for night classes twice a week to get a master's degree in business, her husband said.

The best mother, an inspirational friend, the ultimate woman, Mr. Rivera said, his wife was also a survivor. After the first plane hit, he said, she called him as she made her way down and told him she had left her purse behind but had grabbed a gold rosary her mother gave her.

"I know she made it out," he said. "She's out there with amnesia or something."

ISAIAS RIVERA
A Veteran of 1993

In the very same perilous aerie, the 110th-floor television transmission center atop the north tower, Isaias Rivera had lived through it before: the explosion, the smoke, the desperate evacuation.

As a technician for CBS, Mr. Rivera, 51, had been in the center on Feb. 26, 1993, when a bomb went off in the basement. Besides trying to keep WCBS on the air, he also helped in the rescue efforts, working until the next day, recalled William Rodriguez, whose daughter was Mr.

Rivera's godchild. Mr. Rivera had five children of his own and lived in Perth Amboy, N.J. His wife, Nilsa, is a nurse.

He was employed by CBS for 30 years, Mr. Rodriguez said, and was the last veteran of the 1993 bombing still stationed on the 110th floor. "He wasn't the same person after that," Mr. Rodriguez said. "He had fears of those things happening again."

LINDA RIVERA
A Signature Giggle

Everyone who knew Linda Rivera adored her trademark giggle.

"It was very high-pitched, very squeaky," said Dennise Delgado, a close friend who had been laughing with Ms. Rivera since their days at Canarsie High School in Brooklyn. "She'd laugh at everything, even if it wasn't particularly funny."

Ms. Rivera, 26, worked in human resources at Marsh & McLennan but rarely discussed her career with friends and family. Instead, she chattered about her new apartment, her cat and two dogs, her boyfriend of six years and her younger brother, to whom she was so devoted that she attended his parent-teacher conferences.

She grew up in East New York, Brooklyn, the daughter of Puerto Rican parents who spoke little English. More recently, Ms. Rivera had set down roots in Far Rockaway, Queens, where she was making do with hand-me-down furniture until she could afford nice new things. In particular, she was eager to trade her beat-up futon for a plush sofa. Ms. Delgado visited the apartment only after Ms. Rivera died, to help her friend's parents sort through her possessions.

"She was going to do something special when it was all set up," Ms. Delgado said.

DAVID RIVERS
Searching for an Answer

At a movie party in TriBeCa 18 years ago, Ricky Vider Rivers met her future husband, David, a newcomer to New York by way of Massachusetts. Within three weeks, the two had moved in; they'd been together since.

"He was my soul mate, my best friend, my everything," said Mrs. Rivers, a fashion editor. "And I can't believe we won't see him again."

Mr. Rivers, 40, was editorial director at Risk Waters Group, a financial technology company that was sponsoring a conference at Windows on the World on Sept. 11. After the first plane hit, Mr. Rivers called his wife, who had forgotten that he was in the building. "I'm just hoping he was calm in that storm, standing there on the top of the building," she said.

The family held a memorial service for Mr. Rivers on Martha's Vineyard, a treasured place where he spent summers as a boy and later as a husband and father. "We put a box in the ground with a key to the beach in it," Mrs. Rivers said. "Because that's all we have left."

She continued: "Our son James, who is 5 years old, asks 'Why did Daddy have to be there that day?' And I can't answer him."

JOSEPH R. RIVERSO
A Broker Who Tended Bar

You might think a guy who had landed a nice job as a broker at Cantor Fitzgerald would finally give up tending bar. But there was Joe Riverso, four nights a week, pulling taps at the Sports Page in White Plains, where he worked for half his life. For Mr. Riverso, 34, a former all-league lineman and longtime assistant football coach at Archbishop Stepinac High School in White Plains, the Sports Page was where he held court. His former players would stop in for beers. So would just about everybody else.

"He had quite a following," said Mike Hyland, the bar's manager. "He'd always lighten someone's mood. We've had a lot of business solely based on him being here."

In addition to working full time at Cantor, bartending 30 hours a week and coaching at the high school, Mr. Riverso also coached his 7-year-old daughter, Danielle, and her softball team. (Mr. Riverso was divorced, but his ex-wife and Danielle lived nearby.)

"People would say 'How does your brother do it?' " said Ralph Riverso, 32. "He slept like three hours a night."

PAUL V. RIZZA
Harvesting and Cooking

Paul V. Rizza learned to cook from his father. They would cook together on weekends—osso bucco, sauce, pasta from scratch. When Paul cooked Thanksgiving dinner for 20, he worked for days. He hunted down cheesecloth and sent his wife, Elaine, out for a special roasting pan. "Sometimes I would laugh and get frustrated, 'You don't have to be like Martha Stewart,' " she said.

Paul and Elaine had a huge garden in their yard in Park Ridge, N.J. They grew tomatoes, cucumbers, basil, oregano, thyme, mint, chives, jalapeno peppers, all for Paul's cooking. The Sunday before the attack on the World Trade Center, they harvested tomatoes and made sauce together. "He had such a passion for life," Elaine said. "He loved good food."

Paul, who was 34, worked as an investor services officer at Fiduciary Trust in the trade center. Having grown up near the beach in Babylon, N.Y., he loved boating and fishing, as well as skiing and animals. "We never got around to getting a dog," Elaine said. "We just got hardwood floors put in. But if he wasn't watching the Yankees or the Food Network, he'd be watching Animal Planet."

STEPHEN L. ROACH
A Certain Taste in Shoes

He was very cute. And charming. An athletic 6 feet, 200 pounds.

But those white Capezios he was wearing had to go. Isabel Roach didn't change much about her husband, Stephen L. Roach, when they were married 16 years ago. She likes to say that she "polished him up a bit." And she definitely changed his taste in shoes.

They met in Washington. Both were academic interns at the Washington Center, which arranges internships for college students in public and private work. Mr. Roach, a native Bostonian, went to Washington after he graduated from Anselm College in 1986 hoping to meet the woman of his dreams. That turned out to be Isabel Blanco, who loved everything about him, except those shoes.

Known as Roachie to family and friends, Mr. Roach had a taste for fine red wines. He and his father-in-law, Luis, made

James Vigiano at a holiday party the Mets gave at Shea Stadium on December 8 for children who lost parents in the World Trade Center attack. James's father, Detective Joseph Vigiano, and an uncle, Firefighter John Vigiano, died at the trade center. (*Kevin P. Coughlin*)

their own wines. Mr. Roach, 36, was vice president and director of sales for Cantor Fitzgerald on the 105th floor of 1 World Trade Center. Mackenzie, 9, his youngest child, is funny like her father. Eileen, 10, has his smarts. Stephen Jr., 11, his passion for sports. None, so far, have inherited his taste in shoes.

JOSEPH ROBERTO
Man of Many Enthusiasms

When Joseph Roberto first met his wife, Janet, he offered her a ride on his motorcycle, a Suzuki Intruder. She hopped on. Three years later, in May 1998, they married.

Mr. Roberto, who was a bank analyst at Keefe, Bruyette & Woods, was a man of many enthusiasms. He and his wife attended coin conventions. He loved motorcycles; the couple rode his Yamaha Royal Star to Virginia and West Virginia to see battlefields. He also loved wildlife, and they took their son, Joseph, who was 14 months old in September, on three trips to the Bronx Zoo last summer.

"We still hadn't finished the whole park," Mrs. Roberto said. "He had to read every single sign."

Each year, Mr. Roberto, 37, helped his parents put up their Christmas decorations, and he had begun to accumulate his own. The latest holiday acquisitions were two flag-waving Uncle Sams for Memorial Day, Flag Day and the Fourth of July—three-foot figures that lighted up at night. Mrs. Roberto pulled them out again after Sept. 11.

Friends from their motorcycle club, Lost Wheels, are

After they prayed together, a visitor from San Antonio, Robin Holbrook, right, hugged a volunteer missionary, also from Texas, Valerie Broussard. They were at the intersection of Broadway and Fulton Street in lower Manhattan to see the attack site. (*James Estrin*)

helping Mrs. Roberto, who is pregnant, with the Christmas decorations.

LEO A. ROBERTS
Stalking the Sidelines

"Put the jets on, Michael!" Leo A. Roberts would shout from the sidelines at his son's soccer games. "Run faster!"

That was him. Always stalking the sidelines. Always encouraging his four children. Fall meant Michael's soccer matches and Jeffrey's and Daniel's football games. Winter was for Taylor's competitive cheerleading.

"We would get up and we would plan who would be on what field with what kid," said his wife, Debra Roberts, 43. "That is the way we lived. We lived for our kids."

Weekdays were a whirlwind. Mr. Roberts, 44, got the train from Wayne, N.J., at 6 A.M. for his job at Cantor Fitzgerald, on the 104th floor of 1 World Trade Center. He was home for the kids' practices. There was barely time for dinner before the mad rush started again. Once each weekend, Debra and Leo tried to go on a date, usually coffee or a movie. They told the kids it was so Mom and Dad would still be friends when they grew up, went off to college and moved out of the home.

"We tried every weekend to do something by ourselves," said Mrs. Roberts. "But all we talked about were the kids."

MICHAEL EDWARD ROBERTS
Firehouse Psychologist

When Michael Edward Roberts was just 4, his father took him to a firehouse and sat him on a rig parked there. That's all it took. From that moment on, life was a countdown to the Fire Academy. He took time to get a degree in psychology from the State University of New York at Buffalo, but "he knew without a doubt what he was going to do," said his father, Thomas Roberts, a retired New York City fire captain. "He'd say the only decision he needed to make was whether to grow up, or become a firefighter."

Finally, in February 1998, Michael Edward Roberts was formally admitted to the academy. He ended up at Ladder Company 35 near Lincoln Center. "He was so happy," said his sister, Lisa.

Firefighter Roberts continued to live in Pearl River, N.Y., where he grew up and where he mastered tournament darts for a local team. In the firehouse he listened to other people so intently that he came to be known as "the psychologist."

At his memorial service in November, Firefighter Roberts's family finally met the family of another Michael Edward Roberts, a firefighter with Engine Company 214 in

Brooklyn. They exchanged greetings and politely commiserated about the confusion caused by their identical names and backgrounds, both 31, both sons of firefighters.

Then the families brought together by grief went their separate ways, one to Breezy Point, one to Pearl River. And Captain Roberts brought back his son's badge and put it in a frame in the living room. It is badge No. 13392.

MICHAEL EDWARD ROBERTS
Holder of Heirloom

The number of Firefighter Robert Roberts's badge was 6611. When he left the job, the badge was assigned to his brother, John. When Firefighter John Roberts left the job, No. 6611 was passed on again, this time to John Roberts's son, Michael Edward.

No. 6611 was a Roberts family heirloom by then, but Michael Edward Roberts had a habit of misplacing things. So his mother, Veronica, urged him to think about putting the dress badge in a vault and getting "one of those fake ones" for his uniform.

She need not have worried. In nearly four years as a firefighter, Michael Edward Roberts never lost track of that badge. He was as conscientious a recruit as Lt. Michael Bell, an officer of Engine Company 214 in Brooklyn, had ever seen.

Although Firefighter Roberts had transferred there only in March, Lieutenant Bell said, "We could tell he was going to be a star."

Being a fireman was the center of his life, but Firefighter Roberts, 31, was more than that, said his uncle, Assistant Police Chief Joseph Fox. "He had a way of popping into and out of people's lives," Chief Fox said. At times it seemed he was in two places at once because there was another firefighter—same name, same age, same background. The only time their fathers, both former firemen, met was at their sons' funerals. Now John Roberts has badge No. 6611 again.

Firefighter Roberts routinely volunteered to work holidays for colleagues at the firehouse who had families. And he watched out for his younger sister, Karen, always pushing her to finish college.

She will. In January 2002.

CATHERINA ROBINSON
She Was Aunt Patsy

When teacher conferences were scheduled for her brother's children, you could count on Catherina Robinson to be there. She kept in touch with some of her older nieces and nephews by e-mail and rewarded them for good grades.

Ms. Robinson, 45, worked in the securities section of First Union Bank, and shortly before Sept. 11 the company moved its offices to the 47th floor of 1 World Trade Center. She was born and raised in Antigua. Ms. Robinson's husband died in a car accident six months after they married more than a decade ago, but the nine children of her three brothers and two sisters were almost like her own. Aunt Patsy, they called her.

"When her mom was pregnant with her in Antigua, her next-door neighbor looked at her stomach and said, 'Mrs. Henry, that's a little Patsy in there,'" said her sister-in-law, Thora Henry. The two women met as children when they were in grade school in Antigua. Her sister-in-law called her "the sweetest, dearest person that anyone would ever want to be friends with."

Thora Henry said her own children didn't want a Christmas tree this year, only a portrait of their aunt surrounded by gifts.

JEFFREY ROBINSON
Jazz and Model Cars

Jeffrey Robinson was a soft-spoken "everyday guy," said his wife, Millicent, but he had a well-developed ear and a passion for jazz. His wife said that the people who worked with him quickly learned that he was the fellow to call if you needed a new tweeter.

He also had a "guy" hobby that amused his wife: racing miniature model cars. "They were like big kids," Ms. Robinson said of her husband and his racing buddies. "It was like they didn't get train sets when they were little."

But Mr. Robinson, a systems analyst, had four children of his own and wanted easy commuting. When he started working at Marsh & McLennan, his office was in Princeton, N.J., only 10 minutes from his home in South Brunswick. In February, however, his group was transferred to the World Trade Center, lengthening his travel time to an hour and a half or more.

On Sept. 11, Mr. Robinson told his wife he had stayed up until 1 A.M. listening to a Billie Holliday anthology and overslept. Skipping his morning jog, he raced for the train station. "He was running out of the house like a madman," she said.

DONALD ARTHUR ROBSON
A Keeper

Donald Arthur Robson would sometimes look out the tall windows near his trading desk on the 103rd floor of 1 World Trade Center, stretch and say, "Yes, a Canadian can make it here." Or so he told his brother-in-law Bob Kreek.

Kristin Murphy leads a procession for September 11
victims from St. Michael's Roman Catholic Church in
Greenwich, Connecticut, on December 9. (*James Estrin*)

He could also be seen stretching through his drives on
the golf course of the Plandome Country Club in Manhasset, N.Y., of which he was president-elect. "He was a big
presence on the golf course," said Mr. Kreek. "He couldn't
putt, but he was a heck of a golfer."

Mr. Robson, a partner at Cantor Fitzgerald, also seldom
found a crossword puzzle he could not complete. And he and
his wife, Kathy, seldom found a dance floor they couldn't
dominate.

A native of Toronto, Mr. Robson, 52, met his wife of 25
years in his hometown when she was dispatched temporarily
to his office there. Kathy Kreek became convinced that this
man was a keeper, and she did everything in her power to
make him feel the same.

"Once when they were courting, Don was taking Kathy
away to the beach," Mr. Kreek said. "Kathy spent a great deal
of time matching her sunglasses to her bathing suit to her
beach towel, in an effort to secure Don."

She succeeded, but she never did beat him on the
golf course—that honor fell to their sons, Geoffrey and
Scott.

ANTONIO ROCHA
"Big Kid" with a Big Job

For Antonio Rocha, one of the best things
about having kids was that it gave him an
excuse to go back to Disney World. Mr.
Rocha, who brokered bonds at Cantor
Fitzgerald when he was not bonding with
Goofy and Mickey, had made the pilgrimage three times with
his wife, Marilyn, and once with his wife and daughter, Alyssa,
and he looked forward to taking his son, Ethan, who was born
last March.

"He was just a big kid," Ms. Rocha said. "One of the last
things we did together was go down to Point Pleasant"—on
the Jersey Shore—"and he rode on all the rides with Alyssa, the
teacups and everything like that." Mr. Rocha, 34, loved to take
Alyssa riding on the back of his bike near their home in East
Hanover, N.J. He even played with Barbie dolls with her.

Of course Mr. Rocha had some slightly more grownup
interests, too. He traveled all over the country to see Formula
One car races. He loved to golf.

And he even approached his vacations with a certain degree of seriousness, planning every last detail. In mid-September, the Rochas were to take their first trip with Ethan, to St. Lucia. Marilyn Rocha still has the stack of hotel listings and restaurant menus. "I'm going to definitely try to take that trip someday," she said, "stay at the same hotel, eat at the same restaurants. It will be the easiest trip to plan."

RAYMOND J. ROCHA
28 Weddings in Three Years

Everyone Raymond J. Rocha met, it seemed, became part of his large family, and he was constantly in touch. His girlfriend counted 28 weddings they went to in three years. Even his ex-girlfriends came to his sister's wedding or his annual ski trip, where Mr. Rocha bought everyone walkie-talkies because cell phones would not work on the mountain. A prankster, he would leave rubber snakes in people's beds. At a friend's birthday party, he would wear a silly costume.

But he would also bake a beautiful cake. The youngest of five and a new bond trader at Cantor Fitzgerald, Mr. Rocha was cooking and balancing bank statements at an early age, in part because his mother, Ann Rocha, was losing her sight.

"I loved to go shopping with him because he was very patient with me," she said. "He would read me every ingredient."

It was easy to tell when Mr. Rocha had been around. People would find that someone had marked March 27 on their calendars "Ray Day." Plans were already under way for the next Ray Day, when Mr. Rocha would have turned 30.

LAURA ROCKEFELLER
Her World a Stage

Laura Rockefeller's parents in White Plains got sympathy letters from people who knew her only as J.T.'s mom, one of the regulars at the dog run in Riverside Park, where a bench will be dedicated in her name.

Ms. Rockefeller's animal-loving friends were the first to figure out that she might be among the missing at the World Trade Center, although she did not work there. If she was even 15 minutes late to walk J.T., a shepherd mix named for James Taylor, or feed her two cats, Uff and Parker, something was surely wrong.

Ms. Rockefeller, 41, was an aspiring actress, singer and director who paid the rent on her one-bedroom apartment on West 85th Street with freelance work for Risk Waters, a London-based company that produces seminars for financial managers. On Sept. 11, she was stage-managing one at Windows on the World.

But Ms. Rockefeller's passion, in addition to her animals, was musical theater. She fell in love with the stage as a child when her mother ran a children's theater and her father was a television director. In New York, she went to plays as often as she could afford and often broke into spontaneous song.

Because she was not an employee at the World Trade Center, it took a full day for Ms. Rockefeller's sister Terry and her parents to figure out she had been there and was surely dead. But J.T. continues to resist the finality, running to the door in White Plains, ears perked, each time a car approaches.

JOHN RODAK
His Daughters in White

While driving nearly two dawn-streaked hours from his home in Mantua, N.J., to 2 World Trade Center, where he was a managing director at Sandler O'Neill & Partners, John Rodak would plan his workday and get revved. After the markets closed, he would drive two hours back, letting go of work in the traffic and evening darkness. By the time he walked through the door again, arms open, he was completely ready for his wife and two daughters. He was there.

Mr. Rodak, 39, gravitated toward activities requiring a patient, meditative discipline. Years ago, he would hunt deer and duck. Later he took up golf, then karate, which he practiced with his 10-year-old, Chelsea.

Finally it was deep-sea fishing, which he shared with Devon, 5. He came across as a man without worries, with plenty of time to chat with small children, buy drinks for strangers at a bar or, on that last weekend, to make dinner for his family.

For their 14th anniversary in 2000, Mr. Rodak gave his wife, Joyce, two crystal goblets. He also bought two sets to put aside for his daughters as a surprise on their wedding days. He chose a onetime pattern from Waterford's Millennium collection. It is called "Happiness."

ANTONIO RODRIGUES
"Where Is Your Rock?"

Antonio Rodrigues painted what he liked and he liked the water, so he painted scenes of the beach and of boats. He grew up in Portugal, in a town perched on the coast. When he married and settled near New York, he and his wife, Cristina, chose Port Washington, on Long Island, because they wanted to be near the balm of the water. Their two children, Sara and Adam, had no complaints.

Mr. Rodrigues, 35, had been a transit officer in New York but joined the Port Authority police force in 2001. He designed a T-shirt for his graduating class, with a logo on one side and caricatures of graduates on the back.

He had been stationed at the Port Authority bus terminal, and when the attack occurred, he and 14 other officers commandeered one of the regular commuter buses and raced down to the trade center. Much as he relished painting, Mr. Rodrigues had not done many canvases in a few years. Instead, he drew cartoons about his job.

"He found a lot of things funny with his job," Mrs. Rodrigues said. For instance, she said, one of the other officers at the academy was assigned to carry around a rock and take care of it. It became a running joke to inquire of this officer, "Where is your rock?"

So Mr. Rodrigues drew a cartoon about the officer and the rock. In sorting through the cartoons, Mrs. Rodrigues has decided to give some of them away to officers she feels would appreciate them. The officer with the rock is getting his.

ANTHONY RODRIGUEZ
On His Way to a Dream

Anthony Rodriguez was a probie and he loved it.

"There wasn't a day he didn't come in through the door without saying 'I have the best job in the world,' " said his mother, Brunilda Rodriguez.

At 36, Mr. Rodriguez was one of the oldest probies, or probationary firefighters, in his class at the Fire Academy. He had already spent a full decade in the Navy as a radioman first class, and several years on top of that as an elevator mechanic and independent contractor.

Becoming a fireman was a dream realized, an exciting way to help people and provide a steady income to support his wife, Evelyn, and their growing family, which included children from a previous marriage, a 3-year-old son and a baby due in mid-September.

In the months before his formal graduation, Mr. Rodriguez was assigned to Engine Company 279 in Brooklyn. He was on his way home to Staten Island when the first plane struck the trade center. He called to tell everyone not to worry. When the second building was hit, he called again and said he was going back. "That's what he enjoyed doing," his mother said. "That made Anthony happy."

Mr. Rodriguez's daughter, Morgan Antoinette, was born on Sept. 14, while the search for her father was still going on.

At graduation ceremonies on Nov. 1, Mr. Rodriguez was posthumously made a firefighter. Firefighter Rodriguez's empty chair was one of six draped in mourning bunting that day.

RICHARD RODRIGUEZ
Like Hitting the Jackpot

It can't be said with certainty that Richard Rodriguez was the only Puerto Rican man ever to parade around in a skirt and enjoy it. But his family is certain that no one could have reveled in doing so more than he did.

A member of the Port Authority Police Department and a drummer in its Emerald Society Pipes and Drums, he was as proud of being a police officer as he was of his Latin heritage. And he didn't mind putting on a kilt, even if it was rather unusual for someone of his background to do so. "He used to say he was breaking barriers," said his wife, Cindy.

Before joining the force, Officer Rodriguez went to school for technical drafting—and hated it. But the more time he spent with the volunteer first-aid squad in Perth Amboy, N.J., where he grew up, the more his career interests shifted to public service.

When the Port Authority police offered him a position eight years ago, he told everyone he had won the lottery. He was first assigned to Newark Airport, where he trained for special duty protecting the president when Air Force One landed there.

Three years ago he started teaching at the Port Authority Police Academy, which was in Sea Girt until it moved to Jersey City in August. When the planes hit on Sept. 11, Officer

Members of the family of Captain Frank J. Callahan, who belonged to Ladder Company 35 of the New York Fire Department, lead a procession past an honor guard of firefighters before a December 10 memorial service in Alice Tully Hall at Lincoln Center. (*Don Hogan Charles*)

Rodriguez and the other officers rushed through the Holland Tunnel.

The Port Authority Emerald Society, missing one drummer, played at his memorial service.

MATT ROGAN
A Sneaky Sense of Humor

He did not particularly like Christmas. Too commercial. Hated his birthday. Too much attention. He watched the History Channel. He knew instinctively how to trim back a plant, and his first crop of grapes was so bountiful that he and his wife, Melissa, thought that next year they would try to make wine.

He took his children backpacking in the Adirondacks. His family lived in the same house in West Islip, N.Y., in which he had grown up. But that accumulation of low-key details does not translate into Matt Rogan, quiet, retiring guy. A firefighter like his father and brother before him, he was 37 and had a sneaky sense of humor. Once, after he had minor surgery on his chest, he told his nieces and nephews that he had had a third nipple removed.

When he ate dates covered in nuts, he claimed that they came from the cat's litter box. With the children no longer babies, the couple were planning a more luxurious future. When he retired, he dreamed, they would ride motorcycles across the country. "He wasn't sentimental; I was the sentimental one," said Mrs. Rogan. "He always said if he won the Lotto, he would sell the house in a second and move upstate."

JEAN ROGÉR
Finding Joy in the Sky

You can call just about anybody a people person. People who were close to Jean Rogér say they know this. But what can they do? It is, they say, the best way to describe her.

And it is why Ms. Rogér, who was 24, became a flight attendant two years ago after attending Penn State.

"After four and a half years of college, she wanted to be a flight attendant," said her father, Tom Rogér. "She enjoyed traveling and meeting people, from children to 90-year-old adults; she loved them all."

One person was especially important—her boyfriend, Kevin Dowd, a Boston-area stockbroker whom she had been dating for about two years. The night before Ms. Rogér reported for duty on American Airlines Flight 11 to Los Angeles she celebrated Mr. Dowd's 30th birthday, just the two of them strolling through Boston.

That night Ms. Rogér gave Mr. Dowd a card that, he said, summed up her general life philosophy. "She wished me to have love, happiness and peace of mind because really, everything else just comes and goes," Mr. Dowd said. Despite a late night, the following morning "she went to work with a smile on her face," Mr. Dowd said. "She was happy as could be."

SCOTT W. ROHNER
A Dream Life Cut Short

He played Prince Charming when his fourth-grade class staged "Cinderella," and Scott W. Rohner led a charmed life until his death at 22, just two paychecks into what, had he been given more time to shine as a foreign exchange trader, might have become a dream job at Cantor Fitzgerald.

"He lived an exceptional life and died an exceptional death," said his mother, Kathy Rohner of River Edge, N.J., where busy Route 17 was briefly closed the day of his funeral to accommodate the stream of mourners. Mr. Rohner had countless buddies.

After scoring a job on his first interview after graduating from Hobart College, Mr. Rohner had just bought a cellphone, acquired his own credit card and moved to Hoboken, N.J., rent-free, house-sitting for his uncle. He was already hobnobbing with Cantor clients, but with a twist: instead of heading out for martinis, they hit the court for three-on-three basketball. A natural athlete, he was captain of his football and basketball teams at River Dell High School, which plans to retire his jersey.

Golf was another game that came easily; he took it up as a teenager at Ridgewood Country Club, where he worked as a caddie and locker room attendant. There was a single plot left in the cemetery abutting the fourth fairway: the club deemed it Mr. Rohner's.

JOE ROMAGNOLO
Phones and Family

There were hundreds of telephones at the bond-trading firm of Cantor Fitzgerald and it was Joe Romagnolo's job to keep them working.

Mr. Romagnolo, 37, had a knack for troubleshooting. He was the foreman. But his wife, Sandy, and their four children came first. They lived in Coram, on Long Island. He and his wife, whom he had known since childhood, went to Disney World for their honeymoon; their taste in music ran from heavy metal to Glenn Miller.

Mr. Romagnolo's father, Sal, was a phone technician and

got him started in the business. He lived near his father and his mother, Maria; his sister Michele was nearby, too, and often helped out with his children.

Joe Romagnolo wore an American eagle belt buckle and insisted on buying only American-made products. He drove a Dodge pickup truck and rooted for the Yankees and the Giants, and his best friends were the guys he grew up with. He hunted deer with his brother Steven and rode his Harley-Davidson alone. But he had decided to sell the bike. The brothers were both going to buy house trailers so they could take outings with their wives and children.

EFRAIN FRANCO ROMERO
A Lifetime of Building

Some people like to build things as a hobby. Efrain Franco Romero built, repaired and renovated things as a way of life. He built a pond in the backyard of the house in Hazleton, Pa., where his family lives, along with a balcony.

In the weeks leading up to Sept. 11, he was in the process of building a garage, said his son, Frank Jr. He would work on it when he came home on the weekends from his job at Fine Painting, in the World Trade Center.

"You name it and he did it. My father is definitely the jack of all trades and master of anything you can imagine," Mr. Romero said. He recalled that the pond his father built started out as a minor project to set up a small water fountain, the kind found at any Wal-Mart; that fountain became a pond with a waterfall and populated by small fish.

"He made modifications to our hedge clipper, to the point that I couldn't use it anymore," Mr. Romero said. "It was so powerful it would shake out of my hand."

His father, who was 57, was always a fixer-upper, he said. "As far as I know, he's been doing this since he was old enough to pick up a hammer."

ELVIN ROMERO
A Daughter's Questions

Now that her father, Elvin Romero, is gone, Gabriella, who is 5, wants to know everything about him. "Did Daddy stay up late after I fell asleep?" she will ask her mother, Diane Romero. What was his favorite color? Would he have liked the song playing on the radio now?

For Gabriella, grief is the stringing together of facts, like the beads of a necklace. For her mother, grief is the anguish of recalling all the details that each year brought her and her husband closer together, and made them more of a family. Their son Alexander, who is 2, is just waiting for his father to come home.

Mr. Romero and his wife met in a restaurant in Brooklyn, when he was on a date with someone else. Her girlfriend knew

him, and stopped to say hello. He looked up his future wife later, and asked her for a date, and for the first four months they saw each other every day. They married seven years ago.

Mr. Romero, who was 34 and lived with his family in Matawan, N.J., was a vice president of international equities at Cantor Fitzgerald. He and his wife would talk on the telephone every day when he was at work, sometimes just a short call, because work was often hectic. " 'Love you,' and then he'd hang up," Ms. Romero recalled. "Or, 'Give the kids a hug for me,' and then hang up."

When he called on Sept. 11, she had time to tell him that Gabriella had not cried that day at kindergarten. "It looks like we're going to have a great day," he said to her before the call was cut off.

JAMES A. ROMITO
Water and the Woods

On his 50th birthday in 2000, James A. Romito and his fiancée, Mary Pat Brew Sturdy, had just opened a bottle of wine when his beeper went off: an attempted hijacking at Kennedy Airport. Mr. Romito, the chief of the Port Authority Police Department, answered the call, returning home only at 7 the next morning.

It was typical of the way his sense of duty and public service had structured his life, Ms. Sturdy said. "He would be in the midst of everything," she said. In 30 years with the Port Authority, he had handled crises, including the 1993 bombing of the World Trade Center, and quieter challenges, like how to humanely deal with the homeless at the Port Authority Bus Terminal.

Outside of work, he wanted to be just a regular person. He had Mary Pat and her son, Bobby; he had his daughter, Ellen. Ms. Sturdy said most of the people at their favorite bar, Poor Henry's, did not even know what he did.

He loved the water and the woods. There were times when the beeper would go off, and it would be something he could handle from home. The screened-in back porch would become a command center, and there he and Mary Pat would sit—dealing with the crisis, and looking at the woods.

SEAN ROONEY
A Man of the Kitchen

The kitchen in the house of Sean Rooney and his wife, Beverly Eckert, in Stamford, Conn., reminds her of him for several reasons. First, Mr. Rooney loved to cook. Even more, he loved to have his friends and family, and their conversation and laughter, in the kitchen with him when he did.

But there is another reason that Ms. Eckert likes to sit in their kitchen these days: The hardwood floors beneath her, the cabinets around her, the island in the middle and even the maple dining-room table were all built by Mr. Rooney, by hand. "When I sit there I'm completely surrounded by him," she said. "That makes me feel happy."

Mr. Rooney taught himself carpentry. And somehow, with the demands of commuting and his job as a vice president at Aon, he found time to make the kinds of tangible objects that were such a contrast to the abstractions of insurance.

Mr. Rooney and Ms. Eckert met when they were 16, at a high school dance. In 2001, they turned 50 together. And though they were very different, the words "Bev and Sean" were often spoken as one instead of three. On their second date, they went to see the movie *Camelot*. From then on, they always felt that they were "happily-ever-aftering," as the song says.

"What I miss," his wife said, "is having him come through the door saying, 'Where's my hug?'"

AIDA ROSARIO
Working Hard for Her Girls

Aida Rosario's family always knew when she was around: she was playing her music loud, or laughing hard, or leaving for work with a crying 3-year-old in tow on the way to day care.

Ms. Rosario, an assistant manager in the re-insurance division of Marsh & McLennan, shared a three-story family house in Jersey City with her mother, two brothers and a sister-in-law. She occupied the top floor with her daughters Amy, 14, and Jasmine, 3, and a 6-month-old granddaughter, Marilyn.

"She was very excited about having a granddaughter, although she was very unhappy about the fact that her 14-year-old was having a baby," said her sister-in-law, Minerva Rosario. "She worked very hard so the children would be provided for."

When Ms. Rosario had started working on the 94th floor of 1 World Trade Center three years earlier, her family questioned her wisdom in light of the previous terrorist attack. "She said, 'I have to feed my daughters,'" her sister-in-law said. "She said: 'So what? If the building's on fire I'll jump out the window.'" But it was a joke. Ms. Rosario, 42 and divorced, never dwelled on the potential danger, instead focusing her energies on taking care of her girls.

Now her family is haunted by speculation about what really happened to her. "You just wonder," Minerva Rosario said.

MARK H. ROSEN
Thrilled by Twirls

As a partner at Sandler O'Neill, Mark H. Rosen knew investment banking. As a father, he knew baton twirling.

His daughter, Amanda, now 13, got the twirling bug early, becoming a member of the PAL Sparklers, a club in Brentwood, N.Y., near the family's home in West Islip. For a couple of years, no family vacation was complete without at least a few days spent in some out-of-the-way place at a competition.

"He was quite happy to sit in hot gymnasiums in places like Grand Rapids or Dubuque and watch his daughter twirl," his wife, Patti, recalled.

Twirling also aided Mr. Rosen, 45, in fulfilling another familial obligation, playing Santa Claus at annual holiday school breakfasts. Mrs. Rosen is Catholic, and the children—Amanda, Matthew, 12, and Bryan, 16—were raised in the church. Mr. Rosen was Jewish, but that did not matter. "We talked him into it," Mrs. Rosen said.

He borrowed the red suit from the Sparklers, who also recruited him to play Santa in some local twirling shows. He would be surrounded by jumping girls, with batons constantly whizzing past his nose, but he never flinched, having removed his glasses for that authentic Claus look. "He couldn't see a thing without them," Mrs. Rosen said.

BROOKE ROSENBAUM
Reading at the Station

Every morning, Brooke Rosenbaum would leave the house early. He wanted to have the train station to himself for a little while, so he could read and sort things out for the day ahead. He loved to hang out, to have friends over to watch sports, said Elsa Cordero, his Long Island roommate of seven years, but mostly he loved to read, to the tune of two books and about 15 magazines a week.

"He just read tons of them," she said. "He was always great to talk to because he was just so well informed about everything."

A decade ago, Ms. Cordero said, the two dated and then went their separate ways, but somehow they rediscovered each other and settled into a close friendship. On Monday, Sept. 10, Ms. Cordero said, Mr. Rosenbaum was sick, and she tried to persuade him to stay home the next day. Ever stubborn, he told her that if he did not go in to his job at Cantor Fitzgerald, "literally the whole place would fall apart."

And so, as usual, Mr. Rosenbaum left early Tuesday morning so he would have time to read at the station before catching his train to the city.

SHERYL ROSENBAUM
Doing What She Wanted

Sometime back, Sheryl Rosenbaum filled out an e-mail questionnaire, which her friends passed on to her mother, Bobbie Rosner, after her death. One answer stands out for Mrs. Rosner, who cannot speak of her daughter, the oldest of three children, without weeping.

What job would you want if you could have any one in the world? The one she had, wrote Mrs. Rosenbaum, 33, an accountant and partner at Cantor Fitzgerald. Mrs. Rosenbaum followed her father into accounting, knowing since childhood, when she helped out in his office, that this was what she wanted to do. She met her husband, Mark, when both worked for Arthur Andersen. November 2001 would have been their seventh anniversary.

By the time Mrs. Rosenbaum decided to quit and start a family, she had made herself so valuable at Cantor Fitzgerald that her supervisors wouldn't hear of it. Instead, they changed her hours and permitted her a four-day week, so she could stay and have children—Hannah, now 3, and Sam, 17 months. But even on the mommy track, her talents and diligence earned her bonuses and a partnership, her mother said.

But not at the expense of family and friends. The last weekend of her life was typical. One day was spent traveling from New Jersey, where the Rosenbaums were building a house, to Long Island, for the baby shower of her college roommate. The other was spent at a mall with her mother and 82-year-old grandmother, shopping for jeans and tops.

"And laughing," her mother said. "We always laughed."

LLOYD ROSENBERG
A Mother's World

A mother laments. For her, Lloyd Rosenberg was not just a son, but a close friend. She remembers doing everything for young Lloyd: Little League, Cub Scouts, Boy Scouts, summer camp, guitar lessons. When the family moved to Staten Island and Lloyd disliked his new high school, his mother arranged for him to continue going to his old high school in Sheepshead Bay, Brooklyn.

"Lloyd was my life," his mother, Michele Rosenberg, said. "There wasn't one thing that I wouldn't do for him and his sister, Lorene. He was everything in the world to me, even more than my husband. He was a wonderful son. If he did anything wrong, he always apologized."

She was proud of his success as a bond trader at Cantor Fitzgerald, where he began in the mailroom and quickly ascended. His mother, a teacher, and his father, Larry, a Transit Authority electrician, were delighted that he earned far more than they did. With that money, he bought a handsome home in Morganville, N.J., where he and his wife, Glenna, were raising three daughters, Samantha, 5, Kaylee, 3, and Alyssa, 1.

"Both of us were civil service, and that's good, but we felt if you could do better, go for it," his mother said. "You always want better for your children."

"All I can tell you is I love him very much," she added. "I'm looking at his picture right now. Not only did I lose a good friend, I lost my baby."

MARK L. ROSENBERG
Saving Gas, and the World

Mark L. Rosenberg met his future wife, Jennifer, in 1995 on a seven-hour bus ride to Richmond, Va., for a Jewish youth program. He was trying to shine a flashlight on a book and turn the pages at the same time. She sat behind him, and finally offered to hold the flashlight. He gratefully accepted.

"I thought he was really cute," said Mrs. Rosenberg, who recalled being smitten by his green-blue eyes and smile.

Mr. Rosenberg, 26, a software developer for Marsh & McLennan, was no stranger to buses, or subways, for that matter. His friends called him "Mr. Public Transportation" because he favored mass transit over driving, out of concern for the environment. His wife recalls him hailing a cab only three times during their courtship and marriage.

An avid cyclist, Mr. Rosenberg also used to ride from his home in Teaneck, N.J., over the George Washington Bridge and down to Central Park on Sunday mornings.

"He loved the city," his wife said. "He never wanted to go anywhere else."

ANDREW I. ROSENBLUM
Love Was All Around

As a lawyer, Andrew I. Rosenblum grew frustrated with defending the guilty and, sometimes, seeing the innocent convicted. So he left the law and entered the world of finance, eventually becoming a vice president at Cantor Fitzgerald.

When entertaining clients, he had a knack for listening and making people feel comfortable. "Andrew was always able to make people feel at ease," said his wife, Jill.

He took his sons, Jordan, 14, and Kyle, 11, to Islanders hockey games and made sure they got to meet the players. He took them to a concert and there was Jordan, on stage with Elton John. "There was something magical about my brother," said Adam Rosenblum, the youngest of Andrew's three siblings. "All I ever wanted to do was be just like him."

In May, Mr. Rosenblum, 45, had a near-death experience during surgery for a herniated disk in his neck. To celebrate his recovery, the family held a huge barbecue, with a magician and "I Survived Andy's Surgery" T-shirts, at their home in Rockville Centre, on Long Island. Afterward, Mrs.

Rosenblum said, "He told me he never realized how many people loved him."

JOSHUA M. ROSENBLUM
A "Keeper" for Little Zoe

Two weeks before Joshua M. Rosenblum's and Gina Hawryluk's Sept. 15 wedding date, the couple rented a dinghy in Point Pleasant, N.J., and took Ms. Hawryluk's 5-year-old daughter, Zoe, crabbing. At first the crabs they found were too small. Then Zoe caught one, and Mr. Rosenblum pronounced it big enough to keep.

"Zoe threw up her arms and said, 'I got a keeper!' and his face was like a proud father," Ms. Hawryluk said. "I will always remember the look on his face. He was so sweet and gentle."

Mr. Rosenblum, 28, met Ms. Hawryluk at Cantor Fitzgerald, where he was an assistant trader and she was a trader, and three years ago Mr. Rosenblum moved in with Ms. Hawryluk and Zoe at their home in Hoboken, N.J. "When you think of your kid, sometimes you can't envision them as a parent," said Susan Rosenblum, Mr. Rosenblum's mother. "But he adored that child and it was just as clear Zoe adored him. She called him 'my Josh.' "

On Sept. 11, Ms. Hawryluk stayed home from Cantor Fitzgerald to make the final preparations for the big day. But Mr. Rosenblum went into work, intending to put in one last shift before his wedding.

JOSH ROSENTHAL
A Man and Sister Grow Up

Last Sunday night, Josh Rosenthal went out for dinner with his sister, Helen, and her family to celebrate the coming of fall and the fact that they were all together again after being apart over the summer.

"He had just picked up *Catcher in the Rye* again,' " she said. "And he was just adorable about the relationship between Holden and his sister."

A portfolio manager at Fiduciary Trust, Mr. Rosenthal most liked "to play with his nieces, but of course I would say that," Ms. Rosenthal said. "He would tease them mercilessly, just like he would tease me when I was a little girl." He would also bring them gifts from his many travels, like a stamp with their names in Japanese or beautiful Chinese robes.

Ms. Rosenthal, who described her only sibling as her best friend, said that the two had been especially close since a two-month trip they took together through southeast Asia about 15 years ago, where they discovered each other as adults. "He wasn't teasing me anymore," she said.

RICHARD D. ROSENTHAL
With That Devilish Grin

Richard D. Rosenthal was not a daredevil, but he did have a childlike adventurous streak. "My older daughter called him a man-kid," said his sister, Audrey Model. His 40th birthday party had a *Three Stooges* theme. For his 50th birthday party in May 2001, Ms. Model toasted her brother, saying she hoped he would remain a man-kid.

And Mr. Rosenthal, of Fair Lawn, N.J., did so, on family vacations with his wife, Loren, and sons Evan, 18, and Seth, 14. He coaxed his wife into trying white-water rafting on a cruise last summer. "He always had a devilish grin on his face because he knew I was scared," she said.

But the Rosenthals made a great team, said Ms. Model, dealing with their elder son's familial dysautonomia, a serious genetic disease. Mr. Rosenthal served as the treasurer of the Dysautonomia Foundation for 15 years; he had been a vice president at Cantor Fitzgerald for just six months.

Ms. Model had a hand in building that team: when her brother was younger, she taught him how to dance, and by consensus he had all the right moves. "He was a person that everybody would notice at the dance, because he danced that well," said his wife, who met him at a school dance when she was 14 and he was 17. This month, they would have been married for 24 years. "We spent more time together than we did not," said Mrs. Rosenthal.

PHILIP M. ROSENZWEIG
You Could Count on Him

Philip M. Rosenzweig was the reliable one in the family. He kept his papers in order, and he never missed appointments. He even remembered to call his parents, Harold and Evelyn, once a week and send them cards for their anniversary and birthdays. "He was a very methodical person," said his father. "His whole life."

Mr. Rosenzweig, 47, a vice president with Sun Microsystems, was aboard American Airlines Flight 11. A native of Long Island, he was the older of two boys and graduated from the Rochester Institute of Technology. He lived with his wife, Lauren, and two sons, Jeremy and Max, in Acton, Mass.

In his free time, Mr. Rosenzweig liked to drive sports cars, and once even took lessons at a racetrack in Connecticut. He also bought a silver Porsche Cabriolet convertible, and joined a club for Porsche owners. But when he returned home, he could always be counted on to put his car away. And even though he parked in the garage, he would drape a cover over it.

DANIEL ROSSETTI
His Days on the Water

Daniel Rossetti was a carpenter by trade, but he loved and lived to fish. Mr. Rossetti loved his days on the water so much that, from boyhood, he stuffed mementos of his trips—and his luck—in a zipper-lined photo album. Years later, at the age of 32, he was still doing that. But the album, full of pictures and newspaper clippings, has disappeared.

"That album was old, kind of falling apart, but it was his pride and joy," said Christine Bennett, Mr. Rossetti's fiancée and the mother of Justin, their 15-month-old son. "It is killing us, because we knew how important it was to him."

On Sept. 11, Mr. Rossetti, who lived in Bloomfield, N.J., was finishing up a two-day job at Aon, the insurance company, on the 105th floor of 2 World Trade Center. That day he had taken the train into Manhattan.

"We found his car that night," said his sister-in-law, Nancy Rossetti. "He was considerate. He was always around. He always had a fishing pole with him. But that album is missing in action."

NORMAN ROSSINOW
Adventure, Always

That was the funny thing about Norman Rossinow: he was so much the insurance man, asking friends if they had proper coverage for life's unforeseen whammies, a reserved, even shy, sweetly gentle type who was a risk manager for Aon Corporation. Yet when his buddy, John Williamson, thinks of him, the first thing that comes to mind is "the adventure around the corner."

Mr. Rossinow, 39, who grew up in suburban North Caldwell, N.J., and lived in suburban Cedar Grove, N.J., had a surging affinity for scuba diving, schlepping through Minnesota back country carrying a canoe, and attending an unseemly number of Santana concerts. He would not spend $100 on a pair of pants but would happily plow the same money into food ingredients, loving the challenge of re-creating a restaurant dish.

In June, he embarked on his greatest adventure: marriage. During a business trip this summer, when the executives at a round table had to do the warm and fuzzy by announcing the best thing that ever happened to them, he said that would be his wife, Susan.

On that last September morning, the newlyweds exchanged a frantic flurry of phone calls. Mr. Rossinow said he would wait out the mayhem. During their final exchange, he relented, saying, in his warm, calming way, "If you tell me you love me, I'll come home.'"

NICHOLAS ROSSOMANDO
In Awe of "Nicky Love"

He loved karate and he was good at it. His karate teacher, Dr. Gene Isola, speaks in awe about one of Nicholas Rossomando's feats: he put a six-inch pile of wood on two cinder blocks and then smashed the pile with his fist.

"He hit it so hard that he also broke the cinder blocks on one side," Dr. Isola said. "We have it on film. The guy was built like a steel tank."

That feat, Dr. Isola said, exemplified the gusto that was Nicholas Rossomando. He loved working as a firefighter. He loved to cook—for his girlfriend, for his parents, for his buddies at Rescue Company 5. He loved carpentry; as a volunteer he built 80 percent of the interior of the karate school.

"He had an overwhelming enthusiasm about life, not just 100 percent, but 1,000 percent," Dr. Isola said. "From the way he smiled and hugged you, to the way he made a meal, to the way he did martial arts, it was done with enthusiasm and passion. There was no halfway with Nicky."

"At the karate school," Dr. Isola continued, "everyone had nicknames. There was Crazy Eye Joe, Jazzy Jeff, but Nicky's nickname was Nicky Love."

MICHAEL ROTHBERG
Analytical and Autonomous

Do you know what bothered Michael Rothberg about his stationery? It listed a phone number for Cantor Fitzgerald, where he was the director of program trading, with a 1 followed by the area code and phone number. No adult sophisticated enough to call a bond-trading firm needs to be told to dial 1 before the area code, he reasoned.

This qualm was a source of amusement, not ire, and it was a small, silly display of his analytical mind. Put to serious pursuits, as it often was, this inclination was a formidable skill, and Mr. Rothberg shared its benefits with family and friends.

"When Mike made a decision, you knew it was a good one," said Susan McDermott, the wife of Matthew McDermott, who worked for Mr. Rothberg.

Mr. Rothberg understood the computer systems used for program trading and the communications skills used for relating to clients. He learned at his first firm, Bear, Stearns, that leading a team offered more pay and autonomy than working behind a leader. He moved to Kidder Peabody & Company to become a leader, and later took his employees, whom he called colleagues, along to Cantor Fitzgerald.

With that experience gained, Mr. Rothberg listened three years ago as his sister Rhonda complained about running a business for a salary while the owner reaped larger profits. He encouraged her to strike out on her own, and within four months she was a business owner.

"He was looking out for people," said Jamie Bolton, a friend.

MATTHEW McDERMOTT's portrait appears on page 321.

DONNA M. ROTHENBERG
Filling in the Gaps

As a birthday present a decade ago, a friend placed an inquiry in a New York magazine, seeking a proper suitor for Donna M. Rothenberg, a widow in her early 40s. A gentleman named Edward Schmall responded with a letter carefully crafted to attract her interest. It changed his life.

When Ms. Rothenberg eventually moved into Mr. Schmall's apartment in the Flatiron district, she brought more than two cats. She brought wondrous experiences from having lived in Europe, Asia, and South America. She brought a gift for cooking. She brought a zest for life that was reflected in her colorful wardrobe; "She wasn't somebody who wore a lot of black," remembered her cousin, Susan Sullivan.

She also brought the reassurance that she would be there for crises small and large, from Mr. Schmall's battle against smoking to his sudden collapse while in California.

Ms. Rothenberg, a global affairs executive for the Aon Corporation, was 53 when she died, and the man she met through a personals ad so long ago now struggles to reconcile his blessing and his loss. "What I couldn't do, she did well; what I did well, she did better," he said. "She filled in all my gaps."

NICHOLAS ROWE
Charlie and an Angel

Friends said it seemed as if Nicholas Charles Alexander Rowe came out of every cafe, every bar, every experience with new friends—and he kept in touch with all of them.

"He used to go out on a Friday or Saturday night and when he got home he would phone South Africa, and his friends here would be asleep after an equally riotous night," recalled his mother, Judy Rowe, who lives in Johannesburg. In South Africa, it would already be early morning, she said.

It was at a Halloween party three years ago that Mr. Rowe met Michelle P. Baker, his girlfriend. She was dressed as one of Charlie's Angels; he arrived from work, wearing a suit. "We tagged him as Charlie at that point," she said, adding, "I was in love instantly."

Mr. Rowe's parents, who met Ms. Baker last Christmas,

observed that the feeling was mutual. "We hoped that the next family get-together would be for the wedding," Mrs. Rowe said.

On Sept. 11 Mr. Rowe, who worked for a company called Umevoice that designs speech recognition software, was participating in a conference at Windows on the World. He was 28.

RONALD J. RUBEN
A House in His Memory

Ronald J. Ruben did not mind getting his hands dirty. When he was not trading equities on Wall Street, he was fixing old cars, or building toy boxes, tables and chairs. He was a people person, though his hobbies required him to spend long stretches alone, said his sister, Leslie Dillon.

"He would always be there to fix things and carry things for people," Mrs. Dillon said. "I know people say this all the time, but he was one of the good guys."

Before the attacks, Mr. Ruben, 36, of Hoboken, N.J., had worked for seven months for Keefe, Bruyette & Woods as vice president of equity trading. He had agonized for days over whether he should leave his longtime job at another financial company, she said. But once he started at Keefe, he expressed no regrets.

As a memorial, family and friends are having a Habitat for Humanity house built in Mr. Ruben's name.

JOANNE RUBINO
A Mother's Dream

Hers was a life of simplicity and devotion. She worked, she came home, and she took care of her mother. Austere, perhaps, but Joanne Rubino never made it seem that she was missing anything important.

"My Joanne really was happy being how she was," said her mother, Antoinette. "She wasn't asking for much in life."

Besides heading to her office in the tax department of Marsh & McLennan for more than 20 years, Ms. Rubino, 45, rarely left her mother. On weekends they went to crafts shows. In the fall, they drove through upstate New York, enjoying the scenery, the fresh air, and each other's company.

"I used to tell her, 'Every mother should have a daughter like you,'" said Mrs. Rubino, 74. "So thoughtful, and to other people too."

Ms. Rubino couldn't pass a homeless person without giving money. One blustery winter day she gave a street person her scarf. "She figured he needed it more than she did," Mrs. Rubino said. When her mother became seriously ill a few years ago, Ms. Rubino had to stop visiting her brother, Anthony, in Louisville, Ky.

"She thought of the family before she thought of herself," Mr. Rubino said. "That's the most outstanding point I can make about Joanne."

BART J. RUGGIERE
Every Day a Celebration

Bart J. Ruggiere was a quintessential New Yorker. He dined in fine restaurants, proposed in Central Park and was married in St. Patrick's Cathedral. In the first days after the attack, his family thought he would turn up, said his wife, Claudia.

"His sister Cathleen asked me whether Bart would consider moving out of the city. I said, no way. He belonged here."

On Sept. 10, the couple had dinner at an Italian restaurant in Greenwich Village. "It was a Monday night, and for no reason, he made the reservation," Mrs. Ruggiere said, "because he believed every day is worth celebrating." He had lamb chops for an entree and chocolate soufflé for dessert.

Rich food was his standard fare. A frequent host of dinner parties at their Upper East Side apartment, Mr. Ruggiere, 32, a trader at Cantor Fitzgerald, usually served steaks, mashed potatoes and chocolate soufflés. For breakfast, he usually had Krispy Kreme doughnuts or bacon, egg and cheese sandwiches. "No vegetables, no fish," his wife said. "He didn't deny himself anything. He just lived the life he wanted to live." Although he did not exercise at all, he stood 6-foot-1 and weighed 165 pounds.

A fire truck from Engine Company 55 carries the coffin of Firefighter Robert Lane, who died in the collapse of the World Trade Center, to the New Dorp Moravian Church in Staten Island for Firefighter Lane's funeral on December 11.

(*Keith Meyers*)

"After 9/11, I got a lot of letters from his friends, and many of them said they wanted to live their lives more like Bart had lived his."

ADAM RUHALTER
His Necklace Was His Life

Adam Ruhalter wore symbols of the things he cared about on a chain around his neck. There was a small mezuza case for his Jewish heritage. A miniature drumstick for his love of music. An F for Fern, his wife. Pictures of his children, Danica and Ethan. And an eagle for strength.

The necklace was not long enough to hold pictures of all of the children in Plainview, N.Y., but they belonged on it. Their parents remember Mr. Ruhalter from Saturday morning soccer matches, running from one sideline to the other to cheer on both teams.

Even if they were losing, Mr. Ruhalter would yell, "You're doing a great job! You guys are outstanding! What a great game!" said Arnie Price, a friend.

Mr. Ruhalter, 41, had given up dreams of playing the drums professionally and made a career in finance at his wife's request, as a controller at Cantor Fitzgerald. But he found ways to be a wild man, at parties and on the sporting fields.

"He died with very valuable things, valuable things in terms of his life," his wife said. "He had his children around his neck."

GILBERT RUIZ Sr.
Supported His Siblings

Gilbert Ruiz Sr. grew up on Park Avenue in Harlem, one of seven children. His mother had come to New York from Puerto Rico, his half-brother, William Torres Sr., said. After William's father was shot dead on East 112th Street, his mother was left to raise the children alone, William said. So Gilbert dropped out of high school to support the family.

Mr. Ruiz started out as a messenger, his brother said. In those days, the soles of his shoes were perpetually patched with cardboard. Over the years, he worked in a thread factory, the garment district, the kitchen of the Carlyle Hotel and, for the last five years, in the kitchen at Windows on the World. The father of two grown children, he lived alone in the West Bronx.

"Everybody chipped in, but not like my brother Gilbert," Mr. Torres said, looking back on their childhood together. Mr. Ruiz laid down the law in the family, and was respected for it. "We come from a rough neighborhood. But he always tried to do everything that was possible to stay away from all that," Mr. Torres said. Then he added, "That's all he know how to do, just work."

OBDULIO RUIZ-DIAZ
Dreams Come True

Obdulio Ruiz-Diaz talked often of mis sueños—"my dreams." He had come to the United States from Paraguay and said that he wanted a good job, a family and a good home for them.

He dedicated his life to realizing all three goals, said his wife, Rosa Villalba. He brought her to the United States from Paraguay and they had three children: Vanessa, 10, Pamela, 8, and Bryan, 6. Trained as an architect, he found work that he enjoyed as a draftsman and project manager at a New York company, Bronx Builders. And, at 44, he found the house of his dreams, in Valley Stream, N.Y.; they closed the deal on Sept. 6.

"Todos mis sueños se estan haciendo realidad," he said. "All of my dreams are coming true."

With the help of family and friends, Ms. Villalba and her children moved into the house on Sept. 14, but without Mr. Ruiz-Diaz. They celebrated Christmas with the family of his best friend, Manuel DaMota, who was working with him on a project at Windows on the World on Sept. 11. The families set aside two empty chairs in their memory. "Everybody had wet eyes that night," Ms. Villalba said.

MANUEL DaMOTA's portrait appears on page 116.

STEPHEN P. RUSSELL
Taming Fire and Water

Stephen P. Russell was a firefighter who worked wonders with wood. He built furniture and cabinets and once even made a wave-skipping hydroplane that he raced around Jamaica Bay.

Firefighter Russell, of Engine Company 55, also built a display case at his fire station in Little Italy that became a memorial to him and four colleagues who died at the World Trade Center. Black-framed pictures of them now hang there.

Firefighter Russell, 40, grew up in Rockaway Beach, Queens, in a house on the edge of the bay, and he loved the water. He sailed. He water-skied. He became a master scuba diver. The youngest of three sons, he was close to his parents, Marie and Clifford Russell, and except for one brief time when he tried selling penny stocks, he never moved out of the family home.

One New Year's Eve, he began a long romance with Rhonda Cohen, an administrative assistant at Ernst & Young. They traveled to Las Vegas and New Orleans, and

they both loved the cockatiel that he had taught to whistle "Tequila." They never made it to the altar. But they were as much of a couple as a couple could be.

STEVEN H. RUSSIN
A Childlike Wonder

There was something about Steven H. Russin that made his wife, Andrea, think of Tom Hanks's character in the movie *Big*.

"He always saw things a little bit off, like a child would," she said.

She recalled a visit to a gallery in Sarasota, Fla. The couple had no intention of buying any of the expensive artwork, but that did not stop Mr. Russin from questioning the sales staff so intently that they took the couple for serious buyers and invited them to a special back room. There, they drank Champagne.

"The rest of us would've walked on and gotten ice cream," she said. "Steve was the type of person who would start asking all sorts of questions, like a child."

He had plenty of practice with questions from one particular child, his 2-year-old son, Alec Joseph, and he was very excited that Mrs. Russin was pregnant with twins, who were born on Sept. 15.

Early in the morning of Sept. 11, before Mr. Russin went to work at Cantor Fitzgerald, Mrs. Russin sent him to get her a glass of water. Of course, one glass was not enough, she said, laughing.

A mural on the wall of Buddy's Hardware and Yacht at City Island Avenue and Carroll Street in City Island, the Bronx, one of many that appeared throughout the city, as if to replace holiday decorations. This one was painted by Jane Curtin of City Island. (*Angel Franco*)

"He said, 'I probably should've brought the pitcher,' " Mrs. Russin said. "I told him, 'That's O.K., you'll get it next time.' That was the last thing that I said to him."

MICHAEL RUSSO
"I'll Always Come Home"

If storybooks are written about the lives lived before Sept. 11, "Michael and Theresa" will make a good one.

Lt. Michael Russo, 44, was a good-looking man assigned to the elite Squad 1 unit in Park Slope, Brooklyn. His wife, Theresa, is a nurse. Their child, Michael Jr., was born on the same day as his father.

"A fireman and a nurse, it sounds like a big joke," she said. "But I understood his life and he understood mine."

When asked to think back on their life together, Mrs. Russo talked about the time they sang together in the rain. The sails they took together on their little sailboat in the Long Island Sound. The motorcycle rides along the North Shore when the sun shone in their faces and they were happy and knew God had given them something wonderful. "I remember crab cakes and Corona beer and laughing and talking about the future and how good life was," she said.

She visited the wreckage of the World Trade Center the other evening for the first time. She looked at the smoldering pile and thought about what he once told her: "Don't worry, I'll always come home." "Even the day after, I thought he would," she explained. "I looked at the pile and I knew he was home.'"

WAYNE ALAN RUSSO
A Trip Unrealized

Wayne Alan Russo never got to Egypt. He had been to China, Japan, Russia, all over Europe—he was planning his eighth trip to Italy for early November—and returned on Sept. 2 from India. But some sort of trouble always blocked the trip to the pyramids.

At home, he led an organized life. He gave blood several times a year, and supported a child in Africa. He took the bus from Union, N.J., where he lived with his parents, every morning at 6:30 to arrive early for his accountant's job at Marsh & McLennan. He went to almost every Giants' home game since Giants Stadium opened in 1976 with his father, Arthur Russo. And there were the Yankees. He and his family saw them beat the Red Sox on Sept. 8.

On Sept. 11 Mr. Russo, 37, was to have had dinner with Cheryl Marx, who had been in the group that went to New Delhi, Jaipur and Agra. They never got to exchange photos. But they did receive each other's postcards, sent from India on that last trip. Each said "Egypt next year."

JOHN J. RYAN Jr.
A Born Equity Trader

For John J. Ryan Jr., going to work on Wall Street was a natural: his father, John Sr., had been an equity trader. So, in due course, was his younger brother Patrick.

"It was in the blood," said Patrick Ryan, who works for J. P. Morgan. "We all have the personality where we get on with people, which you need. That and a sense of humor. And I guess we all like the energy you get on Wall Street."

John Ryan Jr.—known to his friends as J.R.—began his lifelong commute to downtown Manhattan at the age of 14, when he traveled from Suffern, N.Y., to attend Xavier High School on West 16th Street. Later, after graduating from Holy Cross College, he began work at a bank. At age 45, he was still commuting, from West Windsor, N.J., where he lived with his wife, Patricia, and their three children, to a job as an equity sales trader for Keefe, Bruyette & Woods.

In an age of electronic trading, Mr. Ryan prided himself on an old-fashioned relationship with his long-standing clients. "He was very customer-oriented," said Mrs. Ryan, who also once worked on a Wall Street trading desk. "He learned the right way, from the old school."

Those clients may not have known a few other things about Mr. Ryan: his fanatical devotion to the rock band the Who, or how he could easily have become a history teacher or a high school coach. He may have worked hard, but he was still a "hands-on father," Patrick Ryan said.

JONATHAN S. RYAN
The Envelope Please

Colin Jonathan Ryan was born on Oct. 2, 2001. He will never know his father, Jonathan S. Ryan, who died at the World Trade Center on Sept. 11, 2001.

Mr. Ryan, 32, who worked at Euro Brokers and lived in Bayville, on Long Island, wanted a name for his boy that had his initials, J.S.R.—like Jake Spencer Ryan or some such. In his absence, his wife, Maria, chose Colin.

"Our daughter, Autumn, just started calling her unborn brother Baby Colin," she said. "It seemed to fit." There are many things Mrs. Ryan is going to tell her son about his father.

"I want him to know how many people his dad touched," said Mrs. Ryan, 31. "Daddy played lacrosse at college. Daddy was a bond broker. Daddy just went to work as usual, trying to make a living for his family."

He was excited that you were coming. He knew you were a boy, but he wasn't sure if he wanted to know. This is how he found out: The doctor wrote down your sex and put it in a sealed envelope. A week later we went out for dinner for our fourth wedding anniversary. He needed two martinis before he could open it.

"When he did he screamed, 'It's a boy!'"

KRISTY IRVINE RYAN
Powers of Persuasion

It was not that Kristy Irvine Ryan was bossy, so much as irresistible. In college, if a friend was homesick, Ms. Ryan would drag him out for a beer. If someone was tired on a Sunday morning, it was Ms. Ryan who persuaded her to go to church.

When her best friend, Meredith O'Neill, said she wanted to get pregnant as soon as she was married, Ms. Ryan ordered her to wait until next June, when she and her husband, Brendan Ryan, were planning to conceive.

"She said she could see the two of us sitting by the pool, in our ninth month, when you're allowed to have a glass of wine," Ms. O'Neill said.

June would have been one year after the Ryans' wedding, which came after years of courtship.

"Are you sure you're going to go through with this?" the men on Ms. Ryan's trading desk at Sandler O'Neill & Partners would tease when her future husband called. "Dead man walking," they would say jokingly, knowing how tough Ms. Ryan, 30, could be.

There was never a question that the two, who grew up in Huntington Bay, N.Y., would be married, even though Ms. Ryan had left the area for college. Right after graduation, she informed her friends. "But you're not even dating Brendan Ryan," Ms. O'Neill pointed out.

The two of them went to Europe for the summer. When they returned, Ms. O'Neill recalled, there was Mr. Ryan at the airport, flowers in hand.

MATTHEW RYAN
Calming Instructions

Since his birth early in 2000, Michael Quinn has learned to enjoy many things, but moments with his grandfather Matthew Ryan were highlights. The two played ball. They walked. They collaborated in the gloriously messy business of washing cars, outside the Ryan home in Seaford, N.Y.

Mr. Ryan's wife, Margaret, said Michael "would take the hose, squirt it all around, squirt the car, squirt Grandpa. Mostly he just got himself soaked."

Matthew Ryan, 54, loved all things Irish and all things family. He also loved to listen to the disc jockey Vin Scelsa play classic rock on the *Idiot's Delight* show on radio, and loved playing or watching hockey.

Matthew Ryan's 28-year career took him from Engine Company 280 in Brooklyn, to Engine Company 43 in the Bronx, where he was a lieutenant, back to Engine Company 280 as captain and then to Manhattan in September 2000 as a battalion chief. In the heat of a fire, he would whisper calming instructions in younger firefighters' ears, Mrs. Ryan said. "They always felt more confident when Matty was on duty."

On Saturday evenings, many members of Engine 280 still listen to *Idiot's Delight*.

THIERRY SAADA
Belly Button Melodies

When Thierry Saada came to New York in 1999 from Paris, he sublet Delphine Zana's apartment through mutual friends in the Sephardic Jewish community. Both their families were originally from Tunisia, but moved to France after Tunisian independence. Mr. Saada was tall, handsome, and "sportif," she said, and they fell in love.

In November 2000, they married, and Mrs. Saada became pregnant. Mr. Saada was so excited he played Tunisian music and sacred Sephardic melodies for his unborn child, and he would "talk to my belly button," she said. Mrs. Saada was scared about the delivery, but "he said we would be together, that he would push with me."

On Sept. 11, Mr. Saada, 26, a trader at Cantor Fitzgerald, was on the 104th floor of 1 World Trade Center. The baby was due on Sept. 16, but Mrs. Saada did not go into labor. "I was hoping he would come back," she said. In the end, the labor was induced, and on Sept. 27, their son, Lior—"my light" in Hebrew—was born, with Mrs. Saada's mother, Dolly, and sister-in-law, Carole, at her side.

THOMAS SABELLA
No Stranger to Heroism

Thomas Sabella, a firefighter with Ladder Company 13, was no stranger to heroism. In 1998, he ran up six flights of stairs in a burning Upper East Side tenement and rescued a man who was leaning out of a fifth-floor window. The city honored him for his bravery the following year.

His wife, Diana, who met her husband at Susan Wagner High School in Staten Island when she was just 16, accepted his choice of a high-risk occupation. "I never really worried," she said. "I always knew that he knew what he was doing, and that he would do his best."

Mr. Sabella, 44, had many hobbies. He went skiing and snowboarding with his daughter Nicole, 10. He grew tomatoes and cucumbers in his Staten Island garden, and he made his own red wine, giving away bottles as holiday gifts.

Their son James, 6, used to have an ambition shared by many little boys. These days, his mother said, "he says, 'I was going to be a fireman, but I don't know, now.'"

SCOTT SABER
Driven to Make Friends

Scott Saber was not famous, and he was probably not even the biggest spender at Wollensky's Grill in Midtown, one of his favorite spots for entertaining clients. But when news spread around the restaurant that he had been on the 106th floor of 1 World Trade Center on Sept. 11 and was among the missing, several members of the staff wrote memorial notes to send to his family. It wasn't a surprise.

"I'm sure that nearly everybody in that restaurant knew him by name because he schmoozed with all of them, from the busboys on up," said Mr. Saber's oldest brother, Bruce. "That was Scott."

It was a kind of theme in Mr. Saber's life. When he made acquaintances, it was not casually. When he made friends, they became like family. A friend recently became ill during a trip to Boston, and Mr. Saber, who worked for UBS Warburg, offered to drive up and get him.

"He was not kidding," said his brother. When it came to his family, Mr. Saber, 37, was unwavering. His other

Sixth-grade students from St. Jude's School in Manhattan sing for firefighters at Engine Company 84 on 161st Street on December 13, and give them gifts of appreciation. (*Matt Moyer*)

brother, Brian, recently adopted a baby from Vietnam. Upon returning to the city, Brian Saber learned that he was not going to be able to return to his own apartment. So for six months, Mr. Saber had shared his small, two-bedroom apartment on the Upper East Side with his brother and the 6-month-old baby.

JOSEPH SACERDOTE
Sadness for a Family Man

Friends and family called him Joe Sas, a way around a mouthful of syllables. Joseph Sacerdote was a Brooklyn boy who loved to joke, a guy who ate a dozen garlic cloves on a bond trader's dare and who called a cousin's neighbor named Crystal "Cut Glass." His sister Jane McMillan said he would call her at work and pretend he was a nut on the phone, or leave an urgent message to call back and, when reached, would ask, "The word accommodate, one M or two?"

A vice president of Cantor Fitzgerald's eSpeed division, Mr. Sacerdote, 48, loved going on offbeat vacations with his wife, Arlene, and daughters, Alison and Andrea, like the visit to Dollywood, Dolly Parton's theme park in Pigeon Forge, Tenn. The family obsession was roller coasters. His was karate, and he was proud of his black belt. His locker at Hwang Karate in Freehold, N.J., has been retired.

It would be nice to say that Mr. Sacerdote died the same happy-go-lucky man. But he did not. Alison, 15, died of a brain tumor last April despite 21 operations and Mr. Sacerdote's wild determination to find a cure.

Her husband was not the same, Mrs. Sacerdote said. "He tried, but everybody knew it was just a front."

JESSICA SACHS
Determined to Succeed

Jessica Sachs's schedule since her December 2000 graduation from the University of Massachusetts at Amherst was exhausting.

She had accepted a job at PricewaterhouseCoopers as an accountant and was working long hours there. Every Saturday she went to an eight-hour course for the C.P.A. exam. And on Sundays, as usual, she attended services at New Colony Baptist Church in Billerica, Mass.

"She complained," said Stephen Sachs, her father. "But she did well."

Despite the workload, she did not sleep in on Sunday mornings. She had never let churchgoing slide, even in college. When she realized that UMass, with 26,000 students, had no Southern Baptist ministry, she helped establish Mercy House on campus.

She was equally determined to succeed in worldly terms. She applied for only two jobs, at the first- and second-largest accounting companies, and was offered a place at each. On Sept. 11, she was flying from Boston to Los Angeles on business, her first trip out West.

FRANK JOHN SADOCHA
Nearing a Longtime Dream

Frank John Sadocha was weeks away from his dream of opening his own restaurant on Long Island. He was training people to take over for him as manager of the food services division of Cantor Fitzgerald when the World Trade Center was attacked.

"All he tried to do was to get us ahead," said his wife, Nancy. Mr. Sadocha, who lived in Huntington with his wife and two daughters, did the catering for a local temple on weekends and sometimes weeknights, in addition to his job in the city.

"He was very much in charge, and he knew catering so well," his wife said. But as hard as he worked, Mr. Sadocha, 41, always had time for his daughters, Ashley, 5, and Kristy, 4. In late summer, after they had enrolled the girls on soccer teams, Ashley said she didn't want to play, that she wasn't any good at soccer. Her father took her outside and worked with her.

"He boosted her confidence," Mrs. Sadocha said. "By the end of the weekend she said she couldn't wait to play, and she told me, 'Daddy said I was good.' "

JUDE SAFI
A Heart in the '50s

Jude Safi used to say he wished he had been born in the 1950s. He loved Elvis and Frank Sinatra and vintage clothing. He bought a 1957 Chevrolet pickup a few years ago and restored it, painting it silver.

A few weeks before the World Trade Center was attacked he attended a concert at Madison Square Garden where Elvis's old band played, in front of film clips of the King shimmying and gyrating.

Mr. Safi was only 24, but he had a '50s sensibility, his brother, John, said.

"He knew the words to all the Sinatra and Elvis songs; he watched all their movies. He loved the movies. He knows every movie that's ever been out."

Mr. Safi had been working as a trader for Cantor Fitzgerald for only four months when the towers went down. He got his job through a friend he had known since kindergarten in the Dyker Heights section of Brooklyn, where Mr. Safi still lived with his family. Another childhood friend worked there, too. None of the three have been seen since, John Safi said.

"We didn't just lose my brother, we lost his friends, too," he said.

BROCK J. SAFRONOFF
A Passion for the Lions

Tara Neelakantappa introduced Brock J. Safronoff to classical music; his compact disc collection quickly surpassed hers. She turned him on to reading on the loftier side of Stephen King, and he packed Kafka in their honeymoon suitcase.

"I would introduce him to something and before I knew it he was telling me everything about it," said the woman who on Aug. 4 became Mrs. Safronoff. There was one passion that consumed Mr. Safronoff, 26, long before his freshman year at Amherst College, when he and his future wife were physics lab partners. It was his devotion to the Detroit Lions, which stemmed from his upbringing in Traverse City, Mich., and which required the strength to withstand continual heartbreak, said Michael A. Cohen, a friend and fellow fan.

Their friendship was based on a shared fantasy that the Lions would one day make it to the Super Bowl. When they met to watch games at an Upper East Side bar, they rarely discussed work. Mr. Cohen, in fact, had forgotten Mr. Safronoff worked as a computer programmer at Marsh & McLennan.

"I had to look up on his wedding announcement where it was that he worked," Mr. Cohen said. "I remember now that he told me he had this great view."

EDWARD SAIYA
Minor Fame, Major Fun

The Saiya brothers have a place among the countless lesser-known Brooklyn legends. Frank, Art, Mike and Eddie were known as the Fame Brothers of Dayhill Road, based on the first letters of their names.

The Saiyas were tough boys. They went to Catholic school and they liked their beer. They served in Vietnam. But they were not so tough that they could not say they loved each other. Mike Saiya died a few years ago of liver cancer. Eddie Saiya, 49, was a communications engineer who worked on the 110th floor of 2 World Trade Center.

"He called me that morning from the roof, calm as could be, and told me to turn on the TV," Frank Saiya said. "The first building had been hit. He thought it was an accident."

Edward Saiya had two children, Katherine, 16, and Shawn, 11. Their mother, who has Alzheimer's disease, sometime asks how Eddie is doing, Frank Saiya said. They tell her just fine.

Frank, 60, is the eldest Fame brother. He now lives in Topeka, Kans., and has 20 pounds of the trade center rubble in his home. "Maybe part of Eddie is in there," he said. He's got that and the memory of Eddie Saiya in 1969 chasing down two thieves who had stolen his car. "He wasn't wearing anything but his skivvies."

JOHN P. SALAMONE
Scoring One for Dad

The death of John P. Salamone is hard for his wife and worse for his children. He had three: Alex, 6, Aidan, 4, and Anna 3. "They have their good days and bad days," said his wife, Mary Ellen. "Halloween was awful. John did the trick-or-treating. They missed him. Alex told his teacher that mom tried to make it a happy day for him but he couldn't help but be sad. He missed his dad."

So their mother took them to the hockey game as their father used to do—she thought that would be nice. Then the boys had to go to the bathroom. They just looked at her. "It was like, 'What do we do now?'"

Mr. Salamone, 37, brokered preferred stocks for Cantor Fitzgerald. "He actually loved his job, loved the guys he worked with. But he didn't love anything more than his kids," she said.

He coached the boys soccer team in West Essex, N.J., as well. And it was hard for the boys to look on the sideline and not see their father there. The league shut down for two weeks in honor of his memory. When play resumed, Alex scored the first goal.

HERNANDO R. SALAS
Following His Dream

Hernando R. Salas used to dream of New York City. Back in Cartagena, Colombia, he longed to see the Statue of Liberty. So he and his wife moved here in the 1960s. Their two children quickly followed.

"He was here when they started building the World Trade Center," said their son Carlos. "He always dreamed of working close over there. When he got the job, he was so happy."

Mr. Salas, 71, had worked part time for the past five years as a clerk for the Civilian Complaint Review Board, on the third floor of 40 Rector Street just south of the trade center. Upbeat and gregarious, he never wanted to retire. People who did nothing risked getting Alzheimer's disease, he told Carlos. He didn't want that. He wanted to stay tuned in.

A week before the attack, Mr. Salas visited relatives in Florida. He returned home to Elmhurst, Queens, saying Florida depressed him. It rained all day there, he said; in New York, it rains for a while, then it lifts.

Mr. Salas was found in the street outside the Rector Street building and was taken to New York University

Downtown Hospital, Carlos said. There, he suffered a heart attack and died.

ESMERLIN SALCEDO
Even Off-Duty, a Rescuer

"He said he was sacrificing for the future," said Raysa Rodriguez. By that, she meant her 36-year-old brother, Esmerlin Salcedo, was spending so much time at school and at work that he rarely saw his three young children, Amber, 5, Kayla, 4, and Markos, 1. He left his Bronx home at 7 each morning, arriving downtown an hour later for six hours of computer classes. Afterward, he worked the 3-to-11 shift as a $10.51-an-hour security guard at the World Trade Center.

"He was to graduate in three weeks, with a certificate in computer programming," his sister said. He was in class when the first plane hit, but then he sprinted to the trade center's underground command station. A co-worker, Roselyn Braud, praised him for leading her to safety before disappearing back into the building. "He loved computers, but he really went into computer programming because of the money," his sister said.

"He was supporting four kids—he had a daughter from his first marriage in Florida—and he needed to make a decent living. He was going to give my husband his résumé to give to his employer. But it's still in my computer. He never printed it out."

JOHN S. SALERNO Jr.
Full of Vim and Humor

"Now that I look back, he wasn't cocky, he was just very sure of himself," Danielle Salerno said of her husband, John S. Salerno Jr., a broker at Cantor Fitzgerald. Back in high school, he was the last person she would have said she wanted to date. He was not shy. Once at a New Year's Eve party, she walked past and he pinched her. When she gave him a how-dare-you look, he said, "You liked that, didn't you?"

They both laughed.

Danielle married Pepe (a childhood nickname, inspired by his superabundance of pep). He was loyal and funny; he was generous; and he knew what he wanted. He wanted a family. Ms. Salerno held off for five years while they were living abroad in London and Tokyo. Now their first child is due in March.

"Every night, he'd kiss my belly," Ms. Salerno said.

A few weekends ago, the Salernos, who lived in Westfield, N.J., were in the Hamptons. Someone who knew them well observed that Mr. Salerno, who recently turned 31, was

such a wise guy sometimes, it was a miracle that he had not gotten his tail kicked.

And, Ms. Salerno recalled, "His best friend, Thomas, said that was because, by the end of the night, the guys who wanted to beat him up were buying him shots."

RICHARD SALINARDI
Back Home Every Summer

His parents took a young Richie Salinardi out of New York, but nobody took his New York—the Yankees, the Rangers, the beach—out of the boy. He came home from St. Louis every summer to hang out with his cousins at Point Pleasant Beach, N.J. When the Rangers were winning the Stanley Cup in 1994, he drove up from Washington.

"We couldn't get tickets, but we finally found a bar that was showing it," said a cousin, Rocco Minervini. St. Louis was hardly irrelevant to the life of Richard Salinardi, 32. He was working for Ogden Food Services there in 1992 when a college student, Brittley Wise, asked for a job so she could earn $600 for a trip to Mexico. She got the job, made her trip and three years later they married.

On Sept. 11, Mr. Salinardi was the Aramark Corporation's general manager for food services in the south tower. Instead of pushing his way onto a crowded elevator, he told a co-worker, Gary Angelica, that he and his staff would catch the next one. He was last seen joking with John Gamboni, probably about their plans to fly to Ecuador the next day to see Mr. Gamboni's parents.

PAUL SALVIO
Brooklyn Kid with Heart

Paul Salvio was a neighborhood kid. And if there were two things he got from the neighborhood, they were a street-corner sense of humor and the belief that you don't get something for nothing.

"Paulie shouldn't have been at work that day," said his friend Sandy Mastropaolo. "He was having some minor surgery that afternoon, but he said he was going to the office to tie up a few ends anyhow."

Mr. Salvio, 27, was a broker with Carr Futures on the 92nd floor of 1 World Trade Center. He was a funny man and had no quarrel with anyone, Ms. Mastropaolo said. He paid for his oil and gas, and he was a victim in a war that he had nothing to do with.

He lived with his grandmother in Bensonhurst, Brooklyn. His grandmother says her heart is gone now. There will be no more answering machine tapes filled with Paulie's prank calls, no more video tapes of him clowning at a wedding.

But the family will not cry, Ms. Mastropaolo said. "Paulie's mother told me that if he knew he was going to die, he'd want to do it in a big way, like this."

SAM SALVO
A Soft Spot for His Dogs

Sam Salvo loved his Stoli on the rocks and he loved good food. "He was a hefty guy, he could eat a lot," said his daughter, Sue. "He knew the best restaurants, everything." "Anything he does is the best," Ms. Salvo said with a fond laugh, speaking of her father as if he were still alive.

Mr. Salvo, 59, had reason to feel confident. He had worked his way up from nothing to become a vice president of Aon, the insurance company that had offices on the 105th floor of 2 World Trade Center.

But Mr. Salvo had his soft side, too. He was almost ridiculously fond of his dogs. There was Dallas, the Weimaraner who, when she stood on her hind legs, was nearly 5 feet 10 inches, and then there was the mutt, Amber.

The Salvo children are grown: David is 29 and Sue is 27. So on weekends, Mr. Salvo would take the dogs instead of the kids on car rides, and at night he and his wife, Gladys, would let the dogs sleep on the bed. "The two dogs were like his little babies," his daughter said.

RENA SAM-DINNOO
A Full Life, Each Second

Her day would start at 4 A.M., when she would rise to make coffee for her husband before he left for work, and would not end until after she had watched the 10 o'clock news. In the intervening hours, Rena Sam-Dinnoo would study for her undergraduate degree at Pace University, cook some dinner for her husband, Andy, work a full day in the accounting division of Marsh & McLennan and attend classes at night.

It was not that she was without help—except for the cooking, her husband, who races horses professionally, would do all the housework. It was simply that she "was a very hardworking person," in the words of her sister, Gina Sam. Originally from Trinidad, Ms. Sam-Dinnoo had just finished her degree and was looking forward to going on to a master's and becoming an accountant, her relatives said.

"She was never a dull person," Mr. Dinnoo said. "She is well educated, and loved to talk, really about anything." He said that he and his wife had not seen much of each other lately because he had been away on business for the six weeks

before Labor Day, and then she had gone to Boston that last weekend to pick apples with relatives.

"We went shopping together to buy groceries on Monday night," he said. "Monday night is the last time we went out together."

MICHAEL SAN PHILLIP
A Grandfather-to-Be

On Memorial Day, Michael San Phillip got the news he had waited years to hear. His oldest daughter, married 11 years, was about to make him a grandfather for the first time. The discovery reduced him to tears, no small task for a man who had spent 34 years rising in the rough and tumble world of Wall Street finance.

Though he had catapulted himself to vice president at Sandler O'Neill & Partners, an investment house on the 104th floor at 2 World Trade Center, the title he craved was that of grandfather. It was as big a moment as if he had won one of his beloved tennis and paddle matches, the ones he has for decades been so devoted to organizing. Folks in Ridgewood, N.J., had nicknamed him Captain Paddle.

"He was really looking forward to seeing his first grandchild in December," said Jill Abbott, Mr. San Phillip's daughter. "He had the hope in his heart that it would be a little boy, a little Mikey."

SYLVIA SAN PIO RESTA's portrait appears with John Resta on page 417.

HUGO SANAY-PENAFIEL
Famous for His Lechon

In his native Ecuador, Hugo Sanay-Penafiel's great enjoyment came not from his job as a firefighter, but from the free hours at home when he could cook. He was a family celebrity for his lechon, a dish in which pork is prepared with spices and condiments the day before the meal and then spends four or more hours in an oven. On special occasions involving his grandmother, he would make the dish for 20 or more relatives and friends.

In 1986, he and his wife, Clara Rosas, decided to seek a better life in the United States. She arrived first and got a job sewing sweaters in a factory in Brooklyn. Two years later, when he arrived, his wife's friend found him a job cooking. Mr. Sanay-Penafiel, 41, last worked as a chef for the Wood Dining Service, which fed workers at 2 World Trade Center.

"They lived in an apartment in Brooklyn," said his niece,

Jenny Sanay. "It was not really big: one bedroom for him and his wife, a living room that served as a bedroom for the three children. His dream was to buy a house. He was talking to a broker. They were very close to a house."

JACQUELYN SANCHEZ
T-Shirts for C.J.

When she called her mother as smoke rose around her on the 104th floor at 1 World Trade Center, Jacquelyn Sanchez said she was scared, that she could hardly breathe. Then she asked for her baby.

"She asked me 'Where's my baby?'" her mother, Kim Coleman, said. "I told her, 'I have your baby. Just get out of there.'"

At 23, Ms. Sanchez had a baby boy, Cedric Pitt Jr., a full-time job as compliance assistant with Cantor Fitzgerald and a strong desire to be a criminal defense lawyer. She attended John Jay College of Criminal Justice on weekends in pursuit of a bachelor's degree and planned to go to law school, her mother said.

"That was my child," Ms. Coleman said. "She felt like she needed to save the world."

Ms. Sanchez lived with her son and boyfriend in Manhattan. She had planned a big first birthday celebration for her son, who turned 1 year old on Sept. 17. She had sent out 50 invitations, hired a clown, ordered a cake and had T-shirts made.

When the day came, a smaller-scale party took place in a hallway of her building with children from the neighborhood. There was no clown but they still got the T-shirts.

They read: "I partied at C.J.'s first birthday."

ERIC SAND
Equity-Trading Philosopher

In his college days, Eric Sand was a philosopher and a Deadhead, voted by his fraternity brothers "most likely to come back as an abstract thought." So when he started as a clerk on the floor of the New York Stock Exchange in the mid-'90s, he found the culture a bit jarring. "He hated it," said his long-time best friend, Roger Weisman. "He said a lot of the people were ignorant, obnoxious, boorish."

Before long, however, Mr. Sand "came to understand the mind-set a little better," Mr. Weisman said. It helped that he moved quickly up the ladder and was soon a trader himself.

Last January, Mr. Sand, 36, took a job at Cantor Fitzgerald, trading equities but hoping to move into management, where he could deal more with people and less with numbers, said his wife, Michele Sand. Mr. Sand liked his job, but one of his favorite things about it was that it usually let him get home to Hawthorne in Westchester County in time to tuck in his son, Aaron, who was 18 months old the last time he saw his father.

"He did bedtime five nights a week," Ms. Sand said. "His attitude was, 'You get him all day. I want to play with him, I want to put him to bed.'"

STACY SANDERS
An Expanding Circle

When Stacy Sanders was captain of the crew and swim teams at Andover, she was famous for her "psych notes." They were short missives to her teammates, sent before big meets. They were all meant to uplift, but each one contained a personal detail. They were all signed with a heart next to her name. To her father, John, the notes were one of the many ways she went the extra distance to make others feel at home.

"She went out of her way to make other people feel comfortable," Mr. Sanders said. "With her friends, she would always end their conversations with, 'I love you.' Many of them learned to say that."

She had a large circle of friends, he said. But Ms. Sanders, 25, who had been working on a technology project for Marsh & McLennan at the World Trade Center, also had a knack for befriending her friends' parents, their sisters and brothers, even their grandparents. It was not uncommon, Mr. Sanders said, for her to spend an evening having dinner and seeing a movie with her boyfriend's grandmother, for instance.

Ms. Sanders and her boyfriend, Bryan Koplin, were shopping for rings and considering marriage. "She had an incredible capacity to make herself a part of their families," Mr. Sanders said. "As a consequence, we all became a part of so many families."

HERMAN S. SANDLER
Card Tables and Confidence

Herman S. Sandler was a presence, Thomas F. O'Neill said yesterday. When he walked into a room, you could not fail to notice. He had enormous confidence and a wonderful laugh. He looked like Daddy Warbucks: a tall man with a shaved head. He loved being out on the water—in the Hamptons, in Palm Beach, on his boat. He had a permanent tan.

Mr. Sandler and Mr. O'Neill left Bear, Stearns in 1988 and started their own investment banking firm, Sandler O'Neill & Partners. It opened in a little office on lower Broadway in 1988. The office was furnished with card tables; you unplugged the copying machine to make coffee. When Mr. O'Neill's father, a retired police officer, first laid eyes on it, he said, "You sure you guys aren't making book here?"

Sandler O'Neill grew from seven guys in a makeshift office to some 170 employees occupying the 104th floor of 2 World Trade Center. Mr. O'Neill credits in large part Mr. Sandler's confidence that the firm would succeed.

"He had a favorite expression and he named his boat after it," Mr. O'Neill said. "His favorite expression was 'No problem.' It's just that simple. No problem. That's exactly what he meant.'"

JAMES SANDS Jr.
Underwater Encounters

The four-foot-long grouper was guarding her baby as James Sands Jr. and his wife, Jennifer, swam by in their scuba-diving suits earlier this year, 75 feet below the surface of the Caribbean Sea at Grand Cayman. It was a tense moment, both for the grouper and for Mr. Sands, a budding underwater photographer. The mother fish gave what is known as a grouper shimmy, and the Sandses took their leave, but not before Mr. Sands captured the rare moment on film.

The picture joined a gallery of his work that included a close-up of a barracuda and a portrait of a moray eel baring its teeth.

Mr. Sands, 38, spent most days well above sea level on the 103rd floor of 1 World Trade Center, where he worked as a software engineer for eSpeed. But he was happiest underwater.

The Sandses lived blocks from each other most of their lives but didn't meet until a dating service set them up on a blind date in 1995. They began diving about three years ago, and Mr. Sands had only recently discovered his flair for photographing fish. "They basically just posed for him; it was amazing to watch," Mrs. Sands said.

AYLEEN SANTIAGO
A Family's Compass

Ayleen Arroyo lost her compass on Sept. 11: her mother, Ayleen Santiago. The 15-year-old remembers what her mother taught her: Depend on yourself.

"She was so proud of her daughter, seeing her make something of herself," said Carlos Albert, Ms. Santiago's brother. "The proudest moment of her life was watching Ayleen go off to Brooklyn Tech high school. There aren't too many Hispanics there, and she made it beyond the odds."

Ms. Santiago, 40, of Brooklyn, was a mother of two, including a 16-month-old boy, and a computer consultant at Blue Cross and Blue Shield. She was the daughter of a single mother of four. She grew up in Park Slope and Sunset Park, and watched her mother work hard without

breaking. Seeing that made her a steely woman, Mr. Albert said.

She was a good parent. She was strict about her curfew, and limited the blocks her daughter could travel. "I tell my niece, 'Keep doing it like your mother was still here,'" Mr. Albert said. "Her dream was for my niece to become a lawyer."

KIRSTEN R. SANTIAGO
Kindness for Strange Dogs

Perhaps Kirsten R. Santiago's favorite wedding gift from her husband was Lady Sailor, a good-natured American bulldog. Her husband, Peter, later adopted a second dog to keep Sailor company; the couple took the dogs everywhere.

One Sunday every month Mrs. Santiago, 26, who worked for Insurance Overload Systems in the World Trade Center, drove Sailor from their home in the Bronx to the Hudsonview Nursing Home in North Bergen, N.J., to play with patients and try to help them recover.

Sailor had been certified by Bright and Beautiful Therapy Dogs Inc., as sufficiently well trained and friendly to play safely with people suffering from Alzheimer's and other illnesses, said June Golden, founder and president of the company. Mrs. Santiago was one of the most reliable volunteers, Ms. Golden said. Several of the therapy dogs attended a memorial service for Mrs. Santiago on Saturday, Ms. Golden said.

Now, Mr. Santiago said, he has to take care of two dogs by himself. "It's a big challenge," he said. "But I can't let them go."

MARIA THERESA SANTILLAN
Busy with Wedding Plans

Maria Theresa Santillan, known to her family as Maritess, was the meticulous, well-organized type. A customer service representative with eSpeed, she had been busy since the previous November planning a wedding scheduled for May 2002.

Her mother, Ester Santillan, said her 27-year-old daughter had filled up a binder with information about every detail—music, reception, flowers, photographer, wedding gown, church—and by the time she disappeared from the 103rd floor of 1 World Trade Center everything except for the invitations was set.

"She was smart, beautiful, a very loving daughter," said her mother. "She had the kind of smile that lit up a room whenever she walked in."

Ms. Santillan, who had two younger brothers and still lived in the family home in Morris Plains, N.J., planned to invite 250 people to celebrate her wedding to Darren Sasso, a civil engineer who had been her boyfriend since high school. The wedding was to have taken place at the Cathedral Basilica of the Sacred Heart in Newark.

Ms. Santillan had wanted to release doves after her wedding to symbolize love and peace. After her memorial service, six doves were released into the sky.

CHRISTOPHER SANTORA
Like Father, Like Son

Like his buddies, Christopher Santora played stickball and basketball growing up in Long Island City. Unlike them, he rooted not for the Mets or the Yankees but for the Toronto Blue Jays. He thrived on holding different opinions—"He would always argue," said his father, Al Santora. And he traded friendly putdowns, as Richard Grech, his oldest friend, remembered. "If you said something stupid, he was all over you."

The other thing he loved was being a firefighter, following his father, a retired deputy chief. After he graduated from Queens College, he was a substitute teacher. But he turned down a permanent job at Junior High School 10.

His hard training helped him earn a perfect score on the Fire Department's physical exam, to go with the 100 on the written test. He joined the department in February. Just after 9 A.M. on Sept. 11 his father took a call from Engine Company 54, saying he should come back to work.

But even though his shift had just ended, Firefighter Santora, 23, had already jumped back on his truck and set off for the World Trade Center.

JOHN, SANTORE
Spoiling the Girls

When the Santores traveled, a few things always accompanied them: candles and two Champagne glasses wrapped in a towel. The candles were store-bought; the glasses were a relic. They were the same glasses John A. Santore and Frances Scarselli used to drink to their happiness the night he asked her to marry him. Mr. Santore asked the waiter if he could keep them.

Both the candles and the glasses were necessary tools for Mr. Santore, a firefighter with Ladder Company 5 on Staten Island, the father of two girls, 20 and 13, and a romantic.

"He would set the table with the candles and the flowers and the wine and then cook for us," Mrs. Santore said. "We are three girls in the home, so he would always spoil us."

On weekend mornings, Mr. Santore would run to a deli to buy coffee and croissants for the family so they would not have to cook. During the week, he would often surprise his wife with a bunch of wildflowers.

When someone mentioned the need for a maritime museum on Staten Island to honor John Noble, a famed local artist, Mr. Santore, 49, formed what he called the Noble Crew to build it, his wife said. "He was wonderful with his hands," she said. 'There was nothing he couldn't do."

ROY SANTOS
Still a Tourist

Roy Santos was a perpetual tourist in the city that he loved. He had lived in New York for nearly six years, but still relished it. His mother, Aurora, called him "a Broadway addict." He had to get tickets to all the latest shows, loved *The Producers,* loved *The Lion King.* On the memorial Web page Mr. Santos's friends created, there are photographs of him against the New York skyline, the Statue of Liberty, the World Trade Center.

Over Christmas 2000, his brother Ronald and Ronald's wife, Rosemary, stayed with him on the Upper East Side. It was a typical Roy good time. They saw *Cabaret,* had Christmas brunch at the Marriott Hotel's revolving restaurant, and spent the rest of the day in Central Park, playing in the snow. On New Year's Eve they were supposed to go to Times Square, but Roy Santos got the flu.

It was the second year in a row that he had gotten sick and missed it. "Next year, I'll be ready," he told his brother. On Sept. 11, Mr. Santos, 37, was at the trade center again. This time, Mr. Santos, a computer consultant for Accenture, was working.

VICTOR J. SARACINI
Making Moments Count

As a veteran pilot for United Airlines, Victor J. Saracini placed great stock in paying attention to time. But as a father to his two daughters, the concept of time—or rather, maximizing the limited amount of it he had—took on an almost transcendent meaning.

Thank goodness, then, that Mr. Saracini, 51, a former Navy pilot, was about the most reliable person you could ever meet, and always thinking of his daughters, Kirsten, 13, and Brielle, 10, according to his in-laws, Bernard F. and Bernadette G. Hildebrand. "He taught them computers even before they could count, basically," Mrs. Hildebrand said about Mr. Saracini, who was the pilot of United Airlines Flight 175.

Once, Kirsten used her allowance money to buy a souvenir in Pennsylvania. After she paid for the item, she counted the change. Satisfied, she said, "Thank you," and picked up the package. "What kid would do that?" Mrs. Hildebrand said.

Mr. Saracini beamed, too, when his daughters did practice flight plans with him, or learned to read a compass. "He was very thorough with everything," Mr. Hildebrand said. "One time, he called to say, 'You won't have to worry about a thing if anything ever happens to me. The girls will be taken care of.'"

KALYAN K. SARKAR
Building Bridges and Family

The idea of constructing things for the Port Authority of New York and New Jersey was so fundamental to Kalyan K. Sarkar, a 53-year-old civil engineer, he would have found the destruction of two skyscrapers unimaginable.

"He is a man who spent his life building—bridges and tunnels and just about anything the Port Authority put up," said his son Kishan, who was looking forward to his father's birthday party two Saturdays from now.

The family finds some hope in the fact that Mr. Sarkar really knew buildings. He phoned his wife, Anarkali, from Tower 1 to explain that he and 12 of his co-workers were trapped on the 64th floor, the elevators were sealed, and they were headed to the stairs. Then he was cut off. Kishan, a computer programmer in New Jersey, is grateful that his father asked him to leave work early Monday night to come to their home in Westwood, N.J., to help his father with some Web site work.

"I was lucky to be there," he said.

GREGORY SAUCEDO
Speaking His Mind

Gregory Saucedo was marching in the St. Patrick's Day Parade last year when he came across some men he knew. "He said, 'This guy's a great guy, this guy's a great guy, this guy I just don't like,'" said Dave Simoes, a childhood friend and fellow firefighter.

Firefighter Saucedo, who happened to be the self-proclaimed bench-press champ of the Ladder Company 5 station house in SoHo, was not much of a diplomat. But "he was much the same way in telling you that he did like you and what he did like about you," Firefighter Simoes said.

After losing both his parents, Firefighter Saucedo drew strength from ties to his three older brothers. On his muscular arm he displayed a tattoo of a gnarly oak tree with four outsized branches, and in his life he displayed absolute candor. Strength and devotion are cousins, and Firefighter Saucedo was the kind of guy who would jog with a hangover.

Now his brothers collect scraps of information about the time Firefighter Saucedo spent inside the World Trade Center, documenting the way that cultivated strength was put to its final use. "The last 90 minutes of his life were extremely important," said Christopher Saucedo. "The family is wrapped up in that moment of terrible sadness and tremendous pride."

At least, he said, there is "nobody wondering, 'How did Greg feel about me?'"

SUSAN SAUER
An Inveterate Traveler

Susan Sauer set goals for herself, and that applied to her wanderlust. She decided that she was going to have visited 50 countries by the time she turned 50. That meant by November of this year. By her count, she had been to 48 by last summer.

And an itinerary was in hand for a trip last fall that would have put her over the top. Her good friend, Clare Doyle, had to admit it was perhaps the wackiest itinerary she had ever heard of, but it did the job. Ms. Sauer was going to fulfill one dream by attending cooking school in Italy, a country she had already been to, then was going to stop for one day in Hungary, which would be number 49, before winding up in Wales, number 50.

Ms. Doyle teased her about whether Wales, being part of the United Kingdom, could rightfully count as a separate country, but she pointed out that Ms. Sauer had been to Czechoslovakia when it was one country, so maybe the math was O.K.

Ms. Sauer, a managing director at Marsh Inc., lived in Chicago and was attending a meeting at the World Trade Center on Sept. 11. She had five nephews, whom she adored and treated as the perfect aunt would. A new interest was golf, which she had taken up a couple of years ago, in part stimulated by the fact that one nephew was in college on a golf scholarship. She was planning to participate in a golf trip to the Dominican Republic this month, and by then who knew how many countries she would have been to.

ANTHONY SAVAS
Refusing to Retire

Anthony Savas had seen a lot as a young man. He had served in Korea, where he saved a friend who stepped on a land mine. "He wasn't one who wanted to see the world particularly," said Phaedra, his wife of 42 years. "He had seen enough of it."

Instead, Mr. Savas was content moving between his home in Astoria, Queens, his job as a construction inspector with the Port Authority and his beach house on Long

Island's North Fork. "He was 72, but he refused to retire," Mrs. Savas said. "Every couple of years he'd tell me that he'd retire in a couple of years."

He looked at least a decade younger than his age. He worked out on a rowing machine. He loved cigars. He woke at 5:45 every morning to head for work.

"He was a very up guy," his wife said. "If I fought with him, he would never stay angry. He would come back with something to make me laugh and forget about it."

Most of all he loved going to his beach house with his three children and two grandchildren. "Every morning when we were there, he would march to the flagpole with Jessica—she's almost 3—and they'd plant the flag," Mrs. Savas said. "He used to just put out the flag on holidays, but when he was with Jessie he'd do it every day. I don't know why. Sure, he was patriotic, but I guess it was also a way to bond with Jessie. We're trying to save pictures and mementos to keep him alive for her."

VLADIMIR SAVINKIN
Young but Mature

When Vladimir Savinkin came to the United States almost six years ago from Ukraine, attending Pace University at 16, none of his friends knew his real age, said his father, Valeriy Savinkin. "He was more mature than all his friends, who were actually 19 or 20," he said. "He was very, very responsible and reliable."

Olga Lerman, Vladimir Savinkin's girlfriend of four

years, said they met in a Russian chat room on the Internet. "I really liked how he was talking. He was very polite. I liked that in a guy," she said. When they met three weeks later, "It was love in the first place."

Their birthdays are a day apart in May, so they always celebrated together. They had spoken about marriage, she said, and had planned a vacation to Odessa, the city they were from. "He was the leader of our group," she said, the one who most often made the plans for their clique of four young couples.

Mr. Savinkin, 21, was an accountant with Cantor Fitzgerald, and lived with his parents and sister in Midwood, Brooklyn. He had recently bought a new Acura, impressing his father.

ROBERT SCANDOLE
An Emptiness at Halloween

This year, Sheila Scandole carved the pumpkin for Halloween, a job that had always fallen to her husband, Robert Scandole. But he is not here anymore, so with a little help, she carefully etched a spider on a pumpkin.

And when she took their two daughters out trick-or-treating in their Pelham Manor neighborhood in Westchester County, she could not help but think about him. "He would have been right there with us," she said. "I felt horrible, but I tried to carve the pumpkin the best that I could. I wanted to make it real special."

Mr. Scandole, 36, a trader with Cantor Fitzgerald, doted on the girls, Emma, 4, and Katie, 2. He worked on Wall Street, but he always clung to his old neighborhood, in Breezy Point, Queens, even taking part in a basketball league with some of the guys he grew up with. He and Sheila met at Breezy Point, where their parents still live. "I lost the greatest love of my life," she said.

JOHN G. SCHARF
The Big Kid of the Family

At a family reunion in Manorville, N.Y., last summer, John G. Scharf was sprayed in the face from a watergun-waving posse of young, giggling cousins. A former Marine Corps sergeant, Mr. Scharf couldn't let them get away with that.

"It wasn't just retaliation, it was double retaliation," said his sister-in-law, Kim Scharf. "He wouldn't let the kids win." At 29, Mr. Scharf was the second oldest of five children, but he remained the "big kid" of the family.

His encounters with life constantly earned their laughter. A favorite tale is the one about how he tangoed with a squirrel while trying to place a birdhouse in a tree in the backyard.

At 11:03 A.M. on December 14, a fire call came over the radio, and firefighters from Ladder Company 29 and Engine Company 83 rushed from the Bronx school auditorium, leaving Battalion Chief John Quevedo with students honoring the fallen of September 11. (*Don Hogan Charles*)

He dangled back and forth from a limb, with the squirrel on his face, before finally getting the birdhouse just right. The squirrel survived, too.

FRED SCHEFFOLD
After the Shift Ended

Over dinner, Fred Scheffold, chief of the 12th Battalion in Harlem, liked to laugh about fighting fires. Like the time he fell off a fire escape or the time he rescued the skinny man and left the fat one for his partner.

"He never told us the bad stuff," said Kim Scheffold, a daughter. "He loved going into fires and rescuing people and he loved his men."

At home in Piermont, in Rockland County, Chief Scheffold skied, golfed, ran marathons and read everything. He also sculptured logs with a chainsaw, painted furniture in crazy-quilt colors and taught his three daughters to reach high and not give up.

His shift had just ended when the station alarm rang Tuesday morning, Sept. 11, but he jumped into the truck with the others. At 1 World Trade Center, he pushed through crowds to the staircase, intending to climb to the top. The building rumbled. "Doesn't sound good," he said to a friend. But he kept on pushing forward.

SCOTT SCHERTZER
Fan of Phish and Cowboys

Scott Schertzer was a master of many environments. He moved as easily within the dress-casual world of Cantor Fitzgerald's corporate office as he did on the basketball court. He was equally at home in the parking lot at a Phish concert as he was in the rowdy seats at a Dallas Cowboys game. What's that? A New Jersey native rooting for the Cowboys?

"I have been racking my brains for years trying to figure that out," said his father, Paul Schertzer, who still keeps his son's bedroom in Edison exactly as he left it—swathed in Cowboys paraphernalia. "It was a love of his."

Mr. Schertzer, 28, followed Phish to Vermont, Las Vegas and Florida, and amassed hundreds of cassette tapes of concerts.

Mr. Schertzer worked in the human resources department at Cantor Fitzgerald, and had a part in the immediate layoffs of a group of workers on Sept. 10, said his sister, Lori Schertzer. Those employees did not return to work the next day.

At a memorial for victims of his company, Ms. Schertzer said one guest wrote a message above a picture of her brother on the wall: "My hero."

JON SCHLISSEL
A Believer in Fitness

There were a lot of sides to Jon Schlissel, and he was passionate about every one of them. He was religious about maintaining his health, and he exercised nearly every day. At 51, Mr. Schlissel had washboard abs and a physique that was the envy of his friends. He was also a dedicated naturist.

To people who toured historic homes in Jersey City, Mr. Schlissel was the man who owned a 14-room Victorian-style brownstone, painstakingly restored and furnished with items from the Victorian era.

His co-workers at the New York State Department of Taxation and Finance, where Mr. Schlissel worked for 29 years, knew him as a dedicated employee. He last worked as a mediator for the agency, but he also knew how to stir things up. He challenged politicians on a variety of issues, including civil rights for gays, and was the kind of advocate who refused to let term limits stop him from serving in his neighborhood civic association.

"Even when he couldn't be in it anymore, he'd be the one making sure that there was ketchup for everyone when they had a potluck dinner," said his brother, Laurence.

Jon Schlissel was faithful to his 80-year-old mother, Ruth, calling her every Saturday morning and visiting her in Florida twice a year. "My son Larry used to talk from 10 to 11, and then I'd talk to Jonny," his mother said. Now, she said, "At 11, I cry. My nieces and nephews call. They try. No one's going to take Jonny's place."

IAN SCHNEIDER
Loud and Caring

Lost: Ian Schneider, 45, of Short Hills, N.J., a husband, a father of three, a loving son and brother, a quick wit, a Wall Street executive, a swimmer and a golfer, a Brooklyn native who loved the Yankees.

Not least, a mensch who coached boys' and girls' teams and magically touched the lives of hundreds of children with his big, bluff voice and his gentle, understanding guidance.

After 23 years with Cantor Fitzgerald, he was a senior managing director, running staffs of bond traders on the 104th floor of 1 World Trade Center.

But family was his fulcrum—his children, Rachel, 10, Jake, 9, and Sophie, 7; his fraternal twin, Joel, his mother, Terry. But they all had to share him.

For four years, he had coached Little League baseball and the soccer, basketball and softball teams of the Millburn-Short Hills Recreation Department.

"On the field, he had a loud, boisterous voice," recalled

his wife, Cheryl. "You always knew he was out there. But he never lost his temper with the children. He always positively reinforced them. He sent them e-mails with pointers after the games. He complimented kids on other teams. When a kid got hurt, he was the first one on the field. People just felt good being around him."

FRANK SCHOTT
In the Garden, at the Stove

Dina Schott could set her watch by her husband's daily routine. Every morning, Frank Schott was up at 5:20 A.M., on the train to his job in Manhattan at 6:09 A.M., and opening the front door again of their home in Massapequa Park, N.Y., at 7:00 P.M. Then, after working for 10 hours as the assistant vice president for technology at Marsh & McLennan, Mr. Schott began his first chore of the evening.

"He would come home, take off his work clothes, put on a pair of shorts—not even tie his sneakers—and he was out there picking his vegetables," Mrs. Schott said. "I always knew where to find him. The man never rested."

While his wife bathed their three children and put them to bed, Mr. Schott, 39, prepared dinner. Some nights it was Indian food; other nights he made a Spanish entree or a Chinese dish. "I got used to it very quickly," Mrs. Schott said. "What woman wouldn't?"

On weekends, Mr. Schott jogged, rode his bicycle and spent time with his children—sometimes taking them into the office with him if he worked on Saturdays because they loved to ride the trains.

"If he had survived what happened and knew of the hate that I have for what these people did, he'd say, 'Ah, don't be so hard on them,'" Mrs. Schott said. "He would always say, 'You can't judge a whole group of people for the actions of a couple of bad apples.' I know that's what he would say."

GERARD P. SCHRANG
Raising the Roof

Gerard P. Schrang's fantasy from an early age was to say the words "I'm on the job" as a New York City firefighter, according to his wife, Denise Schrang. A few years after high school he made that come true. He went on his last job, with Rescue Company 3 in the Bronx, at age 45 on Sept. 11.

"We were happy," Mrs. Schrang said. "His life was to save and help other people. "He was a simple guy. He loved his family. His idea of a good life was stability, a roof over our head, no fighting," she said of her husband of 25 years, the father of Jacqueline, 22, and Brian Patrick, 19. "On May 10 of 2000, we bought our dream house in upstate New York. We had started the second phase of life."

Mrs. Schrang said she could not bear the thought of going to the house without her husband, an avid hunter and fisherman. But she has gone twice since Sept. 11 and found peace.

"If I give that up, I give up on him and the kids," she said. "We promised each other we would live to be 90. He only made half of that."

Jim Rocchio, a friend, remembers the time that the two of them gave Mrs. Schrang a fit by literally taking the roof off the Schrang home in Holbrook, on Long Island, in a home improvement venture.

Firefighter Schrang was quiet and generous, Mr. Rocchio said. "Here he is, a paid fireman, and he comes out here to help out his community as a volunteer firefighter. He was a good father and a real good friend."

JEFFREY SCHREIER
Adversities Conquered

On Sept. 11, Jeffrey Schreier pushed a mail cart out of the Church Street post office. It was 7 A.M. No time to chat, he told the counterman. He had to get to the Cantor Fitzgerald mailroom. (Mr. Schreier was rarely late in his 19 years as a messenger and mailroom employee there.)

On Sept. 11, Mr. Schreier was a happy man. And he was a successful man, brilliantly so. He was married, quietly but happily, to Phyllis. They lived a simple life in her apartment in Sheepshead Bay, Brooklyn.

"Taking a walk on the boardwalk, or seeing a movie, or seeing a sports game on television, was enough to make him incredibly happy," said his sister, Janice Hart.

He made others happy with his imitations (Shemp of the *Three Stooges* was a specialty) and his dazzling dancing at Cantor holiday parties. Winter was his favorite season, but his personality was like the summer. Maybe the only dark spot was not being able to have children.

Mr. Schreier was brilliantly successful because he had conquered the severe learning disabilities he was born with, unable even to feed himself as a child. But his parents, Holocaust survivors, sent him away to a special school, and he learned to take care of himself. He had a knack for getting from one place to another, hence the messenger job.

"He was so self-sufficient and so independent," Mrs. Hart said. "He wanted to prove to people he could do everything himself."

Then, a wonderful achievement: he earned his high school equivalency diploma. "Next to getting married, that was the greatest thing in his life," Mrs. Hart said.

It hangs, laminated, in a quiet living room.

JOHN T. SCHROEDER
A Sharp Sense of Humor

Everyone at Princeton, it seemed, knew him as Stinky. The nickname was applied to John T. Schroeder, for reasons now unclear, when he visited the campus as a high school lacrosse recruit. In the first week of freshman year, "he was introduced to me as Stinky," a classmate, David Shefferman, recalled, "and I thought he must have been at least a sophomore." The two later played on a national championship team.

Eventually the nickname became the norm. An eating club friend once pointed out the prevalence of nicknames on the lacrosse team and said, "Stinky, you're the only one who doesn't have a nickname."

The nickname stuck as Mr. Schroeder, 31, played lacrosse for clubs while he worked on Wall Street; he joined Fred Alger Management as an equity trader in July. "There were different sides to him and they were all a lot of fun," Mr. Shefferman said.

Friends recall his sharp wit, which he often turned on himself. When his Princeton class wore basketball outfits in a reunion parade, he donned oversize glasses and wildly dribbled a basketball in goofy tribute to a former professional basketball player, Kurt Rambis of the Los Angeles Lakers. One Halloween he was Paul Stanley of the rock band Kiss; another time he made an Elvis costume and found many other excuses to wear it, said his roommate, Kevin Coulter.

"He seemed to celebrate Halloween throughout the year," Mr. Coulter said.

SUSAN L. SCHULER
Working the Land

Many Americans cherish a pampered, well-fed lawn; to Susan L. Schuler, a luxuriant patch of grass was a shameful waste of space. Over the years, Ms. Schuler gradually transformed her standard-issue, quarter-acre backyard in Allentown, N.J., into a dazzling botanical paradise. With help from her husband, Jim, she replaced most of the Kentucky bluegrass with raspberry and blackberry bushes, hordes of climbing roses and row upon row of savory vegetables.

"She was a great nurturer, and gardening was her passion," Mr. Schuler said. "She used me as a soil mover, and I was happy to do it."

A consultant to the securities industry, Ms. Schuler, 55, would put in a full day of work and then plunge into her yard, emerging with armfuls of cut flowers and the ingredients for an elaborate evening meal. On weekends, she would churn out strawberry jam, jalapeño jelly or sinus-clearing

horseradish. An extra freezer held whatever produce the Schulers did not give away.

She would travel into the city most Tuesdays to see one of her clients, Sandler O'Neill, in the World Trade Center. For weeks after Sept. 11, Mr. Schuler could not bear to step into the garden, but as the air grew crisp, he knew he had a duty to fulfill. "I just couldn't let it go," he said. He has since pulled the last of the carrots, tilled the beds and blanketed the asparagus patch with a protective layer of straw.

EDWARD W. SCHUNK
His Turn to Wait

On her way to work each morning, Lisa Schunk would drop off her husband, Edward W. Schunk, at the Baldwin, N.Y., train station in time for the 6:20 to Manhattan. Her car would be there each night as well, waiting as the 6:05 pulled in. Though life was hectic at Cantor Fitzgerald, where her husband worked as a broker, he stepped off the train as if his day were just beginning.

"He would be walking this John Wayne walk," she said. "He was the best-looking man getting off that train, because he would just glow."

Mrs. Schunk spent many of the hours in between preparing meals as a corporate chef. Yet she was still delighted to serve up her husband's favorite Italian dinner by candlelight when they got home. Dessert was typically chocolate pudding or cookie-dough ice cream. "He'd always get three scoops, and I'd say, 'get one-and-a-half,' " she recalled—not that he listened.

They had no children, but at 54, he was often the only adult using the slide at his country club's pool, and he played Santa for his eight nieces at Christmas. No pillow was necessary, thanks to all that ice cream. His wife says that he must be in heaven. "I know he's waiting for me until we meet again," she said.

CLARIN SIEGEL SCHWARTZ
The Family Fixer

Clarin Siegel Schwartz's family expected maybe 200 people at her memorial service; about 700 came. Such was the personal magnetism of Ms. Schwartz, 51, a senior vice president at Aon Consulting Inc. in the World Trade Center.

She was the consummate organizer, always helping others. She was the one who assembled her colleagues at work to go to the gym. (They don't go nearly as often now.) When someone had a sick goldfish, she found goldfish medicine. When someone needed a high-quality florist in Illinois, she found one. When someone was out of a job, she helped there, too, picking up the phone and networking. Her family jokingly called her the fixer, or "consigliere."

"She knew how to get things done and where there were interesting things to do," said her brother, Shepherd Siegel, at her memorial service. He said she knew everything from the best museum exhibits to what to do about jury duty to where to get shoes repaired.

A tax lawyer, Ms. Schwartz liked precision and figuring things out, but she also liked red cars, red dresses, jazz, jelly beans and having fun. She would bake for weeks for her annual balloon party, when people jammed her West 77th Street apartment for a bird's-eye view of the balloons being inflated for the Thanksgiving Day parade. She had season tickets to the ballet and the symphony, but she also adored Rocky and Bullwinkle.

"She never lost her joy and wonder," said her sister, Dr. Hudie Siegel. "She was someone who definitely believed that living well was the best revenge."

JOHN SCHWARTZ
A Lifelong New Yorker

John Schwartz may have spent his childhood in the suburbs, on a rustic property in Alpine, N.J., but by the time he was grown it was clear to his family that he would be a lifelong New Yorker. "It was hard to drag him out to the country to see Mom and Dad," his mother, Joyce, recalled, "because there was always so much in the city that interested him."

He frequented museums and took long walks along the river with his wife, Ching-Ping Peng. In warm weather he could be found on the roof of his apartment house on the Upper West Side, sometimes with a glass of wine in hand, always gazing out at the urban panorama below.

He loved art and music and history. When he traveled abroad, he always knew more about historic sites than most of the other people visiting them.

"If he went to an old monastery, he would walk in and he already knew what to look for, or he recognized the old masters on the walls," his mother said.

MARK SCHWARTZ
"I Could Go to Him"

The hours were grueling: up at 4:30 A.M., home at 7:30 P.M. during the week, plus an overnight shift on Friday and back to work on Saturday at 3 P.M., until 7 A.M. Sunday. But Mark Schwartz, 50, an emergency medical technician, needed money for the house, the family's first, bought three years ago in West Hempstead, N.Y., and the vacations once a year with his wife, Patricia, and two children. The Schwartzes would have been married 25 years on Sept. 19, said their daughter, Jennifer, 23.

"I always knew that I could go to him if I had something

wrong with me, and he'd know a little bit more about it than I did," Jennifer Schwartz said. "It was just like a thrill; he'd get so excited when he was going to help somebody."

Her brother, Andrew, 20, is studying to be a paramedic. "Dad always wanted to be a paramedic, but he never had time to go to school for it," she said. "My brother's going to fulfill his dream."

"It's just hard because my dad went to work that day, and he wasn't sick," she said. "He was going to come home. I guess that wasn't in his plan."

ADRIANE SCIBETTA
Saving a Day for Halloween

Adriane Scibetta was supposed to be on vacation on Sept. 11, the last day of a weeklong break from her job in the accounting department at Cantor Fitzgerald. But she decided to return to work ahead of schedule and save the day to spend Halloween with her children.

She told her older brother, Salvatore Venuto, of her plan in a telephone conversation on Monday night. That his sister was in her office in the World Trade Center that fateful Tuesday was typical of her, Mr. Venuto said, because she had chosen to do something special with her children, 4-year-old Gabriella and 15-month-old Vincent.

Mrs. Scibetta, 31, and her husband, Charles, 35, a mason for the Metropolitan Transportation Authority, settled in Staten Island once they could afford to buy a house. But their ties were still in the old neighborhood—Bensonhurst, Brooklyn—where they were raised and where they met on the playground of Seth Low Junior High School.

Each morning, on the way to work in Astoria, Queens, Mr. Scibetta left the children at his mother-in-law's house, where Italian remains the first language 35 years after Caterina and Petro Venuto emigrated from Calabria. The day before the attack, Gabriella started prekindergarten, with her mother in attendance for the first day of school. That was Mrs. Scibetta's last earthly pleasure, which she recounted with joy to her brother.

" 'She's getting used to it already,' " he said she told him that Monday night. " 'She's such a big girl.' "

RANDOLPH SCOTT
A Motorcycle Payback

For a first date, Randolph Scott splurged. A Broadway show, then a nice restaurant, and then, after learning that his date had a sweet tooth, a trip to Juniors in Brooklyn for cheesecake. "When I was cutting the cheesecake he said, 'By the way, I'm never getting married,' " said his date, known less than two years later as

Denise Scott. He even sold his motorcycle to buy the engagement ring.

A broker-dealer with Eurobrokers in 2 World Trade Center, Mr. Scott lived in Stamford, Conn. He and his wife had three daughters, Rebecca, 18, Jessica, 16, and Alexandra, 12. Their boyfriends called him Big Randy, the fun-loving parent who watched sports on television with them and chaperoned co-ed sleepovers.

Two years ago, Big Randy received a big present. Mrs. Scott, who never forgot his love-inspired sacrifice, gave him a motorcycle for their 20th wedding anniversary. He loved riding it so much, Mrs. Scott said, that during a summer trip to Canada she rode in a van with the girls and his sister's family while he followed behind—"freezing" on his bike.

Mrs. Scott said her husband seemed like such a kid that many people were surprised to learn he was 48. Some people teased him about being the only man in a house with four women (and a female dog, Whitney). Mr. Scott, who grew up with his mother and four older sisters in Brooklyn, would reply, "As long as I have my own bathroom, I'm fine."

CHRISTOPHER JAY SCUDDER
The Gadget Guru

Christopher Jay Scudder loved his gadgets. He had two Palm Pilots and a Handspring Visor. He had music mixers, printers, a digital camera, four computers, two cellphones and eyes on more.

"He was a gadget guru," said Naomi Lauture, his girlfriend of two years. "You talk about someone who was into gadgets."

When Ms. Lauture got an iPaq hand-held computer for work, Mr. Scudder set it up for her and began playing with it. Three days later he had one of his own.

Mr. Scudder, 34, worked as a computer technician for EnPointe Technologies and spent two days a week in the trade center working for a client there. He grew up in Spring Valley and lived in Monsey with Salisha, his daughter from a previous relationship. Salisha is now being raised by his mother, Elzoria, said Adriane Scudder, his sister.

"He was the mother and the father," Ms. Scudder said. "He went to the PTA meetings. He took her to church two, maybe three services on Sunday. He wanted to make sure his daughter got the best of everything."

ARTHUR WARREN SCULLIN
A Schmoozer Extraordinaire

Arthur Warren Scullin schmoozed with everyone, even telemarketers. "He never hung up on them," said Mr. Scullin's widow, Cathy. "He'd ask them where they were calling from. He would ask them what the weather was like, what time it was."

His gregariousness could get on the nerves of his chil-

dren, Warren, Jim and Nora, when they were younger. When everyone else was, say, cruising through the tollbooth at the Throgs Neck Bridge, they would be sitting there because their father was chatting up the toll taker.

As a senior vice president and director of taxes at Marsh Inc., Mr. Scullin, 57, traveled all over the world. Naturally, he talked to everyone he met. "He would ask people, 'Do you know anybody in New York?' " Mrs. Scullin recalled. "If they said no, he would say, 'You do now,' and he'd give them his business card."

Born in Woodside, Queens, Mr. Scullin met his wife at the Lowery Street subway station of the Flushing IRT 36 years ago, and together they migrated to Auburndale, Queens. Every week, Mr. Scullin would return to Woodside to visit his mother, Ethel, 90. "He used to say that when he retired, he was going to move back to an apartment in Woodside so he could return to his roots," Mrs. Scullin said. "I would say, 'I'll send you a postcard from Arizona.' "

MICHAEL SEAMAN
Smile at the Finish Line

Swimming was not among the many talents of Michael Seaman. He was a runner, a basketball player, a tennis player—and a gifted father, husband and friend. But a swimmer? Uh, no.

So when he told people that he was taking swimming lessons—at age 40—to compete in a triathlon last summer, his good friend Tommy Corrigan razzed him a bit. "I said, 'Michael, you don't take lessons to compete in a triathlon; you take them to learn to swim,' " Mr. Corrigan recalled. "And he said, 'Yeah, I know. But I'm going to do it.' "

That answer might as well have been Mr. Seaman's mission statement. It was how he excelled at Cantor Fitzgerald, how he could afford a house in Manhasset, on Long Island, for his wife and three children. "He had a pretty disciplined, strict regimen," said his wife, Dara Seaman. "But he did it all with a smile."

The Seaman family now cherishes a photograph taken at the finish line of the Montauk Triathlon, which includes a one-mile swim. It captures the smile that Michael Seaman allowed himself for another goal met.

Mrs. Seaman said: "The whole zeal—it's on his face."

MARGARET SEELIGER
A Mother's Leanings

Margaret Seeliger gave up her place on a crowded elevator leaving the 100th floor of 2 World Trade Center to two colleagues, an act of generosity that surprised neither her husband nor the oldest of her eight siblings. Worrying about others was her way.

Mrs. Seeliger, 34, worked long hours as head of the student health division for Aon Insurance. Yet most weekends she and her husband, Bruce, were on a plane—either to Buffalo to visit her mother, 64, who is in the advanced stages of Alzheimer's disease, or to Rochester, Philadelphia, Atlanta or California to see one of her 11 nieces and nephews—whoever had a special soccer game or a role in a play.

With her 40-year-old sister, Beth Schlehr, who lives in Georgia, Mrs. Seeliger saw to the smallest details of her mother's care: manicure appointments, clothes shopping and maintaining family traditions. She so fully filled her mother's shoes—and so resembled her—that Mrs. Seeliger was known to her nieces and nephews as "grandma."

"She doted on those kids," Bruce Seeliger said.

She even served as delivery-room coach when Mrs. Schlehr had the first of her three children.

Mr. Seeliger said that he and his wife had not yet made "the kiddie decision" because of the demands of their jobs and the cost of life in Manhattan.

But Mrs. Schlehr knew better. Margaret Seeliger, precise in all things, had intended to start trying to get pregnant in November and had already laid claim to the cribs and baby clothes in her sister's basement.

JASON SEKZER
Campers, United

Jason Sekzer started going to Camp Sussex as a boy, one of hundreds of city children who grabbed the chance to spend part of each summer in the country in New Jersey. Then, bit by bit, the camp became an ever larger part of his life. He graduated from camper to waiter, waiter to kitchen helper and finally to chef.

"He used to say that he could cook for 400 but he couldn't cook for 2," recalled Robert Silver, executive vice president of Camp Sussex.

After he got a job at Cantor Fitzgerald, and could no longer spend summers at the camp, Mr. Sekzer joined its board of directors.

"It was something special," said his wife, Natalie Makshanov-Sekzer, 31, whom he had met there; the couple married in January. "The camp and the friends we made there were a major support to me after Sept. 11," she said.

Mr. Sekzer, 31, the son of a New York City police officer, began at Cantor Fitzgerald as a clerk and worked his way up to vice president.

"Every year he got promoted; he was doing very well," his wife said.

Once a year, Mr. Sekzer combined his job and his camp: he invited executives from Cantor Fitzgerald to play in a charity golf tournament raising money for Camp Sussex.

MATTHEW SELLITTO
Letters to a Son

She uses a black fountain pen or a red quill. Loreen D. Sellitto fills the white pages of a journal with words to her son, Matthew, 23, who traded his snowboard for Brooks Brothers suits when he went to work for Cantor Fitzgerald in February on the 105th floor of 1 World Trade Center.

Sept. 22: It's been two weeks since that terrible day. Even when the towers collapsed, I felt you were out. After all, you are strong, young and determined. Matthew, you are my first born and my strength and my hero.

Oct. 2: Please guide me in finding ways to honor your values and determination the best way possible. We owe you this. I love you, Mom.

Oct. 9: Remember, you were the kid who always beat the odds? You were so savvy and smooth, always thinking out the consequences before acting or not acting. I always marveled at your ability to choose right.

Oct. 11: Can you see me? My heart aches like nothing I have ever experienced.

Now, Matthew's black Labrador, Cassie, fills his parents' house in Harding Township, N.J., with occasional barks. His father remembers his last phone call. His mother wears his sterling money clip, with its St. Christopher medal, close to her heart and sometimes hums the Grateful Dead song they played at his memorial Mass.

HOWARD SELWYN
An Accent on Soccer

Howard Selwyn and his wife, Ruth, talked funny because they were from England. At least that was the explanation that their two sons, who were raised on Long Island, would often give to friends when they felt the situation required an explanation.

"It's very strange for two Brits to have these all-American kids," said Ruth Selwyn, Mr. Selwyn's wife, laughing.

The couple moved from London to New York in 1981, originally planning to stay for two years. Two decades later, Hewlett, N.Y., is home for Mrs. Selwyn and sons James, 19, and Alex, 10.

Mr. Selwyn's accent became more Americanized over time, but he never lost his British craze for soccer. At times he would slip and call it football. When he was not working at Maxcor/Eurobrokers, it was all soccer all the time. Weekends were devoted to coaching in his sons' league and playing goalie on an over-40 team called the Blue Baldies. He followed his favorite team, Leeds United, on cable. When he could not find a game elsewhere, he would tune into the Spanish-language channels.

Mr. Selwyn, 47, and a partner opened a soccer store in Hewlett called Soccer Central on Aug. 30. "It was a dream fulfilled," Mrs. Selwyn said. "As a family we want to continue it for him."

FRANKIE SERRANO
Anything for His Dog

When Frankie Serrano went shopping for Dino, he spared no expense. "He totally spoiled Dino," said Mr. Serrano's girlfriend, Kristen Gasiorowski. "All the toys he bought him, you can't imagine. It was like it was his child." In fact, Dino was a dog, a year-old Neopolitan mastiff who weighed in at 109 pounds and slept in a king-size dog bed.

Mr. Serrano, a telecommunications technician at Genuity, a network services provider, lived in Elizabeth, N.J., with his mother and his sister Angie. The three of them were to go to Puerto Rico on Sept. 14 to visit relatives, but Mr. Serrano was going to be back by Sept. 23, to spend his 25th birthday with Miss Gasiorowski.

His sport was bowling: he was a member of four leagues in Roselle, N.J. He liked music from the '50s and '60s, rooted for the Mets and the Giants, preferred to eat at McDonald's and dressed only in Ralph Lauren.

"Anything else he wouldn't wear," said Ms. Gasiorowski, who now takes care of Dino. "It was kind of crazy and expensive."

It would take Mr. Serrano about half an hour, and four elevators, to get from the basement of 1 World Trade Center to his job on the 110th floor, where he worked in a room without windows. "We were the highest around-the-clock tenants," said his supervisor, Joseph Conti. "We were up there 365 days a year."

ALENA SESINOVA
When in Doubt, Serve Tuna

Alena Sesinova never fully mastered English, a trait that her friends found endlessly endearing. She dispensed entirely with certain articles of speech, like the word "the," and when she had had a glass of red wine or two her Czechoslovakian accent would grow thicker still.

When she arrived alone in New York in the early 1970s from Prague and landed a job at the Macy's cafeteria, she would serve a tuna sandwich to any customer she couldn't understand.

"She was a survivor—she'd made it in America, and she loved this country," said her friend of 25 years, Nanette Shaw.

Ms. Shaw said she sometimes kidded Ms. Sesinova for always having an American flag in her car, and always the response was the same: America, Ms. Sesinova would say, was the land that had given her her life, and that was not to be forgotten.

Ms. Sesinova, 57, had been trained as an engineer under the Communist regime, and made the transition to computer work in the 1970s, and later information technology at Marsh Inc.

She lived in Brooklyn Heights and after many years had attained what she considered the highest symbol of making it in New York: a seven-room apartment.

SITA SEWNARINE
Sadness and a Changed Life

If you talk to her friends and relatives, it is pretty clear Sita Sewnarine's life changed when she was pregnant with her daughter, Victoria, who will be 6 on her next birthday.

In her seventh month, Ms. Sewnarine's relationship with the child's father, whom she had expected to marry, suddenly went totally, irreconcilably wrong.

Before that, Ms. Sewnarine worked hard, but she liked to step out, too, for dinner or an evening at a comedy club. But after her breakup she found solace and comfort in the Pentecostal Bethlehem Church of God, and that was that. "It wasn't a complete transformation," said Mike Kimball, who used to work and go to parties with Ms. Sewnarine and is married to her sister, Mary. "But she did change."

"She doted on her daughter, but her whole life was the church," Mary Kimball said. "She was married to the church."

Ms. Sewnarine, who was born in Guyana and moved with her family to the United States about 20 years ago, worked as a disaster recovery agent for the Fiduciary Trust Company in the World Trade Center. "She would talk about religion as she saw fit," said Mike Henken, a co-worker who managed to get out on Sept. 11. "She believed that you never know when your day is going to come."

KAREN LYNN SEYMOUR
Confectioner Extraordinaire

Karen Lynn Seymour's idea of a proper ending to a dinner party was a hand-made candy tower with brown-and-white chocolate walls filled with chocolate mousse and garnished with strawberry and blueberry coulis. Not long ago, she completed a 600-hour course at the French Culinary Institute, graduating first in her class. And she did it while working full time as a technology specialist at Garban Intercapital in the World Trade Center.

"She got home at 1:30," said William Dietrich, her husband. "And got up at 5:30."

Ms. Seymour, he said, took her passions seriously. She met Mr. Dietrich, her future husband, a bicycle racer, while pedaling in Millington, N.J. She started racing with him and wound up as New Jersey's fifth-ranked woman cyclist. When she and Mr. Dietrich rode a tandem cycle, she steered.

Three and a half years ago, she had twins. She had a lot of plans for them, said Mr. Dietrich. "She wanted to take them bicycling and skiing and on trips to Europe, he said. "She couldn't wait," he said.

DAVIS G. SEZNA Jr.
An Enthusiastic Trainee

Davis G. Sezna Jr.—known to his family and friends as Deeg—was in New York for boot camp, his basic training in the world of finance. A freshly minted graduate of Vanderbilt University, Mr. Sezna was ecstatic about his job at Sandler O'Neill & Partners on the 104th floor of 2 World Trade Center. He showed up for work early, insisted on wearing business suits in an office where business casual was the attire du jour, and refused to call his boss by his first name.

Sept. 11 was Mr. Sezna's sixth day on the job, but already Jimmy Dunne, a managing principal at Sandler O'Neill, knew that he would succeed. "He was high energy, a hard worker," Mr. Dunne said. "He knew he was fortunate to have a job, and he was going to make this shot work."

Twice a day, Mr. Sezna, 22, and his father, Davis G. Sezna Sr., spoke about their lives and their game plan—the crux of which consisted of the younger Mr. Sezna's leaving the West Village and coming home to Delaware to run the family's hospitality business, which owns golfing clubs and restaurants.

"He was a very, very intelligent guy who had a bulldog's tenacity when he believed in something," Mr. Sezna said.

THOMAS JOSEPH SGROI
A Man of Many Loyalties

Thomas Sgroi liked to keep his world around him. He was a picture taker.

Not that he was a camera buff, said his former wife, Laraine. "He just wanted to have pictures so we'd have the memories."

Mr. Sgroi, 45, who worked for Marsh & McLennan on the 95th floor of the World Trade Center, moved from Brick Township, N.J., to Staten Island after his divorce in 1999, but the family remained close. He and his former wife exchanged e-mail frequently on the subject of their two sons, Michael, 20, and Nicholas, 14.

"Everyone in the family counted on him," Mrs. Sgroi said. "He was the rock."

He was the kind of guy, she said, who had kept all his friends from high school in Borough Park, Brooklyn, where his parents still live in the house where he grew up, the kind of guy who liked doing home improvements, the kind of guy you wanted at your party and who liked throwing a party himself, the kind of guy who prized loyalty.

"He was a major Jets fan," Mrs. Sgroi said. "I'm trying to continue that tradition," she said. "I was never into football, but now I feel like I have to be. For him."

JAYESH SHAH
Provider of Memories

Jayesh Shah and his brother were always close, whether the family lived in India or Wisconsin or Tulsa or Houston.

They went to the same college. They took computer science classes together in graduate school. "I was a terrible note-taker, and Jayesh was a great note-taker," said Niloy Shah, his brother, younger by a year. And when Jay Shah got married, the newlyweds lived with the younger brother and his wife for months.

Even after Jayesh Shah moved to New York last year, to work at eSpeed International, the brothers talked almost every day.

Mr. Shah, a strong believer in education, wanted to be sure the move would not disrupt his children's schooling, so Mrs. Shah and the children remained in Houston until school was out. Each child has a favorite memory of time with their father. Nikita, 10, loved horseback riding in Yosemite. Sonia, 8, loved the "Sling Shot" ride at Seaside Heights. Kevin, 6, loved wrestling with his dad.

They and their mother—and Mr. Shah's mother, who is staying with them—will return to Houston. But education remains a family value, and they will not leave for Texas until June.

GARY SHAMAY
Upward, Ever Upward

Gary Shamay was a young man on his way up. After graduating at 16 from Sheepshead Bay High School in Brooklyn, he plunged into the corporate workplace at an age when most of his peers were far from making career decisions.

By Sept. 11, he was 23, and had already made his mark as a computer specialist, working for Allstate Insurance, Deutsche Bank, CIBC Oppenheimer and, since August 2000, Cantor Fitzgerald. He was single and living with his parents in Mill Basin, but his work assignments had taken him to Cantor's offices in Los Angeles, San Francisco, Chicago and other cities.

"We were very proud of him," said Mr. Shamay's mother, Zoya Shamay, who said his career goals centered on his computer skills. While working long hours in the office, sometimes starting as early as 5:30 A.M., he was completing college course work at night toward a bachelor's degree in computer engineering.

Mr. Shamay was born in Uzbekistan, and immigrated to Brooklyn when he was 2 years old with Mrs. Shamay and her husband, Beniamim. He had two younger brothers, ages 16 and 8, for whom "he always had advice," his mother said.

NEIL SHASTRI
Tiger Woods, Meet My Wife

Neil Shastri married his college sweetheart, Kruti, in June 2001. The wedding pictures had not even come in yet, but married life had already changed the man. Mr. Shastri was called a "big health freak" by his relatives, a man who lived on PowerBars, played basketball and golf religiously and wanted a Tiger Woods poster on the living room wall. His wife said no.

On Sept. 11, at 9 A.M., Mr. Shastri, 25, called her, according to his twin brother, Jay, who was putting up missing-person posters on Lexington Avenue the next Friday. Mr. Shastri told his wife there was a lot of smoke, that he was having trouble breathing. Then he hung up. An information technology consultant, Mr. Shastri had been working in the offices of one of his clients, Cantor Fitzgerald, on the 103rd floor of 1 World Trade Center.

Jay Shastri said his twin immediately befriended people. "It might sound cliché-ish right now," he began.

His sister-in-law, Priti Naik, 28, finished for him. "If you met right now, he'd be your best friend by the end of the evening."

KATHRYN ANNE SHATZOFF
When Not Collecting, Giving

Kathryn Anne Shatzoff was not a collector, really, but her husband, Neil, the owner of a comic-book shop, was. So a few years ago, he got her started collecting Barbie dolls. He gave her an I Love Lucy doll as a gift, and now he's lost count of all the fancy dolls in their Riverdale home.

"We ran out of shelf space," said Mr. Shatzoff, chuckling.

In fact, Mrs. Shatzoff had carried a torch for Barbie since childhood, said her mother, Anne Davidson. A Manhattan native, Mrs. Shatzoff, 37, was an assistant in the risk management division of Marsh & McLennan, but spent a lot of her free time doing crafts and buying gifts for other people—no occasion necessary.

"She was the kind of person that would talk you into wanting something, just so she could go and buy it for you," said her husband. Christmas, Mrs. Shatzoff's favorite holiday, will not be the same this year.

"I used to surprise her with stuff," said Mr. Shatzoff. "Every Christmas, we'd say, let's not buy each other anything, it's too much."

But then he would buy gifts for her anyway. And even though he did it every year, every year she was still surprised. And she did the same for him.

JEFFREY SHAW
A Third Son to Die

Mid-November was when Jeffrey Shaw, his brother and a friend would head upstate to go deer hunting—a tradition that began long ago when Mr. Shaw's father organized the trips.

"He loved his hunting, he loved his golf, but there was no single thing about Jeff that stuck out," said his wife, Debra. "What made Jeff was just everything. He was my right arm, and he would do anything for his kids. If one of the kids had a basketball game, he'd be there. And last year, he took a referee course, so he'd be able to ref at their games this year. He worked and then he came home to us. That was what he lived for."

Mr. Shaw, 42, an electrician from Levittown, N.Y., whose work took him to the World Trade Center on Sept. 11, was the second of six children—and the third son to die. "I lost one son when he was hit by a car," said his mother, Gerry Shaw. "Another had spina bifida and died. And now we miss Jeff so much. We still call his cell phone, to tell him how our days are going."

ROBERT J. SHAY Jr.
New Baby Has Dad's Eyes

One of eight children, Robert J. Shay Jr. thrived in the company of his large, fun-loving family. And with his wife, Dawn, he was happily creating his own big brood. Just 27, he was already the devoted father of Robert, 5, and Ryan, 2. He did not get to meet his third son, Jonathan Robert, who was born Oct. 22, 2001. The newest Shay came with a head of thick black hair and his dad's eyes, ears and legs, said Eileen Shay, Robert's sister.

Mr. Shay was a bond broker at Cantor Fitzgerald, which he joined in 1993 right after high school, starting in maintenance and working his way up. He was a Mets fan practically from birth, Ms. Shay said. "As far back as we can find pictures of him, he's in his Mets gear."

Mr. Shay was always up and always watching out for others. He lived on Staten Island, just 15 minutes from his parents, whom he called many times each day. Around 8:40 A.M. on Sept. 11, he made a quick call to his wife to see how their son Robert's introduction to kindergarten was going.

Recently, young Robert put some Halloween stickers on his bedroom window. Eileen said that he explained, "I put up stars so my daddy can see where I am."

DANIEL SHEA and JOSEPH SHEA
Two Brothers on Two Floors

For a time, Daniel James Shea would not work at Cantor Fitzgerald. His older brother, Joseph Patrick Shea, was pretty high up there, and he did not want anyone to think he had zipped in on his brother's coattails.

Then he relented.

Joseph Shea, 47, a senior managing director, was on the 105th floor of the first building to be hit. Daniel, 37, was on the 104th. At home in Pelham, N.Y., seven children are without fathers.

Three thousand people turned out for the brothers' joint funeral service at St. Ignatius Loyola Church in Manhattan. One reason, perhaps, was the brothers' generosity. Joseph Shea donated generously to the hockey team of his alma mater, Georgetown University, and coached local youth hockey and baseball teams.

When three New York City firefighters were killed on the job on Father's Day 2001, Daniel Shea contributed his day's commissions to their families and persuaded other men on his floor to do the same.

They raised $15,000.

"Cantor set up at the Pierre and the F.B.I. guy told us no one above the plane would have lived," said their sister, referring to a family service center the company had set up at the hotel after the attack.

"They were all alive for a while. Danny didn't have his cell, but his friend Tommy did. They couldn't call out, but when Tommy's girlfriend called, Danny said, 'Call my wife and tell her how much I love her.' "

Joseph called his wife and said, "A plane just hit the building." She said, "What about Danny?" He said, "I'm just going down to find him."

LINDA SHEEHAN
A Social Shopper

She had a zest for living. She worked hard, worked out hard, but when she had fun, she had fun. That was Linda Sheehan.

Ms. Sheehan, 40, a vice president at Sandler O'Neill & Partners, lived in Manhattan with her two cats, Spanky and Tamara. Her hobby of choice was shopping. But it was not just shopping for shopping's sake, or shopping for sport, but also shopping as social event. She would do it every Saturday, all day, with two of her closest friends, Vivian Urrutia and Gregory Orenstein.

Her favorite store was probably Bergdorf's. She favored Jeffrey for shoes, and she was a regular at the flea market on 26th Street, where she hunted for antiques for her apartment. She had a particular weakness for boots, and her rule with shoes was, the higher the heel, the better.

HAGAY SHEFI
A True Partnership

Hagay Shefi, son of a retired Israeli brigadier general, Dov Shefi, moved to the United States from Tel Aviv in 1992 and co-founded GoldTier Technologies, a communications company in Mount Olive, N.J. So renowned was his expertise that he was both a featured speaker and a panelist at the Risk Waters conference in Windows on the World on the 106th Floor of 1 World Trade Center on the morning of the terrorist attack.

"People say how ironic it is, that he is from Israel, but I don't see that," said his wife, Sigal. "People from every country were in the trade center that day. Terror can happen anywhere in the world, and it is nothing that you can predict."

Since the funeral, she had been remembering what a true partner he was in raising their children, ages 5 and 3, in Tenafly, N.J.—"he helped with everything around the house," she said—and how, despite the long hours at his start-up company, he spent all his spare time with them. "I am thinking he holds me now," Mrs. Shefi said of her husband. "And I am going to keep him, and his way of thinking, in me."

ATSUSHI SHIRATORI
New York Adrenaline

Atsushi Shiratori was not a New Yorker by birth. But he was a New Yorker to the bone.

A trader of dollar/yen options at Cantor Fitzgerald and one of the firm's partners, Mr. Shiratori, 36, was addicted to the city. Sure, he was passionate about his job, and so obsessed with the stock market that he once spent a two-week vacation in a day-trading salon, buying and selling stocks.

But it was New York that really started his engines. Peter Douglas, a friend who sat with Mr. Shiratori on the trading desk a few years ago, said: "He loved, loved, loved New York. Everything about it. The pulse of it, the intensity, the energy. He loved looking sharp, having the style. Going out to dinner with friends, nights on the town. Sucking it in, 24 hours a day."

Magali Somers lived with Mr. Shiratori for the last three years. He recently helped her open a furniture restoration shop. "He had a huge social life and he would always live for the present," she said. "He would always enjoy the moment, and that's what impressed me about him the most."

A memorial Mass for Raymond M. Downey, a deputy fire chief who died in the trade center attack, was celebrated December 15 in Deer Park, New York. Chief Downey led the Special Operations Command and was an expert on rescue operations at collapsed buildings. (*Kevin P. Coughlin*)

MARK SHULMAN
No Average Joe

Mark Shulman was a "kind of quiet guy who loved sports," said his wife, Lori, suggesting the personality profile of an average Joe. But there was more.

He was, undeniably, a sports fan, attending Giants and Rangers games as often as possible, or taking them in on television at home in Old Bridge, N.J. But overriding all was a dedication to his daughters, Jamie, 13, and Melissa, 17, in whom he instilled a zest for accomplishment.

Mr. Shulman was the coach of Jamie's soccer team, the Old Bridge Road Runners, spending weekends traveling to games across central New Jersey. He had been looking forward to Jamie's bat mitzvah, which was celebrated on Nov. 17, a day Mrs. Shulman recalls as "bittersweet."

He was also working closely with Melissa, a high school senior, on college applications. His advice was "go for the best," Mrs. Shulman said, adding that "he would have been so proud" when news came in December of Melissa's early admission to Princeton.

A 47-year-old mechanical engineer, Mr. Shulman worked as a fire protection specialist for Marsh & McClennan on the 100th floor of the World Trade Center.

"He did evacuation plans for clients," Mrs. Shulman said. "If anybody knew how to get out, he would have been the one."

ALLAN SHWARTZSTEIN
No Clothes Horse, He

After 15 years on Wall Street, Allan Shwartzstein still wore the watch he had received for his bar mitzvah. He preferred ratty denim shirts and hole-ridden khakis to the cuff links and starched collars more typical of Cantor Fitzgerald equities traders. That is what he wore on his second date with his wife, Amy, and still she married him.

He promptly lost his wedding ring. "It just wasn't him," she said. "He was somebody that, what you saw was what you got," she added. "This was not the guy that was going to hold the door open or worry about what came out of his mouth, or worry about what I looked like. He was genuine."

Mr. Shwartzstein was the kind of man for whom other people had a hard time buying presents, but who would always remember when it was time to buy them for others. "He would call and say: 'Don't tell him I told you, but it's John's birthday. Call him,' " said Jay Scharf, a best friend.

Even as a child, he seemed older than his years. "When he came home, he did not go straight to the friends to play with them," said his father, Avi. "He would stand first with the parents and have a mature conversation." Allan Shwartzstein, 37 and the father of two, was named after an uncle who was killed in Israel in 1948.

The uncle's body has never been found, Avi Shwartzstein said. Neither has Allan's.

JOHANNA SIGMUND
A Kindness to a Stranger

Ruth Sigmund loves the story her daughter Johanna's friends tell of how she used to joke around at field hockey practices at Fairfield University. "After hours of practice, she would do a little dance and just crack everybody up," her mother said. "She would keep up everybody's spirits."

Johanna Sigmund, 25, ran in the New York Marathon, blared Janet Jackson and U2 at all-night parties, bought meals for a homeless couple who lived near her and regularly cooked breakfast for her three roommates. Her friendliness and ease served her well in her job as a liaison to investors at Fred Alger Management.

Not long after Sept. 11, a stranger wrote to her parents. The letter writer had been thrown out of a taxi after it collided with a car in Hoboken. The taxi driver sped off, leaving the woman on the street, bleeding. Johanna Sigmund rushed over, cleaned the woman up, took her to the emergency room and held her hand while she had stitches.

"I saw Johanna's picture on a Web site recently, and I immediately recognized her as the angel that helped me out that night," the woman wrote. "I lost many friends in the Sept. 11 tragedy. I now add Johanna's name to my list of friends in heaven."

GREGORY R. SIKORSKY
Taking Little Brother Along

There was the time that Gregory R. Sikorsky decided to take his youngest brother, Perry, up in a four-seater Cessna. But after they got up at 6 A.M., after they had driven an hour to the airport, the plane's battery turned out to be dead. So he drove his truck onto the highway and jump-started the plane. Then they took off.

Below them was Spring Valley, N.Y., where they and two other brothers had grown up, where their parents lived, where Gregory Sikorsky, 34, was raising a 3-year-old son with his wife, Marie.

"I've never seen Rockland County from the air before," his brother said. "He showed me our parent's house and the garage. He even let me fly the plane. It really was amazing."

Gregory Sikorsky. Licensed pilot. Firefighter with Squad 41 in the South Bronx. Ex-marine. Harley-Davidson rider. Skydiver. Skier. Automobile mechanic. Licensed tractor-trailer driver. He took his youngest brother with him on many of his adventures, sometimes for company, sometimes for competition. After Firefighter Sikorsky finished a year at auto-body school in Colorado, the two drove back to New York together in a Chevy Blazer.

They took their first skydiving trip together. And they recently rode in a Harley-Davidson rally from New York to a drive-in diner in New Jersey.

STEVE SILLER
A Verse for the Fallen

Steve Siller was an orphan at age 10—his mother died of cancer, his father from a blood clot—and he spent his childhood in the care of his sisters and brothers.

"He accepted what was handed to him," said his wife, Sally. "He lived life to its fullest. People meant everything to him."

A typical day for Mr. Siller, 34, went something like this: work a 24-hour shift and then golf with his brothers; go home and have lunch with his wife; take the children to the park; help the neighbor with a flat and then go to bed.

He was a fireman with the Squad 1 company in Park Slope, Brooklyn, who died helping people. He was last seen running through the Brooklyn-Battery Tunnel on Sept. 11 with his bunker gear under his arm. His brother George wrote a poem for his memorial. It reads, in part:

What to say to his five children and wife?
How do I try to explain what's ahead in their life?
I'll tell them their father was a saint and a hero,
Who fought courageously, the battle at ground zero.

DAVID SILVER
Flowers on Friday

David Silver had a 2-year-old daughter, Rachel. The shape of her eyes and nose are his. She is going to be tall just like her father, said her mother, who is nine months pregnant. "She is asking about him constantly. 'Where is Daddy? I miss Daddy. How come Daddy is not coming home?' " Holli Silver said. "When the garage door opens, she thinks he's home."

Mr. Silver, 35, was a quiet, private man. And the family's split-level home in New Rochelle was the place he most preferred to be. He doted on his daughter, eager to brag about her exploits in nursery school or camp. He and his wife already had a name chosen for their unborn daughter. Now, Mrs. Silver says she will name the newborn after her husband.

While devoted to his family, Mr. Silver also was committed to his job as vice president of eSpeed in 1 World Trade Center. Every workday, he boarded the 5:09 A.M. train and did not return home until 7:30 P.M. On Friday nights, he often surprised his wife with a luscious bouquet of fresh flowers that he had bought at Grand Central Terminal. "It's like Friday night and I expect him to come with a bunch of flowers. It's hard."

CRAIG SILVERSTEIN
Fatherhood on a New Level

Gabriella Silverstein's first day of first grade was Sept. 6. Her father, Craig, knew that it might be tough starting out in a new school, so he took the day off from his job as an equities trader at Sandler O'Neill.

When Gabriella emerged from the school building, there he was, a big smile on his face and a bouquet held out in his hand.

Mr. Silverstein adored his wife, Maria, whom he met when she was 13 and he was 14, sending her e-mail messages again and again from the office every day; he always ended by telling her how much he loved her.

But when it came to his children, his devotion reached a whole new level. Pooh Fish was his pet name for Gabriella, who is 5½. He called her brother Cameron, 4, Handsome Man. He took them to the park near their home in Wyckoff, N.J., and to the movies. He loved to buy them ice cream and toys.

Recently, Cameron has been spending time looking out of the window "to see if he could see heaven, because then maybe he'd be able to see my husband," Mrs. Silverstein said.

The other day, Gabriella asked if she could send her father a letter. "She wanted to use a rocket," Mrs. Silverstein said, "but I convinced her that a balloon might be a better idea."

BRUCE SIMMONS
Chef of the Wee Hours

Kathy Simmons awoke to the smell of onions cooking.

Onions? At 5:30 A.M. on a Saturday? Downstairs, her husband, Bruce, was happily sautéing 200 of them.

That weekend, as a trustee of the Maroons Soccer Club in Ridgewood, N.J., he would oversee food concessions at the annual tournament. Mrs. Simmons realized, laughing, that the passion he brought as a partner to Sandler O'Neill & Partners compelled him to seek the next

level, even when it came to hamburgers and hot dogs. He wanted sautéed onions too.

Mr. Simmons had taken a year off in college to try being a chef, and had honed that skill. He could make a surprise spice cake for his wife's birthday, or a treat for his daughter Emma, 2. And he could teach Meghan, 13, to make beef Wellington.

He brought the same enthusiasm to coaching soccer. Mrs. Simmons saw this 41-year-old man running with his son Jack, 10, and the other little boys as if he were a boy himself. Their team reached first place last spring, but it was never just about winning. He wanted each child to do his best, have fun and learn how to recover from a loss. Smiling, he put onions into crockpots.

"You're mad," she said, and loved him for it.

ARTHUR SIMON
Not Afraid to Commit

Arthur Simon was an equities trader for Fred Alger Management on the 93rd floor of 1 World Trade Center. His oldest child, Kenneth, had a similar job at Cantor Fitzgerald a few flights up.

Arthur Simon, 57, had many passions: his four children; the Jets and the Mets; Atlantic City; doo-wop music (especially the song "Runaround Sue"). But the principal love story of his life began 38 years ago when he was a librarian at the Brooklyn Public Library's Canarsie branch and went to a party where he met another librarian, Susan Bloch, who was then just 16. Both were great dancers, the kind that other dancers stepped back to make room for. They became inseparable.

"He always wanted to get married young and start a family," Mrs. Simon said recently. "It didn't matter that there was no money. He wasn't afraid to make a commitment."

Kenneth was born when his parents were living in Canarsie; then came Jennifer, who is a biology teacher in Chappaqua, N.Y. The family moved to Rockland County where Todd, who became a top high school wrestler and wide receiver, was born, along with Mandy, who grew up to be a homecoming queen.

"Arthur was very, very proud of all of them," Mrs. Simon said. And it all began in Brooklyn. "He chased after me," she said. "And I let him catch me."

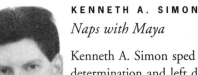

KENNETH A. SIMON
Naps with Maya

Kenneth A. Simon sped through life with determination and left delight bobbing in his wake. "Everyone loved Kenny," said his wife, Karen.

He could cook chocolate chip pancakes for a crowd and thrill a small cousin by juggling balls, beanbags and finally, flaming sticks. He cheered for the Yankees, and when asked when he met his wife, would typically reply: "1996, the year the Yankees won the World Series." And when did they get married? "1998, the year the Yankees won the World Series."

But his fondest moments were those spent with his baby daughter, Maya. He napped on the couch, cradling her on his chest, Mrs. Simon said, and they took her on walks nearly every night, their dog Bailey close behind. Over Labor Day weekend, the Simons took Maya, then 4 months old, to South Street Seaport and showed her the very spot where they got engaged.

"Here's the reason we all loved Kenny so much," one of his aunts wrote for his memorial service in September. "From the first to the very last day, seeing how very, very much he loved Karen and Maya. Seeing the look on his face whenever one of them would come into the room, and seeing how happy he made them every single day, is something we will never forget."

Mr. Simon, 34, was an equities trader for Cantor Fitzgerald in 1 World Trade Center, where his father, Arthur, worked a few flights down.

MICHAEL J. SIMON
A Passionate Sportsman

These are the totems Michael J. Simon's three young children decided to place alongside an urn containing ashes from the World Trade Center at the memorial service for their father, an energy broker for Cantor Fitzgerald:

A bathing suit and a bicycle helmet worn by Tyler during lessons from Dad that helped him master swimming and cycling; a softball trophy won by his daughter, Brittany; and the favorite golf club, a driver with accurate aim, which he used on outings with Michael Jr.

Their father was a sportsman whose passions rubbed off on them; though lacrosse and hockey had been Michael's activities in college, and golf and tennis were his weekend-warrior pursuits after graduating to Wall Street, he set aside time to coach the soccer teams of all three children, and a fourth squad.

No wonder 1,100 mourners showed up at his memorial.

His dream was to start a lacrosse league in Harrington Park, N.J., where he and his wife, Eileen, bought a house 13 years ago. He had not yet made it come true, but he was only 40; he imagined he would get around to it.

"He lived life with no regrets," his wife said.

MARIANNE SIMONE
Still Young at Heart

Marianne Simone had the comic sense of a Lucille Ball. "If you were in a room with her, you would be laughing," said Teresa Hargrave, her daughter.

Once, Mrs. Simone, 62, a communications specialist at Cantor Fitzgerald, dyed her hair and scrunched it up, and went to work with hair as orange as a carrot. Another time she ordered a tree from a gardening catalog, decided she didn't like it, and insisted on dragging it back to the post office so she could return it.

Then there was the time she was in a Duane Reade store in her $5,000 mink coat and a lipstick got caught in the cuff without her realizing it. She set off the theft alarm, and the guard took a mug shot of her with the lipstick she had supposedly stolen underneath. Mrs. Simone loved to tell people she could not go back to Duane Reade for months after.

She was in many ways still a teenager. Recently, she stayed up till 2 A.M. at her daughter's, playing poker with Mrs. Hargrave's husband, Bradley. "They were laughing and yelling," said Mrs. Hargrave. "She said he was cheating. He said she was cheating." Mrs. Hargrave had to tell the two of them to keep it down, as if they were a couple of kids.

BARRY SIMOWITZ
Of Cats and Cashmere

Not every cat is presented with its own futon. But then, not every cat owner is as devoted as Barry Simowitz was to Wanda June, the brown-and-white beauty with whom he shared the last five years.

The pair could often be found in the living room of Mr. Simowitz's apartment on the Lower East Side—Wanda June on her futon, Mr. Simowitz in his favorite chair from Pottery Barn—listening to opera on his high-end stereo system. "Animals were his main passion," said Mr. Simowitz's sister, Laurie. "And he really, really loved Wanda June."

Mr. Simowitz, an auditor for the New York State Department of Taxation and Finance, also had a thing for luxurious clothing. "He left about 100 cashmere sweaters in his closet, all different colors," Laurie Simowitz said. "You name an expensive store, my brother shopped there."

He loved his job in the World Trade Center, where he showed off his impeccable fashion sense and answered colleagues' questions about their cats. His mother, Mollie, stopped working at 83, and Mr. Simowitz, who was 64, had every intention of following her example.

Mollie Simowitz, now 93, misses her only son fiercely.

KHAMLADAI SINGH and
ROSHAN SINGH
Making Things Perfect

It was essential for both of the Singh children to leave very early on the day of the attack—by 6:20 A.M.—because their roles were so crucial at the conference breakfast at Windows on the World.

Holiday lights on a median at Broadway and 140th Street in Manhattan pay tribute to the World Trade Center towers and other buildings that were destroyed on September 11. (*Ting-Li Wang*)

Khamladai, 25, as an assistant banquet manager, would be greeting the participants at 8 A.M.; her little brother, Roshan, 21, was arranging the audio-visual presentation. There were 600 guests, after all, and preparations had to be flawless. So they left the family home in Woodhaven, Queens, together as they always did, caught the A train and arrived by 7 A.M.

If brother and sister were extremely close, doing just about everything together, it is true that Khamladai often had the tighter schedule: after her day at Windows, she studied computer programming full time at Borough of Manhattan Community College. There were times, though, when Roshan was equally pressed, thanks to his duties in the Army National Guard.

Now their mother, Toolsiedai Seepersaud, waits in a quiet house for her only children with their stepfather, Jamil Awan. "I am just hoping they are together," she said.

THOMAS E. SINTON 3rd
What a Find

More than three weeks had passed since Thomas E. Sinton 3rd, a senior vice president at Cantor Fitzgerald, was lost in the collapse of the World Trade Center. But his wife could still hear the sound of his laughter: deep, loud and irrepressible. "He had a great laugh," said Cathy Carilli, a portfolio manager at U.S. Trust. "And he never held it back. He was like a sunny day."

Mr. Sinton's pleasures came in doing for others: helping a stranded driver on the highway. Helping a client plan a birthday party for his wife. Doing the chores at the couple's Westchester home when his wife was building her career and going to school at the same time. Sharing a love of the Knicks and Rangers with his 11-year-old daughter from an earlier marriage.

Ms. Carilli recalled how they met 10 years ago, when

both were 31 years old and beginning their Wall Street careers. She had become friendly with a colleague of Mr. Sinton's on a vacation. Later, he asked her to fix him up with one of her girlfriends.

"You're not good enough," she told the man, with the snide repartee that Wall Street types are famous for. "Why don't you fix me up with one of your friends?"

The words were barely out of her mouth, when he shouted across the bond desk: "Hey, Tom, pick up the phone." Now, Ms. Carilli's pleasure in telling the tale was as full-throated as her husband's laughter.

"That was the greatest sale I ever closed," she said.

PETER SIRACUSE
Game Day, Every Day

Peter Siracuse lived for competition. As a child he jockeyed for attention with his three older brothers. As a young adult, he took his aggression out on the gridiron and in lacrosse. He also played football in college.

So when Mr. Siracuse, 29, became a teacher and a coach at Bethpage High School on Long Island right after college, his family thought he was a natural, since he also loved children. A little over a year ago, he married his high school sweetheart, Alana, and had a child of his own, Ryan Joseph, now 9 months.

"He was just so excited that he had a son and a child," said Matthew Siracuse, one of Mr. Siracuse's brothers. "That was probably the biggest thing in his life at this time."

Four years ago, Mr. Siracuse left the blackboard for the brokerage house. He quickly developed an affinity for his new job as a bond broker at Cantor Fitzgerald.

"He loved it; it was like game day every day," said George Siracuse, another of his brothers. "He loved the whole camaraderie of his co-workers. He loved the competition. He thrived on it."

MURIEL SISKOPOULOS
Always Checking on Family

Muriel Siskopoulos's hobby was knitting for her son, three daughters and two grandsons. She made herself a sweater once, but didn't like it and gave it away. She never knitted anything for her husband, Mark, but he didn't complain. "She spoiled them," Mark said. "And I spoiled her. That's the way it went."

Mrs. Siskopoulos, 60, worked as a secretary for Keefe, Bruyette & Woods. A meticulous dresser, she always made sure that her shoes and handbag matched when she left her home in Bay Ridge, Brooklyn.

She liked to shop, but often bought clothes that were too small just so she could hand them down to her children. She liked to travel, too, but often took the rest of the family

along. The Siskopouloses made eight trips to Disney World in the last 10 years, including one last year with their grandchildren.

And no matter where she was, Mrs. Siskopoulos had to check on her family every day. Usually more than once. "She was generous with herself and her time," her husband said. "They were her life."

JOSEPH SISOLAK
Helping Others to Think

When there was a problem in the e-mail system at Marsh & McClennan in the World Trade Center, someone would call Joseph Sisolak at home in Cobble Hill, Brooklyn, no matter what the hour. Mr. Sisolak, a 35-year-old senior vice president in charge of the e-mail system, would listen but would not hand out an answer. He would tell the caller to think the problem through, a technique that colleagues said made them better at their jobs.

"He just wanted to do the best he could," said his wife, Suzanne. "I think that's why golf appealed to him so much. You had to keep score."

Husband and wife took up golf three years ago, and last summer they played every weekend. Last spring, he joined 20 other men on an annual golf outing to Myrtle Beach, S.C. He was the newcomer, and he brought his enthusiasm to the game. When he parred a hole, he would dance around. He was so excited that he asked to return. Now next spring's getaway has a name: the Joseph Sisolak Memorial Outing.

JOHN SKALA
Always Time for His Friends

John Skala enjoyed himself, but it was important that he made sure everyone else was having fun before he could get comfortable. "He loved making people laugh," said his sister, Irene Lesiw. "If he didn't see you smiling, he would try to make you smile before he would smile."

Officer Skala, 31, lived in Clifton, N.J., and was a Port Authority police officer assigned to the Lincoln Tunnel, and also worked part-time as a paramedic in New Jersey. He was called to the trade center after the towers were attacked.

Yash, as his friends called him, was well known for his good humor and hospitality. He would put in a 48-hour shift but still find the time to have some fun with his friends. He could not hold a tune, but he loved to sing. At karaoke bars or at weddings, he would grab the microphone and break into song. Every year, he threw a Christmas party at his house open to everyone and anyone.

When he was young, he had a propensity for getting into

mischief, like sneaking out in the middle of the night and driving around in his parents' car before he was even 16. "He was ahead of his time," said his sister.

PAUL ALBERT SKRZYPEK
The Backup Man

Paul Albert Skrzypek was constantly in motion. He ran with the bulls in Pamplona, he completed the Chicago Triathlon and the New York Marathon, and he Rollerbladed, biked and skied his way through the changing seasons. The only things he would sit still for, friends joked, were New York sporting events.

After Sept. 11, some wondered if he had, on some level, known that his time was limited. Over the summer he had rented not one but two beach houses. He had backup plans to back up his backup plans. "It was almost like he had an innate crystal ball," his friend James Schuette wrote in a letter to Mr. Skrzypek's parents, Edith and Albert. "He lived two lifetimes in 37 years."

Back in his hometown of Montville, N.J., Mr. Skrzypek's parents and younger sister have heard countless friends recall his generosity, fearlessness and athleticism. It is nothing they didn't know. Until recently, his parents were still watching him play in a local lacrosse league. "I remember we were walking to a game," his mother said. "Bert said, 'Are we going to be going to his games until we're 80?'"

In July, when Mr. Skrzypek became a broker with eSpeed, he told his father that he had finally gotten his career on track. The only area in which he lagged behind his friends was marriage. "Paul sought the relationship he saw in his parents," Mr. Schuette wrote, "and those are very hard to come by."

CHRISTOPHER SLATTERY
The Man Behind the Fun

Fog cloaked the treacherous Colorado slope; a half-dozen skiers couldn't see past their ski tips. Then, through the soup, came a rhythmic clattering: Christopher Slattery, an expert skier, was banging his poles, leading them to safety.

To an ever-expanding circle of friends and relatives, Mr. Slattery, 31, a trader at Cantor Fitzgerald, was a leader and a catalyst. After college, he pulled together six guys to share a Manhattan apartment. Later, he took a caravan to the Kentucky Derby and two dozen Ranger fans to Montreal. At Giants tailgate parties, you never knew how many friends he'd arrive with.

But for a fellow who majored in fun, Mr. Slattery was remarkably thoughtful. Arranging a job for this acquaintance; paying for a room at the Plaza for that young woman

to sleep it off. The exquisite toy horse that delighted his 3-year-old niece; the miniature color television set for his father to wear around his neck during Giants games.

A dying neighbor leaves Mr. Slattery's sister's wedding early: Mr. Slattery chats with him. Women tug at Mr. Slattery's sleeve: come dance! No, says Mr. Slattery, I want to talk with this gentleman. The ill neighbor chooses to stay. Mr. Slattery has compelled him to celebrate the good times a little longer.

VINCENT SLAVIN
Outgoing and Outdoor Type

Vincent Slavin's fiancée called him "very outgoing, high energy, someone who walked to his own beat and never slowed down." His best friend, Tom Robinson, called him "a real New Yorker, a guy you couldn't put anywhere else."

Mr. Slavin, 41, was an equity trader and partner at Cantor Fitzgerald. He and his fiancée, Anna Baez, lived in Belle Harbor, Queens, three houses from the ocean.

Last year, he bought a vacation home on Stratton Mountain in Vermont. He and Ms. Baez drove there with their Rottweiler and their golden retriever on winter weekends for skiing and on summer weekends for biking and canoeing. There were also trips to the Cayman Islands or Belize for scuba diving.

Mr. Robinson, a private investor, and his wife often traveled with Mr. Slavin and Ms. Baez. "He brought everyone into his world," Mr. Robinson said. "Once, a co-worker mentioned in conversation that she would love to see the Oscars in person. Just like that, he got her tickets. He used to introduce me as his brother from another mother. I was proud of that."

ROBERT SLIWAK
A Toast from the Children

Ryan, who just turned 8, inherited Daddy's easygoing nature and athletic ability. Of the twins, who are almost 4, Kyle has Daddy's rascally sense of humor and, it must be said, his tendency to approach chores with a certain lack of urgency. And Nicole has his smile and love of song.

"Her personality is mine, poor thing," said Susan Sliwak, their mother.

Robert Sliwak, who was a bond broker at Cantor Fitzgerald, lives on in his three children. That's what his wife says to help them, and her, get through these days.

Ryan understands what has happened, and has become more introverted. Mrs. Sliwak is working with a child psychologist at his school. Kyle has become more clingy; when his mother went from their home in Wantagh, N.Y., to visit the site, he pleaded with her not to go. Nicole was upset at first, but her mother has encouraged her to think of happier times.

October 26, 2001 was their father's birthday—he would have been 43—and they went out for pizza to celebrate. The kids all had soda, a special treat, and they raised their glasses and toasted him.

PAUL K. SLOAN
Always There for You

Big, sweet, enthusiastic, driven—those are just a few of the words his family and friends use to describe Paul K. Sloan, 26, who worked for Keefe Bruyette & Woods.

Growing up in Novato, Calif., he was an ardent follower of the San Francisco Giants and played offensive lineman for the Brown University football team. Mr. Sloan was adamant about his belief that the Beatles produced the best music ever, and worked hard to convert a lot of his friends to that way of thinking.

He was a dedicated collector of articles and e-mail messages that he would forward to people that he thought might be interested, said his sister, Sarah Funk. Once he forced himself to buy a copy of *People* magazine, even though Julia Roberts, whom he disliked, was on the cover, because there was an article inside about his brother, who works in Hollywood.

"He wasn't the most recognized on the field, but he took his athletic career the farthest," his friend Andrew Pridgeon wrote not long after Sept. 11 in an op-ed article published in the *Marin Independent Journal.* "He wasn't the funniest, but he made you laugh the hardest. He never had the most time, but he was always the one who was there."

STANLEY SMAGALA Jr.
Looking Forward to Baby

Her joke about Firefighter Stanley Smagala was that he was a good wife, said his wife, Dena Smagala. He cooked. He cleaned. He was handy. He was looking forward to having a family.

Firefighter Smagala's first child is due on Jan. 11, four months to the day he died at the World Trade Center as part of the team from Engine Company 226 in Brooklyn. He was 36.

"He loved kids and wanted a big family," Mrs. Smagala said. "He was very much looking forward to this baby."

Her husband's best qualities, his sense of humor and ease with people, were on display when he came to speak about fire safety to the fourth-grade class she taught in Seaford, on Long Island. "He'd act like a little kid," she said. "He had a big heart for children."

Michael Mason, a firefighter at Engine Company 226, said: "He was a real sweetheart, Stan. He was a good fireman. He cared about people and wasn't afraid to do the job." Firefighter Mason recalled that Firefighter Smagala, a big golfer and softball player, had a reputation as a Ping-Pong player.

"He'd always joke around, even at the worst of times," Firefighter Mason said. "I understand that he was laughing that day, on the way to the towers. He was a real good guy."

CATHERINE SMITH
Pepe Le Pew and Penelope

Catherine Smith and her companion, Elba Cedeno, fancied themselves Pepe Le Pew and Penelope from the Looney Tunes cartoon. Ms. Smith, a vice president at Marsh & McLennan, was the persistent skunk, pursuing a reluctant cat. Ms. Cedeno played hard to get for as long as she could. But when she fell, she fell hard.

They had known each other, in passing, for 20-odd years, both frequenting the same bar in Rockland County. A half-dozen years ago, when each of them was newly out of a relationship, they were formally introduced and delighted to have a shoulder to cry on. Friendship quickly turned to love.

"She conquered me," Ms. Cedeno said, breaking into a tearful chorus of "I didn't want to do it; I didn't want to do it."

Ms. Smith, 44, was a ray of sunshine, Ms. Cedeno said. She had an adorable smile and a sense of humor that turned crankiness to laughter. She drove a canary yellow Volkswagon and "she fit in that car so cute." She rooted for the Yankees, had an unexplained devotion to Dan Marino of the Miami Dolphins, traded baseball and football cards on eBay and loved to travel.

The couple was hoping for an early retirement and had recently built a beach house in Manahawkin, on the Jersey Shore, around the corner from Ms. Smith's mother. They were already talking about a trip to Italy three years hence, to celebrate Ms. Cedeno's 50th birthday. "We had so many goals," she said. "So many plans."

GEORGE SMITH
Crazy for His Grandmother

George Smith did a lot of things that would make a mother proud. He worked his way through college. He landed a good job as a senior business analyst at SunGard Asset Management. He even became the deacon of his local church.

But he was not a mama's boy. Instead, he would have been proud if you called him a grandma's boy.

Mr. Smith, 38, and his two sisters, Deborah Sallad and Christine Jackson, were raised by their grandmother, Marion Thomas, who held two jobs while making sure that the children went to church and Christian summer camps near their home in Phoenixville, Pa. Indeed, Mr. Smith was so devoted to his grandmother that he never wanted to leave, Mrs. Sallad said.

Even when he decided more than a decade ago to work in New York City, Mr. Smith chose to endure a rough commute—traveling three hours or so by train from his home in West Chester, Pa., on Sunday nights, staying in a corporate apartment during the week, then traveling back to Pennsylvania for the weekend—to be close to his grandmother.

"When he went to college, he told my grandma that I will always take care of you," Mrs. Sallad said about their grandmother, who is now 89 and battling uterine cancer. "He told her, 'You will have nothing to worry about.' "

JAMES GREGORY SMITH
"Ready to Bite a Bear"

Maybe James Gregory Smith's knack for finance began with the paper-route money he stashed in his Cap'n Crunch Treasure Box for safekeeping. Instead of frittering his funds away, he stockpiled them. From then on, he always held after-school jobs. A stalwart Islanders fan, he kept himself in hockey skates during high school in Hicksville, N.Y., helped put himself through college, and used contacts supplied by his uncle to land a series of jobs on Wall Street, the last at Cantor Fitzgerald.

He once told his sister, Barbara-Jayne Lewthwaite, that a successful trader needed to get up each morning "ready to bite a bear." Which he happily did. She suspects that in a less capitalistic landscape he might have preferred to run a little wine shop—he was a budding collector—or coach hockey.

"But he felt lucky to have his job; we grew up in a working-class family, and Jimmy's career choice turned out to be such a lucrative one," said Ms. Lewthwaite. It bought him and his wife, Donna, a home in Garden City. It meant he was able to take ski vacations with friends, and to take his four children on annual treks to Disney World. Recently it had allowed him to indulge, at age 43, in a sporty Saab convertible he wryly called his "change-of-life" mobile or, whenever he and Donna needed a night out on the town, his "date car."

JEFFREY RANDALL SMITH
Miami and Medieval Poems

Jeffrey Randall Smith met his wife, Ellen Bakalian, eight years ago, while on a diving vacation on Turks and Caicos Islands. Later, he taught her to hunt lobsters and she taught him to sail. She shared her love of medieval poetry; he reciprocated with an appreciation of the Hurricanes, the University of Miami football team.

He lived in Florida, she lived in New York. Hired in 1996 by Sandler O'Neill, Mr. Smith, an equity research analyst, moved to Manhattan. He loved showing friends the view from his office on the 104th floor of 2 World Trade Center.

After Mr. Smith, 36, and Ms. Bakalian were married in 1997, parenthood was the next great exploration. Daughter Margaret was born in 1998, and two years later came Charlotte. Both are November babies.

The family traveled to Europe and went camping, though perhaps their fondest memories are of summers spent sailing, swimming and canoeing at Green Pond in New Jersey. "We were going to put Maggie on skis this year and I'm still going to do it," Ms. Bakalian said.

KARL SMITH
Boating and Breakfast

Karl Smith liked all things active: he got his wife, Joanne, started on running, and when they were first dating, they took karate together.

Mr. Smith loved going to the beach and taking out his Hobie Cat boat. And he loved his sons, Karl Jr., 19, and Bradford, 16.

Most mornings, Mr. Smith, 44, had to wake up early for the long commute from Little Silver, N.J., to his job as a municipal bond broker at Cantor Fitzgerald in the World Trade Center.

But on weekends, he took on a different job: "He had this special thing, on weekends, when there would be a bunch of boys sleeping over," said his brother, Buddy Smith. "It might be 12 or 15 hungry young men from the swim team. Karl would make these breakfast menus and type them up, and pass them out the night before. Around election time, I remember, he had a dish on there called the W. In the morning, he'd get up early and make everyone what they wanted."

SANDRA FAJARDO SMITH
Happy in New York

When Sandra Fajardo Smith heard that her dear cousin, Wanda Fajardo, was feeling lonely and wanted to return to their native Brazil to celebrate her 43rd birthday, she would have none of it. Stay in New York, she told Wanda. Let me organize a birthday party. Trust me, you'll have a good time.

Ms. Smith was right. She was good at cheering people up. She was effervescent, always smiling. She loved her job as an accountant at Marsh & McLennan, loved working out at the gym, loved all of the city's cultural offerings.

But she especially loved her cousin. The two had grown up together, in a small inland town, and had come to New

The family of a New York City firefighter, Jonathan Lee Ielpi, arrive for his funeral on December 17 at St. Aloysius Roman Catholic Church in Great Neck, Long Island. Firefighter Ielpi was one of 343 firefighters killed on September 11 at the World Trade Center. (*Kevin P. Coughlin*)

York more than a decade ago. And even though Ms. Smith was seven years younger, Ms. Fajardo relied increasingly on Ms. Smith for advice.

"Sandra was so strong, so mature, and there was no one that I trusted more," said Ms. Fajardo, whose birthday party took place on Sept. 9. "She was like my therapist. I told her everything. Now, I don't know who I'm going to talk to."

ROCHELLE M. SNELL
A Guilty Pleasure: Wrestling

Rochelle M. Snell was a woman of passionate interests. She had this thing for Japanese films. She also loved everything Scottish and Irish. And she had a secret passion, too: wrestling. She had snared tickets to a couple of matches at Madison Square Garden, where she and her sister Shala d'Aquilar made a vow.

"It was like, 'We can't let people know we came,' " her sister said. "Where did this fascination come from?" asked Ms. d'Aguilar, who recalled a sweet-natured kid sister, nearly twice her size, who loved to squeeze her tight. "We're like Jamaican-American."

Ms. Snell was an administrative assistant and a whiz on computers at Regus, an office-leasing company in the south tower. She shared a house with her sister and mother in Mount Vernon, N.Y., where rose bushes and marigolds brighten the front yard. She rented stacks of foreign movies every week, cajoling her sister into watching them with her.

LEONARD JOSEPH SNYDER
Risky Work, Risky Play

He may have been a risk-management insurer, but Leonard Joseph Snyder was hardly averse to risk. He loved to ski and hunt, and spent many a weekend in dicey weather fishing with his father on the family boat off Long Beach Island in New Jersey.

But one of his greatest aspirations was so very much more tame: "He really wants to be a Little League coach when his children are old enough," said his mother-in-law, Kathleen Marquet. That would be the twins, Jason and Matthew, 2, and his 3-year-old daughter, Lauren.

Mr. Snyder, 34, a vice president at Aon Consultants on the 101st floor of 2 World Trade Center, loved nothing more than "carrying his sons around on his shoulders," she said. It says much about Mr. Snyder, of Cranford, N.J., that his large family and many friends have been distributing leaflets bearing his picture as they journey from hospital to hospital, "looking for Lenny," Mrs. Marquet said. "We won't say that it's too late."

ASTRID SOHAN
Fashion Enthusiast

Astrid Sohan could not sit still for college. Five times she enrolled and five times she dropped out. She wanted to get going on life, not listen to professors. She went to work, learned computer operating at I.B.M. and Johnson & Johnson and was hired to manage the technical support department at Marsh & McLennan. Her salary there let her do what she loved most: shop.

"Expensive clothes," said Clive Sohan, her father. "Ann Taylor. Talbots. Shoes—she had too many." Ms. Sohan, 33, learned about tailoring and natural fabrics from Barbara Sohan, her mother, a dressmaker in Hazlet, N.J. She liked simple leather pumps and classic tailored suits of cotton, silk or wool. She especially loved the jewelry—like a diamond-chip monkey pendant and a pair of black pearl earrings—that her mother had brought back from China and Hong Kong.

The other passion she shared with her mother was travel in hot countries. And even in beach towns, her clothes had flair. "She asked me to make a blouse that's unfinished," Mrs. Sohan said. "Purple. Cotton pique, with short sleeves. Just a little summer shirt to wear with jeans."

SUSHIL SOLANKI
"Comedian in the Family"

There are probably three things one needs to know about Sushil Solanki. He adored a good game of cricket, he doted on his 4-year-old son, Brendon, and at a meeting shortly before Sept. 11 with his family and a minister from his native India, he devoted himself to God.

"He was a cheerful, sensitive person," said Amit Macwan, who was married to Mr. Solanki's sister Sunita. "He was very, very close to his son. They often played cricket together. Brendon called him Sus—I never heard him call him Dad."

Mr. Solanki, 35, worked as a computer operator for Can-

tor Fitzgerald. He and his wife, Lynette, lived near his sister and her family on Staten Island. He was the kind of guy, Mr. Macwan recalled, who stopped by the house on Sept. 10 to ask why his pregnant sister's car was sitting in the driveway in the rain. He took the key and put the car in the garage.

"He told me, 'Don't drive anymore,' " Mrs. Macwan recalled. "He was very soft-hearted, the comedian in the family. His way of talking made people laugh."

NAOMI SOLOMON
Friends from Coast to Coast

Naomi Solomon was originally from California, Los Altos Hills to be exact, and was a graduate of Stanford University, class of 1971. But her West Coast pedigree did not stop her from being a "New Yorker through and through," said her first cousin Vivian Banta.

As the vice president for business development for Callixa, a California-based software company, Ms. Solomon, 52, frequently traveled to her home state, where her parents and two brothers still live.

"But she was always happy to come home to the city, to be in the middle of the energy and the activity," Ms. Banta said.

She loved theater and music, and was herself a classical pianist. She traveled frequently to Israel, and recently became involved with the Simon Wiesenthal Center, where, at a recent conference, she learned about the threat of terrorism in the United States.

Ms. Solomon lived on East 56th Street, not far from her Midtown office. On Sept. 11, she had gone to a technology conference at Windows on the World. When Ms. Banta first heard that her cousin was scheduled to be at the World Trade Center that morning, her only hope was that Ms. Solomon had been late, as usual. But on that day, she had arrived on time.

"She was very giving, very intuitive, a good listener and very generous of herself, very caring of her friends," Ms. Banta said. "She had more friends than you can imagine."

DANNY SONG
A Brother's Love

Danny Song was a sociable guy, a back-slapping bond broker at Cantor Fitzgerald and a former captain of his college football team who liked hanging out with his clients and spent a lot of time with his girlfriend, Mi Hyon Pak. But much more than your average 34-year-old, Mr. Song, who emigrated from South Korea as a child, was dedicated to keeping his nuclear family together.

He lived two blocks from his sister in TriBeCa. He made it financially possible for the family to buy a house in West

Orange, N.J., over the summer so that his parents could finally move out from Wisconsin, where he was raised. And he was particularly close to his brother, Frank, 37.

The brothers had lived together in New York since 1990. When Danny Song first moved to the city and Frank Song was working as a bond trader, Frank Song carried him through the lean years. When Frank Song decided he wanted to become an actor, his brother returned the favor. The brothers would do anything for each other.

"He's my soul mate," Frank Song said, "my partner in life." Now, Frank Song has quit acting and taken on a new role: Danny's job as a bond broker, at a different firm but with many of the same clients, who encouraged him to step into his brother's shoes. "It's kind of a way to remain close to my brother," he said.

As an adult, living in the city and working as a bond salesman at Keefe Bruyette & Woods, Greg Spagnoletti was a problem-solver, caretaker and coach, checking in on his kid brother every day, helping his dad with his finances, organizing an ice hockey team at Chelsea Piers and dropping in on Anthony, the neighborhood tailor, with a cup of coffee.

And Mr. Spagnoletti, who would have turned 33 on Oct. 18, remained as neat and particular as ever. Two years ago, he bought a 1,200-square-foot apartment on West 72nd Street. It was perfectly livable, but he and his fiancée, Gretchen Zurn, spent nine months gutting it to its slab and girders and putting it back together again.

"When all was said and done, he was so proud of it," Paul Spagnoletti said. "It would take him 45 minutes to give you the tour."

TIMOTHY P. SOULAS
Raising a Family of Friends

Timothy P. Soulas was director of Cantor Fitzgerald's foreign currency desk in New York, but his life revolved around his family. He was one of five children who were best friends with one another, and he and his wife, Katy, who met during a history class at Cardinal O'Hara High School in Springfield, Pa., wanted their family to be the same way.

They had five children—a sixth is due in March—and Mr. Soulas coached many of their teams. He coached ice hockey last year, T-ball last spring, roller hockey during the summer and football in the fall. For his wife's 35th birthday in June, Mr. Soulas surprised her with a barbecue for 100 people in their backyard in Basking Ridge, N.J. To get her out of the house, he gave her a day at Elizabeth Arden. To "get back at him" on his 35th birthday in August, Mrs. Soulas surprised him with a chocolate Labrador puppy. She brought it to a football game and asked someone else to hold the leash. Mr. Soulas looked longingly at the dog. "Isn't it beautiful?" he asked.

Mrs. Soulas told him to pick a name, because the puppy was his, but Mr. Soulas thought she was joking. "I gave him a kiss and said, 'He really is yours,' " she said. "It was awesome."

He named the dog Boomer.

DONALD F. SPAMPINATO Jr.
Family and Triathlon Man

Donald F. Spampinato Jr., 39, was in very good shape, so good that he once qualified for the famous Iron Man triathlon in Hawaii. When he became a husband and a father, he continued to compete, but he made sure his training never got in the way of time with his wife, Laurie, and three sons, Donald, 6, David, 4, and Peter, 22 months.

"He would go for a swim in the morning before work at the pool club up the street, or he would go for a run in the evening after the kids were in bed," his wife said. "It was important that we have dinner together every night, that he give the boys their bath. If he trained in the morning, he would always be back in time for breakfast."

Before trying his hand at Wall Street, Mr. Spampinato, a lifelong resident of Manhasset, N.Y., had worked as a high school teacher and coach. As a corporate bond trader at Cantor Fitzgerald, he was at his desk on the 104th floor of the World Trade Center's north tower every morning at 7:30. He had signed up to coach his older sons' soccer teams this fall. On Sept. 8, he had completed a triathlon—a competition that includes swimming, biking and running—at Point Lookout on Long Island.

GREGORY SPAGNOLETTI
The Meticulous Brother

Most kids hate hand-me-downs. But Paul Spagnoletti did not mind wearing his brother Gregory's, because the clothes always seemed practically new, arriving spotless and crisply folded. Greg was the third of the four Spagnoletti brothers—best friends and hockey fanatics all—and he was utterly meticulous. He was also, as Paul Spagnoletti put it, "definitely the responsible one."

ROBERT W. SPEAR Jr.
Always Giving 150 Percent

When the Spear family had not heard from "Robbie," as they called 30-year-old Robert W. Spear Jr., a firefighter, by late afternoon on Sept. 11, they began to worry. He was always in constant contact with his wife and mother, sometimes having rushed cell phone conversations from the back of a speeding fire truck.

The family's thoughts had been centered on Timothy A.

Haviland, Firefighter Spear's brother-in-law, whose office on the 96th floor in tower one of the trade center they saw burning on television.

"I didn't think my son was there," said Irene Spear DeSantis, Firefighter Spear's mother. "But of course he would have been there. This is a man who took a sizable pay cut to join the Fire Department. Anything he did, he did 150 percent."

Firefighter Spear took the entrance test for the Fire Department almost 10 years ago, but it was not hiring at the time, his mother said, so he climbed the ranks in other occupations instead. When the department finally did call, there was no hesitation.

"And he loved it," his mother said of his job with Engine Company 26 in the South Bronx. "He loved the camaraderie."

TIMOTHY A. HAVILAND's portrait appears on page 211.

MAYNARD S. SPENCE Jr.
Stealth Love Notes

Barbara Spence was thumbing through a cookbook in the fall of 2001, when she noticed a note stuck between the pages among the cookie recipes. It read, "I love you, M."

The M was Maynard S. Spence Jr., 42, her husband, a man with a deep devotion and a flair for the romantic. A few years earlier, Mr. Spence had exhausted an entire pad of sticky notes to his wife and hidden them around the house; even today, Mrs. Spence is finding them.

His love notes may have been stealth, but his presence was not. His laugh was big and deep, and colleagues at the Marsh & McLennan office in Atlanta—a construction safety consultant, he was at the World Trade Center on Sept. 11 for a meeting—always knew when the gregarious, seemingly perpetually happy Mr. Spence was in the vicinity.

"It was the most honest laugh you could imagine," his manager, Gary L. Pohlmann, said of Mr. Spence, whom family and friends also remember for his love of barbecue and pickup basketball. The laugh, Mr. Pohlmann said, was one that "everybody in our office continues to wait to hear."

GEORGE E. SPENCER III
Chase Dreams, He Taught

Fifty years ago, when George E. Spencer was born, he was the third person in his family to carry that name. So his parents immediately branded him Twig, the newest branch on the family tree.

The nickname stuck. With the exception of his colleagues at Euro Brokers, which Mr. Spencer joined earlier this year, he was Twig to all.

In spite of his button-down style, Mr. Spencer liked to shock. Living in London during the 1980s, he startled his neighbors by barbecueing in the rain. He stunned conservative colleagues by wearing a pink oxford-cloth shirt to work one Friday, a color no Briton dared to don. Soon every Friday was a pink-shirt day.

A veteran of several Wall Street firms, Mr. Spencer hoped to retire and teach history, his wife, Cathy, said. He liked to combine exercise and adventure—climbing, mountain biking, body surfing, sailing.

Most important, Mr. Spencer always encouraged his wife, daughter and son to chase their dreams. "He was always a lot prouder of me than I was," Mrs. Spencer said. On the morning of Sept. 11, he left her a note on the kitchen counter of their West Norwalk, Conn., home. "Stop being critical of yourself," it said. "Enjoy life. Today is another day. Chance to live a little."

ROBERT SPENCER
A Breath of Salt Air

After the four-hour drive to Bethany Beach, Del., Christine Spencer was eager to unpack the car. But her husband, Robert Andrew Spencer, never let her. "Not until we feel the sand on our feet," he would say, and then he would lead the way, galloping down the beach and plunging headfirst into the salt spray.

Mr. Spencer, known to everyone as either Andy or Spence, had grown up with the smell of salt air and was determined to pass along his love of the shore to his children. "He was sort of like the Pied Piper," said his brother, Michael. He would lead Addison, 5, and Kathryn, 3, into

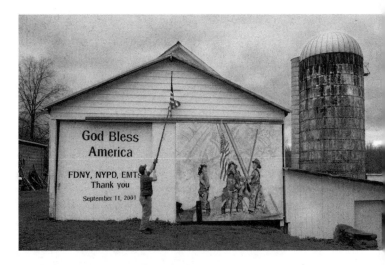

On the Manno family farm in Warwick, New York, a mural by Rocco Manno, a high school art teacher, remembers September 11. A cousin, Jason Makuch, unfurls a flag. (*Chris Ramirez*)

the water at full speed. Then he might drape a strand of seaweed over his ears to keep them laughing. "The guy had a lot of positive energy," said John Greeley, a friend. "He was one of those people who just don't sit down."

Mr. Spencer, 35, left his Middletown, N.J., home at 5 A.M. to get to his job as a foreign exchange broker at Cantor Fitzgerald. He usually returned home a little after 6 P.M., in time to put the girls to bed. A third child, Robert Philip, was born on Aug. 16.

In what she called a celebration of life, Mrs. Spencer decided to have the baby's baptism and her husband's memorial service on the same day.

MARY RUBINA SPERANDO
Her First Trade Show

Mary Rubina Sperando managed her different roles with an easy grace: working days, going to school at night for her master's degree, modeling on the side, while staying close to her parents, her cousins, her friends.

"She was professional, organized and beautiful, inside and out," said her cousin, Catherine Lamonica. "She did for everyone, and she was always grace under fire."

Ms. Sperando, 39, known to almost everyone as Mitzi, loved the job she got last summer, as director of marketing and communications at Encompys, a high-tech company. Her poised presence in the office was hard to miss: even in the August heat, her colleagues remember, the new marketing director always made an impeccable fashion statement.

Members of Hadassah took gifts to Engine Company 23 in Manhattan on December 20. The company lost five members on September 11. (*Edward Keating*)

She was excited about her first trade show for the company—Sept. 11, at the World Trade Center—and so proud of the new sign for the Encompys booth that she invited the whole office to a 4 P.M. unveiling celebration, where as usual, she brought and served her favorite cheesecake, from Junior's.

"You name the bakery, the candy shop, she knew where it was," said her cousin. "She loved to share whatever she found."

FRANK J. SPINELLI
Family, First and Foremost

For much of the year, it was still dark when Frank J. Spinelli, 44, boarded the morning train at Short Hills, N.J., for the commute to Manhattan. A foreign exchange broker, he was usually at work by 6 A.M., tracking overseas markets, and his workday was often not over at 5 P.M. There were clients to wine and dine. He had been doing it for 20 years on Wall Street, though only the last seven months for Cantor Fitzgerald, on the 105th floor of 1 World Trade Center.

On weekends, he and his wife, Michelle, were on the sidelines cheering at the soccer, lacrosse, track and football games of their three children, Nicole, 17, Christopher, 14, and Danielle, 8.

"He was dedicated to his family, to the children," Mrs. Spinelli said. "That was his main focus. Many of the letters we received from his colleagues said the same thing—that his family was the most important thing in his life."

On Sept. 11, Mr. Spinelli called home and left a message. "He knew a plane had struck the building and said he was going to try to get out. The end of the message was, 'I love you and I'll see you later.'" There was no panic in his voice; he had been a volunteer emergency medical technician for five years.

His body was found two weeks later.

JOSEPH P. SPOR Jr.
Like Father, Like Son

Joseph P. Spor Jr. followed in his father's footsteps from the day he was born, which happened to be his father's birthday.

Like his father, he became a firefighter in the Bronx. Like his father, he also worked as a contractor, skilled enough to raise the roof on his Cape Cod house in Somers, N.Y. And in August, Firefighter Spor, 35, was assigned to the same company, Rescue 3 in the Bronx, where his father had worked. "He was ecstatic," said his wife, Colleen. "He was practicing every night on ropes to get all the different knots he'd be tested on."

Before joining the Fire Department in 1994, Firefighter Spor had an office job in Manhattan. But as the youngest of six children, and the only boy, the pull of his father's boots was irresistible. "He was never all that cut out for a suit and tie," said Michael Griffin, a close friend.

When he wasn't at the firehouse, Firefighter Spor usually strapped on his tool belt. His neighbor Michael Hurson was building a deck in his backyard when they first met. "He came nosing down the driveway and said, 'Show me what you're doing,'" Mr. Hurson said. "Then he brought over his own lunch bucket and helped me finish."

Firefighter Spor never got to complete the remodeling of his own house. His Fire Department colleagues took care of the siding. And his father finished the deck.

SARANYA SRINUAN
A Special Style

While Saranya Srinuan was dressing for her 23rd birthday in August, her best friend couldn't help admiring her long, straight hair and model's figure, accentuated by stylish black pants and a white blouse.

"You remind me of Samantha from *Sex and the City*," Jan Julsuwan remembers telling her. Ms. Srinuan just laughed.

Ms. Srinuan always looked impossibly chic to her friends. She had modeled a little before taking a job as a bond trader after college, and confided that she wanted to work in the fashion industry some day. She loved to shop at Banana Republic and French Connection. And this week, she had planned to attend a runway show.

But her family and friends counted on more than her good taste.

"I could share really, really personal stuff with her," said Ms. Julsuwan, who grew up with her in the same building. "We just understood each other."

FITZROY ST. ROSE
Dominica, Oh, Dominica

Fitzroy St. Rose displayed the national flag of his island country, Dominica, on the bedroom wall of his sparsely furnished apartment in the East Bronx. He was constantly trying to set people straight about the Commonwealth of Dominica, part of the Windward Islands.

No, he told them, it's not the Dominican Republic, where even Dominica's postal mail is sometimes sent.

He was so loyal to his impoverished homeland that last year he helped organize a group, the Exodus Club, to raise money for its hospitals and other institutions. The club often met in his small apartment.

His loved ones gathered there for a prayer meeting Saturday night, returning to clean up Sunday morning.

Mr. St. Rose, 40 and single, was a computer technician

for General Telecom in 1 World Trade Center. He had a shy smile and an upbeat stride. He seemed to stand a bit taller, one close friend said, when he was doing things out of the goodness of his heart.

"Ninety people in the world would say he's my best friend," says Irving Guye, the friend. "That's how connected he was to the rest of the world."

MICHAEL STABILE
With Just One Look

At the Staten Island Catholic Youth Organization, Michael Stabile was known as "a go-to guy," a referee who would come to a basketball game on a moment's notice, who would work two games a night if asked.

"He was the type of guy I could always call," said Tony Navarino, Staten Island C.Y.O. director. "He just loved doing it for the kids."

Roseanna Stabile met her husband when he was playing football for the Brooklyn Hurricanes, and she had come with friends from Sheepshead Bay to watch a game in Marine Park. They were both 16.

"With the first look, we were attracted to each other," she said, "and 30 years later, we were still together."

After they were married but before they moved to Staten Island, the Stabiles lived in an apartment in Brooklyn which would fill up on Saturday nights—with the boys he was coaching in football, and the girls she was teaching to be cheerleaders. "There would be about 30 kids in the apartment," Mrs. Stabile recalled.

"It was a way of keeping them off the streets."

While his children, Michele, Robert and Lauren, were still in school, Mr. Stabile, 50, tried his hand at coaching basketball and soccer. He had his day job—most recently as a currency broker at Euro Brokers. But besides the Mets ("he didn't want to hear anything about the Yankees," said his wife), he was most devoted to the C.Y.O. basketball games. "He lived to referee," she said.

TIMOTHY STACKPOLE
Back at Work, as a Captain

After the floor collapsed in the East New York inferno of June 5, 1998, leaving two firefighters dead and Lt. Timothy Stackpole severely burned on his arms, legs, stomach and back, he worried that he might never work again. But he threw himself into months of treatment and physical therapy, encouraged by his wife, Tara, and his five children, who now range in age from 7 to 18. And he used the seemingly endless recuperation time to finish his bachelor's degree in education at St. Francis College in Brooklyn.

After some months of light duty at Ladder 103 in Brooklyn, "he felt it was a tremendous victory when he came back to the firehouse to full duty a few months ago," said the Rev. Jim Cunningham, the Stackpoles' parish priest in Marine Park, Brooklyn. The Thursday before the terrorist attack, Lieutenant Stackpole was promoted to captain. And on the Saturday before the disaster, Captain Stackpole was named Irishman of the Year at the Great Irish Fair in Brooklyn, Father Cunningham said.

On Sept. 11, Captain Stackpole had just finished duty, but with the first news of the calamity he rushed to the trade center, "and he perished there," Father Cunningham said. "Tara knows that Timmy died doing what he wanted to do, serving the people of his city."

ERIC A. STAHLMAN
Selling "Bird Burgers"

Eric Adam Stahlman's parents often had exchange students from South America living at their home in Patchogue, on Long Island. Eric and his buddy Gary were fascinated and decided they would marry South American women. Eric did. Blanca is from Ecuador. They were married eight years and had two children, Allison, 7, and Jacob, 4.

Mr. Stahlman, 43, worked hard: out of the house by 6 A.M. to get to jobs in banking, and eventually, money trading at Cantor Fitzgerald. But one interlude stands out for his big sister Kathy: for a few months when he was out of a job that called for a suit and tie, he helped her sell "bird burgers" from a pushcart in Manhattan. Occasionally he promoted the business in a chicken costume, learning the ways of the pushcart business, from not taking a competitor's spot to feeding the homeless quickly so they would not drive other customers away.

He loved the city, glorying in new restaurants, the Yankees, the Giants and the Islanders, and his friends. His lifelong buddy, Gary Meo, said "You always had to fight him for a dinner check or a bar bill or a greens fee."

GREGORY STAJK
Sports Hero? No, Real One

As a student at C. W. Post on Long Island, Gregory Stajk dreamed of becoming a major league pitcher. He went further than most, landing a couple of tryouts, but did not make a team. Instead, Mr. Stajk, 46, the nephew of a firefighter, fulfilled another boyhood ambition, and would have celebrated his 20th anniversary with the Fire Department of New York early next year.

"He used to say, 'I could retire but Mom, I love my job,'" said his mother, Marge Stajk.

A bachelor, Firefighter Stajk had an oceanfront condo in Long Beach, on Long Island, and often went cycling and running on the boardwalk. He was also a trivia buff and a caricaturist. "There are not a lot of people in this world who have as many passions as my brother," said a sister, Jean Somerville.

Firefighter Stajk, who was called Bro around the firehouse, always worked on holidays, his family said, so that firefighters with children could have the day off.

And unlike many single people, Firefighter Stajk did not mind cooking for himself, his mother said. On Sept. 10, she could tell from a receipt lying on his kitchen counter, he made himself a beef stew. Enough for the next night's meal was in the refrigerator.

MARY STANLEY
Modest Helpmate

Mary Stanley was not the kind to go on and on about herself. Even her closest friend, Bunny Johnson, did not know until after her death that Mrs. Stanley was a vice president at Marsh & McLennan. Nor did Mrs. Johnson know what had brought her from the Midwest to New York as a teenager, with just a high school diploma, or why she was out of touch with most of her family.

But Mrs. Johnson, who grew up in Bedford Stuyvesant with Mrs. Stanley's husband, Paul, did not care. It was enough for her that "every important occasion, there was Mary." When the Johnsons' landmark home was gutted by fire, for example, Mrs. Stanley was at her friend's side, on nights and weekends for nearly a year, sifting through debris, restoring ruined woodwork and helping to replace what was lost with a steady stream of gifts.

Mrs. Stanley, 53, was equally steadfast when her husband, 14 years her senior, had a brain embolism more than two decades ago. Mrs. Johnson said that everyone "gave Paul up for dead, but he survived because of Mary." She became the family breadwinner, while Mr. Stanley was the cook. She also was in charge of technology, as she was at work. Mr. Stanley does not even know how to turn on the answering machine, Mrs. Johnson said. So these days the phone just rings and rings.

ANTHONY STARITA
Relaxing with a Cigar

Cigars were a necessary accessory for Anthony Starita. He had one in his mouth when he went to beach, when he puttered around his backyard in Westfield, N.J., and when he relaxed on his deck every night after dinner. "He liked the flavor," said his wife, Diane Starita. "He didn't always actually smoke them, but he would just have one in his mouth to sort of chew on."

Mr. Starita, 35, also chewed on coffee straws, mostly when he got nervous about a deal at his job as a government bond trader at Cantor Fitzgerald. "When he got a little nervous he put the straws in his mouth and he would start wiping his hands with napkins," said Eddie De Castro, Mr. Starita's longtime friend and former trading partner. "Those were his two things."

Last year, Mr. Starita gave up his full-time golf membership at a country club so that he could spend more time with his wife and two children, Kaila, 6, and Jason, 3.

After the terrorist attacks, Mrs. Starita told the children that their father had gone to heaven. Kaila wondered why "does he have to be with God?" Mrs. Starita said. "My 3-year-old wanted to know if we could call Daddy in heaven."

JEFFREY STARK
A Thoughtful Boyfriend

Let's make one thing clear: Firefighter Jeffrey Stark did the chest-thumping things, too.

He went hunting and fly-fishing, he golfed and did carpentry—some activities with distinction, others with good humor. Relatively new to the department, and with two older brothers already there, he had some catching up to do, so he was always trying to hone his skills. Fires made him nervous but what he really dreaded, he told his girlfriend, was making mistakes in front of the other firefighters at Engine Company 230 in Brooklyn.

Tough-guy credentials established.

Because another truth about Firefighter Stark was that he must have dropped down here from Boyfriend Heaven.

Consider: he drove his girlfriend, Katharine Suarez, home every night after law school so she would not have to take the train; took her food when she was studying; dropped off her laundry and picked it up; made three trips to the paint store without complaining when she changed her mind about the kitchen color; went out at 4 A.M. on a New Year's Eve looking for Band-Aids for her nasty cut; and researched recipes to entice her to eat her broccoli.

He was 30, he looked after his widowed mother, Rosemary, in Staten Island, and he had a quiet, unassuming way about him.

And a startling, melodic, high-pitched laugh.

DEREK J. STATKEVICUS
Father-and-Son Dog Lovers

Derek J. Statkevicus was never a dog person. For one thing, he did not like dog hair everywhere, said his wife, Kimberley Young Statkevicus. When she finally persuaded him that she needed a pet, he decided on a basset hound because he thought it would look goofy and just sit around (she wanted something more high-energy, like a retriever).

Then came Squirt: half basset, half yellow Lab, very cute (and house-trained to boot). "He totally fell in love with that dog," Mrs. Statkevicus said, "even to having her on the bed!"

Though he commuted an hour and a half each way from Norwalk, Conn., to his job as an equity analyst at Keefe, Bruyette & Woods, Mrs. Statkevicus said, "Derek would take her on walks, play ball with her, give her baths and stuff."

And a good thing, too, because Tyler, their son, was born in August 2000, a year after Squirt arrived, and another baby is due in January. (Mr. Statkevicus, 30, loved being a father.)

These days, Squirt gets her exercise in the backyard, sometimes with Tyler, who loves to climb on her. In addition to adoring Squirt, Tyler takes after his father in other ways, Mrs. Statkevicus said: "He's very active, very smart."

CRAIG STAUB
He Had Two Birthdays Coming

A new wife, a new house and, almost, a new baby. "He got married last year and he had just had their house built for them" in New Jersey, Ken Donohue said of his younger brother, Craig Staub, who had worked at the World Trade Center long enough to be there the first time it was attacked. On Sept. 11, Craig Staub's wife, Stacey, who is due on her husband's birthday, Sept. 22, 2001, with the couple's first child, sat at home, unable to watch the news, wearing her husband's slippers, bathrobe and a T-shirt he had gotten that read, "I survived the World Trade Center bombing."

Mr. Donohue said his only hope that his brother was still alive lay in a joke the two shared. Watching a horror movie, he explained, when the monster burst in, they would turn to each other and say, "Time for self," which meant, "There was no time to say goodbye, it was just time to run," Mr. Donohue said. "Like I said to Stacey, Craig knew what time for self was."

WILLIAM STECKMAN
Neither Wind nor Hail

For most of the 35 years that William Steckman worked for NBC, he tended the company's transmitter in 1 World Trade Center, and worked the night shift just about all that time. None of the wild weather—the lashing hailstorms, passing hurricanes or strokes of lightning—really bothered him, "because he was so confident in the strength of that building, he knew nothing could happen to it," said Jerry Vandagna, his father-in-law.

Furthermore, Mr. Steckman, a 56-year-old audio engineer, liked the night shift not only because it let him spend time during the day in West Hempstead, N.Y., with his five children, but also because it gave him a chance to fix everything around the house.

"He could fix absolutely anything," Mr. Vandagna said.

Knowing that, his boss phoned and asked if he could stay after his shift ended at 6 A.M. on the morning of Sept. 11. He always stayed whenever new equipment was being installed. After the first plane crashed, Mr. Steckman phoned his boss and said, "I'll power down and get out."

ERIC STEEN
Man for All Callings

Eric Steen spent his days as a bond trader for Euro Brokers in 2 World Trade Center. But he had a secret desire to make his mark in the arts, and that is why he was working on a screenplay, finishing a novel and launching a film-production company in his spare time.

"He didn't want to divulge that until it was all finished," said his friend David Hegarty, who attended Garden City High School with him. "He was a pretty deep thinker, and he was very well read, so that was a whole other area where he could feel fulfilled outside of Wall Street."

Mr. Steen, 32, who had moved from Cantor Fitzgerald to Euro Brokers in 2001, was also an athlete who ran five miles a day, skied, kayaked, snowboarded and surfed, said his mother, Blanche. Surfing was a recent passion, and Mr. Hegarty said he had been teaching him in the waves off Breezy Point in Queens.

On December 21, visitors stop by a memorial in Battery Park City to victims of the September 11 terrorist attack on the World Trade Center. Past visitors left a Canadian flag, flowers and messages of healing at the site. (*Ruby Washington*)

"He always wanted to try new things."

Mr. Steen took a line from *Fast Times at Ridgemont High* and made it his own. Whenever they made plans to do something together, Mr. Steen would finish up by saying, "I'll pick you up in the van, dude."

ALEX STEINMAN
Bells Ring for Alumnus

Alex Steinman grew up in Staten Island and went to boarding school when he was 14. A few months earlier, his mother had died in a car accident, and when he arrived he was "totally lost and just looking for something solid," said his wife, Tracy Orr-Steinman.

For his first two years at Suffield Academy, in the hills of northern Connecticut, he struggled just to get his work done. But in his junior year, he was elected class president, and from then on was a leader and a force at the school, where he also played soccer and football. At a memorial for him there, Mr. Steinman, a 32-year-old from Hoboken, N.J., who worked on the equity sales desk at Cantor Fitzgerald, was remembered by a former headmaster for "his charisma, his sense of humor and his ability to bring people together and inspire a sense of teamwork and family," said Ms. Tracy Orr-Steinman, who met him when both were students at the school.

In the center of the campus is Bell Hill, topped with a bronze bell that is rung only on special occasions, like when the soccer team wins a game. Once a year, it is also rung in honor of alumni who have died. After the memorial for Alex Steinman, the headmaster explained the significance of the bell and then invited Mr. Steinman's family and friends to ring it. One by one, people stepped forward and the bell clanged again and again, echoing over the playing fields that unfold below the hill.

ANDREW STERN
A Circle of Life

How to fathom the circuitous and horrifying symmetry of the twin towers in the story of Andrew Stern, a Cantor Fitzgerald broker.

"Our lives started together in the World Trade Center and now they have ended with it," said his wife, Katie. The couple met there in 1986. That was at Dean Witter Reynolds, as it was then called, when it was in 2 World Trade Center. He was a trader. She was a sales assistant. "I didn't really know him well," she said. "We met at the copy machine."

Hindsight reveals how perceptibly, but inevitably, photocopying led to dating, and marriage, and children—Danny is 7, Emma is 4—"and as the years went by, I fell in love with him more and more," his wife said. They both moved on, and out, of the trade center, but Mr. Stern returned—this time to 1 World Trade Center—to be a broker in Cantor Fitzgerald's municipal bond department on the 104th floor.

And so it happened that Saturday, Sept. 8, they drove in from Bellmore, N.Y., to attend a Manhattan wedding, and stayed overnight in the Roosevelt Hotel. "I'm so glad to have a memory of that romantic evening," his wife said. But when they left on that beautiful Sunday morning, they walked down Fifth Avenue toward Pennsylvania Station, "and we could both see the trade center, right there before us."

MICHAEL JAMES STEWART
His Favorite Talent

When Michael James Stewart came to New York 20 years ago, he joined the Old Blue rugby club, one of the best clubs on the East Coast. He was an immediate star, but some of the other players did not know what to make of him.

"He looked like a skinny, little guy with crazy sideburns and a goatee, and he wore all black," recalled Greg Finn, a good friend and former teammate. "He looked like a punk rocker; he didn't look athletic. People looked at him and wondered, 'Who is this guy?' I think Michael enjoyed that. He believed you couldn't judge a book by its cover."

Mr. Stewart, 42, was not easy to figure out. He was a Protestant born in Belfast, Ireland, but one of his best friends at the University of Stirling in Scotland was Catholic. He was a poetry major who later earned an M.B.A. He broke his nose, his ribs and his collar bone playing rugby, but was extremely gentle with his three sons. And he continued to wear earrings in both ears even as he worked in banking and finance, most recently at Carr Futures on the 92nd floor of 1 World Trade Center.

Despite Mr. Stewart's love for rugby and other sports, his love for his sons was greater. His fiancée, Kristin Galusha-Wild, said that once, on a car trip, she had asked him what talent he was most proud of. "Being a dad," he answered.

RICHARD STEWART
Looking for Meaning

Hockey brought him records and rings, but Richard Stewart did not think of those times as his glory days, because he had set his eyes on a new goal after moving to New York. Mr. Stewart, 35, involved himself in St. James Episcopal Church on the Upper East Side, where he lived. He served meals to the homeless on Friday nights and was active in the church's young adult group.

"It was fairly clear to us that Rich was looking for more meaning in his life," said the Rev. Craig Townsend, associate rector of St. James. "Most people here didn't know anything about his being a hockey star."

Mr. Stewart started skating at 4, and by the time he was 16 had set the season record for goals scored at the Upland Country Day School in Kennett Square, Pa., a record that lasted 13 years. He went on to become a part of the St. Lawrence University hockey team that made it to the National Collegiate Athletic Association finals in 1988, and is in the university's hall of fame.

Mr. Stewart remained a hockey fan when he started working as a broker for Cantor Fitzgerald six years ago. He put away his skates, but not the helping hand.

"Richie was always helping people, no matter who they were," said his mother, Joan. "He lived a spiritual life and always tried to find the bright side of a situation."

DOUGLAS STONE
Perfect Business Partner

To know Douglas Stone was to know his distinctive brand of humor. "Cynical and dry" his son Zachary called it. "When he got going, everyone would be in tears." His business partner, Tad Parker, recalled the day that Mr. Stone, after dealing with some prickly personnel issue, sat down, looked up at the ceiling and stretched his arms out. "Can you feel the love?" he said, adding: "Human resources isn't my forte. Let's go have a toddy."

Mr. Parker and Mr. Stone, 54, owned Odyssey Press, in Dover, N.H., and to Mr. Parker it was "a professional marriage made in heaven." Mr. Stone, he said, was a master at sniffing out problems that might spell trouble later.

Mr. Stone was divorced, but stayed connected with Zachary, who lived in California with his mother. Theirs "was better than a lot of father-son relationships; he was one of my best friends," said Zachary, who flew East every summer. "I worked in his printshop from the time I was tall enough to stand on a skid."

Mr. Stone flew to California often, and was on hand to watch his son break two minutes in the 800-meter run—"one of the best things I got to share with him," Zachary said.

Although Mr. Stone's trip, on Flight 11, was for business, he also planned to help Zachary settle in at U.C.L.A. for his freshman year.

LONNY STONE
Life Is Like a Good Burger

Sometimes, the family of Lonny Stone would lie on top of one another to make a hamburger. Lonny, at the bottom, was half the bun.

His sons, Joshua, 9, and Alex, 12, were the meat and the pickle. His wife, Stacey,

was the top of the bun, and their dog, Sammy, was the coleslaw.

As for real hamburgers, Mr. Stone stopped eating them and other meat three years ago, when he turned 40. He started jogging, eating organic foods and thinking about the yin and yang of things.

"In the last year or so, he would always tell me, 'Live for the moment, dear,' " his wife said. "We'd be watching the boys play in the garden and he would say, 'Take a picture of it in your mind.' "

She did, and not just of the boys. "We'd been together so long, but when the dog and I would stand at the door waiting for him to get out of the car, my heart would still skip a beat," she said.

Two years ago, life became even sweeter when Mr. Stone landed a dream job as operations manager at Carr Futures. "He loved going to work," Mrs. Stone said. He even made good use of the commute from Bellmore, N.Y. On Aug. 23, their 15th anniversary, his wife came home to find a two-page letter he had written on the train, full of hearts and smiley faces and loving sentiments.

"Maybe he knew something, 'cause it wasn't like him to write a letter," she said. "That letter was like he was saying good-bye to me."

JIMMY N. STOREY
A Reader of Mysteries

Jimmy N. Storey's wife, Pam, does not believe the way her husband died makes him an automatic hero. But the flood of letters she received after Sept. 11 from people whose lives he had touched and careers he had mentored as far back as the 1970s made her deeply proud of the heroic figure he had been during his life.

A senior vice president for Marsh & McLennan based in Houston, Mr. Storey was visiting the company's offices in the World Trade Center on Sept. 11. After his death, Ms. Storey said, letters poured in from as far away as Spokane, Wash., where the couple lived 22 years ago when Mr. Storey worked for Aetna Insurance.

Mr. Storey, 58, was a voracious reader of mysteries, an avid history buff and a doting father and grandfather. His daughter Cynthia used to call him daily with problems and questions about personal and world events. Often, he picked up her children from the day care center near his Houston office when she needed help.

Jeri Riggs holds a quilt she made to commemorate the September 11 terror attacks. In it, a skeletal piece of the World Trade Center overlays a traditional Islamic screen pattern. (*Joyce Dopkeen*)

His other daughter, Tracey, recalls his lending her money to open her first bank account—and taking it away after she spent it, violating the terms of the loan. Ms. Storey took to heart the lesson about trust and its boundaries. "It takes a certain love and respect for your children to be able to teach them things like that," she said.

THOMAS S. STRADA
"Sky Was the Limit"

What made Terry Strada fall fast in love with her husband, Thomas, when they met 20 years ago? "Oh my God, he was the most fun person I ever knew," Mrs. Strada said. "He would take me out, and the sky was the limit. Limos, dinners. I said I liked the Boston Celtics; he flew me to Boston to see them."

Three months after Mr. Strada's death, his wife is still inundated with calls from people eager to reminisce about thrills they experienced, courtesy of Thomas Strada.

"If they went fishing with him, it was the best fishing trip they ever had," Mrs. Strada said. "If they went to the track with him and he won money, he'd share it and make everyone a winner for the night."

Mr. Strada, 41, a bond broker at Cantor Fitzgerald, also ensured that his son, Thomas, 7, and daughter, Kaitlyn, 4, experienced as much exhilaration as they could handle. The family visited Disney World three times since Tommy was born. Just 10 days before his death, Mr. Strada helped the boy catch his first bass.

There is one family member, however, who has missed out on the joy of life with Mr. Strada. He is Justin Thomas, Mr. Strada's third child. He was just four days old on Sept. 11.

JAMES J. STRAINE Jr.
Pleasure from Fishing

Last August, the Straine family moved to Oceanport, N.J., so that James Straine, 36, could be near the ocean and the Shrewsbury River. Everywhere you go in Oceanport you can see water, and it was just perfect for his great passion, fishing. He would arrive home from his job as a bond salesman at Cantor Fitzgerald in the World Trade Center, scoop up his son Finn, 3, and off they would go, to fish.

"He and Finn were best friends," said Mr. Straine's wife, Trish. Last summer, Finn caught his first one, a little snapper, and naturally, Mr. Straine took a picture.

Mr. Straine was also dedicated to his job. When his second son, Charlie, was born on Sept. 5, he took one day off, then he worked half-days. Sept. 10 was his first full day back at work. "He should have been home," Mrs. Straine said.

On Sunday, Sept. 9, the Straines and Mrs. Straine's mother, Dolores Carr, went to the park. There were some children fishing, and Mr. Straine helped them bait and cast their lines. "He just loved that," Mrs. Straine said. "That's exactly why we moved down there. It was a perfect day."

GEORGE J. STRAUCH
Did It "All the Way"

George J. Strauch was, in the words of one friend, "just a regular, great guy" who never did anything halfway.

Mr. Strauch, 53, worked as an insurance broker at Aon at 2 World Trade Center. He commuted there each day from Avon-By-the-Sea in New Jersey because he loved the water and almost any sport connected to water. He was an avid sportsman (golf, fishing, sailing) who often included his wife and daughter on his outings.

"I met him at 17, married him at 22 and never looked back," said his wife, Virginia. "He listened to people. He was a wonderful boss. He loved the Yankees. The rest of it is he and his daughter, the center of his world."

Mrs. Strauch said that Mr. Strauch taught their daughter, Hilary, 12, to play golf so they could play together. He also coached her school basketball team.

Tom Kenny, the friend who called Mr. Strauch "regular and great," said that Hilary's birth after 15 years of marriage completed Mr. Strauch's life. He already had career success, a good marriage, his sports. He brought the same intensity to parenting that he brought to everything else.

"Whatever he got into, he got into it all the way," Mr. Kenny said.

EDWARD STRAUSS
Eagles and Baseball Caps

Edward Strauss loved the eagle. He was captivated by its appearance, its bearing, what it stood for. "He felt it was a majestic animal," said his widow, Jane. "And he was a patriot."

Thus Mr. Strauss, 44, a Port Authority manager, maintained a collection of eagles—the porcelain kind. Most of the replicas he kept in a curio cabinet at his home, but he always had a few on display in his office. He liked to gaze at them and have them nearby for others to see.

A devotee of *Star Trek,* he also had a thing about baseball caps. When he saw a cap, he bought it. Dozens of them accumulated. Caps bearing Looney Tunes characters were a particular weakness. He was a big man (size 22 neck). "Finding a cap that fit his head was amazing," Mrs. Strauss said.

Mr. Strauss was particular about dividing home tasks fairly with his wife. He insisted on doing all the food shopping (his wife cooked). Why? He was expert at detecting the best bargains.

"He would cut out coupons and everything," Mrs. Strauss said. "He did the food shopping with his mother, so he really knew how to do it."

STEVEN STRAUSS
Contentment by the Surf

A bench on the boardwalk in Long Beach, N.Y., now has Steven Strauss's name on it.

It is only steps away from the building where Mr. Strauss's daughter, Melanie, lives, and a Frisbee toss from the spot on the beach where she announced her engagement at a family picnic over the Labor Day weekend. Mr. Strauss brought Champagne to celebrate.

The bench faces the endless ocean that Mr. Strauss never tired of, no matter how many vacations he spent listening to the surf.

"He could sit on the beach for 100 days straight and still want more," said Robert Chaikin, a close friend who often vacationed with Mr. Strauss and his family. "He loved to fish. He loved to boat. He loved anything that had to do with the water."

Mr. Strauss, 51, worked at the Morgan Stanley Dean Witter offices in the World Trade Center as an electrical foreman for the Petrocelli Electric Company. "This is a business where people don't usually get close," said Mr. Chaikin, also an electrician. "But when this happened, everybody in the electric business called Steve's house and offered to help out."

Mr. Strauss had planned to move someday from Fresh Meadows, N.Y., to somewhere nearer the water, perhaps even Long Beach, where the bench with his name on it also bears a plaque: "In the celebration of your life, let the ocean embrace you."

STEVEN STROBERT
Knew When She Met Him

The woman was pregnant and frightened. It was during the 1993 World Trade Center bombing. Steven Strobert, a hefty 6-foot bond broker for Cantor Fitzgerald, put one big arm around her and guided her down a hundred flights of stairs.

"He was so modest, he never really told me much," recalled his wife Tara. "I didn't know about it till later. His mother brought it up. He just said, 'Yeah.' "

They met on St. Patrick's Day 1999 at the Plank Road Inn in his hometown of Secaucus, N.J., "I just walked up to him and announced, 'Everybody, I found my husband,' " she recalls. "He just turned around and laughed." After dinner a week later, he kissed her good night on the cheek. "Wow!" she thought. "He's the greatest guy I've ever met."

Mr. Strobert, 33, married her in October 2000, and they bought a house in Ridgewood, N.J., and had a son, Frankie. "He would come home with a bottle of wine or flowers and was very generous with his time," she recalls. "We were together a very short time, but we lived a very full life in two and a half years."

WALWYN STUART
When the Hugs Ran Out

Oh, the mouth he had, that Walwyn Stuart.

His smile was incandescent, and his kisses ever-flowing. His wife, Thelma, used to chide him over his enthusiasm for his newborn daughter—You're going to smother her!—and Mrs. Stuart didn't much like it when he came after her with his hugs and smooches. Well, actually, she did. Just not all the time.

Mr. Stuart, 28, was a Port Authority police officer who loved his family, chess and the Lord. He had been a narcotics detective with the New York City police, but switched jobs after Mrs. Stuart became pregnant because he wanted a safer assignment. He became a father last year, and when he worked late, nothing meant more to him than returning home to Valley Stream, N.Y., and holding little Amanda. He was great with children, but Mrs. Stuart would sometimes look on, just a little worried.

"I would be like, 'Honey, that's enough,' " Mrs. Stuart said. "He once said to me, 'You know, you never know when the day is going to come and you are going to want that hug from me and I'm not going to be there for you.' "

BENJAMIN SUAREZ
"I Have to Help the People"

On one arm, Benjamin Suarez had a tattoo of his wife's name, Sally. On the other was a tattoo of a dragon entwined with the emblem of the New York Fire Department. They spoke of his two great loves.

Sally Suarez said her husband, 35, was about to end a 24-hour shift with Ladder Company 21, at 38th Street, when he called to tell her he would be late getting back to their home in Brooklyn because "I have to help the people." It was the last she heard of him.

Mrs. Suarez spends her days remembering how open and generous he was. "Everybody loved him," she said. "There was not one place we would go that people didn't know him. I loved that."

Because she worked six days a week and his schedule was more flexible, he tended to accompany their three children to school events like plays or football games. "Sometimes he would take the whole company with him," she recalled.

And he was romantic with his wife of eight years, reminding her of anniversaries that she sometimes forgot. He wanted to buy a house, but because she was so picky, they had spent two years looking, she said.

"He told me, 'I could live in a cardboard box, but I have to make sure you have the house you want.' "

DAVID SUAREZ
Time for the Needy

David Suarez cared. He cared about people who did not have his opportunities, people who did not have his education, people who had to struggle.

"He reached out to people in a very warm and genuine way," said Ted Suarez, his father. "Everyone remembered his smile. From a little boy, he had a smile that was very endearing."

Mr. Suarez, 24, was a systems consultant who worked for Deloitte Consulting. He reported each day to the office of his client, Marsh & McLennan, in the World Trade Center. He was in the process of sending out applications to colleges, because next fall he wanted to embark on an M.B.A. before returning to Deloitte. His hope was to go to Harvard.

But he always made time for the needy. Social concern was a family tradition. He volunteered for the nonprofit group New York Cares. He worked in soup kitchens and tutored high school students for their college entrance exams.

He always gave the disadvantaged the benefit of the doubt. Friends told a story about how they found him once talking to some beggars outside a bar. Mr. Suarez asked one of the beggars, who was in a wheelchair, "What would it take to make you happy?"

The man said, "Give me $20." Mr. Suarez gave him $20. The beggar got up, folded up his wheelchair and walked off. Mr. Suarez was not angry. The episode did not make him jaded. He shrugged it off. By his thinking, he would rather lose $20 here and there to an impostor than risk spurning someone who really needed his help. He kept on giving.

RAMON SUAREZ
Ultimate Public Servant

Carmen and Ramon Suarez were all dressed up for a party when they saw a few teenagers pummeling a man across the street from their home in Ridgewood, Queens. Mrs. Suarez's husband, a New York City police officer, gave her one of his looks and took off running, dress shoes and all.

Minutes later a patrol car found Officer Suarez and the teenagers he had apprehended. "I don't know how my husband used to do this," Mrs. Suarez said. "He must have had wings."

Officer Suarez could run like the wind because, at 45, he still worked out twice a day in the gym. He also ran and coached the track team at his daughter Jillian's elementary school. And he was a physical fitness guru who chided those who sinned.

"He would tease you and say, 'Instead of having that doughnut, why don't you have a power bar or something,' " said Officer Suarez's partner of 11 years, Officer Steven Rentas. He said Officer Suarez was a perfectionist about his uniform, his appearance, his performance on the job.

On the morning of Sept. 11, Officer Suarez was on transit duty at the Delancey Street subway station. He commandeered a cab and rushed to the World Trade Center, where he was photographed helping people out of one of the buildings. "Ray basically symbolized the essence of what the Police Department is looking for in its officers," Officer Rentas said.

WILLIAM CHRISTOPHER SUGRA
The City to Its Fullest

William Christopher Sugra was born and raised in Pennsylvania and started working in computers there. But when his company moved him to New York last year, he wanted to explore the whole city. He and his girlfriend, Suzanne Dinnie, went to the opera and to museums. They went kayaking and rode their bikes.

"We were interested in doing everything we could," Ms. Dinnie said. "He never took the city for granted. We always joked that we were tourists every day, and we did so many of the typical New York tourist things."

Every couple of months when Mr. Sugra's parents came to visit, he would give them a tour of a different part of the city. Once he took them to see his office at Cantor Fitzgerald's eSpeed subsidiary at the World Trade Center, where he was responsible for the e-mail system. They had to get special passes to be allowed upstairs. His office had no view, but he loved working there. Afterward, they went upstairs to Windows on the World.

The last time his parents visited was in August, to celebrate his birthday (he turned 30) and Miss Dinnie's (she turned 27). They had drinks at the Boathouse in Central Park, went to dinner at the Atlantic Grill, and finished up at the Blue Elephant on the Upper East Side, where the owner treated them to a round of drinks because theirs were so slow in coming. Mr. Sugra's mother, El Sugra, said they had hoped to visit Chinatown together on a trip, but never made it.

DANIEL SUHR
"He Kept Everyone Safe"

Daniel Suhr was the recipient of many nicknames. Captain America was one. Whenever he went out with friends, he would point to exit doors and tell them where to meet him if anything happened. "He kept everyone safe," said his wife, Nancy.

A firefighter, Daniel Suhr was rushing to the trade center when someone tumbled out of the sky and on top of him. "The other firefighters stayed with him because they wouldn't leave him behind," his wife said. "Because they didn't go in, he saved their lives."

Firefighter Suhr, 37, loved his job at Engine Company 216. His father was a firefighter and his brother is one. He grew up in Brooklyn, where he was the captain of both the baseball and football teams at James Madison High School. He and his wife began dating when they were in grammar school. Their home is in Rockaway Park, Queens.

Even though he was considered this big, brave firefighter, he could get fairly mushy over his 2-year-old daughter, Briana. He was terrified when she did things like run toward him too fast. "He loved her more than life itself," Nancy said.

DAVID MARC SULLINS
Benefits of the Job

He was a used car salesman, and for fun, he liked tooling around on motorcycles with a bunch of friends who called themselves the Lost Boyz, after the characters in *Peter Pan,* the ones who never wanted to grow up.

By 1995, though, David Marc Sullins thought he ought to do more with his life. So he signed up for night school at Queensborough Community College and at the age of 24 began a new chapter as a paramedic, said his wife, Evelyn.

The work was strenuous but worth it, Mr. Sullins told his wife, who recalls that he was soon packing Matchbox cars and Barbie figurines in his trauma bag to calm the children in his care. One 5-year-old whom he had brought to St. Vincent's with stomach pains was so enamored that when she spotted him later at the hospital, she handed him a lollipop from her pocket.

Another fringe benefit was his ability to work double shifts on Mondays and Tuesdays so that he could have the next three days and alternate weekends off to be with his sons Julian, 4, and Cristian, nearly 2.

On Sept. 11, Mr. Sullins's ambulance sped from Cabrini Medical Center to the trade center. Colleagues say he made at least three trips to local hospitals with injured people he had pulled from the buildings before he re-entered the south tower moments before its collapse.

CHRISTOPHER SULLIVAN
True Partner at Home

Christopher and Dolores Sullivan were high school sweethearts, and he gave her a happy ending with a modern twist. She got a prince who was never too tired to play with their sons, Sean, 6, and Brian, 4 or to prepare her lunch for work. Mr. Sullivan, 39, was a firefighter at Ladder 11 and Engine 214 in Brooklyn.

"The main thing about him was that he was an excellent father," Mrs. Sullivan said. "He'd come home after working 24 hours and they would want to play and he played. He took them hiking and camping. He also did everything at home, from cooking to cleaning. We were a real team."

"The kids didn't have their Dad long, but they got a lot from him," Mrs. Sullivan said.

Jim Sullivan, Christopher's father, said his son "had a heart of gold but no one pushed him around," which made him perfect for firefighting. "Chris loved his job so much. We really respected the men he worked with."

Firefighter Sullivan also loved nature. He planted a pumpkin for the first time this year, and it grew. The family used it to make pumpkin bread at Thanksgiving.

THOMAS G. SULLIVAN
Talking About the Family

If you got to talking with Thomas G. Sullivan about his two young sons or his wife, Deirdre, his high school sweetheart and the "rock" of his life, as one friend said, chances are you would find yourself on the telephone for a long time. "You could walk off the phone, make yourself a cup of coffee and he'd still be talking about them," said Aidan Whitehead, a close friend who once worked for Mr. Sullivan, known as Tommy, a stockbroker who was a partner at Harvey Young Yurman.

As much as Mr. Sullivan, 38, who was having a breakfast meeting on Sept. 11 at Windows on the World with several colleagues from his company, thought and talked about his family, he still had plenty of room in his mind for others. He had an uncanny ability to remember faces, names and important dates. "And once he met somebody, he was their friend forever," Mr. Whitehead said.

Mr. Sullivan, an avid jazz drummer, was game for just about anything and a quick study. Mr. Whitehead, who is Irish, once brought Mr. Sullivan an Irish drum, called a bodhran, to hang on his wall.

"He had no interest in hanging it on the wall," Mr. Whitehead said. "He had never played one before, but soon enough he was the best bodhran player I'd ever heard."

LARRY SUMAYA
The Ski Club Ambassador

Larry Sumaya's friends and family had a lot of names for him. Like Phil, short for Filipino, his ethnicity. Or Horatio, because Hilario was the first name on his birth certificate. Or Gooch and Clem, for reasons no one can quite recall.

Then there was, um, Christie. He got that one after showing up on the slopes wearing a black-and-pink skiing outfit. Unfortunately for Mr. Sumaya, the color scheme was a tad too unisex.

"There was a nice-looking girl wearing the same jacket," said Bob Sitar, a friend and fellow member of Mr. Sumaya's ski club. "It was pretty funny, and we teased him about it."

But the good-natured Mr. Sumaya, 42, took the kidding in stride, always ready to tackle the steep fast curves of the mountain, the rolling greens of the golf course, the waves of the Jersey shore, the social currents of big-city bachelor life. "He was always smiling, very outgoing," said his sister Charito LeBlanc.

Mrs. LeBlanc and her husband, Joseph, miss him the most on Sundays, because that was the day Mr. Sumaya would spend time at their home near his in Staten Island, watching sports, smoking a cigar in the backyard, firing up the barbecue.

Mr. Sumaya, a technology manager at Marsh & McLennan, liked to talk politics and knew how to press home a point. "He was tough to argue with," said another friend, Tom Todaro. But he was also slow to anger, and played the ambassador in his ski club, putting newcomers at ease.

COLLEEN SUPINSKI
Mutual Inspiration Society

For a few years, when they were growing up in eastern Pennsylvania, they shared a room. After college, she went to work in the financial district of New York City, and when it was his turn, he came, too. For a time, they lived three blocks apart in Hoboken. They talked to each other every day, and made a point of getting together at least once a week. Her friends were his friends. Colleen and Benjamin Supinski were brother and sister, but they were each other's inspiration, too.

"She would soften me up a little bit, and I would try to harden her up a little," he said.

When terrorists struck the World Trade Center, both were in danger. But only one of them made it to safety.

Colleen, 27, worked as an assets trader for Sandler O'Neill & Partners, with offices on the 104th floor of 2 World Trade Center. From his offices at Barclays Capital, a few blocks away, where he is a manager, Mr. Supinski saw the first attack, and called to tell her about it. Little more than an hour later, he saw her building collapse.

Mr. Supinski said his sister loved her job, she loved running—she ran track in college—but mostly she loved her family. Their youngest brother, Nathan, 20, an international-business major, was talking about joining his siblings in New York. "I believe that wherever she is, God's taking care of her," Benjamin Supinski said. "She's up there taking care of me, and of the rest of the family."

ROBERT SUTCLIFFE
A Pair of Gifts Left Behind

Robert Sutcliffe enjoyed the chaos of the floor of the New York Stock Exchange, where he worked as a broker for Harvey, Young & Yurman. He was awake and ready to go at 5 every morning. But he was not a hard-charging corporate type. At 39, he was a serene man, content with his life as it was.

He would call his wife, Margaret, from work with a teasing "Do you miss me?" that invariably made her laugh. His early morning hours were private time to be spent with his daughter, Kara Patricia, 3, his "little devil," visiting Dunkin' Donuts, Home Depot and his parents and grandmother, who live near the Sutcliffes' home in Huntington, N.Y.

"People have a hard time finding time in their lives," said Mr. Sutcliffe's sister-in-law Katherine Korz. "Bob never let his friendships or his relationship with his parents and grandmother slip. Everybody misses him. But no one regrets not having had enough time with him. They did."

On Sept. 11, Mr. Sutcliffe was at a meeting at Windows on the World. His father, Robert Sutcliffe Sr., learned later that he had made a habit of gathering uneaten lunches at work and distributing them to street people on his way home. "I never knew this until he died," the father said.

Margaret Sutcliffe is pregnant with twins, due in February. "Bob knew they were coming," Mrs. Korz said. "It's almost like a gift that was left behind."

JOHN SWAINE
Sharing the Wealth

John Swaine was the consummate Wall Street bond trader: "Aggressive and full of boundless energy," said his brother-in-law, Richard McGuire. He worked at Cantor Fitzgerald for about 10 years.

"He really loved his work," Mr. McGuire said. "He worked hard and played hard."

But he wanted to share the wealth. He helped his brother-in-law, John Reo, get a job at Cantor, trading bonds. They worked and died together on the 104th floor.

Mr. Swaine, 37, of Larchmont, N.Y., may have loved the Street but he did not fall for the trappings. He preferred to help his extended family, and to spend money on his wife of 13 years, Suzanne, and three daughters.

"He rarely spent any money on himself," Mr. McGuire said. "He provided his family with a beautiful home. But he was unassuming. He didn't have fancy cars or suits. He took the subway from the train every day. Everything he did, he did it for his family."

JOHN REO's portrait appears on page 415.

KRISTINE SWEARSON
Sister, Cousin, Girlfriend

Kristine Swearson's search for her family roots led her to North Dakota two years ago. She found long-lost cousins who embraced her and set up a family Web site to stay in touch. And she found love with a young man who turned out not to be a relation of any kind.

"I gave her a hard time about it," said her sister, Kerri Roberts. "I asked her, 'Are you sure he's not a cousin, or a cousin of a cousin?'" Ms. Swearson just laughed and kept the boyfriend.

Ms. Swearson, 34, began her adventures in San Jose, Calif. As teenagers, the Swearson sisters would choreograph dances to their favorite disco tunes and perform in the family's garage. They even charged the neighborhood children a quarter for the show.

In later years, the disco gave way to yoga and a Web-design job with eSpeed. But Ms. Swearson never forgot to call or write her disco partner every day. "I was extremely proud of her," Ms. Roberts said. "I couldn't have had a better sister."

MADELINE AMY SWEENEY
The Final Call

Madeline Amy Sweeney never went looking for fame, but fame found her on Sept. 11. Her 15 minutes were the last of her life.

Mrs. Sweeney, known as Amy, was a flight attendant aboard American Airlines Flight 11, the first plane to strike the trade center. She called a ground supervisor by air phone and relayed information about the hijackers that gave the F.B.I. a head start on the investigation.

Mrs. Sweeney's grace under pressure did not surprise her husband, Michael Sweeney, of Acton, Mass. "She would have said she was just doing her job," he said.

Congressional and state officials in Massachusetts have written letters to President Bush, asking that Mrs. Sweeney be awarded the nation's highest civilian honor. With it, Mr. Sweeney hopes to be able to tell his children, Jack, 4, and Anna, 6, about their mother's bravery that day.

Her career took her to Bali and Hong Kong, but she also found adventure on Colorado ski slopes and Cape Cod beaches. With Flight 11, nonstop to Los Angeles, she kept a standing date for lunch with Lynn Blaylock of Irvine, Calif., who was supposed to meet her at the airport that morning.

"She was an amazing, amazing woman," Mrs. Blaylock said, remembering their devil-may-care road trip out West after college.

On Dec. 14, Mrs. Sweeney would have turned 36, so those who miss her gathered at her favorite Mexican restaurants on two coasts. In California, they reflected on the woman who always saw the silver lining. And in New Hampshire, Melanie Bergerson collected paper messages to her oldest friend and put them inside a balloon, then set it free to touch the sky.

KENNETH SWENSON
Man of Inner Peace

Leslie Swenson's favorite memory of her husband, Kenneth Swenson, is the day of the balloons. It was late May or early June, and the couple and their two sons, 10-year-old Kyle and 13-year-old Eric, were at a local field in Chatham, N.J., kicking a ball around. Suddenly, balloons of all colors floated from the sky and landed on the field.

"He brought them over to me and said, 'I ordered these for you,' " Mrs. Swenson said. Mr. Swenson, 40, was a vice president at Cantor Fitzgerald. "He was a great father to our two sons," his wife said. "He enjoyed taking them on camping trips. That was their father-son activity."

There was not much spare time in Mr. Swenson's life, but on Saturday nights he was a volunteer medical technician with Chatham's emergency squad, just like his father before him. Richard Rosenblum, a friend, said that Mr. Swenson was one of the first to marry, because he wanted a family.

He also retained his baby face long after the rest of them fought hair loss and weight gain. "He was like a piece of buttered bread," he said of Mr. Swenson. "No friction, no hassle. He was a peaceful guy, but no one took advantage of him. He was a man about things."

THOMAS F. SWIFT
Master of Factoids

When Thomas F. Swift was around, no one wanted to play Trivial Pursuit or any game that relied on factoids and cultural flotsam. That was because Mr. Swift, whose brothers called him "the book of useless information," knew a bit about all kinds of things, maybe because of those childhood years reading encyclopedias at night for fun.

Mr. Swift, who was 30, worked as an assistant vice president at Morgan Stanley in the World Trade Center. He worked long days, said his wife, Jill, but he managed to be well-rounded. He used to unwind by spending hours listening to music, any kind of music.

The Swifts had been married five years. They celebrated Mrs. Swift's 30th birthday in June by going to the Bahamas with a group of friends. "He was a die-hard Yankees fan," Mrs. Swift said of the man she met when they were both high school students. "He yelled at a lot of TV's because of it. I had to become a Yankees fan before we married. My family was National League, they like the Mets, but it was a deal I had to make."

DEREK SWORD
A New Yorker at Heart

As a teenager, Derek Sword played tennis for Scotland's team, but as an adult it was squash that led him to his fiancée, Maureen Sullivan. They met at a dinner of the New York Athletic Club, where he played squash three times a week, and they planned to marry next year.

Mr. Sword, 29, moved to New York City from Scotland six years ago to work as an equities sales analyst for Keefe Bruyette & Woods, a securities firm. The job took him to Britain every six weeks. That allowed him to see his family often, but he loved New York and did not want to live anywhere else.

"He fell into the routine rather quickly," Ms. Sullivan said. "He loved the quick pace, going to restaurants, being out and about."

On the morning of the attacks, Mr. Sword, who worked on the 89th floor of 2 World Trade Center, made three calls to his fiancée and one to his parents in Scotland to reassure them that he was fine.

GINA SZTEJNBERG
A Life Spent in Motion

Gina Sztejnberg's life was one of journeys. Born in Poland to a Jewish couple who had fled to Russia to escape the Holocaust, and then returned to Poland, she came as a girl to the United States in the early 1960s. Later, travel became a major pastime, and, with her husband and children, she toured much of the United States and more than a dozen countries.

At Erasmus High School in Brooklyn, she renewed acquaintances with a boy from her village, Michael Sztejnberg (pronounced Steinberg). They eventually married, settled in Ridgewood, N.J., and became inseparable traveling companions, even commuting together to their jobs.

Every day, Mr. Sztejnberg, 55, a senior vice president with J. P. Morgan in lower Manhattan, drove Mrs. Sztejnberg, 52, a database architect consultant, to the World Trade Center, where she worked on a project for Marsh & McLennan on the 96th floor of the north tower.

They visited countries in Europe and the Far East, and two summers ago—with daughters Laura, 26, and Julie, 22—she went to her native city, Wroclaw, for the first time.

"My mom always put everything together," Laura said. "She planned everything, from what to see to what maps to carry. She was the perfect traveling companion."

NORBERT SZURKOWSKI
On the Verge

Norbert Szurkowski, the son of a bicycle racer, was on his first visit to New York when he met Ursula Lesniak. It was 1992 and she was a student at Fort Hamilton High School in Brooklyn.

"We just enjoyed seeing each other," she said. Three years to the day after they met, Mr. Szurkowski—always attentive to such details as proper timing—proposed. The City Hall wedding two weeks later was a prelude to the festivities in their native country, Poland: three days of visiting and feasting with relatives.

Back home in Bensonhurst, Mr. Szurkowski walked right up and faced his future without the slightest doubt that he would do well. This past year was bearing out his confidence. His wife was graduating from nursing school and pregnant with their second child, and he was about to be promoted to full-fledged mechanic.

"This was the year," Mrs. Szurkowski said, "that we were supposed to get everything back."

Meanwhile, Mr. Szurkowski, 31, was earning extra money by wallpapering the Cantor Fitzgerald offices. The best part about it was the hours—by shortly after 9 A.M., he was usually out and on his way home.

T

HARRY TABACK
Bound Remembrances

Harry Taback dedicated his professional life at Marsh & McLennan to helping companies plan for disasters, and his personal life to making sure his wife, Jean, and their three daughters had everything they needed.

"People around the company said if they died, they wanted to come back as one of Harry's daughters," said Cheryl Taback, the middle one, who often accompanied him to his beloved New York Giants games.

A low-key, sandy-haired chemical engineer, Mr. Taback, 56, worked on the 100th floor of 1 World Trade Center. After the Sept. 11 attack, one of his colleagues solicited letters from more than 70 people who had worked with him around the world and compiled them in binders for his family. His wife died last year, and the children lived with him or nearby in Staten Island.

"A few people wrote that he was very fair and understanding, and said that your family comes before your job responsibilities," Ms. Taback said. One couple wrote that they had named their dog Harry, after her father, "because of how much he did for them."

Another letter was from a woman who had come for a job interview when she was eight months pregnant, and Mr. Taback had voted to hire. "Many thought this crazy," she wrote. "Many thought it wonderful."

JOANN TABEEK
Tough Cookie, Soft Heart

JoAnn Tabeek worked in the World Trade Center for more than 20 years, always for Cantor Fitzgerald.

"She was dedicated to her job," said Vincent Milotta, Ms. Tabeek's fiancé. "But she wanted to get out and retire in three years. We had already gone to Florida to look around for a place."

When she wasn't working, Ms. Tabeek, who was 41,

spent time with Krystal, her 11-year-old daughter from her first marriage. She liked to shop for clothes. Often, on weekends when Krystal was with her father, Ms. Tabeek and Mr. Milotta would motor to Atlantic City.

"We liked to go down and see a show and eat," he said. "We liked being together."

At work, Ms. Tabeek was all business. But appearances often deceive.

"The first impression was of one tough cookie," said Jennifer Megna, a friend and former co-worker at Cantor Fitzgerald. "But once you got to know her she would give you her heart. You could call at 3 or 4 in the morning and talk to her for hours."

On Sept. 13, Ms. Tabeek's body was found, one of only seven to be recovered thus far from Cantor's offices.

"I have her engagement ring around my neck," Mr. Milotta said. "She is with me all the time."

MICHAEL TADDONIO
Many Best Friends

To be Michael Taddonio's best friend was not such a singular achievement. He collected best friends, from Locust Valley High School on Long Island, where he was class president, to Siena College in Loudonville, N.Y., where his rugby teammates called him Cool.

If someone was planning a trip to Disney World, said his older brother, Richard, "he'd call up, 'Oh my best friend runs the hotel down in Disney.'"

His friendliness was an asset when he, like his older brother and his younger brother, Marc, followed in the footsteps of his grandfather and his father to work on Wall Street, becoming a bond broker for Euro Brokers in 2 World Trade Center.

"He was really a family guy," Richard Taddonio said of his 39-year-old brother, who lived in Huntington, N.Y. "When I was in New York, he'd come over every weekend. His youngest, little Mikey, was always hanging on his shoulder. He always took Mikey on the errands runs with him.

You know, because weekends he'd pick up his laundry and do the food shopping and Mikey was always attached to him." His last phone call was to his mother, from the 91st floor. He told her to tell his three children he loved them.

KEIICHIRO TAKAHASHI
A Comfortable Homebody

As a senior vice president at Euro Brokers, Keiichiro Takahashi had the résumé of a high-flying businessman: lots of travel, lots of responsibility, an office in the World Trade Center. But in reality, he was most comfortable as a homebody who loved the simple life and exuded low-key stability.

On weekends, he liked to stroll the streets of his adopted hometown, Port Washington, N.Y., with his wife, Harumi, whom he met in glee club when they were students at International Christian University in Tokyo. He liked to see science fiction movies—anything with *Star Wars* or *Jurassic Park* in the title—with his wife, his son, Hiroyuki, 26, and his daughter, Akiko, 19.

Mr. Takahashi, 53, enjoyed tending to his backyard garden of flowers, tomatoes and Japanese herbs and vegetables. He was such the quintessence of domestic stability and equilibrium, in fact, that after 28 years of marriage, Mrs. Takahashi said that she had never seen her husband raise his voice. He was, however, getting excited about something else: in a few years, after his daughter graduated from Tufts, he was probably going to retire, and enjoy his home life full-time.

PHYLLIS TALBOT
Cajun and Chaos

Phyllis Talbot grew up in the tiny town of Chataignier, La., population around 383. She picked cotton before and after school, and later told her only child, Keith, that even if her family never had any money, they always had everything they needed.

"From the time she was a little girl she dreamed of living in New York," Mr. Talbot said. "When she moved there it was one of her goals fulfilled." And she loved looking out the window of her office at the World Trade Center, where she was a vice president at Marsh USA, to see the Statue of Liberty.

Ms. Talbot, 53, enjoyed traveling and taking in shows and flea markets in Manhattan, where she lived. She spoke enough Cajun French to get around Paris, and she liked to be challenged, especially at work.

"When all hell was breaking loose, that's when she was in her element," Mr. Talbot said. "That's when she did her best. She was definitely adept at putting out fires."

"She was tough. She was extremely tough, and I thank her every minute," he said of his mother, who raised him alone

most of his life. That toughness, instilled in her son, has helped him since Sept. 11. "A lot of people I think have noticed how trying the events have been of the last three months, and how well I've handled it. I owe it all to her. I think my mother, and her whipping me into shape, helped a lot."

SEAN PATRICK TALLON
Awaiting Fresh Challenges

Sean Patrick Tallon, 26, was a reservist in the United States Marine Corps, a former emergency medical technician and a probationary firefighter with Ladder Company 10 just a few weeks away from the end of his training. He was tough, but he always wondered whether he measured up.

"That's the way he was," said his older sister, Rosaleen DaRos. "He always thought everybody else was capable, but he was just as capable."

Take the button accordion that Mr. Tallon loved to play. He would bring out his instrument and play Irish favorites for relatives at family gatherings, with his sister on the piano accordion. But he rarely played for friends; some of them didn't even know he could play an instrument.

When he left for work from his home in Yonkers on Sept. 11, headed for the fire station that was among the first to respond to the trade center attack, he seemed in a buoyant mood. His probationary period was almost over and a new challenge lay ahead.

"He wanted to find Mrs. Right," Mrs. DaRos said. "That is what he said was his next mission. He said his probie year was almost finished and he wanted to start with the rest of his life. Everything was just all ready. He had just blossomed."

PAUL TALTY
Following a Master Plan

Paul and Barbara Talty's Cape Cod in Wantagh, N.Y., was already crowded when there were just two children, Paul Jr. and Lauren. With a third on the way, it was time to raise the roof.

Having worked as an electrician and carpenter before joining the New York City Police Department in 1993, Officer Talty tackled most of the work himself.

He built a full second-story addition, working after his shift and on days off to get the place ready for Kelly, who was born in August. Officer Talty built his career the way he remodeled his house—combining disparate elements in a master plan.

"Paul wasn't driven to be a hero like some others on the force," said his sister-in-law Lisa Talty. There are many teachers in his family, but no policemen. "He became a policeman because he wanted to take care of his family," Ms. Talty said.

A model for a sculpture honoring fallen firefighters was unveiled on December 21. (See also photo on page 494.) The sculpture is adapted from a photograph by Thomas Franklin of *The Record* of Hackensack, New Jersey. (*Edward Keating*)

Officer Talty was nonetheless dedicated to police work, especially after joining the emergency services unit.

"You knew that if it came down to it, Paul would do whatever needed to be done," said his friend Joseph McAuliffe.

Officer Talty, 40, loved the beach, and looked forward to vacationing in Naples, Fla., each winter. He considered taking the police officer's test there, and going into teaching after he retired.

"Paul would have made a great teacher," said his wife, Barbara. "I always said: 'I wish you were a teacher. It's a much less dangerous career.'"

RACHEL TAMARES
"She Spoke Her Mind"

"Whatever."

Anyone who worked at Aon Financial Services Group with Rachel Tamares will tell you that that was her favorite response when anyone disagreed with her.

But "whatever" did not mean that Ms. Tamares did not care. Quite the opposite. She was known as a fastidious worker, an administrative associate who kept a tidy desk. Rather, said Julia Akinwunmi, a co-worker for 12 years, "whatever" reflected Ms. Tamares's positive attitude toward work, toward friends, and toward most aspects of her life.

"The thing about Rachel is that she spoke her mind," Ms. Akinwunmi said. "She'd say 'Why do you have that on? You know that color is not good for you.' And people appreciated that. If they didn't, and disagreed, Rachel's response would be 'whatever.'"

Ms. Tamares, 30, married John Bruno when she was 16. She was such a traditional and devoted mother to their two boys, Jason, 11, and Robert, 6, that her friends sometimes called her grandma. On weekends, she took the children on excursions to Sesame Place or Dorney Park in Pennsylvania. Sometimes she invited her sister, Jenny, 15, and their mother, Maria Paulino, to come along.

In June, after her mother and sister had to leave their

house, Ms. Tamares invited them to come live in her already crowded two-bedroom apartment in the Bronx until they could find a new place to live.

HECTOR TAMAYO
Evenings Spent in Song

Hector Tamayo loved to sing: Engelbert Humperdinck and Elton John, country music and campfire favorites, especially the one that begins, "Today, while the blossom still clings to the vine . . ." At home in Holliswood, Queens, he had a karaoke machine with thousands of songs.

"He had a lot of friends, most of them are relatives, and on Friday nights and Saturday nights and sometimes week-nights they would drink together and sing together," said his sister-in-law, Sylvia Mercene.

Many of those relatives lived with Mr. Tamayo at some point, because he opened his house to family and friends when they came to the United States from Aklan province in the Philippines, as he had in 1980.

"As a joke we call his house the Ellis Island," Ms. Mercene said. Five of his six siblings are now in the United States, as are his wife, Evelyn, and their two children, Ian, 20, and Pamela, 16.

A civil engineer, Mr. Tamayo, 51, was working in 2 World Trade Center on Sept. 11.

His family remembers him as a happy person who loved jokes, his family and, of course, to sing: "A million tomorrows will all pass away / Ere I forget all the joys that were mine today."

MICHAEL A. TAMUCCIO
A Bud in Any Season

Michael A. Tamuccio was a true guy's guy, which is why his friends knew that Kathleen Horner was "the one" when the couple showed up at a Halloween party in Raggedy Ann and Andy costumes.

This was a man who had dressed as a bottle of Budweiser the previous year, who was a World War II buff and once an Eagle scout. A man who, as a student at Fordham University, wrestled down a mugger, grabbed his weapon (a sock filled with quarters) and then used the change to do laundry for the next few weeks.

A vice president for equities trading at Fred Alger Management, Mr. Tamuccio, 37, was known for helping others find work on Wall Street. If the job did not work out, he told them, we will still be friends.

Mr. Tamuccio was thrilled with the view from his office on the 93rd floor of 1 World Trade Center. But his favorite lookout point was White Face Mountain, in the Adirondacks, where he and Kathleen, his wife since 1996, would go to ski, and to marvel at the rugged beauty of the mountains and swirling snow.

DENNIS G. TAORMINA Jr.
Casual Everydays

Dennis G. Taormina Jr., vice president for finance at Marsh & McLennan, was not one to put on airs.

"Every day when he came home from work, the suit came off, and the Fire Department T-shirt and the Cowboys shorts came on," Diane Taormina said.

Her husband, who was 36 and a member of the East Rutherford volunteer Fire Department, was a huge Cowboys fan, she said. "My husband wasn't into fancy cars or clothes. He was just low-key."

Mr. Taormina, whom his wife described as quiet, also liked to draw, and had a garage full of woodworking tools at their Montville, N.J., home that he used to make her a Chippendale mirror and a desk for their daughter with Queen Anne legs. For their 10th wedding anniversary on Sept. 7, the Taorminas and their children—Meghan, 9, and Jenna, 5—went out to dinner. Mr. Taormina and his wife had picked out a diamond ring for her to commemorate the event, but it wasn't ready immediately.

At the memorial service for her husband, her parents gave it to her, a ring with round and baguette diamonds. "It's the last thing he gave me," she said.

KENNETH J. TARANTINO
The Christmas Connection

Kenneth J. Tarantino was known around Bayonne High School in New Jersey as "the cute sub." He worked there as a substitute teacher while going to college, and among his students in English class was the woman who would later become his wife.

"He was just so charming," said Jennifer Tarantino, 32. "All he had to do was smile."

Mr. Tarantino, 39, eventually got his bachelor's degree in marketing; two years ago, he went to work as a broker for Cantor Fitzgerald, on the 105th floor of 1 World Trade Center. He was very successful, Mrs. Tarantino said, but was always humble and sought only simple pleasures—golf, the Yankees, a beach house every summer on the Jersey shore. Mr. Tarantino also had a warm, friendly way about him that made him a social magnet. Friends described him as the one everybody wanted to hang out with.

At a wedding, he caught the garter and wore it on his head the rest of the evening, and by the end of the night even the band wanted to take him on the road with them.

The Tarantinos had moved to a bigger house in Bayonne, N.J., last February with their 3-year-old son, Kenneth, and were expecting a second child, who is due December 24. Mrs. Tarantino said she hopes the baby comes one day late.

Her husband was a Christmas baby, she said, and "I'd love to have him on Christmas Day."

ALLAN TARASIEWICZ
Attracted by Challenges

"He always wanted more action," said Patricia Tarasiewicz, describing her husband of 24 years, Firefighter Allan Tarasiewicz. So it is no surprise that he reported for work on Sept. 11, the day the couple had planned to leave for a scuba diving vacation in Mexico.

Mr. Tarasiewicz, 45, became a firefighter at 33, already having traveled widely and honed many skills. A Staten Island native, he met Patricia while stationed in Italy with the marines. He went on to work as a sheet metal worker in California, a coal miner in Colorado. The New York Fire Department, Mrs. Tarasiewicz said, was his ultimate goal, or nearly so, since he kept volunteering for more challenging duty.

His last assignment, with Rescue Company 5 on Staten Island, came after he used his free time to learn advanced scuba skills.

There was also his work at home, a weathered, 100-year-old house that he and Patricia, a flight attendant, bought two years ago to be close to the firehouse, a block away. By Sept. 11, he had rewired the place and remodeled the kitchen, bathroom and two bedrooms. His fellow firefighters have pitched in to finish the job.

MICHAEL TARROU's portrait appears with Amy King on page 258.

DONNIE TAYLOR
Military Air in Fatherhood

In the Taylor family, Donnie Taylor played the bad cop. He had spent four years with the Air Force and there was a certain military bent to his parenting of Donnie Jr. and Simone, his 16-year-old son and 14-year-old daughter, his widow, Sarah, said. There was only homework, no TV, after school. If Daddy said the sky was blue, it was the shade of blue Daddy said.

"In every household you have a good guy and a bad guy and he was the very stern parent," Mrs. Taylor said. "The children had a lot of respect for him. They really loved their father."

The Taylors, who grew up in Harlem and were high school sweethearts, separated eight years ago, but that did not make Mr. Taylor, 40, an office services assistant with Aon Corporation, any less involved in the lives of his children. When he disappeared in the collapse of 2 World Trade Center, his son was about to go over his list of college picks with his father.

"All it's done is made both children very strong and very determined in what they've set out to do," Mrs. Taylor said of the attacks. "They're not going to let this setback stop them from the dreams they and their father had."

LORISA TAYLOR
Outdancing Her Husband

Lorisa Taylor actually believed the ruse worked. During visits to her mother, Mrs. Taylor would make a great show of looking through expensive new clothes seemingly bought by her sister. Speaking loudly so her husband could overhear, Mrs. Taylor would say to her sister: "You don't want this? Oh thaaaannnnk you!"

Despite her bottomless appetite for shopping, it was tough to stay angry at Mrs. Taylor, who had her purchases delivered to her mother's. She had a charming sunniness, a capacity to be delighted and to delight. That last weekend, the couple celebrated their seventh anniversary in a Brooklyn night club, with Mrs. Taylor, 31, outdancing her husband till they left at 4 A.M., she carrying her shoes, her bare feet tired but twinkling.

Her life outside of work—she was an insurance broker at Marsh & McLennan—revolved around her family in Brooklyn, which included their three girls and relatives.

"She was my best friend," said her mother, Geneva Dunbar. "We would talk about things that mommy and daughters shouldn't even talk about."

On Sept. 11, Mrs. Taylor and her mother took the subway together to their jobs. Mrs. Taylor chatted about her anniversary and her girls, laughing loudly. The doors opened. Her mother stepped out. "I love you!" "I love you!" they called.

As the doors closed, "she was still laughing," her mother said.

MICHAEL M. TAYLOR
Starting a Vineyard

One way to know Michael M. Taylor is to consider the eight-inch stack of index cards he dutifully prepared after deciding to get serious about wine. On the cards he recorded his impression of every bottle he tasted. As his pursuit of fine wines advanced, Mr. Taylor started his own collection. It now numbers more than 600 bottles. "Michael had a passion for

Fire Commissioner Thomas Von Essen and Mayor Rudolph
Giuliani preside at the unveiling of a model for a sculpture
honoring firefighters on December 21. The sculpture is
shown on page 491. (*Edward Keating*)

perfecting anything he set out to do," said his sister Mary
Kaye Crenshaw.

Mr. Taylor, 42, was a high-yield bond broker with
Cantor Fitzgerald. In a highly competitive business, he
helped others get established. "People in the business tend
to chase after people who are already good," said Jerry
Bias, a friend. "I was just getting started and he encouraged me."

From his Manhattan apartment to the Porsche 911 he
drove, Mr. Taylor enjoyed the benefits of a successful Wall
Street career. But recently he had started thinking about a
more tranquil life, especially after he became engaged to
Natalia Telyupa.

To that end, Mr. Taylor and Mr. Bias were starting a
vineyard and winery in Virginia. They planned to create a
cult wine—hand-picked grapes, low yields—just the kind
of wine Mr. Taylor savored. The first bottles will be
shipped in about 18 months. They will be labeled Taylor-
made vintage.

PAUL TEGTMEIER
A Dream Realized Briefly

After watching his number creep up the list
of new recruits for 20 years, Paul Tegtmeier finally got the call in 2000 to
become a New York City firefighter, at the
age of 40. He quit his job as a field technician at Verizon and picked up his crisp uniform.

"He met the age cutoff, from the time that he applied,"
said his wife, Catherine. "His was the last class taken off that
list. Firefighting was something he wanted to do since he
was a toddler and he only wanted to do it in New York
City."

Firefighter Tegtmeier, 41, a father of two, was on his way
to Ladder Company 46 in the Bronx when the first plane
struck 1 World Trade Center. Fire officials say that he likely
reached the firehouse in time to join his colleagues as they
rushed toward the twin towers, Mrs. Tegtmeier said. He

loved firefighting, and was volunteer for more than 20 years at the Roosevelt, N.Y., Fire Department, where he met his wife, also a volunteer firefighter.

His 6-year-old son, Aric, lives very much in his parents' image. A couple of days after the collapse, Aric pulled on his firefighting helmet, coat and boots and fought invisible fires on the front lawn with firefighters who came to mourn the loss of his dad.

YESH M. TEMBE
Gadgets, Shrikhand, *Brahms*

Precision mattered to Yesh M. Tembe, an accountant working for the New York State Department of Taxation and Finance, and it showed in his fondness for high-tech gadgets. On the Saturday before the terror attacks, he showed his nephew Cyrus Meherji a new, blue cellular phone—although, despite their excitement, the two could not figure out how to activate the voice mail.

Mr. Tembe, 59, a classical music aficionado, also cooked, specializing in an Indian sweet called *shrikhand,* made with sour cream. It was popular with Mr. Meherji's children, who often came with their parents to visit Mr. Tembe and his wife, Coomi, in Piscataway, N.J. "They'd go for that," Mr. Meherji said. The two men used to meet every few weeks for lunch downtown near Mr. Tembe's office in the World Trade Center. They would sample the cuisine of different restaurants, sometimes Thai, Greek, Turkish or Indian.

"New York was the right place for him," Mr. Meherji said. "We liked everything."

DOROTHY TEMPLE
There for Support

Dorothy Temple, who moved to New York from Montgomery, Ala., as a child, never had children of her own, but she had a large extended family.

"Anytime anything happened with a relative anywhere, Dorothy was there to support them," said a niece, Falana Temple, who lived with her aunt in Bushwick, Brooklyn, after her mother died.

Ms. Temple, 50, a longtime employee of the State Department of Taxation and Finance, lavished attention on her nieces and nephews, taking them on trips to Disney World, Mexico and San Francisco, and keeping up with their accomplishments.

She had a number of friends, many of them in Albany, but for the most part "she was a very private person," said another niece, Jada Temple. Ms. Temple, who walked with a cane because of an old knee injury and weighed more than 200 pounds, used a van service for the disabled to get to work. She told her relatives that she planned to retire soon because of her condition.

DAVID TENGELIN
All That the City Offered

Shakespeare in the Park? David Tengelin was the one who would wait in Central Park to get the tickets. Monday movies in Bryant Park? Mr. Tengelin would also be there first, showing up hours before the show to stake out a spot for himself and his friends. Soccer anyone? Every Sunday evening in Prospect Park, like clockwork.

Friends called Mr. Tengelin Swede because he was Swedish, but a more apt name would have been Mr. New York.

"He loved the city more than anything," said a friend, Michael Peck.

Mr. Tengelin, whose family is split between Sweden and Britain, arrived in the city in 1999 fresh out of Northern Arizona University in Flagstaff to try his luck, with no job or place to live. He stayed in a youth hostel for the first months, then a room with no kitchen, and most recently an apartment near Gramercy Park that he shared with two roommates. His friends insisted that he could afford better places in Brooklyn, but he was stuck on Manhattan, where he walked everywhere.

"He asked very little out of life, yet took as much as he possibly could," Mr. Peck said.

An accountant for Marsh & McLennan, Mr. Tengelin, 25, bragged about one thing—working on the 100th floor of 1 World Trade Center.

"He was right where he wanted to be in life—on a top floor in one of the tallest buildings in New York City," Mr. Peck said.

BRIAN TERRENZI
New Home and First Baby

Everything was going just right for Brian Terrenzi. In February 2001, he started a new job as a global network manager in the treasurer's office of Cantor Fitzgerald. In April, he and his wife, Jane, bought their first home, in Hicksville, N.Y., and found out that she was going to have their first baby.

And in July, the couple learned it would be a girl. "There's no girls in the Terrenzi family," said Mrs. Terrenzi, 28, who is eight months' pregnant. "He was just so excited. He would have made the best father."

Mr. Terrenzi, 28, an avid skier and sportsman, used to

call his wife five times during the day from his office on the 101st floor of 1 World Trade Center to check up on her. Now, she says, "the phone doesn't ring."

Mrs. Terrenzi, a kindergarten teacher, said she would name her daughter Elizabeth, after her husband's mother, as he had wanted. But Elizabeth will also have a middle name, Brian, after her own father.

LISA MARIE TERRY
The Equestrian Life

Not long ago, Lisa Marie Terry's days revolved around her horses and horse competitions—an undertaking only slightly less demanding than caring for twin 2-year-olds.

"The horses eat before the people eat," said Sarah Tupper, a horsewoman and friend. "The stalls are cleaned before the beds are made." On weekends, Ms. Terry, 42, was up by 5 A.M. for shows.

But she had drawn away from the horse world. Smoke, her favorite mare, died. "She bought Smoke as a teenager," Ms. Tupper said. "In those days, riding was about saddling Smoke, meeting your best friend and trail riding all afternoon."

The pressure at work—she was a vice president at Marsh & McLennan's Michigan office—had increased. She was away on business more often. On Sept. 11, her work took her to the World Trade Center.

Two years ago, she sold the farm. But last summer, she was horse shopping again. She missed the riding life and the company of horse people. "We always end up at somebody's barn," Ms. Tupper said. "People have great houses. But we sit in the barn, drink a beer and talk about horses."

GOUMATIE THACKURDEEN
A Vivacious Traveler

All the Thackurdeens—Goumatie, her three brothers and two sisters and most of her 12 nieces and nephews—had settled in South Ozone Park in Queens, where they grew up. Goumatie, at 34 the youngest, moved easily between domesticity and aunthood and the cosmopolitan life of a world traveler.

Small, slim and lively, she was a vice president at Fiduciary Trust who traveled for business and vacations. On the Stockholm-to-Helsinki ferry, she met Stefan Hellman, a Finnish salesman, who accompanied her through Europe and California and visited the home she shared with her mother.

On weekends, she took two or three children to the park or zoo or home to bake cakes. To the grown ones she was a confidante and model of glamor and independence.

On holidays, she often invited everybody—23 relatives and assorted friends—for dinners of dishes from France, Italy, America and Trinidad and Tobago, the Thackurdeens' native land.

THOMAS THEURKAUF Jr.
The Time He Was Caught

The head of the sunfish was attached to one side of the hook. The other side of the lure was embedded in Thomas Theurkauf Jr.'s hand. His son Henry, 9, frantically rowed the boat to shore, making a few erratic circles. Mr. Theurkauf waved his hand wildly, trying to shake the fish and hook from his hand. Mr. Theurkauf's wife, Robin, severed the fish head and rushed him to the hospital.

"They successfully treated Tom," his brother Bill said at a recent memorial service. "The fish didn't make it."

But, oh, how Mr. Theurkauf loved to tell the tale of the one that would not go away.

As an analyst at Keefe, Bruyette & Woods, which had offices on the 89th floor of 2 World Trade Center, Mr. Theurkauf gave countless television and newspaper interviews. In 2001 the *Wall Street Journal* named him the top banking analyst in the country. But his family and friends remember the less serious side.

"He loved to make his friends and family laugh," Bill Theurkauf said. "And was more than willing to laugh at himself."

CLIVE THOMPSON
Many Worlds, No Colliding

As an international currency broker, Clive Thompson, who was known to almost everyone as Ian, did not fit the stodgy profile of high finance. Among fellow volunteers on the first-aid squad in his hometown, Summit, N.J., he was one of the guys, just more fun than most.

"He would make himself the fall guy," said Daniel MacMahon, a friend and fellow volunteer, who recalled Mr. Thompson's being thrown into a swimming pool, and stepping up to be the target of water balloons, at Fourth of July picnics.

"He was a magical person," said Mr. Thompson's wife, Lucy, with whom he immigrated to New York in 1992 from southern England, bringing a zest for work, friends, food and good wine. "He was living in the fast lane, and always thinking of other people, not himself."

Mr. Thompson, 43, worked pressure-laden hours at Euro Brokers, but by starting at 5 A.M., he managed to retain afternoons for other interests. There were the carpet-cleaning company that he founded, his volunteer work as an emergency medical technician and the meals he prepared for his wife and children, Ella, 13, and Rachel, 10.

He had "so many worlds that did not collide," his wife said. Mr. MacMahon put it differently: "Ian was a Renaissance man."

GLENN THOMPSON
"My Mountain Man"

Glenn Thompson loved to be outdoors. He hiked. He fished. He biked. He skied. He climbed Mount Kilimanjaro.

And in October 2000, on a mountain pass in the Colorado Rockies, he got down on his knees in the snow (he was wearing shorts) and asked Kai Wittmann to marry him. Mrs. Thompson, as she became when they married in April, has the altitude—11,820 feet—engraved in her engagement ring.

Mr. Thompson, 44, worked at Cantor Fitzgerald on the 104th floor of 1 World Trade Center. While he enjoyed the camaraderie and the adrenaline rush of trading, his wife said, his work was really a means to an end. His dream was to retire early and move to Colorado.

"He was my mountain man," she said. "He was a bond trader and damn good at it. But his heart and soul were outdoors."

NIGEL BRUCE THOMPSON
A Walk Across the Bridge

Many mornings and evenings, to work out and to reflect, Nigel Bruce Thompson walked across the Brooklyn Bridge from his Brooklyn Heights apartment to 1 World Trade Center, where he was a senior broker at Cantor Fitzgerald.

At age 33, Mr. Thompson was a newlywed who would have celebrated his first anniversary on Oct. 21. His wife, Rosana, recalled being smitten with Mr. Thompson when they met in 1997 because he was handsome and had an off-color, British sense of humor. He proposed on bended knee over Peking duck. The wedding album is full of photographs of friends from Cantor Fitzgerald, many of whom were killed on Sept. 11.

"In my little group, we've lost 23 friends," Mrs. Thompson said.

Mr. Thompson's identical twin, Neal, said his brother was his opposite: a good-dresser, a physical fitness buff, tidy. They came to New York in the '90s from England and Nigel pushed him to be his best.

"He was a go-getter," Neal Thompson recalled.

Nick Boski, a good friend, said he and Mr. Thompson got together every Sunday night to watch *The Sopranos.* Or they would go down to the Brooklyn Heights promenade and smoke cigars from Mr. Thompson's collection.

"You could see the World Trade Center," Mr. Boski said of the view. "I still go down there to feel connected to him."

PERRY ANTHONY THOMPSON
A Low-Key Approach

Often, Perry Anthony Thompson would spend some of his spare time photographing the occasional celebrity—like Michael Jackson, Janet Jackson and Whitney Houston—at parties, concerts, and sometimes in his photo studio at home in Williamstown, N.J., for teenage music magazines. His approach was low-key.

"He wasn't pushy," said his wife, Charlette, who sometimes went with him backstage after a concert, when she wasn't home with their two daughters, Ashley, 7, and Chelsea, 3. "He'd say, 'Hi, my name is Perry Thompson, and I'm shooting for such-and-such a magazine.' "

When he was assigned to do a portrait at his home, he rummaged through the props he had in his 4,400-square-foot house set on a half-acre of land. Mr. Thompson, 36, had dozens of painted backdrops in every color. "Purple, green, orange, yellow, two-tone ones, yellow turning into red, silk drops, paper drops, black ones, white ones," Mrs. Thompson said.

He was no less meticulous when it came to photographing his children. On Christmas Eves, he spent hours posing them in front of the tree. This year, Mrs. Thompson was to be the photographer. "I have to carry on the tradition and do it myself," she said. "He would have wanted it."

VANAVAH THOMPSON
Humming the Day Away

It didn't matter whether he was alone in the shower, or riding a crowded subway; Vanavah Thompson would hum the reggae tunes that he so loved. A native of Guyana, he came to New York City with his mother and two sisters in 1989. He sported dreadlocks halfway down his back, and sometimes tucked them into a striped knit hat like his favorite musicians.

Mr. Thompson, 26, was a maintenance worker at the World Trade Center. But at night, he would sing and dance his way through the clubs of Brooklyn and Queens.

"I feel that wherever he is right now, he'll sing to himself to keep strong," said his sister, Tsahai Thompson. The one that he always sang, she said, began with the wistful line: "Remember the days when people on the East Side used to go on the West Side and live in peace."

WILLIAM HARRY THOMPSON
The Stair Climber

Capt. William Harry Thompson never took the elevator. He taught at the court officers' academy on the 12th floor at 123 Williams Street. Every morning, Captain Thompson, 51, would walk up the stairs to the academy.

If he went out to lunch, he would climb the stairs to go back to work. When he would take the recruits, most of them less than half his age, out for runs three times a week, they would climb the stairs after the runs were over. He would be the only one not out of breath.

"His physical regimen would make you cry," said Deputy Chief Jewel Williams, of the New York State Courts, who was his commander at the academy.

On the job, Captain Thompson was spit and polish. At 6-foot-2, with a booming voice, he could easily get people's attention. "I know it sounds corny—he gave the appearance of being hard as nails—but he was so easygoing," Chief Williams said. "He was the type that carried family pictures around with him in his wallet and when they opened up, there were 25 different shots."

Captain Thompson was one of three court officers who died on Sept. 11 when they ran to the World Trade Center. His oldest son, Michael, often finds himself thinking about how his father did things.

"I have been faced with a lot of decisions to make, decisions that I don't want to make. I pause before I decide and I think about the approach he would take."

ERIC THORPE
Ball Carrier on Wall Street

The booming voice, competitiveness and self-assurance that helped Eric Thorpe become the star quarterback of his undefeated high school football team in Wilbraham, Mass., served him well on Wall Street.

Mr. Thorpe, 35, known as Rick, was one of the top salesmen at Keefe, Bruyette & Woods. But Mr. Thorpe kept business success in perspective. He helped run a soup kitchen during college, served as a Big Brother and participated in Hands Together, an antipoverty program in Haiti.

Having grown up in a close family—he referred to his father, Raymond, as his best friend and called him nearly every day—Mr. Thorpe was thrilled when his wife, Linda, gave birth to their daughter, Alexis, last year.

Through it all coursed a nonstop sense of humor. Not even Mr. Thorpe's parents escaped his fondness for nicknames, and he enjoyed initiating phone calls with a disguised voice.

"He teased everyone, including me," said Thomas Michaud, Mr. Thorpe's boss.

JOHN PATRICK TIERNEY
Dedicated to Firefighting

On Father's Day 2001, as Helen Tierney heard the news that three firefighters in Queens had been killed on the job, her heart broke. For the men who died, she cried. For her son John Patrick Tierney, 27, a probationary firefighter training in Queens at the time, she rejoiced that he had had that day off.

"He always said, 'Don't worry, Ma. Everything will be fine.' And it was."

So, on Sept. 11, when his unit, Ladder Company 9 in Manhattan, was called to the World Trade Center, she clung once again to her youngest son's words. Her prayer was that he had headed home to Staten Island that morning. But Mr. Tierney had hopped a fire truck so crowded that he was forced to sit in a colleague's lap.

"The other guys told him he didn't have to come," Mrs. Tierney said. "But from the first day he went to probie school, he worked hard, he really wanted to be part of the Fire Department."

And he was, for six weeks.

WILLIAM R. TIESTE
A Mystery Maven

When B. C. Tieste was in third grade, he was told to bring a picture to school of what he wanted to be when he grew up. It had a guy holding a briefcase; he wanted to sell stocks like his father.

Now 22, he still does: "It's a job where you can be financially secure and still have time to be with your wife and kids."

His father, William R. Tieste, 54, was executive vice president of equity sales at Cantor Fitzgerald. After B.C. went away to school, Mr. Tieste and his wife, Debby, bought their dream house—a five-bedroom, customized colonial with a pool, in Harding, N.J. Last summer, Mr. Tieste would stand in the pool and lean on the ledge reading a book. He liked mysteries.

Although the Tiestes had lived there for more than a year, they were still finishing things, like a game room with a big screen television and a pool table where family and friends could congregate on holidays. Thanksgiving was Mr. Tieste's favorite holiday. He said he liked the "four F's"—family, friends, food and football.

"What was difficult this Thanksgiving was that we used to cook together," Mrs. Tieste said. "But I had to laugh. When his mother was alive, she used to bring peas and carrots in cream sauce. I never could get it right. This year I finally got it right. Everything was right. It was almost as if he was standing there beside me, guiding me."

KEN TIETJEN
He Claimed the Respirator

As a boy, the two things that scared Ken Tietjen most were fire trucks and police cars. So he took some ribbing from his family when, as an adult, he chose a job that required him to ride in both.

Mr. Tietjen, a Port Authority police officer, was at the 33rd Street PATH station when he heard about the terrorist attack, said Laurie Quinn, his sister. Mr. Tietjen commandeered a taxi, banished the driver to the backseat, and drove to ground zero. He rushed into the north tower and helped people down, but when he emerged to get a new respirator, only one remained, his partner recalled.

Smiling, Mr. Tietjen said, "Seniority rules," took the respirator and ran into the south tower. Moments later, the building fell.

Typical, said Ms. Quinn, noting his commendation for bravery this year, received for tackling a man who had stabbed the sergeant he worked with. As a firefighter several years back, he returned to a burning building to rescue an unconscious colleague.

One of those Mr. Tietjen rescued on Sept. 11 attended his memorial Mass. But he did not stay because he became overwhelmed.

Ms. Quinn said: "My brother had a choice whether to go back and he chose to go back in. I wouldn't expect anything less from him."

STEPHEN EDWARD TIGHE
A Soccer Coach in a Suit

Stephen Edward Tighe loved coaching school soccer so much that he considered quitting his job at Cantor Fitzgerald when he took on yet another team last August. He had begun to tire of the financial world, and he loved working with children more than doing anything else.

Mr. Tighe, 41, never screamed at his players the way some coaches do. "Unlucky" was his harshest word. When they played well, he would reward them with by shouting, "Magic!"

It was a tough schedule: there was his son Patrick's team,

the Rockville Centre Revolution, which he coached twice a week; his son Michael's intramural team once a week; and on weekends the children's games, which he attended faithfully.

When he became junior varsity soccer coach at the Kellenberg Memorial High School in August, his bosses at Cantor said he could work half days instead of quitting. He would leave the World Trade Center every day at 3 P.M. to go back to Rockville Centre, on Long Island, where he grew up and still lived with his wife and four children, to coach the high school kids.

"He treated everybody's kid like they were his own," said his wife, Kathleen Tighe.

SCOTT TIMMES
Big Dreams, Small Pleasures

Kristine Timmes did not even get to kiss Scott Timmes at the New Year's Eve party where they met in 1995. She left before midnight to be with her family.

No matter. "I knew we would get married," she said, recalling how she was immediately taken with his smile and sense of humor. "He said funny things. He made me laugh."

Mr. Timmes, 28, of Queens, worked as a commodities customer service clerk with Carr Futures, the global futures trading firm, on the 92nd floor of 1 World Trade Center. He wanted to move up the corporate ladder and make a name for himself, his wife said, but he also "loved to bowl, loved the Mets and loved his daughter," 14-month-old Sydney.

"He loved to sing and dance, specially the oldies," Mrs. Timmes said. "When he sang along to a song and didn't know some of the words, he would make them up as he went along until he got to a part he knew again."

"Basically, he was one of the happiest people you could ever meet in your life."

MICHAEL E. TINLEY
A Prolific Traveler

Michael E. Tinley had visited Marsh & McLennan's conference room in the World Trade Center dozens of times. But it wasn't until Sept. 11 that he mentioned the view to his sister.

"He called me and said, 'I'm up here on the 100th floor and I can see your building,'" said Suzanne Tinley, who lives in TriBeCa. "I turned to my son, Henry, and said, 'Uncle Mike is waving at you.'"

That was at 7:47 A.M.

Mike Tinley, 56, was a vice president at Marsh & McLennan based in Dallas, a job that kept him on the road.

He was a prolific traveler, the kind of man who would meet his daughters, Lisa and Jenna, during airport layovers or drive from Los Angeles to San Francisco for a date.

New York was one of his favorite towns, and here's Mike Tinley doing the Big Apple: Stay at the Marriott downtown. Hang out at Cafe Dante in the Village. Catch a performance of *Saturday Night Fever*. Walk the streets with a digital camera pressed to his eye. "He could get along with anybody," Lisa said.

"When he went to Hawaii, he became friends with the guy who did the luau and cooked the pig."

ROBERT TIPALDI
Eager to Share the Wealth

At 25, Robert Tipaldi was generous in success, his relatives say. In August 2001, he bought a summer home in New Jersey, where he loved to entertain family and friends. In 2002, he planned to buy a boat for his 40-foot dock at the house.

"He wanted to enjoy everything and have everybody enjoy his fortune as well," said his stepfather, Gerard Lombardo.

Mr. Tipaldi rode a motorcycle, went skydiving, played ice hockey and planned to become engaged to his girlfriend next year. He lived in Bellmore, N.Y., with his mother, Stella Lombardo, and his stepfather. Mr. Tipaldi was an assistant trader with Cantor Fitzgerald on the 104th floor of 1 World Trade Center. He cherished the job for its intensity and excitement, Mr. Lombardo said.

On the morning of the attacks, his mother heard from Mr. Tipaldi one last time. He told her he loved her and to tell everybody he loved them, too.

JOHN TIPPING 2nd
Carrier of the Skiing Bug

For the first half-dozen years after he lurched through college, John Tipping 2nd was still deciding what he wanted out of a career. But he always knew what he wanted out of a weekend: biking and skiing. Especially skiing.

The four Tipping children—John was the third, and the only boy—were half-grown when their father, John, bought a cabin at Lake Placid. As one February vacation followed another, the son outgrew the father's intermediate slopes and moved to expert runs.

Six years ago, Mr. Tipping found the career he wanted. At the suggestion of his father, a retired firefighter, he joined the New York Fire Department and was assigned to Engine Company 54, Ladder Company 4.

"He matured as a person when he was in the Fire Department," his father said.

Firefighter Tipping, 33, also moved from skis to a snowboard. Last winter he enticed his father, who had lost the skiing bug, to join him in Vermont. Two John Tippings, the younger mastering his snowboard, the older getting the rust out of his turns, were back on the intermediate runs. "I got my enthusiasm back," the father said.

On Thanksgiving, the Tipping family lit a candle for their son, brother, uncle and cousin. And the older John Tipping made plans to buy new skis.

DAVID TIRADO
Anything for His Mother

"There is only one man who gave the order to fly those planes into the twin towers, and I want the United States to get him," Barbara Tirado, 50, said of Osama bin Laden as she wept. "He killed my son. I've never had this much hate in my heart, but it's all I've got right now."

Her son, David, 26, a computer technician who lived in Mill Basin, Brooklyn, was at 1 World Trade Center on Sept. 11 to deliver and install a personal computer on the 106th floor. At first, he and his supervisor from Rent-a-PC in Midtown were turned away by security and told they could not park near the building. But Mr. Tirado volunteered to set up the computer while his supervisor found a parking space.

Mr. Tirado grew up in Sheepshead Bay, Brooklyn. He enjoyed watching the Mets play and going to Coney Island, Brighton Beach and Manhattan Beach. He helped elderly women carry their groceries and he gave neighbors a ride to work in his green Jeep Cherokee.

The older of two boys, he was born on Valentine's Day. His mother doted on him, and he on her. "The only words I can remember him saying were, 'Anything for my Mom,' " Mrs. Tirado said.

HECTOR TIRADO Jr.
Firefighter and Model

Of his three jobs, Hector Tirado Jr. liked firefighting work the best.

A former emergency medical technician, he was lured to the New York Fire Department less than two years ago by the excitement and the opportunity to help people, said his uncle, Robert Tirado.

The divorced father of five children, Mr. Tirado, 30, also worked as a waiter and, occasionally, as a model. His latest shoot was posing in casual clothes for a Latino firefighters calendar that was due out sometime this year.

His uncle said, "I'd walk on the street with him in the summer and the girls would give him their number."

Mr. Tirado, who lived in the Bronx and was a member of Engine 23 in Manhattan, did not shy away from the attention, but was blasé about it, his uncle said.

His main focus was to support his children—a 7-year-old daughter and four boys, ages 11, 10, 6 and 5—who lived in Ohio with their mother. Mr. Tirado visited them every month, and they spent summers with him in the city.

"As long as it's legitimate and I make money for my children," he told his uncle about the modeling, "I don't care."

MICHELLE L. TITOLO
An Angel Between Sisters

Michelle L. Titolo's sister, Kim Jelley, was starting to get that churning sensation in her stomach. It was her first art show. She had paid for a table at a hotel in New Jersey. But no one was buying her sculptures.

Then in walked Ms. Titolo. She said she wanted to buy a 10-inch-high angel. Take it for free, Ms. Jelley said. Ms. Titolo vigorously shook her head.

"The only thing she ever bought from me was the angel," Ms. Jelley, 38, said. "She just loved and really inspired me to pursue my art. She bragged to everybody about it."

The two had grown up together on Long Island, only four years apart, living with their divorced mother. Ms. Jelley was the elder one, the self-admitted "disorganized" artist. Ms. Titolo was the one with a business degree, a new house and a job as an equity controller at Cantor Fitzgerald in 1 World Trade Center.

As children they danced together in their mother's house to disco music. As adults they went to hip-hop clubs on Long Island. Those were let's-put-on-lipstick-and-stay-up-till-dawn kinds of nights. They also had their subdued moments. After Ms. Jelley gave her sister a tea set for her birthday a couple of years ago, they occasionally sipped afternoon tea together. (Ms. Titolo had returned from a trip to England an unabashed Anglophile.)

For one of Ms. Jelley's recent birthdays, Ms. Titolo gave her older sister a card on which she had written, "Don't worry, I'm going to grow old and fat with you."

RICHARD TODISCO
Paintball with Son's Team

Richard Todisco loved sports. He once played sandlot baseball in Brooklyn with Joe Torre and was invited by the Phillies for a tryout as a pitcher. But what he really loved, his widow, Anne, said, was watching his children, Lisa, 21, and Greg, 19, play sports, develop into respectful, disciplined people, and carry themselves with the same happy, family-oriented attitude that he deemed paramount.

Mr. Todisco, known as Dick, was a vice president at the investment firm of Sandler O'Neill & Partners. Even though he was older than the parents of his children's friends, he had just as much enthusiasm, if not more—particularly when it came to Greg's soccer career.

Once, his son's soccer coach arranged that the team participate in a weekend of paintball with their parents. Mr. Todisco was not initially thrilled. It was hot. The outfits were uncomfortable. And by the end, he was physically spent and his back was throbbing.

Mr. Todisco's reaction: "We had a great, great time."

STEPHEN TOMPSETT
Family, Faith and Job

In summer, Stephen Tompsett liked to build sand castles on the beach with his 10-year-old daughter. But because he was a math whiz, his sand constructions were a bit different.

"They were elaborate sand castles with moats," said Dr. Geralyn Szuba, his sister-in-law. "And I swear, they were timed with the tides. As soon as he finished, the tides would come in and fill the moats."

Mr. Tompsett, 39, a computer scientist and senior vice president at the Instinet Corporation who was attending a meeting at Windows on the World on Sept. 11, was a rare combination of brilliant, easygoing and religious, she said. Raised in Australia, he came to New York 15 years ago on business, promptly fell in love—with the city and his future wife—and settled in.

Instinet employees celebrated when he became their boss. When he attended meetings, they could dispense with note-taking. "Stephen," Dr. Szuba said, "would remember everything verbatim." And he gave everybody the same advice: " 'Your family comes first. Then your faith. Then your job.' How often do you hear that—especially on Wall Street?"

AMY E. TOYEN
A Proposal in Ireland

To catch her early flight on Sept. 11, Amy E. Toyen arose in Boston at 4 A.M. so she could arrive in New York City at 6:45 A.M., in plenty of time to attend the trade show in Windows on the World at 1 World Trade Center. Ms. Toyen, 24, was demonstrating a software product of her company, Thomson Financial in Boston, when her fiancé, Jeffrey Gonski, got a call at 8:58 A.M.—his caller ID showed it was her cell phone—but when he answered, no one was there.

They were engaged to be married next June 16. Mr. Gonski had met Ms. Toyen at their alma mater, Bentley College in Waltham, Mass., and had managed to pull off an elaborate proposal. Last spring he planned a vacation with her to Canada, then surprised her at the airport with a flight for two to Ireland—her favorite place. Then he stunned her again by proposing there, in a romantic locale on the Dingle Peninsula. How could she possibly have said no?

"We had just ordered her wedding dress," said her father, Martin Toyen. "She was so happy in her life—a woman in love, who loved her job."

DAN TRANT
All-American Money

Michael Jordan was third—that is how good the N.B.A. draft was that year. Dan Trant was 228th. Last pick, last round. Last laugh, too, sometimes. When Mr. Trant, a bond trader for Cantor Fitzgerald, and his best friend, Lance Faniel, joined the bruising pickup games down on West Fourth Street years later, players chose Mr. Faniel first.

"They'd look at Danny and they'd look at me," Mr. Faniel said, noting that he is black and had a few inches and pounds on the white friend he called Money. Then Money got his turn, and players saw what the Celtics had seen in the All-American guard they had picked but could not place, maybe because of those inches he did not have.

"We'd walk away laughing," Mr. Faniel said.

"He was able to exceed his All-American status as a father," said Mr. Faniel, who spent Mr. Trant's last night with him and the Trant boys—Daniel, 12, and Alex, 10—waiting for the rain to stop at Yankee Stadium. Mr. Trant, 40, and his wife, Kathy, also had a daughter, Jessica, 19, whom he coached in soccer.

He loved sports, but "he loved me more," Mrs. Trant said. He quit professional basketball in Ireland to marry her, and turned down seats to a Knicks game offered by a job interviewer. Can't, got to baby-sit, he had said, Kathy is going to the Grammys. He was hired.

ABDOUL KARIM TRAORÉ
Success in America

Abdoul Karim Traoré was intent on being a good provider. When his grain-and-beans shop went under in the Ivory Coast, he made a huge decision, immigrating to New York in 1993 while leaving his pregnant wife behind.

"It was the only possibility he had for a better life," said his wife, Hadidjatou Karamoko Traoré.

Like many other illegal immigrants from West Africa, he first worked as a supermarket deliveryman. Next he became a dishwasher. But five years ago he hit the big time, becoming a banquet cook at Windows on the World, a steady job that provided health insurance and other benefits. Each day he rose at 3 A.M. to deliver *USA Today* before reporting to work

at the restaurant. There, he took regular breaks for his daily Muslim prayers.

His wife immigrated in 1997, but because of visa complications, their daughter, Djenebou, now 8, has not been able to come. In New York, the couple had two more children, Souleymane, 3, and Hassan, 1, and with his earnings, Mr. Traoré took a bold leap toward the middle class, putting down a large down payment on a three-family house in the Bronx.

At Windows on the World, a United Nations of 450 workers from dozens of countries, Mr. Traoré, 40, was elected a union shop steward. Although he was one of the few Africans there, other workers, impressed by his intelligence and forcefulness, looked to him to present their case to management.

"Everybody liked him," his wife said. "He was respected."

GLENN TRAVERS
Planning for His Wedding

Diana Sherwood met Glenn Travers—or Saint Glenn, as her parents later called him—on a plane she was not on. He was seated by her friend, who insisted he meet Ms. Sherwood. That was nine years ago.

Mr. Travers, a World Trade Center electrician, bought a house with her in Tenafly, N.J., and embraced her three children. He did not just toss them baseballs—he taught them the skills of the game. He taught Mrs. Sherwood, a lawyer, to fish. He paid close attention to 14-year-old David, who was "floundering and confused" at first. The son of a Navy sailor, Mr. Travers taught David about battleships.

"This isn't the bachelor life," he would say. But he was comfortable with children, having raised two sons alone. He loved being outdoors and drove the family through the countryside to the bay or the Hudson River on Sunday afternoons. He and Mrs. Sherwood postponed marriage because each had been through a tough divorce, she said. But they were finally ready. Mrs. Sherwood wanted a church wedding. It was scheduled for January.

FELICIA TRAYLOR-BASS
Devoted to Children

Felicia Traylor-Bass was an only child who found a way to be an aunt anyway, playing the role with zest for the children of her five cousins.

"She loved dancing and music," said one of them, La-Rae Shelton, recalling the rose tattoo on her cousin's left shoulder and her very short, chic haircut. "She really liked children, but she wanted to wait to get her career started before having a child."

She did just that. After half a dozen years of marriage to Andrew Bass and a career that had taken her to Alliance

Consulting, on the 102nd floor of the World Trade Center's second tower, she and Mr. Bass had a son, Sebastian. He is now almost 2 years old.

"She loved being a mom," Ms. Shelton said. "All her co-workers heard about her baby, the hair stylists, everybody."

Still, Ms. Traylor-Bass, 38, made time for dancing after work, before heading home to Brooklyn. She took classes at Dance Space, on Broadway and Canal Street. "They did a dance tribute to her, as a memorial," Ms. Shelton said.

Sebastian may be too young to remember that, but a generation of cousins who loved his mother will be sure to tell him.

JAMES A. TRENTINI and MARY B. TRENTINI
To See the Grandchildren

In retirement, James and Mary Trentini traveled at every opportunity, wherever their fancy took them. But in particular they liked to go to California to see their daughter Patti in Irvine.

Patti was the mother of three of their grandchildren, ages 2 to 7, and it was great fun to haul the grandchildren off to the beach or to soccer games or, most of all, to Disneyland.

Mr. Trentini, 65, a former school-teacher, and Mrs. Trentini, 67, a former school secretary, lived in Everett, Mass. But every Christmas would find them in Irvine and sometimes they would linger there for weeks, lavishing attention on the grandchildren while waiting for the warmth of spring to return to New England.

This year they headed out to California early. Patti had called to say that she and her husband, Donald Paris, were planning to take a couple of weeks of vacation back east on Martha's Vineyard and would "Grandpa" and "Mimmie" mind flying out to the West Coast to baby-sit?

The Trentinis immediately booked a flight for Los Angeles: American Airlines Flight 11, the flight they always took west. They were scheduled to fly out Sept. 10, and had so many presents for the grandchildren that they needed an extra suitcase. Then Mr. Trentini was summoned for a day of jury duty on the 10th. They rebooked for Sept. 11.

LISA L. TREROTOLA
Surviving Ills, One at a Time

After Lisa L. Trerotola's appointment with the oncologist, she went to her mother's house and burst into tears. Lisa was not a complainer, and her mother feared the worst, that the thyroid cancer was terminal.

"No, no!" Lisa said. She was sobbing because her treatment required isolation, which meant, "I'm going to have to leave my babies for two whole weeks!"

Mrs. Trerotola's family was rocked by her cancer, but she went through treatment keeping her eyes on the prize: her twins, now 3½ years old, whom she had struggled for years to conceive with her husband, Michael. Life kept road-testing Mrs. Trerotola, 36, of Hazlet, N.J.

In addition to cancer and infertility, she had prevailed over other health problems, including a chronic bronchial condition that she believed was triggered by fumes from the 1993 bombing of the World Trade Center, where she worked as an administrative assistant at the Port Authority.

"You know the sweetest thing my sister did?" said her brother, Paul Spina. "She was planning a surprise party Oct. 6 for my brother-in-law's 40th birthday. Sent the invitations and everything. He has no idea. Would you put that in the newspaper? I don't have the heart to tell him."

MICHAEL A. TRINIDAD
Staying Friends

When Michael A. Trinidad and Monique Ferrer divorced three years ago, they stayed friends. Ms. Ferrer got the custody of their two children, Thea, then 7, and Timothy, then 6, and it was understood that the children were "theirs"—not "his" or "hers." Every other Friday, Mr. Trinidad would come to pick up the children for the weekend.

"He was like a big kid," Ms. Ferrer said. "He would take them to the park, play ball games, call them silly names and just act silly." The three also went apple picking in upstate New York and sunbathing on the Jersey shore.

After the first plane hit the trade center on Sept. 11, Mr. Trinidad, 33, who was working in telecommunications accounting for Cantor Fitzgerald, called Ms. Ferrer to say good-bye. " 'What good-bye?' I asked him. 'Are you going anywhere?' " Ms. Ferrer recalled asking him, unaware of the disaster. " 'I love you, and I love the kids,' he said. 'I am not going to make it out.' Then he asked to talk to my husband," Ms. Ferrer said.

"Michael asked my husband to be his children's father and love them for him."

JOSEPH TROMBINO
Close Calls Never Counted

Three people were killed in the 1981 Brink's robbery in Nanuet, N.Y., and Joseph Trombino barely escaped being the fourth. He was shot in the shoulder; his left arm hung by

only a thread. It was sewn back on in three operations. He returned to work as an armed guard two years later.

"He'd done that for so long," said his wife, Jean, "it was like he didn't know what else to do."

Joseph never spoke about the danger involved in his job. In 1993, he had been making deliveries to the World Trade Center just hours before it was bombed. A close call, but after the 1981 robbery, close calls didn't really count.

Now 68, he was at last planning to retire in a year or so, his wife said. But on Sept. 11, as ever, he was up at 2:30 A.M. and out by 3:30 A.M., to make it to work in Brooklyn by 5 A.M. A little after 9 A.M., he was waiting in the armored truck in the basement of the trade center for his three fellow guards to return from the 11th floor.

They made it to safety. Joseph called into Brink's from a pay phone, his wife said, to say a policeman had told him to move the truck. The building was shaking and water was cascading down, Joseph said, before the line went dead.

GREGORY TROST
A Human Jukebox

Whenever he was at a party, Gregory Trost would invariably be asked to perform the Creep.

The dance he invented involved shrugging his shoulders, slithering across the room and other aspects of creepiness rendered with bellyaching hilarity by Mr. Trost, said his sister, Jeanne Trost. Mr. Trost, 26, was a research analyst for Keefe, Bruyette & Woods.

"He had a sense of humor that set the gauge for everyone else," said Ms. Trost, who is two years younger than her brother. "What he found funny, it somehow always became funny."

Ms. Trost, who described her brother as her best friend, said he was a natural entertainer, a "human jukebox," who could recite the words to just about any song, from his favorite musician, Neil Young, to Johnny Cash.

Mr. Trost "loved everything from Broadway shows to Nascar racing," said his father, George Trost, who added that he and his son had begun a tradition three years ago of going to the auto races every year on Father's Day.

"His smile was one of the best characteristics," Ms. Trost said. "He had this laugh that came from so deep within him. I know everybody who has lost somebody—they were special. I don't know, not to be clichéd, but he really was the

most unbelievable person. He was just a really caring, generous, loving person, son, friend, brother."

WILLIAM TSELEPIS Jr.
"A Graceful Soul"

William Tselepis Jr. grew up in a family that stressed loyalty, and he applied that value to just about everything he did. Mr. Tselepis, 33, a Chicago native, never wavered in his devotion to all of its sports teams. His best friend and frequent golfing partner was his older brother, Peter.

He married his college sweetheart. He followed his older brother to New York and became a foreign exchange broker. He worked for almost 10 years at Cantor Fitzgerald, mainly trading foreign exchange options. He spent all of his free time on his wife, Mary, and daughter, Katie, now 3½. And without a doubt, his older brother said, Mr. Tselepis, known as Billy, would have doted on the son he never knew, Will, born on Oct. 5.

In late fall, a group of Mr. Tselepis's Kappa Sigma fraternity brothers gave Peter Tselepis a scrapbook with pictures, notes and other ephemera related to their buddy Billy, and asked that the book be turned over to Mr. Tselepis's children "so that they would know their father better," Peter Tselepis said.

Everyone, he added, said that they were still trying to cope with Mr. Tselepis's absence.

"The predominant description from men and women was that Billy was gentle, caring and generally always good to be around. People wanted to be around Billy. He was just a graceful soul."

ZHANETTA TSOY
Her First Day at Work

On Sept. 11 at 9 A.M., Zhanetta Tsoy's life was to begin anew. It was Day 1 of a new job in a new country, a place where she and her husband believed their futures were as big and bright as the New York skyline.

Fresh from Kazakhstan, Ms. Tsoy, 32, could hardly believe she was about to go to work in one of the world's tallest buildings, as an accountant for Marsh & McLennan. She was so excited that shortly after arriving in America, on Aug. 23, Ms. Tsoy dragged her husband and 4-year-old daughter on a sightseeing trip to the World Trade Center. Her husband, Vyacheslav Ligay, said she was "very hurried" when she left for her first morning of work.

"She was afraid that she can't be late," he said. "Zhanetta wanted very much to make a good start."

In the days since the towers collapsed, Mr. Ligay has looked for the words to explain the disaster to their daughter,

A handmade sign greets people arriving in Bedford, New York. Patriotic displays proliferated in communities across the country after the September 11 terror attacks. *(Joyce Dopkeen)*

Alexandra. He has searched for the photos of their trip to the trade center, but they have also disappeared. Family members want him and Alexandra to go home to Kazakhstan. Mr. Ligay cannot.

"Dead or alive, this is where my wife is," he said. "As long as we are here, she is with us."

PAULINE TULL-FRANCIS
Singer with Dance Moves

Pauline Tull-Francis lent her operatic soprano voice to her church and largely reserved her dance moves for family gatherings, where she would be on the dance floor the first chance she got, said her daughter, Debby Williams. A native of Barbados, Ms. Tull-Francis, 56, was partial to reggae, calypso and other rhythms of the Caribbean, but she could also groove to Ella Fitzgerald and Celine Dion.

Ms. Tull-Francis, who lived in Brooklyn with her husband and had four grown children and five grandchildren, was also a nurturer with a big, radiant smile.

"She was always feeding someone," Ms. Williams said. "She just had to cook."

A food-service employee at Cantor Fitzgerald, she also helped feed traders on the 104th floor of 1 World Trade Center, where she started her workday at 6 A.M. Among the condolences that poured in after her body was recovered a week after the attacks, one in particular touched her family deeply. It came from a woman who had never met her but whose husband, a broker who was also killed, had often told her how wonderful Ms. Tull-Francis was.

"That was confirmation of the kind of person my mom was," Ms. Williams said. "She had a big heart. She hated to see people hungry."

LANCE TUMULTY
Tamed by Love

At Matawan High School in New Jersey, Lance Tumulty was the captain of the football team and dated cheerleaders. Naturally, Cynthia, his future wife, knew who he was. But she was shy and avoided cliques. At 22, when they met again, he asked her out, repeatedly, but she refused, thinking he would soon dump her.

"He had a reputation in high school," she said. Finally she consented to a double date. They wound up talking until dawn. "He wasn't anything like I thought," she said.

Ten years later, they had a home in Bridgewater, N.J.,

and two daughters—Sara, 3, and Caroline, 4 months. He had just started a new job as a trader at Euro Brokers, which he had dreamed of and worked toward. On weekends, he fished or hunted—deer in New Jersey, elk in Montana—and he was looking forward to teaching his daughters about mountains when they were older. Several of their friends are Matawan High School classmates the Tumultys had rediscovered.

They call Mrs. Tumulty "the one who finally tamed him."

DONALD JOSEPH TUZIO
A Buyout and a Fateful Day

For 15 years, Donald Joseph Tuzio worked for Bear, Stearns as a systems programmer. He liked the work and he liked his colleagues. He would go to Yankee games with co-workers and he managed the office softball and soccer teams.

"He enjoyed that kind of stuff," said his wife, Rosemary Tuzio. "And he always had to run a party at the end."

Last summer, for the first time in a decade, Mr. Tuzio, who was 51 and lived in Goshen, N.Y., did not manage the softball team. He was leaving the firm. He had escaped layoffs in March, but feared he might not be so fortunate. He took a buyout in June.

"He not only liked the extracurricular activities, he really liked his job," Mrs. Tuzio said. "A lot of people did not have that luxury. He thought he was going to retire from there. He just belonged there."

His last day was July 31. Then he took a short vacation to Niagara Falls with his wife and daughter and his sister and her family. He also began to send out his résumé, but did not plan to start a serious search until after a job-hunting workshop that was part of his buyout package. It started Sept. 11 at the World Trade Center.

ROBERT TWOMEY
A History and Science Buff

There were no limits to Robert Twomey's love for history and science. Botany, entomology, viniculture, the Civil War: he was always reading something and loved talking about it.

"He retained everything," said his wife, Marie Twomey.

Mr. Twomey, 48, did graduate work in biology in his 20s, but never finished his dissertation and got into finance when he and his wife had the first of their two boys 18 years ago. He worked as a trader on the American Stock

Exchange with Ric Harvey, his brother-in-law, at Harvey Young Yurman, and dreamed of retiring to teach in public school.

On Sept. 11, he was at a weekly breakfast meeting at Windows on the World.

When he was not reading, he loved to ride his bike from his home in Sheepshead Bay, Brooklyn, to Breezy Point, Queens. He knew a lot about Sheepshead Bay, where his family had lived for more than a century. It was one of the many things he shared with his wife, whom he married when they were both 19.

"I'm living in the house my grandparents bought in 1905," Mrs. Twomey said. "Bob's father played in the construction site of this house."

JOHN UELTZHOEFFER
A Super Bowl Family

Super Bowl Sunday was a family holiday for the Ueltzhoeffers. After all, John Ueltzhoeffer's first date with his wife, Uschi, was a Super Bowl XXIV party at his parents' house in 1990. More important, the first of the couple's three children, Sarah, was born on Super Bowl Sunday in 1994.

"I'm in labor and John and the doctor are discussing the Super Bowl," Uschi Ueltzhoeffer recalled.

Sarah came into the world at 5 A.M. "We would always tell Sarah that she came a week late, that she waited for the Super Bowl," Ms. Ueltzhoeffer said. The couple watched the Super Bowl from the hospital. Uschi was wide awake after giving birth, but John kept falling asleep on the couch after the all-nighter. Sarah was followed by Jacob, 4, and Rebekah, 3—neither of them born on Super Bowl Sunday.

Every year, the Ueltzhoeffers have a Super Bowl party at their house—sometimes it coincides with Sarah's birthday party and they celebrate with cake. Uschi Ueltzhoeffer, who is from Austria, has developed a better understanding of football and the Super Bowl since her first date with the man who would become her husband. "We'll keep watching it," she said. "Just for the kids, we'll keep some traditions to remember."

TYLER UGOLYN
A Dream Job, with a Smile

On Tyler Ugolyn's Web site is a handwritten note from his grandmother: "Yesterday is history. Tomorrow a mystery. Today is a gift from God!"

The words resounded through the life of Mr. Ugolyn, a 23-year-old Columbia University graduate who started his dream job last summer as a research associate with Fred Alger Management Inc., in the World Trade Center. At 6-foot-4, he was an accomplished athlete who played basketball for Columbia before being injured. Not to be defined by any one thing, he was well known for a constant smile and infectious, if offbeat, laugh. He helped start a youth basketball program in Harlem, but was also known for his love for his 1992 GMC Typhoon (also featured prominently on the Web site).

"He did many things diligently and with passion," said Zachary Schiller, a friend and teammate at Columbia. "The way he ran drills in basketball. The way he went to church every Sunday. He did it without complaining and would sort of remind everyone through his effort and example."

MICHAEL A. ULIANO
Pleasures of Shore and Stage

Michael A. Uliano, a broker for Cantor Fitzgerald, never changed much from the grinning 10-year-old boy who was profiled in 1969 by his Canton, Mass., paper for snagging a 20-pound bass off Cape Cod. That he had just recovered from a broken wrist only added to his reputation for athleticism.

For the next 32 years, relatives recall, Mr. Uliano returned often to the Cape to dig clams and test out fishing lures he fashioned from chenille and Krazy Glue. He rode the dunes in a 1973 Jeep whose grille he painted to look like a shark's mouth.

Work eventually brought Mr. Uliano to New York, and though he enjoyed being a broker for Cantor Fitzgerald, he really wanted to act. So much, said his sister, Martha King, that he even endured teasing as a student at Ithaca College when he took ballet lessons as a way to improve his football game and prepare for a possible theatrical career.

When he met Linda Buffa in Bay Ridge in 1993, she took note of his Boston accent. He ribbed her about her Noo Yawk habit of talking while chewing gum. They were married in 1996 in Las Vegas, with an Elvis impersonator giving away the bride.

Life had darker moments, too. In March, Ms. Buffa learned she had breast cancer. "Thank God, he was here for that," she said. Daily radiation treatments kept her from attending a ceremony in his honor in which the Canton high school retired the number 10, which he wore as its quarterback.

JONATHAN UMAN
An Artist of Fun and Play

A friend's first impression of Jonathan Uman was that perhaps the man was heavily medicated. Why else would anyone be so happy?

Mr. Uman, 33, made life-play an art. He had a remote-control toy boat for the pool; that it also delighted Alex, 3, and Anna, 11 months, was a happy coincidence. He loved to entertain—"Who's coming over this weekend, Jule?" he would shout on Fridays to his wife, Julie—and was tickled that their pool bash this year featured a real Good Humor man and truck. He was an amateur actor who listened to Shakespeare as he drove his new toy, a Porsche, from Westport, Conn., to eSpeed, where he was a managing director.

A music maker, he had an earnestly mediocre way with a bass guitar that almost made his band a local bar success. He was a hugger and kisser, who held his wife's hand on top of restaurant tables, not under. You could tease him about any of this and it would roll off him, for Mr. Uman, who felt incredulous and grateful about his good fortune, was unashamed of his passions.

He even painted. He did a portrait of Julie's golden retriever, making the dog green. Happy Mr. Uman didn't care: he was color-blind.

ANIL UMARKAR
He Believed in America

Here is how to spell the name of Anil Umarkar's 14-month-old daughter, his most precious achievement, as specified by his wife, Priti: "V for victory; o for ocean; m for Mickey; i for ice cream; k for kite and a for America."

Although Mr. Umarkar, a computer programmer, is missing from the 103rd floor of the World Trade Center, where he worked for eSpeed, his wife is determined that his ambition for his daughter, Vomika, will live on. America, as in the last letter of Vomika, is the place where her father dreamed that she would get an advanced college degree. Although Mr. Umarkar, 34, will not be there to see it, Mrs. Umarkar hopes that victory, as in the first letter of Vomika, will come out of all the loss.

Two and a half years ago, Mrs. Umarkar, who has a master's degree in zoology, "left all that" in her hometown, Nagpur, India, so her husband could pursue his career. He loved football and had taken up jogging in Hackensack, N.J., where they lived.

"He was intelligent, he was very loving, he was a very thorough gentleman, and his work was his only hobby, just to work," Mrs. Umarkar said.

DIANE URBAN
You Knew Where She Stood

It was her best trait and her worst: Diane Urban said what she thought, whether you wanted to hear it or not. The habit was so well known that a relative suggested at her memorial service that they all get T-shirts saying, "Diane Urban Told Me Off."

Sometimes the target of her sharp tongue was an underperforming subordinate at the New York State Department of Taxation, where she rose to No. 2 in the income tax division. Sometimes it was her superiors. Once, she told them she was sick of training accountants only to have them leave for better salaries. "If I wanted to be a teacher, I would have been one," she said.

Ms. Urban, 50 and divorced for more than 20 years, could also be tart with the men in her life. And she tested the patience of her sister, Terry Corio, who withdrew from their relationship for a few years, drained by Ms. Urban's truthtelling. "She never backed down," Mrs. Corio said. "She was a pistol."

But the sisters always loved each other, Mrs. Corio said, and reunited last year. Ms. Urban had recently realized her dream of buying a home on Long Island, not far from her sister and brother-in-law. The sisters had their nails done together, recently splurging an extra $5 to have tiny flowers painted on their wine-colored toes. They were looking forward to pizza and rented movies on Saturday nights the next winter.

V

BRADLEY H. VADAS
Chasing the Best Deal

Bradley H. Vadas's former landlord in Manhattan came to his memorial service—not to sing praises about what a sweet tenant Mr. Vadas had been, but about what a great negotiator he was. "He had an intense desire to be fair, but also to get what he wanted at the minimal cost," said Mr. Vadas's fiancée, Kris McFerren. "He was good at making you want to give him a good deal."

Mr. Vadas, 37, a senior vice president at Keefe, Bruyette & Woods, was regularly one of the firm's top traders, perhaps because it involved the same rough-and-tumble strategizing that he found in his Sunday pickup softball games and online chess—and negotiating his rights as a tenant.

He and Ms. McFerren, who had known each other for nine years, recently made plans to be married. They attended a wedding in Lenox, Mass., over Labor Day weekend. One of his last single boyhood friends had finally made the leap, and on the drive home they had decided that they would, too, next spring. "We talked about going shopping for an engagement ring for Kris in the weeks to come," said a friend, Tom Gallagher.

WILLIAM VALCARCEL
A Life Without Life's Limits

As ever, William Valcarcel was in his wheelchair that Tuesday in his office on the 87th floor of 2 World Trade Center. "He used crutches at home, but in the office it was always the chair," said his 22-year-old daughter, Melissa. "Everything he did in his life was very hard."

Mr. Valcarcel, 54, grew up in a Spanish-speaking household in Brooklyn, and was hospitalized for polio so severe that, for years, he was unable to go to school. That delayed his learning English but did not stop him from swimming, or learning to drive, or from earning an accounting degree and a job with New York State during a time when few Puerto Ricans were being hired. "He overcame everything," his daughter said. "He is a fighter. He always said to us, 'Never give up.'"

MAYRA VALDES-RODRIGUEZ
Contagious Laughter

Friends remember Mayra Valdes-Rodriguez for her beautiful teeth, her unmanageable hair and her laugh. "Her laugh would make you laugh," said Louis Mercado, a friend.

She loved salsa dancing, music and annual trips to Cancún, but she lived for her son, Elias. "Everything she did was for him," said Millie Valdez, her sister. Whether it was something simple like going bowling or venturing off to bigger events like the Ice Capades at Madison Square Garden or vacationing at Disney World, she wanted Elias, 12, to have everything he wanted. When he asked her to try walking the tightrope during a visit to Disney World, she didn't disappoint.

"My sister loved life," Ms. Valdez said.

A 17-year employee of the Aon Corporation, Ms. Valdes-Rodriguez, 39, was a volunteer fire warden on the 103rd floor of the south tower. Co-workers told the family that on Sept. 11 they had seen her on the 78th floor hustling people toward a staircase. The family holds on to the hope she may only be missing. "She was very level-headed," her sister said.

FELIX VALE and IVAN VALE
Brothers in a Big Family

Jose Quintana's youngest brothers, Felix, top, and Ivan Vale, were 8 and 10 years younger, but he understood them pretty well. The older one, Felix, loved children, wanted marriage and loved nothing more than family.

Commuters at Grand Central Terminal pass beneath a
flag-and-laser-light ceiling display offering patriotic
holiday greetings. (*James Estrin*)

"If it was between spending the day in Hollywood with Jennifer Lopez, or having a family gathering over here, he would definitely pick us," Mr. Quintana said. "He was actually the soul of the family." The family included four brothers and one sister, plus dozens of cousins and others from New Jersey, Los Angeles, Puerto Rico, or Connecticut.

Felix Vale, 29, lived in East New York with his mother, whom he supported with his job as a manager at Cantor Fitzgerald. "Felix was the type that if he met you five minutes ago and you needed somebody to help you do your move, he was there," Mr. Quintana said.

He helped his brother, Ivan Vale, 27, get a job at eSpeed, part of Cantor Fitzgerald. He did well there, surviving a round of layoffs on Sept. 10. Ivan Vale had been married to his wife, Lucy, for three years.

"They didn't have any kids; what they had was a zoo," Mr. Quintana said, listing the couple's pets: six to eight rabbits, four or five lizards, two cats, one dog.

"Ivan was a little off center; he loved these weird things,"

Mr. Quintana said. "Ivan loved skeletons, he loved swords, and the stuff with the animals. He painted his room black one time. Once he had a lizard, an alligator, I'm not sure what the heck it was, and he divided his room in half. He gave the lizard half, in its cage, and the other half was for him."

"They're Brooklyn kids who never got into trouble," Mr. Quintana said. "They were doing fine. They were doing O.K."

BENITO VALENTIN
"Our Life of the Party"

Anyone who ever heard the message on Benito Valentin's cell phone knows something about how he chose to live life, always looking for a laugh and a little fun. Ever the comedian, Mr. Valentin, 31, who worked for American Express, teased his callers with a message that said: "Hello, hello, how you doing? Oh, this is a recording."

Now Grissel Valentin, the woman he married on Valentine's Day 11 years earlier, the mother of his three girls, calls to hear his voice two, sometimes three, times a day. It is a link to the man who, when he was not making people laugh, rushed home from work to talk baseball and dance salsa with his daughters, Danyelle, Jailene and Alyssa. "He was our life of the party," Mrs. Valentin said. "As long as I can hear his voice, I have hope that he isn't lying somewhere crushed but just trapped. We miss him too much to believe he's gone."

SANTOS VALENTIN Jr.
A Sharpshooter and a Joker

There is a saying among police officers: "When people are in trouble, they call the cops. When cops are in trouble, they call Emergency Service." Santos Valentin Jr., a member of the New York Police Department's Emergency Service Squad 7, answered the call on Sept. 11.

Officer Valentin was a sharpshooter trained in counter-terrorism tactics, said his sister, Sgt. Denise Valentin, and his family thought that if anyone could come out alive in this attack, it would be him.

What have lived on are the memories—of the jokes he played on his colleagues, of how he loved his dog, Luger (so much that he would leave the Animal Planet channel on for him when he was not home), of his love for family and friends, and of his bravery. Officer Valentin was not afraid of death, but he did hate funerals. So, a few days ago, his family gave him a send-off at the rubble of the World Trade Center, where he was last seen. He loved his Budweiser, so they poured him a can and said their goodbyes.

CARLTON F. VALVO II
Traveler First Class

At the memorial service for Carlton F. Valvo II, friends gave his daughter letters describing an adventure-packed life.

At Northwestern University in Evanston, Ill., when other students were heading home for spring break, Mr. Valvo was jetting off to Sri Lanka, because he somehow had a friend whose father knew the ambassador. "When Carl traveled, he traveled first class," said a college friend, Mitchell Barnett.

On one of his weeks off, Mr. Valvo and his mother, Coletta, met in Manhattan to drop in on the art auctions. He enjoyed them enough that later, when he moved to New York, he often volunteered to check out paintings in Sotheby's catalog that his mother was considering. Working as a vice president at Cantor Fitzgerald just gave Mr. Valvo more ways to see the world. He visited dozens of countries in his 38 years.

Mr. Valvo met his wife, Lori Rossiter, while attending an opera performance. Their daughter, Dante, 7, is already like her dad in her ability to take in the U.S. Open one weekend and a Jets game the next.

For the holidays, Lori and Dante have an invitation to visit the Valvos' ski home in Oregon. But then, they also have an offer to go abroad. You see, Mr. Valvo had a friend whose brother is married to a Pakistani maharani living in Morocco . . .

ERICA VAN ACKER
A Self-Made Woman

In 1971, Erica Van Acker was the subject of *No Tears for Rachel,* a public television documentary about a woman who had been raped—how she was treated and how she responded. It was Ms. Van Acker's story, without her name.

Ms. Van Acker, 62, had an English mother and a French father. She was born in Manhattan but spent much of her childhood in Europe. Despite schooling in drama, she turned to business when she returned to the United States in the 1960s.

She worked for the Off-Track Betting Corporation, Citibank and Aon Consulting in the trade center. Along the way, she also had her own human resources consulting firm, called VASA, and started a restaurant staffed entirely by women, the Station Bistro, in Water Mill on Long Island. She had homes in Manhattan and Sag Harbor, N.Y.

"She was a self-made person who had to overcome a lot to get where she got," said Susan Thompson, a friend since the 1970s.

"People were Erica's bottom line, always, and that was reflected in all of her projects," Ms. Thompson added. "Whether her task was to introduce automated systems to parimutuels at the racetrack or to create workshops for middle managers in crises, her goal was to reach each individual to help them adapt—and she succeeded beautifully."

KENNETH VAN AUKEN
An Arbor of Memories

Kenneth Van Auken's job as a bond broker bought him the house with the yard in East Brunswick, N.J. But his passions for carpentry and gardening built the cedarwood arbor in the yard where his widow, Lorie Van Auken, now goes to grieve.

Mr. Van Auken, 47, who worked at Cantor Fitzgerald and left two children, finished the arbor a week before he died. In October, the clematis plants that the Van Aukens picked out together for the arbor came in the mail. Mrs. Van Auken planted them with a friend at hand to keep her from crying too hard.

Not far from where the pink flowers will crawl up the

arbor, a big old maple stands dying, its leaves brown for months. But it is being allowed to stay for now. "My husband loved this tree," Mrs. Van Auken said.

"We had decided to wait till spring to cut it down. Give it one more chance to go green again." While Mrs. Van Auken is gardening to confront her loss, their 12-year-old daughter, Sarah, has written and recorded a song, "Daddy's Little Girl," that has been played on pop radio stations.

"Daddy, are you there?" the song goes. " 'Cause I've, I've looked everywhere."

"Maybe you'll appear, somehow whisper in my ear."

RICHARD BRUCE VAN HINE
An Avid Outdoorsman

Richard Bruce Van Hine, known to all as Bruce, had been a firefighter for 12 years, most recently with Squad 41 in the South Bronx. The father of Meghan, 14, and Emily, 17, he was one of six men lost from the squad on Sept. 11.

Firefighter Van Hine, 48, had always wanted to be a firefighter, said Ann, his wife of 21 years.

"He was on the list to be a firefighter for seven years," she said. "I am a firm believer in following your dreams, so I encouraged him." But Firefighter Van Hine also loved the outdoors. Even though he took only day hikes, he had completed the New Jersey, New York and Connecticut legs of the Appalachian Trail.

A prized memory, Mrs. Van Hine said, was of a five-week camping trip the family took four years ago that included the Badlands of South Dakota, the Grand Tetons, Yellowstone National Park and the Rocky Mountains.

BRADLEY VAN HOORN
"A Lot of Kid in Him"

Bradley Van Hoorn showed up for his sophomore year at Yale with a mounted caribou head, a loan from his father. The two, along with Mr. Hoorn's mother and sister, crammed the head into a van with Mr. Hoorn's luggage and drove from Richland, near Kalamazoo, Mich., to New Haven.

Mr. Hoorn had warned his roommates.

"These city slicker kids that lived with him thanked us for the moose we brought," his mother, Kathy, recalled. "I don't think they knew the difference between a moose, an elk and a caribou, but they were wonderful kids."

After graduation, Mr. Hoorn, 22, worked as a research analyst in training for Fred Alger Management on the 93rd floor of the World Trade Center's north tower. He saw the city as an adventure, but lamented the lack of tennis courts.

He hoped to eventually head back west in his red Porsche (another loan from his father), and maybe even someday become a teacher, like his mother.

She remembers his sheepish grins when she caught her son reading novels while he was supposed to be studying. In one sitting, Mr. Hoorn could finish a Grisham or a Clancy, and he devoured the Harry Potters.

"There was a lot of kid in him," she said.

DANIEL VAN LAERE
Glen Rock, and Beyond

When Daniel Van Laere was a kid in Glen Rock, N.J., his hero was a neighbor who was a volunteer firefighter. "We grew up seeing Bobby Barton running off to fires all the time," said Mr. Van Laere's brother, Paul, "and I guess it just captured Dan's imagination. He loved the whole aspect of it—the trucks, the equipment, the potential of fighting fires and helping people."

At 18, Daniel Van Laere became a Glen Rock firefighter. Soon he was teaching rescue courses at the Bergen County Fire Academy. But Mr. Van Laere did not go to the trade center on Sept. 11 as part of the rescue effort. He was simply putting in another day at the office. Mr. Van Laere, 46, was a risk analyst and underwriter at Aon Insurance, inspecting big buildings and resorts and writing reports on their fire safety.

His work took him all over the globe, from Texas to the Caribbean to Belgium. For a while, he had a 31-foot boat he kept at the Jersey shore, and he and a former girlfriend and their golden Labrador lived on it in the summertime, ranging up to Rhode Island and down to Cape May.

But he never moved out of Glen Rock, where he bought a house and lived with his fiancée, and his family still remembers him as a local hero. On the wall of his mother's house hangs a photo of a raging fire in a lumber yard. The picture shows Mr. Van Laere in the basket of a 60-foot boom atop a truck, feeding water down onto the flames.

EDWARD R. VANACORE
A Sunset Hog in the Rain

Eddie Vanacore had a smile that made everyone around him happy. He was also the youngest of six, and he learned early to be persistent in getting what he wanted. "He was a pain in the neck," said his brother John, the next oldest in the family.

There was the time when Eddie Vanacore was 5 or 6, and the family went to Amish country in Pennsylvania. They happened to drive past a place that sold minibikes, and for the rest of the trip Eddie repeated, "I want a minibike," over and over again.

"He was a great kid," said John Vanacore.

His persistence helped him go far, and won him a job as a stock analyst for Fiduciary Trust International on the 94th floor of 2 World Trade Center.

And eventually, Eddie Vanacore, 29, got the bike of his dreams, a sunset orange Harley-Davidson. He would ride it through rain and snow from Jersey City, where he lived, to see his girlfriend in Albany. Sometimes, "he would just get on it for a couple of hours and head out into the sunset," his brother remembered. Their parents worried about it. "They figured if he was going to get killed, that was how," his brother said.

JON VANDEVANDER
A Widow's Wish

There is a peacefulness in Anne Vandevander's voice, the serenity of someone who has known happiness and accepted a fate that robbed her of some of it. Anne's husband, Jon, worked as a trader for Carr Futures Inc., on the 92d floor of 1 World Trade Center. She talked to him several times after the tower was hit, until about 10 minutes before the building collapsed.

"He said 'I love you and tell the kids I love them,'" she said. A week later, a police officer came to her door to say they had found his body. She buried him in a cemetery in Ridgewood, N.J., where they lived with their three children. "Most wives will never get that opportunity," she said of the others who are still searching for missing relatives. "I have him back in Ridgewood. My one wish that morning was to have his wedding band back, and now I'm wearing it."

Jon Vandevander, 44, loved his job and died with men he had worked with for 4 years at Carr, and for 10 years before that when their division was owned by Dean Witter.

He played soccer in college, and coached his children's soccer, baseball, softball and basketball teams. He loved taking his two oldest children golfing at the Ridgewood Country Club. "He was a great dad," she said. "I feel very fortunate."

FREDERICK VARACCHI
Teeing Off at 6 A.M.

Although Frederick Varacchi was best known in the finance world as chief operating officer of Cantor Fitzgerald and president of its electronic trading platform, eSpeed Inc., he might better be remembered as a dedicated family man who would play a round of golf at 6 A.M. on a Saturday so he could be home before his three children got up.

"Our families would go on vacation together, and he and my husband would be the first ones running to the rides," said Jayne O'Toole of Melville, N.Y., who has been friends with Mr. Varacchi since they went to kindergarten together in Syosset. In high school, he told Ms. O'Toole how he had

met his future wife, Eileen, in biology class. "He knew she was it from the minute he saw her," she said.

Mr. Varacchi, who was 35 and lived in Greenwich, Conn., brought that same enthusiasm and determination to fatherhood. "I can remember just a couple months ago, he was looking at the kids, saying, 'Gosh, I can't wait till the kids grow up and we can go to their wedding. Gosh, it's going to be such a blast,'" Ms. O'Toole said. "He said, 'Can you imagine?'"

GOPAL VARADHAN
Mathematical Musician

An old neighbor of Gopal Varadhan's said she first knew him through his music. It was like that with everyone around Mr. Varadhan, said his mother, Vasu. He was so dedicated to playing his acoustic guitar that, as a teenager, he lined the walls of his bedroom with egg cartons, hoping it would soundproof the room, rather than strum more softly.

He started a ska-inspired band, City Beat, while attending the Bronx High School of Science during the 1980s, cutting a record and playing CBGB in lower Manhattan.

As it turned out, Mr. Varadhan also had an affinity for numbers and became a successful trader on Wall Street. After starting an unsuccessful Internet company in 2000, he joined Cantor Fitzgerald's eSpeed division in June.

Mr. Varadhan, 32, never forgot his music. He wrote songs for which his girlfriend, Valerie Toscano, was to compose lyrics.

"He thought that would have been our ultimate collaboration," Ms. Toscano said. "I thought marriage would have been the ultimate collaboration."

DAVID VARGAS
Giving Each Other a Leg Up

When she saw the ball of smoke and fire behind her on Sept. 11 as she was being evacuated from the Bank of New York downtown, Rosa Caicedo had only one thought: "My husband was back there, and I feared that my children would be left without any parents if I didn't save myself. So I ran as fast as I could."

Her husband, David Vargas, worked on the 101st floor of 2 World Trade Center. He was a customer service manager at Pitney Bowes, and Ms. Caicedo worked part time as a checks processor a few blocks away, in a third-floor office. When a co-worker told her about the the plane hitting the first tower, she called her husband. "Get out, get out now," she said she told him.

"My children do not accept that he is dead," she said of

her daughter, Leslie, 14, and her son, Kevin, 12. "They have not seen his body; we haven't been able to bury him, so they say that he is missing." Mr. Vargas and his wife met when they had both been in this country about a year. He was from Bolivia, she is from Ecuador.

"I felt like I had known him all of my life. He was such a good person," she said. They married 17 years ago. He got his associate's degree in computer programming at LaGuardia Community College, and when he finished, he encouraged her to go. "He told me, now it is your turn," Mrs. Caicedo said.

SCOTT C. VASEL
Second Day in a New Job

In June, Scott C. Vasel, 32, moved into a new home in Park Ridge, N.J., with his wife, Amy, and his two sons, Ryan, 4, and Matthew, 2. Then he took the summer off to spend it with his family—at the zoo, at the beach, in Vermont. And on Sept. 10 he started a job at the World Trade Center as a disaster recovery specialist with Marsh & McLennan, the insurance brokerage company.

"He said he had a great cubicle right against the window and he could see a great view of the Hudson," said Jenny Frantin, his sister-in-law. "He was looking forward to the job. They had a great summer and he was ready."

Now Mr. Vasel's new neighbors on Pine Drive have stood by his family. They have brought over food, hired a cleaning woman and a lawn service, offered to baby-sit and shop. "They're making dinners from here through Thanksgiving," Ms. Frantin said.

The neighbors set aside a spot in the grass for a shrine with candles and flowers. They also put up a flag-shaped wooden sign. "God Bless America and Our Neighbor," it reads.

ARCANGEL VAZQUEZ
Devout and Helpful

Arcangel Vazquez usually stayed for three Masses every Sunday at St. Barbara's Roman Catholic Church in Brooklyn. He had attended the church since he was young, and at 47 he was an active member: an usher, a catechist, a leader of the men's program.

"He could never say no," said his friend Diane Munez, the secretary of St. Barbara's. "He always wanted to be in the middle of everything."

Mr. Vazquez, who had a 21-year-old daughter and grandchildren, worked in maintenance on the upper floors of 2 World Trade Center. He was last seen helping people leave the 96th and 97th floors.

At his church, where co-workers noted the aptness of his first name, no one expected otherwise. "That was like him," Ms. Munez said, calling him "a comforting friend for everybody."

"Always listening," she said of him. "He always had this smile on his face. The most beautiful teeth."

PETER A. VEGA
Always Ready to Help

Regan Grice-Vega was pregnant and was on the way to the doctor for a checkup with her husband, Peter Vega, when they spotted a car stalled on the side of the road. In it was a woman who had been rushing to the hospital to see her husband, who had had a heart attack. Mr. Vega pushed her car to a safe spot and then drove her to the hospital.

"We were late for our appointment, as usual, but that is the kind of person Peter was," Mrs. Grice-Vega said. "If he was cleaning out our gutter, he would clean the neighbor's, too."

Mr. Vega, 36, a firefighter who was a member of Ladder Company 118 in Brooklyn Heights, called his wife just before he left for the World Trade Center on Sept. 11. They had been married five years. She was a fervent Knicks fan, and he proposed to her at Madison Square Garden with a message on the big screen at half time.

On Nov. 10, she returned to the Garden for the first time since Sept. 11, for a Knicks game against Golden State. Her father-in-law got her two seats on the floor, and she took her twin brother. "When I went with Peter, we were always up," Mrs. Grice-Vega said. "My father-in-law was on a mission to make sure I had a good night." "It was bittersweet," she added. "It was fun—but hard."

SANKARA VELAMURI
Well Read and Well Spoken

Listening to Sankara Velamuri speak was a pleasure, said Vijaya Sonti, a younger sister. His enunciation was distinct, his words precise and his diction elegant. He often quoted a bit of the English or Sanskrit literature he read voraciously. "Poetry," she said. "Religion. He had an excellent memory."

Mr. Velamuri, who grew up in Orissa, India, and worked previously in London, lived in Edison, N.J., with his wife, Avenal. When he immigrated, 30 years ago, he switched from metallurgy to accounting and found work at the New York State Department of Taxation and Finance. The second oldest of 10 children, he was patient and learned, said Mrs. Sonti, a computer specialist with a master's degree in mathematics.

"Growing up," she said, "he taught me algebra one summer. That created my interest in mathematics."

Mr. Velamuri loved company and good conversation, but also studied Hindu scriptures, attended temple and meditated at home.

JORGE VELAZQUEZ
Feeding the Hungry

Jorge Velazquez was always looking for one more hungry soul to feed.

This was in the mid-1990s. Mr. Velazquez, a deeply religious man from Puerto Rico, had founded a program to feed the homeless at his Seventh-day Adventist church, and commuting home to Spanish Harlem from a shipping job in a shoulder-pad factory, he would keep an eye out for the down-and-out, recalled his longtime friend Anthony Salcedo.

Mr. Velazquez and his wife, Consuelo, would cook big pots of rice and beans and stew, and on Saturdays, they would pile their four kids into the car, make the rounds of some of Manhattan's saddest spots and ladle out hot dinners. "I'd ask him where he found these people and he'd say, 'Coming home from work I saw someone walking around and I got out of my car and followed them to where they were,' " Mr. Salcedo said. "He was a very determined man."

Determined to make things better for his family, Mr. Velazquez, 47, landed a job as a security guard for Morgan Stanley Dean Witter in the trade center in 1999, and he quickly worked his way up to security specialist. He had just bought a house in Passaic, N.J., and was moonlighting as a security guard to help pay for it. Now his family members are starting a program to feed the homeless at their local church.

LAWRENCE VELING
Father's "Blue" Period

It can be surprising what latent talents fathers discover when they want to make their kids happy.

Last Christmas, Lawrence Veling found he had a knack for drawing characters from the Nickelodeon show *Blue's Clues.* He had never sketched or doodled, and couldn't draw anything else. But for his 2-year-old son Kevin, he could churn out remarkable likenesses of Blue, Mr. Salt, Mrs. Pepper, Slippery Soap and Tickety Tock in rapid succession as Kevin cried "More!" Even the neighbors were impressed when they saw Mr. Veling's chalk drawings on the sidewalk.

Mr. Veling, 44, worked two jobs—one as a fireman with Engine 235 in Bedford-Stuyvesant, Brooklyn, and one as a high school custodian in Manhattan—so his scarce time at home was devoted to his three children, Ryan, 7, Cynthia, 6, and Kevin.

He colored in coloring books. He played Junior Monopoly. He went to school in his full uniform for fire safety week.

"I knew my kids would grow up to be great adults because they had a great father," said Dianne Veling, his wife.

Mrs. Veling says her own sketches of *Blue's Clues* characters are inconsistent. "A couple of times I was impressed with myself, but I forgot how I did it."

DAVID VERA
Point Man in a Clinch

At the end of every day, David Vera and his daughter, Jennica, greeted each other with a scream. Their salutation was always the same: "I love you twice as much as anything you could say, universe, infinity and beyond the galaxies to the fifth dimension."

Now, when the door opens, Ms. Vera, who came from Puerto Rico two years ago to live with her father, still expects to hear his voice.

She will remember him most for his strict parenting. On her prom night, Ms. Vera's date had to grasp her father's keys so that Mr. Vera would have copies of the young man's fingerprints. "He would always say he trusted me, but he didn't trust the world," said Ms. Vera, 18. "He was very overprotective."

Mr. Vera, 41, who lived in Brooklyn, was the senior telecommunications technician at Euro Brokers. He also had a sacred fitness ritual. He exercised every day, but reserved Saturdays for pickup basketball games in Park Slope. "He wasn't too much of a dribbler, but if you left him alone he'd burn you," said a longtime friend, Eddie Claudio. "He was a go-to guy. The type of guy that if you needed help he was there in clinch time."

CHRISTOPHER VIALONGA
Cool Guy, Warm Heart

Hey. To be 30, single, a sharp dresser, with a front pocket full of cash and a back pocket full of friends and family? Little brother, your married-with-children two older brothers think you're having too much fun! Even though he meant to settle down (no serious contenders for the wife title, so far), Christopher Vialonga, a foreign exchange trader with Carr Futures, was having a great time flying solo.

A big, good-looking guy and former offensive tackle, he whistled everybody together for Jets tailgate parties and organized the tee-off times on Sundays for a gang of six. He always arrived a half-hour early, because he was so revved. Johnnie Juicebag, they called him, Johnnie Black Shoes.

The money spilled from his pockets. Yes, it went for the black BMW and those clothes—forgetting to pack ski clothes for a Lake Tahoe trip, dropping $1,000 on new stuff—but it flowed like crazy for his niece and nephews ("Chris, you're spoiling them!")

A full-tilt guy, who happened to be a sweetheart. He was worrying about his mother, Katherine, who struggled with widowhood. So at the beginning of September, he moved home to Demarest, N.J., to help around the house, just for a little while.

MATTHEW VIANNA

Wit and a Well-Knotted Tie

When Matthew Vianna wore a tie, it was always properly centered, with a tight knot and a tasteful pattern.

Even the T-shirts he wore kayaking were crisp and spotless. "Matthew loved to dress up," said Marilynda Vianna, his mother. "The shirt. The tie. The jacket—always polished. Even when he was casual, he looked nice."

On Sept. 11, he dressed with particular care for a sales meeting. "Blue shirt," Mrs. Vianna said. "Blue eyes. I told him, 'You look so beautiful.' It was the last time I saw him."

Mr. Vianna, 23, from Manhasset, N.Y., learned the importance of details and the pleasures of formality at nearby Chaminade High School. That stood him in good stead at Villanova University, where, his mother said, he found a "real community of friends," and at Cantor Fitzgerald. But he was also perfectly happy rooting for the Giants and the Yankees and making quiet remarks that made his friends howl with laughter. "He always had the perfect, perfect comeback," Mrs. Vianna said.

ROBERT VICARIO

Instant Friends

Robert Vicario saved everything. He saved souvenirs from the vacations that he would take with his wife, Jill, to Jamaica. He saved a lock of her hair from the first time they met 10 years ago. He saved match-books and Playbills. He even saved the umbilical cord stump from their daughter, Savannah Rose, who was born three months before the attack.

Mr. Vicario, 40, made people laugh; he never had a bad word to say. Everyone he met became an instant friend. The toll taker. The grocery clerk. The homeless man. The gas station attendant. The fellow contractors with whom he had just started a new job in early September at Cantor Fitzger-

ald. He liked them all, and he wanted to invite them all to his wedding or to his house in Weehawken, N.J.

He was particularly friendly with those he met in Jamaica. In fact, he liked to take photos with these new friends, then mail copies of the photos along with a note. Thus another friendship was notched, forever.

"It was like, 'Rob, you know the entire world,'" Mrs. Vicario used to tell her husband (who was actually called Bobby by everyone else). "'Is there anybody you don't know?'"

JOANNA VIDAL

A Conference and a Call

On the Monday night before the terrorist attack, Joanna Vidal, a 26-year-old event coordinator for Risk Waters, the London-based financial publishing house, was ecstatic. The first day of the company's conference at Windows on the World, an event she had helped create, had been a brilliant success. And at dinner with her father, Enrique, and her mother, Lesbia, in their Yonkers home, "she was so hurried, making her preparations, that she was eating standing up," Mr. Vidal recalled.

In fact, the first day had gone so smoothly that Ms. Vidal was hoping to leave the conference after the first speaker; after all, so much work was waiting on her desk in her office at 270 Lafayette Street. And so on Tuesday morning she hurried to the trade center at 5:30 A.M. After the attack, "she called from the conference and said the building was on fire," Mr. Vidal said. "She said, 'I want you to know that no matter what happens, I love you.' And then she was cut off."

JOHN VIGIANO and JOSEPH VIGIANO

Growing Up Right

Maybe there was something in the water.

For some reason, perhaps a dozen men who came of age during the 1970s and '80s in Deer Park, N.Y., developed an appetite for civic duty. They became New York City police officers and firefighters in their professional lives, and volunteer firefighters with Engine Company No. 2 in Deer Park in their personal ones. They called it the Deer Park Connection, and Firefighter John Vigiano, top, and Detective Joseph Vigiano, two of the tightest brothers you could ever find, were among the best-liked and most accomplished members.

Both followed the unwritten manual on growing up right in Deer Park, said their father, John Vigiano, a retired captain in the New York City Fire Department. They were active in sports. They became Eagle Scouts. They hatched pranks that were wicked in their creativity but gentle in their impact.

"They never embarrassed me," said Captain Vigiano. "They were good fathers, good husbands and they were good men."

John Vigiano, at 36, was older by two years, though his brother never let him forget that he was also four inches shorter and maybe 30 pounds lighter, too. John was the quieter of the two, and spent as much time as possible with his two young daughters, his father said. He was a terrific hockey player (and rabid Rangers fan) and he would occasionally rent out an entire rink for his family, his brother's family and a few other friends.

Joseph Vigiano, who was known as Joey, loved to mug for the cameras and played lacrosse on the Police Department team, said his wife, Kathy, a fellow police officer. On the job, he was commended for his bravery: he survived being shot on three different occasions. At home, he taught his two boys how to build pinewood derby cars. Eventually, he was going to do the same with his youngest son, who was 3 months old in September.

For now, the Vigianos are collecting anecdotes and tributes from friends and relatives on a new Web site, www.vigiano.com. Here, presumably, is one of the last stories: On the Sunday before Sept. 11, Kathy Vigiano returned home after the first game of the season in her soccer league, bruised and tired. She was prepared to make dinner, but instead, she saw that her husband had fixed prime rib, Caesar salad, mashed potatoes, and broccoli with cheese—while watching their baby, too. All this from a guy who had previously insisted that he only knew how to make spaghetti sauce.

FRANK J. VIGNOLA Jr.
A Kid's Man

Their house in Merrick, N.Y., was the playground, and Frank J. Vignola Jr. was the leader to the kids. "Our gate is like a revolving door, and sometimes I answered the phone, 'Grand Central,' " said his wife, Lynn Vignola. On the weekends, more than a half-dozen kids—the couple's children, nieces and nephews—kept the gate swinging.

Mr. Vignola, 6-foot-1, would try to make the biggest splash in the swimming pool. He would play Monopoly and Battleship, and run electric trains, with the kids.

For his own children—Sarah, 13, and Anthony, 8— weekends were "Daddy Time." When a new *Star Wars* movie or an *X-Men* came out, he would get up at 6 A.M. and

go to the theater with them to wait in line. Anthony would follow Daddy like a shadow, even when he ran errands.

Weekends are a lot quieter now. "When I asked my son 'Want to play with Mom?' he said, 'No, you don't have imagination,' " Mrs. Vignola said.

Mr. Vignola, 44, was a senior vice president and partner at Cantor Fitzgerald.

SERGIO VILLANUEVA
Soccer Lover

It was Sunday afternoon, Sept. 9, and the game was scoreless with just minutes left to play. Suddenly Sergio Villanueva sped down the field, whacked the ball with his foot, and goal! The Fire Department won, 1-0.

A native of Argentina, Firefighter Villanueva, 33, loved soccer. Tanya Villanueva, his fiancée, used to have to put on a special hat with bells dangling from it, as well as a jersey from an Argentine team, and run through the house shouting, "Goal!" when an important match was on television. "He was a huge soccer fan," she said.

He also enjoyed a fine cigar and knew his red wines, and around Ladder Company 132 in Brooklyn, he made a name for himself in the kitchen. While "firehouse cuisine" can be an oxymoron, when it was Firefighter Villanueva's turn at the stove, his company feasted on pasta, chicken and other Italian dishes. As a child, he had learned to cook at his father's restaurant, Piccolo San Marino in Bayside, and remembered the recipes (along with the words to all of Barry Manilow's songs) all his life.

Before becoming a firefighter, he spent eight years as a police officer, battling robbers and drug dealers. One of his partners in the Bronx precinct where he started out thought of him as the consummate transplanted New Yorker. "He loved New York, loved his country, loved Queens," said Lt. Rick Miller, "and he would go hoarse for three days after an Argentine soccer game."

MELISSA VINCENT
Doing All Things New York

Melissa Vincent was infatuated with New York, but just couldn't find an apartment here when she moved from LeRoy, N.Y., near Rochester, a few years ago.

So she settled for Hoboken, N.J., and immediately began doing all the New York things: opera and movies, of course, but she also went to as many Yankee games as she could, and to Broadway shows whenever she could get tickets.

Meanwhile, to her surprise, she found herself really liking Hoboken; what's more, she absolutely loved the new job she found in 2000 at Alliance Consulting Group, on the 102nd floor of 1 World Trade Center. As a recruiter, she specialized in locating technical personnel, especially those in the arcane universe of software engineering. Ms. Vincent's career was rising quickly, not unlike the elevators that whooshed her to the office every day.

"She truly loved Hoboken," said her brother, Matthew, "but it really wasn't close enough to New York. She wanted to get closer. She was hoping to move in."

FRANCINE VIRGILIO
A Cool Aunt in Demand

One Christmas, Francine Virgilio treated her nephews to a show with the Rockettes at Radio City Music Hall and dinner afterward at Mickey Mantle's. She even hired a limousine to take them around.

Though Ms. Virgilio, 48, never married or had children of her own, she was always in demand. She was the cool aunt, the one who knew how to have a good time without embarrassing them in front of their friends. "She was just so generous," said her sister-in-law, Susan Virgilio. "Not just with her money, but with her time."

An Aon executive, Ms. Virgilio started out as a secretary after high school and worked her way up. She was just as disciplined about her favorite team, the Yankees. She followed them through the bad years, and kept an autographed photo of Lou Piniella on her desk. In 2000, she snagged a ticket to the Subway Series and had it framed for a place in her home on Staten Island.

LAWRENCE JOSEPH VIRGILIO
A Firefighter by Choice

Given his two bachelor's degrees, Lawrence Joseph Virgilio did not have to be a firefighter. He had a physical therapy degree from New York University, and found great satisfaction in rehabilitating cardiac and pulmonary patients. And as part of his minor in dance at Queens College, he had trained in classical ballet and performed in community theater. But he loved responding to crises as an advanced rescue specialist at Squad 18 in Manhattan, and he loved the firehouse camaraderie.

After 13 years as a firefighter, he had just been given the honor of training to become a member of the elite Fire Department team that travels to other cities in times of disaster. And so, when Mr. Virgilio, 38, called his girlfriend of six years, Abigail Francis, from his fire truck on the morning of the attack, "he knew the situation was dire, because he had always been worried about a terrorist attack in the city," she said.

All seven men on his truck are believed to have perished;

so far, four, including Mr. Virgilio, have been recovered. "He told me he loved me," Ms. Francis said. "That message was a great gift."

JOSEPH VISCIANO
Always the Best Man

Fresh out of Boston College, where he graduated magna cum laude with a degree in finance, Joseph Visciano told relatives he loved his new job as a trader for Keefe, Bruyette & Woods, a securities company at 2 World Trade Center. Mr. Visciano, 22 and single, had promised his mother that he would someday give her a granddaughter, but first he wanted to focus on his career, save money and go for an M.B.A.

"His career was really very important to him," said Bill Matarazzo, a cousin, adding that Mr. Visciano had been an overachiever since kindergarten.

Mr. Matarazzo and Mr. Visciano grew up like brothers across the street from each other in Staten Island, and worked through their teenage years in the family business—an auto parts wholesale company where they did everything from inventory to sales. When Mr. Matarazzo planned his wedding, he asked his cousin Joe to be his best man.

Mr. Matarazzo acquiesced to his extended family's wishes to go on with the wedding on Oct. 6. Mr. Visciano's younger brother, Jason, would stand in as honorary groomsman. "No one can take his place," Mr. Matarazzo, 24, said of Mr. Visciano, who worked at the trade center for only six weeks. "He will always be my best man."

JOSHUA VITALE
Love with No Regrets

Joshua Vitale and Ina Weintraub had been best friends since they were seventh graders in Syosset, on Long Island. In 1999, when they were 26, Mr. Vitale made a confession as they left the movies.

"He said he'd been in love with me for many years and that if he didn't tell me this now he would always regret it," Ms. Weintraub said. "I was so blown away I didn't talk to him for three months."

When the dust settled, the couple's life together quickly fell into place. They got engaged and moved into an apartment in Great Neck, N.Y. Mr. Vitale, who had been a wanderer, a party animal and something of a lost soul for much of his 20s, got a job at Cantor Fitzgerald's trading desk.

"Once we got together it was like we were shooting for the stars," Ms. Weintraub said. "We were so happy."

Two days before Sept. 11, the couple tried to get tickets to the United States Open tennis tournament, without success. "Josh said: 'Forget the Open. Why don't we go to the zoo?' "

Ms. Weintraub said. The couple communed with the gorillas at the Bronx Zoo, and then Mr. Vitale, his wandering instincts intact, found a path where they had a picnic together.

"There was nothing left unsaid between us," Ms. Weintraub said. "He knew how much I loved him and I will always know how much he loved me."

MARIA PERCOCO VOLA
Combing the City for Her

Maria Percoco Vola's relatives are still combing the city, and peering at every photograph they see of the World Trade Center attacks, looking for a sign that she made it to safety. Ms. Vola, who worked as an administrative assistant in the claims department for Aon, the insurance broker, had called her sister Tilly twice to tell her about the attacks on Sept. 11.

"Maybe she's in a daze, maybe she was hit by something," said her father, John Vola.

There was some dark irony in Ms. Vola being the victim of a sweeping tragedy. Her family said that when she was 12, and heard about an earthquake in Italy, she took it upon herself to go around the neighborhood to collect money for the victims. Now 36, Ms. Vola would show up at Aon at 8 A.M. when she did not have to be there for another hour. She also taught aerobics classes at two different dance studios.

And every Friday night, Ms. Vola, who lived in Bay Ridge, Brooklyn, baby-sat for her sister Tilly's two children.

"How can this be happening?" Mr. Vola asked.

LYNETTE VOSGES
A Special Party

Last February, Lynette Vosges invited about 100 of her closest friends to a party to celebrate the 15 years she and her friend, Maurice, had been living together. Once everyone had gathered at a New Rochelle banquet hall, she announced the surprise. The party was a really a wedding.

She and Maurice then exchanged marriage vows in front of a guest who was a justice of the peace.

The daughter of immigrants from Guadeloupe, Lynette Vosges grew up in Queens and studied English at Queens College, without graduating. Her first real job was at Guy Carpenter & Company, working in the claims department.

Later, she moved to Aon Insurance, where she was eventually promoted to senior vice president of reinsurance, at a six-figure salary. She and Maurice bought a home in the Douglaston section of Queens, which they were renovating and redecorating.

Lately, she would return home in the evening and immerse herself in fabric swatches and paint samples.

GARO VOSKERIJIAN
Everyone's Favorite Santa

Garo Voskerijian was like this, said his friend Shemavon Atamian: every year at the Holy Martyrs Armenian Day School in Bayside, Queens, where their children were enrolled, he had to play Santa Claus, by popular acclaim.

Mr. Voskerijian, 43, was tall and husky, but beyond that, he had the attitude of a Kris Kringle. He hated to see anyone unhappy, and spent untold hours trying to unravel problems for friends, loved ones and co-workers at Marsh & McLennan, where he worked in global technology services.

"He was madly in love with his work and with his company," said his widow, Nayda, who was introduced to him in 1985 after Mr. Voskerijian's mother spotted her at a party. "He would create outings, whether bowling or baseball, and just lift up the morale of his whole department."

Mr. Voskerijian became famous for his memos praising someone else's accomplishments. "I felt he truly cared about his workers," said Randi Abraham, a longtime colleague, "and it's not often that you find that."

Everyone in the office also knew how he felt about his wife and his children, 12, 8 and 6. "I used to say, if I ever got married I would want to have a marriage like his," Ms. Abraham said. "He seemed so genuinely happy."

ALFRED VUKOSA
A Meeting of Families

His family was from Croatia. Hers was from Guyana. They lived in Brooklyn and met on the floor of the New York Mercantile Exchange.

In the genre of "only in New York," Alfred Vukosa, 37, and his wife, Annette, 34, lived the dream. Their two families were nearby as well—a dense, extended old-fashioned network of aunts, uncles, grandparents and cousins that could be fully several hundred strong when assembled.

Alfred and Annette, along with his parents, Sam and Irma, and his sister Sonja, all lived in the same building in Kensington, Brooklyn. Annette Vukosa's family—including four sisters and a brother—were almost as close at hand, in Queens.

Mr. Vukosa, who worked for Cantor Fitzgerald as an information technology specialist, had to be at his desk in the World Trade Center by 7 A.M. When he would arrive home every day about 4, another family tradition would unfold: a walk with his two boys—Austin, 7, and Adam, 2. "The children would wait for him to come," said his wife.

W

GREGORY WACHTLER
I.D. and Aspirations

On Sept. 9, Gregory Wachtler took his father and a cousin from Belgium up to his office on the 93rd floor of 1 World Trade Center. It was Sunday and the building was closed, but Mr. Wachtler flashed his company I.D. to the guard. A research associate at Fred Alger Management, he had his run of the place.

They stared out at Manhattan from the conference room. Floor-to-ceiling glass windows. The Empire State Building across the way. A bird's-eye view of the street in SoHo where Mr. Wachtler had begun renting a studio only eight months earlier. This was the outlook on life that Mr. Wachtler had at age 25.

"He became really responsible, very conscious of what he was doing," his father, Paul Wachtler, said. "It was a nice life for him."

Gregory Wachtler had finally made the big leap across the Hudson River, from the suburbs of New Jersey to the electric dance of Manhattan. He went club-hopping. He went in-line skating along the Hudson. He played tennis at Chelsea Piers. Just a year ago, he and his father went to see a Pink Floyd concert. The city seemed to be full of music.

His father recently began clearing out his son's apartment. Mr. Wachtler was just settling in, and a bed he had ordered was still en route. His tennis rackets were nowhere to be found. But his body has been recovered, along with the I.D. that always got him into the World Trade Center.

MARY ALICE WAHLSTROM
Unstoppable 78

She extracted the maximum out of life. Up at 5 in the morning, reading, traveling, debating current events, going to the movies. As Scott Wahlstrom said about his mother, Mary Alice Wahlstrom, "She was a ball of fire."

She was 78.

"She could have lived another 25 years," he said. "I have no doubt about it."

Mrs. Wahlstrom, a retired loan officer, lived in Kaysville, Utah, with her husband, Norman. She loved to travel, but had been reluctant to leave home because he was recovering from a heart attack. Still, she had gone with her daughter, Carolyn Beug, to help settle Mrs. Beug's twin daughters into the Rhode Island School of Design. Mrs. Wahlstrom and Mrs. Beug were returning to Los Angeles, where Mrs. Beug lived, via American Airlines Flight 11.

The energized matriarch of a family of five children and 16 grandchildren, Mrs. Wahlstrom subscribed to about 20 magazines. She read books that she then sent off to her children, and still occasionally played golf. She might never have broken 100, but she did score two holes in one.

CAROLYN BEUG's portrait appears on page 41.

GABRIELA S. WAISMAN
Living for the Moment

Gabriela S. Waisman loved to pamper herself. Weekends were reserved for manicures and pedicures, trips to the hair salon, movies or museums. With an infectious laugh, a childlike sense of humor and a penchant for spontaneous trips, she believed in living for the moment.

Should someone suggest that a trip might be too costly, she would respond, "You never know when you're going to be gone," said Janet Perez, a longtime friend.

Her zest for life carried over into her work at Sybase, an enterprise software company. At 33 and living in Queens, she had recently been promoted to operations manager and had volunteered to help set up a trade show at the World Trade Center.

On the Friday before the attack she stopped by the downtown office of Andrea Treble, her sister, to give her some pictures. As they parted, her sister remembered her not so much walking as dancing down Broadway, like John Travolta in *Saturday Night Fever*. "I said, 'Gaby, what are you doing?' " Ms. Treble said. "She just walked on laughing."

WENDY WAKEFORD
A Secret Organizer

Ada Rosario Dolch knew that her younger sister, Wendy Wakeford, was a busy person, working as an assistant to a top broker at Cantor Fitzgerald and taking up running earlier this year to stay in shape at age 40. But she had no idea that her sister was supremely organized, too.

Upon visiting Ms. Wakeford's new house in Freehold, N.J., shortly after the terrorist attacks, Mrs. Dolch, a high school principal in Manhattan, discovered that her sister had kept a copy of a letter to a Brooklyn landlord. It was 15 years old. She found meticulous files on stocks, 401(k) records, taxes, company records, insurance records.

"Everything, dated," Mrs. Dolch marveled. It wasn't all business, either. "We found calendars, almost like little diaries, where she would record what we thought was the most insignificant things: what she wore, etc. She had met this wonderful young man—his name is Gary—and she wrote about 'The first time I went out with Gary. The first time Gary sent me flowers.' This organization thing has knocked us all for a loop. Who would've known? To me, she'll always be my kid sister."

COURTNEY WALCOTT
Uncovering a Busy Life

After the attack, Delano Walcott learned two things about his quiet, unassuming eldest brother, Courtney, a manager at IQ Financial Systems in 2 World Trade Center.

First: Courtney, 37, was the most organized man in the solar system. In his Hackensack, N.J., apartment, the bills were in sequence and organized by category; his shirts were separated into short-sleeve, long-sleeve and dress; the khakis sorted by shade, the shoes by season, the sneakers by sport and the sock drawers by type and color.

Second: Courtney Walcott had good reason to keep his life uncluttered. He was too busy to waste time hunting for socks that matched.

Delano Walcott knew about the regular visits his brother made to their parents in Queens and their grandmother in Hempstead. He also knew about the peewee football camp he helped coach at his alma mater, Hofstra, every summer, where he supervised one godson; and the basketball team he coached in Hackensack, where he watched over another.

But as he sat at the memorial service at the Allen A.M.E. Church in Jamaica, Queens, Mr. Walcott learned that every Monday and Friday after work, his brother would drive to the church to be a mentor to teenage boys, counseling them, getting them jobs at Shea Stadium. Then he would drive home to New Jersey. At least 30 boys told the Walcotts how Courtney Walcott, who was divorced and longed for children of his own, had graced their lives. The family had had no idea.

VICTOR WALD
A Knack for Languages

Victor Wald performed ably as a stockbroker, his wife, Rebecca, recalled, but he seemed miscast in the role.

"I think he missed his calling," she said. "If he had to do his life over again, he would not be a stockbroker. He would have an academic job."

Long bedridden with rheumatic fever as a child, Mr. Wald came to love reading and books. His Upper West Side apartment was stuffed with them, Mrs. Wald said, especially histories and Judaica. He had an uncanny mastery of foreign languages, opera librettos, sports statistics. After college, he tried to write a book about religion.

"He really had a passion for the Jewish religion," Mrs. Wald said. "He knew more than the rabbis did."

But there were two young daughters to raise, and so, to Wall Street. In 1992, Mr. Wald helped found a specialty investment bank, which later closed. Late in August, he took a job at Avalon Partners, which had just moved to new offices on the north tower's 84th floor.

"He was working out of home for a while," Mrs. Wald said. "I said, 'Go! Go to your office. You'll get more done there.' "

He was buried on Nov. 23, what would have been his 50th birthday.

KENNETH WALDIE
The Oldest Teammate

Carol Waldie thought of her husband as her fifth child. "Just what I needed," she said. Kenneth Waldie wanted to do everything the kids did, especially their sporting activities.

For instance, his daughter, Meredith, 17, plays on the varsity basketball team, wearing No. 44. Mr. Waldie was at games so often that the coaches referred to him as No. 44½. After he died, the coaches had his number put on shirts and presented them to Mrs. Waldie.

Since he admired Joe Paterno and his brother had gone to Penn State, Mr. Waldie was fanatical about the Penn State football team, and sometimes took his son J.T., 14, to games. He kept himself as fit as a professional athlete. He jogged and worked out every day, and at work, he always skipped lunch so he could go on long walks with colleagues.

On frigid days, he would be the only one out there. Mrs. Waldie said that at 46 he looked the same as he did at 20.

Mr. Waldie lived in Methuen, Mass., and his other children are Andrew, 24, and Jeff, 21. A senior quality control engineer at Raytheon, he was headed to California on a business trip.

Around work, his colleagues referred to him as 911, because of his generosity whenever someone needed help, and there it was that he died on 9/11. His favorite number happened to be 11, and he was on Flight 11 when it crashed on the 11th.

BENJAMIN JAMES WALKER
"I Want Daddy"

After her father died on Sept. 11, adults kept telling Samantha Walker, 4, that her daddy, Benjamin James Walker, would always be in her heart.

"She said, 'I don't want Daddy to be in my heart. I want Daddy to be in my house,' " said Laura Walker, her mother.

One night when Samantha was curling up in bed with her mother, she broke into tears. Daddy had promised to teach her to play soccer once she turned 5. Her brothers, Henry, 9, and Christopher, 7, assured her that they would.

But the boys have their moments, too. In November, after Henry scored a 63-yard touchdown in a football game in Rockland County, where they live, Henry came off the field in tears, because Daddy wasn't there to watch him.

Their father, who was 41, worked as an insurance broker for Marsh & McLennan and doubled as a local soccer league coach on weekends.

"Ben made pancakes every Saturday morning," Mrs. Walker said. "Now they have to make do with mine, and mine are not as good."

GLEN J. WALL
"Our Uncle, Our Friend"

The last person that Glen J. Wall would usually think of doing a favor for was Glen J. Wall. A senior vice president at Cantor Fitzgerald who lived in Rumson, N.J., Mr. Wall served as a cheerful, unofficial ticket broker, maître d'hôtel and savings and loan association (even though he let many a loan slide). But Mr. Wall, 39, was most in his element when he spent time with, or just talked to acquaintances about, his two daughters, Payton, 4, and Avery, 3.

"He needed nothing," said his wife, Diane. "It was all for his girls."

A few of his nieces even wrote a poem about Mr. Wall for his memorial service that conveyed his zest for life:

His piggyback rides and dances
Had everyone waiting for a turn
Music from our hands
Was just one thing he helped us learn.
But the most important thing he taught us
Was to live life on the "Bright Side of the Road"
And enjoy it while you can
You'll always be in our hearts and minds
Our uncle, our friend, Glen.

MITCHEL WALLACE
"I Have to Help"

On Sept. 11, Mitchel Wallace, a court officer in State Supreme Court, was arriving for work at 111 Centre Street when he saw a plane hit the World Trade Center. He ran to help.

It was a typical reaction for Mr. Wallace, 34. He had saved lives before.

Trained as an emergency medical technician, Mr. Wallace had saved his fiancée, Noreen McDonough, three years ago by dragging her to the hospital after he noticed her exhibiting symptoms of a stroke.

Then, in 2000, Mr. Wallace was on his way home on the Long Island Rail Road when a man on the train went into cardiac arrest. Mr. Wallace performed C.P.R. for more than 25 minutes, and the man survived. Mr. Wallace received an award for heroism from Judith S. Kaye, New

At St. Paul's Chapel, near the World Trade Center site, a memorial for victims of the September 11 attack continued to attract the curious on December 24. Passersby stopped to look at the flags and banners, and to read notes that had been fastened to the churchyard fence. *(Fred R. Conrad)*

York's chief judge, and moved from family court to the Supreme Court.

On that morning in September, when Mr. Wallace arrived at the World Trade Center, he called Ms. McDonough to tell her that there had been a terrible accident. She told him that it was not an accident but a terrorist attack and told him to get away.

He replied: "I can't. There are bodies everywhere. I have to help."

After Mr. Wallace disappeared, Judge Kaye went over to the apartment of Ms. McDonough and Mr. Wallace with a large bag of jelly beans and sat down with her. She said, "We are going to sit here and eat jelly beans until he comes home.'"

PETER G. WALLACE
Opa's Second Chance

Peter G. Wallace believed that being a grandparent was a better deal than being a parent—all of the love and almost none of the work.

"We get a second chance," said his wife, Charlotte. "We may not have the energy, but we have a lot of patience." Mr. Wallace had five second chances—Andy, Zachary, Kristen, Lauren and Benjamin. They called him Opa and Pa.

Mr. Wallace, 66, still worked as a vice president at Marsh & McLennan, but he always had enough time to read to his grandchildren. The titles he read were the same enduring Dr. Seuss classics from his daughters' childhood—*The Cat in the Hat* and *Green Eggs and Ham*. When one grandson wanted a story read, he would pull the glasses out of Peter's shirt pocket and hand them to him.

A few days after Sept. 11, Zachary, 5, looked up and exclaimed that he saw a star against the daytime sky. His skeptical father looked up, and surprisingly enough there was a shimmering white speck fixed against the blue. What could that be, asked the father. The boy responded confidently, "That's a star from God to show that we miss Pa."

ROBERT WALLACE
Humor Against Adversity

Nancy Wallace remembers Robert, her husband of 21 years, for his wacky sense of humor and the way he took every little car breakdown in stride. And there were many.

"We put three engines in it, and two trannies," she said of the family's Jeep Wagoneer. "Half the time we didn't make it to where we were going."

She remembers him trudging through the snow to buy baby aspirin when the family was stuck in a snowstorm in the early 1980s. And she remembered how after those babies

had turned into teenagers, the whole family—their four children and a nephew—slept in the broken-down Wagoneer on the highway because nearby hotels were full.

Lieutenant Wallace, 43, followed his father into firefighting, and was known for pointing at the sky above Engine Company 205 in Brooklyn Heights, just to get people to look up, too.

"My family used to tease him," Mrs. Wallace recalled, "and he'd say, 'No, I'm going off to fight fires and save the people of New York.' " "We'd say, 'Oh, get outta here,' and he'd say, 'I'm going to go fight fires and save the people of New York.' "

ROY WALLACE
Love and Understanding

Scene from a courtship: Three months after they met at a group share in the Hamptons, Susan Rhoades left her job as an emergency room nurse so she could follow Roy Wallace to Tokyo, where he had taken a job as a broker.

An optimum situation for cementing a fledgling relationship it was not. Ms. Rhoades spent her days waiting for Mr. Wallace to come home from work.

"Some nights I'd be crying when he walked in," she said. "I'd say: 'I have to go back. I need my friends.' He didn't say: 'This is too much pressure for me. Why don't you go back to New York?' He didn't say, 'Snap out of it.' He was understanding."

They were married within the year, and two years later they came home. Mr. Wallace, 42, worked as a broker with Cantor Fitzgerald. They bought a home in Wyckoff, N.J., and had two children, Mallory, 6, and Caroline, 3.

Scene from a marriage: "He used to say, 'I don't know about you, but I'm not going anywhere,' " Mrs. Wallace, 41, said. "I was so happy to be married. I just loved having an adult person to hang out with. We just laughed about the same things."

Scene from a family: "Mallory had just started soccer. He took her to her first game the Saturday before he died. I've never seen him so proud. He's walking around with his camera, saying, 'This is great!' She just ran around aimlessly and had fun. He went on and on about it: 'I loved the soccer game!' " Mallory played out all 10 weeks of soccer.

JEANMARIE WALLENDORF
The Worries Had Ended

"This is the first time in my life that I wasn't worried about her," Christine Barton said of her daughter, Jeanmarie Wallendorf. "Before, I would always worry about who she was with. But since this relationship, I knew she was with someone who could take care of her."

Ms. Wallendorf, 23, whom her family nicknamed Miss Sephora after her love of cosmetics shopping, met her boyfriend when they both worked at a financial company. She left to work in the equity trading department at Keefe, Bruyette & Woods because the couple decided it would be better for their relationship, Ms. Barton said. The two were always out, traveling on vacation, going to weddings, hanging out with friends, but Ms. Wallendorf still found time to keep in touch. Once, her mother said, the couple was stuck in the air for hours, a source of great anxiety for Ms. Barton.

"She called me from the plane just to tell me she was all right," she said. Ms. Wallendorf was particularly looking forward to the birth of her boyfriend's sister's baby, Ms. Barton said, adding, "I've been waiting for her to give me one, but they wanted to wait, to make sure everything was right."

MATTHEW BLAKE WALLENS
"That Was Fun, Wasn't It?"

When Matthew Blake Wallens had lunch at his favorite pizza place with his wife, Raina Wallens, it was his habit to turn to her when she was finished.

"He would say, 'That was fun, wasn't it?'" Mrs. Wallens recalled. "I would say, 'Yeah.' And he would say, 'That is what we do, we have fun.'"

That was the spirit Mr. Wallens, 31, created wherever he went, no matter what he did. So when he fell in the mud, it was the greatest mud in the world, said his father, Dr. Donald Wallens.

"He found something to grab hold of in all life's experiences," Dr. Wallens said. Known to all as Blake, Mr. Wallens was a senior vice president at Cantor Fitzgerald whose contagious enthusiasm made his clients look forward to his calls, knowing he could make a bad day good and a good day better.

"There are things in life you need," his father said. "You need to work and you need to play and you need to love. He did them all in an extremely satisfying way."

JOHN WALLICE Jr.
Christening Loved Ones

It is something of a toss-up as to which game John Wallice Jr. liked better: golf or bear. He was a long-shooter on the links with the habit of putting from crazy angles. His handicap was five or six, though it would sometimes fluctuate depending on who he was playing.

Bear was a different sort of game, played on the fairways of Mr. Wallice's backyard in Huntington Bay, N.Y., during family cookouts. He would rise from the table, spread his arms wide, make scary noises and chase the children around the yard.

Mr. Wallice, 43, was an international equities trader at Cantor Fitzgerald, but despite his success he saved his finest work for home. He loved to swim in Huntington Bay, and his three boys—Jack, 9; Christian, 7; and Patrick, 4—would tag along as he dipped into the water.

"They were like three tails everywhere he went," said his wife, Allison.

John Wallice had that knack for putting people at ease. He did it simply: he gave out nicknames to everyone he loved. His sister, Kim, was Red for her red hair. Another sister, Pam, was Mo. His third sister, Amy, was known as Baby, and Paul, his brother, somehow went by Joe.

His wife and sons had too many names to count. "That was his way to connect," Mrs. Wallice said. "Once you got a name, it was almost like you'd been christened."

BARBARA WALSH
She Bound a Family

The glue that held the family together, that's how relatives talk about Barbara Walsh. Her son-in-law, Paul Landstrom, said that Ms. Walsh, 59, was planning to have everyone over to the house in Staten Island on Tuesday to discuss a family vacation.

"She was talking with her husband at 8:30 about what she was going to make for dinner for us that night," Mr. Landstrom said of his mother-in-law, an administrative assistant at Marsh & McLennan. Making dinner for everyone was a pleasure, not a chore—she loved to cook.

A finicky eater, Mr. Landstrom said that he had once mentioned, casually, that he liked a green bean casserole his mother-in-law made. "Well, there wasn't a Thanksgiving for the next 10 years that there wasn't string-bean casserole on the table."

Once, when his wife was a child, Mr. Landstrom said, Ms. Walsh fell through the ice of a neighborhood pond, nicknamed the Unknown, trying to get her daughter Jennifer off it. There had been no real danger, Mr. Landstrom said. It was simply an unacceptable situation. "All she thought was, 'Get the kid out of the Unknown.'"

JEFFREY WALZ
The Magic of Thursday

Jeffrey Walz and his wife were told they could not have a child, so when they had Bradley, he was something of a miracle to them. Mr. Walz doted on the boy, and made sure he did something special with his son every Thursday, his day off from Ladder 9, Engine 33—the zoo, a museum, a baseball game, an afternoon in the park.

Firefighter Walz, 37, grew up in Staten Island and lived

in Tuckahoe, N.Y. He was the son of a fireman, and it was as a fireman that he met his wife, Rani. She was at a Halloween party in the East Village that was so good that the Fire Department was called, and when Mr. Walz arrived and saw her in costume, they posed for a photo together, naturally.

"I was dressed as a Dalmatian," she said. She sent it to him, with her number.

Bradley, now 3½ and the family's "little linebacker," has begun to resemble his father in small ways. He's big, like his father, and to his mother's frustration, he has picked up her husband's habit of separating his peanut butter sandwiches from his jelly sandwiches—never together.

And Bradley has suddenly become interested in his father's profession. "Not until any of this happened," Ms. Walz said, "has my son showed any interest in fire trucks."

WEIBIN WANG
Living the American Dream

Weibin Wang and Wen Shi met as students in Beijing, and married three years later. A few months after the wedding in 1986, Mr. Wang left for the United States to study geophysics, at Yale and then at Columbia. Ms. Shi followed a year later.

"We were very happy," she recalled. "We were finally able to be together. We were working hard, trying to realize our American dream."

And they did. He did research at Columbia's Lamont-Doherty Earth Observatory in Palisades, N.Y., and then shifted into computer systems to provide better for his wife and three children, working the last two years for Cantor Fitzgerald at 1 World Trade Center. The family moved to a house in Orangeburg in Rockland Country, where every weekend he cooked dumplings, noodles, even lasagna. On Saturdays he took his children to piano lessons, art school and karate; on Sundays he took them to a school in Fort Lee, N.J., where they studied Chinese reading, writing and culture. The family visited China when they were able.

"We want to instill a lot of learning and a lot of Chinese traditions," Ms. Shi said. But Mr. Wang, 41, was also committed to his new country. In March, he became an American citizen.

Cody Rodgers, nine, gives a gift bag to Terry Damin, a city sanitation worker, lower right, at Nino's restaurant Christmas Day near the site of the World Trade Center. Cody and forty-four others from the River of Life Church in Kansas City, Missouri, came to New York to volunteer. *(Ting-Li Wang)*

MICHAEL WARCHOLA
The Name Meant Something

When Lt. Michael Warchola was a child in Greenpoint, Brooklyn, his grandmother brought British tabloid newspapers into the house. Paging through the tales of three-headed babies and ichthyological anthropomorphism, he developed a passion for reading and a flair for the bizarre.

He parlayed his appetite for books into a teaching certificate, and he joined the New York Fire Department in 1977, after five years on the waiting list. "It was dangerous, but it was a good job," said his father, Michael Warchola. It also helped pay for his trips to the strange and historical sites he read about.

As he neared retirement, Lieutenant Warchola, 51, who was divorced, devoted more time to tending his garden at his home in Middle Village, Queens, where he made elaborate drawings of Venus flytraps, but he kept a Godzilla poster on his wall.

The attack of Sept. 11 spread his name around the world, as it did those of many other victims. One who noticed the name was Prime Minister Mikulas Dzurinda of Slovakia, and when he came here recently to run in the New York Marathon, he sought out Lieutenant Warchola's older brother Denis, who was only vaguely aware of the family's central European ancestry. Mr. Dzurinda took home a picture of Lieutenant Warchola and held it aloft during a television appearance.

"Everybody in the country saw my brother's picture," Denis Warchola said.

The brother, a retired firefighter himself, had a chance for the most intimate of farewells. After his brother was dead, "I got to put my hands on my brother's arm."

STEPHEN WARD

A Devil Boy, With Glee

"He was an airplane-rides-around-the-living-room-until-you-want-to-throw-up kind of an uncle," said Susan Moore of her younger brother, Stephen Ward, who had just moved to Manhattan. "I call him a devil boy, one of those little devilish, impish-looking people, blond-haired, blue-eyed. He looked like an angel, but then he'd give you that grin and uh-oh!"

"How do you put someone's humanity into words? He was wonderful, smart, funny and vivacious, and infuriating," she said. "He followed me on my first date."

Ms. Moore found it strange that her brother, 33, an accountant at Cantor Fitzgerald, was really an adult. "He would talk to me about grown-up stuff, 401(k)s, and 'Do you have a Roth I.R.A. or a regular I.R.A.?' and I was like, 'Are you for real?' " she said. "But to my younger sister—she's the youngest—he was her big brother, he was a god. It's interesting for the two of us, we have the two perspectives. For me, he's a little kid, how could he be gone? For her, he's the great big strong big brother, how could he be gone?"

TIMOTHY RAY WARD

The Valentine's Child

Timothy Ray Ward came into the world on Valentine's Day in 1963, and immediately became the love of his mother's life.

"He was everything to me," said his mother, Susie Ward Baker.

Mr. Ward, 38, lived in Scripps Ranch, Calif., with his companion, Linda Brewton, and worked for Rubio's Baja Grill, a chain of Mexican restaurants based in Carlsbad, Calif. He was a systems administrator overseeing the chain's computer networks. On Sept. 11, he was aboard United Airlines Flight 175, heading home from a long weekend on the East Coast.

The tall, blond Mr. Ward loved animals, his mother said, starting with his shaggy white West Highland terrier, Sherman. He was a devoted fan of the San Diego State Aztecs, and would travel around to their football games even after he graduated. At the tailgate parties, people knew to check out what Mr. Ward was serving. He was an accomplished cook, who might pack two kinds of caviar in his picnic basket, along with a chocolate confection he had whipped up himself.

Next year, Valentine's Day will be painful for his mother. "I usually bought him a heart-shaped cake," she said.

JAMES WARING

The Joys of Fatherhood

When James Waring's first child, Jessica, was born 14 years ago his sister, Mary Jane Edgar, wondered what kind of a dad he would be.

Her brother, after all, once bought 30 bottles of Charlie perfume to give to all his girlfriends and never outgrew his love of the Animals, the Rolling Stones, the Kinks and all the other bands he played on his white Fender Stratocaster in high school bands. Might he find fatherhood a bit dull?

Not a chance. Mr. Waring, the 49-year-old director of security for Cantor Fitzgerald, did everything his way, growing up in New York rooting for the White Sox and the Packers.

But he found his greatest joy in being with his four daughters. His wife, Maria, worked at night, so he was home at 5:15 every afternoon taking the girls to dance lessons or playing softball with them. He took them to the beach every summer and had just taught the youngest, 5-year-old Jamie, to swim.

Mr. Waring took his daughters to 13 Yankee games last summer and had one more coming up, Sept. 12, against the White Sox, where he planned to show up as usual in his White Sox jacket and cap, calling out a cheery, "How you doing, babe?" to everyone he met. He had the tickets with him at work on Sept. 11.

BRIAN WARNER

Inspector Gadget

They called Brian Warner Inspector Gadget. He specialized in fixing things for others—cars, televisions, plumbing, computers. He was the good Samaritan who always stopped to help a stranded driver change a flat tire. If a neighbor's driveway needed plowing, Mr. Warner was there. He spent hours on the phone talking friends and colleagues through computer problems.

He was good at fixing human beings, too. At his memorial service, his friend Brian Potopowitz remembered how back in high school Mr. Warner had coaxed him out of his shell with Dr. Pepper and *Star Trek* get-togethers at his house.

Mr. Warner, who was 32 and the senior computer technician at Cantor Fitzgerald's eSpeed division, loved to share his knowledge of how things worked. Lucky for him he had a son Allen, 3½, Junior Inspector Gadget.

"On Saturday mornings the two of them would get dressed in jeans, work boots and T-shirts," said Mr. Warner's wife, Patricia, who also has a 5-month-old daughter, Kathryn. "They'd put their baseball hats on, and go out and work on a project—fixing the lawn tractor, the car, building a shed." "If Brian had to go to Home Depot, Allen would be right there with him," Mrs. Warner said. "When Brian was installing a ceiling fan up in Allen's room, and he was doing the wiring, Allen crawled right up there with his plastic tools, pretending he's doing the same as Daddy."

DERRICK C. WASHINGTON
Love at Romeo and Juliet

It was an unlikely romance. She lived way out on Long Island; he lived in Brooklyn. They went to different high schools and probably would never have otherwise met. But one magical day 15 years ago—a day neither of them would ever forget—each went on a class trip to Hofstra University to see a production of *Romeo and Juliet.*

"I don't think I was paying attention to the play," said Keisha Washington, who fell in love with Derrick C. Washington that Monday: March 10, 1986, a day they continued to celebrate every year. They eventually married and had three children: Christopher, 13, Devin, 8, and Malik, 3.

A devoted husband, father and son, Mr. Washington, 33, enjoyed shopping for groceries and mowing the lawn with his sons. On a typical weekday, he would drive from his home in Calverton on Long Island, park at his mother's house in Brooklyn, and then continue by subway to his technician's job for Verizon on the 110th floor of 2 World Trade Center. Normally, he did not arrive at his office until 9 A.M. But on Sept. 10, Mr. Washington decided to sleep at his mother's house so he could help her install window blinds. The next morning he got to work early.

CHARLIE WATERS
A Father and Son's Bond

Charlie Waters left a wife, three children and his parents in Bethpage on Long Island. But Mr. Waters, 44, a vice president at Cantor Fitzgerald, got to take the memory of something very precious with him.

It was a letter from his 14-year-old son, also Charlie. Mr. Waters loved his 11-year-old twin daughters, Jaclyn and Allison, very much, but the bond between father and son was special, said Mr. Waters's wife, Barbara. Big Charlie turned little Charlie on to the Grateful Dead. Son turned father on to Metallica. Charlie the son took up the guitar, and when his band, Dormant Virus, played last year, he wore his father's old Grateful Dead T-shirt beneath his Giants jersey.

Last spring, when the family debated where young Charlie should go to high school, the boy gave his father a letter.

"Dear Dad," it read. "I feel like you would do anything just to make me happy for a split second, and you do. I just wish I got to spend more time with you. I want to thank you because I know that whatever high school I would have chosen you would have been behind me 100 percent. You're also the easiest person I know to talk to. That's what I think I love about you the most."

Charlie Waters cried when he read that letter.

JAMES T. WATERS Jr.
Breaking the Banker Mold

James T. Waters Jr. did not quite fit the mold.

"He was definitely out of step with what you would think of as a conservative investment banker," said Steve Watson, a friend since boyhood. "He was generous to the core."

Mr. Waters, 39, had succeeded in the pressurized world of finance, working as a bond trader at Keefe, Bruyette & Woods. But he is remembered vividly far from the office.

Over the years, he had volunteered long hours in Republican Party campaigns. He routinely gave food and money to the homeless, and was in constant touch with family and friends, keeping a battered 1983 Saab for frequent trips from his one-bedroom apartment on the Upper East Side to Litchfield, Conn., his hometown.

"He always brought his baseball glove," said his sister, Karen Smart, whose 13-year-old son was forced to miss Little League over the summer because of a broken ankle. In response, she said, Mr. Waters offered the services of a sports medicine specialist, and drove to Litchfield two weeks before the trade center attack to see the boy return to the field.

Mr. Watson, who in 1990 made an unsuccessful run for one of Connecticut's seats in Congress, said Mr. Waters left his job at the time—at Bear, Stearns—and slept on a foldout couch in Mr. Watson's living room to help run the campaign. "He would drop everything to be at the side of a friend," Mr. Watson said.

PATRICK WATERS
Coffee and Nerves of Steel

You knew that Patrick Waters was on duty if there was a phenomenal amount of coffee brewing in the firehouse kitchen. Captain Waters, 44, always seemed to have a cup of the stuff in his hand.

He was what firemen call "a good fireman," graceful under pressure, passionate about the job and everything it entails—from battling flames to filing reports (his were always spelled correctly). In 1998, he was on duty at Ladder Company 106 in Queens when the India Street

After September 12, the site of the World Trade Center
drew throngs of people to lower Manhattan to look at
the remnants, to take pictures and, often, simply to
come to grips with the September 11 terrorist attacks.
Hundreds of people gathered on Broadway on
December 26. (*James Estrin*)

pier collapsed, hurling eight people into the turbulent East
River. There was no time to don protective gear; Captain
Waters, whose father, Patrick, taught him to swim at the Jersey shore, jumped in and kept a woman afloat until she could
be hauled in safely.

"That was a great day," remembered Lt. Mike Kenney,
a friend, who still has a picture of Captain Waters, soaked
and freezing. "Eight people went home to their families
that day." Off duty, Captain Waters coached his sons, 10
and 14, in basketball and hockey and ran their school
PTA.

On Sept. 11, he was at the Fire Department's medical
office, having a routine physical with four firefighters from
his hazardous-materials unit, when they heard about the
attack. They ran out the door and over the Brooklyn Bridge
to the trade center.

"I've never met anybody who loved going to work as
much as he did," said his wife, Janice. The coffee was only
part of it.

NATHANIEL WEBB
The Path of Righteousness

In the garden was an apple tree, and they
were forbidden to eat of the fruit of that
tree. Nathaniel Webb and his cousins
picked his grandfather's still-green apples
anyway. When the old man saw that the
apples were missing he demanded to know who had disobeyed him.

"We didn't tell the truth," said Delores Matthews, Mr.
Webb's cousin. "But when he was cornered, Nathaniel
always got teary-eyed and told the truth. Then we all got
punished, but he never did."

From that almost biblical beginning, Mr. Webb
remained on the side of authority for the rest of his life. He
was a Port Authority police officer for 28 years and, said Mrs.
Matthews, "he was always trying to keep everyone else on the
straight and narrow."

His friends and colleagues knew Officer Webb as a righteous and generous man. He took care of his housebound mother, stopping in several times a week to spend time with her. Sometimes, when a few officers went out for drinks or dinner after work, he would pick up the tab.

Officer Sharon Feoktistov, who worked with Officer Webb at the Holland Tunnel, said that once when she was stuck in Brooklyn with a flat tire, he drove from his home in Jersey City just to sit with her and wait for the tow truck. "And the thing was," she said, "I didn't even have to ask."

WILLIAM M. WEEMS
Always Using Kindness

William M. Weems paid attention to the small things in life, right down to the white tennis shoes he always wore.

Gifts were more than presents, they were always a little part of himself: the lighter used in *Blood Simple* he gave to his movie buddy, or the steel theme (to represent the 10th anniversary) he built on last year—down to the antique steel pens used to write the menu—to celebrate his marriage to his wife, Lisa.

"His life was really based on what he could do to enhance the lives of others," said friend Cynthia Gardner. "Most importantly his wife and daughter Zoe."

"Love my girls," he said as he headed out for United Flight 175 a day earlier than necessary to accompany clients to Los Angeles and see relatives. A 46-year-old freelance commercial producer, who lived in Marblehead, Mass., went against type.

"He always did things with kindness," said Dan Lincoln, the movie buddy who worked with him since 1986, "and a nice word.'

JOANNE WEIL
An Array of Friends

Judy and Floyd Weil knew that their daughter Joanne had accumulated a wide range of friends over her 39 years, from her tennis-playing childhood in Armonk, N.Y., to her days as a French major (and emergency medical technician) at Brown University, to her days (and nights) as a securities lawyer for Harris Beach in the World Trade Center.

But only after Joanne died did her parents learn the depth of those friendships.

In letters, phone calls and personal visits, the Weils have heard from the friends, who said that they would have gladly traded their lives for hers. They have learned that Ms. Weil's friends also miss her full-bodied, make-you-smile laugh. They have even learned that their only child once turned

down a sensitive government job that would have required her to limit her contact with her parents.

"What she cared about, and who she cared about, were what was important to her," Mrs. Weil said. "She was not a dabbler."

Perhaps one letter, Mrs. Weil added, summed up her daughter best. It came from a longtime friend of Ms. Weil's who now lives in California.

"I've been told that the measure of a person's life is not the distance they traveled but the heights they reached," the friend wrote. "Joanne soared, and I am both blessed and grateful to have shared even a part of her life, and to have her consider me a friend."

MICHAEL T. WEINBERG
A Model and a Firefighter

She was standing on the Brooklyn Bridge when the first tower fell. Everyone around her was madly dialing cellphones with no success. Suddenly, her own phone started ringing.

"It was my older brother," recalled Patricia Gambino, who had just escaped from the 72nd floor of the south tower. "He said: 'Thank God. You're all right, and Michael is on vacation.' "

Little did either of them realize that at that precise moment their younger brother, Michael T. Weinberg, 34—the stunningly handsome baby of the family, a part-time model who had played minor league baseball for the Detroit Tigers organization and was now a firefighter—had just arrived at the World Trade Center. As the first tower collapsed, he had taken cover under a fire truck. His was among the first bodies found.

An avid golfer, he had planned to spend that morning on the golf course. His tee time was 9:08 A.M. But when news arrived, he threw his clubs into his car and raced toward Manhattan. His car was eventually found by the side of the highway, where he had apparently abandoned it to hitch a ride with an emergency rescue vehicle.

"He loved to help people," his sister said.

STEVEN WEINBERG
He Never Lost a Friend

Steven Weinberg was not a cook, but he loved to go to the supermarket. He was not a collector, but he was nonetheless a familiar figure at garage sales in New City, N.Y.

As his family's social secretary, an assistant basketball coach for his children, a man of 41 who kept every friend he ever made, all the way back to childhood, Mr. Weinberg never passed up an opportunity to run into someone he knew.

He enjoyed his position as an accounting manager at Baseline Financial Services, but it was as Laurie Weinberg's husband of 14 years; as the father of Lindsay, 12, Samuel, 8, and Jason, 6; and as a people magnet that Mr. Weinberg glowed. His wife said he had a distinct relationship with each of his children but a single message for all: "Stop fighting." He planned every family outing with other families. Seven hundred people attended his memorial service.

SCOTT WEINGARD
The Man on the Trapeze

A fantastic athlete he was, but "a gymnast trapeze stuntman he was not," Marc Shapiro recalled about his friend, Scott Weingard. But being the daring sort of person who would squeeze in an adventure whenever he could, Mr. Weingard gladly volunteered to fly with the professional trapeze team while on vacation at a Club Med resort a few years ago.

"There he was, swinging along, doing his thing with his lanky body while we were cheering him on," Mr. Shapiro said, laughing.

Friends began to call Mr. Weingard First Time Scottie because he was so often in the position of doing something totally out of the ordinary and new. He was also known for making friends, and keeping them. While still at the resort, Mr. Weingard, a trader at Cantor Fitzgerald who would have been 30 on Sept. 23, disappeared for a while. Where did he go?

"We found him befriending the whole island," recalled Mr. Shapiro, a buddy since their kindergarten days in Dix Hills, on Long Island. His girlfriend, Julie Kaufmann, called him an angel. His cousin, Jeff Honigstock, interviewed on a recent Thursday, said: "I'm missing him today. It would have been a perfect day for happy hour with Scottie."

SIMON V. WEISER
Medieval History Buff

Simon V. Weiser was born in Kiev, Ukraine, in 1936. For most of the next 36 years, his family says, he tried to leave. Finally, his opportunity came, in a brief warming of the cold war in 1972, when some Jews were allowed to emigrate to Israel. His wife and son followed in 1974; the family moved to the United States in 1978—to Canarsie, Brooklyn.

Mr. Weiser, who had been an engineer in the Soviet Union, eventually worked in power-distribution engineering for the Port Authority of New York and New Jersey at its office in the World Trade Center. At the same time, Mr. Weiser filled his house with thousands of books on scores of subjects—history, religion, photography, genetics. Over the years, he managed to collect several dozen books just on hypnosis.

Mr. Weiser loved inventing, too. As a medieval history buff, he had become engrossed with crossbows and their trigger mechanisms. He built 40 fully functioning crossbows, most of them patented.

"He wanted me to become a patent lawyer," recalled his son, Anatoly Weiser, 41, of San Diego. And he did.

Mr. Weiser's family remembers how, living in Kiev, he would listen to the Voice of America. "Even in the Soviet Union, my father was an American," his son said.

DAVID MARTIN WEISS
All Muscle and Heart

David Martin Weiss, a New York City firefighter, was built like a fireplug. He stood 5-foot-9 and weighed 225 pounds. He was all muscle, with biceps as big as the thigh of a medium-build woman. He was bulldozer strong. He looked as tough as he sounded. His head was shaved and his body was covered in tattoos. He drove Harleys.

He was an ironworker before he became a firefighter 13 years ago. He blended both experiences to become a member of the Fire Department's elite force. He joined Rescue Company 1 in Times Square about six years ago after receiving a medal for a rescue attempt: a man's car careered off Franklin D. Roosevelt Drive and plunged into the East River. Mr. Weiss, off duty, stopped his car, climbed down the iron trestles of the elevated highway and jumped into the river to rescue the driver, whose heart had given out.

"He just jumped, knowing that he was the person's only hope," said Thor Johannessen, a firefighter. Mr. Weiss, 41, of Maybrook, N.Y., had a mean sense of humor. "If he saw a thread, he knew how to pull it to unravel the whole shirt," said Joel Kanasky, another firefighter. "He was the king of that."

CHRISTIAN WEMMERS
Off the Mountaintop

Christian Wemmers moved from Ahrensburg, a town outside Hamburg, Germany, to Jackson, Mich., when he was a 16-year-old exchange student, and he never went back for long.

"When he was a little boy, he already knew that one day he wanted to live in California because of the sunny climate," said Sibylle Dircks, his sister, in an e-mail message from Germany. "He always enjoyed the American way of life, the friendly, polite people, who were so different to Germans."

Mr. Wemmers, 42, lived in San Francisco and worked as director of product management for Callixa, a software company. He was at the World Trade Center for a trade show on Sept. 11.

A friend, Rebecca Cleff, recalled that he loved San

Francisco because "he could go for a 10-mile hike through the forest, over hills and to the ocean during the day, and then a great restaurant and show in the evening."

Ms. Cleff remembers how he told another friend that if he had to die, he'd prefer to just go to the top of a mountain and disappear. "Chris vanished on top of an urban mountain," she wrote in an e-mail message, "an incredible metaphoric combination of his favorite places."

VANESSA WEN
Learning Self-Sufficiency

Since they were little girls growing up in Taiwan, Vanessa and Sarah Wen were taught to be self-sufficient. Their parents, teachers who ran an import-export business, traveled frequently with the daughters. In Hong Kong, they explained the mass transit system to the girls when Sarah was 10.

"They told us how to do it, and then from there, we knew what to do," Sarah said.

When Sarah was 20 and Vanessa 18, their parents took them to Texas, staying with them for a week, then left them there, where the girls attended the University of Texas at Arlington. Just before she graduated in 2000, Vanessa was offered a job as a programmer for Cantor Fitzgerald.

The night before the trade center attack, the sisters talked by telephone. Sarah, who still lives in Texas, said Vanessa, 23, told her that the company had laid off several people in her department.

"She told me she was going to be very busy," Sarah said, "and that's why she had to leave early the next morning to get to the office."

Children from a day care center at Riverview Medical Center in Red Bank, New Jersey, at a memorial for trade center victims on December 27. (*Dith Pran*)

OLEH WENGERCHUK
Soul Mates from Age 2

Oleh Wengerchuk and his wife, Oksana, met as children, when their families were interned at a German displacement camp when they were toddlers. Their families were Ukrainian.

"I don't remember him from that time," Mrs. Wengerchuk said. "My mother used to tell me that we would play together all the time, he and his brother and I. We were like the three musketeers. We were only 2 or 3 years old."

Through the years, and in the turmoil after the war, the two families kept in touch. Hers ended up in South Bend, Ind., while his immigrated to New York a year later. When her father died, her family moved to Trenton, N.J., and they visited the Wengerchuks. Oleh Wengerchuk was in the Army. "We fell in love, which wasn't planned," Mrs. Wengerchuk said. "We had a long history. We were like soul mates."

Fast-forward to the year 2001. He was a transportation designer for the Washington Group International, with an office on the 91st floor of 2 World Trade Center. The couple had a nice home in Centerpoint, N.Y., on Long Island. They loved to entertain.

One of Mr. Wengerchuk's passions was going sailing with his brother. The Wengerchuks had a daughter, Andrea, who is 23, and just out of college. She had come home to live with her parents again; father and daughter were forging an adult friendship.

The weekend before Sept. 11, the couple had friends over for dinner. At the end, as they sat in the twilight, Mr. Wengerchuk, 56, took his wife's hand and kissed it, as he often did after these nights of wine and good conversation.

"He told me, 'I just want you to know how much I appreciate everything you do for me. If one of us has to go first, I hope it's me because I can't imagine life without you.' "

PETER M. WEST
Terms of the Deal

For Eileen West, there was always "the deal" she had with her husband, Peter M. West. The deal was an agreement that spontaneity had its time and its place, and that Mrs. West was the one to say, gently, when and where. On vacations, Mr. West, a municipal bond broker at Cantor Fitzgerald, could do his latest daredevil thrill, like skydiving or hang-gliding.

"But never on the first day of vacation," said Mrs. West, a hospital administrator, "always on the last." A lifelong fan of James Dean, Mr. West, 54, wanted a motorcycle. "But the deal was, only when the kids were finished with college," Mrs. West recalled.

So in 1997, days after their daughter, Meredith, graduated

from college (they also have a son, Matthew), Mr. West bought a starter motorcycle, a Yamaha. In 2000, he bought his dream machine, a Harley-Davidson Softail Deuce. It was a black and chrome beauty that Mr. West got at a special auction; his bid was far higher than the motorcycle's usual $16,000 price tag.

On weekends, Mr. West, in leather chaps, would roar off from the couple's home in Pottersville, N.J., sometimes for hours. One day, a police officer asked Mr. West who was following him in the blue Audi. "My wife," he replied.

MEREDITH LYNN WHALEN
Cruising Between Dreams

Meredith Lynn Whalen wanted to be a successful portfolio manager and then the owner of a horse farm in Kentucky. And between those goals, she planned to cram in a lot of travel, including many cruises. Ms. Whalen, 23, was a research associate at Fred Alger Management on the 93rd floor of 1 World Trade Center.

She grew up in Canton, Mich., where she learned to ride and cheerfully cleaned out stalls. She graduated from the University of Michigan Business School in 2000. She had worked the summer before her senior year at Goldman Sachs in London but decided she wanted to work for a smaller firm, where she thought she would get more intense training.

"It was her dream job," said her mother, Pat. "My daughter loved the fast-paced life of the city and enjoyed all it had to offer, from the plays to the parks and museums and the night life."

Although she had been working just 15 months, Ms. Whalen was the frontline person for researching eBay, the Internet auction company, one of Alger's top holdings.

Ms. Whalen was already a veteran of four cruises. Her first, in the early 1990s on the *Sovereign of the Sea*, was delayed because of a fire while it was docked in San Juan, P.R. She had planned to leave from Barcelona, Spain, on Sept. 15 for a 12-night Mediterranean cruise with her mother.

EUGENE WHELAN
Guilty of Serial Hugging

"He was no saint!" said Eugene Whelan's mother, Joan, her laughter bubbling up. "Yeah, he could be a giant pain!" her husband, Alfred, added, chuckling about the ninth of their 10 children.

But examples eluded them.

While Firefighter Whelan, 31, undoubtedly jettisoned saint eligibility at some Rockaway pub or Grateful Dead concert—a captain called him "the king of fun"—he was still terrific. He kept extra winter jackets in his Jeep in case he spotted a shivering homeless person. He was a persistent serial hugger, spreading those burly embraces known as "Eugene hugs."

He was a Mr. Fix-it and human Velcro to kids. In Bedford-Stuyvesant, Brooklyn, the neighborhood served by Engine Company 230, children would arrive at the firehouse with broken bicycles for Firefighter Whelan to make whole.

During a school visit, he asked why one child was left in the bus. The child was paralyzed, a teacher replied. Mr. Whelan carried the child to the fire truck.

"He understood what life was really about," said his father, "so we feel pretty good about him."

ADAM WHITE
Days Filled with Surprises

Growing up in Atlanta, Adam White was like an electron zinging through an always-interesting orbit, or maybe several orbits at once.

"He was an exhausting child," said his stepmother, Georgia, who joined the family when Adam was 4. And also a charming one, who packed more into his waking hours than anyone she knew.

He loved surprises and drama and being the star of the show. When his high school put on a production of *Amadeus,* he landed the role of Mozart, playing all the piano passages himself. He had hundreds of friends, scattered all over the world, and dozens of interests, like mountain climbing and traveling and oratory, into which he poured his heart.

Adult life took him to San Francisco, and then to New York, where Mr. White, 26, was developing an electronic trading program in carbon dioxide for Cantor Fitzgerald.

"The bigger the city, the better for him," Mrs. White said. "His brothers used to go and visit him, wherever he was, and say afterwards that they felt like they had been there for a month when it had only been a few days.

"His dad went up to visit him in New York for a weekend last year, and when he got back he had to rest for a couple of days before he could go back to work. Everything was so exciting with Adam."

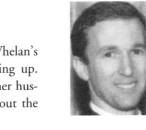

JAMES PATRICK WHITE
Braving the Bulls

James Patrick White was sitting over a beer in a bar in Hoboken, N.J., with two high school buddies when they got the idea. They would take off for Spain and run with the bulls at Pamplona.

The night before the run they drank a lot of beer and were so worried they would oversleep and miss the bulls that they slept on the street in their clothes. Somehow, they survived the stampede.

"It was very scary," said Tom Kane, one of the friends. "We kind of leaned on each other to get the courage to do it."

Mr. White, 34, a Cantor Fitzgerald bond broker, was the

oldest of five children, three of them boys. He played varsity tennis in high school in Hightstown, N.J., skiied, rode mountain bikes and ran the New York City Marathon three times, twice with his brother Mike. It took him 4 hours, 40 minutes the first time. Then four hours. "The third time we were lazy," said Mike, who had run one year with their brother Greg.

"Our time wasn't so good. But we finished."

JOHN WHITE
The Mark of a Helpful Man

For John White, life was all about helping. If a friend's bathroom pipes backed up, he soon arrived to fix them. If co-workers needed a 5 A.M. ride to work, he picked them up. If his supervisor needed him to stay until midnight on his job operating elevators at the World Trade Center, he unfailingly said yes.

Once, while he and some friends were painting the facade of a church in Brooklyn, an elderly driver crashed into some young toughs, who jumped out of their car and began pummeling the older man.

Mr. White and his friends ran over and pulled them off the driver, enraging them.

A half-hour later, the men returned with guns and started shooting, killing one of Mr. White's friends and hitting Mr. White.

"He still had a bullet in his spine," said Elsa McCaw, his sister. "He was just a happy, good person," she said. "He was always ready to help. He's someone you want around if you're ever stuck somewhere."

Mr. White, 48, emigrated from Jamaica in 1973 and lived in Brooklyn. But his wife, Enid, disliked New York's cold, so she moved to Florida several years ago. The high points of his year were his three annual trips to Florida for a reunion with his wife and daughters, Maxine and Denise.

"He was working at the trade center for 27 years, and he was seriously thinking of retiring and moving to Florida, maybe this winter," his sister said. "He missed his family very much."

KEN WHITE
View from a Sailboat

Whenever Ken White had a spare minute last summer, he was likely to head for his sailboat at the Richmond County Yacht Club in Staten Island. He had not had the boat long, and sometimes he and his wife, Catherine, would just sit on it at the mooring and talk and gaze at the Manhattan skyline.

A business in Peekskill, New York, shows patriotic fervor in its window December 28. (*Joyce Dopkeen*)

Mr. White, 50, was a telephone technician at Cantor Fitzgerald. When his four children were growing up, he coached Little League and soccer. He went to his daughter Kristen's dance recitals and cheered his daughter Allison at gymnastics.

Mr. White met his wife at the United States Air Force base in Wiesbaden, Germany. She was a secretary, he a sergeant. They were married in her hometown in Ireland in 1973 and lived there for more than a year before settling in Staten Island. There were woods near their house in New York and he used to go in and gather wildflowers for her.

"Kenny was a hard-working guy," said Mike Campbell, his childhood friend and grown-up horseshoe league partner. "He was always competing with himself. He always liked to do better, whatever he was doing."

LEONARD ANTHONY WHITE
Passionate about New York

Leonard Anthony White loved beautiful things. He collected West African art to decorate his Brooklyn apartment, wore designer shirts, and cooked foods that were delicious to both the taste buds and the eyes.

And he was a big fan of everything that went on at Lincoln Center, "the ballets, the operas, the shows, you know," said Shirley Nottingham, his older sister. "He always bought the season tickets."

The only one of eight siblings who had left their hometown, Norfolk, Va., Mr. White traveled often between his birthplace and New York City.

"He had a real attachment to home," said Mrs. Nottingham. "He would come and do things for our 100-year-old neighbor. He called me very often and sometimes held the phone to a speaker to have me listen to his favorite arias."

Single and without children, Mr. White, 57, a Verizon technician at the World Trade Center, paid college tuition for some of his nephews and nieces and never missed their weddings in Virginia. "But he loved New York so much," said Mrs. Nottingham, "I didn't bug him about retiring in Norfolk."

MALISSA WHITE
Caretaker of the Family

When Malissa White was growing up in Bald Knob, Ark., strangers assumed she was the eldest child in the family, even though she was not. If anyone asked her older sister a question, she would answer.

"She was like the caretaker of the whole family, the spokesperson, the whole lot," said her brother Marc.

When Ms. White married Rocky Higgins in 1996 and they set up house together in East Flatbush, she became a mother to his two sons. Marlon, the older of the two, played basketball at his high school in Queens. Ms. White kept in contact with his coaches and college scouts, making it possible for him to win a basketball scholarship to Talladega College in Alabama. She found summer jobs for Mr. Higgins's nieces.

"She was a real family person," Mr. Higgins said of his wife, who was 36 and worked in the human resources department of Marsh & McLennan. Ms. White was a mentor in her church. When members of the congregation were burned out of their homes, she took them in.

"All I can say is that she is the best thing that happened to me," Mr. Higgins said.

WAYNE WHITE
"Stay in School"

Wayne White's mantra for his sons, Terrell, 18, and Wayne Jr., 16, was simple: "Stay in school." He believed it strongly because he had not followed his own advice. "He would tell them, 'Finish high school, go to college, girls can come later,' " said Hilda Ventura, Mr. White's oldest sister.

Mr. White, of Brooklyn, dropped out of high school in the 11th grade. Terrell was born when his father was 20. Mr. White subsequently received a G.E.D.

" 'I should have waited,' he would tell me. 'I should have finished school first,' " said Ms. Ventura. Urging his sons to focus on their studies, he set an example by returning to school himself. A mailroom manager at Marsh and McLennan, Mr. White, 38, had registered to take college-level computer science courses this fall.

"It's never too late. That you get to a certain age doesn't mean you cannot learn," he told his sister.

MARK WHITFORD
Seeker of Solace Outdoors

Screaming sirens. Thick coats with broad yellow stripes. Strong arms, sharp eyes, stoic indifference to danger. A winter's day. Evergreen needles trapped in a wisp of snow. Skies cleared by cold and a vista open to all possibility, all hope.

At his core, Mark Whitford, 31, was a New York City fireman. And tempting though it is to let that description stand for the man, those who knew him said it should be noted that he also was a man who sought solace in the outdoors.

"If he had a bed of grass under his feet and a bit of sky above his head, he was happy," said his wife, Rene.

Firefighter Whitford, a captain in the Army Reserve, drove a rig at Engine Company 23. It was his life's dream.

"When you hear of a guy born to be a fireman, that was Mark," said his brother Dennis.

After Firefighter Whitford's twins, Timothy and Matthew, were born in the summer of 2000, he moved closer to the trails at Bear Mountain. His favorite spot was the lookout atop the mountain known as Anthony's Nose. He and Ms. Whitford hiked up in February.

"It was very cold," she recalled. "It just felt peaceful there. The world was shut out. We were together, and we didn't have to worry about anything."

MARY LENZ WIEMAN
Energy, Loyalty, Parties

Mary L. Wieman was strong and hard-charging, a business executive and mother who more than once caught the red-eye home to New York from California, cooked breakfast for her husband and three children, then shot off to work at the Aon Corporation.

She orchestrated insurance coverage for major American corporations and she was so devoted to detail that early on Sept. 11, as she was preparing to run a meeting on the 105th floor of 2 World Trade Center, she polished the office furniture.

"There were no insurmountable problems for her," said her husband, Marc Wieman.

Ms. Wieman, 43, loved dancing and throwing big parties for work and at home, and the loyalty she generated led people to congregate in her office when there was time to catch a breath. She kept trim by working out nearly every morning. When word came to evacuate, she walked down to the 78th floor. Then, inexplicably, she decided to take the elevator, colleagues told her husband.

"That decision was perfectly in character," Mr. Wieman said. "It was just like her to say, 'I'm not taking the stairs.' And that would be it."

JEFFREY WIENER
A Proposal in a Toy Store

Jeffrey and Heidi Wiener became engaged at F.A.O. Schwarz, in front of the big clock. The couple had first gone to the toy store on an early date, when they were living in Philadelphia, where they met.

"We were taking the elevator down and he told me he knew that someday we would bring our kids there," Mrs. Wiener recalled.

A few years later, when they were visiting New York because Mr. Wiener was running in the New York City marathon, he took her to F.A.O. Schwarz again, and asked her to marry him.

"I laughed and I cried and I hugged him and somewhere in there I said 'yes,' " she said. "And then we went for a carriage ride in Central Park."

Mr. Wiener, 33, could be serious and studious—he had degrees in aerospace engineering and business from Princeton, the University of Pennsylvania and New York University—but he never forgot how to have fun. He grew up in Trumbull, Conn., and was manager of the risk-technologies group at Marsh & McLennan. For Mr. Wiener and his wife, another favorite spot was just a few blocks from F.A.O Schwarz—the Central Park Zoo.

"He used to say that if he ever won the lottery, he would spend time working at the zoo or an aquarium," she said. "He loved animals."

WILLIAM WIK
He Helped the Rescuers

When William Joseph Wik called his wife, Kathleen, shortly after the first attack on Sept. 11, her message was emphatic:

"I told him, 'Get out!' " she said. Her husband, 44, an assistant director in the risk management service department of the Aon Corporation, on the 92nd floor of 2 World Trade Center, said, " 'No, I can't do that, there are still people here,' " she recalled. "I wasn't surprised. Billy wasn't the type to turn his back on someone who needed help."

She, and the city officials who have examined his remains, believe that he joined the rescue workers, "possibly showing them where the other workers were," said Mrs. Wik, who lives in Yonkers. Her husband's body was discovered in a pocket of rubble along with the bodies of five firefighters. Mr. Wik was wearing work gloves and a mask and had an Emergency Medical Service flashlight in his hand; the equipment was probably handed over by rescue workers as he assisted them.

Mrs. Wik said she believes that for her and their three children, ranging in age from 8 to 16, "the fact that he was located, and that we got his wedding ring and wallet; well, those are little miracles—a sense of closure for me and the kids."

ALISON M. WILDMAN
Life on an Uptick

Alison Wildman's e-mail one-liners could send friends into hysterics at their desk. Her phone calls, as frequent as they were brief, punctuated the days of her parents and close friends with doses of humor, gossip, stock market updates.

"She'd call just to say 'Hi, I'm busy, I'll call you later,' " her mother, June Wildman, said. "It was a little bit of contact every day."

Ms. Wildman, 30, was a broker at Carr Futures. She enjoyed kayaking, skiing, running with her two dogs, Molly and Shannon, and horseback riding. Such activities, however, had to be scheduled around manicure appointments. Ms. Wildman, who wore little makeup and whose long blonde hair was the envy of some of her friends, was a bit obsessive about her nails.

Ms. Wildman's life was "on an uptick" just before Sept. 11, said her friend Annmarie Cunningham. She had just met a nice man. And the results of her test for a certified financial analyst's license had arrived—although she had not yet garnered the strength to look at them. After Ms. Wildman's death, her sister opened the envelope. She had passed.

GLENN WILKINSON
Athletic Family Man

Glenn Wilkinson was 46, but he could act like a youngster when he was with his three children. At the dinner table, his wife would admonish one of their children for doing something inappropriate.

"I'd turn around and he would be doing the same thing," said Margie Wilkinson.

He was a lieutenant with Engine Company 238 of the New York City Fire Department. And sometimes, he did not get home to Bayport, N.Y., until very late. Still, his 13-year-old daughter, Kelsie, a straight-A student, would wait up for him. He would sit by her side, happily going over homework she had already finished.

He was solidly built and athletic. He used to curl his arms into a swing for his little ones. As the kids grew older, and heavier, they were reluctant to give up on that bit of fun. In the last year, though, his 12-year-old son, Craig, joined him running. His 8-year-old son, Kevin, rode a bicycle to keep up. On Tuesday morning, the youngest son asked his mother whether the family would have to change its last name now.

"He has no idea if anything is going to remain the same," she said.

JOHN CHARLES WILLETT
One Who Spoke His Mind

John Charles Willett was the youngest county treasurer in the history of Missouri. Mr. Willett, fresh out of college, was appointed in 1993 by the governor to mind the finances of Taney County. The county is almost all Republican, and when young Mr. Willett, a Democrat, asked prosecutors to investigate the Republican county clerk and tax collector, his political fate was sealed (though the clerk and collector also lost their bids for re-election). Mr. Willett returned to school and got a master's degree. In January, he began working at Cantor Fitzgerald.

Mr. Willett, 29, lived in Jersey City and called his parents three times a week, said his father, Ron Willett. One of Ron Willett's favorite memories came from the heady days when his son was Treasurer Willett.

"I was standing on the courthouse lawn with him one day," the elder Willett recalled, "and a citizen recognized him as working for the county. The man came up to him and just laid into him unmercifully. John listened very patiently, and then asked the man, 'Did you vote?' The guy said no, and John said, 'Then I don't want to hear it' and turned and walked away. I felt like I was about 10 feet tall."

BRIAN P. WILLIAMS
Honest Abe from Kentucky

Brian P. Williams found stardom at Covington Catholic High School, in Kentucky. He won the "That's My Boy" award, given by northern Kentucky football coaches to the best scholar-player-leader (a prize now named after him). Columbia University recruited him for football. In New York, he acted as unofficial tourist bureau for visiting Kentuckians.

Those are the memories of Kenneth Williams Sr., a man who has lost two sons—Kenneth Jr., who died in 1994 after three years in a coma caused by a fall, and now Brian.

The father adds another college-era memory, to show his son's generosity. As a college senior, Brian Williams used his emergency credit card to pay a bar bill for three cash-strapped buddies. He sent a check to repay his father, with a note explaining the charge. "I figured that was an emergency," the note said.

Brian Williams, 29, worked as a bond trader at Cantor Fitzgerald, with the ultimate plan of returning to the Cincinnati area near his family's home in Edgewood.

Kenneth Williams goes back to the day he drove off after delivering his son to start college in the big city.

"When I looked back in the rearview mirror, he was standing in 115th Street about two houses off Broadway and he looked like a deer in the headlights," Mr. Williams said. "On the road home I was half-talking to myself and said, 'I'm going back to get that country bumpkin.' "

CANDACE LEE WILLIAMS
On the Way to Hollywood

How to comprehend the terrible symmetry that returned Candace Lee Williams to the place of her triumph, the World Trade Center? A 20-year-old student in the cooperative work-study program at Northeastern University in Boston, she toiled from January to June at Merrill Lynch as an intern on the 14th floor of 1 World Trade Center.

"They loved her there so much, they took her out to din-

ner on her last day, and sent her home in a limousine," said her mother, Sherri. "Then they wrote Northeastern a letter saying, 'Send us five more like Candace.' "

After finishing midterm exams in her June-to-December schedule, instead of returning home to Danbury, Conn., Ms. Williams agreed to meet her Northeastern roommate, Erin, at her home in California.

"They'd rented a convertible preparing for the occasion, and Candace wanted her picture taken with that Hollywood sign," her mother said. So on Sept. 11 in Boston, Candace boarded Flight 11, which was then hijacked and sent crashing into the same trade center tower where she had worked.

"The airline told us she was seated next to an 80-year-old grandmother on the plane," her mother said, "and I know that Candace was consoling that woman to the last."

CROSSLEY WILLIAMS Jr.
Converted Parents to Karate

When the first plane hit the World Trade Center, Crossley Williams Jr. immediately called his father at his office in Queens. His father called his wife, who was working at her office in Manhattan, and arranged a three-way conversation.

"He told us he saw two bodies falling out of the window of the first building," the father said. His son, a financial analyst for Fiduciary Trust, worked in the south tower. "His mother urged him to get out immediately. I told him: 'You heard what your mother said. Call me when you get out.' That was our last conversation."

An only child, the younger Mr. Williams, 28, was always close to his parents. When he was 10 and "chubby," as his father described him, they enrolled him in martial arts classes. He eventually became a black belt. Because he seemed to enjoy it, his father and his mother, Valrie, started studying karate, too, and earned their black belts.

Mr. Williams lived with his parents in Uniondale, on Long Island, and most Fridays and Saturdays, he went out to dinner with them. "He enjoyed our company and we did his," his father said.

KEVIN M. WILLIAMS
Waiting for Wedding Bells

In 2000 Kevin M. Williams decided to pop the big question and ask Jillian Volk, his high school sweetheart, to marry him. Mr. Williams, 24, a bond salesman at Sandler O'Neill on the 104th floor of the south tower, took her to Macy's just before Christmas. Together on Santa's lap, he asked.

"She had tears of joy," said Dan Williams, his uncle.

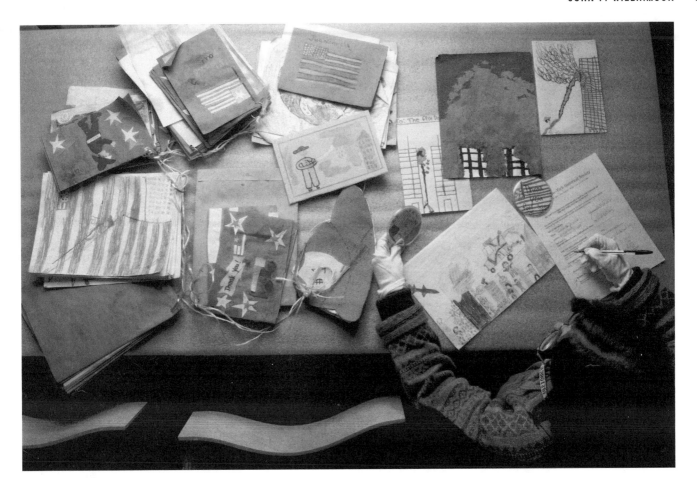

Amy A. Weinstein of the New-York Historical Society, cataloging some of the drawings and letters that children from across the country have sent to New York City firehouses since the Fire Department lost 343 members at the World Trade Center on September 11. (Fred R. Conrad)

"Kevin always had a knack to do something a little extra, to make those special occasions something a little extra."

Since that day at Macy's, the wedding, scheduled for December, was all Mr. Williams talked about, even at a party in June for his brother's high school graduation. "These were young people in love," his uncle said.

LOUIE ANTHONY WILLIAMS
Love Notes on the Pillow

Louie Anthony Williams wrote his wife the kinds of letters that make women proud and bashful. Mornings did not pass without his sitting at his desk on the 66th floor of 1 World Trade Center and sending pages to his wife in a special code all their own.

If Deborah Perkins-Williams saw 381 come across her pager, she knew it was an "I love you." And if Louie, 44, typed 3814, as he did Tuesday morning, she could almost hear his voice saying, "I love you forever." "He just liked to let you know you were loved," she said. "I'd come home from work and there was always a note on the pillow telling me to enjoy the snack he prepared for me. He was a devoted husband."

Nine years of love letters by her side, she clings to the hope that it is not too late, that the "love of her life" will soon come home. "He lived by the Bible, so I know he probably just got trapped trying to comfort someone else."

JOHN P. WILLIAMSON
"A True Renaissance Man"

John P. Williamson was not a casual golfer. He signed up for golf lessons, practiced in his yard and even made a player of his son, Marc. The pair routinely disappeared for hours on a golf course.

"He was just so focused," said his wife, Mary. "He was able to do anything."

Battalion Chief Williamson, 46, showed the same dedication to his job and family. In his 23 years with the New York Fire Department, he rose through the ranks to become chief of Battalion 6 in lower Manhattan. And at home in Warwick, N.Y., he designed and built a wood-and-glass house for his family. He made the furniture, too.

Chief Williamson later added a basketball court for his daughter, Jessica, and rearranged his schedule so that he could attend all her school games. He kept lunch dates with his mother, Lucy, even when he was busy.

"He was a true Renaissance man," his wife said. "We got a lot of work out of him in the winter when there was too much frost on the ground to play golf."

DONNA WILSON
Staying in Touch

In almost every circle of friends there is someone like Donna Wilson. Ms. Wilson was the person who kept track of co-workers and classmates, passing bits of news and gossip between them. "She was the one who kept us all in touch with each other," said Francine Awad, Ms. Wilson's friend since the two women were freshmen at St. Vincent Ferrer High School in Manhattan.

"She was the focal point between people."

Co-workers said Ms. Wilson, 48, an assistant vice president at Aon, always tried to make people feel valued and was very diligent. When she fretted over a small discrepancy on a balance sheet, a colleague mailed her a five-dollar bill to make up the difference.

Ms. Wilson rose early to get to work, then sped home to Williston Park, in Nassau County, to take care of her 75-year-old mother, Patricia.

"Donna was a good worker, she did her job and took care of our mother," said Linda Wilson, her sister. "She made a living, took care of her family and tried to lead a good life."

WILLIAM E. WILSON
Equally Matched Golfers

Many husbands and wives do not golf together because their skills are too different. But William E. Wilson had a handicap of 20, and his wife, Ann Payne, had a 22, and they played together nearly every weekend from April through October.

"On any given day, I could beat him or he could beat me," Ms. Payne said, "and we loved playing together."

Eight years ago, for his 50th birthday, they took a golf cruise through the Caribbean. It was his idea and he loved it—each day they got off their ship and played golf on a different island.

A marine insurance broker with Aon, Mr. Wilson sometimes played during the week, too, taking clients to his private club's monthly beefsteak lunch and the tournament that followed. In August, he won the tournament for the first time; he was scheduled to play in the next one Sept. 12.

Ms. Payne said that playing without her husband was difficult, but she is doing it. "It's not quite the same," she said. "But I love it and felt like I had to get back."

DAVID H. WINTON
The Staunch Provider

For many people, investment banking is just a job where you can make good money. For David Winton, banking was practically a calling.

As an undergraduate at Fordham University's business school, Mr. Winton was the chief executive of the student-run federal credit union. He recruited his roommate Gregory Moundas to be president, and, volunteering 30 hours a week, the two of them turned around a troubled institution and doubled its assets in two years, Mr. Moundas said. Even as Mr. Winton rose to vice president at Keefe, Bruyette & Woods, where he was a research analyst, he made frequent trips back to Fordham to be on the student bank's supervisory committee.

Mr. Winton, 29, inherited some of his head for finance from his mother, a retired bank officer. But Mr. Moundas said a lot of his friend's ardor for banking grew out of a protective love for his family.

"His father died when he was in high school and he wanted to provide for his mom and his sister," Mr. Moundas said. "He never really talked about it, but that was one of the things that really motivated him."

On weekends, Mr. Winton frequently made the two-hour trip from Brooklyn Heights to his mother's house near Hartford, usually taking along his fiancée (they were to be married Nov. 17).

"After we lost his father, he said, 'I'll never leave you, Mom,' " Joan Winton said. "He never did."

GLENN WINUK
Sprinting Toward Danger

As a boy, his dream was to be a firefighter, a hero. As a man, Glenn Winuk became a prominent Manhattan lawyer, but he used his lifelong interest in fighting fires as a volunteer in his hometown, Jericho, N.Y. He was so committed, such a natural, the town named him fire commissioner.

So on Sept. 11, Mr. Winuk, 40, did what he, as a firefighter, had been trained to do. First, he escorted people from his law firm, Holland & Knight, a block and a half from the trade center. He was last seen headed for the towers.

"If I had been there with him that day, I wouldn't have been able to stop him from trying to help," said Mr. Winuk's older brother, Jay. "Even though he became a lawyer, my brother always saw himself as a firefighter. It was a passion for him, the chance to help someone."

When terrorists bombed the World Trade Center in 1993, Mr. Winuk, still dressed in a suit, rushed to help, too. "If it has to be that he did not survive this time," Jay Winuk said, "then in our eyes, he went down being an American hero. We're proud of him."

FRANK T. WISNIEWSKI
Permanent Party at Home

Frank T. Wisniewski loved his new house so much he cut short a family beach vacation this summer to come home. That was understandable. Home was a house on the edge of the woods in Basking Ridge, N.J., with a creek nearby where Mr. Wisniewski and his son and daughter liked to catch crayfish and put them in an aquarium.

Mr. Wisniewski, 54, a vice president in Cantor Fitzgerald's municipal bonds division who was known to friends and family as Paul, would often say things like, "Let's take a walk and look at all the flowers," said his wife, Carol Wisniewski.

Mr. Wisniewski, a big, gregarious man, made his home into a permanent party. When the children, now 13 and 11, were younger, Mr. Wisniewski would blast oldies on the radio and the whole family would dance around the house. In early September, Mr. Wisniewski had a barbecue at the house for a bunch of friends, and was singing along with the radio at the top of his lungs.

"The neighbors said 'The Wisniewskis are having a party with a karaoke machine,'" Carol Wisniewski said, "but it was just Paul and the radio."

DAVID WISWALL
Vacuuming the Yard

David Wiswall was a nice, easygoing guy, but he could get very excited about a patch of lush green grass.

"When he wasn't out playing golf, he was out in the yard," said his wife, Pat Wiswall. "He was just a fanatic about his lawn."

One time when the Wiswalls were getting ready for a party at their house in North Massapequa, on Long Island, their son, Keith, looked out the window and saw his father vacuuming the lawn. Berries from a tree on a neighbor's yard had been falling onto the grass.

"Being married to him so many years, I understood," Pat Wiswall said. "He liked things a certain way."

Recently, with their two children grown and out of the house, the Wiswalls had been making the most of their empty nest. They played a lot of golf, both on Long Island and in North Carolina, and went out to dinner often with close friends, most of them people David Wiswall had known since grammar school.

Mr. Wiswall, a senior vice president at Aon Insurance in the World Trade Center, was 54. He and Pat were looking forward to his retiring in about six years so they could move down to North Carolina, where they planned to play even more golf.

"We were enjoying it so much," Ms. Wiswall said. "Just the fact that we were free to go out and do things. It's just another nice stage of life."

MICHAEL R. WITTENSTEIN
Every Day a Casual Day

Michael R. Wittenstein loved game shows, the Jets and Mets, and good—or, truth to tell, bad—jokes. When he graduated from the State University of New York at Albany 13 years ago, he told friends he planned to be a proctologist or a game show host. Don't ask.

Instead, he became a bond trader for Cantor Fitzgerald, working in London and California, as well as New York. He was delighted when the firm did away with its dress code; ever after, he was sighted only in khakis and polo shirt.

He was on the phone with a client in California when an explosion rocked the skyscraper. He called back to apologize that the phone had been disconnected.

In April, he moved out of his parents' home in Seaford, on Long Island, to live with his fiancée, Carrie Bernstein, in Hoboken, N.J. They were supposed to be married in October. Ms. Bernstein went to a Devils-Rangers hockey game that month with his brother Jeffrey.

"She seems all right," he said.

CHRISTOPHER W. WODENSHEK
A Long Drive Home

Christopher W. Wodenshek would joke ruefully with his wife, Anne, about the demands of his work heading the electricity brokerage department at Cantor Fitzgerald. He had been there less than two years, after all, and he and his family had just moved from Connecticut to Ridgewood, N.J.

"He'd say, 'I wish I could be at your tennis game, but I have this thing called work,'" Mrs. Wodenshek said. "He was very dedicated to it."

Yet with five young children, aged 2 to 9, Mr. Wodenshek, 35, also found ways to meet the demands of fatherhood. For example, Mrs. Wodenshek and her children summered on Martha's Vineyard, and Mr. Wodenshek would fly up on weekends. When work kept him from flying one Friday night for the end-of-vacation drive home in 2000, he drove up the next day and surprised Mrs. Wodenshek and the children at the ferry.

"Then he took the kids and the big car and turned around and drove home with them, so I could have a peaceful drive home," Mrs. Wodenshek said. "He did it for me."

MARTIN WOHLFORTH
Snapshots of a Family

Susan Telesco, a Vassar woman, had been invited to a football game by a Princeton man, but she found herself hoping Martin Wohlforth, another Princeton guy whom everybody called Buff, would be there. He was. They would have celebrated their 21st wedding anniversary on Sept. 13.

Susan's memories of Sept. 11 are that she had gone to her Junior League office in Greenwich, Conn., of which she is president, and heard that the second tower, where her husband worked, had been attacked. Trying to drive home, so she could be found, she pulled over and threw up.

Mr. Wohlforth, 45, was a managing director in the bond department of Sandler O'Neill, on the 104th floor. He caught the 5:55 A.M. train to New York, or on rare occasions the 6:05, but was always home for dinner with Susan and their daughter Chloe, now 16.

"I have a picture of him holding our daughter for the first time in the hospital with a mask on," Susan said. "Playing with her on the beach in Nantucket, his pants are rolled up and wet, she is 7 or 8, and he is tossing her a ball. I've got pictures of him carving pumpkins with her every year. Every year, when they carved their pumpkins, homely or gorgeous, and they were never gorgeous. I knew he loved me very, very much. I was very secure in our marriage. We were blessed."

KATHERINE WOLF
Standing Up for Beliefs

There is a 37-year-old home recording of the voice of Katherine Wolf, as a 3-year-old girl in Wales, telling her "mummy and daddy" that she would "like to sing 'All Things Bright and Beautiful.' "

It was a promising start to a lifelong avocation. Mrs. Wolf became a classically trained pianist, and an accompanist for the Philbeach Society, an amateur operetta group in London.

Her musicianship led her to America in 1988, when the ensemble staged a joint production with the Village Light Opera Group in Manhattan. Charles Wolf, a member of the

opera group, recalled the night he met her that year and said to a colleague: "Who is that woman? I have got to get to know her." They had been together ever since.

Mrs. Wolf worked for years at Schroders, a British asset management company in Midtown. And just three weeks before Sept. 11, she began a new job at Marsh & McLennan, on the 97th floor of 1 World Trade Center.

"You couldn't let her reserved exterior fool you—she'd stand up to anyone for something or someone who she believed in," said her friend Jean Orr.

JENNIFER Y. WONG
Duty to God and Family

Home, family and church were important to Jennifer Y. Wong. She knew how to have fun, but duty to God and family were what motivated her, said her friend Sandra Mark.

Ms. Wong, 26, worked for Marsh & McLennan, in client services for the risk management division. She and Ms. Mark became fast friends when they met at church in Chinatown seven years ago.

"She had a contagious laugh," Ms. Mark said. "She was a Christian, and her whole house was very Christian. She was very active in the church."

She had a brother and a sister, and lived with her parents in Queens. Ms. Mark said her friend's family was extremely private, but they wanted people to know what a dutiful daughter Ms. Wong was. "She knew where she stood in life, and that was pleasing God," Ms. Mark said. "You could tell by her actions. She was always helpful. She didn't have a bad bone in her body. She thought of other people before she thought of herself."

JENNY LOW WONG
A Reunion Too Soon

Jenny Low Wong came to live with an aunt in New York City when she was 12 years old, because her family in Venezuela thought there was more opportunity for her here. And there was, although she ended up finding success by looking back at the part of the world she came from.

Ms. Wong, at 25, had just been promoted to assistant vice president of Marsh & McLennan, in the market information group. Ms. Wong, fluent in English, Spanish and Cantonese, was in charge of analyzing the Latin American market.

Her parents were originally from China, said her sister, Mary Low Wong, and moved to Venezuela as children with their parents. One by one, their three children came to the United States. Ms. Wong and her brother, William, planned to go to San Francisco, where Mary Low Wong moved this summer, to spend Thanksgiving together. Instead, the family had an unplanned reunion after Sept. 11. Ms. Wong's parents came from Venezuela, and her maternal grandmother from Hong Kong.

YIN PING WONG
Hong Kong on Canal Street

The crooning ballads by Cantonese pop stars reminded Yin Ping Wong of his childhood in Hong Kong. Mr. Wong, known to his friends as Steven, immigrated with his family in the late 1970s to Bensonhurst, Brooklyn, from Hong Kong. He was 12 years old, the sixth of seven children and spoke only a little English. It was a difficult transition for a boy with a gentle soul.

At that time, Brooklyn's Chinese-American population had not congealed yet and Manhattan's Chinatown was smaller than it is today. But as the community grew, Hong Kong culture became more accessible, and Yin Ping would buy CDs and rent concert videos of his favorite singers. He liked Alan Tam and Sam Hui for their poignant lyrics and robust voices.

"He liked people who really can sing," said Nicole Wong, Yin Ping's younger sister. "He preferred voice over looks."

Bensonhurst now has its own thriving Chinese community, but Canal Street in Manhattan remains the bustling commercial center of choice. Yin Ping would stop by its fruit stands, bakeries and video stores on the way home from Aon. His mother loved to watch serialized Chinese dramas, but when new episodes were not available, he would bring home American movies.

BRENT J. WOODALL
A Present That Will Live On

Brent J. Woodall always loved children and looked forward to having his own. But when his wife tried to announce the good news subtly a few weeks before Sept. 11, Mr. Woodall missed the point entirely. As a surprise for their first wedding anniversary, Tracy Pierce Woodall gave her husband a book about what expectant fathers should expect.

"He was like, O.K., thanks honey," said Annalisa Fredrickson, a friend visiting the couple's home in Oradell, N.J. "That will come in handy someday."

Mr. Woodall, a trader at Keefe, Bruyette & Woods on the 87th floor of the south tower, spoke with his wife three times on Sept. 11. In their last conversation, he said he was headed downstairs. "He is someone you always turned to in a jam, a really reliable guy," Ms. Fredrickson said. "He probably stopped to help someone."

Mrs. Woodall was eight weeks pregnant on Sept. 11.

JAMES WOODS
Close to Family, Literally

James Woods stuck by his friends, his family and his sports teams, even when they were in the doghouse. When the Jets were the team everyone loved to hate, Mr. Woods would climb up to the nosebleed season-ticket seats he and his father returned to year after year.

His roommate on the Upper East Side, Jared Leschner, was his best friend from fifth grade. And while not many 26-year-olds would relish the idea of living next door to their older sister, Mr. Woods did.

"We were like best friends," said Eileen Woods, 29. "We'd go out all the time. Jogging in Central Park. Barhopping. Concerts. We were always close, but the older we got, the closer we got."

A trader's assistant at Cantor Fitzgerald, Mr. Woods worked hard, but played even harder, going on trips with his family to Ireland, golf outings to South Carolina with his college buddies, summer weekends on Fire Island. Since Sept. 11, his father, John, has been giving his Jets tickets away.

"He won't go back to a Jets game," Ms. Woods said of her father, a retired firefighter who rescued more than a dozen people during the 1993 bombing of the World Trade Center. "He can't go back without Jimmy."

PATRICK WOODS
The 5 A.M. Bagel Call

Patrick Woods's friends were accustomed to his distinctive style. Pretty much every weekend, he would call them up at some ungodly hour brimming with a plan. "Let's go get bagels," he'd say. It would be 5 A.M., or even earlier.

"People sleep on Saturday and Sunday, but he didn't," said his friend, Joe Dallesandro. "He was always doing something." If Mr. Dallesandro's machine picked up, Mr. Woods, who was known as Patty, would croon the song "Pretty Patty" into the tape.

Mr. Woods, 36, spent a lot of time with Raven, his Doberman pinscher. He liked to take her to the beach near his home in the Dongan Hills neighborhood of Staten Island, and sometimes he drove her into the city to see the sights. On Sept. 11, Mr. Woods was part of a seven-man team, all members of Local 608 of the carpenters' union, building desks and cubicles for Aon Insurance on the 103rd floor of 2 World Trade Center.

His career evolved naturally, from a skill he seemed to have been born with. He could fix everything, from cars to electrical wiring, and neighbors called on him for help.

"He'd rip half the wall down until he got it perfect," said his brother Thomas. "He knew what he was doing with a lot of things, a lot more than me and my other brother. We've got a lot of projects started, and now we've got to get someone in to finish them."

DAVID T. WOOLEY
A Decorating Officer

Anyone could see that it was a strange combination of jobs, fighting fires and interior decorating. But not David T. Wooley. Captain of Ladder Company 4 in Midtown Manhattan: he also put up wallpaper on the side, turning it into a family affair that included his son, brother and cousin.

"He did that because my mother was always asking him to decorate around the house," said his son, David Jr. "He changed the wallpaper so often, and he was so good at it, that he decided to make it his second career. He did it since 1985 or 1986."

Sure, hanging wallpaper did not quite pack the rush of running into a blaze. But in Captain Wooley's crew were his brother Burt (another firefighter), his cousin Jeff and his son. "It was time we spent together, and it was almost like not working," David Wooley Jr. said.

As they beautified houses, Captain Wooley, 53, would tune in to a politically conservative radio station. Then his son would switch the dial to a liberal station. That was how it went between the two of them—listen to politics, debate about it, laugh over it.

Captain Wooley's son made fun of him when he took a job putting up wallpaper in the Westchester home of Bill and Hillary Clinton. Meeting them did not change the captain's political leanings. But Captain Wooley was what his son called a "people person," and he told his son afterward that the Clintons were "nice and personable."

JOHN B. WORKS
A Love of Books

John B. Works always had his nose in a book. Or books—he usually had three or four going at a time, said his wife, Pamela Block Works. History books. Gold books. Economics books. Philosophy books. Historical fiction. (Dorothy Dunnett and Patrick O'Brian were favorites.)

"And lots of junk—*Star Trek*," she said.

On his bedside table are *Cryptonomicon*, Neal Stephenson's novel about making and breaking codes, and Jack D. Schwager's *New Market Wizards: Conversations with America's Top Traders*. Mr. Works, 36, had recently become a trader himself; in March, he rejoined the investment firm of Keefe, Bruyette & Woods, where he had started his career as an analyst.

To house all those books, as well as their 3-year-old, Allison, the Workses were building a house on the site in Rowayton, Conn., where Mr. Works grew up. On weekends this summer, he would climb a ladder to the third floor, with its view of Long Island Sound. That floor was going to be his library, Mrs. Works said, "with a large porch off it, because he always wanted a widow's walk."

RODNEY J. WOTTON
A Death, and a New Life

Patricia Greene-Wotton is planning a memorial service and a baptism. Her husband, Rodney J. Wotton, disappeared in the attacks on Sept. 11, and their son, Rodney Patrick, was born eight days later.

"It's like death and resurrection," she said. "The baptism was to have been a happy occasion, but it's a sad thing knowing that Rod will not be there for the baby's baptism."

Mr. Wotton, 36, who worked at Fiduciary Trust, never found out whether his child was a girl or a boy. At the couple's request, the doctor who performed the sonogram wrote the sex on a piece of paper and sealed it in an envelope. Meanwhile, the Wottons picked names for a girl and a boy: Amanda Helga and Brendan Stewart. Now, the baby is named for his missing father.

Mr. Wotton loved children. He had a daughter, Dorothea Jean, 2, whom he loved to bathe and tuck in at night. Five years ago, he and his wife looked at 65 houses before settling on a ranch-style home on two acres in Middletown, N.J.

"It's our dream house," she said. "It has a big yard that we thought would be nice for the children. It has a big garden that he put in because he loved gardening. A couple of weeks ago, I gave Dorothea watermelon that her dad grew. She loved it."

WILLIAM WREN
Sharp-Dressed Hero

Bill Wren fought fires for 25 years, raised two sons and when they began thinking about careers, said: "You want something that you love, that you're waking up in the morning and looking forward to."

That is how Mr. Wren felt about being a firefighter in Coney Island. His family shared good times—friendships with firefighting families, barbecues where the men cooked. But they never heard about the danger and exhaustion. After retiring, he became the the World Trade Center's fire safety director. When visiting firefighters saw him in a suit, "they'd rag on him for dressing so sharp," said his son Christopher.

Off duty, he went to art museums and watched Sister Wendy's art lectures on TV. He grew vegetables and cooked for himself and Pat, his wife. A trip to Ireland got him interested in his forebears.

"He was understated," Christopher said. "But in control—the voice of reason and calm. In a family emergency, we'd look to him. Now we're asking: 'What are we going to do now?' "

JOHN W. WRIGHT Jr.
A Younger Big Brother

It wasn't exactly a feminist household, but it didn't revolve around the only boy in the family, either. A shy kid at first who suffered through "the hormonal rages" of three sisters growing up, John W. Wright Jr. finally put his foot down at 15, when it became chic for girls to wear boxer shorts.

"They are stealing my underwear," he complained to his father. "Don't I have a right to have underwear?"

Nonetheless, or maybe as a result, John grew up to be a staunch family man, remaining devoted to his mother and, despite the demands of being a managing director at Sandler O'Neill, always finding time to help with the care of his three children, frequently taking them to visit relatives to give his wife some time to herself.

"He was a very devoted father," his father said. "I was so proud of him for that." And, adolescent chafing aside, his sisters now realize how much they looked up to him.

"They would never let him be the big brother," his father said, "although now, from what they're telling me, he was the big brother all along."

NEIL R. WRIGHT
A Contrarian Humor

Whether it was his English accent, self-confident manner or natural gift of humor, Neil Wright was always able to draw laughter from the crowd at the Mountain View Chalet, a local bar and restaurant in Asbury, N.J.

Carol Vaughn, a friend and neighbor, remembers meeting Mr. Wright for the first time at the Chalet on a night when she was feeling down. Within minutes of talking to him, she was filled with "the kind of laughing that makes your face hurt," she said.

As a young child, Mr. Wright demonstrated a certain contrarian outlook that may have been the key to his humor. Left to his own devices while the adults chattered in the garden, he painted the family's black Labrador white: "White looks much nicer than black," his mother, Mary Wright, recalls him explaining.

Mr. Wright, 30, moved to the United States five years ago after his employer in London, Cantor Fitzgerald, asked him to transfer to its office in the World Trade Center. He loved his new home, although he told friends he missed certain English foods, like Yorkshire pudding.

After he and his wife divorced, Mr. Wright won sole custody of his children, Daniel, 5, and Jack, 3, and his mother moved here to help take care of them.

His favorite way to relax was to ride his canary yellow Aprilla motorcycle. "I used to say, 'Please don't ride that thing; think of me and the children if anything happened,' " his mother said.

SANDRA WRIGHT
Have Daughter, Will Travel

Growing up in Bucks County, Pa., Sandra Wright was the oldest girl among nine children and the biggest adventurer. When divorce left her to raise her own daughter alone in New Jersey, she did it with gusto.

"We drove across the country in a camper when I was just a little tot," recalled her daughter, Shelli, who gave birth to her mother's only grandchild in the summer of 2001. "We went to Paris, skiing in Europe. Most of her family never went into New York."

In 1992, mother and daughter both worked in Rockefeller Center, reveling in the glamour of pedicure lunch hours and "window shopping in the stores we couldn't afford." When Shelli went to college, though, her mother moved from New Jersey back to her hometown of Langhorne, Pa., where her family gathers 150 strong every holiday. In 2000 she was married there to Steven Cartledge, a man she met at a church dance.

Ms. Wright, 57, had a round-trip commute of four hours between Langhorne and Aon in the World Trade Center.

"She never complained about it," her daughter said, "because she loved New York City and she loved her family, and she got to have both."

JUPITER YAMBEM
Holding On to India

Jupiter Yambem was born and raised on the other side of the world, in the remote state of Manipur in the northeast corner of India. At the age of 21 he came to the United States and promptly took up a career in some of New York City's most famous restaurants, including the Rainbow Room and then Windows on the World, where he worked as a banquet manager.

But even as he planted hardy roots here—marrying a woman from Syracuse, settling down in Beacon, N.Y., joining an environmental group dedicated to protecting the Hudson River, becoming friends with Pete Seeger, signing on as assistant coach for his 5-year-old son Santi's soccer team—Mr. Yambem, 41, held fast to his Indian past. Retaining his Indian citizenship, he co-founded the North American Manipur Association, a small group of Manipur families that sought to promote and preserve the culture of their homeland over here.

He had two purposes, said his wife, Nancy Yambem. He wanted his son to know something of his heritage—to see the dances and hear the music and taste the food. But he also wanted to construct a bridge, however modest, between two vastly different cultures.

The strands of Mr. Yambem's life came together at his memorial service. His friends gathered at Beacon Riverfront Park on the banks of the Hudson River. They had a potluck dinner and Mr. Seeger sang "Turn, Turn, Turn." Later, they released hundreds of small paper boats onto the river, each with a candle inside. Mr. Yambem's ashes were returned to Manipur and scattered over a lake.

MATTHEW YARNELL
A Merry Prankster

More than once, Matthew Yarnell's mother hung up on him. He would call, disguising his voice, and try to sell her a random product—pool supplies, anything. "Sorry, I'm not interested," Michele Yarnell would say and hang up before she realized who was calling.

"He liked to have fun," Ms. Yarnell said wistfully. Mr. Yarnell, 26, an assistant vice president for technology at Fiduciary Trust Company, took his job seriously enough that he was promoted three times in the year and a half he was there.

But he crammed plenty of fun into his life.

Last spring, on a blind date with Angela Tsuei, the two found themselves without a plan after dinner.

"Matthew said, 'Well, the Duane Reade in the World Trade Center is open,' " Ms. Tsuei recalled.

In the store, they split up and bought each other gifts. Mr. Yarnell got his date animal stickers for her nails. She bought him a rubber ducky.

At Pier 94 in Manhattan, where an assistance center has been helping the families of World Trade Center attack victims, a block-long wall came to resemble a memorial. It is dotted with missing-person posters depicting the faces of hundreds of lost loved ones. (*James Estrin*)

In the months to come, they would spend hours in Mr. Yarnell's apartment in Jersey City, giggling and goofing.

"When we got down to the end of the paper towel roll, we would end up smacking each other with it allnight," Ms. Tsuei said. "We would be just howling with laughter."

MYRNA YASKULKA
Dressing to Be Noticed

Myrna Yaskulka's family called her the bag lady—she was rarely without bulging shopping bags from Strawberry and Century 21. To her granddaughters, the clothes they contained were more thrilling than a new Barbie outfit. There was, for instance, her metallic gold raincoat. And her FUBU pantsuit. And leopard-skin everything—pants, earrings, photo frames.

"Not the sorts of things," said Jay Yaskulka, her son, "you would normally see on a woman her age." But Ms. Yaskulka, 59 and a size 8, was as chic as a downtown hipster. She was such an ardent shopper that store managers called her about new shipments. She was confident enough to wear outrageous things, like pink rhinestone-studded sunglasses, and carry it off.

She commuted from Staten Island to her secretarial job at Fred Alger Management in 1 World Trade Center. Often, Mr. Yaskulka passed beneath her windows when he took Brianna, 8, and Shannon, 4, to the city. "When we drove by the World Trade Center," he said, "they would look up at the 93rd floor and yell, 'Hi, Grandma!' "

KEVIN P. YORK
Man with Snowblower

After a big snow last winter, the serene streets of Kevin P. York's neighborhood in Princeton were tucked under a thick blanket of snow. His new snowblower made easy work of his driveway. Then he wheeled it to a neighbor's driveway and cleared that one, too. And then he did another, and another, all day until the light gave out.

That's the way Mr. York, 41, was. He liked to buy things, often the best available, but his greatest enjoyment came from using them to take care of others, especially his wife and two sons.

"For Kevin, working in New York meant prosperity," said his wife, Chiemi. "He didn't come from a wealthy family, but he always thought that someday he was going to have anything that he could imagine wanting."

Long hours and hard work paid off, and as he progressed to senior vice president at Euro Brokers, Mr. York kept to his lifelong plan. A few years ago, he and Mrs. York incorporated their visions of stability and elegance into the house they built in Princeton. "The house was tangible proof of what he was doing for us," Mrs. York said.

Mr. York left the house early for the long commute to New York, but when he got off the train in the late afternoon his focus shifted from finance to family. Aidan, 1, is too young to understand, but Connor, 6, is upset because, he said, "Daddy didn't get to teach me everything."

RAYMOND R. YORK
"He Always Was My Hero"

Raymond R. York spent nearly two decades fighting blazes and loving the New York Fire Department when a shoulder injury in 2000 forced him into light duty. But he found a second calling, teaching children about fire safety at the Fire Zone at Rockefeller Center. There, he was Fireman Ray to the youngsters whom he captivated.

But on Sept. 11, he learned of the World Trade Center attack from a television crew that was doing a story on the Fire Zone, jumped onto a nearby fire truck and headed downtown. After traffic held him up, he hitched a ride on an ambulance and reached the Fire Department's command post at the trade center.

"We're so proud and we just want everybody to know what a great guy Ray was," his wife, Joan, said. "Everybody's saying, 'He's a hero, he's a hero.' He always was my hero. Now the world knows he's a hero."

She described her husband as a man in love with life, a man who insisted on flying the flag. "He was a Little League coach, he was a scout leader—when it came to his kids, he was there for everything," she said. That included building an ice skating rink in the backyard of their Valley Stream, N.Y., home when his son, one of four children, wanted to learn how to skate.

BARRINGTON L. YOUNG Jr.
A Clear Line of Sight

From her office at J.P. Morgan Chase's offices in Garden City, on Long Island, Margaret Foster Young had a good view on clear days all the way to the World Trade Center, where her husband, Barrington L. Young Jr., managed the telecommunications systems for Euro Brokers.

When she got to her desk, she would wave and imagine her 6-foot-3, 270-pound bear of a man waving back from the 84th floor of the south tower. Her office mates could not resist teasing her.

"You must really love that man!" they would say. True enough, although it had taken her awhile to realize it. Originally, he was just Barry, the big brother of her junior-high friend Grace, and one of their close-knit crowd of young Jehovah's Witnesses in the Laurelton neighborhood of Queens. He had been married and divorced, and she had been engaged to someone else, before they clicked for good in 1995.

Mr. Young, 35, was last seen tarrying to gather papers.

"I was hoping he wouldn't be himself for once," said Mrs. Young, who imagined her husband encouraging others to go before him. "I could see the flash when the second plane hit and when the buildings collapsed. I wish it had been a cloudy day."

JACQUELINE YOUNG
Avoiding Noise, Not Music

Jacqueline Young, known as Jakki, hated noise. She hated it so much that she moved to Staten Island, even though she had no relatives there, for some quiet. Raised in South Carolina, Ms. Young, 37, who worked for Marsh & McLennan, often talked about moving out of the city altogether and searched for jobs in other states.

"She wanted to be where life was at a slower pace, where it was not so hectic all the time," said her mother, LaBertha McKenly-Williams.

Ms. Young's brother, James McKenly, accompanied her to a job interview in Virginia in 2000, and when the hotel they were staying in proved too noisy, she insisted they move to another one.

It was about 20 miles away, he said. Despite her need for quiet, Ms. Young, who was unmarried, often took her nieces and nephews on excursions and loved to dance.

In July, she danced at the wedding of another brother in Brooklyn. "She was so happy for him," Mr. McKenly said.

ELKIN YUEN
Creative Vacationer

Wall Street brokers often complain about how much work they have to do in such little time that they can't even contemplate taking a vacation. But not Elkin Yuen, who worked for Carr Futures.

Every year, he and his wife, Cella, took two major vacations and plenty of smaller ones, to get away from the city they grew up in. It was important, he always told his wife, to have fun, to live in the moment. (And to play golf, go to the beach and gamble, if at all possible.) Even when his wife had the urge to save money more quickly to buy a house, "he'd rather spend a few thousand dollars going away for a week than save the money," his wife recalled. And with that perpetual smile and infectious joie de vivre, who could say no?

Hawaii, Cancún, Las Vegas, Myrtle Beach, Lake Tahoe, St. Maartens, Walt Disney World: they all made their way into the overflowing photo albums in the Yuens' Flushing home. Oh, and Aruba, twice. "I'm so glad he pushed me," Mrs. Yuen said. "I would have lost all that time with him."

Perhaps the only thing Mr. Yuen loved more than going on vacation was doting on his daughter, Nicole, now 3. These days, Nicole is still not sure what happened, but she does miss her father. She sometimes tells her mother: "I want Daddy to come home. Daddy used to take me to Chuck E. Cheese."

A display at the firehouse in Tinton Falls, New Jersey, pays tribute to the uniformed personnel—police officers, firefighters and emergency service workers—lost on September 11. (*Dith Pran*)

Z

JOSEPH ZACCOLI
The Little Miracles

Joseph Zaccoli's wife, Helen, teaches theology to schoolchildren and, a few days after her husband's body was found, she went to her children's school, Holy Name of Mary, in their community of Valley Stream, N.Y., to talk. "These kids are so traumatized, not just mine," said Helen, who is mother to three, all under 14. "I was trying to say that they had to look for miracles beyond the building, little miracles that are happening all over the place."

She listed some.

"A woman I don't even know at Jamaica Hospital made red, white and blue ribbon pins and sold them and gave me all the money. Every day for the last 15 years, my husband brought me coffee and a muffin. I was telling people that was one of the things that I was going to miss. Yesterday, somebody left coffee and a muffin outside my door."

Mr. Zaccoli, 39, was a municipal bond broker at Cantor Fitzgerald who somehow found the time to coach five different elementary school athletic teams. Another thing his wife counts as a little miracle—they found his wedding ring. "His ring said, 'Till death,' mine said, 'Till us part,' " she said. "He was on the 104th floor. With all that debris, I can't even fathom how they found it."

ADEL ZAKHARY
Studying the Saints

Adel and Nagat Zakhary immigrated from Egypt 17 years ago to escape the terrorism aimed at Coptic Christians. "Every year," said George, their 21-year-old son, "there would be bombs on Christian buses going to monasteries."

In North Arlington, N.J., the Zakharys centered their lives on St. Mark's and St. Anthony's Church. Mr. Zakhary studied the Bible, the lives of the saints and books by Bishop David, a friend and church leader.

But Mr. Zakhary, 50, had a sharp side. "He was sarcastic to the point you couldn't tell if he was serious," George Zakhary said.

The family was intensely close. An accountant at Carr Futures, Mr. Zakhary worked nights and cooked the dinner. "Cheesecake with strawberries," his son said. "Chicken cordon bleu." When anyone went to the doctor, Mr. Zakhary took a day off to accompany them. Mrs. Zakhary startled the doctor in September when she turned up for her appointment alone.

ARKADY ZALTSMAN
A Man of Many Views

If you were Arkady Zaltsman's guest in New York, you could be sure he would take you to the esplanade at Brooklyn Heights. And you could be sure he would be beaming as he showed off that vista. It was his favorite view.

Then again, Mr. Zaltsman, an architect, had lots of favorite views. "He loved New York so much," said his wife, Zhanna Galperina. "He was very proud to live here." With their daughter, Laura, the couple immigrated in 1990 from Moldova (then the Moldavian Soviet Socialist Republic) and settled in Midwood, Brooklyn. But they did not come until he could see his most important project to completion: the House of Parliament in Chisinau.

Mr. Zaltsman reached two milestones in 2000. He was hired by Skidmore, Owings & Merrill—"He used to tell me that S.O.M. is mentioned in every book on architecture," Ms. Galperina said. And he turned 45. Rather than wait until his 50th birthday for a blow-out party, Mr. Zaltsman celebrated his 45th in grand style, with nearly 100 friends, colleagues and clients.

Though he dreamed of beautifying Brooklyn, especially the Russian quarter in Brighton Beach, much of Mr. Zaltsman's work took place in the towers of Manhattan. He was at a meeting with the Aon Corporation in 2 World Trade Center on Sept. 11.

ROBERT A. ZAMPIERI
Trader Relished Privacy

"Dad, someday I'm going to tell you to wear a tuxedo, and that will be my wedding," Robert A. Zampieri once said. "You won't even meet the girl before."

Robbie, as everyone called him, was shy and private. Now the father, a dentist who is also named Robert, has been moved to make his son's life a little more public. Dr. Zampieri is finishing a newsletter devoted to the life of his son. He has been writing such letters to his patients for 30 years, but never one so personal.

Robbie Zampieri, 30, a trader on the foreign exchange floor for Carr Futures, was low man on the totem pole, working the swing shift. The week before Sept. 11, he had been on nights. That week, he was moved to days on the 92nd floor of the north tower.

He grew up in Saddle River, N.J., the oldest of three children, and attended St. Francis College in Loretto, Pa. He loved his dog, Daisy. They ate and slept together, and played in the ocean. He and his father were buddies. They played golf every Friday.

Robbie loved to surprise his mother. He cut the hedges just the way she liked them. He cleaned the gutters. Despite the memorial service, his father has not said good-bye. "He's not gone," Dr. Zampieri said. "It's just that I can't hug him anymore."

MARK ZANGRILLI
Solicitous of All

Mark and Jill Zangrilli met as teenagers working at Fortunoff's in Wayne, N.J., and began a happily-ever-after life that was the envy of all who knew them. Until Mr. Zangrilli's death, while attending a business meeting in the World Trade Center, he kissed his sleeping wife each and every morning and she greeted him at the front door each and every night.

Without a peep of complaint, Mr. Zangrilli, 36, would go to the pharmacy in the middle of the night if his wife had cramps or a cold. He praised her meals even when they were mediocre and never said a word if she put on a few extra pounds. If 3-year-old Alexander or 18-month-old Nicholas woke in the night, he was right there beside her in the family room with the fussy child.

Such solicitude extended to his four siblings, his parents and his in-laws. Mrs. Zangrilli says she knew he was a keeper when she watched him, at 19, put drops in his mother's eyes. Mr. Zangrilli's sisters, 30-year old twins, remember him teaching them to ride bicycles he had built from scrap parts

and tolerating their screechy violin concerts when he came home with a date.

If there is consolation amid sorrow, Mrs. Zangrilli said, it is that their feelings for each other never went unexpressed. On their last weekend together, on the beach at the Jersey shore with the children playing at their feet, "we got choked up talking about how lucky we were," she said. And they decided to try for another baby come spring.

CHRISTOPHER R. ZARBA
A Curious Mind

Christopher R. Zarba Jr. was just a baby when the Boston Pops performed a piece composed by his father, "Palm Sunday," in 1954. The younger Mr. Zarba inherited his family's musical genes, and grew up to be a talented pianist and French horn player who performed with local symphonies in his free time. He even married a fellow horn player, Sheila Kiernan.

Mr. Zarba, 47, lived with his wife and young son, Christopher James, in Hopkinton, Mass., before he boarded American Airlines Flight 11. A software engineer by profession, he also painted, gardened, and learned to speak German and Italian fluently. He was perpetually curious, even keeping algebra and calculus books around the house to read for pleasure.

"He was always investigating," said his only brother, Joe Zarba.

To remember Mr. Zarba, his father, wife and brother-in-law performed "Palm Sunday" in November with the Thayer Symphony Orchestra in Fitchburg, Mass. His uncle sang the national anthem. Mr. Zarba, who had played with the symphony for more than a decade, had talked about performing his father's work, but never got the chance.

"I think Chris would have just loved it," Mrs. Zarba said.

IRA ZASLOW
Anywhere for Paddleball

The closer it got to Saturday, the more excited Ira Zaslow would become. At 55, a financial analyst for Lehman Brothers, he was like a boy about the weekend. He would call Bryan, his eldest son, to say: "This weekend is going to be great!"

For Mr. Zaslow, weekends meant paddleball. "He had a passion for it," said Bryan Zaslow. "It was pure happiness for him to wake up at 6 on Saturdays and Sundays and meet the same paddleball friends. He went anywhere to play." An argument over a foul ball? Play it over, he would say. "Anything," Bryan Zaslow said, "to play more."

His other passions were equally homey: a good nap on

the couch. Listening to the car radio while Felicia, his wife of 31 years, shopped at the mall. The pizza at a place in North Woodmere, his Long Island hometown.

A quiet man, he went out of his way to lend a hand, while deflecting the credit. When New York University rejected a young Lehman employee, he made a call or two and got her in. Then he congratulated her. "He had time for everybody," his son said. " 'Whatever you want,' he'd say."

ABE ZELMANOWITZ
A Friend to the End

Abe Zelmanowitz's family used to nag him about not being married. But although he never found a mate, he did not miss out on the experience of raising children. Living with his older brother Jack in Brooklyn, Uncle Avremel, as Mr. Zelmanowitz, 55, was known within the family, was deeply involved in the upbringing of his nieces and nephews.

"My children were his children," his brother said. "My grandchildren were his grandchildren." When their parents were alive, Mr. Zelmanowitz, an Orthodox Jew, thought nothing of walking three miles each way to visit them on the Sabbath.

He loved music—everything from Andrea Bocelli to the Beatles—and he was so handy that he could build a sukkah, a temporary hut for the festival of Sukkot, without using nails.

In death, Mr. Zelmanowitz has been celebrated by President Bush and people around the world for remaining with his quadriplegic friend and colleague, Edward Beyea, after the attack on the World Trade Center, where they worked as computer programmers at Empire Blue Cross and Blue Shield.

But to his family, this sacrifice was typical of Mr. Zelmanowitz's nature. "Had it been a casual acquaintance," his brother said, "he would have done the same thing. He could never turn his back on another human being."

ZHE ZENG
"Completely Selfless Person"

Zhe Zeng was safe. The first plane struck the north tower as he was leaving the Brooklyn Bridge subway stop, and he could have stayed in his Barclay Street office, blocks away from the carnage, at the Bank of New York, where he was project manager for American depositary receipts.

But Mr. Zeng, 29, who was known as Zack, was also a certified emergency medical technician, and after stopping

by his office for some supplies, he plunged into the maelstrom of dust and ash. A news video broadcast later that day showed him working, still in his business suit, over a prostrate form. But he has not been seen since.

"It didn't surprise anybody who knew him," said Peggy Farrell, his supervisor. "He was a completely selfless person—he was just someone who would automatically volunteer his assistance. To me it was a truly heroic display."

MARC ZEPLIN
He Shoots! He Scores!

When Marc Zeplin was 4, his father took him to his first Rangers game. There, he found his calling.

Throughout his childhood, his mother would come upon him in the living room, playing an entire hockey game by himself while calling the play-by-play. He would hit the puck and run to the other side of the room to protect the goal. Meanwhile, he would announce his moves at the top of his lungs. Afterward, at the dinner table, he would recap the game in his imitation of Howard Cosell's grating baritone.

When he went to the University of Michigan, he broadcast the games on the school radio station. His dream, said Leona Zeplin, his mother, was to be a professional sportscaster. But he was enough of a realist to know how slim his chances at success were.

Instead, he became a trader at Cantor Fitzgerald, entertaining clients with his sports chatter. He and Debra, his wife, had two sons—1-year-old Ethan and 3-year-old Ryan. He looked forward to sharing years of Rangers games and sports talk with them. Already, he was making plans to take Ryan to his first Rangers game.

JUSTIN ZHAO
Easing Parents' Burden

Justin Zhao earned good grades as a student and never rebelled, even as a teenager. After starting to work for Aon as a computer technician, Mr. Zhao, 26, whose given name in China was Jieyao, frequently gave his parents money and always bought them cakes and fruits.

This year was the first time that the Zhaos found their financial burden lightened since they immigrated to the United States 15 years ago from Guangzhou, China. At first, they lived in a basement apartment in Woodside, Queens. The father, Qixuan Zhao, waited on tables in Chinese restaurants, and the mother, Shuzhen Zhao, sewed clothes in Chinese garment factories.

Then in 2001, their sons, Jimmy and Justin, both City University of New York graduates, found well-paying jobs. Suddenly, taking vacations and enjoying retirement no longer seemed like preposterous goals.

"But who knew this would happen?" said Jimmy Zhao, Justin's older brother. "We just cannot accept the reality. We are still in denial."

MICHAEL ZINZI Jr.
Life as a Joyride

The progress of Michael Zinzi Jr.'s life could be measured in Harley-Davidson motorcycles.

There was his first, a 1956 K model, beautiful but no shocks, that he rebuilt with his father in Texas when he was 18 and finally picked up 15 years later on a trip home with his new wife, Dyan.

Then there was the Heritage, a burnt-orange 1340-cc monster that he paid for with his savings from his job at Marsh & McLennan, where he eventually became a vice president, and bought in 1998 after three years on a waiting list. The only thing that Mr. Zinzi wanted more than that bike was a child. But by then, his wife wanted to do some serious riding herself.

"A happy wife is a happy life," Mr. Zinzi always said.

So in January 1999, they got her a Harley Sportster. The couple rode everywhere together, all around their home in hilly Newfoundland, N.J., and as far as Vermont.

In the fall of 2000, Dyan Zinzi agreed to lay down her helmet for a while, and in July, Dean was born, the joy of his 37-year-old father's life.

On Sept. 9, the couple went riding together for the first time since before the baby, a charity run from Parsippany to Newark.

"It was just wonderful," Ms. Zinzi said. "Doing that again. Together."

JULIE ZIPPER
Defining Her Own Style

For most college students, a nice dinner out is a burrito and a beer. But not for Julie Zipper and Rick Klein, who met at the State University of New York at Binghamton. At a time when brown rice and steamed veggies were in vogue, they went to the nicest French restaurants they could afford.

Even then, Ms. Zipper had style, said Mr. Klein, who married her 24 years ago. She was a passionate shopper who bought clothes on sale just before they were cleared out, when the markdown was lowest. She wore them to Sun-guard, a brokerage software company, and to parties, where she talked with everybody.

Ms. Zipper and Mr. Klein went to Europe on their honeymoon and returned later with their children, 4 and 12. The children, it seems, have style, too. They were as happy in northern Italy as they were at Disney World. Their favorite food, Mr. Klein said, is salmon—the same as their mother's.

SALVATORE ZISA
The Top Priority

When traveling on business, as he often did, Salvatore Zisa, 45, would almost invariably take the red-eye flight home from the West Coast. From the airport, he would then typically proceed directly into the office at Marsh Inc., where he was a senior vice president, arriving at his desk as though he had slept in a bed like everyone else. This pattern repeated itself again and again over the years.

Workaholic? Maybe. Or maybe just a father who wanted to make sure he could get home to Hawthorne, N.J., in time for a soccer game where his daughter Christina, 16, or his son Joseph, 12, would expect to look up and see him cheering.

"His priority was making sure he got to his kids' games on time, that he didn't miss anything," said his brother, Tony Zisa. "He traveled a lot, but he would work his schedule around making sure he was home for the important things. He was always there for our parents, and for his kids, and for his wife."

PAUL ZOIS
Games as Sacred Rites

For Paul Zois, his children's ball games were sacred rites—events that took precedence over practically everything. He emmigrated from Greece at the age of 9, and was poor: he had never had time to play. As soon as his children—Stefania and Theo—were able to toddle, he began to make up for it. He coached their soccer and basketball teams year-round. Nearly every night, after work, he went to a practice or game. Frequently, he did not get home for dinner until 10 or 11, said his wife, Dorota.

"You should see our backyard," she said. "We have more balls and nets than you can imagine. He would never come home without new sports socks or sports gear he had picked up in the city."

The Friday before Sept. 11, Theo asked for a new pair of high-quality soccer shoes. The stores did not carry them, so

Painted plywood letters spell out AMERICA beside the Garden
State Parkway in Holmdel, New Jersey, not far from the
PNC Bank Arts Center. Cars pulled over frequently so
people could write messages, draw symbols or simply
sign their names in tribute to the victims of September
11. (*Dith Pran*)

Mr. Zois, 46, ordered them from a catalog. Meanwhile, since
the soccer season was starting, he screwed new nubs into
Theo's old shoes.

Wednesday, Sept. 12, the shoes arrived, Mrs. Zois said.
Theo sat on the bed, crying and cradling them.

ANDREW ZUCKER
A Blessing on the Way

In the Jewish religion, funerals generally
take place within 24 hours of death. That
leaves little time for writing eulogies, or
ruminating on the special meaning of a
life. But Andrew Zucker's family had the
better part of five weeks to prepare, waiting for the Jewish
holy days to pass and for a ruling from a rabbinical council as
to whether an Orthodox funeral could take place without a
body.

During those weeks, Mr. Zucker's siblings, parents and
friends huddled at the home of a brother, Stuart Zucker, on
Long Island. A similar vigil took place in Riverdale, N.Y., for
Mr. Zucker's wife, Erica. When it was finally time to remem-
ber Andrew, 28, a new associate at the law firm of Harris
Beach, 1,500 people swarmed the Riverdale Jewish Center.

By then the Zuckers had figured out that Mr. Zucker
remained in touch with virtually everyone he had ever
known. High school classmates came. So did members of his
Chabad group at the State Univeristy of New York at Binghamton and his law school class at Cardozo. There were wor-
shippers from the synagogue where Mr. Zucker prayed every
morning before work. And Harris Beach colleagues, who
said they were alive because of his help.

In those weeks, Erica, 25, had also shared a secret with
her parents and her husband's family. A baby is expected in
March. Last April, an earlier pregnancy had ended in a still-
birth. The family gasped at the news and then saw it might

be a blessing. Stuart Zucker is assembling a photo album so there will be "something to show this baby."

IGOR ZUKELMAN
Ugly Car, Beautiful Dream

Nobody but a scrap-yard scout would give it a second look, but to Igor Zukelman, the rather tired eight-year-old Toyota Cressida was a steel chariot, a three-dimensional symbol of his cherished dream of becoming an American.

Mr. Zukelman, 29, had saved money from the moment he landed in New York in 1992 after leaving his native Ukraine. The day he bought the Toyota—his first car—he knew he had embarked on the American dream. He splurged on vanity license plates, a little joke if you knew Ukrainian.

The plate said Melkey, the Ukrainian equivalent of Tiny. Mr. Zukelman weighed more than 230 pounds. A few minutes after he took the citizenship oath earlier this year, he called his mother, Mara, in Brooklyn and told her, "You can congratulate me now, I'm already a citizen," she said.

Mr. Zukelman enrolled in a computer school, married and had a son, Allan, now 3. The family was moving from Queens to Brooklyn in September. He had a job with the Fiduciary Trust Company and thought that working at the World Trade Center was marvelous.

"He was proud that he worked on the 97th floor where he could see the whole city," said Alexander Shetman, Mr. Zukelman's brother-in-law. In April 2001, a driver jumped a curb on Ocean Parkway, killing Mr. Shetman's two daughters. He said Mr. Zukelman helped him get through those days, staying with him overnight at the hospital, organizing the funerals, and telling him that everything would be all right.

Acknowledgments

If there has ever been a sustained mobilization at the *New York Times* to match the effort required to produce the "Portraits of Grief," nobody at the newspaper can remember it. One hundred forty-three writers—along with eleven researchers, three photo editors, three news assistants, three assigning editors and a couple dozen copy editors—worked over three and one-half months to give *Times* readers glimpses of 1,910 of the lives lost in the attack on the World Trade Center.

Some reporters wrote one profile. Three reporters—Jan Hoffman, N. R. Kleinfield and Barbara Stewart—wrote more than seventy-five each. All approached this daunting and emotionally wrenching assignment with an extraordinary sense of mission and remarkable skill. Some contributed in particularly distinctive ways.

Diane Cardwell, Glenn Collins, Winnie Hu, Andrew Jacobs, Lynda Richardson, Janny Scott and Joyce Wadler wrote the first day's portraits, creating a style and tone that was imitated and even, occasionally, improved upon for the rest of the year. Steven Greenhouse used contacts from his labor beat to find people who might have otherwise fallen between the cracks—dishwashers, carpenters, elevator operators, security guards. Kirk Johnson wrote with remarkable grace. Andy Newman showed in his profiles that grief leaves room for a chuckle, or even a belly laugh.

The project was supervised by the metropolitan news department, but it could not have succeeded without contributions of reporters' time by the heads of nearly every other desk at the *Times*. Glenn Kramon, the business editor, provided sixteen reporters. Neil Amdur, the sports editor, John Darnton, the cultural news editor and Katy Roberts, the national editor, also contributed members of their staffs.

Five members of the News Research staff—Jack Begg, Alain Delaqueriere, Judy Greenfeld, Linda Lake and Carolyn Wilder—spent weeks wrestling with fragmentary and often inaccurate listings of the missing to provide the writers with over one thousand telephone numbers of next-of-kin. The news assistants Ben Sisario, Seth Solomonow and Tarannum Kamlani culled lists of the missing and also helped reporters make the necessary contacts.

The difficult task of collecting snapshots of the victims fell to Stella Kramer, Yolanda Andrews and Carol Whaley of the photography desk. Although the vast majority of photographs were supplied by family members, a number of Web sites were also kind enough to supply pictures of victims. These Web sites included those of the New York City police and fire departments, the Vulcan Society, the Associated Press, *Newsday*, CNN, CBS2, WNBC and Aon.

Wendell Jamieson, an editor on the metro desk, skillfully handled the day-to-day management of the "Portraits of Grief" with help from his colleague Patrick Farrell.

But the crucial inspiration came from Christine Kay, an assistant metropolitan editor, who understood before anyone else that these profiles must be about life, not death; that they should be snapshots, not obituaries. It was she who implored reporters to discover the one story people like to remember about their missing loved-one, or the single characteristic that most stands out in their memories.

And so they are portraits of joy as well as grief. Through them, we have come to understand what was lost.

These writers contributed profiles:

Abelson, Reed	Bagdorf, Jessica	Barboza, David	Belkin, Lisa
Applebome, Peter	Bahrampour, Tara	Barnes, Julian E.	Berenson, Alex
Archibold, Randal C.	Baker, Al	Barringer, Felicity	Bernstein, Nina
Arenson, Karen W.	Banerjee, Neela	Barry, Dan	Bohlen, Celestine
Ayres Jr., B. Drummond	Baranauckas, Carla	Barstow, David	Boxer, Sarah

Brick, Michael
Burkhart, Ford
Cardwell, Diane
Chen, David W.
Christian, Nichole M.
Clymer, Adam
Collins, Glenn
Cowan, Alison Leigh
Day, Sherri
DePalma, Anthony
Dewan, Shaila K.
Dunlap, David W.
Dunning, Jennifer
Dwyer, Jim
Eakin, Emily
Eaton, Leslie
Fabrikant, Geraldine
Farrell, Patrick
Feder, Barnaby J.
Feuer, Alan
Finn, Robin
Flanders, Stephanie
Flynn, Kevin
Fountain, Henry
Fried, Joseph P.
Fuerbringer, Jonathan
Gilpin, Kenneth N.
Glater, Jonathan D.
Goodnough, Abby
Gootman, Elissa
Greenhouse, Steven

Gross, Jane
Hakim, Danny
Halbfinger, David M.
Hanley, Robert
Harmon, Amy
Harshaw, Tobin
Hartocollis, Anemona
Hays, Constance L.
Henriques, Diana B.
Herring, Hubert B.
Hershey Jr., Robert D.
Hoffman, Jan
Holland, Jenny
Holloway, Lynette
Hu, Winnie
Hyland, John
Iovine, Julie V.
Ives, Nat
Jacobs, Andrew
James, George
Johnson, Kirk
Johnston, David Cay
Kelley, Tina
Kennedy, Randy
Kershaw, Sarah
Kleiman, Dena
Kleinfield, N.R.
Kocieniewski, David
LeDuff, Charlie
Lee, Felicia R.
Lee, Jennifer

Leland, John
Leonhardt, David
Levy, Clifford J.
Lewin, Tamar
Litsky, Frank
Longman, Jere
Louie, Elaine
Lueck, Thomas J.
Martin, Douglas
McClain, Dylan Loeb
McElroy. Kathleen
McFadden, Robert D.
Minunni, Debra
Molotsky, Irvin
Molyneux, Michael
Morgenson, Gretchen
Murphy, Dean E.
Murphy, Mary Jo
Navarro, Mireya
Newman, Andy
Newman, Maria
Niebuhr, Gustav
Norris, Floyd
Ojito, Mirta
Petersen, Melody
Peterson, Iver
Pollak, Michael
Pristin, Terry
Purnick, Joyce
Ramirez, Anthony
Richardson, Lynda

Richtel, Matthew
Rimer, Sara
Roberts, Karin
Rutenburg, Jim
Ryzik, Melena Z.
Salamon, Julie
Saulny, Susan
Schwartz, John
Scott, Janny
Sengupta, Somini
Sisario, Ben
Smith, Dinitia
Solomonow, Seth
Stellin, Susan
Stewart, Barbara
Treaster, Joseph B.
Wadler, Joyce
Wakin, Daniel J.
Waldman, Amy
Walsh, Mary Williams
Wayne, Leslie
Weber, Bruce
West, Debra
Whitaker, Barbara
Williams, Lena
Wong, Edward
Worth, Robert F.
Wyatt, Edward
Zernike, Kate
Zhao, Yilu

—Jonathan Landman,
Metropolitan Editor

Converting 132 newspaper pages of "Portraits of Grief" into a 550-page book worthy of the occasion turned out to be a tricky process, demanding more time, patience and ingenuity than we anticipated at the start. In the end, though, disasters were averted, deadlines were conquered and *Portraits 9/11/01* emerged in record time as a heartbreaking, life-affirming testament to 1,910 victims of the terrorist assault on the World Trade Center. Thanks to the New York Times Foundation and its president, Jack Rosenthal, each victim's family will receive a complimentary copy of the book; and profits from its publication will go to the New York Times 9/11 Neediest Fund.

We regret that the book, tied to a tight production schedule, does not include portraits published in the *Times* after February 3. In the event of a second edition we will bring the roster up to date, completing the work that remains under way in the newspaper.

Along with our fine publishing partners at Times Books/Henry Holt, a small cadre at the *Times*—several of them veterans of the original "Portraits" team—made this book possible. Wendell Jamieson, Tarannum Kamlani, Michael Pollak, Campbell Robertson, Melena Ryzik, Ben Sisario and Seth Solomonow worked tirelessly to perfect the text, from alphabetizing and checking every entry to copyediting and proofreading. Yolanda Andrews, Stella Kramer, Art Mulford, Jesse Ruiz, Peter Simmons, Megan Sullivan and Phil Ventricelli carefully filed, retrieved, cropped and processed the photographs. Appreciation is also due to the freelance photographers who donated their outstanding work.

Finally, special thanks to Jim Mones, my colleague on this project as head of the New York Times Photo Archives, and to Nancy Lee and Tom Carley of the News Services division for their generous support and good advice.

—Mitchel Levitas,
Editorial Director, Book Development